THE
WINCHESTER READER

Edited by

Donald McQuade
University of California, Berkeley

Robert Atwan

D0075115

Bedford Books *of* **St. Martin's Press**
Boston

For Bedford Books

Publisher: Charles H. Christensen
Associate Publisher: Joan E. Feinberg
Managing Editor: Elizabeth M. Schaaf
Developmental Editor: Ellen Darion
Production Editor: Tara L. Masih
Copyeditors: Dan Otis and Kathleen F. Kent
Text Design: Melinda Grosser for *silk*
Cover Design: Hannus Design Associates
Cover Art: Photograph © 1990 Jeffrey Becom, courtesy of
Abbeville Press Inc., New York, publishers of *Mediterranean
Color*, © 1990 Cross River Press Ltd.

For information, write: St. Martin's Press, Inc.
175 Fifth Avenue, New York, NY 10010

Editorial Offices: Bedford Books *of* St. Martin's Press
29 Winchester Street, Boston, MA 02116

ISBN: 0-312-04880-7

Acknowledgments

Paula Gunn Allen, "Where I Come from Is Like This." From *The Sacred Hoop* by Paula Gunn Allen. Copyright © 1986 by Paula Gunn Allen. Reprinted by permission of Beacon Press.
Dorothy Allison, "Don't Tell Me You Don't Know." From *Trash* by Dorothy Allison. Copyright © 1988 by Dorothy Allison. Reprinted by permission of Firebrand Books, Ithaca, New York.
Rudolfo A. Anaya, "B. Traven Is Alive and Well in Cuernavaca." From *Cuentos Chicanos: A Short Story Anthology*, ed. Rudolfo A. Anaya and A. Marquez. Copyright © 1984 by Rudolfo A. Anaya. Reprinted by permission of the author.
Sherwood Anderson, "Discovery of a Father." Copyright 1939 by The Reader's Digest. Copyright renewed 1966 by Eleanor Copenhaver Anderson. Reprinted by permission of Harold Ober Associates Incorporated.
Maya Angelou, "What's Your Name, Girl?" From *I Know Why the Caged Bird Sings* by Maya Angelou. Copyright © 1969 by Maya Angelou. Reprinted by permission of Random House Inc.
Max Apple, "Bridging." From *Free Agents* by Max Apple. Copyright © 1984 by Max Apple. Reprinted by permission of HarperCollins Publishers.
Michael J. Arlen, "Ode to Thanksgiving." From *The Camera Age* by Michael J. Arlen. Originally appeared in *The New Yorker*. Copyright © 1978, 1981 by Michael J. Arlen. Reprinted by permission of Farrar, Straus and Giroux, Inc.

Acknowledgments and copyrights are continued at the back of the book on pages 996–999, which constitute an extension of the copyright page.

 The text of this book has been printed on recycled paper.

Preface for Instructors

The Winchester Reader is a large, thematically arranged anthology of prose intended for use in first-year composition classes. Such textbooks have been around for much of this century, of course, distinguished from one another by (1) the selections they reprint, (2) the arrangement of the selections, and (3) the additional material accompanying the selections. As the latest entry in the field, *The Winchester Reader* differs significantly from its contemporaries—and, indeed, its forebears—in each of these elements.

DIVERSE SELECTIONS

More than half of the 124 selections in *The Winchester Reader* are by women and minorities and were written since 1980. These are much higher proportions than in any similar anthology. The collection is ample enough, however, to ensure that writers from within the literary and cultural mainstream are also well represented. The book's twelve short stories reflect the same variety.

Thematic juxtapositions make the most of the selections' diversity. Mainstream writers and hitherto marginalized writers appear together. Older and newer selections confront each other. Moreover, the high proportion of very recent selections that directly address contemporary concerns and values ensures that these juxtapositions are also provocative.

We think this diverse mixture offers at least two instructional advantages. First, it creates *inside the book* an intense dialogue among authors from widely divergent cultures and backgrounds. Second, these interactions help create *outside the book* a productive community of diverse readers and writers. We hope this collection will encourage your students to see that their reading and writing can help them establish individual voices in the university community.

The diversity and interaction of voices in *The Winchester Reader* are not limited to the essays and stories, for the book also features 139 quotations by nearly as many writers. "I have always been fond of the books that have little quotations at the head of each chapter," wrote Gertrude Stein in "What Is English Literature?" "I like it particularly when the quotations are very varied and many of them of more or less important writers." We think Gertrude Stein might have enjoyed this book. The many quotations range over cultures and historical periods from ancient Greece to contemporary Africa, and represent creative writers, philosophers, and specialists in varied disciplines. Drawn from works not included in the book and often of paragraph length, the quotations in themselves compose a miniature browsing anthology. But they serve deliberate purposes, too, starting students thinking about the issues that follow and thickening the texture of voices and ideas.

MULTIPLE THEMATIC CHAPTERS

The multicultural interaction of *The Winchester Reader* benefits from a distinctive organization. Like many thematic readers, this one is divided into large categories (in this case, seven) reflecting general topics and academic disciplines. But unlike other thematic readers, *The Winchester Reader* is further divided into forty-one "bite-size"chapters, each containing about three selections and each focusing on a specific theme or topic. These small chapters, we believe, will help you reconcile two instructional ideals that frequently conflict—focus and freedom. The small number of selections per theme promotes focused reading and writing, yet the large number of topics offers a wide choice for the classroom. By being simultaneously narrow and broad, the book can accommodate immensely varied juxtapositions. Here is the new with the familiar (June Jordan and George Orwell on the English language), the multicultural with the traditonal (Ishmael Reed and Crèvecoeur on American identity), the factual with the fictional (David Elkind and Joyce Carol Oates on adolescence).

With its variety and focus, *The Winchester Reader* actually comprises a sampler of composition readers that allows you to shape a text for your own pedagogical interests and purposes. Among the many possible combinations of topics and selections are these:

Multicultural or cross-cultural readings
Cross-curricular readings
Opposing arguments
Readings in "great ideas"
Readings in contemporary issues and events
Readings in language

Comparisons of fiction and nonfiction
Comparisons of expository and experiential nonfiction
Comparisons of humorous and serious writing

Suggestions for creating such combinations appear in the accompanying Resources for Teaching *The Winchester Reader.*

ABSENCE OF CONVENTIONAL APPARATUS

In contrast to its contemporaries, there is one thing *The Winchester
Reader* does not contain: instructional apparatus. No chapter introduc-
tions, headnotes, discussion questions, or writing assignments prejudice
students' responses to what they read. We believe this openness facili-
tates an unencumbered dialogue between writers and readers—as well
as between one selection and another. For information's sake, however,
we have unobtrusively included biographical notes on the writers at the
back of the book.

RESOURCES FOR TEACHING *THE WINCHESTER READER*

Though free of apparatus, *The Winchester Reader* comes with an
unusually extensive instructor's manual. Each of the forty-one topical
chapters and each of the individual selections receive detailed attention. The suggested teaching strategies interweave successful class-
discussion practices and more speculative ideas for using the chapters
and selections. Reflecting the book's spirit, the manual includes a
Writing-before-Reading exercise for each chapter. Students assigned
these exercises will explore their views of a theme before they see how
the professionals did it. They will then read the selections with a writer's
eye, having already contributed to the same subject.

ACKNOWLEDGMENTS

The Winchester Reader began several years ago in a series of spirited
conversations about broadening the range of material presented to
composition students as occasions for reading and writing. From its
inception, then, *The Winchester Reader* has been a collaborative enterprise. We are grateful to the dedicated staff of Bedford Books of St.
Martin's Press for their innumerable contributions to this project. Our
editor Ellen Darion guided us through every stage of the book's development. She is the kind of editor any writer might hope to work with:
intelligent, imaginative, patient, and thoroughly reliable in her judgment. We could not have completed this project without her advice and
support. Jane Betz also served as a crucial resource, reading and re-

sponding to selections as well as suggesting new ones. Ellen Kuhl skillfully choreographed the procedures for securing permissions for the selections. Tara Masih steered the book safely through a seemingly endless maze of production decisions and recastings. She did so with great intelligence and imagination, and we enjoyed her good humor and engaging professionalism.

Chuck Christensen, the publisher of Bedford Books, gave us rigorous comments and encouraging advice. He urged us to take the kinds of risks that would make our purposes clearer and more useful to students and teachers. We quickly came to appreciate the assistance that associate publisher Joan Feinberg offered throughout the process of converting pedagogical principles into sound practice.

We are also grateful to Dick Hannus and Melinda Grosser for the simple and elegant look of the book's cover and text design. In addition, we would like to express our gratitude to the other accomplished people at Bedford Books who helped us in more ways than we can recount: Kimberly Chabot, Laura McCready, Beth Castrodale, Frank Dumais, and Constance Mayer.

Alix Schwartz and Greg Mullins contributed their time, energy, and intelligence to virtually every aspect of this enormous project. We are especially indebted to Alix Schwartz for her knowledge of the literature of minorities and other marginalized Americans, and for her experience as an innovative and accomplished teacher and scholar. Greg Mullins's skills as a researcher and his resourcefulness as a reader and writer contributed in several important ways to the distinctiveness of *The Winchester Reader*. His thumbnail biographical sketches at the end of the book are engaging invitations to further reading.

The book profits enormously from Julia Sullivan's participation. She and Alix Schwartz helped us prepare Resources for Teaching *The Winchester Reader*. They made it a comprehensive resource for exploring the pedagogical richness of the entire collection. We gratefully acknowledge their contributions. In addition, we would like to acknowledge the advice and assistance of friends and colleagues at Berkeley and across the nation who generously shared with us ideas and experiences: Mitchell Breitwieser, Beverly Crawford, Carolyn Dinshaw, Cindy Franklin, Marty Gaetjens, Deborah Holdstein, Kristin Mahlis, Michael McSpedon, Frann Michel, Charles O'Neill, Aron Roberts, Jack Roberts, Carol Snow, Sue Schweik, Jackie Stevens, Sherwood Williams, and Rob Birle of the Pacific Center, as well as the National Gay and Lesbian Task Force.

Finally, we invite Helene, Gregory, and Emily Atwan and Susanne, Christine, and Marc McQuade to share our satisfaction as this project goes into print.

Contents

——— PART TWO ———
THE SOCIAL FABRIC

14
Public Space   325
Jane Jacobs, Richard Sennett, Liu Binyan,
Fran Lebowitz

15
On Holidays   342
Charles Dickens, Jeijun, Gwendolyn Brooks

16
Consumer Culture   350
Thorstein Veblen, Sir Thomas More, Ellen Willis

17
The National Pastime   365
Eve Babitz, Roger Angell, Elting E. Morison,
Bud Abbott and Lou Costello

25
The Debate on Abortion 531
Carl Sagan and Ann Druyan, Anna Quindlen,
Ernest Hemingway, Florynce C. Kennedy

26
Freedom of Expression 561
Michel de Montaigne, Carl L. Becker, Bertrand Russell,
John Stuart Mill and Harriet Taylor

27
Denigrating the Species 574
H. L. Mencken, Taylor Caldwell, Thomas Hobbes

28
Visions of the Land 599
Heinmot Tooyalaket (Chief Joseph), Noel Perrin,
Brigid Brophy

29
Environmental Action   631
Joy Williams, Aldo Leopold, J. E. Lovelock

PART SIX
THE POWER OF LANGUAGE

30
The Languages of Home   657
Barbara Mellix, Richard Rodriguez,
An-Thu Quang Nguyen, Edmund Wilson

31
Bilingualism   691
Tina Bakka, S. I. Hayakawa, Oscar Hijuelos

32
Language and Politics   701
Walt Whitman, Randall Jarrell, James Baldwin

41

The Act of Reading   937

Malcolm X, Henry David Thoreau, Vladimir Nabokov,
Edna Buchanan

The First-Person Singular

1

Writing for Oneself

Joan Didion, On Keeping a Notebook

Toi Derricotte, Diary: At an Artist's Colony

William Safire, On Keeping a Diary

Saturday, 20 June, 1942

I haven't written for a few days, because I wanted first of all to think about my diary. It's an odd idea for someone like me to keep a diary; not only because I have never done so before, but because it seems to me that neither I—nor for that matter anyone else—will be interested in the unbosomings of a thirteen-year-old schoolgirl. Still, what does that matter? I want to write, but more than that, I want to bring out all kinds of things that lie buried deep in my heart.

There is a saying that "paper is more patient than man"; it came back to me on one of my slightly melancholy days, while I sat chin in hand, feeling too bored and limp even to make up my mind whether to go out or stay at home. Yes, there is no doubt that paper is patient and as I don't intend to show this cardboard-covered notebook, bearing the proud name of "diary," to anyone, unless I find a real friend, boy or girl, probably nobody cares. And now I come to the root of the matter, the reason for my starting a diary: it is that I have no such real friend.

Anne Frank, from *Diary of a Young Girl*

May 31st, 1889

I think that if I get into the habit of writing a bit about what happens, or rather doesn't happen, I may lose a little of the sense of loneliness and desolation which abides with me. My circumstances allowing of nothing but the ejaculation of one-syllabled reflections, a written monologue by that most interesting being, *myself*, may have its yet to be discovered consolations. I shall at least have it all my own way and it may bring relief as an outlet to that geyser of emotions, sensations, speculations and reflections which ferments perpetually within my poor old carcass for its sins; so here goes, my first Journal!

Alice James, from *The Diaries of Alice James*

To set down such choice experiences that my own writings may inspire me and at last I may make wholes of parts. Certainly it is a distinct profession to rescue from oblivion and to fix the sentiments and thoughts which visit all men more or less generally, that the contempla-tion of the unfinished picture may suggest its harmonious completion. Associate reverently and as much as you can with your loftiest thoughts. Each thought that is welcomed and recorded is a nest egg, by the side of which more will be laid. Thoughts accidentally thrown together become a frame in which more may be developed and exhibited. Perhaps this is the main value of a habit of writing, of keeping a journal—that so we remember our best hours and stimulate ourselves. My thoughts are my company. They have a certain individuality and separate existence, aye, personality. Having by chance recorded a few disconnected thoughts and then brought them into juxtaposition, they suggest a whole new field in which it was possible to labor and to think. Thought begat thought.

Henry David Thoreau, from *Journal* **(1852)**

Women diarists typically located themselves in relation to space and time—often taking care to note where they were sitting, what they had been doing, and what was going on around them as they wrote. "The sun is shining bright and warm, and a cool breeze blowing makes it very nice indeed, and it seems very much like home. . . . Oh, they are starting, so I must stop for today. . . . Trying to write walking, but it won't do." Most women did not go into quite the detail Agnes Stewart included in this passage, but men, by contrast, were likely not to bother with any of these, content to assume that the fact of writing itself established a sufficient identifying framework.

Men's writing was usually plain, unadorned, and terse.

John Mack Faragher, from *Women and Men on the Overland Trail*

Joan Didion

On Keeping a Notebook

"'That woman Estelle,'" the note reads, "'is partly the reason why George Sharp and I are separated today.' *Dirty crepe-de-Chine wrapper, hotel bar, Wilmington RR, 9:45 a.m. August Monday morning.*"

Since the note is in my notebook, it presumably has some meaning to me. I study it for a long while. At first I have only the most general notion of what I was doing on an August Monday morning in the bar of the hotel across from the Pennsylvania Railroad station in Wilmington, Delaware (waiting for a train? missing one? 1960? 1961? why Wilmington?), but I do remember being there. The woman in the dirty crepe-de-Chine wrapper had come down from her room for a beer, and the bartender had heard before the reason why George Sharp and she were separated today. "Sure," he said, and went on mopping the floor. "You told me." At the other end of the bar is a girl. She is talking, pointedly, not to the man beside her but to a cat lying in the triangle of sunlight cast through the open door. She is wearing a plaid silk dress from Peck & Peck, and the hem is coming down.

Here is what it is: the girl has been on the Eastern Shore, and now she is going back to the city, leaving the man beside her, and all she can see ahead are the viscous summer sidewalks and the 3 A.M. long-distance calls that will make her lie awake and then sleep drugged through all the steaming mornings left in August (1960? 1961?). Because she must go directly from the train to lunch in New York, she wishes that she had a safety pin for the hem of the plaid silk dress, and she also wishes that she could forget about the hem and the lunch and stay in the cool bar that smells of disinfectant and malt and make friends with the woman in the crepe-de-Chine wrapper. She is afflicted by a little self-pity, and she wants to compare Estelles. That is what that was all about.

Why did I write it down? In order to remember, of course, but exactly what was it I wanted to remember? How much of it actually happened? Did any of it? Why do I keep a notebook at all? It is easy to deceive oneself on all those scores. The impulse to write things down is a peculiarly compulsive one, inexplicable to those who do not share it, useful only accidentally, only secondarily, in the way that any compulsion tries to justify itself. I suppose that it begins or does not begin in the cradle. Although I have felt compelled to write things down since I was five years old, I doubt that my daughter ever will, for she is a singularly blessed and accepting child, delighted with life exactly as life presents itself to her, unafraid to go to sleep and unafraid to wake up. Keepers of private notebooks are a different breed altogether, lonely

and resistant rearrangers of things, anxious malcontents, children afflicted apparently at birth with some presentiment of loss.

My first notebook was a Big Five tablet, given to me by my mother
with the sensible suggestion that I stop whining and learn to amuse
myself by writing down my thoughts. She returned the tablet to me a
few years ago; the first entry is an account of a woman who believed
herself to be freezing to death in the Arctic night, only to find, when
day broke, that she had stumbled onto the Sahara Desert, where she
would die of the heat before lunch. I have no idea what turn of a five-
year-old's mind could have prompted so insistently "ironic" and exotic
a story, but it does reveal a certain predilection for the extreme which
has dogged me into adult life; perhaps if I were analytically inclined I
would find it a truer story than any I might have told about Donald
Johnson's birthday party or the day my cousin Brenda put Kitty Litter in
the aquarium.

So the point of my keeping a notebook has never been, nor is it now,
to have an accurate factual record of what I have been doing or thinking. That would be a different impulse entirely, an instinct for reality
which I sometimes envy but do not possess. At no point have I ever been
able successfully to keep a diary; my approach to daily life ranges from
the grossly negligent to the merely absent, and on those few occasions
when I have tried dutifully to record a day's events, boredom has so
overcome me that the results are mysterious at best. What is this business about "shopping, typing piece, dinner with E, depressed"? Shopping for what? Typing what piece? Who is E? Was this "E" depressed, or
was I depressed? Who cares?

In fact I have abandoned altogether that kind of pointless entry;
instead I tell what some would call lies. "That's simply not true," the
members of my family frequently tell me when they come up against my
memory of a shared event. "The party was *not* for you, the spider was *not*
a black widow, *it wasn't that way at all.*" Very likely they are right, for not
only have I always had trouble distinguishing between what happened
and what merely might have happened, but I remain unconvinced that
the distinction, for my purposes, matters. The cracked crab that I recall
having for lunch the day my father came home from Detroit in 1945
must certainly be embroidery, worked into the day's pattern to lend
verisimilitude; I was ten years old and would not now remember the
cracked crab. The day's events did not turn on cracked crab. And yet it
is precisely that fictitious crab that makes me see the afternoon all over
again, a home movie run all too often, the father bearing gifts, the child
weeping, an exercise in family love and guilt. Or that is what it was to
me. Similarly, perhaps it never did snow that August in Vermont;
perhaps there never were flurries in the night wind, and maybe no one

else felt the ground hardening and summer already dead even as we pretended to bask in it, but that was how it felt to me, and it might as well have snowed, could have snowed, did snow.

How it felt to me: that is getting closer to the truth about a notebook. I sometimes delude myself about why I keep a notebook, imagine that some thrifty virtue derives from preserving everything observed. See enough and write it down, I tell myself, and then some morning when the world seems drained of wonder, some day when I am only going through the motions of doing what I am supposed to do, which is write—on that bankrupt morning I will simply open my notebook and there it will all be, a forgotten account with accumulated interest, paid passage back to the world out there: dialogue overheard in hotels and elevators and at the hatcheck counter in Pavillon (one middle-aged man shows his hat check to another and says, "That's my old football number"); impressions of Bettina Aptheker and Benjamin Sonnenberg and Teddy ("Mr. Acapulco") Stauffer; careful *aperçus* about tennis bums and failed fashion models and Greek shipping heiresses, one of whom taught me a significant lesson (a lesson I could have learned from F. Scott Fitzgerald, but perhaps we all must meet the very rich for ourselves) by asking, when I arrived to interview her in her orchid-filled sitting room on the second day of a paralyzing New York blizzard, whether it was snowing outside.

I imagine, in other words, that the notebook is about other people. But of course it is not. I have no real business with what one stranger said to another at the hatcheck counter in Pavillon; in fact I suspect that the line "That's my old football number" touched not my own imagination at all, but merely some memory of something once read, probably "The Eighty-Yard Run." Nor is my concern with a woman in a dirty crepe-de-Chine wrapper in a Wilmington bar. My stake is always, of course, in the unmentioned girl in the plaid silk dress. *Remember what it was to be me:* that is always the point.

It is a difficult point to admit. We are brought up in the ethic that others, any others, all others, are by definition more interesting than ourselves; taught to be diffident, just this side of self-effacing. ("You're the least important person in the room and don't forget it," Jessica Mitford's governess would hiss in her ear on the advent of any social occasion; I copied that into my notebook because it is only recently that I have been able to enter a room without hearing some such phrase in my inner ear.) Only the very young and the very old may recount their dreams at breakfast, dwell upon self, interrupt with memories of beach picnics and favorite Liberty lawn dresses and the rainbow trout in a creek near Colorado Springs. The rest of us are expected, rightly, to affect absorption in other people's favorite dresses, other people's trout.

And so we do. But our notebooks give us away, for however dutifully we record what we see around us, the common denominator of
all we see is always, transparently, shamelessly, the implacable "I."
We are not talking here about the kind of notebook that is patently for
public consumption, a structural conceit for binding together a series of
graceful *pensées*;[1] we are talking about something private, about bits of
the mind's string too short to use, an indiscriminate and erratic as-
semblage with meaning only for its maker.

And sometimes even the maker has difficulty with the meaning. 12
There does not seem to be, for example, any point in my knowing for
the rest of my life that, during 1964, 720 tons of soot fell on every square
mile of New York City, yet there it is in my notebook, labeled "FACT." Nor
do I really need to remember that Ambrose Bierce liked to spell Leland
Stanford's name "£eland $tanford" or that "smart women almost always
wear black in Cuba," a fashion hint without much potential for practical
application. And does not the relevance of these notes seem marginal at
best?:

> In the basement museum of the Inyo County Courthouse in Indepen-
> dence, California, sign pinned to a mandarin coat: "This MANDARIN COAT
> was often worn by Mrs. Minnie S. Brooks when giving lectures on her
> TEAPOT COLLECTION."
>
> Redhead getting out of car in front of Beverly Wilshire Hotel,
> chinchilla stole, Vuitton bags with tags reading:
>> MRS LOU FOX
>>
>> HOTEL SAHARA
>>
>> VEGAS

Well, perhaps not entirely marginal. As a matter of fact, Mrs. Minnie S. Brooks and her MANDARIN COAT pull me back into my own childhood, for although I never knew Mrs. Brooks and did not visit Inyo
County until I was thirty, I grew up in just such a world, in houses
cluttered with Indian relics and bits of gold ore and ambergris and the
souvenirs my Aunt Mercy Farnsworth brought back from the Orient. It
is a long way from that world to Mrs. Lou Fox's world, where we all live
now, and is it not just as well to remember that? Might not Mrs. Minnie
S. Brooks help me to remember what I am? Might not Mrs. Lou Fox help
me to remember what I am not?

But sometimes the point is harder to discern. What exactly did I
have in mind when I noted down that it cost the father of someone I
know $650 a month to light the place on the Hudson in which he lived
before the Crash? What use was I planning to make of this line by Jimmy

---

[1]*pensées*: Thoughts or reflections (French).—EDS.

Hoffa: "I may have my faults, but being wrong ain't one of them"? And although I think it interesting to know where the girls who travel with the Syndicate have their hair done when they find themselves on the West Coast, will I ever make suitable use of it? Might I not be better off just passing it on to John O'Hara? What is a recipe for sauerkraut doing in my notebook? What kind of magpie keeps this notebook? *"He was born the night the Titanic went down."* That seems a nice enough line, and I even recall who said it, but is it not really a better line in life than it could ever be in fiction?

But of course that is exactly it: not that I should ever use the line, but that I should remember the woman who said it and the afternoon I heard it. We were on her terrace by the sea, and we were finishing the wine left from lunch, trying to get what sun there was, a California winter sun. The woman whose husband was born the night the *Titanic* went down wanted to rent her house, wanted to go back to her children in Paris. I remember wishing that I could afford the house, which cost $1,000 a month. "Someday you will," she said lazily. "Someday it all comes." There in the sun on her terrace it seemed easy to believe in someday, but later I had a low-grade afternoon hangover and ran over a black snake on the way to the supermarket and was flooded with inexplicable fear when I heard the checkout clerk explaining to the man ahead of me why she was finally divorcing her husband. "He left me no choice," she said over and over as she punched the register. "He has a little seven-month-old baby by her, he left me no choice." I would like to believe that my dread then was for the human condition, but of course it was for me, because I wanted a baby and did not then have one and because I wanted to own the house that cost $1,000 a month to rent and because I had a hangover.

It all comes back. Perhaps it is difficult to see the value in having 16 one's self back in that kind of mood, but I do see it; I think we are well advised to keep on nodding terms with the people we used to be whether we find them attractive company or not. Otherwise they turn up unannounced and surprise us, come hammering on the mind's door at 4 A.M. of a bad night and demand to know who deserted them, who betrayed them, who is going to make amends. We forget all too soon the things we thought we could never forget. We forget the loves and the betrayals alike, forget what we whispered and what we screamed, forget who we were. I have already lost touch with a couple of people I used to be; one of them, a seventeen-year-old, presents little threat, although it would be of some interest to me to know again what it feels like to sit on a river levee drinking vodka-and-orange-juice and listening to Les Paul and Mary Ford and their echoes sing "How High the Moon" on the car radio. (You see I still have the scenes, but I no longer perceive myself among those present, no longer could even improvise the dialogue.)

The other one, a twenty-three-year-old, bothers me more. She was always a good deal of trouble, and I suspect she will reappear when I least want to see her, skirts too long, shy to the point of aggravation, always the injured party, full of recriminations and little hurts and stories I do not want to hear again, at once saddening me and angering me with her vulnerability and ignorance, an apparition all the more insistent for being so long banished.

It is a good idea, then, to keep in touch, and I suppose that keeping in touch is what notebooks are all about. And we are all on our own when it comes to keeping those lines open to ourselves: your notebook will never help me, nor mine you. *"So what's new in the whiskey business?"* What could that possibly mean to you? To me it means a blonde in a Pucci bathing suit sitting with a couple of fat men by the pool at the Beverly Hills Hotel. Another man approaches, and they all regard one another in silence for a while. "So what's new in the whiskey business?" one of the fat men finally says by way of welcome, and the blonde stands up, arches one foot and dips it in the pool, looking all the while at the cabaña where Baby Pignatari is talking on the telephone. That is all there is to that, except that several years later I saw the blonde coming out of Saks Fifth Avenue in New York with her California complexion and a voluminous mink coat. In the harsh wind that day she looked old and irrevocably tired to me, and even the skins in the mink coat were not worked the way they were doing them that year, not the way she would have wanted them done, and there is the point of the story. For a while after that I did not like to look in the mirror, and my eyes would skim the newspapers and pick out only the deaths, the cancer victims, the premature coronaries, the suicides, and I stopped riding the Lexington Avenue IRT because I noticed for the first time that all the strangers I had seen for years—the man with the seeing-eye dog, the spinster who read the classified pages every day, the fat girl who always got off with me at Grand Central—looked older than they once had.

It all comes back. Even that recipe for sauerkraut: even that brings it back. I was on Fire Island when I first made that sauerkraut, and it was raining, and we drank a lot of bourbon and ate the sauerkraut and went to bed at ten, and I listened to the rain and the Atlantic and felt safe. I made the sauerkraut again last night and it did not make me feel any safer, but that is, as they say, another story.   *1966*

Toi Derricotte

Diary: At an Artist's Colony

BLACK ARMS

A group of us are sitting around the TV room. Ray, a painter from the South, is talking about how hard his mother works. He says: "I told her all you need is a pair of good black arms." The others snicker.

I am new here. All I want to do is get along. I say nothing, though now I know there is a part of me that is a joke to this man—my washerwoman great-grandmother, my cook grandmother.

I will be silent. I want him to like me. I want to tell him how he hurts me. I want to speak. But then the colonists will say: "You know how sensitive they are." I will be labled. And for six weeks, the only black person, I will never be able to sit at the dinner table without "Black Arms."

DINNER TIME

Last night at the dinner table, John, a man who didn't know I'm black, noticed the book of women's diary writing which has a section of *The Black Notebooks* in it.

He asked me to see the book, and when he took it, I could see he wasn't going to just skim over the table of contents. He went directly for my story, putting down his fork, and began to read. I felt a coldness, like a breeze ruffling a curtain on a line. The other dinner tables were quiet; many of the colonists don't know I'm black. I could just hear him blurt loudly, "I didn't know you're black. You don't look black. How did you get that color?"

I don't like to lose control of my identity that way. I fear being the center of attention, like an animal in a cage prodded and poked by on-lookers.

The man, fortunately, kept his comments to the quality of the work. "This is great. It sent a shiver up my spine. It's dramatic."

The other people at the table didn't know the content. Not that I mind every person at the colony knowing I'm black. I don't care, and I am proud of my work. But when several come at me from all sides, I don't know which way to turn. Heaven help me if I should show anger or be defensive.

John wouldn't let it alone. Later, as several of us were sitting around the fireplace, he said, "You should read this article in *The Times*. You'll like it. It reminds me of your book." I hadn't seen the article, but I knew it must be about black people. As soon as he knew I was black, I became

a category, and anything he reads by or about a black person reminds
him of me.

A Chinese man who has also read my book said, "This article is
nothing like the writing in Toi's book." I was glad he spoke, defending
the uniqueness of my experience.

Later, John was playing pool. I was sitting twenty feet away and
noticed him staring at me. I thought he was thinking I was attractive and
was beginning to feel flattered. Suddenly he yelled across the room,
"You really should read that article. You'll find it interesting. It's really
timely."

Another man in the room called: "What's the article about?"　　　12

"Racism," he yelled back.

The people in the room looked up. I felt the conversation go out of
my hands.

The other man said, "That isn't timely. It's ongoing and eternal."

I was glad somebody spoke and it wasn't me.　　　　　　　　16

THE TESTIMONY OF INNOCENCE

Last night I went over to Marty's studio to share my work. She read
some of my diary entries and I read some of her poems. She said she felt
my diary entries were extremely important. She asked me who they
were addressed to, and I read her the diary entry which describes my
audience: all the people in my past, black and white, who represent the
internalized process of racism within me.

In 1976, when I began writing *The Black Notebooks*, I wrote mainly to
myself, although at the back of my mind was an idea that maybe
someday, I would get the courage to make it public. The idea was to tell
the truth as deeply as I could, however painful, but also to write for the
larger human community. I know that sounds ridiculously grandiose,
but I felt an honest confession would have merit. My negative self-
concept made me trust myself to be more egoless than some writers
whose descriptions of racism seem to be testimonies of their own
innocence—and I have always distrusted that, both from whites and
blacks.

My skin color causes certain problems continuously, problems
which open the issue of racism over and over, like a wound, a chronic
wound—a stigmata. These openings are occasions for reexamination.
My skin color keeps things, literally, from being either black or white.

My decision to make more of my entries public comes from my　20
meeting at the colony with a political activist, Pat, who, when I showed
her my most scary black hatred entries, still loved me, showed me the
mirror of acceptance. How I love her for that!

I'll publish. I'll make a name for myself; I'll make money. I'll win the love of my relatives and get a professorship at a university. I'll win a movie contract and play the heroine of my own story. It seems awful to hope success will come out of such disaster.

Not to worry, Pat says, writing about racism doesn't make you successful, it makes you ignored.

RAY

Yesterday, after breakfast, I saw him lumbering toward his jeep. He looked a little lost; several of his close friends have left the colony. I had heard him say another gem this morning, "I wish I had ten little black women to sew the holes in that canvas . . ."

Every time the opportunity comes to talk to him the time doesn't 24 seem right. Either other people are around or there's another problem. After his art show last night, I stayed longer than anyone, but he seemed depressed with people's reactions. It would have been piling shit on top of shit if I had tried to talk to him; and I don't think he would have heard what I was saying. I found myself listening to his worries, reassuring him, and kicking myself for being a coward.

But this morning was perfect. I know he often goes into town for donuts. I had been on my way to my studio, but I turned in my tracks.

Sitting in the donut shop, I waited for a relaxed moment. The comforting cups of coffee were placed before us. He lit a cigarette. "There's something I have to tell you," I said. "I'm black, and last week when you made that comment about black arms, it made me feel bad. And this morning you said something else about little black women sewing holes in the canvas." I didn't say it in a mean voice, just a human voice, one on one. (Inside, I'm saying, Why can't I just blurt it out? Why do I have to be so careful?)

I tried not to look at his face so I could get my words out, but I caught a glimpse and saw a muscle twitching in his cheek, his mouth was slightly open, and he was listening to me intently. I went on, "You see, I wanted to say something to you when this happened last week, but I didn't want to say something that would make people look at me as if I'm different. Sometimes when people find out I'm black, they treat me differently from then on. So when people say things that hurt me, I don't know what to do. I want to tell them. But, at the same time, I'm afraid I'll be hurt even more if I do."

He started to explain, "When I said that about 'black arms,' I was 28 repeating something my mother-in-law said, and I was repeating it because I was horrified by it. What you feel must be similar to what I feel at my wife's house, because I am the only goy." I was happy that he was identifying with me, but I didn't want him to spend fifteen minutes explaining his life. I just wanted to tell him my pain and make sure he got my message. "Please, I don't want to put you on the spot. I just want you to understand my feelings. Do you understand? What do you hear me saying?" He said, "I hear you saying that certain comments which other people make without sensitivity have great poignancy to you because you are black." That wasn't exactly what I was saying, but it seemed close. Besides, it had taken all the bravery I could muster to come this far, I couldn't press him further.

In the past, I have left conversations like this empty, not getting what I wanted. I thought it was rage I wanted to vent. But yesterday, because he listened, because I had waited for the right moment and asked for what I wanted, I thought, maybe I've found the answer. From now on, if I just wait, if I just talk about my feelings honestly, if I don't expect the person to say something to take my pain away, if I just ask him or her to repeat back what I said until they've understood, then everything will be fine.

I want so much to find a formula! Of course, there is none. Sometimes it will come out OK, like yesterday, and sometimes I will walk away with a hole in my heart that all the little black women in the world cannot sew up.

SATURDAY NIGHT

Several colonists sat around trying to have fun on a Saturday night. We miss New York, movies, Chinese restaurants. We talked about feminism, about how, these days, many of the young girls have babies while in high school.

A southern lady said, "That's what black girls have been doing for 32 years. They have babies and their families raise them. Maybe it's catching up with white girls." This is the same woman who three days ago was talking about how black people have "funny" names. "They name their kids the strangest things." I thought about the twins in New Jersey whose mother had honored the doctor who had delivered them by giving them names he suggested: Syphily and Gonorra.

This woman loves to talk about black people. She's our resident expert. She said, "There aren't any black people here. I haven't seen any."

"Yes there are," I said, smiling.

"Who?"

"You're looking at one."   36

"You're not really black. Just an eighth or something."

"I don't know how black I am, but I am black."

"Was your mother black?"

"My mother, my father, my grandparents. They are black, and they 40 look just like me."

"How do you know you're black?"

"I'm black because black people were the first people I touched and loved."

A woman at the table said, "Did you read the article in *The New York Times* that said if they were strict about genetics, sixty percent of the people in the United States would be classified as black?"

I looked around the table. I was laughing. The others were not. They 44 were worried about how black I was and they should be worrying about how black *they* are.

I thought of all the little white children, the light of their mothers' and fathers' eyes, in Montana, in flat Wyoming, in Idaho, in lake-filled Michigan; I thought of that "funny" blackness inside of them, a kernel in each little heart put there, somehow in the night, like a visit from the tooth fairy.

I thought of the layers of lies of the first generation which covered that mystery up, the layers of repressed questions in the second generation which decomposed into layers of unconsciousness. Layer after layer, till one day little children walk around with unconsciousness laid over their minds like shrouds, pretty little children in pinafores with a nigger maid who has a funny name. Somewhere babies are popping out of women and no one understands where they come from.

I smile at the little heart of darkness in sixty out of a hundred babies. The drop of blood that can't lie to statistics, that will be bled out, measured, and put in a crystal tube.

That blood gives those little ones a special light. Wherever I look I 48 see brothers, sisters, who want to break out of their cramped skins, singing with love.

THAT

Marty said yesterday she was surprised that Pat had called the colony a "white establishment," and said she was uncomfortable with some of the people. Marty hadn't noticed any of "that." Had I noticed any of "that"?

I was on guard. So many times if a black person admits discomfort, the white person then says that the black person must be "sensitive— paranoid"—not responding to the present environment, which is safe and friendly, but responding to something in the past. They want to hear that the white people in this environment (themselves) are fine. It's the black person who is crazy.

I said, "It is not something that is done consciously; but most of the white people here have had limited exposure to blacks; there are bound to be great problems in communication. There are some people who hate and fear blacks and don't want to be under the same roof. For

example, Jan told me that Sandra said, when she saw no black people in
the dining room, 'Good. I'm glad there are no black people. After New
York, this is refreshing.'"

Marty said sometimes when she is with black people, she doesn't   52
know what to do; no matter what she does it seems to be the wrong
thing.

She told me how she had invited a black woman, a lawyer, over to
her house for dinner and during the dinner conversation, the guests at
the table started talking about Arabs raising the price of everything in
England. Marty said she didn't think they were saying anything racist,
and even if they were, what did the Arabs have to do with this black
woman? But the woman stood up from the table and said, "I'm sorry, I
find this conversation extremely embarrassing." Marty asked me did I
think the woman was right to do that?

I told her, "Marty, frequently white people who have been made
uncomfortable by something a black person says or does, go to another
black person to try to ease the pain, to feel vindicated. First of all, I
wasn't there, so I don't know what she responded to. Secondly, there
would be no way to find out unless both of you could sit down and
really talk to each other."

Marty said, "That will never happen because she has never asked
me out, and when I called her she was cold."

I said, "Black people don't like pain either."   56

I thought of how sad it is—how a black person and a white person
are not just two individuals who have to decide whether they like each
other, but representatives carrying huge expectations, stereotypes they
must scale like dangerous mountains trying to reach each other.

JAN'S STUDIO

I visited Jan yesterday. I went there feeling greatly honored that she
had asked me, since most artists prize their time alone and don't want to
be disturbed. I had just come into her room, sat down on the mattress,
received a cup of tea, when she took off Mozart and asked me if I
wanted to hear one of her favorite records, a record about Attica. The
hair on the back of my neck stood up. What connection had she made
between me and Attica?

Give her a chance, I thought, calming myself, maybe it's just a
coincidence.

It was atrocious. A white band had taken the departing words of a   60
prisoner and repeated them over and over as if we were certain to catch
the significance. Atonal music played in the background; everything got
louder and crashed to an end.

I sat there feeling the need to receive her gift with enthusiasm. She
waited. The only word that came to my mind was "interesting."

After she took the record off, she started flipping through her collection of classical music to find something else especially for me. "I have a record by Paul Robeson. Would you like to hear that?" Oh God, I thought, it wasn't a coincidence. Give up hope all you who enter.

"No, thank you."

She seemed puzzled and at a loss. Finally, she asked, "There is a   64 picture around here of a black man I liked. I slept with him. Would you like to see that?"

I gaped at her innocent face: Jan, the woman whom I head toward at dinner time because she is not pompous or intimidating, one of the only people here I feel comfortable with.

I told her that just because I am black doesn't mean I am one-dimensional. I am interested in many things, just as she is. I like classical music and know quite a bit about it. She said, "But my other black friends like it when I play those records." She looked genuinely hurt.

I told her all black people are different. She said, "But I've tried so hard. I'm tired of always trying to please them." She looked at me in anger. I was one more proof of her inadequacy. I should have taken whatever was offered and let her feel generous and good.

I left abruptly, sorry for my anger, sorry for what I had learned   68 about her, sorry that she had lost her feeling of closeness, however illusory, to black people—sorry, sorry, sorry—and somehow to blame. I had felt close to her, now I distrusted my instincts, and dreaded a deeper isolation here than ever before.

JAZZ

Now that I am the "known" black here, everything with a tinge of blackness on it is delivered to me.

Mark, the composer, who has been talking about Mozart at the dinner table for days, comes running up to me this afternoon when he sees me on the path, his face lit like a beacon. He doesn't even bother with a greeting.

"Guess what I've been doing today?" he blurts out.

I can't imagine.   72

"I've been writing JAZZ," he presents, as if it is a Cartier jewel on a silver platter.

What am I supposed to say? You must be a really nice white guy? Thanks for taking us seriously?

"Good for you," I answer, and walk on as quickly as possible.

CRAZY THOUGHTS

How beautiful the view from my desk of wild flowers through the   76 cathedral-tall window. I watch the lovely black birds. How kind the lunch on my doorstep, the vegetable torte with white cream sauce, the chocolate cake. How pleasing the flower on the table, the yellow Victorian sofa, the barn of colorful chickens. Kind and specific the words in the office, the locks on my doors. I am treated like a queen. But when the lights go off, I face my fears.

Why is my stomach in knots? Why do I fear that during the night I'll be smothered? I think poison gas will come out of the register. I think the people are monsters, not artists, and during the night they will implant a small radio in my brain. How can I think this? Memory of my father being smothered by a pillow my grandmother put over his head when he was three? In the morning I am ashamed.

I try desperately to make friends, hoping I will actually feel that trust that makes the knots in my stomach loosen. I was terrified to come here; I always feel frightened, except when I'm near home. I trust no one—especially not myself.

I try to do my work. This is a perfect environment. No cleaning. No cooking. I needn't even go to get my lunch; it is placed in a basket outside my door by a man on tiptoes. Wood is stacked. I make a fire. I sit in the sun. I want to be grateful. I am grateful. But the sickness of fear backs up in my throat like phlegm.

In the kitchen the cook speaks softly. I want to sit by her all day and   80
stay away from the roads on which I have been hurt by a word. But she is cooking and I don't want to bother her.

Please, let me not bother anyone or anything. Let me leave the tub without a hair. Let me not speak to those who turn their bodies slightly away from me. I must notice this.

No one can help. Only I, myself. But how can I let go? My face is a mask, like Uncle Tom's, my heart twisted in rage and fear.

AFTER

After I came back I was sick for several weeks. I felt completely wrung out, run down. I had left smiling, beaming, thanking everyone: the kitchen help, the office help, the yard help, everyone for their kindness. My friend came to pick me up. The night before we were to drive home, I sat with her in the restaurant—the first black face I had seen in weeks—and, for an instant, I felt my body falling under me, as if I had slipped under the wheels of a train. I had almost made it until the last minute, keeping a stiff upper lip, and here I was, so close to the end, finally about to lose it.

They were so sorry to see me go they offered me a stay of two more   84
weeks. If I stayed I would prove my desperate bravery to myself. But I declined. I was tired of feeling frightened and wanted to go home where I felt safe.

A Jewish activist friend returned from the colony shortly after and asked me to please write a letter telling them how hard it was to be the only black person there. She had found the same token black during her stay. I postponed it and postponed it. I didn't want to do it. I had been a success—I had gone some place far from home and stayed four weeks without having a nervous breakdown. And they had tried to do everything to please me—cook, clean after me, put wood in my fireplace. I didn't have the heart to tell them I had been miserable and frightened all the time. Besides, I wanted to be a "successful" black person, a person whom they would ask back, a person who would ease the way for other blacks. "See, we're not as bad as you thought."

The day my friend returned from the colony she was full of news about how she had written a letter to the board, sent names and addresses of black artists. The president had talked to her for a half hour about how pleased he was with her efforts. The next day she called me, despondent. Her editor had called her from her large publishing house—they were remaindering her last book. I felt so sorry for her. I told my husband about her efforts at the colony, and how she had come home to this big disappointment. "I'm not surprised," he said. "Somebody from the colony must have gotten to somebody at her publishing house and iced her." I looked at my husband angrily. "Oh, that's silly, I said. One has nothing to do with the other." But I felt the ground under me sinking.   *1988*

William Safire

On Keeping a Diary

Diaries are no longer dear; as the invention of the telephone began the decline of letter writing, the invention of the tape recorder has led to the atrophy of the personal diary. Many of us record our words but few of us record our thoughts.

Why is a diary stereotyped today as the gushing of a schoolgirl or the muttering of a discontented politician, unworthy of the efforts of a busy person? Perhaps because we are out of the habit of writing, or have fallen into the habit of considering our lives humdrum, or have become fearful of committing our thoughts to paper. . . .

Diaries remind us of details that would otherwise fade from memory and make less vivid our recollection. Navy Secretary Gideon Welles, whose private journal is an invaluable source for Civil War historians, watched Abraham Lincoln die in a room across the street from Ford's Theater and later jotted down a detail that puts the reader in the room: "The giant sufferer lay extended diagonally across the bed, which was not long enough for him . . ."

Diaries can be written in psychic desperation, intended to be   4
burned, as a hold on sanity: "I won't give up the diary again," wrote novelist Franz Kafka; "I must hold on here, it is the only place I can." Or written in physical desperation, intended to be read, as in the last entry in Arctic explorer Robert Scott's diary: "For God's sake look after our people."

But what of people who are neither on trial nor freezing to death, neither witnesses to great events nor participants in momentous undertakings? To most of us, a diary presents a terrible challenge: "Write down in me something worth remembering," the neatly dated page says; "prove that this day was not a waste of time."

For people intimidated by their own diaries, here are a handful of rules:

1. *You own the diary, the diary doesn't own you.* There are many days in all our lives about which the less written the better. If you are the sort of person who can only keep a diary on a regular schedule, filling up two pages just before you go to bed, become another sort of person.

2. *Write for yourself.* The central idea of a diary is that you are not   8
writing for critics or for posterity but are writing a private letter to your future self. If you are petty, or wrongheaded, or hopelessly emotional, relax—if there is anybody who will understand and forgive, it is your future self.

3. *Put down what cannot be reconstructed.* You are not a newspaper of record, obligated to record every first time that man walks on the moon. Instead, remind yourself of the poignant personal moment, the remark you wish you had made, your predictions about the outcome of your own tribulations.

4. *Write legibly.* This sounds obvious, but I have pages of scribblings by a younger me who was infuriatingly illiterate. Worse, to protect the innocent, I had encoded certain names and then misplaced my Rosetta Stone; now I will never know who "JW" was in my freshman year at college, and she is a memory it might be nice to have.

Four rules are enough rules. Above all, *write about what got to you that day*, the way a parched John Barrymore did during a trip to Mexico in 1926 when he discovered a bar that to him was an oasis:

"The beer arrived—*draft* beer—in a tall, thin, clean crystal of Grecian proportions, with a creamy head on it. I tasted it. . . . The planets seemed to pause a moment in their circling to breathe a benediction on that Mexican brewer's head. . . . Then the universe went on its wonted way again. Hot Dog! But that *was* a glass of beer!"

That is the art of the diarist in its pure form, unafraid, intimate, 12 important in its insignificance, ringingly free. Who can compare Barrymore's frothy recall with the insecure jottings-down of most of us on little expense ledgers?

Wish I still kept a diary. But you see, I get very tired at the end of the day, and besides, nothing interesting happens any more. And so to bed. . . .   *1974*

2

Ambitions

Frederick Douglass, Learning to Read
and Write

Russell Baker, Gumption

Amy Tan, Two Kinds

As a child I had the usual dreams. I wanted to be handsome, specifically
as cowboy stars in movies were handsome. I wanted to be a killer hero
in a worldwide war. Or if no wars came along (our teachers told us
another was impossible), I wanted at the very least to be a footloose
adventurer. Then I branched out and thought of being a great artist,
and then, getting ever more sophisticated, a great criminal.

My mother, however, wanted me to be a railroad clerk. And that was
her *highest* ambition; she would have settled for less. At the age of
sixteen when I let everybody know that I was going to be a great writer,
my friends and family took the news quite calmly, my mother included.
She did not become angry. She quite simply assumed that I had gone off
my nut. She was illiterate and her peasant life in Italy made her believe
that only a son of the nobility could possibly be a writer. Artistic beauty
after all could spring only from the seedbed of fine clothes, fine food,
luxurious living. So then how was it possible for a son of hers to be an
artist? She was not too convinced she was wrong even after my first two
books were published many years later. It was only after the commercial
success of my third novel [*The Godfather*] that she gave me the title of
poet.

Mario Puzo, from *Choosing a Dream: Italians in Hell's Kitchen*

Someone is always at my elbow reminding me that I am the granddaughter of slaves. It fails to register depression with me. Slavery is sixty
years in the past. The operation was successful and the patient is doing

well, thank you. The terrible struggle that made me an American out of a potential slave said "On the line!" The Reconstruction said "Get set!"; and the generation before said "Go!" I am off to a flying start and I must not halt in the stretch to look behind and weep. Slavery is the price I paid for civilization, and the choice was not with me. It is a bully adventure and worth all that I have paid through my ancestors for it. No one on earth ever had a greater chance for glory. The world to be won and nothing to be lost. It is thrilling to think—to know that for any act of mine, I shall get twice as much praise or twice as much blame. It is quite exciting to hold the center of the national stage, with the specta-tors not knowing whether to laugh or to weep.

Zora Neale Hurston, from *How It Feels to Be Colored Me*

The point is that if we are to have a rich and full life in which all are to share and play their parts, if the American dream is to be a reality, our communal spiritual and intellectual life must be distinctly higher than elsewhere, where classes and groups have their separate interests, habits, markets, arts, and lives. If the dream is not to prove possible of fulfillment, we might as well become stark realists, become once more class-conscious, and struggle as individuals or classes against one an-other. If it is to come true, those on top, financially, intellectually, or otherwise, have got to devote themselves to the "Great Society," and those who are below in the scale have got to strive to rise, not merely economically, but culturally. We cannot become a great democracy by giving ourselves up as individuals to selfishness, physical comfort, and cheap amusements. The very foundation of the American dream of a better and richer life for all is that all, in varying degrees, shall be capable of wanting to share in it. It can never be wrought into a reality by cheap people or by "keeping up with the Joneses." There is nothing whatever in a fortune merely in itself or in a man merely in himself. It all depends on what is made of each. Lincoln was not great because he was born in a log cabin, but because he got out of it—that is, because he rose above the poverty, ignorance, lack of ambition, shiftlessness of character, contentment with mean things and low aims which kept so many thousands in the huts where they were born.

James Truslow Adams, from *The Epic of America*

Personally, I like my little book of poems, "The Black Riders," better than I do "The Red Badge of Courage." The reason is, I suppose, that the former is the more ambitious effort. In it I aim to give my ideas of life as a whole, so far as I know it, and the latter is a mere episode—an amplification. Now that I have reached the goal for which I have been working ever since I began to write, I suppose I ought to be contented; but I am not. I was happier in the old days when I was always dreaming of the thing I have now attained. I am disappointed with success. Like many things we strive for, it proves when obtained to be an empty and a fleeting joy.

Stephen Crane, from *A Letter* (1896)

Frederick Douglass
Learning to Read and Write

I lived in Master Hugh's family about seven years. During this time, I succeeded in learning to read and write. In accomplishing this, I was compelled to resort to various stratagems. I had no regular teacher. My mistress, who had kindly commenced to instruct me, had, in compliance with the advice and direction of her husband, not only ceased to instruct, but had set her face against my being instructed by anyone else. It is due, however, to my mistress to say of her, that she did not adopt this course of treatment immediately. She at first lacked the depravity indispensable to shutting me up in mental darkness. It was at least necessary for her to have some training in the exercise of irrespon-sible power, to make her equal to the task of treating me as though I were a brute.

My mistress was, as I have said, a kind and tender-hearted woman; and in the simplicity of her soul she commenced, when I first went to live with her, to treat me as she supposed one human being ought to treat another. In entering upon the duties of a slaveholder, she did not seem to perceive that I sustained to her the relation of a mere chattel, and that for her to treat me as a human being was not only wrong, but dangerously so. Slavery proved as injurious to her as it did to me. When I went there, she was a pious, warm, and tender-hearted woman. There was no sorrow or suffering for which she had not a tear. She had bread for the hungry, clothes for the naked, and comfort for every mourner that came within her reach. Slavery soon proved its ability to divest her of these heavenly qualities. Under its influence, the tender heart became stone, and the lamblike disposition gave way to one of tiger-like fierceness. The first step in her downward course was in her ceasing to instruct me. She now commenced to practise her husband's precepts. She finally became even more violent in her opposition than her husband himself. She was not satisfied with simply doing as well as he had commanded; she seemed anxious to do better. Nothing seemed to make her more angry than to see me with a newspaper. She seemed to think that here lay the danger. I have had her rush at me with a face made all up of fury, and snatch from me a newspaper, in a manner that fully revealed her apprehension. She was an apt woman; and a little experience soon demonstrated, to her satisfaction, that education and slavery were incompatible with each other.

From this time I was most narrowly watched. If I was in a separate room any considerable length of time, I was sure to be suspected of having a book, and was at once called to give an account of myself. All this, however, was too late. The first step had been taken. Mistress, in teaching me the alphabet, had given me the *inch*, and no precaution could prevent me from taking the *ell*.

The plan which I adopted, and the one by which I was most success- 4 ful, was that of making friends of all the little white boys whom I met in the street. As many of these as I could, I converted into teachers. With their kindly aid, obtained at different times and in different places, I finally succeeded in learning to read. When I was sent of errands, I always took my book with me, and by going one part of my errand quickly, I found time to get a lesson before my return. I used also to carry bread with me, enough of which was always in the house, and to which I was always welcome; for I was much better off in this regard than many of the poor white children in our neighborhood. This bread I used to bestow upon the hungry little urchins, who, in return, would give me that more valuable bread of knowledge. I am strongly tempted to give the names of two or three of those little boys, as a testimonial of the gratitude and affection I bear them; but prudence forbids—not that it would injure me, but it might embarrass them; for it is almost an unpardonable offence to teach slaves to read in this Christian country. It is enough to say of the dear little fellows, that they lived on Philpot Street, very near Durgin and Bailey's ship-yard. I used to talk this matter of slavery over with them. I would sometimes say to them, I wished I could be as free as they would be when they got to be men. "You will be free as soon as you are twenty-one, *but I am a slave for life!* Have not I as good a right to be free as you have?" These words used to trouble them; they would express for me the liveliest sympathy, and console me with the hope that something would occur by which I might be free.

I was now about twelve-years-old, and the thought of being *a slave for life* began to bear heavily upon my heart. Just about this time, I got hold of a book entitled "The Columbian Orator." Every opportunity I got, I used to read this book. Among much of other interesting matter, I found in it a dialogue between a master and his slave. The slave was represented as having run away from his master three times. The dialogue represented the conversation which took place between them, when the slave was retaken the third time. In this dialogue, the whole argument in behalf of slavery was brought forward by the master, all of which was disposed of by the slave. The slave was made to say some very smart as well as impressive things in reply to his master—things which had the desired though unexpected effect; for the conversation resulted in the voluntary emancipation of the slave on the part of the master.

In the same book, I met with one of Sheridan's[1] mighty speeches on and in behalf of Catholic emancipation. These were choice documents to me. I read them over and over again with unabated interest. They gave tongue to interesting thoughts of my own soul, which had frequently flashed through my mind, and died away for want of utterance. The moral which I gained from the dialogue was the power of truth over the conscience of even a slaveholder. What I got from Sheridan was a bold denunciation of slavery, and a powerful vindication of human rights. The reading of these documents enabled me to utter my thoughts, and to meet the arguments brought forward to sustain slavery; but while they relieved me of one difficulty, they brought on another even more painful than the one of which I was relieved. The more I read, the more I was led to abhor and detest my enslavers. I could regard them in no other light than a band of successful robbers, who had left their homes, and gone to Africa, and stolen us from our homes, and in a strange land reduced us to slavery. I loathed them as being the meanest as well as the most wicked of men. As I read and contemplated the subject, behold! that very discontentment which Master Hugh had predicted would follow my learning to read had already come, to torment and sting my soul to unutterable anguish. As I writhed under it, I would at times feel that learning to read had been a curse rather than a blessing. It had given me a view of my wretched condition, without the remedy. It opened my eyes to the horrible pit, but to no ladder upon which to get out. In moments of agony, I envied my fellow-slaves for their stupidity. I have often wished myself a beast. I preferred the condition of the meanest reptile to my own. Anything, no matter what, to get rid of thinking! It was this everlasting thinking of my condition that tormented me. There was no getting rid of it. It was pressed upon me by every object within sight or hearing, animate or inanimate. The silver trump of freedom had roused my soul to eternal wakefulness. Freedom now appeared, to disappear no more forever. It was heard in

---

[1]Richard Brinsley Butler Sheridan (1751–1816), Irish dramatist and orator.—Eds.

every sound, and seen in every thing. It was ever present to torment me with a sense of my wretched condition. I saw nothing without seeing it, I heard nothing without hearing it, and felt nothing without feeling it. It looked from every star, it smiled in every calm, breathed in every wind, and moved in every storm.

I often found myself regretting my own existence, and wishing myself dead; and but for the hope of being free, I have no doubt but that I should have killed myself, or done something for which I should have been killed. While in this state of mind, I was eager to hear anyone speak of slavery. I was a ready listener. Every little while, I could hear something about the abolitionists. It was some time before I found what the word meant. It was always used in such connections as to make it an interesting word to me. If a slave ran away and succeeded in getting clear, or if a slave killed his master, set fire to a barn, or did anything very wrong in the mind of a slaveholder, it was spoken of as the fruit of *abolition.* Hearing the word in this connection very often, I set about learning what it meant. The dictionary afforded me little or no help. I found it was "the act of abolishing"; but then I did not know what was to be abolished. Here I was perplexed. I did not dare to ask anyone about its meaning, for I was satisfied that it was something they wanted me to know very little about. After a patient waiting, I got one of our city papers, containing an account of the number of petitions from the North, praying for the abolition of slavery in the District of Columbia, and of the slave trade between the States. From this time I understood the words *abolition* and *abolitionist,* and always drew near when that word was spoken, expecting to hear something of importance to myself and fellow-slaves. The light broke in upon me by degrees. I went one day down on the wharf of Mr. Waters; and seeing two Irishmen unloading a scow of stone, I went, unasked, and helped them. When we had finished, one of them came to me and asked me if I were a slave. I told him I was. He asked, "Are ye a slave for life?" I told him that I was. The good Irishman seemed to be deeply affected by the statement. He said to the other that it was a pity so fine a little fellow as myself should be a slave for life. He said it was a shame to hold me. They both advised me to run away to the North; that I should find friends there, and that I should be free. I pretended not to be interested in what they said, and treated them as if I did not understand them; for I feared they might be treacherous. White men have been known to encourage slaves to escape, and then, to get the reward, catch them and return them to their masters. I was afraid that these seemingly good men might use me so; but I nevertheless remembered their advice, and from that time I resolved to run away. I looked forward to a time at which it would be safe for me to escape. I was too young to think of doing so immediately; besides, I wished to learn how to write, as I might have occasion to write my own pass. I consoled myself with the hope that I should one day find a good chance. Meanwhile, I would learn to write.

The idea as to how I might learn to write was suggested to me by 8 being in Durgin and Bailey's shipyard, and frequently seeing the ship carpenters, after hewing, and getting a piece of timber ready for use, write on the timber the name of that part of the ship for which it was intended. When a piece of timber was intended for the larboard side, it would be marked thus—"L." When a piece was for the starboard side, it would be marked thus—"S." A piece for the larboard side forward, would be marked thus—"L.F." When a piece was for starboard side forward, it would be marked thus—"S.F." For larboard aft, it would be marked thus—"L.A." For starboard aft, it would be marked thus—"S.A." I soon learned the names of these letters, and for what they were intended when placed upon a piece of timber in the shipyard. I immediately commenced copying them, and in a short time was able to make the four letters named. After that, when I met with any boy who I knew could write, I would tell him I could write as well as he. The next word would be, "I don't believe you. Let me see you try it." I would then make the letters which I had been so fortunate as to learn, and ask him to beat that. In this way I got a good many lessons in writing, which it is quite possible I should never have gotten in any other way. During this time, my copy-book was the board fence, brick wall, and pavement; my pen and ink was a lump of chalk. With these, I learned mainly how to write. I then commenced and continued copying the Italics in *Webster's Spelling Book*, until I could make them all without looking on the book. By this time, my little Master Thomas had gone to school, and learned how to write, and had written over a number of copy-books. These had been brought home, and shown to some of our near neighbors, and then laid aside. My mistress used to go to class meeting at the Wilk Street meeting-house every Monday afternoon, and leave me to take care of the house. When left thus, I used to spend the time in writing in the spaces left in master Thomas's copy-book, copying what he had written. I continued to do this until I could write a hand very similar to that of Master Thomas. Thus, after a long, tedious effort for years, I finally succeeded in learning how to write. *1845*

Russell Baker

Gumption

I began working in journalism when I was eight years old. It was my mother's idea. She wanted me to "make something" of myself and, after a levelheaded appraisal of my strengths, decided I had better start young if I was to have any chance of keeping up with the competition.

The flaw in my character which she had already spotted was lack of "gumption." My idea of a perfect afternoon was lying in front of the radio rereading my favorite Big Little Book, *Dick Tracy Meets Stooge Viller*. My mother despised inactivity. Seeing me having a good time in repose, she was powerless to hide her disgust. "You've got no more gumption than a bump on a log," she said. "Get out in the kitchen and help Doris do those dirty dishes."

My sister Doris, though two years younger than I, had enough gumption for a dozen people. She positively enjoyed washing dishes, making beds, and cleaning the house. When she was only seven she could carry a piece of short-weighted cheese back to the A&P, threaten the manager with legal action, and come back triumphantly with the full quarter-pound we'd paid for and a few ounces extra thrown in for forgiveness. Doris could have made something of herself if she hadn't been a girl. Because of this defect, however, the best she could hope for was a career as a nurse or schoolteacher, the only work that capable females were considered up to in those days.

This must have saddened my mother, this twist of fate that had   4
allocated all the gumption to the daughter and left her with a son who was content with Dick Tracy and Stooge Viller. If disappointed, though, she wasted no energy on self-pity. She would make me make something of myself whether I wanted to or not. "The Lord helps those who help themselves," she said. That was the way her mind worked.

She was realistic about the difficulty. Having sized up the material the Lord had given her to mold, she didn't overestimate what she could do with it. She didn't insist that I grow up to be president of the United States.

Fifty years ago parents still asked boys if they wanted to grow up to be president, and asked it not jokingly but seriously. Many parents who were hardly more than paupers still believed their sons could do it. Abraham Lincoln had done it. We were only sixty-five years from Lincoln. Many a grandfather who walked among us could remember Lincoln's time. Men of grandfatherly age were the worst for asking if you wanted to grow up to be president. A surprising number of little boys said yes and meant it.

I was asked many times myself. No, I would say, I didn't want to grow up to be president. My mother was present during one of these interrogations. An elderly uncle, having posed the usual question and exposed my lack of interest in the presidency, asked, "Well what *do* you want to be when you grow up?"

I loved to pick through trash piles and collect empty bottles, tin   8
cans with pretty labels, and discarded magazines. The most desirable job on earth sprang instantly to mind. "I want to be a garbage man," I said.

My uncle smiled, but my mother had seen the first distressing evidence of a bump budding on a log. "Have a little gumption, Russell," she said. Her calling me Russell was a signal of unhappiness. When she approved of me I was always "Buddy."

When I turned eight years old she decided that the job of starting me on the road toward making something of myself could no longer be safely delayed. "Buddy," she said one day, "I want you to come home right after school this afternoon. Somebody's coming and I want you to meet him."

When I burst in that afternoon she was in conference in the parlor with an executive of the Curtis Publishing Company. She introduced me. He bent low from the waist and shook my hand. Was it true as my mother had told him, he asked, that I longed for the opportunity to conquer the world of business?

My mother replied that I was blessed with a rare determination to   12
make something of myself.

"That's right," I whispered.

"But have you got the grit, the character, the never-say-quit spirit it takes to succeed in business?"

My mother said I certainly did.

"That's right," I said.   16

He eyed me silently for a long pause, as though weighing whether I could be trusted to keep his confidence, then spoke man-to-man. Before taking a crucial step, he said, he wanted to advise me that working for the Curtis Publishing Company placed enormous responsibility on a young man. It was one of the great companies of America. Perhaps the greatest publishing house in the world. I had heard, no doubt, of the *Saturday Evening Post?*

Heard of it? My mother said that everyone in our house had heard of the *Saturday Post* and that I, in fact, read it with religious devotion.

Then doubtless, he said, we were also familiar with those two monthly pillars of the magazine world, the *Ladies Home Journal* and the *Country Gentleman.*

Indeed we were familiar with them, said my mother.   20

Representing the *Saturday Evening Post* was one of the weightiest honors that could be bestowed in the world of business, he said. He was personally proud of being a part of that great corporation.

My mother said he had every right to be.

Again he studied me as though debating whether I was worthy of a knighthood. Finally: "Are you trustworthy?"

My mother said I was the soul of honesty.   24

"That's right," I said.

The caller smiled for the first time. He told me I was a lucky young man. He admired my spunk. Too many young men thought life was all play. Those young men would not go far in this world. Only a young man willing to work and save and keep his face washed and his hair neatly combed could hope to come out on top in a world such as ours. Did I truly and sincerely believe that I was such a young man?

"He certainly does," said my mother.

"That's right," I said.   28

He said he had been so impressed by what he had seen of me that he was going to make me a representative of the Curtis Publishing Company. On the following Tuesday, he said, thirty freshly printed copies of the *Saturday Evening Post* would be delivered at our door. I would place these magazines, still damp with the ink of the presses, in a handsome canvas bag, sling it over my shoulder, and set forth through the streets to bring the best in journalism, fiction, and cartoons to the American public.

He had brought the canvas bag with him. He presented it with reverence fit for a chasuble. He showed me how to drape the sling over my left shoulder and across the chest so that the pouch lay easily accessible to my right hand, allowing the best in journalism, fiction, and cartoons to be swiftly extracted and sold to a citizenry whose happiness and security depended upon us soldiers of the free press.

The following Tuesday I raced home from school, put the canvas bag over my shoulder, dumped the magazines in, and, tilting to the left to balance their weight on my right hip, embarked on the highway of journalism.

We lived in Belleville, New Jersey, a commuter town at the northern 32 fringe of Newark. It was 1932, the bleakest year of the Depression. My father had died two years before, leaving us with a few pieces of Sears, Roebuck furniture and not much else, and my mother had taken Doris and me to live with one of her younger brothers. This was my Uncle Allen. Uncle Allen had made something of himself by 1932. As salesman for a soft-drink bottler in Newark, he had an income of $30 a week; wore pearl-gray spats, detachable collars, and a three-piece suit; was happily married; and took in threadbare relatives.

With my load of magazines I headed toward Belleville Avenue. That's where the people were. There were two filling stations at the intersection with Union Avenue, as well as an A&P, a fruit stand, a bakery, a barber shop, Zuccarelli's drugstore, and a diner shaped like a railroad car. For several hours I made myself highly visible, shifting position now and then from corner to corner, from shop window to shop window, to make sure everyone could see the heavy black lettering on the canvas bag that said THE SATURDAY EVENING POST. When the angle of the light indicated it was suppertime, I walked back to the house.

"How many did you sell, Buddy?" my mother asked.

"None."

"Where did you go?" 36

"The corner of Belleville and Union Avenues."

"What did you do?"

"Stood on the corner waiting for somebody to buy a *Saturday Evening Post*."

"You just stood there?" 40

"Didn't sell a single one."

"For God's sake, Russell!"

Uncle Allen intervened. "I've been thinking about it for some time," he said, "and I've about decided to take the *Post* regularly. Put me down as a regular customer." I handed him a magazine and he paid me a nickel. It was the first nickel I earned.

Afterwards my mother instructed me in salesmanship. I would have 44 to ring doorbells, address adults with charming self-confidence, and break down resistance with a sales talk pointing out that no one, no matter how poor, could afford to be without the *Saturday Evening Post* in the home.

I told my mother I'd changed my mind about wanting to succeed in the magazine business.

"If you think I'm going to raise a good-for-nothing," she replied, "you've got another think coming." She told me to hit the streets with the canvas bag and start ringing doorbells the instant school was out next day. When I objected that I didn't feel any aptitude for salesman-ship, she asked how I'd like to lend her my leather belt so she could whack some sense into me. I bowed to superior will and entered jour-nalism with a heavy heart.

My mother and I had fought this battle almost as long as I could remember. It probably started even before memory began, when I was a country child in northern Virginia and my mother, dissatisfied with my father's plain workman's life, determined that I would not grow up like him and his people, with calluses on their hands, overalls on their backs, and fourth-grade educations in their heads. She had fancier ideas of life's possibilities. Introducing me to the *Saturday Evening Post*, she was trying to wean me as early as possible from my father's world where men left with their lunch pails at sunup, worked with their hands until the grime ate into the pores, and died with a few sticks of mail-order furniture as their legacy. In my mother's vision of the better life there were desks and white collars, well-pressed suits, evenings of reading and lively talk, and perhaps—if a man were very, very lucky and hit the jackpot, really made something important of himself—perhaps there might be a fantastic salary of $5,000 a year to support a big house and a Buick with a rumble seat and a vacation in Atlantic City.

And so I set forth with my sack of magazines. I was afraid of the 48 dogs that snarled behind the doors of potential buyers. I was timid about ringing the doorbells of strangers, relieved when no one came to the door, and scared when someone did. Despite my mother's instructions, I could not deliver an engaging sales pitch. When a door opened I simply asked, "Want to buy a *Saturday Evening Post?*" In Belleville few persons did. It was a town of thirty thousand people, and most weeks I rang a fair majority of its doorbells. But I rarely sold my thirty copies. Some weeks I canvassed the entire town for six days and still had four or five unsold magazines on Monday evening; then I dreaded the coming of Tuesday morning, when a batch of thirty fresh *Saturday Evening Post*s was due at the front door.

"Better get out there and sell the rest of those magazines tonight," my mother would say.

I usually posted myself then at a busy intersection where a traffic light controlled commuter flow from Newark. When the light turned red I stood on the curb and shouted my sales pitch at the motorists.

"Want to buy a *Saturday Evening Post?*"

One rainy night when car windows were sealed against me I came 52 back soaked and with not a single sale to report. My mother beckoned to Doris.

"Go back down there with Buddy and show him how to sell these magazines," she said.

Brimming with zest, Doris, who was then seven years old, returned with me to the corner. She took a magazine from the bag, and when the light turned red she strode to the nearest car and banged her small fist against the closed window. The driver, probably startled at what he took to be a midget assaulting his car, lowered the window to stare, and Doris thrust a *Saturday Evening Post* at him.

"You need this magazine," she piped, "and it only costs a nickel."

Her salesmanship was irresistible. Before the light changed half a 56 dozen times she disposed of the entire batch. I didn't feel humiliated. To the contrary. I was so happy I decided to give her a treat. Leading her to the vegetable store on Belleville Avenue, I bought three apples, which cost a nickel, and gave her one.

"You shouldn't waste your money," she said.

"Eat your apple." I bit into mine.

"You shouldn't eat before supper," she said. "It'll spoil your appetite."

Back at the house that evening, she dutifully reported me for 60 wasting a nickel. Instead of a scolding, I was rewarded with a pat on the back for having the good sense to buy fruit instead of candy. My mother reached into her bottomless supply of maxims and told Doris, "An apple a day keeps the doctor away."

By the time I was ten I had learned all my mother's maxims by heart. Asking to stay up past normal bedtime, I knew that a refusal would be explained with, "Early to bed and early to rise, makes a man healthy, wealthy, and wise." If I whimpered about having to get up early in the morning, I could depend on her to say, "The early bird gets the worm."

The one I most despised was, "If at first you don't succeed, try, try again." This was the battle cry with which she constantly sent me back into the hopeless struggle whenever I moaned that I had rung every doorbell in town and knew there wasn't a single potential buyer left in Belleville that week. After listening to my explanation, she handed me the canvas bag and said, "If at first you don't succeed . . ."

Three years in that job, which I would gladly have quit after the first day except for her insistence, produced at least one valuable result. My mother finally concluded that I would never make something of myself by pursuing a life in business and started considering careers that demanded less competitive zeal.

One evening when I was eleven I brought home a short "composi- 64 tion" on my summer vacation which the teacher had graded with an A. Reading it with her own schoolteacher's eye, my mother agreed that it was top-drawer seventh grade prose and complimented me. Nothing more was said about it immediately, but a new idea had taken life in her mind. Halfway through supper she suddenly interrupted the conversation.

"Buddy," she said, "maybe you could be a writer."

I clasped the idea to my heart. I had never met a writer, had shown no previous urge to write, and hadn't a notion how to become a writer, but I loved stories and thought that making up stories must surely be almost as much fun as reading them. Best of all, though, and what really gladdened my heart, was the ease of the writer's life. Writers did not have to trudge through the town peddling from canvas bags, defending themselves against angry dogs, being rejected by surly strangers. Writers did not have to ring doorbells. So far as I could make out, what writers did couldn't even be classified as work.

I was enchanted. Writers didn't have to have any gumption at all. I did not dare tell anybody for fear of being laughed at in the schoolyard, but secretly I decided that what I'd like to be when I grew up was a writer. *1982*

Amy Tan

Two Kinds

My mother believed you could be anything you wanted to be in America. You could open a restaurant. You could work for the government and get good retirement. You could buy a house with almost no money down. You could become rich. You could become instantly famous.

"Of course, you can be prodigy, too," my mother told me when I was nine. "You can be best anything. What does Auntie Lindo know? Her daughter, she is only best tricky."

America was where all my mother's hopes lay. She had come to San Francisco in 1949 after losing everything in China: her mother and father, her family home, her first husband, and two daughters, twin baby girls. But she never looked back with regret. Things could get better in so many ways.

We didn't immediately pick the right kind of prodigy. At first my 4
mother thought I could be a Chinese Shirley Temple. We'd watch Shirley's old movies on TV as though they were training films. My mother would poke my arm and say, "*Ni kan*. You watch." And I would see Shirley tapping her feet, or singing a sailor song, or pursing her lips into a very round O while saying "Oh, my goodness."

"*Ni kan*," my mother said, as Shirley's eyes flooded with tears. "You already know how. Don't need talent for crying!"

Soon after my mother got this idea about Shirley Temple, she took me to the beauty training school in the Mission District and put me in the hands of a student who could barely hold the scissors without shaking. Instead of getting big fat curls, I emerged with an uneven mass of crinkly black fuzz. My mother dragged me off to the bathroom and tried to wet down my hair.

"You look like Negro Chinese," she lamented, as if I had done this on purpose.

The instructor of the beauty training school had to lop off these 8
soggy clumps to make my hair even again. "Peter Pan is very popular these days," the instructor assured my mother. I now had hair the length of a boy's, with curly bangs that hung at a slant two inches above my eyebrows. I liked the haircut, and it made me actually look forward to my future fame.

In fact, in the beginning I was just as excited as my mother, maybe even more so. I pictured this prodigy part of me as many different images, and I tried each one on for size. I was a dainty ballerina girl standing by the curtain, waiting to hear the music that would send me floating on my tiptoes. I was like the Christ child lifted out of the straw manger, crying with holy indignity. I was Cinderella stepping from her pumpkin carriage with sparkly cartoon music filling the air.

In all my imaginings I was filled with a sense that I would soon become perfect. My mother and father would adore me. I would be beyond reproach. I would never feel the need to sulk, or to clamor for anything.

But sometimes the prodigy in me became impatient. "If you don't hurry up and get me out of here, I'm disappearing for good," it warned. "And then you'll always be nothing."

Every night after dinner my mother and I would sit at the Formica-   12
topped kitchen table. She would present new tests, taking her examples from stories of amazing children that she had read in *Ripley's Believe It or Not* or *Good Housekeeping*, *Reader's Digest*, or any of a dozen other magazines she kept in a pile in our bathroom. My mother got these magazines from people whose houses she cleaned. And since she cleaned many houses each week, we had a grest assortment. She would look through them all, searching for stories about remarkable children.

The first night she brought out a story about a three-year-old boy who knew the capitals of all the states and even of most of the European countries. A teacher was quoted as saying that the little boy could also pronounce the names of the foreign cities correctly. "What's the capital of Finland?" my mother asked me, looking at the story.

All I knew was the capital of California, because Sacramento was the name of the street we lived on in Chinatown. "Nairobi!" I guessed, saying the most foreign word I could think of. She checked to see if that might be one way to pronounce *Helsinki* before showing me the answer.

The tests got harder—multiplying numbers in my head, finding the queen of hearts in a deck of cards, trying to stand on my head without using my hands, predicting the daily temperatures in Los Angeles, New York, and London. One night I had to look at a page from the Bible for three minutes and then report everything I could remember. "Now Jehoshaphat had riches and honor in abundance and . . . that's all I remember, Ma," I said.

And after seeing, once again, my mother's disappointed face, some-   16
thing inside me began to die. I hated the tests, the raised hopes and failed expectations. Before going to bed that night I looked in the mirror above the bathroom sink, and when I saw only my face staring back—and understood that it would always be this ordinary face—I began to cry. Such a sad, ugly girl! I made high-pitched noises like a crazed animal, trying to scratch out the face in the mirror.

And then I saw what seemed to be the prodigy side of me—a face I had never seen before. I looked at my reflection, blinking so that I could see more clearly. The girl staring back at me was angry, powerful. She and I were the same. I had new thoughts, willful thoughts—or, rather, thoughts filled with lots of won'ts. I won't let her change me, I promised myself. I won't be what I'm not.

So now when my mother presented her tests, I performed listlessly, my head propped on one arm. I pretended to be bored. And I was. I got so bored that I started counting the bellows of the foghorns out on the bay while my mother drilled me in other areas. The sound was comforting and reminded me of the cow jumping over the moon. And the next day I played a game with myself, seeing if my mother would give up on me before eight bellows. After a while I usually counted only one bellow, maybe two at most. At last she was beginning to give up hope.

Two or three months went by without any mention of my being a prodigy. And then one day my mother was watching the *Ed Sullivan Show* on TV. The TV was old and the sound kept shorting out. Every time my mother got halfway up from the sofa to adjust the set, the sound would come back on and Sullivan would be talking. As soon as she sat down, Sullivan would go silent again. She got up—the TV broke into loud piano music. She sat down—silence. Up and down, back and forth, quiet and loud. It was like a stiff, embraceless dance between her and the TV set. Finally, she stood by the set with her hand on the sound dial.

She seemed entranced by the music, a frenzied little piano piece 20 with a mesmerizing quality, which alternated between quick, playful passages and teasing, lilting ones.

"*Ni kan*," my mother said, calling me over with hurried hand gestures. "Look here."

I could see why my mother was fascinated by the music. It was being pounded out by a little Chinese girl, about nine years old, with a Peter Pan haircut. The girl had the sauciness of a Shirley Temple. She was proudly modest, like a proper Chinese child. And she also did a fancy sweep of a curtsy, so that the fluffy skirt of her white dress cascaded to the floor like the petals of a large carnation.

In spite of these warning signs, I wasn't worried. Our family had no piano and we couldn't afford to buy one, let alone reams of sheet music and piano lessons. So I could be generous in my comments when my mother badmouthed the little girl on TV.

"Play note right, but doesn't sound good!" my mother complained. 24 "No singing sound."

"What are you picking on her for?" I said carelessly. "She's pretty good. Maybe she's not the best, but she's trying hard." I knew almost immediately that I would be sorry I had said that.

"Just like you," she said. "Not the best. Because you are not trying." She gave a little huff as she let go of the sound dial and sat down on the sofa.

The little Chinese girl sat down also, to play an encore of "Anitra's Tanz," by Grieg. I remember the song, because later on I had to learn how to play it.

Three days after watching the *Ed Sullivan Show* my mother told me 28 what my schedule would be for piano lessons and piano practice. She had talked to Mr. Chong, who lived on the first floor of our apartment building. Mr. Chong was a retired piano teacher, and my mother had traded housecleaning services for weekly lessons and a piano for me to practice on every day, two hours a day, from four until six.

When my mother told me this, I felt as though I had been sent to hell. I whined, and then kicked my foot a little when I couldn't stand it anymore.

"Why don't you like me the way I am?" I cried. "I'm *not* a genius! I can't play the piano. And even if I could, I wouldn't go on TV if you paid me a million dollars!"

My mother slapped me. "Who ask you to be genius?" she shouted. "Only ask you be your best. For you sake. You think I want you to be genius? Hnnh! What for! Who ask you!"

"So ungrateful," I heard her mutter in Chinese. "If she had as much 32 talent as she has temper, she'd be famous now."

Mr. Chong, whom I secretly nicknamed Old Chong, was very strange, always tapping his fingers to the silent music of an invisible orchestra. He looked ancient in my eyes. He had lost most of the hair on the top of his head, and he wore thick glasses and had eyes that always looked tired. But he must have been younger than I thought, since he lived with his mother and was not yet married.

I met Old Lady Chong once, and that was enough. She had a peculiar smell, like a baby that had done something in its pants, and her fingers felt like a dead person's, like an old peach I once found in the back of the refrigerator; its skin just slid off the flesh when I picked it up.

I soon found out why Old Chong had retired from teaching piano. He was deaf. "Like Beethoven!" he shouted to me. "We're both listening only in our head!" And he would start to conduct his frantic silent sonatas.

Our lessons went like this. He would open the book and point to 36 different things, explaining their purpose: "Key! Treble! Bass! No sharps or flats! So this is C major! Listen now and play after me!"

And then he would play the C scale a few times, a simple chord, and then, as if inspired by an old unreachable itch, he would gradually add more notes and running trills and a pounding bass until the music was really something quite grand.

I would play after him, the simple scale, the simple chord, and then just play some nonsense that sounded like a cat running up and down on top of garbage cans. Old Chong would smile and applaud and say, "Very good! But now you must learn to keep time!"

So that's how I discovered that Old Chong's eyes were too slow to keep up with the wrong notes I was playing. He went through the motions in half time. To help me keep rhythm, he stood behind me and pushed down on my right shoulder for every beat. He balanced pennies on top of my wrists so that I would keep them still as I slowly played scales and arpeggios. He had me curve my hand around an apple and keep that shape when playing chords. He marched stiffly to show me how to make each finger dance up and down, staccato, like an obedient little soldier.

He taught me all these things, and that was how I also learned I could be lazy and get away with mistakes, lots of mistakes. If I hit the wrong notes because I hadn't practiced enough, I never corrected myself. I just kept playing in rhythm. And Old Chong kept conducting his own private reverie. 40

So maybe I never really gave myself a fair chance. I did pick up the basics pretty quickly, and I might have become a good pianist at that young age. But I was so determined not to try, not to be anybody different, that I learned to play only the most ear-splitting preludes, the most discordant hymns.

Over the next year I practiced like this, dutifully in my own way. And then one day I heard my mother and her friend Lindo Jong both talking in a loud, bragging tone of voice so that others could hear. It was after church, and I was leaning against a brick wall, wearing a dress with stiff white petticoats. Auntie Lindo's daughter, Waverly, who was my age, was standing farther down the wall, about five feet away. We had grown up together and shared all the closeness of two sisters, squabbling over crayons and dolls. In other words, for the most part, we hated each other. I thought she was snotty. Waverly Jong had gained a certain amount of fame as "Chinatown's Littlest Chinese Chess Champion."

"She bring home too many trophy," Auntie Lindo lamented that Sunday. "All day she play chess. All day I have no time do nothing but dust off her winnings." She threw a scolding look at Waverly, who pretended not to see her.

"You lucky you don't have this problem," Auntie Lindo said with a sigh to my mother. 44

And my mother squared her shoulders and bragged: "Our problem worser than yours. If we ask Jing-mei wash dish, she hear nothing but music. It's like you can't stop this natural talent."

And right then I was determined to put a stop to her foolish pride.

A few weeks later Old Chong and my mother conspired to have me play in a talent show that was to be held in the church hall. By then my parents had saved up enough to buy me a secondhand piano, a black Wurlitzer spinet with a scarred bench. It was the showpiece of our living room.

For the talent show I was to play a piece called "Pleading Child," 48 from Schumann's *Scenes From Childhood*. It was a simple, moody piece that sounded more difficult than it was. I was supposed to memorize the whole thing. But I dawdled over it, playing a few bars and then cheating, looking up to see what notes followed. I never really listened to what I was playing. I daydreamed about being somewhere else, about being someone else.

The part I liked to practice best was the fancy curtsy: right foot out, touch the rose on the carpet with a pointed foot, sweep to the side, bend left leg, look up, and smile.

My parents invited all the couples from their social club to witness my debut. Auntie Lindo and Uncle Tin were there. Waverly and her two older brothers had also come. The first two rows were filled with children either younger or older than I was. The littlest ones got to go first. They recited simple nursery rhymes, squawked out tunes on miniature violins, and twirled hula hoops in pink ballet tutus, and when they bowed or curtsied, the audience would sigh in unison, "*Awww*," and then clap enthusiastically.

When my turn came, I was very confident. I remember my childish excitement. It was as if I knew, without a doubt, that the prodigy side of me really did exist. I had no fear whatsoever, no nervousness. I remember thinking. This is it! This is it! I looked out over the audience, at my mother's blank face, my father's yawn, Auntie Lindo's stiff-lipped smile, Waverly's sulky expression. I had on a white dress, layered with sheets of lace, and a pink bow in my Peter Pan haircut. As I sat down, I envisioned people jumping to their feet and Ed Sullivan rushing up to introduce me to everyone on TV.

And I started to play. Everything was so beautiful. I was so caught 52 up in how lovely I looked that I wasn't worried about how I would sound. So I was surprised when I hit the first wrong note. And then I hit another, and another. A chill started at the top of my head and began to trickle down. Yet I couldn't stop playing, as though my hands were bewitched. I kept thinking my fingers would adjust themselves back, like a train switching to the right track. I played this strange jumble through to the end, the sour notes staying with me all the way.

When I stood up, I discovered my legs were shaking. Maybe I had just been nervous, and the audience, like Old Chong, had seen me go through the right motions and had not heard anything wrong at all. I swept my right foot out, went down on my knee, looked up, and smiled. The room was quiet, except for Old Chong, who was beaming and shouting. "Bravo! Bravo! Well done!" But then I saw my mother's face, her stricken face. The audience clapped weakly, and as I walked back to my chair, with my whole face quivering as I tried not to cry, I heard a little boy whisper loudly to his mother, "That was awful," and the mother whispered back, "Well, she certainly tried."

And now I realized how many people were in the audience—the whole world, it seemed. I was aware of eyes burning into my back. I felt the shame of my mother and father as they sat stiffly through the rest of the show.

We could have escaped during intermission. Pride and some strange sense of honor must have anchored my parents to their chairs. And so we watched it all: The eighteen-year-old boy with a fake moustache who did a magic show and juggled flaming hoops while riding a unicycle. The breasted girl with white makeup who sang an aria from *Madame Butterfly* and got an honorable mention. And the eleven-year-old boy who won first prize playing a tricky violin song that sounded like a busy bee.

After the show the Hsus, the Jongs, and the St. Clairs, from the Joy Luck Club, came up to my mother and father.

"Lots of talented kids," Auntie Lindo said vaguely, smiling broadly.

"That was somethin' else," my father said, and I wondered if he was referring to me in a humorous way, or whether he even remembered what I had done.

Waverly looked at me and shrugged her shoulders. "You aren't a genius like me," she said matter-of-factly. And if I hadn't felt so bad, I would have pulled her braids and punched her stomach.

But my mother's expression was what devastated me: a quiet, blank look that said she had lost everything. I felt the same way, and everybody seemed now to be coming up, like gawkers at the scene of an accident, to see what parts were actually missing.

When we got on the bus to go home, my father was humming the busy-bee tune and my mother was silent. I kept thinking she wanted to wait until we got home before shouting at me. But when my father unlocked the door to our apartment, my mother walked in and went straight to the back, into the bedroom. No accusations. No blame. And in a way, I felt disappointed. I had been waiting for her to start shouting, so that I could shout back and cry and blame her for all my misery.

I had assumed that my talent-show fiasco meant that I would never have to play the piano again. But two days later, after school, my mother came out of the kitchen and saw me watching TV.

"Four clock," she reminded me, as if it were any other day. I was stunned, as though she were asking me to go through the talent-show torture again. I planted myself more squarely in front of the TV.

"Turn off TV," she called from the kitchen five minutes later.   64

I didn't budge. And then I decided. I didn't have to do what my mother said anymore. I wasn't her slave. This wasn't China. I had listened to her before, and look what happened. She was the stupid one.

She came out from the kitchen and stood in the arched entryway of the living room. "Four clock," she said once again, louder.

"I'm not going to play anymore," I said nonchalantly. "Why should I? I'm not a genius."

She stood in front of the TV. I saw that her chest was heaving up and 68 down in an angry way.

"No!" I said, and I now felt stronger, as if my true self had finally emerged. So this was what had been inside me all along.

"No! I won't!" I screamed.

She snapped off the TV, yanked me by the arm and pulled me off the floor. She was frighteningly strong, half pulling, half carrying me toward the piano as I kicked the throw rugs under my feet. She lifted me up and onto the hard bench. I was sobbing by now, looking at her bitterly. Her chest was heaving even more and her mouth was open, smiling crazily as if she were pleased that I was crying.

"You want me to be someone that I'm not!" I sobbed. "I'll never be 72 the kind of daughter you want me to be!"

"Only two kinds of daughters, she shouted in Chinese. "Those who are obedient and those who follow their own mind! Only one kind of daughter can live in this house. Obedient daughter!"

"Then I wish I weren't your daughter. I wish you weren't my mother," I shouted. As I said these things I got scared. It felt like worms and toads and slimy things crawling out of my chest, but it also felt good, that this awful side of me had surfaced, at last.

"Too late change this," my mother said shrilly.

And I could sense her anger rising to its breaking point. I wanted to 76 see it spill over. And that's when I remembered the babies she had lost in China, the ones we never talked about. "Then I wish I'd never been born!" I shouted. "I wish I were dead! Like them."

It was as if I had said magic words. Alakazam!—her face went blank, her mouth closed, her arms went slack, and she backed out of the room, stunned, as if she were blowing away like a small brown leaf, thin, brittle, lifeless.

It was not the only disappointment my mother felt in me. In the years that followed, I failed her many times, each time asserting my will, my right to fall short of expectations. I didn't get straight As. I didn't become class president. I didn't get into Stanford. I dropped out of college.

Unlike my mother, I did not believe I could be anything I wanted to be. I could only be me.

And for all those years we never talked about the disaster at the   80 recital or my terrible declarations afterward at the piano bench. Neither of us talked about it again, as if it were a betrayal that was now unspeakable. So I never found a way to ask her why she had hoped for something so large that failure was inevitable.

And even worse, I never asked her about what frightened me the most: Why had she given up hope? For after our struggle at the piano, she never mentioned my playing again. The lessons stopped. The lid to the piano was closed, shutting out the dust, my misery, and her dreams.

So she surprised me. A few years ago she offered to give me the piano, for my thirtieth birthday. I had not played in all those years. I saw the offer as a sign of forgiveness, a tremendous burden removed.

"Are you sure?" I asked shyly. "I mean, won't you and Dad miss it?"

"No, this your piano," she said firmly. "Always your piano. You only   84 one can play."

"Well, I probably can't play anymore," I said. "It's been years."

"You pick up fast," my mother said, as if she knew this was certain. "You have natural talent. You could be genius if you want to."

"No, I couldn't."

"You just not trying," my mother said. And she was neither angry   88 nor sad. She said it as if announcing a fact that could never be disproved. "Take it," she said.

But I didn't at first. It was enough that she had offered it to me. And after that, every time I saw it in my parents' living room, standing in front of the bay window, it made me feel proud, as if it were a shiny trophy that I had won back.

Last week I sent a tuner over to my parents' apartment and had the piano reconditioned, for purely sentimental reasons. My mother had died a few months before, and I had been getting things in order for my father, a little bit at a time. I put the jewelry in special silk pouches. The sweaters she had knitted in yellow, pink, bright orange—all the colors I hated—I put in mothproof boxes. I found some old Chinese silk dresses, the kind with little slits up the sides. I rubbed the old silk against my skin, and then wrapped them in tissue and decided to take them home with me.

After I had the piano tuned, I opened the lid and touched the keys. It sounded even richer than I remembered. Really, it was a very good piano. Inside the bench were the same exercise notes with handwritten scales, the same secondhand music books with their covers held together with yellow tape.

I opened up the Schumann book to the dark little piece I had played at the recital. It was on the left-hand page, "Pleading Child." It looked more difficult than I remembered. I played a few bars, surprised at how easily the notes came back to me.

And for the first time, or so it seemed, I noticed the piece on the right-hand side. It was called "Perfectly Contented." I tried to play this one as well. It had a lighter melody but with the same flowing rhythm and turned out to be quite easy. "Pleading Child" was shorter but slower; "Perfectly Contented" was longer but faster. And after I had played them both a few times, I realized they were two halves of the same song.   *1989*

3

Moments of Recognition

George Orwell, Shooting an Elephant

Langston Hughes, Salvation

John Updike, A & P

By an epiphany he meant a sudden spiritual manifestation, whether in the vulgarity of speech or of gesture or in a memorable phase of the mind itself. He believed that it was for the man of letters to record these epiphanies with extreme care, seeing that they themselves are the most delicate and evanescent of moments.

James Joyce, from *Stephen Hero*

In most cultures, adulthood is equated with self-reliance and responsibility, yet often Americans do not achieve this status until we are in our late twenties or early thirties—virtually the entire average life-span of a person in a traditional non-Western society. We tend to treat prolonged adolescence as a warm-up for real life, as a wobbly suspension bridge between childhood and legal maturity. Whereas a nineteenth-century Cheyenne or Lakota teenager was expected to alter self-conception in a split-second vision, we often meander through an analogous rite of passage for more than a decade—through high school, college, graduate school.

Though he had never before traveled alone outside his village, the Plains Indian male was expected at puberty to venture solo into the wilderness. There he had to fend for and sustain himself while avoiding the menace of unknown dangers, and there he had absolutely to remain until something happened that would transform him. Every human being, these tribes believed, was entitled to at least one moment of personal, enabling insight.

Michael Dorris, from *Life Stories*

For groups, as well as for individuals, life itself means to separate and to be reunited, to change form and condition, to die and to be reborn. It is to act and to cease, to wait and rest, and then to begin acting again, but in a different way. And there are always new thresholds to cross: the thresholds of summer and winter, of a season or a year, of a month or a night; the thresholds of birth, adolescence, maturity, and old age; the threshold of death and that of the afterlife—for those who believe in it.

Arnold Van Gennep, from *The Rites of Passage*

George Orwell

Shooting an Elephant

In Moulmein, in Lower Burma, I was hated by large numbers of people—the only time in my life that I have been important enough for this to happen to me. I was subdivisional police officer of the town, and in an aimless, petty kind of way anti-European feeling was very bitter. No one had the guts to raise a riot, but if a European woman went through the bazaars alone somebody would probably spit betel juice over her dress. As a police officer I was an obvious target and was baited whenever it seemed safe to do so. When a nimble Burman tripped me up on the football field and the referee (another Burman) looked the other way, the crowd yelled with hideous laughter. This happened more than once. In the end the sneering yellow faces of young men that met me everywhere, the insults hooted after me when I was at a safe distance, got badly on my nerves. The young Buddhist priests were the worst of all. There were several thousands of them in the town and none of them seemed to have anything to do except stand on street corners and jeer at Europeans.

All this was perplexing and upsetting. For at that time I had already made up my mind that imperialism was an evil thing and the sooner I chucked up my job and got out of it the better. Theoretically—and secretly, of course—I was all for the Burmese and all against the oppressors, the British. As for the job I was doing, I hated it more bitterly than I can perhaps make clear. In a job like that you see the dirty work of Empire at close quarters. The wretched prisoners huddling in the stinking cages of the lockups, the grey, cowed faces of the long-term convicts, the scarred buttocks of the men who had been flogged with bamboos—all these oppressed me with an intolerable sense of guilt. But I could get nothing into perspective. I was young and ill-educated and I had had to think out my problems in the utter silence that is imposed on every Englishman in the East. I did not even know that the British Empire is dying, still less did I know that it is a great deal better than the younger empires that are going to supplant it. All I knew was that I was stuck between my hatred of the empire I served and my rage against the evil-spirited little beasts who tried to make my job impossible. With one part of my mind I thought of the British Raj[1] as an unbreakable tyranny, as something clamped down, in *saecula saeculorum*,[2] upon the will of prostrate peoples; with another part I thought that the greatest joy in the world would be to drive a bayonet into a Buddhist priest's guts. Feelings like these are the normal by-products of imperialism; ask any Anglo-Indian official, if you can catch him off duty.

One day something happened which in a roundabout way was enlightening. It was a tiny incident in itself, but it gave me a better glimpse than I had had before of the real nature of imperialism—the real motives for which despotic governments act. Early one morning the subinspector at a police station the other end of town rang me up on the phone and said that an elephant was ravaging the bazaar. Would I please come and do something about it? I did not know what I could do, but I wanted to see what was happening and I got on to a pony and started out. I took my rifle, an old .44 Winchester and much too small to kill an elephant, but I thought the noise might be useful *in terrorem*.[3] Various Burmans stopped me on the way and told me about the elephant's doings. It was not, of course, a wild elephant, but a tame one which had gone "must."[4] It had been chained up, as tame elephants always are when their attack of "must" is due, but on the previous night it had broken its chain and escaped. Its mahout,[5] the only person who could manage it when it was in that state, had set out in pursuit, but had taken the wrong direction and was now twelve hours' journey away, and in the morning the elephant had suddenly reappeared in the town. The Burmese population had no weapons and were quite helpless against it. It had already destroyed somebody's bamboo hut, killed a cow, and raided some fruit stalls and devoured the stock; also it had met the municipal rubbish van and, when the driver jumped out and took to his heels, had turned the van over and inflicted violences upon it.

[1]**Raj**: The British administration.—EDS.
[2]*saecula saeculorum*: Forever and ever (Latin).—EDS.
[3]*in terrorem*: As a warning (Latin).—EDS.
[4]**"must"**: Sexual arousal.—EDS.
[5]**mahout**: Keeper (Hindi).—EDS

The Burmese subinspector and some Indian constables were wait- 4
ing for me in the quarter where the elephant had been seen. It was a very
poor quarter, a labyrinth of squalid bamboo huts, thatched with palm-
leaf, winding all over a steep hillside. I remember that it was a cloudy,
stuffy morning at the beginning of the rains. We began questioning the
people as to where the elephant had gone and, as usual, failed to get any
definite information. That is invariably the case in the East; a story
always sounds clear enough at a distance, but the nearer you get to the
scene of events the vaguer it becomes. Some of the people said that the
elephant had gone in one direction, some said that he had gone in
another, some professed not even to have heard of any elephant. I had
almost made up my mind that the whole story was a pack of lies, when
we heard yells a little distance away. There was a loud, scandalized cry of
"Go away, child! Go away this instant!" and an old woman with a switch
in her hand came round the corner of a hut, violently shooing away a
crowd of naked children. Some more women followed, clicking their
tongues and exclaiming; evidently there was something that the children ought not to have seen. I rounded the hut and saw a man's dead
body sprawling in the mud. He was an Indian, a black Dravidian[6]
coolie, almost naked, and he could not have been dead many minutes.
The people said that the elephant had come suddenly upon him round
the corner of the hut, caught him with its trunk, put its foot on his back,
and ground him into the earth. This was the rainy season and the
ground was soft, and his face had scored a trench a foot deep and a
couple of yards long. He was lying on his belly with arms crucified and
head sharply twisted to one side. His face was coated with mud, the eyes
wide open, the teeth bared and grinning with an expression of unen-
durable agony. (Never tell me, by the way, that the dead look peaceful.
Most of the corpses I have seen looked devilish.) The friction of the
great beast's foot had stripped the skin from his back as neatly as one
skins a rabbit. As soon as I saw the dead man I sent an orderly to a
friend's house nearby to borrow an elephant rifle. I had already sent
back the pony, not wanting it to go mad with fright and throw me if it
smelled the elephant.

The orderly came back in a few minutes with a rifle and five
cartridges, and meanwhile some Burmans had arrived and told us that
the elephant was in the paddy fields below, only a few hundred yards
away. As I started forward practically the whole population of the
quarter flocked out of the houses and followed me. They had seen
the rifle and were all shouting excitedly that I was going to shoot the
elephant. They had not shown much interest in the elephant when he
was merely ravaging their homes, but it was different now that he was

[6]**Dravidian**: A populous Indian group.—EDS.

going to be shot. It was a bit of fun to them, as it would be to an English crowd; besides they wanted the meat. It made me vaguely uneasy. I had no intention of shooting the elephant—I had merely sent for the rifle to defend myself if necessary—and it is always unnerving to have a crowd following you. I marched down the hill, looking and feeling a fool, with the rifle over my shoulder and an ever-growing army of people jostling at my heels. At the bottom, when you got away from the huts, there was a metalled road and beyond that a miry waste of paddy fields a thousand yards across, not yet ploughed but soggy from the first rains and dotted with coarse grass. The elephant was standing eight yards from the road, his left side towards us. He took not the slightest notice of the crowd's approach. He was tearing up bunches of grass, beating them against his knees to clean them and stuffing them into his mouth.

I had halted on the road. As soon as I saw the elephant I knew with perfect certainty that I ought not to shoot him. It is a serious matter to shoot a working elephant—it is comparable to destroying a huge and costly piece of machinery—and obviously one ought not to do it if it can possibly be avoided. And at that distance, peacefully eating, the elephant looked no more dangerous than a cow. I thought then and I think now that his attack of "must" was already passing off; in which case he would merely wander harmlessly about until the mahout came back and caught him. Moreover, I did not in the least want to shoot him. I decided that I would watch him for a little while to make sure that he did not turn savage again, and then go home.

But at that moment, I glanced round at the crowd that had followed me. It was an immense crowd, two thousand at the least and growing every minute. It blocked the road for a long distance on either side. I looked at the sea of yellow faces above the garish clothes—faces all happy and excited over this bit of fun, all certain that the elephant was going to be shot. They were watching me as they would watch a conjuror about to perform a trick. They did not like me, but with the magical rifle in my hands I was momentarily worth watching. And suddenly I realized that I should have to shoot the elephant after all: The people expected it of me and I had got to do it; I could feel their two thousand wills pressing me forward, irresistibly. And it was at this moment, as I stood there with the rifle in my hands, that I first grasped the hollowness, the futility of the white man's dominion in the East. Here was I, the white man with his gun, standing in front of the unarmed native crowd—seemingly the leading actor of the piece; but in reality I was only an absurd puppet pushed to and fro by the will of those yellow faces behind. I perceived in this moment that when the white man turns tyrant it is his own freedom that he destroys. He becomes a sort of hollow, posing dummy, the conventionalized figure of a sahib. For it is the condition of his rule that he shall spend his life in trying to impress the "natives," and so in every crisis he has got to do what the "natives" expect of him. He wears a mask, and his face grows to fit it. I had got to shoot the elephant. I had committed myself to doing it when I sent for the rifle. A sahib has got to act like a sahib; he has got to appear resolute, to know his own mind and do definite things. To come all that way, rifle in hand, with two thousand people marching at my heels, and then to trail feebly away, having done nothing—no, that was impossible. The crowd would laugh at me. And my whole life, every white man's life in the East, was one long struggle not to be laughed at.

But I did not want to shoot the elephant. I watched him beating his   8 bunch of grass against his knees, with that preoccupied grandmotherly air that elephants have. It seemed to me that it would be murder to shoot him. At that age I was not squeamish about killing animals, but I had never shot an elephant and never wanted to. (Somehow it always seems worse to kill a *large* animal.) Besides, there was the beast's owner to be considered. Alive, the elephant was worth at least a hundred pounds; dead, he would only be worth the value of his tusks, five pounds, possibly. But I had got to act quickly. I turned to some experienced-looking Burmans who had been there when we arrived, and asked them how the elephant had been behaving. They all said the same thing: He took no notice of you if you left him alone, but he might charge if you went too close to him.

It was perfectly clear to me what I ought to do. I ought to walk up to within, say, twenty-five yards of the elephant and test his behavior. If he charged, I could shoot; if he took no notice of me, it would be safe to leave him until the mahout came back. But also I knew that I was going to do no such thing. I was a poor shot with a rifle and the ground was soft mud into which one would sink at every step. If the elephant charged and I missed him, I should have about as much chance as a toad under a steamroller. But even then I was not thinking particularly of my own skin, only of the watchful yellow faces behind. For at that moment, with the crowd watching me, I was not afraid in the ordinary sense, as I would have been if I had been alone. A white man mustn't be frightened in front of "natives"; and so, in general, he isn't frightened. The sole thought in my mind was that if anything went wrong those two thousand Burmans would see me pursued, caught, trampled on, and reduced to a grinning corpse like that Indian up the hill. And if that happened it was quite probable that some of them would laugh. That would never do. There was only one alternative. I shoved the cartridges into the magazine and lay down on the road to get a better aim.

The crowd grew very still, and a deep, low, happy sigh, as of people who see the theatre curtain go up at last, breathed from innumerable throats. They were going to have their bit of fun after all. The rifle was a beautiful German thing with cross-hair sights. I did not then know that in shooting an elephant one would shoot to cut an imaginary bar running from ear-hole to ear-hole. I ought, therefore, as the elephant was sideways on, to have aimed straight at his ear-hole; actually I aimed several inches in front of this, thinking the brain would be further forward.

When I pulled the trigger I did not hear the bang or feel the kick—one never does when a shot goes home—but I heard the devilish roar of glee that went up from the crowd. In that instant, in too short a time, one would have thought, even for the bullet to get there, a mysterious, terrible change had come over the elephant. He neither stirred nor fell, but every line of his body had altered. He looked suddenly stricken, shrunken, immensely old, as though the frightful impact of the bullet had paralyzed him without knocking him down. At last, after what seemed a long time—it might have been five seconds, I dare say—he sagged flabbily to his knees. His mouth slobbered. An enormous senility seemed to have settled upon him. One could have imagined him thousands of years old. I fired again into the same spot. At the second shot he did not collapse but climbed with desperate slowness to his feet and stood weakly upright, with legs sagging and head drooping. I fired a third time. That was the shot that did for him. You could see the agony of it jolt his whole body and knock the last remnant of strength from his legs. But in falling he seemed for a moment to rise, for as his hind legs collapsed beneath him he seemed to tower upward like a huge rock toppling, his trunk reaching skywards like a tree. He trumpeted, for the first and only time. And then down he came, his belly towards me, with a crash that seemed to shake the ground even where I lay.

I got up. The Burmans were already racing past me across the mud. 12 It was obvious that the elephant would never rise again, but he was not dead. He was breathing very rhythmically with long rattling gasps, his great mound of a side painfully rising and falling. His mouth was wide open. I could see far down into caverns of pale pink throat. I waited a long time for him to die, but his breathing did not weaken. Finally, I fired my two remaining shots into the spot where I thought his heart must be. The thick blood welled out of him like red velvet, but still he did not die. His body did not even jerk when the shots hit him, the tortured breathing continued without a pause. He was dying, very slowly and in great agony, but in some world remote from me where not even a bullet could damage him further. I felt I had got to put an end to that dreadful noise. It seemed dreadful to see the great beast lying there, powerless to move and yet powerless to die, and not even to be able to finish him. I sent back for my small rifle and poured shot after shot into his heart, and down his throat. They seemed to make no impression. The tortured gasps continued as steadily as the ticking of a clock.

In the end I could not stand it any longer and went away. I heard later that it took him half an hour to die. Burmans were bringing dahs[7] and baskets even before I left, and I was told they had stripped his body almost to the bones by the afternoon.

Afterwards, of course, there were endless discussions about the shooting of the elephant. The owner was furious, but he was only an Indian and could do nothing. Besides, legally I had done the right thing, for a mad elephant has to be killed, like a mad dog, if its owner fails to control it. Among the Europeans opinion was divided. The older men said I was right, the younger men said it was a damn shame to shoot an elephant for killing a coolie, because the elephant was worth more than any damn Coringhee coolie. And afterwards I was very glad that the coolie had been killed; it put me legally in the right and it gave me sufficient pretext for shooting the elephant. I often wondered whether any of the others grasped that I had done it solely to avoid looking a fool.   *1936*

Langston Hughes

Salvation

I was saved from sin when I was going on thirteen. But not really saved. It happened like this. There was a big revival at my Auntie Reed's church. Every night for weeks there had been much preaching, singing, praying, and shouting, and some very hardened sinners had been brought to Christ, and the membership of the church had grown by leaps and bounds. Then just before the revival ended, they held a special meeting for children, "to bring the young lambs to the fold." My aunt spoke of it for days ahead. That night I was escorted to the front row and placed on the mourners' bench with all the other young sinners, who had not yet been brought to Jesus.

My aunt told me that when you were saved you saw a light, and something happened to you inside! And Jesus came into your life! And God was with you from then on! She said you could see and hear and feel Jesus in your soul. I believed her. I had heard a great many old people say the same thing and it seemed to me they ought to know. So I sat there calmly in the hot, crowded church, waiting for Jesus to come to me.

[7]**dahs**: Large knives.—EDS.

The preacher preached a wonderful rhythmical sermon, all moans and shouts and lonely cries and dire pictures of hell, and then he sang a song about the ninety and nine safe in the fold, but one little lamb was left out in the cold. Then he said: "Won't you come? Won't you come to Jesus? Young lambs, won't you come?" And he held out his arms to all us young sinners there on the mourners' bench. And the little girls cried. And some of them jumped up and went to Jesus right away. But most of us just sat there.

A great many old people came and knelt around us and prayed, old 4 women with jet-black faces and braided hair, old men with work-gnarled hands. And the church sang a song about the lower lights are burning, some poor sinners to be saved. And the whole building rocked with prayer and song.

Still I kept waiting to *see* Jesus.

Finally all the young people had gone to the altar and were saved, but one boy and me. He was a rounder's son named Westley. Westley and I were surrounded by sisters and deacons praying. It was very hot in the church, and getting late now. Finally Westley said to me in a whisper: "God damn! I'm tired o' sitting here. Let's get up and be saved." So he got up and was saved.

Then I was left all alone on the mourners' bench. My aunt came and knelt at my knees and cried, while prayers and song swirled all around me in the little church. The whole congregation prayed for me alone, in a mighty wail of moans and voices. And I kept waiting serenely for Jesus, waiting, waiting—but he didn't come. I wanted to see him, but nothing happened to me. Nothing! I wanted something to happen to me, but nothing happened.

I heard the songs and the minister saying: "Why don't you come? My 8 dear child, why don't you come to Jesus? Jesus is waiting for you. He wants you. Why don't you come? Sister Reed, what is this child's name?"

"Langston," my aunt sobbed.

"Langston, why don't you come? Why don't you come and be saved? Oh, Lamb of God! Why don't you come?"

Now it was really getting late. I began to be ashamed of myself, holding everything up so long. I began to wonder what God thought about Westley, who certainly hadn't seen Jesus either, but who was now sitting proudly on the platform, swinging his knickerbockered legs and grinning down at me, surrounded by deacons and old women on their knees praying. God had not struck Westley dead for taking his name in vain or for lying in the temple. So I decided that maybe to save further trouble, I'd better lie, too, and say that Jesus had come, and get up and be saved.

So I got up. 12

Suddenly the whole room broke into a sea of shouting, as they saw me rise. Waves of rejoicing swept the place. Women leaped in the air. My aunt threw her arms around me. The minister took me by the hand and led me to the platform.

When things quieted down, in a hushed silence, punctuated by a few ecstatic "Amens," all the new young lambs were blessed in the name of God. Then joyous singing filled the room.

That night, for the first time in my life but one—for I was a big boy twelve years old—I cried. I cried, in bed alone, and couldn't stop. I buried my head under the quilts, but my aunt heard me. She woke up and told my uncle I was crying because the Holy Ghost had come into my life, and because I had seen Jesus. But I was really crying because I couldn't bear to tell her that I had lied, that I had deceived everybody in the church, that I hadn't seen Jesus, and that now I didn't believe there was a Jesus anymore, since he didn't come to help me.   *1940*

John Updike

A & P

In walks these three girls in nothing but bathing suits. I'm in the third checkout slot, with my back to the door, so I don't see them until they're over by the bread. The one that caught my eye first was the one in the plaid green two-piece. She was a chunky kid, with a good tan and a sweet broad soft-looking can with those two crescents of white just under it, where the sun never seems to hit, at the top of the backs of her legs. I stood there with my hand on a box of HiHo crackers trying to remember if I rang it up or not. I ring it up again and the customer starts giving me hell. She's one of these cash-register-watchers, a witch about fifty with rouge on her cheekbones and no eyebrows, and I know it made her day to trip me up. She'd been watching cash registers for fifty years and probably never seen a mistake before.

By the time I got her feathers smoothed and her goodies into a bag—she gives me a little snort in passing, if she'd been born at the right time they would have burned her over in Salem—by the time I get her on her way the girls had circled around the bread and were coming back, without a pushcart, back my way along the counters, in the aisle between the checkouts and the Special bins. They didn't even have shoes on. There was this chunky one, with the two-piece—it was bright green and the seams on the bra were still sharp and her belly was still pretty pale so I guessed she just got it (the suit)—there was this one, with one of those chubby berry-faces, the lips all bunched together under her nose, this one, and a tall one, with black hair that hadn't quite frizzed right, and one of these sunburns right across under the eyes, and a chin that was too long—you know, the kind of girl other girls think is very "striking" and "attractive" but never quite makes it, as they very well know, which is why they like her so much—and then the third one, that wasn't quite so tall. She was the queen. She kind of led them, the other two peeking around and making their shoulders round. She didn't look around, not this queen, she just walked straight on slowly, on these long white prima-donna legs. She came down a little hard on her heels, as if she didn't walk in her bare feet that much, putting down her heels and then letting the weight move along to her toes as if she was testing the floor with every step, putting a little deliberate extra action into it. You never know for sure how girls' minds work (do you really think it's a mind in there or just a little buzz like a bee in a glass jar?) but you got the idea she had talked the other two into coming in here with her, and now she was showing them how to do it, walk slow and hold yourself straight.

She had on a kind of dirty pink—beige maybe, I don't know— bathing suit with a little nubble all over it and, what got me, the straps were down. They were off her shoulders looped loose around the cool tops of her arms, and I guess as a result the suit had slipped a little on her, so all around the top of the cloth there was this shining rim. If it hadn't been there you wouldn't have known there could have been anything whiter than those shoulders. With the straps pushed off, there was nothing between the top of the suit and the top of her head except just *her*, this clean bare plane of the top of her chest down from the shoulder bones like a dented sheet of metal tilted in the light. I mean, it was more than pretty.

She had sort of oaky hair that the sun and salt had bleached, done   4 up in a bun that was unraveling, and a kind of prim face. Walking into the A & P with your straps down, I suppose it's the only kind of face you *can* have. She held her head so high her neck, coming up out of those white shoulders, looked kind of stretched, but I didn't mind. The longer her neck was, the more of her there was.

She must have felt in the corner of her eye me and over my shoulder Stokesie in the second slot watching, but she didn't tip. Not this queen. She kept her eyes moving across the racks, and stopped, and turned so slow it made my stomach rub the inside of my apron, and buzzed to the other two, who kind of huddled against her for relief, and then they all three of them went up the cat-and-dog-food-breakfast-cereal-macaroni-rice - raisins - seasonings - spreads - spaghetti - soft - drinks - crackers-and-cookies aisle. From the third slot I look straight up this aisle to the meat counter, and I watched them all the way. The fat one with the tan sort of fumbled with the cookies, but on second thought she put the package back. The sheep pushing their carts down the aisle—the girls were walking against the usual traffic (not that we have one-way signs or any-thing)—were pretty hilarious. You could see them, when Queenie's white shoulders dawned on them, kind of jerk, or hop, or hiccup, but their eyes snapped back to their own baskets and on they pushed. I bet you could set off dynamite in an A & P and the people would by and large keep reaching and checking oatmeal off their lists and muttering "Let me see, there was a third thing, began with A, asparagus, no, ah, yes, applesauce!" or whatever it is they do mutter. But there was no doubt, this jiggled them. A few houseslaves in pin curlers even looked around after pushing their carts past to make sure what they had seen was correct.

You know, it's one thing to have a girl in a bathing suit down on the beach, where what with the glare nobody can look at each other much anyway, and another thing in the cool of the A & P, under the fluores-cent lights, against all those stacked packages, with her feet paddling along naked over our checkerboard green-and-cream rubber-tile floor.

"Oh Daddy," Stokesie said beside me. "I feel so faint."

"Darling," I said. "Hold me tight." Stokesie's married, with two babies chalked up on his fuselage already, but as far as I can tell that's the only difference. He's twenty-two, and I was nineteen this April. 8

"Is it done?" he asks, the responsible married man finding his voice. I forgot to say he thinks he's going to be manager some sunny day, maybe in 1990 when it's called the Great Alexandrov and Petrooshki Tea Company or something.

What he meant was, our town is five miles from a beach, with a big summer colony out on the Point, but we're right in the middle of town, and the women generally put on a shirt or shorts or something before they get out of the car into the street. And anyway these are usually women with six children and varicose veins mapping their legs and nobody, including them, could care less. As I say, we're right in the middle of town, and if you stand at our front doors you can see two banks and the Congregational church and the newspaper store and three real-estate offices and about twenty-seven old freeloaders tearing up Central Street because the sewer broke again. It's not as if we're on the Cape, we're north of Boston and there's people in this town haven't seen the ocean for twenty years.

The girls had reached the meat counter and were asking McMahon something. He pointed, they pointed, and they shuffled out of sight behind a pyramid of Diet Delight peaches. All that was left for us to see was old McMahon patting his mouth and looking after them sizing up their joints. Poor kids, I began to feel sorry for them, they couldn't help it.

Now here comes the sad part of the story, at least my family says it's 12 sad, but I don't think it's so sad myself. The store's pretty empty, it being Thursday afternoon, so there was nothing much to do except lean on the register and wait for the girls to show up again. The whole store was like a pinball machine and I didn't know which tunnel they'd come out of. After a while they come around out of the far aisle, around the light bulbs, records at discount of the Caribbean Six or Tony Martin Sings or some such gunk you wonder they waste the wax on, six-packs of candy bars, and plastic toys done up in cellophane that fall apart when a kid looks at them anyway. Around they come, Queenie still leading the way, and holding a little gray jar in her hands. Slots Three through Seven are unmanned and I could see her wondering between Stokes and me, but Stokesie with his usual luck draws an old party in baggy gray pants who stumbles up with four giant cans of pineapple juice (what do these bums *do* with all that pineapple juice? I've often asked myself). So the girls come to me. Queenie puts down the jar and I take it into my fingers icy cold. Kingfish Fancy Herring Snacks in Pure Sour Cream: 49¢. Now her hands are empty, not a ring or a bracelet, bare as God made them, and I wonder where the money's coming from. Still with that prim look she lifts a folded dollar bill out of the hollow at the center of her nubbled pink top. The jar went heavy in my hand. Really, I thought that was so cute.

Then everybody's luck begins to run out. Lengel comes in from haggling with a truck full of cabbages on the lot and is about to scuttle into that door marked MANAGER behind which he hides all day when the girls touch his eye. Lengel's pretty dreary, teaches Sunday school and the rest, but he doesn't miss that much. He comes over and says, "Girls, this isn't the beach."

Queenie blushes, though maybe it's just a brush of sunburn I was noticing for the first time, now that she was so close. "My mother asked me to pick up a jar of herring snacks." Her voice kind of startled me, the way voices do when you see the people first, coming out so flat and dumb yet kind of tony, too, the way it ticked over "pick up" and "snacks." All of a sudden I slid right down her voice into the living room. Her father and the other men were standing around in ice-cream coats and bow ties and the women were in sandals picking up herring snacks on toothpicks off a big glass plate and they were all holding drinks the color of water with olives and sprigs of mint in them. When my parents have somebody over they get lemonade and if it's a real racy affair Schlitz in tall glasses with "They'll Do It Every Time" cartoons stenciled on.

"That's all right," Lengel said. "But this isn't the beach." His repeating this struck me as funny, as if it had just occurred to him, and he had been thinking all these years the A & P was a great big dune and he was the head lifeguard. He didn't like my smiling—as I say he doesn't miss much—but he concentrates on giving the girls that sad Sunday-school-superintendent stare.

Queenie's blush is no sunburn now, and the plump one in plaid, 16 that I liked better from the back—a really sweet can—pipes up, "We weren't doing any shopping. We just came in for the one thing."

"That makes no difference," Lengel tells her, and I could see from the way his eyes went that he hadn't noticed she was wearing a two-piece before. "We want you decently dressed when you come in here."

"We *are* decent," Queenie says suddenly, her lower lip pushing, getting sore now that she remembers her place, a place from which the crowd that runs the A & P must look pretty crummy. Fancy Herring Snacks flashed in her very blue eyes.

"Girls, I don't want to argue with you. After this come in here with your shoulders covered. It's our policy." He turns his back. That's policy for you. Policy is what the kingpins want. What the others want is juvenile delinquency.

All this while, the customers had been showing up with their carts 20 but, you know, sheep, seeing a scene, they had all bunched up on Stokesie, who shook open a paper bag as gently as peeling a peach, not wanting to miss a word. I could feel in the silence everybody getting nervous, most of all Lengel, who asks me, "Sammy, have you rung up their purchase?"

I thought and said "No" but it wasn't about that I was thinking. I go through the punches, 4, 9, GROC. TOT—it's more complicated than you think, and after you do it often enough, it begins to make a little song, that you hear words to, in my case "Hello *(bing)* there, you *(gung)* hap-py pee-pul *(splat)!*"—the *splat* being the drawer flying out. I uncrease the bill, tenderly as you may imagine, it just having come from between the two smoothest scoops of vanilla I had ever known were there, and pass a half and a penny into her narrow pink palm, and nestle the herrings in a bag and twist its neck and hand it over, all the time thinking.

The girls, and who'd blame them, are in a hurry to get out, so I say "I quit" to Lengel quick enough for them to hear, hoping they'll stop and watch me, their unsuspected hero. They keep right on going, into the electric eye; the door flies open and they flicker across the lot to their car. Queenie and Plaid and Big Tall Goony Goony (not that as raw

material she was so bad), leaving me with Lengel and a kink in his
eyebrow.

"Did you say something, Sammy?"

"I said I quit."   24

"I thought you did."

"You didn't have to embarrass them."

"It was they who were embarrasing us."

I started to say something that came out "Fiddle-de-doo." It's a   28
saying of my grandmother's, and I know she would have been pleased.

"I don't think you know what you're saying," Lengel said.

"I know you don't," I said. "But I do." I pull the bow at the back of
my apron and start shrugging it off my shoulders. A couple customers
that had been heading for my slot begin to knock against each other,
like scared pigs in a chute.

Lengel sighs and begins to look very patient and old and gray. He's
been a friend of my parents for years. "Sammy, you don't want to do this
to your mom and dad," he tells me. It's true, I don't. But it seems to me
that once you begin a gesture it's fatal not to go through with it. I fold
the apron, "Sammy" stitched in red on the pocket, and put it on the
counter, and drop the bow tie on top of it. The bow tie is theirs, if you've
ever wondered. "You'll feel this for the rest of your life," Lengel says,
and I know that's true, too, but remembering how he made the pretty
girl blush makes me so scrunchy inside I punch the No Sale tab and the
machine whirs "pee-pul" and the drawer splats out. One advantage to
this scene taking place in summer, I can follow this up with a clean exit,
there's no fumbling around getting your coat and galoshes. I just saun-
ter into the electric eye in my white shirt that my mother ironed the
night before, and the door heaves itself open, and outside the sunshine
is skating around on the asphalt.

I look around for my girls, but they're gone, of course. There wasn't   32
anybody but some young married screaming with her children about
some candy they didn't get by the door of a powder-blue Falcon station
wagon. Looking back in the big windows, over the bags of peat moss and
aluminum lawn furniture stacked on the pavement, I could see Lengel
in my place in the slot, checking the sheep through. His face was dark
gray and his back stiff, as if he'd just had an injection of iron, and my
stomach kind of fell as I felt how hard the world was going to be to me
hereafter.   *1961*

4

Places in the Heart

E. B. White, Once More to the Lake
Gretel Ehrlich, The Solace of Open Spaces
David Bradley, Ringgold Street

This is the most beautiful place on earth.

There are many such places. Every man, every woman, carries in heart and mind the image of the ideal place, the right place, the one true home, known or unknown, actual or visionary. A houseboat in Kashmir, a view down Atlantic Avenue in Brooklyn, a gray gothic farmhouse two stories high at the end of a red dog road in the Allegheny Mountains, a cabin on the shore of a blue lake in spruce and fir country, a greasy alley near the Hoboken waterfront, or even, possibly, for those of a less demanding sensibility, the world to be seen from a comfortable apartment high in the tender, velvety smog of Manhattan, Chicago, Paris, Tokyo, Rio or Rome—there's no limit to the human capacity for the homing sentiment. Theologians, sky pilots, astronauts have even felt the appeal of home calling to them from up above, in the cold black outback of interstellar space.

Edward Abbey, from *The First Morning*

Every continent has its own great spirit of place. Every people is polarized in some particular locality, which is home, the homeland. Different places on the face of the earth have different vital effluence, different vibration, different chemical exhalation, different polarity with different stars: call it what you like. But the spirit of place is a great reality.

D. H. Lawrence, from *The Spirit of Place*

I think the sense of place is as essential to good and honest writing as a logical mind; surely they are somewhere related. It is by knowing where you stand that you grow able to judge where you are. Place absorbs our earliest notice and attention, it bestows on us our original awareness; and our critical powers spring up from the study of it and the growth of experience inside it. It perseveres in bringing us back to earth when we fly too high. It never really stops informing us, for it is forever astir, alive, changing, reflecting, like the mind of man itself. One place comprehended can make us understand other places better. Sense of place gives equilibrium; extended, it is sense of direction too. Carried off we might be in spirit, and should be, when we are reading or writing something good; but it is the sense of place going with us still that is the ball of golden thread to carry us there and back and in every sense of the word to bring us home.

Eudora Welty, from Place in Fiction

E. B. White

Once More to the Lake

One summer, along about 1904, my father rented a camp on a lake in Maine and took us all there for the month of August. We all got ringworm from some kittens and had to rub Pond's Extract on our arms and legs night and morning, and my father rolled over in a canoe with all his clothes on; but outside of that the vacation was a success and from then on none of us ever thought there was any place in the world like that lake in Maine. We returned summer after summer—always on August 1st for one month. I have since become a salt-water man, but sometimes in summer there are days when the restlessness of the tides and the fearful cold of the sea water and the incessant wind that blows across the afternoon and into the evening make me wish for the placidity of a lake in the woods. A few weeks ago this feeling got so strong I bought myself a couple of bass hooks and a spinner and returned to the lake where we used to go, for a week's fishing and to revisit old haunts.

I took along my son, who had never had any fresh water up his nose and who had seen lily pads only from train windows. On the journey

over to the lake I began to wonder what it would be like. I wondered
how time would have marred this unique, this holy spot—the coves and
streams, the hills that the sun set behind, the camps and the paths
behind the camps. I was sure that the tarred road would have found it
out and I wondered in what other ways it would be desolated. It is
strange how much you can remember about places like that once you
allow your mind to return into the grooves that lead back. You
remember one thing, and that suddenly reminds you of another thing. I
guess I remembered clearest of all the early mornings, when the lake
was cool and motionless, remembered how the bedroom smelled of the
lumber it was made of and of the wet woods whose scent entered
through the screen. The partitions in the camp were thin and did not
extend clear to the top of the rooms, and as I was always the first up I
would dress softly so as not to wake the others, and sneak out into the
sweet outdoors and start out in the canoe, keeping close along the shore
in the long shadows of the pines. I remembered being very careful never
to rub my paddle against the gunwale for fear of disturbing the stillness
of the cathedral.

The lake had never been what you would call a wild lake. There
were cottages sprinkled around the shores, and it was in farming country although the shores of the lake were quite heavily wooded. Some of
the cottages were owned by nearby farmers, and you would live at the
shore and eat your meals at the farmhouse. That's what our family did.
But although it wasn't wild, it was a fairly large and undisturbed lake
and there were places in it which, to a child at least, seemed infinitely
remote and primeval.

I was right about the tar: it led to within half a mile of the shore. But   4
when I got back there, with my boy, and we settled into a camp near a
farmhouse and into the kind of summertime I had known, I could tell
that it was going to be pretty much the same as it had been before—I
knew it, lying in bed the first morning, smelling the bedroom, and
hearing the boy sneak quietly out and go off along the shore in a boat. I
began to sustain the illusion that he was I, and therefore, by simple
transposition, that I was my father. This sensation persisted, kept crop-
ping up all the time we were there. It was not an entirely new feeling,
but in this setting it grew much stronger. I seemed to be living a dual
existence. I would be in the middle of some simple act, I would be
picking up a bait box or laying down a table fork, or I would be saying
something, and suddenly it would be not I but my father who was saying
the words or making the gesture. It gave me a creepy sensation.

We went fishing the first morning. I felt the same damp moss
covering the worms in the bait can, and saw the dragonfly alight on the
tip of my rod as it hovered a few inches from the surface of the water. It
was the arrival of this fly that convinced me beyond any doubt that

everything was as it always had been, that the years were a mirage and there had been no years. The small waves were the same, chucking the rowboat under the chin as we fished at anchor, and the boat was the same boat, the same color green and the ribs broken in the same places, and under the floor-boards the same fresh-water leavings and debris— the dead hellgrammite, the wisps of moss, the rusty discarded fishhook, the dried blood from yesterday's catch. We stared silently at the tips of our rods, at the dragonflies that came and went. I lowered the tip of mine into the water, tentatively, pensively dislodging the fly, which darted two feet away, poised, darted two feet back, and came to rest again a little farther up the rod. There had been no years between the ducking of this dragonfly and the other one—the one that was part of memory. I looked at the boy, who was silently watching his fly, and it was my hands that held his rod, my eyes watching. I felt dizzy and didn't know which rod I was at the end of.

We caught two bass, hauling them in briskly as though they were mackerel, pulling them over the side of the boat in a businesslike manner without any landing net, and stunning them with a blow on the back of the head. When we got back for a swim before lunch, the lake was exactly where we had left it, the same number of inches from the dock, and there was only the merest suggestion of a breeze. This seemed an utterly enchanted sea, this lake you could leave to its own devices for a few hours and come back to, and find that it had not stirred, this constant and trustworthy body of water. In the shallows, the dark, water-soaked sticks and twigs, smooth and old, were undulating in clusters on the bottom against the clean ribbed sand, and the track of the mussel was plain. A school of minnows swam by, each minnow with its small individual shadow, doubling the attendance, so clear and sharp in the sunlight. Some of the other campers were in swimming, along the shore, one of them with a cake of soap, and the water felt thin and clear and unsubstantial. Over the years there had been this person with the cake of soap, this cultist, and here he was. There had been no years.

Up to the farmhouse to dinner through the teeming, dusty field, the road under our sneakers was only a two-track road. The middle track was missing, the one with the marks of the hooves and splotches of dried, flaky manure. There had always been three tracks to choose from in choosing which track to walk in; now the choice was narrowed down to two. For a moment I missed terribly the middle alternative. But the way led past the tennis court, and something about the way it lay there in the sun reassured me; the tape had loosened along the backline, the alleys were green with plantains and other weeds, and the net (installed in June and removed in September) sagged in the dry noon, and the whole place steamed with midday heat and hunger and emptiness. There was a choice of pie for dessert, and one was blueberry and one was apple, and the waitresses were the same country girls, there having been no passage of time, only the illusion of it as in a dropped curtain— the waitresses were still fifteen; their hair had been washed, that was the only difference—they had been to the movies and seen the pretty girls with the clean hair.

Summertime, oh summertime, pattern of life indelible, the fade-   8 proof lake, the woods unshatterable, the pasture with the sweetfern and the juniper forever and ever, summer without end; this was the back-ground, and the life along the shore was the design, the cottages with their innocent and tranquil design, their tiny docks with the flagpole and the American flag floating against the white clouds in the blue sky, the little paths over the roots of the trees leading from camp to camp and the paths leading back to the outhouses and the can of lime for sprinkling, and at the souvenir counters at the store the miniature birch-bark canoes and the post cards that showed things looking a little better than they looked. This was the American family at play, escaping the city heat, wondering whether the newcomers in the camp at the head of the cove were "common" or "nice," wondering whether it was true that the people who drove up for Sunday dinner at the farmhouse were turned away because there wasn't enough chicken.

It seemed to me, as I kept remembering all this, that those times and those summers had been infinitely precious and worth saving. There had been jollity and peace and goodness. The arriving (at the beginning of August) had been so big a business in itself, at the railway station the farm wagon drawn up, the first smell of the pine-laden air, the first glimpse of the smiling farmer, and the great importance of the trunks and your father's enormous authority in such matters, and the feel of the wagon under you for the long ten-mile haul, and at the top of the last long hill catching the first view of the lake after eleven months of not seeing this cherished body of water. The shouts and cries of the other campers when they saw you, and the trunks to be unpacked, to give up their rich burden. (Arriving was less exciting nowadays, when you sneaked up in your car and parked it under a tree near the camp and took out the bags and in five minutes it was all over, no fuss, no loud wonderful fuss about trunks.)

Peace and goodness and jollity. The only thing that was wrong now, really, was the sound of the place, an unfamiliar nervous sound of the outboard motors. This was the note that jarred, the one thing that would sometimes break the illusion and set the years moving. In those other summertimes all motors were inboard; and when they were at a little distance, the noise they made was a sedative, an ingredient of summer sleep. They were one-cylinder and two-cylinder engines, and some were make-and-break and some were jump-spark, but they all made a sleepy sound across the lake. The one-lungers throbbed and fluttered, and the twin-cylinder ones purred and purred, and that was a quiet sound too. But now the campers all had outboards. In the daytime, in the hot mornings, these motors made a petulant, irritable sound; at night, in the still evening when the afterglow lit the water, they whined about one's ears like mosquitoes. My boy loved our rented outboard, and his great desire was to achieve singlehanded mastery over it, and authority, and he soon learned the trick of choking it a little (but not too much), and the adjustment of the needle valve. Watching him I would remember the things you could do with the old one-cylinder engine with the heavy flywheel, how you could have it eating out of your hand if you got really close to it spiritually. Motor boats in those days didn't have clutches, and you would make a landing by shutting off the motor at the proper time and coasting in with a dead rudder. But there was a way of reversing them, if you learned the trick, by cutting the switch and putting it on again exactly on the final dying revolution of the flywheel, so that it would kick back against compression and begin reversing. Approaching a dock in a strong following breeze, it was difficult to slow up sufficiently by the ordinary coasting method, and if a boy felt he had complete mastery over his motor, he was tempted to keep it running beyond its time and then reverse it a few feet from the dock. It took a cool nerve, because if you threw the switch a twentieth of a second too soon you could catch the flywheel when it still had speed enough to go up past center, and the boat would leap ahead, charging bull-fashion at the dock.

We had a good week at the camp. The bass were biting well and the sun shone endlessly, day after day. We would be tired at night and lie down in the accumulated heat of the little bedrooms after the long hot day and the breeze would stir almost imperceptibly outside and the smell of the swamp drift in through the rusty screens. Sleep would come easily and in the morning the red squirrel would be on the roof, tapping out his gay routine. I kept remembering everything, lying in bed in the mornings—the small steamboat that had a long rounded stern like the lip of a Ubangi, and how quietly she ran on the moonlight sails, when the older boys played their mandolins and the girls sang and we ate doughnuts dipped in sugar, and how sweet the music was on the water in the shining night, and what it had felt like to think about girls then. After breakfast we would go up to the store and the things were in the same place—the minnows in a bottle, the plugs and spinners disarranged and pawed over by the youngsters from the boys' camp, the Fig Newtons and the Beeman's gum. Outside, the road was tarred and cars stood in front of the store. Inside, all was just as it had always been, except there was more Coca-Cola and not so much Moxie and root beer and birch beer and sarsaparilla. We would walk out with a bottle of pop apiece and sometimes the pop would backfire up our noses and hurt.

We explored the streams, quietly, where the turtles slid off the sunny logs and dug their way into the soft bottom; and we lay on the town wharf and fed worms to the tame bass. Everywhere we went I had trouble making out which was I, the one walking at my side, the one walking in my pants.

One afternoon while we were there at that lake a thunderstorm 12 came up. It was like the revival of an old melodrama that I had seen long ago with childish awe. The second-act climax of the drama of the electrical disturbance over a lake in America had not changed in any important respect. This was the big scene, still the big scene. The whole thing was so familiar, the first feeling of oppression and heat and a general air around camp of not wanting to go very far away. In midafter-noon (it was all the same) a curious darkening of the sky, and a lull in everything that had made life tick; and then the way the boats suddenly swung the other way at their moorings with the coming of a breeze out of the new quarter, and the premonitory rumble. Then the kettle drum, then the snare, then the bass drum and cymbals, then crackling light against the dark, and the gods grinning and licking their chops in the hills. Afterward the calm, the rain steadily rustling in the calm lake, the return of light and hope and spirits, and the campers running out in joy and relief to go swimming in the rain, their bright cries perpet-uating the deathless joke about how they were getting simply drenched, and the children screaming with delight at the new sensation of bathing in the rain, and the joke about getting drenched linking the generations in a strong indestructible chain. And the comedian who waded in carrying an umbrella.

When the others went swimming my son said he was going in too. He pulled his dripping trunks from the line where they had hung all through the shower, and wrung them out. Languidly, and with no thought of going in, I watched him, his hard little body, skinny and bare, saw him wince slightly as he pulled up around his vitals the small, soggy, icy garment. As he buckled the swollen belt suddenly my groin felt the chill of death.   *1941*

Gretel Ehrlich

The Solace of Open Spaces

It's May and I've just awakened from a nap, curled against sagebrush the way my dog taught me to sleep—sheltered from wind. A front is pulling the huge sky over me, and from the dark a hailstone has hit me on the head. I'm trailing a band of two thousand sheep across a stretch of Wyoming badlands, a fifty-mile trip that takes five days because sheep shade up in hot sun and won't budge until it's cool. Bunched together now, and excited into a run by the storm, they drift across dry land, tumbling into draws like water, and surge out again onto the rugged, choppy plateaus that are the building blocks of this state.

The name Wyoming comes from an Indian word meaning "at the great plains," but the plains are really valleys, great arid valleys, sixteen hundred square miles, with the horizon bending up on all sides into mountain ranges. This gives the vastness a sheltering look.

Winter lasts six months here. Prevailing winds spill snowdrifts to the east, and new storms from the northwest replenish them. This white bulk is sometimes dizzying, even nauseating, to look at. At twenty, thirty, and forty degrees below zero, not only does your car not work, but neither do your mind and body. The landscape hardens into a dungeon of space. During the winter, while I was riding to find a new calf, my jeans froze to the saddle, and in the silence that such cold creates I felt like the first person on earth, or the last.

Today the sun is out—only a few clouds billowing. In the east, where the sheep have started off without me, the benchland tilts up in a series of eroded red-earthed mesas, planed flat on top by a million years of water; behind them, a bold line of muscular scarps rears up ten thousand feet to become the Big Horn Mountains. A tidal pattern is engraved into the ground, as if left by the sea that once covered this state. Canyons curve down like galaxies to meet the oncoming rush of flat land.

To live and work in this kind of open country, with its hundred-mile views, is to lose the distinction between background and foreground. When I asked an older ranch hand to describe Wyoming's openness, he said, "It's all a bunch of nothing—wind and rattlesnakes—and so much of it you can't tell where you're going or where you've been and it don't make much difference." John, a sheepman I know, is tall and handsome and has an explosive temperament. He has a perfect intuition about people and sheep. They call him "Highpockets," because he's so long-legged; his graceful stride matches the distances he has to cover. He says, "Open space hasn't affected me at all. It's all the people moving in on it." The huge ranch he was born on takes up much of one county and spreads into another state; to put 100,000 miles on his pickup in three years and never leave home is not unusual. A friend of mine has an aunt who ranched on Powder River and didn't go off her place for eleven years. When her husband died, she quickly moved to town, bought a car, and drove around the States to see what she'd been missing.

Most people tell me they've simply driven through Wyoming, as if there were nothing to stop for. Or else they've skied in Jackson Hole, a place Wyomingites acknowledge uncomfortably because its green beauty and chic affluence are mismatched with the rest of the state. Most of Wyoming has a "lean-to" look. Instead of big, roomy barns and Victorian houses, there are dugouts, low sheds, log cabins, sheep camps, and fence lines that look like driftwood blown haphazardly into place. People here still feel pride because they live in such a harsh place, part of the glamorous cowboy past, and they are determined not to be the victims of a mining-dominated future.

Most characteristic of the state's landscape is what a developer euphemistically describes as "indigenous growth right up to your front door"—a reference to waterless stands of salt sage, snakes, jackrabbits, deerflies, red dust, a brief respite of wildflowers, dry washes, and no trees. In the Great Plains the vistas look like music, like Kyries of grass, but Wyoming seems to be the doing of a mad architect—tumbled and twisted, ribboned with faded, deathbed colors, thrust up and pulled down as if the place had been startled out of a deep sleep and thrown into a pure light.

I came here four years ago. I had not planned to stay, but I couldn't 8 make myself leave. John, the sheepman, put me to work immediately. It was spring, and shearing time. For fourteen days of fourteen hours each, we moved thousands of sheep through sorting corrals to be sheared, branded, and deloused. I suspect that my original motive for coming here was to "lose myself" in new and unpopulated territory. Instead of producing the numbness I thought I wanted, life on the sheep ranch woke me up. The vitality of the people I was working with flushed out what had become a hallucinatory rawness inside me. I threw away my clothes and bought new ones; I cut my hair. The arid country was a clean slate. Its absolute indifference steadied me.

Sagebrush covers 58,000 square miles of Wyoming. The biggest city has a population of fifty thousand, and there are only five settlements that could be called cities in the whole state. The rest are towns, scattered across the expanse with as much as sixty miles between them, their populations two thousand, fifty, or ten. They are fugitive-looking, perched on a barren, windblown bench, or tagged onto a river or a railroad, or laid out straight in a farming valley with implement stores and a block-long Mormon church. In the eastern part of the state, which slides down into the Great Plains, the new mining settlements are boomtowns, trailer cities, metal knots on flat land.

Despite the desolate look, there's a coziness to living in this state. There are so few people (only 470,000) that ranchers who buy and sell cattle know one another statewide; the kids who choose to go to college usually go to the state's one university, in Laramie; hired hands work their way around Wyoming in a lifetime of hirings and firings. And despite the physical separation, people stay in touch, often driving two ee hours to another ranch for dinner.

Seventy-five years ago, when travel was by buckboard or horseback, cowboys who were temporarily out of work rode the grub line—drifting from ranch to ranch, mending fences or milking cows, and receiving in exchange a bed and meals. Gossip and messages traveled this slow circuit with them, creating an intimacy between ranchers who were three and four weeks' ride apart. One old-time couple I know, whose turn-of-the-century homestead was used by an outlaw gang as a relay station for stolen horses, recall that if you were traveling, desperado or not, any lighted ranch house was a welcome sign. Even now, for someone who lives in a remote spot, arriving at a ranch or coming to town for supplies is cause for celebration. To emerge from isolation can be disorienting. Everything looks bright, new, vivid. After I had been herding sheep for only three days, the sound of the camp tender's pickup flustered me. Longing for human company, I felt a foolish grin take over my face; yet I had to resist an urgent temptation to run and hide.

Things happen suddenly in Wyoming, the change of seasons and 12 weather; for people, the violent swings in and out of isolation. But good-naturedness is concomitant with severity. Friendliness is a tradition. Strangers passing on the road wave hello. A common sight is two pickups stopped side by side far out on a range, on a dirt track winding through the sage. The drivers will share a cigarette, uncap their Thermos bottles, and pass a battered cup, steaming with coffee, between windows. These meetings summon up the details of several generations, because, in Wyoming, private histories are largely public knowledge.

Because ranch work is a physical and, these days, economic strain, being "at home on the range" is a matter of vigor, self-reliance, and common sense. A person's life is not a series of dramatic events for which he or she is applauded or exiled but a slow accumulation of days, seasons, years, fleshed out by the generational weight of one's family and anchored by a land-bound sense of place.

In most parts of Wyoming, the human population is visibly outnumbered by the animal. Not far from my town of fifty, I rode into a narrow valley and startled a herd of two hundred elk. Eagles look like small people as they eat car-killed deer by the road. Antelope, moving in small, graceful bands, travel at sixty miles an hour, their mouths open as if drinking in the space.

The solitude in which westerners live makes them quiet. They telegraph thoughts and feelings by the way they tilt their heads and listen; pulling their Stetsons into a steep dive over their eyes, or pigeon-toeing one boot over the other, they lean against a fence with a fat wedge of Copenhagen beneath their lower lips and take in the whole scene. These detached looks of quiet amusement are sometimes cynical, but they can also come from a dry-eyed humility as lucid as the air is clear.

Conversation goes on in what sounds like a private code; a few 16 phrases imply a complex of meanings. Asking directions, you get a curious list of details. While trailing sheep I was told to "ride up to that kinda upturned rock, follow the pink wash, turn left at the dump, and then you'll see the water hole." One friend told his wife on roundup to "turn at the salt lick and the dead cow," which turned out to be a scattering of bones and no salt lick at all.

Sentence structure is shortened to the skin and bones of a thought. Descriptive words are dropped, even verbs; a cowboy looking over a corral full of horses will say to a wrangler, "Which one needs rode?" People hold back their thoughts in what seems to be a dumbfounded silence, then erupt with an excoriating perceptive remark. Language, so compressed, becomes metaphorical. A rancher ended a relationship with one remark: "You're a bad check," meaning bouncing in and out was intolerable, and even coming back would be no good.

What's behind this laconic style is shyness. There is no vocabulary for the subject of feelings. It's not a hangdog shyness, or anything coy— always there's a robust spirit in evidence behind the restraint, as if the earth-dredging wind that pulls across Wyoming had carried its people's voices away but everything else in them had shouldered confidently into the breeze.

I've spent hours riding to sheep camp at dawn in a pickup when nothing was said; eaten meals in the cookhouse when the only words spoken were a mumbled "Thank you, ma'am" at the end of dinner. The silence is profound. Instead of talking, we seem to share one eye. Keenly observed, the world is transformed. The landscape is engorged with detail, every movement on it chillingly sharp. The air between people is charged. Days unfold, bathed in their own music. Nights become hallu-cinatory; dreams, prescient.

Spring weather is capricious and mean. It snows, then blisters with 20 heat. There have been tornadoes. They lay their elephant trunks out in the sage until they find houses, then slurp everything up and leave. I've noticed that melting snowbanks hiss and rot, viperous, then drip into calm pools where ducklings hatch and livestock, being trailed to sum-mer range, drink. With the ice cover gone, rivers churn a milkshake brown, taking culverts and small bridges with them. Water in such an arid place (the average annual rainfall where I live is less than eight inches) is like blood. It festoons drab land with green veins; a line of cottonwoods following a stream; a strip of alfalfa; and, on ditch banks, wild asparagus growing.

I've moved to a small cattle ranch owned by friends. It's at the foot of the Big Horn Mountains. A few weeks ago, I helped them deliver a calf who was stuck halfway out of his mother's body. By the time he was freed, we could see a heartbeat, but he was straining against a swollen tongue for air. Mary and I held him upside down by his back feet, while Stan, on his hands and knees in the blood, gave the calf mouth-to-mouth resuscitation. I have a vague memory of being pneumonia-choked as a child, my mother giving me her air, which may account for my romance with this windswept state.

If anything is endemic to Wyoming, it is wind. This big room of space is swept out daily, leaving a bone yard of fossils, agates, and carcasses in every stage of decay. Though it was water that initially shaped the state, wind is the meticulous gardener, raising dust and pruning the sage.

I try to imagine a world in which I could ride my horse across uncharted land. There is no wilderness left; wildness, yes, but true wilderness has been gone on this continent since the time of Lewis and Clark's overland journey.

Two hundred years ago, the Crow, Shoshone, Arapaho, Cheyenne, 24 and Sioux roamed the intermountain West, orchestrating their movements according to hunger, season, and warfare. Once they acquired horses, they traversed the spines of all the big Wyoming ranges—the Absarokas, the Wind Rivers, the Tetons, the Big Horns—and wintered on the unprotected plains that fan out from them. Space was life. The world was their home.

What was life-giving to Native Americans was often nightmarish to sodbusters who had arrived encumbered with families and ethnic pasts to be transplanted in nearly uninhabitable land. The great distances, the shortage of water and trees, and the loneliness created unexpected hardships for them. In her book *O Pioneers!*, Willa Cather gives a settler's version of the bleak landscape:

> The little town behind them had vanished as if it had never been, had fallen behind the swell of the prairie, and the stern frozen country received them into its bosom. The homesteads were few and far apart; here and there a windmill gaunt against the sky, a sod house crouching in a hollow.

The emptiness of the West was for others a geography of possibility. Men and women who amassed great chunks of land and struggled to preserve unfenced empires were, despite their self-serving motives, unwitting geographers. They understood the lay of the land. But by the 1850s the Oregon and Mormon trails sported bumper-to-bumper traffic. Wealthy landowners, many of them aristocratic absentee landlords, known as remittance men because they were paid to come West and get out of their families' hair, overstocked the range with more than a million head of cattle. By 1885 the feed and water were desperately

short, and the winter of 1886 laid out the gaunt bodies of dead animals
so closely together that when the thaw came, one rancher from Kaycee
claimed to have walked on cowhide all the way to Crazy Woman Creek,
twenty miles away.

Territorial Wyoming was a boy's world. The land was generous with
everything but water. At first there was room enough, food enough, for
everyone. And, as with all beginnings, an expansive mood set in. The
young cowboys, drifters, shopkeepers, schoolteachers, were heroic, lawless, generous, rowdy, and tenacious. The individualism and optimism
generated during those times have endured.

John Tisdale rode north with the trail herds from Texas. He was a 28
college-educated man with enough money to buy a small outfit near the
Powder River. While driving home from the town of Buffalo with a
buckboard full of Christmas toys for his family and a winter's supply of
food, he was shot in the back by an agent of the cattle barons who
resented the encroachment of small-time stockmen like him. The
wealthy cattlemen tried to control all the public grazing land by restrict-
ing membership in the Wyoming Stock Growers Association, as if it
were a country club. They ostracized from roundups and brandings
cowboys and ranchers who were not members, then denounced them as
rustlers. Tisdale's death, the second such cold-blooded murder, kicked
off the Johnson County cattle war, which was no simple good-guy-bad-
guy shoot-out but a complicated class struggle between landed gentry
and less affluent settlers—a shocking reminder that the West was not an
egalitarian sanctuary after all.

Fencing ultimately enforced boundaries, but barbed wire abrogated
space. It was stretched across the beautiful valleys, into the mountains,
over desert badlands, through buffalo grass. The "anything is possible"
fever—the lure of any new place—was constricted. The integrity of the
land as a geographical body, and the freedom to ride anywhere on it,
were lost.

I punched cows with a young man named Martin, who is the great-
grandson of John Tisdale. His inheritance is not the open land that
Tisdale knew and prematurely lost but a rage against restraint.

Wyoming tips down as you head northeast; the highest ground—the
Laramie Plains—is on the Colorado border. Up where I live, the Big
Horn River leaks into difficult, arid terrain. In the basin where it's
dammed, sandhill cranes gather and, with delicate legwork, slice
through the stilled water. I was driving by with a rancher one morning
when he commented that cranes are "old-fashioned." When I asked why,
he said, "Because they mate for life." Then he looked at me with a
twinkle in his eyes, as if to say he really did believe in such things but
also understood why we break our own rules.

In all this open space, values crystalize quickly. People are strong on 32 scruples but tenderhearted about quirky behavior. A friend and I found one ranch hand, who's "not quite right in the head," sitting in front of the badly decayed carcass of a cow, shaking his finger and saying, "Now, I don't want you to do this ever again!" When I asked what was wrong with him, I was told, "He's goofier than hell, just like the rest of us." Perhaps because the West is historically new, conventional morality is still felt to be less important than rock-bottom truths. Though there's always a lot of teasing and sparring, people are blunt with one another, sometimes even cruel, believing honesty is stronger medicine than sympathy, which may console but often conceals.

The formality that goes hand in hand with the rowdiness is known as the Western Code. It's a list of practical dos and don'ts, faithfully observed. A friend, Cliff, who runs a trapline in the winter, cut off half his foot while chopping a hole in the ice. Alone, he dragged himself to his pickup and headed for town, stopping to open the ranch gate as he left, and getting out to close it again, thus losing, in his observance of rules, precious time and blood. Later, he commented, "How would it look, them having to come to the hospital to tell me their cows had gotten out?"

Accustomed to emergencies, my friends doctor each other from the vet's bag with relish. When one old-timer suffered a heart attack in hunting camp, his partner quickly stirred up a brew of red horse liniment and hot water and made the half-conscious victim drink it, then tied him onto a horse and led him twenty miles to town. He regained consciousness and lived.

The roominess of the state has affected political attitudes as well. Ranchers keep up with world politics and the convulsions of the economy but are basically isolationists. Being used to running their own small empires of land and livestock, they're suspicious of big government. It's a "don't fence me in" holdover from a century ago. They still want the elbow room their grandfathers had, so they're strongly conservative, but with a populist twist.

Summer is the season when we get our "cowboy tans"—on the lower 36 parts of our faces and on three fourths of our arms. Excessive heat, in the nineties and higher, sends us outside with the mosquitoes. In winter we're tucked inside our houses, and the white wasteland outside appears to be expanding, but in summer all the greenery abridges space. Summer is a go-ahead season. Every living thing is off the block and in the race: battalions of bugs in flight and biting; bats swinging around my log cabin as if the bases were loaded and someone had hit a home run. Some of the summer's high-speed growth is ominous: larkspur, death camas, and green greasewood can kill sheep—an ironic idea, dying in this desert from eating what is too verdant. With sixteen hours of daylight, farmers and ranchers irrigate feverishly. There are first, second, and third cuttings of hay, some crews averaging only four hours of sleep a night for weeks. And, like the cowboys who in summer ride the night rodeo circuit, nighthawks make daredevil dives at dusk with an eerie whirring sound like a plane going down on the shimmering horizon.

In the town where I live, they've had to board up the dance-hall windows because there have been so many fights. There's so little to do except work that people wind up in a state of idle agitation that becomes fatalistic, as if there were nothing to be done about all this untapped energy. So the dark side to the grandeur of these spaces is the small-mindedness that seals people in. Men become hermits; women go mad. Cabin fever explodes into suicides, or into grudges and lifelong family feuds. Two sisters in my area inherited a ranch but found they couldn't get along. They fenced the place in half. When one's cows got out and mixed with the other's, the women went at each other with shovels. They ended up in the same hospital room but never spoke a word to each other for the rest of their lives.

After the brief lushness of summer, the sun moves south. The range grass is brown. Livestock is trailed back down from the mountains. Water holes begin to frost over at night. Last fall Martin asked me to accompany him on a pack trip. With five horses, we followed a river into the mountains behind the tiny Wyoming town of Meeteetse. Groves of aspen, red and orange, gave off a light that made us look toasted. Our hunting camp was so high that clouds skidded across our foreheads, then slowed to sail out across the warm valleys. Except for a bull moose who wandered into our camp and mistook our black gelding for a rival, we shot at nothing.

One of our evening entertainments was to watch the night sky. My dog, a dingo bred to herd sheep, also came on the trip. He is so used to the silence and empty skies that when an airplane flies over he always looks up and eyes the distant intruder quizzically. The sky, lately, seems to be much more crowded than it used to be. Satellites make their silent passes in the dark with great regularity. We counted eighteen in one hour's viewing. How odd to think that while they circumnavigated the planet, Martin and I had moved only six miles into our local wilderness and had seen no other human for the two weeks we stayed there.

At night, by moonlight, the land is whittled to slivers—a ridge, a 40 river, a strip of grassland stretching to the mountains, then the huge sky. One morning a full moon was setting in the west just as the sun was rising. I felt precariously balanced between the two as I loped across a meadow. For a moment, I could believe that the stars, which were still visible, work like cooper's bands, holding together everything above Wyoming.

Space has a spiritual equivalent and can heal what is divided and burdensome in us. My grandchildren will probably use space shuttles for a honeymoon trip or to recover from heart attacks, but closer to home we might also learn how to carry space inside ourselves in the effortless way we carry our skins. Space represents sanity, not a life purified, dull, or "spaced out" but one that might accommodate intelligently any idea or situation.

From the clayey soil of northern Wyoming is mined bentonite, which is used as a filler in candy, gum, and lipstick. We Americans are great on fillers, as if what we have, what we are, is not enough. We have a cultural tendency toward denial, but, being affluent, we strangle ourselves with what we can buy. We have only to look at the houses we build to see how we build *against* space, the way we drink against pain and loneliness. We fill up space as if it were a pie shell, with things whose opacity further obstructs our ability to see what is already there.

1981

David Bradley

Ringgold Street

Eight-ten in the morning. The 700 block of North Ringgold Street. Bright September sunshine and a hint of breeze; not enough to stir the immature trees struggling to shade the traditional two- and three-story red-brick row houses that line the west side of the street. The street is narrow—two lanes only, one for traffic, one for parking—and short; from a vantage point at this block's northern end, where it intersects Brown, North Ringgold Street seems to vanish at the southern end, dissolving into Aspen Street and a pair of neat Georgian houses, which lie on its far side.

Not that Ringgold Street has entirely eluded modern architecture. The balconied bulk of a high-rise apartment house called The Philadelphian looms behind the Georgians, in eerie domination of the Ringgold Street scene, and on the east side of the street squat twenty futuristic three- and four-story houses joined together in a seamless mass. These houses have a certain uniformity; each is built of brick the color of watered blood, is trimmed in a standard chocolate brown, and has a garage. The clearest variation, apart from height, is that the taller houses—those at the lower, southern end of the block—have square, metal bays on the third story and equally angular dormers on the fourth. The number of doors also varies; the houses at the upper end are duplexes and have two doors (not counting the garage door). Those at the lower end are single-family townhouses, and have only one door. The doors represent not just the sole variation in features the houses offer at street level, but the sole feature as well—on the east side of Ringgold Street there are no windows, no stoops.

A bearded black man turns onto the bottom of Ringgold Street, ducking his head as the No. 48 bus roars by behind him on Aspen. Balding, a bit paunchy, wearing raggedy sweat pants and a T-shirt bearing the faded logo of a recently popular Canadian lager, he is carrying a white plastic shopping bag. A few yards up the block, a pretty, dark-haired woman, her skin tinged with summer tan, leans against the jamb of a row house doorway, spooning yogurt from a container. She appears younger than the bearded black—perhaps thirty to his forty or so—and while she too is clad in sweat pants, hers are neat and set off by a matching sweat shirt. She calls a greeting to the bearded black, who stops to chat. Just then a large dog comes panting off Aspen Street, dragging after him another woman, thin, young, with gold-rimmed glasses, a strong jaw, and bright eyes. She is wearing running shoes but otherwise is dressed for business in skirt and blouse, the latter having broad pink and white stripes. The bearded black barely has time to tease her about looking like she works at Kentucky Fried Chicken before the dog pulls her on up the block to another row house, the bricks of which were at one time painted an unwise vanilla-yellow. The blank and dusty windows on the house's lower floor suggest that renovations are in progress and, as if to confirm that, when the woman reemerges, reshod, she steps gingerly, as if avoiding internal chaos. Behind her comes a man, her match in age and physique, wearing a tan suit and a button-down shirt. Juggling briefcase and keys, he follows her back down the block. As he passes the pair in sweat pants, the bearded black reminds him that he is without a tie; the young man pulls one from an inner pocket as if showing ID, then follows his companion around the corner.

Across the street, two doors, one to a house, the other to a garage,   4 open almost simultaneously. From the garage comes a brand-new Mercedes Benz 190 in a striking shade of blue. The man at the wheel, all but obscured by the tinted glass, waves absently to the sweat-panted pair, his attention first on the maneuvering required to get the Mercedes into the narrow street unscathed, and then on triggering the remote control for his garage door. From the other door comes a woman, a zaftig beauty in a pink summery dress, who, were she not carrying a slim leather briefcase, could be mistaken for the bride in a peasant wedding. She waves to the pair across the street and then heads toward Brown Street, cocking her head to listen for a bus. As she vanishes around the corner another garage opens, this one belonging to one of the duplexes. Through it comes a mustachioed man dressed in tweed jacket, corduroy pants, and a clerical collar, wheeling a bicycle. Closing the garage, he mounts his bike and coasts toward Aspen, calling a greeting to the bearded black and the woman in sweat pants. As if reminded of neglected duty, the woman finishes her yogurt and pulls back inside her house. The bearded black man pauses to contemplate the cryptic message painted on the woman's door: How's THIS COLOR? LET ME KNOW. Then he picks up his bag and makes his way up the block to the duplex from which the mustachioed minister has come. As he opens his door, an elderly woman, her stocky body encased in a cotton housedress, her sturdy legs in stockings knotted at the top, comes out of the row house next door and begins to sweep the steps. As the man goes inside, she favors his closing door with a look of vague suspicion, as if wondering why he is not going to work like everybody else.

In the spring of 1981 I got tired of commuting from New York City, where I was living, to Philadelphia, where I was teaching, so I went looking for an apartment in the Art Museum area. I knew the district was considered ritzy and would probably be overpriced, but I am a runner and was willing to pay for the pleasure of jogging along the Schuylkill. Eventually I rented the upper apartment in a duplex in the 700 block of North Twenty-fourth Street, which was not really in the Art Museum area, but in a less-ritzy district called Fairmount, as the real estate agent candidly admitted just prior to socking me with the Art Museum–style price.

My new apartment was indeed new—part of a two- or three-year-old development the agent called "Aspen Park." It was open and spacious, built on two levels, with the living room occupying half of the building's second floor, and the kitchen, bath, dining area, and two bedrooms taking up all of the third. Though somewhat featureless, it was rescued from sterility by a cunning use of light—8-foot-high windows in the living room, which overlooked the street, a skylight in a sloping ceiling over the dining area, and bedroom windows that overlooked a sort of courtyard. Delighted with the seclusion provided by the floor plan, I set up my desk facing the window in the smaller bedroom. Then I discovered that, while the place was essentially cut off from the sights and sounds of Twenty-fourth Street, it was fully exposed to those of a row of apparently identical houses about 30 yards away, the back windows of which looked onto the courtyard.

I was not so much upset by this intimacy as curious, so I went around the corner to have a look at the street on which those houses fronted. There was not much to see. No businesses or bars, no mailbox. It was an unlovely little street, its corners between bus stops, and its name—Ringgold—was not only unlovely, but also apparently undistinguished, as I discovered when I returned home and tried to look it up in *Street Names of Philadelphia*. I did not think then that, seen from my windows, Ringgold Street might present a different aspect than it did from the corner of Ringgold and Brown.

Let me be clear about this: I never *observed* the people of Ringgold   8 Street. I just saw and heard them, as you catch glimpses and snippets of sound through windows as you walk down a street. But I saw them often enough to begin to think of them as my *real* neighbors. I had no chance to meet them (what was I to do, ring a doorbell and say, "Hi, I've seen you through your bedroom window, and I wanted to get acquainted"?), yet I became so familiar with them I had no choice but to give them names. There was, for example, "The Parisian," a rail-thin man who, each morning at precisely 7:15, would sit, wearing white shirt, tie, and vest, at a glass-topped table (his was a lower unit, with its dining area in the rear), partaking of Blue Mountain coffee (I was sure it was Blue Mountain) and a croissant. There was also "The Sunbather," a lush-figured woman who passed spring and summer mornings in her portion of the courtyard, lying on a chaise lounge in a brilliant white swimsuit. Eventually (and, I suppose, inevitably) I began to react to them emotionally. I had no use for "The Champagne Klansman," who played Lawrence Welk music and whose bedroom was draped with an enormous Confederate flag. I grew fond, though, of "The Working Couple," whose spare bedroom was aburst with books, and who often spent winter evenings reading them while holding hands and lying side by side in a big brass bed.

I never saw the people of Ringgold Street doing anything scandalous; I did not want to. My only interest was to follow their lives, to see how their stories played out over time.

That of The Sunbather was perhaps the most conventionally titillating; she acquired a lover. I never saw him, but on several occasions I glimpsed a man's jacket tossed carelessly across her bed, and during my second summer noted sunny mornings when she failed to appear, as if she had spent the night elsewhere. The Parisian just . . . loosened up a little, started wearing colored shirts and apparently acquired a taste for the music of Merle Haggard, which he played at an increasingly confident volume. The Champagne Klansman seemed to be constantly in financial difficulties; I often saw him late at night at the desk in his spare bedroom, working with a calculator and a yellow legal pad, the pages of which he kept balling up and throwing away. Lots of things, it seemed, were happening on Ringgold Street; in fact, I would have begun to feel that life was passing me by had it not been for The Working Couple, whose lives seemed as unchanging as my own. Then one rainy but warm October night, as I lay on the verge of sleep, I heard what at first seemed to be a cry of pain, or a call for help. I sat up in bed, my heart pounding, wondering who was hurt or in trouble. And then it came to me what that sound had been: a woman's love cry. Not a rutting mutter or a chanting of explicit words, but a high, pure call of ecstasy that went beyond ecstasy, a sound you simply could not describe with any but reverent tones. It was not the first time I had heard people making love in Aspen Park, but it was the first and only time I heard anything so intense and *loving*. For a while I lay there wondering which apartment it had come from. Then, somehow, I knew. And I also knew that, from that moment on, Ringgold Street would never again seem unlovely.

Noon on Ringgold Street. The breeze has died. A few clouds cross the sun—a pity, since the street is so narrow and has few hours of direct light. It has plenty of sound, though: the chiming of the carillons of the neighborhood churches; the chatter of a group of youngsters carrying books and dressed in green parochial school uniforms who come up the block on their way to homes in other streets; a bit of subdued bonging as a few of the children ring the doorbells of Aspen Park; the haunting music of a bassoon that drifts out through an upper-story window of one of the row houses and hangs in the air like tangy smoke. Behind the children comes a bespectacled black woman with a harried look and bulging mailbag. She eyes Aspen Park as if it were an enemy, and, unlike the children, turns her attention first to the older houses.

As the mail carrier nears the middle of the block, the bearded black, 12 clad in running shoes and shorts, emerges from his duplex and begins to do stretching exercises. At the same time, a rather plain but vital-looking woman, dressed in tailored slacks and matching sweater and leading a child of two or three emerges from the duplex next door. The bearded black suspends his stretching to greet the woman and to beam almost parentally at the toddler. The mother responds, but gives a more forceful greeting to the mail carrier, whom she accosts with a complaint regarding irregularities in delivery. The mail carrier sighs and makes a weary note. The bearded black completes his stretching and sets off at an easy jog. Two-thirds of the way down the block he passes another mother, this one a bit younger, a bit hipper, and dressed a bit more haphazardly, who is struggling her way out of a row house while encumbered with a toddler, an infant, a stroller, a huge box of Huggies. Across from this young mother, the door of a townhouse opens and a small dog comes trotting out. He eyes the passing black, then sets off in pursuit. An older woman, perhaps in her sixties, with tastefully applied makeup and carefully coiffed hair, steps into the street, calling after the departing canine: "Pooper. Here, Pooper." The dog trots to the bottom of the street, where he stands gazing after the departing black. Satisfied that the man has no intention of returning, the dog emits one short triumphant bark and then lives up to his name.

Fate brought me to live on Ringgold Street. At least, it wasn't planning. I had moved out of my apartment on Twenty-fourth Street, had traveled around the world, had lived in Virginia and in California, before events brought me back to Philadelphia. Even then, although I wanted to buy a house in Fairmount, I never thought of Ringgold Street. But something made me walk by on Brown Street, and there was a FOR SALE sign on an Aspen Park duplex, and suddenly I saw *myself* living on Ringgold Street. I think the realtor saw it, too; I was fortunate that she did not take unfair advantage. After the closing, I got a couple of bottles of Moosehead and sat in what was suddenly *my* living room, looking out on what was suddenly *my* street. Bassoon music floated inexplicably in the air. I felt like Jonah, fresh from the whale's belly, alive and free upon his destined shore.

But this Ringgold Street was a different creature than the one I had seen from Twenty-fourth, for the quirks of architecture that had afforded me my old insights were reversed; I could see into Twenty-fourth Street apartments—into, in fact, the one where I used to live—but into none on Ringgold. Living on Ringgold Street made it impossible for me to experience it as I had before. Of course I could have shifted my vantage point from my study to my living room, which would have allowed me to look into the row houses across the street, but that would have been an actual prying into people's lives. I had no desire to do that, especially considering the effects of the architecture. From my windows on Twenty-fourth Street, I had looked into houses of identical height and similar floor plan, so there was nothing I could see of others that they could not see of me. But from my upstairs living room on Ringgold, I would have been looking down into the bedrooms of the row houses; the angle and the differing nature of the rooms would have made it unfair.

And it wasn't very sporting, either. Because while the security-conscious design of Aspen Park made finding out what went on inside the houses a challenge, almost a dare, these row houses were, well, *trusting.* They had windows at street level; *anybody* could look in. They had stoops on which people were *supposed* to stand to exchange information. Then, too, a lot of the residents of the row houses were older folk who, although they had probably spent their lives gossiping, being nosy, butting into each other's business, had done so to people whose religion and ethnic identity and values they shared; it felt wrong for me, a raw newcomer of doubtful religion and an ethnic identity that made some of them uneasy, to sit in my house, rendered invulnerable by architecture, looking down on their lives. Perhaps the first important thing that happened to me on Ringgold Street was realizing something that, in the wider context of Twenty-fourth Street, had escaped me: If you anthropomorphized the houses of Aspen Park, you would see that they were turning their backs on the row houses on the opposite side of the street. And if you considered the placement of the garage doors, it was equally obvious that it was not the tops of their backs, either.

Back when I was growing up, my family subscribed to *The Reader's* 16 *Digest.* I hated the *Digest,* but loved the puzzles it sometimes had, in which you would be given clues about a block of houses and then you would deduce the missing information, like who smoked Old Golds, who drank orange juice, and who owned the zebra? Once I realized I could no longer catch glimpses of Ringgold Street, I turned it into the setting for one of those puzzles. I even named it: *Who Plays the Bassoon?*

I didn't immediately attack that ultimate mystery, however; I started with the cars. Who, I wondered, owned the red Lancia with the ripped top, and did they live in a townhouse, a row house, or a duplex? Was the owner of the brown Toyota with the Drexel U sticker and the art supplies scattered over the back seat the same person who walked the big dog? Did the little dog belong to the driver of the dirty white Cadillac, or perhaps the marine-blue Mercedes? And who drove the taxicab?

I found some clues in the garbage set out carefully each Thursday night, which I could easily match up with the houses to learn who paid top dollar at Klein's Supermarket at the Philadelphian (which gave out white plastic shopping bags), and who made the trek north to Girard Avenue and the less expensive Brewerytown Shop 'n Bag. I learned who subscribed to the *Inky* and/or the *Jewish Exponent,* who read *Sports Illustrated, Newsweek, Time,* who drank Moosehead, Schaeffer, Piels, and who was watching his waistline by drinking Budweiser Light.

It was more than a game, it was a kind of sociological investigation. The cars supported case studies. When the taxicab disappeared, I decided that somebody no longer needed an extra job to get along. And when the brown Toyota with the Drexel sticker was replaced by a gray Cressida, I rejoiced that the artist had graduated and got a good job. The garbage was a barometer of trends. The Aspen Park duplexes, for example, tended toward transcience; there you found your cartons emblazoned with the logo of North American, Allied, Mayflower Van

Lines, and almost never saw discarded the boxes from stereo equipment or TVs. The townhouses to the south were a lot more permanent; folks there did not hesitate to throw out the box. The west side of Ringgold Street bought American, the east side foreign. The east side had Cuisinarts, the west side Mixmasters and Osterizers. The west side was not into high tech, the east side . . . well, they had cordless phones, home computers, answering machines, remote-controlled VCRs. Which might have made me think that the east side was cold and mechanical, if I had not also learned that the east side had the ghosts.

The first hint of ghosts I saw I did not recognize as such—I was 20 concentrating on cars and trash and this was just a note pasted to the door of a duplex instructing the mail carrier: "Do not deliver mail for so-and-so, so-and-so, or so-and-so." I did not know then that, unlike Twenty-fourth Street, whose mail carrier has for years been a learned gentleman named Frederick who knows his route's residents by sight as well as by name, Ringgold Street seems never to have had the pleasure of a permanent mail carrier, but has instead endured a succession of temporary assignees. This (combined with the Poplar Street post office's blend of inefficiency and arrogant bureaucracy) has produced poltergeists at Ringgold Street's transient upper end. Never mind what forms you file, once you have lived on Ringgold Street in body you tend to linger there in third-class mail.

My house, I discovered, has three ghosts. There is Ira, who, fittingly, had (has?) an IRA with Delaware Cash Reserve and subscribed at one time to the *Jewish Exponent* and several business magazines. There is Leesa, who owned property in Avalon, New Jersey, about which the Avalon authorities seem concerned—at least, they send envelopes with warnings printed on them—and who seemed to have something to do with fashion or design, if you could believe the people who sent her cards announcing gala openings. And then there is Mary, who once had a subscription to *Better Homes and Gardens*, which the publisher seems anxious to have her renew.

For a while I took mail for Ira, Leesa, and Mary, wrote "Not at this address" on it and dropped it into a mailbox, but half the time the same mail was redelivered, and I always got more. For a while I just kept it. Finally I realized I should do what Ira, Leesa, and Mary would probably have done: throw it away. (If Mary wanted to renew her subscription she would have done it, don't you think?) After that I began to enjoy getting mail for Ira, Leesa, and Mary, began to wonder what they looked like, began to wonder if I had ever glimpsed one of them when I lived on Twenty-fourth Street. I decided Ira was, of course, a nice Jewish boy, careful to save his money and date only Jewish girls. Mary . . . well, what can you say about a woman who *ever* subscribed to *Better Homes and Gardens*, even if she didn't renew? Ah, but Leesa. There was a woman you might like to meet—artistic but businesslike, and not intimidated by the dunning of authority. Of course it was all a game. Until one night, when I was sitting in my living room sipping gin and listening to the BSO on WFLN and I got this strange, wonderful feeling that I was not alone. "Ira?" I said. There was no reply. Well, who needed male companionship anyway? "Leesa?" I whispered, my heart pounding in anticipation. Still no reply. Just my luck, I thought. Mary.

Six P.M. on Ringgold Street. The clouds have thickened and the street is darker than the hour and season warrant. The bassoon music still drifts between the houses, adding haunting timbre to the growing gloom. The bearded black man comes out of his house dressed in a sports jacket and blue jeans and carrying a battered leather shoulder bag. He pauses to listen to the sound of the woodwind but then, harkening to the roar of a bus Center City–bound on Brown, trots toward the corner, slowing only to wave in the general direction of a gray sedan that turns off Brown Street and picks its way down the block, parking at last before the row house with the cryptic door. The sweat-suited woman, dressed now in a neat navy suit, climbs out, juggling an artist's portfolio and a purse. The blue Mercedes appears at the upper end, glides down almost soundlessly, then slips into the garage that opens magically before it.

When I had spent a year living on Ringgold Street, I decided that all 24 my games were at least silly and probably evidence of a serious personality disorder. Who, I asked myself, wants to know his neighbors by their garbage or their vehicles? What decent person looks in other peoples' windows, for that matter? And so I tried to get to know about my neighbors by asking questions. I got answers, of course—I was not asking for scandal, simply information—but they seemed, well, *wrong*. Still, I persisted. Until the night I met the bassoonist.

It was a Thursday, and I was coming home late from a night class. I had the seat behind him on the 48 bus. I *knew* he was the bassoonist, although he carried no instrument, but when he got off at Twenty-fourth Street and headed east I trailed him silently, unwilling to commit myself lest I myself be committed. Just as I expected, he turned up Ringgold Street and stopped before the proper door. I stepped out of the shadows and asked if he was the person who played the bassoon. He admitted, a little defensively, that he was. He said he hoped the sound had not disturbed me, and went on to explain apologetically that it was audition season and he needed to practice a lot. I assured him that his playing gave me only pleasure, but I didn't think he believed me.

Later I sat feeling guilty, wondering if the bassoonist would from now on worry about me listening and perhaps not practice as diligently, or fail to give a phrase its proper emphasis for fear of disturbing. And what of me? Would the sense of magic and permanence I felt when I heard that music floating over Ringgold Street vanish now that I knew that the sound was in part generated by the dutifulness of practice and the anxiety of a looming audition?

This was not simply a matter of bassoonists. It came down to the question of where I wanted to live: in a real place with real people or in a place that I loved but which was largely fantasy. I was not deluding myself. I knew, had always known, that Ringgold Street's reality was less magical than I imagined it; knew that The Working Couple's child was probably conceived not in a pure moment of elemental passion, but a few nights before, when the carefully plotted chart of body temperature indicated that the hour of ovulation was at hand; that the Champagne Klansman belonged to the ACLU; that the owner of the jacket in The Sunbather's bedroom was a brother, not a lover; that the Parisian had been drinking Maxwell House; that all those folks had left Ringgold Street long ago, and existed there now only as ghostly third-class mail. But I didn't like it that way. I didn't really believe it, either. I believed that Ringgold Street was magic, even as it was mundane; that if you kept your eyes and ears open to it you could learn almost anything about people whose lives would be fascinating if you took the time to think about them.

And so I resolved to leave off questioning; to leave reality alone. To 28 watch the cars and the garbage, to note the little details that make people people instead of statistics: how they wear their hair, what beer they drink, and the silly names they give their dogs.

Eleven P.M. on Ringgold Street. Rain is falling, and light from the streetlamps glimmers dimly on the wet pavement and the cars parked tightly along the west side of the street. From the row houses, cheery light; the glow of incandescent bulbs, the blue flicker of TVs. Aspen Park is dark, almost menacing, closed, aloof. But before each Ringgold Street home, be it row house, townhouse, or duplex, is the garbage, bagged or boxed or cloaked in plastic, waiting for collection, full of clues. And over it all hovers the haunting sound of a confident, un-muffled bassoon.   *1985*

5

The Power of Names

Maya Angelou, "What's Your Name, Girl?"
Mary McCarthy, Names
Paul Gruchow, Seeing the Elephant

JULIET: O Romeo, Romeo! wherefore art thou Romeo?
Deny thy father, and refuse thy name;
Or, if thou wilt not, be but sworn my love,
And I'll no longer be a Capulet.
ROMEO: [*Aside.*] Shall I hear more, or shall I speak at
this?
JULIET: 'Tis but thy name that is my enemy;
Thou art thyself though, not a Montague.
What's Montague? it is nor hand, nor foot,
Nor arm, nor face, nor any other part
Belonging to a man. O! be some other name:
What's in a name? that which we call a rose
By any other name would smell as sweet;
So Romeo would, were he not Romeo call'd,
Retain that dear perfection which he owes
Without that title. Romeo, doff thy name;
And for that name, which is no part of thee,
Take all myself.
ROMEO: I take thee at thy word.
Call me but love, and I'll be new baptiz'd;
Henceforth I never will be Romeo.

William Shakespeare, from *Romeo and Juliet*

"Sticks and stones may break my bones, but words can never hurt me."
To accept this adage as valid is sheer folly. "What's in a name? that

which we call a rose by any other name would smell as sweet." The answer to Juliet's question is "Plenty!" and to her own response to the question we can only say that this is by no means invariably true. The importance, significance, and ramifications of naming and defining people cannot be over-emphasized. From *Genesis* and beyond, to the present time, the power which comes from naming and defining people has had positive as well as negative effects on entire populations.

Haig A. Bosmajian, from *The Language of Oppression*

After the coming of freedom there were two points upon which practically all the people on our place were agreed, and I find that this was generally true throughout the South: that they must change their names, and that they must leave the old plantation for at least a few days or weeks in order that they might really feel sure that they were free.

In some way a feeling got among the colored people that it was far from proper for them to bear the surname of their former owners, and a great many of them took other surnames. This was one of the first signs of freedom. When they were slaves, a colored person was simply called "John" or "Susan." There was seldom occasion for more than the use of the one name. If "John" or "Susan" belonged to a white man by the name of "Hatcher," sometimes he was called "John Hatcher," or as often "Hatcher's John." But there was a feeling that "John Hatcher" or "Hatcher's John" was not the proper title by which to denote a freeman; and so in many cases "John Hatcher" was changed to "John S. Lincoln" or "John S. Sherman," the initial "S" standing for no name, it being simply a part of what the colored man proudly called his "entitles."

Booker T. Washington, from *Up From Slavery*

At the end of a period varying in length, the newborn child is at last transformed into a definite human being. Ceremonies, differing according to the tribes, play their part in this event. As a rule the most important of these consists in giving the infant a name or, as they often put it, in "discovering" what its name is—that is, which member of the family is reincarnated in him. Thus we can understand that the name is not . . . merely "a label," but a constituent and "individuating" element of the personality. To the primitive's mind, being reckoned among the number of human beings can only signify being a member of the social group. How may this newborn infant, who is not yet a member, become one? He has no power of himself to enter their ranks, for the mystic virtue that is necessary is not his. He acquires it, however, at the moment when he is given the name of an ancestor. This latter, who, in a certain sense, lives again in him, has been and, though dead, still is, a member of the group. In other words, the bestowal of a name makes the child an integral part of his group, though in an indirect fashion, through the intervention of the ancestor.

Lucien Lévy-Bruhl, from *The "Soul" of the Primitive*

Maya Angelou

"What's Your Name, Girl?"

Recently a white woman from Texas, who would quickly describe herself as a liberal, asked me about my hometown. When I told her that in Stamps my grandmother had owned the only Negro general merchandise store since the turn of the century, she exclaimed. "Why, you were a debutante." Ridiculous and even ludicrous. But Negro girls in small Southern towns, whether poverty-stricken or just munching along on a few of life's necessities, were given as extensive and irrelevant preparations for adulthood as rich white girls shown in magazines. Admittedly the training was not the same. While white girls learned to waltz and sit gracefully with a tea cup balanced on their knees, we were lagging behind, learning the mid-Victorian values with very little money to indulge them. (Come and see Edna Lomax spending the money she made picking cotton on five balls of ecru tatting thread. Her fingers are bound to snag the work and she'll have to repeat the stitches time and time again. But she knows that when she buys the thread.)

We were required to embroider and I had trunkfuls of colorful dishtowels, pillowcases, runners, and handkerchiefs to my credit. I mastered the art of crocheting and tatting, and there was a lifetime's supply of dainty doilies that would never be used in sacheted dresser drawers. It went without saying that all girls could iron and wash, but the finer touches around the home, like setting a table with real silver, baking roasts, and cooking vegetables without meat, had to be learned elsewhere. Usually at the source of those habits. During my tenth year, a white woman's kitchen became my finishing school.

Mrs. Viola Cullinan was a plump woman who lived in a three-bedroom house somewhere behind the post office. She was singularly unattractive until she smiled, and then the lines around her eyes and mouth which made her look perpetually dirty disappeared, and her face looked like the mask of an impish elf. She usually rested her smile until late afternoon when her women friends dropped in and Miss Glory, the cook, served them cold drinks on the closed-in porch.

The exactness of her house was inhuman. This glass went here and   4
only here. That cup had its place and it was an act of impudent rebellion to place it anywhere else. At twelve o'clock the table was set. At 12:15 Mrs. Cullinan sat down to dinner (whether her husband had arrived or not). At 12:16 Miss Glory brought out the food.

It took me a week to learn the difference between a salad plate, a bread plate, and a dessert plate.

Mrs. Cullinan kept up the tradition of her wealthy parents. She was from Virginia. Miss Glory, who was a descendant of slaves that had worked for the Cullinans, told me her history. She had married beneath her (according to Miss Glory). Her husband's family hadn't had their money very long and what they had "didn't 'mount to much."

As ugly as she was, I thought privately, she was lucky to get a husband above or beneath her station. But Miss Glory wouldn't let me say a thing against her mistress. She was very patient with me, however, over the housework. She explained the dishware, silverware, and servants' bells.

The large round bowl in which soup was served wasn't a soup bowl,   8
it was a tureen. There were goblets, sherbet glasses, ice-cream glasses, wine glasses, green glass coffee cups with matching saucers, and water glasses. I had a glass to drink from, and it sat with Miss Glory's on a separate shelf from the others. Soup spoons, gravy boat, butter knives, salad forks, and carving platter were additions to my vocabulary and in fact almost represented a new language. I was fascinated with the novelty, with the fluttering Mrs. Cullinan and her Alice-in-Wonderland house.

Her husband remains, in my memory, undefined. I lumped him with all the other white men that I had ever seen and tried not to see.

On our way home one evening, Miss Glory told me that Mrs. Cullinan couldn't have children. She said that she was too delicate-boned. It was hard to imagine bones at all under those layers of fat. Miss Glory went on to say that the doctor had taken out all her lady organs. I reasoned that a pig's organs included the lungs, heart, and liver, so if Mrs. Cullinan was walking around without these essentials, it explained why she drank alcohol out of unmarked bottles. She was keeping herself embalmed.

When I spoke to Bailey[1] about it, he agreed that I was right, but he also informed me that Mr. Cullinan had two daughters by a colored lady and that I knew them very well. He added that the girls were the spitting image of their father. I was unable to remember what he looked like, although I had just left him a few hours before, but I thought of the Coleman girls. They were very light-skinned and certainly didn't look very much like their mother (no one ever mentioned Mr. Coleman).

My pity for Mrs. Cullinan preceded me the next morning like the 12 Cheshire cat's smile. Those girls, who could have been her daughters, were beautiful. They didn't have to straighten their hair. Even when they were caught in the rain, their braids still hung down straight like tamed snakes. Their mouths were pouty little cupid's bows. Mrs. Cullinan didn't know what she missed. Or maybe she did. Poor Mrs. Cullinan.

For weeks after, I arrived early, left late, and tried very hard to make up for her barrenness. If she had had her own children, she wouldn't have had to ask me to run a thousand errands from her back door to the back door of her friends. Poor old Mrs. Cullinan.

Then one evening Miss Glory told me to serve the ladies on the porch. After I set the tray down and turned toward the kitchen, one of the women asked, "What's your name, girl?" It was the speckled-faced one. Mrs. Cullinan said, "She doesn't talk much. Her name's Margaret."

"Is she dumb?"

"No. As I understand it, she can talk when she wants to but she's 16 usually quiet as a little mouse. Aren't you, Margaret?"

I smiled at her. Poor thing. No organs and couldn't even pronounce my name correctly.

"She's a sweet little thing, though."

"Well, that may be, but the name's too long. I'd never bother myself. I'd call her Mary if I was you."

I fumed into the kitchen. That horrible woman would never have 20 the chance to call me Mary because if I was starving I'd never work for her. I decided I wouldn't pee on her if her heart was on fire. Giggles drifted in off the porch and into Miss Glory's pots. I wondered what they could be laughing about.

Whitefolks were so strange. Could they be talking about me? Everybody knew that they stuck together better than the Negroes did. It was possible that Mrs. Cullinan had friends in St. Louis who heard about a girl from Stamps being in court and wrote to tell her. Maybe she knew about Mr. Freeman.[2]

[1] **Bailey**: Her brother.—Eds.

[2] **Mr. Freeman**: A friend of Angelou's mother; he was convicted of raping Angelou when she was a child.—Eds.

My lunch was in my mouth a second time and I went outside and relieved myself on the bed of four-o'clocks. Miss Glory thought I might be coming down with something and told me to go on home, that Momma would give me some herb tea, and she'd explain to her mistress.

I realized how foolish I was being before I reached the pond. Of course Mrs. Cullinan didn't know. Otherwise she wouldn't have given me the two nice dresses that Momma cut down, and she certainly wouldn't have called me a "sweet little thing." My stomach felt fine, and I didn't mention anything to Momma.

That evening I decided to write a poem on being white, fat, old, and 24
without children. It was going to be a tragic ballad. I would have to watch her carefully to capture the essence of her loneliness and pain.

The very next day, she called me by the wrong name. Miss Glory and I were washing up the lunch dishes when Mrs. Cullinan came to the doorway. "Mary?"

Miss Glory asked, "Who?"

Mrs. Cullinan, sagging a little, knew and I knew. "I want Mary to go down to Mrs. Randall's and take her some soup. She's not been feeling well for a few days."

Miss Glory's face was a wonder to see. "You mean Margaret, ma'am. 28
Her name's Margaret."

"That's too long. She's Mary from now on. Heat that soup from last night and put it in the china tureen and, Mary, I want you to carry it carefully."

Every person I knew had a hellish horror of being "called out of his name." It was a dangerous practice to call a Negro anything that could be loosely construed as insulting because of the centuries of their having been called niggers, jigs, dinges, blackbirds, crows, boots, and spooks.

Miss Glory had a fleeting second of feeling sorry for me. Then as she handed me the hot tureen she said, "Don't mind, don't pay that no mind. Sticks and stones may break your bones, but words . . . You know, I been working for her for twenty years."

She held the back door open for me. "Twenty years. I wasn't much 32
older than you. My name used to be Hallelujah. That's what Ma named me, but my mistress give me 'Glory,' and it stuck. I likes it better too."

I was in the little path that ran behind the houses when Miss Glory shouted. "It's shorter too."

For a few seconds it was a tossup over whether I would laugh (imagine being named Hallelujah) or cry (imagine letting some white woman rename you for her convenience). My anger saved me from either outburst. I had to quit the job, but the problem was going to be how to do it. Momma wouldn't allow me to quit for just any reason.

"She's a peach. That woman is a real peach." Mrs. Randall's maid was talking as she took the soup from me, and I wondered what her name used to be and what she answered to now.

For a week I looked into Mrs. Cullinan's face as she called me Mary.   36 She ignored my coming late and leaving early. Miss Glory was a little annoyed because I had begun to leave egg yolk on the dishes and wasn't putting much heart in polishing the silver. I hoped that she would complain to our boss, but she didn't.

Then Bailey solved my dilemma. He had me describe the contents of the cupboard and the particular plates she liked best. Her favorite piece was a casserole shaped like a fish and the green glass coffee cups. I kept his instructions in mind, so on the next day when Miss Glory was hanging out clothes and I had again been told to serve the old biddies on the porch, I dropped the empty serving tray. When I heard Mrs. Cullinan scream, "Mary!" I picked up the casserole and two of the green glass cups in readiness. As she rounded the kitchen door I let them fall on the tiled floor.

I could never absolutely describe to Bailey what happened next, because each time I got to the part where she fell on the floor and screwed up her ugly face to cry, we burst out laughing. She actually wobbled around on the floor and picked up shards of the cups and cried, "Oh, Momma. Oh, dear Gawd. It's Momma's china from Virginia. Oh, Momma, I sorry."

Miss Glory came running in from the yard and the women from the porch crowded around. Miss Glory was almost as broken up as her mistress. "You mean to say she broke our Virginia dishes? What we gone do?"

Mrs. Cullinan cried louder. "That clumsy nigger. Clumsy little black   40 nigger."

Old speckled-face leaned down and asked, "Who did it, Viola? Was it Mary? Who did it?"

Everything was happening so fast I can't remember whether her action preceded her words, but I know that Mrs. Cullinan said, "Her name's Margaret, goddamn it, her name's Margaret!" And she threw a wedge of the broken plate at me. It could have been the hysteria which put her aim off, but the flying crockery caught Miss Glory right over her ear and she started screaming.

I left the front door wide open so all the neighbors could hear. Mrs. Cullinan was right about one thing. My name wasn't Mary.   44

1969

Mary McCarthy

Names

Anna Lyons, Mary Louise Lyons, Mary von Phul, Emilie von Phul, Eugenia McLellan, Marjorie McPhail, Marie-Louise L'Abbé, Mary Danz, Julia Dodge, Mary Fordyce Blake, Janet Preston—these were the names (I can still tell them over like a rosary) of some of the older girls in the convent: the Virtues and Graces. The virtuous ones wore wide blue or green moire good-conduct ribbons, bandoleer-style, across their blue serge uniforms; the beautiful ones wore rouge and powder or at least were reputed to do so. Our class, the eighth grade, wore pink ribbons (I never got one myself) and had names like Patricia ("Pat") Sullivan, Eileen Donohoe, and Joan Kane. We were inelegant even in this respect; the best name we could show, among us, was Phyllis ("Phil") Chatham, who boasted that her father's name, Ralph, was pronounced "Rafe" as in England.

Names had a great importance for us in the convent, and foreign names, French, German, or plain English (which, to us, were foreign, because of their Protestant sound), bloomed like prize roses among a collection of spuds. Irish names were too common in the school to have any prestige either as surnames (Gallagher, Sheehan, Finn, Sullivan, McCarthy) or as Christian names (Kathleen, Eileen). Anything exotic had value: an "olive" complexion, for example. The pet girl of the convent was a fragile Jewish girl named Susie Lowenstein, who had pale red-gold hair and an exquisite retroussé nose, which, if we had had it, might have been called "pug." We liked her name too and the name of a child in the primary grades: Abbie Stuart Baillargeon. My favorite name, on the whole, though, was Emilie von Phul (pronounced "Pool"); her oldest sister, recently graduated, was called Celeste. Another name that appealed to me was Genevieve Albers, Saint Genevieve being the patron saint of Paris who turned back Attila from the gates of the city.

All these names reflected the still-pioneer character of the Pacific Northwest. I had never heard their like in the parochial school in Minneapolis, where "foreign" extraction, in any case, was something to be ashamed of, the whole drive being toward Americanization of first name and surname alike. The exceptions to this were the Irish, who could vaunt such names as Catherine O'Dea and the name of my second cousin, Mary Catherine Anne Rose Violet McCarthy, while an unfortunate German boy named Manfred was made to suffer for his. But that was Minneapolis. In Seattle, and especially in the convent of the Ladies of the Sacred Heart, foreign names suggested not immigration but emigration—distinguished exile. Minneapolis was a granary; Seattle

was a port, which had attracted a veritable Foreign Legion of adventurers—soldiers of fortune, younger sons, gamblers, traders, drawn
by the fortunes to be made in virgin timber and shipping and by the
Alaska Gold Rush. Wars and revolutions had sent the defeated out to
Puget Sound, to start a new life; the latest had been the Russian
Revolution, which had shipped us, via Harbin, a Russian colony, complete with restaurant, on Queen Anne Hill. The English names in the
convent, when they did not testify to direct English origin, as in the case
of "Rafe" Chatham, had come to us from the South and represented a
kind of internal exile; such girls as Mary Fordyce Blake and Mary
McQueen Street (a class ahead of me; her sister was named Francesca)
bore their double-barreled first names like titles of aristocracy from the
ante-bellum South. Not all our girls, by any means, were Catholic; some
of the very prettiest ones—Julia Dodge and Janet Preston, if I remember
rightly—were Protestants. The nuns had taught us to behave with special courtesy to these strangers in our midst, and the whole effect was of
some superior hostel for refugees of all the lost causes of the past
hundred years. Money could not count for much in such an atmosphere;
the fathers and grandfathers of many of our "best" girls were ruined
men.

Names, often, were freakish in the Pacific Northwest, particularly 4
girls' names. In the Episcopal boarding school I went to later, in Ta-
coma, there was a girl called De Vere Utter, and there was a girl called
Rocena and another called Hermonie. Was Rocena a mistake for
Rowena and Hermonie for Hermione? And was Vere, as we called her,
Lady Clara Vere de Vere? Probably. You do not hear names like those
often, in any case, east of the Cascade Mountains; they belong to the
frontier, where books and libraries were few and memory seems to have
been oral, as in the time of Homer.

Names have more signficance for Catholics than they do for other
people; Christian names are chosen for the spiritual qualities of the
saints they are taken from; Protestants used to name their children out
of the Old Testament and now they name them out of novels and plays,
whose heroes and heroines are perhaps the new patron saints of a
secular age. But with Catholics it is different. The saint a child is named
for is supposed to serve, literally, as a model or pattern to imitate; your
name is your fortune and it tells you what you are or must be. Catholic
children ponder their names for a mystic meaning, like birthstones; my
own, I learned, besides belonging to the Virgin and Saint Mary of Egypt,
originally meant "bitter" or "star of the sea." My second name, Thérèse,
could dedicate me either to Saint Theresa or to the saint called the
Little Flower, Soeur Thérèse of Lisieux, on whom God was supposed to
have descended in the form of a shower of roses. At Confirmation, I had
added a third name (for Catholics then rename themselves, as most

nuns do, yet another time, when they take orders); on the advice of a
nun, I had taken "Clementina," after Saint Clement, an early pope—a
step I soon regretted on account of "My Darling Clementine" and her
number nine shoes. By the time I was in the convent, I would no longer
tell anyone what my Confirmation name was. The name I had nearly
picked was "Agnes," after a little Roman virgin martyr, always shown
with a lamb, because of her purity. But Agnes would have been just as
bad, I recognized in Forest Ridge Convent—not only because of the
possibility of "Aggie," but because it was subtly, indefinably *wrong* in
itself. Agnes would have made me look like an ass.

The fear of appearing ridiculous first entered my life, as a governing motive, during my second year in the convent. Up to then, a desire
for prominence had decided many of my actions and, in fact, still
persisted. But in the eighth grade, I became aware of mockery and
perceived that I could not seek prominence without attracting laughter.
Other people could, but I couldn't. This laughter was proceeding, not
from my classmates, but from the girls of the class just above me, in
particular from two boon companions. Elinor Heffernan and Mary
Harty, a clownish pair—oddly assorted in size and shape, as teams of
clowns generally are, one short, plump, and baby-faced, the other tall,
lean, and owlish—who entertained the high-school department by calling attention to the oddities of the younger girls. Nearly every school
has such a pair of satirists, whose marks are generally low and who are
tolerated just because of their laziness and nonconformity; one of them
(in this case, Mary Harty, the plump one) usually appears to be half
asleep. Because of their low standing, their indifference to appearances,
the sad state of their uniforms, their clowning is taken to be harmless,
which, on the whole, it is, their object being not to wound but to divert;
such girls are bored in school. We in the eighth grade sat directly in
front of the two wits in study hall, so that they had us under close
observation; yet at first I was not afraid of them, wanting, if anything, to
identify myself with their laughter, to be initiated into the joke. One of
their specialties was giving people nicknames, and it was considered an
honor to be the first in the eighth grade to be let in by Elinor and Mary
on their latest invention. This often happened to me; they would tell
me, on the playground, and I would tell the others. As their intermedi-
ary, I felt myself almost their friend and it did not occur to me that I
might be next on their list.

I had achieved prominence not long before by publicly losing my
faith and regaining it at the end of a retreat. I believe Elinor and Mary
questioned me about this on the playground, during recess, and listened with serious, respectful faces while I told them about my conversations with the Jesuits. Those serious faces ought to have been an
omen, but if the two girls used what I had revealed to make fun of me, it

must have been behind my back. I never heard any more of it, and yet just at this time I began to feel something, like a cold breath on the nape of my neck, that made me wonder whether the new position I had won for myself in the convent was as secure as I imagined. I would turn around in study hall and find the two girls looking at me with specula-tion in their eyes.

It was just at this time, too, that I found myself in a perfectly absurd 8 situation, a very private one, which made me live, from month to month, in horror of discovery. I had waked up one morning, in my convent room, to find a few small spots of blood on my sheet; I had somehow scratched a trifling cut on one of my legs and opened it during the night. I wondered what to do about this, for the nuns were fussy about bedmaking, as they were about our white collars and cuffs, and if we had an inspection those spots might count against me. It was best, I decided, to ask the nun on dormitory duty, tall, stout Mother Slattery, for a clean bottom sheet, even though she might scold me for having scratched my leg in my sleep and order me to cut my toenails. You never know what you might be blamed for. But Mother Slattery, when she bustled in to look at the sheet, did not scold me at all; indeed, she hardly seemed to be listening as I explained to her about the cut. She told me to sit down: she would be back in a minute. "You can be excused from athletics today," she added, closing the door. As I waited, I consid-ered this remark, which seemed to me strangely munificent, in view of the unimportance of the cut. In a moment, she returned, but without the sheet. Instead, she produced out of her big pocket a sort of cloth girdle and a peculiar flannel object which I first took to be a bandage, and I began to protest that I did not need or want a bandage; all I needed was a bottom sheet. "The sheet can wait," said Mother Slattery, succinctly, handing me two large safety pins. It was the pins that abruptly enlight-ened me; I saw Mother Slattery's mistake, even as she was instructing me as to how this flannel article, which I now understood to be a sanitary napkin, was to be put on.

"Oh, no, Mother," I said, feeling somewhat embarrassed. "You don't understand. It's just a little cut, on my leg." But Mother, again, was not listening; she appeared to have grown deaf, as the nuns had a habit of doing when what you were saying did not fit in with their ideas. And now that I knew what was in her mind, I was conscious of a funny constraint; I did not feel it proper to name a natural process, in so many words, to a nun. It was like trying not to think of their going to the bathroom or trying not to see the straggling iron-gray hair coming out of their coifs (the common notion that they shaved their heads was false). On the whole, it seemed better just to show her my cut. But when I offered to do so and unfastened my black stocking, she only glanced at my leg, cursorily. "That's only a scratch, dear," she said. "Now hurry up and put this on or you'll be late for chapel. Have you any pain?" "No, no, Mother!" I cried. "You don't understand!" "Yes, yes, I understand," she replied soothingly, "and you will too, a little later. Mother Superior will tell you about it some time during the morning. There's nothing to be afraid of. You have become a woman."

"I know all about that," I persisted. "Mother, please listen. I just cut my leg. On the athletic field. Yesterday afternoon." But the more ex-cited I grew, the more soothing, and yet firm, Mother Slattery became. There seemed to be nothing for it but to give up and do as I was bid. I was in the grip of a higher authority, which almost had the power to persuade me that it was right and I was wrong. But of course I was not wrong; that would have been too good to be true. While Mother Slattery waited, just outside my door, I miserably donned the equipment she had given me, for there was no place to hide it, on account of drawer inspection. She led me down the hall to where there was a chute and explained how I was to dispose of the flannel thing, by dropping it down the chute into the laundry. (The convent arrangements were very old-fashioned, dating back, no doubt, to the days of Louis Philippe.)

The Mother Superior, Madame MacIllvra, was a sensible woman, and all through my early morning classes, I was on pins and needles, chafing for the promised interview with her which I trusted would clear things up. "*Ma Mère*," I would begin, "Mother Slattery thinks. . . ." Then I would tell her about the cut and the athletic field. But precisely the same impasse confronted me when I was summoned to her office at recess-time. *I* talked about my cut, and *she* talked about becoming a woman. It was rather like a round, in which she was singing "Scotland's burning, Scotland's burning," and I was singing "Pour on water, pour on water." Neither of us could hear the other, or, rather, I could hear her, but she could not hear me. Owing to our different positions in the convent she was free to interrupt me, whereas I was expected to remain silent until she had finished speaking. When I kept breaking in, she hushed me, gently, and took me on her lap. Exactly like Mother Slattery, she attributed all my references to the cut to a blind fear of this new, unexpected reality that had supposedly entered my life. Many young girls, she reassured me, were frightened if they had not been prepared. "And you, Mary, have lost your dear mother, who could have made this easier for you." Rocked on Madame MacIllvra's lap, I felt paralysis overtake me and I lay, mutely listening, against her bosom, my face being tickled by her white, starched, fluted wimple, while she explained to me how babies were born, all of which I had heard before.

There was no use fighting the convent. I had to pretend to have 12 become a woman, just as, not long before, I had had to pretend to get my faith back—for the sake of peace. This pretense was decidedly awkward. For fear of being found out by the lay sisters downstairs in the laundry (no doubt an imaginary contingency, but the convent was so very thorough), I reopened the cut on my leg, so as to draw a little blood to stain the napkins, which were issued me regularly, not only on this occasion, but every twenty-eight days thereafter. Eventually, I abandoned this bloodletting, for fear of lockjaw, and trusted to fate. Yet I was in awful dread of detection; my only hope, as I saw it, was either to be released from the convent or to become a woman in reality, which might take a year at least, since I was only twelve. Getting out of athletics once a month was not sufficient compensation for the farce I was going through. It was not my fault; they had forced me into it; nevertheless, it was I who would look silly—worse than silly; half mad—if the truth ever came to light.

I was burdened with this guilt and shame when the nickname finally found me out. "Found me out," in a general sense, for no one ever did learn the particular secret I bore about with me, pinned to the linen band. "We've got a name for you," Elinor and Mary called out to me, one day on the playground. "What is it?" I asked half hoping, half fearing, since not all their sobriquets were unfavorable. "Cye," they answered, looking at each other and laughing. "Si?" I repeated, supposing that it was based on Simple Simon. Did they regard me as a hick? "C.Y.E.," they elucidated, spelling it out in chorus. "The letters stand for something. Can you guess?" I could not and I cannot now. The closest I could come to it in the convent was "Clean Your Ears." Perhaps that was it, though in later life I have wondered whether it did not stand, simply, for "Clever Young Egg" or "Champion Young Eccentric." But in the convent I was certain that it stood for something horrible, something even worse than dirty ears (as far as I knew, my ears were clean), something I could never guess because it represented some aspect of myself that the world could see and I couldn't, like a sign pinned on my back. Everyone in the convent must have known what the letters stood for, but no one would tell me. Elinor and Mary had made them promise. It was like halitosis; not even my best friend, my deskmate, Louise, would tell me, no matter how much I pleaded. Yet everyone assured me that it was "very good," that is, very apt. And it made everyone laugh.

This name reduced all my pretensions and solidifed my sense of *wrongness*. Just as I felt I was beginning to belong to the convent, it turned me into an outsider, since I was the only pupil who was not in the know. I liked the convent, but it did not like me, as people say of certain foods that disagree with them. By this, I do not mean that I was actively unpopular, either with the pupils or with the nuns. The Mother Superior cried when I left and predicted that I would be a novelist, which surprised me. And I had finally made friends; even Emilie von Phul smiled upon me softly out of her bright blue eyes from the far end of the study hall. It was just that I did not fit into the convent pattern;

the simplest thing I did, like asking for a clean sheet, entrapped me in consequences that I never could have predicted. I was not bad; I did not consciously break the rules; and yet I could never, not even for a week, get a pink ribbon, and this was something I could not understand, because I was trying as hard as I could. It was the same case as with the hated name; the nuns, evidently, saw something about me that was invisible to me.

The oddest part was all that pretending. There I was, a walking mass of lies, pretending to be a Catholic and going to confession while really I had lost my faith, and pretending to have monthly periods by cutting myself with nail scissors; yet all this had come about without my volition and even contrary to it. But the basest pretense I was driven to was the acceptance of the nickname. Yet what else could I do? In the convent, I could not live it down. To all those girls, I had become "Cye McCarthy." That was who I was. That was how I had to identify myself when telephoning my friends during vacations to ask them to the movies: "Hello, this is Cye." I loathed myself when I said it, and yet I succumbed to the name totally, making myself over into a sort of hearty to go with it—the kind of girl I hated. "Cye" was my new patron saint. This false personality stuck to me, like the name, when I entered public high school, the next fall, as a freshman, having finally persuaded my grand-parents to take me out of the convent, although they could never get to the bottom of my reasons, since, as I admitted, the nuns were kind, and I had made many nice new friends. What I wanted was a fresh start, a chance to begin life over again, but the first thing I heard in the corridors of the public high school was that name called out to me, like the warmest of welcomes: "Hi, there, Si!" That was the way they thought it was spelled. But this time I was resolute. After the first weeks, I dropped the hearties who called me "Si" and I never heard it again. I got my own name back and sloughed off Clementina and even Thérèse—the names that did not seem to me any more to be mine but to have been imposed on me by others. And I preferred to think that Mary meant "bitter" rather than "star of the sea."   *1957*

Paul Gruchow

Seeing the Elephant

By the time you reached western Nebraska on the Oregon Trail—by the time you had passed the Trail's first great landmark, Chimney Rock—the landscape had turned hard and bitter. You were at the edge of the acrid desert, and the spring had worn into summer. The trees had vanished; from horizon to horizon, not a spot of shade fell. Good water was hard to find. The water in the naked marshes was nauseatingly alkaline. It gave you a miserable attack of diarrhea. It made the oxen bloat and die. Sometimes you couldn't find a place to camp at night away from the stench of their rotting carcasses. The alkali dust stuck in your nostrils and collected in your lungs. You knew the claustrophobia of not being able to catch your breath.

Probably somebody in your party had already died: had been crushed under the wheel of a wagon or caught cholera along the polluted Platte, had collapsed from exhaustion or fallen victim to the careless gunshot of a wagon mate. The wagon trains set out loaded like armadas, their organizers fearful of Indian attack. The Indians didn't attack; the wars with them came after the westward movement. They had subtler methods. They would greet you at a river crossing, help you ford, ask for a little food in return, and disappear in the night with your best horses. So the whites, loaded to the gills with ammunition, got gun-happy and, more frequently than one might guess, killed and maimed each other accidentally. The slow progress across the prairies, 12 or 15 miles a day, had become a drudging routine. It must have seemed as if you had been traveling forever. You made the miles pass by counting gravestones and praying for a diversion: the sight of a buffalo, the relief of a cottonwood tree, anything to break the monotony of the way ahead.

And now you were crossing sagebrush country—sparse in forage for the horses and mules; abounding in rattlesnakes and lizards; where coyotes barked and wolves howled in the night, where the heat of the midday sun radiated from the scorching earth like the embers of an old fire.

The farther west you traveled, the less distinct the trail became, the less reliable was the advice of fellow travelers, the more recklessly you were inclined to try ill-fated shortcuts. Soon you would be beyond the Platte, and after that you might have only the vaguest idea how to proceed. You might know that you wanted to continue westward until you came to some other kind of country—some green mountain valley, or the sea—and nothing more. The landscape itself offered fewer and fewer clues—just an endless line of distant hills and mountains; the gray-green monotony of the arid flora; the continual parade of clouds from which no rain fell; the unceasing undulation of the earth like the waves of the sea, each new wave identical to the last.

Perhaps you undertook the journey in hope and determination, sustained by the promise of gold or of a farm at the end of the trail. Perhaps you traveled in desperation, seeing the trip as the last or best hope, as the inevitable choice among the one or two available. Perhaps you didn't know why you went, but simply had the itch to be a part of what the newspaper writers back east were calling the nation's manifest destiny. Perhaps you followed out of wifely duty, indulging a husband's dream in which you could not share. However you set out, you were certain to meet fear along the way. There were so many things to fear:

Every strange noise in the night;

Every twist in a river's current;

Every sharply angled hillside upon which a narrow wagon might   8
overturn;

Every nightfall;

Snakes lurking in the grass;

Wolves and bears;

Every bird bursting unexpectedly from beneath your feet;   12

Every moment when you remembered that you were unlikely ever
to see again the relatives and friends you had left behind;

The midday heat;

Every fresh grave along the way;

Every fever or festering wound;   16

Every round of rifle fire heard over the next horizon;

Every juncture in the trail, that you might now have chosen the right
way;

Thunderstorms;

The possibility that no water might be found tomorrow;   20

The possibility that you would run out of breast milk for the baby.

But fear is its own antidote. You face a fear long enough, and you learn to accept it. This is why you can get into an automobile in the morning and drive to work along the freeway without a paralyzing and altogether sensible fear of dying. Oregon Trail travelers had a wonderful name for it. They called it the elephant. You got to a certain point in the journey, and you said that now you had seen the elephant. It was a metaphor, one historian has suggested, with origins in the circus: Once you had seen the elephant, you had seen all the circus had to offer.

As a nation, we have been both too constantly on the move and too relentlessly utilitarian to think very deeply about the qualities of place. But even we now and then recognize some particular place as having unique powers, as possessing magical charms and persuasions. Independence Rock is such a place.

There were other celebrated landmarks along the Oregon Trail. By 24
the time its travelers arrived at Independence Rock, they had already passed, among others, Courthouse and Jailhouse rocks, Chimney Rock, and Scottsbluff—but these were places notable more for their physical than for their spiritual qualities. They were impressive in size, as visual links with the world back home, and for their instant recognizability—not for anything they might say in themselves to the people headed west. From a distance, Courthouse and Jailhouse rocks do look remarkably like a pair of familiar county-government buildings. Chimney Rock

reminded travelers of the obelisk on Beacon Hill in Boston; it presented a nostalgic encounter with the civilized East. By the narrowness of the pass through it, Scottsbluff was a kind of gateway into the semiarid West—a point of no return; by the impression it gave from a distance, it was an apparition of Europe. Scottsbluff looked like a pair of enormous castles somehow raised and then abandoned upon the wild plains.

Independence Rock is something different. It is not especially big; it covers about 25 acres and is 193 feet high at its peak. It reminded travelers of nothing in the East or in Europe. Diarists saw it as a mammoth egg half-buried, a turtle, a bowl turned upside-down, a sleeping hippopotamus, a whale. To me, it looks like a petrified brain—and it is one, in a way. It is the bald granite peak of an old mountain, its base buried in the wash of debris that accompanied the geologic revolution that formed the Rocky Mountains, a monument to the impermanence even of mountains in the vast scale of time.

Independence Rock came to mean what it did, I think, because of two felicities of timing. First, it lay at the point along the trail where familiarity had finally overcome fear, where the journey west had ceased to be a journey and had begun to seem its own occupation. By the time you reached it, you had probably already seen the elephant. Second, as it worked out, travelers could expect to reach Independence Rock by the Fourth of July. So it came to be a temporal landmark as well as a physical one, and the temporal symbolism was doubly rich: One could simultaneously celebrate the nation's independence and the independence one was privately seeking. The rock offered itself as a faith stone, as an occasion for reaffirming the promise of the West.

You affirmed that faith by a ritual act as old as human culture. You approached the rock and made your mark. Some people stood at the very base of the rock and scrawled their names in charcoal or paint; those names washed away in the first rain. Some scratched their names along the most exposed surfaces of the rock—eager, perhaps, to be visible; their scratchings wore away in the rains of decades. Some carved their names deeply, taking a whole day at it, and in seventy-five years the lichens covered them. Some chiseled their names in bold, deep letters, adding curlicues and flourishes, and more than a century later their marks endure. They have gained at least so much immortality. By 1855, this being America, you could hire a Mormon to do the job for you at $1 to $4 a name.

When the explorer John C. Fremont visited the rock in 1842, he [28] carried the practice of inscribing it to a new height: "I engraved on this rock of the far West, a symbol of Christian faith . . . a large cross, which I covered with a black preparation of India rubber well calculated to resist the influence of wind and rain." But the symbol did disappear, probably in a blast of gunpowder set off by a party of one thousand immigrants gathered there on July 4, 1847. And when Fremont later sought the presidency, his cross helped to defeat him. He was Catholic; therefore, his etching was a defilement of a national symbol, and it was used to turn Protestant voters against him. Frivolous considerations of "character" are nothing new in our politics.

I climbed the rock myself one August day to have a look at the marks the travelers had left behind. I had spent the morning in pursuit of antelopes and lizards. I had gone on foot to get some idea of what it might have been like to travel that country in a wagon; had walked its yellow earth, rich in minerals but poor in humus; had felt its heat in the soles of my feet; had climbed and descended its labyrinth of arroyos and hills, never seeming to come any closer to the long line of blue mountains to the north and west. By midday, although the air tempera-ture was only eighty-five degrees, my pocket thermometer registered almost one hundred degrees at ground level. The only shade was cast by the brim of my hat (shade barely adequate to reach my eyes, into which my sweat ran) and by the woody stems of the sagebrushes and the paddles of the pear cactuses—shade enough for the tiny lizards that abounded there, appealing little creatures that coquettishly cocked their heads and stared at me out of one eye.

I climbed Independence Rock late in the afternoon, when there was already some purple in the lines of the mountains visible on every side and the shadows in the hills were beginning to cast the landscape into relief. I had approached it around a bend in the highway; the instant I saw it, I knew what it was. I tried to measure the pleasure of my own sense of having arrived against the great joy that Oregon Trail travelers must have known upon encountering it: something familiar and antici-pated in the midst of so much that was strange, new, unexpected. I thought I could feel vicariously, even across the space of a century, the relief, the momentary rush of calm, the excitement of turning around the bend in the valley and seeing the rock and knowing that you were much of the way west and all was well. "Cold chills come over me and tears would flow in spite of all my efforts to repress them," Harriet Sherril Ward wrote upon coming around that bend in 1853.

People lingered there for a day or two and made friends with fellow travelers. In such circumstances, friendships come easily. There was music, dancing, conversation around campfires late into the night. There were stories about the trip, the beginning of the fabrication of a memory of the trail, the first telling of events one would alter, embel-lish, polish through a hundred more tellings in the years ahead. New alliances were forged, with fractious trail mates parting ways and join-ing new companies. Teams fragmented by death, fights, or second thoughts merged into new traveling units. There was time for rest and repairs, for swapping lore, for pooling information about the way ahead. Perhaps there was a message from home or from a friend who had passed earlier; the rock was used as a bulletin board. And there was time to climb Independence Rock, hammer and chisel in hand, to make your mark or the mark of your family on what the Jesuit missionary Father P. J. De Smet, who signed it in 1840, called "the great registery of the desert."

I climbed the rock. It was steeper than it looked from the parking 32 lot, but you could ascend it simply by walking up the dome over a surface almost as smooth as a city sidewalk. From the peak of the dome, despite the mountains towering around me, I felt the familiar force of a mountaintop. The place had a summit's constricted sense of space in the context of so much visible landscape. Here was a rare instance where the geologic fact—the top of a buried mountain—was reinforced, made believable by my own sensations.

There were five other people on the summit when I arrived, an enthusiastic family of vacationers scrambling here and there and call-ing to each other: "Here! Look here! Here's one from 1847!" "I've got an 1842 over here! Come quick, John! Get a picture of it!" "Oh, wow! Look at this one!" I tried to get out of their way—to stay on some unoccupied corner of the rock, out of the way of the incessant clicking of the motor-driven camera—but it was almost impossible. They were everywhere at once and, it seemed, getting noisier all the time. I suppose I ought to have been amused at their shaky, typically American sense of history— "What do all these dates mean, Mom?" "They are the dates when these people died, Terry."—or thrilled that a group of young children could be so excited about a historic site, or charmed by how much they seemed to be enjoying themselves. But I did not feel anything of the sort. I felt about them the way one feels about the revelers in the next hotel room at 2:30 A.M. I wished that they would all shut up and go away. Eventually they did. I watched them climb down the rock, wondering what they knew about the elephant, whether any of them had ever seen it. And then, regretting the harshness of my mood, I sat on a point of rock and waited for the spirit of the place, the spirit I had briefly caught on achieving the summit, to return.

The shadows began to lengthen radically. The first tinges of the color salmon began to show in the western sky. In the prelude to twilight, the ruts of the wagon wheels, still showing faintly in the patch of grass just north of the rock, emerged vividly: two dark green scratches in the silver-green vegetation. I imagined that I could hear the wheels of wagons clattering and creaking over those ruts; the cries of drivers shouting to horses and mules, drawing them into a circle along the Sweetwater River below, commanding them to halt: "Wagons ho!" I imagined that I could smell the smoke of camp fires, that I could see children playing, that I could hear the crowing of caged roosters, that I was surrounded by the evidence of a temporary village taking shape in the valley below.

But it was, in fact, very quiet. Occasionally a car passed on the highway, shining like a silver ribbon—but passed noiselessly like a phantom. There were still a few visitors in the parking lot reading the signs explaining the geology of the rock, but they, too, were beyond hearing. I got up from my perch and began to wander over the summit, inspecting the names inscribed in its face. These were the names of survivors, not of casualties, but looking at them had the same overpowering effect on me as looking at the names inscribed on the black marble wall of the Vietnam memorial in Washington, D.C. There were no names with which I could make any personal connection. I was looking for no name in particular, the name of no relative or historical figure, for no particular date or place of origin. I wandered vaguely and without precise purpose, simply letting the names and dates and places accumulate, the array of national origins, the expanse of years, the rich melody of the names themselves—names like Obadiah and Jeremiah, Elias and Ezekiel, Ruth and Elizabeth, Opal and Beulah, names speaking in the calico colors of another age. I saw names washing away in the rains of a century; names chipped away in a hundred years of freezes and thaws; names slowly being engulfed in the advance of lichens; names carved with bravado to last for the ages, and still enduring. For every name I saw, I knew that another hundred had already faded away and run down the side of the ancient mountaintop to become part of the meager soil in which the sagebrush desert now took root. There was defiance in those names, and pride; determination and hope; resignation and prayer.

I saw in those names the beginnings of many other names, of a new 36 generation of names born in the West: the names of mountains, of lakes and streams, of fledgling towns, of roads and passes, of children born along the trail, or on new farms, or in mining camps—children destined to make of a wide and nameless place a new and richly designated one. It is how we lay claim to anything—to a place, or a plant, or a person, or an idea: We give it a name; and it is, perhaps, a uniquely human handicap that if we do not know the name of a thing, we cannot know anything else worth knowing about it.

That is the power of the Vietnam wall: It names a war, names it as precisely as such an experience can be named, and makes it possible for us to know its full meaning. Independence Rock worked on me in the fading light of an August day when the merciful shadows of evening were falling. Here was the westward expansion given a name, the American dream of independence translated from concept into a knowable place, a place with a name, the place of the elephant. I wandered among all those names on Independence Rock, skirting around them, preserving them from the impact of my feet, as one avoids the mound behind a gravestone, and while I was wandering among them, seeing over and over again the juxtaposition of a name, a place, and a date, July 4, 18—, the weight of their accumulation rose like a bubble in the well of my throat, and it did not burst until I was long down the road past the monument, following the eastern flank of the Wind River Mountains through the oil fields, a new dream as capricious as the last, and had switched on my headlights to see the road ahead to Thermopolis. I was headed by then, alone, into grizzly country, in search, I suddenly understood, of my own elephant. *1987*

6

Divided Identities

Kesaya E. Noda, Growing Up Asian
in America

Adrienne Rich, Split at the Root: An Essay
on Jewish Identity

Shelby Steele, On Being Black and
Middle Class

I must register a certain impatience with the faddish equation . . . of the
term identity with the question "Who am I?" This question nobody
would ask himself except in a more or less transient morbid state, in a
creative self-confrontation, or in an adolescent state sometimes combining both; wherefore on occasion I find myself asking a student who
claims that he is in an "identity crisis" whether he is complaining or
boasting. The pertinent question, if it can be put into the first person at
all, would be, "What do I want to make of myself, and what do I have to
work with?"

Erik H. Erikson, from *Identity: Youth and Crisis*

British feminist Jacqueline Rose has argued for recognition of a *"resistance to identity"* which lies at the very heart of psychic life." Basing her
discussion on elements of Freudian and subsequent psychoanalytic
theory, she paints a picture of identity as a deceptively smooth facade
hiding an endless turmoil of contradictory impulses and desires. Socially powerful groups have a stake in promoting the illusion of uncon-
flicted identity because the maintenance of their power depends on
keeping in place a constellation of apparently fixed, "natural," immutable social relationships and psychological postures. She spots an irony
in the feminist tendency to view psychic conflict as "either an accident

106

or an obstacle on the path to psychic and sexual continuity—a continuity which we, as feminists, recognize as a myth of our culture only to
reinscribe it in a different form on the agenda. . . ."

Jan Clausen, from *My Interesting Condition*

The act of writing is the act of making soul, alchemy. It is the quest for
the self, for the center of the self, which we women of color have come to
think as "other"—the dark, the feminine. Didn't we start writing to
reconcile this other within us? We knew we were different, set apart,
exiled from what is considered "normal," white-right. And as we internalized this exile, we came to see the alien within us and too often, as a
result, we split apart from ourselves and each other. Forever after we
have been in search of that self, that "other" and each other. And we
return, in widening spirals and never to the same childhood place
where it happened, first in our families, with our mothers, with our
fathers. The writing is a tool for piercing that mystery but it also shields
us, gives a margin of distance, helps us survive. And those that don't
survive? The waste of ourselves: so much meat thrown at the feet of
madness or fate or the state.

Gloria Anzaldúa, from *Speaking in Tongues:*
A Letter to Third World Women Writers

Kesaya E. Noda

Growing Up Asian in America

Sometimes when I was growing up, my identity seemed to hurtle
toward me and paste itself right to my face. I felt that way, encountering
the stereotypes of my race perpetuated by non-Japanese people (primarily white) who may or may not have had contact with other Japanese
in America. "You don't like cheese, do you?" someone would ask. "I
know your people don't like cheese." Sometimes questions came making allusions to history. That was another aspect of the identity. Events
that had happened quite apart from the me who stood silent in that
moment connected my face with an incomprehensible past. "Your parents were in California? Were they in those camps during the war?" And

sometimes there were phrases or nicknames: "Lotus Blossom." I was sometimes addressed or referred to as racially Japanese, sometimes as Japanese-American, and sometimes as an Asian woman. Confusions and distortions abounded.

How is one to know and define oneself? From the inside—within a context that is self-defined, from a grounding in community and a connection with culture and history that are comfortably accepted? Or from the outside—in terms of messages received from the media and people who are often ignorant? Even as an adult I can still see two sides of my face and past. I can see from the inside out, in freedom. And I can see from the outside in, driven by the old voices of childhood and lost in anger and fear.

I AM RACIALLY JAPANESE

A voice from my childhood says: "You are other. You are less than. You are unalterably alien." This voice has its own history. We have indeed been seen as other and alien since the early years of our arrival in the United States. The very first immigrants were welcomed and sought as laborers to replace the dwindling numbers of Chinese, whose influx had been cut off by the Chinese Exclusion Act of 1882. The Japanese fell natural heir to the same anti-Asian prejudice that had arisen against the Chinese. As soon as they began striking for better wages, they were no longer welcomed.

I can see myself today as a person historically defined by law and   4 custom as being forever alien. Being neither "free white," nor "African," our people in California were deemed "aliens, ineligible for citizenship," no matter how long they intended to stay here. Aliens ineligible for citizenship were prohibited from owning, buying, or leasing land. They did not and could not belong here. The voice in me remembers that I am always a *Japanese*-American in the eyes of many. A third-generation German-American is an American. A third-generation Japanese-American is a Japanese-American. Being Japanese means being a danger to the country during the war and knowing how to use chopsticks. I wear this history on my face.

I move to the other side. I see a different light and claim a different context. My race is a line that stretches across ocean and time to link me to the shrine where my grandmother was raised. Two high, white banners lift in the wind at the top of the stone steps leading to the shrine. It is time for the summer festival. Black characters are written against the sky as boldly as the clouds, as lightly as kites, as sharply as the big black crows I used to see above the fields in New Hampshire. At festival time there is liquor and food, ritual, discipline, and abandonment. There is music and drunkenness and invocation. There is hope. Another season has come. Another season has gone.

I am racially Japanese. I have a certain claim to this crazy place where the prayers intoned by a neighboring Shinto priest (standing in for my grandmother's nephew who is sick) are drowned out by the rehearsals for the pop singing contest in which most of the villagers will compete later that night. The village elders, the priest, and I stand respectfully upon the immaculate, shining wooden floor of the outer shrine, bowing our heads before the hidden powers. During the patchy intervals when I can hear him, I notice the priest has a stutter. His voice flutters up to my ears only occasionally because two men and a women are singing gustily into a microphone in the compound, testing the sound system. A prerecorded tape of guitars, samisens, and drums accompanies them. Rock music and Shinto prayers. That night, to loud applause and cheers, a young man is given the award for the most *netsuretsu*—passionate, burning—rendition of a song. We roar our approval of the reward. Never mind that his voice had wandered and slid, now slightly above, now slightly below the given line of the melody. Netsuretsu. Netsuretsu.

In the morning, my grandmother's sister kneels at the foot of the stone stairs to offer her morning prayers. She is too crippled to climb the stairs, so each morning she kneels here upon the path. She shuts her eyes for a few seconds, her motions as matter of fact as when she washes rice. I linger longer than she does, so reluctant to leave, savoring the connection I feel with my grandmother in America, the past, and the power that lives and shines in the morning sun.

Our family has served this shrine for generations. The family's need 8 to protect this claim to identity and place outweighs any individual claim to any individual hope. I am Japanese.

I AM A JAPANESE-AMERICAN

"Weak." I hear the voice from my childhood years. "Passive," I hear. Our parents and grandparents were the ones who were put into those camps. They went without resistance; they offered cooperation as proof of loyalty to America. "Victim," I hear. And, "Silent."

Our parents are painted as hard workers who were socially uncomfortable and had difficulty expressing even the smallest opinion. Clean, quiet, motivated, and determined to match the American way; that is us, and that is the story of our time here.

"Why did you go into those camps?" I raged at my parents, frightened by my own inner silence and timidity. "Why didn't you do anything to resist? Why didn't you name it the injustice it was?" Couldn't our parents even think? Couldn't they? Why were we so passive?

I shift my vision and my stance. I am in California. My uncle is in 12 the midst of the sweet potato harvest. He is pressed, trying to get the harvesting crews onto the field as quickly as possible, worried about the flow of equipment and people. His big pickup is pulled off to the side, motor running, door ajar. I see two tractors in the yard in front of an old shed; the flatbed harvesting platform on which the workers will stand has already been brought over from the other field. It's early morning. The workers stand loosely grouped and at ease, but my uncle looks as harried and tense as a police officer trying to unsnarl a New York City traffic jam. Driving toward the shed, I pull my car off the road to make way for an approaching tractor. The front wheels of the car sink lux- uriously into the soft, white sand by the roadside and the car slides to a dreamy halt, tail still on the road. I try to move forward. I try to move back. The front bites contentedly into the sand, the back lifts itself at a jaunty angle. My uncle sees me and storms down the road, running. He is shouting before he is even near me.

"What's the matter with you?" he screams. "What the hell are you doing?" In his frenzy, he grabs his hat off his head and slashes it through the air across his knee. He is beside himself. "Don't you know how to drive in sand? What's the matter with you? You've blocked the whole roadway. How am I supposed to get my tractors out of here? Can't you use your head? You've cut off the whole roadway, and we've got to get out of here."

I stand on the road before him helplessly thinking, "No, I don't know how to drive in sand. I've never driven in sand."

"I'm sorry, uncle," I say, burying a smile beneath a look of sincere apology. I notice my deep amusement and my affection for him with great curiosity. I am usually devastated by anger. Not this time.

During the several years that follow I learn about the people and the place, and much more about what has happened in this California village where my parents grew up. The issei, our grandparents, made this settlement in the desert. Their first crops were eaten by rabbits and ravaged by insects. The land was so barren that men walking from house to house sometimes got lost. Women came here too. They bore children in 114-degree heat, then carried the babies with them into the fields to nurse when they reached the end of each row of grapes or other truck-farm crops.

I had had no idea what it meant to buy this kind of land and make it grow green. Or how, when the war came, there was no space at all for the subtlety of being who we were—Japanese-Americans. Either/or was the way. I hadn't understood that people were literally afraid for their lives then, that their money had been frozen in banks; that there was a five- mile travel limit; that when the early evening curfew came and they were inside their houses, some of them watched helplessly as people they knew went into their barns to steal their belongings. The police were patrolling the road, interested only in violators of curfew. There was no help for them in the face of thievery. I had not been able to imagine before what it must have felt like to be an American—to know absolutely that one is an American—and yet to have almost everyone else deny it. Not only deny it, but challenge that identity with machine guns and troops of white American soldiers. In those circumstances it was difficult to say, "I'm a Japanese-American." "American" had to do.

But now I can say that I am a Japanese-American. It means I have a place here in this country, too. I have a place here on the East Coast, where our neighbor is so much a part of our family that my mother never passes her house at night without glancing at the lights to see if she is home and safe; where my parents have hauled hundreds of pounds of rocks from fields and arduously planted Christmas trees and blueberries, lilacs, asparagus, and crab apples; where my father still dreams of angling a stream to a new bed so that he can dig a pond in the field and fill it with water and fish. "The neighbors already came for their Christmas tree?" he asks in December. "Did they like it? Did they like it?"

I have a place on the West Coast where my relatives still farm, where I heard the stories of feuds and backbiting, and where I saw that people survived and flourished because fundamentally they trusted and relied upon one another. A death in the family is not just a death in a family; it is a death in the community. I saw people help each other with money, materials, labor, attention, and time. I saw men gather once a year, without fail, to clean the grounds of a ninety-year-old woman who had helped the community before, during, and after the war. I saw her remembering them with birthday cards sent to each of their children.

I come from a people with a long memory and a distinctive grace. 20 We live our thanks. And we are Americans. Japanese-Americans.

I AM A JAPANESE-AMERICAN WOMAN

Woman. The past piece of my identity. It has been easier by far for me to know myself in Japan and to see my place in America than it has been to accept my line of connection with my own mother. She was my dark self, a figure in whom I thought I saw all that I feared most in myself. Growing into womanhood and looking for some model of strength, I turned away from her. Of course, I could not find what I sought. I was looking for a black feminist or a white feminist. My mother is neither white nor black.

My mother is a woman who speaks with her life as much as with her tongue. I think of her with her own mother. Grandmother had Parkinson's disease and it had frozen her gait and set her fingers, tongue, and feet jerking and trembling in a terrible dance. My aunts and uncles wanted her to be able to live in her own home. They fed her, bathed her, dressed her, awoke at midnight to take her for one last trip to the bathroom. My aunts (her daughters-in-law) did most of the care, but my mother went from New Hampshire to California each summer to spend a month living with Grandmother, because she wanted to and because she wanted to give my aunts at least a small rest. During those hot summer days, mother lay on the couch watching the television or reading, cooking foods that Grandmother liked, and speaking little. Grandmother thrived under her care.

The time finally came when it was too dangerous for Grandmother to live alone. My relatives kept finding her on the floor beside her bed when they went to wake her in the mornings. My mother flew to California to help clean the house and make arrangements for Grandmother to enter a local nursing home. On her last day at home, while Grandmother was sitting in her big, overstuffed armchair, hair combed and wearing a green summer dress, my mother went to her and knelt at her feet. "Here, Mamma," she said. "I've polished your shoes." She lifted Grandmother's legs and helped her into the shiny black shoes. My Grandmother looked down and smiled slightly. She left her house walking, supported by her children, carrying her pocket book, and wearing her polished black shoes. "Look, Mamma," my mom had said, kneeling. "I've polished your shoes."

Just the other day, my mother came to Boston to visit. She had 24 recently lost a lot of weight and was pleased with her new shape and her feeling of good health. "Look at me, Kes," she exclaimed, turning toward me, front and back, as naked as the day she was born. I saw her small breasts and the wide, brown scar, belly button to pubic hair, that marked her because my brother and I were both born by Caesarean section. Her hips were small. I was not a large baby, but there was so little room for me in her that when she was carrying me she could not even begin to bend over toward the floor. She hated it, she said.

"Don't I look good? Don't you think I look good?"

I looked at my mother, smiling and as happy as she, thinking of all the times I have seen her naked. I have seen both my parents naked throughout my life, as they have seen me. From childhood through adulthood we've had our naked moments, sharing baths, idle conversations picked up as we moved between showers and closets, hurried moments at the beginning of days, quiet moments at the end of days.

I know this to be Japanese, this ease with the physical, and it makes me think of an old Japanese folk song. A young nursemaid, a fifteen-year-old girl, is singing a lullaby to a baby who is strapped to her back. The nursemaid has been sent as a servant to a place far from her own home. "We're the beggars," she says, "and they are the nice people. Nice people wear fine sashes. Nice clothes."

If I should drop dead,
bury me by the roadside!

I'll give a flower
to everyone who passes.

What kind of flower?
The cam-cam-camellia [tsun-tsun-tsubaki]
watered by Heaven:
alms water.

The nursemaid is the intersection of heaven and earth, the intersec-   28
tion of the human, the natural world, the body, and the soul. In this
song, with clear eyes, she looks steadily at life, which is sometimes so
very terrible and sad. I think of her while looking at my mother, who is
standing on the red and purple carpet before me, laughing, without any
clothes.

I am my mother's daughter. And I am myself.

I am a Japanese-American woman.

EPILOGUE

I recently heard a man from West Africa share some memories of his
childhood. He was raised Muslim, but when he was a young man, he
found himself deeply drawn to Christianity. He struggled against his
inner impulse for years, trying to avoid the church yet feeling pushed to
return to it again and again. "I would have done *anything* to avoid the
change," he said. At last, he became Christian. Afterwards he was afraid
to go home, fearing that he would not be accepted. The fear was
groundless, he discovered, when at last he returned—he had separated
himself, but his family and friends (all Muslim) had not separated
themselves from him.

The man, who is now a professor of religion, said that in the Africa   32
he knew as a child and a young man, pluralism was embraced rather
than feared. There was "a kind of tolerance that did not deny your
particularity," he said. He alluded to zestful, spontaneous debates that
would sometimes loudly erupt between Muslims and Christians in the
village's public spaces. His memories of an atheist who harangued the
villagers when he came to visit them once a week moved me deeply.
Perhaps the man was an agricultural advisor or inspector. He harrassed
the women. He would say: "Don't go to the fields! Don't even bother to
go to the fields. Let God take care of you. He'll send you the food. If you
believe in God, why do you need to work? You don't need to work! Let
God put the seeds in the ground. Stay home."

The professor said, "The women laughed, you know? They just
laughed. Their attitude was, 'Here is a child of God. When will he come
home?' "

The storyteller, the professor of religion, smiled a most fantastic
tender smile as he told this story. "In my country, there is a deep

affirmation of the oneness of God," he said. "The atheist and the women were having quite different experiences in their encounter, though the atheist did not know this. He saw himself as quite separate from the women. But the women did not see themselves as being separate from him. 'Here is a child of God,' they said. 'When will he come home?'"   *1989*

Adrienne Rich

Split at the Root:
An Essay on Jewish Identity

For about fifteen minutes I have been sitting chin in hand in front of the typewriter, staring out at the snow. Trying to be honest with myself, trying to figure out why writing this seems to be so dangerous an act, filled with fear and shame, and why it seems so necessary. It comes to me that in order to write this I have to be willing to do two things: I have to claim my father, for I have my Jewishness from him and not from my gentile mother, and I have to break his silence, his taboos; in order to claim him I have in a sense to expose him.

And there is, of course, the third thing: I have to face the sources and the flickering presence of my own ambivalence as a Jew; the daily, mundane anti-Semitisms of my entire life.

These are stories I have never tried to tell before. Why now? Why, I asked myself sometime last year, does this question of Jewish identity float so impalpably, so ungraspably around me, a cloud I can't quite see the outlines of, which feels to me to be without definition?

And yet I've been on the track of this longer than I think.   4

In a long poem written in 1960, when I was thirty-one years old, I described myself as "Split at the root, neither Gentile nor Jew,/Yankee nor Rebel."[1] I was still trying to have it both ways: to be neither/nor, trying to live (with my Jewish husband and three children more Jewish

[1]Adrienne Rich, "Readings of History," in *Snapshots of a Daughter-in-Law* (New York: W. W. Norton, 1967), pp. 36–40. [Author's note]

in ancestry than I) in the predominantly gentile Yankee academic world of Cambridge, Massachusetts.

But this begins, for me, in Baltimore, where I was born in my father's workplace, a hospital in the black ghetto, whose lobby contained an immense white marble statue of Christ.

My father was then a young teacher and researcher in the department of pathology at the Johns Hopkins Medical School, one of the very few Jews to attend or teach at that institution. He was from Birmingham, Alabama; his father, Samuel, was Ashkenazic,[2] an immigrant from Austria-Hungary and his mother, Hattie Rice, a Sephardic[3] Jew from Vicksburg, Mississippi. My grandfather had had a shoe store in Birmingham, which did well enough to allow him to retire comfortably and to leave my grandmother income on his death. The only souvenirs of my grandfather, Samuel Rich, were his ivory flute, which lay on our living-room mantel and was not to be played with; his thin gold pocket watch, which my father wore; and his Hebrew prayer book, which I discovered among my father's books in the course of reading my way through his library. In this prayer book there was a newspaper clipping about my grandparents' wedding, which took place in a synagogue.

My father, Arnold, was sent in adolescence to a military school in   8
the North Carolina mountains, a place for training white southern Christian gentlemen. I suspect that there were few, if any, other Jewish boys at Colonel Bingham's, or at "Mr. Jefferson's university" in Charlottesville, where he studied as an undergraduate. With whatever conscious forethought, Samuel and Hattie sent their son into the dominant southern WASP culture to become an "exception," to enter the professional class. Never, in describing these experiences, did he speak of having suffered—from loneliness, cultural alienation, or outsiderhood. Never did I hear him use the word *anti-Semitism*.

It was only in college, when I read a poem by Karl Shapiro beginning "To hate the Negro and avoid the Jew / is the curriculum," that it flashed on me that there was an untold side to my father's story of his student years. He looked recognizably Jewish, was short and slender in build with dark wiry hair and deep-set eyes, high forehead, and curved nose.

My mother is a gentile. In Jewish law I cannot count myself a Jew. If it is true that "we think back through our mothers if we are women"

[2]**Ashkenazic:** Descendants of the Jews, generally Yiddish-speaking, who settled in middle and northern Europe.—Eds.
[3]**Sephardic:** Descendants of the Jews who settled for the most part in Spain, Portugal, and northern Africa.—Eds.

(Virginia Woolf)—and I myself have affirmed this—then even according to lesbian theory, I cannot (or need not?) count myself a Jew.

The white southern Protestant woman, the gentile, has always been
there for me to peel back into. That's a whole piece of history in itself,
for my gentile grandmother and my mother were also frustrated artists
and intellectuals, a lost writer and a lost composer between them.
Readers and annotators of books, note takers, my mother a good pianist
still, in her eighties. But there was also the obsession with ancestry, with
"background," the southern talk of family, not as people you would
necessarily know and depend on, but as heritage, the guarantee of
"good breeding." There was the inveterate romantic heterosexual fantasy, the mother telling the daughter how to attract men (my mother
often used the word "fascinate"); the assumption that relations between
the sexes could only be romantic, that it was in the woman's interest to
cultivate "mystery," conceal her actual feelings. Survival tactics of a
kind, I think today, knowing what I know about the white woman's
sexual role in the southern racist scenario. Heterosexuality as protection, but also drawing white women deeper into collusion with white
men.

It would be easy to push away and deny the gentile in me—that
white southern woman, that social christian. At different times in my
life I have wanted to push away one or the other burden of inheritance,
to say merely *I am a woman; I am a lesbian.* If I call myself a Jewish lesbian,
do I thereby try to shed some of my southern gentile white woman's
culpability? If I call myself only through my mother, is it because I pass
more easily through a world where being a lesbian often seems like
outsiderhood enough?

According to Nazi logic, my two Jewish grandparents would have
made me a *Mischling, first-degree*—nonexempt from the Final Solution.[4]

The social world in which I grew up was christian virtually without
needing to say so—christian imagery, music, language, symbols, assumptions everywhere. It was also a genteel, white, middle-class world
in which "common" was a term of deep opprobrium. "Common" white
people might speak of "niggers"; *we* were taught never to use that
word—*we* said "Negroes" (even as we accepted segregation, the eating
taboo, the assumption that black people were simply of a separate
species). Our language was more polite, distinguishing us from the "rednecks" or the lynch-mob mentality. But so charged with negative meaning was even the word "Negro" that as children we were taught never to
use it in front of black people. We were taught that any mention of skin

---

[4]**Final Solution:** The Nazi plan to exterminate all members of the Jewish race.—EDS.

color in the presence of colored people was treacherous, forbidden ground. In a parallel way, the word *Jew* was not used by polite gentiles. I sometimes heard my best friend's father, a Presbyterian minister, allude to "the Hebrew people" or "people of the Jewish faith." The world of acceptable folk was white, gentile (christian, really), and had "ideals" (which colored people, white "common" people, were not supposed to have). "Ideals" and "manners" included not hurting someone's feelings by calling her or him a Negro or a Jew—naming the hated identity. This is the mental framework of the 1930s and 1940s in which I was raised.

(Writing this, I feel dimly like the betrayer: of my father, who did not speak the word; of my mother, who must have trained me in the messages; of my caste and class; of my whiteness itself.)

Two memories: I am in a play reading at school of *The Merchant of* 16 *Venice*. Whatever Jewish law says, I am quite sure I was *seen* as Jewish (with a reassuringly gentile mother) in that double vision that bigotry allows. I am the only Jewish girl in the class, and I am playing Portia. As always, I read my part aloud for my father the night before, and he tells me to convey, with my voice, more scorn and contempt with the word *Jew*: "Therefore, Jew . . . ." I have to say the word out, and say it loudly. I was encouraged to pretend to be a non-Jewish child acting a non-Jewish character who has to speak the word *Jew* emphatically. Such a child would not have had trouble with the part. But *I* must have had trouble with the part, if only because the word itself was really taboo. I can see that there was a kind of terrible, bitter bravado about my father's way of handling this. And who would not dissociate from Shylock in order to identify with Portia? As a Jewish child who was also a female, I loved Portia—and, like every other Shakespearean heroine, she proved a treacherous role model.

A year or so later I am in another play, *The School for Scandal*, in which a notorious spendthrift is described as having "many excellent friends . . . among the Jews." In neither case was anything explained, either to me or to the class at large, about this scorn for Jews and the disgust surrounding Jews and money. Money, when Jews wanted it, had it, or lent it to others, seemed to take on a peculiar nastiness; Jews and money had some peculiar and unspeakable relation.

At this same school—in which we had Episcopalian hymns and prayers, and read aloud through the Bible morning after morning—I gained the impression that Jews were in the Bible and mentioned in English literature, that they had been persecuted centuries ago by the wicked Inquisition, but that they seemed not to exist in everyday life. These were the 1940s, and we were told a great deal about the Battle of Britain, the noble French Resistance fighters, the brave, starving Dutch—but I did not learn of the resistance of the Warsaw ghetto until I left home.

I was sent to the Episcopal church, baptized and confirmed, and attended it for about five years, though without belief. That religion seemed to have little to do with belief or commitment; it was liturgy that mattered, not spiritual passion. Neither of my parents ever entered that church, and my father would not enter *any* church for any reason— wedding or funeral. Nor did I enter a synagogue until I left Baltimore. When I came home from church, for a while, my father insisted on reading aloud to me from Thomas Paine's *The Age of Reason*—a diatribe against institutional religion. Thus, he explained, I would have a balanced view of these things, a choice. He—they—did not give me the choice to be a Jew. My mother explained to me when I was filling out forms for college that if any question was asked about "religion," I should put down "Episcopalian" rather than "none"—to seem to have no religion was, she implied, dangerous.

But it was white social christianity, rather than any particular chris- 20
tian sect, that the world was founded on. The very word *Christian* was used as a synonym for virtuous, just, peace-loving, generous, etc., etc.[5] The norm was christian: "religion: none" was indeed not acceptable. Anti-Semitism was so intrinsic as not to have a name. I don't recall exactly being taught that the Jews killed Jesus—"Christ killer" seems too strong a term for the bland Episcopal vocabulary—but certainly we got the impression that the Jews had been caught out in a terrible mistake, failing to recognize the true Messiah, and were thereby less advanced in moral and spiritual sensibility. The Jews had actually allowed *moneylenders in the Temple* (again, the unexplained obsession with Jews and money). They were of the past, archaic, primitive, as older (and darker) cultures are supposed to be primitive; christianity was lightness, fairness, peace on earth, and combined the feminine appeal of "The meek shall inherit the earth" with the masculine stride of "Onward, Christian Soldiers."

Sometime in 1946, while still in high school, I read in the newspaper that a theater in Baltimore was showing films of the Allied liberation of the Nazi concentration camps. Alone, I went downtown after school one afternoon and watched the stark, blurry, but unmistakable newsreels. When I try to go back and touch the pulse of that girl of sixteen, growing up in many ways so precocious and so ignorant, I am overwhelmed by a memory of despair, a sense of inevitability more enveloping than any I had ever known. Anne Frank's diary and many other personal narratives of the Holocaust were still unknown or unwritten. But it came to me that every one of those piles of corpses,

---

[5]In a similar way the phrase *That's white of you* implied that you were behaving with the superior decency and morality expected of white but not of black people. [Author's note]

mountains of shoes and clothing had contained, simply, individuals, who had believed, as I now believed of myself, that they were intended to live out a life of some kind of meaning, that the world possessed some kind of sense and order; yet *this* had happened to them. And I, who believed my life was intended to be so interesting and meaningful, was connected to those dead by something—not just mortality but a taboo name, a hated identity. Or was I—did I really have to be? Writing this now, I feel belated rage that I was so impoverished by the family and social worlds I lived in, that I had to try to figure out by myself what this did indeed mean for me. That I had never been taught about resistance, only about passing. That I had no language for anti-Semitism itself.

When I went home and told my parents where I had been, they were not pleased. I felt accused of being morbidly curious, not healthy, sniffing around death for the thrill of it. And since, at sixteen, I was often not sure of the sources of my feelings or of my motives for doing what I did, I probably accused myself as well. One thing was clear: there was nobody in my world with whom I could discuss those films. Probably at the same time, I was reading accounts of the camps in magazines and newspapers; what I remember were the films and having questions that I could not even phrase, such as *Are those men and women "them" or "us"?*

To be able to ask even the child's astonished question *Why do they hate us so?* means knowing how to say "we." The guilt of not knowing, the guilt of perhaps having betrayed my parents or even those victims, those survivors, through mere curiosity—these also froze in me for years the impulse to find out more about the Holocaust.

1947: I left Baltimore to go to college in Cambridge, Massachusetts, 24 left (I thought) the backward, enervating South for the intellectual, vital North. New England also had for me some vibration of higher moral rectitude, of moral passion even, with its seventeenth-century Puritan self-scrutiny, its nineteenth-century literary "flowering," its abolitionist righteousness, Colonel Shaw and his black Civil War regiment depicted in granite on Boston Common. At the same time, I found myself, at Radcliffe, among Jewish women. I used to sit for hours over coffee with what I thought of as the "real" Jewish students, who told me about middle-class Jewish culture in America. I described my background— for the first time to strangers—and they took me on, some with amusement at my illiteracy, some arguing that I could never marry into a strict Jewish family, some convinced I didn't "look Jewish," others that I did. I learned the names of holidays and foods, which surnames are Jewish and which are "changed names"; about girls who had had their noses "fixed," their hair straightened. For these young Jewish women, students in the late 1940s, it was acceptable, perhaps even necessary, to

strive to look as gentile as possible; but they stuck proudly to being
Jewish, expected to marry a Jew, have children, keep the holidays, carry
on the culture.

I felt I was testing a forbidden current, that there was danger in
these revelations. I bought a reproduction of a Chagall portrait of a
rabbi in striped prayer shawl and hung it on the wall of my room. I was
admittedly young and trying to educate myself, but I was also doing
something that *is* dangerous: I was flirting with identity.

One day that year I was in a small shop where I had bought a dress
with a too-long skirt. The shop employed a seamstress who did altera-
tions, and she came in to pin up the skirt on me. I am sure that she was a
recent immigrant, a survivor. I remember a short, dark woman wearing
heavy glasses, with an accent so foreign I could not understand her
words. Something about her presence was very powerful and disturbing
to me. After marking and pinning up the skirt, she sat back on her
knees, looked up at me, and asked in a hurried whisper: "You Jewish?"
Eighteen years of training in assimilation sprang into the reflex by
which I shook my head, rejecting her, and muttered, "No."

What was I actually saying "no" to? She was poor, older, struggling
with a foreign tongue, anxious; she had escaped the death that had been
intended for her, but I had no imagination of her possible courage and
foresight, her resistance—I did not see in her a heroine who had
perhaps saved many lives, including her own. I saw the frightened
immigrant, the seamstress hemming the skirts of college girls, the
wandering Jew. But I was an American college girl having her skirt
hemmed. And I was frightened myself, I think, because she had recognized me ("It takes one to know one," my friend Edie at Radcliffe had
said) even if I refused to recognize myself or her, even if her recognition
was sharpened by loneliness or the need to feel safe with me.

But why should she have felt safe with me? I myself was living with a   28
false sense of safety.

There are betrayals in my life that I have known at the very moment
were betrayals: this was one of them. There are other betrayals committed so repeatedly, so mundanely, that they leave no memory trace
behind, only a growing residue of misery, of dull, accreted self-hatred.
Often these take the form not of words but of silence. Silence before the
joke at which everyone is laughing: the anti-woman joke, the racist joke,
the anti-Semitic joke. Silence and then amnesia. Blocking it out when
the oppressor's language starts coming from the lips of one we admire,
whose courage and eloquence have touched us: *She didn't really mean that;
he didn't really say that.* But the accretions build up out of sight, like scale
inside a kettle.

1948: I come home from my freshman year at college, flaming with new insights, new information. I am the daughter who has gone out into the world, to the pinnacle of intellectual prestige, Harvard, fulfilling my father's hopes for me, but also exposed to dangerous influences. I have already been reproved for attending a rally for Henry Wallace[6] and the Progressive party. I challenge my father: "Why haven't you told me that I am Jewish? Why do you never talk about being a Jew?" He answers measuredly, "You know that I have never denied that I am a Jew. But it's not important to me. I am a scientist, a deist. I have no use for organized religion. I choose to live in a world of many kinds of people. There are Jews I admire and others whom I despise. I am a person, not simply a Jew." The words are as I remember them, not perhaps exactly as spoken. But that was the message. And it contained enough truth—as all denial drugs itself on partial truth—so that it remained for the time being unanswerable, leaving me high and dry, split at the root, gasping for clarity, for air.

At that time Arnold Rich was living in suspension, waiting to be appointed to the professorship of pathology at Johns Hopkins. The appointment was delayed for years, no Jew ever having held a profes-sional chair in that medical school. And he wanted it badly. It must have been a very bitter time for him, since he had believed so greatly in the redeeming power of excellence, of being the most brilliant, inspired man for the job. With enough excellence, you could presumably make it stop mattering that you were Jewish; you could become the *only* Jew in the gentile world, a Jew so "civilized," so far from "common," so attrac-tively combining southern gentility with European cultural values that no one would ever confuse you with the raw, "pushy" Jews of New York, the "loud, hysterical" refugees from eastern Europe, the "overdressed" Jews of the urban South.

We—my sister, mother, and I—were constantly urged to speak 32 quietly in public, to dress without ostentation, to repress all vividness or spontaneity, to assimilate with a world which might see us as too flamboyant. I suppose that my mother, pure gentile though she was, could be seen as acting "common" or "Jewish" if she laughed too loudly or spoke aggressively. My father's mother, who lived with us half the year, was a model of circumspect behavior, dressed in dark blue or lavender, retiring in company, ladylike to an extreme, wearing no jewelry except a good gold chain, a narrow brooch, or a string of pearls. A few times, within the family, I saw her anger flare, felt the passion she was repressing. But when Arnold took us out to a restaurant or on a trip,

[6]**Henry Wallace:** (1888–1965), American journalist, agriculturalist, and politician. Was the 1948 Progressive party's candidate for the presidency.—EDS.

the Rich women were always tuned down to some WASP level my father
believed, surely, would protect us all—maybe also make us unrecogniz-
able to the "real Jews" who wanted to seize us, drag us back to the *shtetl*,
the ghetto, in its many manifestations.

For, yes, that *was* a message—that some Jews would be after you,
once they "knew," to rejoin them, to re-enter a world that was messy,
noisy, unpredictable, maybe poor—"even though," as my mother once
wrote me, criticizing my largely Jewish choice of friends in college,
"some of them will be the most brilliant, fascinating people you'll ever
meet." I wonder if that isn't one message of assimilation—of America—
that the unlucky or the unachieving want to pull you backward, that to
identify with them is to court downward mobility, lose the precious
chance of passing, of token existence. There was always within this
sense of Jewish identity a strong class discrimination. Jews might be
"fascinating" as individuals but came with huge unruly families who
"poured chicken soup over everyone's head" (in the phrase of a white
southern male poet). Anti-Semitism could thus be justified by the bad
behavior of certain Jews; and if you did not effectively deny family and
community, there would always be a remote cousin claiming kinship
with you who was the "wrong kind" of Jew.

I have always believed his attitude toward other Jews depended on who they
were. . . . It was my impression that Jews of this background looked down on
Eastern European Jews, including Polish Jews and Russian Jews, who generally
were not as well educated. This from a letter written to me recently by a
gentile who had worked in my father's department, whom I had asked
about anti-Semitism there and in particular regarding my father. This
informant also wrote me that it was hard to perceive anti-Semitism in
Baltimore because the racism made so much more intense an impression: *I would almost have to think that blacks went to a different heaven than the*
whites, because the bodies were kept in a separate morgue, and some white persons
did not even want blood transfusions from black donors. My father's mind was
predictably racist and misogynist; yet as a medical student he noted in
his journal that southern male chivalry stopped at the point of any
white man in a streetcar giving his seat to an old, weary black woman
standing in the aisle. Was this a Jewish insight—an outsider's insight,
even though the outsider was striving to be on the inside?

Because what isn't named is often more permeating than what is, I
believe that my father's Jewishness profoundly shaped my own identity
and our family existence. They were shaped both by external anti-
Semitism and my father's self-hatred, and by his Jewish pride. What
Arnold did, I think, was call his Jewish pride something else: achievement, aspiration, genius, idealism. Whatever was unacceptable got left
back under the rubric of Jewishness or the "wrong kind" of Jews—
uneducated, aggressive, loud. The message I got was that we were really

superior: nobody else's father had collected so many books, had traveled so far, knew so many languages. Baltimore was a musical city, but
for the most part, in the families of my school friends, culture was for
women. My father was an amateur musician, read poetry, adored en-
cyclopedic knowledge. He prowled and pounced over my school papers,
insisting I use "grown-up" sources; he criticized my poems for faulty
technique and gave me books on rhyme and meter and form. His
investment in my intellect and talent was egotistical, tyrannical, opinionated, and terribly wearing. He taught me, nevertheless, to believe in
hard work, to mistrust easy inspiration, to write and rewrite; to feel that
I *was* a person of the book, even though a woman; to take ideas seriously.
He made me feel, at a very young age, the power of language and that I
could share in it.

The Riches were proud, but we also had to be very careful. Our   36
behavior had to be more impeccable than other people's. Strangers
were not to be trusted, nor even friends; family issues must never go
beyond the family; the world was full of potential slanderers, betrayers,
people who could not understand. Even within the family, I realize that I
never in my whole life knew what my father was really feeling. Yet he
spoke—monologued—with driving intensity. You could grow up in such
a house mesmerized by the local electricity, the crucial meanings assumed by the merest things. This used to seem to me a sign that we were
all living on some high emotional plane. It was a difficult force field for
a favored daughter to disengage from.

Easy to call that intensity Jewish; and I have no doubt that passion is
one of the qualities required for survival over generations of persecution. But what happens when passion is rent from its original base,
when the white gentile world is softly saying "Be more like us and you
can be almost one of us"? What happens when survival seems to mean
closing off one emotional artery after another? His forebears in Europe
had been forbidden to travel or expelled from one country after another, had special taxes levied on them if they left the city walls, had
been forced to wear special clothes and badges, restricted to the poorest
neighborhoods. He had wanted to be a "free spirit," to travel widely,
among "all kinds of people." Yet in his prime of life he lived in an
increasingly withdrawn world, in his house up on a hill in a neighborhood where Jews were not supposed to be able to buy property, depending almost exclusively on interactions with his wife and daughters to
provide emotional connectedness. In his home, he created a private
defense system so elaborate that even as he was dying, my mother felt
unable to talk freely with his colleagues or others who might have
helped her. Of course, she acquiesced in this.

The loneliness of the "only," the token, often doesn't feel like
loneliness but like a kind of dead echo chamber. Certain things that

ought to don't resonate. Somewhere Beverly Smith writes of women of color "inspiring the behavior" in each other. When there's nobody to "inspire the behavior," act out of the culture, there is an atrophy, a dwindling, which is partly invisible.

Sometimes I feel I have seen too long from too many disconnected angles: white, Jewish, anti-Semite, racist, anti-racist, once-married, lesbian, middle-class, feminist, exmatriate southerner, *split at the root*—that I will never bring them whole. I would have liked, in this essay, to bring together the meanings of anti-Semitism and racism as I have experienced them and as I believe they intersect in the world beyond my life. But I'm not able to do this yet. I feel the tension as I think, make notes: *If you really look at the one reality, the other will waver and disperse.* Trying in one week to read Angela Davis and Lucy Davidowicz,[7] trying to hold throughout to a feminist, a lesbian, perspective—what does this mean? Nothing has trained me for this. And sometimes I feel inadequate to make any statement as a Jew; I feel the history of denial within me like an injury, a scar. For assimilation has affected *my* perceptions; those early lapses in meaning, those blanks, are with me still. My ignorance can be dangerous to me and to others.

Yet we can't wait for the undamaged to make our connections for us; we can't wait to speak until we are perfectly clear and righteous. There is no purity and, in our lifetimes, no end to this process.

This essay, then, has no conclusions: it is another beginning for me. Not just a way of saying, in 1982 Right Wing America, *I, too, will wear the yellow star.* It's a moving into accountability, enlarging the range of accountability. I know that in the rest of my life, the next half century or so, every aspect of my identity will have to be engaged. The middle-class white girl taught to trade obedience for privilege. The Jewish lesbian raised to be a heterosexual gentile. The woman who first heard oppression named and analyzed in the black Civil Rights struggle. The woman with three sons, the feminist who hates male violence. The woman limping with a cane, the woman who has stopped bleeding are also accountable. The poet who knows that beautiful language can lie, that the oppressor's language sometimes sounds beautiful. The woman trying, as part of her resistance, to clean up her act.   *1986*

[7]Angela Y. Davis, *Women, Race and Class* (New York: Random House, 1981); Lucy S. Davidowicz, *The War against the Jews 1933–1945* (1975) (New York: Bantam, 1979). [Author's note]

Shelby Steele

On Being Black and Middle Class

Not long ago a friend of mine, black like myself, said to me that the term "black middle class" was actually a contradiction in terms. Race, he insisted, blurred class distinctions among blacks. If you were black, you were just black and that was that. When I argued, he let his eyes roll at my naiveté. Then he went on. For us, as black professionals, it was an exercise in self-flattery, a pathetic pretention, to give meaning to such a distinction. Worse, the very idea of class threatened the unity that was vital to the black community as a whole. After all, since when had white America taken note of anything but color when it came to blacks? He then reminded me of an old Malcolm X line that had been popular in the sixties. Question: What is a black man with a Ph.D.? Answer: A nigger.

For many years I had been on my friend's side of this argument. Much of my conscious thinking on the old conundrum of race and class was shaped during my high school and college years in the race-charged sixties, when the fact of my race took on an almost religious significance. Progressively, from the mid-sixties on, more and more aspects of my life found their explanation, their justification, and their motivation in race. My youthful concerns about career, romance, money, values, and even styles of dress became a subject to consultation with various oracular sources of racial wisdom. And these ranged from a figure as ennobling as Martin Luther King, Jr., to the underworld elegance of dress I found in jazz clubs on the South Side of Chicago. Everywhere there were signals, and in those days I considered myself so blessed with clarity and direction that I pitied my white classmates who found more embarrassment than guidance in the face of *their* race. In 1968, inflated by my new power, I took a mischievous delight in calling them culturally disadvantaged.

But now, hearing my friend's comment was like hearing a priest from a church I'd grown disenchanted with. I understood him, but my faith was weak. What had sustained me in the sixties sounded monotonous and off the mark in the eighties. For me, race had lost much of its juju, its singular capacity to conjure meaning. And today, when I honestly look at my life and the lives of many other middle-class blacks I know, I can see that race never fully explained our situation in American society. Black though I may be, it is impossible for me to sit in my single-family house with two cars in the driveway and a swing set in the back yard and *not* see the role class has played in my life. And how can my friend, similarly raised and similarly situated, not see it?

Yet despite my certainty I felt a sharp tug of guilt as I tried to   4
explain myself over my friend's skepticism. He is a man of many
comedic facial expressions and, as I spoke, his brow lifted in extreme
moral alarm as if I were uttering the unspeakable. His clear implication
was that I was being elitist and possibly (dare he suggest?) antiblack—
crimes for which there might well be no redemption. He pretended to
fear for me. I chuckled along with him, but inwardly I did wonder at
myself. Though I never doubted the validity of what I was saying, I felt
guilty saying it. Why?

After he left (to retrieve his daughter from a dance lesson) I realized
that the trap I felt myself in had a tiresome familiarity and, in a sort of
slow-motion epiphany, I began to see its outline. It was like the suddenly
sharp vision one has at the end of a burdensome marriage when all the
long-repressed incompatibilities come undeniably to light.

What became clear to me is that people like myself, my friend, and
middle-class blacks generally are caught in a very specific double bind
that keeps two equally powerful elements of our identity at odds with
each other. The middle-class values by which we were raised—the work
ethic, the importance of education, the value of property ownership, of
respectability, of "getting ahead," of stable family life, of initiative, of
self-reliance, etc.—are, in themselves, raceless and even assimilationist.
They urge us toward participation in the American mainstream, toward
integration, toward a strong identification with the society—and toward the entire constellation of qualities that are implied in the word
"individualism." These values are almost rules for how to prosper in a
democratic, free-enterprise society that admires and rewards individual
effort. They tell us to work hard for ourselves and our families and to
seek our opportunities whenever they appear, inside or outside the
confines of whatever ethnic group we may belong to.

But the particular pattern of racial identification that emerged in
the sixties and that still prevails today urges middle-class blacks (and all
blacks) in the opposite direction. This pattern asks us to see ourselves as
an embattled minority, and it urges an adversarial stance toward the
mainstream, an emphasis on ethnic consciousness over individualism.
It is organized around an implied separatism.

The opposing thrust of these two parts of our identity results in the   8
double bind of middle-class blacks. There is no forward movement on
either plane that does not constitute backward movement on the other.
This was the familiar trap I felt myself in while talking with my friend.
As I spoke about class, his eyes reminded me that I was betraying race.
Clearly, the two indispensable parts of my identity were a threat to each
other.

Of course when you think about it, class and race are both similar in
some ways and also naturally opposed. They are two forms of collective

identity with boundaries that intersect. But whether they clash or peace-fully coexist has much to do with how they are defined. Being both black and middle class becomes a double bind when class and race are defined in sharply antagonistic terms, so that one must be repressed to appease the other.

But what is the "substance" of these two identities, and how does each establish itself in an individual's overall identity? It seems to me that when we identify with any collective we are basically identifying with images that tell us what it means to be a member of that collective. Identity is not the same thing as the fact of membership in a collective; it is, rather, a form of self-definition, facilitated by images of what we wish our membership in the collective to mean. In this sense, the images we identify with may reflect the aspirations of the collective more than they reflect reality, and their content can vary with shifts in those aspirations.

But the process of identification is usually dialectical. It is just as necessary to say what we are *not* as it is to say what we are—so that finally identification comes about by embracing a polarity of positive and negative images. To identify as middle class, for example, I must have both positive and negative images of what being middle class entails; then I will know what I should and should not be doing in order to be middle class. The same goes for racial identity.

In the racially turbulent sixties the polarity of images that came to 12 define racial identification was very antagonistic to the polarity that defined middle-class identification. One might say that the positive images of one lined up with the negative images of the other, so that to identify with both required either a contortionist's flexibility or a dangerous splitting of the self. The double bind of the black middle class was in place.

The black middle class has always defined its class identity by means of positive images gleaned from middle- and upper-class white society, and by means of negative images of lower-class blacks. This habit goes back to the institution of slavery itself, when "house" slaves both mimicked the whites they served and held themselves above the "field" slaves. But in the sixties the old bourgeois impulse to dissociate from the lower classes (the "we-they" distinction) backfired when racial identity suddenly called for the celebration of this same black lower class. One of the qualities of a double bind is that one feels it more than sees it, and I distinctly remember the tension and strange sense of dishonesty I felt in those days as I moved back and forth like a bigamist between the demands of class and race.

Though my father was born poor, he achieved middle-class standing through much hard work and sacrifice (one of his favorite words) and by identifying fully with solid middle-class values—mainly hard work, family life, property ownership, and education for his children (all four of whom have advanced degrees). In his mind these were not so much values as laws of nature. People who embodied them made up the positive images in his class polarity. The negative images came largely from the blacks he had left behind because they were "going nowhere."

No one in my family remembers how it happened, but as time went on, the negative images congealed into an imaginary character named Sam, who, from the extensive service we put him to, quickly grew to mythic proportions. In our family lore he was sometimes a trickster, sometimes a boob, but always possessed of a catalogue of sly faults that gave up graphic images of everything we should not be. On sacrifice: "Sam never thinks about tomorrow. He wants it now or he doesn't care about it." On work: "Sam doesn't favor it too much." On children: "Sam likes to have them but not to raise them." On money: "Sam drinks it up and pisses it out." On fidelity: "Sam has to have two or three women." On clothes: "Sam features loud clothes. He likes to see and be seen." And so on. Sam's persona amounted to a negative instruction manual in class identity.

I don't think that any of us believed Sam's faults were accurate 16 representations of lower-class black life. He was an instrument of self-definition, not of sociological accuracy. It never occurred to us that he looked very much like the white racist stereotype of blacks, or that he might have been a manifestation of our own racial self-hatred. He simply gave us a counterpoint against which to express our aspirations. If self-hatred was a factor, it was not, for us, a matter of hating lower-class blacks but of hating what we did not want to be.

Still, hate or love aside, it is fundamentally true that my middle-class identity involved a dissociation from images of lower-class black life and a corresponding identification with values and patterns of responsibility that are common to the middle class everywhere. These values sent me a clear message: be both an individual and a responsible citizen; understand that the quality of your life will approximately reflect the quality of effort you put into it; know that individual responsibility is the basis of freedom and that the limitations imposed by fate (whether fair or unfair) are no excuse for passivity.

Whether I live up to these values or not, I know that my acceptance of them is the result of lifelong conditioning. I know also that I share this conditioning with middle-class people of all races and that I can no more easily be free of it than I can be free of my race. Whether all this got started because the black middle class modeled itself on the white middle class is no longer relevant. For the middle-class black, conditioned by these values from birth, the sense of meaning they provide is as immutable as the color of his skin.

I started the sixties in high school feeling that my class-conditioning was the surest way to overcome racial barriers. My racial identity was pretty much taken for granted. After all, it was obvious to the world that I was black. Yet I ended the sixties in graduate school a little embarrassed by my class background and with an almost desperate need to be "black." The tables had turned. I knew very clearly (though I struggled to repress it) that my aspirations and my sense of how to operate in the world came from my class background, yet "being black" required certain attitudes and stances that made me feel secretly a little duplicitous. The inner compatibility of class and race I had known in 1960 was gone.

For blacks, the decade between 1960 and 1969 saw racial identification undergo the same sort of transformation that national identity undergoes in times of war. It became more self-conscious, more narrowly focused, more prescribed, less tolerant of opposition. It spawned an implicit party line, which tended to disallow competing forms of identity. Race-as-identity was lifted from the relative slumber it knew in the fifties and pressed into service in a social and political war against oppression. It was redefined along sharp adversarial lines and directed toward the goal of mobilizing the great mass of black Americans in this warlike effort. It was imbued with a strong moral authority, useful for denouncing those who opposed it and for celebrating those who honored it as a positive achievement rather than as a mere birthright.

The form of racial identification that quickly evolved to meet this challenge presented blacks as a racial monolith, a singular people with a common experience of oppression. Differences within the race, no matter how ineradicable, had to be minimized. Class distinctions were one of the first such differences to be sacrificed, since they not only threatened racial unity but also seemed to stand in contradiction to the principle of equality which was the announced goal of the movement for racial progress. The discomfort I felt in 1969, the vague but relentless sense of duplicity, was the result of a historical necessity that put my race and class at odds, that was asking me to cast aside the distinction of my class and identify with a monolithic view of my race.

If the form of this racial identity was the monolith, its substance was victimization. The civil rights movement and the more radical splinter groups of the late sixties were all dedicated to ending racial victimization, and the form of black identity that emerged to facilitate this goal made blackness and victimization virtually synonymous. Since it was our victimization more than any other variable that identified and unified us, moreover, it followed logically that the purest black was the poor black. It was images of him that clustered around the positive pole of the race polarity; all other blacks were, in effect, required to identify with him in order to confirm their own blackness.

Certainly there were more dimensions to the black experience than victimization, but no other had the same capacity to fire the indignation needed for war. So, again out of historical necessity, victimization became the overriding focus of racial identity. But this only deepened the double bind for middle-class blacks like me. When it came to class we were accustomed to defining ourselves against lower-class blacks and identifying with at least the values of middle-class whites; when it came to race we were now being asked to identify with images of lower-class blacks and to see whites, middle class or otherwise, as victimizers. Negative lining up with positive, we were called upon to reject what we had previously embraced and to embrace what we had previously rejected. To put it still more personally, the Sam figure I had been raised to define myself against had now become the "real" black I was expected to identify with.

The fact that the poor black's new status was only passively earned 24 by the condition of his victimization, not by assertive, positive action, made little difference. Status was status apart from the means by which it was achieved, and along with it came a certain power—the power to define the terms of access to that status, to say who was black and who was not. If a lower-class black said you were not really "black"—a sellout, an Uncle Tom—the judgment was all the more devastating because it carried the authority of his status. And this judgment soon enough came to be accepted by many whites as well.

In graduate school I was once told by a white professor, "Well, but . . . you're not really black. I mean, you're not disadvantaged." In his mind my lack of victim status disqualified me from the race itself. More recently I was complimented by a black student for speaking reasonably correct English, "proper" English as he put it. "But I don't know if I really want to talk like that," he went on. "Why not?" I asked. "Because then I wouldn't be black no more," he replied without a pause.

To overcome his marginal status, the middle-class black had to identify with a degree of victimization that was beyond his actual experience. In college (and well beyond) we used to play a game called "nap matching." It was a game of one-upmanship, in which we sat around outdoing each other with stories of racial victimization, symbolically measured by the naps of our hair. Most of us were middle class and so had few personal stories to relate, but if we could not match naps with our own biographies, we would move on to those legendary tales of victimization that came to us from the public domain.

The single story that sat atop the pinnacle of racial victimization for us was that of Emmett Till, the Northern black teenager who, on a visit to the South in 1955, was killed and grotesquely mutilated for supposedly looking at or whistling at (we were never sure which, though we argued the point endlessly) a white woman. Oh, how we probed his story, finding in his youth and Northern upbringing the quintessential embodiment of black innocence, brought down by a white evil so portentous and apocalyptic, so gnarled and hideous, that it left us with a feeling not far from awe. By telling his story and others like it, we came to *feel* the immutability of our victimization, its utter indigenousness, as a thing on this earth like dirt or sand or water.

Of course, these sessions were a ritual of group identification, a means by which we, as middle-class blacks, could be at one with our race. But why were we, who had only a moderate experience of victimization (and that offset by opportunities our parents never had), so intent on assimilating or appropriating an identity that in so many ways contradicted our own? Because, I think, the sense of innocence that is always entailed in feeling victimized filled us with a corresponding feeling of entitlement, or even license, that helped us endure our vulnerability on a largely white college campus. 28

In my junior year in college I rode to a debate tournament with three white students and our faculty coach, an elderly English professor. The experience of being the lone black in a group of whites was so familiar to me that I thought nothing of it as our trip began. But then halfway through the trip the professor casually turned to me and, in an isn't-the-world-funny sort of tone, said that he had just refused to rent an apartment in a house he owned to a "very nice" black couple because their color would "offend" the white couple who lived downstairs. His eyebrows lifted helplessly over his hawkish nose, suggesting that he too, like me, was a victim of America's racial farce. His look assumed a kind of comradeship: he and I were above this grimy business of race, though for expediency we had occasionally to concede the world its madness.

My vulnerability in this situation came not so much from the professor's blindness to his own racism as from his assumption that I would participate in it, that I would conspire with him against my own race so that he might remain comfortably blind. Why did he think I would be amenable to this? I can only guess that he assumed my middle-class identity was so complete and all-encompassing that I would see his action as nothing more than a trifling concession to the folkways of our land, that I would in fact applaud his decision not to disturb propriety. Blind to both his own racism and to me—one blindness serving the other—he could not recognize that he was asking me to betray my race in the name of my class.

His blindness made me feel vulnerable because it threatened to expose my own repressed ambivalence. His comment pressured me to choose between my class identification, which had contributed to my being a college student and a member of the debating team, and my desperate desire to be "black." I could have one but not both; I was double-bound.

Because double binds are repressed there is always an element of 32 terror in them: the terror of bringing to the conscious mind the buried duplicity, self-deception, and pretense involved in serving two masters. This terror is the stuff of vulnerability, and since vulnerability is one of the least tolerable of all human feelings, we usually transform it into an emotion that seems to restore the control of which it has robbed us; most often, that emotion is anger. And so, before the professor had even finished his little story, I had become a furnace of rage. The year was 1967, and I had been primed by endless hours of nap-matching to feel, at least consciously, completely at one with the victim-focused black identity. This identity gave me the license, and the impunity, to unleash upon this professor one of those volcanic eruptions of racial indigna- tion familiar to us from the novels of Richard Wright. Like Cross Damon in *Outsider*, who kills in perfectly righteous anger, I tried to annihilate the man. I punished him not according to the measure of his crime but according to the measure of my vulnerability, a measure set by the cumulative tension of years of repressed terror. Soon I saw that terror in *his* face, as he stared hollow-eyed at the road ahead. My white friends in the back seat, knowing no conflict between their own class and race, were astonished that someone they had taken to be so much like themselves could harbor a rage that for all the world looked murderous.

Though my rage was triggered by the professor's comment, it was deepened and sustained by a complex of need, conflict, and repression in myself of which I had been wholly unaware. Out of my racial vulnerability I had developed the strong need of an identity with which to defend myself. The only such identity available was that of me as victim, him as victimizer. Once in the grip of this paradigm, I began to do far more damage to myself than he had done.

Seeing myself as a victim meant that I clung all the harder to my racial identity, which, in turn, meant that I suppressed my class identity. This cut me off from all the resources my class values might have offered me. In those values, for instance, I might have found the means to a more dispassionate response, the response less of a victim attacked by a victimizer than of an individual offended by a foolish old man. As an individual I might have reported this professor to the college dean. Or I might have calmly tried to reveal his blindness to him, and possibly won a convert. (The flagrancy of his remark suggested a hidden guilt and even self-recognition on which I might have capitalized. Doesn't confession usually signal a willingness to face oneself?) Or I might have simply chuckled and then let my silence serve as an answer to his provocation. Would not my composure, in any form it might take, deflect into his own heart the arrow he'd shot at me?

Instead, my anger, itself the hair-trigger expression of a long-repressed double bind, not only cut me off from the best of my own resources, it also distorted the nature of my true racial problem. The righteousness of this anger and the easy catharsis it brought buoyed the delusion of my victimization and left me as blind as the professor himself.

As a middle-class black I have often felt myself *contriving* to be 36 "black." And I have noticed this same contrivance in others—a certain stretching away from the natural flow of one's life to align oneself with a victim-focused black identity. Our particular needs are out of sync with the form of identity available to meet those needs. Middle-class blacks need to identify racially; it is better to think of ourselves as black and victimized than not black at all; so we contrive (more unconsciously than consciously) to fit ourselves into an identity that denies our class and fails to address the true source of our vulnerability.

For me this once meant spending inordinate amounts of time at black faculty meetings, though these meetings had little to do with my real racial anxieties or my professional life. I was new to the university, one of two blacks in an English department of over seventy, and I felt a little isolated and vulnerable, though I did not admit it to myself. But at these meetings we discussed the problems of black faculty and students within a framework of victimization. The real vulnerability we felt was covered over by all the adversarial drama the victim/victimized polarity inspired, and hence went unseen and unassuaged. And this, I think, explains our rather chronic ineffectiveness as a group. Since victimization was not our primary problem—the university had long ago opened its doors to us—we had to contrive to make it so, and there is not much energy in contrivance. What I got at these meetings was ultimately an object lesson in how fruitless struggle can be when it is not grounded in actual need.

At our black faculty meetings, the old equation of blackness with victimization was ever present—to be black was to be a victim; therefore, not to be a victim was not to be black. As we contrived to meet the terms of this formula there was an inevitable distortion of both ourselves and the larger university. Through the prism of victimization the university seemed more impenetrable than it actually was, and we more limited in our powers. We fell prey to the victim's myopia, making the university an institution from which we could seek redress but which we could never fully join. And this mind-set often led us to look more for compensations for our supposed victimization than for opportunities we could pursue as individuals.

The discomfort and vulnerability felt by middle-class blacks in the sixties, it could be argued, was a worthwhile price to pay considering the progress achieved during that time of racial confrontation. But what may have been tolerable then is intolerable now. Though changes in American society have made it an anachronism, the monolithic form of racial identification that came out of the sixties is still very much with us. It may be more loosely held, and its power to punish heretics has probably diminished, but it continues to catch middle-class blacks in a double bind, thus impeding not only their own advancement but even, I would contend, that of blacks as a group.

The victim-focused black identity encourages the individual to feel 40
that his advancement depends almost entirely on that of the group. Thus he loses sight not only of his own possibilities but of the inextricable connection between individual effort and individual advancement. This is a profound encumbrance today, when there is more opportunity for blacks than ever before, for it reimposes limitations that can have the same oppressive effect as those the society has only recently begun to remove.

It was the emphasis on mass action in the sixties that made the victim-focused black identity a necessity. But in the eighties and beyond, when racial advancement will come only through a multitude of individual advancements, this form of identity inadvertently adds itself to the forces that hold us back. Hard work, education, individual initiative, stable family life, property ownership—these have always been the means by which ethnic groups have moved ahead in America. Regardless of past or present victimization, these "laws" of advancement apply absolutely to black Americans also. There is no getting around this. What we need is a form of racial identity that energizes the individual by putting him in touch with both his possibilities and his responsibilities.

It has always annoyed me to hear from the mouths of certain arbiters of blackness that middle-class blacks should "reach back" and pull up those blacks less fortunate than they—as though middle-class status were an unearned and essentially passive condition in which one needed a large measure of noblesse oblige to occupy one's time. My own image is of reaching back from a moving train to lift on board those who have no tickets. A noble enough sentiment—but might it not be wiser to show them the entire structure of principles, efforts, and sacrifice that puts one in a position to buy a ticket any time one likes? This, I think, is something members of the black middle class can realistically offer to other blacks. Their example is not only a testament to possibility but also a lesson in method. But they cannot lead by example until they are released from a black identity that regards that example as suspect, that sees them as "marginally" black, indeed that holds *them* back by catching them in a double bind.

To move beyond the victim-focused black identity we must learn to make a difficult but crucial distinction: between actual victimization, which we must resist with every resource, and identification with the victim's status. Until we do this we will continue to wrestle more with ourselves than with the new opportunities which so many paid so dearly to win.   *1988*

The Social Fabric

7

What Is an American?

J. Hector St. Jean de Crèvecoeur, What Is
an American?

Ishmael Reed, America:
The Multinational Society

Mary Gordon, More than Just a Shrine:
Paying Homage to the Ghosts of Ellis Island

Man is the most composite of all creatures. . . . Well, as in the old
burning of the Temple at Corinth, by the melting and intermixture of
silver and gold and other metals a new compound more precious than
any, called Corinthian brass, was formed; so in this continent—asylum
of all nations—the energy of Irish, Germans, Swedes, Poles, and Cos-
sacks, and all the European tribes—of the Africans, and of the Poly-
nesians—will construct a new race, a new religion, a new state, a new
literature, which will be as vigorous as the new Europe which came out
of the smelting-pot of the Dark Ages, or that which earlier emerged
from the Pelasgic and Etruscan barbarism.

Ralph Waldo Emerson, from *Journals*

The melting pot was one of those metaphors that turned out only to be
partly true, and recent years have seen an astonishing repudiation of
the whole conception. Many Americans today righteously reject the
historic goal of "a new race of man." The contemporary ideal is not
assimilation but ethnicity. The escape from origins has given way to the
search for "roots." "Ancient prejudices and manners"—the old-time
religion, the old-time diet—have made a surprising comeback.

    These developments portend a new turn in American life. Instead
of a transformative nation with a new and distinctive identity, America

139

increasingly sees itself as preservative of old identities. We used to say *e pluribus unum*. Now we glorify *pluribus* and belittle *unum*.

Arthur Schlesinger, Jr., from *When Ethnic Studies Are Un-American*

Whence all this passion toward conformity anyway?—diversity is the word. Let man keep his many parts and you'll have no tyrant states. Why, if they follow this conformity business they'll end up by forcing me, an invisible man, to become white, which is not a color but the lack of one. Must I strive toward colorlessness? But seriously, and without snobbery, think of what the world would lose if that should happen. America is woven of many strands; I would recognize them and let it so remain. It's "winner take nothing" that is the great truth of our country or of any country. Life is to be lived, not controlled; and humanity is won by continuing to play in face of certain defeat. Our fate is to become one, and yet many——This is not prophecy, but description. Thus one of the greatest jokes in the world is the spectacle of the whites busy escaping blackness and becoming blacker every day, and the blacks striving toward whiteness, becoming quite dull and gray. None of us seems to know who he is or where he's going.

Ralph Ellison, from *Invisible Man*

During this phase of my childhood the cultural tug of war known as "Americanization" almost pulled me apart. There were moments when I would identify completely with the gringo world (what could have been more American than my earnest high-voiced portrayal of George Washington, however ridiculous the cotton wig my mother had fashioned for me?); then quite suddenly I would feel so acutely Mexican that I would stammer over the simplest English phrase. I was so ready to take offense at the slightest slur against Mexicans that I would imagine prejudice where none existed. But on other occasions, in full confidence of my belonging, I would venture forth into social areas that I should have realized were clearly forbidden to little chicanos from Curtis Park. The inevitable rebuffs would leave me floundering in self-pity; it was small comfort to know that other minority groups suffered even worse rebuffs than we did.

Enrique López, from *Back to Bachimba*

J. Hector St. Jean de Crèvecoeur
What Is an American?

I wish I could be acquainted with the feelings and thoughts which must agitate the heart and present themselves to the mind of an enlightened Englishman, when he first lands on this continent. He must greatly rejoice that he lived at a time to see this fair country discovered and settled; he must necessarily feel a share of national pride, when he views the chain of settlements which embellishes these extended shores. When he says to himself, this is the work of my countrymen, who, when convulsed by factions, afflicted by a variety of miseries and wants, restless and impatient, took refuge here. They brought along with them their national genius, to which they principally owe what liberty they enjoy, and what substance they possess. Here he sees the industry of his native country displayed in a new manner, and traces in their works the embryos of all the arts, sciences, and ingenuity which flourish in Europe. Here he beholds fair cities, substantial villages, extensive fields, an immense country filled with decent houses, good roads, orchards, meadows, and bridges, where a hundred years ago all was wild, woody, and uncultivated! What a train of pleasing ideas this fair spectacle must suggest; it is a prospect which must inspire a good citizen with the most heartfelt pleasure. The difficulty consists in the manner of viewing so extensive a scene. He is arrived on a new continent; a modern society offers itself to his contemplation, different from what he had hitherto seen. It is not composed, as in Europe, of great lords who possess every thing, and of a herd of people who have nothing. Here are no aristocratical families, no courts, no kings, no bishops, no ecclesiastical dominion, no invisible power giving to a few a very visible one; no great manufacturers employing thousands, no great refinements of luxury. The rich and the poor are not so far removed from each other as they are in Europe. Some few towns excepted, we are all tillers of the earth, from Nova Scotia to West Florida. We are a people of cultivators, scattered over an immense territory, communicating with each other by means of good roads and navigable rivers, united by the silken bands of mild government, all respecting the laws, without dreading their power, because they are equitable. We are all animated with the spirit of an industry which is unfettered and unrestrained, because each person works for himself. If he travels through our rural districts he views not the hostile castle, and the haughty mansion, contrasted with the clay-built hut and miserable cabin, where cattle and men help to keep each other warm, and dwell in meanness, smoke, and indigence. A pleasing uniformity of decent competence appears throughout our habitations.

The meanest of our loghouses is a dry and comfortable habitation. Lawyer or merchant are the fairest titles our towns afford; that of a farmer is the only appellation of the rural inhabitants of our country. It must take some time ere he can reconcile himself to our dictionary; which is but short in words of dignity, and names of honor. There, on a Sunday, he sees a congregation of respectable farmers and their wives, all clad in neat homespun, well mounted, or riding in their own humble wagons. There is not among them an esquire, saving the unlettered magistrate. There he sees a parson as simple as his flock, a farmer who does not riot on the labor of others. We have no princes, for whom we toil, starve, and bleed: we are the most perfect society now existing in the world. Here man is free as he ought to be; nor is this pleasing equality so transitory as many others are. Many ages will not see the shores of our great lakes replenished with inland nations, nor the unknown bounds of North America entirely peopled. Who can tell how far it extends? Who can tell the millions of men whom it will feed and contain? for no European foot has as yet traveled half the extent of this mighty continent! . . .

In this great American asylum, the poor of Europe have by some means met together; and in consequence of various causes; to what purpose should they ask one another what countrymen they are? Alas, two-thirds of them had no country. Can a wretch who wanders about, who works and starves, whose life is a continual scene of sore affliction or pinching penury; can that man call England or any other kingdom his country? A country that had no bread for him, whose fields procured him no harvest, who met with nothing but the frowns of the rich, the severity of the laws, with jails and punishments; who owned not a single foot of the extensive surface of this planet? No! Urged by a variety of motives, here they came. Every thing has tended to regenerate them; new laws, a new mode of living, a new social system; here they are become men: in Europe they were as so many useless plants, wanting vegetative mold, and refreshing showers; they withered, and were mowed down by want, hunger, and war; but now by the power of transplantation, like all other plants they have taken root and flourished! Formerly they were not numbered in any civil lists of their country, except in those of the poor; here they rank as citizens. By what invisible power has this surprising metamorphosis been performed? By that of the laws and that of their industry. The laws, the indulgent laws, protect them as they arrive, stamping on them the symbol of adoption; they receive ample rewards for their labors; these accumulated rewards procure them lands; those lands confer on them the title of freemen, and to that title every benefit is affixed which men can possibly require. This is the great operation daily performed by our laws. From whence proceed these laws? From our government. Whence the government? It is derived from the original genius and strong desire of the people ratified and confirmed by the crown. This is the great chain which links us all. . . .

What attachment can a poor European emigrant have for a country where he had nothing? The knowledge of the language, the love of a few kindred as poor as himself, were the only cords that tied him: his country is now that which gives him land, bread, protection, and consequence: *Ubi panis ibi patria*,[1] is the motto of all emigrants. What then is the American, this new man? He is either a European, or the descendant of a European, hence that strange mixture of blood, which you will find in no other country. I could point out to you a family whose grandfather was an Englishman, whose wife was Dutch, whose son married a French woman, and whose present four sons have now four wives of different nations. *He* is an American, who leaving behind him all his ancient prejudices and manners, receives new ones from the new mode of life he has embraced, the new government he obeys, and the new rank he holds. He becomes an American by being received in the broad lap of our great *Alma Mater*.[2] Here individuals of all nations are melted into a new race of men, whose labors and posterity will one day cause great changes in the world. Americans are the western pilgrims, who are carrying along with them that great mass of arts, sciences, vigor, and industry which began long since in the east; they will finish the great circle. The Americans were once scattered all over Europe; here they are incorporated into one of the finest systems of population which has ever appeared, and which will hereafter become distinct by the power of the different climates they inhabit. The American ought therefore to love this country much better than that wherein either he or his forefathers were born. Here the rewards of his industry follow with equal steps the progress of his labor; his labor is founded on the basis of nature, *self-interest*; can it want a stronger allurement? Wives and children, who before in vain demanded of him a morsel of bread, now, fat and frolicsome, gladly help their father to clear those fields whence exuberant crops are to arise to feed and to clothe them all; without any part being claimed, either by a despotic prince, a rich abbot, or a mighty lord. Here religion demands but little of him; a small voluntary salary to the minister, and gratitude to God; can he refuse these? The American is a new man, who acts upon new principles; he must therefore entertain new ideas, and form new opinions. From involuntary idleness, servile dependence, penury, and useless labor, he has passed to toils of a very different nature, rewarded by ample subsistence. This is an American. . . .

---

[1] **Ubi panis ibi patria:** "Where there is bread, there is our country."—Eds.
[2] **Alma Mater:** Literally "fostering mother." Commonly used to refer to one's school.—Eds.

Men are like plants; the goodness and flavor of the fruit proceeds   4
from the peculiar soil and exposition[3] in which they grow. We are
nothing but what we derive from the air we breathe, the climate we
inhabit, the government we obey, the system of religion we profess, and
the nature of our employment. Here you will find but few crimes; these
have acquired as yet no root among us. I wish I were able to trace all my
ideas; if my ignorance prevents me from describing them properly, I
hope I shall be able to delineate a few of the outlines, which are all I
propose.

Those who live near the sea, feed more on fish than on flesh, and
often encounter that boisterous element. This renders them more bold
and enterprising; this leads them to neglect the confined occupations of
the land. They see and converse with a variety of people; their intercourse with mankind becomes extensive. The sea inspires them with a
love of traffic, a desire of transporting produce from one place to
another; and leads them to a variety of resources which supply the place
of labor. Those who inhabit the middle settlements, by far the most
numerous, must be very different; the simple cultivation of the earth
purifies them, but the indulgences of the government, the soft re-
monstrances of religion, the rank of independent freeholders, must
necessarily inspire them with sentiments, very little known in Europe
among people of the same class. What do I say? Europe has no such class
of men; the early knowledge they acquire, the early bargains they make,
give them a great degree of sagacity. As freemen they will be litigious;
pride and obstinacy are often the cause of lawsuits; the nature of our
laws and governments may be another. As citizens it is easy to imagine,
that they will carefully read the newspapers, enter into every political
disquisition, freely blame or censure governors and others. As farmers
they will be careful and anxious to get as much as they can, because
what they get is their own. As northern men they will love the cheerful
cup. As Christians, religion curbs them not in their opinions; the general indulgence leaves every one to think for themselves in spiritual
matters; the laws inspect our actions, our thoughts are left to God.
Industry, good living, selfishness, litigiousness, country politics, the
pride of freemen, religious indifference, are their characteristics. If you
recede still farther from the sea, you will come into more modern
settlements; they exhibit the same strong lineaments, in a ruder appearance. Religion seems to have still less influence, and their manners
are less improved.

Now we arrive near the great woods, near the last inhabited districts; there men seem to be placed still farther beyond the reach of
government, which in some measure leaves them to themselves. How

---

[3]**exposition:** In this context refers to exposure to the sun.—Eds.

can it pervade every corner; as they were driven there by misfortunes, necessity of beginnings, desire of acquiring large tracts of land, idleness, frequent want of economy, ancient debts; the reunion of such people does not afford a very pleasing spectacle. When discord, want of unity and friendship; when either drunkenness or idleness prevail in such remote districts; contention, inactivity, and wretchedness must ensue. There are not the same remedies to these evils as in a long-established community. The few magistrates they have, are in general little better than the rest; they are often in a perfect state of war; that of man against man, sometimes decided by blows, sometimes by means of the law; that of man against every wild inhabitant of these venerable woods, of which they are come to dispossess them. There men appear to be no better than carnivorous animals of a superior rank, living on the flesh of wild animals when they can catch them, and when they are not able, they subsist on grain. He who would wish to see America in its proper light, and have a true idea of its feeble beginnings and barbarous rudiments, must visit our extended line of frontiers where the last settlers dwell, and where he may see the first labors of settlement, the mode of clearing the earth, in all their different appearances; where men are wholly left dependent on their native tempers, and on the spur of uncertain industry, which often fails when not sanctified by the efficacy of a few moral rules. There, remote from the power of example, and check of shame, many families exhibit the most hideous parts of our society. They are a kind of forlorn hope, preceding by ten or twelve years the most respectable army of veterans which come after them. In that space, prosperity will polish some, vice and the law will drive off the rest, who uniting again with others like themselves will recede still farther; making room for more industrious people, who will finish their improvements, convert the log house into a convenient habitation, and rejoicing that the first heavy labors are finished, will change in a few years that hitherto barbarous country into a fine, fertile, well-regulated district. Such is our progress, such is the march of the Europeans toward the interior parts of this continent. In all societies there are offcasts; this impure part serves as our precursors or pioneers; my father himself was one of that class, but he came upon honest principles, and was therefore one of the few who held fast; by good conduct and tem-perance, he transmitted to me his fair inheritance, when not above one in fourteen of his contemporaries had the same good fortune.

Forty years ago this smiling country was thus inhabited; it is now purged, a general decency of manners prevails throughout, and such has been the fate of our best countries. . . .

But to return to our back settlers. I must tell you, that there is 8 something in the proximity of the woods, which is very singular. It is with men as it is with the plants and animals that grow and live in the forest; they are entirely different from those that live in the plains. I will candidly tell you all my thoughts but you are not to expect that I shall advance any reasons. By living in or near the woods, their actions are regulated by the wildness of the neighborhood. The deer often come to eat their grain, the wolves to destroy their sheep, the bears to kill their hogs, the foxes to catch their poultry. This surrounding hostility, immediately puts the gun into their hands; they watch these animals, they kill some; and thus by defending their property, they soon become professed hunters; this is the progress; once hunters, farewell to the plough. The chase renders them ferocious, gloomy, and unsociable; a hunter wants no neighbor, he rather hates them, because he dreads the compe tition. In a little time their success in the woods makes them neglect their tillage. They trust to the natural fecundity of the earth, and therefore do little; carelessness in fencing, often exposes what little they sow to destruction; they are not at home to watch; in order therefore to make up the deficiency, they go oftener to the woods. That new mode of life brings along with it a new set of manners, which I cannot easily describe. These new manners being grafted on the old stock, produce a strange sort of lawless profligacy, the impressions of which are indelible. The manners of the Indian natives are respectable, compared with this European medley. Their wives and children live in sloth and inactivity; and having no proper pursuits, you may judge what education the latter receive. Their tender minds have nothing else to contemplate but the example of their parents; like them they grow up a mongrel breed, half civilized, half savage, except nature stamps on them some constitutional propensities. That rich, that voluptuous sentiment is gone that struck them so forcibly; the possession of their freeholds no longer conveys to their minds the same pleasure and pride. To all these reasons you must add, their lonely situation, and you cannot imagine what an effect on manners the great distances they live from each other has! . . .

There is no wonder that this country has so many charms, and presents to Europeans so many temptations to remain in it. A traveler in Europe becomes a stranger as soon as he quits his own kingdom; but it is otherwise here. We know, properly speaking, no strangers; this is every person's country; the variety of our soils, situations, climates, governments, and produce, hath something which must please every body. No sooner does a European arrive, no matter of what condition, than his eyes are opened upon the fair prospect; he hears his language spoke, he retraces many of his own country manners, he perpetually hears the names of families and towns with which he is acquainted; he sees happiness and prosperity in all places disseminated; he meets with hospitality, kindness, and plenty every where; he beholds hardly any poor, he seldom hears of punishments and executions; and he wonders at the elegance of our towns, those miracles of industry and freedom. He cannot admire enough our rural districts, our convenient roads, good taverns, and our many accommodations; he involuntarily loves a country where every thing is so lovely. When in England, he was a mere Englishman; here he stands on a larger portion of the globe, not less than its fourth part, and may see the productions of the north, in iron and naval stores; the provisions of Ireland, the grain of Egypt, the indigo, the rice of China. He does not find, as in Europe, a crowded society, where every place is overstocked; he does not feel that perpetual collision of parties, that difficulty of beginning, that contention which oversets so many. There is room for every body in America; has he any particular talent, or industry? he exerts it in order to procure a livelihood, and it succeeds. Is he a merchant? the avenues of trade are infinite; is he eminent in any respect? he will be employed and respected. Does he love a country life? pleasant farms present themselves; he may purchase what he wants, and thereby become an American farmer. Is he a laborer, sober and industrious? he need not go many miles, nor receive many informations before he will be hired, well fed at the table of his employer, and paid four or five times more than he can get in Europe. Does he want uncultivated lands? thousands of acres present themselves, which he may purchase cheap. Whatever be his talents or inclinations, if they are moderate, he may satisfy them. I do not mean that every one who comes will grow rich in a little time; no, but he may procure an easy, decent maintenance, by his industry. Instead of starving he will be fed, instead of being idle he will have employment; and these are riches enough for such men as come over here. The rich stay in Europe, it is only the middling and the poor that emigrate. Would you wish to travel in independent idleness, from north to south, you will find easy access, and the most cheerful reception at every house; society without ostentation, good cheer without pride, and every decent diversion which the country affords, with little expense. It is no wonder that the European who has lived here a few years, is desirous to remain; Europe with all its pomp, is not to be compared to this continent, for men of middle stations, or laborers. . . .

This great continent must in time absorb the poorest part of Europe; . . . and this will happen in proportion as it becomes better known; and as war, taxation, oppression, and misery increase there. The Hebrides appear to be fit only for the residence of malefactors, and it would be much better to send felons there than either to Virginia or Maryland. What a strange compliment has our mother country paid to two of the finest provinces in America! England has entertained in that respect very mistaken ideas; what was intended as a punishment, is become the good fortune of several; many of those who have been transported as felons, are now rich, and strangers to the stings of those

wants that urged them to violations of the law: they are become industrious, exemplary, and useful citizens. The English government should
purchase the most northern and barren of those islands; it should send
over to us the honest, primitive Hebrideans, settle them here on good
lands, as a reward for their virtue and ancient poverty; and replace
them with a colony of her wicked sons. The severity of the climate, the
inclemency of the seasons, the sterility of the soil, the tempestuousness
of the sea, would afflict and punish enough. Could there be found a
spot better adapted to retaliate the injury it had received by their
crimes? Some of those islands might be considered as the hell of Great
Britain, where all evil spirits should be sent. Two essential ends would
be answered by this simple operation. The good people, by emigration,
would be rendered happier; the bad ones would be placed where they
ought to be. In a few years the dread of being sent to that wintry region
would have a much stronger effect, than that of transportation. This is
no place for punishment; were I a poor hopeless, breadless Englishman,
and not restrained by the power of shame, I should be very thankful for
the passage. It is of very little importance how, and in what manner an
indigent man arrives; for if he is but sober, honest, and industrious, he
has nothing more to ask of heaven. Let him go to work, he will have
opportunities enough to earn a comfortable support, and even the
means of procuring some land; which ought to be the utmost wish of
every person who has health and hands to work. I knew a man who
came to this country, in the literal sense of the expression, stark naked; I
think he was a Frenchman, and a sailor on board an English man of war.
Being discontented, he had stripped himself and swam ashore; where
finding clothes and friends, he settled afterwards at Maraneck, in the
county of Chester, in the province of New York: he married and left a
good farm to each of his sons. I knew another person who was but
twelve years old when he was taken on the frontiers of Canada, by the
Indians; at his arrival at Albany he was purchased by a gentleman, who
generously bound him apprentice to a tailor. He lived to the age of
ninety, and left behind him a fine estate and a numerous family, all well
settled; many of them I am acquainted with. Where is then the industrious European who ought to despair?

    After a foreigner from any part of Europe is arrived, and become a
citizen, let him devoutly listen to the voice of our great parent, which
says to him, "Welcome to my shores, distressed European; bless the hour
in which thou didst see my verdant fields, my fair navigable rivers, and
my green mountains! If thou wilt work, I have bread for thee; if thou wilt
be honest, sober, and industrious, I have greater rewards to confer on
thee—ease and independence. I will give thee fields to feed and clothe
thee; a comfortable fireside to sit by, and tell thy children by what
means thou hast prospered; and a decent bed to repose on. I shall

endow thee beside with the immunities of a freeman. If thou wilt carefully educate thy children, teach them gratitude to God, and reverence to that government, that philanthropic government, which has collected here so many men and made them happy, I will also provide for the progeny; and to every good man this ought to be the most holy, the most powerful, the most earnest wish he can possibly form, as well as the most consolatory prospect when he dies. Go thou and work and till; thou shalt prosper, provided thou be just, grateful, and industrious." *1782*

Ishmael Reed

America: The Multinational Society

At the annual Lower East Side Jewish Festival yesterday, a Chinese woman ate a pizza slice in front of Ty Thuan Duc's Vietnamese grocery store. Beside her a Spanish-speaking family patronized a cart with two signs: "Italian Ices" and "Kosher by Rabbi Alper." And after the pastrami ran out, everybody ate knishes.
—*New York Times*, 23 June 1983

On the day before Memorial Day, 1983, a poet called me to describe a city he had just visited. He said that one section included mosques, built by the Islamic people who dwelled there. Attending his reading, he said, were large numbers of Hispanic people, forty thousand of whom lived in the same city. He was not talking about a fabled city located in some mysterious region of the world. The city he'd visited was Detroit.

A few months before, as I was leaving Houston, Texas, I heard it announced on the radio that Texas's largest minority was Mexican-American, and though a foundation recently issued a report critical of bilingual education, the taped voice used to guide the passengers on the air trams connecting terminals in Dallas Airport is in both Spanish and English. If the trend continues, a day will come when it will be difficult to travel through some sections of the country without hearing commands in both English and Spanish; after all, for some western states, Spanish was the first written language and the Spanish style lives on in the western way of life.

Shortly after my Texas trip, I sat in an auditorium located on the campus of the University of Wisconsin at Milwaukee as a Yale professor—whose original work on the influence of African cultures upon those of the Americas has led to his ostracism from some monocultural intellectual circles—walked up and down the aisle, like an old-time southern evangelist, dancing and drumming the top of the lectern, illustrating his points before some serious Afro-American intellectuals and artists who cheered and applauded his performance and his mastery of information. The professor was "white." After his lecture, he joined a group of Milwaukeeans in a conversation. All of the participants spoke Yoruban, though only the professor had ever traveled to Africa.

One of the artists told me that his paintings, which included African and Afro-American mythological symbols and imagery, were hanging in the local McDonald's restaurant. The next day I went to McDonald's and snapped pictures of smiling youngsters eating hamburgers below paintings that could grace the walls of any of the country's leading museums. The manager of the local McDonald's said, "I don't know what you boys are doing, but I like it," as he commissioned the local painters to exhibit in his restaurant.

Such blurring of cultural styles occurs in everyday life in the United States to a greater extent than anyone can imagine and is probably more prevalent than the sensational conflict between people of different backgrounds that is played up and often encouraged by the media. The result is what the Yale professor, Robert Thompson, referred to as a cultural bouillabaisse, yet members of the nation's present educational and cultural Elect still cling to the notion that the United States belongs to some vaguely defined entity they refer to as "Western civilization," by which they mean, presumably, a civilization created by the people of Europe, as if Europe can be viewed in monolithic terms. Is Beethoven's Ninth Symphony, which includes Turkish marches, a part of Western civilization, or the late nineteenth- and twentieth-century French paintings, whose creators were influenced by Japanese art? And what of the cubists, through whom the influence of African art changed modern painting, or the surrealists, who were so impressed with the art of the Pacific Northwest Indians that, in their map of North America, Alaska dwarfs the lower forty-eight in size?

Are the Russians, who are often criticized for their adoption of "Western" ways by Tsarist dissidents in exile, members of Western civilization? And what of the millions of Europeans who have black African and Asian ancestry, black Africans having occupied several countries for hundreds of years? Are these "Europeans" members of Western civilization, or the Hungarians, who originated across the Urals in a place called Greater Hungary, or the Irish, who came from the Iberian Peninsula? Even the notion that North America is part of Western civilization because our "system of government" is derived from Europe is being challenged by Native American historians who say that the founding fathers, Benjamin Franklin especially, were actually influenced by the system of government that had been adopted by the Iroquois hundreds of years prior to the arrival of large numbers of Europeans.

Western civilization, then, becomes another confusing category like Third World, or Judeo-Christian culture, as man attempts to impose his small-screen view of political and cultural reality upon a complex world. Our most publicized novelist recently said that Western civilization was the greatest achievement of mankind, an attitude that flourishes on the street level as scribbles in public restrooms: "White Power," "Niggers and Spics Suck," or "Hitler was a prophet," the latter being the most telling, for wasn't Adolph Hitler the archetypal monoculturalist who, in his pigheaded arrogance, believed that one way and one blood was so pure that it had to be protected from alien strains at all costs? Where did such an attitude, which has caused so much misery and depression in our national life, which has tainted even our noblest achievements, begin? An attitude that caused the incarceration of Japanese-American citizens during World War II, the persecution of Chicanos and Chinese-Americans, the near-extermination of the Indians, and the murder and lynchings of thousands of Afro-Americans.

Virtuous, hard-working, pious, even though they occasionally would wander off after some fancy clothes, or rendezvous in the woods with the town prostitute, the Puritans are idealized in our schoolbooks as "a hardy band" of no-nonsense patriarchs whose discipline razed the forest and brought order to the New World (a term that annoys Native American historians). Industrious, responsible, it was their "Yankee ingenuity" and practicality that created the work ethic. They were simple folk who produced a number of good poets, and they set the tone for the American writing style, of lean and spare lines, long before Hemingway. They worshiped in churches whose colors blended in with the New England snow, churches with simple structures and ornate lecterns.

The Puritans were a daring lot, but they had a mean streak. They hated the theater and banned Christmas. They punished people in a cruel and inhuman manner. They killed children who disobeyed their parents. When they came in contact with those whom they considered heathens or aliens, they behaved in such a bizarre and irrational manner that this chapter in the American history comes down to us as a late-movie horror film. They exterminated the Indians, who taught them how to survive in a world unknown to them, and their encounter with the calypso culture of Barbados resulted in what the tourist guide in Salem's Witches' House refers to as the Witchcraft Hysteria.

The Puritan legacy of hard work and meticulous accounting led to the establishment of a great industrial society; it is no wonder that the American industrial revolution began in Lowell, Massachusetts, but there was the other side, the strange and paranoid attitudes toward those different from the Elect.

The cultural attitudes of that early Elect continue to be voiced in 12 everyday life in the United States: the president of a distinguished university, writing a letter to the *Times*, belittling the study of African civilizations; the television network that promoted its show on the Vatican art with the boast that this art represented "the finest achievements of the human spirit." A modern up-tempo state of complex rhythms that depends upon contacts with an international community can no longer behave as if it dwelled in a "Zion Wilderness" surrounded by beasts and pagans.

When I heard a schoolteacher warn the other night about the invasion of the American educational system by foreign curriculums, I wanted to yell at the television set, "Lady, they're already here." It has already begun because the world is here. The world has been arriving at these shores for at least ten thousand years from Europe, Africa, and Asia. In the late nineteenth and early twentieth centuries, large numbers of Europeans arrived, adding their cultures to those of the European, African, and Asian settlers who were already here, and recently millions have been entering the country from South America and the Caribbean, making Yale Professor Bob Thompson's bouillabaisse richer and thicker.

One of our most visionary politicians said that he envisioned a time when the United States could become the brain of the world, by which he meant the repository of all of the latest advanced information systems. I thought of that remark when an enterprising poet friend of mine called to say that he had just sold a poem to a computer magazine and that the editors were delighted to get it because they didn't carry fiction or poetry. Is that the kind of world we desire? A humdrum homogeneous world of all brains and no heart, no fiction, no poetry; a world of robots with human attendants bereft of imagination, of culture? Or does North America deserve a more exciting destiny? To become a place where the cultures of the world crisscross. This is possible because the United States is unique in the world: The world is here.   *1988*

Mary Gordon

More than Just a Shrine: Paying Homage to the Ghosts of Ellis Island

I once sat in a hotel in Bloomsbury trying to have breakfast alone. A Russian with a habit of compulsively licking his lips asked if he could join me. I was afraid to say no; I thought it might be bad for détente. He explained to me that he was a linguist, and that he always liked to talk to Americans to see if he could make any connection between their speech and their ethnic background. When I told him about my mixed ancestry—my mother is Irish and Italian, my father a Lithuanian Jew— he began jumping up and down in his seat, rubbing his hands together, and licking his lips even more frantically.

"Ah," he said, "so you are really somebody who comes from what is called the boiling pot of America." Yes, I told him, yes I was, but I quickly rose to leave. I thought it would be too hard to explain to him the relation of the boiling potters to the main course, and I wanted to get to the British Museum. I told him that the only thing I could think of that united people whose backgrounds, histories, and points of view were utterly diverse was that their people had landed at a place called Ellis Island.

I didn't tell him that Ellis Island was the only American landmark I'd ever visited. How could I describe to him the estrangement I'd always felt from the kind of traveler who visits shrines to America's past greatness, those rebuilt forts with muskets behind glass and sabers mounted on the walls and gift shops selling maple sugar candy in the shape of Indian headdresses, those reconstructed villages with tables set for fifty and the Paul Revere silver gleaming? All that Americana— Plymouth Rock, Gettysburg, Mount Vernon, Valley Forge—it all inhabits for me a zone of blurred abstraction with far less hold on my imagination than the Bastille or Hampton Court. I suppose I've always known that my uninterest in it contains a large component of the willed: I am American, and those places purport to be my history. But they are not mine.

Ellis Island is, though; it's the one place I can be sure my people are 4 connected to. And so I made a journey there to find my history, like any Rotarian traveling in his Winnebago to Antietam to find his. I had become part of that humbling democracy of people looking in some site for a past that has grown unreal. The monument I traveled to was not, however, a tribute to some old glory. The minute I set foot upon the island I could feel all that it stood for: insecurity, obedience, anxiety, dehumanization, the terrified and careful deference of the displaced. I hadn't traveled to the Battery and boarded a ferry across from the

Statue of Liberty to raise flags or breathe a richer, more triumphant air. I wanted to do homage to the ghosts.

I felt them everywhere, from the moment I disembarked and saw the building with its high-minded brick, its hopeful little lawn, its ornamental cornices. The place was derelict when I arrived; it had not functioned for more than thirty years—almost as long as the time it had operated at full capacity as a major immigration center. I was surprised to learn what a small part of history Ellis Island had occupied. The main building was constructed in 1892, then rebuilt between 1898 and 1900 after a fire. Most of the immigrants who arrived during the latter half of the nineteenth century, mainly northern and western Europeans, landed not at Ellis Island but on the western tip of the Battery at Castle Garden, which had opened as a receiving center for immigrants in 1855.

By the 1880s the facilities at Castle Garden had grown scandalously inadequate. Officials looked for an island on which to build a new immigration center because they thought that on an island immigrants could be more easily protected from swindlers and quickly transported to railroad terminals in New Jersey. Bedloe's Island was considered, but New Yorkers were aghast at the idea of a "Babel" ruining their beautiful new treasure, "Liberty Enlightening the World." The statue's sculptor, Frédéric Auguste Bartholdi, reacted to the prospect of immigrants landing near his masterpiece in horror; he called it a "monstrous plan." So much for Emma Lazarus.

Ellis Island was finally chosen because the citizens of New Jersey petitioned the federal government to remove from the island an old naval powder magazine that they thought dangerously close to the Jersey shore. The explosives were removed; no one wanted the island for anything. It was the perfect place to build an immigration center.

I thought about the island's history as I walked into the building 8 and made my way to the room that was the center in my imagination of the Ellis Island experience: the Great Hall. It had been made real for me in the stark, accusing photographs of Louis Hine and others who took those pictures to make a point. It was in the Great Hall that everyone had waited—waiting, always, the great vocation of the dispossessed. The room was empty, except for me and a handful of other visitors and the park ranger who showed us around. I felt myself grow insignificant in that room, with its huge semicircular windows, its air, even in dereliction, of solid and official probity.

I walked in the deathlike expansiveness of the room's disuse and tried to think of what it might have been like, filled and swarming. More than sixteen million immigrants came through that room; approximately 250,000 were rejected. Not really a large proportion, but the implications for the rejected were dreadful. For some, there was nothing to go back to, or there was certain death; for others, who left as adventurers, to return would be to adopt in local memory the fool's role, and the failure's. No wonder that the island's history includes reports of three thousand suicides.

Sometimes immigrants could pass through Ellis Island in mere hours, though for some the process took days. The particulars of the experience in the Great Hall were often influenced by the political events and attitudes on the mainland. In the 1890s and the first years of the new century, when cheap labor was needed, the newly built receiving center took in its immigrants with comparatively little question. But as the century progressed, the economy worsened, eugenics became both scientifically respectable and popular, and World War I made American xenophobia seem rooted in fact.

Immigration acts were passed; newcomers had to prove, besides moral correctness and financial solvency, their ability to read. Quota laws came into effect, limiting the number of immigrants from southern and eastern Europe to less than 14 percent of the total quota. Intelligence tests were biased against all non-English-speaking persons and medical examinations became increasingly strict, until the machinery of immigration nearly collapsed under its own weight. The Second Quota Law of 1924 provided that all immigrants be inspected and issued visas at American consular offices in Europe, rendering the center almost obsolete.

On the day of my visit, my mind fastened upon the medical inspec-   12
tions, which had always seemed to me most emblematic of the ignominy and terror the immigrants endured. The medical inspectors, sometimes dressed in uniforms like soldiers, were particularly obsessed with a disease of the eyes called trachoma, which they checked for by flipping back the immigrants' top eyelids with a hook used for buttoning gloves—a method that sometimes resulted in the transmission of the disease to healthy people. Mothers feared that if their children cried too much, their red eyes would be mistaken for a symptom of the disease and the whole family would be sent home. Those immigrants suspected of some physical disability had initials chalked on their coats. I remembered the photographs I'd seen of people standing, dumbstruck and innocent as cattle, with their manifest numbers hung around their necks and initials marked in chalk upon their coats: "E" for eye trouble, "K" for hernia, "L" for lameness, "X" for mental defects, "H" for heart disease.

I thought of my grandparents as I stood in the room; my seventeen-year-old grandmother, coming alone from Ireland in 1896, vouched for by a stranger who had found her a place as a domestic servant to some Irish who had done well. I tried to imagine the assault it all must have been for her; I've been to her hometown, a collection of farms with a main street—smaller than the athletic field of my local public school. She must have watched the New York skyline as the first- and second-class passengers were whisked off the gangplank with the most cursory of inspections while she was made to board a ferry to the new immigration center.

What could she have made of it—this buff-painted wooden structure with its towers and its blue slate roof, a place *Harper's Weekly* described as "a latter-day watering place hotel"? It would have been the first time she'd have heard people speaking something other than English. She would have mingled with people carrying baskets on their heads and eating foods unlike any she had ever seen—dark-eyed people, like the Sicilian she would marry ten years later, who came over with his family, responsible even then for his mother and sister. I don't know what they thought, my grandparents, for they were not expansive people, nor romantic; they didn't like to think of what they called "the hard times," and their trip across the ocean was the single adventurous act of lives devoted after landing to security, respectability, and fitting in.

What is the potency of Ellis Island for someone like me—an American, obviously, but one who has always felt that the country really belonged to the early settlers, that, as J. F. Powers wrote in "Morte D'Urban," it had been "handed down to them by the Pilgrims, George Washington and others, and that they were taking a risk in letting you live in it." I have never been the victim of overt discrimination; nothing I have wanted has been denied me because of the accidents of blood. But I suppose it is part of being an American to be engaged in a somewhat tiresome but always self-absorbing process of national definition. And in this process, I have found in traveling to Ellis Island an important piece of evidence that could remind me I was right to feel my differentness. Something had happened to my people on that island, a result of the eternal wrongheadedness of American protectionism and the predictabilities of simple greed. I came to the island, too, so I could tell the ghosts that I was one of them, and that I honored them—their stoicism, and their innocence, the fear that turned them inward, and their pride. I wanted to tell them that I liked them better than the Americans who made them pass through the Great Hall and stole their names and chalked their weaknesses in public on their clothing. And to tell the ghosts what I have always thought: that American history was a very classy party that was not much fun until they arrived, brought the good food, turned up the music, and taught everyone to dance.   *1985*

8

Bridging Distances

James Baldwin, Stranger in the Village

Jonathan Kozol, Distancing the Homeless

Sallie Tisdale, Neither Morons
nor Imbeciles nor Idiots: In the Company
of the Mentally Retarded

A society can be judged by the way it treats its most disadvantaged, its least beloved, its mad. As things now stand, we must be judged a poor lot, and it is time to mend our ways.

Lewis Thomas, from *On the Need for Asylums*

I don't then regard tolerance as a great eternally established divine principle, though I might perhaps quote "In My Father's House are many mansions" in support of such a view. It is just a makeshift, suitable for an overcrowded and overheated planet. It carries on when love gives out, and love generally gives out as soon as we move away from our home and our friends, and stand among strangers in a queue for potatoes. Tolerance is wanted in the queue; otherwise we think, "Why will people be so slow?"; it is wanted in the tube, or "Why will people be so fat?"; it is wanted at the telephone, or "Why are they so deaf?" or conversely, "Why do they mumble?" It is wanted in the street, in the office, at the factory, and it is wanted above all between classes, races, and nations. It's dull. And yet it entails imagination. For you have all the time to be putting yourself in someone else's place. Which is a desirable spiritual exercise.

E. M. Forster, from *Tolerance*

But it is not really difference the oppressor fears so much as similarity. He fears he will discover in himself the same aches, the same longings as those of the people he has shitted on. He fears the immobilization threatened by his own incipient guilt. He fears he will have to change his life once he has seen himself in the bodies of the people he has called different.

Cherrie Moraga, from *La Güera*

Now the peculiar thing about Them is that They are created only by each one of us repudiating his own identity. When we have installed Them in our hearts, we are only a plurality of solitudes in which what each person has in common is his allocation to the other of the necessity for his own actions. Each person, however, as other to the other, is the other's necessity. Each denies any internal bond with the others; each person claims his own inessentiality: "I just carried out my orders. If I had not done so, someone else would have." "Why don't you sign? Everyone else has," etc. Yet although I can make no difference, I cannot act differently. No single other person is any more necessary to me than I claim to be to Them. But just as he is "one of Them" to me, so I am "one of Them" to him. In this collection of reciprocal indifference, of reciprocal inessentiality and solitude, there appears to exist no freedom. There is conformity to a *presence* that is everywhere *elsewhere*.

R. D. Laing, from *Us and Them*

James Baldwin
Stranger in the Village

From all available evidence no black man had ever set foot in this tiny Swiss village before I came. I was told before arriving that I would probably be a "sight" for the village; I took this to mean that people of my complexion were rarely seen in Switzerland, and also that city people are always something of a "sight" outside of the city. It did not occur to me—possibly because I am an American—that there could be people anywhere who had never seen a Negro.

It is a fact that cannot be explained on the basis of the inaccessibility of the village. The village is very high, but it is only four hours from Milan and three hours from Lausanne. It is true that it is virtually unknown. Few people making plans for a holiday would elect to come here. On the other hand, the villagers are able, presumably, to come and go as they please—which they do: to another town at the foot of the mountain, with a population of approximately five thousand, the nearest place to see a movie or go to the bank. In the village there is no movie house, no bank, no library, no theater; very few radios, one jeep, one station wagon; and, at the moment, one typewriter, mine, an invention which the woman next door to me here had never seen. There are about six hundred people living here, all Catholic—I conclude this from the fact that the Catholic church is open all year round, whereas the Protestant chapel, set off on a hill a little removed from the village, is open only in the summertime when the tourists arrive. There are four or five hotels, all closed now, and four or five bistros, of which, however, only two do any business during the winter. These two do not do a great deal, for life in the village seems to end around nine or ten o'clock. There are a few stores, butcher, baker, *épicerie*,[1] a hardware store, and a money-changer—who cannot change travelers' checks, but must send them down to the bank, an operation which takes two or three days. There is something called the *Ballet Haus*, closed in the winter and used for God knows what, certainly not ballet, during the summer. There seems to be only one schoolhouse in the village, and this for the quite young children; I suppose this to mean that their older brothers and sisters at some point descend from these mountains in order to complete their education—possibly, again, to the town just below. The landscape is absolutely forbidding, mountains towering on all four sides, ice and snow as far as the eye can reach. In this white wilderness, men and women and children move all day, carrying washing, wood, buckets of milk or water, sometimes skiing on Sunday afternoons. All week long boys and young men are to be seen shoveling snow off the rooftops, or dragging wood down from the forest in sleds.

The village's only real attraction, which explains the tourist season, is the hot spring water. A disquietingly high proportion of these tourists are cripples, or semi-cripples, who come year after year—from other parts of Switzerland, usually—to take the waters. This lends the village, at the height of the season, a rather terrifying air of sanctity, as though it were a lesser Lourdes. There is often something beautiful, there is always something awful, in the spectacle of a person who has lost one of his faculties, a faculty he never questioned until it was gone, and who struggles to recover it. Yet people remain people, on crutches or indeed

---

[1] *épicerie*: A grocery (French).—EDS.

on deathbeds; and wherever I passed, the first summer I was here, among the native villagers or among the lame, a wind passed with me— of astonishment, curiosity, amusement, and outrage. That first summer I stayed two weeks and never intended to return. But I did return in the winter, to work; the village offers, obviously, no distractions whatever and has the further advantage of being extremely cheap. Now it is winter again, a year later, and I am here again. Everyone in the village knows my name, though they scarcely ever use it, knows that I come from America—though, this, apparently, they will never really believe: black men come from Africa—and everyone knows that I am the friend of the son of a woman who was born here, and that I am staying in their chalet. But I remain as much a stranger today as I was the first day I arrived, and the children shout *Neger! Neger!* as I walk along the streets.

It must be admitted that in the beginning I was far too shocked to   4
have any real reaction. In so far as I reacted at all, I reacted by trying to be pleasant—it being a great part of the American Negro's education (long before he goes to school) that he must make people "like" him. This smile-and-the-world-smiles-with-you routine worked about as well in this situation as it had in the situation for which it was designed, which is to say that it did not work at all. No one, after all, can be liked whose human weight and complexity cannot be, or has not been, ad-mitted. My smile was simply another unheard-of phenomenon which al-lowed them to see my teeth—they did not, really, see my smile and I began to think that, should I take to snarling, no one would notice any difference. All of the physical characteristics of the Negro which had caused me, in America, a very different and almost forgotten pain were nothing less than miraculous—or infernal—in the eyes of the village people. Some thought my hair was the color of tar, that it had the texture of wire, or the texture of cotton. It was jocularly suggested that I might let it all grow long and make myself a winter coat. If I sat in the sun for more than five minutes some daring creature was certain to come along and gingerly put his fingers on my hair, as though he were afraid of an electric shock, or put his hand on my hand, astonished that the color did not rub off. In all of this, in which it must be conceded there was the charm of genuine wonder and in which there was cer-tainly no element of intentional unkindness, there was yet no sugges-tion that I was human: I was simply a living wonder.

I knew that they did not mean to be unkind, and I know it now; it is necessary, nevertheless, for me to repeat this to myself each time I walk out of the chalet. The children who shout *Neger!* have no way of knowing the echoes this sound raises in me. They are brimming with good humor and the more daring swell with pride when I stop to speak with them. Just the same, there are days when I cannot pause and smile, when I have no heart to play with them; when, indeed, I mutter sourly to myself, exactly as I muttered on the streets of a city these children have never seen, when I was no bigger than these children are now: *Your mother was a nigger.* Joyce is right about history being a nightmare—but it may be the nightmare from which no one *can* awaken. People are trapped in history and history is trapped in them.

There is a custom in the village—I am told it is repeated in many villages—of "buying" African natives for the purpose of converting them to Christianity. There stands in the church all year round a small box with a slot for money, decorated with a black figurine, and into this box the villagers drop their francs. During the *carnaval* which precedes Lent, two village children have their faces blackened—out of which bloodless darkness their blue eyes shine like ice—and fantastic horse-hair wigs are placed on their blond heads; thus disguised, they solicit among the villagers for money for the missionaries in Africa. Between the box in the church and the blackened children, the village "bought" last year six or eight African natives. This was reported to me with pride by the wife of one of the bistro owners and I was careful to express astonishment and pleasure at the solicitude shown by the village for the souls of black folk. The bistro owner's wife beamed with a pleasure far more genuine than my own and seemed to feel that I might now breathe more easily concerning the souls of at least six of my kinsmen.

I tried not to think of these so lately baptized kinsmen, of the price paid for them, or the peculiar price they themselves would pay, and said nothing about my father, who having taken his own conversion too literally never, at bottom, forgave the white world (which he described as heathen) for having saddled him with a Christ in whom, to judge at least from their treatment of him, they themselves no longer believed. I thought of white men arriving for the first time in an African village, strangers there, as I am a stranger here, and tried to imagine the astounded populace touching their hair and marveling at the color of their skin. But there is a great difference between being the first white man to be seen by Africans and being the first black man to be seen by whites. The white man takes the astonishment as tribute, for he arrives to conquer and to convert the natives, whose inferiority in relation to himself is not even to be questioned; whereas I, without a thought of conquest, find myself among a people whose culture controls me, has even, in a sense, created me, people who have cost me more in anguish and rage than they will ever know, who yet do not even know of my existence. The astonishment with which I might have greeted them, should they have stumbled into my African village a few hundred years ago, might have rejoiced their hearts. But the astonishment with which they greet me today can only poison mine.

And this is so despite everything I may do to feel differently,   8
despite my friendly conversations with the bistro owner's wife, despite

their three-year-old son who has at last become my friend, despite the *saluts* and *bonsoirs* which I exchange with people as I walk, despite the fact that I know that no individual can be taken to task for what history is doing, or has done. I say that the culture of these people controls me—but they can scarcely be held responsible for European culture. America comes out of Europe, but these people have never seen America, nor have most of them seen more of Europe than the hamlet at the foot of their mountain. Yet they move with an authority which I shall never have; and they regard me, quite rightly, not only as a stranger in their village but as a suspect latecomer, bearing no credentials, to everything they have—however unconsciously—inherited.

For this village, even were it incomparably more remote and incredibly more primitive, is the West, the West onto which I have been so strangely grafted. These people cannot be, from the point of view of power, strangers anywhere in the world; they have made the modern world, in effect, even if they do not know it. The most illiterate among them is related, in a way that I am not, to Dante, Shakespeare, Michelangelo, Aeschylus, Da Vinci, Rembrandt, and Racine; the cathedral at Chartres says something to them which it cannot say to me, as indeed would New York's Empire State Building, should anyone here ever see it. Out of their hymns and dances come Beethoven and Bach. Go back a few centuries and they are in their full glory—but I am in Africa, watching the conquerors arrive.

The rage of the disesteemed is personally fruitless, but it is also absolutely inevitable; this rage, so generally discounted, so little understood even among the people whose daily bread it is, is one of the things that makes history. Rage can only with difficulty, and never entirely, be brought under the domination of the intelligence and is therefore not susceptible to any arguments whatever. This is a fact which ordinary representatives of the *Herrenvolk*, having never felt this rage and being unable to imagine it, quite fail to understand. Also, rage cannot be hidden, it can only be dissembled. This dissembling deludes the thoughtless, and strengthens rage, and adds, to rage, contempt. There are, no doubt, as many ways of coping with the resulting complex of tensions as there are black men in the world, but no black man can hope ever to be entirely liberated from this internal warfare—rage, dissembling, and contempt having inevitably accompanied his first realization of the power of white men. What is crucial here is that, since white men represent in the black man's world so heavy a weight, white men have for black men a reality which is far from being reciprocal; and hence all black men have toward all white men an attitude which is designed, really, either to rob the white man of the jewel of his naïveté, or else to make it cost him dear.

The black man insists, by whatever means he finds at his disposal, that the white man cease to regard him as an exotic rarity and recognize him as a human being. This is a very charged and difficult moment, for there is a great deal of will power involved in the white man's naïveté. Most people are not naturally reflective any more than they are naturally malicious, and the white man prefers to keep the black man at a certain human remove because it is easier for him thus to preserve his simplicity and avoid being called to account for crimes committed by his forefathers, or his neighbors. He is inescapably aware, nevertheless, that he is in a better position in the world than black men are, nor can he quite put to death the suspicion that he is hated by black men therefor. He does not wish to be hated, neither does he wish to change places, and at this point in his uneasiness he can scarcely avoid having recourse to those legends which white men have created about black men, the most usual effect of which is that the white man finds himself enmeshed, so to speak, in his own language which describes hell, as well as the attributes which lead one to hell, as being as black as night.

Every legend, moreover, contains its residuum of truth, and the root 12 function of language is to control the universe by describing it. It is of quite considerable significance that black men remain, in the imagination, and in overwhelming numbers in fact, beyond the disciplines of salvation; and this despite the fact that the West has been "buying" African natives for centuries. There is, I should hazard, an instantaneous necessity to be divorced from this so visibly unsaved stranger, in whose heart, moreover, one cannot guess what dreams of vengeance are being nourished; and, at the same time, there are few things on earth more attractive than the idea of the unspeakable liberty which is allowed the unredeemed. When, beneath the black mask, a human being begins to make himself felt one cannot escape a certain awful wonder as to what kind of human being it is. What one's imagination makes of other people is dictated, of course, by the laws of one's own personality and it is one of the ironies of black-white relations that, by means of what the white man imagines the black man to be, the black man is enabled to know who the white man is.

I have said, for example, that I am as much a stranger in this village today as I was the first summer I arrived, but this is not quite true. The villagers wonder less about the texture of my hair than they did then, and wonder rather more about me. And the fact that their wonder now exists on another level is reflected in their attitudes and in their eyes. There are the children who make those delightful, hilarious, sometimes astonishing grave overtures of friendship in the unpredictable fashion of children; other children, having been taught that the devil is a black man, scream in genuine anguish as I approach. Some of the older women never pass without a friendly greeting, never pass, indeed, if it seems that they will be able to engage me in conversation; other women look down or look away or rather contemptuously smirk. Some of the men drink with me and suggest that I learn how to ski—partly, I gather, because they cannot imagine what I would look like on skis—and want to know if I am married, and ask questions about my métier. But some of the men have accused *le sale nègre*—behind my back—of stealing wood and there is already in the eyes of some of them that peculiar intent, paranoiac malevolence which one sometimes surprises in the eyes of American white men when, out walking with their Sunday girl, they see a Negro male approach.

There is a dreadful abyss between the streets of this village and the streets of the city in which I was born, between the children who shout *Neger!* today and those who shouted *Nigger!* yesterday—the abyss is experience, the American experience. The syllable hurled behind me today expresses, above all, wonder: I am a stranger here. But I am not a stranger in America and the same syllable riding on the American air expresses the war my presence has occasioned in the American soul.

For this village brings home to me this fact: that there was a day, and not really a very distant day, when Americans were scarcely Americans at all but discontented Europeans, facing a great unconquered conti-nent and strolling, say, into a marketplace and seeing black men for the first time. The shock this spectacle afforded is suggested, surely, by the promptness with which they decided that these black men were not really men but cattle. It is true that the necessity on the part of the settlers of the New World of reconciling their moral assumptions with the fact—and the necessity—of slavery enhanced immensely the charm of this idea, and it is also true that this idea expresses, with a truly American bluntness, the attitude which to varying extents all masters have had toward all slaves.

But between all former slaves and slave-owners and the drama 16 which begins for Americans over three hundred years ago at James-town, there are at least two differences to be observed. The American Negro slave could not suppose, for one thing, as slaves in past epochs had supposed and often done, that he would ever be able to wrest the power from his master's hands. This was a supposition which the mod-ern era, which was to bring about such vast changes in the aims and dimensions of power, put to death; it only begins, in unprecedented fashion, and with dreadful implications, to be resurrected today. But even had this supposition persisted with undiminished force, the Amer-ican Negro slave could not have used it to lend his condition dignity, for the reason that this supposition rests on another: that the slave in exile yet remains related to his past, has some means—if only in memory—of revering and sustaining the forms of his former life, is able, in short, to maintain his identity.

This was not the case with the American Negro slave. He is unique among the black men of the world in that his past was taken from him, almost literally, at one blow. One wonders what on earth the first slave found to say to the first dark child he bore. I am told that there are Haitians able to trace their ancestry back to African kings, but any American Negro wishing to go back so far will find his journey through time abruptly arrested by the signature on the bill of sale which served as the entrance paper for his ancestor. At the time—to say nothing of the circumstances—of the enslavement of the captive black man who was to become the American Negro, there was not the remotest pos-sibility that he would ever take power from his master's hands. There was no reason to suppose that his situation would ever change, nor was there, shortly, anything to indicate that his situation had ever been different. It was his necessity, in the words of E. Franklin Frazier, to find a "motive for living under American culture or die." The identity of the American Negro comes out of this extreme situation, and the evolution of this identity was a source of the most intolerable anxiety in the minds and the lives of his masters.

For the history of the American Negro is unique also in this: that the question of his humanity, and of his rights therefore as a human being, became a burning one for several generations of Americans, so burning a question that it ultimately became one of those used to divide the nation. It is out of this argument that the venom of the epithet *Nigger!* is derived. It is an argument which Europe has never had, and hence Europe quite sincerely fails to understand how or why the argument arose in the first place, why its effects are so frequently disastrous and always so unpredictable, why it refuses until today to be entirely settled. Europe's black possessions remained—and do remain—in Europe's colonies, at which remove they represented no threat to European identity. If they posed any problem at all for the European conscience, it was a problem which remained comfortingly abstract: in effect, the black man, *as a man*, did not exist for Europe. But in America, even as a slave, he was an inescapable part of the general social fabric and no American could escape having an attitude toward him. Americans attempt until today to make an abstraction of the Negro, but the very nature of these abstractions reveals the tremendous effects the presence of the Negro has had on the American character.

When one considers the history of the Negro in America it is of the greatest importance to recognize that the moral beliefs of a person, or a people, are never really as tenuous as life—which is not moral—very often causes them to appear; these create for them a frame of reference

and a necessary hope, the hope being that when life has done its worst
they will be enabled to rise above themselves and to triumph over life.
Life would scarcely be bearable if this hope did not exist. Again, even
when the worst has been said, to betray a belief is not by any means to
have put oneself beyond its power; the betrayal of a belief is not the
same thing as ceasing to believe. If this were not so there would be no
moral standards in the world at all. Yet one must also recognize that
morality is based on ideas and that all ideas are dangerous—dangerous
because ideas can only lead to action and where the action leads no man
can say. And dangerous in this respect: that confronted with the impossibility of remaining faithful to one's beliefs, and the equal impossibility
of becoming free of them, one can be driven to the most inhuman
excesses. The ideas on which American beliefs are based are not,
though Americans often seem to think so, ideas which originated in
America. They came out of Europe. And the establishment of democracy on the American continent was scarcely as radical a break with the
past as was the necessity, which Americans faced, of broadening this
concept to include black men.

   This was, literally, a hard necessity. It was impossible, for one thing,   20
for Americans to abandon their beliefs, not only because these beliefs
alone seemed able to justify the sacrifices they had endured and the
blood that they had spilled, but also because these beliefs afforded
them their only bulwark against a moral chaos as absolute as the
physical chaos of the continent it was their destiny to conquer. But in
the situation in which Americans found themselves, these beliefs threatened an idea which, whether or not one likes to think so, is the very
warp and woof of the heritage of the West, the idea of white supremacy.

   Americans have made themselves notorious by the shrillness and
the brutality with which they have insisted on this idea, but they did not
invent it; and it has escaped the world's notice that those very excesses
of which Americans have been guilty imply a certain, unprecedented
uneasiness over the idea's life and power, if not, indeed, the idea's
validity. The idea of white supremacy rests simply on the fact that white
men are the creators of civilization (the present civilization, which is the
only one that matters; all previous civilizations are simply "contributions" to our own) and are therefore civilization's guardians and defenders. Thus it was impossible for Americans to accept the black man
as one of themselves, for to do so was to jeopardize their status as white
men. But not so to accept him was to deny his human reality, his human
weight and complexity, and the strain of denying the overwhelmingly
undeniable forced Americans into rationalizations so fantastic that they
approached the pathological.

   At the root of the American Negro problem is the necessity of the
American white man to find a way of living with the Negro in order to

be able to live with himself. And the history of this problem can be reduced to the means used by Americans—lynch law and law, segregation and legal acceptance, terrorization and concession—either to come to terms with this necessity, or to find a way around it, or (most usually) to find a way of doing both these things at once. The resulting spectacle, at once foolish and dreadful, led someone to make the quite accurate observation that "the Negro-in-America is a form of insanity which overtakes white men."

In this long battle, a battle by no means finished, the unforeseeable effects of which will be felt by many future generations, the white man's motive was the protection of his identity; the black man was motivated by the need to establish an identity. And despite the terrorization which the Negro in America endured and endures sporadically until today, despite the cruel and totally inescapable ambivalence of his status in his country, the battle for his identity has long ago been won. He is not a visitor to the West, but a citizen there, an American, as American as the Americans who despise him, the Americans who fear him, the Americans who love him—the Americans who became less than themselves, or rose to be greater than themselves by virtue of the fact that the challenge he represented was inescapable. He is perhaps the only black man in the world whose relationship to white men is more terrible, more subtle, and more meaningful than the relationship of bitter possessed to uncertain possessor. His survival depended, and his development depends, on his ability to turn his peculiar status in the Western world to his own advantage and, it may be, so the very great advantage of that world. It remains for him to fashion out of his experience that which will give him sustenance, and a voice.

The cathedral of Chartres, I have said, says something to the people 24 of this village which it cannot say to me; but it is important to understand that this cathedral says something to me which it cannot say to them. Perhaps they are struck by the power of the spires, the glory of the windows; but they have known God, after all, longer than I have known him, and in a different way, and I am terrified by the slippery bottomless well to be found in the crypt, down which heretics were hurled to death, and by the obscene, inescapable gargoyles jutting out of the stone and seeming to say that God and the devil can never be divorced. I doubt that the villagers think of the devil when they face a cathedral because they have never been identified with the devil. But I must accept the status which myth, if nothing else, gives me in the West before I can hope to change the myth.

Yet, if the American Negro has arrived at his identity by virtue of the absoluteness of his estrangement from his past, American white men still nourish the illusion that there is some means of recovering the European innocence, of returning to a state in which black men do not exist. This is one of the greatest errors Americans can make. The identity they fought so hard to protect has, by virtue of that battle, undergone a change: Americans are as unlike any other white people in the world as it is possible to be. I do not think, for example, that it is too much to suggest that the American vision of the world—which allows so little reality, generally speaking, for any of the darker forces in human life, which tends until today to paint moral issues in glaring black and white—owes a great deal to the battle waged by Americans to maintain between themselves and black men a human separation which could not be bridged. It is only now beginning to be borne in on us—very faintly, it must be admitted, very slowly, and very much against our will—that this vision of the world is dangerously inaccurate, and perfectly useless. For it protects our moral high-mindedness at the terrible expense of weakening our grasp of reality. People who shut their eyes to reality simply invite their own destruction, and anyone who insists on remaining in a state of innocence long after that innocence is dead turns himself into a monster.

The time has come to realize that the interracial drama acted out on the American continent has not only created a new black man, it has created a new white man, too. No road whatever will lead Americans back to the simplicity of this European village where white men still have the luxury of looking on me as a stranger. I am not, really, a stranger any longer for any American alive. One of the things that distinguishes Americans from other people is that no other people has ever been so deeply involved in the lives of black men, and vice versa. This fact faced, with all its implications, it can be seen that the history of the American Negro problem is not merely shameful, it is also something of an achievement. For even when the worst has been said, it must also be added that the perpetual challenge posed by this problem was always, somehow, perpetually met. It is precisely this black-white experience which may prove of indispensable value to us in the world we face today. This world is white no longer, and it will never be white again.

1953

Jonathan Kozol

Distancing the Homeless

It is commonly believed by many journalists and politicians that the homeless of America are, in large part, former patients of large mental hospitals who were deinstitutionalized in the 1970s—the consequence, it is sometimes said, of misguided liberal opinion, which favored the treatment of such persons in community-based centers. It is argued that this policy, and the subsequent failure of society to build such centers or to provide them in sufficient number, is the primary cause of homelessness in the United States.

Those who work among the homeless do not find that explanation satisfactory. While conceding that a certain number of the homeless are, or have been, mentally unwell, they believe that, in the case of most unsheltered people, the primary reason is economic rather than clinical. The cause of homelessness, they say with disarming logic, is the lack of homes and of income with which to rent or acquire them.

They point to the loss of traditional jobs in industry (two million every year since 1980) and to the fact that half of those who are laid off end up in work that pays a poverty-level wage. They point to the parallel growth of poverty in families with children, noting that children, who represent one quarter of our population, make up forty percent of the poor: since 1968, the number of children in poverty has grown by three million, while welfare benefits to families with children have declined by 35 percent.

And they note, too, that these developments have coincided with a   4
time in which the shortage of low-income housing has intensified as the gentrification of our major cities has accelerated. Half a million units of low-income housing have been lost each year to condominium conversion as well as to arson, demolition, or abandonment. Between 1978 and 1980, median rents climbed 30 percent for people in the lowest income sector, driving many of these families into the streets. After 1980, rents rose at even faster rates. In Boston, between 1982 and 1984, over 80 percent of the housing units renting below three hundred dollars disappeared, while the number of units renting above six hundred dollars nearly tripled.

Hard numbers, in this instance, would appear to be of greater help than psychiatric labels in telling us why so many people become homeless. Eight million American families now pay half or more of their income for rent or a mortgage. Six million more, unable to pay rent at all, live doubled up with others. At the same time, federal support for low-income housing dropped from $30 billion (1980) to $9 billion (1986). Under Presidents Ford and Carter, five hundred thousand subsidized private housing units were constructed. By President Reagan's second term, the number had dropped to twenty-five thousand. "We're getting out of the housing business, period," said a deputy assistant secretary of the Department of Housing and Urban Development in 1985.

One year later, the *Washington Post* reported that the number of homeless families in Washington, D.C., had grown by 500 percent over the previous twelve months. In New York City, the waiting list for public housing now contains two hundred thousand names. The waiting is eighteen years.

Why, in the face of these statistics, are we impelled to find a psychiatric explanation for the growth of homelessness in the United States?

A misconception, once it is implanted in the popular imagination, 8 is not easy to uproot, particularly when it serves a useful social role. The notion that the homeless are largely psychotics who belong in institutions, rather than victims of displacement at the hands of enterprising realtors, spares us from the need to offer realistic solutions to the fact of deep and widening extremes of wealth and poverty in the United States. It also enables us to tell ourselves that the despair of homeless people bears no intimate connection to the privileged existence we enjoy— when, for example, we rent or purchase one of those restored town-houses that once provided shelter for people now huddled in the street.

But there may be another reason to assign labels to the destitute. Terming economic victims "psychotic" or "disordered" helps to place them at a distance. It says that they aren't quite like us—and, more important, that we could not be like them. The plight of homeless families is a nightmare. It may not seem natural to try to banish human beings from our midst, but it *is* natural to try to banish nightmares from our minds.

So the rituals of clinical contamination proceed uninterrupted by the economic facts described above. Research that addresses homeless-ness as an *injustice* rather than as a medical *misfortune* does not win the funding of foundations. And the research which *is* funded, defining the narrowed borders of permissible debate, diverts our attention from the antecedent to the secondary cause of homelessness. Thus it is that perfectly ordinary women whom I know in New York City—people whose depression or anxiety is a realistic consequence of months and even years in crowded shelters or the streets—are interrogated by invasive research scholars in an effort to decode their poverty, to find clinical categories for their despair and terror, to identify the secret failing that lies hidden in their psyche.

Many pregnant women without homes are denied prenatal care because they constantly travel from one shelter to another. Many are anemic. Many are denied essential dietary supplements by recent federal cuts. As a consequence, some of their children do not live to see their second year of life. Do these mothers sometimes show signs of stress? Do they appear disorganized, depressed, disordered? Frequently. They are immobilized by pain, traumatized by fear. So it is no surprise that when researchers enter the scene to ask them how they "feel," the resulting reports tell us that the homeless are emotionally unwell. The reports do not tell us we have *made* these people ill. They do not tell us that illness is a natural response to intolerable conditions. Nor do they tell us of the strength and the resilience that so many of these people still retain despite the miseries they must endure. They set these men and women apart in capsules labeled "personality disorder" or "psychotic," where they no longer threaten our complacence.

I visited Haiti not many years ago, when the Duvalier family was 12 still in power. If an American scholar were to have made a psychological study of the homeless families living in the streets of Port-au-Prince— sleeping amidst rotten garbage, bathing in open sewers—and if he were to return to the United States to tell us that the reasons for their destitution were "behavioral problems" or "a lack of mental health," we would be properly suspicious. Knowledgeable Haitians would not merely be suspicious. They would be enraged. Even to initiate such research when economic and political explanations present themselves so starkly would appear grotesque. It is no less so in the United States.

One of the more influential studies of this nature was carried out in 1985 by Ellen Bassuk, a psychiatrist at Harvard University. Drawing upon interviews with eight homeless parents, Dr. Bassuk contends, according to the *Boston Globe*, that "90 percent [of these people] have problems other than housing and poverty that are so acute they would be unable to live successfully on their own." She also precludes the possibility that illness, where it does exist, may be provoked by destitution. "Our data," she writes, "suggest that mental illness tends to precede homelessness." She concedes that living in the streets can make a homeless person's mental illness worse; but she insists upon the fact of prior illness.

The executive director of the Massachusetts Commission on Children and Youth believes that Dr. Bassuk's estimate is far too high. The staff of Massachusetts Human Services Secretary Phillip Johnston believes the appropriate number is closer to 10 percent.

In defending her research, Bassuk challenges such critics by claiming that they do not have data to refute her. This may be true. Advocates for the homeless do not receive funds to defend the sanity of the people they represent. In placing the burden of proof upon them, Dr. Bassuk has created an extraordinary dialectic: How does one prove that people aren't unwell? What homeless mother would consent to enter a procedure that might "prove" her mental health? What overburdened shelter operator would divert scarce funds to such an exercise? It is an unnatural, offensive, and dehumanizing challenge.

Dr. Bassuk's work, however, isn't the issue I want to raise here; the 16 issue is the use or misuse of that work by critics of the poor. For example, in a widely syndicated essay published in 1986, the newspaper columnist Charles Krauthammer argued that the homeless are essentially a deranged segment of the population and that we must find the "political will" to isolate them from society. We must do this, he said, "whether they like it or not." Arguing even against the marginal benefits of homeless shelters, Krauthammer wrote: "There is a better alternative, however, though no one dares speak its name." Krauthammer dares: that better alternative, he said, is "asylum."

One of Mr. Krauthammer's colleagues at the *Washington Post*, the columnist George Will, perceives the homeless as a threat to public cleanliness and argues that they ought to be consigned to places where we need not see them. "It is," he says, "simply a matter of public hygiene" to put them out of sight. Another journalist, Charles Murray, writing from the vantage point of a social Darwinist, recommends the restoration of the almshouses of the 1800s. "Granted Dickensian horror stories about almshouses," he begins, there were nonetheless "good almshouses"; he proposes "a good correctional 'halfway house'" as a proper shelter for a mother and child with no means of self-support.

In the face of such declarations, the voices of those who work with and know the poor are harder to hear.

Manhattan Borough President David Dinkins made the following observation on the basis of a study commissioned in 1986: "No facts support the belief that addiction or behavioral problems occur with more frequency in the homeless family population than in a similar socioeconomic population. Homeless families are not demographically different from other public assistance families when they enter the shelter system. . . . Family homelessness is typically a housing and income problem: the unavailability of affordable housing and the inadequacy of public assistance income."

In a "hypothetical world," write James Wright and Julie Lam of the 20
University of Massachusetts, "where there were no alcoholics, no drug addicts, no mentally ill, no deinstitutionalization, . . . indeed, no personal social pathologies at all, there would still be a formidable homelessness problem, simply because at this stage in American history, there is not enough low-income housing" to accommodate the poor.

New York State's respected commissioner of social services, Cesar Perales, makes the point in fewer words: "Homelessness is less and less a result of personal failure, and more and more is caused by larger forces. There is no longer affordable housing in New York City for people of poor and modest means."

Even the words of medical practitioners who care for homeless people have been curiously ignored. A study published by the Massachusetts Medical Society, for instance, has noted that the most frequent illnesses among a sample of the homeless population, after alcohol and drug use, are trauma (31 percent), upper respiratory disorders (28 percent), limb disorders (19 percent), mental illness (16 percent), skin diseases (15 percent), hypertension (14 percent), and neurological illnesses (12 percent). (Excluded from this tabulation are lead poisoning, malnutrition, acute diarrhea, and other illnesses especially common among homeless infants and small children.) Why, we may ask, of all these calamities, does mental illness command so much political and press attention? The answer may be that the label of mental illness places the destitute outside the sphere of ordinary life. It personalizes an anguish that is public in its genesis; it individualizes a misery that is both general in cause and general in application.

The rate of tuberculosis among the homeless is believed to be ten times that of the general population. Asthma, I have learned in countless interviews, is one of the most common causes of discomfort in the shelters. Compulsive smoking, exacerbated by the crowding and the tension, is more common in the shelters than in any place that I have visited except prison. Infected and untreated sores, scabies, diarrhea, poorly set limbs, protruding elbows, awkwardly distorted wrists, bleeding gums, impacted teeth, and other untreated dental problems are so common among children in the shelters that one rapidly forgets their presence. Hunger and emaciation are everywhere. Children as well as adults can bring to mind the photographs of people found in camps for refugees of war in 1945. But these miseries bear no stigma, and mental illness does. It conveys a stigma in the Soviet Union. It conveys a stigma in the United States. In both nations the label is used, whether as a matter of deliberate policy or not, to isolate and treat as special cases those who, by deed or word or by sheer presence, represent a threat to national complacence. The two situations are obviously not identical, but they are enough alike to give Americans reason for concern.

Last summer, some twenty-eight thousand homeless people were 24 afforded shelter by the city of New York. Of this number, twelve thousand were children and six thousand were parents living together in families. The average child was six years old, the average parent twenty-seven. A typical homeless family included a mother with two or three children, but in about one-fifth of these families two parents were present. Roughly ten thousand single persons, then, made up the remainder of the population of the city's shelters.

These proportions vary somewhat from one area of the nation to another. In all areas, however, families are the fastest-growing sector of the homeless population, and in the Northeast they are by far the largest sector already. In Massachusetts, three-fourths of the homeless now are families with children; in certain parts of Massachusetts—Attleboro and Northampton, for example—the proportion reaches ninety percent.

Two-thirds of the homeless children studied recently in Boston were less than five years old.

Of an estimated two to three million homeless people nationwide, about 500,000 are dependent children, according to Robert Hayes, counsel to the National Coalition for the Homeless. Including their parents, at least 750,000 homeless people in America are family members.

What is to be made, then, of the supposition that the homeless are primarily the former residents of mental hospitals, persons who were carelessly released during the 1970s? Many of them are, to be sure. Among the older men and women in the streets and shelters, as many as one-third (some believe as many as one-half) may be chronically disturbed, and a number of these people were deinstitutionalized during the 1970s. But in a city like New York, where nearly half the homeless are small children with an average age of six, to operate on the basis of such a supposition makes no sense. Their parents, with an average age of twenty-seven, are not likely to have been hospitalized in the 1970s, either.

Nor is it easy to assume, as was once the case, that single men—those 28 who come closer to fitting the stereotype of the homeless vagrant, the drifting alcoholic of an earlier age—are the former residents of mental hospitals. The age of homeless men has dropped in recent years; many of them are only twenty-one to twenty-eight years old. Fifty percent of homeless men in New York City shelters in 1984 were there for the first time. Most had previously had homes and jobs. Many had never before needed public aid.

A frequently cited set of figures tells us that in 1955, the average daily census of nonfederal psychiatric institutions was 677,000, and that by 1984, the number had dropped to 151,000. Subtract the second number from the first, conventional logic tells us, and we have an explanation for the homelessness of half a million people. A closer look at the same number offers us a different lesson.

The sharpest decline in the average daily census of these institutions occurred prior to 1978, and the largest part of that decline, in fact, appeared at least a decade earlier. From 677,000 in 1955, the census dropped to 378,000 in 1972. The 1974 census was 307,000. In 1976 it was 230,000; in 1977 it was 211,000; and in 1978 it was 190,000. In no year since 1978 has the average daily census dropped by more than 9,000 persons, and in the six-year period from 1978 to 1984, the total decline was 39,000 persons. Compared with a decline of 300,000 from 1955 to 1972, and of nearly 200,000 more from 1972 to 1978, the number is small. But the years since 1980 are the period in which the present homeless crisis surfaced. Only since 1983 have homeless individuals overflowed the shelters.

If the large numbers of the homeless lived in hospitals before they reappeared in subway stations and in public shelters, we need to ask where they were and what they had been doing from 1972 to 1980. Were they living under bridges? Were they waiting out the decade in the basements of deserted buildings?

No. The bulk of those who had been psychiatric patients and were 32 released from hospitals during the 1960s and early 1970s had been living in the meantime in low-income housing, many in skid-row hotels or boarding houses. Such housing—commonly known as SRO (single-room occupancy) units—was drastically diminished by the gentrification of our cities that began in 1970. Almost 50 percent of SRO housing was replaced by luxury apartments or by office buildings between 1970 and 1980, and the remaining units have been disappearing at even faster rates. As recently as 1986, after New York City had issued a prohibition against conversion of such housing, a well-known developer hired a demolition team to destroy a building in Times Square that had previously been home to indigent people. The demolition took place in the middle of the night. In order to avoid imprisonment, the developer was allowed to make a philanthropic gift to homeless people as a token of atonement. This incident, bizarre as it appears, reminds us that the profit motive for displacement of the poor is very great in every major city. It also indicates a more realistic explanation for the growth of homelessness during the 1980s.

Even for those persons who are ill and were deinstitutionalized during the decades before 1980, the precipitating cause of homelessness in 1987 is not illness but loss of housing. SRO housing, unattractive as it may have been, offered low-cost sanctuaries for the homeless, providing a degree of safety and mutual support for those who lived within them. They were a demeaning version of the community health centers that society had promised; they were the de facto "halfway houses" of the 1970s. For these people too, then—at most half of the homeless single persons in America—the cause of homelessness is lack of housing.

A writer in the *New York Times* describes a homeless woman standing on a traffic island in Manhattan. "She was evicted from her small room in the hotel just across the street," and she is determined to get revenge. Until she does, "nothing will move her from that spot. . . . Her argumentativeness and her angry fixation on revenge, along with the apparent absence of hallucinations, mark her as a paranoid." Most physicians, I imagine, would be more reserved in passing judgment with so little evidence, but this author makes his diagnosis without hesitation. "The paranoids of the street," he says, "are among the most difficult to help."

Perhaps so. But does it depend on who is offering the help? Is anyone offering to help this woman get back her home? Is it crazy to seek vengeance for being thrown into the street? The absence of anger, some psychiatrists believe, might indicate much greater illness.

The same observer sees additional symptoms of pathology ("nega- 36 tive symptoms," he calls them) in the fact that many homeless persons demonstrate a "gross deterioration in their personal hygiene" and grooming, leading to "indifference" and "apathy." Having just identi- fied one woman as unhealthy because she is so far from being "indif- ferent" as to seek revenge, he now sees apathy as evidence of illness; so consistency is not what we are looking for in this account. But how much less indifferent might the homeless be if those who decide their fate were less indifferent themselves? How might their grooming and hygiene be improved if they were permitted access to a public toilet?

In New York City, as in many cities, homeless people are denied the right to wash in public bathrooms, to store their few belongings in a public locker, or, in certain cases, to make use of public toilets al- together. Shaving, cleaning of clothes, and other forms of hygiene are prohibited in the men's room of Grand Central Station. The terminal's three hundred lockers, used in former times by homeless people to secure their goods, were removed in 1986 as "a threat to public safety," according to a study made by the New York City Council.

At one-thirty every morning, homeless people are ejected from the station. Many once attempted to take refuge on the ramp that leads to Forty-second Street because it was protected from the street by wooden doors and thus provided some degree of warmth. But the station man- agement responded to this challenge in two ways. The ramp was mopped with a strong mixture of ammonia to produce a noxious smell, and when the people sleeping there brought cardboard boxes and newspapers to protect them from the fumes, the entrance doors were chained wide open. Temperatures dropped some nights to ten degrees. Having driven these people to the streets, city officials subsequently determined that their willingness to risk exposure to cold weather could be taken as further evidence of mental illness.

At Pennsylvania Station in New York, homeless women are denied the use of toilets. Amtrak police come by and herd them off each hour on the hour. In June 1985, Amtrak officials issued this directive to police: "It is the policy of Amtrak to not allow the homeless and undesirables to remain. . . . Officers are encouraged to eject all undesir- ables. . . . Now is the time to train and educate them that their presence will not be tolerated as cold weather sets in." In an internal memo, according to CBS, an Amtrak official asked flatly: "Can't we get rid of this trash?"

I have spent many nights in conversation with the women who are 40
huddled in the corridors and near the doorway of the public toilets in
Penn Station. Many are young. Most are cogent. Few are dressed in the
familiar rags suggested by the term *bag ladies*. Unable to bathe or use the
toilets in the station, almost all are in conditions of intolerable physical
distress. The sight of clusters of police officers, mostly male, guarding a
toilet from use by homeless women speaks volumes about the public
conscience of New York.

Where do these women defecate? How do they bathe? What will we
do when, in her physical distress, a woman finally disrobes in public
and begins to urinate right on the floor? "Gross deterioration," someone will call it, evidence of mental illness. In the course of an impromptu survey in the streets last September, Mayor Koch observed a
homeless woman who had soiled her own clothes. Not only was the
woman crazy, said the mayor, but those who differed with him on his
diagnosis must be crazy, too. "I am the number one social worker in this
town—with sanity," said he.

It may be that this woman was psychotic, but the mayor's comment
says a great deal more about his sense of revulsion and the moral
climate of a decade in which words like these may be applauded than
about her mental state.

A young man who had lost his job, then his family, then his home,
all in the summer of 1986, spoke with me for several hours in Grand
Central Station on the weekend following Thanksgiving. "A year ago,"
he said, "I never thought that somebody like me would end up in a
shelter. Nothing you've ever undergone prepares you. You walk into
the place [a shelter on the Bowery]—the smell of sweat and urine hits
you like a wall. Unwashed bodies and the look of absolute despair on
many, many faces there would make you think you were in Dante's
Hell. . . . What you fear is that you will be here forever. You do not
know if it is ever going to end. You think to yourself: it is a dream
and I will awake. Sometimes I think: it's an experiment. They are
watching you to find out how much you can take. . . . I was a pretty
stable man. Now I tremble when I meet somebody in the ordinary
world. I'm trembling right now. . . . For me, the loss of work and loss
of wife had left me rocking. Then the welfare regulations hit me. I
began to feel that I would be reduced to trash. . . . Half the people
that I know are suffering from chest infections and sleep deprivation.
The lack of sleep leaves you debilitated, shaky. You exaggerate your
fears. If a psychiatrist came along he'd say that I was crazy. But I was
an ordinary man. There was nothing wrong with me. I lost my kids. I
lost my home. Now would you say that I was crazy if I told you I was
feeling sad?"

"If the plight of homeless adults is the shame of America," writes 44
Fred Hechinger in the *New York Times*, "the lives of homeless children
are the nation's crime."

In November 1984, a fact already known to advocates for the homeless was given brief attention by the press. Homeless families, the *New
York Times* reported, "mostly mothers and young children, have been
sleeping on chairs, counters, and floors of the city's emergency welfare
offices." Reacting to such reports, the mayor declared: "The woman is
sitting on a chair or on a floor. It is not because we didn't offer her a
bed. We provide a shelter for every single person who knocks on our
door." On the same day, however, the city reported that in the previous
eleven weeks it had been unable to give shelter to 153 families, and in
the subsequent year, 1985, the city later reported that about two thousand children slept in welfare offices because of lack of shelter space.

Some eight hundred homeless infants in New York City, reported
the National Coalition for the Homeless, "routinely go without sufficient food, cribs, health care, and diapers." The lives of these children
"are put at risk," while "high-risk pregnant women" are repeatedly
forced to sleep in unsafe "barracks shelters" or welfare offices called
Emergency Assistance Units (EAUs). "Coalition monitors, making spo-
radic random checks, found eight women in their *ninth* month of pregnancy sleeping in EAUs. . . . Two women denied shelter began having
labor contractions at the EAU." In one instance, the Legal Aid Society
was forced to go to court after a woman lost her child by miscarriage
while lying on the floor of a communal bathroom in a shelter which the
courts had already declared unfit to house pregnant women.

The coalition also reported numerous cases in which homeless
mothers were obliged to choose between purchasing food or diapers for
their infants. Federal guidelines issued in 1986 deepened the nutrition
crisis faced by mothers in the welfare shelters by counting the high rent
paid to the owners of the buildings as a part of family income, rendering their residents ineligible for food stamps. Families I interviewed
who had received as much as $150 in food stamps monthly in June 1986
were cut back to $33 before Christmas.

"Now you're hearing all kinds of horror stories," said President 48
Reagan, "about the people that are going to be thrown out in the snow
to hunger and [to] die of cold and so forth. . . . We haven't cut a single
budget." But in the four years leading up to 1985, according to the *New
Republic*, Aid to Families with Dependent Children had been cut by $4.8
billion, child nutrition programs by $5.2 billion, food stamps by $6.8
billion. The federal government's authority to help low-income families
with housing assistance was cut from $30 billion to $11 billion in

Reagan's first term. In his fiscal 1986 budget, the president proposed to cut that by an additional 95 percent.

"If even one American child is forced to go to bed hungry at night," the president said on another occasion, "that is a national tragedy. We are too generous a people to allow this." But in the years since the president spoke these words, thousands of poor children in New York alone have gone to bed too sick to sleep and far too weak to rise the next morning to attend a public school. Thousands more have been unable to attend school at all because their homeless status compels them to move repeatedly from one temporary shelter to another. Even in the affluent suburbs outside New York City, hundreds of homeless children are obliged to ride as far as sixty miles twice a day in order to obtain an education in the public schools to which they were originally assigned before their families were displaced. Many of these children get to school too late to eat their breakfast; others are denied lunch at school because of federal cuts in feeding programs.

Many homeless children die—and others suffer brain damage—as a direct consequence of federal cutbacks in prenatal programs, maternal nutrition, and other feeding programs. The parents of one such child shared with me the story of the year in which their child was delivered, lived, and died. The child, weighing just over four pounds at birth, grew deaf and blind soon after, and for these reasons had to stay in the hospital for several months. When he was released on Christmas Eve of 1984, his mother and father had no home. He lived with his parents in the shelters, subways, streets, and welfare offices of New York City for four winter months, and was readmitted to the hospital in time to die in May 1985.

When we met and spoke the following year, the father told me that his wife had contemplated and even attempted suicide after the child's death, while he had entertained the thought of blowing up the welfare offices of New York City. I would tell him that to do so would be illegal and unwise. I would never tell him it was crazy.

"No one will be turned away," says the mayor of New York City, as 52 hundreds of young mothers with their infants are turned from the doors of shelters season after season. That may sound to some like denial of reality. "Now you're hearing all these stories," says the president of the United States as he denies that anyone is cold or hungry or unhoused. On another occasion he says that the unsheltered "are homeless, you might say, by choice." That sounds every bit as self-deceiving.

The woman standing on the traffic island screaming for revenge until her room has been restored to her sounds relatively healthy by comparison. If three million homeless people did the same, and all at the same time, we might finally be forced to listen.   *1988*

Sallie Tisdale

Neither Morons nor Imbeciles nor Idiots: In the Company of the Mentally Retarded

I went dancing one night last September with a glad crowd of nearly a thousand merrymakers at one of the Red Lion hotels in Portland, Oregon. The dance was the climactic event of a Labor Day weekend convention, following a formal dinner and day of workshops and lost hotel registrations. The conventioneers were members of an organization called People First, and almost all of them were mentally retarded.

The band wore Hawaiian shirts and played loud sixties music, and I stood to one side, clutching a glass but already punch-drunk with the day's events. Excited people in their best holiday clothes paced in and out of the huge room, and the rest of them danced, alone and cheek-to-cheek, in groups and in wheelchairs and balanced on one foot, waggling their heads and shaking with palsied fervor. And after a while I danced, too: the twist, the frug, and new dances never done before.

When I was a child there were few words more insulting than *retard* (*ree*-tard). At lunch hour each school day a certain group of children appeared. Tall and splayed, or fat, given to hand twiddling and rocking in place, they had mussed hair and bottle-bottom glasses and dangling lower lips. And even now I remember them as being much older than me but, even so, lost in an eternal babyhood, stirring the peas into the mashed potatoes and drooling in the soup. They were gawked at; and if they showed their faces at any other time, they were jeered at—"Hey, *ree*-tard!"

The difference between *them* and *us* was a gulf that could not be   4 bridged.

In recent years that gulf has shrunk. My fears about the retarded— inarticulate fears of derangement, impulsiveness, the uncivilized id— almost disappeared. I found myself wanting the company of the retarded without knowing who, exactly, the retarded were. The People First convention was the beginning of a trip I made around the country, a search for some understanding of the fit between *them* and *me*.

The Red Lion–Lloyd Center is a showy complex filled with brass, mirrors, and flocked wallpaper in shades of rust and maroon. Two glass elevators reflect the hundreds of tiny light bulbs in the lobby; they rise and fall slowly like drifting leaves. I had parked that morning in the hotel's lot and passed a bright, white room lined with shining sports cars guarded by stout young men in red blazers; young people were just beginning to arrive for another event, something called an All-British Field Car Rally.

Crossing the lot, where vans with wheelchair lifts were parked beside BMWs, I'd joined the People First crowd in the lobby. It took my breath away, that crowd: I leaned against a wall, washed in a wave of people, hundreds of people, as varied and multiple as the blooms of a wild field. There was a pretty, plump, dark woman in a tight purple swimsuit and neon green stretch shorts; a few nattily dressed men with briefcases, talking earnestly among themselves; a man who looked just like Peter Boyle; a fat woman in a short blue skirt and white snow boots, taking pictures with a pink Instamatic. Wheelchairs filled with plump and lumpy bodies—some twitching, others with bent, bowed heads and shut eyes—slid gently past people in helmets with bite guards. I saw the familiar hand twiddling and more: drooling, scratching, finger wiggling, lip diddling, rhythmic rocking, head nodding, hair twirling, face stroking, head holding, tongue chewing, ear poking, all taking place in a jumble of round, wide-eyed faces, low shelving brows, receding chins, crooked noses, misaligned teeth, short legs, bowed legs, amputated legs, misshapen hands, crossed eyes. I saw a wide variety of hats.

People wandered in and out all day; every now and then someone spotted a friend and shouted out a name or a sound—a holler of guttural, inarticulate voice. There was a schedule: a slide show, a panel discussion, a sing-along down one wing. But hardly anyone stuck to it. The halls were difficult to negotiate; I'd had to slip past people limping, running, stumbling, greeting each other with rude noises made against the back of their hands. From time to time a great fat man in overalls asked the room at large when dinner would be served. Men my age with bad haircuts sprawled on big red couches, smoking luxuriously. Later, men in tuxedos and women in evening dresses passed through, giggling loudly and staring, looking for the Field Car Rally formal.

Not long before the dance began I had stopped for a few moments in an open-air bar, to make notes and take a breath. The man on the stool next to me—a short, grizzled fellow in an ill-fitting suit—said something nonsensical; a few minutes later, distracted, I responded with an appropriate nonsense answer, only to turn and see a different man, a "regular" patron; he looked at me and looked at my People First name tag and picked up his beer and left.

A few weeks after the dance I flew east and visited a dim and cluttered group home in Brooklyn, one of twelve run by the Association for Children with Retarded Mental Development (ACRMD), one of the oldest and biggest New York–area agencies serving retarded adults. The house in Brooklyn is longer than it is wide, with many square rooms; it faces a weary strip of grass, a wide avenue, and a store called Brain Damage Comics. The rooms are outfitted with rummage-sale furniture. The few people in them strayed from armchair to couch to armchair

again, looking out windows, watching television. In the kitchen, under a
single fluorescent light, a gray-haired woman rocked from foot to foot,
growling; she paid no attention to me.

"That's Maggie," Arthur Palevsky said after we'd walked by. "She
does that."

Palevsky was my guide in Brooklyn; he is a young, fast-talking man   12
who runs the residential programs for the ACRMD. Besides the group
homes, the ACRMD runs three apartment houses and five day-
treatment centers. The waiting list for group homes, Palevsky told me, is
more than a thousand names long. Getting neighborhoods to accept the
ACRMD group homes and apartment houses is the main problem.
Palevsky says he hears the same thing whenever he holds a neighborhood hearing on a new site. People fear, he said, everything: crime,
molestation, indecent exposure, drunkenness, plummeting property
values.

We walked upstairs, through big bedrooms and small, past posters
of sports cars and rock stars and shelves upon which many stuffed
animals were neatly displayed. Palevsky had to make a phone call, and I
waited in the cramped upstairs hallway, in shadow.

A man came to the doorway of his room near the stairs; he was short
and middle-aged, with a big square head and jowly unshaven cheeks.
When I turned my face toward him he came up to me fast and silent on
big flat feet and grabbed my hand, looking at me with wide watery eyes.
He held his face close to mine, my hand in both of his. His mouth was
full of crooked yellow teeth.

An aide, sitting at a nearby desk, said, "That's Donald."

Donald nodded several times, still holding my hand in both of his;   16
he was so much shorter than me that I found myself bending over.

"Ee teep dah," he said. "Ee teep dah!"

Again the aide spoke up. "He sleeps there. That's his bed."

And Donald was pulling me into the room and pointing at the
nearer of twin beds covered with a crooked pink chenille bedspread, at
a white dresser with the drawers slightly awry, at a cheap poster of a
snow-covered mountain. I nodded, he nodded. I nodded and smiled, he
nodded and smiled. Palevsky had disappeared, and I stood in Donald's
silent room, in the milky light of an early fall day filtered through white
curtains, waiting until it seemed possible to go. And then I moved
toward the steep, dark stairway—and Donald moved with me in shuf-
fling concert, as though we were chained at the ankle.

He looked up at me hopefully and said, "Teeeee?"   20

"You go ask Anna. She'll make you a cup of tea," the aide said,
without looking up from his paperwork, and Donald and I descended
the stairs together, hand in hand, one narrow step at a time. I didn't
know how to say good-bye to someone like Donald, who is almost

unbearably used to hearing it. Later in my travels I heard a story of a man, somewhat like Donald, who couldn't say good-bye; he would stand in a doorway or on a sidewalk talking about whatever came to mind, as though afraid to stop. All he needed, in the end, was to be taught to wave: to make meaningful the experience of farewell.

At the base of the stairs we turned a corner and found the common area, a worn-looking room with a television playing quietly in the corner. Several people sat on tired chairs, and Arthur Palevsky chatted softly with a young woman I took to be Anna. The scene was terribly mundane. Donald made no sound at all but at once dropped my hand and moved to a seat beside the wall, his chin tucked in against his chest. He didn't look up again, as though he'd known all along I wasn't going to stay.

The subject of mental retardation is encumbered with conventional wisdom, small beliefs we cling to from childhood and large ideas that fuel the social machine. The main piece of fiction under which we labor, I think, is that we know what mental retardation is. We know that it exists: permanent, irreversible, tragic. Thousands of pages, dozens of definitions, have been written about retardation, but nothing comes close to defining it. And I can't write my own definition, either; when I try, I find myself relying on nothing more lucid than *difference from myself*. This is what drives the desire to define in the first place: These people are so unlike me, behave so unlike me, they must be something else altogether.

Less than a hundred years ago people we now call mentally re- 24
tarded were labeled by researchers as morons, imbeciles, and idiots—
each term referring to a different degree of defect—and were thought
to be all of a type. They were considered incomplete humans, unable to
feel pain, perhaps mad or possessed, and certainly dangerous. People
called them the feebleminded, cretins, simpletons, dullards. Now we are
to call them people-with-mental-retardation. I sometimes wonder what,
left alone, the retarded would call themselves. And what would they call
me? The word *retardation* only means delay, and in that sense it may be
perfectly descriptive. It means the slowing down of something's course:
A car's timing is retarded, and so is a flow of liquid, a tumor's growth. It
is a vague and almost poetic word. And the rest—"mental"—is indefin-
able, a foggy reference to the life behind the eyes, impossible to measure and dangerous to judge.

The official definition of mental retardation today is one formulated by the American Association on Mental Retardation (AAMR). The
AAMR carries out research, studies the results, asks for expert opinions.
In its current form the definition of mental retardation has three parts:
subnormal intellectual function, defined as an intelligence quotient

(IQ) at least two standard deviations below the mean; poor adaptive behavior; and symptoms of retardation that appear during the developmental period. Based on the AAMR definition, between 2 and 3 percent of the population are retarded—five and a half to seven million people. This statistic remains fairly steady for reasons unclear. According to the AAMR, about 89 percent of this group are "mildly retarded." But here the plot begins to thicken.

There are two widely accepted categories of retardation: organic and nonorganic. Organic retardation has more than 250 known causes, among them Down syndrome and other chromosomal disorders, metabolic imbalances, tumors, brain malformations, and trauma. But researchers in the field commonly hold that only about 20 percent of all the people called retarded have an organic problem.

The remaining 80 percent are affected by nonorganic retardation—retardation caused by, say, parental neglect or abuse, or by a baby's having eaten lead paint—and there is nothing physiologically wrong with them. Almost all of the people classified as mildly retarded are considered to be nonorganically retarded. One of the more controversial questions in the field of mental retardation right now is whether the nonorganically retarded are—or should be labeled—retarded at all.

For years the measurement of one's IQ figured most significantly in   28 our description of who is and who is not mentally retarded. IQ is a measurement of mental age divided by chronological age; a child of six who has the mental abilities of a six-year-old has an IQ of 100, the American mean. (About 50 percent of Americans are thought to have an IQ between 90 and 110). An IQ of 70 is two standard deviations below the mean and is, therefore, the cutoff for defining retardation.

Because IQ tests are woefully inadequate—measuring a person's fund of information with little regard for the quality of one's mind or one's ability to learn—IQ as the primary measure of retardation has been slowly but surely disappearing. This has had a very real impact on a particular population—the enormous number of people called borderline, whose IQ scores hover between 70 and 85. In 1959 the two-standard-deviations qualification was changed by the AAMR to one standard deviation. The number of retarded increased fivefold in one fell swoop; millions of people who until that moment had enjoyed official normality were reclassified as retarded. In 1973 the definition returned to two standard deviations, and all those people, in one stroke, became normal again.

I was skimming back issues of *The American Journal of Mental Deficiency* not long ago when I found a story written in 1961 titled "A Provocative Case of Over-Achievement by a Mongoloid." The brief, scholarly article described a thirty-six-year-old man who had been diagnosed mongoloid at an early age and had lived his whole life with his mother. For the last years of her life the woman was an invalid, and her son was responsible for the household—he took care of housework, shopping, errands, finances, laundry, his own and her personal care. He also played the piano, read books and kept a journal, and made money by selling small homemade items in the neighborhood. The neighbors knew he was retarded, but no one seemed to care.

When his mother died he was committed to a "training school," where the author of the story found him. The man, called only E., was tested on entry and found to have an IQ of barely 28. The author seemed unwilling to admit that there might be something wrong with the test. "If there is a lesson to be learned," he wrote, it is not to rely solely on IQ scores to predict outcomes. *If* there is a lesson. In other words, the test is not wrong in labeling the man profoundly retarded; it is E. who has been mistaken, who has "overachieved," as though he had gorged himself on skills. With the arid lack of narrative so common in these journals, the writer never reveals E.'s fate. I can't help but fear the obvious: that he never escaped the system he had until then so successfully confounded. He was, after all, profoundly retarded; his IQ made him so, and I imagine he was kept in the institution until he died.

The mental-retardation field is full of stories about retarded people 32 who have gotten lost in the regular world for one reason or another and never been found again, so successfully did they *pretend* to be normal. The psychologist Robert Edgerton has followed a group of mentally retarded men who left an institution and entered the community as normal people more than twenty years ago; he finds them unusually optimistic in the face of adversity and no less able than their neighbors to get by. They are, he writes, hidden in "a cloak of competence," and he suggests that their unwillingness to be called retarded has kept them normal.

Most researchers in the field don't talk much at all about intelligence. Educators, for their part, talk about "delays." (One of the more consistent observations about the population called retarded is that they learn more slowly and tend to forget information more quickly than the rest of us.) A lot of people, especially those concerned with housing and employment, talk about "function." Experts refer to the mentally retarded who are able to care for themselves personally and socially as being "high function." Retarded people complimented by the accolade "high function" move in the world and take care of business in the same sorts of ways that you and I do. They are said to exhibit "adaptive behavior" as opposed to "adaptive failure."

One afternoon in San Francisco I was introduced to a middle-aged man named Gary. Gary looks an awful lot like Humphrey Bogart, with a stubborn pugilist's face and a capacity for long, full silences. He will say nothing at all, then he will say much that isn't relevant, until he feels prepared to answer the question at hand. Gary was kept at home for many years, unused to the world, unskilled, a kind of Kaspar Hauser.

"I used to give Gary Coca-Colas, and he always put them in his bag with his other possessions," a recreational therapist who works with Gary told me. "And one day it dawned on me that maybe he can't open a Coca-Cola can. So I introduced him to the idea of prying open the cap, and he said, 'Oh!' and that world opened up, that problem was solved."

This therapist was going to drive me to where I was staying, and 36 Gary home, after our talk, and Gary and I had to wait in a cold parking lot, after dark, for him to come and unlock the car doors. While we stood in the drizzle under the streetlights, Gary began to talk to himself. He wondered out loud where he would sit, where he *should* sit, whether he should put on his seat belt.

He shifted his weight from foot to foot, murmuring over and over, "I'll just ask him to repeat it." When we all got in the car Gary ran through his questions several times, until the therapist's patient, repetitive answers relieved him, and he settled back for the ride. So Gary—actually, by definition, an adaptive failure of magnificent proportions—makes his way in the world with constant, unshakable dignity.

On the same gray fall day that Arthur Palevsky showed me around the group home where I met Donald, he took me to the Lubin Center, occupying two attached brownstones in Carroll Gardens, a mostly Italian neighborhood in Brooklyn. At the Lubin Center there are twenty-four apartments for retarded adults living on their own. Among the residents, there was one recently married couple—both the husband and wife in wheelchairs—and two single parents, one of whom had just given birth to her second child. All Lubin Center residents work, some in "real world" jobs, others in workshops. All pay 30 percent of their income for rent.

"This is our first venture where we don't know where people are all the time," said Palevsky. "They can go out at three in the morning and get a hooker, and we don't know."

Palevsky took me through the empty foyer and the neat common 40 room up to the fourth floor. He wanted me to meet Debbie, and I could tell by his manner that he felt an almost paternal pride in her. Debbie, thirty-one, is a slim, gracious black woman. As she opened the door, I could see a dark bathroom and a long white hall leading to a single, large white room, where an older man with white hair sat at a small kitchen table. He rose in silent alarm and slipped past us, like a ghost.

"That's Alan," Palevsky told me in a stage whisper loud enough for Debbie to hear. "He and Debbie are romantically involved. He's afraid we're going to kick him out of the building if we find out they're sleeping together. I've told him we won't, but he doesn't believe me."

Debbie, dressed in slacks and a flannel shirt, with a bandanna on her head, smiled at his remark and invited me to sit down at the table. "I like it here," she then said. "The rent is feasible." And her use of that word startled me.

"Debbie is very modest," Palevsky said. "She's a very capable woman, who not only cooks, cleans, and cares for herself but probably handles her personal affairs better than most people ever hope to do." Debbie grinned, clearly pleased, and got up from the table to turn off the radio near her double bed. She moved around the apartment in a waddle, limping from side to side, the result of a recent hip replacement.

"Oh, Aww-thuh," she said. Her pronunciation of his name was 44 curious and pleasing. "I'm going to be calling the Holiday Inn about their new hotel, which is on Forty-eighth Street in Manhattan, to work in the kitchen, the cafeteria there. I used to do that, you know, learn how to do things in the kitchen." She turned back toward me. "I take the train."

"One of the things we liked when we bought this building is that it's a one-fare commute," said Palevsky. "It's the second subway stop from lower Manhattan."

"No, Arthur, it's the third stop." She wagged her finger and beckoned me down the hall, where she showed me her elaborate subway maps. She opened a closet to show Palevsky her Great Adventure amusement park T-shirt, boasting about her bravery in riding the giant roller coaster there.

Listening to Debbie, not wanting to leave her affable, gentle company, I thought how odd it is that people tend to think of retardation as a kind of disease, having in mind "victims" of retardation who are "suffering." (People uneasy with his programs have told Palevsky they thought you could *catch* retardation from being near it, the way you catch a cold.) When we say Debbie is retarded—she of the subway maps and clean apartment and roller-coaster rides—we mean it as a wrongness in Debbie. We say it with a hint of pity. I want to say that Debbie is not the same as the retarded kids I remember from school; I want to point out the many and essential differences. But to a large extent the world throws them all together, pea-stirrers and Debbie alike. What humbles me now, in the moment of writing this, is believing that Debbie is kinder than me: She wouldn't be ashamed to be thrown in with the pea-stirrers.

Debbie walked us to the elevator and then headed down the hall, 48 banging on the door at the far end. As we began to descend, I could hear her shout: "It's all right, Alan! You can come out now!"

Beginning in the late nineteenth century and continuing for about sixty years, it was generally held that entire family lines were tainted by retardation and that it would be best—for society, for these families themselves—if family members were prevented from procreating. In 1927 Supreme Court Justice Oliver Wendell Holmes wrote the majority opinion in the case *Buck* v. *Bell*, a ruling in which the Court let stand a Virginia court decision ordering an institutionalized mentally retarded young woman to be sterilized. "She is the daughter of a feebleminded mother in the same institution, and the mother of an illegitimate feeble-minded child," Holmes wrote. "We have seen more than once that the public welfare may call upon the best citizens for their lives. It would be strange if it could not call upon those who already sap the strength of the State for these lesser sacrifices. . . . Three generations of imbeciles are enough." Twenty years before, Indiana had passed a law permitting authorities to order compulsory sterilization (vasectomy, tubal ligation) for, among others, "idiots" and "imbeciles." Nor has such thinking disappeared altogether. In 1985 Canada allowed the hysterectomy of a mentally retarded ten-year-old girl, at her parents' request; the couple felt their daughter simply could not cope with the demands of men-struation. And in England as many as ninety sterilizations a year are performed on retarded teenagers.

No one knows how many retarded parents there are, but there are quite a few, and experts believe that the number is growing. To meet with retarded parents, I traveled to Los Angeles to learn about the SHARE/UCLA Parenting Program, one of the original intensive-education programs aimed specifically at retarded parents. The Parent-ing Program was designed by Dr. Alexander Tymchuk, a psychologist who teaches in the clinical psychiatry departmant at UCLA and who remains appalled at the lack of knowledge nationwide about retarded parents. Last year he wrote to dozens of private and governmental agencies in each state, trying to get a sense of how much the population of retarded parents has grown; the result, he said, was remarkable. Alaska reported one retarded parent; and Louisiana, Mississippi, and Alabama reported none at all.

The Parenting Program has several combination support-education groups in various neighborhoods of Los Angeles; I went to a Thursday morning class on a chilly October day at a community center in the mid-Wilshire area. I was early, but Wilma and Rashida were already at the center when I arrived. Wilma is a large black woman with a short, flattened head; her face is slightly squashed, like a bulldog's, and her voice is slow and lazy and soft. She stayed very near her daughter, a small girl wearing a very short cotton smock, with her kinky hair twisted into plastic barrettes. Rashida is Wilma's second child; neither Rashida nor her older sister is retarded. Wilma followed Rashida on an aimless toddler's path around the small, cement-floored room, with its small tables and chairs, its blackboard, its many posters of puppies and kittens.

Before long Delores, a Hispanic woman in her forties, arrived with 52 her son Jesse. Delores also has an older, normal child. But Jesse is at least moderately retarded; he is a short, curly-haired boy, almost completely silent, with the characteristic features of Down syndrome: epicanthal folds, a protruding tongue, short fingers. He is four years old and still in diapers.

Two other mothers arrived, both quiet, well-dressed black women. (The Parenting Program is mostly a project for retarded mothers.) Cynthia has two daughters, six and eight, both diagnosed as mildly retarded, and Sue has an eight-month-old infant who is normal. Last to arrive was Linda Andron, a social worker who administers the Parenting Program. A fast-talking, gregarious woman of middle age, she carried with her a giant plastic tub filled with puppets, dolls, toys, and art supplies. As Andron spread out paper and glue and precut teddy-bear silhouettes, she spoke to each child in turn, patting one on the head, chucking another's chin.

There is a weariness in Andron's voice. The mothers she works with are dogged by predictions of failure, by their own lack of education and training. (Education for the mentally retarded wasn't required by federal law until the early 1970s.) It is especially difficult for Andron when one of the mothers in the program becomes pregnant: A maze of regulations restricts the advice she can give in such a situation, particularly the suggestion of an abortion. How, I wonder, would such a thing be put to a retarded woman, obvious as its advantages might at first appear? How does one advise her to consider an abortion—by pointing out how ill-prepared she is, how, well, *retarded* she is? Does one mention the possibility that the infant could be just like her?

I asked Andron if it was possible these mothers might be better parents because of their retardation.

"In some ways Delores is probably a better mother for Jesse than 56 someone who has high expectations," she said. "He's just Jesse, that's her kid. She makes the other one do the homework, and she has people all through the building who help her. But Jesse's not any less worthwhile to her."

Part of the Thursday morning ritual is a walk to the grocery store. While Andron returned to the children, helping them with an art project, Wilma, Sue, Delores, Cynthia, and I walked to the nearby 7-Eleven, where we bought cheese puffs, doughnuts, soft drinks, nachos with squirts of processed cheese and chili, and little bags of Fritos for the children. It was a desultory, languid hour, our conversation the same simple chat of any group of women with little in common but their children. On the walk back to the center I asked Delores about Jesse; she described the day and night of his birth at length, but she never mentioned the fact that he is retarded. A while later, when I sat on a bench outside with Linda Andron, Delores walked by on the way to catch a taxi. Jesse gave Linda a hug, a vague smile, his eyes not quite meeting hers. Then he said his first words of the morning, "Bye-bye," and marched off to school.

That afternoon I drove to another neighborhood of Los Angeles, the industrial area called Culver City, to tour what is known as a sheltered workshop. Run by PAR (Production and Rehabilitation) Services, a division of the Exceptional Children's Foundation, the biggest agency for the retarded in Los Angeles, this particular workshop—PAR Westside—produces folding accordian tiles on a contract with the General Services Administration. It's a good contract, and the one hundred employees start at minimum wage and can make up to six dollars per hour; the operation, though, is still running at a loss after three years of production.

In the front office of PAR Westside there is a series of neat cubicles for the secretarial staff, employee counselors, and supervisors. This is only a small part of a rambling building leading far back from the street, most of which is actual warehouse: cement floors, high open ceilings, fluorescent lights. Moving toward the rear, I saw several long counters, and along each counter were a dozen people on stools. Each person was sorting pencils into groups according to the shape and color of the erasers. At the front counter were the people who could count to two and sorted pairs; at the rear counter people could count to six, and they sorted by the half-dozen. I passed between counters, and in passing I crossed through uplifted faces and outstretched hands and greetings and queries of every kind. "Hello." "Halloo." "Name?" "Good day."

I chatted with a supervisor, a stout, radiant blond woman who 60 became teary all at once when she mentioned a worker who had been promoted to the back room, out of her area. She missed him, she said, though he was only fifty yards away. A short bald man, leaning on a four-footed walker near the candy machines, planted himself in front of me and closed his eyes and held out one pale hand until I took it for a moment.

The file folders are made in the last room, a huge space thick with the smell of hot glue and the huffing of hydraulics. Each step in the making of an accordian folder is done separately: The pieces of cardboard are scored in one place, folded in another, then labeled, glued, sorted, and so on. The center of the room is given over to four conveyor belts run at different speeds. Cardboard dividers labeled with different letters of the alphabet slide on the belts past the workers, who must find the correct letter and slip each divider into the correct slot of the folder. These employees are given a commission by the piece on top of their basic wage; they are trained on the slow belt and eventually graduate to faster speeds. The inspectors and supervisors are not retarded, but I was surprised to learn that a few of the line employees aren't either; because of another handicap or, in some cases, the inability to speak English, this is the best job they can find.

The trend in work for the retarded is toward something called supported employment, which takes place not in workshops but in the general sector. A job coach—paid by an agency like the Exceptional Children's Foundation, not the employer—first learns the necessary skill, then teaches it to the retarded employee on the job, staying beside the recruit as long as necessary. Employers who have tried it like supported employment, because the costs are low and the responsibility for training lies with the agency. The retarded are considered good workers, capable of productivity approaching 100 percent of their nonretarded counterparts, with lower absentee rates. The foundation is moving into supported employment slowly, unwilling, at present, to close the sheltered workshops run by PAR Services, which employ hundreds of people who are unlikely to be successful in other jobs. And all of these considerations pale next to the desire of the retarded to have work—to act in the world and be rewarded for the effort.

The Recreation Center for the Handicapped is a maze of buildings connected by corridors on a hill above the San Francisco Zoo. Ron Jones, forty-eight, with pale hair and a florid face, has been a specialist at the Rec Center for twelve years, teaching physical recreation and coaching a basketball team sanctioned by the Special Olympics. Jones says the Special Olympics officials aren't very fond of his team, because they aren't strong competitors in any conventional sense. With what he calls a "political attitude," he decided long ago that on *his* basketball team anyone could play and everyone could win. Every game, he fields between fifty and sixty players, divided into different squads by the color of their jerseys. There are almost as many women as men playing, and everyone is retarded; a few use crutches or wheelchairs, and a few are blind or deaf.

The Wildcats play a full and lusty season against a stunning array of 64 opponents, including the San Francisco Police Department, the Salvation Army, a team made up of prisoners, and, once, the Chinese Consulate team. Ron Jones and the Wildcats are a cult legend of sorts in San Francisco, and I'd been wanting to play a game with them ever since I read *B-Ball*, Jones's memoir about the team. This was my chance, and I had recruited about a dozen people to be the Wildcats' first opponents of the season.

I arrived early for a pregame dinner in the cafeteria of the Rec Center and followed a step or two behind Jones as he entered the crowded room. A half-dozen people leapt from their seats to grasp his shoulder or slap him high-fives; almost everyone was wearing a head-band labeled Wildcats.

At my table sat a man named Michael Rice, one of the main characters I knew from *B-Ball*. Michael is in his forties, a bear of a man with a lumpy, crooked face, shaggy hair, and a huge, deep laugh. He is one of the veteran players, a bit of a star. He seems to keep his mouth perpetually half-open, set to holler his agreement—or his derisive disagreement—with whatever you're about to say. Rice can't tell time. Clocks, watches, the analog concept—these mean nothing to him. But Michael Rice is never late; he runs his life and his days by the passage of buses along certain routes, by radio shows, by the regular schedules of people who do use watches. When Michael's aging parents die, Ron Jones and his wife will become his guardians.

After dinner I lay on the wooden stage at one end of the room and watched the crowd. They cleared their dishes, scraped their plates, carried milk cartons and bowls of leftover mashed potatoes back to the kitchen. There were no straight lines, no efficiency; people were grinning and stumbling into each other for hugs, to slap backs, and, again and again, to slap hands in the high-five. The room was full of people acting like they'd just won a grand prize, and I thought about how little etiquette there is among the retarded. One only needs not to be mean. Watching them, I was watching myself released.

The game was preceded by a rally and warm-up. One corner of the   68
gym had been given over to a disc jockey, spinning and scratching at rap records while a full complement of cheerleaders—male and female staff in rally skirts, with pom-poms—practiced their routines. Squad after squad of players, in purple or red jerseys, took their places under the baskets, tripping through the time-honored routines of shoot and run, catch and pass.

I stood in the doorway, mentally reviewing the little I knew about basketball. Ron Jones, a few yards away, was suddenly accosted by a pudgy-faced Chinese man wearing a red jersey. "Wha' team?" the man asked with urgency, pointing at the practice.

"*Our* team! We're the Wildcats."

"Wildcats?" the man asked again.

"Wildcats." Jones was definitive this time.   72

"Wildcats?"

"*Wildcats.*"

"Wildcats! Aww *right!*" And he threw up his hand for a high-five.

A short while later a man named Vincent joined me. We'd met at   76
dinner. Vincent has a long, narrow face under a shock of brown hair. He shook my hand enthusiastically and for a long time.

"Can I be on your team?" he asked, and I couldn't imagine why not. So Vincent defected from the Wildcats, with predictions of astonishing prowess, and in a moment of abandon he was joined by his friend Michelle. Michelle is a woman in her late twenties, short and heavy-chested, with a mouthful of crazy white teeth.

The half-dozen cheerleaders formed a tunnel of arms and pom-poms beneath one basket, and with a roar the Wildcats ran (stumbled, limped, rolled) through the tunnel and past their opponents, slapping hands. Midway through the line came a small pale man with almond eyes and a few brief strings of hair combed sideways. My hands were open for another high-five slap, but instead he grabbed my hand, turned it over, and delicately pressed his dry lips to it in a kiss.

The buzzer sounded and the game began. I was careful of the half-court line, careful to avoid the dreaded double dribble. A few minutes into the game, Jones, acting as referee and final authority, called time-out and required us to substitute players. Our starting five took seats, and we dispatched our other squad. A few moments later Jones called time again, and everyone stood there, waiting for an explanation. A young man with bent legs, in a purple jersey, wobbled slowly onto the court, dropped his crutches, and shot twice. Only when the ball fell short the second time did Jones whistle again and allow the players to move.

One of the fans on our side of the gym brushed the lint off his suit 80 and joined the cheerleaders; another onlooker quietly opened a little suitcase and took out a trumpet. Jones was in and out of everything, dashing to and fro, whistling madly and switching players apparently at random. He's been known to bring a ringing phone onto the court, and a ladder; he's played with dogs, handcuffs, and bicycles. Last year Art Agnos, the mayor of San Francisco, played on a team fielded by state assembly speaker Willie Brown, and Jones gave Agnos a technical foul for the color of his shorts.

When a man in a wheelchair, pushed up and down the court by a staff member, finally reached the basket with a ball in his hands, I stopped and stared at that high, high basket; but then a woman from the sidelines ran out and made a circle of her arms near his lap. He shot, and he hit. It wasn't competition anymore but play. It felt reck-less, almost naughty; I was hiccuping with laughter. Then I was fouled with a bear hug from Michael Rice, and I had to turn around and shoot backward, over my head, with the whole room upside down and chanting.

Later, from nowhere, Michelle, sidling away from the other play-ers, threw the ball with a wild two-handed shove. It fell through the net with a swish. Her jaw dropped and she clapped her hands to her cheeks, mouth wide with stupefied amazement, and the crowd of players surrounded her a moment to slap her back; then all the players on both teams ran in a stumbling ballet to the other end.

All players, that is, but Michelle; she stood transfixed by her own astonishing feat.

Just before the basketball game I was sitting with Jones in his little office, hearing the distant splash of swimmers in the therapy pool. A young man about to play his first game with the Wildcats stood just outside the door, looking in mournfully, waiting for the coach to tell him when to change his clothes. We had been talking about the qualities of retardation, and what it was, and what it meant to the rest of us: to the nonretarded.

"I think they offer something different from what I offer to the world," he said after a moment. "What do they give back to us? If they give back a sense of trust, and joy, and courage—well, these are things I'd think the world would be hungry for. Do you want miracles in your life? Are you going to get them anywhere else?"   *1990*

9

Affirmations of Love

George Weinberg, The Madness and Myths
of Homophobia

David Leavitt, Territory

Dorothy Allison, Don't Tell Me You
Don't Know

Proposition 4
Society does not hate us because
we hate ourselves; we hate
ourselves because we grew up
and live in a society that hates us.

Michael Denneny, from *Gay Politics*

Medieval inquisitors used the label *witch* to reinforce the normative
boundaries of their community, to unite that community against the
perceived source of its problems, and to eliminate completely women
who seemed to threaten the social order. Currently, the word *lesbian* is
used not only to describe women who love other women but also to
censure women who overstep the bounds of the traditional female role
and to teach all women that such behavior will not be tolerated. Feminists, women athletes, professional women, and others risk being labeled lesbian for their actions and beliefs. Awareness of the potential
social consequences of that label exerts significant pressure on all
women to remain in their traditional roles.

Rose Weitz, from *What Price Independence?*
Social Reactions to Lesbians, Spinsters, Widows, and Nuns

Publications on homosexuality usually do not distinguish clearly enough between the questions of the choice of object, on the one hand, and of the sexual characteristics and sexual attitude of the subject, on the other, as though the answer to the former necessarily involved the answers to the latter. Experience, however, proves the contrary: a man with predominantly male characteristics and also masculine in his love-life may still be inverted in respect to his object, loving only men instead of women. A man in whose character feminine attributes evidently predominate, who may, indeed, behave in love like a woman, might be expected, from this feminine attitude, to choose a man for his love-object; but he may nevertheless be heterosexual, and show no more inversion in respect of his object than an average normal man. The same is true of women; here also mental sexual character and object-choice do not necessarily coincide. The mystery of homosexuality is therefore by no means so simple as it is commonly depicted in popular expositions, *e.g.*, a feminine personality, which therefore has to love a man, is unhappily attached to a male body; or a masculine personality, irresistibly attracted by women, is unfortunately cemented to a female body.

Sigmund Freud, from *The Psychogenesis of a Case of Homosexuality in a Woman*

George Weinberg

The Madness and Myths of Homophobia

Most gay people in the United States imagine that they would receive better treatment in England than in their own country. After all, forty-five of the fifty states[1] still have laws according to which adult men and women who engage in consenting sexual acts in private may be imprisoned, in some states for as long as ten years, even for a first offense. By contrast, it is known that the 1967 Sexual Offenses Act permits adults to engage in homosexual acts in private in England. And people assume that this implies greater freedom of spirit toward homosexuals and more permissiveness generally. The assumption is dead wrong. In

[1]In 1990, that number is twenty-six.—EDS.

the States, gay people get the chance to present their case for decent treatment on television, even national television, and on radio regularly.

In Chicago, while I was on television promoting a book, a woman called in and asked me whether I thought it would be all right for her to be a lesbian. It was a long-distance call. Can you imagine asking a person who doesn't know you and is a thousand miles away for permission to use your own body as you please? I answered that it was unwarranted and silly for anyone to ask someone else such a question, and said that matters of taste could never be decided by other people. The next call came from a man who accused me of promoting homosexuality, and threatened me. The only other time I was threatened was when a man called up a radio show. He seemed to be crying with rage. He stammered out the story that someone had tried to suck him off in a movie theater when he was fourteen. I asked him what happened, and he said he refused. But then he added that the next year he was "forced into it," also in a theater. I responded that if he did it, he must have thought at the time he would enjoy it. And at that he said he would come down to the station and kill me. A couple of tough women from the Chicago Gay Alliance provided me an escort back to my hotel.

FANCY, NEGATIVE PSYCHOLOGY

As for the psychology profession, it is interesting to compare the branches in the two countries. Psychologists on both sides of the Atlantic spend too many waking hours (1) wondering how people get to be homosexual; (2) trying to figure out how to detect homosexuals; (3) warning homosexuals of the dire dangers that supposedly will dog them till their dying days unless they give up homosexuality and either become heterosexuals or give up sex entirely; (4) inventing techniques for converting homosexuals, none of which work, but many of which brutalize the poor victims. As a result, sometimes the persecuted homosexual (nearly always a man) *says* he sees the folly of his ways and is no longer homosexual. The torture therapist then reports his "cure" in some psychological or medical journal, and gains status in the field.

I want to look at the four issues briefly. First, the eternal wonderment on the part of psychologists and medical people as to how people become homosexual.   4

1. SPECULATIONS ABOUT ORIGIN

The most salient thing to consider with regard to this question is that the very asking of it presupposes in nearly every case that it is bad to be homosexual. The question of how people get to be heterosexual is not similarly asked, though there is nothing more known about the origins of heterosexuality than of homosexuality. The real question, if anyone were truly interested, would be "How do sexual preferences develop?"

Also, behind the relentless curiosity of many experts to account for homosexuality is the desire to stamp out the causes, to be sure that future generations do not produce homosexuals as the past ones have. Thus the homosexual man or woman who becomes preoccupied with wondering how he or she got that way is playing right into the hands of those who condemn homosexuality. Asking how I got this way is a fancy, intellectual way of bemoaning the fact that one is homosexual.

Think about it. Suppose I asked you persistently "how did you get a nose like that?" You would know that I thought you had a strange looking nose, an undesirable nose. The very fact that you have to explain your nose puts you on the defensive. Knowledge is never bad to have, but it should not be a special burden of gay people, not incumbent on heteros, to explain the origin of their tastes.

Also behind the question is the misconception that heterosexuality 8 is natural and that homosexuality is a departure from nature. Homosexuality abounds in the animal kingdom, and there is nothing unnatural about it there or with humans. Nor is it a deviancy. The question of how did one get that way is like the question "What pebble diverted the stream?" No stream has been diverted. There is no departure from a natural course and no need for explanation.

The most popular theory about how people become homosexual is taken from psychoanalysis. It pertains to homosexual men. (Men bear the brunt of most attacks because their desire not to seek the usual "masculine" satisfactions is feared as undermining to society. In contrast, a woman who is thought of as trying to be like a man is misread as merely seeking a man's social advantages. Her imagined desire to be independent and strong is not considered as threatening as a man's readiness to give up his power. There is little more threatening than the repudiation of power. For this to become contagious would undermine our whole competitive social structure, and make it impossible to motivate multitudes.) In any event, the psychoanalytic theory is that a "weak father" and a "strong mother" cause homosexuality.

A vicious article in the British magazine *Climax: The Journal of Sexual Perfection* sums up every documented assault on homosexuals ever made, and pretends to be factual. Such a magazine, if it appeared in the States, would be greeted by a mob scene of gays parading in front of its offices. The name of the article is "Homosexuals—They Mock Sex." As to origins, the article says: "The homosexual grows up with his fear of castration, should he sleep with a woman. A man is safe because he can say to his father, 'Look I am no threat to you, I don't want mama . . .'"

The article goes on to say that he admires his mother and loathes his father for not being more of a man. This idea has been used to instill guilt in mothers who tried to be forceful people, to break down the stereotype for women. In effect, the "weak mother" theory says to women, "be subservient or you will produce homosexual sons."

Thus it is aimed at killing two birds with one stone: at keeping 12 women in their place and calling homosexuals a form of monster, of whom their own parents should be ashamed. Time and again we see the coupling of sexism and anti-gay attitudes. A woman who courageously fought for feminist rights in the last century, Sarah Grimké, once said, "Whatever it is morally right for a man to do, it is morally right for a woman to do." Perhaps she did not have in mind making love to women. But this too, in whatever measure it is right for a man to do, it is right for a woman to do. The desperate study of how homosexuals "got that way" will doubtless go on until gay groups have forced the acceptance of homosexuality on Western culture. Already in the United States, there is a diminution in the concern with origins, and perhaps this is beginning to be true in England too.

2. THE DETECTION OF HOMOSEXUALS

Again, one naturally asks, "why should anyone care?" The exception is the case of a gay man or woman who wants to know about the potentiality for a love affair and isn't sure of the other person.

Techniques designed by experts have been various. Some employ a sequence of pictures of nudes of both sexes, and a device to measure the amount of time spent by men gazing at the two kinds of pictures. Others actually put his penis into an apparatus and study whether it swells at the sight of men or women. Others study the urine of people to detect supposed differences in the androsterone/etiocholanolone balance, on the theory that detection can be made this way. For the last fifty years, different studies have reported biochemical discrepancies of one kind or another. But none has been supported by follow-up studies, and there is absolutely no general conviction among medical people that any such studies work.

The usual reasons for the half-cocked and mistaken conclusions of success drawn by the medical doctors here and in the United States are statistical errors. Take any group of people and study them on numerous possible attributes. For instance, if they are measured on half a dozen different characteristics that might conceivably distinguish, it is likely that in a small group, one of them will separate the two groups, though imperfectly, by sheer chance. The true test is what statisticians call cross-validation. Does the method truly distinguish among large groups of people? If hundreds of researchers look for some difference between groups, some are bound to find what they are looking for in their particular groups. These are the experts who write up their find-ings, and the others do not. So instead of publishing that fifty different hospital teams looked for some distinguishing trait, and forty-eight failed to find such a trait, the medical journals write merely that the trait was found twice.

My own field at one time was statistics, and I wrote a text book on 16 statistics that has been used by over a million students in the United States, and is still going strong. And I can tell you that the most slip-shod research done statistically appears in medical journals in connec-tion with sex research of all kinds.

A study in the *British Medical Journal* that appeared in July 1973, reports a finding to the effect that discrimination can be made between homosexuals and heterosexuals using the androsterone/etiocholano-lone ratios. The experimenters made numerous statistical errors, using devices that loaded the dice in their favor. They had a small sample, looked for various differentiators, and found one that seemed to dis-tinguish *on their particular group*. Instead of using statistical devices that took into account their employment of many possible distinguishing characteristics, they used tests that assumed they had looked for only one distinction. The details of their ignorance get technical; and their statistics were fancy. But they have far from proved anything. Curiously, they also concluded that homosexuals had more homosexual relatives in their "immediate and extended families" than heterosexuals did. As everyone knows, gay people are far more apt to know who is gay and who isn't, in their families and elsewhere. A heterosexual would very likely report that a brother or sister, mother or father is also heterosex-ual than a gay person would, even if the whole family was loaded with homosexuals. To most heterosexuals, it would be abhorrent to think of someone close in the family as gay. Moreover, confessions, or profes-sions, of homosexuality are often exchanged, and thus this conclusion should be taken with a grain of salt. The trouble is that such studies often go into the popular press and gain attention. Later when other researchers fail to get the same findings, nothing is said. One never sees a retraction in the popular press, or a statement that some psychological or medical theory about homosexuals is now believed wrong. Theories replace one another, each believed for a time. Only the status of the professionals as experts is a constant.

3. WARNINGS ON THE DIRE DANGERS THAT ACCOMPANY A HOMOSEXUAL LIFESTYLE

The third preoccupation of the so-called expert is with warning people that if they become homosexual, they will suffer till their dying days. In place of the burning lakes, which preachers have used for millennia, the experts warn gays that they will suffer an incomplete sex life, a loss of satisfaction, and a terrible response from society.

Here the experts try to make their own prophecies come true. They do their best to persuade parents that if their sons or daughters are homosexual, they are sick, diseased, miserable. They then make the case that homosexuals find themselves without an ally in society. In the article "Homosexuals—They Mock Sex," already mentioned, the author maintains that homosexuals engage in "excessive watchfulness, excessive worry that the other gets fed properly, clothed properly, sent on his daily tasks properly." Instead of viewing this as evidence of genuine caring, of love in many cases, it is seen as a dire consequence, something that homosexuals ought to worry about.

In England it is well recognised that gay people have many friends 20 in the heterosexual world, many people who feel genuine outrage at the abuses of civil liberties against homosexuals. Gay people have allies among heteros in the States too. But the gay groups are much slower to acknowledge this fact. Their attitude generally is very unfortunate. On television shows, and on radio, gay people talk too often as if they have no friends except for other gays. One result is that whenever a heterosexual speaks up for gay rights, he is called homosexual, not just by the general public, but by the gays themselves. This is a bias, and in many cases is probably a deterrent to getting allies.

The real danger that homosexuals have to fear is what will result if gay men or women make a serious effort to change, as in psychotherapy or by any of the other "recommended" techniques. Here I would like to quote from my own book, *Society and the Healthy Homosexual*: "The harm done to a homosexual man or woman by the persons trying to convert is multifold. Homosexuals should be warned. First of all, the venture is almost certain to fail, and you will lose time and money. But this is the least of it. In trying to convert, you will deepen your belief that you are one of nature's misfortunes. You will intensify your clinging to conventionality, enlarge your fear and guilt and regret. You will be voting in your own mind for the premise that people should all act and feel the same ways. You will stultify your fantasy . . . and undermine your sense of the right to give and receive love . . . in the manner you wish to."

4. ATTEMPTS AT CONVERSION

As for techniques designed with the aim of converting homosexuals, all of them are failures, and do harm in the process of tampering with the patient. A great range of them have been attempted. Several teams of doctors tried the method of getting gay patients to look at pictures and masturbate at the same time. Just before reaching orgasm the patient was to give notice, and the experts switched on a light behind a picture of a person of the opposite sex. The attempt to condition people in this way failed utterly. Other experts have tried using various kinds of poison, called emetics, which were supposed to get the patient to loathe the sight of his lover whose picture he was looking at. The subjects were all males in these studies.

A doctor named Fritz Roeder tried brain surgery, and psychologists have tried using electric shock as a punishment technique. The long-term methods of psychotherapy have included strictly psychoanalytic methods and also therapy which was little more than persuasion. The therapist would compliment his male patient every time he said something hostile about his gay friends, and would lecture him on the evils of going back to homosexual bars. Drugs, truth serums, all sorts of the newest devices have been tried, to no avail.

By the way, as a therapist, I am sometimes called up by the parent of 24 a gay who wants the young person to be given more of some desired hormone. If it is a gay man, the parent asks me if giving him more male hormone will help. If a woman, female hormone is asked about by the parent. Were the study cited earlier from the *British Medical Journal* correct, then this method might be of advantage. But as it is, giving a male hormone to a man will simply heighten his sexual urge for whomever he now feels urges for. It will make him *more* homosexual, not less.

THE REAL PROBLEM

The real problems are none of those which the so-called experts invent, or spend their time at trying to solve. The real problem is an illness, which we call "homophobia." The word *homophobia* has become very popular in the United States. It refers to the morbid and irrational fear of homosexuals, and the hatred of them.

If a heterosexual person can't get to sleep downstairs because he keeps thinking of the two gay people upstairs making love, and if he wants them evicted for the sake of his own calm, he is a "homophobe." He is the one who needs the help, not they. "Homophobia" is a term everyone should know. The failure of most people in the profession to take it seriously, to see where the danger truly lies, bespeaks their own homophobia.

The chief origins of "homophobia" are: (*a*) the teachings of religion, and the Bible in particular; (*b*) the secret fear in many heterosexuals that they themselves are homosexual; (*c*) repressed envy (remember H. L. Mencken's line that puritanism is "the lurking fear that someone, somewhere is happy"[2]); (*d*) the threat to people's sense that all of

---

[2]Apparently, Weinberg accidentally misquoted Mencken here; Mencken actually wrote: "Puritanism: the haunting fear that someone, somewhere, may be happy."—EDs.

humankind must struggle toward conventionality; and (*e*) the recognition that there are people brave enough to live their lives on earth without feeling the necessity of having children. Of course, many gay people do have children. But the homophobe does not think of this. Many people are constantly afraid to die, and are unable to take their lives as present experiences. They have children so that they can enjoy a sense of "vicarious immortality" after they die. They would like all others to do the same. The idea that gay people are living now, and not later, troubles them.

In sum, "homophobia" is a form of acute conventionality. We 28 should do our best to help humankind over this illness, since heterosexuals who are free of it tend to have much better lives than heterosexuals who are not.   *1973*

David Leavitt

Territory

Neil's mother, Mrs. Campbell, sits on her lawn chair behind a card table outside the food co-op. Every few minutes, as the sun shifts, she moves the chair and table several inches back so as to remain in the shade. It is a hundred degrees outside, and bright white. Each time someone goes in or out of the co-op a gust of air-conditioning flies out of the automatic doors, raising dust from the cement.

Neil stands just inside, poised over a water fountain, and watches her. She has on a sun hat, and a sweatshirt over her tennis dress; her legs are bare, and shiny with cocoa butter. In front of her, propped against the table, a sign proclaims: MOTHERS, FIGHT FOR YOUR CHILDREN'S RIGHTS— SUPPORT A NONNUCLEAR FUTURE. Woman dressed exactly like her pass by, notice the sign, listen to her brief spiel, finger pamphlets, sign petitions or don't sign petitions, never give money. Her weary eyes are masked by dark glasses. In the age of Reagan, she has declared, keeping up the causes of peace and justice is a futile, tiresome, and unrewarding effort; it is therefore an effort fit only for mothers to keep up. The sun bounces off the window glass through which Neil watches her. His own reflection lines up with her profile.

Later that afternoon, Neil spreads himself out alongside the pool and imagines he is being watched by the shirtless Chicano gardener. But the gardener, concentrating on his pruning, is neither seductive nor seducible. On the lawn, his mother's large Airedales—Abigail, Lucille, Fern—amble, sniff, urinate. Occasionally, they accost the gardener, who yells at them in Spanish.

After two years' absence, Neil reasons, he should feel nostalgia, 4 regret, gladness upon returning home. He closes his eyes and tries to muster the proper background music for the cinematic scene of return. His rhapsody, however, is interrupted by the noises of his mother's trio—the scratchy cello, whining violin, stumbling piano—as she and Lillian Havalard and Charlotte Feder plunge through Mozart. The tune is cheery, in a Germanic sort of way, and utterly inappropriate to what Neil is trying to feel. Yet it *is* the music of his adolescence; they have played it for years, bent over the notes, their heads bobbing in silent time to the metronome.

It is getting darker. Every few minutes, he must move his towel so as to remain within the narrowing patch of sunlight. In four hours, Wayne, his lover of ten months and the only person he has ever imagined he could spend his life with, will be in this house, where no lover of his has ever set foot. The thought fills him with a sense of grand terror and curiosity. He stretches, tries to feel seductive, desirable. The gardener's shears whack at the ferns; the music above him rushes to a loud premature conclusion. The women laugh and applaud themselves as they give up for the day. He hears Charlotte Feder's full nasal twang, the voice of a fat woman in a pink pants suit—odd, since she is a scrawny, arthritic old bird, rarely clad in anything other than tennis shorts and a blouse. Lillian is the fat woman in the pink pants suit; her voice is thin and warped by too much crying. Drink in hand, she calls out from the porch, "Hot enough!" and waves. He lifts himself up and nods to her.

The women sit on the porch and chatter; their voices blend with the clink of ice in glasses. They belong to a small circle of ladies all of whom, with the exception of Neil's mother, are widows and divorcées. Lillian's husband left her twenty-two years ago, and sends her a check every month to live on; Charlotte has been divorced twice as long as she was married, and has a daughter serving a long sentence for terrorist acts committed when she was nineteen. Only Neil's mother has a husband, a distant sort of husband, away often on business. He is away on business now. All of them feel betrayed—by husbands, by children, by history.

Neil closes his eyes, tries to hear the words only as sounds. Soon, a new noise accosts him: his mother arguing with the gardener in Spanish. He leans on his elbows and watches them; the syllables are loud, heated, and compressed, and seem on the verge of explosion. But the argument ends happily; they shake hands. The gardener collects his check and walks out the gate without so much as looking at Neil.

He does not know the gardener's name; as his mother has reminded 8
him, he does not know most of what has gone on since he moved away.
Her life has gone on, unaffected by his absence. He flinches at his own
egoism, the egoism of sons.

"Neil! Did you call the airport to make sure the plane's coming in
on time?"

"Yes," he shouts to her. "It is."

"Good. Well, I'll have dinner ready when you get back."

"Mom—"   12

"What?" The word comes out in a weary wail that is more of an
answer than a question.

"What's wrong?" he says, forgetting his original question.

"Nothing's wrong," she declares in a tone that indicates that everything is wrong. "The dogs have to be fed, dinner has to be made, and
I've got people here. Nothing's wrong."

"I hope things will be as comfortable as possible when Wayne gets 16
here."

"Is that a request or a threat?"

"Mom—"

Behind her sunglasses, her eyes are inscrutable. "I'm tired," she
says. "It's been a long day. I . . . I'm anxious to meet Wayne. I'm sure
he'll be wonderful, and we'll all have a wonderful, wonderful time. I'm
sorry. I'm just tired."

She heads up the stairs. He suddenly feels an urge to cover himself; 20
his body embarrasses him, as it has in her presence since the day she saw
him shirtless and said with delight, "Neil! You're growing hair under
your arms!"

Before he can get up, the dogs gather round him and begin to sniff
and lick at him. He wriggles to get away from them, but Abigail, the
largest and stupidest, straddles his stomach and nuzzles his mouth. He
splutters and, laughing, throws her off. "Get away from me, you goddamn dogs," he shouts, and swats at them. They are new dogs, not the
dog of his childhood, not dogs he trusts.

He stands, and the dogs circle him, looking up at his face expect-
antly. He feels renewed terror at the thought that Wayne will be here so
soon: Will they sleep in the same room? Will they make love? He has
never had sex in his parents' house. How can he be expected to be a
lover here, in this place of his childhood, of his earliest shame, in this
household of mothers and dogs?

"Dinnertime! Abbylucyferny, Abbylucyferny, dinnertime!" His
mother's litany disperses the dogs, and they run for the door.

"Do you realize," he shouts to her, "that no matter how much those 24
dogs love you they'd probably kill you for the leg of lamb in the
freezer?"

Neil was twelve the first time he recognized in himself something like sexuality. He was lying outside, on the grass, when Rasputin—the dog, long dead, of his childhood—began licking his face. He felt a tingle he did not recognize, pulled off his shirt to give the dog access to more of him. Rasputin's tongue tickled coolly. A wet nose started to sniff down his body, toward his bathing suit. What he felt frightened him, but he couldn't bring himself to push the dog away. Then his mother called out, "Dinner," and Rasputin was gone, more interested in food than in him.

It was the day after Rasputin was put to sleep, years later, that Neil finally stood in the kitchen, his back turned to his parents, and said, with unexpected ease, "I'm a homosexual." The words seemed insufficient, reductive. For years, he had believed his sexuality to be detachable from the essential him, but now he realized that it was part of him. He had the sudden, despairing sensation that though the words had been easy to say, the fact of their having been aired was incurably damning. Only then, for the first time, did he admit that they were true, and he shook and wept in regret for what he would not be for his mother, for having failed her. His father hung back, silent; he was absent for that moment as he was mostly absent—a strong absence. Neil always thought of him sitting on the edge of the bed in his underwear, captivated by something on television. He said, "It's OK, Neil." But his mother was resolute; her lower lip didn't quaver. She had enormous reserves of strength to which she only gained access at moments like this one. She hugged him from behind, wrapped him in the childhood smells of perfume and brownies, and whispered, "It's OK, honey," For once, her words seemed as inadequate as his. Neil felt himself shrunk to an embarrassed adolescent, hating her sympathy, not wanting her to touch him. It was the way he would feel from then on whenever he was in her presence—even now, at twenty-three, bringing home his lover to meet her.

All through his childhood, she had packed only the most nutritious lunches, had served on the PTA, had volunteered at the children's library and at his school, had organized a successful campaign to ban a racist history textbook. The day after he told her, she located and got in touch with an organization called the Coalition of Parents of Lesbians and Gays. Within a year, she was president of it. On weekends, she and the other mothers drove their station wagons to San Francisco, set up their card tables in front of the Bulldog Baths, the Liberty Baths, passed out literature to men in leather and denim who were loath to admit they even had mothers. These men, who would habitually do violence to each other, were strangely cowed by the suburban ladies with their informational booklets, and bent their heads. Neil was a sophomore in college then, and lived in San Francisco. She brought him pamphlets

detailing the dangers of bathhouses and back rooms, enemas and poppers, wordless sex in alleyways. His excursion into that world had been
brief and lamentable, and was over. He winced at the thought that she
knew all his sexual secrets, and vowed to move to the East Coast to
escape her. It was not very different from the days when she had
campaigned for a better playground, or tutored the Hispanic children
in the audiovisual room. Those days, as well, he had run away from her
concern. Even today, perched in front of the co-op, collecting signatures
for nuclear disarmament, she was quintessentially a mother. And if the
lot of mothers was to expect nothing in return, was the lot of sons to
return nothing?

Driving across the Dumbarton Bridge on his way to the airport, Neil   28
thinks, I have returned nothing; I have simply returned. He wonders if
she would have given birth to him had she known what he would grow
up to be.

Then he berates himself: Why should he assume himself to be the
cause of her sorrow? She has told him that her life is full of secrets.
She has changed since he left home—grown thinner, more rigid,
harder to hug. She has given up baking, taken up tennis; her skin has
browned and tightened. She is no longer the woman who hugged him
and kissed him, who said, "As long as you're happy, that's all that's
important to us."

The flats spread out around him; the bridge floats on purple and
green silt, and spongy bay fill, not water at all. Only ten miles north, a
whole city has been built on gunk dredged up from the bay.

He arrives at the airport ten minutes early, to discover that the
plane has landed twenty minutes early. His first view of Wayne is from
behind, by the baggage belt. Wayne looks as he always looks—slightly
windblown—and is wearing the ratty leather jacket he was wearing the
night they met. Neil sneaks up on him and puts his hands on his
shoulders; when Wayne turns around, he looks relieved to see him.

They hug like brothers; only in the safety of Neil's mother's car do   32
they dare to kiss. They recognize each other's smells, and grow comfortable again. "I never imagined I'd actually see you out here," Neil says,
"but you're exactly the same here as there."

"It's only been a week."

They kiss again. Neil wants to go to a motel, but Wayne insists on
being pragmatic. "We'll be there soon. Don't worry."

"We could go to one of the bathhouses in the city and take a room
for a couple of aeons," Neil says. "Christ, I'm hard up. I don't even know
if we're going to be in the same bedroom."

"Well, if we're not," Wayne says, "we'll sneak around. It'll be ro-   36
mantic."

They cling to each other for a few more minutes, until they realize that people are looking in the car window. Reluctantly, they pull apart. Neil reminds himself that he loves this man, that there is a reason for him to bring this man home.

He takes the scenic route on the way back. The car careers over foothills, through forests, along white four-lane highways high in the mountains. Wayne tells Neil that he sat next to a woman on the plane who was once Marilyn Monroe's psychiatrist's nurse. He slips his foot out of his shoe and nudges Neil's ankle, pulling Neil's sock down with his toe.

"I have to drive," Neil says. "I'm very glad you're here."

There is a comfort in the privacy of the car. They have a common 40 fear of walking hand in hand, of publicly showing physical affection, even in the permissive West Seventies of New York—a fear that they have admitted only to one another. They slip through a pass between two hills, and are suddenly in residential Northern California, the land of expensive ranch-style houses.

As they pull into Neil's mother's driveway, the dogs run barking toward the car. When Wayne opens the door, they jump and lap at him, and he tries to close it again. "Don't worry. Abbylucyferny! Get in the house, damn it!"

His mother descends from the porch. She has changed into a blue-flower-print dress, which Neil doesn't recognize. He gets out of the car and halfheartedly chastises the dogs. Crickets chirp in the trees. His mother looks radiant, even beautiful, illuminated by the headlights, surrounded by the now quiet dogs, like a Circe with her slaves. When she walks over to Wayne, offering her hand, and says, "Wayne, I'm Barbara," Neil forgets that she is his mother.

"Good to meet you, Barbara," Wayne says, and reaches out his hand. Craftier than she, he whirls her around to kiss her cheek.

Barbara! He is calling his mother Barbara! Then he remembers that 44 Wayne is five years older than he is. They chat by the open car door, and Neil shrinks back—the embarrassed adolescent, uncomfortable, unwanted.

So the dreaded moment passes and he might as well not have been there. At dinner, Wayne keeps the conversation smooth, like a captivated courtier seeking Neil's mother's hand. A faggot son's sodomist—such words spit into Neil's head. She has prepared tiny meatballs with fresh coriander, fettucine with pesto. Wayne talks about the street people in New York; El Salvador is a tragedy; if only Sadat had lived; Phyllis Schlafly—what can you do?

"It's a losing battle," she tells him. "Every day I'm out there with my card table, me and the other mothers, but I tell you, Wayne, it's a losing battle. Sometimes I think us old ladies are the only ones with enough patience to fight."

Occasionally, Neil says something, but his comments seem stupid and clumsy. Wayne continues to call her Barbara. No one under forty has ever called her Barbara as long as Neil can remember. They drink wine; he does not.

Now is the time for drastic action. He contemplates taking Wayne's 48 hand, then checks himself. He has never done anything in her presence to indicate that the sexuality he confessed to five years ago was a reality and not an invention. Even now, he and Wayne might as well be friends, college roommates. Then Wayne, his savior, with a single, sweeping gesture, reaches for his hand, and clasps it, in the midst of a joke he is telling about Saudi Arabians. By the time he is laughing, their hands are joined. Neil's throat contracts; his heart begins to beat violently. He notices his mother's eyes flicker, glance downward; she never breaks the stride of her sentence. The dinner goes on, and every taboo nurtured since childhood falls quietly away.

She removes the dishes. Their hands grow sticky; he cannot tell which fingers are his and which Wayne's. She clears the rest of the table and rounds up the dogs.

"Well, boys, I'm very tired, and I've got a long day ahead of me tomorrow, so I think I'll hit the sack. There are extra towels for you in Neil's bathroom, Wayne. Sleep well."

"Good night, Barbara," Wayne calls out. "It's been wonderful meeting you."

They are alone. Now they can disentangle their hands. 52

"No problem about where we sleep, is there?"

"No," Neil says. "I just can't imagine sleeping with someone in this house."

His leg shakes violently. Wayne takes Neil's hand in a firm grasp and hauls him up.

Later that night, they lie outside, under redwood trees, listening to 56 the hysteria of the crickets, the hum of the pool cleaning itself. Redwood leaves prick their skin. They fell in love in bars and apartments, and this is the first time that they have made love outdoors. Neil is not sure he has enjoyed the experience. He kept sensing eyes, imagined that the neighborhood cats were staring at them from behind a fence of brambles. He remembers he once hid in this spot when he and some of the children from the neighborhood were playing sardines, remembers the intoxication of small bodies packed together, the warm breath of suppressed laughter on his neck. "The loser had to go through the spanking machine," he tells Wayne.

"Did you lose often?"

"Most of the time. The spanking machine never really hurt—just a whirl of hands. If you moved fast enough, no one could actually get you. Sometimes, though, late in the afternoon, we'd get naughty. We'd chase each other and pull each other's pants down. That was all. Boys and girls together!"

"Listen to the insects," Wayne says, and closes his eyes.

Neil turns to examine Wayne's face, notices a single, small pimple. 60 Their lovemaking usually begins in a wrestle, a struggle for dominance, and ends with a somewhat confusing loss of identity—as now, when Neil sees a foot on the grass, resting against his leg, and tries to determine if it is his own or Wayne's.

From inside the house, the dogs begin to bark. Their yelps grow into alarmed falsettos. Neil lifts himself up. "I wonder if they smell something," he says.

"Probably just us," says Wayne.

"My mother will wake up. She hates getting waked up."

Lights go on in the house; the door to the porch opens. 64

"What's wrong, Abby? What's wrong?" his mother's voice calls softly.

Wayne clamps his hand over Neil's mouth. "Don't say anything," he whispers.

"I can't just—" Neil begins to say, but Wayne's hand closes over his mouth again. He bites it, and Wayne starts laughing.

"What was that?" Her voice projects into the garden. "Hello?" she 68 says.

The dogs yelp louder. "Abbylucyferny, it's OK, it's OK." Her voice is soft and panicked. "Is anyone there?" she asks loudly.

The brambles shake. She takes a flashlight, shines it around the garden. Wayne and Neil duck down; the light lands on them and hovers for a few seconds. Then it clicks off and they are in the dark—a new dark, a darker dark, which their eyes must readjust to.

"Let's go to bed, Abbylucyferny," she says gently. Neil and Wayne hear her pad into the house. The dogs whimper as they follow her, and the lights go off.

Once before, Neil and his mother had stared at each other in the 72 glare of bright lights. Four years ago, they stood in the arena created by the headlights of her car, waiting for the train. He was on his way back to San Francisco, where he was marching in a Gay Pride Parade the next day. The train station was next door to the food co-op and shared its parking lot. The co-op, familiar and boring by day, took on a certain mystery in the night. Neil recognized the spot where he had skidded on his bicycle and broken his leg. Through the glass doors, the brightly lit interior of the store glowed, its rows and rows of cans and boxes forming their own horizon, each can illuminated so that even from outside Neil could read the labels. All that was missing was the ladies in tennis dresses and sweatshirts, pushing their carts past bins of nuts and dried fruits.

"Your train is late," his mother said. Her hair fell loosely on her shoulders, and her legs were tanned. Neil looked at her and tried to imagine her in labor with him—bucking and struggling with his birth. He felt then the strange, sexless love for women which through his whole adolescence he had mistaken for heterosexual desire.

A single bright light approached them; it preceded the low, haunting sound of the whistle. Neil kissed his mother, and waved good-bye as he ran to meet the train. It was an old train, with windows tinted a sort of horrible lemon-lime. It stopped only long enough for him to hoist himself on board, and then it was moving again. He hurried to a window, hoping to see her drive off, but the tint of the window made it possible for him to make out only vague patches of light—street lamps, cars, the co-op.

He sank into the hard, green seat. The train was almost entirely empty; the only other passenger was a dark-skinned man wearing blue jeans and a leather jacket. He sat directly across the aisle from Neil, next to the window. He had rough skin and a thick mustache. Neil discovered that by pretending to look out the window he could study the man's reflection in the lemon-lime glass. It was only slightly hazy—the quality of a bad photograph. Neil felt his mouth open, felt sleep closing in on him. Hazy red and gold flashes through the glass pulsed in the face of the man in the window, giving the curious impression of muscle spasms. It took Neil a few minutes to realize that the man was staring at him, or, rather, staring at the back of his head—staring at his staring. The man smiled as though to say, I know exactly what you're staring at, and Neil felt the sickening sensation of desire rise in his throat.

Right before they reached the city, the man stood up and sat down 76 in the seat next to Neil's. The man's thigh brushed deliberately against his own. Neil's eyes were watering; he felt sick to his stomach. Taking Neil's hand, the man said, "Why so nervous, honey? Relax."

Neil woke up the next morning with the taste of ashes in his mouth. He was lying on the floor, without blankets or sheets or pillows. Instinctively, he reached for his pants, and as he pulled them on came face to face with the man from the train. His name was Luis; he turned out to be a dog groomer. His apartment smelled of dog.

"Why such a hurry?" Luis said.

"The parade. The Gay Pride Parade. I'm meeting some friends to march."

"I'll come with you," Luis said. "I think I'm too old for these things, 80 but why not?"

Neil did not want Luis to come with him, but he found it impossible to say so. Luis looked older by day, more likely to carry diseases. He dressed again in a torn T-shirt, leather jacket, blue jeans. "It's my everyday apparel," he said, and laughed. Neil buttoned his pants, aware that they had been washed by his mother the day before. Luis possessed the peculiar combination of hypermasculinity and effeminacy which exemplifies faggotry. Neil wanted to be rid of him, but Luis's mark was on him, he could see that much. They would become lovers whether Neil liked it or not.

They joined the parade midway. Neil hoped he wouldn't meet anyone he knew; he did not want to have to explain Luis, who clung to him. The parade was full of shirtless men with oiled, muscular shoulders. Neil's back ached. There were floats carrying garishly dressed prom queens and cheerleaders, some with beards, some actually looking like women. Luis said, "It makes me proud, makes me glad to be what I am." Neil supposed that by darting into the crowd ahead of him he might be able to lose Luis forever, but he found it difficult to let him go; the prospect of being alone seemed unbearable.

Neil was startled to see his mother watching the parade, holding up a sign. She was with the Coalition of Parents of Lesbians and Gays; they had posted a huge banner on the wall behind them proclaiming: OUR SONS AND DAUGHTERS, WE ARE PROUD OF YOU. She spotted him; she waved, and jumped up and down.

"Who's that woman?" Luis asked.   84

"My mother. I should go say hello to her."

"OK," Luis said. He followed Neil to the side of the parade. Neil kissed his mother. Luis took off his shirt, wiped his face with it, smiled.

"I'm glad you came," Neil said.

"I wouldn't have missed it, Neil. I wanted to show you I cared."   88

He smiled, and kissed her again. He showed no intention of introducing Luis, so Luis introduced himself.

"Hello, Luis," Mrs. Campbell said. Neil looked away. Luis shook her hand, and Neil wanted to warn his mother to wash it, warned himself to check with a VD clinic first thing Monday.

"Neil, this is Carmen Bologna, another one of the mothers," Mrs. Campbell said. She introduced him to a fat Italian woman with flushed cheeks, and hair arranged in the shape of a clamshell.

"Good to meet you, Neil, good to meet you," said Carmen Bologna.   92
"You know my son, Michael? I'm so proud of Michael! He's doing so well now. I'm proud of him, proud to be his mother I am, and your mother's proud, too!"

The woman smiled at him, and Neil could think of nothing to say but "Thank you." He looked uncomfortably toward his mother, who stood listening to Luis. It occurred to him that the worst period of his life was probably about to begin and he had no way to stop it.

A group of drag queens ambled over to where the mothers were standing. "Michael! Michael!" shouted Carmen Bologna, and embraced a sticklike man wrapped in green satin. Michael's eyes were heavily dosed with green eyeshadow, and his lips were painted pink.

Neil turned and saw his mother staring, her mouth open. He marched over to where Luis was standing, and they moved back into the parade. He turned and waved to her. She waved back; he saw pain in her face, and then, briefly, regret. That day, he felt she would have traded him for any other son. Later, she said to him, "Carmen Bologna really was proud, and, speaking as a mother, let me tell you, you have to be brave to feel such pride."

Neil was never proud. It took him a year to dump Luis, another year to leave California. The sick taste of ashes was still in his mouth. On the plane, he envisioned his mother sitting alone in the dark, smoking. She did not leave his mind until he was circling New York, staring down at the dawn rising over Queens. The song playing in his earphones would remain hovering on the edges of his memory, always associated with her absence. After collecting his baggage, he took a bus into the city. Boys were selling newspapers in the middle of highways, through the windows of stopped cars. It was seven in the morning when he reached Manhattan. He stood for ten minutes on East Thirty-fourth Street, breathed the cold air, and felt bubbles rising in his blood.

Neil got a job as a paralegal—a temporary job, he told himself. When he met Wayne a year later, the sensations of that first morning returned to him. They'd been up all night, and at six they walked across the park to Wayne's apartment with the nervous, deliberate gait of people aching to make love for the first time. Joggers ran by with their dogs. None of them knew what Wayne and he were about to do, and the secrecy excited him. His mother came to mind, and the song, and the whirling vision of Queens coming alive below him. His breath solidified into clouds, and he felt happier than he had ever felt before in his life.

The second day of Wayne's visit, he and Neil go with Mrs. Campbell to pick up the dogs at the dog parlor. The grooming establishment is decorated with pink ribbons and photographs of the owner's champion pit bulls. A fat, middle-aged woman appears from the back, leading the newly trimmed and fluffed Abigail, Lucille, and Fern by three leashes. The dogs struggle frantically when they see Neil's mother, tangling the woman up in their leashes. "Ladies, behave!" Mrs. Campbell commands, and collects the dogs. She gives Fern to Neil and Abigail to Wayne. In the car on the way back, Abigail begins pawing to get on Wayne's lap.

"Just push her off," Mrs. Campbell says. "She knows she's not supposed to do that."

"You never groomed Rasputin," Neil complains.

"Rasputin was a mutt."

96

100

"Rasputin was a beautiful dog, even if he did smell."

"Do you remember when you were a little kid, Neil, you used to make Rasputin dance with you? Once you tried to dress him up in one of my blouses."

"I don't remember that," Neil says.   104

"Yes. I remember," says Mrs. Campbell. "Then you tried to organize a dog beauty contest in the neighborhood. You wanted to have runners-up—everything."

"A dog beauty contest?" Wayne says.

"Mother, do we have to—"

"I think it's a mother's privilege to embarrass her son," Mrs. Camp-   108
bell says, and smiles.

When they are about to pull into the driveway, Wayne starts scream-ing, and pushes Abigail off his lap. "Oh, my God!" he says, "The dog just pissed all over me."

Neil turns around and sees a puddle seeping into Wayne's slacks. He suppresses his laughter, and Mrs. Campbell hands him a rag.

"I'm sorry, Wayne," she says. "It goes with the territory."

"This is really disgusting," Wayne says, swatting at himself with the   112
rag.

Neil keeps his eyes on his own reflection in the rearview mirror and smiles.

At home, while Wayne cleans himself in the bathroom, Neil watches his mother cook lunch—Japanese noodles in soup. "When you went off to college," she says, "I went to the grocery store. I was going to buy you ramen noodles, and I suddenly realized you weren't going to be around to eat them. I started crying right then, blubbering like an idiot."

Neil clenches his fists inside his pockets. She has a way of telling him little sad stories when he doesn't want to hear them—stories of dolls broken by her brothers, lunches stolen by neighborhood boys on the way to school. Now he has joined the ranks of male children who have made her cry.

"Mama, I'm sorry," he says.   116

She is bent over the noodles, which steam in her face. "I didn't want to say anything in front of Wayne, but I wish you had answered me last night. I was very frightened—and worried."

"I'm sorry," he says, but it's not convincing. His fingers prickle. He senses a great sorrow about to be born.

"I lead a quiet life," she says. "I don't want to be a disciplinarian. I just don't have the energy for these—shenanigans. Please don't frighten me that way again."

"If you were so upset, why didn't you say something?"   120

"I'd rather not discuss it. I lead a quiet life. I'm not used to getting woken up late at night. I'm not used—"

"To my having a lover?"

"No, I'm not used to having other people around, that's all. Wayne is charming. A wonderful young man."

"He likes you, too."   124

"I'm sure we'll get along fine."

She scoops the steaming noodles into ceramic bowls. Wayne returns, wearing shorts. His white, hairy legs are a shocking contrast to hers, which are brown and sleek.

"I'll wash those pants, Wayne," Mrs. Campbell says. "I have a special detergent that'll take out the stain."

She gives Neil a look to indicate that the subject should be dropped. 128 He looks at Wayne, looks at his mother; his initial embarrassment gives way to a fierce pride—the arrogance of mastery. He is glad his mother knows that he is desired, glad it makes her flinch.

Later, he steps into the backyard; the gardener is back, whacking at the bushes with his shears. Neil walks by him in his bathing suit, imagining he is on parade.

That afternoon, he finds his mother's daily list on the kitchen table:

TUESDAY

7:00—breakfast
Take dogs to groomer
Groceries (?)

Campaign against Draft—4–7

Buy underwear
Trios—2:00
Spaghetti
Fruit
Asparagus if sale
Peanuts
Milk

Doctor's Appointment (make)
Write Cranston/Hayakawa
re disarmament

Handi-Wraps
Mozart
Abigail
Top Ramen
Pedro

Her desk and trash can are full of such lists; he remembers them from the earliest days of his childhood. He had learned to read from them. In his own life, too, there have been endless lists—covered with check marks and arrows, at least one item always spilling over onto the next day's agenda. From September to November, "Buy plane ticket for Christmas" floated from list to list.

The last item puzzles him: Pedro. Pedro must be the gardener. He observes the accretion of names, the arbitrary specifics that give a sense of his mother's life. He could make a list of his own selves: the child, the adolescent, the promiscuous faggot son, and finally the good son, settled, relatively successful. But the divisions wouldn't work; he is today and will always be the child being licked by the dog, the boy on the floor with Luis; he will still be everything he is ashamed of. The other lists— the lists of things done and undone—tell their own truth: that his life is measured more properly in objects than in stages. He knows himself as "jump rope," "book," "sunglasses," "underwear."

"Tell me about your family, Wayne," Mrs. Campbell says that night, 132 as they drive toward town. They are going to see an Esther Williams movie at the local revival house: an underwater musical, populated by mermaids, underwater Rockettes.

"My father was a lawyer," Wayne says. "He had an office in Queens, with a neon sign. I think he's probably the only lawyer in the world who had a neon sign. Anyway, he died when I was ten. My mother never remarried. She lives in Queens. Her great claim to fame is that when she was twenty-two she went on *The $64,000 Question*. Her category was mystery novels. She made it to sixteen thousand before she got tripped up."

"When I was about ten, I wanted you to go on *Jeopardy*," Neil says to his mother. "You really should have, you know. You would have won."

"You certainly loved *Jeopardy*," Mrs. Campbell says. "You used to watch it during dinner. Wayne, does your mother work?"

"No," he says. "She lives off investments." 136

"You're both only children," Mrs. Campbell says. Neil wonders if she is ruminating on the possible connection between that coincidence and their "alternative life-style."

The movie theater is nearly empty. Neil sits between Wayne and his mother. There are pillows on the floor at the front of the theater, and a cat is prowling over them. It casts a monstrous shadow every now and then on the screen, disturbing the sedative effect of water ballet. Like a teenager, Neil cautiously reaches his arm around Wayne's shoulder. Wayne takes his hand immediately. Next to them, Neil's mother breathes in, out, in, out. Neil timorously moves his other arm and lifts it behind his mother's neck. He does not look at her, but he can tell from her breathing that she senses what he is doing. Slowly, carefully, he lets his hand drop on her shoulder; it twitches spasmodically, and he jumps, as if he had received an electric shock. His mother's quiet breathing is broken by a gasp; even Wayne notices. A sudden brightness on the screen illuminates the panic in her eyes, Neil's arm frozen above her, about to fall again. Slowly, he lowers his arm until his fingertips touch her skin, the fabric of her dress. He has gone too far to go back now; they are all too far.

Wayne and Mrs. Campbell sink into their seats, but Neil remains stiff, holding up his arms, which rest on nothing. The movie ends, and they go on sitting just like that.

"I'm old," Mrs. Campbell says later, as they drive back home. "I remember when those films were new. Your father and I went to one on our first date. I loved them, because I could pretend that those women underwater were flying—they were so graceful. They really took advantage of Technicolor in those days. Color was something to appreciate. You can't know what it was like to see a color movie for the first time, after years of black-and-white. It's like trying to explain the surprise of snow to an East Coaster. Very little is new anymore, I fear."

Neil would like to tell her about his own nostalgia, but how can he explain that all of it revolves around her? The idea of her life before he was born pleases him. "Tell Wayne how you used to look like Esther Williams," he asks her.

She blushes, "I was told I looked like Esther Williams, but really more like Gene Tierney," she says. "Not beautiful, but interesting. I like to think I had a certain magnetism."

"You still do," Wayne says, and instantly recognizes the wrongness of his comment. Silence and a nervous laugh indicate that he has not yet mastered the family vocabulary.

When they get home, the night is once again full of the sound of crickets. Mrs. Campbell picks up a flashlight and calls the dogs. "Abbylucyferny, Abbylucyferny," she shouts, and the dogs amble from their various corners. She pushes them out the door to the backyard and follows them. Neil follows her. Wayne follows Neil, but hovers on the porch. Neil walks behind her as she tramps through the garden. She holds out her flashlight, and snails slide from behind bushes, from under rocks, to where she stands. When the snails become visible, she crushes them underfoot. They make a wet, cracking noise, like eggs being broken.

"Nights like this," she says, "I think of children without pants on, in hot South American countries. I have nightmares about tanks rolling down our street."

"The weather's never like this in New York," Neil says. "When it's hot, it's humid and sticky. You don't want to go outdoors."

"I could never live anywhere else but here. I think I'd die. I'm too used to the climate."

"Don't be silly."

"No, I mean it," she says. "I have adjusted too well to the weather."

The dogs bark and howl by the fence. "A cat, I suspect," she says. She aims her flashlight at a rock, and more snails emerge—uncountable numbers, too stupid to have learned not to trust light.

"I know what you were doing at the movie," she says.

"What?"   152

"I know what you were doing."

"What? I put my arm around you."

"I'm sorry, Neil," she says. "I can only take so much. Just so much."

"What do you mean?" he says. "I was only trying to show affection." 156

"Oh, affection—I know about affection."

He looks up at the porch, sees Wayne moving toward the door, trying not to listen.

"What do you mean?" Neil says to her.

She puts down the flashlight and wraps her arms around herself. "I 160 remember when you were a little boy," she says. "I remember, and I have to stop remembering. I wanted you to grow up happy. And I'm very tolerant, very understanding. But I can only take so much."

His heart seems to have risen into his throat. "Mother," he says, "I think you know my life isn't your fault. But for God's sake, don't say that your life is my fault."

"It's not a question of fault," she says. She extracts a Kleenex from her pocket and blows her nose. "I'm sorry, Neil. I guess I'm just an old woman with too much on her mind and not enough to do." She laughs halfheartedly. "Don't worry. Don't say anything," she says. "Abbylucyferny, Abbylucyferny, time for bed!"

He watches her as she walks toward the porch, silent and regal. There is the pad of feet, the clinking of dog tags as the dogs run for the house.

He was twelve the first time she saw him march in a parade. He 164 played the tuba, and as his elementary-school band lumbered down the streets of their then small town she stood on the sidelines and waved. Afterward, she had taken him out for ice cream. He spilled some on his red uniform, and she swiped at it with a napkin. She had been there for him that day, as well as years later, at that more memorable parade; she had been there for him every day.

Somewhere over Iowa, a week later, Neil remembers this scene, remembers other days, when he would find her sitting in the dark, crying. She had to take time out of her own private sorrow to appease his anxiety. "It was part of it," she told him later. "Part of being a mother."

"The scariest thing in the world is the thought that you could unknowingly ruin someone's life," Neil tells Wayne. "Or even change

someone's life. I hate the thought of having such control. I'd make a
rotten mother."

"You're crazy," Wayne says. "You have this great mother, and all you
do is complain. I know people whose mothers have disowned them."

"Guilt goes with the territory," Neil says.   168

"Why?" Wayne asks, perfectly seriously.

Neil doesn't answer. He lies back in his seat, closes his eyes, imagines he grew up in a house in the moutains of Colorado, surrounded by
snow—endless white snow on hills. No flat places, and no trees; just
white hills. Every time he has flown away, she has come into his mind,
usually sitting alone in the dark, smoking. Today she is outside at dusk,
skimming leaves from the pool.

"I want to get a dog," Neil says.

Wayne laughs. "In the city? It'd suffocate."   172

The hum of the airplane is druglike, dazing. "I want to stay with you
a long time," Neil says.

"I know." Imperceptibly, Wayne takes his hand.

"It's very hot there in the summer, too. You know, I'm not thinking
about my mother now."

"It's OK."   176

For a moment, Neil wonders what the stewardess or the old woman
on the way to the bathroom will think, but then he laughs and relaxes.

Later, the plane makes a slow circle over New York City, and on it
two men hold hands, eyes closed, and breathe in unison.   *1985*

Dorothy Allison

Don't Tell Me You Don't Know

I came out of the bathroom with my hair down wet on my shoulders.
My Aunt Alma, my mama's oldest sister, was standing in the middle of
Casey's dusty hooked rug looking like she had just flown in on it, her
gray hair straggling out of its misshapen bun. For a moment I was so
startled I couldn't move. Aunt Alma just stood there looking around at
the big bare room with its two church pews bracketing the only other
furniture—a massive pool table. I froze while the water ran down from
my hair to dampen the collar of the oversized tuxedo shirt I used for a
bathrobe.

"Aunt Alma," I stammered, "well . . . welcome. . . ."

"You really live here?" she breathed, as if, even for me, such a situation was quite past her ability to believe. "Like this?"

I looked around as if I were seeing it for the first time myself,   4
shrugged and tried to grin. "It's big," I offered, "lots of space, four porches, all these windows. We get along well here, might not in a smaller place." I looked back through the kitchen to Terry's room with its thick dark curtains covering a wall of windows. Empty. So was Casey's room on the other side of the kitchen. It was quiet and still, with no one even walking through the rooms overhead.

"Thank God," I whispered to myself. Nobody else was home.

Aunt Alma turned around slowly and stepped over to the mantel with the old fly-spotted mirror over it. She pushed a few of her loose hairs back and then laid her big rattan purse up by a stack of fliers Terry had left there, brushing some of the dust away first.

"My God," she echoed, "dirtier than we ever lived. Didn't think you'd turn out like this."

I shrugged again, embarrassed and angry and trying not to show it.   8
Well hell, what could I do? I hadn't seen her in so long. She hadn't even been around that last year I'd lived with Mama, and I wasn't sure I particularly wanted to see her now. But why was she here anyway? How had she found me?

I closed the last two buttons on my shirt and tried to shake some of the water out of my hair. Aunt Alma watched me through the dark spots of the mirror, her mouth set in an old familiar line. "Well," I said, "I didn't expect to see you." I reached up to push hair back out of my eyes. "You want to sit down?"

Aunt Alma turned around and bumped her hip against the pool table. "Where?" One disdainful glance rendered the pews for what they were—exquisitely uncomfortable even for my hips. Her expression reminded me of my Uncle Jack's jokes about her, about how she refused to go back to church till they put in rocking chairs.

"No rocking chairs here," I laughed, hoping she'd laugh with me. Aunt Alma just leaned forward and rocked one of the balls on the table against another. Her mouth kept its flat, impartial expression. I tried gesturing across the pool table to my room and the big waterbed outlined in sunlight and tree shade from the three windows overlooking it.

"It's cleaner in there," I offered, "it's my room. This is our collective   12
space." I gestured around.

"Collective," my aunt echoed me again, but the way she said the word expressed clearly her opinion of such arrangements. She looked toward my room with its narrow cluttered desk and stacks of books, then turned back to the pool table as by far the more interesting view.

She rocked the balls again so that the hollow noise of the thump resounded against the high, dim ceiling.

"Pitiful," she sighed, and gave me a sharp look, her washed-out blue eyes almost angry. Two balls broke loose from the others and rolled idly across the matted green surface of the table. The sunlight reflecting through the oak leaves outside made Aunt Alma's face seem younger than I remembered it, some of the hard edge eased off the square jaw.

"Your mama is worried about you."

"I don't know why." I turned my jaw to her, knowing it would   16
remind her of how much alike we had always been, the people who had said I was more her child than my mama's. "I'm fine. Mama should know that. I spoke to her not too long ago."

"How long ago?"

I frowned, mopped at my head some more. Two months, three, last month? "I'm not sure . . . Reese's birthday. I think it was Reese's birthday."

"Three months." My aunt rocked one ball back and forth across her palm, a yellow nine ball. The light filtering into the room went a shade darker. The –9– gleamed pale through her fingers. I looked more closely at her. She looked just as she had when I was thirteen, her hair gray in that loose bun, her hands large and swollen, her body straining the seams of the faded print dress. She'd worn her hair short for a while, but it was grown long again now, and the print dress under her coat could have been any dress she'd worn in the last twenty years. She'd gotten old, suddenly, after the birth of her eighth child, but since then she seemed not to change at all. She looked now as if she would go on forever—a worn stubborn woman who didn't care what you saw when you looked at her.

I drew breath in slowly, carefully. I knew from old experience to use   20
caution in dealing with any of my aunts, and this was the oldest and most formidable. I'd seen grown men break down and cry when she'd kept that look on them too long; little children repent and swear to change their ways. But I'd also seen my other aunts stare her right back, and like them I was a grown woman minding my own business. I had a right to look her in the eye, I told myself. I was no wayward child, no half-drunk, silly man. I was her namesake, my mama's daughter. I had to be able to look her in the eye. If I couldn't, I was in trouble, and I didn't want that kind of trouble here, five hundred miles and half a lifetime away from my aunts and the power of their eyes.

Slow, slow, the balls rocked one against the other. Aunt Alma looked over at me levelly. I let the water run down between my breasts, looked back at her. My mama's sister. I could feel the tears pushing behind my eyes. It had been so long since I'd seen her or any of them! The last time I'd been to Old Henderson Road had been years back. Aunt Alma had stood on that sagging porch and looked at me, memorizing me, both of us knowing we might not see each other again. She'd moved her mouth and I'd seen the pain there, the shadow of the nephew behind her— yet another one she was raising since her youngest son, another cousin of mine, had run off and left the girl who'd birthed that boy. The pain in her eyes was achingly clear to me, the certain awful knowledge that measured all her children and wrenched her heart.

Something wrong with that boy, my uncles had laughed.

Yeah, something. Dropped on his head one too many times, you think?

I think.

24

My aunt, like my mama, understood everything, expected nothing, and watched her own life like a terrible fable from a Sunday morning sermon. It was the perspective that all those women shared, the view that I could not, for my life, accept. I believed, I believed with all my soul that death was behind it, that death was the seed and the fruit of that numbed and numbing attitude. More than anything else, it was my anger that had driven me away from them, driven them away from me— my unpredictable, automatic anger. Their anger, their hatred, always seemed shielded, banked and secret, and because of that—shameful. My uncles were sudden, violent, and daunting. My aunts wore you down without ever seeming to fight at all. It was my anger that my aunts thought queer, my wild raging temper they respected in a boy and discouraged in a girl. That I slept with girls was curious, but not dangerous. That I slept with a knife under my pillow and refused to step aside for my uncles was more than queer. It was crazy.

Aunt Alma's left eye twitched, and I swallowed my tears, straightened my head, and looked her full in the face. I could barely hold myself still, barely return her look. Again those twin emotions, the love and the outrage that I'd always felt for my aunt, warred in me. I wanted to put out my hand and close my fingers on her hunched, stubborn shoulder. I wanted to lay my head there and pull tight to her, but I also wanted to hit her, to scream and kick and make her ashamed of herself. Nothing was clean between us, especially not our love.

Between my mama and Aunt Alma there were five other sisters. The most terrible and loved was Bess, the one they swore had always been so smart. From the time I was eight Aunt Bess had a dent in the left side of her head—a shadowed dent that emphasized the twitch of that eye, just like the twitch Aunt Alma has, just like the twitch I sometimes get, the one they tell me is nerves. But Aunt Bess wasn't born with that twitch as we were, just as she wasn't born with that dent. My uncle, her husband, had come up from the deep dust on the road, his boots damp from the river, picking up clumps of dust and making mud, knocking it off on her steps, her screen door, her rug, the back rung of a kitchen chair. She'd shouted at him, "Not on my clean floor!" and he'd swung the bucket, river-stained and heavy with crawfish. He'd hit her in the side of the head—dented her into a lifetime of stupidity and half-blindness. Son of a bitch never even said he was sorry, and all my childhood he'd laughed at her, the way she'd sometimes stop in the middle of a sentence and grope painfully for a word.

None of them had told me that story. I had been grown and out of the house before one of the Greenwood cousins had told it so I understood, and as much as I'd hated him then, I'd raged at them more.

"You let him live?" I'd screamed at them. "He did that to her and you did nothing! You did nothing to him, nothing for her."

"What'd you want us to do?"

My Aunt Grace had laughed at me. "You want us to cut him up and feed him to the river? What good would that have done her or her children?"

She'd shaken her head, and they had all stared at me as if I were still a child and didn't understand the way the world was. The cold had gone through me then, as if the river were running up from my bowels. I'd felt my hands curl up and reach, but there was nothing to reach for. I'd taken hold of myself, my insides, and tried desperately to voice the terror that was tearing at me.

"But to leave her with him after he did that, to just let it stand, to let him get away with it." I'd reached and reached, trying to get to them, to make them feel the wave moving up and through me. "It's like all of it, all you let them get away with."

"Them?" My mama had watched my face as if afraid of what she might find there. "Who do you mean? And what do you think we could do?"

I couldn't say it. I'd stared into Mama's face, and looked from her to all of them, to those wide, sturdy cheekbones, those high, proud eyebrows, those set and terrible mouths. I had always thought of them as mountains, mountains that everything conspired to grind but never actually broke. The women of my family were all I had ever believed in. What was I if they were not what I had shaped them in my own mind? All I had known was that I had to get away from them—all of them—the men who could do those terrible things and the women who would let it happen to you. I'd never forgiven any of them.

It might have been more than three months since I had talked to Mama on the telephone. It had been far longer than that since I had been able to really talk to any of them. The deepest part of me didn't believe that I would ever be able to do so. I dropped my eyes and pulled myself away from Aunt Alma's steady gaze. I wanted to reach for her, touch her, maybe cry with her, if she'd let me.

"People will hurt you more with pity than with hate," she'd always told me. "I can hate back, or laugh at them, but goddamn the son of a bitch that hands me pity."

No pity. Not allowed. I reached to rock a ball myself.

"Want to play?" I tried looking up into her eyes again. It was too close. Both of us looked away.

"I'll play myself." She set about racking up the balls. Her mouth was   40
still set in that tight line. I dragged a kitchen stool in and sat in the doorway out of her way, telling myself I had to play this casually, play this as family, and wait and see what the point was.

"Where's Uncle Bill?" I was rubbing my head again and trying to make conversation.

"What do you care? I don't think Bill said ten words to you in your whole life." She rolled the rack forward and back, positioning it per-fectly for the break. " 'Course he didn't say many more to anybody else either." She grinned, not looking at me, talking as if she were pouring tea at her own kitchen table. "Nobody can say I married that man for his conversation."

She leaned into her opening shot, and I leaned forward in apprecia-tion. She had a great stance, her weight centered over her massive thighs. My family runs to heavy women, gravy-fed working women, the kind usually seen in pictures taken at mining disasters. Big women, all of my aunts move under their own power and stalk around telling everybody else what to do. But Aunt Alma was the prototype, the one I had loved most, starting back when she had given us free meals in the roadhouse she'd run for a while. It had been one of those bad times when my stepfather had been out of work and he and Mama were always fighting. Mama would load us all in the Pontiac and crank it up on seventy-five cents worth of gas, just enough to get to Aunt Alma's place on the Eustis Highway. Once there, we'd be fed on chicken gravy and biscuits, and Mama would be fed from the well of her sister's love and outrage.

You tell that bastard to get his ass out on the street. Whining don't make   44
money. Cursing don't get a job . . .

Bitching don't make the beds and screaming don't get the tomatoes planted.
They had laughed together then, speaking a language of old stories and older jokes.

You tell him.

I said.

Now girl, you listen to me.   48

The power in them, the strength and the heat! How could anybody not love my mama, my aunts? How could my daddy, my uncles, ever stand up to them, dare to raise hand or voice to them? They were a power on the earth.

I breathed deep, watching my aunt rock on her stance, settling her eye on the balls, while I smelled chicken gravy and hot grease, the close thick scent of love and understanding. I used to love to eat at Aunt Alma's house, all those home-cooked dinners at the roadhouse; pinto beans with peppers for fifteen, nine of them hers. Chow-chow on a clean white plate passed around the table while the biscuits passed the other way. My aunt always made biscuits. What else stretched so well? Now those starch meals shadowed her loose shoulders and dimpled her fat white elbows.

She gave me one quick glance and loosed her stroke. The white ball punched the center of the table. The balls flew to the edges. My sixty-year-old aunt gave a grin that would have scared piss out of my Uncle Bill, a grin of pure, fierce enjoyment. She rolled the stick in fingers loose as butter on a biscuit, laughed again, and slid her palms down the sides of polished wood, while the anger in her face melted into skill and concentration.

I rocked back on my stool and covered my smile with my wet hair.   52
Goddamn! Aunt Alma pushed back on one ankle, swung the stick to follow one ball, another, dropping them as easily as peas on potatoes. Goddamn! She went after those balls like kids on a dirt yard, catching each lightly and dropping them lovingly. Into the holes, move it! Turning and bracing on ankles thickened with too many years of flour and babies, Aunt Alma blitzed that table like a twenty-year-old hustler, not sparing me another glance.

Not till the eighth stroke did she pause and stop to catch her breath.

"You living like this—not for a man, huh?" she asked, one eyebrow arched and curious.

"No," I shrugged, feeling more friendly and relaxed. Moving like that, aunt of mine I wanted to say, don't tell me you don't understand.

"Your mama said you were working in some photo shop, doing shit   56
work for shit money. Not much to show for that college degree, is that?"

"Work is work. It pays the rent."

"Which ought not to be much here."

"No," I agreed, "not much. I know," I waved my hands lightly, "it's a wreck of a place, but it's home. I'm happy here. Terry, Casey, and everybody—they're family."

"Family." Her mouth hardened again. "You have a family, don't you   60
remember? These girls might be close, might be important to you, but they're not family. You know that." Her eyes said more, much more. Her eyes threw the word *family* at me like a spear. All her longing, all her resentment of my abandonment was in that word, and not only hers, but Mama's and my sisters' and all the cousins' I had carefully not given my new address.

"How about a beer?" I asked. I wanted one myself. "I've got a can of Pabst in the icebox."

"A glass of water," she said. She leaned over the table to line up her closing shots.

I brought her a glass of water. "You're good," I told her, wanting her to talk to me about how she had learned to play pool, anything but family and all this stuff I so much did not want to think about.

"Children," she stared at me again. "What about children?" There was something in her face then that waited, as if no question were more important, as if she knew the only answer I could give.   64

Enough, I told myself, and got up without a word to get myself that can of Pabst. I did not look in her eyes. I walked into the kitchen on feet that felt suddenly unsteady and tender. Behind me, I heard her slide the cue stick along the rim of the table and then draw it back to set up another shot.

Play it out, I cursed to myself, just play it out and leave me alone. Everything is so simple for you, so settled. Make babies. Grow a garden. Handle some man like he's just another child. Let everything come that comes, die that dies, let everything go where it goes. I drank straight from the can and watched her through the doorway. All my uncles were drunks, and I was more like them than I had ever been like my aunts.

Aunt Alma started talking again, walking around the table, measuring shots and not even looking in my direction. "You remember when ya'll lived out on Greenlake Road? Out on that dirt road where that man kept that old egg-busting dog? Your mama couldn't keep a hen to save her life till she emptied a shell and filled it again with chicken shit and baby piss. Took that dog right out of himself when he ate it. Took him right out of the taste for hens and eggs." She stopped to take a deep breath, sweat glittering on her lip. With one hand she wiped it away, the other going white on the pool cue.

"I still had Annie then. Lord, I never think about her anymore."   68

I remembered then the last child she had borne, a tiny girl with a heart that fluttered with every breath, a baby for whom the doctors said nothing could be done, a baby they swore wouldn't see six months. Aunt Alma had kept her in an okra basket and carried her everywhere, talking to her one minute like a kitten or a doll and the next minute like a grown woman. Annie had lived to be four, never outgrowing the vegetable basket, never talking back, just lying there and smiling like a wise old woman, dying between a smile and a laugh while Aunt Alma never interrupted the story that had almost made Annie laugh.

I sipped my beer and watched my aunt's unchanging face. Very slowly she swung the pool cue up and down, not quite touching the table. After a moment she stepped in again and leaned half her weight on the table. The 5-ball became a bird murdered in flight, dropping suddenly into the far right pocket.

Aunt Alma laughed out loud, delighted. "Never lost it," she crowed. "Four years in the roadhouse with that table set up in the back. Every one of them sons of mine thought he was going to make money on it. Lord those boys! Never made a cent." She swallowed the rest of her glass of water.

"But me," she wiped the sweat away again. "I never would have done   72
it for money. I just loved it. Never went home without playing myself three or four games. Sometimes I'd set Annie up on the side and we'd pretend we was playing. I'd tell her when I was taking her shots. And she'd shout when I'd sink 'em. I let her win most every time."

She stopped, put both hands on the table, closed her eyes.

" 'Course, just after we lost her, we lost the roadhouse." She shook her head, eyes still closed. "Never did have anything fine that I didn't lose."

The room was still, dust glinted in the sunlight past her ears. She opened her eyes and looked directly at me.

"I don't care," she began slowly, softly. "I don't care if you're queer   76
or not. I don't care if you take puppydogs to bed, for that matter, but your mother was all my heart for twenty years when nobody else cared what happened to me. She stood by me. I've stood by her and I always thought to do the same for you and yours. But she's sitting there, did you know that? She's sitting there like nothing's left of her life, like . . . like she hates her life and won't say shit to nobody about it. She wouldn't tell me. She won't tell me what it is, what has happened."

I sat the can down on the stool, closed my own eyes, dropped my head. I didn't want to see her. I didn't want her to be there. I wanted her to go away, disappear out of my life the way I'd run out of hers. Go away, old woman. Leave me alone. Don't talk to me. Don't tell me your stories. I an't a baby in a basket, and I can't lie still for it.

"You know. You know what it is. The way she is about you. I know it has to be you—something about you. I want to know what it is, and you're going to tell me. Then you're going to come home with me and straighten this out. There's a lot I an't never been able to fix, but this time, this thing, I'm going to see it out. I'm going to see it fixed."

I opened my eyes and she was still standing there, the cue stick shiny in her hand, her face all flushed and tight.

"Go," I said and heard my voice, a scratchy, strangling cry in the big   80
room. "Get out of here."

"What did you tell her? What did you say to your mama?"

"Ask her. Don't ask me. I don't have nothing to say to you."

The pool cue rose slowly, slowly till it touched the right cheek, the

fine lines of broken blood vessels, freckles, and patchy skin. She shook
her head slowly. My throat pulled tighter and tighter until it drew my
mouth down and open. Like a shot the cue swung. The table vibrated
with the blow. Her cheeks pulled tight, the teeth all a grimace. The cue
split and broke. White dust rose in a cloud. The echo hurt my ears while
her hands rose up as fists, the broken cue in her right hand as jagged as
the pain in her face.

"Don't you say that to me. Don't you treat me like that. Don't you   84
know who I am, what I am to you? I didn't have to come up here after
you. I could have let it run itself out, let it rest on your head the rest of
your life, just let you carry it—your mama's life. YOUR MAMA'S LIFE,
GIRL. Don't you understand me? I'm talking about your mama's life."

She threw the stick down, turned away from me, her shoulders
heaving and shaking, her hands clutching nothing. "I an't talking about
your stepfather. I an't talking about no man at all. I'm talking about
your mama sitting at her kitchen table, won't talk to nobody, won't eat,
won't listen to nothing. What'd she ever ask from you? Nothing. Just
gave you your life and everything she had. Worked herself ugly for you
and your sister. Only thing she ever hoped for was to do the same for
your children, someday to sit herself back and hold her grandchildren
on her lap. . . ."

It was too much. I couldn't stand it.

"GODDAMN YOU!" I was shaking all over. "CHILDREN! All you
ever talk about—you and her and all of you. Like that was the end-all
and be-all of everything. Never mind what happens to them once
they're made. That don't matter. It's only the getting of them. Like some
goddamned crazy religion. Get your mother a grandchild and solve all
her problems. Get yourself a baby and forget everything else. It's what
you were born for, the one thing you can do with no thinking about it at
all. Only I can't. To get her a grandchild, I'd have to steal one!"

I was wringing my own hands, twisting them together and pulling   88
them apart. Now I swung them open and slapped down at my belly,
making my own hollow noise in the room.

"No babies in there, aunt of mine, and never going to be. I'm sterile
as a clean tin can. That's what I told Mama, and not to hurt her. I told
her because she wouldn't leave me alone about it. Like you, like all of
you, always talking about children, never able to leave it alone." I was
walking back and forth now, unable to stop myself from talking. "Never
able to hear me when I warned her to leave it be. Going on and on till I
thought I'd lose my mind."

I looked her in the eye, loving her and hating her, and not wanting
to speak, but hearing the words come out anyway. "Some people never
do have babies, you know. Some people get raped at eleven by a
stepfather their mama half-hates but can't afford to leave. Some people

then have to lie and hide it 'cause it would make so much trouble. So nobody will know, not the law and not the rest of the family. Nobody but the women supposed to be the ones who take care of everything, who know what to do and how to do it, the women who make children who believe in them and trust in them, and sometimes die for it. Some people never go to a doctor and don't find out for ten years that the son of a bitch gave them some goddamned disease."

I looked away, unable to stand how gray her face had gone.

"You know what it does to you when the people you love most in the world, the people you believe in—cannot survive without believing in—when those people do nothing, don't even know something needs to be done? When you cannot hate them but cannot help yourself? The hatred grows. It just takes over everything, eats you up and makes you somebody full of hate."

I stopped. The roar that had been all around me stopped, too. The cold was all through me now. I felt like it would never leave me. I heard her move. I heard her hip bump the pool table and make the balls rock. I heard her turn and gather up her purse. I opened my eyes to see her moving toward the front door. That cold cut me then like a knife in fresh slaughter. I knew certainly that she'd go back and take care of Mama, that she'd never say a word, probably never tell anybody she'd been here. 'Cause then she'd have to talk about the other thing, and I knew as well as she that however much she tried to forget it, she'd really always known. She'd done nothing then. She'd do nothing now. There was no justice. There was no justice in the world.

When I started to cry it wasn't because of that. It wasn't because of babies or no babies, or pain that was so far past I'd made it a source of strength. It wasn't even that I'd hurt her so bad, hurt Mama when I didn't want to. I cried because of the things I hadn't said, didn't know how to say, cried most of all because behind everything else there was no justice for my aunts or my mama. Because each of them to save their lives had tried to be strong, had become, in fact, as strong and determined as life would let them. I and all their children had believed in that strength, had believed in them and their ability to do anything, fix anything, survive anything. None of us had ever been able to forgive ourselves that we and they were not strong enough, that strength itself was not enough.

Who can say where that strength ended, where the world took over and rolled us all around like balls on a pool table? None of us ever would. I brought my hands up to my neck and pulled my hair around until I clenched it in my fists, remembering how my aunt used to pick up Annie to rub that baby's belly beneath her chin—Annie bouncing against her in perfect trust. Annie had never had to forgive her mama anything.

"Aunt Alma, wait. Wait!"   96

She stopped in the doorway, her back trembling, her hands gripping the doorposts. I could see the veins raised over her knuckles, the
cords that stood out in her neck, the flesh as translucent as butter beans
cooked until the skins come loose. Talking to my mama over the phone,
I had not been able to see her face, her skin, her stunned and haunted
eyes. If I had been able to see her, would I have ever said those things to
her?

"I'm sorry."

She did not look back. I let my head fall back, rolled my shoulders
to ease the painful clutch of my own muscles. My teeth hurt. My ears
stung. My breasts felt hot and swollen. I watched the light as it moved on
her hair.

"I'm sorry. I would . . . I would . . . anything. If I could change   100
things, if I could help. . . ."

I stopped. Tears running down my face. My aunt turned to me, her
wide pale face as wet as mine. "Just come home with me. Come home for
a little while. Be with your mama a little while. You don't have to forgive
her. You don't have to forgive anybody. You just have to love her the way
she loves you. Like I love you. Oh girl, don't you know how we love you!"

I put my hands out, let them fall apart on the pool table. My aunt
was suddenly across from me, reaching across the table, taking my
hands, sobbing into the cold dirty stillness—an ugly sound, not softened by the least self-consciousness. When I leaned forward, she leaned
to me and our heads met, her gray hair against my temple brightened
by the sunlight pouring in the windows.

"Oh, girl! Girl, you are our precious girl."

I cried against her cheek, and it was like being five years old again   104
in the roadhouse, with Annie's basket against my hip, the warmth in the
room purely a product of the love that breathed out from my aunt and
my mama. If they were not mine, if I was not theirs, who was I? I opened
my mouth, put my tongue out, and tasted my aunt's cheek and my own.
Butter and salt, dust and beer, sweat and stink, flesh of my flesh.

"Precious," I breathed back to her.

"Precious."   *1988*

10

Crises of Adolescence

David Elkind, *From* Teenagers in Crisis
Joyce Carol Oates, Shopping

If adolescents are only plunged into difficulties and distress because of
conditions in their social environment, then by all means let us so
modify that environment as to reduce this stress and eliminate this
strain and anguish of adjustment. But, unfortunately, the conditions
which vex our adolescents are the flesh and bone of our society, no
more subject to straightforward manipulation upon our part than is the
language which we speak. We can alter a syllable here, a construction
there; but the great and far-reaching changes in linguistic structure (as
in all parts of culture) are the work of time, a work in which each
individual plays an unconscious and inconsiderable part. The principal
causes of our adolescents' difficulty are the presence of conflicting
standards and the belief that every individual should make his or her
own choices, coupled with a feeling that choice is an important matter.
Given these cultural attitudes, adolescence, regarded now not as a
period of physiological change, for we know that physiological puberty
need not produce conflict, but as the beginning of mental and emotional maturity, is bound to be filled with conflicts and difficulties. A
society which is clamoring for choice, which is filled with many articulate groups, each urging its own brand of salvation, its own variety of
economic philosophy, will give each new generation no peace until all
have chosen or gone under, unable to bear the conditions of choice. The
stress is in our civilization, not in the physical changes through which
our children pass, but it is none the less real nor the less inevitable in
twentieth-century America.

Margaret Mead, from *Coming of Age in Samoa*

Before eighteen, the motto is loud and clear: "I have to get away from my parents." But the words are seldom connected to action. Generally still safely part of our families, even if away at school, we feel our autonomy to be subject to erosion from moment to moment.

After eighteen, we begin Pulling Up Roots in earnest. College, military service, and short-term travels are all customary vehicles our society provides for the first round trips between family and a base of one's own. In the attempt to separate our view of the world from our family's view, despite vigorous protestations to the contrary—"I know exactly what I want!"—we cast about for any beliefs we can call our own. And in the process of testing those beliefs we are often drawn to fads, preferably those most mysterious and inaccessible to our parents.

Gail Sheehy, from *Passages*

My own studies point to early adolescence—the years from ten to thirteen—as a period of special strain between parents and children. But more intriguing, perhaps, is that these studies reveal that puberty plays a central role in triggering parent-adolescent conflict. Specifically, as youngsters develop toward physical maturity, bickering and squabbling with parents increase. If puberty comes early, so does the arguing and bickering; if it is late, the period of heightened tension is delayed. Although many other aspects of adolescent behavior reflect the intertwined influences of biological and social factors, this aspect seems to be directly connected to the biological event of puberty; something about normal physical maturation sets off parent-adolescent fighting. It's no surprise that they argue about overflowing trash cans, trails of dirty laundry, and blaring stereos. But why should teenagers going through puberty fight with their parents more often than youngsters of the same age whose physical development is slower? More to the point: if puberty is inevitable, does this mean that parent-child conflict is, too?

Laurence Steinberg, from *Bound to Bicker*

David Elkind

From Teenagers in Crisis

There is no place for teenagers in American society today—not in our homes, not in our schools, and not in society at large. This was not always the case: barely a decade ago, teenagers had a clearly defined position in the social structure. They were the "next generation," the "future leaders" of America. Their intellectual, social, and moral development was considered important, and therefore it was protected and nurtured. The teenager's occasional foibles and excesses were excused as an expression of youthful spirit, a necessary Mardi Gras before assuming adult responsibility and decorum. Teenagers thus received the time needed to adapt to the remarkable transformations their bodies, minds, and emotions were undergoing. Society recognized that the transition from childhood to adulthood was difficult and that young people needed time, support, and guidance in this endeavor.

In today's rapidly changing society, teenagers have lost their once privileged position. Instead, they have had a premature adulthood thrust upon them. Teenagers now are expected to confront life and its challenges with the maturity once expected only of the middle-aged, without any time for preparation. Many adults are too busy retooling and retraining their own job skills to devote any time to preparing the next generation of workers. And some parents are so involved in reordering their own lives, managing a career, marriage, parenting, and leisure, that they have no time to give their teenagers; other parents simply cannot train a teenager for an adulthood they themselves have yet to attain fully. The media and merchandisers, too, no longer abide by the unwritten rule that teenagers are a privileged group who require special protection and nurturing. They now see teenagers as fair game for all the arts of persuasion and sexual innuendo once directed only to adult audiences and consumers. High schools, which were once the setting for a unique teenage culture and language, have become miniatures of the adult community. Theft, violence, sex, and substance abuse are now as common in the high schools as they are on the streets.

It is true, of course, that many parents and other adults are still committed to giving teenagers the time, protection, and guidance they require to traverse this difficult period. But these well-meaning adults meet almost insurmountable barriers in today's society, and many feel powerless to provide the kind of guidance they believe teenagers need. For example, a mother of a teenager asked me recently what to do with her fourteen-year-old son who was staying up late to watch X-rated movies on cable television. I suggested that if she did not want him to see the movies, she should not permit him to do so and should give him her reasons for the prohibition. Her next question surprised me. She asked me what she should do if he watches them after she goes to bed. It was clear that the mother felt helpless to monitor her son's TV watching. For this youth, as for many others, premature adulthood is gained by default.

In today's society we seem unable to accept the fact of adolescence,   4 that there are young people in transition from childhood to adulthood who need adult guidance and direction. Rather, we assume the teenager is a kind of adult. Whether we confer premature adulthood upon teenagers because we are too caught up in our own lives to give them the time and attention they require or because we feel helpless to provide them with the safe world they need, the end result is the same: teenagers have no place in this society. They are not adults capable of carrying the adult responsibilities we confer upon them. And they are not children whose subservience to adults can be taken for granted. We expect them to be grown up in all those domains where we cannot or do not want to maintain control. But in other domains, such as attending school, we expect our teenagers to behave like obedient children.

Perhaps the best word to describe the predicament of today's teen-agers is "unplaced." Teenagers are not displaced in the sense of having been put in a position they did not choose to be in (a state sometimes called anomie). Nor are they misplaced in the sense of having been put in the wrong place (a state sometimes called alienation). Rather, they are unplaced in the sense that there is no place for a young person who needs a measured and controlled introduction to adulthood. In a rapidly changing society, when adults are struggling to adapt to a new social order, few adults are genuinely committed to helping teenagers attain a healthy adulthood. Young people are thus denied the special recognition and protection that society previously accorded their age group. The special stage belonging to teenagers has been excised from the life cycle, and teenagers have been given a pro forma adulthood, an adulthood with all of the responsibilities but few of the prerogatives. Young people today are quite literally all grown up with no place to go.

The imposition of premature adulthood upon today's teenagers affects them in two different but closely related ways. First, because teenagers need a protected period of time within which to construct a personal identity, the absence of that period impairs the formation of that all-important self-definition. Having a personal identity amounts to having an abiding sense of self that brings together, and gives mean-ing to, the teenager's past while at the same time giving him or her guidance and direction for the future. A secure sense of self, of personal identity, allows the young person to deal with both inner and outer demands with consistency and efficiency. This sense of self is thus one of the teenager's most important defenses against stress. By impairing his or her ability to construct a secure personal identity, today's society leaves the teenager more vulnerable and less competent to meet the challenges that are inevitable in life.

The second effect of premature adulthood is inordinate stress: teenagers today are subject to more stress than were teenagers in previous generations. This stress is of three types. First, teenagers are confronted with many more freedoms today than were available to past generations. Second, they are experiencing losses, to their basic sense of security and expectations for the future, that earlier generations did not encounter. And third, they must cope with the frustration of trying to prepare for their life's work in school settings that hinder rather than facilitate this goal. Any one of these new stresses would put a heavy burden on a young person; taken together, they make a formidable demand on the teenager's ability to adapt to new demands and new situations.

Contemporary American society has thus struck teenagers a double   8
blow. It has rendered them more vulnerable to stress while at the same time exposing them to new and more powerful stresses than were ever faced by previous generations of adolescents. It is not surprising, then, to find that the number of stress-related problems among teenagers has more than trebled in the last decade and a half. Before we examine in more detail the predicament of today's teenagers, we need to look at some of the frightening statistics in order to understand both the seriousness and the magnitude of the problem.

A GENERATION UNDER STRESS

Substance abuse is now the leading cause of death among teenagers and accounts for more than ten thousand deaths each year. Although the use of drugs has leveled off after a threefold rise in the last decade and a half, alcohol use is becoming more widespread and is appearing among younger age groups. According to a recent survey of junior high school students, 65 percent of the thirteen-year-olds had used alcohol at least once that year, some 35 percent used it once a month, and 20 percent used it once a week. Thirty-five percent of the thirteen-year-olds queried said that it was fun and all right to get drunk. The National Institute on Alcohol Abuse and Alcoholism reports, conservatively, that 1.3 million teenagers between the ages of twelve and seventeen have serious drinking problems. According to a 1981 report from the Department of Health, Education and Welfare, more than three million youths nationwide have experienced problems at home, in school, or on the highways as a result of drinking.[1] In my own travels throughout this

[1]N. Cobb. "Who's Getting High on What?" *Boston Globe*, October 10, 1982.

country I have found that it is commonplace for beer to be available at parties for twelve- and thirteen-year-olds. It is often provided by parents, who, relieved that the youngsters are not into drugs, appear to consider alcohol benign by comparison.

Sexual activity, at least among teenage girls, has more than tripled over the last two decades. In contrast to the 1960s, when only about 10 percent of teenage girls were sexually active, more than 50 percent are sexually active today. By the age of nineteen at least 70 percent of young women have had at least one sexual experience. Among young women who are sexually active, four out of ten will become pregnant before they leave their teens. Currently about 1.3 million teenagers become pregnant each year, and more than a third of them are choosing to have and to keep their babies.[2] Although young women may be able to conceive an infant, the pelvic girdle does not attain its full size until the age of seventeen or eighteen. This puts the young teenage mother and her infant at physical risk. The data also indicate that the infants of teenage mothers are more at risk for child abuse and for emotional problems than are the children of more mature mothers.

Suicide rates for teenagers have climbed at a fearful pace. Five thousand teenagers commit suicide each year, and for each of these suicides fifty to one hundred youngsters make an unsuccessful attempt.[3] Sex differences in mode of suicide are changing. Girls, who in the past resorted to pills and slashing their wrists, are now using the more violent means often employed by boys, namely, hanging and shooting. In addition, many "accidental" teenage deaths are regarded by experts as being, in part at least, suicidal.

Crime rates have increased dramatically among juveniles. For many   12 children, crime is a regular part of their lives, in both the home and the school.

> Every month, secondary schools experience 2.4 million thefts, almost 300,000 assaults and over 100,000 robberies. Criminal behavior starts early, usually in school, and peaks quickly. More 17 to 20 year old males are arrested for virtually every class of crime (including homicide) than males in any other age group. But the record of children under 10 (55,000 arrests in 1980) is itself sobering and it gets seven times worse by age 14.[4]

[2]M. Zelnick and J. Kantner, "Sexuality, Contraception and Pregnancy among Young Unwed Females in the United States," *Research Reports*, Commission on Population Growth and the American Future, vol. 1 (Washington, D.C.: Government Printing Office, 1980).

[3]C. L. Tishler, "Adolescent Suicide: Prevention, Practice and Treatment," *Feelings and Their Medical Significance* 23, no. 6 (November–December 1981).

[4]C. Murphy, "Kids Today," *Wilson Quarterly*, Autumn 1982.

To these alarming statistics we must add that over one million children run away from home each year, and an indeterminate number of these are forced into prostitution or pornography, or both.[5]

These statistics define the gravity of the problems resulting from teenage stress. Now we need to examine some of the social changes that have taken place in this country and how they have led us to deny, ignore, or abdicate our responsibilities toward youth.

SOCIAL CHANGE AND TEENAGE IDENTITY

It is generally agreed today, following the original work of the psychoanalyst Erik Erikson, that the primary task of the teenage years is to construct a sense of personal identity.[6] In Erikson's view, the teenager's task is to bring together all of the various and sometimes conflicting facets of self into a working whole that at once provides continuity with the past and focus and direction for the future. This sense of personal identity includes various roles (son or daughter, student, athlete, musician, artist, and so on), various traits and abilities (quiet, outgoing, timid, generous, high-strung), as well as the teenager's personal tableau of likes and dislikes, political and social attitudes, religious orientation, and much more.

It is clear from this description that the task of forming an identity 16 is a difficult and complex one. It is not undertaken until the teen years in part because the young person has not accumulated all the necessary ingredients until this time, and in part because prior to adolescence young people lack the mental abilities required for the task. The late Jean Piaget demonstrated that it is not until the teen years that young people are capable of constructing theories.[7] And it is not unreasonable to characterize identity as a theory of oneself. Forming an identity, like building a theory, is a creative endeavor that takes much time and concentrated effort. That is why Erikson has suggested that teenagers either make or find a "moratorium," a period of time for themselves during which they can engage in the task of identity formation.

In the past, a clearly demarcated period of development, called adolescence, gave young people the needed respite before assuming adult responsibility and decision making. But this period is no longer available. The current generation of young people is being denied the time needed to put together a workable theory of self. The issue, it should be said, is not one of leisure or free time. Many teenagers today

[5]"Shelters and Streets Draw Throw-away Kids," *New York Times*, June 3, 1983.
[6]E. Erikson, *Childhood and Society* (New York: Norton, 1950).
[7]J. Piaget, *The Psychology of Intelligence* (London: Routledge & Kegan Paul, 1950).

have that. Rather, what is lacking is *pressure-free* time, time that is free of the burdens designated properly for adults. Even at their leisure teen-agers carry with them the adult expectation that they will behave as if they were already fully grown and mature. It is because young people today carry with them, and are often preoccupied by, adult issues that they do not have the time to deal with properly teenage concerns, namely, the construction of a personal definition of self.

It is not only time that is missing. Teenagers also need a clearly defined value system against which to test other values and discover their own. But when the important adults in their lives don't know what their own values are and are not sure what is right and what is wrong, what is good and what is bad, the teenagers' task is even more difficult and more time-consuming. The process of constructing an identity is adversely affected because neither the proper time nor the proper ingredients are available. Let us consider how the very process of identity formation is affected by the teenager's being "unplaced" in the society.

SOCIAL CHANGE AND PARENTING

In the last thirty years our society has undergone more change, at a faster rate, than during any other period. We are now moving rapidly from an industrial to a postindustrial or information society:

> Twenty-five years ago, the nation's work force was about equally di-vided between white-collar and blue-collar jobs, between goods and service industries. There are now more people employed full time in our colleges and universities than are employed in agriculture. In 1981, white-collar jobs outnumbered blue-collar jobs by three to two. And the number of people employed by U.S. Steel is smaller than the number of employees at McDonald's.[8]

The nature of the work force has changed as well. Over half of the twenty-five million women with children in the United States are work-ing outside the home, compared with 20 percent in 1950.

Although the changes relating to work are significant, even greater 20 changes have come about in our values and social philosophy. Daniel Yankelovich has likened this shift to the major changes in the earth's crust as a result of shifts of the tectonic plates deep in the earth's interior. Yankelovich argues that we are rapidly moving away from the "social role" orientation that once dominated American society.[9] He describes the old "social role" (give-and-take) philosophy this way:

[8]E. L. Boyer, *Highschool* (New York: Harper & Row, 1983), p. 4.
[9]D. Yankelovich, *New Rules* (New York: Bantam, 1981).

I give hard work, loyalty and steadfastness, I swallow my frustrations and suppress my impulse to do what I would enjoy, and do what is expected of me instead. I do not put myself first; I put the needs of others ahead of my own. I give a lot, but what I get in return is worth it. I receive an ever growing standard of living, and a family life with a devoted spouse and decent kids. Our children will take care of us in our old age if we really need it, which thank goodness we will not. I have a nice home, a good job, the respect of my friends and neighbors, a sense of accomplishment at having made something of my life. Last but not least, as an American I am proud to be a citizen of the finest country in the world.[10]

That is the philosophy most of today's parents grew up with, and it is the one most adults today recognize as familiar and generally their own. But over the last twenty years a new philosophy has emerged to vie with the older social role orientation. This new philosophy has been variously called the "culture of narcissism" or the "me generation" or more kindly by Yankelovich as a "search for self-fulfillment." According to numerous surveys by Yankelovich and others, this new philosophy now fully pervades our society:

> By the late seventies . . . seven out of ten Americans (72 percent) [were] spending a great deal of time thinking about themselves and their inner lives, this in a nation once notorious for its impatience with inwardness. The rage for self-fulfillment . . . has now spread to virtually the entire U.S. population.[11]

The changes we are undergoing today in American society have been described in somewhat different terms by John Naisbitt in his book *Megatrends*.[12] He argues that the "basic building block of the society is shifting from the family to the individual" and that we are changing from a "fixed option" to a "multiple option" society. Choices in the basic areas of family and work have exploded into a multitude of highly individual arrangements and life-styles. And the basic idea of a multiple option society has spilled over into other important areas of our lives: religion, the arts, music, food, entertainment, and, finally, the extent to which cultural, ethnic, and racial diversity are now celebrated in the United States. Both Yankelovich and Naisbitt suggest that there are many pluses and minuses to the new self-fulfillment philosophy, just as there were for the social role orientation. Moreover, it may be, as Naisbitt suggests, that an individual-oriented social philosophy is better suited than a role-oriented social philosophy to the requirements of an information society.

[10]Ibid., p. 7.
[11]Ibid., p. 3.
[12]J. Naisbitt, *Megatrends* (New York: Warner, 1982).

However that may be, the important point here is not that one philosophy is good and the other is bad, but rather that we as adults and parents are caught in the crossfire of these two social philosophies. Sexual values are a case in point. As parents and adults, we have the values we learned as children; as members of a modern society, we recognize that values have changed and a new set of values is followed. The conflict arises when we as adults must confront the new values rather than merely tolerate them. Recently a father admitted to me that his daughter is living with a man. The father grew up when I did, and at that time a young woman who lived with a man would most probably be disowned by her family. But such behavior is the norm today, and though the father may feel deeply that what his daughter is doing is wrong, the contemporary value system supports it. After all, isn't everyone else doing it? This father must now cope with two conflicting value systems—his own and his daughter's.

Parents who, like this father, would like to protect and shield their offspring feel overwhelmed by the pressure to accept the new social code. If they openly challenge the new values, they are sure to be labeled, and dismissed, as old-fashioned and stuffy. Ellen Goodman put the dilemma of the committed parent in a time of changing values this way:

> I belong to a whole generation of people who grew up under traditional rules about sex. We heard all about the rights and wrongs, shoulds and shouldn'ts, do's and don'ts. As adults we have lived through a time when all these rules were questioned, when people were set "free" to discover their own sexuality and their own definition of morality. Whether we observed this change from the outside or were part of it, we were nevertheless affected by it. Now, with all of our ambivalence and confusion, we are the new generation of parents raising the next generation of adults. Our agenda is a complicated one, because we do not want to be the new guardians of sexual repression. Nor are we willing to define sexual freedom as the children's right to do it. We are equally uncomfortable with notions that sex is evil and sex is groovy.[13]

In times of rapid social change, even committed parents are confused about what limits to set and what values to advocate and to enforce. For us adults this is a time to give serious thought to our values and principles, just as it is a time to struggle for greater tolerance. Ironically, our responses may only make matters worse for teenagers. Caught between two value systems, parents become ambivalent, and teenagers perceive their ambivalence as license. Failing to act, we force our teenagers to do so, before they are ready. Because we are reluctant

[13]E. Goodman, "The Turmoil of Teenage Sexuality," *Ms.*, July 1983, pp. 37–41.

to take a firm stand, we deny teenagers the benefit of our parental concern and we impel them into premature adulthood. We say, honestly, "I don't know," but teenagers hear, "They don't care."

Parents who are themselves awash in the tide of social change and are looking for self-fulfillment may have a different reaction to the teenager. A parent going through a "midlife" crisis may be too self-absorbed with his or her own voyage of personal discovery to appreciate fully and support the needs of a teenage son or daughter. Similarly, parents who are undergoing a divorce (as more than one million couples a year do) may be too caught up in the turbulence of their own lives to be of much help to a teenager with his or her own kind of life change. Other parents, who may be learning new job skills such as those involved in using computers, may look upon teenagers as having the advantage. Such parents may feel that the teenager has more knowledge and technological sophistication than they have and therefore that teenagers have it made. It may be hard for these parents to see the teenager's need for a special time and for support and guidance.

Still other parents and adults find the pace of social change too much to take and are overwhelmed by it. While their mates may have found the new social philosophy liberating and challenging, they find it frightening and isolating. If divorce comes, they feel adrift and alone, lost in a world they did not bargain for and do not want to participate in. It is a great temptation for these parents to reverse roles and look to their teenagers for support and guidance. Here again, the impact of social change is to deny the teenager the time and freedom to be a teenager in order to prepare for adulthood; the teenager is rushed from childhood to adulthood in order to meet the needs of a troubled parent.

Rapid social change, particularly from one social philosophy to another, inevitably affects parental attitudes toward teenagers. Although different parents are affected in different ways, the end result is always the same. For one reason or another, in one way or another, teenagers are denied the protection, guidance, and instruction they desperately need in order to mature. As we shall see in later chapters, it is not only parents but society as a whole that is unplacing teenagers. Perhaps this is why Hermann Hesse in *Steppenwolf* described the plight of youth caught between social philosophies in this way:

> Every age, every culture, every custom and tradition has its own character, its own weaknesses and its own strength, its beauties and ugliness; accepts certain sufferings as matters of course, puts up patiently with certain evils. Human life is reduced to real suffering, to real hell only when two ages, two cultures and religions overlap. . . . Now there are times when a whole generation is caught in this way between two ages, two modes of life with the consequence that it loses all power to

understand itself, and has no standard, no security, no simple acquiescence.[14]

If we put Hesse's last sentence in contemporary terms, we would say
that youths caught between two cultures have a weak sense of identity
(no standard, no security) and self-definition and are thus more vulnerable to stress. Clearly our situation today is not unique; there have been
comparable periods in history. But that does not make our present
situation any more tolerable. Today's teenager must struggle to achieve
a sense of self, a sense of personal identity, if she or he is going to go on
to build a full life as a mature and complete adult. But by bestowing a
premature mantle of adulthood upon teenagers, we as parents and
adults impair the formation of their sense of identity and render them
more vulnerable to stress. We thus endanger their future and society's as
well.

TWO WAYS OF GROWING

When we talk about a "mature" person, we are talking in part about
the healthy sense of identity and of self developed during the teen years.
This sense of personal identity is constructed by one of two methods,
either by differentiation (the process of discriminating or separating
out) and higher-order integration (or simply integration) or by substitution. The kind of parenting a teenager receives and the social climate in
which he or she grows up are critical in determining which of these two
paths of development a young person will follow, and what sort of self-
definition he or she will attain.

Growth by *integration* is conflictual, time-consuming, and laborious.
A child who is acquiring the concept of squareness, for example, must
encounter a variety of different shapes before he or she can separate
squareness from roundness or pointedness. In addition, the child must
see many different square things such as boxes, dice, sugar cubes, and
alphabet blocks before he or she can arrive at a higher-order notion of
squareness that will allow him or her to differentiate a square from all
other shapes and to integrate all square things, regardless of size, color,
or any other features, into the same concept.

The principles of differentiation and integration operate in the 32
social realm as well. To acquire a consistent sense of self, we must
encounter a great number of different experiences within which we can
discover how our feelings, thoughts, and beliefs are different from
those of other people. At the same time, we also need to learn how
much we are like other people. We need to discover that other people

[14]H. Hesse, *Steppenwolf* (New York: Rinehart, 1963), p. 24.

don't like insults any more than we do and that other people appreciate compliments just as we do. As a result of this slow process of differentiating ourselves from others, in terms of how we are alike and yet different from them, we gradually arrive at a stable and unique perception of our self.

Once growth by integration has occurred, it is difficult if not impossible to break down. After a child has acquired the concept of squareness, for example, he or she will not lose it; the concept becomes a permanent part of the self and a consistent way of seeing reality. The same is true in the social realm. People who have a strong sense of self do not lose it even under the most trying circumstances. Survivors of concentration camps and of brainwashing had such strong concepts of self that even extreme stress, exposure, starvation, torture, did not break them.

Mental structures achieved by differentiation and integration also conserve energy and reduce stress. Once we know what a square is we can identify it immediately; we don't have to go through a laborious process of differentiation and integration in order to recognize it again. In the same way, once we have an integrated sense of self, we know what to do in different situations. A well-defined sense of self and identity provides us with effective strategies for managing psychological stress— the major stress in our society. . . .

The second way in which growth occurs is by *substitution*. Consider the transition we have all made from making a phone call by turning a wheel several times to getting the same number by pushing buttons. Learning to dial a number by turning a wheel is not a preparation for getting that number by pushing buttons. Both actions have the same result, but the first skill is neither required to learn the second nor incorporated within it. Both exist independently and side by side. Either skill can be drawn upon if needed. This type of learning is clearly of value, particularly in a society with a rapidly changing technology. In adapting to new technology, it is an advantage to be able to replace old habits quickly with new ones.

The same principles, again, can be followed in social growth. In- 36 deed, substitution is the kind of growth suggested by the well-known adage "When in Rome do as the Romans do." In some social situations, particularly those in which we don't know the rules, it is generally considered wise to adapt and to follow the example of others who are familiar with the situation. But such learning is not adaptive when it comes to constructing a sense of personal identity. A sense of self constructed by the simple addition of feelings, thoughts, and beliefs copied from others amounts to a *patchwork* self. A person who has constructed a self in this way is not in touch with the deeper core of his or her being. Young people who have a self constructed by substitution are easily swayed and influenced by others because they do not have a clear definition of their own self. In addition, they are more vulnerable to stress than teenagers with an integrated sense of self because each new situation is a new challenge. Teenagers with a patchwork self have not developed an inner core of consistency and stability that allows them to deal with new situations in terms of past experiences.

These two different kinds of growth account for the two quite different types of teenagers we see. Teenagers who have acquired an integrated sense of identity are able to postpone immediate gratification in order to attain long-range goals. They are future-oriented and inner-directed. In contrast, teenagers who have grown by substitution and have only a patchwork self are less able to postpone immediate gratification. They are present-oriented and other-directed, easily influenced by others. By encouraging teenagers to choose growth by substitution and the development of a patchwork self, contemporary society has rendered teenagers more vulnerable to stress and denied them the full development of their personality and character.   *1984*

Joyce Carol Oates

Shopping

An old ritual, Saturday morning shopping. Mother and daughter. Mrs. Dietrich and Nola. Shops in the village, stores and boutiques at the splendid Livingstone Mall on Route 12. Bloomingdale's, Saks, Lord & Taylor, Bonwit's, Neiman-Marcus: and the rest. Mrs. Dietrich would know her way around the stores blindfolded but there is always the surprise of lavish seasonal displays, extraordinary holiday sales, the openings of new stores at the Mall like Laura Ashley, Paraphernalia. On one of their Mall days Mrs. Dietrich and Nola would try to get there at midmorning, have lunch around 1 P.M. at one or another of their favorite restaurants, shop for perhaps an hour after lunch, then come home. Sometimes the shopping trips were more successful than at other times but you have to have faith, Mrs. Dietrich tells herself. Her interior voice is calm, neutral, free of irony. Ever since her divorce her interior voice has been free of irony. You have to have faith.

Tomorrow morning Nola returns to school in Maine; today will be a day at the Mall. Mrs. Dietrich has planned it for days. At the Mall, in such crowds of shoppers, moments of intimacy are possible as they rarely are at home. (Seventeen-year-old Nola, home on spring break for a brief eight days, seems always to be *busy*, always out with her *friends*— the trip to the Mall has been postponed twice.) But Saturday, 10:30 A.M., they are in the car at last headed south on Route 12, a bleak March morning following a night of freezing rain, there's a metallic cast to the air and no sun anywhere in the sky but the light hurts Mrs. Dietrich's eyes just the same. "Does it seem as if spring will ever come?—it must be twenty degrees colder up in Maine," she says. Driving in heavy traffic always makes Mrs. Dietrich nervous and she is overly sensitive to her daughter's silence, which seems deliberate, perverse, when they have so little time remaining together—not even a full day.

Nola asks politely if Mrs. Dietrich would like her to drive and Mrs. Dietrich says no, of course not, she's fine, it's only a few more miles and maybe traffic will lighten. Nola seems about to say something more, then thinks better of it. So much between them that is precarious, chancy—but they've been kind to each other these past seven days. Mrs. Dietrich loves Nola with a fierce unreasoned passion stronger than any she felt for the man who had been her husband for thirteen years, certainly far stronger than any she ever felt for her own mother. Sometimes in weak despondent moods, alone, lonely, self-pitying, when she has had too much to drink, Mrs. Dietrich thinks she is in love with her daughter—but this is a thought she can't contemplate for long. And how Nola would snort in amused contempt, incredulous, mocking—"Oh *Mother!*"—if she were told.

Mrs. Dietrich tries to engage her daughter in conversation of a   4 harmless sort but Nola answers in monosyllables, Nola is rather tired from so many nights of partying with her friends, some of whom attend the local high school, some of whom are home for spring break from prep schools—Exeter, Lawrenceville, Concord, Andover, Portland. Late nights, but Mrs. Dietrich doesn't consciously lie awake waiting for Nola to come home: they've been through all that before. Now Nola sits beside her mother looking wan, subdued, rather melancholy. Thinking her private thoughts. She is wearing a bulky quilted jacket Mrs. Dietrich has never liked, the usual blue jeans, black calfskin boots zippered tightly to midcalf. Mrs. Dietrich must resist the temptation to ask, "Why are you so quiet, Nola? What are you thinking?" They've been through all that before.

Route 12 has become a jumble of small industrial parks, high-rise office and apartment buildings, torn-up landscapes—mountains of raw earth, uprooted trees, ruts and ditches filled with muddy water. There is no natural sequence to what you see—buildings, construction work, leveled woods, the lavish grounds owned by Squibb. Though she has driven this route countless times, Mrs. Dietrich is never quite certain

where the Mall is and must be prepared for a sudden exit. She remembers getting lost the first several times, remembers the excitement she
and her friends felt about the grand opening of the Mall, stores worthy
of serious shopping at last. Today is much the same. No, today is worse.
Like Christmas when she was a small child, Mrs. Dietrich thinks. She'd
hoped so badly to be happy she'd felt actual pain, a constriction in her
throat like crying.

"*Are* you all right, Nola?—you've been so quiet all morning," Mrs.
Dietrich asks, half-scolding. Nola stirs from her reverie, says she's fine, a
just perceptible edge to her reply, and for the remainder of the drive
there's some stiffness between them. Mrs. Dietrich chooses to ignore it.
In any case she is fully absorbed in driving—negotiating a tricky exit
across two lanes of traffic, then the hairpin curve of the ramp, the
numerous looping drives of the Mall. Then the enormous parking lot,
daunting to the inexperienced, but Mrs. Dietrich always heads for the
area behind Lord & Taylor on the far side of the Mall, Lot D; her luck
holds and she finds a space close in. "Well—we made it," she says,
smiling happily at Nola. Nola laughs in reply—what does a seventeen-
year-old's laughter *mean?*—but she remembers, getting out, to lock both
doors on her side of the car. The smile Nola gives Mrs. Dietrich across
the car's roof is careless and beautiful and takes Mrs. Dietrich's breath
away.

The March morning tastes of grit with an undercurrent of something acrid, chemical; inside the Mall, beneath the first of the elegant
brass-buttressed glass domes, the air is fresh and tonic, circulating from
invisible vents. The Mall is crowded, rather noisy—it *is* Saturday
morning—but a feast for the eyes after that long trip on Route 12. Tall
slender trees grow out of the mosaic-tiled pavement, there are beds of
Easter lilies, daffodils, jonquils, tulips of all colors. Mrs. Dietrich smiles
with relief. She senses that Nola too is relieved, cheered. It's like coming
home.

The shopping excursions began when Nola was a small child but 8
did not acquire their special significance until she was twelve or thirteen years old and capable of serious, sustained shopping with her
mother. This was about the time when Mr. Dietrich moved out of the
house and back into their old apartment in the city—a separation, he'd
called it initially, to give them perspective—though Mrs. Dietrich had
no illusions about what "perspective" would turn out to entail—so the
shopping trips were all the more significant. Not that Mrs. Dietrich and
Nola spent very much money—they really didn't, *really* they didn't, when
compared to friends and neighbors.

At seventeen Nola is shrewd and discerning as a shopper, not easy
to please, knowledgeable as a mature woman about certain aspects of

fashion, quality merchandise, good stores. Her closets, like Mrs. Dietrich's, are crammed, but she rarely buys anything that Mrs. Dietrich
thinks shoddy or merely faddish. Up in Portland, at the Academy, she
hasn't as much time to shop but when she is home in Livingstone it isn't
unusual for her and her girlfriends to shop nearly every day. Like all
her friends she has charge accounts at the better stores, her own credit
cards, a reasonable allowance. At the time of their settlement Mr.
Dietrich said guiltily that it was the least he could do for them—if Mrs.
Dietrich wanted to work part-time, she could (she was trained, more or
less, in public relations of a small-scale sort); if not, not. Mrs. Dietrich
thought, It's the most you can do for us too.

Near Bloomingdale's entrance mother and daughter see a disheveled woman sitting by herself on one of the benches. Without seeming
to look at her, shoppers are making a discreet berth around her, a
stream following a natural course. Nola, taken by surprise, stares. Mrs.
Dietrich has seen the woman from time to time at the Mall, always
alone, smirking and talking to herself, frizzed gray hair in a tangle,
puckered mouth. Always wearing the same black wool coat, a garment of
fairly good quality but shapeless, rumpled, stained, as if she sleeps in it.
She might be anywhere from forty to sixty years of age. Once Mrs.
Dietrich saw her make menacing gestures at children who were teasing
her, another time she'd seen the woman staring belligerently at *her*. A
white paste had gathered in the corners of her mouth. . . . "My God, that
poor woman," Nola says. "I didn't think there were people like her
here—I mean, I didn't think they would allow it."

"She doesn't seem to cause any disturbance," Mrs. Dietrich says.
"She just sits—Don't stare, Nola, she'll see you."

"You've seen her here before? Here?"   12

"A few times this winter."

"Is she always like that?"

"I'm sure she's harmless, Nola. She just *sits*."

Nola is incensed, her pale blue eyes like washed glass. "I'm sure *she's* 16
harmless, Mother. It's the harm the poor woman has to endure that is
the tragedy."

Mrs. Dietrich is surprised and a little offended by her daughter's
passionate tone but she knows enough not to argue. They enter Bloomingdale's, taking their habitual route. So many shoppers!—so much
merchandise! Nola speaks of the tragedy of women like that woman—
the tragedy of the homeless, the mentally disturbed—bag ladies out on
the street—outcasts of an affluent society—but she's soon distracted by
the busyness on all sides, the attractive items for sale. They take the
escalator up to the third floor, to the Juniors department where Nola
often buys things. From there they will move on to Young Collector,
then to New Impressions, then to Petites, then one or another boutique
and designer—Liz Claiborne, Christian Dior, Calvin Klein, Carlos

Falchi, and the rest. And after Bloomingdale's the other stores await, to
be visited each in turn. Mrs. Dietrich checks her watch and sees with
satisfaction that there's just enough time before lunch but not *too* much
time. She gets ravenously hungry, shopping at the Mall.

Nola is efficient and matter-of-fact about shopping, though she acts
solely upon instinct. Mrs. Dietrich likes to watch her at a short
distance—holding items of clothing up to herself in the three-way
mirrors, modeling things she thinks especially promising. A twill blazer
with rounded shoulders and blouson jacket, a funky zippered jumpsuit
in white sailcloth, a pair of straight-leg Evan-Picone pants, a green
leather vest: Mrs. Dietrich watches her covertly. At such times Nola is
perfectly content, fully absorbed in the task at hand; Mrs. Dietrich
knows she isn't thinking about anything that would distress her. (Like
Mr. Dietrich's betrayal. Like Nola's difficulties with her friends. Like her
difficulties at school—as much as Mrs. Dietrich knows of them.) Once,
at the Mall, perhaps in this very store in this very department, Nola saw
Mrs. Dietrich watching her and walked away angrily and when Mrs.
Dietrich caught up with her she said, "I can't stand it, Mother." Her
voice was choked and harsh, a vein prominent in her forehead. "Let me
go. For Christ's sake will you let me go." Mrs. Dietrich didn't dare touch
her though she could see Nola was trembling. For a long terrible moment mother and daughter stood side by side near a display of bright
brash Catalina beachwear while Nola whispered, "Let me go. *Let me go.*"

Difficult to believe that girl standing so poised and self-assured in
front of the three-way mirror was once a plain, rather chunky, unhappy
child. She'd been unpopular at school. Overly serious. Anxious. Quick
to tears. Aged eleven she hid herself away in her room for hours at a
time, reading, drawing pictures, writing little stories she could sometimes be prevailed upon to read aloud to her mother, sometimes even
to her father, though she dreaded his judgment. She went through a
"scientific" phase a while later—Mrs. Dietrich remembers an ambitious
bas-relief map of North America, meticulous illustrations for "photosynthesis," a pastel drawing of an eerie ball of fire labeled "Red Giant"
(a dying star?) which won a prize in a state competition for junior high
students. Then for a season it was stray facts Nola confronted them with,
often at the dinner table. Interrupting her parents' conversation to say
brightly: "Did you know that Nero's favorite color was green?—he
carried a giant emerald and held it up to his eye to watch Christians
being devoured by lions." And once at a large family gathering: "Did
you know that last week downtown a little baby's nose was chewed off by
rats in his crib?—a little *black* baby?" Nola meant only to call attention
to herself but you couldn't blame her listeners for being offended. They
stared at her, not knowing what to say. What a strange child! What queer

glassy-pale eyes! Mr. Dietrich told her curtly to leave the table—he'd had enough of the game she was playing and so had everyone else.

Nola stared at him, her eyes filling with tears. Game?   20

When they were alone Mr. Dietrich said angrily to Mrs. Dietrich: "Can't you control her in front of other people at least?" Mrs. Dietrich was angry too, and frightened. She said "I *try*."

They sent her off aged fourteen to the Portland Academy up in Maine and without their help she matured into a girl of considerable beauty. A heart-shaped face, delicate features, glossy red-brown hair scissor-cut to her shoulders. Five feet seven inches tall, weighing less than one hundred pounds—the result of constant savage dieting. (Mrs. Dietrich, who has weight problems herself, doesn't dare to inquire as to details. They've been through that already.) Thirty days after they'd left her at the Portland Academy Nola telephoned home at 11:00 P.M. one Sunday giggly and high telling Mrs. Dietrich she adored the school she adored her suite mates she adored most of her teachers particularly her riding instructor Terri, Terri the Terrier they called the woman because she was so fierce, such a character, eyes that bore right through your skull, wore belts with the most amazing silver buckles! Nola loved Terri but she wasn't *in* love—there's a difference!

Mrs. Dietrich broke down weeping, *that* time.

Now of course Nola has boyfriends. Mrs. Dietrich has long since 24 given up trying to keep track of their names. There is even one "boy"— or young man—who seems to be married: who seems to be, in fact, one of the junior instructors at the school. (Mrs. Dietrich does not eavesdrop on her daughter's telephone conversations but there are things she cannot help overhearing.) Is your daughter on the Pill? the women in Mrs. Dietrich's circle asked one another for a while, guiltily, surreptitiously. Now they no longer ask.

But Nola has announced recently that she loathes boys—she's fed up.

She's never going to get married. She'll study languages in college, French, Italian, something exotic like Arabic, go to work for the American foreign service. Unless she drops out of school altogether to become a model.

"Do you think I'm fat, Mother?" she asks frequently, worriedly, standing in front of the mirror twisted at the waist to reveal her small round belly which, it seems, can't help being round: she bloats herself on diet Cokes all day long. "Do you think it *shows*?"

When Mrs. Dietrich was pregnant with Nola she'd been twenty-nine 28 years old and she and Mr. Dietrich had tried to have a baby for nearly five years. She'd lost hope, begun to despise herself, then suddenly it happened: like grace. Like happiness swelling so powerfully it can barely be contained. I can hear its heartbeat! her husband exclaimed.

He'd been her lover then, young, vigorous, dreamy. Caressing the rock-hard belly, splendid white tight-stretched skin. Mr. Dietrich gave Mrs. Dietrich a reproduction on stiff glossy paper of Dante Gabriel Rossetti's *Beata Beatrix*, embarrassed, apologetic, knowing it was sentimental and perhaps a little silly but that was how he thought of her—so beautiful, rapturous, pregnant with their child. She told no one but she knew the baby was to be a girl. It would be herself again, reborn and this time perfect.

"Oh, Mother—isn't it *beautiful?*" Nola exclaims.

It is past noon. Past twelve-thirty. Mrs. Dietrich and Nola have made the rounds of a half-dozen stores, traveled countless escalators, one clothing department has blended into the next and the chic smiling saleswomen have become indistinguishable and Mrs. Dietrich is beginning to feel the urgent need for a glass of white wine. Just a glass. "Isn't it beautiful?—it's *perfect*," Nola says. Her eyes glow with pleasure, her smooth skin is radiant. As Nola models in the three-way mirror a queer little yellow-and-black striped sweater with a ribbed waist, punk style, mock-cheap, Mrs. Dietrich feels the motherly obligation to register a mild protest, knowing that Nola will not hear. She must have it and will have it. She'll wear it a few times, then retire it to the bottom of a drawer with so many other novelty sweaters, accumulated since sixth grade. (She's like her mother in that regard—can't bear to throw anything away.)

"*Isn't* it beautiful?" Nola demands, studying her reflection in the mirror.

Mrs. Dietrich pays for the sweater on her charge account.   32

Next, they buy Nola a good pair of shoes. And a handbag to go with them. In Paraphernalia, where rock music blasts overhead and Mrs. Dietrich stands to one side, rather miserable, Nola chats companionably with two girls—tall, pretty, cutely made up—she'd gone to public school in Livingstone with, says afterward with an upward rolling of her eyes, "God, I was afraid they'd latch on to us!" Mrs. Dietrich has seen women friends and acquaintances of her own in the Mall this morning but has shrunk from being noticed, not wanting to share her daughter with anyone. She has a sense of time passing ever more swiftly, cruelly.

She watches Nola preening in a mirror, watches other shoppers watching her. My daughter. Mine. But of course there is no connection between them—they don't even resemble each other. A seventeen-year-old, a forty-seven-year-old. When Nola is away she seems to forget her mother entirely—doesn't telephone, certainly doesn't write. It's the way all their daughters are, Mrs. Dietrich's friends tell her. It doesn't *mean* anything. Mrs. Dietrich thinks how when she was carrying Nola, those nine long months, they'd been completely happy—not an instant's doubt or hesitation. The singular weight of the body. A trancelike state you are tempted to mistake for happiness because the body is incapable of thinking, therefore incapable of anticipating change. Hot rhythmic blood, organs, packed tight and moist, the baby upside down in her sac in her mother's belly, always present tense, always *now*. It was a shock when the end came so abruptly but everyone told Mrs. Dietrich she was a natural mother, praised and pampered her. For a while. Then of course she'd had her baby, her Nola. Even now Mrs. Dietrich can't really comprehend the experience. *Giving birth. Had a baby. Was born.* Mere words, absurdly inadequate. She knows no more of how love ends than she knew as a child, she knows only of how love begins—in the belly, in the womb, where it is always present tense.

The morning's shopping has been quite successful but lunch at La Crêperie doesn't go well for some reason. La Crêperie is Nola's favorite Mall restaurant—always amiably crowded, bustling, a simulated side-walk café with red-striped umbrellas, wrought-iron tables and chairs, menus in French, music piped in overhead. Mrs. Dietrich's nerves are chafed by the pretense of gaiety, the noise, the openness onto one of the Mall's busy promenades where at any minute a familiar face might emerge, but she is grateful for her glass of chilled white wine. She orders a small tossed salad and a creamed-chicken crepe and devours it hungrily—she *is* hungry. While Nola picks at her seafood crepe with a disdainful look. A familiar scene: mother watching while daughter pushes food around on her plate. Suddenly Nola is tense, moody, corners of her mouth downturned. Mrs. Dietrich wants to ask, What's wrong? She wants to ask, Why are you unhappy? She wants to smooth Nola's hair back from her forehead, check to see if her forehead is overly warm, wants to hug her close, hard. Why, why? What did I do wrong? Why do you hate me?

Calling the Portland Academy a few weeks ago Mrs. Dietrich sud-   36
denly lost control, began crying. She hadn't been drinking and she hadn't known she was upset. A girl unknown to her, one of Nola's suite mates, was saying "Please, Mrs. Dietrich, it's all right, I'm sure Nola will call you back later tonight, or tomorrow, Mrs. Dietrich?—I'll tell her you called, all right?—Mrs. Dietrich?" as embarrassed as if Mrs. Dietrich had been her own mother.

How love begins. How love ends.

Mrs. Dietrich orders a third glass of wine. This is a celebration of sorts isn't it?—their last shopping trip for a long time. But Nola resists, Nola isn't sentimental. In casual defiance of Mrs. Dietrich she lights up a cigarette—yes, Mother, Nola has said ironically, since *you* stopped smoking *everybody* is supposed to stop—and sits with her arms crossed, watching streams of shoppers pass. Mrs. Dietrich speaks lightly of

practical matters, tomorrow morning's drive to the airport, and will
Nola telephone when she gets to Portland to let Mrs. Dietrich know she
has arrived safely?

Then with no warning—though of course she'd been planning this
all along—Nola brings up the subject of a semester in France, in Paris
and Rouen, the fall semester of her senior year it would be; she has put
in her application, she says, and is waiting to hear if she's been accepted. She smokes her cigarette calmly, expelling smoke from her
nostrils in a way Mrs. Dietrich thinks particularly coarse. Mrs. Dietrich,
who believed that particular topic was finished, takes care to speak
without emotion. "I just don't think it's a very practical idea right now,
Nola" she says. "We've been through it haven't we? I—"

"I'm going," Nola says.   40

"The extra expense, for one thing. Your father—"

"If I get accepted, I'm going."

"Your father—"

"The hell with him too."   44

Mrs. Dietrich would like to slap her daughter's face. Bring tears to
those steely eyes. But she sits stiff, turning her wine glass between her
fingers, patient, calm, she's heard all this before; she says, "Surely this
isn't the best time to discuss it, Nola."

Mrs. Dietrich is afraid her daughter will leave the restaurant, simply
walk away, that has happened before and if it happens today she doesn't
know what she will do. But Nola sits unmoving; her face closed, impas-
sive. Mrs. Dietrich feels her quickened heartbeat. Once after one of
their quarrels Mrs. Dietrich told a friend of hers, the mother too of a
teenage daughter, "I just don't know her any longer, how can you keep
living with someone you don't know?" and the woman said, "Eventually
you can't."

Nola says, not looking at Mrs. Dietrich: "Why don't we talk about it,
Mother?"

"Talk about what?" Mrs. Dietrich asks.   48

"You know."

"The semester in France? Again?"

"No."

"What, then?   52

"You *know*."

"I don't know, really. Really!" Mrs. Dietrich smiles, baffled. She feels
the corners of her eyes pucker white with strain.

Nola says, sighing, "How exhausting it is."

"How *what*?"   56

"How exhausting it is."

"What is?"

"You and me—"

"What?" 60
"Being together—"
"Being together how—?"
"The two of us, like this—"
"But we're hardly ever together, Nola," Mrs. Dietrich says. 64

Her expression is calm but her voice is shaking. Nola turns away, covering her face with a hand, for a moment she looks years older than her age—in fact exhausted. Mrs. Dietrich sees with pity that her daughter's skin is fair and thin and dry—unlike her own, which tends to be oily—it will wear out before she's forty. Mrs. Dietrich reaches over to squeeze her hand. The fingers are limp, ungiving. "You're going back to school tomorrow, Nola," she says. "You won't come home again until June 12. And you probably will go to France—if your father consents."

Nola gets to her feet, drops her cigarette to the flagstone terrace and grinds it beneath her boot. A dirty thing to do, Mrs. Dietrich thinks, considering there's an ashtray right on the table, but she says nothing. She dislikes La Crêperie anyway.

Nola laughs, showing her lovely white teeth. "Oh, the hell with him," she says. "Fuck Daddy, right?"

They separate for an hour, Mrs. Dietrich to Neiman-Marcus to buy a 68 birthday gift for her elderly aunt, Nola to the trendy new boutique Pour Vous. By the time Mrs. Dietrich rejoins her daughter she's quite angry, blood beating hot and hard and measured in resentment, she has had time to relive old quarrels between them, old exchanges, stray humiliating memories of her marriage as well, these last-hour disagreements are the cruelest and they are Nola's specialty. She locates Nola in the rear of the boutique amid blaring rock music, flashing neon lights, chrome-edged mirrors, her face still hard, closed, prim, pale. She stands beside another teenage girl looking in a desultory way through a rack of blouses, shoving the hangers roughly along, taking no care when a blouse falls to the floor. As Nola glances up, startled, not prepared to see her mother in front of her, their eyes lock for an instant and Mrs. Dietrich stares at her with hatred. Cold calm clear unmistakable hatred. She is thinking, Who are *you*? What have I to do with *you*? I don't know *you*, I don't love *you*, why should I?

Has Nola seen, heard?—she turns aside as if wincing, gives the blouses a final dismissive shove. Her eyes look tired, the corners of her mouth downturned. Anxious, immediately repentant, Mrs. Dietrich asks if she has found anything worth trying on. Nola says with a shrug, "Not a thing, Mother."

On their way out of the Mall Mrs. Dietrich and Nola see the disheveled woman in the black coat again, this time sitting prominently on a

concrete ledge in front of Lord & Taylor's busy main entrance. Shopping bag at her feet, shabby purse on the ledge beside her. She is
shaking her head in a series of annoyed twitches as if arguing with
someone but her hands are loose, palms up, in her lap. Her posture is
unfortunate—she sits with her knees parted, inner thighs revealed,
fatty, dead white, the tops of cotton stockings rolled tight cutting into
the flesh. Again, streams of shoppers are making a careful berth around
her. Alone among them Nola hesitates, seems about to approach the
woman—Please don't, Nola! please! Mrs. Dietrich thinks—then changes
her mind and keeps on walking. Mrs. Dietrich murmurs isn't it a pity,
poor thing, don't you wonder where she lives, who her family is, but
Nola doesn't reply. Her pace through the first door of Lord & Taylor is
so rapid that Mrs. Dietrich can barely keep up.

But Nola's upset. Strangely upset. As soon as they are in the car,
packages and bags in the backseat, she begins crying.

It's childish helpless crying, as though her heart is broken. But Mrs. 72
Dietrich knows it isn't broken, she has heard these very sobs before.
Many times before. Still she comforts her daughter, embraces her, hugs
her hard, hard. A sudden fierce passion. Vehemence. "Nola honey, Nola
dear, what's wrong, dear, everything will be all right, dear," she says,
close to weeping herself. She would embrace Nola even more tightly
except for the girl's quilted jacket, that bulky L. L. Bean thing she has
never liked, and Nola's stubborn lowered head. Nola has always been
ashamed, crying, frantic to hide her face. Strangers are passing close by
the car, curious, staring. Mrs. Dietrich wishes she had a cloak to draw
over her daughter and herself, so that no one else would see.   *1987*

11

A National Obsession

Marie Winn, TV Addiction
Pete Hamill, Crack and the Box

The average household has its television sets on approximately seven hours a day. The average American child watches 5000 hours of television before he or she ever gets to school; about 16,000 hours by high school's end. The only activity that occupies more of an American youth's time than TV-viewing is sleeping. Americans who have reached the age of forty will have seen over one million television commercials, and can expect to see another million before their first retirement check arrives.

Television in America, it would appear, is the *soma* of Huxley's *Brave New World*. But let me hasten to say that America's immersion in television is not to be taken as an attempt by a malevolent government or an avaricious corporate state to employ the age-old trick of distracting the masses with circuses. The problem is more serious than that, and far from being age-old. The problem is not that TV presents the masses with entertaining subject matter, but that television presents all subject matter as entertaining. What is dangerous about television is not its junk. Every culture can absorb a fair amount of junk, and, in any case, we do not judge a culture by its junk but by how it conducts its serious public business. What is happening in America is that television is transforming all serious public business into junk.

Neil Postman, from *Amusing Ourselves to Death*

There is a kind of young television watcher seeing old movies for the first time who is surprisingly sensitive to their values and responds almost with the intensity of a moviegoer. But he's different from the moviegoer. For one thing, he's housebound, inactive, solitary. Unlike a moviegoer, he seems to have no need to discuss what he sees. The kind of television watcher I mean (and the ones I've met are all boys) seems to have extreme empathy with the material in the box (new TV shows as well as old movies, though rarely news), but he may not know how to enter into a conversation, or even how to come into a room or go out of it. He fell in love with his baby-sitter, so he remains a baby. He's unusually polite and intelligent, but in a mechanical way—just going through the motions, without interest. He gives the impression that he wants to withdraw from this human interference and get back to real life—the box. He is like a prisoner who has everything he wants in prison and is content to stay there.

Pauline Kael, from *Movies to Television*

There are other points to consider in relationship to this narcotisizing aspect of the medium's power. In conjunction with TV's tendency to isolate and its potential for, in effect, drugging people not to care, there is also the real danger of much personal, internal conflict resulting from heavy exposure. Constantly shifting between what is and what is not; between shows, ideas, images, and channels literally is enough to push some people over the "deep end" or to make them nervous temperamentally. So much TV is based upon illusion and fantasy that it becomes very difficult at times to know what is truth and what is not. This is especially true of young children, who have not yet accumulated a vast catalogue of personal experiences against which to evaluate TV content.

Maurine Doerken, from *Classroom Combat: Teaching and Television*

Television watching became an addiction comparable only to life itself. If the set was not on, Americans began to feel that they had missed what was "really happening." And just as it was axiomatic that it was better to be alive than to be dead, so it became axiomatic that it was better to be watching *something* than to be watching nothing at all. When there was "nothing on TV tonight," there was a painful void. No wonder, then, that Americans revised their criteria for experience. Even if a firsthand experience was not worth having, putting it on TV might make it so.

Daniel J. Boorstin, from *The Americans*

Marie Winn

TV Addiction

The word "addiction" is often used loosely and wryly in conversation. People will refer to themselves as "mystery book addicts" or "cookie addicts." E. B. White writes of his annual surge of interest in gardening: "We are hooked and are making an attempt to kick the habit." Yet nobody really believes that reading mysteries or ordering seeds by catalogue is serious enough to be compared with addictions to heroin or alcohol. The word "addiction" is here used jokingly to denote a tendency to overindulge in some pleasurable activity.

People often refer to being "hooked on TV." Does this, too, fall into the lighthearted category of cookie eating and other pleasures that people pursue with unusual intensity, or is there a kind of television viewing that falls into the more serious category of destructive addiction?

When we think about addiction to drugs or alcohol, we frequently focus on negative aspects, ignoring the pleasures that accompany drinking or drug-taking. And yet the essence of any serious addiction is a pursuit of pleasure, a search for a "high" that normal life does not supply. It is only the inability to function without the addictive substance that is dismaying, the dependence of the organism upon a certain experience and an increasing inability to function normally without it. Thus a person will take two or three drinks at the end of the day not merely for the pleasure drinking provides, but also because he "doesn't feel normal" without them.

An addict does not merely pursue a pleasurable experience and   4
need to experience it in order to function normally. He needs to *repeat* it again and again. Something about that particular experience makes life without it less than complete. Other potentially pleasurable experiences are no longer possible, for under the spell of the addictive experience, his life is peculiarly distorted. The addict craves an experience and yet he is never really satisfied. The organism may be temporarily sated, but soon it begins to crave again.

Finally a serious addiction is distinguished from a harmless pursuit of pleasure by its distinctly destructive elements. A heroin addict, for instance, leads a damaged life: his increasing need for heroin in increasing doses prevents him from working, from maintaining relationships, from developing in human ways. Similarly an alcoholic's life is narrowed and dehumanized by his dependence on alcohol.

Let us consider television viewing in the light of the conditions that define serious addictions.

Not unlike drugs or alcohol, the television experience allows the participant to blot out the real world and enter into a pleasurable and passive mental state. The worries and anxieties of reality are as effectively deferred by becoming absorbed in a television program as by going on a "trip" induced by drugs or alcohol. And just as alcoholics are only inchoately aware of their addiction, feeling that they control their drinking more than they really do ("I can cut it out any time I want—I just like to have three or four drinks before dinner"), people similarly overestimate their control over television watching. Even as they put off other activities to spend hour after hour watching television, they feel they could easily resume living in a different, less passive style. But somehow or other while the television set is present in their homes, the click doesn't sound. With television pleasures available, those other experiences seem less attractive, more difficult somehow.

A heavy viewer (a college English instructor) observes: "I find   8
television almost irresistible. When the set is on, I cannot ignore it. I can't turn it off. I feel sapped, will-less, enervated. As I reach out to turn off the set, the strength goes out of my arms. So I sit there for hours and hours."

The self-confessed television addict often feels he "ought" to do other things—but the fact that he doesn't read and doesn't plant his garden or sew or crochet or play games or have conversations means that those activities are no longer as desirable as television viewing. In a way a heavy viewer's life is as imbalanced by his television "habit" as a drug addict's or an alcoholic's. He is living in a holding pattern, as it were, passing up the activities that lead to growth or development or a sense of accomplishment. This is one reason people talk about their television viewing so ruefully, so apologetically. They are aware that it is an unproductive experience, that almost any other endeavor is more worthwhile by any human measure.

Finally it is the adverse effect of television viewing on the lives of so many people that defines it as a serious addiction. The television habit distorts the sense of time. It renders other experiences vague and curiously unreal while taking on a greater reality for itself. It weakens relationships by reducing and sometimes eliminating normal opportunities for talking, for communicating.

And yet television does not satisfy, else why would the viewer continue to watch hour after hour, day after day? "The measure of health," writes Lawrence Kubie, "is flexibility . . . and especially the freedom to cease when sated." But the television viewer can never be sated with his television experiences—they do not provide the true nourishment that satiation requires—and thus he finds that he cannot stop watching.   *1977*

Pete Hamill

Crack and the Box

One sad rainy morning last winter, I talked to a woman who was addicted to crack cocaine. She was twenty-two, stiletto-thin, with eyes as old as tombs. She was living in two rooms in a welfare hotel with her children, who were two, three, and five years of age. Her story was the usual tangle of human woe: early pregnancy, dropping out of school, vanished men, smack and then crack, tricks with johns in parked cars to pay for the dope. I asked her why she did drugs. She shrugged in an empty way and couldn't really answer beyond "makes me feel good." While we talked and she told her tale of squalor, the children ignored us. They were watching television.

Walking back to my office in the rain, I brooded about the woman, her zombielike children, and my own callous indifference. I'd heard so many versions of the same story that I almost never wrote them any-more; the sons of similar women, glimpsed a dozen years ago, are now in Dannemora or Soledad or Joliet; in a hundred cities, their daughters are moving into the same loveless rooms. As I walked, a series of homeless men approached me for change, most of them junkies. Others sat in doorways, staring at nothing. They were additional casualties of our time of plague, demoralized reminders that although this country holds only 2 percent of the world's population, it consumes 65 percent of the world's supply of hard drugs.

Why, for God's sake? Why do so many millions of Americans of all ages, races, and classes choose to spend all or part of their lives stu-pefied? I've talked to hundreds of addicts over the years; some were my friends. But none could give sensible answers. They stutter about the pain of the world, about despair or boredom, the urgent need for magic or pleasure in a society empty of both. But then they just shrug. Americans have the money to buy drugs; the supply is plentiful. But almost nobody in power asks, *Why*? Least of all, George Bush and his drug warriors.

William Bennett talks vaguely about the heritage of sixties per-   4
missiveness, the collapse of Traditional Values, and all that. But he and Bush offer the traditional American excuse: It Is Somebody Else's Fault. This posture set the stage for the self-righteous invasion of Panama, the bloodiest drug arrest in world history. Bush even accused Manuel Nori-ega of "poisoning our children." But he never asked *why* so many Americans demand the poison.

And then, on that rainy morning in New York, I saw another one of those ragged men staring out at the rain from a doorway. I suddenly remembered the inert postures of the children in that welfare hotel, and I thought: *television.*

Ah, no, I muttered to myself: too simple. Something as complicated as drug addiction can't be blamed on television. Come on. . . . but I remembered all those desperate places I'd visited as a reporter, where there were no books and a TV set was always playing and the older kids had gone off somewhere to shoot smack, except for the kid who was at the mortuary in a coffin. I also remembered when I was a boy in the forties and early fifties, and drugs were a minor sideshow, a kind of dark little rumor. And there was one major difference between that time and this: television.

We had unemployment then; illiteracy, poor living conditions, racism, governmental stupidity, a gap between rich and poor. We didn't have the all-consuming presence of television in our lives. Now two generations of Americans have grown up with television from their earliest moments of consciousness. Those same American generations are afflicted by the pox of drug addiction.

Only thirty-five years ago, drug addiction was not a major problem   8 in this country. There were drug addicts. We had some at the end of the nineteenth century, hooked on the cocaine in patent medicines. During the placid fifties, Commissioner Harry Anslinger pumped up the budget of the old Bureau of Narcotics with fantasies of reefer madness. Heroin was sold and used in most major American cities, while the bebop generation of jazz musicians got jammed up with horse.

But until the early sixties, narcotics were still marginal to American life; they weren't the $120-billion market they make up today. If anything, those years have an eerie innocence. In 1955 there were 31,700,000 TV sets in use in the country (the number is now past 184 million). But the majority of the audience had grown up without the dazzling new medium. They embraced it, were diverted by it, perhaps even loved it, but they weren't *formed* by it. That year, the New York police made a mere 1,234 felony drug arrests; in 1988 it was 43,901. They confiscated ninety-seven *ounces* of cocaine for the entire year; last year it was hundreds of pounds. During each year of the fifties in New York, there were only about a hundred narcotics-related deaths. But by the end of the sixties, when the first generation of children *formed* by television had come to maturity (and thus to the marketplace), the number of such deaths had risen to 1,200. The same phenomenon was true in every major American city.

In the last Nielsen survey of American viewers, the average family was watching television seven hours a day. This has never happened before in history. No people has ever been entertained for seven hours a *day.* The Elizabethans didn't go to the theater seven hours a day. The pre-TV generation did not go to the movies seven hours a day. Common sense tells us that this all-pervasive diet of instant imagery, sustained now for forty years, must have changed us in profound ways.

Television, like drugs, dominates the lives of its addicts. And though some lonely Americans leave their sets on without watching them, using them as electronic companions, television usually absorbs its viewers the way drugs absorb their users. Viewers can't work or play while watching television; they can't read; they can't be out on the streets, falling in love with the wrong people, learning how to quarrel and compromise with other human beings. In short they are asocial. So are drug addicts.

One Michigan State University study in the early eighties offered a 12 group of four- and five-year-olds the choice of giving up television or giving up their fathers. Fully one third said they would give up Daddy. Given a similar choice (between cocaine or heroin and father, mother, brother, sister, wife, husband, children, job), almost every stoned junkie would do the same.

There are other disturbing similarities. Television itself is a consciousness-altering instrument. With the touch of a button, it takes you out of the "real" world in which you reside and can place you at a basketball game, the back alleys of Miami, the streets of Bucharest, or the cartoony living rooms of Sitcom Land. Each move from channel to channel alters mood, usually with music or a laugh track. On any given evening, you can laugh, be frightened, feel tension, thump with excitement. You can even tune in *MacNeil/Lehrer* and feel sober.

But none of these abrupt shifts in mood is *earned*. They are attained as easily as popping a pill. Getting news from television, for example, is simply not the same experience as reading it in a newspaper. Reading is *active*. The reader must decode little symbols called words, then create images or ideas and make them connect; at its most basic level, reading is an act of the imagination. But the television viewer doesn't go through that process. The words are spoken to him by Dan Rather or Tom Brokaw or Peter Jennings. There isn't much decoding to do when watching television, no time to think or ponder before the next set of images and spoken words appears to displace the present one. The reader, being active, works at his or her own pace; the viewer, being passive, proceeds at a pace determined by the show. Except at the highest levels, television never demands that its audience take part in an act of imagination. Reading always does.

In short, television works on the same imaginative and intellectual level as psychoactive drugs. If prolonged television viewing makes the young passive (dozens of studies indicate that it does), then moving to drugs has a certain coherence. Drugs provide an unearned high (in contrast to the earned rush that comes from a feat accomplished, a human breakthrough earned by sweat or thought or love).

And because the television addict and the drug addict are alienated 16
from the hard and scary world, they also feel they make no difference in
its complicated events. For the junkie, the world is reduced to him and
the needle, pipe, or vial; the self is absolutely isolated, with no desire for
choice. The television addict lives the same way. Many Americans who
fail to vote in presidential elections must believe they have no more
control over such a choice than they do over the casting of *L. A. Law.*

The drug plague also coincides with the unspoken assumption of
most television shows: Life should be *easy.* The most complicated events
are summarized on TV news in a minute or less. Cops confront murder,
chase the criminals, and bring them to justice (usually violently) within
an hour. In commercials, you drink the right beer and you get the girl.
Easy! So why should real life be a grind? Why should any American have
to spend years mastering a skill or a craft, or work eight hours a day at
an unpleasant job, or endure the compromises and crises of a marriage?
Nobody *works* on television (except cops, doctors, and lawyers). Love
stories on television are about falling in love or breaking up; the long,
steady growth of a marriage—its essential *dailiness*—is seldom explored,
except as comedy. Life on television is almost always simple: good guys
and bad, nice girls and whores, smart guys and dumb. And if life in the
real world isn't that simple, well, hey, man, have some dope, man, be
happy, feel good.

The doper always whines about how he *feels*; drugs are used to
enhance his feelings or obliterate them, and in this the doper is very
American. No other people on earth spend so much time talking about
their feelings; hundreds of thousands go to shrinks, they buy self-help
books by the millions, they pour out intimate confessions to virtual
strangers in bars or discos. Our political campaigns are about emotional issues now, stated in the simplicities of adolescence. Even alleged
statesmen can start a sentence, "I feel that the Sandinistas should . . ."
when they once might have said, "I *think.* . . ." I'm convinced that this
exaltation of cheap emotions over logic and reason is one by-product of
hundreds of thousands of hours of television.

Most Americans under the age of fifty have now spent their lives
absorbing television; that is, they've had the structures of drama
pounded into them. Drama is always about conflict. So news shows,
politics, and advertising are now all shaped by those structures. Nobody
will pay attention to anything as complicated as the part played by
Third World debt in the expanding production of cocaine; it's much
easier to focus on Manuel Noriega, a character right out of *Miami Vice*,
and believe that even in real life there's a Mister Big.

What is to be done? Television is certainly not going away, but its 20
addictive qualities can be controlled. It's a lot easier to "just say no" to
television than to heroin or crack. As a beginning, parents must take

immediate control of the sets, teaching children to watch specific television *programs*, not "television," to get out of the house and play with other kids. Elementary and high schools must begin teaching television as a subject, the way literature is taught, showing children how shows are made, how to distinguish between the true and the false, how to recognize cheap emotional manipulation. All Americans should spend more time reading. And thinking.

For years, the defenders of television have argued that the networks are only giving the people what they want. That might be true. But so is the Medellín cartel.   *1990*

12

Family Stories

Elizabeth Stone, Stories Make a Family

Judith Ortiz Cofer, *Casa*: A Partial
Remembrance of a
Puerto Rican Childhood

Maxine Hong Kingston, No Name Woman

Itabari Njeri, Granddaddy

I'm glad Uncle Bob was unconcerned with "redundancy" and told those stories over and over. I never tired of them. They were about someone in my family, and thus also about me. In defining my family's history, Uncle Bob was defining me. Without him and his stories, I would be different than I am.

Clyde Edgerton, from *A Four-Blade Case*

Communal storytelling was a self-correcting process in which listeners were encouraged to speak up if they noted an important fact or detail omitted. The people were happy to listen to two or three different versions of the same event or the same humma-hah story. Even conflicting versions of an incident were welcomed for the entertainment they provided. Defenders of each version might joke and tease one another, but seldom were there any direct confrontations. Implicit in the Pueblo oral tradition was the awareness that loyalties, grudges, and kinship must always influence the narrator's choices as she emphasizes to listeners this is the way *she* has always heard the story told. The ancient Pueblo people sought a communal truth, not an absolute. For them this truth lived somewhere within the web of differing versions, disputes over minor points, outright contradictions tangling with old feuds and village rivalries.

Leslie Marmon Silko, from *Landscape, History, and the Pueblo Imagination*

It is a skill we learn early, the art of inventing stories to explain away the fearful sacred strangeness of the world. Storytelling and make-believe, like war and agriculture, are among the arts of self-defense, and all of them are ways of enclosing otherness and claiming ownership.

William Kittredge, from *Home*

Then one Saturday in 1965 I happened to be walking past the National Archives building in Washington. Across the interim years I had thought of Grandma's old stories—otherwise I can't think what diverted me up the Archives' steps. And when a main reading room desk attendant asked if he could help me, I wouldn't have dreamed of admitting to him some curiosity hanging on from boyhood about my slave forebears. I kind of bumbled that I was interested in census records of Alamance County, North Carolina, just after the Civil War.

Alex Haley, from *"My Furthest-Back Person—The African"*

Elizabeth Stone

Stories Make a Family

In the beginning, as far back in my family as anyone could go, was my great-grandmother, and her name was Annunziata. In the next generation, it would be my grandmother's name, in the generation after that (in its Anglicized form, Nancy) it would be my aunt's first name and my mother's middle name, and in the generation after that, my sister's middle name as well.

As for that first Annunziata, I never met her, but my mother often told me a family story about her that I knew as well as I knew the story of Cinderella. I don't remember my mother or grandmother actually telling me this story, or the others I heard. I only remember listening to them and feeling lucky because of them—though I couldn't know then how deeply etched they were in my imagination. To me, my ancestors were like characters out of a fairy tale. The stories they told me were the prologue to my life, stories I would live by.

Annunziata was the daughter of a rich landowner in Messina, Sicily, so the story went, and she fell in love with the town postman, a poor man but talented, able to play any musical instrument he laid eyes on. Her father heard about this romance and forbade them to see each other. So one night in the middle of the night—and then came the line I always waited for with a thrill of pleasure—she ran off with him in her shift.

I didn't know what a shift was and didn't want my version of the story disrupted by any new information. I loved the scene as I saw it: In the background was the house with the telltale ladder leaning against the second-story window. In the foreground was my great-grandmother, like some pre-Raphaelite maiden, dressed in a flowing white garment, holding the hand of her beloved as she ran through a field at dawn, toward her future and toward me.

The story of my grandmother's generation began with another marriage, only it wasn't really a love story, or at least that's not why it was still told three-quarters of a century later. In 1890, my grandfather, Gaetano Bongiorno, came to New York from the Lipari Islands, off the coast of Sicily. He was a young man of eighteen, serious and somewhat stolid but also strong and hardworking.

Like so many Southern Italian men of the time, he was a "bird of passage" who had come here to work so he could earn money for his family back home. Over the years, he had a variety of jobs: he piloted a barge and worked as a longshoreman, loading and unloading the ships that came into Brooklyn harbor.

After work he would go home to Union Street in Brooklyn, where he lived with the members of his family who had preceded him there— namely two married sisters. It was even cozier than that. Gaetano's two sisters had married two brothers, and those brothers also happened to be their first cousins.

The years went by, and Gaetano showed no sign of wanting to return to Italy or of marrying and settling down. By 1905, he was already thirty-three. One day in the mail, however, a letter came. Along with it was a photograph of his cousin Annunziata, the youngest sister of his sisters' husbands.

Gaetano was taken with the photograph of this young woman, and as his sisters had been badgering him to marry, he decided to try to arrange a marriage with her. And so Gaetano sailed to Sicily, went to his uncle, Annunziata's father, and asked for permission to marry her. My grandmother was willing. She was fifteen: the idea of marriage seemed very grown-up and the prospect of coming to live in America was exciting. Besides, my grandfather's looks—he was tall, red-headed, and blue-eyed—appealed to my grandmother. So the betrothal was arranged and the marriage soon followed. When my grandmother left for America, her mother gave her a silk handkerchief, the edges scalloped with pastel flowers she had embroidered herself.

When my grandfather returned to Union Street with his bride in 1905, they moved in with his two sisters and two brothers-in-law, and there they all lived until Annunziata and Gaetano could find a place of their own on Union Street. And thus it was that two brothers and a sister married two sisters and a brother and all came to live in the same house.

The story of how my grandparents had come to marry was often told in my family, and what it said to me was that the family was so important that one should even try to marry within it. I remember at the age of four or five having already decided which of my male first cousins I would eventually marry. The nuclear family—a couple and their children—belonged to the larger unit. If you'd asked me then how many people there were in my family, I would have said twenty-five: my grandmother, my parents, my aunts and uncles, my sister, and my cousins. That was what family meant.

My grandfather, despite his surname, was not a true Bongiorno. He 12 died when my mother was twelve, and was reputed to have been a rather phlegmatic man who sat enveloped in great clouds of cigar smoke. The true Bongiorno was my grandmother, the first Annunziata's last child.

My grandmother was the hub of the family's collective life. She lived in the upstairs of a two-family house on East Fifth Street in Brooklyn with my Aunt Jean and her family; downstairs lived my Uncle Joe and his family. When I think of my grandmother now, I still remember her the way I did when I was young. My memories are all physical and sensuous—the elderly smoothness of her fleshy arms, the soft feel of her dark flowered print dresses, the hazy aura of Old Spice that always enveloped her.

She was supposed to have had a terrible temper when she was young. I never saw any sign of it—by the time I knew her everyone said she had "mellowed." But this temper was one of several traits that

defined us as Bongiornos—sort of like the Hapsburg lip. One story I
heard often as a child was about the time she was serving soup to her six
children. As she circled the big round dining room table, ladling the
soup, a quarrel broke out between two of them, Nancy and Bart. My
grandmother tried to stop their squabbling, but with no success. Exasperated, she took the soup tureen and upended it over Bart's head.

The primary heir to the Bongiorno temper in the next generation
was my Aunt Nancy, my grandmother's third child. My aunt had a
mauve hat that she wore to work every day, rain or shine. Whenever
she'd had a bad day, she would put her hat on backward and word would
go around: "Nancy's got her hat on backward. You'd better leave her
alone."

I used to wonder why my family treasured this image of themselves 16
as splenetic people. Maybe they saw a volatile temper as evidence of
their *élan vital*, their stamina and vitality, the living proof that they
weren't cowed or intimidated by anything—though from my perspective as an adult, they were actually rather gentle people. Or maybe it
had to do with the organization of power in the three generations of this
family. To say that there was a "Bongiorno temper" was to say that my
once-volatile grandmother (and not her late and laconic husband) was
the center of the family, just as her mythic and strong-willed mother had
been before her. In our family, temper was an inherited trait.

The happiest Bongiorno stories were the ones in which my mother
and her brothers and sisters were at home together on Vanderbilt Street
in Brooklyn, making fun of their piano teacher, Miss Asquith (whom
they referred to as "Miss Broadbottom"), or teaching Brother Joe how to
pronounce the "t's" in "butter," or playing charades based on lines from
Edna St. Vincent Millay.

It was only when they had to go out into the world that they found it
unfriendly. For my mother's family, one of the central and abiding
preoccupations was the pain of being Italian in America, a country that
executed Sacco and Vanzetti, that equated Italians, as it still does, with
mafiosi, and had a closetful of derogatory terms to call them. Our
family stories often tried tacitly to counteract what the culture said
about Italians—that we were coarse and stupid and short and dark. (My
grandmother and all her six children *were* short and dark, which didn't
help matters any.)

My grandparents moved to Flatbush when my mother was four or
five. Once they got there, to Vanderbilt Street, they named their cats
George Washington and Abraham Lincoln. And after their rather conservative father, Gaetano, died, the process of assimilation speeded up
immeasurably. From then on, it was Joe, the oldest son, who made the
decisions. No more *DeNobili* cigars and no more *Il Progressos*. Everyone in

the house spoke English. The younger children barely understood Italian—and prided themselves on the fact. They rushed to Anglicize their names—Giovanna, Giuseppe, Annunziata, Bartolomeo, and Maria Elena became Jean, Joe, Nancy, Bart, and Ellen. Even my grandmother anglicized her name. Only my mother, Aurora, kept her name, and that was because the only alternative that occurred to her—Rory—would have been worse than what she started with.

In many ways, the Bongiornos of my mother's generation were 20 unusual for their time and place. The oldest boy, Joe, wrote poetry and sent it off regularly to the *Brooklyn Eagle*, where it was eventually published. Then he moved on to fiction—detective novels, historical novels—and much of this was published, too.

My mother's younger sister, Ellen, trained as a nurse. During World War II, when she was still only in her early twenties, she went overseas as an officer in the Nursing Corps. While Ellen studied nursing, my mother, a year and a half older, went to Hunter College, and then, during her junior year, left to play ingénue roles in summer stock in Mount Kisco.

During the late 1930s, she found a haven among left-wing theater people from old families. She joined a repertory company led by a Russian émigré late of the Moscow Art Theater who had studied with a disciple of Stanislavsky's. They did Maxwell Anderson, Clifford Odets, and Thornton Wilder Off Broadway, and once even got to Broadway, where they did Strindberg.

Toward the end of the 1930s, because my mother was talented, there were screen tests. She was decidedly Mediterranean-looking—beautiful in a sulky, innocent way, small with very dark hair, very dark eyes, a full mouth and a nose that she thought altogether too broad. They were looking for something else. What they wanted was a pert nose and blue eyes and strawberry hair, and height.

My mother stayed with her repertory company until World War II 24 dispersed it. After the war she didn't go back to acting. There is no story about why, and when I ask, even now, her explanation never explains.

Many families build self-esteem through stories about money and self-made men. But in my family there wasn't a single story like that. What the Bongiornos substituted was a sense that they came from a long line of people with talent, a talent that was innate, nearly genetic. Their celebration of the artist and their conviction that art was in their blood dated back to an unnamed (and probably apocryphal) court musician who had lived before the beginning of family time. And of course this talent was invoked again in the story in which my great-grandmother, the tale's moral center, fell in love with that poor but talented musical postman.

The motif of art and talent was too important and too powerful a symbol to live in those two stories alone, and so it flourished in many. One of the oldest stories in our family was about my great-grandfather long after his elopement. He could play any instrument he laid eyes on, it was said. And so could his sons who, like my grandmother, inherited his musical genes. In the evenings after dinner, he and his sons would go into the courtyard, each with his instrument, and play music together for several hours. People would come "from miles around" just to listen.

My grandmother, the youngest of his children, had a lovely singing voice, and this was the subject of one very important family story set during her childhood in Sicily. One day she was at home with her mother, singing as she did some chore around the house. Suddenly, her mother looked out the window and saw the parish priest ambling up the road. "Be quiet! Be quiet!" she hissed to my grandmother. "The padre will hear you singing, and he will again tell us that we must send you to Rome for singing lessons, and you know we don't have the money for that."

My grandmother never did have voice lessons, but thirty years later 28 she was still singing. By then, she and her six children were living on Vanderbilt Street in a second-floor apartment over a grocery store run by a man named Mr. Peterson. Every Friday morning, my grandmother would get down on her hands and knees and wash the tile floor in the first-floor entry hall. She loved opera, and as she scrubbed the floor, she would sing one aria or another. As the story goes, Mr. Peterson would invariably stop whatever he was doing and hush his customers in order to listen to her without interruption.

I wonder about these stories now. How could a man with a post-man's income afford to buy all those instruments? And would a nineteenth-century parish priest in a small Sicilian village really encourage a family to send their preadolescent daughter hundreds of miles away to Rome? And would he do it for as secular an undertaking as singing lessons? And did Mr. Peterson really stop everything to listen?

No one ever noticed the oddities in these stories. In part, it was because they inhabited a strangely protected realm, half real, half fanciful; they were too useful for us to question whether they were true or not. But literal truth was never the point. What all these stories did was give us something strong and important to hold onto for as long as we needed it—a sense of belonging in the world. When I was growing up, my sense of what the future might hold was shaped by the stories I'd heard about our past.

The particular spirit of a family is newly imagined every generation, with old family stories disappearing or coming to mean something different, and new ones being coined. My husband and I have two sons of our own now, and we live in a new family. The storytelling goes on, parent to child, as ever. Only now I'm the teller. Already my five-year-old son, Paul, is eager to listen. He knows about the magic tricks performed by a grandfather he never knew, and how his parents met at Lenny and Bella's Christmas party, and how there was a big blizzard on the April morning we first brought him home from the hospital three days after he was born.

The evidence of his family past is everywhere. Just this afternoon, 32 he raced over to me from the rocket ship he was building out of his younger brother Gabriel's empty diaper box. "You know that handkerchief of your grandmother's?" He meant the one her mother had given her when she got married and came to America. "Can I use it?" he asked. "My astronaut needs a parachute." *1986*

Judith Ortiz Cofer

Casa: A Partial Remembrance of a Puerto Rican Childhood

At three or four o'clock in the afternoon, the hour of *café con leche*, the women of my family gathered in Mamá's living room to speak of important things and retell familiar stories meant to be overheard by us young girls, their daughters. In Mamá's house (everyone called my grandmother Mamá) was a large parlor built by my grandfather to his wife's exact specifications so that it was always cool, facing away from the sun. The doorway was on the side of the house so no one could walk directly into her living room. First they had to take a little stroll through and around her beautiful garden where prize-winning orchids grew in the trunk of an ancient tree she had hollowed out for that purpose. This room was furnished with several mahogany rocking chairs, acquired at the births of her children, and one intricately carved rocker that had passed down to Mamá at the death of her own mother.

It was on these rockers that my mother, her sisters, and my grandmother sat on these afternoons of my childhood to tell their stories, teaching each other, and my cousin and me, what it was like to be a woman, more specifically, a Puerto Rican woman. They talked about life on the island, and life in *Los Nueva Yores,* their way of referring to the United States from New York City to California: the other place, not home, all the same. They told real-life stories though, as I later learned, always embellishing them with a little or a lot of dramatic detail. And they told *cuentos*, the morality and cautionary tales told by the women in our family for generations: stories that became a part of my sub-conscious as I grew up in two worlds, the tropical island and the cold city, and that would later surface in my dreams and in my poetry.

One of these tales was about the woman who was left at the altar. Mamá liked to tell that one with histrionic intensity. I remember the rise and fall of her voice, the sighs, and her constantly gesturing hands, like two birds swooping through her words. This particular story usually would come up in a conversation as a result of someone mentioning a forthcoming engagement or wedding. The first time I remember hear-ing it, I was sitting on the floor at Mamá's feet, pretending to read a comic book. I may have been eleven or twelve years old, at that difficult age when a girl was no longer a child who could be ordered to leave the room if the women wanted freedom to take their talk into forbidden zones, nor really old enough to be considered a part of their conclave. I could only sit quietly, pretending to be in another world, while absorb-ing it all in a sort of unspoken agreement of my status as silent auditor. On this day, Mamá had taken my long, tangled mane of hair into her ever-busy hands. Without looking down at me and with no interruption of her flow of words, she began braiding my hair, working at it with the quickness and determination that characterized all her actions. My mother was watching us impassively from her rocker across the room. On her lips played a little ironic smile. I would never sit still for *her* ministrations, but even then, I instinctively knew that she did not possess Mamá's matriarchal power to command and keep everyone's attention. This was never more evident than in the spell she cast when telling a story.

"It is not like it used to be when I was a girl," Mamá announced. 4 "Then, a man could leave a girl standing at the church altar with a bouquet of fresh flowers in her hands and disappear off the face of the earth. No way to track him down if he was from another town. He could be a married man, with maybe even two or three families all over the island. There was no way to know. And there were men who did this. Hombres with the devil in their flesh who would come to a pueblo, like this one, take a job at one of the haciendas, never meaning to stay, only to have a good time and to seduce the women."

The whole time she was speaking, Mamá would be weaving my hair into a flat plait that required pulling apart the two sections of hair with little jerks that made my eyes water; but knowing how grandmother detested whining and *boba* (sissy) tears, as she called them, I just sat up as straight and stiff as I did at La Escuela San Jose, where the nuns enforced good posture with a flexible plastic ruler they bounced off of slumped shoulders and heads. As Mamá's story progressed, I noticed how my young Aunt Laura lowered her eyes, refusing to meet Mamá's meaningful gaze. Laura was seventeen, in her last year of high school, and already engaged to a boy from another town who had staked his claim with a tiny diamond ring, then left for Los Neuva Yores to make his fortune. They were planning to get married in a year. Mamá had expressed serious doubts that the wedding would ever take place. In Mamá's eyes, a man set free without a legal contract was a man lost. She believed that marriage was not something men desired, but simply the price they had to pay for the privilege of children and, of course, for what no decent (synonymous with "smart") woman would give away for free.

"María La Loca was only seventeen when *it* happened to her." I listened closely at the mention of this name. María was a town character, a fat middle-aged woman who lived with her old mother on the outskirts of town. She was to be seen around the pueblo delivering the meat pies the two women made for a living. The most peculiar thing about María, in my eyes, was that she walked and moved like a little girl though she had the thick body and wrinkled face of an old woman. She would swing her hips in an exaggerated, clownish way, and sometimes even hop and skip up to someone's house. She spoke to no one. Even if you asked her a question, she would just look at you and smile, showing her yellow teeth. But I had heard that if you got close enough, you could hear her humming a tune without words. The kids yelled out nasty things at her, calling her *La Loca*, and the men who hung out at the bodega playing dominoes sometimes whistled mockingly as she passed by with her funny, outlandish walk. But María seemed impervious to it all, carrying her basket of *pasteles* like a grotesque Little Red Riding Hood through the forest.

María La Loca interested me, as did all the eccentrics and crazies of our pueblo. Their weirdness was a measuring stick I used in my serious quest for a definition of normal. As a Navy brat shuttling between New Jersey and the pueblo, I was constantly made to feel like an oddball by my peers, who made fun of my two-way accent: a Spanish accent when I spoke English, and when I spoke Spanish I was told that I sounded like a *Gringa*. Being the outsider had already turned my brother and me into cultural chameleons. We developed early on the ability to blend into a crowd, to sit and read quietly in a fifth story apartment building for days and days when it was too bitterly cold to play outside, or, set free, to run wild in Mamá's realm, where she took charge of our lives, releasing Mother for a while from the intense fear for our safety that our father's absences instilled in her. In order to keep us from harm when Father was away, Mother kept us under strict surveillance. She even walked us to and from Public School No. 11, which we attended during the months we lived in Paterson, New Jersey, our home base in the states. Mamá freed all three of us like pigeons from a cage. I saw her as my liberator and my model. Her stories were parables from which to glean the *Truth*.

"María La Loca was once a beautiful girl. Everyone thought she 8 would marry the Méndez boy." As everyone knew, Rogelio Méndez was the richest man in town. "But," Mamá continued, knitting my hair with the same intensity she was putting into her story, "this *macho* made a fool out of her and ruined her life." She paused for the effect of her use of the word "macho," which at that time had not yet become a popular epithet for an unliberated man. This word had for us the crude and comical connotation of "male of the species," stud; a *macho* was what you put in a pen to increase your stock.

I peeked over my comic book at my mother. She too was under Mamá's spell, smiling conspiratorially at this little swipe at men. She was safe from Mamá's contempt in this area. Married at an early age, an unspotted lamb, she had been accepted by a good family of strict Spaniards whose name was old and respected, though their fortune had been lost long before my birth. In a rocker Papá had painted sky blue sat Mamá's oldest child, Aunt Nena. Mother of three children, step-mother of two more, she was a quiet woman who liked books but had married an ignorant and abusive widower whose main interest in life was accumulating wealth. He too was in the mainland working on his dream of returning home rich and triumphant to buy the *finca* of his dreams. She was waiting for him to send for her. She would leave her children with Mamá for several years while the two of them slaved away in factories. He would one day be a rich man, and she a sadder woman. Even now her life-light was dimming. She spoke little, an aberration in Mamá's house, and she read avidly, as if storing up spiritual food for the long winters that awaited her in Los Nueva Yores without her family. But even Aunt Nena came alive to Mamá's words, rocking gently, her hands over a thick book in her lap.

Her daughter, my cousin Sara, played jacks by herself on the tile porch outside the room where we sat. She was a year older than I. We shared a bed and all our family's secrets. Collaborators in search of answers, Sara and I discussed everything we heard the women say, trying to fit it all together like a puzzle that, once assembled, would reveal life's mysteries to us. Though she and I still enjoyed taking part in boys' games—chase, volleyball, and even *vaqueros*, the island version of cowboys and Indians involving cap-gun battles and violent shoot-outs under the mango tree in Mamá's backyard—we loved best the quiet hours in the afternoon when the men were still at work, and the boys had gone to play serious baseball at the park. Then Mamá's house belonged only to us women. The aroma of coffee perking in the kitchen, the mesmerizing creaks and groans of the rockers, and the women telling their lives in *cuentos* are forever woven into the fabric of my imagination, braided like my hair that day I felt my grandmother's hands teaching me about strength, her voice convincing me of the power of storytelling.

That day Mamá told how the beautiful María had fallen prey to a man whose name was never the same in subsequent versions of the story; it was Juan one time, José, Rafael, Diego, another. We understood that neither the name nor any of the *facts* were important, only that a woman had allowed love to defeat her. Mamá put each of us in María's place by describing her wedding dress in loving detail: how she looked like a princess in her lace as she waited at the altar. Then, as Mamá approached the tragic denouement of her story, I was distracted by the sound of my Aunt Laura's violent rocking. She seemed on the verge of tears. She knew the fable was intended for her. That week she was going to have her wedding gown fitted, though no firm date had been set for the marriage. Mamá ignored Laura's obvious discomfort, digging out a ribbon from the sewing basket she kept by her rocker while describing María's long illness, "a fever that would not break for days." She spoke of a mother's despair: "that woman climbed the church steps on her knees every morning, wore only black as a *promesa* to the Holy Virgin in exchange for her daughter's health." By the time María returned from her honeymoon with death, she was ravished, no longer young or sane. "As you can see, she is almost as old as her mother already," Mamá lamented while tying the ribbon to the ends of my hair, pulling it back with such force that I just knew I would never be able to close my eyes completely again.

"That María is getting crazier every day." Mamá's voice would take a lighter tone now, expressing satisfaction, either for the perfection of my braid, or for a story well told—it was hard to tell. "You know that tune María is always humming?" Carried away by her enthusiasm, I tried to nod, but Mamá still had me pinned between her knees.

"Well, that's the wedding march." Surprising us all, Mamá sang out, "Da, da, dara . . . da, da, dara." Then lifting me off the floor by my skinny shoulders, she would lead me around the room in an impromptu waltz—another session ending with the laughter of women, all of us caught up in the infectious joke of our lives.   *1989*

Maxine Hong Kingston
No Name Woman

"You must not tell anyone," my mother said, "what I am about to tell you. In China your father had a sister who killed herself. She jumped into the family well. We say that your father has all brothers because it is as if she had never been born.

"In 1924 just a few days after our village celebrated seventeen hurry-up weddings—to make sure that every young man who went 'out on the road' would responsibly come home—your father and his brothers and your grandfather and his brothers and your aunt's new husband sailed for America, the Gold Mountain. It was your grand-father's last trip. Those lucky enough to get contracts waved good-bye from the decks. They fed and guarded the stowaways and helped them off in Cuba, New York, Bali, Hawaii. 'We'll meet in California next year,' they said. All of them sent money home.

"I remember looking at your aunt one day when she and I were dressing; I had not noticed before that she had such a protruding melon of a stomach. But I did not think, 'She's pregnant,' until she began to look like other pregnant women, her shirt pulling and the white tops of her black pants showing. She could not have been pregnant, you see, because her husband had been gone for years. No one said anything. We did not discuss it. In early summer she was ready to have the child, long after the time when it could have been possible.

"The village had also been counting. On the night the baby was to be born the villagers raided our house. Some were crying. Like a great saw, teeth strung with lights, files of people walked zigzag across our land, tearing the rice. Their lanterns doubled in the disturbed black water, which drained away through the broken bunds. As the villagers closed in, we could see that some of them, probably men and women we knew well, wore white masks. The people with long hair hung it over their faces. Women with short hair made it stand up on end. Some had tied white bands around their foreheads, arms, and legs.

"At first they threw mud and rocks at the house. Then they threw eggs and began slaughtering our stock. We could hear the animals scream their deaths—the roosters, the pigs, a last great roar from the ox. Familiar wild heads flared in our night windows; the villagers encircled us. Some of the faces stopped to peer at us, their eyes rushing like searchlights. The hands flattened against the panes, framed heads, and left red prints.

"The villagers broke in the front and the back doors at the same time, even though we had not locked the doors against them. Their knives dripped with the blood of our animals. They smeared blood on the doors and walls. One woman swung a chicken, whose throat she had slit, splattering blood in red arcs about her. We stood together in the middle of our house, in the family hall with the pictures and tables of the ancestors around us, and looked straight ahead.

"At that time the house had only two wings. When the men came back, we would build two more to enclose our courtyard and a third one to begin a second courtyard. The villagers pushed through both wings, even your grandparents' rooms, to find your aunt's, which was also mine until the men returned. From this room a new wing for one of the younger families would grow. They ripped up her clothes and shoes and broke her combs, grinding them underfoot. They tore her work from the loom. They scattered the cooking fire and rolled the new weaving in it. We could hear them in the kitchen breaking our bowls and banging the pots. They overturned the great waist-high earthenware jugs; duck eggs, pickled fruits, vegetables burst out and mixed in acrid torrents. The old woman from the next field swept a broom through the air and loosed the spirits-of-the-broom over our heads. 'Pig.' 'Ghost.' 'Pig,' they sobbed and scolded while they ruined our house.

"When they left, they took sugar and oranges to bless themselves. 8 They cut pieces from the dead animals. Some of them took bowls that were not broken and clothes that were not torn. Afterward we swept up the rice and sewed it back up into sacks. But the smells from the spilled preserves lasted. Your aunt gave birth in the pigsty that night. The next morning when I went up for the water, I found her and the baby plugging up the family well.

"Don't let your father know that I told you. He denies her. Now that you have started to menstruate, what happened to her could happen to you. Don't humiliate us. You wouldn't like to be forgotten as if you had never been born. The villagers are watchful."

Whenever she had to warn us about life, my mother told stories that ran like this one, a story to grow up on. She tested our strength to establish realities. Those in the emigrant generations who could not reassert brute survival died young and far from home. Those of us in the first American generations have had to figure out how the invisible world the emigrants built around our childhoods fit in solid America.

The emigrants confused the gods by diverting their curses, mislead-ing them with crooked streets and false names. They must try to confuse their offspring as well, who, I suppose, threaten them in similar ways— always trying to get things straight, always trying to name the unspeak-able. The Chinese I know hide their names; sojourners take new names when their lives change and guard their real names with silence.

Chinese-Americans, when you try to understand what things in you 12 are Chinese, how do you separate what is peculiar to childhood, to poverty, insanities, one family, your mother who marked your growing with stories, from what is Chinese? What is Chinese tradition and what is the movies?

If I want to learn what clothes my aunt wore, whether flashy or ordinary, I would have to begin, "Remember Father's drowned-in-the-well sister?" I cannot ask that. My mother has told me once and for all the useful parts. She will add nothing unless powered by Necessity, a riverbank that guides her life. She plants vegetable gardens rather than lawns; she carries the odd-shaped tomatoes home from the fields and eats food left for the gods.

Whenever we did frivolous things, we used up energy; we flew high kites. We children came up off the ground over the melting cones our parents brought home from work and the American movie on New Year's Day—*Oh, You Beautiful Doll* with Betty Grable one year, and *She Wore a Yellow Ribbon* with John Wayne another year. After the one carnival ride each, we paid in guilt; our tired father counted his change on the dark walk home.

Adultery is extravagance. Could people who hatch their own chicks and eat the embryos and the heads for delicacies and boil the feet in vinegar for party food, leaving only the gravel, eating even the gizzard lining—could such people engender a prodigal aunt? To be a woman, to have a daughter in starvation time was a waste enough. My aunt could not have been the lone romantic who gave up everything for sex. Women in the old China did not choose. Some man had commanded her to lie with him and be his secret evil. I wonder whether he masked himself when he joined the raid on her family.

Perhaps she encountered him in the fields or on the mountain   16 where the daughters-in-law collected fuel. Or perhaps he first noticed her in the marketplace. He was not a stranger because the village housed no strangers. She had to have dealings with him other than sex. Perhaps he worked an adjoining field, or he sold her the cloth for the dress she sewed and wore. His demand must have surprised, then terrified her. She obeyed him; she always did as she was told.

When the family found a young man in the next village to be her husband, she stood tractably beside the best rooster, his proxy, and promised before they met that she would be his forever. She was lucky that he was her age and she would be the first wife, an advantage secure now. The night she first saw him, he had sex with her. Then he left for America. She had almost forgotten what he looked like. When she tried to envision him, she only saw the black and white face in the group photograph the men had had taken before leaving.

The other man was not, after all, much different from her husband. They both gave orders: she followed. "If you tell your family, I'll beat you. I'll kill you. Be here again next week." No one talked sex, ever. And she might have separated the rapes from the rest of living if only she did not have to buy her oil from him or gather wood in the same forest. I want her fear to have lasted just as long as rape lasted so that the fear could have been contained. No drawn-out fear. But women at sex hazarded birth and hence lifetimes. The fear did not stop but permeated everywhere. She told the man, "I think I'm pregnant." He organized the raid against her.

On nights when my mother and father talked about their life back home, sometimes they mentioned an "outcast table" whose business they still seemed to be settling, their voices tight. In a commensal tradition, where food is precious, the powerful older people made wrongdoers eat alone. Instead of letting them start separate new lives like the Japanese, who could become samurais and geishas, the Chinese family, faces averted but eyes glowering sideways, hung on to the offenders and fed them leftovers. My aunt must have lived in the same house as my parents and eaten at an outcast table. My mother spoke about the raid as if she had seen it, when she and my aunt, a daughter-in-law to a different household, should not have been living together at all. Daughters-in-law lived with their husbands' parents, not their own; a synonym for marriage in Chinese is "taking a daughter-in-law." Her husband's parents could have sold her, mortgaged her, stoned her. But they had sent her back to her own mother and father, a mysterious act hinting at disgraces not told me. Perhaps they had thrown her out to deflect the avengers.

She was the only daughter; her four brothers went with her father, 20 husband, and uncles "out on the road" and for some years became western men. When the goods were divided among the family, three of the brothers took land, and the youngest, my father, chose an education. After my grandparents gave their daughter away to her husband's family, they had dispensed all the adventure and all the property. They expected her alone to keep the traditional ways, which her brothers, now among the barbarians, could fumble without detection. The heavy, deep-rooted women were to maintain the past against the flood, safe for returning. But the rare urge west had fixed upon our family, and so my aunt crossed boundaries not delineated in space.

The work of preservation demands that the feelings playing about in one's guts not be turned into action. Just watch their passing like cherry blossoms. But perhaps my aunt, my forerunner, caught in a slow life, let dreams grow and fade and after some months or years went toward what persisted. Fear at the enormities of the forbidden kept her desires delicate, wire and bone. She looked at a man because she liked the way the hair was tucked behind his ears, or she liked the question-mark line of a long torso curving at the shoulder and straight at the hip. For warm eyes or a soft voice or a slow walk—that's all—a few hairs, a line, a brightness, a sound, a pace, she gave up family. She offered us up for a charm that vanished with tiredness, a pigtail that didn't toss when the wind died. Why, the wrong lighting could erase the dearest thing about him.

It could very well have been, however, that my aunt did not take subtle enjoyment of her friend, but, a wild woman, kept rollicking company. Imagining her free with sex doesn't fit, though. I don't know any women like that, or men either. Unless I see her life branching into mine, she gives me no ancestral help.

To sustain her being in love, she often worked at herself in the mirror, guessing at the colors and shapes that would interest him, changing them frequently in order to hit on the right combination. She wanted him to look back.

On a farm near the sea, a woman who tended her appearance 24 reaped a reputation for eccentricity. All the married women blunt-cut their hair in flaps about their ears or pulled it back in tight buns. No nonsense. Neither style blew easily into heart-catching tangles. And at their weddings they displayed themselves in their long hair for the last time. "It brushed the backs of my knees," my mother tells me. "It was braided, and even so, it brushed the backs of my knees."

At the mirror my aunt combed individuality into her bob. A bun could have been contrived to escape into black streamers blowing in the wind or in quiet wisps about her face, but only the older women in our picture album wear buns. She brushed her hair back from her forehad, tucking the flaps behind her ears. She looped a piece of thread, knotted into a circle between her index fingers and thumbs, and ran the double strand across her forehead. When she closed her fingers as if she were making a pair of shadow geese bite, the string twisted together catching the little hairs. Then she pulled the thread away from her skin, ripping the hairs out neatly, her eyes watering from the needles of pain. Opening her fingers, she cleaned the thread, then rolled it along her hairline and the tops of her eyebrows. My mother did the same to me and my sisters and herself. I used to believe that the expression "caught by the short hairs" meant a captive held with a depilatory string. It especially hurt at the temples, but my mother said we were lucky we didn't have to have our feet bound when we were seven. Sisters used to sit on their beds and cry together, she said, as their mothers or their slave removed the bandages for a few minutes each night and let the blood gush back into their veins. I hope that the man my aunt loved appreciated a smooth brow, that he wasn't just a tits-and-ass man.

Once my aunt found a freckle on her chin, at a spot that the almanac said predestined her for unhappiness. She dug it out with a hot needle and washed the wound with peroxide.

More attention to her looks than these pullings of hairs and pickings at spots would have caused gossip among the villagers. They owned work clothes and good clothes, and they wore good clothes for feasting the new seasons. But since a woman combing her hair hexes beginnings, my aunt rarely found an occasion to look her best. Women looked like great sea snails—the corded wood, babies, and laundry they carried were the whorls on their backs. The Chinese did not admire a bent back; goddesses and warriors stood straight. Still there must have been a marvelous freeing of beauty when a worker laid down her burden and stretched and arched.

Such commonplace loveliness, however, was not enough for my aunt. She dreamed of a lover for the fifteen days of New Year's, the time for families to exchange visits, money, and food. She plied her secret comb. And sure enough she cursed the year, the family, the village, and herself.

Even as her hair lured her imminent lover, many other men looked at her. Uncles, cousins, nephews, brothers would have looked, too, had they been home between journeys. Perhaps they had already been restraining their curiosity, and they left, fearful that their glances, like a field of nesting birds, might be startled and caught. Poverty hurt, and that was their first reason for leaving. But another, final reason for leaving the crowded house was the never-said.

She may have been unusually beloved, the precious only daughter, spoiled and mirror-gazing because of the affection the family lavished on her. When her husband left, they welcomed the chance to take her back from the in-laws; she could live like the little daughter for just a while longer. There are stories that my grandfather was different from other people, "crazy ever since the little Jap bayoneted him in the head." He used to put his naked penis on the dinner table, laughing. And one day he brought home a baby girl, wrapped up inside his brown western-style greatcoat. He had traded one of his sons, probably my father, the youngest, for her. My grandmother made him trade back. When he finally got a daughter of his own, he doted on her. They must have all loved her, except perhaps my father, the only brother who never went back to China, having once been traded for a girl.

Brothers and sisters, newly men and women, had to efface their sexual color and present plain miens. Disturbing hair and eyes, a smile like no other, threatened the ideal of five generations living under one roof. To focus blurs, people shouted face to face and yelled from room to room. The immigrants I know have loud voices, unmodulated to American tones even after years away from the village where they called their friendships out across the fields. I have not been able to stop my mother's screams in public libraries or over telephones. Walking erect (knees straight, toes pointed forward, not pigeon-toed, which is Chinese-feminine) and speaking in an inaudible voice, I have tried to turn myself American-feminine. Chinese communication was loud, public. Only sick people had to whisper. But at the dinner table, where the family members came nearest one another, no one could talk, not the outcasts nor any eaters. Every word that falls from the mouth is a coin lost. Silently they gave and accepted food with both hands. A preoccupied child who took his bowl with one hand got a sideways glare. A complete moment of total attention is due everyone alike. Children and lovers have no singularity here, but my aunt used a secret voice, a separate attentiveness.

She kept the man's name to herself throughout her labor and dying; she did not accuse him that he be punished with her. To save her inseminator's name she gave silent birth.

He may have been somebody in her own household, but intercourse with a man outside the family would have been no less abhorrent. All the village were kinsmen, and the titles shouted in loud country voices never let kinship be forgotten. Any man within visiting distance would have been neutralized as a lover—"brother," "younger brother," "older brother"—115 relationship titles. Parents researched birth charts probably not so much to assure good fortune as to circumvent incest in a population that has but one hundred surnames. Everybody has eight million relatives. How useless then sexual mannerisms, how dangerous.

As if it came from an atavism deeper than fear, I used to add "brother" silently to boys' names. It hexed the boys, who would or would not ask me to dance, and made them less scary and as familiar and deserving of benevolence as girls.

But, of course, I hexed myself also—no dates. I should have stood up, both arms waving, and shouted out across libraries, "Hey, you! Love me back." I had no idea, though, how to make attraction selective, how to control its direction and magnitude. If I made myself American-pretty so that the five or six Chinese boys in the class fell in love with me, everyone else—the Caucasian, Negro, and Japanese boys—would too. Sisterliness, dignified and honorable, made much more sense.

Attraction eludes control so stubbornly that whole societies designed to organize relationships among people cannot keep order, not even when they bind people to one another from childhood and raise them together. Among the very poor and the wealthy, brothers married their adopted sisters, like doves. Our family allowed some romance, paying adult brides' prices and providing dowries so that their sons and daughters could marry strangers. Marriage promises to turn strangers into friendly relatives—a nation of siblings.

In the village structure, spirits shimmered among the live creatures, balanced and held in equilibrium by time and land. But one human being flaring up into violence could open up a black hole, a maelstrom that pulled in the sky. The frightened villagers, who depended on one another to maintain the real, went to my aunt to show her a personal, physical representation of the break she made in the "roundness." Misallying couples snapped off the future, which was to be embodied in true offspring. The villagers punished her for acting as if she could have a private life, secret and apart from them.

If my aunt had betrayed the family at a time of large grain yields and peace, when many boys were born, and wings were being built on many houses, perhaps she might have escaped such severe punishment. But the men—hungry, greedy, tired of planting in dry soil, cuckolded—had been forced to leave the village in order to send food-money home. There were ghost plagues, bandit plagues, wars with the Japanese, floods. My Chinese brother and sister had died of an unknown sickness. Adultery, perhaps only a mistake during good times, became a crime when the village needed food.

The round moon cakes and round doorways, the round tables of graduated size that fit one roundness inside another, round windows and rice bowls—these talismans had lost their power to warn this family of the law: a family must be whole, faithfully keeping the descent line by having sons to feed the old and the dead who in turn look after the family. The villagers came to show my aunt and lover-in-hiding a broken house. The villagers were speeding up the circling of events because she was too shortsighted to see that her infidelity had already harmed the village, that waves of consequences would return unpredictably, sometimes in disguise, as now, to hurt her. This roundness had to be made coin-sized so that she would see its circumference: punish her at the birth of her baby. Awaken her to the inexorable. People who refused fatalism because they could invent small resources insisted on culpability. Deny accidents and wrest fault from the stars.

After the villagers left, their lanterns now scattering in various 40 directions toward home, the family broke their silence and cursed her. "Aiaa, we're going to die. Death is coming. Death is coming. Look what you've done. You've killed us. Ghost! Dead Ghost! Ghost! You've never been born." She ran out into the fields, far enough from the house so that she could no longer hear their voices, and pressed herself against the earth, her own land no more. When she felt the birth coming, she thought that she had been hurt. Her body seized together. "They've hurt me too much," she thought. "This is gall, and it will kill me." With forehead and knees against the earth, her body convulsed and then relaxed. She turned on her back, lay on the ground. The black well of sky and stars went out and out forever; her body and her complexity seemed to disappear. She was one of the stars, a bright dot in blackness, without home, without a companion, in eternal cold and silence. An agoraphobia rose in her, speeding higher and higher, bigger and bigger; she would not be able to contain it; there would be no end to fear.

Flayed, unprotected against space, she felt pain return, focusing her body. This pain chilled her—a cold, steady kind of surface pain. Inside, spasmodically, the other pain, the pain of the child, heated her. For hours she lay on the ground, alternately body and space. Sometimes a vision of normal comfort obliterated reality: she saw the family in the evening gambling at the dinner table, the young people massaging their elders' backs. She saw them congratulating one another, high joy on the mornings the rice shoots came up. When these pictures burst, the stars drew yet further apart. Black space opened.

She got to her feet to fight better and remembered that old-fashioned women gave birth in their pigsties to fool the jealous, pain-dealing gods, who do not snatch piglets. Before the next spasms could stop her, she ran to the pigsty, each step a rushing out into emptiness. She climbed over the fence and knelt in the dirt. It was good to have a fence enclosing her, a tribal person alone.

Laboring, this woman who had carried her child as a foreign growth that sickened her every day, expelled it at last. She reached down to touch the hot, wet, moving mass, surely smaller than anything human, and could feel that it was human after all—fingers, toes, nails, nose. She pulled it up on to her belly, and it lay curled there, butt in the air, feet precisely tucked one under the other. She opened her loose shirt and buttoned the child inside. After resting, it squirmed and thrashed and she pushed it up to her breast. It turned its head this way and that until it found her nipple. There, it made little snuffling noises. She clenched her teeth at its preciousness, lovely as a young calf, a piglet, a little dog.

She may have gone to the pigsty as a last act of responsibility: she 44 would protect this child as she had protected its father. It would look after her soul, leaving supplies on her grave. But how would this tiny child without family find her grave when there would be no marker for her anywhere, neither in the earth nor the family hall? No one would give her a family hall name. She had taken the child with her into the wastes. At its birth the two of them had felt the same raw pain of separation, a wound that only the family pressing tight could close. A child with no descent line would not soften her life but only trail after her, ghostlike, begging her to give it purpose. At dawn the villagers on their way to the fields would stand around the fence and look.

Full of milk, the little ghost slept. When it awoke, she hardened her breasts against the milk that crying loosens. Toward morning she picked up the baby and walked to the well.

Carrying the baby to the well shows loving. Otherwise abandon it. Turn its face into the mud. Mothers who love their children take them along. It was probably a girl; there is some hope of forgiveness for boys.

"Don't tell anyone you had an aunt. Your father does not want to hear her name. She has never been born." I have believed that sex was unspeakable and words so strong and fathers so frail that "aunt" would do my father mysterious harm. I have thought that my family, having settled among immigrants who had also been their neighbors in the ancestral land, needed to clean their name, and a wrong word would incite the kinspeople even here. But there is more to this silence: they want me to participate in her punishment. And I have.

In the twenty years since I heard this story I have not asked for details nor said my aunt's name; I do not know it. People who comfort the dead can also chase after them to hurt them further—a reverse ancestor worship. The real punishment was not the raid swiftly inflicted by the villagers, but the family's deliberately forgetting her. Her betrayal so maddened them, they saw to it that she would suffer forever, even after death. Always hungry, always needing, she would have to beg food from other ghosts, snatch and steal it from those whose living descendants give them gifts. She would have to fight the ghosts massed at crossroads for the buns a few thoughtful citizens leave to decoy her away from village and home so that the ancestral spirits could feast unharassed. At peace, they could act like gods, not ghosts, their descent lines providing them with paper suits and dresses, spirit money, paper houses, paper automobiles, chicken, meat, and rice into eternity— essences delivered up in smoke and flames, steam and incense rising from each rice bowl. In an attempt to make the Chinese care for people outside the family, Chairman Mao encourages us now to give our paper replicas to the spirits of outstanding soldiers and workers, no matter whose ancestors they may be. My aunt remains forever hungry. Goods are not distributed evenly among the dead.

My aunt haunts me—her ghost drawn to me because now, after fifty years of neglect, I alone devote pages of paper to her, though not origamied into houses and clothes. I do not think she always means me well. I am telling on her, and she was a spite suicide, drowning herself in the drinking water. The Chinese are always very frightened of the drowned one, whose weeping ghost, wet hair hanging and skin bloated, waits silently by the water to pull down a substitute.   *1975*

48

Itabari Njeri

Granddaddy

I drove along a road in southern Georgia. It was a night without a moon. Beyond the pine trees and farmland I could see fire in the distance. Farmers had torched their fields to clear the earth for planting. Bark and grass smoldered at the edge of the road. I saw a tall pine ablaze, and I could not suppress the thought of a burning cross as I drove to the house of the man who killed my grandfather twenty-three years ago.

I had heard the tale all of my life: Drunken white boys drag racing through a small southern town in 1960 had killed my granddaddy. Nobody, I was told, knew their names. Nobody, I was told, knew what happened to them. Things were hushed up. Those were the rumors. What everyone knew was this: Granddaddy was a black doctor in Bainbridge, Georgia. Late on the night of October 30 his phone rang. It was an emergency. A patient was gravely ill. Granddaddy left his home in his robe and pajamas, drove to the small infirmary he ran in town, and treated his patient. As he was returning home, a car collided with his. My grandfather was thrown to the pavement. His ribs were broken; his skull was cracked.

Several hours later, the telephone call came to my parents' apartment in Harlem. Granddaddy was dead.

During my childhood, my grandfather was the only adult male I   4 remember openly loving me. Yet, oddly, I seemed unable to absorb the meaning of his death. I felt no grief. Nineteen sixty had been filled with confusing events that disturbed the calm childhood I had known. The distant and accidental violence that took my grandfather's life could not compete with the psychological terror that had begun to engulf my own. The year my grandfather died, my own father returned, and I began to sleep each night with a knife under my pillow.

As I grew older, my grandfather assumed mythic proportions in my imagination. Even in absence, he filled my room like music and watched over me when I was fearful. His fantasized presence diverted thoughts of my father's drunken rages. With age, my fantasizing ceased, the image of my grandfather faded. What lingered was the memory of his caress, the pain of something missing in my life, wrenched away by reckless white youths. I had a growing sense—the beginning of an inevitable comprehension—that this society deals blacks a disproportionate share of pain and denial.

With time, I felt compelled to find out what really happened in Bainbridge that night in 1960.

My family wasn't much help. My stepgrandmother, Madelyn, had suffered a nervous breakdown after the accident and to this day is unyielding in her refusal to discuss it. "It's been twenty-three years," she says. "It took me a long time to get past that. I don't want to open old wounds."

She also feared that, if I stirred things up, "they might desecrate"   8 my granddaddy's grave. If she still held such fears after so much time, I needed no other reason to return to Bainbridge, and so I did.

Black people in Bainbridge had told me my grandfather was buried in Pineview Cemetery. "It's the black cemetery in the white part of town," said Anne Smith, seventy-eight, an elegant, retired school-teacher. Granddaddy had delivered her baby. "The white cemetery is in the black part of town," she said.

I headed for the white part of town.

The streets were unfamiliar. I had only been to Bainbridge twice before, in 1957 and 1958.

Mama and I had flown to Tallahassee from New York City. Grand-daddy had picked us up and driven the 42 miles north to Bainbridge, Georgia's "first inland port," population 12,714, then. The town lies in the southwest corner of the state, north of Attapulgus, south of Camilla.

My grandfather had moved there in 1935 after his residency at Brewster Hospital in Jacksonville, Florida. Shortly before, he'd divorced my Jamaican-born grandmother, Ruby Duncombe Lord, to marry Madelyn Parsons, a much younger woman. Ruby never had a kind word to say about Granddaddy. Their marital problems were myriad, but among them was her refusal to move to the Jim Crow South from New York. "I'll not step aside for any white people," she boldly claimed. What she really felt, I suspect, was justifiable fear of a life filled with terrorism. But Bainbridge needed a black doctor, so Granddaddy went.

I spent two summers with my grandfather, and a few holidays. I was about four the first time we met, and properly outfitted for the occasion in a brilliant yellow, silk- and satin-trimmed peignoir. I believed myself devastating. But the straps kept slipping. The sleeves kept sliding. I didn't care. Granddaddy hugged me and chased me in circles around the house till we fell down laughing on the floor.

"Oh, Granddaddy, I don't feel so well," I'd tease.

"We can't have that," he'd say, then run and get his black bag and pretend to prepare an injection.

"No, no. I'm fine, Grandpa." He'd chase me again.

"Sure you're fine now?"

"I'm sure." I squealed and ran myself silly. He'd catch me, hug me, and tickle me to tears.

Now I was searching for his grave.

The weather was windy, cold, very gray. In the car, outside the cemetery, I sat searching for my sunglasses. I kept fumbling for them, in my purse, under the seat. I had not cried once.

It was my third day in town. I had talked to dozens of people who knew him, trying to reconstruct his life and death. I wanted to be professionally detached, unemotional. I cursed the missing sunglasses.

Thirteen minutes later I gave up and stepped out of the rented car.

I began walking around the southern rim of the graveyard. His would be a big tombstone, I was sure.

"Was he good?" repeated L.H.B. Foote incredulously. "One of the best. He never stopped trying to learn medicine and that makes any doctor good." Leonard Hobson Buchanan Foote, M.D., did not look his eighty-five years. We had sat in his Tallahassee home on the Florida A&M University campus. For forty years he had been the director of student medical services there. He had been one of my grandfather's closest friends.

They entered Howard University the same year. "The freshman class of 1918," Foote said. The year before, my grandfather had immigrated to the United States from Georgetown, Guyana, then a British colony.

"I was just a boy from Maryland," Foote said, "born and reared just north of Baltimore." Granddaddy, he recalled, "was tall, slender, a nice-looking young colored man with a foreign accent. I'd say, 'Man, I can't understand you. What are you saying?' He'd say, 'You just listen real good. I speak the King's English.' I said, 'What king?' He said, 'The King of England.' 'You're one of those West Indians, huh?' 'Yeah, what's wrong with that?' 'Not a thing,' I said. 'Welcome here, brother.'

"I felt like I had lost a brother when he died. He had a lot of whites who were his friends, some of them were his patients."   28

But, he said, Granddaddy had been the object of some resentment. There are, explained Foote, "three things that the southern white man has tried over the years to keep out of the hands of blacks—education, money, and social rank. Your grandfather had all that."

As I walked to the western edge of the graveyard, I heard voices nearby. Several houses lined the western perimeter of the cemetery. I stared at the windows looking out on the tombstones.

"Rumor was, one of the boys in the car could look out of his kitchen window and see Daddy's grave," my aunt Earlyne had told me.

I searched for nearly an hour. Finally, I reached the north end.   32
About fifty feet ahead of me I spotted a gray marble headstone.

I stepped closer to the tombstone, a solitary monument in a twenty-foot-square plot. It was the biggest headstone in the cemetery: The Family of Dr. E A R Lord.

I stared standing in the cold. I wiped my nose. In the crevice of the chiseled letters that formed the word "of," dirt and rain had left a sooty streak. It was the only smudge on the stone. Unconsciously, I leaned forward and began to wipe the stain with the pink Kleenex in my hand. I rubbed hard against the marble. The tissue frayed and disintegrated in the wind.

On the slab of marble that covered his grave was the symbol of the medical profession, the caduceus with its entwined serpents on a winged staff. Engraved in the stone was his full name: Edward Adolphus Rufus Lord Sr. M.D.

They called him Earl Lord for short. He was born July 26, 1897, in   36
Georgetown, Guyana. He died October 30, 1960, in Bainbridge, Georgia.

"Wasn't from around here," Bernice Busbee drawled. The man across from her stood gnomelike behind the rocking chair in his office, smiled like Puck and softly proclaimed himself "the oldest living white person in Bainbridge." Then Mortimer Alfred Ehrlich, M.D., eighty-nine, sat down and rocked.

He was retired. As a younger man Dr. Ehrlich had often come to my grandfather's infirmary to help with surgery. He was one of the few whites in Bainbridge whom my family thought of as a genuine friend.

I told him only that I was a newspaper reporter doing a story about small-town doctors; I wanted him to speak freely. Then I asked him about Dr. Lord.

Dr. Ehrlich regarded me thoughtfully.   40

"I don't want to talk bad of the dead," he said. I switched off the tape recorder and smiled my encouragement.

"He was a bad man," Ehrlich finally said. The old chair groaned with each rock.

"Blacks didn't like him either," Busbee offered. She had been Ehrlich's receptionist for thirty-one years. Now they spent their days making quilts for comfort when it's cold. "He was an undermining, sneaky fellow," she said. "He tried to bring the NAACP in here."

"Lord was for integration," Ehrlich elaborated.   44

"He just didn't fit in," she said. "Didn't understand the people. Didn't know our ways. We were all glad when he was gone."

My smile was beginning to ache.

"If he hadn't been killed in the accident, he would have been shot," Ehrlich said. "Better he was killed that way so we didn't have the bother of a trial for whoever shot him."

We spoke for a few more minutes. Then I rose to leave and shake his   48
hand. He offered the tips of his fingers.

I left him rocking.

That old white southerners would have believed that the NAACP was subversive, and condemned my grandfather for belonging to it, did not surprise me. That my grandfather was political at all did.

I had thought my family in Bainbridge to be insulated, apolitical members of the southern black bourgeoisie under segregation. I recall going to a movie theater with my uncle Paul and my aunt Pat, the youngest of the five children Granddaddy had with Madelyn. I wandered to the "wrong" side of the theater lobby to read the posters advertising the coming attractions.

"No, come here," Aunt Pat said, tugging me gently.   52

"Why?" I boomed, pulling her to where I wanted to be.

"You just can't," Uncle Paul told me with no further explanation. He was tall, handsome, and dark brown like Granddaddy, while Aunt Pat was so pale she could have gone into the "whites only" section of the theater unnoticed. But I

recall no signs that announced the Jim Crow seating plan. I had never heard of him, and my aunt had to put a hand over my mouth to quiet my protests from the balcony.

"Why are we up here? Why can't we sit downstairs?"

I remembered that night in the theater when I called Aunt Earlyne to tell her   56
I was going back to Bainbridge.

"We always grew up so secure," she insisted. "We could just walk into any store and say 'Charge it.'" As she spoke, I envisioned the delicate string of pearls, my first and only, that she sent to me when I was just a toddler. The Lords, she said, could take clothes out of a store on approval at any time. This was when most southern blacks weren't allowed to try on a pair of shoes. You bought them and suffered if they didn't fit. "We never really felt any open hostility toward us," she mused. "But it was always something you knew was there. You knew how far you could go in raising an issue. Some things you could get away with. Others, you knew you could not. It was a KKK city and KKK members ran it along with a few politicians from the town's first families."

I would find out later that my grandfather had spoken out for equal pay for black and white teachers in Bainbridge long before the 1954 U.S. Supreme Court ruled that separate could not be equal. He wanted black and white students to use the same textbooks. He wanted black students to ride buses, not walk miles to school.

"All of these inequities were addressed by Doctor Lord," said S. B. Bryant, the retired assistant principal of Hutto High, once all black. Now it is an integrated junior high school. He is seventy-one and blind.

"No one liked the disparities, but there were those who sat supinely   60
by and took it. And there were those, like Doctor Lord, who were concerned." As schoolteachers, "we couldn't openly contribute to the NAACP and keep our jobs.

"Doctor Lord, however, *stayed* in the superintendent's office pleading the cause, so much so that when they got ready to name the swimming pool, it was named after him."

It was the only city-owned swimming facility that allowed blacks. It wasn't integrated until 1970.

There was also a street named after him, in the black part of town. Lord Avenue. It's still there. Still in the black part of town.

Granddaddy's name is still painted on the window of the infirmary   64
he once ran. It is a flophouse now.

Bainbridge seemed a little town locked in time.

The downtown streets were mostly vacant, empty of traffic. An old white man sat on a bench, muttering to himself in front of the gazebo.

The city built the latticed structure a few years ago. In chamber of commerce literature costumed southern belles adorn it, but on this day no one was there but the self-absorbed old man and some goldfish. The fish swam in a pool at the base of a statue of a Confederate soldier. Along the marble rim of the pool in gold was: BAINBRIDGE, INCORPORATED 1829.

I felt like an alien there. 68

I was born in Brooklyn, the daughter of a Marxist historian and a nurse. I had studied most of my life to be a musician, an opera singer. In the 1970s I embraced what was considered to be radical black politics. I rejected my slave name for an African one. I began to wear only traditional African clothes. I abandoned classical music because it was incompatible with my newly aroused sense of cultural identity. In time I would come to see that black nationalism almost inevitably leads to a kind of cultural chauvinism indistinguishable from racism, the very thing I thought I was fighting.

But no moderation of my political views could make me tolerate the stifling atmosphere of Bainbridge. On my first day in town I spoke with some of the city's young blacks. They spoke with bitterness about the professional opportunities denied them in their hometown. And they laughed dryly at the social outlets Bainbridge offered them: Skatetown, the roller rink, its six nights of rock set aside for soul on Sundays, the unspoken invitation that let blacks know that night—and only that night—was theirs. Meanwhile, their white counterparts got to go to the country club, to which no black belonged. And like the generations of blacks who lived there during and before my grandfather's day, they all said: What do you do if you're black in Bainbridge and you've got ambition? Go to Tallahassee.

"Some nights, a chilling silence would fall on the town," my mother told me, recalling one particularly stark image she maintained of Bainbridge. "It was that time of evening after supper, when the dishes were done and families would gather in the parlor before bed." It seemed as though the town had gasped, held its breath, then minutes later released it with a shudder, she said. "The next morning, word would come that someone had been lynched."

As I walked through the town, I imagined how much more cruel a 72 place it was when my grandfather, elegant and worldly, lived and died there.

I remembered his house on Planter Street in the way a child recalls a beautiful, festive dream. All the room! Lots of space to dance whenever music played; music that poured down on me from above. Granddaddy had installed an elaborate music system with speakers in the ceiling of each room.

In the front of the house was a circular driveway that led to the porch. A dark blue canopy stretched from the front door to the street, to protect guests from inclement weather. Art deco glass bricks framed the windows in each room. A glass brick bar stood on the circular patio in the rear of the house. Four giant white columns grandly marked the boundaries of his property.

What an impertinence that house must have been for a black man in Bainbridge in 1942.

I wondered how many whites in Bainbridge had mourned his 76 death? Who among them would have stepped forward to demand punishment for his killers?

How do you unlock a twenty-three-year-old mystery? Without much hope, I visited the newspaper, the *Bainbridge Post-Searchlight*, published twice weekly, to see if their morgue contained any reference to my grandfather's death, any leads I could follow. I expected to find nothing, but I was wrong.

On the front page, November 3, 1960, where a week later the newspaper would report the election of John F. Kennedy, was a four-paragraph story:

"Doctor E.A.R. Lord, well known colored physician, died early Sunday . . ." My eyes raced down the column. ". . . enroute to Memorial Hospital of injuries sustained . . . The accident, according to Bainbridge police officers, occurred . . . intersection of Planter and Scott . . .

"Doctor Lord, driving a '53 Ford . . . The other vehicle . . . '57 80 Dodge driven by . . ."

Nothing quite registered. I had always been told no one ever found out who did it, that the killer had been protected by the white establishment.

But here was his name, on the front page.

John Lawrence Harper, twenty-two.

I jumped for the phone book. Harper wasn't listed, but I felt it 84 didn't matter. If he was still alive, I knew I could find him.

And ask him—what?

I needed more information before I could confront him. How had the accident happened? Was he drunk? If his name was known, might he even have been punished?

With a name, I thought I could find these things out. I hurried across the street to the courthouse.

The files for 1960 showed that John Lawrence Harper had never 88 been charged with a crime. Expecting nothing, I checked the civil court records. A clerk pulled the dockets for the 1960–61 term for me. There was a case styled *Madelyn P. Lord* vs. *John Lawrence Harper*.

I stared at the page in disbelief.

My grandmother, who had been silent all these years, had not only known the identity of the driver, but sued for damages in 1961. One hundred thousand dollars in damages.

In the file, I found a police report. Under the "apparent cause of accident," it said Harper was "exceeding lawful speed." There was no mention of alcohol.

The case had gone to trial. Harper had alleged the accident was my   92
grandfather's fault; my grandmother had claimed Harper was to blame. On May 5, 1961, a jury had reached a verdict: six thousand dollars for Madelyn Lord.

I called my aunt Earlyne. She was shocked. She knew nothing about a civil suit. She only knew her mother never tried to press any criminal charges both because she was so "traumatized" by Granddaddy's death and because of "politics." It was a Klan town, she reminded me.

But if my grandmother was so traumatized, how did she find the wherewithal to proceed with a civil suit?

Her friends pressed her to do it, said Anne Smith, the retired teacher who told me where to find my grandfather's grave. My grand-mother was so upset, she recounted, she let strangers take my grand-father's car away.

My aunt recalled the same story. "Someone took it after the acci-   96
dent, fixed it up, and was driving around town in it."

After Granddaddy died, Smith said, my grandma Madelyn was still going into stores charging things for which she could not pay. "I'd go to the house, get the jewelry, and have to take it back to the store," Smith said. My grandmother lived in a daze, she told me.

I knew the fog had lifted for my grandmother, but not the fear.

I searched for transcripts of the trial. If they ever existed, they were gone. All that was left, except for routine paperwork, was the list of jurors.

They would be all white. Blacks weren't called for jury duty in   100
Bainbridge, Georgia, in 1961. How would these jurors react to me, a black woman from Miami, on their doorstep asking questions about the local boy who had killed her grandfather?

I wanted the truth, and in this particular town complete honesty didn't seem to be the way to get it. As with Dr. Ehrlich, I decided not to mention I was Dr. Lord's granddaughter. Further, I decided to interview the jurors by telephone. I did not want them to know I was black.

I wanted to be fair. But more important, I wanted the truth.

I wanted to know why Granddaddy died.

Juror James F. Steadham, now seventy-four: 104

"It was the middle of the night," he remembered. "Lord was half drunk, half asleep. . . . The boys had gone out to the Dog and Gun Club and I think they were about half drunk and they just run together . . ." How good was his memory? The police report made no allegations about alcohol. There was no mention of a blood test for Harper or an autopsy report for my grandfather. I thought it unlikely that Granddaddy had been drinking. He had been aroused from bed by a phone call, had driven to the infirmary and treated a patient. Would he have stopped at a bar on the way home in his pajamas?

I asked Steadham if he knew Dr. Lord.

"Yeah, I just knew him when I saw him. He was a nigger and . . . wasn't much association between white and niggers at that time. I had nigger friends that I think just about as much of as white friends."

But "Lord," he said, "was kinda arrogant. Sooner or later somebody   108 would have shot him. He didn't understand the people here. . . . Bainbridge was a good town to live in for both black and white. He just didn't get along too well with the public. I think he must of come in from the North."

How, I asked him, was the six-thousand-dollar figure arrived at? It seemed a small sum to me even for 1961.

"We kicked that around a bit. Money was scarce and hard to get," he said. He said he thought the award was just. The jury had discussed it, he said, and one juror had pointed out: " 'Never saw a hundred-thousand-dollar nigger.' "

In the next few days I would reach four other jurors, Bainbridge police chief James "Jabbo" Duke, the lawyer who had represented my grandmother in the suit, the former police officer who had investigated the accident, the former district attorney.

No one agreed on anything.   112

Two of the four jurors I could still find said they remembered nothing of the case. The third said my grandfather had been at fault. The fourth said Harper had been at fault. My grandmother's former lawyer remembered almost nothing about the case, nor did the cop on the scene ("I can hardly remember what happened a week ago"). Chief Duke was also hazy, but he remembered my grandfather well. He said he had been well respected by blacks and whites alike, and a fine doctor.

It was the first kind word about my grandfather that I had heard from a white person, but I could not shake off a skepticism about his sincerity. He hadn't offered his hand to me when we met or parted, either; nor had I offered mine to him.

The police accident report listed two witnesses, though it didn't specify how they happened to be involved. One had left Bainbridge. "That's my son you're talking about," said Benson Woodbery's mother. "No one knows where he is. When the accident happened, he was living with his grandmother." Last she heard, he was living in Florida. ". . . But he's just the kind that drifts," the mother said.

The other witness was Lee Parker, Bainbridge's postmaster. I called   116
him.

"I don't know why they would have my name as a witness. I passed by the accident after it happened. Maybe a half hour, an hour later. Yes, I knew Larry Harper. I grew up in Bainbridge. His father still lives here," Parker told me. The father's name was C. E. Harper.

A short, plump, white-haired man answered the door. He looked like a man perpetually on the verge of telling a joke. In his living room he pointed to a plaster of paris bust swathed with red cloth. He undraped it. It was a woman with cascading, shoulder-length hair and bare breasts big enough to suckle a nation. He laughed. His wife covered it again.

The father of the man who killed my grandfather was sixty-nine. He seemed genuinely friendly, but clearly uncomfortable. Again, I told him only that I was a reporter writing about small-town doctors, and that during my interviews, Earl Lord's name had been mentioned repeatedly as a physician who'd had some influence in Bainbridge. I asked about Dr. Lord's death.

He said he didn't remember much about the accident. I asked if he knew of any witnesses.

"Lee Parker was in the car with Larry," he volunteered.

Lee Parker. The man who'd been listed as a witness to the accident but denied knowing anything about it. What was he hiding?

I said nothing.

Harper's wife, Estelle, sat staring at the black reporter and white photographer in her living room.

"This isn't going to stir up any racial thing?" Harper asked. He looked genuinely concerned.

"I used to sell insurance, you know," he went on. "I have lots of black friends. Always got along well. I called Larry to tell him you were coming. He wasn't home. He's in Albany, Georgia, now, selling insurance.

"This is not going to stir up a black-white thing?" he asked again. "I know Larry really hated it when it happened," the father assured me.

Perhaps he really did, I thought, looking at the genial man who was his father, a man who had never been deliberately unkind to a black person in his life, probably. Perhaps his son was like him. Probably. Perhaps.

I went back to my motel room and telephoned John Lawrence Harper in Albany.

I kept rehearsing my tone of voice—calm, businesslike, detached. I was trying to keep the nerves and anger out.

His voice was pleasant, youthful. I said that in the course of my story on doctors I had become interested in Dr. Lord, and that I was trying to reconstruct the events of his life and the accident that caused his death.

"So . . . what do you want from me?"   132
"I'm trying to find out what happened," I told him.
"I wouldn't even be interested, it happened so long ago."
I asked if he ever thought about the accident.
"Naw," he said. "The case that happened then was then. I had a lot   136
of feelings then, none now."
I told him there are no official records explaining what actually
happened.
"Yeah, probably never will be either, will it?" he tossed out cockily.
". . . Probably wasn't important enough to."
I stiffened. "Someone *did* die."
"So, people die in accidents every day."   140
"What were the circumstances?" I repeated.
"Oh, gosh, it could be a million circumstances. . . . Good heav-
ens . . ."
There was a click. The line went dead. I called back.
"I thought we were through. It's so irrelevant now. You think there's   144
some mystery here to be unwound. I was in a car. Another man was in a
car. We met under a red light . . ."
"Your father . . . told me that Mr. Parker was in the car with you."
"He remembers more about it than I do."
"Why did Mr. Parker say he wasn't involved then?"
"I'm sure he looks back on that thing . . ." He paused. "It was a   148
trying experience for all of us. I don't imagine he *wanted* to be involved
at the time, and his feelings, probably, when you called him, came back.
He probably doesn't recollect the event hardly either.
"There was nobody in the car with me," he said.
"So your father was incorrect?"
"Ah, probably so if he said that."
"So Mr. Parker was not there?"   152
"Uh, when did you talk to Daddy, today?"
"Yes."
"Yeah, he remembers more about it than I do," Harper repeated
sarcastically.
He was understandably defensive, shaken to have an incident half   156
his lifetime old resurrected. That was the reason for the cockiness, the
sarcasm, I tried to convince myself. I knew I was upsetting him badly
but still I pressed him.
"Do you go to bed with a clear conscience about this?"
"Clear conscience—now wait a minute . . ." He raised his voice for
the first time. "You went too far there. That thing was cleared up twenty-
three years ago and you're asking me something about a conscience.
Hey, don't call me anymore." He hung up.

I sat there on the bed of my motel room, trembling. Around me were all my pens and notebooks, all the trappings of the dispassionate journalist.

No, Harper was wrong. It was not "cleared up."   160

I had to see him in person.

We drove past one-blink-and-gone towns built around railroad tracks, grazing cows, and pecan orchards to get to Albany. It was close to dusk when we arrived. The only gas station open downtown had no maps of the city. I found Harper's address in an old phone book at the service station and asked for directions. We got sent to an area of dilapidated shacks near an old railroad station. It was the wrong place.

We turned back toward town and checked into a Holiday Inn. A more recent telephone directory had a different address.

The house was in a well-to-do subdivision with nicely trimmed 164 lawns and lamps at the front door. No lights were on at Harper's address. It was 9:10 P.M. We drove around and returned twenty minutes later. The house was still dark. The photographer stayed in the car while I got out to look closer. The house was empty, recently vacated, it appeared. Newspapers were still in the driveway.

Frustrated, I returned to the motel and dialed information. The operator gave me the same telephone number for Harper that was listed in the current phone directory, but at another address. I resorted to a cab company for directions.

We drove miles past the city limits unable to find it. The absent moon and clouds made the night sky seem opaque. The sudden flicker of light in the woods was startling. I'd never seen torched farmland before. The deeper we drove into the countryside, the more widespread the flames. The fields the farmers set afire posed no danger on the damp earth. It was the glowing branches at the road's edge, overlapping like a cross, that made me shudder . . . drift . . . into a psychic film noir replay of the past twenty-three years.

We had driven twenty miles and were lost. We turned back. Fifteen miles toward town, I spotted it, Harper's street, just before a railroad crossing. The house was in a tract of modest single-family homes and duplexes. It was midnight. We'd have to return in the morning.

We went back to the Holiday Inn. I drank a shot of cognac and 168 smoked half a pack of cigarettes. I don't care much for liquor. I don't smoke.

At 7:40 A.M., I stepped from my car into the rain at the home of the man I wanted to see. The photographer remained in the car. We knew a camera would make things more difficult.

The house was divided into two apartments. Harper's was on the left. The heels of my black pumps sank in the red mud that covered what should have been a lawn. I entered a dark foyer and pressed the bell. Gloria Harper, his wife, answered the door. I told her my name and gave her my card.

"We have nothing to say to you." She was five feet two inches at most, plump, had brown hair and wore glasses. She pulled the floor-length robe tighter around her.

I told her only her husband could tell me what happened the night 172 of the accident. She stared at me as I stood in the dimly lit hallway dressed all in black, my hands in my pockets, the collar of my coat turned toward by beige cheeks.

"My husband's getting dressed for work. He has nothing to say to you." She shut the door in my face. I stood there for a few moments, breathed deeply, then pressed the bell again.

"Look, I told you—"

I interrupted. I told her what I had heard about the accident.

She stood there framed by the open door. A young boy walked 176 behind her and stood slightly to her left. He was not more than sixteen, bare-chested and dressed in jeans. His hair looked ash blond. One could not be sure in the pale light. But his face was clearly beautiful. He looked pained and perplexed at my presence.

"I'd like to hear your husband's version of what happened."

"He has nothing to tell you," she said.

"Let *him* tell me that, Mrs. Harper." Then I told them. "I'm not interested just as a reporter," I said. "I am Doctor Lord's granddaughter."

"I knew it," Harper exclaimed. He had been standing at the side of 180 the door, out of sight, listening.

He had on a yellow shirt and tan slacks and wore glasses. He looked older than forty-five. Perhaps because his hair was so white. His wife and son formed a zigzag line of defense in front of him.

"I knew it had to be someone from the family," he said excitedly. His hands were stiffly at his sides. He stared at me from behind his child. I realized my stance may have looked threatening. I took my hands out of my pockets.

"You just stay right there," the wife said. "We're calling the police."

"I knew it, I knew it . . ." Harper kept saying. I heard him pick up 184 the phone. The wife shut the door in my face again. I stood there for a moment, wondering what would happen to me if I stayed to be taken to some small southern city jail. I left.

We drove past groves of nut trees in the drizzling rain and away from Albany. The landscape and the graying light pushed thoughts of John Lawrence Harper from my mind. And my heart slowed, enough for me to think and take stock of what had happened.

I had stood on a man's doorstep and humiliated him in front of his wife and child.

For what? What had he done?

Twenty-three years ago he had the misfortune to be in an auto 188 accident that claimed a life.

The rumors had been wrong. There was no evidence of drag racing, none I could find. If there had been a cover-up, it had been pretty inept. Harper's name was front-page news in the local paper. If there had been an injustice, hadn't it been mitigated by a six-thousand-dollar award by a white jury to a black woman?

Despite the pain that induced it, hadn't my grandmother's silence for twenty-three years kept alive in my family a hurtful distortion?

And yet I felt like screaming. Because nothing was resolved, nothing was settled. Absolutely nothing.

I came to Bainbridge, Georgia, hoping to find and expose a killer 192 who had been protected by a white racist society for twenty-three years. That, or something else: to discover that the man who killed Grand-daddy had been punished, and that he and the people of his town, whites and blacks, had mourned the loss of a man such as E.A.R. Lord.

But I found neither thing. I found no clear-cut guilt or innocence, nor did I find my grandfather warmly remembered.

In Bainbridge, Georgia, 1983, I found a town that had changed very little in the last twenty-three years, one that had entered this quarter century only reluctantly, dragged by the courts, pouting, without guilt. Yes, it does have integrated schools and a lone black city councilman. And it named a street after a dead black doctor. But it is still strangled by plantation-style racism: gentle-voiced, genteel whites unabashedly talking of niggers, white people still so contemptuous of blacks that they would not soil their hands by touching mine. There is still a black part of town and a white part of town. A black cemetery and a white cemetery. Skatetown rock on weekdays and Skatetown soul on Sundays. Opportunities for whites, a bus ticket out of town for blacks.

And who is to blame?

I came, tried to find blame, and I failed. I wanted to stay in 196 Bainbridge longer. I wanted to go back once I returned to Miami. With more reporting, I argued, I could find an answer; the truth. My editors said no. Then they suggested that Bill Rose, a white reporter born and raised in the South, try to talk to Harper, just to see if he'd feel less threatened. I agreed.

Harper ran to the men's room in his office building when Rose came to see him and would not talk.

At the paper, we struggled with this story for months, arguing over its point of view and the need to dig deeper. It was the only way to find the truth, I bellowed. Finally, I was compelled to write.

A woman whose family had lived in Bainbridge walked into the newsroom months after my return. She was a Miami writer. She told an editor she had something to tell me. Her uncle had been killed by "rednecks" in the town, she said. They had found him walking in the woods, beat him, and left him to die. It was the 1930s, she said; about the time my grandfather came to Bainbridge; about the time my mother remembers the chilling silence that fell on the town some evenings. Her uncle's murder, said the woman, almost destroyed her grandmother's life, contributed to her own mother's mental breakdown. The pain becomes "generational," said Marjorie Klein, whose uncle was a Jew.

There is so much blood on the land, who will ever know The Truth? 200

And so, as a matter of law and justice, I am compelled to consider the whites of Bainbridge to be innocent: the man who drove the car, the jurors who had "never seen a hundred-thousand-dollar nigger" and awarded six thousand dollars, the white town that did not prosecute.

Yet I cannot.

In the absence of proof of guilt, I need some proof of innocence. Or I am left, against the backdrop of my life and the lives of so many others, to wariness.

Would John Lawrence Harper have been prosecuted had he been 204 black and my grandfather white? Can you really expect me to assume otherwise? On that night in Bainbridge, Georgia, twenty-three years ago, even if just for a moment, did John Lawrence Harper heave a sigh of relief that it was only a black man who had died?

How could I assume otherwise?

I feel the suspicion in me. I feel the hatred creeping up. Those feelings are so powerful, they cannot be extinguished by trustingly extending to the town, to the man, the benefit of a doubt. Trust requires more than a failure to prove guilt; it requires a belief in innocence.

The night my grandfather's skull cracked against the pavement, my grandmother Madelyn flew through the street, her white nightgown, her pale, pale skin streaks of light against the darkness. She tried to push through the crowd, a witness told me months after I returned from Bainbridge. A white cop pushed her back gently. "Don't worry yourself, ma'am," he told her. "It's just a nigger."

Against a backdrop of personal loss, against the evidence of history 208 that fills me with a knowledge of the hateful behavior of whites toward blacks, I see the people of Bainbridge. And I cannot trust them. I cannot absolve them.

Perhaps you will argue that this is intemperate. Perhaps you will call me a racist. I do not think that I am.

But I am weary of the collective amnesia of most white Americans. I am not responsible for what Daddy or Granddaddy did, they say; and as long as they are innocent of perpetuating the evils of the past, they are right. I read history as a child, not fiction. I understand how insidious was the impersonal social system that had coldly denied opportunity to blacks, and seemingly left no one to blame, as if systems do not bear the marks of their creators.

I saw what it did to my father. It helped shatter him, a classical scholar with a doctorate in philosophy and few options for a black intellectual in America in the 1930s. He spent his life writing about liberty denied because of race and class. He spent his life galled that he was confined to traditional Negro colleges, unrecognized as an important scholar by the white academic establishment, his intellect always defined by the parameters of race.

I found him naked and bloated, lying on his apartment floor, dying, 212 an alcoholic in a diabetic coma, the bills from the liquor store stuck in the pages of his books. I was twenty-five and he was sixty-nine, the anger between us unresolved at his death. I am bitter when I think what society denied him and me. And I am bitter when I think of my grandfather, and the white people of Bainbridge.

In going back to Bainbridge I felt I was tracking down a thousand anonymous bigots whose acts would never be known, whose guilt or innocence would never be judged. Men who killed a black man and laughed. Even men who, without malice, killed a black man and sighed, knowing it ultimately did not matter.

When I returned home, my aunt Earlyne told me that if she met Harper today, she would shake his hand. "That's what Daddy would have wanted," she said. "Turn the other cheek. We can't live in this world with hate."

I know no such charity.

I want a thousand anonymous bigots to know that somebody's 216 grandchild might someday knock at their door, too. *1982*

Everyday Life

13

Anxieties of Appearance

Alice Walker, Beauty: When the Other Dancer
Is the Self

Nora Ephron, A Few Words about Breasts

John Updike, At War with My Skin

Two out of every three adults in the United States say they fidget, fuss, take furtive glances in windows and mirrors, and study other people's reactions to the way they look. It is not overstating it to report that a solid majority of the American people are close to being obsessed with their physical appearance.

Louis Harris, from *Inside America*

She knew the meaning of the word heart. Her heart grew so big she thought the moon fell from the heavens and resided inside. The moon-beams became her longings, her wishes, as they shot at her from within her body, her red, red heart. And so she dreamed of becoming heroic, not like Wonder Woman who fought America's enemies with her steel bracelets and short, short skirt, but more like Marilyn Monroe, perhaps, with a mouth that invited touch. Touching lived as far away as a distant cousin in China from this woman's heart. Her fingers were too dry, she insisted. Her knuckles were too big, too ugly, and so she taught herself that her fingers and body weren't hers. They belonged outside to the world, detached from her person, her dry skin, her eyes that danced on top of her hand, as she saw herself lying on a beach in St. Tropez with the sun blazing on a body that she would never have. She was a woman who had learned to live under cover and under cover pointed the toes of a dancer thudding against her wild heart.

Nellie Wong, from *Broad Shoulders*

We all proceed on the basis of the unspoken rule that every man *is* as he *looks*: this is a correct rule; the difficulty lies in applying it. The capacity for doing so is in part inborn, in part to be gained through experience, but no one ever perfects it: even the most practiced detect errors in themselves. Yet the face does not lie: it is we who read what is not written there. In any event, the deciphering of the face is a great and difficult art.

Arthur Schopenhauer, from *On Physiognomy*

Alice Walker

Beauty: When the Other Dancer Is the Self

It is a bright summer day in 1947. My father, a fat, funny man with beautiful eyes and a subversive wit, is trying to decide which of his eight children he will take with him to the county fair. My mother, of course, will not go. She is knocked out from getting most of us ready: I hold my neck stiff against the pressure of her knuckles as she hastily completes the braiding and the beribboning of my hair.

My father is the driver for the rich old white lady up the road. Her name is Miss Mey. She owns all the land for miles around, as well as the house in which we live. All I remember about her is that she once offered to pay my mother thirty-five cents for cleaning her house, raking up piles of her magnolia leaves, and washing her family's clothes, and that my mother—she of no money, eight children, and a chronic earache—refused it. But I do not think of this in 1947. I am two-and-a-half years old. I want to go everywhere my daddy goes. I am excited at the prospect of riding in a car. Someone has told me fairs are fun. That there is room in the car for only three of us doesn't faze me at all. Whirling happily in my starchy frock, showing off my biscuit-polished patent-leather shoes and lavender socks, tossing my head in a way that makes my ribbons bounce, I stand, hands on hips, before my father. "Take me, Daddy," I say with assurance; "I'm the prettiest!"

Later, it does not surprise me to find myself in Miss Mey's shiny black car, sharing the back seat with the other lucky ones. Does not surprise me that I thoroughly enjoy the fair. At home that night I tell the unlucky ones all I can remember about the merry-go-round, the man who eats live chickens, and the teddy bears, until they say: that's enough, baby Alice. Shut up now, and go to sleep.

It is Easter Sunday, 1950. I am dressed in a green, flocked,   4 scalloped-hem dress (handmade by my adoring sister, Ruth) that has its own smooth satin petticoat and tiny hot-pink roses tucked into each scallop. My shoes, new T-strap patent leather, again highly biscuit-polished. I am six years old and have learned one of the longest Easter speeches to be heard that day, totally unlike the speech I said when I was two: "Easter lilies / pure and white / blossom in / the morning light." When I rise to give my speech I do so on a great wave of love and pride and expectation. People in the church stop rustling their new crino-lines. They seem to hold their breath. I can tell they admire my dress, but it is my spirit, bordering on sassiness (womanishness), they secretly applaud.

"That girl's a little *mess*," they whisper to each other, pleased.

Naturally I say my speech without stammer or pause, unlike those who stutter, stammer, or, worst of all, forget. This is before the word "beautiful" exists in people's vocabulary, but "Oh, isn't she the *cutest* thing!" frequently floats my way. "And got so much sense!" they grate-fully add . . . for which thoughtful addition I thank them to this day.

It was great fun being cute. But then, one day, it ended.

I am eight years old and a tomboy. I have a cowboy hat, cowboy   8 boots, checkered shirt and pants, all red. My playmates are my brothers, two and four years older than I. Their colors are black and green, the only difference in the way we are dressed. On Saturday nights we all go to the picture show, even my mother; Westerns are her favorite kind of movie. Back home, "on the ranch," we pretend we are Tom Mix, Hopalong Cassidy, Lash LaRue (we've even named one of our dogs Lash LaRue); we chase each other for hours rustling cattle, being outlaws, delivering damsels from distress. Then my parents decide to buy my brothers guns. These are not "real" guns. They shoot BBs, copper pellets my brothers say will kill birds. Because I am a girl, I do not get a gun. Instantly I am relegated to the position of Indian. Now there appears a great distance between us. They shoot and shoot at everything with their new guns. I try to keep up with my bow and arrows.

One day while I am standing on top of our makeshift "garage"—pieces of tin nailed across some poles—holding my bow and arrow and looking out toward the fields, I feel an incredible blow in my right eye. I look down just in time to see my brother lower his gun.

Both brothers rush to my side. My eye stings, and I cover it with my hand. "If you tell," they say, "we will get a whipping. You don't want that to happen, do you?" I do not. "Here is a piece of wire," says the older brother, picking it up from the roof; "say you stepped on one end of it and the other flew up and hit you." The pain is beginning to start. "Yes," I say. "Yes, I will say that is what happened." If I do not say this is what happened, I know my brothers will find ways to make me wish I had. But now I will say anything that gets me to my mother.

Confronted by our parents we stick to the lie agreed upon. They place me on a bench on the porch and I close my left eye while they examine the right. There is a tree growing from underneath the porch that climbs past the railing to the roof. It is the last thing my right eye sees. I watch as its trunk, its branches, and then its leaves are blotted out by the rising blood.

I am in shock. First there is intense fever, which my father tries to 12 break using lily leaves bound around my head. Then there are chills: my mother tries to get me to eat soup. Eventually, I do not know how, my parents learn what has happened. A week after the "accident" they take me to see a doctor. "Why did you wait so long to come?" he asks, looking into my eye and shaking his head. "Eyes are sympathetic," he says. "If one is blind, the other will likely become blind too."

This comment of the doctor's terrifies me. But it is really how I look that bothers me most. Where the BB pellet struck there is a glob of whitish scar tissue, a hideous cataract, on my eye. Now when I stare at people—a favorite pastime, up to now—they will stare back. Not at the "cute" little girl, but at her scar. For six years I do not stare at anyone, because I do not raise my head.

Years later, in the throes of a mid-life crisis, I ask my mother and sister whether I changed after the "accident." "No," they say, puzzled. "What do you mean?"

What do I mean?

I am eight, and, for the first time, doing poorly in school, where I 16 have been something of a whiz since I was four. We have just moved to the place where the "accident" occurred. We do not know any of the people around us because this is a different county. The only time I see the friends I knew is when we go back to our old church. The new school is the former state penitentiary. It is a large stone building, cold and drafty, crammed to overflowing with boisterous, ill-disciplined children. On the third floor there is a huge circular imprint of some partition that has been torn out.

"What used to be here?" I ask a sullen girl next to me on our way past it to lunch.

"The electric chair," says she.

At night I have nightmares about the electric chair, and about all the people reputedly "fried" in it. I am afraid of the school, where all the students seem to be budding criminals.

"What's the matter with your eye?" they ask, critically. 20

When I don't answer (I cannot decide whether it was an "accident" or not), they shove me, insist on a fight.

My brother, the one who created the story about the wire, comes to my rescue. But then brags so much about "protecting" me, I become sick.

After months of torture at the school, my parents decide to send me back to our old community, to my old school. I live with my grand-parents and the teacher they board. But there is no room for Phoebe, my cat. By the time my grandparents decide there *is* room, and I ask for my cat, she cannot be found. Miss Yarborough, the boarding teacher, takes me under her wing, and begins to teach me to play the piano. But soon she marries an African—a "prince," she says—and is whisked away to his continent.

At my old school there is at least one teacher who loves me. She is 24 the teacher who "knew me before I was born" and bought my first baby clothes. It is she who makes life bearable. It is her presence that finally helps me turn on the one child at the school who continually calls me "one-eyed bitch." One day I simply grab him by his coat and beat him until I am satisfied. It is my teacher who tells me my mother is ill.

My mother is lying in bed in the middle of the day, something I have never seen. She is in too much pain to speak. She has an abscess in her ear. I stand looking down on her, knowing that if she dies, I cannot live. She is being treated with warm oils and hot bricks held against her cheek. Finally a doctor comes. But I must go back to my grandparents' house. The weeks pass but I am hardly aware of it. All I know is that my mother might die, my father is not so jolly, my brothers still have their guns, and I am the one sent away from home.

"You did not change," they say.

Did I imagine the anguish of never looking up?

I am twelve. When relatives come to visit I hide in my room. My 28 cousin Brenda, just my age, whose father works in the post office and whose mother is a nurse, comes to find me. "Hello," she says. And then she asks, looking at my recent school picture, which I did not want taken, and on which the "glob," as I think of it, is clearly visible, "You still can't see out of that eye?"

"No," I say, and flop back on the bed over my book.

That night, as I do almost every night, I abuse my eye. I rant and rave at it, in front of the mirror. I plead with it to clear up before morning. I tell it I hate and despise it. I do not pray for sight. I pray for beauty.

"You did not change," they say.

I am fourteen and baby-sitting for my brother Bill, who lives in   32 Boston. He is my favorite brother and there is a strong bond between us. Understanding my feelings of shame and ugliness he and his wife take me to a local hospital, where the "glob" is removed by a doctor named O. Henry. There is still a small bluish crater where the scar tissue was, but the ugly white stuff is gone. Almost immediately I become a different person from the girl who does not raise her head. Or so I think. Now that I've raised my head I win the boyfriend of my dreams. Now that I've raised my head I have plenty of friends. Now that I've raised my head classwork comes from my lips as faultlessly as Easter speeches did, and I leave high school as valedictorian, most popular student, and *queen,* hardly believing my luck. Ironically, the girl who was voted most beautiful in our class (and was) was later shot twice through the chest by a male companion, using a "real" gun, while she was pregnant. But that's another story in itself. Or is it?

"You did not change," they say.

It is now thirty years since the "accident." A beautiful journalist comes to visit and to interview me. She is going to write a cover story for her magazine that focuses on my latest book. "Decide how you want to look on the cover," she says. "Glamorous, or whatever."

Never mind "glamorous," it is the "whatever" that I hear. Suddenly all I can think of is whether I will get enough sleep the night before the photography session: if I don't, my eye will be tired and wander, as blind eyes will.

At night in bed with my lover I think up reasons why I should not   36 appear on the cover of a magazine. "My meanest critics will say I've sold out," I say. "My family will now realize I write scandalous books."

"But what's the real reason you don't want to do this?" he asks.

"Because in all probability," I say in a rush, "my eye won't be straight."

"It will be straight enough," he says. Then, "Besides, I thought you'd made your peace with that."

And I suddenly remember that I have.   40

I remember:

I am talking to my brother Jimmy, asking if he remembers anything unusual about the day I was shot. He does not know I consider that day the last time my father, with his sweet home remedy of cool lily leaves, chose me, and that I suffered and raged inside because of this. "Well," he says, "all I remember is standing by the side of the highway with Daddy, trying to flag down a car. A white man stopped, but when Daddy said he needed somebody to take his little girl to the doctor, he drove off."

I remember:

I am in the desert for the first time. I fall totally in love with it. I am 44 so overwhelmed by its beauty, I confront for the first time, consciously, the meaning of the doctor's words years ago: "Eyes are sympathetic. If one is blind, the other will likely become blind too." I realize I have dashed about the world madly, looking at this, looking at that, storing up images against the fading of the light. *But I might have missed seeing the desert!* The shock of that possibility—and gratitude for over twenty-five years of sight—sends me literally to my knees. Poem after poem comes—which is perhaps how poets pray.

ON SIGHT

I am so thankful I have seen
The Desert
And the creatures in the desert
And the desert Itself.

The desert has its own moon
Which I have seen
With my own eye.
There is no flag on it.

Trees of the desert have arms
All of which are always up
That is because the moon is up
The sun is up
Also the sky
The Stars
Clouds
None with flags.

If there were flags, I doubt
the trees would point.
Would you?

But mostly, I remember this:
I am twenty-seven, and my baby daughter is almost three. Since her birth I have worried about her discovery that her mother's eyes are different from other people's. Will she be embarrassed? I think. What will she say? Every day she watches a television program called *Big Blue Marble.* It begins with a picture of the earth as it appears from the moon. It is bluish, a little battered-looking, but full of light, with whitish clouds swirling around it. Every time I see it I weep with love, as if it is a picture of Grandma's house. One day when I am putting Rebecca down for her

nap, she suddenly focuses on my eye. Something inside me cringes, gets ready to try to protect myself. All children are cruel about physical differences, I know from experience, and that they don't always mean to be is another matter. I assume Rebecca will be the same.

But no-o-o-o. She studies my face intently as we stand, her inside and me outside her crib. She even holds my face maternally between her dimpled little hands. Then, looking every bit as serious and law-yerlike as her father, she says, as if it may just possibly have slipped my attention: "Mommy, there's a *world* in your eye." (As in, "Don't be alarmed, or do anything crazy.") And then, gently, but with great inter-est: "Mommy, where did you *get* that world in your eye?"

For the most part, the pain left then. (So what, if my brothers grew 48 up to buy even more powerful pellet guns for their sons and to carry real guns themselves. So what, if a young "Morehouse man" once nearly fell off the steps of Trevor Arnett Library because he thought my eyes were blue.) Crying and laughing I ran to the bathroom, while Rebecca mumbled and sang herself to sleep. Yes indeed, I realized, looking into the mirror. There *was* a world in my eye. And I saw that it was possible to love it: that in fact, for all it had taught me of shame and anger and inner vision, I *did* love it. Even to see it drifting out of orbit in boredom, or rolling up out of fatigue, not to mention floating back at attention in excitement (bearing witness, a friend has called it), deeply suitable to my personality, and even characteristic of me.

That night I dream I am dancing to Stevie Wonder's song "Always" (the name of the song is really "As," but I hear it as "Always"). As I dance, whirling and joyous, happer than I've ever been in my life, another bright-faced dancer joins me. We dance and kiss each other and hold each other through the night. The other dancer has obviously come through all right, as I have done. She is beautiful, whole and free. And she is also me.   *1983*

Nora Ephron
A Few Words about Breasts

I have to begin with a few words about androgyny. In grammar school, in the fifth and sixth grades, we were all tyrannized by a rigid set of rules that supposedly determined whether we were boys or girls. The episode in *Huckleberry Finn* where Huck is disguised as a girl and gives himself away by the way he threads a needle and catches a ball—that kind of thing. We learned that the way you sat, crossed your legs, held a cigarette, and looked at your nails—the way you did these things in-stinctively was absolute proof of your sex. Now obviously most children did not take this literally, but I did. I thought that just one slip, just one incorrect cross of my legs or flick of an imaginary cigarette ash would turn me from whatever I was into the other thing; that would be all it took, really. Even though I was outwardly a girl and had many of the trappings generally associated with girldom—a girl's name, for exam-ple, and dresses, my own telephone, an autograph book—I spent the early years of my adolescence absolutely certain that I might at any point gum it up. I did not feel at all like a girl. I was boyish. I was athletic, ambitious, outspoken, competitive, noisy, rambunctious. I had scabs on my knees and my socks slid into my loafers and I could throw a football. I wanted desperately not to be that way, not to be a mixture of both things, but instead just one, a girl, a definite indisputable girl. As soft and as pink as a nursery. And nothing would do that for me, I felt, but breasts.

I was about six months younger than everyone else in my class, and so for about six months after it began, for six months after my friends had begun to develop (that was the word we used, develop), I was not particularly worried. I would sit in the bathtub and look down at my breasts and know that any day now, any second now, they would start growing like everyone else's. They didn't. "I want to buy a bra," I said to my mother one night. "What for?" she said. My mother was really hateful about bras, and by the time my third sister had gotten to the point where she was ready to want one, my mother had worked the whole business into a comedy routine. "Why not use a Band-Aid in-stead?" she would say. It was a source of great pride to my mother that she had never even had to wear a brassiere until she had her fourth child, and then only because her gynecologist made her. It was in-comprehensible to me that anyone could ever be proud of something like that. It was the 1950s, for God's sake. Jane Russell. Cashmere sweaters. Couldn't my mother see that? *"I am too old to wear an under-shirt."* Screaming. Weeping. Shouting. "Then don't wear an undershirt," said my mother. "But I want to buy a bra." "What for?"

I suppose that for most girls, breasts, brassieres, that entire thing, has more trauma, more to do with the coming of adolescence, with becoming a woman, than anything else. Certainly more than getting your period, although that, too, was traumatic, symbolic. But you could see breasts; they were there; they were visible. Whereas a girl could claim to have her period for months before she actually got it and nobody would ever know the difference. Which is exactly what I did. All you had to do was make a great fuss over having enough nickels for the Kotex machine and walk around clutching your stomach and moaning for three to five days a month about The Curse and you could convince anybody. There is a school of thought somewhere in the women's lib/ women's mag/gynecology establishment that claims that menstrual cramps are purely psychological, and I lean toward it. Not that I didn't have them finally. Agonizing cramps, heating-pad cramps, go-down-to-the-school-nurse-and-lie-on-the-cot cramps. But unlike any pain I had ever suffered, I adored the pain of cramps, welcomed it, wallowed in it, bragged about it. "I can't go. I have cramps." "I can't do that. I have cramps." And most of all, gigglingly, blushingly: "I can't swim. I have cramps." Nobody ever used the hard-core word. Menstruation. God, what an awful word. Never that. "I have cramps."

The morning I first got my period, I went into my mother's bed- 4
room to tell her. And my mother, my utterly-hateful-about-bras mother, burst into tears. It was really a lovely moment, and I remember it so clearly not just because it was one of the two times I ever saw my mother cry on my account (the other was when I was caught being a six-year-old kleptomaniac), but also because the incident did not mean to me what it meant to her. Her little girl, her firstborn, had finally become a woman. That was what she was crying about. My reaction to the event, however, was that I might well be a woman in some scientific, textbook sense (and could at least stop faking every month and stop wasting all those nickels). But in another sense—in a visible sense—I was as androgynous and as liable to tip over into boyhood as ever.

I started with a 28 AA bra. I don't think they made them any smaller in those days, although I gather that now you can buy bras for five-year-olds that don't have any cups whatsoever in them; trainer bras they are called. My first brassiere came from Robinson's Department Store in Beverly Hills. I went there alone, shaking, positive they would look me over and smile and tell me to come back next year. An actual fitter took me into the dressing room and stood over me while I took off my blouse and tried the first one on. The little puffs stood out on my chest. "Lean over," said the fitter. (To this day, I am not sure what fitters in bra departments do except to tell you to lean over.) I leaned over, with the fleeting hope that my breasts would miraculously fall out of my body and into the puffs. Nothing.

"Don't worry about it," said my friend Libby some months later, when things had not improved. "You'll get them after you're married."

"What are you talking about?" I said.

"When you get married," Libby explained, "your husband will 8
touch your breasts and rub them and kiss them and they'll grow."

That was the killer. Necking I could deal with. Intercourse I could deal with. But it had never crossed by mind that a man was going to touch my breasts, that breasts had something to do with all that, petting, my God, they never mentioned petting in my little sex manual about the fertilization of the ovum. I became dizzy. For I knew instantly—as naïve as I had been only a moment before—that only part of what she was saying was true: the touching, rubbing, kissing part, not the growing part. And I knew that no one would ever want to marry me. I had no breasts. I would never have breasts.

My best friend in school was Diana Raskob. She lived a block from me in a house full of wonders. English muffins, for instance. The Raskobs were the first people in Beverly Hills to have English muffins for breakfast. They also had an apricot tree in the back, and a badminton court, and a subscription to *Seventeen* magazine, and hundreds of games, like Sorry and Parcheesi and Treasure Hunt and Anagrams. Diana and I spent three or four afternoons a week in their den reading and playing and eating. Diana's mother's kitchen was full of the most colossal assortment of junk food I have ever been exposed to. My house was full of apples and peaches and milk and homemade chocolate-chip cookies—which were nice, and good for you, but-not-right-before-dinner-or-you'll-spoil-your-appetite. Diana's house had nothing in it that was good for you, and what's more, you could stuff it in right up until dinner and nobody cared. Bar-B-Q potato chips (they were the first in them, too), giant bottles of ginger ale, fresh popcorn with melted butter, hot fudge sauce on Baskin-Robbins jamoca ice cream, powdered-sugar doughnuts from Van de Kamp's. Diana and I had been best friends since we were seven; we were about equally popular in school (which is to say, not particularly), we had about the same success with boys (extremely intermittent), and we looked much the same. Dark. Tall. Gangly.

It is September, just before school begins. I am eleven years old, about to enter the seventh grade, and Diana and I have not seen each other all summer. I have been to camp and she has been somewhere like Banff with her parents. We are meeting, as we often do, on the street midway between our two houses, and we will walk back to Diana's and eat junk and talk about what has happened to each of us that summer. I am walking down Walden Drive in my jeans and my father's shirt hanging out and my old red loafers with the socks falling into them and coming toward me is . . . I take a deep breath . . . a young woman. Diana. Her hair is curled and she has a waist and hips and a bust and she is wearing a straight skirt, an article of clothing I have been repeatedly told I will be unable to wear until I have the hips to hold it up. My jaw drops, and suddenly I am crying, crying hysterically, can't catch my breath sobbing. My best friend has betrayed me. She has gone ahead without me and done it. She has shaped up.

Here are some things I did to help: 12
Bought a Mark Eden Bust Developer.
Slept on my back for four years.
Splashed cold water on them every night because some French actress said in *Life* magazine that that was what *she* did for her perfect bustline.

Ultimately, I resigned myself to a bad toss and began to wear 16 padded bras. I think about them now, think about all those years in high school and I went around in them, my three padded bras, every single one of them with different-sized breasts. Each time I changed bras I changed sizes: one week nice perky but not too obtrusive breasts, the next medium-sized slightly pointy ones, the next week knockers, true knockers; all the time, whatever size I was, carrying around this rubberized appendage on my chest that occasionally crashed into a wall and was poked inward and had to be poked outward—I think about all that and wonder how anyone kept a straight face through it. My parents, who normally had no restraints about needling me—why did they say nothing as they watched my chest go up and down? My friends, who would periodically inspect my breasts for signs of growth and reassure me—why didn't they at least counsel consistency?

And the bathing suits. I die when I think about the bathing suits. That was the era when you could lay an uninhabited bathing suit on the beach and someone would make a pass at it. I would put one on, an absurd swimsuit with its enormous bust built into it, the bones from the suit stabbing me in the rib cage and leaving little red welts on my body, and there I would be, my chest plunging straight downward absolutely vertically from my collarbone to the top of my suit and then suddenly, wham, out came all that padding and material and wiring absolutely horizontally.

Buster Klepper was the first boy who ever touched them. He was my boyfriend my senior year of high school. There is a picture of him in my high-school yearbook that makes him look quite attractive in a Jewish, horn-rimmed-glasses sort of way, but the picture does not show the pimples, which were air-brushed out, or the dumbness. Well, that isn't really fair. He wasn't dumb. He just wasn't terribly bright. His mother refused to accept it, refused to accept the relentlessly average report cards, refused to deal with her son's inevitable destiny in some junior college or other. "He was tested," she would say to me, apropos of nothing, "and it came out a hundred and forty-five. That's near-genius." Had the word "underachiever" been coined, she probably would have lobbed that one at me, too. Anyway, Buster was really very sweet—which is, I know, damning with faint praise, but there it is. I was the editor of the front page of the high-school newspaper and he was editor of the back page; we had to work together, side by side, in the print shop, and that was how it started. On our first date, we went to see *April Love*, starring Pat Boone. Then we started going together. Buster had a green coupe, a 1950 Ford with an engine he had hand-chromed until it shone, dazzled, reflected the image of anyone who looked into it, anyone usually being Buster polishing it or the gas-station attendants he constantly asked to check the oil in order for them to be overwhelmed by the sparkle on the valves. The car also had a boot stretched over the back seat for reasons I never understood; hanging from the rearview mirror, as was the custom, was a pair of angora dice. A previous girl friend named Solange, who was famous throughout Beverly Hills High School for having no pigment in her right eyebrow, had knitted them for him. Buster and I would ride around town, the two of us seated to the left of the steering wheel. I would shift gears. It was nice.

There was necking. Terrific necking. First in the car, overlooking Los Angeles from what is now the Trousdale Estates. Then on the bed of his parents' cabana at Ocean House. Incredibly wonderful, frustrating necking, I loved it, really, but no further than necking, please don't, please, because there I was absolutely terrified of the general implications of going-a-step-further with a near-dummy and also terrified of his finding out there was next to nothing there (which he knew, of course; he wasn't that dumb).

I broke up with him at one point. I think we were apart for about 20 two weeks. At the end of that time, I drove down to see a friend at a boarding school in Palos Verdes Estates and a disc jockey played "April Love" on the radio four times during the trip. I took it as a sign. I drove straight back to Griffith Park to a golf tournament Buster was playing in (he was the sixth-seeded teenage golf player in southern California) and presented myself back to him on the green of the eighteenth hole. It was all very dramatic. That night we went to a drive-in and I let him get his hand under my protuberances and onto my breasts. He really didn't seem to mind at all.

"Do you want to marry my son?" the woman asked me.

"Yes," I said.

I was nineteen years old, a virgin, going with this woman's son, this big strange woman who was married to a Lutheran minister in New Hampshire and pretended she was gentile and had this son, by her first husband, this total fool of a son who ran the hero-sandwich concession at Harvard Business School and whom for one moment one December in New Hampshire I said—as much out of politeness as anything else—that I wanted to marry.

"Fine," she said. "Now, here's what you do. Always make sure you're on top of 24
him so you won't seem so small. My bust is very large, you see, so I always lie on
my back to make it look smaller, but you'll have to be on top most of the time."
I nodded. "Thank you," I said.
"I have a book for you to read," she went on. "Take it with you when you
leave. Keep it." She went to the bookshelf, found it, and gave it to me. It was a
book on frigidity.
"Thank you," I said.

That is a true story. Everything in this article is a true story, but I 28
feel I have to point out that that story in particular is true. It happened
on December 30, 1960. I think about it often. When it first happened, I
naturally assumed that the woman's son, my boyfriend, was responsible.
I invented a scenario where he had had a little heart-to-heart with his
mother and had confessed that his only objection to me was that my
breasts were small; his mother then took it upon herself to help out.
Now I think I was wrong about the incident. The mother was acting on
her own, I think: that was her way of being cruel and competitive under
the guise of being helpful and maternal. You have small breasts, she was
saying; therefore you will never make him as happy as I have. Or you
have small breasts; therefore you will doubtless have sexual problems.
Or you have small breasts; therefore you are less woman than I am. She
was, as it happens, only the first of what seems to me to be a never-
ending string of women who have made competitive remarks to me
about breast size. "I would love to wear a dress like that," my friend
Emily says to me, "but my bust is too big." Like that. Why do women say
these things to me? Do I attract these remarks the way other women
attract married men or alcoholics or homosexuals? This summer, for
example. I am at a party in East Hampton and I am introduced to a
woman from Washington. She is a minor celebrity, very pretty and
Southern and blond and outspoken, and I am flattered because she has
read something I have written. We are talking animatedly, we have been
talking no more than five minutes, when a man comes up to join us.
"Look at the two of us," the woman says to the man, indicating me and
her. "The two of us together couldn't fill an A cup." Why does she say
that? It isn't even true, dammit, so why? Is she even more addled than I
am on this subject? Does she honestly believe there is something wrong
with her size breasts, which, it seems to me, now that I look hard at
them, are just right? Do I unconsciously bring out competitiveness in
women? In that form? What did I do to deserve it?
    As for men.
    There were men who minded and let me know that they minded.
There were men who did not mind. In any case, *I* always minded.
    And even now, now that I have been countlessly reassured that my

figure is a good one, now that I am grown-up enough to understand that most of my feelings have very little to do with the reality of my shape, I am nonetheless obsessed by breasts. I cannot help it. I grew up in the terrible fifties—with rigid stereotypical sex roles, the insistence that men be men and dress like men and women be women and dress like women, the intolerance of androgyny—and I cannot shake it, cannot shake my feelings of inadequacy. Well, that time is gone, right? All those exaggerated examples of breast worship are gone, right? Those women were freaks, right? I know all that. And yet here I am, stuck with the psychological remains of it all, stuck with my own peculiar version of breast worship. You probably think I am crazy to go on like this: here I have set out to write a confession that is meant to hit you with the shock of recognition, and instead you are sitting there thinking I am thoroughly warped. Well, what can I tell you? If I had had them, I would have been a completely different person. I honestly believe that.

After I went into therapy, a process that made it possible for me to 32 tell total strangers at cocktail parties that breasts were the hang-up of my life, I was often told that I was insane to have been bothered by my condition. I was also frequently told, by close friends, that I was extremely boring on the subject. And my girlfriends, the ones with nice big breasts, would go on endlessly about how their lives had been far more miserable than mine. Their bra straps were snapped in class. They couldn't sleep on their stomachs. They were stared at whenever the word "mountain" cropped up in geography. And *Evangeline*, good God what they went through every time someone had to stand up and recite the Prologue to Longfellow's *Evangeline*: ". . . stand like druids of eld . . . / With beards that rest on their bosoms." It was much worse for them, they tell me. They had a terrible time of it, they assure me. I don't know how lucky I was, they say.

I have thought about their remarks, tried to put myself in their place, considered their point of view. I think they are full of shit.   *1972*

John Updike
At War with My Skin

My mother tells me that up to the age of six I had no psoriasis; it came on strong after an attack of measles in February of 1938, when I was in kindergarten. The disease—"disease" seems strong, for a condition that is not contagious, painful, or debilitating; yet psoriasis has the volatility of a disease, the sense of another presence coöccupying your body and singling you out from the happy herds of healthy, normal mankind—first attached itself to my memory while I was lying on the upstairs side porch of the Shillington house, amid the sickly, oleaginous smell of Siroil, on fuzzy sun-warmed towels, with my mother, sun-bathing. We are both, in my mental picture, not quite naked. She would have been still a youngish woman at the time, and I remember being embarrassed by something, but whether by our being together this way or simply by my skin is not clear in this mottled recollection. She, too, had psoriasis; I had inherited it from her. Siroil and sunshine and not eating chocolate were our only weapons in our war against the red spots, ripening into silvery scabs, that invaded our skins in the winter. Siroil was the foremost medication available in the thirties and forties: a bottled preparation the consistency of pus, tar its effective ingredient and its drippy texture and bilious color and insinuating odor deeply involved with my embarrassment. Yet, as with our own private odors, those of sweat and earwax and even of excrement, there was also something satisfying about this scent, an intimate rankness that told me who I was.

One dabbed Siroil on; it softened the silvery scales but otherwise did very little good. Nor did abstaining from chocolate and "greasy" foods like potato chips and french fries do much visible good, though as with many palliations there was no knowing how much worse things would be otherwise. Only the sun, that living god, had real power over psoriasis; a few weeks of summer erased the spots from all of my responsive young skin that could be exposed—chest, legs, and face. Inspecting the many photographs taken of me as a child, including a set of me cavorting in a bathing suit in the back yard, I can see no trace of psoriasis. And I remember, when it rained, going out in a bathing suit with friends to play in the downpour and its warm puddles. Yet I didn't learn to swim, because of my appearance; I stayed away from "the Porgy," the dammed pond beyond the poorhouse, and from the public pool in West Reading, and the indoor pool at the Reading "Y," where my father in winter coached the high-school swimming team. To the travails of my freshman year at Harvard was added the humiliation of learning at last to swim, with my spots and my hydrophobia, in a class of quite naked boys. Recently the chunky, mild-spoken man who taught that class over thirty years ago came up to me at a party and pleasantly identified himself; I could scarcely manage politeness, his face so sharply brought back that old suppressed rich mix of chlorine and fear and brave gasping and naked, naked shame.

Psoriasis is a metabolic disorder that causes the epidermis, which normally replaces itself at a gradual, unnoticeable rate, to speed up the process markedly and to produce excess skin cells. The tiny mechanisms gone awry are beyond the precise reach of internally taken medicine; a derivative of vitamin A, etretinate, and an anticancer drug, methotrexate, are effective but at the price of potential side-effects to the kidneys and liver more serious than the disease, which is, after all, superficial—too much, simply, of a good thing (skin). In the 1970s, dermatologists at Massachusetts General Hospital developed PUVA, a controlled light treatment: fluorescent tubes radiate long-wave ultraviolet (UV-A) onto skin sensitized by an internal dose of methoxsalen, a psoralen (the "P" of the acronym) derived from a weed, *Ammi majus*, which grows along the river Nile and whose sun-sensitizing qualities were known to the ancient Egyptians. So a curious primitivity, a savor of folk-medicine, clings to this new cure, a refinement of the old sun-cure. It is pleasant, once or twice a week, to stand nearly naked in a kind of glowing telephone booth. It was pleasant to lie on the upstairs porch, hidden behind the jigsawed wooden balusters, and to feel the slanting sun warm the fuzzy towel while an occasional car or pack of children crackled by on Shilling Alley. One became conscious, lying there trying to read, of bird song, of distant shouts, of a whistle calling men back to work at the local textile factory, which was rather enchantingly called the Fairy Silk Mill.

My condition forged a hidden link with things elemental—with the 4 seasons, with the sun, and with my mother. A tendency to psoriasis is inherited—only through the maternal line, it used to be thought. My mother's mother had had it, I was told, though I never noticed anything wrong with my grandmother's skin—just her false teeth, which slipped down while she was napping in her rocking chair. Far in the future, I would marry a young brunette with calm, smooth, deep-tanning skin and was to imagine that thus I had put an end to at least my particular avenue of genetic error. Alas, our fourth child inherited my complexion and, lightly, in her late teens, psoriasis. The disease favors the fair, the dry-skinned, the pallid progeny of cloud-swaddled Holland and Ireland and Germany. Though my father was not red-haired, his brother Arch was, and when I grew a beard, as my contribution to the revolutionary sixties, it came in reddish. And when I shaved it off, red spots had thrived underneath.

Psoriasis keeps you thinking. Strategies of concealment ramify, and self-examination is endless. You are forced to the mirror, again and again; psoriasis compels narcissism, if we can suppose a Narcissus who did not like what he saw. In certain lights, your face looks passable; in slightly different other lights, not. Shaving mirrors and rearview mirrors in automobiles are merciless, whereas the smoky mirrors in airplane bathrooms are especially flattering and soothing: one's face looks as tawny as a movie star's. Flying back from the Caribbean, I used to admire my improved looks; years went by before I noticed that I looked equally good, in the lavatory glow, on the flight down. I cannot pass a reflecting surface on the street without glancing in, in hopes that I have somehow changed. Nature and the self, the great moieties of earthly existence, are each cloven in two by a fascinated ambivalence. One hates one's abnormal, erupting skin but is led into a brooding, solic-itous attention toward it. One hates the Nature that has imposed this affliction, but only this same Nature can be appealed to for erasure, for cure. Only Nature can forgive psoriasis; the sufferer in his self-contempt does not grant to other people this power. Perhaps the unease of my first memory has to do with my mother's presence; I wished to be alone with the sun, the air, the distant noises, the possibility of my hideousness eventually going away.

I recall remarkably few occasions when I was challenged, in the brute world of childhood, about my skin. In the second grade, perhaps it was, the teacher, standing above our obedient rows, rummaged in my hair and said aloud, "Good heavens, child, what's this on your head?" I can hear these words breaking into the air above me and see my mother's face when, that afternoon, I recounted them to her, probably with tears; her eyes took on a fanatic glare and the next morning, like an arrow that had fixed her course, she went to the school to "have it out" with the teacher who had heightened her defective cub's embarrass-ment. Our doctor, Doc Rothermel in his big grit-and-stucco house, also, eerily, had psoriasis; far from offering a cure out of his magical expand-ing black bag, he offered us the melancholy confession that he had felt prevented, by his scaly wrists, from rolling back his sleeves and becoming—his true ambition—a surgeon. " 'Physician, heal thyself,' they'd say to me," he said. I don't, really, know how bad I looked, or how many conferences among adults secured a tactful silence from above. My peers (again, as I remember, which is a choosing to remember) either didn't notice anything terrible about my skin or else neglected to comment upon it. Children are frank, as we know from the taunts and nicknames they fling at one another; but also they all feel imperfect and vulnerable, which works for mutual forbearance. In high school, my gym class knew how I looked in the locker room and shower. Once, a boy from a higher class came up to me with an exclamation of cheerful disgust, touched my arm, and asked if I had syphilis. But my classmates held their tongues, and expressed no fear of contagion.

I participated, in gym shorts and tank top, in the annual gym exhibitions. Indeed, as the tallest of the lighter boys, I stood shakily on top of "Fats" Sterner's shoulders to make the apex of our gymnastics pyramid. I braved it through, inwardly cringing, prisoner and victim of my skin. It was not really *me*, was the explanation I could not shout out. Like an obese person (like good-natured Fats so sturdy under me, a human rock, his hands gripping my ankles while I fought the sensation that I was about to lurch forward and fly out over the heads of our assembled audience of admiring parents), and unlike someone with a withered arm, say, or a port-wine stain splashed across his neck and cheek, I could change—every summer I *did* become normal and, as it were, beautiful. An overvaluation of the normal went with my ailment, a certain idealization of everyone who was not, as I felt myself to be, a monster.

Because it came and went, I never settled in with my psoriasis, 8 never adopted it as, inevitably, part of myself. It was temporary and in a way illusionary, like my being poor, and obscure, and (once we moved to the farm) lonely—a spell that had been put upon me, a test, as in a fairy story or one of those divinely imposed ordeals in the Bible. "Where's my public?" I used to ask my mother, coming back from the empty mailbox, by this joke conjuring a public out of the future.

My last public demonstration of my monstrosity, in a formal social setting, occurred the day of my examination for the draft, in the summer of 1955. A year in England, with no sun, had left my skin in bad shape, and the examining doctor took one glance up from his plywood table and wrote on my form, "4-F: Psoriasis." At this point in my young life I had a job offer in New York, a wife, and an infant daughter, and was far from keen to devote two years to the national defense; I had never gone to summer camp, and pictured the Army as a big summer camp, with extra-rough bullies and extra-cold showers in the morning. My trepidation should be distinguished from political feelings; I had absolutely no doubts about my country's need, from time to time, to fight, and its right to call me to service. So suddenly and emphatically excused, I felt relieved, guilty, and above all ashamed at being singled out; the naked American men around me had looked at my skin with surprise and now were impressed by the exemption it had won me. I had not foreseen this result; psoriasis would handicap no killing skills and, had I reported in another season, might have been nearly invisible. My wife, when I got back to my parents' house with my news, was naturally delighted; but my mother, always independent in her moods, seemed saddened, as if she had laid an egg which, when candled by the government, had been pronounced rotten.

It pains me to write these pages. They are humiliating—"scab-picking," to use a term sometimes leveled at modern autobiographical writers. I have written about psoriasis only twice before: I gave it to Peter Caldwell in *The Centaur* and to an anonymous, bumptious ceramicist in the short story "From the Journal of a Leper." I expose it this third time only in order to proclaim the consoling possibility that whenever in my timid life I have shown some courage and originality it has been because of my skin. Because of my skin, I counted myself out of any of those jobs—salesman, teacher, financier, movie star—that demand being presentable. What did that leave? Becoming a craftsman of some sort, closeted and unseen—perhaps a cartoonist or a writer, a worker in ink who can hide himself and send out a surrogate presence, a signature that multiplies even while it conceals. Why did I marry so young? Because, having once found a comely female who forgave me my skin, I dared not risk losing her and trying to find another. Why did I have children so young? Because I wanted to surround myself with people who did not have psoriasis. Why, in 1957, did I leave New York and my nice employment there? Because my skin was bad in the urban shadows, and nothing, not even screwing a sunlamp bulb into the socket above my bathroom mirror, helped. Why did I move, with my family, all the way to Ipswich, Massachusetts? Because this ancient Puritan town happened to have one of the great beaches of the Northeast, in whose dunes I could, like a sin-soaked anchorite of old repairing to the desert, bake and cure myself.   *1985*

14

Public Space

Desmond Morris, Territorial Behavior

Susan Jacoby, Unfair Game

Brent Staples, Just Walk on By:
A Black Man Ponders His Power to
Alter Public Space

A city street equipped to handle strangers, and to make a safety asset, in itself, out of the presence of strangers, as the streets of successful city neighborhoods always do, must have three main qualities:

First, there must be a clear demarcation between what is public space and what is private space. Public and private spaces cannot ooze into each other as they do typically in suburban settings or in projects.

Second, there must be eyes upon the street, eyes belonging to those we might call the natural proprietors of the street. The buildings on a street equipped to handle strangers and to insure the safety of both residents and strangers, must be oriented to the street. They cannot turn their backs or blank sides on it and leave it blind.

And third, the sidewalk must have users on it fairly continuously, both to add to the number of effective eyes on the street and to induce the people in buildings along the street to watch the sidewalks in sufficient numbers. Nobody enjoys sitting on a stoop or looking out a window at an empty street. Almost nobody does such a thing. Large numbers of people entertain themselves, off and on, by watching street activity.

Jane Jacobs, from *The Uses of Sidewalks*

Sennett: The Greeks had a notion of public space as a place for political education. We've lost the sense of the social life of the city as an

educative process. It survives vestigially in the *idea* of the town meeting. But for Americans today, the public realm is a silent realm, which
is not the way it once was. In the eighteenth century, both men and
women were very verbal in public. The public places—coffeehouses,
assembly rooms, court halls—were sociable places. Silence began
during the Industrial Revolution, when women were driven from the
public realm. Their presence in public was suddenly considered
unseemly, unladylike, particularly for middle-class women. They
were confined to the home. In the 1880s, when women began to
return to the public space, it was only in terms of consumption—
going to stores, shopping. That was a time when women couldn't talk
to strangers, a time of great isolation and silence. Gradually, those
became the terms for men as well. Our public realm is still largely a
silent one.

Richard Sennett, from *Harper's Forum,*
"Whatever Became of the Public Square?"

The thing that first caught my attention in Iowa City was how much
space the people of this tiny city of sixty thousand enjoy. On both sides
of the quiet, clean streets are house after house, each quaint and
distinctive with little repetition of color or style. The one-family houses
have a certain space between them; each house has its own personality, whether grand and elegant or bright and light-hearted, while it
strives to be distinctive with its style of roof, doorway, porch, and windows. For a moment I felt I had fallen into a world of moving color
pictures. . . .

Comparing this with the suffocating pressure of a typical big American city like New York or San Francisco leads one inevitably to the
thought that people need a certain space.

Liu Binyan, from *America, Spacious Yet Confining*

Music in Public Places Such as Restaurants,
Supermarkets, Hotel Lobbies, Airports, Etc.
When I am in any of the above-mentioned places I am not there to hear
music. I am there for whatever reason is appropriate to the respective
place. I am no more interested in hearing "Mack the Knife" while

waiting for the shuttle to Boston than someone sitting ringside at the Sands Hotel is interested in being forced to choose between sixteen varieties of cottage cheese.

Fran Lebowitz, from *The Sound of Music:*
Enough Already

Desmond Morris

Territorial Behavior

A territory is a defended space. In the broadest sense, there are three kinds of human territory: tribal, family, and personal.

It is rare for people to be driven to physical fighting in defense of these "owned" spaces, but fight they will, if pushed to the limit. The invading army encroaching on national territory, the gang moving into a rival district, the trespasser climbing into an orchard, the burglar breaking into a house, the bully pushing to the front of a queue, the driver trying to steal a parking space, all of these intruders are liable to be met with resistance varying from the vigorous to the savagely violent. Even if the law is on the side of the intruder, the urge to protect a territory may be so strong that otherwise peaceful citizens abandon all their usual controls and inhibitions. Attempts to evict families from their homes, no matter how socially valid the reasons, can lead to siege conditions reminiscent of the defense of a medieval fortress.

The fact that these upheavals are so rare is a measure of the success of Territorial Signals as a system of dispute prevention. It is sometimes cynically stated that "all property is theft," but in reality it is the opposite. Property, as owned space which is *displayed* as owned space, is a special kind of sharing system which reduces fighting much more than it causes it. Man is a co-operative species, but he is also competitive, and his struggle for dominance has to be structured in some way if chaos is to be avoided. The establishment of territorial rights is one such structure. It limits dominance geographically. I am dominant in my territory and you are dominant in yours. In other words, dominance is shared out spatially, and we all have some. Even if I am weak and unintelligent and you can dominate me when we meet on neutral ground, I can still enjoy a thoroughly dominant role as soon as I retreat to my private base. Be it ever so humble, there is no place like a home territory.

Of course, I can still be intimidated by a particularly dominant   4 individual who enters my home base, but his encroachment will be dangerous for him and he will think twice about it, because he will know that here my urge to resist will be dramatically magnified and my usual subservience banished. Insulted at the heart of my own territory, I may easily explode into battle—either symbolic or real—with a result that may be damaging to both of us.

In order for this to work, each territory has to be plainly advertised as such. Just as a dog cocks its leg to deposit its personal scent on the trees in its locality, so the human animal cocks its leg symbolically all over his home base. But because we are predominantly visual animals we employ mostly visual signals, and it is worth asking how we do this at the three levels: tribal, family, and personal.

First: the Tribal Territory. We evolved as tribal animals, living in comparatively small groups, probably of less than a hundred, and we existed like that for millions of years. It is our basic social unit, a group in which everyone knows everyone else. Essentially, the tribal territory consisted of a home base surrounded by extended hunting grounds. Any neighboring tribe intruding on our social space would be repelled and driven away. As these early tribes swelled into agricultural super-tribes, and eventually into industrial nations, their territorial defense systems became increasingly elaborate. The tiny, ancient home base of the hunting tribe became the great capital city, the primitive warpaint became the flags, emblems, uniforms, and regalia of the specialized military, and the war-chants became national anthems, marching songs, and bugle calls. Territorial boundary-lines hardened into fixed borders, often conspicuously patrolled and punctuated with defensive structures—forts and lookout posts, checkpoints and great walls, and, today, customs barriers.

Today each nation flies its own flag, a symbolic embodiment of its territorial status. But patriotism is not enough. The ancient tribal hunter lurking inside each citizen finds himself unsatisfied by member-ship in such a vast conglomeration of individuals, most of whom are totally unknown to him personally. He does his best to feel that he shares a common territorial defense with them all, but the scale of the operation has become inhuman. It is hard to feel a sense of belonging with a tribe of fifty million or more. His answer is to form sub-groups, nearer to his ancient pattern, smaller, and more personally known to him—the local club, the teenage gang, the union, the specialist society, the sports association, the political party, the college fraternity, the social clique, the protest group, and the rest. Rare indeed is the individual who does not belong to at least one of these splinter groups, and take from it a sense of tribal allegiance and brotherhood. Typical of all these groups is the development of Territorial Signals—badges, costumes, headquarters, banners, slogans, and all the other displays of group identity. This is where the action is, in terms of tribal territorialism, and only when a major war breaks out does the emphasis shift upwards to the higher group level of the nations.

Each of these modern pseudo-tribes sets up its own special kind of home base. In extreme cases non-members are totally excluded, in others they are allowed in as visitors with limited rights and under a control system of special rules. In many ways they are like miniature nations, with their own flags and emblems and their own border guards. The exclusive club has its own "customs barrier": the doorman who checks your "passport" (your membership card) and prevents strangers from passing in unchallenged. There is a government: the club committee; and often special displays of the tribal elders: the photographs or portraits of previous officials on the walls. At the heart of the specialized territories there is a powerful feeling of security and importance, a sense of shared defense against the outside world. Much of the club chatter, both serious and joking, directs itself against the rottenness of everything outside the club boundaries—in that "other world" beyond the protected portals.

In social organizations which embody a strong class system, such as military units and large business concerns, there are many territorial rules, often unspoken, which interfere with the official hierarchy. High-status individuals, such as officers or managers, could in theory enter any of the regions occupied by the lower levels in the peck order, but they limit this power in a striking way. An officer seldom enters a sergeant's mess or a barrack room unless it is for a formal inspection. He respects those regions as alien territories even though he has the power to go there by virtue of his dominant role. And in businesses, part of the appeal of unions, over and above their obvious functions, is that with their officials, headquarters, and meetings they add a sense of territorial power for the staff workers. It is almost as if each military organization and business concern consists of two warring tribes: the officers versus the other ranks, and the management versus the workers. Each has its special home base within the system, and the territorial defense pattern thrusts itself into what, on the surface, is a pure social hierarchy. Negotiations between managements and unions are tribal battles fought out over the neutral ground of a boardroom table, and are as much concerned with territorial display as they are with resolving problems of wages and conditions. Indeed, if one side gives in too quickly and accepts the other's demands, the victors feel strangely

8

cheated and deeply suspicious that it may be a trick. What they are missing is the protracted sequence of ritual and counter-ritual that keeps alive their group territorial identity.

Likewise, many of the hostile displays of sports fans and teenage gangs are primarily concerned with displaying their group image to rival fan-clubs and gangs. Except in rare cases, they do not attack one another's headquarters, drive out the occupants, and reduce them to a submissive, subordinate condition. It is enough to have scuffles on the borderlands between the two rival territories. This is particularly clear at football matches, where the fan-club headquarters becomes temporarily shifted from the club-house to a section of the stands, and where minor fighting breaks out at the unofficial boundary line between the massed groups of rival supporters. Newspaper reports play up the few accidents and injuries which do occur on such occasions, but when these are studied in relation to the total numbers of displaying fans involved it is clear that the serious incidents represent only a tiny fraction of the overall group behavior. For every actual punch or kick there are a thousand war-cries, war dances, chants, and gestures.

Second: the Family Territory. Essentially, the family is a breeding unit and the family territory is a breeding ground. At the center of this space, there is the nest—the bedroom—where, tucked up in bed, we feel at our most territorially secure. In a typical house the bedroom is upstairs, where a safe nest should be. This puts it farther away from the entrance hall, the area where contact is made, intermittently, with the outside world. The less private reception rooms, where intruders are allowed access, are the next line of defense. Beyond them, outside the walls of the building, there is often a symbolic remnant of the ancient feeding grounds—a garden. Its symbolism often extends to the plants and animals it contains, which cease to be nutritional and become merely decorative—flowers and pets. But like a true territorial space it has a conspicuously displayed boundary-line, the garden fence, wall, or railings. Often no more than a token barrier, this is the outer territorial demarcation, separating the private world for the family from the public world beyond. To cross it puts any visitor or intruder at an immediate disadvantage. As he crosses the threshold, his dominance wanes, slightly but unmistakably. He is entering an area where he senses that he must ask permission to do simple things that he would consider a right elsewhere. Without lifting a finger, the territorial owners exert their dominance. This is done by all the hundreds of small ownership "markers" they have deposited on their family territory: the ornaments, the "possessed" objects positioned in the rooms and on the walls; the furnishings, the furniture, the colors, the patterns, all owner-chosen and all making this particular home base unique to them.

It is one of the tragedies of modern architecture that there has been 12
a standardization of these vital territorial living units. One of the most
important aspects of a home is that it should be similar to other homes
only in a general way, and that in detail it should have many differences,
making it a *particular* home. Unfortunately, it is cheaper to build a row
of houses, or a block of flats, so that all the family living-units are
identical, but the territorial urge rebels against this trend and house-
owners struggle as best they can to make their mark on their mass-
produced properties. They do this with garden-design, with front-door
colors, with curtain patterns, with wallpaper and all the other decorative elements that together create a unique and different family environment. Only when they have completed this nest-building do they
feel truly "at home" and secure.

When they venture forth as a family unit they repeat the process in
a minor way. On a day-trip to the seaside, they load the car with
personal belongings and it becomes their temporary, portable territory.
Arriving at the beach they stake out a small territorial claim, marking it
with rugs, towels, baskets, and other belongings to which they can
return from their seaboard wanderings. Even if they all leave it at once
to bathe, it retains a characteristic territorial quality and other family
groups arriving will recognize this by setting up their own "home" bases
at a respectful distance. Only when the whole beach has filled up with
these marked spaces will newcomers start to position themselves in such
a way that the inter-base distance becomes reduced. Forced to pitch
between several existing beach territories they will feel a momentary
sensation of intrusion, and the established "owners" will feel a similar
sensation of invasion, even though they are not being directly inconve-
nienced.

The same territorial scene is being played out in parks and fields
and on riverbanks, wherever family groups gather in their clustered
units. But if rivalry for spaces creates mild feelings of hostility, it is true
to say that, without the territorial system of sharing and space-limited
dominance, there would be chaotic disorder.

Third: the Personal Space. If a man enters a waiting-room and sits at
one end of a long row of empty chairs, it is possible to predict where the
next man to enter will seat himself. He will not sit next to the first man,
nor will he sit at the far end, right away from him. He will choose a
position about halfway between these two points. The next man to enter
will take the largest gap left, and sit roughly in the middle of that, and so
on, until eventually the latest newcomer will be forced to select a seat
that places him right next to one of the already seated men. Similar
patterns can be observed in cinemas, public urinals, airplanes, trains,
and buses. This is a reflection of the fact that we all carry with us,

everywhere we go, a portable territory called a Personal Space. If people move inside this space, we feel threatened. If they keep too far outside it, we feel rejected. The result is a subtle series of spatial adjustments, usually operating quite unconsciously and producing ideal compromises as far as this is possible. If a situation becomes too crowded, then we adjust our reactions accordingly and allow our personal space to shrink. Jammed into an elevator, a rush-hour compartment, or a packed room, we give up altogether and allow body-to-body contact, but when we relinquish our Personal Space in this way, we adopt certain special techniques. In essence, what we do is to convert these other bodies into "nonpersons." We studiously ignore them, and they us. We try not to face them if we can possibly avoid it. We wipe all expressiveness from our faces, letting them go blank. We may look up at the ceiling or down at the floor, and we reduce body movements to a minimum. Packed together like sardines in a tin, we stand dumbly still, sending out as few social signals as possible.

Even if the crowding is less severe, we still tend to cut down our 16 social interactions in the presence of large numbers. Careful observations of children in play groups revealed that if they are high-density groupings there is less social interaction between the individual children, even though there is theoretically more opportunity for such contacts. At the same time, the high-density groups show a higher frequency of aggressive and destructive behavior patterns in their play. Personal Space—"elbow room"—is a vital commodity for the human animal, and one that cannot be ignored without risking serious trouble.

Of course, we all enjoy the excitement of being in a crowd, and this reaction cannot be ignored. But there are crowds and crowds. It is pleasant enough to be in a "spectator crowd," but not so appealing to find yourself in the middle of a rush-hour crush. The difference between the two is that the spectator crowd is all facing in the same direction and concentrating on a distant point of interest. Attending a theater, there are twinges of rising hostility toward the stranger who sits down immediately in front of you or the one who squeezes into the seat next to you. The shared armrest can become a polite, but distinct, territorial boundary-dispute region. However, as soon as the show begins, these invasions of Personal Space are forgotten and the attention is focused beyond the small space where the crowding is taking place. Now, each member of the audience feels himself spatially related, not to his cramped neighbors, but to the actor on the stage, and this distance is, if anything, too great. In the rush-hour crowd, by contrast, each member of the pushing throng is competing with his neighbors all the time. There is no escape to a spatial relation with a distant actor, only the pushing, shoving bodies all around.

Those of us who have to spend a great deal of time in crowded conditions become gradually better able to adjust, but no one can ever become completely immune to invasions of Personal Space. This is because they remain forever associated with either powerful hostile or equally powerful loving feelings. All through our childhood we will have been held to be loved and held to be hurt, and anyone who invades our Personal Space when we are adults is, in effect, threatening to extend his behavior into one of these two highly charged areas of human interaction. Even if his motives are clearly neither hostile nor sexual, we still find it hard to suppress our reactions to his close approach. Unfortunately, different countries have different ideas about exactly how close is close. It is easy enough to test your own "space reaction": when you are talking to someone in the street or in any open space, reach out with your arm and see where the nearest point on his body comes. If you hail from western Europe, you will find that he is at roughly fingertip distance from you. In other words, as you reach out, your fingertips will just about make contact with his shoulder. If you come from eastern Europe you will find you are standing at "wrist distance." If you come from the Mediterranean region you will find that you are much closer to your companion, at little more than "elbow distance."

Trouble begins when a member of one of these cultures meets and talks to one from another. Say a British diplomat meets an Italian or an Arab diplomat at an embassy function. They start talking in a friendly way, but soon the fingertips man begins to feel uneasy. Without knowing quite why, he starts to back away gently from his companion. The companion edges forward again. Each tries in his way to set up a Personal Space relationship that suits his own background. But it is impossible to do. Every time the Mediterranean diplomat advances to a distance that feels comfortable for him, the British diplomat feels threatened. Every time the Briton moves back, the other feels rejected. Attempts to adjust this situation often lead to a talking pair shifting slowly across a room, and many an embassy reception is dotted with western-Europe fingertip-distance men pinned against the walls by eager elbow-distance men. Until such differences are fully understood and allowances made, these minor differences in "body territories" will continue to act as an alienation factor which may interfere in a subtle way with diplomatic harmony and other forms of international transaction.

If there are distance problems when engaged in conversation, then there are clearly going to be even bigger difficulties where people must work privately in a shared space. Close proximity of others, pressing against the invisible boundaries of our personal body-territory, makes it

difficult to concentrate on nonsocial matters. Flat-mates, students sharing a study, sailors in the cramped quarters of a ship, and office staff in
crowded work-places, all have to face this problem. They solve it by
"cocooning." They use a variety of devices to shut themselves off from
the others present. The best possible cocoon, of course, is a small
private room—a den, a private office, a study, or a studio—which
physically obscures the presence of other nearby territory-owners. This
is the ideal situation for non-social work, but the space-sharers cannot
enjoy this luxury. Their cocooning must be symbolic. They may, in
certain cases, be able to erect small physical barriers, such as screens
and partitions, which give substance to their invisible Personal Space
boundaries, but when this cannot be done, other means must be sought.
One of these is the "favored object." Each space-sharer develops a
preference, repeatedly expressed until it becomes a fixed pattern, for a
particular chair, or table, or alcove. Others come to respect this, and
friction is reduced. This system is often formally arranged (this is my
desk, that is yours), but even where it is not, favored places soon
develop. Professor Smith has a favorite chair in the library. It is not
formally his, but he always uses it and others avoid it. Seats around a
mess-room table, or a boardroom table, become almost personal property for specific individuals. Even in the home, father has his favorite
chair for reading the newspaper or watching television. Another device
is the blinkers-posture. Just as a horse that over-reacts to other horses
and the distractions of the noisy race-course is given a pair of blinkers
to shield its eyes, so people studying privately in a public place put on
pseudo-blinkers in the form of shielding hands. Resting their elbows on
the table, they sit with their hands screening their eyes from the scene
on either side.

A third method of reinforcing the body-territory is to use personal
markers. Books, papers, and other personal belongings are scattered
around the favored site to render it more privately owned in the eyes of
companions. Spreading out one's belongings is a well-known trick in
public-transport situations, where a traveler tries to give the impression
that seats next to him are taken. In many contexts carefully arranged
personal markers can act as an effective territorial display, even in the
absence of the territory owner. Experiments in a library revealed that
placing a pile of magazines on the table in one seating position successfully reserved that place for an average of 77 minutes. If a sports-
jacket was added, draped over the chair, then the "reservation effect"
lasted for over two hours.

In these ways, we strengthen the defenses of our Personal Spaces,
keeping out intruders with the minimum of open hostility. As with all
territorial behavior, the object is to defend space with signals rather
than with fists and at all three levels—the tribal, the family, and the

personal—it is a remarkably efficient system of space-sharing. It does not always seem so, because newspapers and newscasts inevitably magnify the exceptions and dwell on those cases where the signals have failed and wars have broken out, gangs have fought, neighboring families have feuded, or colleagues have clashed, but for every territorial signal that has failed, there are millions of others that have not. They do not rate a mention in the news, but they nevertheless constitute a dominant feature of human society—the society of a remarkably territorial animal.

1977

Susan Jacoby

Unfair Game

My friend and I, two women obviously engrossed in conversation, are sitting at a corner table in the crowded Oak Room of the Plaza[1] at ten o'clock on a Tuesday night. A man materializes and interrupts us with the snappy opening line, "A good woman is hard to find."

We say nothing, hoping he will disappear back into his bottle. But he fancies himself as our genie and asks, "Are you visiting?" Still we say nothing. Finally my friend looks up and says, "We live here." She and I look at each other, the thread of our conversation snapped, our thoughts focused on how to get rid of this intruder. In a minute, if something isn't done, he will scrunch down next to me on the banquette and start offering to buy us drinks.

"Would you leave us alone, please," I say in a loud but reasonably polite voice. He looks slightly offended but goes on with his bright social patter. I become more explicit. "We don't want to talk to you, we didn't ask you over here, and we want to be alone. Go away." This time he directs his full attention to me—and he is mad. "All right, all right, *excuse me.*" He pushes up the corners of his mouth in a Howdy Doody smile. "You ought to try smiling. You might even be pretty if you smiled once in a while."

At last the man leaves. He goes back to his buddy at the bar. I watch them out of the corner of my eye, and he gestures angrily at me for at

4

---

[1]The famous New York City luxury hotel.—EDS.

least fifteen minutes. When he passes our table on the way out of the
room, this well-dressed, obviously affluent man mutters, "Good-bye,
bitch," under his breath.

Why is this man calling me names? Because I have asserted my right
to sit at a table in a public place without being drawn into a sexual
flirtation. Because he has been told, in no uncertain terms, that two
attractive women prefer each other's company to his.

This sort of experience is an old story to any woman who travels,
eats, or drinks—for business or pleasure—without a male escort. In
Holiday Inns and at the Plaza, on buses and airplanes, in tourist and
first class, a woman is always thought to be looking for a man in
addition to whatever else she may be doing. The man who barged in on
us at the bar would never have broken into the conversation of two men,
and it goes without saying that he wouldn't have imposed himself on a
man and a woman who were having a drink. But two women at a table
are an entirely different matter. Fair game.

This might be viewed as a relatively small flaw in the order of the
universe—something in a class with an airline losing luggage or a
computer fouling up a bank statement. Except a computer doesn't foul
up your bank account every month and an airline doesn't lose your
suitcase every time you fly. But if you are an independent woman, you
have to spend a certain amount of energy, day in and day out, in order
to go about your business without being bothered by strange men.

On airplanes, I am a close-mouthed traveler. As soon as the "No   8
Smoking" sign is turned off, I usually pull some papers out of my
briefcase and start working. Work helps me forget that I am scared of
flying. When I am sitting next to a woman, she quickly realizes from my
monosyllabic replies that I don't want to chat during the flight. Most
men, though, are not content to be ignored.

Once I was flying from New York to San Antonio on a plane that
was scheduled to stop in Dallas. My seatmate was an advertising executive who kept questioning me about what I was doing and who remained undiscouraged by my terse replies until I ostentatiously covered myself with a blanket and shut my eyes. When the plane started its
descent into Dallas, he made his move.

"You don't really have to get to San Antonio today, do you?"

"Yes."

"Come on, change your ticket. Spend the evening with me here. I'm   12
staying at a wonderful hotel, with a pool, we could go dancing . . ."

"No."

"Well, you can't blame a man for trying."

I do blame a man for trying in this situation—for suggesting that a
woman change her work and travel plans to spend a night with a perfect

stranger in whom she had displayed no personal interest. The "no personal interest" is crucial; I wouldn't have blamed the man for trying if I had been stroking his cheek and complaining about my dull social life.

There is a nice postscript to this story. Several months later, I was 16 walking my dog in Carl Schurz Park when I ran into my erstwhile seatmate, who was taking a stroll with his wife and children. He recognized me, all right, and was trying to avoid me when I went over and courteously reintroduced myself. I reminded him that we had been on the same flight to Dallas. "Oh yes," he said. "As I recall you were going on to somewhere else." "San Antonio," I said. "I was in a hurry that day."

The code of feminine politeness, instilled in girlhood, is no help in dealing with the unwanted approaches of strange men. Our mothers didn't teach us to tell a man to get lost; they told us to smile and hint that we'd be just delighted to spend time with the gentleman if we didn't have other commitments. The man in the Oak Room bar would not be put off by a demure lowering of eyelids; he had to be told, roughly and loudly, that his presence was a nuisance.

Not that I am necessarily against men and women picking each other up in public places. In most instances, a modicum of sensitivity will tell a woman or a man whether someone is open to approaches.

Mistakes can easily be corrected by the kind of courtesy so many people have abandoned since the "sexual revolution." One summer evening, I was whiling away a half hour in the outdoor bar of the Stanhope Hotel. I was alone, dressed up, having a drink before going on to meet someone in a restaurant. A man at the next table asked, "If you're not busy, would you like to have a drink with me?" I told him I was sorry but I would be leaving shortly. "Excuse me for disturbing you," he said, turning back to his own drink. Simple courtesy. No insults and no hurt feelings.

One friend suggested that I might have avoided the incident in the 20 Oak Room by going to the Palm Court[2] instead. It's true that the Palm Court is a traditional meeting place for unescorted ladies. But I don't like violins when I want to talk. And I wanted to sit in a large, comfortable leather chair. Why should I have to hide among the potted palms to avoid men who think I'm looking for something else?   *1978*

---

[2]Another restaurant at the Plaza.—Eds.

Brent Staples

Just Walk on By:
A Black Man Ponders His Power
to Alter Public Space

My first victim was a woman—white, well dressed, probably in her early twenties. I came upon her late one evening on a deserted street in Hyde Park, a relatively affluent neighborhood in an otherwise mean, impoverished section of Chicago. As I swung onto the avenue behind her, there seemed to be a discreet, uninflammatory distance between us. Not so. She cast back a worried glance. To her, the youngish black man—a broad six feet two inches with a beard and billowing hair, both hands shoved into the pockets of a bulky military jacket—seemed menacingly close. After a few more quick glimpses, she picked up her pace and was soon running in earnest. Within seconds she disappeared into a cross street.

That was more than a decade ago. I was twenty-two years old, a graduate student newly arrived at the University of Chicago. It was in the echo of that terrified woman's footfalls that I first began to know the unwieldy inheritance I'd come into—the ability to alter public space in ugly ways. It was clear that she thought herself the quarry of a mugger, a rapist, or worse. Suffering a bout of insomnia, however, I was stalking sleep, not defenseless wayfarers. As a softy who is scarcely able to take a knife to a raw chicken—let alone hold it to a person's throat—I was surprised, embarrassed, and dismayed all at once. Her flight made me feel like an accomplice in tyranny. It also made it clear that I was indistinguishable from the muggers who occasionally seeped into the area from the surrounding ghetto. That first encounter, and those that followed, signified that a vast, unnerving gulf lay between nighttime pedestrians—particularly women—and me. And I soon gathered that being perceived as dangerous is a hazard in itself. I only needed to turn a corner into a dicey situation, or crowd some frightened, armed person in a foyer somewhere, or make an errant move after being pulled over by a policeman. Where fear and weapons meet—and they often do in urban America—there is always the possibility of death.

In that first year, my first away from my hometown, I was to become thoroughly familiar with the language of fear. At dark, shadowy inter-sections in Chicago, I could cross in front of a car stopped at a traffic light and elicit the *thunk, thunk, thunk, thunk* of the driver—black, white, male, or female—hammering down the door locks. On less traveled streets after dark, I grew accustomed to but never comfortable with people who crossed to the other side of the street rather than pass me.

Then there were the standard unpleasantries with police, doormen, bouncers, cabdrivers, and others whose business is to screen out trou- blesome individuals *before* there is any nastiness.

I moved to New York nearly two years ago and I have remained an   4 avid night walker. In central Manhattan, the near-constant crowd cover minimizes tense one-on-one street encounters. Elsewhere—visiting friends in SoHo,[1] where sidewalks are narrow and tightly spaced build- ings shut out the sky—things can get very taut indeed.

Black men have a firm place in New York mugging literature. Norman Podhoretz[2] in his famed (or infamous) 1963 essay, "My Negro Problem—And Ours," recalls growing up in terror of black males; they "were tougher than we were, more ruthless," he writes—and as an adult on the Upper West Side of Manhattan, he continues, he cannot con- strain his nervousness when he meets black men on certain streets. Similarly, a decade later, the essayist and novelist Edward Hoagland extols a New York where once "Negro bitterness bore down mainly on other Negroes." Where some see mere panhandlers, Hoagland sees "a mugger who is clearly screwing up his nerve to do more than just *ask* for money." But Hoagland has "the New Yorker's quick-hunch posture for broken-field maneuvering," and the bad guy swerves away.

I often witness that "hunch posture," from women after dark on the warrenlike streets of Brooklyn where I live. They seem to set their faces on neutral and, with their purse straps strung across their chests ban- dolier style, they forge ahead as though bracing themselves against being tackled. I understand, of course, that the danger they perceive is not a hallucination. Women are particularly vulnerable to street vio- lence, and young black males are drastically overrepresented among the perpetrators of that violence. Yet these truths are no solace against the kind of alienation that comes of being ever the suspect, against being set apart, a fearsome entity with whom pedestrians avoid making eye contact.

It is not altogether clear to me how I reached the ripe old age of twenty-two without being conscious of the lethality nighttime pedes- trians attributed to me. Perhaps it was because in Chester, Pennsylvania, the small, angry industrial town where I came of age in the 1960s, I was scarcely noticeable against a backdrop of gang warfare, street knifings, and murders. I grew up one of the good boys, had perhaps a half-dozen fistfights. In retrospect, my shyness of combat has clear sources.

Many things go into the making of a young thug. One of those   8 things is the consummation of the male romance with the power to

---

[1]A district of lower Manhattan known for its art galleries.—EDS.

[2]A well-known literary critic and editor of *Commentary* magazine.—EDS.

intimidate. An infant discovers that random flailings send the baby bottle flying out of the crib and crashing to the floor. Delighted, the joyful babe repeats those motions again and again, seeking to duplicate the feat. Just so, I recall the points at which some of my boyhood friends were finally seduced by the perception of themselves as tough guys. When a mark cowered and surrendered his money without resistance, myth and reality merged—and paid off. It is, after all, only manly to embrace the power to frighten and intimidate. We, as men, are not supposed to give an inch of our lane on the highway; we are to seize the fighter's edge in work and in play and even in love; we are to be valiant in the face of hostile forces.

Unfortunately, poor and powerless young men seem to take all this nonsense literally. As a boy, I saw countless tough guys locked away; I have since buried several, too. They were babies, really—a teenage cousin, a brother of twenty-two, a childhood friend in his mid-twenties—all gone down in episodes of bravado played out in the streets. I came to doubt the virtues of intimidation early on. I chose, perhaps even unconsciously, to remain a shadow—timid, but a survivor.

The fearsomeness mistakenly attributed to me in public places often has a perilous flavor. The most frightening of these confusions occurred in the late 1970s and early 1980s when I worked as a journalist in Chicago. One day, rushing into the office of a magazine I was writing for with a deadline story in hand, I was mistaken for a burglar. The office manager called security and, with an ad hoc posse, pursued me through the labyrinthine halls, nearly to my editor's door. I had no way of proving who I was. I could only move briskly toward the company of someone who knew me.

Another time I was on assignment for a local paper and killing time before an interview. I entered a jewelry store on the city's affluent Near North Side. The proprietor excused herself and returned with an enormous red Doberman pinscher straining at the end of a leash. She stood, the dog extended toward me, silent to my questions, her eyes bulging nearly out of her head. I took a cursory look around, nodded, and bade her good night. Relatively speaking, however, I never fared as badly as another black male journalist. He went to nearby Waukegan, Illinois, a couple of summers ago to work on a story about a murderer who was born there. Mistaking the reporter for the killer, police hauled him from his car at gunpoint and but for his press credentials would probably have tried to book him. Such episodes are not uncommon. Black men trade tales like this all the time.

In "My Negro Problem—And Ours," Podhoretz writes that the 12 hatred he feels for blacks makes itself known to him through a variety of avenues—one being his discomfort with that "special brand of paranoid touchiness" to which he says blacks are prone. No doubt he is speaking here of black men. In time, I learned to smother the rage I felt at so often being taken for a criminal. Not to do so would surely have led to madness—via that special "paranoid touchiness" that so annoyed Podhoretz at the time he wrote the essay.

I began to take precautions to make myself less threatening. I move about with care, particularly late in the evening. I give a wide berth to nervous people on subway platforms during the wee hours, particularly when I have exchanged business clothes for jeans. If I happen to be entering a building behind some people who appear skittish, I may walk by, letting them clear the lobby before I return, so as not to seem to be following them. I have been calm and extremely congenial on those rare occasions when I've been pulled over by the police.

And on late-evening constitutionals along streets less traveled by, I employ what has proved to be an excellent tension-reducing measure: I whistle melodies from Beethoven and Vivaldi and the more popular classical composers. Even steely New Yorkers hunching toward night-time destinations seem to relax, and occasionally they even join in the tune. Virtually everybody seems to sense that a mugger wouldn't be warbling bright, sunny selections from Vivaldi's *Four Seasons*. It is my equivalent of the cowbell that hikers wear when they know they are in bear country.   *1986*

15

On Holidays

Russell Baker, Happy New Year?

Michael Arlen, Ode to Thanksgiving

Nikki Giovanni, On Holidays and How to
Make Them Work

Who can be insensible to the outpourings of good feeling, and the honest interchange of affectionate attachment, which abound at this season of the year? A Christmas family party! We know nothing in nature more delightful! There seems a magic in the very name of Christmas. Petty jealousies and discords are forgotten; social feelings are awakened in bosoms to which they have long been strangers; father and son, or brother and sister, who have met and passed with averted gaze or a look of cold recognition for months before, proffer and return the cordial embrace, and bury their past animosities in their present happiness. Kindly hearts that have yearned toward each other, but have been withheld by false notions of pride and self-dignity, are again reunited, and all is kindness and benevolence! Would that Christmas lasted the whole year through (as it ought), and that the prejudices and passions which deform our better nature were never called into action among those to whom they should ever be strangers!

Charles Dickens, from "A Christmas Dinner"

Christmas, which comes once a year, is a big event in an American family. Like other families, the Whites excitedly bought gifts, decorated the house, went to the post office to mail cards and packages—not until the day before Christmas could the arrangements be considered more or less complete. Once this activity had stopped, however, the house was so dull and cheerless as to seem strange and even depressing. Old Mrs.

White sat on the sofa sadly watching the snowflakes flutter outside the window; nestled against her, the big calico cat slept soundly. Even the mischievous Anna, Wendy, and Shirley were surprisingly quiet, lying on the rug as gently as the cat, listening to "White Christmas" over and over with their eyes open. A big Christmas tree standing in the corner was dressed up like a young lady in her best attire, a shining gold star on her head, countless silver paper necklaces around her neck, and spread all over her skirt colored lights and silver stars and snowflakes—so beautiful, proudly standing in the corner like a lone flower appreciating itself. Mr. White strolled out of the study, a magazine in his hand, and looked around the living room. "Where has everyone gone?" he asked, his voice betraying impatience. He wanted the children to come see the goldfish tank he had just bought. Mr. White was probably already finding vacation at home empty and dull.

Jeijun, from *Land Without Ghosts*

Yes, needed is a holiday for blacks everywhere, a Black World Day, with black excitement and black trimmings in honor of the astounding strength and achievement of black people. A yearly Black People's Day—akin, perhaps, to the black concept Kwanza, which, based on a traditional African holiday, is considered by many black people an alternative to commercial Christmas; for the week beginning December twenty-sixth, homes are decorated in red and black and green, the black representing the black nation, the red representing our shed blood, the green featured as a symbol of land for nation-establishment and a symbol, too, for live faith in our young.

Gwendolyn Brooks, from "Dreams of a Black Christmas"

Russell Baker

Happy New Year?

New Year's Day is always a depressing holiday, and for good reason. For one thing, it comes in January, and to those who ask, "If January comes, can spring be far behind?" my answer is yes, two months and three weeks behind, including February, a month that never fails to last at least nine years.

For another thing, New Year's Day is when the annual hike in Social Security taxes always starts to erode your standard of living. For a third thing, the day is a nightmare of football.

All right, nobody has to watch the football orgies, but suppose you don't. Without any television narcotic to paralyze the brain, you are vulnerable to the fourth horror of New Year's Day. This is the irresistible impulse to think about your bad habits.

I suppose people would think about their bad habits on New Year's   4
Day no matter what day it was held on. The very idea of a "new year" makes our calendar-ridden minds dwell upon the past and how our missteps back there can be corrected to improve the future. It is this impulse that accounts for New Year's resolutions, at least among the young, who are too inexperienced to realize that habit's iron grip is unbreakable by an oath taken on a dark day in January.

With age, each new year's arrival merely mocks you with the memory of all the bad habits you've failed to break and forces you to concede that you are, among other things, the sum of your bad habits.

One of my bad habits, for example, is cutting my fingernails in the living room. Because my fingernails are extremely hard, they snap off like flying pellets when the clipper jaws are applied, zoom through the air and end up scattered all over the rug.

Socially this creates hardship. Many times I have caught guests glancing at the rug and exchanging meaningful glances that said, "What are we doing trafficking with people who have fingernail clippings all over the rug?"

After years of futile effort to break the habit, I decided to make the   8
most of it. Would I, after all, still be the authentic individual I am, without a rug bearing fingernail clippings? Of course not. I would be an eccentric who went outside and sat on the curb every time I wanted to cut my nails.

And yet, every New Year's Day, dwelling on bad habits out of ancient instinct, I am depressed by the realization that this habit has beaten me.

Humans are the only creatures who allow themselves to be made morose by the turning of the calendar. Some years ago, when I yearned to hold dominion over beasts, I maintained a cat whose habits were far from impeccable.

Among many idiosyncrasies which made that cat unique was the habit of getting into the salad bowl and shedding cat hair in it. It was an unbreakable compulsion, and the cat accepted it as such and lived with it.

Did the cat, on New Year's Day, sit around the hearth looking   12
miserable because she faced another year in which she would be unable to stop shedding hair in the salad bowl? Neither on New Year's Day nor

any other day of the year did that cat ever show one instant of depression about her evil habit.

Well, of course, the cat didn't know New Year's Day from a July afternoon in Key West. Lacking the slightest understanding of the solar system's mechanics, she was not emotionally enslaved to the dictates of a calendar.

Humans treat time as a map and always know where they are located on it and respond with the appropriate emotion. If it's the Fourth of July we are happy to eat hot dogs, and if it's Thanksgiving we are unhappy to eat hot dogs. If it's May we are saddened by the sight of a lovely tree chopped down, and if it's December we gather in delighted merriment around a lovely tree chopped off in the bloom of youth.

If it's New Year's Day we feel the depressing weight of the new rising tax and lurch toward despair at thoughts of the frigid Sahara separating us from spring. We sit in the parlor, powerless to stop ourselves from clipping fingernails into the rug, our spirit soured with envy of the cat shedding hair into the salad without the slightest twinge of self-loathing.

These are the curses of our intellectual superiority to all other 16 creatures, whose intelligence is as dim as though their brains had been marinated in sixteen hours of televised football. This is why I usually spend sixteen hours of New Year's Day in front of the television set watching the football.   *1984*

Michael Arlen

Ode to Thanksgiving

It is time, at last, to speak the truth about Thanksgiving, and the truth is this. Thanksgiving is really not such a terrific holiday. Consider the traditional symbols of the event: Dried corn husks hanging on the door! Terrible wine! Cranberry jelly in little bowls of extremely doubtful provenance which everyone is required to handle with the greatest of care! Consider the participants, the merrymakers: men and women (also children) who have survived passably well throughout the years, mainly as a result of living at considerable distances from their dear parents and beloved siblings, who on this feast of feasts must apparently forgather (as if beckoned by an aberrant fairy godmother), usually by circuitous routes, through heavy traffic, at a common meeting place, where the very moods, distempers, and obtrusive personal habits that have kept them all happily apart since adulthood are then and there encouraged to slowly ferment beneath the corn husks, and gradually rise with the aid of the terrible wine, and finally burst forth out of control under the stimulus of the cranberry jelly! No, it is a mockery of a holiday. For instance: *Thank you, O Lord, for what we are about to receive.* This is surely not a gala concept. There are no presents, unless one counts Aunt Bertha's sweet rolls a present, which no one does. There is precious little in the way of costumery: miniature plastic turkeys and those witless Pilgrim hats. There is no sex. Indeed, Thanksgiving is the one day of the year (a fact known to everybody) when all thoughts of sex completely vanish, evaporating from apartments, houses, condominiums, and mobile homes like steam from a bathroom mirror.

Consider also the nowhereness of the time of year: the last week or so in November. It is obviously not yet winter: winter, with its death-dealing blizzards and its girls in tiny skirts pirouetting on the ice. On the other hand, it is certainly not much use to anyone as fall: no golden leaves or Oktoberfests, and so forth. Instead, it is a no-man's-land between the seasons. In the cold and sobersides northern half of the country, it is a vaguely unsettling interregnum of long, mournful walks beneath leafless trees: the long, mournful walks following the midday repast with the dread inevitability of pie following turkey, and the leafless trees looming or standing about like eyesores, and the ground either as hard as iron or slightly mushy, and the light snow always beginning to fall when one is halfway to the old green gate—flecks of cold, watery stuff plopping between neck and collar, for the reason that, it being not yet winter, one has forgotten or not chosen to bring along a muffler. It is a corollary to the long, mournful Thanksgiving walk that the absence of this muffler is quickly noticed and that four weeks or so later, at Christmastime, instead of the Sony Betamax one had secretly hoped the children might have chipped in to purchase, one receives another muffler: by then the thirty-third. Thirty-three mufflers! Some walk! Of course, things are more fun in the warm and loony southern part of the country. No snow there of any kind. No need of mufflers. Also, no long, mournful walks, because in the warm and loony southern part of the country everybody drives. So everybody drives over to Uncle Jasper's house to watch the Cougars play the Gators, a not entirely unimportant conflict which will determine whether the Gators get a Bowl bid or must take another postseason exhibition tour of North Korea. But no sooner do the Cougars kick off (an astonishing end-over-end squiggly thing that floats lazily above the arena before plummeting down toward K. C. McCoy and catching him on the helmet) than Auntie Em starts hustling turkey. Soon Cousin May is slamming around the bowls and platters, and Cousin Bernice is oohing and ahing about "all

the fixin's," and Uncle Bob is making low, insincere sounds of appreciation: "Yummy, yummy, Auntie Em, I'll have me some more of these
delicious yams!" Delicious yams? Uncle Bob's eyes roll wildly in his
head. Billy Joe Quaglino throws his long bomb in the middle of
Grandpa Morris saying grace, Grandpa Morris speaking so low nobody
can hear him, which is just as well, since he is reciting what he can
remember of his last union contract. And then, just as J. B. (Speedy)
Snood begins his ninety-two-yard punt return, Auntie Em starts dealing
everyone second helpings of her famous stuffing, as if she were pushing
a controlled substance, which it well might be, since there are no easily
recognizable ingredients visible to the naked eye.

Consider for a moment the Thanksgiving meal itself. It has become
a sort of refuge for endangered species of starch: cauliflower, turnips,
pumpkin, mince (whatever "mince" is), those blessed yams. Bowls of
luridly colored yams, with no taste at all, lying torpid under a lava flow
of marshmallow! And then the sacred turkey. One might as well try to
construct a holiday repast around a fish—say, a nice piece of haddock.
After all, turkey tastes very similar to haddock; same consistency, same
quite remarkable absence of flavor. But then, if the Thanksgiving pièce
de résistance were a nice piece of boiled haddock instead of turkey,
there wouldn't be all that fun for Dad when Mom hands him the
sterling-silver, bone-handled carving set (a wedding present from her
parents and not sharpened since) and then everyone sits around pretending not to watch while he saws and tears away at the bird as if he
were trying to burrow his way into or out of some grotesque, fowllike
prison.

What of the good side to Thanksgiving, you ask. There is always a 4
good side to everything. Not to Thanksgiving. There is only a bad side
and then a worse side. For instance, Grandmother's best linen tablecloth
is a bad side: the fact that it is produced each year, in the manner of a
red flag being produced before a bull, and then is always spilled upon
by whichever child is doing poorest at school that term and so is in need
of greatest reassurance. Thus, "Oh, my God, *Veronica*, you just spilled
grape juice [or plum wine or tar] on Grandmother's best linen tablecloth!" But now comes worse. For at this point Cousin Bill, the one who
lost all Cousin Edwina's money on the car dealership three years ago
and has apparently been drinking steadily since Halloween, bizarrely
chooses to say: "Seems to me those old glasses are always falling over."
To which Auntie Meg is heard to add: "Somehow I don't remember
receivin' any of those old glasses." To which Uncle Fred replies: "That's
because you and George decided to go on vacation to Hawaii the
summer Grandpa Sam was dying." Now Grandmother is sobbing,
though not so uncontrollably that she can refrain from murmuring: "I
think that volcano painting I threw away by mistake got sent me from

Hawaii, heaven knows why." But the gods are merciful, even the Pilgrim-hatted god of corn husks and soggy stuffing, and there is an end to everything, even to Thanksgiving. Indeed, there is a grandeur to the feelings of finality and doom which usually settle on a house after the Thanksgiving celebration is over, for with the completion of Thanksgiving Day the year itself has been properly terminated: shot through the cranium with a high-velocity candied yam. At this calendrical nadir, all energy on the planet has gone, all fun has fled, all the terrible wine has been drunk.

But then, overnight, life once again begins to stir, emerging, even by the next morning, in the form of Japanese window displays and Taiwanese Christmas lighting, from the primeval ooze of the nation's department stores. Thus, a new year dawns, bringing with it immediate and cheering possibilities of extended consumer debt, office-party flirtations, good—or, at least, mediocre—wine, and visions of Supersaver excursion fares to Montego Bay. It is worth noting, perhaps, that this true new year always starts with the same mute, powerful mythic ceremony: the surreptitious tossing out, in the early morning, of all those horrid aluminum-foil packages of yams and cauliflowers and stuffing and red, gummy cranberry substance which have been squeezed into the refrigerator as if a reenactment of the siege of Paris were shortly expected. Soon afterward, the phoenix of Christmas can be observed as it slowly rises, beating its drumsticks, once again goggle-eyed with hope and unrealistic expectations.　　　　　*1976*

Nikki Giovanni

On Holidays
and How to Make Them Work

A proper holiday, coming from the medieval "holy day," is supposed to be a time of reflection on great men, great deeds, great people. Things like that. Somehow in America this didn't quite catch on. Take Labor Day. On Labor Day you take the day off, then go to the Labor Day sales and spend your devalued money with a clerk who is working. And organized labor doesn't understand why it suffers declining membership? Pshaw. Who wants to join an organization that makes you work on the day it designates as a day off? Plus, no matter how hidden the agenda, who wants a day off if they make you march in a parade and listen to some politicians talk on and on about nothing.

Hey. I'm a laborer. I used to work in Walgreen's on Linn Street. We were open every holiday and I, being among the junior people, always "got" to work the time-and-a-half holidays. I hated those people who came in. Every fool in the Western world, and probably in this universe, knows that Christmas is December 25. Has been that way for over a thousand years, yet there they'd be, standing outside the door, cold, bleary-eyed, waiting for us to open so they could purchase a present. Memorial Day, which used to be Armistice Day until we got into this situation of continuous war, was the official start of summer. We would want to be out with our boyfriends barbecuing . . . or something, but there we were behind the counter waiting to see who forgot that in order to barbecue you need: (1) a grill, (2) charcoal, (3) charcoal starter. My heart goes out to the twenty-four-hour grocery people, who are probably selling meat!

But hey. It's the American way. The big Fourth of July sales probably reduced the number of fatal injuries as people spent the entire day sober in malls, fighting over markdowns. Minor cuts and bruises were way up, though, I'll bet. And forget the great nonholiday, Presidents' Day. The damned thing could at least have a real name. What does that mean—Presidents' Day? Mostly that we don't care enough to take the time to say to Washington and Lincoln: Well done. But for sure, as a Black American I've got to go for it. Martin Luther King, Jr.'s birthday has come up for the first time as a national holiday. If we are serious about celebrating it, Steinberg's will be our first indication: GHETTO BLASTERS 30% OFF! FREE TAPE OF "I HAVE A DREAM" WITH EVERY VCR PURCHASED AT THE ALL-NEW GIGANTIC MARTY'S BIRTHDAY SALE. Then Wendy's will, just maybe, for Black patrons (and their liberal sympathizers) Burn-A-Burger to celebrate the special day. Procter & Gamble will withhold Clorox for the day, respectfully requesting that those Black spots be examined for their liberating influence. But what we really want, where we can know we have succeeded, is that every Federated department store offers 50 percent off to every colored patron who can prove he or she is black in recognition of the days when colored citizens who were black were not accorded all the privileges of other shoppers. That will be a big help because everybody will want to be Black for a Day. Sun tanneries will make fortunes during the week preceding MLK Day. Wig Salons will reap great benefits. Dentists will have to hire extra help to put that distinctive gap between the middle front teeth. MLK Day will be accepted. And isn't that the heart of the American dream?

I really love a good holiday—it takes the people off the streets and puts them safely in the shopping malls. Now think about it. Aren't you proud to be with Uncle Sam? *1988*

16

Consumer Culture

William Severini Kowinski, Kids in the Mall:
Growing Up Controlled

Phyllis Rose, Shopping and Other Spiritual
Adventures in America Today

Toni Cade Bambara, The Lesson

The desire for wealth can scarcely be satiated in any individual instance, and evidently a satiation of the average or general desire for
wealth is out of the question. However widely, or equally, or "fairly," it
may be distributed, no general increase of the community's wealth can
make any approach to satiating this need, the ground of which is the
desire of every one to excel every one else in the accumulation of goods.
If, as is sometimes assumed, the incentive to accumulation were the
want of subsistence or of physical comfort, then the aggregate economic
wants of a community might conceivably be satisfied at some point in
the advance of industrial efficiency; but since the struggle is substantially a race for reputability on the basis of an invidious comparison, no
approach to a definitive attainment is possible.

Thorstein Veblen, from *The Theory of the Leisure Class*

Each city is divided into four equal parts. In the middle of each pair is a
marketplace for everything. There the produce of each household is
brought and put in certain buildings. Each different kind of product is
put separately into barns. From these each family head seeks what he
and his family need, and he carries off whatever he seeks, without any
money or exchange of any kind. For why should anything be refused
him? There is more than enough of everything and there is no fear that
anyone will ask for more than he needs. For why would he be likely to

seek too much, when he knows for certain that his needs will always be met? A man is made greedy and grasping either by the fear of need (a fear common to all creatures) or else (in man alone) by pride, which thinks it glorious to surpass others in superfluous show. This kind of vice has no place at all in the ways of the Utopians.

Sir Thomas More, from *Utopia*

The profusion of commodities is a genuine and powerful compensation for oppression. It is a bribe, but like all bribes it offers concrete benefits—in the average American's case, a degree of physical comfort unparalleled in history. Under present conditions, people are preoccupied with consumer goods not because they are brainwashed but because buying is the one pleasurable activity not only permitted but actively encouraged by our rulers. The pleasure of eating an ice cream cone may be minor compared to the pleasure of meaningful, autonomous work, but the former is easily available and the latter is not. A poor family would undoubtedly rather have a decent apartment than a new TV, but since they are unlikely to get the apartment, what is to be gained by not getting the TV?

Ellen Willis, from *Women and the Myth of Consumerism*

William Severini Kowinski

Kids in the Mall: Growing Up Controlled

Butch heaved himself up and loomed over the group. "Like it was different for me," he piped. "My folks used to drop me off at the shopping mall every morning and leave me all day. It was like a big free baby-sitter, you know? One night they never came back for me. Maybe they moved away. Maybe there's some kind of a Bureau of Missing Parents I could check with."

—Richard Peck, *Secrets of the Shopping Mall*, a novel for teenagers

From his sister at Swarthmore, I'd heard about a kid in Florida whose mother picked him up after school every day, drove him straight to the mall, and left him there until it closed—all at his insistence. I'd heard about a boy in Washington who, when his family moved from one suburb to another, pedaled his bicycle five miles every day to get back to his old mall, where he once belonged.

These stories aren't unusual. The mall is a common experience for the majority of American youth; they have probably been going there all their lives. Some ran within their first large open space, saw their first fountain, bought their first toy, and read their first book in a mall. They may have smoked their first cigarette or first joint or turned them down, had their first kiss or lost their virginity in the mall parking lot. Teenagers in America now spend more time in the mall than anywhere else but home and school. Mostly it is their choice, but some of that mall time is put in as the result of two-paycheck and single-parent households, and the lack of other viable alternatives. But are these kids being harmed by the mall?

I wondered first of all what difference it makes for adolescents to experience so many important moments in the mall. They are, after all, at play in the fields of its little world and they learn its ways; they adapt to it and make it adapt to them. It's here that these kids get their street sense, only it's mall sense. They are learning the ways of a large-scale artificial environment: its subtleties and flexibilities, its particular pleasures and resonances, and the attitudes it fosters.

The presence of so many teenagers for so much time was not $\quad$ 4 something mall developers planned on. In fact, it came as a big surprise. But kids became a fact of mall life very early, and the International Council of Shopping Centers found it necessary to commission a study, which they published along with a guide to mall managers on how to handle the teenage incursion.

The study found that "teenagers in suburban centers are bored and come to the shopping centers mainly as a place to go. Teenagers in suburban centers spent more time fighting, drinking, littering and walking than did their urban counterparts, but presented fewer overall problems." The report observed that "adolescents congregated in groups of two to four and predominantly at locations selected by them rather than management." This probably had something to do with the decision to install game arcades, which allow management to channel these restless adolescents into naturally contained areas away from major traffic points of adult shoppers.

The guide concluded that mall management should tolerate and even encourage the teenage presence because, in the words of the report, "The vast majority support the same set of values as does shopping center management." *The same set of values* means simply that mall kids are already preprogrammed to be consumers and that the mall can put the finishing touches to them as hard-core, lifelong shoppers just like everybody else. That, after all, is what the mall is about. So it shouldn't be surprising that in spending a lot of time there, adolescents find little that challenges the assumption that the goal of life is to make money and buy products, or that just about everything else in life is to be used to serve those ends.

Growing up in a high-consumption society already adds inestimable pressure to kids' lives. Clothes consciousness has invaded the grade schools, and popularity is linked with having the best, newest clothes in the currently acceptable styles. Even what they read has been affected. "Miss [Nancy] Drew wasn't obsessed with her wardrobe," noted *The Wall Street Journal*. "But today the mystery in teen fiction for girls is what outfit the heroine will wear next." Shopping has become a survival skill and there is certainly no better place to learn it than the mall, where its importance is powerfully reinforced and certainly never questioned.

The mall as a university of suburban materialism, where Valley 8 Girls and Boys from coast to coast are educated in consumption, has its other lessons in this era of change in family life and sexual mores and their economic and social ramifications. The plethora of products in the mall, plus the pressure on teens to buy them, may contribute to the phenomenon that psychologist David Elkind calls "the hurried child": kids who are exposed to too much of the adult world too quickly, and must respond with a sophistication that belies their still-tender emotional development. Certainly the adult products marketed for children—form-fitting designer jeans, sexy tops for preteen girls—add to the social pressure to look like an adult, along with the homegrown need to understand adult finances (why mothers must work) and adult emotions (when parents divorce).

Kids spend so much time at the mall partly because their parents allow it and even encourage it. The mall is safe, it doesn't seem to harbor any unsavory activities, and there is adult supervision; it is, after all, a controlled environment. So the temptation, especially for working parents, is to let the mall be their baby-sitter. At least the kids aren't watching TV. But the mall's role as a surrogate mother may be more extensive and more profound.

Karen Lansky, a writer living in Los Angeles, has looked into the subject and she told me some of her conclusions about the effects on its teenaged denizens of the mall's controlled and controlling environment. "Structure is the dominant idea, since true 'mall rats' lack just that in their home lives," she said, "and adolescents about to make the big leap into growing up crave more structure than our modern society cares to acknowledge." Karen pointed out some of the elements malls supply that kids used to get from their families, like warmth (Strawberry Shortcake dolls and similar cute and cuddly merchandise), old-fashioned mothering ("We do it all for you," the fast-food slogan), and even home cooking (the "homemade" treats at the food court).

The problem in all this, as Karen Lansky sees it, is that while families nurture children by encouraging growth through the assumption of responsibility and then by letting them rest in the bosom of the family from the rigors of growing up, the mall as a structural mother encourages passivity and consumption, as long as the kid doesn't make trouble. Therefore all they learn about becoming adults is how to act and how to consume.

Kids are in the mall not only in the passive role of shoppers—they 12 also work there, especially as fast-food outlets infiltrate the mall's enclosure. There they learn how to hold a job and take responsibility, but still within the same value context. When *CBS Reports* went to Oak Park Mall in suburban Kansas City, Kansas, to tape part of their hour-long consideration of malls, "After the Dream Comes True," they interviewed a teenaged girl who worked in a fast-food outlet there. In a sequence that didn't make the final program, she described the major goal of her present life, which was to perfect the curl on top of the ice-cream cones that were her store's specialty. If she could do that, she would be moved from the lowly soft-drink dispenser to the more prestigious ice-cream division, the curl on top of the status ladder at her restaurant. These are the achievements that are important at the mall.

Other benefits of such jobs may also be overrated, according to Laurence D. Steinberg of the University of California at Irvine's social ecology department, who did a study on teenage employment. Their jobs, he found, are generally simple, mindlessly repetitive, and boring. They don't really learn anything, and the jobs don't lead anywhere. Teenagers also work primarily with other teenagers; even their supervisors are often just a little older than they are. "Kids need to spend time with adults," Steinberg told me. "Although they get benefits from peer relationships, without parents and other adults it's one-sided socialization. They hang out with each other, have age-segregated jobs, and watch TV."

Perhaps much of this is not so terrible or even so terribly different. Now that they have so much more to contend with in their lives, adolescents probably need more time to spend with other adolescents without adult impositions, just to sort things out. Though it is more concentrated in the mall (and therefore perhaps a clearer target), the value system there is really the dominant one of the whole society. Attitudes about curiosity, initiative, self-expression, empathy, and disinterested learning aren't necessarily made in the mall; they are mirrored there, perhaps a bit more intensely—as through a glass brightly.

Besides, the mall is not without its educational opportunities. There are bookstores, where there is at least a short shelf of classics at great prices, and other books from which it is possible to learn more than how to do sit-ups. There are tools, from hammers to VCRs, and products, from clothes to records, that can help the young find and express themselves. There are older people with stories, and places to be alone or to talk one on one with a kindred spirit. And there is always the passing show.

The mall itself may very well be an education about the future. I was 16 struck with the realization, as early as my first forays into Greengate,[1] that the mall is only one of a number of enclosed and controlled environments that are part of the lives of today's young. The mall is just an extension, say, of those large suburban schools—only there's Karmelkorn instead of chem lab, the ice rink instead of the gym: It's high school without the impertinence of classes.

Growing up, moving from home to school to the mall—from enclosure to enclosure, transported in cars—is a curiously continuous process, without much in the way of contrast or contact with unenclosed reality. Places must tend to blur into one another. But whatever differences and dangers there are in this, the skills these adolescents are learning may turn out to be useful in their later lives. For we seem to be moving inexorably into an age of preplanned and regulated environments, and this is the world they will inherit.

Still, it might be better if they had more of a choice. One teenaged girl confessed to *CBS Reports* that she sometimes felt she was missing something by hanging out at the mall so much. "But I'm here," she said, "and this is what I have."　　*1985*

Phyllis Rose

Shopping and Other Spiritual Adventures in America Today

Last year a new Waldbaum's Food Mart opened in the shopping mall on Route 66. It belongs to the new generation of superdupermarkets open twenty-four hours that have computerized checkout. I went to see the place as soon as it opened and I was impressed. There

---

[1]**Greengate:** A mall in Greensburg, Pennsylvania.—EDs.

was trail mix in Lucite bins. There was freshly made pasta. There were coffee beans, four kinds of tahini, ten kinds of herb teas, raw shrimp in shells and cooked shelled shrimp, fresh-squeezed orange juice. Every sophistication known to the big city, even goat's cheese covered with ash, was now available in Middletown, Conn. People raced from the warehouse aisle to the bagel bin to the coffee beans to the fresh fish market, exclaiming at all the new things. Many of us felt elevated, graced, complimented by the presence of this food palace in our town.

This is the wonderful egalitarianism of American business. Was it Andy Warhol who said that the nice thing about Coke is, no can is any better or worse than any other? Some people may find it dull to cross the country and find the same chain stores with the same merchandise from coast to coast, but it means that my town is as good as yours, my shopping mall as important as yours, equally filled with wonders.

Imagine what people ate during the winter as little as seventy-five years ago. They ate food that was local, long-lasting, and dull, like acorn squash, turnips, and cabbage. Walk into an American supermarket in February and the world lies before you: grapes, melons, artichokes, fennel, lettuce, peppers, pistachios, dates, even strawberries, to say nothing of ice cream. Have you ever considered what a triumph of civilization it is to be able to buy a pound of chicken livers? If you lived on a farm and had to kill a chicken when you wanted to eat one, you wouldn't ever accumulate a pound of chicken livers.

Another wonder of Middletown is Caldor, the discount department 4 store. Here is man's plenty: tennis racquets, panty hose, luggage, glassware, records, toothpaste. Timex watches, Cadbury's chocolate, corn poppers, hair dryers, warm-up suits, car wax, light bulbs, television sets. All good quality at low prices with exchanges cheerfully made on defective goods. There are worse rules to live by. I feel good about America whenever I walk into this store, which is almost every midwinter Sunday afternoon, when life elsewhere has closed down. I go to Caldor the way English people go to pubs: out of sociability. To get away from my house. To widen my horizons. For culture's sake. Caldor provides me too with a welcome sense of seasonal change. When the first outdoor grills and lawn furniture appear there, it's as exciting a sign of spring as the first crocus or robin.

Someone told me about a Soviet emigré who practices English by declaiming, at random, sentences that catch his fancy. One of his favorites is, "Fifty percent off all items today only." Refugees from Communist countries appreciate our supermarkets and discount department stores for the wonders they are. An Eastern European scientist visiting Middletown wept when she first saw the meat counter at Waldbaum's. On the other hand, before her year in America was up, her pleasure turned sour. She wanted everything she saw. Her approach to consumer goods was insufficiently abstract, too materialistic. We Americans are beyond a simple, possessive materialism. We're used to abundance and the possibility of possessing things. The things, and the possibility of possessing them, will still be there next week, next year. So today we can walk the aisles calmly.

It is a misunderstanding of the American retail store to think we go there necessarily to buy. Some of us shop. There's a difference. Shopping has many purposes, the least interesting of which is to acquire new articles. We shop to cheer ourselves up. We shop to practice decision-making. We shop to be useful and productive members of our class and society. We shop to remind ourselves how much is available to us. We shop to remind ourselves how much is to be striven for. We shop to assert our superiority to the material objects that spread themselves before us.

Shopping's function as a form of therapy is widely appreciated. You don't really need, let's say, another sweater. You need the feeling of power that comes with buying or not buying it. You need the feeling that someone wants something you have—even if it's just your money. To get the benefit of shopping, you needn't actually purchase the sweater, any more than you have to marry every man you flirt with. In fact, window-shopping, like flirting, can be more rewarding, the same high without the distressing commitment, the material encumbrance. The purest form of shopping is provided by garage sales. A connoisseur goes out with no goal in mind, open to whatever may come his or her way, secure that it will cost very little. Minimum expense, maximum experience. Perfect shopping.

I try to think of the opposite, a kind of shopping in which the object 8 is all-important, the pleasure of shopping at a minimum. For example, the purchase of blue jeans. I buy new blue jeans as seldom as possible because the experience is so humiliating. For every pair that looks good on me, fifteen look grotesque. But even shopping for blue jeans at Bob's Surplus on Main Street—no frills, bare-bones shopping—is an event in the life of the spirit. Once again I have to come to terms with the fact that I will never look good in Levi's. Much as I want to be mainstream, I never will be.

In fact, I'm doubly an oddball, neither Misses nor Junior, but Misses Petite. I look in the mirror, I acknowledge the disparity between myself and the ideal, I resign myself to making the best of it: I will buy the Lee's Misses Petite. Shopping is a time of reflection, assessment, spiritual self-discipline.

It is appropriate, I think, that Bob's Surplus has a communal dressing room. I used to shop only in places where I could count on a private dressing room with a mirror inside. My impulse then was to hide my weaknesses. Now I believe in sharing them. There are other women in the dressing room at Bob's Surplus trying on blue jeans who look as bad as I do. We take comfort from one another. Sometimes a woman will ask me which of two items looks better. I always give a definite answer. It's the least I can do. I figure we are all in this together, and I emerge from the dressing room not only with a new pair of jeans but with a renewed sense of belonging to a human community.

When a Solzhenitsyn rants about American materialism, I have to look at my digital Timex and check what year this is. Materialism? Like conformism, a hot moral issue of the fifties, but not now. How to spread the goods, maybe. Whether the goods are the Good, no. Solzhenitsyn, like the visiting scientist who wept at the beauty of Waldbaum's meat counter but came to covet everything she saw, takes American materialism too materialistically. He doesn't see its spiritual side. Caldor, Waldbaum's, Bob's Surplus—these, perhaps, are our cathedrals.   *1987*

Toni Cade Bambara
The Lesson

Back in the days when everyone was old and stupid or young and foolish and me and Sugar were the only ones just right, this lady moved on our block with nappy hair and proper speech and no makeup. And quite naturally we laughed at her, laughed the way we did at the junk man who went about his business like he was some big-time president and his sorry-ass horse his secretary. And we kinda hated her too, hated the way we did the winos who cluttered up our parks and pissed on our handball walls and stank up our hallways and stairs so you couldn't halfway play hide-and-seek without a goddamn gas mask. Miss Moore was her name. The only woman on the block with no first name. And she was black as hell, cept for her feet, which were fish-white and spooky. And she was always planning these boring-ass things for us to do, us being my cousin, mostly, who lived on the block cause we all moved North the same time and to the same apartment then spread out gradual to breathe. And our parents would yank our heads into some kinda shape and crisp up our clothes so we'd be presentable for travel with Miss Moore, who always looked like she was going to church, though she never did. Which is just one of things the grown-ups talked about when they talked behind her back like a dog. But when she came calling with some sachet she'd sewed up or some gingerbread she'd made or some book, why then they'd all be too embarrassed to turn her down and we'd get handed over all spruced up. She'd been to college and said it was only right that she should take responsibility for the young ones' education, and she not even related by marriage or blood. So they'd go for it. Specially Aunt Gretchen. She was the main gofer in the family. You got some ole dumb shit foolishness you want somebody to go for, you send for Aunt Gretchen. She been screwed into the go-along for so long, it's a blood-deep natural thing with her. Which is how she got saddled with me and Sugar and Junior in the first place while our mothers were in a la-de-da apartment up the block having a good ole time.

So this one day Miss Moore rounds us all up at the mailbox and it's puredee hot and she's knocking herself out about arithmetic. And school suppose to let up in summer I heard, but she don't never let up. And the starch in my pinafore scratching the shit outta me and I'm really hating this nappy-head bitch and her goddamn college degree. I'd much rather go to the pool or to the show where it's cool. So me and Sugar leaning on the mailbox being surly, which is a Miss Moore word. And Flyboy checking out what everybody brought for lunch. And Fat Butt already wasting his peanut-butter-and-jelly sandwich like the pig he is. And Junebug punchin on Q.T.'s arm for potato chips. And Rosie Giraffe shifting from one hip to the other waiting for somebody to step on her foot or ask her if she from Georgia so she can kick ass, preferably Mercedes's. And Miss Moore asking us do we know what money is, like we a bunch of retards. I mean real money, she say, like it's only poker chips or monopoly papers we lay on the grocer. So right away I'm tired of this and say so. And would much rather snatch Sugar and go to the Sunset and terrorize the West Indian kids and take their hair ribbons and their money too. And Miss Moore files that remark away for next week's lesson on brotherhood, I can tell. And finally I say we oughta get to the subway cause it's cooler and besides we might meet some cute boys. Sugar done swiped her mama's lipstick, so we ready.

So we heading down the street and she's boring us silly about what things cost and what our parents make and how much goes for rent and how money ain't divided up right in this country. And then she gets to the part about we all poor and live in the slums, which I don't feature. And I'm ready to speak on that, but she steps out in the street and hails two cabs just like that. Then she hustles half the crew in with her and hands me a five-dollar bill and tells me to calculate 10 percent tip for the driver. And we're off. Me and Sugar and Junebug and Flyboy hangin out the window and hollering to everybody, putting lipstick on each other cause Flyboy a faggot anyway, and making farts with our sweaty armpits. But I'm mostly trying to figure how to spend this money.

But they all fascinated with the meter ticking and Junebug starts laying bets as to how much it'll read when Flyboy can't hold his breath no more. Then Sugar lay bets as to how much it'll be when we get there. So I'm stuck. Don't nobody want to go for my plan, which is to jump out at the next light and run off to the first bar-b-que we can find. Then the driver tells us to get the hell out cause we there already. And the meter reads eight-five cents. And I'm stalling to figure out the tip and Sugar say give him a dime. And I decide he don't need it bad as I do, so later for him. But then he tries to take off with Junebug's foot still in the door so we talk about his mama something ferocious. Then we check out that we on Fifth Avenue and everybody dressed up in stockings. One lady in a fur coat, hot as it is. White folks crazy.

"This is the place," Miss Moore say, presenting it to us in the voice   4
she uses at the museum. "Let's look in the windows before we go in."

"Can we steal?" Sugar asks very serious like she's getting the ground rules squared away before she plays. "I beg your pardon," say Miss Moore, and we fall out. So she leads us around the windows of the toy store and me and Sugar screamin, "This is mine, that's mine, I gotta have that, that was made for me, I was born for that," till Big Butt drowns us out.

"Hey, I'm going to buy that there."

"That there? You don't even know what it is, stupid."

"I do so," he say punchin on Rosie Giraffe. "It's a microscope."   8

"Whatcha gonna do with a microscope, fool?"

"Look at things."

"Like what, Ronald?" ask Miss Moore. And Big Butt ain't got the first notion. So here go Miss Moore gabbing about the thousands of bacteria in a drop of water and the somethinorother in a speck of blood and the million and one living things in the air around us is invisible to the naked eye. And what she say that for? Junebug go to town on that "naked" and we rolling. Then Miss Moore ask what it cost. So we all jam into the window smudgin it up and the price tag say three hundred dollars. So then she ask how long'd take for Big Butt and Junebug to save up their allowances. "Too long," I say. "Yeh," adds Sugar, "outgrown it by that time." And Miss Moore say no, you never outgrow learning instruments. "Why, even medical students and interns and," blah, blah, blah. And we ready to choke Big Butt for bringing it up in the first damn place.

"This here costs four hundred eighty dollars," say Rosie Giraffe. So   12
we pile up all over her to see what she pointin out. My eyes tell me it's a chunk of glass cracked with something heavy, and different-color inks dripped into the splits. then the whole thing put into a oven or something. But for $480 it don't make sense.

"That's a paperweight made of semi-precious stones fused together under tremendous pressure," she explains slowly, with her hands doing the mining and all the factory work.

"So what's a paperweight?" asks Rosie Giraffe.

"To weigh paper with, dumbbell," say Flyboy, the wise man from the East.

"Not exactly," say Miss Moore, which is what she say when you warm   16 or way off too. "It's to weigh paper down so it won't scatter and make your desk untidy." So right away me and Sugar curtsy to each other and then to Mercedes who is more the tidy type.

"We don't keep paper on top of the desk in my class," say Junebug, figuring Miss Moore crazy or lyin one.

"At home, then," she say. "Don't you have a calendar and a pencil case and a blotter and a letter-opener on your desk at home where you do your homework?" And she know damn well what our homes look like cause she nosys around in them every chance she gets.

"I don't even have a desk," say Junebug, "Do we?"

"No. And I don't get no homework neither," says Big Butt.   20

"And I don't even have a home," say Flyboy like he do at school to keep the white folks off his back and sorry for him. Send this poor kid to camp posters, is his specialty.

"I do," says Mercedes. "I have a box of stationery on my desk and a picture of my cat. My godmother bought the stationery and the desk. There's a big rose on each sheet and the envelopes smell like roses."

"Who wants to know about your smelly-ass stationery," say Rosie Giraffe fore I can get my two cents in.

"It's important to have a work area all your own so that . . ."   24

"Will you look at this sailboat, please," say Flyboy, cuttin her off and pointin to the thing like it was his. So once again we tumble all over each other to gaze at this magnificent thing in the toy store which is just big enough to maybe sail two kittens across the pond if you strap them to the posts tight. We all start reciting the price tag like we in assembly. "Handcrafted sailboat of fiberglass at one thousand one hundred ninety-five dollars."

"Unbelievable," I hear myself say and am really stunned. I read it again for myself just in case the group recitation put me in a trance. Same thing. For some reason this pisses me off. We look at Miss Moore and she lookin at us, waiting for I dunno what.

"Who'd pay all that when you can buy a sailboat set for a quarter at Pop's, a tube of glue for a dime, and a ball of string for eight cents? It must have a motor and a whole lot else besides," I say. "My sailboat cost me about fifty cents."

"But will it take water?" say Mercedes with her smart ass.   28

"Took mine to Alley Pond Park once," say Flyboy. "String broke. Lost it. Pity."

"Sailed mine in Central Park and it keeled over and sank. Had to ask my father for another dollar."

"And you got the strap," laugh Big Butt. "The jerk didn't even have a string on it. My old man wailed on his behind."

Little Q.T. was staring hard at the sailboat and you could see he 32 wanted it bad. But he too little and somebody'd just take it from him. So what the hell. "This boat for kids, Miss Moore?"

"Parents silly to buy something like that just to get all broke up," say Rosie Giraffe.

"That much money it should last forever," I figure.

"My father'd buy it for me if I wanted it."

"Your father, my ass," say Rosie Giraffe getting a chance to finally 36 push Mercedes.

"Must be rich people shop here," say Q.T.

"You are a very bright boy," say Flyboy. "What was your first clue?" And he rap him on the head with the back of his knuckles, since Q.T. the only one he could get away with. Though Q.T. liable to come up behind you years later and get his licks in when you half expect it.

"What I want to know is," I says to Miss Moore though I never talk to her, I wouldn't give the bitch that satisfaction, "is how much a real boat costs? I figure a thousand'd get you a yacht any day."

"Why don't you check that out," she says, "and report back to the 40 group?" Which really pains my ass. If you gonna mess up a perfectly good swim day least you could do is have some answers. "Let's go in," she say like she got something up her sleeve. Only she don't lead the way. So me and Sugar turn the corner to where the entrance is, but when we get there I kinda hang back. Not that I'm scared, what's there to be afraid of, just a toy store. But I feel funny, shame. But what I got to be shamed about? Got as much right to go in as anybody. But somehow I can't seem to get hold of the door, so I step away for Sugar to lead. But she hangs back too. And I look at her and she looks at me and this is ridiculous. I mean, damn, I have never ever been shy about doing nothing or going nowhere. But then Mercedes steps up and then Rosie Giraffe and Big Butt crowd in behind and shove, and next thing we all stuffed into the doorway with only Mercedes squeezing past us, smoothing out her jumper and walking right down the aisle. Then the rest of us tumble in like a glued-together jigsaw done all wrong. And people lookin at us. And it's like the time me and Sugar crashed into the Catholic church on a dare. But once we got in there and everything so hushed and holy and the candles and the bowin and the handkerchiefs on all the drooping heads, I just couldn't go through with the plan. Which was for me to run up to the altar and do a tap dance while Sugar played the nose flute and messed around in the holy water. And Sugar kept givin me the elbow. Then later teased me so bad I tied her up in the shower and turned it on and locked her in. And she'd be there till this day if Aunt Gretchen hadn't finally figured I was lyin about the boarder takin a shower.

Same thing in the store. We all walkin on tiptoe and hardly touchin the games and puzzles and things. And I watched Miss Moore who is steady watchin us like she waiting for a sign. Like Mama Drewery watches the sky and sniffs the air and takes note of just how much slant is in the bird formation. Then me and Sugar bump smack into each other, so busy gazing at the toys, 'specially the sailboat. But we don't laugh and go into our fat-lady bump-stomach routine. We just stare at that price tag. Then Sugar ran a finger over the whole boat. And I'm jealous and want to hit her. Maybe not her, but I sure want to punch somebody in the mouth.

"Whatcha bring us here for, Miss Moore?"

"You sound angry, Sylvia. Are you mad about something?" Givin me one of them grins like she tellin a grown-up joke that never turns out to be funny. And she's lookin very closely at me like maybe she plannin to do my portrait from memory. I'm mad, but I won't give her that satisfaction. So I slouch around the store bein very bored and say, "Let's go."

Me an Sugar at the back of the train watchin the tracks whizzin by 44 large then small then gettin gobbled up in the dark. I'm thinkin about this tricky toy I saw in the store. A clown that somersaults on a bar then does chin-ups just cause you yank lightly at his leg. Cost $35. I could see me askin my mother for a $35 birthday clown. "You wanna who that costs what?" she'd say, cocking her head to the side to get a better view of the hole in my head. Thirty-five dollars could buy new bunk beds for Junior and Gretchen's boy. Thirty-five dollars and the whole household could go visit Granddaddy Nelson in the country. Thirty-five dollars would pay for the rent and the piano bill too. Who are these people that spend that much for performing clowns and $1,000 for toy sailboats? What kinda work they do and how they live and how come we ain't in on it? Where we are is who we are, Miss Moore always pointin out. But it don't necessarily have to be that way, she always adds then waits for somebody to say that poor people have to wake up and demand their share of the pie and don't none of us know what kind of pie she talkin about in the first damn place. But she ain't so smart cause I still got her four dollars from the taxi and she sure ain't getting it. Messin up my day with this shit. Sugar nudges me in my pocket and winks.

Miss Moore lines us up in front of the mailbox where we started from, seem like years ago, and I got a headache for thinkin so hard. And we lean all over each other so we can hold up under the draggy-ass lecture she always finishes us off with at the end before we thank her for borin us to tears. But she just looks at us like she readin tea leaves. Finally she say, "Well, what did you think of F.A.O. Schwartz?"

Rosie Giraffe mumbles, "White folks crazy."

"I'd like to go there again when I get my birthday money," says Mercedes, and we shove her out the pack so she has to lean on the mailbox by herself.

"I'd like a shower. Tiring day," says Flyboy.   48

Then Sugar surprises me by sayin, "You know, Miss Moore, I don't think all of us here put together eat in a year what that sailboat costs." And Miss Moore lights up like somebody goosed her. "And?" she say, urging Sugar on. Only I'm standin on her foot so she don't continue.

"Imagine for a minute what kind of society it is in which some people can spend on a toy what it would cost to feed a family of six or seven. What do you think?"

"I think," say Sugar pushing me off her feet like she never done before, cause I whip her ass in a minute, "that this is not much of a democracy if you ask me. Equal chance to pursue happiness means an equal crack at the dough, don't it?" Miss Moore is besides herself and I am disgusted with Sugar's treachery. So I stand on her foot one more time to see if she'll shove me. She shuts up, and Miss Moore looks at me, sorrowfully I'm thinkin. And somethin weird is goin on. I can feel it in my chest.

"Anybody else learn anything today?" lookin dead at me. I walk   52
away and Sugar has to run to catch up and don't even seem to notice when I shrug her arm off my shoulder.

"Well, we got four dollars anyway," she says.

"Uh-hunh."

"We could go to Hascombs and get half a chocolate layer and then go to the Sunset and still have plenty money for potato chips and ice cream sodas."

"Uh-hunh."   56

"Race you to Hascombs," she say.

We start down the block and she gets ahead which is OK by me cause I'm going to the West End and then over to the Drive to think this day through. She can run if she want to and even run faster. But ain't nobody gonna beat me at nuthin.   *1972*

17

The National Pastime

Gerald Early, Baseball:
The Ineffable National Pastime

Doris Kearns Goodwin, From Father,
with Love

Philip Roth, My Baseball Years

Our seats were way up. They were around third base so we could see over the tops of the bleachers on the other side and out to the green hills in the coming twilight beyond. The green hills had violent purple ice plants on them and looked like a scratch in the world bleeding purple blood. The baseball field below was gorgeous. It was the first I'd ever seen, but I'm sure other people must think it's a beautiful one. The grass all mowed in patterns like Japanese sand gardens and the dirt all sculpted in swirling bas-relief.

"It's so beautiful," I gushed.

Eve Babitz, from *Dodger Stadium*

I don't think anyone can watch many baseball games without becoming aware of the fact that the ball, for all its immense energy and unpredictability, very rarely escapes the control of the players. It is released again and again—pitched and caught, struck along the ground or sent high in the air—but almost always, almost instantly, it is recaptured and returned to control and safety and harmlessness. Nothing is altered, nothing has been allowed to happen. This orderliness and constraint are among the prime attractions of the sport; a handful of men, we discover, can police a great green country, forestalling unimaginable disasters. A slovenly, error-filled game can sometimes be exciting, but it never seems serious, and is thus never truly satisfying, for the metaphor of safety—of danger subdued by skill and courage—has been lost. Too much civilization, however, is deadly—in this game, a deadly bore. A deeper need is stifled. The ball looks impetuous and dangerous, but we perceive that in fact it lives in a slow, guarded world of order, vigilance, and rules. Nothing can ever happen here. And then once again the ball is pitched—sent on its quick, planned errand. The bat flashes, there is a new, louder sound, and suddenly we see the ball streaking wild through the air and then bounding along distant and untouched in the sweet green grass. We leap up, thousands of us, and shout for its joyful flight—free, set free, free at last.

Roger Angell, from *The Four Seasons*

I began to feel it might be possible to recover much of the essential information about this country's past through a course on baseball. My project has not been carried forward to so satisfying a culmination as a syllabus and teacher's guide. That is for others to do. But I have some suggestions and observations that might help them with their work.

Because "relevance" is now so large a consideration in the learning process, I suggest that it would be useful to begin with an examination of how deeply the technical terms of the game permeate our language: "Pinch-hit for," "threw me a curve ball," "out in left field," "caught in a squeeze play," "never got to first base," "has two strikes against him," "just a ball-park figure," "fouled out," "touched all bases," "it's a whole new ball game." The list could be continued almost indefinitely.

Why is baseball's terminology so dominant an influence in the language? Does it suggest that the situations that develop as the game is played are comparable to the patterns of our daily work? Does the sport imitate the fundamentals of the national life or is the national life shaped to an extent by the character of the sport? In any case, here is an opportunity to reflect on the meaning of what I think I heard Reggie Jackson say in his spot on a national network in the last World Series: "The country is as American as baseball."

Elting E. Morison, from *Positively the Last Word on Baseball*

LOU: Do you know the fellas' names?
BUD: Well, I should.
LOU: Well, then who's on first?
BUD: Yes.

Lou: I mean the fella's name.
Bud: Who.
Lou: The guy on first.
Bud: Who!
Lou: The first baseman.
Bud: WHO!
Lou: The guy playing first.
Bud: Who is on first.
Lou: I'm asking *you* who's on first.
Bud: That's the man's name.
Lou: That's whose name?
Bud: Yes.

Bud Abbott and Lou Costello, from *Who's On First?*

Gerald Early

Baseball: The Ineffable National Pastime

The most marvelous gift of sports is its faculty for making heroes
of underdogs, of lifting the downtrodden up to solid ground.
—A. S. Young, *Negro Firsts in Sports* (1963)

For they had much rather see us engaged in those degrading
sports, than to see us behaving like intellectual, moral, and
accountable beings.
—Frederick Douglass, *Narrative of the Life of Frederick Douglass,*
An American Slave (1845)

The following tableaus are about baseball, one of the sports I know
best, and one that (along with boxing) perhaps defines and reflects the
complexities of American culture better than any other. There is little
here about the sport itself. The examination is centered on baseball's
political, social, and cultural meaning. I leave it to wiser and more
scholarly heads than mine to talk about sports as philosophy, as play, as
performance, as economic enterprise, or in relation to American history.
    It is one of the persistent ironies in our culture that athletic en-
deavor, such a speechless act, should generate such need for narrative,

for language, for story—from the coach's pep talk to the sportswriter's column; from the television sports announcers who describe actions readily seen to sports talk shows and "open lines" that discuss events which, for the most part, are settled on the field of play. What is remarkable about the rise of professional sports in America (beyond the increasingly exacting specialization among athletes themselves) is that the popularity of athletics would not have been possible without the progressive technology of endlessly reproducing discourse about it: newspapers, radio, television, VCRs. The far-reaching varieties of discourse about sports signify not only our commitment to athletics but also our commitment to language as metaexperience; once the athletic event has ended, the discourse about it displaces the event. The event becomes the shadow.

Everyone knows, for instance, that as a young man Ronald Reagan worked as a baseball announcer. He was a very good one, describing games he himself did not see, simply embellishing stark summations he received off a ticker tape. There he sat at the microphone, speaking threads and threads of narrative, shaping drama like a blind Homer. It is fitting that this collective fantasizing should revolve around baseball, which promotes a gamut of fantasies from old-timers' games and daydreamers' camps to card and board games, from professional sports' most publicized All-Star Games to computer matchups. What Reagan did as a broadcaster is what most rabid baseball fans do; namely, work backward from the facts and statistics and reconstruct the entire narrative structure of ball games, for ball games are insistently and relentlessly narrative. One must not simply *know* baseball; one must *tell* it. Baseball is one of two sports that seek to be an omnipresent—and sometimes ominous—metalanguage. (Boxing is the other.) It is in this maze of fantasy that the hero of Robert Coover's *The Universal Baseball Association, Inc., J. Henry Waugh, Prop.* (1968) finds himself. Our enjoyment of baseball, and of sports generally, is inextricably bound to story, to rhetoric, to conversation, to dialogue, to pure fussing about how the event actually was and how it should be told. The Greeks were right: in a fundamental and timeless way, sports are about our being human, about our being what we are. Only a barbarian would hate sports.

"Sports give people things to talk about other than the inadequacy 4 and unhappiness of their lives," someone once told me. Sports do even more: they give people, specifically men, a language *in* which to talk as well as a language *about* which to prate. Often, sitting in the company of older men during my boyhood, I wondered what would there be to talk about if professional sports did not exist. Discussion and argument were bountiful and eternal about all sorts of questions athletic: how big were Sonny Liston's fists; which was the better local high school basketball team, West Philadelphia or Overbrook; which records did Wilt

Chamberlain set at Overbrook High; were the Washington Redskins a racist team; why did the Philadelphia Eagles trade Sonny Jurgenson; who was the better Eagle running back, Timmy Brown or Tom Woodeshick; why could local light heavyweight Harold Johnson never beat Archie Moore; why could local middleweight Bennie Briscoe never win a title; who was the better center, Bill Russell or Wilt Chamberlain; why was Joey Giardello a pretty good fighter "for a white boy"; who was the better baseball player, Hank Aaron, Willie Mays, or Roberto Clemente; why were the current crop of black ball players (circa the early and middle 1960s) not as good as the old Negro league players; why were current black ball players better than current white ball players; why were old-time Negro league players better than old-time white players; who was the best fighter, Jack Johnson, Sugar Ray Robinson, or Joe Louis?

Around and around the talk went, swirls and eddies, torrents and streams, which, as a youngster, I found both fascinating and enriching, foolish and funny, learned and exhibitionist by turns. "Dammit, nigger, can't you get it through your thick head? Wasn't no way on earth Louis was gonna beat Lil Arthur! Ain't nobody was ever born who was a better defensive fighter than Jack Johnson. Johnson could be hitting you all upside your head and peeling a grape at the same time." "I knows I'm right, man! Josh Gibson got better numbers than Babe Ruth and you can look it up. I got the book at home, man. The book don't lie." "I don't care what nobody say. I *know* that Satchel Paige, in his prime, was a better pitcher than Bob Gibson 'cause I seen 'em both pitch. I know what I'm talking about." "It take about five white guys to bring down Jim Brown excepting maybe Sam Huff. You got to give the devil his due there. That Huff is a bad white boy." "How come ain't no colored middle linebackers is what I wants to know. Some colored boys out there be badder than Huff if they give us the chance."

But I was shaken once when, sitting around with the cronies in the local barbershop, one of the guys, Raymond, I think, jumped up and shouted, "Why y'all always sitting around talkin' about these goddam sports? Why don't you talk about something natural that a man is supposed to talk about—like a woman, or a bottle of Scotch, or how the world ain't treatin' you right? All this here talking about these jocks and these games ain't natural; it ain't a natural way for one man to talk to another." The fact that the vast majority of athletes experience defeat more commonly than they do victory is why the mystical insistence on unnaturalness is sport's great fascination and great virtue. Alas, the athlete replicates a holistic yet puzzling human experience by giving us the male (and some females) whose vocation and condition are identical. There are two explicit and distinct memories I have of baseball and language.

As a child I remember never discussing baseball with my grandfather, a native of the Bahamas, a short, stern, very black man who, I was
told by other family members, was, in his youth, a follower of Marcus
Garvey, although I never heard him utter a political word in his life and
he has seemed a particularly accommodating man around whites. I
recall one incident I was told several times: during the Depression, in
order to feed his quite large family, my grandfather, in desperation,
tried to steal some sausages from the local white grocer by stuffing them
in his pocket. Such ineptitude made his discovery nearly inevitable. It
was painfully embarrassing for him to have to plead his case to the
white grocer because my grandfather has always prided himself on
being an honest man and on being able to feed his family. The grocer
knew my grandfather well and times were hard for everyone, so he did
not have him arrested. He simply sent him home. Family members tell
the story with a great deal of good-natured humor, although he has
never found it funny. I do not recall ever having a real conversation with
my grandfather during my entire life, certainly not during my entire
childhood. I was too afraid of him.

Yet despite the silence of our relationship he took me to profes-   8
sional baseball games every summer as he was an ardent fan of the
sport; in fact, he introduced me to the sport. I remember many a sunny
Sunday afternoon (we always seemed to go on a Sunday after church),
sitting in Connie Mack Stadium's bleacher section, watching the Philadelphia Phillies play: Johnny Callison making grand catches in right
field; Art Mahaffey and his curious windup; Don Demeter fouling balls
off his left foot; Dick Stuart, old "Dr. Strangeglove," hitting a homer; the
voices of Byrum Saam and Bill Campbell, the Phillies sports announcers, on radios around the park; Frank Thomas having a racial run-
in with Richie (later Dick) Allen; the colorful southpaw Bo Belinsky,
who once dated Mamie Van Doren and who, along with pitcher Dean
Chance, was, if not one of the playboys of the Western world, certainly
one of the most publicized playboys of professional baseball; the less
colorful southpaw Dennis Bennet, who never made it; the deadly way
Wes Covington cocked his bat before swinging; the two great years Jack
Baldshun had as a relief pitcher before being traded away to mediocrity
and obscurity.

I hated the Phillies as a boy; virtually every black person I knew felt
the same, recalling how the team had treated Jackie Robinson when he
first broke into the National League. My grandfather, however, silent
and strict-looking, handing out the sandwiches and drinks for our lunch
with his usual authority, liked the Phillies a great deal. Perhaps that is
why we never spoke to each other about the games. Once, during a
twilight double header against the Dodgers (in which Sandy Koufax
pitched the first game, winning six to two), he bought me a Phillies

yearbook. This was unusual for two reasons: first, we almost never went to night games and, second, he almost never bought anything at the ball park. I had ambivalent feelings about the book; I felt especially treated because my grandfather bought it for me, yet I remember always intensely disliking the *smell* of it. The book always smelled new, even after I had had it for several years. I never read that yearbook; I do not recall even opening it except while standing before my grandfather a few moments after he bought it. I thanked him profusely for buying it. My grandfather bought the book because he knew I liked books about baseball. In fact, I liked them almost more than I liked the game itself.

The books that most readily come to mind from my childhood are Dr. Seuss's *The Cat in the Hat*; L. Frank Baum's *The Wizard of Oz*; Edward Ormondroyd's *David and the Phoenix*; and seemingly miles of juvenile baseball biographies. I would occasionally, if only for the sake of variety, read the biography of an athlete from another sport—the lives of Red Grange, Oscar Robertson, Bobby Hull, A. J. Foyt (if one can consider him an athlete), Benny Leonard, and others. But the baseball biographies were my favorites, and having such books written for young boys was, I suppose, a very profitable market for publishers. Henry Aaron, Willie Mays, Babe Ruth, Lou Gehrig, Joe DiMaggio, Ty Cobb, Walter Johnson, Cy Young, Grover Cleveland Alexander, Felipe Alou, Mickey Mantle—all were presented in ghostwritten, antiseptic volumes that were simply longer versions of articles in *The Sporting News* or *Boys' Life* (Many of the books were autobiographies, but I made no distinction as a boy between self-narrative and reportorial narrative; since all were ghostwritten and all were, in some essential ways, fraudulent works, their core attraction was their *narrativity*, not their authenticity. Or let me say that the books' authenticity was located in something far larger and much more gripping than the normal consideration we give to the nature of biographical writing.) During my boyhood and adolescence, my love for these books was so intense that I once had a fistfight with my friend William Bradshaw over a Warren Spahn biography he had been given. I knew he was not interested in baseball and I wanted him to give the book to me. In fact, I demanded it. He refused to give it to me, so we fought. He, being both stronger and bigger, easily beat me. What is so surprising and dismaying about this in retrospect is that I was very shy and timid as a boy. It is still hard for me to comprehend how I could have been so aggressive about something that did not belong to me.

I learned a certain sort of factual information from these books, the sort of information that a boy who loved baseball would want: year-by-year statistics, career statistics, teams played for, best games played, and the like. But it was not for this information alone that I read these books, information that, after all, was condensed on the back of the baseball cards I sometimes collected. It was the sheer redundancy of the paradigmatic lesson, the comfort of knowing that each player's life was like every other player's, that producing the odd oxymoron of dull, rooted inspiration. You had to work hard to succeed, the books taught incessantly. You had to be single-minded and dedicated. You had to live a pure, clean life. You had to marry your teenage sweetheart. If you worked hard, you would be rewarded sooner or later. The books became better, infinitely more interesting than watching the games themselves in which I could see many of these athletes play. The games began to seem, in my youthful mind, like the end product, although I still enjoyed them a lot. It was far more vital to learn the story of how a man became an athlete. Once he achieved success, his story was finished. There was something like the Ben Franklin father-to-son story in all of this, and something that reminded me, years later, of F. Scott Fitzgerald's Jay Gatsby writing out his day's schedule, as a boy, on the cover of *Hopalong Cassidy*. I did something similar, writing out a schedule for success when I was about thirteen, on the cover of a juvenile biography of Roy Campanella.

It did not occur to me until I taught *The Great Gatsby* and Heming- 12 way's *The Sun Also Rises* in a freshman English class that the connection between sports and literature is central to understanding what sports are and why they exist. On one level, those books are about the very imposture of our national character and our national myth: blacks, Jews, and Catholics as athletes and sportsmen in *The Sun Also Rises*; the fake yachtsman, fake polo-player Gatsby, whose name change resonates with ethnic overtones; the rich, hard, Yale football star. Tom Buchanan, self-centered and racist; the woman's golf pro Jordan Baker, who cheats and feels no responsibility for her recklessness. These books are the absolute unraveling (unwriting and rewriting) of the American myth through sports. (It is surely no accident that these books were published in the 1920s, the golden age of American professional and amateur sports, both in terms of mass popularity and the production of mass sportswriting in newspapers.)

Obviously, reading those baseball biographies as a child gave me a very usable mythology of male heroism, much more usable than, say, Greek legends or tall tales of the American frontier. The books also provided me with an orientation toward the culture I was to live in as a man, an orientation that was valuable, if not always honest or harmless. Indeed, the true value of the books as cultural orientation may center in the fact that they are dishonest—one must learn, in some ways, to negotiate their simplistic moralizing, which so distorts the real issues of real life. That I never read sports *fiction* as a child is also quite telling: for me, nothing could be made up that was more exciting than the re-creation of a real athletic career. And the re-creation of that young man-career became, over and over, simply the recitation of games, the story of games. We know that sports are an essential part of our cultural history and social fabric, but it is my contention that the sheer narratability of sports, or, at least, our fixation with their narratability, is, whether we are sports fans or not, the incessant reinvention of ourselves as males in relation to our national myth. The meaning of sports biography (and autobiography) is indelibly tied to its narrative dramatization of our national character as a rite of beautiful young manhood.

About two years ago I saw my grandfather while I was revisiting Philadelphia. It has never been easy for us to talk, but I felt very genial, possibly because my children were with me. I remember turning the conversation to baseball, after he had asked me about living in St. Louis. I talked about the Phillies and was in fact eager to show that I still kept up with the game and even with the local team. When I asked him about their chances that year he gave me a curious, almost childlike look, a wan smile, and said, "Oh, I don't know," as if he hardly thought about baseball anymore. I felt momentarily nonplussed. But his eyes seemed almost sad at my discomfort as our conversation fell away, almost as if he felt sorry for me, as if, in the calm center of wisdom, he knew, always knew from my childhood and before, what I would only come to know years later: What is there to say about games anyway?   *1990*

Doris Kearns Goodwin

From Father, with Love

The game of baseball has always been linked in my mind with the mystic texture of childhood, with the sounds and smells of summer nights and with the memories of my father.

My love for baseball was born on the first day my father took me to Ebbets Field in Brooklyn. Riding in the trolley car, he seemed as excited as I was, and he never stopped talking; now describing for me the street in Brooklyn where he had grown up, now recalling the first game he had been taken to by his own father, now recapturing for me his favorite memories from the Dodgers of his youth—the Dodgers of Casey Stengel, Zach Wheat, and Jimmy Johnston.

In the evenings, when my dad came home from work, we would sit together on our porch and relive the events of that afternoon's game which I had so carefully preserved in the large, red scorebook I'd been given for my seventh birthday. I can still remember how proud I was to have mastered all those strange and wonderful symbols that permitted me to recapture, in miniature form, the every movement of Jackie Robinson and Pee Wee Reese, Duke Snider and Gil Hodges. But the real power of that scorebook lay in the responsibility it entailed. For all through my childhood, my father kept from me the knowledge that the daily papers printed daily box scores, allowing me to believe that without my personal renderings of all those games he missed while he was at work, he would be unable to follow our team in the only proper way a team should be followed, day by day, inning by inning. In other words, without me, his love for baseball would be forever incomplete.

To be sure, there were risks involved in making a commitment as   4 boundless as mine. For me, as for all too many Brooklyn fans, the presiding memory of "the boys of summer" was the memory of the final playoff game in 1951 against the Giants. Going into the ninth, the Dodgers held a 4–1 lead. Then came two singles and a double, placing the winning run at the plate with Bobby Thomson at bat. As Dressen replaced Erskine with Branca, my older sister, with maddening foresight, predicted the forever famous Thomson homer—a prediction that left me so angry with her, imagining that with her words she had somehow brought it about, that I would not speak to her for days.

So the seasons of my childhood passed until that miserable summer when the Dodgers were taken away to Los Angeles by the unforgivable O'Malley, leaving all our rash hopes and dreams of glory behind. And then came a summer of still deeper sadness when my father died. Suddenly my feelings for baseball seemed an aspect of my departing youth, along with my childhood freckles and my favorite childhood haunts, to be left behind when I went away to college and never came back.

Then one September day, having settled into teaching at Harvard, I agreed, half reluctantly, to go to Fenway Park. There it was again: the cozy ballfield scaled to human dimensions so that every word of encouragement and every scornful yell could be heard on the field; the fervent crowd that could, with equal passion, curse a player for today's failures after cheering his heroics the day before; the team that always seemed to break your heart in the last week of the season. It took only a matter of minutes before I found myself directing all my old intensities toward my new team—the Boston Red Sox.

I am often teased by my women friends about my obsession, but just as often, in the most unexpected places—in academic conferences, in literary discussions, at the most elegant dinner parties—I find other women just as crazily committed to baseball as I am, and the discovery creates an instant bond between us. All at once, we are deep in conversation, mingling together the past and the present, as if the history of the Red Sox had been our history too.

There we stand, one moment recollecting the unparalleled per- 8 formance of Yaz in '67, the next sharing ideas on how the present lineup should be changed; one moment recapturing the splendid career of "the Splendid Splinter,"[1] the next complaining about the manager's decision to pull the pitcher the night before. And then, invariably, comes the most vivid memory of all, the frozen image of Carlton Fisk as he rounded first in the sixth game of the '75 World Series, an image as intense in its evocation of triumph as the image of Ralph Branca weeping in the dugout is in its portrayal of heartache.

There is another, more personal memory associated with Carlton Fisk, for he was, after all the years I had followed baseball, the first player I actually met in person. Apparently, he had read the biography I had written on Lyndon Johnson and wanted to meet me. Yet when the meeting took place, I found myself reduced to the shyness of childhood. There I was, a professor at Harvard, accustomed to speaking with presidents of the United States, and yet, standing beside this young man in a baseball uniform, I was speechless.

Finally, Fisk said that it must have been an awesome experience to work with a man of such immense power as President Johnson—and with that, I was at last able to stammer out, with a laugh, "Not as awesome as the thought that I am really standing here talking with you."

Perhaps I have circled back to my childhood, but if this is so, I am certain that my journey through time is connected in some fundamental way to the fact that I am now a parent myself, anxious to share with my three sons the same ritual I once shared with my father.

For in this linkage between the generations rests the magic of 12 baseball, a game that has defied the ravages of modern life, a game that is still played today by the same basic rules and at the same pace as it was played one hundred years ago. There is something deeply satisfying in the knowledge of this continuity.

And there is something else as well which I have experienced sitting in Fenway Park with my small boys on a warm summer's day. If I close my eyes against the sun, all at once I am back at Ebbets Field, a young girl once more in the presence of my father, watching the players of my youth on the grassy field below. There is magic in this moment, for when I open my eyes and see my sons in the place where my father once sat, I feel an invisible bond between our three generations, an anchor of loyalty linking my sons to the grandfather whose face they never saw but whose person they have already come to know through this most timeless of all sports, the game of baseball.   *1986*

---

[1]**Splendid Splinter:** The Hall-of-Fame Red Sox outfielder, Ted Williams.—Eds.

Philip Roth
My Baseball Years

In one of his essays George Orwell writes that, though he was not very good at the game, he had a long, hopeless love affair with cricket until he was sixteen. My relations with baseball were similar. Between the ages of nine and thirteen, I must have put in a forty-hour week during the snowless months over at the neighborhood playfield—softball, hardball, and stickball pick-up games—while simultaneously holding down a full-time job as a pupil at the local grammar school. As I remember it, news of two of the most cataclysmic public events of my childhood—the death of President Roosevelt and the bombing of Hiroshima—reached me while I was out playing ball. My performance was uniformly erratic; generally okay for those easygoing pick-up games, but invariably lacking the calm and the expertise that the naturals displayed in stiff competition. My taste, and my talent, such as it was, was for the flashy, whiz-bang catch rather than the towering fly; running and leaping I loved, all the do-or-die stuff—somehow I lost confidence waiting and waiting for the ball lofted right at me to descend. I could never make the high school team, yet I remember that, in one of the two years I vainly (in both senses of the word) tried out, I did a good enough imitation of a baseball player's *style* to be able to fool (or amuse) the coach right down to the day he cut the last of the dreamers from the squad and gave out the uniforms.

Though my disappointment was keen, my misfortune did not necessitate a change in plans for the future. Playing baseball was not what the Jewish boys of our lower-middle-class neighborhood were expected to do in later life for a living. Had I been cut from the high school itself, *then* there would have been hell to pay in my house, and much confusion and shame in me. As it was, my family took my chagrin in stride and lost no more faith in me than I actually did in myself. They probably would have been shocked if I had made the team.

Maybe I would have been too. Surely it would have put me on a somewhat different footing with this game that I loved with all my heart, not simply for the fun of playing it (fun was secondary, really), but for the mythic and aesthetic dimension that it gave to an American boy's life—particularly to one whose grandparents could hardly speak English. For someone whose roots in America were strong but only inches deep, and who had no experience, such as a Catholic child might, of an awesome hierarchy that was real and felt, baseball was a kind of secular church that reached into every class and region of the nation and bound millions upon millions of us together in common concerns, loyalties, rituals, enthusiasms, and antagonisms. Baseball made me understand what patriotism was about, at its best.

Not that Hitler, the Bataan Death March, the battle for the Solomons, and the Normandy invasion didn't make of me and my contemporaries what may well have been the most patriotic generation of schoolchildren in American history (and the most willingly and successfully propagandized). But the war we entered when I was eight had thrust the country into what seemed to a child—and not only to a child—a struggle to the death between Good and Evil. Fraught with perilous, unthinkable possibilities, it inevitably nourished a patriotism grounded in moral virtue and bloody-minded hate, the patriotism that fixes a bayonet to a Bible. It seems to me that through baseball I was put in touch with a more humane and tender brand of patriotism, lyrical rather than martial or righteous in spirit, and without the reek of saintly zeal, a patriotism that could not so easily be sloganized, or contained in a high-sounding formula to which you had to pledge something vague but all-encompassing called your "allegiance."

To sing the National Anthem in the school auditorium every week, even during the worst of the war years, generally left me cold. The enthusiastic lady teacher waved her arms in the air and we obliged with the words: "See! Light! Proof! Night! There!" But nothing stirred within, strident as we might be—in the end, just another school exercise. It was different, however, on Sundays out at Ruppert Stadium, a green wedge of pasture miraculously walled in among the factories, warehouses, and truck depots of industrial Newark. It would, in fact, have seemed to me an emotional thrill forsaken if, before the Newark Bears took on the hated enemy from across the marshes, the Jersey City Giants, we hadn't first to rise to our feet (my father, my brother, and I—along with our inimical countrymen, the city's Germans, Italians, Irish, Poles, and, out in the Africa of the bleachers, Newark's Negroes) to celebrate the America that had given to this unharmonious mob a game so grand and beautiful.

Just as I first learned the names of the great institutions of higher learning by trafficking in football pools for a neighborhood bookmaker rather than from our high school's college adviser, so my feel for the American landscape came less from what I learned in the classroom about Lewis and Clark than from following the major-league clubs on their road trips and reading about the minor leagues in the back pages of *The Sporting News*. The size of the continent got through to you finally when you had to stay up to 10:30 P.M. in New Jersey to hear via radio "ticker-tape" Cardinal pitcher Mort Cooper throw the first strike of the night to Brooklyn shortstop Pee Wee Reese out in "steamy" Sportsman's Park in St. Louis, Missouri. And however much we might be told by teacher about the stockyards and the Haymarket riot, Chicago only began to exist for me as a real place, and to matter in American history, when I became fearful (as a Dodger fan) of the bat of Phil Cavarretta, first baseman for the Chicago Cubs.

Not until I got to college and was introduced to literature did I find anything with a comparable emotional atmosphere and aesthetic appeal. I don't mean to suggest that it was a simple exchange, one passion for another. Between first discovering the Newark Bears and the Brooklyn Dodgers at seven or eight and first looking into Conrad's *Lord Jim* at age eighteen, I had done some growing up. I am only saying that my discovery of literature, and fiction particularly, and the "love affair"—to some degree hopeless, but still earnest—that has ensued, derives in part from this childhood infatuation with baseball. Or, more accurately perhaps, baseball—with its lore and legends, its cultural power, its seasonal associations, its native authenticity, its simple rules and transparent strategies, its longueurs and thrills, its spaciousness, its suspensefulness, its heroics, its nuances, its lingo, its "characters," its peculiarly hypnotic tedium, its mythic transformation of the immediate—was the literature of my boyhood.

Baseball, as played in the big leagues, was something completely 8 outside my own life that could nonetheless move me to ecstasy and to tears; like fiction it could excite the imagination and hold the attention as much with minutiae as with high drama. Mel Ott's cocked leg striding into the ball, Jackie Robinson's pigeon-toed shuffle as he moved out to second base, each was to be as deeply affecting over the years as that night—"inconceivable," "inscrutable," as any night Conrad's Marlow[1] might struggle to comprehend—the night that Dodger wild man, Rex Barney (who never lived up to "our" expectations, who should have been "our" Koufax), not only went the distance without walking in half a dozen runs, but, of all things, threw a no-hitter. A thrilling mystery, marvelously enriched by the fact that a light rain had fallen during the early evening, and Barney, figuring the game was going to be postponed, had eaten a hot dog just before being told to take the mound.

This detail was passed on to us by Red Barber, the Dodger radio sportscaster of the forties, a respectful, mild southerner with a subtle rural tanginess to his vocabulary and a soft country-parson tone to his voice. For the adventures of "dem bums" of Brooklyn—a region then the very symbol of urban wackiness and tumult—to be narrated from Red Barber's highly alien but loving perspective constituted a genuine triumph of what my English professors would later teach me to call "point of view." James himself might have admired the implicit cultural ironies and the splendid possibilities for oblique moral and social commentary. And as for the detail about Rex Barney eating his hot dog,

---

[1]**Marlow:** The narrator of Joseph Conrad's classic novella, *Heart of Darkness* (1902).—Eds.

it was irresistible, joining as it did the spectacular to the mundane, and furnishing an adolescent boy with a glimpse of an unexpectedly ordinary, even humdrum, side to male heroism.

Of course, in time, neither the flavor and suggestiveness of Red Barber's narration nor "epiphanies" as resonant with meaning as Rex Barney's pre-game hot dog could continue to satisfy a developing literary appetite; nonetheless, it was just this that helped to sustain me until I was ready to begin to respond to the great inventors of narrative detail and masters of narrative voice and perspective like James, Conrad, Dostoevsky, and Bellow.   *1973*

Perspectives on Gender

18

The Feminist Movement Today

Vivian Gornick, Who Says We Haven't
Made a Revolution?:
A Feminist Takes Stock

bell hooks, Feminism:
A Transformational Politic

Nancy Mairs, A Letter to Matthew

Only a funny thing is happening in the women's movement today. The
middle-class movement, which is pretty much the movement as we've
known it, has been showing disturbing signs of lethargy. Meanwhile,
something vast and angry and inspired seems to be brewing among the
women of the pink-collar ghettos and the blue-collar suburbs, the housing developments and the trailer parks. And I think it may be nothing
less than the next great wave of feminism.

> **Barbara Ehrenreich, from** *The Next Wave*

From its inception the feminist movement in the United States has been
predominantly white and middle class. Like blacks, Hispanics, and
other women of color, Asian-American women have not joined white
women and, thus far, have not made a great impact on the movement.
Since the late 1960s, Asian-Americans have begun to organize themselves and build bonds with other women's groups to advocate for their
civil rights as a racial minority and as women. Their relative lack of
political activism stems from cultural, psychological, and social oppressions which historically discouraged them from organizing. This resulted in their apparent political invisibility and powerlessness.

> **Esther Ngan-Ling Chow, from** *The Feminist Movement:*
> *Where Are All the Asian-American Women?*

Being female doesn't stop us from being sexist   we've had to choose
early or late at 7 14 27 56 to think different   dress different   act
different   to struggle   to organize   to picket   to argue   to change other women's minds   to change our own minds
to change our feelings   ours   yours and mine constantly   to
change and change and change   to fight the onslaught   on our
minds and bodies and feelings.

Rosario Morales, from *I Am What I Am*

Women of today are still being called upon to stretch across the gap of
male ignorance, and to educate men as to our existence and our needs.
This is an old and primary tool of all oppressors to keep the oppressed
occupied with the master's concerns. Now we hear that it is the task of
black and Third World women to educate white women, in the face of
tremendous resistance, as to our existence, our differences, our relative
roles in our joint survival. This is a diversion of energies and a tragic
repetition of racist patriarchal thought.

Audre Lorde, from *The Master's Tools Will Never Dismantle
the Master's House*

Vivian Gornick

Who Says We Haven't Made a
Revolution?: A Feminist Takes Stock

Last year I taught at a small liberal-arts college in the West. The
students were intelligent, the teachers conscientious, and the town
quiet to the point of death. Among the faculty was a historian with
whom I fell into friendship. This man found my hunger for the larger
world interesting and was amused that I possessed it while he did not.
We had long talks about work and love, as people do nowadays, and he

startled me by announcing that intimate love had become a paramount value of his. He explained that years ago in pursuit of tenure at a famous university he had ignored the needs of his first marriage and then, when he didn't get the job, saw that he had put real life on hold while he fulfilled the deadly requirements of work. I listened but failed to respond sympathetically. I said work *was* real life; his problem was that academic success did not necessarily equate with real work. We provoked one another. He said worshipfully that intimacy was every-thing. I said recklessly that I could do without. Then we both stared. It wasn't what was being said that astonished, it was who was saying what. Here was a man in his forties romanticizing love, and a woman in her fifties romanticizing work.

We each knew that we had arrived at this moment because twenty years of feminism was in the air we breathed. We also knew this conver-sation had taken place between people like ourselves many times before in modern history. If you read George Gissing's novel *The Odd Women*, written in the 1890s, there we are. If you read Virginia Woolf's *A Room of One's Own*, written in the 1920s, there we are. And yes, it you read Mary Wollstonecraft's *A Vindication of the Rights of Woman*, written in the 1790s, we are there, too; behind that remarkable exposition one can hear the charged, Enlightenment conversation of a handful of women and men.

That's it: a handful. There weren't many of us in 1790, and there aren't that many of us in 1990. A quality of loneliness rises up from these books. I know that loneliness well. *The Odd Women* is exciting to read. And the historian and I, even as we argued our positions, could feel the power of an idea of life that had come and gone and come again, and was alive now in us.

I wrote my first feminist polemic twenty years ago. It appeared   4 in *The Village Voice* and was called "The Next Great Moment in History Is Theirs." I'd been sent out by the *Voice* editors to investigate these "women's libbers" who seemed to have sprung up out of the earth, and I came back converted. In one week I met Ti-Grace Atkinson, Kate Millett, Shulamith Firestone, and Ann Snitow. The next week I met Gloria Steinem, Phyllis Chesler, Ellen Willis, and Alix Kates Shulman. They were all talking at once, and I heard every word each one said.

It was so simple, really: the idea that men by nature take their brains seriously, and women by nature do not, is a learned one; it serves the culture; from that central piece of information all else follows. That fall, listening to a few articulate women speaking in half a dozen apartments in New York City, this insight went into me like a laser beam headed inexorably for the place of injury. Not that the idea was unfamiliar—it wasn't. But now its time had come, and I felt it with the power of original discovery. It shed light and warmth. It healed and explained. It told me who I was in the world as I experienced the world.

That is a moment of joy, when a sufficiently large number of people are galvanized by a social explanation of how their lives have taken shape, and are gathered together in the same place at the same time, speaking the same language, making the same analysis, meeting again and again in restaurants, lecture halls, and apartments for the pleasure of elaborating the insight and repeating the analysis. It is the joy of revolutionary politics, and it was ours. To be a feminist in New York City in the early seventies—bliss was it in that dawn to be alive. Not an I-love-you in the world could touch it. There was no other place to be, except with each other. We lived then, all of us, inside the loose embrace of feminism. It was as though we'd been released from a collective lifetime of silence. Every week, there was a gathering of some sort at which the talk was an exhilaration. There wasn't a woman in the room whose conversation did not engage. Once, after one of these evenings, a friend called me in the morning and sang into the phone, "Everyone was interested, and everyone was interesting." I laughed and sang back, "Everyone was interesting *because* everyone was interested."

We saw our inner lives being permanently marked by the words we spoke. We were changing before each other's eyes, taking our own ideas seriously, becoming other than we had been. We were, in fact, reincarnating as the feminists of previous generations, although what this actually meant was understood only slowly and very imperfectly. I remember reading Elizabeth Cady Stanton and feeling amazed that a hundred years ago she had said exactly what I was now saying. Amazed, and gratified. Not sobered. That would come later.

For most of us, this liveliness went on a good seven or eight years.   8 We wrote, we taught, we marched; and of course we never stopped talking. The newspapers of the world reported on us. We went to Washington, and Washington came to us. We invented consciousness-raising (the personal is political), and we made sexism the natural analogue of racism and homophobia. We gave people sentences with which to frame questions about their lives they would not otherwise have been able to ask. We gave a dimension to American civil rights that helped insure its place in the history of twentieth-century politics.

I know that I, for one, truly believed we were making the revolution. Today, we're hundreds, I thought, tomorrow thousands, and the day after that millions. From week to month to year our numbers were growing. Any minute now the whole country would be converted to the rightness of our cause. After all, it wasn't as if it hadn't all been said before. Now, surely, it was being said fully, freely, and for the last time. Women and men alike would set quickly about correcting the painful imbalance and then, existentially speaking, let the chips fall where they may.

This is what I thought in 1970, and in 1975, and for years after. Then the seventies passed into the eighties, and the revolution began to seem a bit farther off than I'd imagined. I slowed down, and rethought the matter. I remembered my own rhetoric; remembered the times I had spoken glibly of how frightened we *all* are to look clearly at the meaning of sexism, how difficult it is to reverse the emotional habits of centuries, what anxieties the effort induces. I began to see it was going to take longer than any of us had expected. Much longer.

It often seems to me the progress of feminism is very much like that of a psychoanalysis. Roughly speaking, there are two parts to analysis. First comes insight: collecting data on the damage within; then comes extrication from the personality that has developed in response to the damage. The first part is easy, the second part hell. Insight comes in a rush; swift, exciting, dramatic. Extrication is interminable: repetitious, slogging, unesthetic. At least thirty-two times a year for six or seven years the patient repeats original insight as if for the first time. And then, when the analyst can hardly believe this is going to happen again, the patient announces, "Now I see clearly what I have not seen before." The analyst passes a tired hand across a weary brow and replies: "You saw that clearly last month, and last year, and the year before. When are you going to *act* on what you see?"

Indeed. To see is one thing. To release oneself from behaviors that 12 have hardened into emotional necessity is quite another. The analyst and the patient are locked into an act of faith—the necessity will give, on the other side lies freedom—but how long, O Lord, how long?

So it is with feminism and the idea of equal rights for women. We can *see* easily enough what we have done to ourselves, but we cannot act on what we see. The thought of true independence for women arouses fear, as well as desire. From Plato on, the anxiety has been monumental. The insight that women are as real as men comes easily to the rational mind, but to be absorbed into the flesh of social change it must penetrate a resistance that often seems primitive. Eventually, what we see will displace what we fear, but the purgation of fear is an unbelievably longer process than anyone ever dreams it can be. Here, too, an act of faith is required.

The women's movement of the seventies was a moment akin to the one in the analyst's office when the patient says, "Now I see clearly." In reality, feminism saw clearly when Mary Wollstonecraft wrote *A Vindication of the Rights of Woman* in 1792 and then again when Elizabeth Stanton organized the Seneca Falls convention in 1848, and then again when Alice Paul framed the equal rights amendment in 1923. The 1970s

saw yet another rehearsal of fundamentals in this painfully long analysis. We must believe that reiteration of the insight *is* the purge itself;
that after each repeat the patient is, in fact, not the same as before—and
neither is the world. I, for one, do believe that.

It is now 1990. The swirl and excitement of the seventies has, of
necessity, abated. (After all, how many times can original insight make
headlines?) Countless women and men experienced those years as
crucial—feminism gave them an inner clarity that continues to
sustain—but for most people the task of life is overwhelming, and
without the compelling factor of daily activism, hard truths become
blurred, difficult to hold on to. People fall back on the familiar, on that
which gives ready comfort. As feminism appears to lose ground, quie-
tude and inertia fill the vacuum. Quiet brings on anxiety, and anxiety
makes anyone lose his or her nerve. On the right, the loss of nerve is
greeted with relief; on the left, it's an occasion for panic. Orwellian
phrases develop quickly to assure an end to the radical impulse: *post-
feminism, second stage, a different voice.* The words indicate progress but the
meaning is regression. Sociologists write books about the longing for
connection, and novels wink at marriage. Activists wring their hands—
"Everybody's having babies!"—and journalists rush to announce it's all
over, folks.

I listen in amazement. For me, none of it adds up. Between the   16
public statistic and the private reality lies a sea of contradiction in
which these pronouncements drown. Marriage seems to me more
conflict-ridden than ever, and the divorce rate—with or without new
babies in the house—remains constant. The fabric of men-and-women-
as-they-once-were is so thin in places no amount of patching can weave
that cloth together again. The longing for connection may be strong, but
even stronger is the growing perception that only people who are real to
themselves can connect. Two shall be as one is over, no matter how
lonely we get.

Contemporary feminism is a piece of consciousness that can't be
gone back on. It has changed forever the way we think about ourselves.
All over this country people who do not call themselves feminists see
their lives differently because of this second wave of American feminism, and in every part of our national life—in government, business,
the arts, and the academy—the question of sexism remains an influence
on thought and behavior. That influence is there to be seen on the
street, in the movies, in the bedroom; in the books being written, the
conversations overheard, the social responses that surprise. What's astonishing, I think, is how much we *have* accomplished this time around:
how penetrating has been the analysis, how far-reaching the response.

A year ago I marched in Washington for legal abortion. Marching
beside me were the women I marched with in 1970, but all around us

were thousands of women who had never before marched *for anything.*
Feminism had politicized them. Then, in November, when a black man
was elected governor of Virginia because he supported legal abortion, I
thought, who says we haven't made a revolution?

At a family gathering that included men and women ranging in age
from thirty-one to sixty-two, the conversation turned to therapy. A
cousin of mine, a woman in her late forties, said, "Six months after I
entered analysis—this was a good fifteen years ago—my analyst said,
'Ah, I see now. You don't want to *marry* the Great Man, you want to *be* the
Great Man,' as though he'd discovered my dirty little secret." Everyone
at the table shook their heads in routine disbelief. It seemed an ice age
ago, when analysts talked like that to women.

A few months ago a group of academics ran *All About Eve* on the   20
VCR. These people were in their fifties and hadn't seen the movie in
twenty years. When Margo Channing delivered her famous speech
about love and career—the things you drop on your way up, and in the
end, what is a woman without a man? nothing—an English teacher
leaned forward in her seat and cried: "From Congreve to Bette Davis!
Not a line changed." After the movie a long discussion followed on why
it was inconceivable that such a speech would be written into an American movie today.

A book review in *The Nation* caught my attention recently. The book
under discussion was a work of feminist theory. Author and reviewer,
both academic feminists, stood on opposite sides of a philosophic
divide. The review contained no jargon, but it was written as if from
well inside the polemic. I was struck by the editorial assumption that the
general readership was sufficiently conversant to not require an explication of terms. And indeed, conducting an informal poll among non-
academic, nonfeminist readers of the magazine, I discovered everyone
knew what the reviewer was talking about.

A thirty-year-old woman taking a doctorate in political science at an
Ivy League university tells this story: "To come on like a feminist in this
department is to commit professional suicide. No one does it, including
yours truly. Last year I took a course on poverty by one of our brilliant
young men, a guy who thinks of himself as 'sensitive and aware.' At one
session he kept repeating that a major cause of poverty is single parents
on welfare. Not once did he mention that virtually all these single
parents are women. Finally, I raised my hand and said: 'Isn't something
missing from this tale? These parents are nearly all women. Where are
the men? Don't we need to ask that?' Silence. Nobody responded. Then
from the back of the room a woman's voice piped up. 'Child support has
been a black joke for years,' she said. 'You know how many thousands of
women go chasing hopelessly after men who don't pay what the court
awards them? And affordable child care is practically nonexistent.'

Then a *third* voice called out: 'Yes, and when these women do go to work they're not paid as much as men are, even for comparable work. How can we talk about the poverty caused by women without considering women's economic disadvantage?' That class was really something. Not one of those women thought of herself as a feminist, but not one of them could stop herself from analyzing like one."

I was eating lunch in a crowded restaurant on Chambers Street one day while on jury duty. At the next table sat two women I recognized as secretaries from the Criminal Courts Building. One was telling the other that her husband had failed to do the laundry last night, and this morning she was late because she had to go digging for clean under-wear. Her voice was tight and angry as she spoke. "He said to me, 'Why didn't you remind me, or put the laundry bag in the bedroom?' I told him division of labor means I don't have to *think* about laundry. It's *your* job, not mine." Then, with a forkful of tuna salad halfway to her mouth and a quizzical look in her eyes, she said, "He pays lip service to feminism, but he doesn't really get it." *I* stopped eating. Twenty years ago that sentence was continually on my lips. At Upper West Side dinner parties, people looked puzzled when I spoke it. Now it was on the lips of someone in a fast-food restaurant in lower Manhattan, and the person to whom she spoke was nodding her head.

Who says we haven't made a revolution?   24

When I was twenty-one and a student at City College, my friends and I were once invited to a physics department party at Columbia. There we met an Alice Paul suffragist—that is, a supporter of the ERA—a woman in her fifties we thought eccentric. She spoke in deadly earnest about issues we considered over and done with—women's rights, was she kidding?—but we liked her and tried to engage by teasing or cajoling her into some shared amusement that might endear us to her. The boys were gentle and the girls audacious, but in neither key would she lighten up. We needed her to meet us halfway, and this she would not, or could not, do. She had, we agreed, no sense of humor. What more was there to say? Later, when I was leaving the party, I looked for her. She was standing alone, smoking a cigarette, an expression of remote-ness on her face.

A few months ago the relentless suffragist flashed across my mem-ory, and I startled myself by thinking: I have become that woman. Then I laughed out loud. I could afford to.

Remembering the suffragist made me remember the party. That prototypic party. We, the girls from City College, bold, quick-witted, sexy; they, the boys from Columbia, urbane, reserved, serious. We all saw ourselves as intellectuals, of course. but the real agenda for the evening was that we would provoke, and they would respond. The point of being a smart girl was that you could arouse the hunger of boys who would tomorrow be men of power. That was the bottom line, no matter what anyone said. This agenda created energy and excitement, the sexual charge that ran through every party ever given at which men and women gathered. That night on Morningside Heights we were drinking Scotch, up in the Bronx they were drinking beer, and over on the East Side champagne. But the same deal was being cut all over town.

At a gathering of friends, all feminists who went back to 1970 with me—everyone drinking and laughing, the atmosphere, as always among feminists, one of unguarded pleasure and entertainment—I recounted the episode of the suffragist and the Columbia party.

One of us, Karen I think, said with a moan, "My God, parties don't feel like *that* anymore."

"You know why, don't you," said Ann. "Because these days the most interesting people in the room are likely to be the women."

"That's right," said Debra, "and can you picture sexual charge at a party where the women are powerful, and the men hover around them?"

That sobered everyone up. All heads jerked quickly from side to side. "It's never happened," said Doris, "and it's never going to happen."

"Who wants it to happen?" said Alice. "Reversed positions is not what I've been working for."

"Me neither," said Vera. "What we want is a roomful of people in which everyone is sexy, and everyone is powerful."

"Not in my lifetime," said Karen.

She's right, I thought. Not in our lifetime. For a moment I felt like I'd been kicked in the stomach. Making the revolution? Who was *I* kidding? We were only halfway through the analysis.

Ann put her hand on my arm and, ever so lightly, she said, "You're a New Woman of the seventies and eighties. That means intermittent erotic connection, and the company of intelligent women."

I laughed, and came to. "I can live with that," I said. I took a long look around the room. "I've got enough company to live with that."

Elizabeth Cady Stanton was a visionary feminist whose ideas were embraced in radical times and rejected in conservative times. She spent years in political isolation, but she remained alive in mind and spirit and her thought continued to deepen. Enforced solitude made her think hard about the loneliness of existence. She saw that each human being is essentially alone, and *therefore* it was of the greatest importance that each person own as much of him or herself as possible. To die alone, having had no power over one's own life, was a terrible thing.

One of the last talks Stanton gave—delivered at the time into the silence of conservative feminism—is called "The Solitude of the Self." Today it is read as one of the great essays of American literature.

When it was my turn to pick up the book of her life it was the 40 wisdom of the final years that compelled. We were beginning at exactly the place she had left off, and I was grateful that she lived as long as she did.

Feminists of my generation are in a privileged position: we are not alone. We have ourselves, and we have each other. We have the memory of visionary politics alive inside us, and we have the company of ideas in our friendships. When we go out into the world, our point of view may not be welcome, but it is not held to be eccentric. We are not shunted aside, and there is always someone in the room to hear what we are saying.

Radical feminism is not wanted this year, perhaps not this decade. Not, I think, because feminism in our time is over, but because the insights of the seventies are being assimilated in the slow unlovely way of social change: two steps forward, one step back. But who knows? Maybe I'm wrong. Maybe my friends and I are about to find ourselves as isolated as the suffragist at the Columbia party. If so, I hope we have the courage she had to go on speaking hard truths into the rejecting air. I take it as our task to think feminism as deeply as we can, as long as we must, and to live as Elizabeth Stanton did, so that our last words will be useful the next time a New Woman walks through the door to say, "Now I see clearly." As she most surely will. Until everyone in the room is sexy, and everyone is powerful, the analysis is incomplete.   *1990*

bell hooks

Feminism: A Transformational Politic

We live in a world in crisis—a world governed by politics of domina-tion, one in which the belief in a notion of superior and inferior, and its concomitant ideology—that the superior should rule over the inferior—effects the lives of all people everywhere, whether poor or privileged, literate or illiterate. Systematic dehumanization, worldwide famine, eco-logical devastation, industrial contamination, and the possibility of nuclear destruction are realities which remind us daily that we are in crisis. Contemporary feminist thinkers often cite sexual politics as the origin of this crisis. They point to the insistence on difference as that factor which becomes the occasion for separation and domination and suggest that differentiation of status between females and males globally is an indication that patriarchal domination of the planet is the root of the problem. Such an assumption has fostered the notion that elimination of sexist oppression would necessarily lead to the eradication of all forms of domination. It is an argument that has led influential Western white women to feel that feminist movement should be *the* central political agenda for females globally. Ideologically, thinking in this direction enables Western women, especially privileged white women, to suggest that racism and class exploitation are merely the offspring of the parent system: patriarchy. Within feminist movement in the West, this has led to the assumption that resisting patriarchal domination is a more legitimate feminist action than resisting racism and other forms of domination. Such thinking prevails despite radical critiques made by black women and other women of color who question this propostion. To speculate that an oppositional division between men and women existed in early human communities is to impose on the past, on these nonwhite groups, a world view that fits all too neatly within contemporary feminist paradigms that name man as the enemy and woman as the victim.

Clearly, differentiation between strong and weak, powerful and powerless, has been a central defining aspect of gender globally, carrying with it the assumption that men should have greater authority than women, and should rule over them. As significant and important as this fact is, it should not obscure the reality that women can and do participate in politics of domination, as perpetrators as well as victims—that we dominate, that we are dominated. If focus on patriarchal domination masks this reality or becomes the means by which women deflect attention from the real conditions and circumstances of our lives, then women cooperate in suppressing and promoting false consciousness, inhibiting our capacity to assume responsibility for transforming ourselves and society.

Thinking speculatively about early human social arrangement, about women and men struggling to survive in small communities, it is likely that the parent-child relationship with its very real imposed survival structure of dependency, of strong and weak, of powerful and powerless, was a site for the construction of a paradigm of domination. While this circumstance of dependency is not necessarily one that leads to domination, it lends itself to the enactment of a social drama wherein domination could easily occur as a means of exercising and maintaining control. This speculation does not place women outside the practice of domination, in the exclusive role of victim. It centrally names women as agents of domination, as potential theoreticians, and creators of a paradigm for social relationships wherein those groups of individuals designated as "strong" exercise power both benevolently and coercively over those designated as "weak."

Emphasizing paradigms of domination that call attention to woman's   4 capacity to dominate is one way to deconstruct and challenge the simplistic notion that man is the enemy, woman the victim; the notion that men have always been the oppressors. Such thinking enables us to examine our role as women in the perpetuation and maintenance of systems of domination. To understand domination, we must understand that our capacity as women and men to be either dominated or domi- nating is a point of connection, of commonality. Even though I speak from the particular experience of living as a black woman in the United States, a white-supremacist, capitalist, patriarchal society, where small numbers of white men (and honorary "white men") constitute ruling groups, I understand that in many places in the world oppressed and oppressor share the same color. I understand that right here in this room, oppressed and oppressor share the same gender. Right now as I speak, a man who is himself victimized, wounded, hurt by racism and class exploitation, is actively dominating a woman in his life—that even as I speak, women who are ourselves exploited, victimized, are domi- nating children. It is necessary for us to remember, as we think critically about domination, that we all have the capacity to act in ways that oppress, dominate, wound (whether or not that power is institu- tionalized). It is necessary to remember that it is first the potential oppressor within that we must resist—the potential victim within that we must rescue—otherwise we cannot hope for an end to domination, for liberation.

This knowledge seems especially important at this historical mo- ment when black women and other women of color have worked to create awareness of the ways in which racism empowers white women to act as exploiters and oppressors. Increasingly this fact is considered a reason we should not support feminist struggle even though sexism and sexist oppression is a real issue in our lives as black women (see, for example, Vivian Gordon's *Black Women, Feminism, Black Liberation: Which Way?*). It becomes necessary for us to speak continually about the convictions that inform our continued advocacy of feminist struggle. By calling attention to interlocking systems of domination—sex, race, and class—black women and many other groups of women acknowledge the diversity and complexity of female experience, of our relationship to power and domination. The intent is not to dissuade people of color from becoming engaged in feminist movement. Feminist struggle to end patriarchal domination should be of primary importance to women and men globally not because it is the foundation of all other oppressive structures but because it is that form of domination we are most likely to encounter in an ongoing way in everyday life.

Unlike other forms of domination, sexism directly shapes and determines relations of power in our private lives, in familiar social spaces, in that most intimate context—home—and in that most intimate sphere of relations—family. Usually, it is within the family that we witness coercive domination and learn to accept it, whether it be domination of parent over child, or male over female. Even though family relations may be, and most often are, informed by acceptance of a politic of domination, they are simultaneously relations of care and connection. It is this convergence of two contradictory impulses—the urge to promote growth and the urge to inhibit growth—that provides a practical setting for feminist critique, resistance, and transformation.

Growing up in a black, working-class, father-dominated household, I experienced coercive adult male authority as more immediately threatening, as more likely to cause immediate pain than racist oppression or class exploitation. It was equally clear that experiencing exploitation and oppression in the home made one feel all the more powerless when encountering dominating forces outside the home. This is true for many people. If we are unable to resist and end domination in relations where there is care, it seems totally unimaginable that we can resist and end it in other institutionalized relations of power. If we cannot convince the mothers and/or fathers who care not to humiliate and degrade us, how can we imagine convincing or resisting an employer, a lover, a stranger who systematically humiliates and degrades?

Feminist effort to end patriarchal domination should be of primary   8 concern precisely because it insists on the eradication of exploitation and oppression in the family context and in all other intimate relationships. It is that political movement which most radically addresses the person—the personal—citing the need for transformation of self, of relationships, so that we might be better able to act in a revolutionary manner, challenging and resisting domination, transforming the world outside the self. Strategically, feminist movement should be a central component of all other liberation struggles because it challenges each of us to alter our person, our personal engagement (either as victims or perpetrators or both) in a system of domination.

Feminism, as liberation struggle, must exist apart from and as a part of the larger struggle to eradicate domination in all its forms. We must understand that patriarchal domination shares an ideological foundation with racism and other forms of group oppression, that there is no hope that it can be eradicated while these systems remain intact. This knowledge should consistently inform the direction of feminist theory and practice. Unfortunately, racism and class elitism among women have frequently led to the suppression and distortion of this connection so that it is now necessary for feminist thinkers to critique and revise much feminist theory and the direction of feminist move-ment. This effort at revision is perhaps most evident in the current widespread acknowledgement that sexism, racism, and class exploita-tion constitute interlocking systems of domination—that sex, race, and class, and not sex alone, determine the nature of any female's identity, status, and circumstance, the degree to which she will or will not be dominated, the extent to which she will have the power to dominate.

While acknowledgement of the complex nature of woman's status (which has been most impressed upon everyone's consciousness by radical women of color) is a significant corrective, it is only a starting point. It provides a frame of reference which must serve as the basis for thoroughly altering and revising feminist theory and practice. It chal-lenges and calls us to rethink popular assumptions about the nature of feminism that have had the deepest impact on a large majority of women, on mass consciousness. It radically calls into question the notion of a fundamentally common female experience which has been seen as the prerequisite for our coming together, for political unity. Recognition of the interconnectedness of sex, race, and class highlights the diversity of experience, compelling redefinition of the terms for unity. If women do not share "common oppression," what then can serve as a basis for our coming together?

Unlike many feminist comrades, I believe women and men must share a common understanding—a basic knowledge of what feminism is—if it is ever to be a powerful mass-based political movement. In *Feminist Theory: from margin to center*, I suggest that defining feminism broadly as a "movement to end sexism and sexist oppression" would enable us to have a common political goal. We would then have a basis on which to build solidarity. Multiple and contradictory definitions of feminism create confusion and undermine the effort to construct femi-nist movement so that it addresses everyone. Sharing a common goal does not imply that women and men will not have radically divergent perspectives on how that goal might be reached. Because each individ-ual starts the process of engagement in feminist struggle at a unique level of awareness, very real differences in experience, perspective, and knowledge make developing varied strategies for participation and transformation a necessary agenda.

Feminist thinkers engaged in radically revisioning central tenets of 12 feminist thought must continually emphasize the importance of sex, race, and class as factors which *together* determine the social construction of femaleness, as it has been so deeply ingrained in the consciousness of many women active in feminist movement that gender is the sole factor determining destiny. However, the work of education for critical con-sciousness (usually called consciousness-raising) cannot end there.

Much feminist consciousness-raising has in the past focused on identifying the particular ways men oppress and exploit women. Using the paradigm of sex, race, and class means that the focus does not begin with men and what they do to women, but rather with women working to identify both individually and collectively the specific character of our social identity.

Imagine a group of women from diverse backgrounds coming together to talk about feminism. First they concentrate on working out their status in terms of sex, race, and class using this as the standpoint from which they begin discussing patriarchy or their particular relations with individual men. Within the old frame of reference, a discussion might consist solely of talk about their experiences as victims in relationship to male oppressors. Two women—one poor, the other quite wealthy—might describe the process by which they have suffered physical abuse by male partners and find certain commonalities which might serve as a basis for bonding. Yet if these same two women engaged in a discussion of class, not only would the social construction and expression of femaleness differ, so too would their ideas about how to confront and change their circumstances. Broadening the discussion to include an analysis of race and class would expose many additional differences even as commonalities emerged.

Clearly the process of bonding would be more complex, yet this broader discussion might enable the sharing of perspectives and strategies for change that would enrich rather than diminish our understanding of gender. While feminists have increasingly given "lip service" to the idea of diversity, we have not developed strategies of communication and inclusion that allow for the successful enactment of this feminist vision.

Small groups are no longer the central place for feminist consciousness-raising. Much feminist education for cricital consciousness takes place in women's studies classes or at conferences which focus on gender. Books are a primary source of education, which means that already masses of people who do not read have no access. The separation of grass-roots ways of sharing feminist thinking across kitchen tables from the spheres where much of that thinking is generated, the academy, undermines feminist movement. It would further feminist movement if new feminist thinking could be once again shared in small group contexts, integrating critical analysis with discussion of personal experience. It would be useful to promote anew the small group setting as an arena for education for critical consciousness, so that women and men might come together in neighborhoods and communities to discuss feminist concerns.

Small groups remain an important place for education for critical 16 consciousness for several reasons. An especially important aspect of the small group setting is the emphasis on communicating feminist thinking, feminist theory, in a manner that can be easily understood. In small groups, individuals do not need to be equally literate or literate at all because the information is primarily shared through conversation, in dialogue which is necessarily a liberatory expression. (Literacy should be a goal for feminists even as we ensure that it not become a require-ment for participation in feminist education.) Reforming small groups would subvert the appropriation of feminist thinking by a select group of academic women and men, usually white, usually from privileged class backgrounds.

Small groups of people coming together to engage in feminist discussion, in dialectical struggle make a space where the "personal is political" as a starting point for education for critical consciousness can be extended to include politicization of the self that focuses on creat-ing understanding of the ways sex, race, and class together determine our individual lot and our collective experience. It would further fem-inist movement if many well-known feminist thinkers would partici-pate in small groups, critically reexamining ways their works might be changed by incorporating broader perspectives. All efforts at self-transformation challenge us to engage in ongoing, critical self-examination and reflection about feminist practice, about how we live in the world. This individual commitment, when coupled with engage-ment in collective discussion, provides a space for critical feedback which strengthens our efforts to change and make ourselves new. It is in this commitment to feminist principles in our words and deeds that the hope of feminist revolution lies.

Working collectively to confront difference, to expand our aware-ness of sex, race, and class as interlocking systems of domination, of the ways we reinforce and perpetuate these structures, is the context in which we learn the true meaning of solidarity. It is this work that must be the foundation of feminist movement. Without it, we cannot effec-tively resist patriarchal domination; without it, we remain estranged and alienated from one another. Fear of painful confrontation often leads women and men active in feminist movement to avoid rigorous critical encounter, yet if we cannot engage dialectically in a committed, rigorous, humanizing manner, we cannot hope to change the world. True politicization—coming to critical consciousness—is a difficult, "trying" process, one that demands that we give up set ways of thinking and being, that we shift our paradigms, that we open ourselves to the unknown, the unfamiliar. Undergoing this process, we learn what it means to struggle and in this effort we experience the dignity and integrity of being that comes with revolutionary change. If we do not change our consciousness, we cannot change our actions or demand change from others.

Our renewed commitment to a rigorous process of education for critical consciousness will determine the shape and direction of future feminist movement. Until new perspectives are created, we cannot be living symbols of the power of feminist thinking. Given the privileged lot of many leading feminist thinkers, both in terms of status, class, and race, it is harder these days to convince women of the primacy of this process of politicization. More and more, we seem to form select interest groups composed of individuals who share similar perspectives. This limits our capacity to engage in critical discussion. It is difficult to involve women in new processes of feminist politicization because so many of us think that identifying men as the enemy, resisting male domination, gaining equal access to power and privilege is the end of feminist movement. Not only is it not the end, it is not even the place we want revitalized feminist movement to begin. We want to begin as women seriously addressing ourselves, not solely in relation to men, but in relation to an entire structure of domination of which patriarchy is one part. While the struggle to eradicate sexism and sexist oppression is and should be the primary thrust of feminist movement, to prepare ourselves politically for this effort we must first learn how to be in solidarity, how to struggle with one another.

Only when we confront the realities of sex, race, and class, the ways 20 they divide us, make us different, stand us in opposition, and work to reconcile and resolve these issues will we be able to participate in the making of feminist revolution, in the transformation of the world. Feminism, as Charlotte Bunch emphasizes again and again in *Passionate Politics*, is a transformational politics, a struggle against domination wherein the effort is to change ourselves as well as structures. Speaking about the struggle to confront difference, Bunch asserts:

> A crucial point of the process is understanding that reality does not look the same from different people's perspective. It is not surprising that one way feminists have come to understand about differences has been through the love of a person from another culture or race. It takes persistence and motivation—which love often engenders—to get beyond one's ethnocentric assumptions and really learn about other perspectives. In this process and while seeking to eliminate oppression, we also discover new possibilities and insights that come from the experience and survival of other peoples.

Embedded in the commitment to feminist revolution is the challenge to love. Love can be and is an important source of empowerment when we struggle to confront issues of sex, race, and class. Working together to identify and face our differences—to face the ways we dominate and are dominated—to change our actions, we need a mediating force that can sustain us so that we are not broken in this process, so that we do not despair.

Not enough feminist work has focused on documenting and sharing ways individuals confront differences constructively and successfully.

Women and men need to know what is on the other side of the pain experienced in politicization. We need detailed accounts of the ways our lives are fuller and richer as we change and grow politically, as we learn to live each moment as committed feminists, as comrades working to end domination. In reconceptualizing and reformulating strategies for future feminist movement, we need to concentrate on the politicization of love, not just in the context of talking about victimization in intimate relationships, but in a critical discussion where love can be understood as a powerful force that challenges and resists domination. As we work to be loving, to create a culture that celebrates life, that makes love possible, we move against dehumanization, against domination. In *Pedagogy of the Oppressed*, Paulo Freire evokes this power of love, declaring:

> I am more and more convinced that true revolutionaries must perceive the revolution, because of its creative and liberating nature, as an act of love. For me, the revolution, which is not possible without a theory of revolution—and therefore science—is not irreconcilable with love . . . The distortion imposed on the word "love" by the capitalist world cannot prevent the revolution from being essentially loving in character, nor can it prevent the revolutionaries from affirming their love of life.

That aspect of feminist revolution that calls women to love womanness, that calls men to resist dehumanizing concepts of masculinity, is an essential part of our struggle. It is the process by which we move from seeing ourselves as objects to acting as subjects. When women and men understand that working to eradicate patriarchal domination is a struggle rooted in the longing to make a world where everyone can live fully and freely, then we know our work to be a gesture of love. Let us draw upon that love to heighten our awareness, deepen our compassion, intensify our courage, and strengthen our commitment.   *1989*

Nancy Mairs

A Letter to Matthew

July 1983

My Dear Child—

    Last night Daddy and I watched, on William F. Buckley, Jr.'s *Firing Line*, a debate whether women "have it as good as men," and I have been talking to you in my head ever since. Odd not to be able to talk with you in person—I'm not yet used to your absence—but I thought I would put onto paper some of the things I would say if you were here. They are not the sort of things I would say to Mr. Buckley if ever I met him. Mr. Buckley is an elderly man, fixed by his circumstances within a range of experiences so narrow that new ideas and new behaviors cannot squeeze through the boundaries. He is complete as he is. But you are just emerging into young manhood, still fluid, still making the choices that will determine the shape that manhood will take. I, as your mother and as a feminist, hope that the choices you make—you individually and your generation as a whole—will be transformative, that the manhood you develop will be so radically new that the question in Mr. Buckley's debate, smacking as it does of competition for goods and goodness, will no longer have any more meaning than questions like "Do pigs have it as good as fiddlehead ferns?" or, more aptly, "Do pigs have it as good as pigs?"

In many ways, of course, you've dashed my hopes already. You have, after all, lived for fourteen years in a dangerously patriarchal society, and you have put on much of the purple that Mr. Buckley wears with such aplomb. When I find myself disliking you—and I find myself disliking you with about the same regularity, I imagine, as you find yourself disliking me—I can usually tell that I'm responding to some behavior that I identify as peculiarly "masculine." I dislike your cockiness, for instance. When you first began to work with computers, I remember, you immediately assumed the attitude that you knew all that was worth knowing about computers; when you took up racquetball, right away you set yourself up as a champion. This kind of swaggering strikes me as a very old pattern of masculine behavior (I think of Beowulf and Unferth at Heorot), the boast designed to establish superiority and domination, which trigger challenge and thus conflict. Related to your cockiness is your quickness to generalize and, from your generalizations, to pronounce judgments: Calculus is a waste of time; Christians are stupidly superstitious; classical music is boring; Jerry Falwell and the Moral Majority are idiots. This is just the kind of uninformed thinking that empowers Jerry Falwell and the Moral Majority in the first place, of course, this refusal to experience and explore the ambiguities of whatever one is quick to condemn. More seriously, such a pattern of response enables men to create the distinctions between Us and Them—the good guys and the bad guys, the left wing and the right, the Americans and the Russians—that lead to suspicion, fear, hatred, and finally the casting of stones.

Well then, have you shattered *all* my hopes? By no means. For you are not merely arrogant and opinionated. These qualities are overshadowed by another, one I have seldom seen in men: your extraordinary empathic capacity, your willingness to listen for and try to fulfill the needs of others. When Sean was threatening suicide, you were genuinely engaged in his pain. When Katherine needed a male model to encourage her creepy little fifth-grade boys to dance, you leaped in with psychological (if not physical!) grace. When Anne left us for good, I felt your presence supporting and soothing me despite your relief at being an only child at last. Women have long been schooled in this sensitivity to others; but men have been trained to hold themselves aloof, to leave the emotional business of life to their mothers and sisters and wives. I think you are learning to conduct some of that business on your own.

Clearly I believe that the ability to do so is a benefit and not the 4 curse our patriarchal culture has made it out to be. In fact, in an ironic way the answer to Mr. Buckley's question might be that women have it better than men, and it is the fear of such an answer that keeps men nervously posing the question in the first place. You'll remember that Freud ascribed to women a problem he called "penis envy"; a later psychoanalyst, Lacan, called it a "lack." If I've learned anything during the years I've spent in psychotherapy, I've learned that the feelings and motives I ascribe to others tell me little about them but much about myself, for I am projecting my own feelings and motives onto them. Freud ascribed to women penis envy; ascription = projection; therefore Freud was really suffering from womb envy. QED. A man, lacking the womb and yearning to return to his early identity with the mother, tries to hide his pain by denigrating everything associated with the womb: the blood, the babies, the intuitive and nurturing behaviors of child-rearing. The very condition of having a womb in the first place he labels a pathology: hysteria. If I haven't got it, he tells himself, it can't be worth having. (But maybe, he whispers so softly that even he can't hear, maybe it *is*.)

I'm more than half serious, you know, amid this high-flown silliness. But I don't seriously believe, despite some psychological advantages, that in the "real world" women have it as good as men. In some highly visible ways they have it very bad indeed: They are raped, battered, prostituted, abandoned to raise their children in poverty. Less visibly but no less ruinously, they are brainwashed (often by their mothers and sisters as well as their fathers, brothers, lovers, and husbands) into believing that whatever they get is what they deserve, being only women. Imagine this, Matthew, if you can—and maybe you can, since you are just emerging from childhood, and children are often treated like women in our society. Imagine thinking yourself lucky to get *any* job, no matter how servile or poorly paid, *any* partner, no matter how brutal or dull, *any* roof over your head, no matter how costly the psychic mortgage payment. Imagine believing that's what you deserve. Imagine feeling guilty if you fail to feel grateful.

If you have trouble imagining such conditions, I'm not surprised. I have trouble too; and for many years I held back from calling myself a feminist because I couldn't conceive problems I hadn't experienced. The men in our family do not smack their women and children around. They seldom raise their voices, let alone their palms. They are gentle, courteous, witty, companionable, solicitous. And yet, of late, I've begun to recognize in them certain behaviors and attitudes which suggest that they, too, share a set of cultural assumptions about male power and rights which devalue women's lives. But our men worship their women, you may say; they put them right up on what one of my students once called a "pedastool." True enough, but tell me, how much actual living could you get done confined to a tiny platform several feet above the ground, especially if you had acrophobia?

Look, now that you're staying with them, at Aunt Helen and Uncle Ted, for instance. For forty-eight years they have sustained a relationship founded on domination and submission if ever there was one. Daddy has often insisted that their relationship is fine as long as it works for them. For a long time I tried to accept it too, because I believed that he must be right. I tend, as you know, to believe that Daddy is always right: I'm the product of a patriarchal society too, after all. But now I believe that he's wrong. Although I admire much about their marriage, especially its durability and friendliness, I balk at its basis in a kind of human sacrifice. Trying, I suppose, to compensate for not having graduated from high school, Uncle Ted kept Aunt Helen, a college graduate, confined in a life containing only himself, their one son, and the housework to maintain them. She could have worked, of course—she had the education, and they always needed the money—but Uncle Ted's manly pride insisted on his being the breadwinner, and her job became to stretch the crusts and crumbs from one meager meal to the next. So little had she to occupy her that she grieved for years after her child left for college, and clung to her housework to give her days meaning. Once, in the late sixties, I asked her why she didn't replace her old-fashioned washing machine with an automatic (my mother had had one since 1952), and she replied, "But then what would I do on Mondays?" Worse than the deprivation of stimulating activity has been the undermining of her self-confidence. Even her statements sound like questions, and she repeatedly turns to her husband: "Isn't that right, Ted?" She tiptoes through space as through conversation like our Lionel Tigress, cautious, timorous, whiskers twitching, ready to dash under the bed at a strange voice or a heavy footfall. I like to watch her bake a cake. There in her kitchen she plants her feet firmly and even, sometimes, rattles the pans.

Is Uncle Ted then a monster, some Bluebeard glowering and dangling the incriminating key that represents some independent act that will cost Aunt Helen her head? Hardly. He is a man of sincerity and rectitude, who has lived scrupulously, at considerable cost to himself, 8 according to the code by which he was raised, a code that Rudyard Kipling, whom he admires, described as the "white man's burden." In it, women (among others, such as our "darker brethren") require the kind of protection and control they are unable, being more "natural" creatures, to provide themselves. He adores Aunt Helen, I do believe, and wants to do only what's best for her. But he assumes that he knows what's best for her, and so does she. In the name of manhood, he has taken from her the only authentic power a human being can hold: that of knowing and choosing the good. Such theft of power results in mastery. There is no mistressy.

I've been uneasy, as you know, about your spending this summer with them, largely, I suppose, because I don't want Uncle Ted to make a "man" of you. And I've encouraged you to subvert their patterns of interaction in a small way, by helping Aunt Helen with her chores just as you help Uncle Ted with his, even when he tries to divert you and she tells you to run along with him, not so that you can change those patterns (you can't) but so that you'll remain aware of them. You may well be tempted to fall into them because what Uncle Ted construes as "men's work" is infinitely more interesting than "women's work." You already know what a drag it is to set the table knowing that within an hour the dishes will be streaked and gummy, to wash those dishes knowing that they'll go right back on the table for breakfast, to fold a whole line of clothes that will crawl straight back into the hamper, muddy and limp, to be washed and hung out again. How much more pleasant and heartening to tramp through the woods checking the line from the brook, to ride the lawn mower round and round on the sweet falling grass, to plot traps for porcupines and saw down trees and paddle the canoe across the pond spreading algicide and possibly falling in. If everyone washed the dishes together, of course, everyone could go for a walk in the woods. How one would tell the men from the women, though, I'm not sure.

But then, so what if you do fall into the patterns? Surely the world won't end if you and Uncle Ted take the fishing rods down to the Battenkill to catch a few trout for breakfast, leaving Aunt Helen to make the beds? Well yes, I think in a way it will, and that's why I'm writing you this letter. For Aunt Helen and Uncle Ted's marriage is not in the least extraordinary. On the contrary, the interactions between them, despite some idiosyncracies, are being played out in millions of relationships throughout the world, including, in its own way, Daddy's and mine, within which you have lived your whole life. One partner is telling the other (though seldom in words) that she is weaker physically and intellectually, that her concerns are less meaningful to the world at large, that she is better suited (or even formed by God) to serve his needs in the privacy of his home than to confront the tangled problems of the public sphere. And instead of ignoring his transparent tactics for enhancing his uncertain self-image and increasing his own comfort, she is subordinating her needs to his, accepting the limits he decrees, and thereby bolstering the artificial pride that enables him to believe himself a "superior" creature. As soon as he feels superiority, he is capable of dividing his fellow creatures into Us and Them and of trying to dominate Them. That is, he is ready to make war.

This connection—between the private male who rules his roost and keeps his woman, however lovingly, in her place and the public male who imposes his will by keeping blacks poor and pacifying Vietnamese villages and shipping arms and men to Central America—is far from new. Virginia Woolf made it in *Three Guineas* nearly fifty years ago. "The public and the private worlds are inseparably connected," she wrote; "the tyrannies and servilities of the one are the tyrannies and servilities of the other." But *Three Guineas* has been largely ignored or denigrated: One male critic called it "neurotic," "morbid"; another, "cantankerous." (You know, I am sure, that when a man speaks out, he is assertive, forthright; when a woman speaks her "mind," she is sick or bitchy.) Moreover, its feminism has been labeled "old-fashioned," as though already in 1938 the problems Woolf named had been solved. If so, why do we stand today in the same spot she stood then, looking at the same photographs of dead bodies and burned villages? No, her feminism isn't out of date, though such a label shows a desperate attempt to set it aside. Rather, it says something, valid today, that men still do not want to hear: that if humanity—men and women—is to have it any good at all, men must give up their pleasure in domination, their belief in their superiority, the adulation of their fellow creatures, at the personal and private level of their lives. Now. They must stop believing that whoever they love will perish without their "protection," for the act of protecting leads to a sense of possession, and it necessitates enemies to protect from. They must completely and radically revise their relationships with themselves, their wives and children, their business associates, the men and women in the next block, the next city, the next country. They must learn to say to every other who enters their lives not, "You're over there, and you're bad," but, "You're over there, and you're me."

Can they do it? Some feminists think not. They say that we should 12 simply kill men off (except perhaps for the babies) and start fresh. I understand the anger that fuels such a proposal and the desire to sweep the rubbishy world clean. But I reject it because it perpetuates the violence that distinguishes masculine solutions to conflict. Our cultural heritage would still be based on killing, our mythology rooted in massacre.

No, I think that I will let you live. Will you let me live? If so, the terms of your existence must be transformed. What's been good enough for Aunt Helen and Uncle Ted, for Mr. Buckley, for Ronald Reagan and the other men who govern us and every other nation, for the Catholic Church, for the medical and legal professions, for the universities, for all the patriarchy, cannot be good enough for you. (And I address you personally, though obviously I mean all young men everywhere, because moral choice is always a lonely matter. You may all encourage one another—in fact, if the transformation is working, you will—but each will have to choose his way of being for himself.) You must learn to develop your identity through exploring the ways you are like, not different from or better than, others. You must learn to experience power through your connections with people, your ability to support their growth, not through weakening them by ridicule or patronage or deprivation. If this means dancing with the little boys, then dance your heart out; they'll dance on into the future with more assurance because of you. And who can shoot straight while he's dancing?

I am demanding something of you that takes more courage than entering a battle: not to enter the battle. I am asking you to say *no* to the values that have defined manhood through the ages—prowess, competition, victory—and to grow into a manhood that has not existed before. If you do, some men and women will ridicule and even despise you. They may call you spineless, possibly even (harshest of curses) womanish. But your life depends on it. My life depends on it. I wish you well.

Now go help Aunt Helen with the dishes.

I love you—
Mother

1986

19

Mothers

Gloria Steinem, Ruth's Song (Because She
Could Not Sing It)

Alice Walker, In Search of Our
Mothers' Gardens

Barbara Lazear Ascher, Mothers and Sons

Women and men are different, after all. Being a mother isn't the same
as being a father. Motherhood means that a woman gives her body over
to her child, her children; they're on her as they might be on a hill, in a
garden; they devour her, sleep on her; and she lets herself be devoured.
Nothing like that happens with fathers.

Marguerite Duras, from *Practicalities*

A formidable woman. Determined to speak her mind, determined to
have her way, determined to bend those who opposed her. In that time
when I had known her best, my mother had hurled herself at life with
chin thrust forward, eyes blazing, and an energy that made her seem
always on the run.

She ran after squawking chickens, an axe in her hand, determined
on a beheading that would put dinner in the pot. She ran when she
made the beds, ran when she set the table. One Thanksgiving she
burned herself badly when, running up from the cellar oven with the
ceremonial turkey, she tripped on the stairs and tumbled back down,
ending at the bottom in the debris of giblets, hot gravy, and battered
turkey. Life was combat, and victory was not to the lazy, the timid, the
slugabed, the drugstore cowboy, the libertine, the mushmouth afraid to
tell people exactly what was on his mind whether people liked it or not.
She ran.

Russell Baker, from *Growing Up*

407

Women, not men, are considered responsible for the children of Western society and are blamed for our children's fates. Therefore, we have smothering mothers, schizophrenic mothers, mothers who cause anorexia and bulimia, autism, neuroses, and psychoses. And women are still—after decades of feminist agitation—expected to provide the necessary without payment: to do the cooking, the laundry, the cleaning, the marketing, and the childcare. Men who follow these occupations are paid for their work and are considered professionals.

Marilyn French, from *Self-Respect: A Female Perspective*

Gloria Steinem

Ruth's Song
(Because She Could Not Sing It)

Happy or unhappy, families are all mysterious. We have only to imagine how differently we would be described—and will be, after our deaths—by each of the family members who believe they know us. The only question is, Why are some mysteries more important than others?

The fate of my Uncle Ed was a mystery of importance in our family. We lavished years of speculation on his transformation from a brilliant young electrical engineer to the town handyman. What could have changed this elegant, Lincolnesque student voted "Best Dressed" by his classmates to the gaunt, unshaven man I remember? Why did he leave a young son and a first wife of the "proper" class and religion, marry a much less educated woman of the "wrong" religion, and raise a second family in a house near an abandoned airstrip; a house whose walls were patched with metal signs to stop the wind? Why did he never talk about his transformation?

For years, I assumed that some secret and dramatic events of a year he spent in Alaska had made the difference. Then I discovered that the trip had come after his change and probably been made because of it. Strangers he worked for as a much-loved handyman talked about him as one more tragedy of the Depression, and it was true that Uncle Ed's father, my paternal grandfather, had lost his money in the stock-market crash and died of (depending on who was telling the story) pneumonia or a broken heart. But the crash of 1929 also had come long after Uncle Ed's transformation. Another theory was that he was afflicted with a mental problem that lasted most of his life, yet he was supremely competent at his work, led an independent life, and asked for help from no one.

Perhaps he had fallen under the spell of a radical professor in the   4
early days of the century, the height of this country's romance with socialism and anarchism. That was the theory of another uncle on my mother's side. I do remember that no matter how much Uncle Ed needed money, he would charge no more for his work than materials plus 10 percent, and I never saw him in anything other than ancient boots and overalls held up with strategic safety pins. Was he really trying to replace socialism-in-one-country with socialism-in-one man? If so, why did my grandmother, a woman who herself had run for the school board in coalition with anarchists and socialists, mistrust his judgment so much that she left his share of her estate in trust, even though he was over fifty when she died? And why did Uncle Ed seem uninterested in all other political words and acts? Was it true instead that, as another relative insisted, Uncle Ed had chosen poverty to disprove the myths of Jews and money?

Years after my uncle's death, I asked a son in his second family if he had the key to this family mystery. No, he said. He had never known his father any other way. For that cousin, there had been no question. For the rest of us, there was to be no answer.

For many years I also never imagined my mother any way other than the person she had become before I was born. She was just a fact of life when I was growing up; someone to be worried about and cared for; an invalid who lay in bed with eyes closed and lips moving in occasional response to voices only she could hear; a woman to whom I brought an endless stream of toast and coffee, bologna sandwiches and dime pies, in a child's version of what meals should be. She was a loving, intel-ligent, terrorized woman who tried hard to clean our littered house whenever she emerged from her private world, but who could rarely be counted on to finish one task. In many ways, our roles were reversed: I was the mother and she was the child. Yet that didn't help her, for she still worried about me with all the intensity of a frightened mother, plus the special fears of her own world full of threats and hostile voices.

Even then I suppose I must have known that, years before she was thirty-five and I was born, she had been a spirited, adventurous young woman who struggled out of a working-class family and into college, who found work she loved and continued to do, even after she was married and my older sister was there to be cared for. Certainly, our immediate family and nearby relatives, of whom I was by far the youngest, must have remembered her life as a whole and functioning person. She was thirty before she gave up her own career to help my father run the Michigan summer resort that was the most practical of his many dreams, and she worked hard there as everything from bookkeeper to bar manager. The family must have watched this energetic, fun-loving, book-loving woman turn into someone who was afraid to be alone, who could not hang on to reality long enough to hold a job, and who could rarely concentrate enough to read a book.

Yet I don't remember any family speculation about the mystery of   8 my mother's transformation. To the kind ones and those who liked her, this new Ruth was simply a sad event, perhaps a mental case, a family problem to be accepted and cared for until some natural process made her better. To the less kind or those who had resented her earlier independence, she was a willful failure, someone who lived in a filthy house, a woman who simply would not pull herself together.

Unlike the case of my Uncle Ed, exterior events were never suggested as reason enough for her problems. Giving up her own career was never cited as her personal parallel of the Depression. (Nor was there discussion of the Depression itself, though my mother, like millions of others, had made potato soup and cut up blankets to make my sister's winter clothes.) Her fears of dependence and poverty were no match for my uncle's possible political beliefs. The real influence of newspaper editors who had praised her reporting was not taken as seriously as the possible influence of one radical professor.

Even the explanation of mental illness seemed to contain more personal fault when applied to my mother. She had suffered her first "nervous breakdown," as she and everyone else called it, before I was born and when my sister was about five. It followed years of trying to take care of a baby, be the wife of a kind but financially irresponsible man with show-business dreams, and still keep her much-loved job as reporter and newspaper editor. After many months in a sanatorium, she was pronounced recovered. That is, she was able to take care of my sister again, to move away from the city and the job she loved, and to work with my father at the isolated rural lake in Michigan he was trying to transform into a resort worthy of the big dance bands of the 1930s.

But she was never again completely without the spells of depression, anxiety, and visions into some other world that eventually were to turn her into the nonperson I remember. And she was never again without a bottle of dark, acrid-smelling liquid she called "Doc Howard's medicine": a solution of chloral hydrate that I later learned was the main ingredient of "Mickey Finns" or "knockout drops," and that probably made my mother and her doctor the pioneers of modern tranquilizers. Though friends and relatives saw this medicine as one more evidence of weakness and indulgence, to me it always seemed an embarrassing but necessary evil. It slurred her speech and slowed her coordination, making our neighbors and my school friends believe she was a drunk. But without it, she would not sleep for days, even a week at a time, and her feverish eyes began to see only that private world in which wars and hostile voices threatened the people she loved.

Because my parents had divorced and my sister was working in a   12 faraway city, my mother and I were alone together then, living off the meager fixed income that my mother got from leasing her share of the remaining land in Michigan. I remember a long Thanksgiving weekend spent hanging on to her with one hand and holding my eighth-grade assignment of *Tale of Two Cities* in the other, because the war outside our house was so real to my mother that she had plunged her hand through a window, badly cutting her arm in an effort to help us escape. Only when she finally agreed to swallow the medicine could she sleep, and only then could I end the terrible calm that comes with crisis and admit to myself how afraid I had been.

No wonder that no relative in my memory challenged the doctor who prescribed this medicine, asked if some of her suffering and hallucinating might be due to overdose or withdrawal, or even consulted another doctor about its use. It was our relief as well as hers.

But why was she never returned even to that first sanatorium? Or to help that might come from other doctors? It's hard to say. Partly, it was her own fear of returning. Partly, it was too little money, and a family's not-unusual assumption that mental illness is an inevitable part of someone's personality. Or perhaps other family members had feared something like my experience when, one hot and desperate summer between the sixth and seventh grade, I finally persuaded her to let me take her to the only doctor from those sanatorium days whom she remembered without fear.

Yes, this brusque old man told me after talking to my abstracted, timid mother for twenty minutes: She definitely belongs in a state hospital. I should put her there right away. But even at that age, *Life* magazine and newspaper exposés had told me what horrors went on inside those hospitals. Assuming there to be no other alternative, I took her home and never tried again.

In retrospect, perhaps the biggest reason my mother was cared for   16 but not helped for twenty years was the simplest: Her functioning was not that necessary to the world. Like women alcoholics who drink in their kitchens while costly programs are constructed for executives who drink, or like the homemakers subdued with tranquilizers while male patients get therapy and personal attention instead, my mother was not an important worker. She was not even the caretaker of a very young child, as she had been when she was hospitalized the first time. My father had patiently brought home the groceries and kept our odd household going until I was eight or so and my sister went away to college. Two years later when wartime gas rationing closed his summer resort and he had to travel to buy and sell in summer as well as winter, he said: How can I travel and take care of your mother? How can I make a living? He was right. It was impossible to do both. I did not blame him for leaving once I was old enough to be the bringer of meals and answerer of my mother's questions. ("Has your sister been killed in a car crash?" "Are there German soldiers outside?") I replaced my father, my mother was left with one more way of maintaining a sad status quo, and the world went on undisturbed.

That's why our lives, my mother's from forty-six to fifty-three, and my own from ten to seventeen, were spent alone together. There was one sane winter in a house we rented to be near my sister's college in Massachusetts, then one bad summer spent house-sitting in suburbia while my mother hallucinated and my sister struggled to hold down a summer job in New York. But the rest of those years were lived in Toledo where both my mother and father had been born, and on whose city newspapers an earlier Ruth had worked.

First we moved into a basement apartment in a good neighborhood. In those rooms behind a furnace, I made one last stab at being a child. By pretending to be much sicker with a cold than I really was, I hoped my mother would suddenly turn into a sane and cheerful woman bringing me chicken soup à la Hollywood. Of course, she could not. It only made her feel worse that she could not. I stopped pretending.

But for most of those years, we lived in the upstairs of the house my mother had grown up in and that her parents left her—a deteriorating farmhouse engulfed by the city, with poor but newer houses stacked against it and a major highway a few feet from its sagging front porch. For a while, we could rent the two downstairs apartments to a newlywed factory worker and a local butcher's family. Then the health department condemned our ancient furnace for the final time, sealing it so tight that even my resourceful Uncle Ed couldn't produce illegal heat.

In that house, I remember: 20

. . . lying in the bed my mother and I shared for warmth, listening on the early morning radio to the royal wedding of Princess Elizabeth and Prince Philip being broadcast live, while we tried to ignore and thus protect each other from the unmistakable sounds of the factory worker downstairs beating up and locking out his pregnant wife.

. . . hanging paper drapes I had bought in the dime store; stacking books and papers in the shape of two armchairs and covering them with blankets; evolving my own dishwashing system (I waited until all the dishes were dirty, then put them in the bathtub); and listening to my mother's high praise for these housekeeping efforts to bring order from chaos, though in retrospect I think they probably depressed her further.

. . . coming back from one of the Eagles' Club shows where I and other veterans of a local tap-dancing school made ten dollars a night for two shows, and finding my mother waiting with a flashlight and no coat in the dark cold of the bus stop, worried about my safety walking home.

. . . in a good period, when my mother's native adventurousness 24 came through, answering a classified ad together for an amateur acting troupe that performed Biblical dramas in churches, and doing several very corny performances of *Noah's Ark* while my proud mother shook metal sheets backstage to make thunder.

. . . on a hot summer night, being bitten by one of the rats that shared our house and its back alley. It was a terrifying night that turned into a touching one when my mother, summoning courage from some unknown reservoir of love, became a calm, comforting parent who took me to a hospital emergency room despite her terror at leaving home.

. . . coming home from a local library with the three books a week into which I regularly escaped, and discovering that for once there was no need to escape. My mother was calmly planting hollyhocks in the vacant lot next door.

But there were also times when she woke in the early winter dark, too frightened and disoriented to remember that I was at my usual after-school job, and so called the police to find me. Humiliated in front of my friends by sirens and policemen, I would yell at her—and she would bow her head in fear and say "I'm sorry, I'm sorry, I'm sorry," just as she had done so often when my otherwise-kindhearted father had yelled at her in frustration. Perhaps the worst thing about suffering is that it finally hardens the hearts of those around it.

And there were many, many times when I badgered her until her 28 shaking hands had written a small check to cash at the corner grocery and I could leave her alone while I escaped to the comfort of well-heated dime stores that smelled of fresh doughnuts, or to air-conditioned Saturday-afternoon movies that were windows on a very different world.

But my ultimate protection was this: I was just passing through, a guest in the house; perhaps this wasn't my mother at all. Though I knew very well that I was her daughter, I sometimes imagined that I had been adopted and that my real parents would find me, a fantasy I've since discovered is common. (If children wrote more and grownups less, being adopted might be seen not only as a fear but also as a hope.) Certainly, I didn't mourn the wasted life of this woman who was scarcely older than I am now. I worried only about the times when she got worse.

Pity takes distance and a certainty of surviving. It was only after our house was bought for demolition by the church next door, and after my sister had performed the miracle of persuading my father to give me a carefree time before college by taking my mother with him to California for a year, that I could afford to think about the sadness of her life. Suddenly, I was far away in Washington, living with my sister and sharing a house with several of her friends. While I finished high school and discovered to my surprise that my classmates felt sorry for me because my mother *wasn't* there, I also realized that my sister, at least in her early childhood, had known a very different person who lived inside our mother, an earlier Ruth.

She was a woman I met for the first time in a mental hospital near Baltimore, a humane place with gardens and trees where I visited her each weekend of the summer after my first year away in college. Fortunately, my sister hadn't been able to work and be our mother's caretaker, too. After my father's year was up, my sister had carefully researched hospitals and found the courage to break the family chain.

At first, this Ruth was the same abstracted, frightened woman I had 32 lived with all those years; though now all the sadder for being approached through long hospital corridors and many locked doors. But gradually she began to talk about her past life, memories that doctors there must have been awakening. I began to meet a Ruth I had never known.

. . . A tall, spirited, auburn-haired high-school girl who loved basketball and reading; who tried to drive her uncle's Stanley Steamer when it was the first car in the neighborhood; who had a gift for gardening and who sometimes, in defiance of convention, wore her father's overalls; a girl with the courage to go to dances even though her church told her that music itself was sinful, and whose sense of adventure almost made up for feeling gawky and unpretty next to her daintier, dark-haired sister.

. . . A very little girl, just learning to walk, discovering the body places where touching was pleasurable, and being punished by her mother who slapped her hard across the kitchen floor.

. . . A daughter of a handsome railroad-engineer and a schoolteacher who felt she had married "beneath her"; the mother who took her two daughters on Christmas trips to faraway New York on an engineer's free railroad pass and showed them the restaurants and theaters they should aspire to—even though they could only stand outside them in the snow.

. . . A good student at Oberlin College, whose freethinking tradi- 36 tions she loved, where friends nicknamed her "Billy"; a student with a talent for both mathematics and poetry, who was not above putting an invisible film of Karo syrup on all the john seats in her dormitory the night of a big prom; a daughter who had to return to Toledo, live with her family, and go to a local university when her ambitious mother— who had scrimped and saved, ghostwritten a minister's sermons, and made her daughters' clothes in order to get them to college at all—ran out of money. At home, this Ruth became a part-time bookkeeper in a lingerie shop for the very rich, commuting to classes and listening to her mother's harsh lectures on the security of becoming a teacher; but also a young woman who was still rebellious enough to fall in love with my father, the editor of her university newspaper, a funny and charming young man who was a terrible student, had no intention of graduating, put on all the campus dances, and was unacceptably Jewish.

I knew from family lore that my mother had married my father twice: once secretly, after he invited her to become the literary editor of his campus newspaper, and once a year later in a public ceremony, which some members of both families refused to attend as the "mixed marriage" of its day.

And I knew that my mother had gone on to earn a teaching certificate. She had used it to scare away truant officers during the winters when, after my father closed the summer resort for the season, we lived in a house trailer and worked our way to Florida or California and back by buying and selling antiques.

But only during those increasingly adventurous weekend outings from the hospital—going shopping, to lunch, to the movies—did I realize that she had taught college calculus for a year in deference to her mother's insistence that she have teaching "to fall back on." And only then did I realize she had fallen in love with newspapers along with my father. After graduating from the university paper, she wrote a gossip column for a local tabloid, under the name "Duncan Mac-Kenzie," since women weren't supposed to do such things, and soon had earned a job as society reporter on one of Toledo's two big dailies. By the time my sister was four or so, she had worked her way up to the coveted position of Sunday editor.

It was a strange experience to look into those brown eyes I had seen 40 so often and realize suddenly how much they were like my own. For the first time, I realized that she might really be my mother.

I began to think about the many pressures that might have led up to that first nervous breakdown: leaving my sister whom she loved very much with a grandmother whose values my mother didn't share; trying to hold on to a job she loved but was being asked to leave by her husband; wanting very much to go with a woman friend to pursue their own dreams in New York; falling in love with a co-worker at the newspaper who frightened her by being more sexually attractive, more supportive of her work than my father, and perhaps the man she should have married; and finally, nearly bleeding to death with a miscarriage because her own mother had little faith in doctors and refused to get help.

Did those months in the sanatorium brainwash her in some Freudian or very traditional way into making what were, for her, probably the
wrong choices? I don't know. It almost doesn't matter. Without extraordinary support to the contrary, she was already convinced that divorce
was unthinkable. A husband could not be left for another man, and
certainly not for a reason as selfish as a career. A daughter could not be
deprived of her father and certainly not be uprooted and taken off to
an uncertain future in New York. A bride was supposed to be virginal
(not "shopworn," as my euphemistic mother would have said), and if
your husband turned out to be kind, but innocent of the possibility of a
woman's pleasure, then just be thankful for kindness.

Of course, other women have torn themselves away from work and
love and still survived. But a story my mother told me years later has
always symbolized for me the formidable forces arrayed against her.

> "It was early spring, nothing was open yet. There was nobody for miles   44
> around. We had stayed at the lake that winter, so I was alone a lot while
> your father took the car and traveled around on business. You were a
> baby. Your sister was in school, and there was no phone. The last straw
> was that the radio broke. Suddenly it seemed like forever since I'd
> been able to talk with anyone—or even hear the sound of another
> voice.
>
> "I bundled you up, took the dog, and walked out to the Brooklyn
> road. I thought I'd walk the four or five miles to the grocery store, talk
> to some people, and find somebody to drive me back. I was walking
> along with Fritzie running up ahead in the empty road—when sud-
> denly a car came out of nowhere and down the hill. It hit Fritzie head
> on and threw him over to the side of the road. I yelled and screamed at
> the driver, but he never slowed down. He never looked at us. He never
> even turned his head.
>
> "Poor Fritzie was all broken and bleeding, but he was still alive. I
> carried him and sat down in the middle of the road, with his head
> cradled in my arms. I was going to *make* the next car stop and help.
>
> "But no car ever came. I sat there for hours, I don't know how long,
> with you in my lap and holding Fritzie, who was whimpering and
> looking up at me for help. It was dark by the time he finally died. I
> pulled him over to the side of the road and walked back home with you
> and washed the blood out of my clothes.
>
> "I don't know what it was about that one day—it was like a   48
> breaking point. When your father came home, I said: 'From now on,
> I'm going with you. I won't bother you. I'll just sit in the car. But I can't
> bear to be alone again.' "

I think she told me that story to show she had tried to save herself,
or perhaps she wanted to exorcise a painful memory by saying it out
loud. But hearing it made me understand what could have turned her
into the woman I remember: a solitary figure sitting in the car, perspir-

ing through the summer, bundled up in winter, waiting for my father to come out of this or that antique shop, grateful just not to be alone. I was there, too, because I was too young to be left at home, and I loved helping my father wrap and unwrap the newspaper around the china and small objects he had bought at auctions and was selling to dealers. It made me feel necessary and grown-up. But sometimes it was hours before we came back to the car again and to my mother who was always patiently, silently waiting.

At the hospital and later when Ruth told me stories of her past, I used to say, "But why didn't you leave? Why didn't you take the job? Why didn't you marry the other man?" She would always insist it didn't matter, she was lucky to have my sister and me. If I pressed hard enough, she would add, "If I'd left you never would have been born."

I always thought but never had the courage to say: *But you might have been born instead.*

I'd like to tell you that this story has a happy ending. The best I can 52 do is one that is happier than its beginning.

After many months in that Baltimore hospital, my mother lived on her own in a small apartment for two years while I was in college and my sister married and lived nearby. When she felt the old terrors coming back, she returned to the hospital at her own request. She was approaching sixty by the time she emerged from there and from a Quaker farm that served as a halfway house, but she confounded her psychiatrists' predictions that she would be able to live outside for shorter and shorter periods. In fact, she never returned. She lived more than another twenty years, and for six of them, she was well enough to stay in a rooming house that provided both privacy and company. Even after my sister and her husband moved to a larger house and generously made two rooms into an apartment for her, she continued to have some independent life and many friends. She worked part-time as a "sales-girl" in a china shop; went away with me on yearly vacations and took one trip to Europe with relatives; went to women's club meetings; found a multiracial church that she loved; took meditation courses; and enjoyed many books. She still could not bear to see a sad movie, to stay alone with any of her six grandchildren while they were babies, to live without many tranquilizers, or to talk about those bad years in Toledo. The old terrors were still in the back of her mind, and each day was a fight to keep them down.

It was the length of her illness that had made doctors pessimistic. In fact, they could not identify any serious mental problem and diagnosed her only as having "an anxiety neurosis": low self-esteem, a fear of being dependent, a terror of being alone, a constant worry about money. She also had spells of what now would be called agoraphobia, a problem almost entirely confined to dependent women: fear of going outside the house, and incapacitating anxiety attacks in unfamiliar or public places.

Would you say, I asked one of her doctors, that her spirit had been broken? "I guess that's as good a diagnosis as any," he said. "And it's hard to mend anything that's been broken for twenty years."

But once out of the hospital for good, she continued to show flashes 56 of the different woman inside; one with a wry kind of humor, a sense of adventure, and a love of learning. Books on math, physics, and mysticism occupied a lot of her time. ("Religion," she used to say firmly, "begins in the laboratory.") When she visited me in New York during her sixties and seventies, she always told taxi drivers that she was eighty years old ("so they will tell me how young I look"), and convinced theater ticket sellers that she was deaf long before she really was ("so they'll give us seats in the front row"). She made friends easily, with the vulnerability and charm of a person who feels entirely dependent on the approval of others. After one of her visits, every shopkeeper within blocks of my apartment would say, "Oh yes, I know your mother!" At home, she complained that people her own age were too old and stodgy for her. Many of her friends were far younger than she. It was as if she were making up for her own lost years.

She was also overly appreciative of any presents given to her—and that made giving them irresistible. I loved to send her clothes, jewelry, exotic soaps, and additions to her collection of tarot cards. She loved receiving them, though we both knew they would end up stored in boxes and drawers. She carried on a correspondence in German with our European relatives, and exchanges with many other friends, all written in her painfully slow, shaky handwriting. She also loved giving gifts. Even as she worried about money and figured out how to save pennies, she would buy or make carefully chosen presents for grandchildren and friends.

Part of the price she paid for this much health was forgetting. A single reminder of those bad years in Toledo was enough to plunge her into days of depression. There were times when this fact created loneliness for me, too. Only two of us had lived most of my childhood. Now, only one of us remembered. But there were also times in later years when, no matter how much I pled with reporters *not* to interview our friends and neighbors in Toledo, *not* to say that my mother had been hospitalized, they published things that hurt her very much and sent her into a downhill slide.

On the other hand, she was also her mother's daughter, a person with a certain amount of social pride and pretension, and some of her objections had less to do with depression than false pride. She complained bitterly about one report that we had lived in a house trailer. She finally asked angrily: "Couldn't they at least say 'vacation mobile home'?" Divorce was still a shame to her. She might cheerfully tell friends, "I don't know *why* Gloria says her father and I were divorced— we never were." I think she justified this to herself with the idea that they had gone through two marriage ceremonies, one in secret and one in public, but been divorced only once. In fact, they were definitely divorced, and my father had briefly married someone else.

She was very proud of my being a published writer, and we gener- 60 ally shared the same values. After her death, I found a mother-daughter morals quiz I once had written for a women's magazine. In her un- mistakably shaky writing, she had recorded her own answers, her en- tirely accurate imagination of what my answers would be, and a score that concluded our differences were less than those "normal for women separated by twenty-odd years." Nonetheless, she was quite capable of putting a made-up name on her name tag when going to a conservative women's club where she feared our shared identity would bring contro- versy or even just questions. When I finally got up the nerve to tell her I was signing a 1972 petition of women who publicly said we had had abortions and were demanding the repeal of laws that made them illegal and dangerous, her only reply was sharp and aimed to hurt back. "Every starlet says she's had an abortion," she said. "It's just a way of getting publicity." I knew she agreed that abortion should be a legal choice, but I also knew she would never forgive me for embarrassing her in public.

In fact, her anger and a fairly imaginative ability to wound with words increased in her last years when she was most dependent, most focused on herself, and most likely to need the total attention of others. When my sister made a courageous decision to go to law school at the age of fifty, leaving my mother in a house that not only had many loving teenage grandchildren in it but a kindly older woman as a paid compan- ion besides, my mother reduced her to frequent tears by insisting that this was a family with no love in it, no home-cooked food in the refrigerator; not a real family at all. Since arguments about home cooking wouldn't work on me, my punishment was creative and dif- ferent. She was going to call up *The New York Times*, she said, and tell them that this was what feminism did: it left old sick women all alone.

Some of this bitterness brought on by failing faculties was even- tually solved by a nursing home near my sister's house where my mother not only got the twenty-four-hour help her weakening body demanded, but the attention of affectionate nurses besides. She charmed them, they loved her, and she could still get out for an occasional family wedding. If I ever had any doubts about the debt we owe to nurses, those last months laid them to rest.

When my mother died just before her eighty-second birthday in a hospital room where my sister and I were alternating the hours in which her heart wound slowly down to its last sounds, we were alone together for a few hours while my sister slept. My mother seemed bewildered by her surroundings and the tubes that invaded her body, but her consciousness cleared long enough for her to say: "I want to go home. Please take me home." Lying to her one last time, I said I would. "Okay, honey," she said. "I trust you." Those were her last understandable words.

The nurses let my sister and me stay in the room long after there was no more breath. She had asked us to do that. One of her many fears came from a story she had been told as a child about a man whose coma was mistaken for death. She also had made out a living will requesting that no extraordinary measures be used to keep her alive, and that her ashes be sprinkled in the same stream as my father's. 64

Her memorial service was in the Episcopalian church that she loved because it fed the poor, let the homeless sleep in its pews, had members of almost every race, and had been sued by the Episcopalian hierarchy for having a woman priest. Most of all, she loved the affection with which its members had welcomed her, visited her at home, and driven her to services. I think she would have liked the Quaker-style informality with which people rose to tell their memories of her. I know she would have loved the presence of many friends. It was to this church that she donated some of her remaining Michigan property in the hope that it could be used as a multiracial camp, thus getting even with those people in the tiny nearby town who had snubbed my father for being Jewish.

I think she also would have been pleased with her obituary. It emphasized her brief career as one of the early women journalists and asked for donations to Oberlin's scholarship fund so others could go to this college she loved so much but had to leave.

I know I will spend the next years figuring out what her life has left in me.

I realize that I've always been more touched by old people than by children. It's the talent and hopes locked up in a failing body that get to me; a poignant contrast that reminds me of my mother, even when she was strong. 68

I've always been drawn to any story of a mother and a daughter on their own in the world. I saw *A Taste of Honey* several times as both a play and a film, and never stopped feeling it. Even *Gypsy* I saw over and over again, sneaking in backstage for the musical and going to the movie as well. I told myself that I was learning the tap-dance routines, but actually my eyes were full of tears.

I once fell in love with a man only because we both belonged to that large and secret club of children who had "crazy mothers." We traded stories of the shameful houses to which we could never invite our friends. Before he was born, his mother had gone to jail for her pacifist convictions. Then she married the politically ambitious young lawyer who had defended her, stayed home, and raised many sons. I fell out of love when he confessed that he wished I wouldn't smoke or swear, and he hoped I wouldn't go on working. His mother's plight had taught him self-pity—nothing else.

I'm no longer obsessed, as I was for many years, with the fear that I would end up in a house like that one in Toledo. Now, I'm obsessed instead with the things I could have done for my mother while she was alive, or the things I should have said.

I still don't understand why so many, many years passed before I 72 saw my mother as a person and before I understood that many of the forces in her life are patterns women share. Like a lot of daughters, I suppose I couldn't afford to admit that what had happened to my mother was not all personal or accidental, and therefore could happen to me.

One mystery has finally cleared. I could never understand why my mother hadn't been helped by Pauline, her mother-in-law; a woman she seemed to love more than her own mother. This paternal grandmother had died when I was five, before my mother's real problems began but long after that "nervous breakdown," and I knew Pauline was once a suffragist who addressed Congress, marched for the vote, and was the first woman member of a school board in Ohio. She must have been a courageous and independent woman, yet I could find no evidence in my mother's reminiscences that Pauline had encouraged or helped my mother toward a life of her own.

I finally realized that my grandmother never changed the politics of her own life, either. She was a feminist who kept a neat house for a husband and four antifeminist sons, a vegetarian among five male meat eaters, and a woman who felt so strongly about the dangers of alcohol that she used only paste vanilla; yet she served both meat and wine to the men of the house and made sure their lives and comforts were continued undisturbed. After the vote was won, Pauline seems to have stopped all feminist activity. My mother greatly admired the fact that her mother-in-law kept a spotless house and prepared a week's meals at a time. Whatever her own internal torments, Pauline was to my mother a woman who seemed able to "do it all." "Whither thou goest, I shall go," my mother used to say to her much-loved mother-in-law, quoting the Ruth of the Bible. In the end, her mother-in-law may have added to my mother's burdens of guilt.

Perhaps like many later suffragists, my grandmother was a public feminist and a private isolationist. That may have been heroic in itself, the most she could be expected to do, but the vote and a legal right to work were not the only kind of help my mother needed.

The world still missed a unique person named Ruth. Though she 76
longed to live in New York and in Europe, she became a woman who was
afraid to take a bus across town. Though she drove the first Stanley
Steamer, she married a man who never let her drive.

I can only guess what she might have become. The clues are in
moments of spirit or humor.

After all the years of fear, she still came to Oberlin with me when I
was giving a speech there. She remembered everything about its history
as the first college to admit blacks and the first to admit women, and
responded to students with the dignity of a professor, the accuracy of a
journalist, and a charm that was all her own.

When she could still make trips to Washington's wealth of libraries,
she became an expert genealogist, delighting especially in finding the
rogues and rebels in our family tree.

Just before I was born, when she had cooked one more enormous 80
meal for all the members of some famous dance band at my father's
resort and they failed to clean their plates, she had taken a shotgun
down from the kitchen wall and held it over their frightened heads until
they had finished the last crumb of strawberry shortcake. Only then did
she tell them the gun wasn't loaded. It was a story she told with great
satisfaction.

Though sex was a subject she couldn't discuss directly, she had a
great appreciation of sensuous men. When a friend I brought home
tried to talk to her about cooking, she was furious. ("He came out in the
kitchen and talked to me about *stew!*") But she forgave him when we
went swimming. She whispered, "He has wonderful legs!"

On her seventy-fifth birthday, she played softball with her grand-
sons on the beach, and took pride in hitting home runs into the ocean.

Even in the last year of her life, when my sister took her to visit a
neighbor's new and luxurious house, she looked at the vertical stripes of
a very abstract painting in the hallway and said, tartly, "Is that the price
code?"

She worried terribly about being socially accepted herself, but she 84
never withheld her own approval for the wrong reasons. Poverty or style
or lack of education couldn't stand between her and a new friend.
Though she lived in a mostly white society and worried if I went out
with a man of the "wrong" race, just as she had once married a man of
the "wrong" religion, she always accepted each person as an individual.

"Is he *very* dark?" she once asked worriedly about a friend. But when
she met this very dark person, she only said afterward, "What a kind and
nice man!"

My father was the Jewish half of the family, yet it was my mother
who taught me to have pride in that tradition. It was she who encouraged me to listen to a radio play about a concentration camp when I was

little. "You should know that this can happen," she said. Yet she did it just enough to teach, never enough to frighten.

It was she who introduced me to books and a respect for them, to poetry that she knew by heart, and to the idea that you could never criticize someone unless you "walked miles in their shoes."

It was she who sold that Toledo house, the only home she had, with 88 the determination that the money be used to start me in college. She gave both her daughters the encouragement to leave home for four years of independence that she herself had never had.

After her death, my sister and I found a journal she had kept of her one cherished and belated trip to Europe. It was a trip she had described very little when she came home: she always deplored people who talked boringly about their personal travels and showed slides. Nonetheless, she had written a descriptive essay called "Grandma Goes to Europe." She still must have thought of herself as a writer. Yet she showed this long journal to no one.

I miss her, but perhaps no more in death than I did in life. Dying seems less sad than having lived too little. But at least we're now asking questions about all the Ruths and all our family mysteries.

If her song inspires that, I think she would be the first to say: It was worth the singing.   *1983*

Alice Walker

In Search of Our Mothers' Gardens

I described her own nature and temperament. Told how they needed a larger life for their expression. . . . I pointed out that in lieu of proper channels, her emotions had overflowed into paths that dissipated them. I talked, beautifully I thought, about an art that would be born, an art that would open the way for women the likes of her. I asked her to hope, and build up an inner life against the coming of that day. . . . I sang, with a strange quiver in my voice, a promise song.
—"Avey," Jean Toomer, *Cane*
The poet speaking to a prostitute who
falls asleep while he's talking.

When the poet Jean Toomer walked through the South in the early twenties, he discovered a curious thing: black women whose spirituality was so intense, so deep, so *unconscious*, they were themselves unaware of the richness they held. They stumbled blindly through their lives: creatures so abused and mutilated in body, so dimmed and confused by pain, that they considered themselves unworthy even of hope. In the selfless abstractions their bodies became to the men who used them, they became more than "sexual objects," more even than mere women: They became "Saints." Instead of being perceived as whole persons, their bodies became shrines: What was thought to be their minds became temples suitable for worship. These crazy Saints stared out at the world, wildly, like lunatics—or quietly, like suicides; and the "God" that was in their gaze was as mute as a great stone.

Who were these Saints? These crazy, loony, pitiful women?

Some of them, without a doubt, were our mothers and grandmothers.

In the still heat of the post-Reconstruction South, this is how they   4
seemed to Jean Toomer: exquisite butterflies trapped in an evil honey, toiling away their lives in an era, a century, that did not acknowledge them, except as "the *mule* of the world." They dreamed dreams that no one knew—not even themselves, in any coherent fashion—and saw visions no one could understand. They wandered or sat about the countryside crooning lullabies to ghosts, and drawing the mother of Christ in charcoal on courthouse walls.

They forced their minds to desert their bodies and their striving spirits sought to rise, like frail whirlwinds from the hard red clay. And when those frail whirlwinds fell, in scattered particles, upon the ground, no one mourned. Instead, men lit candles to celebrate the emptiness that remained, as people do who enter a beautiful but vacant space to resurrect a God.

Our mothers and grandmothers, some of them: moving to music not yet written. And they waited.

They waited for a day when the unknown thing that was in them would be made known; but guessed, somehow in their darkness, that on the day of their revelation they would be long dead. Therefore to Toomer they walked, and even ran, in slow motion. For they were going nowhere immediate, and the future was not yet within their grasp. And men took our mothers and grandmothers, "but got no pleasure from it." So complex was their passion and their calm.

To Toomer, they lay vacant and fallow as autumn fields, with harvest   8
time never in sight: and he saw them enter loveless marriages, without joy; and become prostitutes, without resistance; and become mothers of children, without fulfillment.

For these grandmothers and mothers of ours were not Saints, but Artists; driven to a numb and bleeding madness by the springs of creativity in them for which there was no release. They were Creators,

who lived lives of spiritual waste, because they were so rich in spirituality—which is the basis of Art—that the strain of enduring their unused
and unwanted talent drove them insane. Throwing away this spirituality
was their pathetic attempt to lighten the soul to a weight their work-
worn, sexually abused bodies could bear.

What did it mean for a black woman to be an artist in our grandmothers' time? In our great-grandmothers' day? It is a question with an
answer cruel enough to stop the blood.

Did you have a genius of a great-great-grandmother who died under
some ignorant and depraved white overseer's lash? Or was she required
to bake biscuits for a lazy backwater tramp, when she cried out in her
soul to paint watercolors of sunsets, or the rain falling on the green and
peaceful pasturelands? Or was her body broken and forced to bear
children (who were more often than not sold away from her)—eight,
ten, fifteen, twenty children—when her one joy was the thought of
modeling heroic figures of rebellion, in stone or clay?

How was the creativity of the black woman kept alive, year after year 12
and century after century, when for most of the years black people have
been in America, it was a punishable crime for a black person to read or
write? And the freedom to paint, to sculpt, to expand the mind with action did not exist. Consider, if you can bear to imagine it, what might have
been the result if singing, too, had been forbidden by law. Listen to the
voices of Bessie Smith, Billie Holiday, Nina Simone, Roberta Flack, and
Aretha Franklin, among others, and imagine those voices muzzled for life.
Then you may begin to comprehend the lives of our "crazy," "Sainted"
mothers and grandmothers. The agony of the lives of women who might
have been Poets, Novelists, Essayists, and Short-Story Writers (over a
period of centuries), who died with their real gifts stifled within them.

And, if this were the end of the story, we would have cause to cry out
in my paraphrase of Okot p'Bitek's great poem:

O, my clanswomen
Let us all cry together!
Come,
Let us mourn the death of our mother,
The death of a Queen
The ash that was produced
By a great fire!
O, this homestead is utterly dead
Close the gates
With lacari *thorns,*
For our mother
The creator of the Stool is lost!
And all the young men
Have perished in the wilderness!

But this is not the end of the story, for all the young women—our mothers and grandmothers, *ourselves*—have not perished in the wilderness. And if we ask ourselves why, and search for and find the answer, we will know beyond all efforts to erase it from our minds, just exactly who, and of what, we black American women are.

One example, perhaps the most pathetic, most misunderstood one, can provide a backdrop for our mothers' work: Phillis Wheatley, a slave in the 1700s.

Virginia Woolf, in her book *A Room of One's Own*, wrote that in order   16 for a woman to write fiction she must have two things, certainly: a room of her own (with key and lock) and enough money to support herself.

What then are we to make of Phillis Wheatley, a slave, who owned not even herself? This sickly, frail black girl who required a servant of her own at times—her health was so precarious—and who, had she been white, would have been easily considered the intellectual superior of all the women and most of the men in the society of her day.

Virginia Woolf wrote further, speaking of course not of our Phillis, that "any woman born with a great gift in the sixteenth century [insert "eighteenth century," insert "black woman," insert "born or made a slave"] would certainly have gone crazed, shot herself, or ended her days in some lonely cottage outside the village, half witch, half wizard [insert "Saint"], feared and mocked at. For it needs little skill and psychology to be sure that a highly gifted girl who had tried to use her gift of poetry would have been so thwarted and hindered by contrary instincts [add "chains, guns, the lash, the ownership of one's body by someone else, submission to an alien religion"], that she must have lost her health and sanity to a certainty."

The key words, as they relate to Phillis, are "contrary instincts." For when we read the poetry of Phillis Wheatley—as when we read the novels of Nella Larsen or the oddly false-sounding autobiography of that freest of all black women writers, Zora Hurston—evidence of "contrary instincts" is everywhere. Her loyalties were completely divided, as was, without question, her mind.

But how could this be otherwise? Captured at seven, a slave of   20 wealthy, doting whites who instilled in her the "savagery" of the Africa they "rescued" her from . . . one wonders if she was even able to remember her homeland as she had known it, or as it really was.

Yet, because she did try to use her gift for poetry in a world that made her a slave, she was "so thwarted and hindered by . . . contrary instincts, that she . . . lost her health. . . ." In the last years of her brief life, burdened not only with the need to express her gift but also with a penniless, friendless "freedom" and several small children for whom she was forced to do strenuous work to feed, she lost her health, certainly. Suffering from malnutrition and neglect and who knows what mental agonies, Phillis Wheatley died.

So torn by "contrary instincts" was black, kidnapped, enslaved Phillis that her description of "the Goddess"—as she poetically called the Liberty she did not have—is ironically, cruelly humorous. And, in fact, has held Phillis up to ridicule for more than a century. It is usually read prior to hanging Phillis's memory as that of a fool. She wrote:

The Goddess comes, she moves divinely fair,
Olive and laurel binds her golden hair.
Wherever shines this native of the skies,
Unnumber'd charms and recent graces rise. [My emphasis]

It is obvious that Phillis, the slave, combed the "Goddess's" hair every morning; prior, perhaps, to bringing in the milk, or fixing her mistress's lunch. She took her imagery from the one thing she saw elevated above all others.

With the benefit of hindsight we ask, "How could she?" 24

But at last, Phillis, we understand. No more snickering when your stiff, struggling, ambivalent lines are forced on us. We know now that you were not an idiot or a traitor; only a sickly little black girl, snatched from your home and country and made a slave; a woman who still struggled to sing the song that was your gift, although in a land of barbarians who praised you for your bewildered tongue. It is not so much what you sang, as that you kept alive, in so many of our ancestors, *the notion of song.*

Black women are called, in the folklore that so aptly identified one's status in society, "the *mule* of the world," because we have been handed the burdens that everyone else—*everyone* else—refused to carry. We have also been called "Matriarchs," "Superwomen," and "Mean and Evil Bitches." Not to mention "Castraters" and "Sapphire's Mama." When we have pleaded for understanding, our character has been distorted; when we have asked for simple caring, we have been handed empty inspirational appellations, then stuck in the farthest corner. When we have asked for love, we have been given children. In short, even our plainer gifts, our labors of fidelity and love, have been knocked down our throats. To be an artist and a black woman, even today, lowers our status in many respects, rather than raises it: And yet, artists we will be.

Therefore we must fearlessly pull out of ourselves and look at and identify with our lives the living creativity some of our great-grandmothers were not allowed to know. I stress *some* of them because it is well known that the majority of our great-grandmothers knew, even

without "knowing" it, the reality of their spirituality, even if they didn't
recognize it beyond what happened in the singing at church—and they
never had any intention of giving it up.

How they did it—those millions of black women who were not 28
Phillis Wheatley, or Lucy Terry or Frances Harper or Zora Hurston or
Nella Larsen or Bessie Smith; or Elizabeth Catlett, or Katherine Dun-
ham, either—brings me to the title of this essay, "In Search of Our
Mothers' Gardens," which is a personal account that is yet shared, in its
theme and its meaning, by all of us. I found, while thinking about the
far-reaching world of the creative black woman, that often the truest
answer to a question that really matters can be found very close.

In the late 1920s my mother ran away from home to marry my
father. Marriage, if not running away, was expected of seventeen-year-
old girls. By the time she was twenty, she had two children and was
pregnant with a third. Five children later, I was born. And this is how I
came to know my mother: She seemed a large, soft, loving-eyed woman
who was rarely impatient in our home. Her quick, violent temper was
on view only a few times a year, when she battled with the white
landlord who had the misfortune to suggest to her that her children did
not need to go to school.

She made all the clothes we wore, even my brothers' overalls. She
made all the towels and sheets we used. She spent the summers canning
vegetables and fruits. She spent the winter evenings making quilts
enough to cover our beds.

During the "working" day, she labored beside—not behind—my
father in the fields. Her day began before sunup, and did not end until
late at night. There was never a moment for her to sit down, undisturbed, to unravel her own private thoughts; never a time free from
interruption—by work or the noisy inquiries of her many children. And
yet, it is to my mother—and all our mothers who were not famous—that
I went in search of the secret of what has fed that muzzled and often
mutilated, but vibrant, creative spirit that the black woman has inherited, and that pops out in wild and unlikely places to this day.

But when, you will ask, did my overworked mother have time to 32
know or care about feeding the creative spirit?

The answer is so simple that many of us have spent years discovering it. We have constantly looked high, when we should have looked
high—and low.

For example: In the Smithsonian Institution in Washington, D.C.,
there hangs a quilt unlike any other in the world. In fanciful, inspired,
and yet simple and identifiable figures, it portrays the story of the
Crucifixion. It is considered rare, beyond price. Though it follows no

known pattern of quilt-making, and though it is made of bits and pieces of worthless rags, it is obviously the work of a person of powerful imagination and deep spiritual feeling. Below this quilt I saw a note that says it was made by "an anonymous Black woman in Alabama, a hundred years ago."

If we could locate this "anonymous" black woman from Alabama, she would turn out to be one of our grandmothers—an artist who left her mark in the only materials she could afford, and in the only medium her position in society allowed her to use.

As Virginia Woolf wrote further, in *A Room of One's Own:*   36

> Yet genius of a sort must have existed among women as it must have existed among the working class. [Change this to "slaves" and "the wives and daughters of sharecroppers."] Now and again an Emily Brontë or a Robert Burns [change this to "a Zora Hurston or a Richard Wright"] blazes out and proves its presence. But certainly it never got itself on to paper. When, however, one reads of a witch being ducked, of a woman possessed by devils [or "Sainthood"], of a wise woman selling herbs [our root workers], or even a very remarkable man who had a mother, then I think we are on the track of a lost novelist, a suppressed poet, or some mute and inglorious Jane Austen. . . . Indeed, I would venture to guess that Anon, who wrote so many poems without signing them, was often a woman. . . .

And so our mothers and grandmothers have, more often than not anonymously, handed on the creative spark, the seed of the flower they themselves never hoped to see: or like a sealed letter they could not plainly read.

And so it is, certainly, with my own mother. Unlike "Ma" Rainey's songs, which retained their creator's name even while blasting forth from Bessie Smith's mouth, no song or poem will bear my mother's name. Yet so many of the stories that I write, that we all write, are my mother's stories. Only recently did I fully realize this: That through years of listening to my mother's stories of her life, I have absorbed not only the stories themselves, but something of the manner in which she spoke, something of the urgency that involves the knowledge that her stories—like her life—must be recorded. It is probably for this reason that so much of what I have written is about characters whose counterparts in real life are so much older than I am.

But the telling of these stories, which came from my mother's lips as naturally as breathing, was not the only way my mother showed herself as an artist. For stories, too, were subject to being distracted, to dying without conclusion. Dinners must be started, and cotton must be gathered before the big rains. The artist that was and is my mother showed itself to me only after many years. This is what I finally noticed:

Like Mem, a character in *The Third Life of Grange Copeland*, my 40
mother adorned with flowers whatever shabby house we were forced to
live in. And not just your typical straggly country stand of zinnias,
either. She planted ambitious gardens—and still does—with over fifty
different varieties of plants that bloom profusely from early March
until late November. Before she left home for the fields, she watered her
flowers, chopped up the grass, and laid out new beds. When she returned from the fields, she might divide clumps of bulbs, dig a cold pit,
uproot and replant roses, or prune branches from her taller bushes or
trees—until night came and it was too dark to see.

Whatever she planted grew as if by magic, and her fame as a grower
of flowers spread over three counties. Because of her creativity with her
flowers, even my memories of poverty are seen through a screen of
blooms—sunflowers, petunias, roses, dahlias, forsythia, spirea, del-
phiniums, verbena . . . and on and on.

And I remember people coming to my mother's yard to be given
cuttings from her flowers; I hear again the praise showered on her
because whatever rocky soil she landed on, she turned into a garden. A
garden so brilliant with colors, so original in its design, so magnificent
with life and creativity, that to this day people drive by our house in
Georgia—perfect strangers and imperfect strangers—and ask to stand
or walk among my mother's art.

I notice that it is only when my mother is working in her flowers that
she is radiant, almost to the point of being invisible—except as Creator:
hand and eye. She is involved in work her soul must have. Ordering the
universe in the image of her personal conception of Beauty.

Her face, as she prepares the Art that is her gift, is a legacy of 44
respect she leaves to me, for all that illuminates and cherishes life. She
has handed down respect for the possibilities—and the will to grasp
them.

For her, so hindered and intruded upon in so many ways, being an
artist has still been a daily part of her life. This ability to hold on, even
in very simple ways, is work black women have done for a very long
time.

This poem is not enough, but it is something, for the woman who
literally covered the holes in our walls with sunflowers:

They were women then
My mama's generation
Husky of voice—Stout of
Step
With fists as well as
Hands
How they battered down
Doors

And ironed
Starched white
Shirts
How they led
Armies
Headragged Generals
Across mined
Fields
Booby-trapped
Kitchens
To discover books
Desks
A place for us
How they knew what we
Must *know*
Without knowing a page
Of it
Themselves

Guided by my heritage of a love of beauty and a respect for strength—in search of my mother's garden, I found my own.

And perhaps in Africa over two hundred years ago, there was just 48 such a mother; perhaps she painted vivid and daring decorations in oranges and yellows and greens on the walls of her hut; perhaps she sang—in a voice like Roberta Flack's—*sweetly* over the compounds of her village; perhaps she wove the most stunning mats or told the most ingenious stories of all the village storytellers. Perhaps she was herself a poet—though only her daughter's name is signed to the poems that we know.

Perhaps Phillis Wheatley's mother was also an artist.

Perhaps in more than Phillis Wheatley's biological life is her mother's signature made clear.   *1974*

Barbara Lazear Ascher

Mothers and Sons

"Mothers raise daughters to be wives,
they raise sons to be sons."
—Sarah Crichton

You realize, of course, that nothing is going to change until mothers start raising their sons differently. Women can sit on corporate boards, remove cancerous spleens, argue cases before the Supreme Court of the United States, but the heart of man will remain the same. Our presence in the boardroom, operating room, courtroom will be tolerated because failure to do so is considered bad form. But this is a case where form has little to do with substance.

The tolerant law firm will promote women to partnership. The tolerant Port Authority will put Sheila Bloom behind the wheel of a city bus. But this has nothing to do with what the tolerant man is saying of these women when he's having a beer with the guys, and it has nothing to do with how he treats his wife, girlfriend, secretary, daughter.

This is the heart of the matter. It is a mother's work to instill in her sons a respect for and understanding of women. Compared with her, we, the women who come along later in their lives, are limited in how much we can affect men's thinking.

Unfortunately, mothers aren't doing so well. Recently I called on a   4 friend who had to have an abortion, a trauma to heart, soul, and body no matter how valid the reason or swift the curette. I arrived with flowers and a bottle of wine, prepared to hold her hand or numb pain with frequently filled glasses. An attractive middle-aged woman opened the door and was introduced as "Phil's mother." It seems that Phil, who was at the office, had asked his mother to accompany his lover to the clinic and to bring her home afterward.

I would wish that that mother had replied, "Look here, Junior, this is a time that you should be standing by." Why did she come running in acquiescence? Because she had too much too lose—her son's gratitude and dependency. Here was a man who thought she was important. She was not about to stand up for what she as a woman knew would be helpful to another woman if she could strengthen the bond between mother and son. Sons are miniature versions of our fathers, the men we first loved and admired. But now there is no mother running inter-ference. Blind love will have its way; over and over again opportunities will present themselves for mothers to teach their sons about women and they will fail to do so.

To us, these objects of a mother's delight are just the men in our lives: the guy who orders two eggs over light, the boss who addresses one as "sweetie," the voice on the other end of the phone saying, "Sell McCrae, buy G.E." Beside these boyfriends, husbands, and guys we left behind are mothers whispering in their ears, "I'm always standing by."

Many women seek to have a closeness with their sons that they don't have with their husbands. This is an opportunity to mold an adoring, noncritical fan. I can see the temptation there and I can also see that the waters of "sisterhood" run shallow when the choice is between "sister" and son. These "sisters," other women who will populate our sons' lives in the form of classmates and teachers in the early years, girlfriends and colleagues later, and then finally lovers and wives, are betrayed by our attitudes.

And it happens in the "best" of homes. In the most liberated of 8 homes. In the best educated of homes. I dined the other night with a friend who is a powerful executive in a major corporation. Her husband is her fan and supporter and her eight-year-old son the apple of her eye. When he appeared to say good night, his mother asked if he had packed for a trip planned for the next morning. "No," was the serious reply. "That's a woman's work." My friend, his mother, laughed.

It's just another example of how we work against ourselves— through communications broad and narrow we do work against ourselves.

Until women truly respect themselves and each other, we will continue to undermine sisterhood through word and example, through the ways we treat our daughters and sons and the way we expect to be treated in return.

Unless daughters are respected, what are sons to think? I know a family that worked hard to win scholarships to private school for their two young boys. They did not feel that the public school was "good enough." Their youngest child, a girl, upon becoming school age was sent to that public school. Not a protest was raised, not a question asked. But what were these parents saying to their boys? That girls are not as important. And this is the lesson with which they will go forth into the world of business, finance, arts, letters, and marriage. These are lessons for life.

How odd that at a time when women are demanding more of their 12 husbands, they don't seem to demand more of their sons. What are we turning over to the future generation of wives and lovers and co-workers? Nothing very different from what was turned over to us. Only mothers can change this course of history, can stop its insistent and stubborn repetition. Mothers are the first beloved female in a boy's life. He is like a puppy in his eagerness to please her. He is ready to learn if she will teach kindness, caring, and generosity of spirit, if she demands it.

A friend who has five children insists that the three boys partake in all household chores, including the traditional "girls' jobs." She does it, she says, "Because my future daughters-in-law deserve something better." All of our daughters and daughters-in-law deserve something better, but they aren't going to get it until we as mothers start delivering a better and stronger message to our sons. Only then will the species become extinct—that species of head-scratching, muttering men who find it in their best interest to feign ignorance and declare that they just don't know what women want. *1982*

20

Fathers

Sherwood Anderson, Discovery of a Father

Max Apple, Bridging

Bharati Mukherjee, Fathering

You don't have to deserve your mother's love. You have to deserve your father's. He's more particular.

Robert Frost, from *Barnes & Nobles Book of Quotations*

I watch today's feminist fathers, their daughters riding in Snuglis on their chests or in knapsacks on their backs, their sticky fingers plunged into Daddy's hair. I see fathers changing diapers, playing catch, dressing their daughters for school, feeding them, waiting at bus stops, teaching them manners and how to fix a car, and I wonder if these daughters who experience their fathers differently than I did will love them differently, too.

Mary-Lou Weisman, from a "Hers" column

Though it is more difficult to write about my father than my mother, since I spent less time with him and knew him less well, it is equally liberating. Partly this is because writing about someone helps us to understand them, and understanding them helps us to accept them as part of ourselves. Since I share so many of my father's characteristics, physical and otherwise, coming to terms with what he has meant to my life is crucial to a full acceptance and love of myself.

Alice Walker, from *Father: For What You Were*

Sherwood Anderson

Discovery of a Father

One of the strangest relationships in the world is that between father and son. I know it now from having sons of my own.

A boy wants something very special from his father. You hear it said that fathers want their sons to be what they feel they cannot themselves be, but I tell you it also works the other way. I know that as a small boy I wanted my father to be a certain thing he was not. I wanted him to be a proud, silent, dignified father. When I was with other boys and he passed along the street, I wanted to feel a glow of pride: "There he is. That is my father."

But he wasn't such a one. He couldn't be. It seemed to me then that he was always showing off. Let's say someone in our town had got up a show. They were always doing it. The druggist would be in it, the shoestore clerk, the horse doctor, and a lot of women and girls. My father would manage to get the chief comedy part. It was, let's say, a Civil War play and he was a comic Irish soldier. He had to do the most absurd things. They thought he was funny, but I didn't.

I thought he was terrible. I didn't see how Mother could stand it. She   4
even laughed with the others. Maybe I would have laughed if it hadn't been my father.

Or there was a parade, the Fourth of July or Decoration Day. He'd be in that, too, right at the front of it, as Grand Marshal or something, on a white horse hired from a livery stable.

He couldn't ride for shucks. He fell off the horse and everyone hooted with laughter, but he didn't care. He even seemed to like it. I remember once when he had done something ridiculous, and right out on Main Street, too. I was with some other boys and they were laughing and shouting at him and he was shouting back and having as good a time as they were. I ran down an alley back of some stores and there in the Presbyterian Church sheds I had a good long cry.

Or I would be in bed at night and Father would come home a little lit up and bring some men with him. He was a man who was never alone. Before he went broke, running a harness shop, there were always a lot of men loafing in the shop. He went broke, of course, because he gave too much credit. He couldn't refuse it and I thought he was a fool. I had got to hating him.

There'd be men I didn't think would want to be fooling around with   8
him. There might even be the superintendent of our schools and a quiet man who ran the hardware store. Once, I remember, there was a white-haired man who was a cashier of the bank. It was a wonder to me they'd

want to be seen with such a windbag. That's what I thought he was. I know now what it was that attracted them. It was because life in our town, as in all small towns, was at times pretty dull and he livened it up. He made them laugh. He could tell stories. He'd even get them to singing.

If they didn't come to our house they'd go off, say at night, to where there was a grassy place by a creek. They'd cook food there and drink beer and sit about listening to his stories.

He was always telling stories about himself. He'd say this or that wonderful thing happened to him. It might be something that made him look like a fool. He didn't care.

If an Irishman came to our house, right away father would say he was Irish. He'd tell what county in Ireland he was born in. He'd tell things that happened there when he was a boy. He'd make it seem so real that, if I hadn't known he was born in southern Ohio, I'd have believed him myself.

If it was a Scotchman, the same thing happened. He'd get a burr 12 into his speech. Or he was a German or a Swede. He'd be anything the other man was. I think they all knew he was lying, but they seemed to like him just the same. As a boy that was what I couldn't understand.

And there was Mother. How could she stand it? I wanted to ask but never did. She was not the kind you asked such questions.

I'd be upstairs in my bed, in my room above the porch, and Father would be telling some of his tales. A lot of Father's stories were about the Civil War. To hear him tell it he'd been in about every battle. He'd known Grant, Sherman, Sheridan, and I don't know how many others. He'd been particularly intimate with General Grant so that when Grant went East, to take charge of all the armies, he took Father along.

"I was an orderly at headquarters and Sam Grant said to me, 'Irve,' he said, 'I'm going to take you along with me.'"

It seems he and Grant used to slip off sometimes and have a quiet 16 drink together. That's what my father said. He'd tell about the day Lee surrendered and how, when the great moment came, they couldn't find Grant.

"You know," my father said, "about General Grant's book, his memoirs. You've read of how he said he had a headache and how, when he got word that Lee was ready to call it quits, he was suddenly and miraculously cured."

"Huh," said Father, "He was in the woods with me.

"I was in there with my back against a tree. I was pretty well cornered. I had got hold of a bottle of pretty good stuff.

"They were looking for Grant. He had got off his horse and come 20 into the woods. He found me. He was covered with mud.

"I had the bottle in my hand. What'd I care? The war was over. I knew we had them licked."

My father said that he was the one who told Grant about Lee. An orderly riding by had told him, because the orderly knew how thick he was with Grant. Grant was embarrassed.

"But, Irve, look at me. I'm all covered with mud," he said to Father.

And then, my father said, he and Grant decided to have a drink 24 together. They took a couple of shots and then, because he didn't want Grant to show up potted before the immaculate Lee, he smashed the bottle against the tree.

"Sam Grant's dead now and I wouldn't want it to get out on him," my father said.

That's just one of the kind of things he'd tell. Of course, the men knew he was lying, but they seemed to like it just the same.

When we got broke, down and out, do you think he ever brought anything home? Not he. If there wasn't anything to eat in the house, he'd go off visiting around at farm houses. They all wanted him. Sometimes he'd stay away for weeks, Mother working to keep us fed, and then home he'd come bringing, let's say, a ham. He'd got it from some farmer friend. He'd slap it on the table in the kitchen. "You bet I'm going to see that my kids have something to eat," he'd say, and Mother would just stand smiling at him. She'd never say a word about all the weeks and months he'd been away, not leaving us a cent for food. Once I heard her speaking to a woman in our street. Maybe the woman had dared to sympathize with her. "Oh," she said, "it's all right. He isn't ever dull like most of the men in this street. Life is never dull when my man is about."

But often I was filled with bitterness, and sometimes I wished he 28 wasn't my father. I'd even invent another man as my father. To protect my mother I'd make up stories of a secret marriage that for some strange reason never got known. As though some man, say the president of a railroad company or maybe a congressman, had married my mother, thinking his wife was dead and then it turned out she wasn't.

So they had to hush it up but I got born just the same. I wasn't really the son of my father. Somewhere in the world there was a very dignified, quite wonderful man who was really my father. I even made myself half believe these fancies.

And then there came a certain night. Mother was away from home. Maybe there was church that night. Father came in. He'd been off somewhere for two or three weeks. He found me alone in the house, reading by the kitchen table.

It had been raining and he was very wet. He sat and looked at me for a long time, not saying a word. I was startled, for there was on his

face the saddest look I had ever seen. He sat for a time, his clothes
dripping. Then he got up.

"Come on with me," he said.   32

I got up and went with him out of the house. I was filled with
wonder but I wasn't afraid. We went along a dirt road that led down into
a valley, about a mile out of town, where there was a pond. We walked in
silence. The man who was always talking had stopped his talking.

I didn't know what was up and had the queer feeling that I was with
a stranger. I don't know whether my father intended it so. I don't think
he did.

The pond was quite large. It was still raining hard and there were
flashes of lightning followed by thunder. We were on a grassy bank at
the pond's edge when my father spoke, and in the darkness and rain his
voice sounded strange.

"Take off your clothes," he said. Still filled with wonder, I began to 36
undress. There was a flash of lightning and I saw that he was already
naked.

Naked, we went into the pond. Taking my hand, he pulled me in. It
may be that I was too frightened, too full of a feeling of strangeness, to
speak. Before that night my father had never seemed to pay any attention to me.

"And what is he up to now?" I kept asking myself. I did not swim
very well, but he put my hand on his shoulder and struck out into the
darkness.

He was a man with big shoulders, a powerful swimmer. In the
darkness I could feel the movements of his muscles. We swam to the
far edge of the pond and then back to where we had left our clothes.
The rain continued and the wind blew. Sometimes my father swam
on his back, and when he did he took my hand in his large powerful
one and moved it over so that it rested always on his shoulder. Sometimes there would be a flash of lightning, and I could see his face quite
clearly.

It was as it was earlier, in the kitchen, a face filled with sadness. 40
There would be the momentary glimpse of his face, and then again the
darkness, the wind and the rain. In me there was a feeling I had never
known before.

It was a feeling of closeness. It was something strange. It was as
though there were only we two in the world. It was as though I had been
jerked suddenly out of myself, out of my world of the schoolboy, out of a
world in which I was ashamed of my father.

He had become blood of my blood; he the strong swimmer and I the
boy clinging to him in the darkness. We swam in silence, and in silence
we dressed in our wet clothes and went home.

There was a lamp lighted in the kitchen, and when we came in, the water dripping from us, there was my mother. She smiled at us. I remember that she called us "boys." "What have you boys been up to?" she asked, but my father did not answer. As he had begun the evening's experience with me in silence, so he ended it. He turned and looked at me. Then he went, I thought, with a new and strange dignity, out of the room.

I climbed the stairs to my room, undressed in darkness and got into 44 bed. I couldn't sleep and did not want to sleep. For the first time I knew that I was the son of my father. He was a storyteller as I was to be. It may be that I even laughed a little softly there in the darkness. If I did, I laughed knowing that I would never again be wanting another father.

1939

Max Apple

Bridging

At the Astrodome, Nolan Ryan is shaving the corners. He's going through the Giants in order. The radio announcer is not even mentioning that by the sixth the Giants haven't had a hit. The Ks mount on the scoreboard. Tonight Nolan passes the Big Train and is now the all-time strikeout king. He's almost as old as I am and he still throws nothing but smoke. His fastball is an aspirin; batters tear their tendons lunging for his curve. Jessica and I have season tickets, but tonight she's home listening and I'm in the basement of St. Anne's Church watching Kay Randall's fingertips. Kay is holding her hands out from her chest, her fingertips on each other. Her fingers move a little as she talks and I can hear her nails click when they meet. That's how close I'm sitting.

Kay is talking about "bridging"; that's what her arched fingers represent.

"Bridging," she says, "is the way Brownies become Girl Scouts. It's a slow steady process. It's not easy, but we allow a whole year for bridging."

Eleven girls in brown shirts with red bandannas at their neck are   4
imitating Kay as she talks. They hold their stumpy chewed fingertips
out and bridge them. So do I.

I brought the paste tonight and the stick-on gold stars and the
thread for sewing buttonholes.

"I feel a little awkward," Kay Randall said on the phone, "asking a
man to do these errands . . . but that's my problem, not yours. Just bring
the supplies and try to be at the church meeting room a few minutes
before seven."

I arrive a half-hour early.

"You're off your rocker," Jessica says. She begs me to drop her at the   8
Astrodome on my way to the Girl Scout meeting. "After the game, I'll
meet you at the main souvenir stand on the first level. They stay open an
hour after the game. I'll be all right. There are cops and ushers every
five yards."

She can't believe that I am missing this game to perform my
functions as an assistant Girl Scout leader. Our Girl Scout battle has
been going on for two months.

"Girl Scouts is stupid," Jessica says. "Who wants to sell cookies and
sew buttons and walk around wearing stupid old badges?"

When she agreed to go to the first meeting, I was so happy I
volunteered to become an assistant leader. After the meeting, Jessica
went directly to the car the way she does after school, after a birthday
party, after a ball game, after anything. A straight line to the car. No
jabbering with girlfriends, no smiles, no dallying, just right to the car.
She slides into the back seat, belts in, and braces herself for destruction.
It has already happened once.

I swoop past five thousand years of stereotypes and accept my   12
assistant leader's packet and credentials.

"I'm sure there have been other men in the movement," Kay says,
"we just haven't had any in our district. It will be good for the girls."

Not for my Jessica. She won't bridge, she won't budge.

"I know why you're doing this," she says. "You think that because I
don't have a mother, Kay Randall and the Girl Scouts will help me.
That's crazy. And I know that Sharon is supposed to be like a mother
too. Why don't you just leave me alone."

Sharon is Jessica's therapist. Jessica sees her twice a week. Sharon   16
and I have a meeting once a month.

"We have a lot of shy girls," Kay Randall tells me. "Scouting brings
them out. Believe me, it's hard to stay shy when you're nine years old
and you're sharing a tent with six other girls. You have to count on each
other, you have to communicate."

I imagine Jessica zipping up in her sleeping bag, mumbling good night to anyone who first says it to her, then closing her eyes and hating me for sending her out among the happy.

"She likes all sports, especially baseball," I tell my leader.

"There's room for baseball in scouting," Kay says. "Once a year the whole district goes to a game. They mention us on the big scoreboard." 20

"Jessica and I go to all the home games. We're real fans."

Kay smiles.

"That's why I want her in Girl Scouts. You know, I want her to go to things with her girlfriends instead of always hanging around with me at ball games."

"I understand," Kay says. "It's part of bridging." 24

With Sharon the term is "separation anxiety." That's the fastball, "bridging" is the curve. Amid all their magic words I feel as if Jessica and I are standing at home plate blindfolded.

While I await Kay and the members of Troop 111, District 6, I eye St. Anne in her grotto and St. Gregory and St. Thomas. Their hands are folded as if they started out bridging, ended up praying.

In October the principal sent Jessica home from school because Mrs. Simmons caught her in spelling class listening to the World Series through an earphone.

"It's against the school policy," Mrs. Simmons said. "Jessica under- 28 stands school policy. We confiscate radios and send the child home."

"I'm glad," Jessica said. "It was a cheap-o radio. Now I can watch the TV with you."

They sent her home in the middle of the sixth game. I let her stay home for the seventh too.

The Brewers are her favorite American League team. She likes Rollie Fingers, and especially Robin Yount.

"Does Yount go in the hole better than Harvey Kuenn used to?" 32

"You bet," I tell her. "Kuenn was never a great fielder but he could hit three hundred with his eyes closed."

Kuenn is the Brewers' manager. He has an artificial leg and can barely make it up the dugout steps, but when I was Jessica's age and the Tigers were my team, Kuenn used to stand at the plate, tap the corners with his bat, spit some tobacco juice, and knock liners up the alley.

She took the Brewers' loss hard.

"If Fingers wasn't hurt they would have squashed the Cards, 36 wouldn't they?"

I agreed.

"But I'm glad for Andujar."

We had Andujar's autograph. Once we met him at a McDonald's. He was a relief pitcher then, an erratic right-hander. In St. Louis he im-proved. I was happy to get his name on a napkin. Jessica shook his hand.

One night after I read her a story, she said, "Daddy, if we were rich   40
could we go to the away games too? I mean, if you didn't have to be at
work every day."

"Probably we could," I said, "but wouldn't it get boring? We'd have
to stay at hotels and eat in restaurants. Even the players get sick of it."

"Are you kidding?" she said. "I'd never get sick of it."

"Jessica has fantasies of being with you forever, following baseball
or whatever," Sharon says. "All she's trying to do is please you. Since she
lost her mother she feels that you and she are alone in the world. She
doesn't want to let anyone or anything else into that unit, the two of you.
She's afraid of any more losses. And, of course, her greatest worry is
about losing you."

"You know," I tell Sharon, "that's pretty much how I feel too."   44

"Of course it is," she says. "I'm glad to hear you say it."

Sharon is glad to hear me say almost anything. When I complain
that her $100-a-week fee would buy a lot of peanut butter sandwiches,
she says she is "glad to hear me expressing my anger."

"Sharon's not fooling me," Jessica says. "I know that she thinks
drawing those pictures is supposed to make me feel better or something. You're just wasting your money. There's nothing wrong with me."

"It's a long, difficult, expensive process," Sharon says. "You and   48
Jessica have lost a lot. Jessica is going to have to learn to trust the world
again. It would help if you could do it too."

So I decide to trust Girl Scouts. First Girl Scouts, then the world. I
make my stand at the meeting of Kay Randall's fingertips. While Nolan
Ryan breaks Walter Johnson's strikeout record and pitches a two-hit
shutout, I pass out paste and thread to nine-year-olds who are sticking
and sewing their lives together in ways Jessica and I can't.

II

Scouting is not altogether new to me. I was a Cub Scout. I owned a
blue beanie and I remember very well my den mother, Mrs. Clark. A den
mother made perfect sense to me then and still does. Maybe that's why I
don't feel uncomfortable being a Girl Scout assistant leader.

We had no den father. Mr. Clark was only a photograph on the
living room wall, the tiny living room where we held our monthly
meetings. Mr. Clark was killed in the Korean War. His son John was in
the troop. John was stocky but Mrs. Clark was huge. She couldn't sit on a
regular chair, only on a couch or a stool without sides. She was the
cashier in the convenience store beneath their apartment. The story we
heard was that Walt, the old man who owned the store, felt sorry for her
and gave her the job. He was her landlord too. She sat on a swivel stool
and rang up the purchases.

We met at the store and watched while she locked the door; then we   52
followed her up the steep staircase to her three-room apartment. She
carried two wet glass bottles of milk. Her body took up the entire width
of the staircase. She passed the banisters the way semi trucks pass each
other on a narrow highway.

We were ten years old, a time when everything is funny, especially
fat people. But I don't remember anyone ever laughing about Mrs.
Clark. She had great dignity and character. So did John. I didn't know
what to call it then, but I knew John was someone you could always
trust.

She passed out milk and cookies, then John collected the cups and
washed them. They didn't even have a television set. The only decoration in the room that barely held all of us was Mr. Clark's picture on the
wall. We saw him in his uniform and we knew he died in Korea
defending his country. We were little boys in blue beanies drinking milk
in the apartment of a hero. Through that aura I came to scouting. I
wanted Kay Randall to have all of Mrs. Clark's dignity.

When she took a deep breath and then bridged, Kay Randall had
noticeable armpits. Her wide shoulders slithered into a tiny rib cage.
Her armpits were like bridges. She said "bridging" like a mantra,
holding her hands before her for about thirty seconds at the start of
each meeting.

"A promise is a promise," I told Jessica. "I signed up to be a leader,   56
and I'm going to do it with you or without you."

"But you didn't even ask me if I liked it. You just signed up without
talking it over."

"That's true; that's why I'm not going to force you to go along. It was
my choice."

"What can you like about it? I hate Melissa Randall. She always has
a cold."

"Her mother is a good leader."   60

"How do you know?"

"She's my boss. I've got to like her, don't I?" I hugged Jessica.
"C'mon, honey, give it a chance. What do you have to lose?"

"If you make me go I'll do it, but if I have a choice I won't."

Every other Tuesday, Karen, the fifteen-year-old Greek girl who lives   64
on the corner, babysits Jessica while I go to the Scout meetings. We talk
about field trips and how to earn merit badges. The girls giggle when
Kay pins a promptness badge on me, my first.

Jessica thinks it's hilarious. She tells me to wear it to work.

Sometimes when I watch Jessica brush her hair and tie her ponytail
and make up her lunch kit I start to think that maybe I should just relax
and stop the therapy and the scouting and all my not-so-subtle attempts
to get her to invite friends over. I start to think that, in spite of

everything, she's a good student and she's got a sense of humor. She's barely nine years old. She'll grow up like everyone else does. John Clark did it without a father; she'll do it without a mother. I start to wonder if Jessica seems to the girls in her class the way John Clark seemed to me: dignified, serious, almost an adult even while we were playing. I admired him. Maybe the girls in her class admire her. But John had that hero on the wall, his father in a uniform, dead for reasons John and all the rest of us understood.

My Jessica had to explain a neurologic disease she couldn't even pronounce. "I hate it when people ask me about Mom," she says. "I just tell them she fell off the Empire State Building."

III

Before our first field trip I go to Kay's house for a planning session.   68
We're going to collect wildflowers in East Texas. It's a one-day trip. I arranged to rent the school bus.

I told Jessica that she could go on the trip even though she wasn't a troop member, but she refused.

We sit on colonial furniture in Kay's den. She brings in coffee and we go over the supply list. Another troop is joining ours so there will be twenty-two girls, three women, and me, a busload among the bluebonnets.

"We have to be sure the girls understand that the bluebonnets they pick are on private land and that we have permission to pick them. Otherwise they might pick them along the roadside, which is against the law."

I imagine all twenty-two of them behind bars for picking bluebon-   72
nets and Jessica laughing while I scramble for bail money.

I keep noticing Kay's hands. I notice them as she pours coffee, as she checks off the items on the list, as she gestures. I keep expecting her to bridge. She has large, solid, confident hands. When she finishes bridging I sometimes feel like clapping the way people do after the national anthem.

"I admire you," she tells me. "I admire you for going ahead with Scouts even though your daughter rejects it. She'll get a lot out of it indirectly from you."

Kay Randall is thirty-three, divorced, and has a Bluebird too. Her older daughter is one of the stubby-fingered girls, Melissa. Jessica is right; Melissa always has a cold.

Kay teaches fifth grade and has been divorced for three years. I am   76
the first assistant she's ever had.

"My husband, Bill, never helped with Scouts," Kay says. "He was pretty much turned off to everything except his business and drinking.

When we separated I can't honestly say I missed him; he'd never been there. I don't think the girls miss him either. He only sees them about once a month. He has girlfriends, and his business is doing very well. I guess he has what he wants."

"And you?"

She uses one of those wonderful hands to move the hair away from her eyes, a gesture that makes her seem very young.

"I guess I do too. I've got the girls and my job. I'm lonesome,   80
though. It's not exactly what I wanted."

We both think about what might have been as we sit beside her glass coffeepot with our lists of sachet supplies. If she was Barbra Streisand and I Robert Redford and the music started playing in the background to give us a clue and there was a long close-up of our lips, we might just fade into middle age together. But Melissa called for Mom because her mosquito bite was bleeding where she scratched it. And I had an angry daughter waiting for me. And all Kay and I had in common was Girl Scouts. We were both smart enough to know it. When Kay looked at me before going to put alcohol on the mosquito bite, our mutual sadness dripped from us like the last drops of coffee through the grinds.

"You really missed something tonight," Jessica tells me. "The Astros did a double steal. I've never seen one before. In the fourth they sent Thon and Moreno together, and Moreno stole home."

She knows batting averages and won-lost percentages too, just like the older boys, only they go out to play. Jessica stays in and waits for me.

During the field trip, while the girls pick flowers to dry and then   84
manufacture into sachets, I think about Jessica at home, probably beside the radio. Juana, our once-a-week cleaning lady, agreed to work on Saturday so she could stay with Jessica while I took the all-day field trip.

It was no small event. In the eight months since Vicki died I had not gone away for an entire day.

I made waffles in the waffle iron for her before I left, but she hardly ate.

"If you want anything, just ask Juana."

"Juana doesn't speak English."   88

"She understands, that's enough."

"Maybe for you it's enough."

"Honey, I told you, you can come; there's plenty of room on the bus. It's not too late for you to change your mind."

"It's not too late for you either. There's going to be plenty of other   92
leaders there. You don't have to go. You're just doing this to be mean to me."

I'm ready for this. I spent an hour with Sharon steeling myself. "Before she can leave you," Sharon said, "you'll have to show her that you can leave. Nothing's going to happen to her. And don't let her be sick that day either."

Jessica is too smart to pull the "I don't feel good" routine. Instead she becomes more silent, more unhappy looking than usual. She stays in her pajamas while I wash the dishes and get ready to leave.

I didn't notice the sadness as it was coming upon Jessica. It must have happened gradually in the years of Vicki's decline, the years in which I paid so little attention to my daughter. There were times when Jessica seemed to recognize the truth more than I did.

As my Scouts picked their wildflowers, I remembered the last out-   96
ing I had planned for us. It was going to be a Fourth of July picnic with some friends in Austin. I stopped at the bank and got $200 in cash for the long weekend. But when I came home Vicki was too sick to move and the air conditioner had broken. I called our friends to cancel the picnic; then I took Jessica to the mall with me to buy a fan. I bought the biggest one they had, a 58-inch oscillating model that sounded like a hurricane. It could cool 10,000 square feet, but it wasn't enough.

Vicki was home sitting blankly in front of the TV set. The fan could move eight tons of air an hour, but I wanted it to save my wife. I wanted a fan that would blow the whole earth out of its orbit.

I had $50 left. I gave it to Jessica and told her to buy anything she wanted.

"Whenever you're sad, Daddy, you want to buy me things." She put the money back in my pocket. "It won't help." She was seven years old, holding my hand tightly in the appliance department at J. C. Penney's.

I watched Melissa sniffle even more among the wildflowers, and I   100
pointed out the names of various flowers to Carol and JoAnne and Sue and Linda and Rebecca, who were by now used to me and treated me pretty much as they treated Kay. I noticed that the Girl Scout flower book had very accurate photographs that made it easy to identify the bluebonnets and buttercups and poppies. There were also several varieties of wild grasses.

We were only 70 miles from home on some land a wealthy rancher long ago donated to the Girl Scouts. The girls bending among the flowers seemed to have been quickly transformed by the colorful meadow. The gigglers and monotonous singers on the bus were now, like the bees, sucking strength from the beauty around them. Kay was in the midst of them and so, I realized, was I, not watching and keeping score and admiring from the distance but a participant, a player.

JoAnne and Carol sneaked up from behind me and dropped some dandelions down my back. I chased them; then I helped the other leaders pour the Kool-Aid and distribute the Baggies and the name tags for each girl's flowers.

My daughter is home listening to a ball game, I thought, and I'm out here having fun with nine-year-olds. It's upside down.

When I came home with dandelion fragments still on my back, 104 Juana had cleaned the house and I could smell the taco sauce in the kitchen, Jessica was in her room. I suspected that she had spent the day listless and tearful, although I had asked her to invite a friend over.

"I had a lot of fun, honey, but I missed you."

She hugged me and cried against my shoulder. I felt like holding her the way I used to when she was an infant, the way I rocked her to sleep. But she was a big girl now and needed not sleep but wakefulness.

"I heard on the news that the Rockets signed Ralph Sampson," she sobbed, "and you hardly ever take me to any pro basketball games."

"But if they have a new center things will be different. With 108 Sampson we'll be contenders. Sure I'll take you."

"Promise?"

"Promise." I promise to take you everywhere, my lovely child, and then to leave you. I'm learning to be a leader.   *1984*

Bharati Mukherjee

Fathering

Eng stands just inside our bedroom door, her fidgety fist on the doorknob which Sharon, in a sulk, polished to a gleam yesterday afternoon.

"I'm starved," she says.

I know a sick little girl when I see one. I brought the twins up without much help ten years ago. Eng's got a high fever. Brownish stains stiffen the nap of her terry robe. Sour smells fill the bedroom.

"For God's sake leave us alone," Sharon mutters under the quilt. She 4 turns away from me. We bought the quilt at a garage sale in Rock Springs the Sunday two years ago when she moved in. "Talk to her."

Sharon works on this near-marriage of ours. I'll hand it to her, she really does. I knead her shoulders, and I say, "Easy, easy," though I really hate it when she treats Eng like a deaf-mute. "My girl speaks English, remember?"

Eng can outcuss any freckle-faced kid on the block. Someone in the killing fields must have taught her. Maybe her mama, the honeyest-skinned bar girl with the tiniest feet in Saigon. I was an errand boy with the Combined Military Intelligence. I did the whole war on Dexedrine. Vietnam didn't happen, and I'd put it behind me in marriage and fatherhood and teaching high school. Ten years later came the screwups with the marriage, the job, women, the works. Until Eng popped up in my life, I really believed it didn't happen.

"Come here, sweetheart," I beg my daughter. I sidle closer to Sharon, so there'll be room under the quilt for Eng.

"I'm starved," she complains from the doorway. She doesn't budge.   8
The robe and hair are smelling something fierce. She doesn't show any desire to cuddle. She must be sick. She must have thrown up all night. Sharon throws the quilt back. "Then go raid the refrigerator like a normal kid," she snaps.

Once upon a time Sharon used to be a cheerful, accommodating woman. It isn't as if Eng was dumped on us out of the blue. She knew I was tracking my kid. Coming to terms with the past was Sharon's idea. I don't know what happened to *that* Sharon. "For all you know, Jason," she'd said, "the baby died of malaria or something." She said, "Go on, find out and deal with it." She said she could handle being a step-mother—better a fresh chance with some orphan off the streets of Saigon than with my twins from Rochester. My twins are being raised in some organic-farming lesbo commune. Their mother breeds Nubian goats for a living. "Come get in bed with us, baby. Let Dad feel your forehead. You burning up with fever?"

"She isn't hungry, I think she's sick," I tell Sharon, but she's already tugging her sleeping mask back on. "I think she's just letting us know she hurts."

I hold my arms out wide for Eng to run into. If I could, I'd suck the virus right out of her. In the jungle, VC mamas used to do that. Some nights we'd steal right up to a hootch—just a few of us intense sons of bitches on some special mission—and the women would be at their mumbo jumbo. They'd be sticking coins and amulets into napalm burns.

"I'm hungry, Dad." It comes out as a moan. Okay, she doesn't run   12
into my arms, but at least she's come as far in as the foot of our bed. "Dad, let's go down to the kitchen. Just you and me."

I am about to let that pass though I can feel Sharon's body go into weird little jerks and twitches when my baby adds with emphatic viciousness, "Not her, Dad. We don't want her with us in the kitchen."

"She loves you," I protest. Love—not spite—makes Eng so ter-ritorial; that's what I want to explain to Sharon. She's a sick, frightened, foreign kid, for Chrissake. "Don't you, Sharon? Sharon's concerned about you."

But Sharon turns over on her stomach. "You know what's wrong with you, Jase? You can't admit you're being manipulated. You can't cut through the 'frightened-foreign-kid' shit."

Eng moves closer. She comes up to the side of my bed, but doesn't 16 touch the hand I'm holding out. She's a fighter.

"I feel fire-hot, Dad. My bones feel pain."

"Sharon?" I want to deserve this woman. "Sharon, I'm so sorry." It isn't anybody's fault. You need uppers to get through peace times, too.

"Dad. Let's go. Chop-chop."

"You're too sick to keep food down, baby. Curl up in here. Just for a 20 bit?"

"I'd throw up, Dad."

"I'll carry you back to your room. I'll read you a story, okay?"

Eng watches me real close as I pull the quilt off. "You got any scars you haven't shown me yet? My mom had a big scar on one leg. Shrapnel. Boom boom. I got scars. See? I got lots of bruises."

I scoop up my poor girl and rush her, terry robe flapping, to her 24 room which Sharon fixed up with white girlish furniture in less compli-cated days. Waiting for Eng was good. Sharon herself said it was good for our relationship. "Could you bring us some juice and aspirin?" I shout from the hallway.

"Aspirin isn't going to cure Eng," I hear Sharon yell. "I'm going to call Doctor Kearns."

Downstairs I hear Sharon on the phone. She isn't talking flu viruses. She's talking social workers and shrinks. My girl isn't crazy; she's picked up a bug in school as might anyone else.

"The child's arms are covered with bruises," Sharon is saying. "Nothing major. They look like . . . well, they're sort of tiny circles and welts." There's nothing for a while. Then she says, "Christ! no, Jason can't do enough for her! That's not what I'm saying! What's happening to this country? You think we're perverts? What I'm saying is the girl's doing it to herself."

"Who are you talking to?" I ask from the top of the stairs. "What 28 happened to the aspirin?"

I lean as far forward over the railing as I dare so I can see what Sharon's up to. She's getting into her coat and boots. She's having trouble with buttons and snaps. In the bluish light of the foyer's broken chandelier, she looks old, harrowed, depressed. What have I done to her?

"What's going on?" I plead. "You deserting me?"

"Don't be so fucking melodramatic. I'm going to the mall to buy some aspirin."

"How come we don't have any in the house?"   32

"Why are you always picking on me?"

"Who was that on the phone?"

"So now you want me to account for every call and every trip?" She ties an angry knot into her scarf. But she tells me. "I was talking to Meg Kearns. She says Doctor Kearns has gone hunting for the day."

"Great!"   36

"She says he has his beeper on him."

I hear the back door stick and Sharon swear. She's having trouble with the latch. "Jiggle it gently," I shout, taking the stairs two at a time. But before I can come down, her Nissan backs out of the parking apron.

Back upstairs I catch Eng in the middle of a dream or delirium. "They got Grandma!" she screams. She goes very rigid in bed. It's a four-poster with canopy and ruffles and stuff that Sharon put on her Master-Card. The twins slept on bunk beds. With the twins it was different, totally different. Dr. Spock can't be point man for Eng, for us.

"She bring me food," Eng's screaming. "She bring me food from the   40
forest. They shoot Grandma! Bastards!"

"Eng?" I don't dare touch her. I don't know how.

"You shoot my grandmother?" She whacks the air with her bony arms. Now I see the bruises, the small welts all along the insides of her arms. Some have to be weeks old, they're that yellow. The twins' scrapes and cuts never turned that ochre. I can't help wondering if maybe Asian skin bruises differently from ours, even though I want to say skin is skin; especially hers is skin like mine.

"I want to be with Grandma. Grandma loves me. I want to be ghost. I don't want to get better."

I read to her. I read to her because good parents are supposed to   44
read to their kids laid up sick in bed. I want to do it right. I want to be a good father. I read from a sci-fi novel that Sharon must have picked up. She works in a camera store in the mall, right next to a B. Dalton. I read three pages out loud, then I read four chapters to myself because Eng's stopped up her ears. Aliens have taken over small towns all over the country. Idaho, Nebraska: No state is safe from aliens.

Some time after two, the phone rings. Since Sharon doesn't answer it on the second ring, I know she isn't back. She carries a cordless phone everywhere around the house. In the movies, when cops have bad news to deliver, they lean on your doorbell; they don't call. Sharon will come back when she's ready. We'll make up. Things will get back to normal.

"Jason?"

I know Dr. Kearns's voice. He saw the twins through the usual immunizations.

"I have Sharon here. She'll need a ride home. Can you drive over?"   48
"God! What's happened?"

"Nothing to panic about. Nothing physical. She came for a consultation."

"Give me a half hour. I have to wrap Eng real warm so I can drag her out in this miserable weather."

"Take your time. This way I can take a look at Eng, too."   52
"What's wrong with Sharon?"

"She's a little exercised about a situation. I gave her a sedative. See you in a half hour."

I ease delirious Eng out of the overdecorated four-poster, prop her against my body while I wrap a blanket around her. She's a tiny thing, but she feels stiff and heavy, a sleepwalking mummy. Her eyes are dry-bright, strange.

It's a sunny winter day, and the evergreens in the front yard are   56
glossy with frost. I press Eng against my chest as I negotiate the front steps. Where the gutter leaks, the steps feel spongy. The shrubs and bushes my ex-wife planted clog the front path. I've put twenty years into this house. The steps, the path, the house all have a right to fall apart.

I'm thirty-eight. I've let a lot of people down already.

The inside of the van is deadly cold. Mid-January ice mottles the windshield. I lay the bundled-up child on the long seat behind me and wait for the engine to warm up. It feels good with the radio going and the heat coming on. I don't want the ice on the windshield to melt. Eng and I are safest in the van.

In the rearview mirror, Eng's wrinkled lips begin to move. "Dad, can I have a quarter?"

"May I, kiddo," I joke.   60

There's all sorts of junk in the pockets of my parka. Buckshot, dimes and quarters for the vending machine, a Blistex.

"What do you need it for, sweetheart?"

Eng's quick. Like the street kids in Saigon who dove for cigarettes and sticks of gum. She's loosened the blanket folds around her. I watch her tuck the quarter inside her wool mitt. She grins. "Thanks, soldier."

At Dr. Kearns's, Sharon is lying unnaturally slack-bodied on the   64
lone vinyl sofa. Her coat's neatly balled up under her neck, like a bolster. Right now she looks amiable, docile. I don't think she exactly recognizes me, although later she'll say she did. All that stuff about Kearns going hunting must have been a lie. Even the stuff about having to buy aspirins in the mall. She was planning all along to get here.

"What's wrong?"

"It's none of my business, Jason, but you and Sharon might try an

honest-to-goodness heart-to-heart." Then he makes a sign to me to lay
Eng on the examining table. "We don't look so bad," he says to my
daughter. Then he excuses himself and goes into a glass-walled cubicle.

Sharon heaves herself into a sitting position of sorts on the sofa.
"Everything was fine until she got here. Send her back, Jase. If you love
me, send her back." She's slouched so far forward, her pointed, sweat-
ered breasts nearly touch her corduroy pants. She looks helpless, pathetic. I've brought her to this state. Guilt, not love, is what I feel.

I want to comfort Sharon, but my daughter with the wild, grieving   68
pygmy face won't let go of my hand. "She's bad, Dad. Send *her* back."

Dr. Kearns comes out of the cubicle balancing a sample bottle of
pills or caplets on a flattened palm. He has a boxer's tough, squarish
hands. "Miraculous stuff, this," he laughs. "But first we'll stick our
tongue out and say *ahh*. Come on, open wide."

Eng opens her mouth real wide, then brings her teeth together,
hard, on Dr. Kearns's hand. She leaps erect on the examining table,
tearing the disposable paper sheet with her toes. Her tiny, funny toes
are doing a frantic dance. "Don't let him touch me, Grandma!"

"He's going to make you all better, baby." I can't pull my alien child
down, I can't comfort her. The twins had diseases with easy names,
diseases we knew what to do with. The thing is, I never felt for them
what I feel for her.

"Don't let him touch me, Grandma!" Eng's screaming now. She's   72
hopping on the table and screaming. "Kill him, Grandma! Get me out of
here, Grandma!"

"Baby, it's all right."

But she looks through me and the country doctor as though we
aren't here, as though we aren't pulling at her to make her lie down.

"Lie back like a good girl," Dr. Kearns commands.

But Eng is listening to other voices. She pulls her mitts off with her   76
teeth, chucks the blanket, the robe, the pajamas to the floor; then,
naked, hysterical, she presses the quarter I gave her deep into the soft
flesh of her arm. She presses and presses that coin, turning it in nasty
half-circles until blood starts to pool under the skin.

"Jason, grab her at the knees. Get her back down on the table."

From the sofa, Sharon moans. "See, I told you the child was crazy.
She hates me. She's possessive about Jason."

The doctor comes at us with his syringe. He's sedated Sharon; now
he wants to knock out my kid with his cures.

"Get the hell out, you bastard!" Eng yells. "*Vamos!* Bang bang!" She's   80
pointing her arm like a semiautomatic, taking out Sharon, then the
doctor. My Rambo. "Old way is good way. Money cure is good cure.
When they shoot my grandma, you think pills do her any good? You

Yankees, please go home." She looks straight at me. "Scram, Yankee bastard!"

Dr. Kearns has Eng by the wrist now. He has flung the quarter I gave her on the floor. Something incurable is happening to my women.

Then, as in fairy tales, I know what has to be done. "Coming, pardner!" I whisper. "I got no end of coins." I jiggle the change in my pocket. I jerk her away from our enemies. My Saigon kid and me: we're a team. In five minutes we'll be safely away in the cold chariot of our van. *1988*

21

Gender Roles and Stereotypes

Alexis de Tocqueville, How the Americans
Understand the Equality of the Sexes

Thomas Edison, The Woman of the Future

Jamaica Kincaid, Girl

Bruce Curtis, The Wimp Factor

The stereotype is the Eternal Feminine. She is the Sexual Object sought by all men, and by all women. She is of neither sex, for she has herself no sex at all. Her value is solely attested by the demand she excites in others. All she must contribute is her existence. She need achieve nothing, for she is the reward of achievement. She need never give positive evidence of her moral character because virtue is assumed from her loveliness and her passivity. If any man who has no right to her be found with her she will not be punished, for she is morally neuter. The matter is solely one of male rivalry. Innocently she may drive men to madness and war. The more trouble she can cause, the more her stocks go up, for possession of her means more the more demand she excites. Nobody wants a girl whose beauty is imperceptible to all but him; and so men welcome the stereotype because it directs their taste into the most commonly recognized areas of value, although they may protest because some aspects of it do not tally with their fetishes. There is scope in the stereotype's variety for most fetishes. The leg man may follow miniskirts, the tit man can encourage see-through blouses and plunging necklines, although the man who likes fat women may feel constrained to enjoy them in secret. There are stringent limits to the variations on the stereotype, for nothing must interfere with her function as sex object. She may wear leather, as long as she cannot actually handle a motorbike: she may wear rubber, but it ought not to indicate that she is an expert diver or waterskier. If she wears athletic clothes the purpose is to underline her unathleticism. She may sit astride a horse, looking soft and curvy, but she must not crouch over its neck with her rump in the air.

Germaine Greer, from *The Stereotype*

It is probably true that very few individuals conform totally to their sex-relevant stereotypes. Roles of all kinds . . . are sociocultural givens, but this is not to say that people play them in the same way. Indeed, individuals, like stage actors and actresses, interpret their roles and create innovations for their "parts." The fact remains that there is a "part" to be played, and it does strongly influence the actual "performance."

It is also important to recall that the precise definitions of gender role stereotypes vary within the broader culture by social class, region, race and ethnicity, and other subcultural categories. Thus, for instance, more than most other Americans, the various Spanish-speaking groups in this country (Mexican-American, Puerto Rican, Cuban) stress domesticity, passivity, and other stereotypical feminine traits, and dominance, aggressiveness, physical prowess, and other stereotypical masculine traits. Indeed, the masculine gender role for this group is generally described by reference to the highly stereotyped notion of *machismo*. In fact, a strong emphasis on masculine aggressiveness and dominance may be characteristic of most groups in the lower ranges of the socio-economic ladder. Conversely, due to historical conditions beyond its control, black America has had to rely heavily on the female as provider and, more often than in the rest of society, as head of the household. Thus, the feminine stereotype discussed above has traditionally been less a part of the cultural heritage of blacks than that of whites. It is also clear that, at least at the verbal level, both gender role stereotypes have historically been taken more seriously in Dixie than elsewhere. Although today this difference is probably declining, along with most other regional differences, personal experience leads me to conclude that it nonetheless remains. The pioneer past of the Far West, where survival relied upon strong, productive, independent females as well as males, may have dampened the emphasis on some aspects of the traditional feminine stereotype in that area of the country.

Janet Saltzman Chafetz, from *Some Individual Costs*
of Gender Role Conformity

In the traditional society, a boy went to work around the age of puberty, and began to earn his own living. It is customary to suppose and to say that when he had arrived at legal majority, and at a stage of sexual maturity and at economic independence, he had become a man. Very often, as it happens, he had indeed become a man, but neither because of sexual maturation nor because of economic earnings; for being a man was something that was *learned* by members of our instinct-deficient species and was not merely *arrived at* by physiological growth, or by getting a job. In fact, the society had a system for training boys to become men, and the completion of this training was nicely timed to coincide with physiological maturation and with the acquisition of earning power. The way that a boy really became a man was, first, by identifying with his father or some substitute authority figure, and thus internalizing the purpose to occupy a man's role; and later by practicing to assume a man's role in a group of young males with whom he formed affiliative ties such that he experienced socialization. Without the internalization of authority, without the purposeful adoption of a role, without the interpersonal relations with other individuals, no amount of elapsed time, sexual potency, or earned income could make him a socialized man. These processes were as vital to the maintenance of the human society as instincts are to animal species. In fact they may be regarded as the equivalents of instinct in providing human beings with a set of the right reactions.

David M. Potter, from *Rejection of the Prevailing American Society*

Probably no man has ever troubled to imagine how strange his life would appear to himself if it were unrelentingly assessed in terms of his maleness; if everything he wore, said, or did had to be justified by reference to female approval; if he were compelled to regard himself, day in day out, not as a member of society, but merely (*salvâ reverentiâ*) as a virile member of society. If the centre of his dress-consciousness were the codpiece, his education directed to making him a spirited lover and meek paterfamilias; his interests held to be natural only in so far as they were sexual. If from school and lecture room, Press and pulpit, he heard the persistent outpouring of a shrill and scolding voice, bidding him remember his biological function. If he were vexed by continual advice how to add a rough male touch to his typing, how to be learned without losing his masculine appeal, how to combine chemical research with seduction, how to play bridge without incurring the suspicion of impotence. If, instead of allowing with a smile that "women prefer cavemen," he felt the unrelenting pressure of a whole social structure forcing him to order all his goings in conformity with that pronouncement.

Dorothy L. Sayers, from *The Human-Not-Quite Human*

Alexis de Tocqueville

How the Americans Understand the Equality of the Sexes

I have shown how democracy destroys or modifies the different inequalities that originate in society; but is this all, or does it not ultimately affect that great inequality of man and woman which has seemed, up to the present day, to be eternally based in human nature? I believe that the social changes that bring nearer to the same level the father and son, the master and servant, and, in general, superiors and inferiors will raise woman and make her more and more the equal of man. But here, more than ever, I feel the necessity of making myself clearly understood; for there is no subject on which the coarse and lawless fancies of our age have taken a freer range.

There are people in Europe who, confounding together the different characteristics of the sexes, would make man and woman into beings not only equal but alike. They would give to both the same functions, impose on both the same duties, and grant to both the same rights; they would mix them in all things—their occupations, their pleasures, their business. It may readily be conceived that by thus attempting to make one sex equal to the other, both are degraded, and from so preposterous a medley of the works of nature nothing could ever result but weak men and disorderly women.

It is not thus that the Americans understand that species of democratic equality which may be established between the sexes. They admit that as nature has appointed such wide differences between the physical and moral constitution of man and woman, her manifest design was to give a distinct employment to their various faculties; and they hold that improvement does not consist in making beings so dissimilar do pretty nearly the same things, but in causing each of them to fulfill their respective tasks in the best possible manner. The Americans have applied to the sexes the great principle of political economy which governs the manufacturers of our age, by carefully dividing the duties of man from those of woman in order that the great work of society may be the better carried on.

In no country has such constant care been taken as in America to   4 trace two clearly distinct lines of action for the two sexes and to make them keep pace one with the other, but in two pathways that are always different. American women never manage the outward concerns of the family or conduct a business or take a part in political life; nor are they, on the other hand, ever compelled to perform the rough labor of the fields or to make any of those laborious efforts which demand the exertion of physical strength. No families are so poor as to form an exception to this rule. If, on the one hand, an American woman cannot escape from the quiet circle of domestic employments, she is never forced, on the other, to go beyond it. Hence it is that the women of America, who often exhibit a masculine strength of understanding and a manly energy, generally preserve great delicacy of personal appearance and always retain the manners of women although they sometimes show that they have the hearts and minds of men.

Nor have the Americans ever supposed that one consequence of democratic principles is the subversion of marital power or the confusion of the natural authorities in families. They hold that every association must have a head in order to accomplish its object, and that the natural head of the conjugal association is man. They do not therefore deny him the right of directing his partner, and they maintain that in the smaller association of husband and wife as well as in the great social community the object of democracy is to regulate and legalize the powers that are necessary, and not to subvert all power.

This opinion is not peculiar to one sex and contested by the other; I never observed that the women of America consider conjugal authority as a fortunate usurpation of their rights, or that they thought themselves degraded by submitting to it. It appeared to me, on the contrary, that they attach a sort of pride to the voluntary surrender of their own will and make it their boast to bend themselves to the yoke, not to shake it off. Such, at least, is the feeling expressed by the most virtuous of their sex; the others are silent; and in the United States it is not the practice for a guilty wife to clamor for the rights of women while she is trampling on her own holiest duties.

It has often been remarked that in Europe a certain degree of contempt lurks even in the flattery which men lavish upon women; although a European frequently affects to be the slave of woman, it may be seen that he never sincerely thinks her his equal. In the United States men seldom compliment women, but they daily show how much they esteem them. They constantly display an entire confidence in the understanding of a wife and a profound respect for her freedom; they have decided that her mind is just as fitted as that of a man to discover the plain truth, and her heart as firm to embrace it; and they have never sought to place her virtue, any more than his, under the shelter of prejudice, ignorance, and fear.

It would seem in Europe, where man so easily submits to the despotic sway of women, that they are nevertheless deprived of some of the greatest attributes of the human species and considered as seductive but imperfect beings; and (what may well provoke astonishment) women ultimately look upon themselves in the same light and almost consider it as a privilege that they are entitled to show themselves futile, feeble, and timid. The women of America claim no such privileges.

Again, it may be said that in our morals we have reserved strange immunities to man, so that there is, as it were, one virtue for his use and another for the guidance of his partner, and that, according to the opinion of the public, the very same act may be punished alternately as a crime or only as a fault. The Americans do not know this iniquitous division of duties and rights; among them the seducer is as much dishonored as his victim.

It is true that the Americans rarely lavish upon women those eager attentions which are commonly paid them in Europe, but their conduct to women always implies that they suppose them to be virtuous and refined; and such is the respect entertained for the moral freedom of the sex that in the presence of a woman the most guarded language is used lest her ear should be offended by an expression. In America a young unmarried woman may alone and without fear undertake a long journey.

The legislators of the United States, who have mitigated almost all the penalties of criminal law, still make rape a capital offense, and no crime is visited with more inexorable severity by public opinion. This may be accounted for; as the Americans can conceive nothing more precious than a woman's honor and nothing which ought so much to be respected as her independence, they hold that no punishment is too severe for the man who deprives her of them against her will. In France, where the same offense is visited with far milder penalties, it is frequently difficult to get a verdict from a jury against the prisoner. Is this a consequence of contempt of decency or contempt of women? I cannot but believe that it is a contempt of both.

Thus the Americans do not think that man and woman have either 12 the duty or the right to perform the same offices, but they show an equal regard for both their respective parts; and though their lot is different, they consider both of them as beings of equal value. They do not give to the courage of woman the same form or the same direction as to that of man, but they never doubt her courage; and if they hold that man and his partner ought not always to exercise their intellect and understanding in the same manner, they at least believe the understanding of the one to be as sound as that of the other, and her intellect to be as clear. Thus, then, while they have allowed the social inferiority of woman to continue, they have done all they could to raise her morally and intellectually to the level of man; and in this respect they appear to me to have excellently understood the true principle of democratic improvement.

As for myself, I do not hesitate to avow that although the women of the United States are confined within the narrow circle of domestic life, and their situation is in some respects one of extreme dependence, I have nowhere seen woman occupying a loftier position; and if I were asked, now that I am drawing to the close of this work, in which I have spoken of so many important things done by the Americans, to what the singular prosperity and growing strength of that people ought mainly to be attributed, I should reply: To the superiority of their women.

1835

Thomas Edison

The Woman of the Future

"The housewife of the future will be neither a slave to servants nor herself a drudge. She will give less attention to the home, because the home will need less; she will be rather a domestic engineer than a domestic laborer, with the greatest of all handmaidens, electricity, at her service. This and other mechanical forces will so revolutionize the woman's world that a large portion of the aggregate of woman's energy will be conserved for use in broader, more constructive fields."

As we talked, Thomas A. Edison, doubtless the greatest inventor of all time, said some things which may offend the woman of now, but he said others so appreciative and inspiring that they surely will wipe offense away. He declared, without reserve, his concord with the suffrage workers; he explained that woman as she is, and speaking generally, is an undeveloped creature and—here is where the women's wrath will rise at first—vastly man's inferior. But he went on to say that anatomical investigation of the female brain has shown it to be finer and more capable of ultimate aesthetic development than man's, and he explained that that development is undoubtedly, at last, well under way.

"It may be a perfectly natural detail of the development of the race that the modern woman not only does not wish to be, but will not be, a servant," Mr. Edison declared. "This has had its really unfortunate effect in that it has led, of late years, to general neglect of woman's work, and has resulted in the refusal, or, at least the failure, of many mothers to rightly teach their daughters. But good will ultimately come of it, for the necessities arising out of womankind's unwillingness, have turned the minds of the inventors toward creation of mechanical devices to perform that work which woman used to do. The first requisite of such machinery was a power which could be easily and economically subdivided into small units. Such a power has been found in electricity, which is now not only available in the cities, where it can be obtained from the great electrical supply concerns, but is becoming constantly more easily available in the rural districts, through the development of the small dynamo and of the gasoline engine and the appreciation and utilization of small water powers which are becoming general even on our farms.

"Electricity will do practically all of the manual work about the　4 home. Just as it has largely supplanted the broom and dustpan, and even the carpet sweeper, by being harnessed to the vacuum cleaner, it will be applied to the hundreds of other littler drudgeries in the house and in the yard. Attached to various simple but entirely effective mechanical contrivances now everywhere upon the market, and many others soon to be there, it will eliminate the task of maintaining cleanliness in other ways as well as in cleaning up dirt. No labor is much worse than sweeping. It has killed many women. Did you ever stop to think what a boon to women the vacuum cleaner really has been?

"Electricity will not only, as now, wash the clothes when turned on in a laundry and plugged into any one of dozens of existent patent washers, but will dry them, gather them, and iron them without the use of the little manual labor even now required in ironing by electrically heated individual irons and by the application of electricity to the other parts of the process. Electricity already dries clothes, after washing, quickly and with great economy of fabric, in easily equipped and inexpensive drying rooms, electrically heated, free from the dust of coal fires and from the winds which tore grandmother's wash to tatters when it was hung upon the outdoor lines of the old days. These electric laundries have already been reduced to what approaches absolute perfection in the larger establishments, such as commercial laundries, hotels, and the more luxurious apartment buildings, but it will not be long before they will be made possible for the small home in the cities or on farms.

"By supplying light through bulbs containing neither wicks to trim nor reservoirs to be filled with dust-accumulating oil, and involving no lamp chimneys to be cleaned of soot, electricity is constantly eliminating one large detail of the old-time household drudgery.

"As improved methods of production are developed, especially as waterpower comes into use for its creation, the electric current is becoming cheaper, so that it is now available, even in the kitchen, as a substitute for coal or oil, or gas in cooking. A vast advantage which comes from it, lies in the fact that it does not heat up a kitchen and that, with nominal expenditure for additional current, ventilators can be arranged and operated which will keep the kitchen absolutely free of fumes. Many a woman's life in old days was shortened; many a woman's life in these days is being shortened, by her presence for long hours

each day in an overheated atmosphere above a cook-stove. The application of electricity to domestic work will do away with this.

"A kitchen in which the cooking is electrically done and in which a   8
ventilation system electrically operated is installed, cannot become
unduly heated even in the worst days of our terrific American summers.
Electricity will cool the room as readily as it will cook the food. The
kitchen of the future will be all electric, and the electric kitchen will be
as comfortable as any room in the house.

"And the electric cooking of the future will, in many instances,
improve the food. It will permit the preparation of many dishes literally
on the dining table, by means of the electric chafing dish, and more
complete utensils, and so reduce the labor of food preparation that
there will be no temptation to prepare it in large quantities and put
parts of it aside for future use, a system which results frequently in sad
deterioration of the food involved.

"And not only will it make cooking simple and economical, but it
will make it better, for electric heat can be locally applied as no other
heat can be. The electrically cooked roast will be the perfect roast. No
part of it need be underdone, no part of it need be burned in the oven.
The housewife's great problem of imperfectly adjusted draughts and
dampers will be solved—indeed, it has been solved—in many kitchens,
for electric cooking is already widely practiced.

"The housewife's work, in days to come, will amount to little more
than superintendence, not of Norah, fresh from Ireland, or Gretchen,
fresh from Germany, but of simplified electrical appliances; and that is
why I said, to start with, that electricity will change the housewives of
the future from drudges into engineers.

"Electricity has already cheapened very greatly; it is getting cheaper   12
every day. It used to cost ten cents a kilowatt hour, but the price has
been reduced to five cents, four cents, even three cents to large consumers of power. An element in the cost is the time at which the current
is consumed. If it is not used at the times known as "peak hours," that is,
at hours when it is most in demand for lighting and for power, it can be
manufactured and served very cheaply.

"The problem of the storage of electricity must enter our calcula-
tions when we endeavor to make predictions of its future cost, and that
is, perhaps, too complicated to go into here; but I do not hesitate to say
that in the not far distant future electricity will be sold in New York City
at 50 percent of its present cost. In cities where water power is available
for its manufacture, the rate already is much lower than it is in New
York City, and it will continue to decrease until electricity becomes the
cheapest power which man has ever known.

"Even as things are now, all sort of minor mechanical appliances
such as brushes to clear the hair from dust in barber shops, factories,
and homes, vacuum cleaners and a hundred other things operated

through air condensed by electricity are in daily and growing use—a use which must be economical or it would not exist. There are lawn mowers which are chargeable 'off the line,' and indeed if I were to attempt to make a catalog of all the minor uses to which electricity is already put, the list would fill a good part of an issue of *Good Housekeeping*. Here is a distinct advance, for everything performing labor without requiring power from human muscles must be regarded as real progress.

"To diminish the necessity for utilizing man himself, or woman herself, as the motor-furnishing force for this life's mechanical tasks, is to increase the potentiality of humanity's brain power. When all our mental energy can be devoted to the highest tasks of which it may be capable, then shall we have made the greatest forward step in this world's history. To so conserve our energy as to trend toward this eventuality is the tendency of the age.

"It is there that electricity will play its greatest part in the develop- 16 ment of womankind. It will not only permit women to more generally exercise their mental force, but will compel this exercise, and thus insure a brain development in them such as has been prevented in the past.

"It will develop woman to that point where she can think straight. Direct thought is not at present an attribute of femininity. In this woman is now centuries, ages, even epochs behind man. That it is true is not her fault, but her misfortune, and the misfortune of the race. Man must accept responsibility for it, for it has been through his superior physical strength that he has held his dominance over woman and delayed her growth. For ages woman was man's chattel, and in such condition progress for her was impossible; now she is emerging into real sex independence, and the resulting outlook is a dazzling one. This must be credited very largely to progression in mechanics; more especially to progression in electrical mechanics.

"Under these new influences woman's brain will change and achieve new capabilities, both of effort and accomplishment. Woman will grow more involved cross fibers and that will mean a new race of mankind.

"Man is at present little, if any, more than half what he might be. The child may be considered the mean between his father and his mother—between the undeveloped female and the developed male. The male has had his full of mental exercise since society first organized; it has been denied the female. To growth, exercise is an essential. An arm which never has been used will show weak muscles. A blacksmith's arm is mighty because it lifts great weights, strikes heavy blows. Development of brain is not so very different from muscular development. The idle brain will atrophy, as will the idle arm.

"The brain of woman in the past has been, to an extent, an idle 20 brain. She has been occupied with petty tasks which, while holding her attention closely, have not given her brain exercise; such thinking as she has had time for, she has very largely found unnecessary because the stronger sex has done it for her. Through exercise men's brains have developed from the low standard of the aborigine to the high standard of the modern man, and if, in the new era which is dawning, woman's mental power increases with as great rapidity as that with which man's has grown, the children of the future—the children of the exercised, developed man, and of the exercised, developed woman—will be of mental power incredible to us today.

"The evolution of the brain of the male human has been the most wonderful of all the various phenomena of nature. When, in the new era of emancipation from the thraldom of the everyday mechanical task, the brain of woman undergoes a similar development, then, and only then, will the race begin to reach its ultimate. Yes, the mental power of the child born in the future will be marvelous, for to it women will make a contribution as great as that of man.

"There never was any need for woman's retardation. Man's selfishness, his lust for ownership, must be held responsible for it. He was not willing to make woman equal partner in his various activities, and so he held her back from an ability to fill an equal partnership.

"Less of this is evident in the development of the Jewish than in that of any other race. The almost supernatural business instinct of the Jew may be, I think, attributed to the fact that the various persecutions of the race have forced it to develop all its strength—its strength of women as well as that of men. Women have, from the beginning, taken part in Jewish councils; Jewish women have shared, always, in the pursuits of Jewish men; especially have they been permitted to play their part in business management. The result is that the Jewish child receives commercial acumen not only from the father's but from the mother's side. This may be taken as an evidence of what may come in future when womankind in general is equally developed with men along all lines.

"This development of woman through the evolution of mechanics 24 will, by means of those mechanics, probably be the quickest which the world has ever seen. The refinements of life in the future will be carried to a point not dreamed of now. I think the time has just arrived when the menial phases of existence may be said to be upon the verge of disappearing. This undoubtedly accounts for the great difficulty we experience now in hiring men, and more especially in hiring women, to do menial labor. The servant girl performs her tasks unwillingly in these days, and when she sees an opportunity, deserts them for the factory, where, through mechanical appliances, her potentiality as a human being finds new effectiveness.

"The drudgery of life will, by and by, entirely disappear. In days to come, through a small outlay of money, both men and women will be gratified by an infinite variety of delightful sights, sounds, and experiences that today are unknown and unimagined.

"An illustration of what may eventually be accomplished has arisen recently in my own experience. I have been once more working on the phonograph, endeavoring to bring it to perfection, and, within a few months, have succeeded in so doing. Here at my laboratory we now know not only that we can make records of and reproduce the finest music which humanity has yet created, but through our work we have discovered imperfections in the music of the past which, now that they have been found out, will be corrected. In a short time it will be possible to produce within the humblest home the best music of the world, and to produce it there as perfectly as it was in its first form. The reproduction will be presented so that any individual listening to it will hear the music to far better advantage than could any individual listening to the original production, unless his seat, while listening, were located in a scientifically determined spot in the auditorium wherein the music was produced. At concerts, now, the listener on one side of the hall hears too much brass. On the other side wood instruments or the strings are dominant.

"In playing for the phonographic records of the future, the orchestras will be so carefully distributed that each instrument will have its uttermost value in relation to the one spot where the phonograph is located and recording. Therefore, the person hearing music reproduced for them by this new instrument will have advantages which hitherto have been among the possibilities for but a small group at each concert. In the phonographic concert of the future, all will be balanced. I am informed that balance is secured in New York's Metropolitan Opera House only in a few seats near the center aisles, back, close to the doors. In front, on either side, and above, the music must, of necessity, be more or less unbalanced, and the cleverest acoustics cannot counteract this.

"In order to learn what was true and what was false about our 28 records, I made a minute microscopical examination of tremendous numbers of them, and eventually reduced music to a minutely measured science. I was enabled to reproduce singers' notes exactly as they had been sung. This gave us all the beauties of the original rendition, but, alas! it gave us all the flaws as well. The latter was appalling, both in number and magnitude. I shall not give a list of the world-famous singers who worked with us, but I shall reveal the surprising fact that the greatest of them dramatically are correspondingly poor vocally. When the tiny dots which register the sound upon a phonographic cylinder can be subjected to a microscopical examination and exact measurement, the slightest falsity is at once scientifically and mathematically discernible.

"The influence of this advance will be to startlingly improve the singing of the world, because it will make possible the discovery of imperfections which in the past have been glossed by emotions. These faults, thus revealed, will undoubtedly be found subject to correction, and thus singing will improve. All this will enormously simplify the labors of anxious mothers and of teachers who strive to impart musical training to the young. I have been studying music with as much intensity, of late, as I ever gave to any task, and I find few instruments, and practically no human voices without glaring imperfections. I have had a great number of teachers in my laboratory, and have found them all at sea. They have had no standards, no measurements. Music has been, like other things, unorganized. Its standardization, its measurement, its organization, were the first steps in our experimenting.

"I have in five months tried nine thousand five hundred tunes or songs in an earnest endeavor to find what it all means, to learn why certain music dies, why other music lives. Once, in a brief period, I studied one thousand seven hundred waltzes, as reproduced day by day without pause on pianos, and at another time seven hundred more. It was only in this way that a real investigation of the facts of music became possible. The study necessitated elaborate investigations of each musical instrument. I knew the mechanics of them, but did not know the musical aesthetics. My investigations have been accurate, for they have been founded upon measurement; actual physical measurement of sound vibrations, as recorded on the phonographic cylinder. Helmholtz in his studies was thrown off badly by the imperfect instruments which he used in experimenting. I have been able to avoid all that. I can make a record, reproduce it, and then examine with a microscope the vibrations of which it is made up, and this makes their measurement quite possible and proves out the quality of tone by actually hearing it. The method was not known to Helmholtz, and he therefore drew many wrong conclusions.

"It will be with music as it has been with electricity. When we first began in electricity we had no measurements; we had to guess at everything. It was only when we reduced currents down to units of measurements such as volts and amperes that measurement was possible, and until measurement was possible, no true knowledge of electricity was possible. Music has, likewise, floundered about, misunderstood, unsystematized. It has been a complicated matter in which the personal equation has played the largest part and in which accuracy—which means Truth—has played a very small part.

"I have gone into this matter of the new phonograph (which has not 32 hitherto been announced) because it indicates advance along those special lines you ask me to consider. It will save the woman of the future one more of those tasks which have absorbed her in the past, and will perform it for her better than she could perform it for herself. It will open to her and her children, at small cost, a vast mass of music which has hitherto been denied them at any price whatever of money or of effort, and will leave no real excuse for such expenditure of mothers' time as has been given to producing for, and teaching to, the children of the past crude music on pianos or what not.

"Science has, by this advance, removed one more of the great time eaters which have so oppressed all women. With the home-picture machine, now well developed, taking moving pictures into the family circle, it will be possible to furnish, quickly and concretely, such knowledge of the wonders of the nature which surrounds us as was impossible for our forefathers to obtain through any means of study. The revelations are illimitable. We could start at eight each morning, and watch films till eight each night for a period of a thousand years, and see new things each moment, without more than slightly touching on the surface of the facts which are available. The moving picture is developing the circumstance that we live in an environment of which we know practically nothing, and of which we even surmise little.

"All these things will do more for the development of women than they will for the development of men, and they are but a few of many influences which now are working toward that end. They occur to me because they are involved in those things which most engage my thought. They will help develop those cells in a woman's mind which have not in the past had opportunity or encouragement to grow. Give them opportunity and encouragement, and they will grow with great rapidity. They are very smart—these little cells! I have not much muscle, because I never have had reason to develop muscle. If I had had to do hard manual labor in the past, my little cells would have built muscle for me.

"The exercise of women's brains will build for them new fibers, new involutions, and new folds. If women had had the same struggle for existence which has confronted men, they would have been physically as strong, as capable of mind. But in the past they were protected, or, if not protected, forced to drudgery. These days are the days of woman's start upon the race—her first fair start.

"More and more she must be pushed, and more and more she will 36 advance herself. It is lack of those brain folds which has made her so illogical. Now, as they begin to come to her she will gain in logic. When she has to meet, in future, the same crises which men in the past have had to meet, the conservation of her time, which modern science has made possible, will have armed her for the encounter. This will make Earth a splendid planet to live upon.

"The development of women will solve many problems which we now deem quite insoluble. When women progress side by side with men, matrimony will become the perfect partnership. This perfect partnership will produce a childhood made up of individuals who

would now be thought not only mental, but physical and moral prod-
igies. There will be no drawbacks to life. We shall stop the cry for more
births and raise instead a cry for better births. We shall wake up
presently to the dire fact that this world is getting settled at a rate which
presently will occupy its total space. The less of that space which is
occupied by the unfit and the imperfect, certainly the better for the
race. The development of women which has now begun and is progress-
ing with such startling speed, will do more to solve this problem than
any other thing could do. What we want now is quality, not quantity. The
woman of the future—the domestic engineer, not the domestic
drudge—the wife, not the dependent; not alone the mother, but the
teacher and developer, will help to bring this quality about."   *1912*

Jamaica Kincaid
Girl

Wash the white clothes on Monday and put them on the stone heap;
wash the color clothes on Tuesday and put them on the clothesline to
dry; don't walk barehead in the hot sun; cook pumpkin fritters in very
hot sweet oil; soak your little clothes right after you take them off; when
buying cotton to make yourself a nice blouse, be sure that it doesn't
have gum on it, because that way it won't hold up well after a wash; soak
salt fish overnight before you cook it; is it true that you sing benna in
Sunday School?; always eat your food in such a way that it won't turn
someone else's stomach; on Sundays try to walk like a lady and not like
the slut you are so bent on becoming; don't sing benna in Sunday
School; you mustn't speak to wharf-rat boys, not even to give directions;
don't eat fruits on the street—flies will follow you; *but I don't sing benna
on Sundays at all and never in Sunday School*; this is how to sew on a button;
this is how to make a buttonhole for the button you have just sewed on;
this is how to hem a dress when you see the hem coming down and so to
prevent yourself from looking like the slut I know you are so bent on
becoming; this is how you iron your father's khaki shirt so that it doesn't
have a crease; this is how you iron your father's khaki pants so that they
don't have a crease; this is how you grow okra—far from the house,
because okra tree harbors red ants; when you are growing dasheen,

make sure it gets plenty of water or else it makes your throat itch when you are eating it; this is how you sweep a corner; this is how you sweep a whole house; this is how you sweep a yard; this is how you smile to someone you don't like too much; this is how you smile to someone you don't like at all; this is how you smile to someone you like completely; this is how you set a table for tea; this is how you set a table for dinner; this is how you set a table for dinner with an important guest; this is how you set a table for lunch; this is how you set a table for breakfast; this is how to behave in the presence of men who don't know you very well, and this way they won't recognize immediately the slut I have warned you against becoming; be sure to wash every day, even if it is with your own spit; don't squat down to play marbles—you are not a boy, you know; don't pick people's flowers—you might catch something; don't throw stones at blackbirds, because it might not be a blackbird at all; this is how to make a bread pudding; this is how to make doukona; this is how to make pepper pot; this is how to make a good medicine for a cold; this is how to make a good medicine to throw away a child before it even becomes a child; this is how to catch a fish; this is how to throw back a fish you don't like, and that way something bad won't fall on you; this is how to bully a man; this is how a man bullies you; this is how to love a man, and if this doesn't work there are other ways, and if they don't work don't feel too bad about giving up; this is how to spit up in the air if you feel like it, and this is how to move quick so that it doesn't fall on you; this is how to make ends meet; always squeeze bread to make sure it's fresh; *but what if the baker won't let me feel the bread?*; you mean to say that after all you are really going to be the kind of woman who the baker won't let near the bread? *1978*

Bruce Curtis

The Wimp Factor

Just before George Bush announced his running mate in 1988, a one-liner going the rounds was that he should choose Jeane Kirkpatrick to add some machismo to the ticket. Until midway through the campaign the embarrassing "fact" about Bush, as revealed in a spate of jokes, cartoons, and anecdotes gleefully reported or generated by the press, was the candidate's "wimpiness." A wimp, of course, is effete, ineffectual, somehow unmanly. Real men, the diametrical opposite of wimps, are war heroes and government leaders, especially combat pilots and spy masters. But wait! Didn't George Bush become a combat pilot at eighteen, fly on fifty-eight missions, and win the Distinguished Flying Cross? And doesn't everyone know he directed the Central Intelligence Agency?

Clearly, the phenomenon of George Bush, Wimp, has been grounded not upon the rock of objective fact but upon treacherous sands of image and modes of masculinity. Clearly, also, as Ronald Reagan recently and often demonstrated, the successful public man will cling to image, leaving fact to shift for itself. To do so is imperative when one's masculine image is at stake. And in American politics, at stake it almost always is. Just as in the presidential campaign of 1988 George Bush fought to assert and reassert his masculinity—to avoid effete gestures and calls for "just another splash" of coffee—so aspiring or established politicians routinely must nurture a masculine image for the public, and especially for the press.

Consider Bush's running mate, the "Veepette" or "Bush Lite," who had to face charges that his National Guard service was combat dodging by a "war wimp," a "sissy rich boy" who was Quayle-ing in the face of danger. Quayle is what you get, reported a foreign observer, when you cross a chicken with a hawk. Even the columnist Richard Cohen, a critic of sexual stereotypes, slipped easily into wimp-baiting, saying that in his debate with Senator Lloyd Bentsen, Quayle "looked like a mamma's boy at a family showdown searching for a sympathetic face." Another liberal, the *Doonesbury* creater Garry Trudeau, suggested in his comic strip that George Bush's late-mushrooming masculinity derived from anabolic steroids.

Governor Michael Dukakis may have seemed manly enough to the   4 casual observer, but Massachusetts pols ten years ago joked that because he dined at home every evening with his family, he was "Kitty-whipped." In 1988 "the Duke" (a nickname that invited unflattering comparisons with John Wayne) took up tank driving and played catch on his front lawn with a baseball pro. Nevertheless, commenting retrospectively, Joseph A. Califano, Jr., regretted that "from the beginning Dukakis had 'wimp on defense' written all over him."

Numerous analyses of comparative masculinity scanned and probed the bodies of the candidates, avoiding only their minds. What did they eat, and why? asked one article. It went on: "This is more than mere trivia. Social scientists agree that the food choices of political candidates can say much more than any speech. . . ." Macho pork rinds were the choice of Bush, who seemed to be baiting his line with them for good-ol'-boy Southern voters. In contrast, Dukakis, the article continued, seemed more "comfortable with his masculinity and sexuality." He did not hesitate to eat that "not macho" "women's food" ice cream, and coffee ice cream at that.

So far as I know, social scientists did not reveal Jesse Jackson's food fetishes, but one analyst of so-called body language intuited easily that Jackson was "the most macho," whereas Dukakis's handshake was "kind of wimpy," and Bush was "more characteristic of women" in multiple movements, especially in "sort of leading with the pelvic region," since "real machos lead with their chests." However, the analyst was quoted, "I am not saying that he is feminine in his carriage." A postelection *New Republic* commentator was less reticent, saying, "Visually the president-elect, I regret to say, sags—sort of the male version of the debutante slouch."

Read his body! Read his menu! When did all this probing of a man's masculinity, all this political wimp-baiting, begin? Conservatives blame Democrats, liberals blame Republicans. William Safire asserts that Ted Kennedy started it with his "Where was George?" cry at the Atlanta convention. But *Time* notes that while the 1988 Republican convention keynoter, Thomas Kean, accused his party's opposition of "pastel patriotism," Jeane Kirkpatrick had in 1984 already labeled them "San Francisco Democrats." That, recall, was the year of "Mondale Eats Quiche" bumper stickers. In 1988 George Bush continued in the grand tradition by attacking Harvard-tainted Dukakis's "boutique" foreign policy.

Political wimp-baiting was new neither in 1988 nor in 1984. It has   8 ever been thus. American politicians and the American press perennially reflect and magnify the public's hopes and fears. The presidential campaign of 1988 only confirmed what a historical perspective reveals: Sweeping changes in American life over decades and centuries have left virtually undampened the burning issue of masculinity; indeed, at times winds of change have fanned the flames. Historically, concern with masculinity has engendered a variant of what in 1969 Kate Millett called "sexual politics"—that is, "power-structured relationships" whereby one group (men) controls another group (women). But American sexual politics has been and is more complex and pervasive than that. Of course, men use sexual politics to control women, but men use sexual politics to control other men as well.

Masculine anxiety attended the birth and growth of American politics. Late in the eighteenth century Thomas Jefferson was accused of "timidity, whimsicalness," "an inertness of mind," "a wavering of disposition," and a weakness for flattery, all stereotypically feminine traits. A late-nineteenth-century historian was more direct: Jefferson had been "womanish" because "he took counsel of his feelings and imagination." Early in the nineteenth century the Indian fighter, war hero, and duelist Andrew Jackson referred to a politician whom he suspected of homosexuality as "Miss Nancy," while another politician called the same man "Aunt Fancy." In the same era, President Van Buren was accused of wearing corsets and taking too many baths, presumably perfumed.

In the game of sexual politics perhaps the most obvious nineteenth-century targets were men—the Alan Aldas of their day—who supported the women's movement. Such weak-minded creatures, said the Albany *Register* in 1854, "tied to the apron-strings" of "strong-minded" but "unsexed" feminists, were "restless men" who "comb their hair smoothly back, and with fingers locked across their stomachs, speak in a soft voice, and with upturned eyes." Similarly the New York *Herald* in 1852 had characterized "mannish" feminist women as "like hens that crow"—while most men who attended feminist conventions were termed "hen-pecked husbands" who ought to "wear petticoats."

The petticoat recalls another antiquated slur that not long ago flowed easily from the pen of George Will, the columnist. Will seems to have inherited the mantle of concern with national toughness and masculinity from the late columnist Joseph Alsop, who was a grand-nephew and spiritual descendant of Theodore Roosevelt. Will, intimating that then presidential candidate Paul Simon's foreign policy would not be tough and manly enough, asserted that Simon had "lifted his pinafore and cried 'Eeek'" when another candidate had "let loose" the "mouse of a thought" that American interests abroad must be defended. With such words, Will managed to insult one man and all women; he may also have intimidated politicians, male or female, who were concerned about the importance of presenting a strong image to the electorate.

In the nineteenth century the prime targets of hypermasculine 12 politicians and journalists were those cultured upper- and middle-class reformers called Mugwumps. The machine spoilsman Roscoe Conkling attacked the leading civil service reformer and editor of *Harper's Weekly* George William Curtis—who was conveniently both a Mugwump and a women's suffragist—by asserting that such effete types "are the man-milliners, the dilettanti and carpet knights of politics" who "forget that parties are not built by deportment, or by ladies' magazines, or by gush. . . ."

These reformers were further denounced as "political hermaphrodites," as "namby-pamby, goody-goody gentlemen" who "sip cold tea." They were, stormed Senator John Ingalls of Kansas to his fellow legislators, "the third sex" and "have two recognized functions. They sing falsetto, and they are usually selected as the guardians of the seraglios of Oriental despots." They were, fulminated the senator in nicely

balanced rhetoric, "effeminate without being either masculine or feminine; unable either to beget or bear; possessing neither fecundity nor
virility; endowed with the contempt of men and the derision of women,
and doomed to sterility, isolation, and extinction."

If the political argot of today and a century ago could have been
conflated in the 1988 election, surely George Bush, with his Ivy League
and Establishment pedigree, would have been labeled a "Mugwimp,"
for, like Bush, the Mugwumps were attacked not only for the substance
of their politics but also for their style and social class. And surely
questions about the manliness of both derived from pervasive unease
about masculinity in both *fin de siècle* eras. The hyperbole of Ingalls and
Conkling suggests that an enduring American male concern with masculinity became inordinate late in the nineteenth century. Indeed,
numerous scholars have discoverd a masculinity crisis in that era of
unsettling change. Why did this crisis develop?

One answer is that by the late nineteenth century not only working-
class, black, and immigrant men but women—especially Anglo-Saxon
women—were demanding a share of the power, prestige, and wealth of
the dominant males. As recognition of their inferior status impelled
women to strive for equality, rapid industrialization and urbanization
created greater opportunities and necessities for them to break from
rigid gender roles. Consequently, a great many men expressed heightened concern to maintain, or restore, or even intensify traditional
gender distinctions and especially insisted upon the crucial importance
of masculine "virility." This was true not only of privileged males but
also of black and immigrant males, who saw their masculinity as one of
their few resources.

When Basil Ransom, the traditionalist Southerner in Henry James's 16
1886 novel *The Bostonians*, speaks to Verena Tarrant about aggressive
feminist women, he says:

> There has been far too much talk about you, and I want to leave you
> alone altogether. My interest is in my own sex; yours evidently can look
> after itself. . . . The whole generation is womanized; the masculine
> tone is passing out of the world; it's a feminine, a nervous, hysterical,
> chattering, canting age. . . . The masculine character, the ability to
> dare and endure, to know and yet not fear reality, to look the world in
> the face and take it for what it is—a very queer and partly very base
> mixture—that is what I want to preserve, or rather, as I may say, to
> recover; and I must tell you that I don't in the least care what becomes
> of you ladies while I make the attempt!

As in fiction, a California newspaper editorialized in the 1890s that
"the ardor and strength of prime manhood is a much needed quality in
American government, especially at this time, when all things political

and all things social are in the transition stage." Then into the masculinity crisis strode Teddy Roosevelt, a weak-eyed Harvard man, to be sure, but a self-made boxer, rancher, and Rough Rider, come to preach the "Strenuous Life" of benevolent expansionism and to shame members of either sex who threatened traditional gender roles. "In the last analysis," Roosevelt asserted in 1899, "a healthy state can exist only when the men and women . . . lead clean, vigorous, healthy lives. . . . The man must be glad to do a man's work, to dare and endure and to labor; to keep himself, and to keep those dependent upon him. The woman must be the housewife, the helpmeet . . . the wise and fearless mother of many healthy children. . . . When men fear work or fear righteous war, when women fear motherhood, they tremble on the brink of doom; and well it is that they should vanish from the earth. . . ." Consistent in such concerns, Roosevelt would later rage that, by not plunging into World War I, President Wilson had "done more to emasculate American manhood . . . than anyone else I can think of. He is a dangerous man . . . for he is a man of brains and he debauches men of brains."

The remarkable fact about Teddy Roosevelt is that despite superior qualities of intelligence and leadership, despite his popularity and power as head of a great and rising imperial nation, when he preaches manhood from his national "bully pulpit," he sounds, to present-day observers, insecure. And if in this he seems a virtual contemporary of politicians we know well, that is perhaps because, a century after the first wave of feminism threatened to inundate Roosevelt and his cohorts, American men are now awash in a second wave. Many men, in a traditionally reactive way, are experiencing another crisis in our enduring historical concern to be masculine enough. That concern, as Richard Hofstadter perceived a quarter-century ago in *Anti-Intellectualism in American Life*, is written into "the national code at large."

The roots of our present masculinity crisis grow deep into American history, but they draw special sustenance from developments of the last half-century—depression, war, cold war, and inflation. In this era traditional gender-role verities have been overridden more than ever by events: widespread male unemployment in the thirties; demand for women workers ever since the forties; revolutionary changes in international relations, in which American power has increased and then diminished; and a revived, broadened women's movement. Especially in the last twenty-five years, masses of women, impelled by personal and family opportunities and necessities, have asserted their rights to work, to freedom, and to sexuality. Even traditional women have been drawn from the domestic into the public sphere.

The reaction of men to this battery of changes in social conditions 20
has been complex, involving confusion, resentment, resistance, and
grudging acquiescence to realities, public and domestic, American and
international. Sometimes men have felt gratitude for being relieved of
manhood's solitary burdens; occasionally they have supported more
egalitarian gender roles and relationships. Many American men,
however, have not yet adjusted to the withering of their self-image as the
husband-father-breadwinner who endures daily battles in the public
jungle for the sake of his loved ones.

What does all of this mean for politics? First that, as feminists have
taught us, the personal is political. But also that the political is personal.
Politicians, unsurprisingly, play to their constituents' gender-image
needs and to their own. Now that the ideal masculine man is farther
removed from reality than ever, many nostalgic men, and not a few
nostalgic women, demand that our public leaders appear more masculine than ever, a demand to which our leaders may personally be
drawn. In 1984 a woman from Warren, Michigan, said that she admired
President Ronald Reagan because he was like John Wayne. That statement must cause one to ponder the irony of a society in which an actor-
turned-politician can be seen as admirable because he is modeled on
another actor. And not just any actor, but on John Wayne, surely the all-
time leading sexual politician among actors. Ironically, also, in his
acting days Ronald Reagan yearned to emulate John Wayne's success as
a tall-walking hero. When asked if he had been nervous after debating
President Carter in 1980, Reagan replied, "Not at all. I've been on the
same stage with John Wayne." The politics of image and masculinity can
hardly be more precisely illustrated.

We can also test the proposition concerning masculinity that the
personal is political and the political personal by examining other
presidential aspirants and officeholders of the last quarter-century.
John Kennedy came to prominence in an era when American manhood, like his own, had recently been validated in battle. Kennedy's was
an era in which the Cold War demanded leaders who were "hard," an
era in which McCarthyites sought to dispose of "fellow travelers" (often
smeared as effeminate or homosexual) who were "soft on" Communism. Inevitably, it was the era of the "egghead," a male whom the
novelist Louis Bromfield defined as "over-emotional and feminine in
reactions to any problem"—meaning, of course, Adlai Stevenson. Stevenson, to whom the New York *Daily News* referred as "Adelaide," was
supported by "Harvard lace-cuff liberals" and "lace-panty diplomats";
he used "teacup words," which his "fruity" voice "trilled," a poor
contrast with Richard Nixon's "manly explanation of his financial affairs."

   Given such a climate, one can hardly be surprised that Kennedy,
whose father had instilled an almost manic competitive masculinity in
his sons, should have sought to assert and reassert his manhood when
faced with older men at home and abroad. The story was reported long
ago in David Halberstam's *The Best and the Brightest* (1969), and reaffirmed in Stanley Karnow's 1983 history of Vietnam, that Kennedy,
after meeting Nikita Khrushchev in Vienna, told *The New York Times*'s
James Reston: "I think he thought that anyone who was so young and
inexperienced as to get into that mess [the Bay of Pigs] could be taken,
and anyone who got into it, and didn't see it through, had no guts. So he
just beat hell out of me. So I've got a terrible problem." Now, Kennedy
told Reston, shifting from singular to plural point of view, "we have a
problem in making our power credible, and Vietnam is the place."

   If the personal was political and the political personal for Kennedy, 24
it was even more nakedly so for his successor. Surely no president has
been more earthily vulgar than Lyndon Johnson, particularly when
comparing unfavorably the masculinity of underlings and opponents
with his own. Reporters have told of repeated instances in which
Johnson asserted dominance over an aide, or Hubert Humphrey, or
even Ho Chi Minh by saying that he had emasculated the man. Politics,
for Lyndon Johnson, could hardly have been more personal, or more
sexual. Such a leader might have appeared comic, except that for a great
many Americans and Vietnamese the political was also intimately personal. Bill Moyers has said of Johnson and Vietnam, "It was almost like a
frontier test, as if he were saying, 'By God, I'm not going to let those
puny brown people push me around.'" Like Kennedy, Johnson person-
alized the Vietnam War. He saw it as a game or a wrestling match in
which he would make Ho Chi Minh cry "uncle."

   One might discuss Richard Nixon in much the same terms, given
his concern with personal crises and with crushing his enemies in the
game of politics. Nixon's masculine metaphors were, of course, from
poker or football or boxing. In *Six Crises*, his encounter as vice president
with Khrushchev in Moscow is reported in heroic underdog images that
any American viewer of ring movies could recognize: "I had had to
counter him like a fighter with one hand tied behind his back. . . .
Khrushchev had started the encounter by knocking me out of the ring.
At the end, I had climbed back in to fight again. And the second round
was still coming up. . . . Now we were going at it toe-to-toe." At the end,
"I felt like a fighter wearing sixteen-ounce gloves and bound by Marquis
of Queensbury rules, up against a bare-knuckle slugger who had
gouged, kneed, and kicked." "It was"—Nixon shifted images—"cold
steel between us all afternoon." In this contest, Nixon wrote, he had had
the facts when he had called Khrushchev, for it would not do to bluff
too often in the poker game of world politics.

Even Jimmy Carter, among recent presidents seemingly the least driven by machismo, revealed during the 1988 campaign his susceptibility to its public demands by remarking that Bush seemed rather "effeminate." Clearly, a major common denominator of recent presidents, and, indeed, as the sociologist Michael Kimmel believes, of most presidential administrations historically, has been an attraction to "compulsive masculinity, a socially constructed gender identity that is manifest both in individual behavior and in foreign and domestic politics."

Compulsive masculinity is most immediately dangerous in foreign politics. Theoretically, warfare is a form of controlled violence in the pursuit of foreign policy. The danger, as in the Vietnam era, is that the symbiotic bond between male leaders and followers will deteriorate into an irrational competition to prove one's manhood or at least to avoid appearing effeminate. Considerable testimony drawn from the memoirs of former Marines—foot soldiers and officers alike—reveals young men determined to be honorable and brave, to prove themselves, to avoid the shame of failing in training or fleeing in battle. They often chose John Wayne as a role model. Their worst fear, also that of their commander in chief, Lyndon Johnson, was that they might cut and run like "nervous Nellies."

The commander in chief of Vietnam-era soldiers, says David 28 Halberstam, believed "all those John Wayne movies, a cliché in which real life had styled itself on image," and so Lyndon Johnson demanded a portrait of himself as "a tall tough Texan in the saddle." Such is the meaning of sexual politics for men. Does a Michigan woman confuse Reagan with John Wayne? Some of us can no longer distinguish between *PT 109* (the movie) and reality. Our leaders and soldiers and image makers are indistinguishable. They are daring each other. And they are macho. They are all John Wayne.

As an actor John Wayne personified in dangerously attractive images the romantic myth that masculine style and substance are indivisible; that to express openly and unashamedly one's emotions of doubt, fear, love, and even (unless goaded unendurably) anger is womanish; that the dominant male must control himself, his environment, and indeed all of life, through action, often violent action in chivalric defense of women, children, and country, action forced upon the good man by evil others; that by willpower, strength, skill, superior technology, and firepower he can prevail over circumstance and chance, over enemies, personal and national, in a world of black-and-white moral choices.

The point is not that the "manly" characteristics of the myth— courage, assertiveness in the face of aggression, righteous defense of the weak—are undesirable or dangerous in themselves. The cinematic myth is dangerous because it is labeled "for men only" and because it may be distorted and debased by actors on the public scene.

The consequences of this sort of obsessive masculinity can perhaps best be understood in a historical context. Speaking in the aftermath of the Spanish-American War, in 1899, Teddy Roosevelt asserted: "I have scant patience with those who fear to undertake the task of governing the Philippines . . . who make a pretense of humanitarianism to hide and cover their timidity, and who cant about 'liberty' and the 'consent of the governed,' in order to excuse themselves for their unwillingness to play the part of men. Their doctrines, if carried out, would make it incumbent upon us to . . . decline to interfere in a single Indian reservation. Their doctrines condemn your forefathers and mine for ever having settled in these United States." Almost a century later Philip Caputo's 1987 novel *Indian Country* would remind us that the practice among American soldiers of referring to hostile territory in Vietnam as Indian country had historical roots.

If the demands of masculinity have burdened men in American 32 politics, they have pressed with special intensity upon trespassing women, who have automatically been tested by masculine standards. If many men are too wimpy for politics, what are men to think about women, and what are women to think of themselves? Pat Schroeder, for example, shed public tears when she withdrew from the presidential race of 1988. By failing to mask her feelings, Schroeder was widely perceived as having joined the ranks of those—like Ed Muskie—who seemed not manly enough for the rough game of high-stakes politics. After all, would you want a leader with a finger on the nuclear button who was suffering from what the nineteenth century called hysteria or from twentieth-century equivalents, such as PMS? That was substantially the question asked of Geraldine Ferraro in her 1984 debate with George Bush. To all appearances, with steely eye and firm response, Ferraro passed the macho test—so much so, in fact, that the next morning Bush felt compelled to affirm that in the debate he had "kicked a little ass."

Women in politics like Ferraro and Schroeder are condemned no matter what they do. If gentle, they are womanish; if tough, they are not womanly. By tradition a female cannot be a courageous, charismatic, wise, effective leader as a woman. Thus one-liners about "macho" Jeane Kirkpatrick, about Indira Gandhi's being the only man in India's government. Thus "Iron Lady" Margaret Thatcher plays the manly role but, to allay fears, must make the point that at home she may relax by ironing her husband's shirts.

So long as the power to define gender characteristics remains a dominant-male prerogative, politics will remain defined as a masculine prerogative, even if women enter politics in considerably increased numbers. For gender definitions are about power relationships, and the power to define is real. Attacks upon Schroeder or Bush as wimps, an earlier attack on Senator Henry Jackson as homosexual, and Senator Orrin Hatch's 1988 smear of the Democrats as "the party of homosexuals" all serve the purpose of excluding or dominating the opposition. Likewise, attacks upon "long-haired men and short-haired women" reformers, a staple of politics since the nineteenth century, seek to limit the range and depth of challenges to established social policy. For according to the masculine logic of sexual politics, all women and all men are relatively "womanized," except the hardest, toughest, most powerful, most masculine.

Postelection commentary on George Bush has seemed to reflect among journalists a masculinity-concerns-as-usual attitude. Murray Kempton wrote in *The New York Review of Books* that "the Quayle selection more than suggested that Bush fears associates too bold for his own peace and comfort; and he proceeded thereafter to submit himself abjectly to the advisers who at once contrived to make him seem tougher but altogether less likeable than previous experience had permitted us to imagine him." Some commentators nevertheless concluded that in fact or in image Bush was no longer a wimp, Tom Wicker noting that the "suspect candidate" had "established by September a satisfactory identification as Ronald Reagan's surrogate, who was not a wimp after all." Humphrey Taylor concurred, reporting in the *National Review* that at the New Orleans convention Bush had "emerged from the shadow of Ronald Reagan as his own man, a fighter not a wimp." In a public letter to "Dear George," Lee Iacocca wrote: "First of all, congratulations! It was a tough campaign, a real street fight toward the end. Nobody will ever call you a wimp again, George. Nice going." *Newsweek* commented: "The new George Bush looks rugged, even macho, standing chest-deep in the Florida surf. . . . Something startling has happened to the man who was once mocked as Ronald Reagan's lap dog. . . . It could be argued, George Bush walked into the polling booth as Clark Kent and emerged as the Beltway equivalent of Superman."

Meanwhile, David Beckwith noted left-handedly in *Time* that the 36 candidate had won "with a toughness that surprised even his friends." Beckwith believed that Bush, having seen aides take credit for Reagan's successes, "is determined not to be similarly emasculated. . . ." To the contrary, Fred Barnes predicted flatly in *The New Republic* that, lacking a mandate, a program, and congressional cooperation, "Bush will be a eunuch on his honeymoon."

Genital imagery and masculine anxiety appeared among journalists all along the main-line political spectrum. In *The New Republic* "TRB" summed up the Reagan presidency as having injected the nation with anabolic steroids, leaving it for the moment "economically and militarily virile. Unfortunately," "TRB" concluded, "steroids, like sedatives, have side effects, and already our national testicles are starting to shrink . . . beginning to emasculate the Pentagon. . . ." With mixed images, the *National Review*'s William F. Buckley, seeking to buck up the president-elect, noted that "to cave in" on the tax issue would "emasculate the presidency. That would give the Democratic Congress a free hand to scrape every last shred of pork out of the barrel, and roll even bigger logs over the taxpayers."

As throughout the history of the Republic, so in the 1988 presidential election's aftermath, concern about the toughness and masculinity of our leaders remained at the center of American politics. Will the media continue to define our leaders, and will leaders and the public continue to allow themselves to be defined, in these narrow terms? Given the persistent masculine tradition in American politics and society, the answer is probably yes. And yet a century or even little more than a generation ago, who would have thought that traditional images of racial superiority and inferiority could be challenged with considerable success, that racist beliefs and practices could be at least diminished?

If we cannot clearly foresee it, we must surely hope for a time when the political leaders of America—and the men of the press who help fashion them—spend less energy defining and defending gendered turf. Should that day come, politicians, the press, and the public will have more energy for more important social issues than the state of American masculinity.   *1989*

22

Resistance to Stereotypes

Virginia Woolf, Thoughts on Peace
in an Air Raid

Judy Brady, I Want a Wife

Bob Greene, Mr. President

The emphasis for the past twenty years has been on women's equality. Not enough has been said about our side of the bargain. You don't have to flutter around men in a mating dance that makes you look like a hyperthyroid toad. You can disagree with them when you feel like it. You don't have to treat their egos as though they were fragile works of art. In short, you can treat men as equals.

Rita Mae Brown, from *Some of My Best Friends Are . . . Men*

"Wall, chilern, whar dar is so much racket dar must be somethin' out o' kilter. I tink dat 'twixt de niggers of de Souf and de womin at de Norf, all talkin' 'bout rights, de white men will be in a fix pretty soon. But what's all dis here talkin' 'bout?

"Dat man ober dar say dat womin needs to be helped into carriages, and lifted ober ditches, and to hab de best place everywhar. Nobody eber helps me into carriages, or ober mud-puddles, or gibs me any best place!" And raising herself to her full height, and her voice to a pitch like rolling thunder, she asked, "And a'n't I a woman? Look at me! Look at my arm! (and she bared her right arm to the shoulder, showing her tremendous muscular power). I have ploughed, and planted, and gathered into barns, and no man could head me! And a'n't I a woman? I could work as much and eat as much as a man—when I could get it—and bear de lash as well! And a'n't I a woman? I have borne thirteen

481

chilern, and seen 'em mos' all sold off to slavery, and when I cried out
with my mother's grief, none but Jesus heard me! And a'n't I a woman?"

Sojourner Truth (as quoted by Frances Dana Barker Gage),
from *And A'n't I a Woman?*

I have always disliked being a man. The whole idea of manhood in
America is pitiful, a little like having to wear an ill-fitting coat for one's
entire life. (By contrast, I imagine femininity to be an oppressive sense
of nakedness.) Even the expression "Be a man!" strikes me as insulting
and abusive. It means: Be stupid, be unfeeling, obedient and soldierly,
and stop thinking. Man means "manly"—how can one think "about
men" without considering the terrible ambition of manliness? And yet
it is part of every man's life. It is a hideous and crippling lie; it not only
insists on difference and connives at superiority, it is also by its very
nature destructive—emotionally damaging and socially harmful.

Paul Theroux, from *The Male Myth*

Virginia Woolf

Thoughts on Peace in an Air Raid

The Germans were over this house last night and the night before
that. Here they are again. It is a queer experience, lying in the dark and
listening to the zoom of a hornet, which may at any moment sting you to
death. It is a sound that interrupts cool and consecutive thinking about
peace. Yet it is a sound—far more than prayers and anthems—that
should compel one to think about peace. Unless we can think peace into
existence we—not this one body in this one bed but millions of bodies
yet to be born—will lie in the same darkness and hear the same death
rattle overhead. Let us think what we can do to create the only efficient
air-raid shelter while the guns on the hill go pop pop pop and the
searchlights finger the clouds and now and then, sometimes close at
hand, sometimes far away, a bomb drops.

Up there in the sky young Englishmen and young German men are
fighting each other. The defenders are men, the attackers men. Arms

are not given to Englishwomen either to fight the enemy or to defend herself. She must lie weaponless tonight. Yet if she believes that the fight going on up in the sky is a fight by the English to protect freedom, by the Germans to destroy freedom, she must fight, so far as she can, on the side of the English. How far can she fight for freedom without firearms? By making arms, or clothes or food. But there is another way of fighting for freedom without arms; we can fight with the mind. We can make ideas that will help the young Englishman who is fighting up in the sky to defeat the enemy.

But to make ideas effective, we must be able to fire them off. We must put them into action. And the hornet in the sky rouses another hornet in the mind. There was one zooming in *The Times* this morning—a woman's voice saying, "Women have not a word to say in politics." There is no woman in the Cabinet; nor in any responsible post. All the idea-makers who are in a position to make ideas effective are men. That is a thought that damps thinking, and encourages irresponsibility. Why not bury the head in the pillow, plug the ears, and cease this futile activity of idea-making? Because there are other tables besides officer tables and conference tables. Are we not leaving the young Englishman without a weapon that might be of value to him if we give up private thinking, tea-table thinking, because it seems useless? Are we not stress-ing our disability because our ability exposes us perhaps to abuse, perhaps to contempt? "I will not cease from mental fight," Blake wrote. Mental fight means thinking against the current, not with it.

That current flows fast and furious. It issues in a spate of words 4 from the loudspeakers and the politicians. Every day they tell us that we are a free people, fighting to defend freedom. That is the current that has whirled the young airman up into the sky and keeps him circling there among the clouds. Down here, with a roof to cover us and a gas-mask handy, it is our business to puncture gas-bags and discover seeds of truth. It is not true that we are free. We are both prisoners tonight—he boxed up in his machine with a gun handy; we lying in the dark with a gas-mask handy. If we were free we should be out in the open, dancing, at the play, or sitting at the window talking together. What is it that prevents us? "Hitler!" the loudspeakers cry with one voice. Who is Hitler? What is he? Aggressiveness, tyranny, the insane love of power made manifest, they reply. Destroy that, and you will be free.

The drone of the planes is now like the sawing of a branch over-head. Round and round it goes, sawing and sawing at a branch directly above the house. Another sound begins sawing its way in the brain. "Women of ability"—it was Lady Astor speaking in *The Times* this morning—"are held down because of a subconscious Hitlerism in the hearts of men." Certainly we are held down. We are equally prisoners tonight—the Englishmen in their planes, the Englishwomen in their beds. But if he stops to think he may be killed; and we too. So let us think for him. Let us try to drag up into consciousness the subconscious Hitlerism that holds us down. It is the desire for aggression; the desire to dominate and enslave. Even in the darkness we can see that made visible. We can see shop windows blazing; and women gazing; painted women; dressed-up women; women with crimson lips and crimson fingernails. They are slaves who are trying to enslave. If we could free ourselves from slavery we should free men from tyranny. Hitlers are bred by slaves.

A bomb drops. All the windows rattle. The anti-aircraft guns are getting active. Up there on the hill under a net tagged with strips of green and brown stuff to imitate the hues of autumn leaves guns are concealed. Now they all fire at once. On the nine o'clock radio we shall be told "Forty-four enemy planes were shot down during the night, ten of them by anti-aircraft fire." And one of the terms of peace, the loudspeakers say, is to be disarmament. There are to be no more guns, no army, no navy, no air force in the future. No more young men will be trained to fight with arms. That rouses another mind-hornet in the chambers of the brain—another quotation. "To fight against a real enemy, to earn undying honour and glory by shooting total strangers, and to come home with my breast covered with medals and decorations, that was the summit of my hope. . . . It was for this that my whole life so far had been dedicated, my education, training, everything. . . ."

Those were the words of a young Englishman who fought in the last war. In the face of them, do the current thinkers honestly believe that by writing "Disarmament" on a sheet of paper at a conference table they will have done all that is needful? Othello's occupation will be gone; but he will remain Othello. The young airman up in the sky is driven not only by the voices of loudspeakers; he is driven by voices in himself—ancient instincts, instincts fostered and cherished by education and tradition. Is he to be blamed for those instincts? Could we switch off the maternal instinct at the command of a table full of politicians? Suppose that imperative among the peace terms was: "Child-bearing is to be restricted to a very small class of specially selected women," would we submit? Should we not say, "The maternal instinct is a woman's glory. It was for this that my whole life has been dedicated, my education, training, everything. . . ." But if it were necessary, for the sake of humanity, for the peace of the world, that childbearing should be restricted, the maternal instinct subdued; women would attempt it. Men would help them. They would honour them for their refusal to bear children. They would give them other openings for their creative power. That too must make part of our fight for freedom. We must help the young Englishmen to root out from themselves the love of medals and decorations. We must create more honourable activities for those who try to conquer in themselves their fighting instinct, their subconscious Hitlerism. We must compensate the man for the loss of his gun.

The sound of sawing overhead has increased. All the searchlights 8 are erect. They point at a spot exactly above this roof. At any moment a bomb may fall on this very room. One, two, three, four, five, six . . . the seconds pass. The bomb did not fall. But during those seconds of suspense all thinking stopped. All feeling, save one dull dread, ceased. A nail fixed the whole being to one hard board. The emotion of fear and of hate is therefore sterile, unfertile. Directly that fear passes, the mind reaches out and instinctively revives itself by trying to create. Since the room is dark it can create only from memory. It reaches out to the memory of other Augusts—in Bayreuth, listening to Wagner; in Rome, walking over the Campagna; in London. Friends' voices come back. Scraps of poetry return. Each of those thoughts, even in memory, was far more positive, reviving, healing, and creative than the dull dread made of fear and hate. Therefore if we are to compensate the young man for the loss of his glory and of his gun, we must give him access to the creative feelings. We must make happiness. We must free him from the machine. We must bring him out of his prison into the open air. But what is the use of freeing the young Englishman if the young German and the young Italian remain slaves?

The searchlights, wavering across the flat, have picked up the plane now. From this window one can see a little silver insect turning and twisting in the light. The guns go pop pop pop. Then they cease. Probably the raider was brought down behind the hill. One of the pilots landed safe in a field near here the other day. He said to his captors, speaking fairly good English, "How glad I am that the fight is over!" Then an Englishman gave him a cigarette, and an Englishwoman made him a cup of tea. That would seem to show that if you can free the man from the machine, the seed does not fall upon altogether stony ground. The seed may be fertile.

At last all the guns have stopped firing. All the searchlights have been extinguished. The natural darkness of a summer's night returns. The innocent sounds of the country are heard again. An apple thuds to the ground. An owl hoots, winging its way from tree to tree. And some half-forgotten words of an old English writer come to mind: "The huntsmen are up in America. . . ." Let us send these fragmentary notes to the huntsmen who are up in America, to the men and women whose sleep has not yet been broken by machine-gun fire, in the belief that they will rethink them generously and charitably, perhaps shape them into something serviceable. And now, in the shadowed half of the world, to sleep.   *1940*

Judy Brady

I Want a Wife

I belong to that classification of people known as wives. I am A Wife. And, not altogether incidentally, I am a mother.

Not too long ago a male friend of mine appeared on the scene fresh from a recent divorce. He had one child, who is, of course, with his ex-wife. He is looking for another wife. As I thought about him while I was ironing one evening, it suddenly occurred to me that I, too, would like to have a wife. Why do I want a wife?

I would like to go back to school so that I can become economically independent, support myself, and, if need be, support those dependent on me. I want a wife who will work and send me to school. And while I am going to school I want a wife to take care of my children. I want a wife to keep track of the children's doctor and dentist appointments. And to keep track of mine, too. I want a wife to make sure my children eat properly and are kept clean. I want a wife who will wash the children's clothes and keep them mended. I want a wife who is a good nurturant attendant to my children, who arranges for their schooling, makes sure that they have an adequate social life with their peers, takes them to the park, the zoo, etc. I want a wife who takes care of the children when they are sick, a wife who arranges to be around when the children need special care, because, of course, I cannot miss classes at school. My wife must arrange to lose time at work and not lose the job. It may mean a small cut in my wife's income from time to time, but I guess I can tolerate that. Needless to say, my wife will arrange and pay for the care of the children while my wife is working.

I want a wife who will take care of *my* physical needs. I want a wife 4 who will keep my house clean. A wife who will pick up after my children, a wife who will pick up after me. I want a wife who will keep my clothes clean, ironed, mended, replaced when need be, and who will see to it that my personal things are kept in their proper place so that I can find what I need the minute I need it. I want a wife who cooks the meals, a wife who is a *good* cook. I want a wife who will plan the menus, do the necessary grocery shopping, prepare the meals, serve them pleasantly, and then do the cleaning up while I do my studying. I want a wife who will care for me when I am sick and sympathize with my pain and loss of time from school. I want a wife to go along when our family takes a vacation so that someone can continue to care for me and my children when I need a rest and change of scene.

I want a wife who will not bother me with rambling complaints about a wife's duties. But I want a wife who will listen to me when I feel the need to explain a rather difficult point I have come across in my course of studies. And I want a wife who will type my papers for me when I have written them.

I want a wife who will take care of the details of my social life. When my wife and I are invited out by my friends, I want a wife who will take care of the baby-sitting arrangements. When I meet people at school that I like and want to entertain, I want a wife who will have the house clean, will prepare a special meal, serve it to me and my friends, and not interrupt when I talk about things that interest me and my friends. I want a wife who will have arranged that the children are fed and ready for bed before my guests arrive so that the children do not bother us. I want a wife who takes care of the needs of my guests so that they feel comfortable, who makes sure that they have an ashtray, that they are passed the hors d'oeuvres, that they are offered a second helping of the food, that their wine glasses are replenished when necessary, that their coffee is served to them as they like it. And I want a wife who knows that sometimes I need a night out by myself.

I want a wife who is sensitive to my sexual needs, a wife who makes love passionately and eagerly when I feel like it, a wife who makes sure that I am satisfied. And, of course, I want a wife who will not demand sexual attention when I am not in the mood for it. I want a wife who assumes the complete responsibility for birth control, because I do not want more children. I want a wife who will remain sexually faithful to me so that I do not have to clutter up my intellectual life with jealousies. And I want a wife who understands that *my* sexual needs may entail more than strict adherence to monogamy. I must, after all, be able to relate to people as fully as possible.

If, by chance, I find another person more suitable as a wife than the wife I already have, I want the liberty to replace my present wife with another one. Naturally, I will expect a fresh, new life; my wife will take the children and be solely responsible for them so that I am left free. [8]

When I am through with school and have a job, I want my wife to quit working and remain at home so that my wife can more fully and completely take care of a wife's duties.

My God, who *wouldn't* want a wife?   *1971*

Bob Greene

Mr. President

"We're going to have spaghetti tonight," said Thomas Lucas on his seventeenth birthday. "My mom makes excellent spaghetti. Especially the sauce. She uses sausage, chicken, mushrooms, peppers—I've only made spaghetti sauce once, but it can't come close to Mom's."

Thomas Lucas was sitting in the wood-paneled living room of his family's home in Salt Rock, West Virginia. He is a big, handsome kid— five feet eleven, 185 pounds—and on top of the television set in the living room was a photograph of him in his red-and-white Barboursville High School football uniform. Last year Thomas was a starting defensive tackle on the team.

But things have changed for Thomas Lucas since last summer. His life will never be the same—and, in at least a minor way, the lives of American high school students will never be the same, either.

Because Thomas Lucas won an election last summer. And he is now   4 the first male to be the national president of Future Homemakers of America.

Thomas Lucas's family lives in the West Virginia hollows. This is Chuck Yeager country, where the men are supposed to be tough, laconic, rugged, and all of the other adjectives that have always added up to a definition of maleness. So it is all the more surprising that the first male president of Future Homemakers of America should come from here.

"In junior high school," Thomas said, "the boys are all required to take home economics as well as shop, and the girls are all required to take shop as well as home economics. In high school you don't have to do that, but when I was a freshman I decided that I'd keep taking home economics. And when the teacher announced that there would be a Future Homemakers of America meeting, I went to it.

"I didn't do it for any particular reason. I just did it to meet some kids. I was the only boy there. But it turned out that I liked it."

Approximately 11 percent of the 315,000 members of Future Home-   8 makers of America nationwide are males. But, until very recently, it was unthinkable for a boy to become president of the forty-one-year-old organization.

"A lot of people define homemaking as just sewing and cooking," Thomas said. "But my definition of a homemaker is someone who contributes to the well-being of the family. That should be a male as well as a female. You have to understand, there was never a time when I thought that men and women weren't equal. I was born in nineteen sixty-nine, and that was at the beginning of the women's movement."

As might be expected, Thomas has taken some teasing from his schoolmates about this whole thing. "Yeah, there have been some re-marks," he said. "The macho image of a lot of high school guys is the same that it has always been. You know, 'I'm tough.' Always getting in fights to prove their masculinity. All this boastfulness about themselves, and putting down other people. They're so locked into that image that they can't associate outside that.

"People couldn't understand that I was a football player and that I was also in FHA. But football and FHA are just two different things that I did. I'm not playing football this year, because of my FHA duties. That's okay with me.

"You hear so much about football being a character builder. If you 12 ask me, football creates animosity between people. I know that it's supposed to develop sportsmanship and develop physical well-being and make you feel good about yourself. But all football was for me was going out there and knocking heads with someone every day. Future Homemakers of America is a hundred times more of a character builder than football, and Future Homemakers of America has offered me a hundred times more good things than football ever could."

Thomas is aware of the modern heroes for young people: Rambo for the boys, Vanna White for the girls. "Look, I saw *Rambo* three times," he said. "I liked the story of it. It was an exciting movie, and very suspense-ful. But it's fantasy. What I'm doing is real."

Thomas's stepfather, Larry Brown, came into the living room. Brown is forty-one years old and a dealer account manager with Ford Motor Credit Company. He is a burly, bearded man, and he listened to his son talking about Future Homemakers of America.

"When I was in high school, something like this would never be done," Brown said. "The boys just didn't take home economics. My conception, when I was growing up, was that the wife was the home-maker and the husband was the provider. And there are still a lot of men who would rather have their son be the football captain than the president of FHA.

"But I'm very proud of Thomas, and the more I learn about what 16 he's doing, the more proud I am. Frankly, if anything, we felt at first that he was a little too dedicated to it. We saw Future Homemakers becom-ing his whole life. But what can we say? He set his sights on becoming national president, and now he is.

"In this day and age, I think it's wrong to want to bring your son up to be macho. I think that what Thomas was just saying about the macho image you get from movies is right. Basically, the macho image is ignorant. The macho guys you see in the movies seem to be playing with about half a deck upstairs.

"What Thomas is doing represents a change for everybody. With more and more women in the work force, men are going to have to adapt, and accept learning skills around the house. They're not going to have any choice."

Thomas cut in. "The real prejudice against what I'm doing doesn't come from kids my own age," he said. "Oh, there's some of that, but I can handle it. But the bad stereotype comes from adults. Not to put down you adults or anything, but teenagers are a little more liberal in their thinking than adults.

"Like at the national convention in Orlando, where I was elected. I 20 had my delegate name tag on, and there was this woman in the lobby of the hotel who was just staying there as a guest—she wasn't a part of the FHA convention. And she looked at me and she looked at my tag, and she said, 'Oh, you're a homemaker, are you?' She kind of snickered. I knew she was making fun."

Thomas's mother, Sue Brown, thirty-eight, walked into the living room for a moment from the kitchen, where she had been preparing dinner.

"I've never believed that a woman should have all the homemaker's chores," she said. "Oh, women do help keep the social aspects of the family going. They send out the greeting cards and buy the presents for Christmas and call people to invite them to things. On things like that, men have to be sort of dragged along. It shouldn't be that way. It's unfair.

"But Thomas—Thomas has done household chores since he was small."

"I mow the yard," Thomas said. "I take out the garbage. I dust. I do 24 the dishes. I make the bed. Mom still does most of the cooking."

"You can be a man and still be like Thomas," his mother said. "Thomas is no sissy. I don't think he's going to be a househusband and just stay home when he gets older. But he's been taught to do his share. And I think his being elected national president proves that it doesn't matter if you're from a hollow in West Virginia. Your mind can go anywhere."

There was a knock at the front door, and Thomas's mother went to answer it. In a few moments a lanky young man walked into the living room. He was Anthony Thompson, a high school buddy of Thomas's, and he had been invited to come over for the birthday dinner.

"Thomas was always a go-getter," Anthony said. "I think it's great that he made it to president."

It didn't seem to occur to Anthony that there was anything par- 28 ticularly unusual about the fact that the group that Thomas had "made it to president" of was the Future Homemakers of America. He seemed simply to admire the accomplishment.

"In junior high school, Thomas and I both ran for student body president, and I won," Anthony said. "But now Thomas has established himself in a far more prestigious position than president of Salt Rock Junior High School."

Anthony said that he had no desire to join FHA. "I guess that I just don't have the interest that Thomas has," he said. "I'm not saying that I think it was a weird thing for him to do. There are a lot of people who would think it would be a feminine move, but I don't think so. I'm sure that there will be some feeling against him in school this year now that he's national president, and that some people will stereotype him. But he can handle it. I know he can.

"People are just brought up in different ways. Take my grandparents. My grandmother waits on my grandfather hand and foot. He wouldn't be able to exist without her. I think all Thomas is saying is that it's about time for boys to learn stuff that has always been thought of as women's stuff."

Anthony said that although he respects what Thomas is doing, he 32 has other goals for himself. "I want to join the Navy," he said.

Thomas said that he had some specific areas on which he wanted to concentrate as national president of FHA. "I want to help develop and expand drug-abuse programs, programs about drinking and driving, programs about teen pregnancies. When people hear about Future Homemakers of America, they tend to think in terms of the cooking and sewing, and think that's it. But cooking and sewing is really only a small part of FHA. Those things are necessary, because everyone should know how to keep their own home going. FHA is really a lot more than that, though.

"I hope to get married and have two or three kids. That's one of the nice things about being one of the few boys in FHA—you really get to meet a lot of girls."

Thomas's mother had gone back into the kitchen, and now she returned to the living room.

"If everyone is ready, dinner is served," she said. 36

One more person had joined the group—Thomas's original home-ec teacher, who was also his FHA adviser. The group sat down around the table.

"Mr. Future Homemaker, I see you're letting your mother do all the work setting the food on the table," Thomas's stepfather said.

Thomas blushed and shook his head.

"Just kidding," his stepfather said.   40

A salad was the first course. Thomas's stepfather dripped some dressing on the table.

"Honey, watch," Thomas's mother said.

The home-ec teacher said, "Thomas, should we tell the story about the Jell-O?"

Thomas didn't say anything.   44

"Should we, Thomas?" she said.

"What story is that?" Thomas's mother said.

"The story about the time that Thomas burned the Jell-O," the home-ec teacher said. "Didn't Thomas ever tell you that story?"

"We don't hear about a lot of the things that Thomas does," his   48 stepfather said, laughing.

"I burned the Jell-O once," Thomas said, not amused.

Out in the living room the radio was still turned on to a country station, and as if by some corny cosmic joke, the song that happened to be playing was the old Johnny Cash number, "A Boy Named Sue." But under the circumstances it seemed terribly out of date and irrelevant— almost like something you would find in a time capsule. The spaghetti was served, and then Thomas's mother brought a cake to the table.

The group began to sing:

Happy birthday to you,
Happy birthday to you,
Happy birthday, President Lucas,
Happy birthday to you.

The cake was cut. "You drink coffee?" Thomas's mother said to   52 Thomas's friend Anthony.

"I do," Anthony said.

"I'm gonna tell your daddy," Thomas's mother said.   *1987*

23

Conflicting Loyalties

June Jordan, Waiting for a Taxi

Paula Gunn Allen, Where I Come from Is Like This

Scott Russell Sanders, The Men We Carry in Our Minds

In adolescence you don't split from your mother because you want to catapult into the outside world, the father's world, in which competitiveness and ambition and making it are the big things. In adolescence you *have* to split off; otherwise, you feel too dependent, too cozy, too loved, too comfortable. It's a search for your own voice. But now the struggle extends far beyond adolescence: it's a mass rejection of a whole generation of women by a younger generation of women. The younger women are often denying the feminine voice, and yet they can't take on the masculine voice either. This has led to tremendous difficulties in marriages—trying to find a new way to be in a relationship that's not the way it was, but has not yet evolved into something different.

Olga Silverstein, from *The Good Mother: An Interview with Olga Silverstein*

The Jewishness inside me is an education. I see more clearly, can think more inventively, because I can think analogously about "them" and "us." That particular knowledge of being one among the many is mine twice over. I have watched masters respond to "them" and "us," and I have learned. I wouldn't have missed being Jewish for the world. It lives in me as a vital subculture, enriching my life as a writer, as an American, and certainly as a woman.

**Vivian Gornick, from "Twice an Outsider:
On Being Jewish and a Woman"**

Psychoanalysis has taught us to look for personal constrictions in three general areas: love, work, and play. In all three areas feminist men regularly report feeling a lack of power and vitality. Many a feminist man is unable to stand up to a woman just when they both need him to. Or the man's lack of vitality might be reflected in his inability to come forth with his feelings and desires. Often the problem surfaces in the emotional turmoil of one or more of the couple's children. For instance, the father—whether living with the mother or divorced—might make a habit of bowing to the mother's will, which leaves the child to experience his father as passive or absent, and his mother as controlling. The man's inability to express his power with the woman is passed on as a problem to another generation. Alternatively, the single man's difficulties finding a partner might be related to the idea that, once he commits himself to a relationship, the partner will gain control of him and he will lose his personal freedom as well as his sense of identity.

Terry Allen Kupers, from *Feminist Men*

June Jordan

Waiting for a Taxi

We weren't doing anything. We hadn't hurt anybody, and we didn't want to. We were on holiday. We had studied maps of the city and taken hundreds of photographs. We had walked ourselves dizzy and stared at the other visitors and stammered out our barely Berlitz versions of a beautiful language. We had marveled at the convenient frequency of the Metro and devoured vegetarian crêpes from a sidewalk concession. Among ourselves, we extolled the seductive intelligence and sensual style of this Paris, this magical place to celebrate the two hundredth anniversary of the French Revolution, this obvious place to sit back with a good glass of wine and think about a world lit by longings for *Liberté, Egalité, Fraternité*.

It was raining. It was dark. It was late. We hurried along, punch-drunk with happiness and fatigue. Behind us, the Cathedral of the Sacred Heart glowed ivory and gorgeous in a flattering wash of artificial, mellow light.

These last hours of our last full day in Paris seemed to roll and slide into pleasure and surprise. I was happy. I was thinking that, as a matter of fact, the more things change, the more things change.

I was thinking that if we, all of us black, all of us women, all of us 4 deriving from connected varieties of peasant/immigrant/persecuted histories of struggle and significant triumph, if we could find and trust each other enough to travel together into a land where none of us belonged, nothing on Earth was impossible anymore.

But then we tried to get a cab to stop for us, and we failed. We tried again, and then again. One driver actually stopped and then, suddenly, he sped away almost taking with him the arm of one of my companions who had been about to open the door to his taxi.

This was a miserable conclusion to a day of so much tourist privilege and delight, a day of feeling powerful because to be a sightseer is to be completely welcome among strangers. And that's the trick of it: No one will say "no" to freely given admiration and respect. But now we had asked for something in return—a taxi. And with that single, ordinary request, the problems of our identity, our problems of power, reappeared and trashed our holiday confidence and joy.

I am looking for a way to catch a taxi. I am looking for an umbrella big enough to overcome the tactical and moral limitations of "identity politics"—politics based on gender, class, or race. I am searching for the language of a new political consciousness of identity.

Many of us function on the basis of habits of thought that automat- 8 ically concede paramount importance to race or class. These habits may, for example, correlate race with class in monolithic, absolute ways: i.e., white people have, black people have not, or, poor people equals black people. Although understandable, these dominating habits of thought tend to deny the full functions of race and class, both.

If we defer mainly to race, then what about realities of class that point to huge numbers of poor white people or severe differences of many kinds among various, sometimes conflicting classes of black people?

Or, if we attend primarily to factors of class, then we may mislead ourselves significantly by ignoring privileges inherent to white identity, per se, or the socially contemptible status of minority-group members regardless of class.

Both forms of analysis encourage exaggerated—or plainly mistaken—suppositions about racial or class grounds for political solidarity. Equally important, any exclusive mode of analysis will overlook, or obviate, the genuine potential for political unity across class and race boundaries.

Habits of racial and class analyses also deny universal functions of 12 gender which determine at least as much, if not more, about any citizen's psychological, economic, and physical life force and well-being. Focusing on racial *or* class *or* gender attributes will yield only distorted and deeply inadequate images of ourselves.

Traditional calls to "unity" on the basis of only one of these factors—race or class or gender—will fail, finally, and again and again, I believe, because no simple one of these components provides for a valid fathoming of the complete individual.

And yet, many of us persist in our race/class habits of thought. And why is that? We know the negative, the evil origins, the evil circumstances that have demanded our development of race and class analyses. For those of us born into a historically scorned and jeopardized status, our bodily survival testifies to the defensively positive meanings of race and class identity because we have created these positive implications as a source of self-defense.

We have wrested, we have invented positive consequences from facts of unequal conflict, facts of oppression. Facts such as I am black, or I do not have much money, or I am Lithuanian, or I am Senegalese, or I am a girl, or my father mends shoes, become necessary and crucial facts of race and class and gender inside the negative contexts of unequal conflict and the oppression of one group by another, the oppression of somebody weak by somebody more powerful.

Race and *class*, then, are not the same kinds of words as *grass* and 16 *stars*. *Gender* is not the same kind of noun as *sunlight*. *Grass*, *stars*, and *sunlight* all enjoy self-evident, positive connotations, everywhere on the planet. They are physical phenomena unencumbered by our knowledge or our experience of slavery, discrimination, rape, and murder. They do not presuppose an evil any one of us must seek to extirpate.

I am wondering if those of us who began our lives in difficult conditions defined by our race or our class or our gender identities, I am wondering if we can become more carefully aware of the limitations of race and class and gender analyses, for these yield only distorted and deeply inadequate images of ourselves.

There is another realm of possibility: political unity and human community based upon concepts that underlie or supersede relatively immutable factors of race, class, and gender: the concept of justice, the concept of equality, the concept of tenderness.

I rejoice to see that last year, more than eight million American voters—black and white and Latino and Asian and Native American and straight and gay and lesbian and working-class and Ivy League—voted for Jesse Jackson.

I rejoice to see that 300,000 people demonstrated for pro-choice 20 rights in Washington, D.C., on April 9, 1989. Of that 300,000, an estimated 100,000 who stood up for women's rights were men.

I rejoice at this good news, this happy evidence of moral and tactical outreach and response beyond identity politics. This is getting us where all of us need to go.

On the other hand, the hideous despoiling of Prince William Sound in Alaska, the Exxon spill of ten million gallons of oil contaminating 3,000 square miles of those previously clear and lovely waters, makes plain the total irrelevance—the dismal inadequacy—of identity politics, or even national politics. From the torn sky of Antarctica to the Port of Valdez in Alaska, we need vigilant, international agencies empowered to assure the survival of our life-supporting environments.

But we are creatures of habit. I consider myself fortunate, therefore, to keep coming upon immediate, personal events that challenge my inclinations toward a politics as preoccupied with the known old enemies as it is alert to the potential for new allies.

Less than a month ago, I traveled to Liverpool, England, for the first 24 time. I brought with me a selection of my poetry that includes poems written during the 1960s, during the civil rights revolution. I had heard about the poverty characteristic of much of Liverpool, but I was not ready for what I encountered face to face.

One of my hosts was Ruth Grosvenor, a young black woman who described herself, at lunch, as a half-caste Irish-Caribbean. I asked her for more detail about her family background, and she told me about her mother, who had grown up in Ireland so poor she regularly used to dig in the pig bins, searching for scraps of edible garbage. And for additional pennies, her mother was given soiled sanitary napkins to launder by hand.

Ruth's mother, of course, is white. I had lost my appetite, by now, completely, and I could not comprehend the evident cheeriness of Ruth, who had moved on in conversation to describe the building success of the Africa Art Collective in Liverpool that she codirects.

"But," I interrupted, "what about your mother? What has happened to her?"

"Oh," Ruth told me, instantly switching subjects but not altering her 28
bright and proselytizing tone, "my mother is very happy. She remarried,
and she has her own little flat, at last. And she has a telephone!"

I felt mortified by the contrast between what would allow me, a
black woman from America, to feel happy and the late and minimal
amenities that could ease the daily experience of a white woman living
in England. To speak with Ruth's mother, to speak for Ruth's mother, I
would certainly have to eschew facile notions of race and class correla-
tion. On the basis of class alone, Ruth's mother might very well distrust
or resent me. On the basis of race alone, I might very well be inclined to
distrust or resent Ruth's mother.

And yet, identity politics aside, we both had infinitely more to gain
as possible comrades joined against socioeconomic inequities than we
could conceivably benefit from hostilities exchanged in serious ignorance of each other.

After our lunch, we drove to the Liverpool public library, where I
was scheduled to read. By then, we were forty-five minutes late, and on
arrival we saw five middle-aged white women heading away toward an
old car across the street. When they recognized me, the women came
over and apologized: They were really sorry, they said, but they had to
leave or they'd get in trouble on the job. I looked at them. Every one of
them was wearing an inexpensive, faded housedress and, over that, a
cheap and shapeless cardigan sweater. I felt honored by their open-
mindedness in having wanted to come and listen to my poetry. I
thought and I said that it was I who should apologize: I was late. It was I
who felt, moreover, unprepared: What in my work, to date, deserves the
open-minded attention of blue-collar white women terrified by the
prospect of overstaying a union-guaranteed hour for lunch?

Two and a half weeks after Liverpool, I sat sorting through my 32
messages and mail at the university where I teach. One message kept
recurring: A young black man—the son, in fact, of a colleague—had
been accused of raping a young white woman. The message, as delivered
by my secretary, was this: Call so and so at once about the young black
man who supposedly raped some white woman.

I was appalled by the accusation leveled against the son of my
colleague. I was stunned to learn that yet another female student, of
whatever color, had been raped. I felt a kind of nausea overtaking me as
I reread the phone messages. They seemed to assume I would commit
myself to one side or the other, automatically. The sides, apparently,
were Young Black Man versus Young White Woman.

I got up from my desk and snatched the nearest newspaper I could
find. I needed to know more. As best I could tell, the young black

student could not have raped anybody; he has several witnesses who establish him off campus throughout the evening of the alleged assault. As far as I can tell, the young white woman had been raped and she was certain, if mistaken, about the face and the voice of her assailant.

I declined to make any public comment: I do not yet know what the truth of this terrible matter may be. I believe there is a likelihood of mistaken identification on the part of the victim. And I believe that such a mistake, if that is the case, will have created a second victim, the wrongly accused black student. But these are my opinions merely. And I cannot comprehend why or how anyone would expect me to choose between my gender and racial identities.

SOLIDARITY

for Angela

Even then
in the attenuated Light
of the Church of Le Sacré Coeur
(early evening and folk songs
on the mausoleum steps)
and armed
only with 2 Instamatic cameras
(not a terrorist among us)
even there
in that Parisian downpour
four
Black women (2 of Asian 2
of African descent)
could not catch a taxi
and
I wondered what umbrella
would be big enough to stop
the shivering
of our collective impotence
up
against such negligent
assault

And I wondered
who would build that shelter
who will build and lift it
high and wide
above
such loneliness.

—June Jordan

I do not agree that rape is less serious than any other heinous felony. 36
I do not agree that the skin color of a female victim shall alienate me
from a gender sense of unity and peril. I do not agree that the mistaken
accusation of a black man is less than a very serious crime. I do not
agree that the genuine gender concerns that I embody shall alienate me
from a racial sense of unity and peril.

But there is a route out of the paralysis of identity politics, even
here, in this ugly, heartbreaking crisis. There is available to me a moral
attachment to a concept beyond gender and race. I am referring to the
concept of justice, which I am prepared to embrace and monitor so that
justice shall equally serve the young black man and the young white
woman. It is that concept and it is on behalf of both the primary and the
possible second victim of yet another on-campus rape that I am willing
to commit my energies and my trust.

Returning to the recent rainy evening in Paris, I am still looking for
an umbrella big enough to overcome the tactical and moral limitations
of identity politics.

Yes, I am exhilarated by the holiday I enjoyed with my friends, and I
am proud of the intimate camaraderie we shared. But somebody, pretty
soon, needs to be talking, sisterly and brotherly, with the taxi drivers of
the world, as well.   *1989*

Paula Gunn Allen

Where I Come from Is Like This

I

Modern American Indian women, like their non-Indian sisters, are
deeply engaged in the struggle to redefine themselves. In their struggle
they must reconcile traditional tribal definitions of women with industrial and postindustrial non-Indian definitions. Yet while these definitions seem to be more or less mutually exclusive, Indian women must
somehow harmonize and integrate both in their own lives.

An American Indian woman is primarily defined by her tribal
identity. In her eyes, her destiny is necessarily that of her people, and
her sense of herself as a woman is first and foremost prescribed by her

tribe. The definitions of woman's roles are as diverse as tribal cultures in the Americas. In some she is devalued, in others she wields considerable power. In some she is a familial/clan adjunct, in some she is as close to autonomous as her economic circumstances and psychological traits permit. But in no tribal definitions is she perceived in the same way as are women in Western industrial and postindustrial cultures.

In the West, few images of women form part of the cultural mythos, and these are largely sexually charged. Among Christians, the Madonna is the female prototype, and she is portrayed as essentially passive: her contribution is simply that of birthing. Little else is attributed to her and she certainly possesses few of the characteristics that are attributed to mythic figures among Indian tribes. This image is countered (rather than balanced) by the witch-goddess/whore characteristics designed to reinforce cultural beliefs about women, as well as Western adversarial and dualistic perceptions of reality.

The tribes see women variously, but they do not question the power 4
of femininity. Sometimes they see women as fearful, sometimes peaceful, sometimes omnipotent and omniscient, but they never portray women as mindless, helpless, simple, or oppressed. And while the women in a given tribe, clan, or band may be all these things, the individual woman is provided with a variety of images of women from the interconnected supernatural, natural, and social worlds she lives in.

As a half-breed American Indian woman, I cast about in my mind for negative images of Indian women, and I find none that are directed to Indian women alone. The negative images I do have are of Indians in general and in fact are more often of males than of females. All these images come to me from non-Indian sources, and they are always balanced by a positive image. My ideas of womanhood, passed on largely by my mother and grandmothers, Laguna Pueblo women, are about practicality, strength, reasonableness, intelligence, wit, and competence. I also remember vividly the women who came to my father's store, the women who held me and sang to me, the women at Feast Day, at Grab Days, the women in the kitchen of my Cubero home, the women I grew up with; none of them appeared weak or helpless, none of them presented herself tentatively. I remember a certain reserve on those lovely brown faces; I remember the direct gaze of eyes framed by bright-colored shawls draped over their heads and cascading down their backs. I remember the clean cotton dresses and carefully pressed hand-embroidered aprons they always wore; I remember laughter and good food, especially the sweet bread and the oven bread they gave us. Nowhere in my mind is there a foolish woman, a dumb woman, a vain woman, or a plastic woman, though the Indian women I have known have shown a wide range of personal style and demeanor.

My memory includes the Navajo woman who was badly beaten by

her Sioux husband; but I also remember that my grandmother abandoned her Sioux husband long ago. I recall the stories about the Laguna
woman beaten regularly by her husband in the presence of her children
so that the children would not believe in the strength and power of
femininity. And I remember the women who drank, who got into fights
with other women and with the men, and who often won those battles. I
have memories of tired women, partying women, stubborn women,
sullen women, amicable women, selfish women, shy women, and aggressive women. Most of all I remember the women who laugh and scold
and sit uncomplaining in the long sun on feast days and who cook
wonderful food on wood stoves, in beehive mud ovens, and over open
fires outdoors.

Among the images of women that come to me from various tribes as
well as my own are White Buffalo Woman, who came to the Lakota long
ago and brought them the religion of the Sacred Pipe which they still
practice; Tinotzin the goddess who came to Juan Diego to remind him
that she still walked the hills of her people and sent him with her
message, her demand, and her proof to the Catholic bishop in the city
nearby. And from Laguna I take the images of Yellow Woman, Coyote
Woman, Grandmother Spider (Spider Old Woman), who brought the
light, who gave us weaving and medicine, who gave us life. Among the
Keres she is known as Thought Woman who created us all and who
keeps us in creation even now. I remember Iyatiku, Earth Woman, Corn
Woman, who guides and counsels the people to peace and who welcomes us home when we cast off this coil of flesh as huskers cast off the
leaves that wrap the corn. I remember Iyatiku's sister, Sun Woman, who
held metals and cattle, pigs and sheep, highways and engines and so
many things in her bundle, who went away to the east saying that one
day she would return.

II

Since the coming of the Anglo-Europeans beginning in the fifteenth   8
century, the fragile web of identity that long held tribal people secure
has gradually been weakened and torn. But the oral tradition has
prevented the complete destruction of the web, the ultimate disruption
of tribal ways. The oral tradition is vital; it heals itself and the tribal web
by adapting to the flow of the present while never relinquishing its
connection to the past. Its adaptability has always been required, as
many generations have experienced. Certainly the modern American
Indian woman bears slight resemblance to her forebears—at least on
superficial examination—but she is still a tribal woman in her deepest
being. Her tribal sense of relationship to all that is continues to flourish. And though she is at times beset by her knowledge of the enormous

gap between the life she lives and the life she was raised to live, and while she adapts her mind and being to the circumstances of her present life, she does so in tribal ways, mending the tears in the web of being from which she takes her existence as she goes.

My mother told me stories all the time, though I often did not recognize them as that. My mother told me stories about cooking and childbearing; she told me stories about menstruation and pregnancy; she told me stories about gods and heroes, about fairies and elves, about goddesses and spirits; she told me stories about the land and the sky, about cats and dogs, about snakes and spiders; she told me stories about climbing trees and exploring the mesas; she told me stories about going to dances and getting married; she told me stories about dressing and undressing, about sleeping and waking; she told me stories about herself, about her mother, about her grandmother. She told me stories about grieving and laughing, about thinking and doing; she told me stories about school and about people; about darning and mending; she told me stories about turquoise and about gold; she told me European stories and Laguna stories; she told me Catholic stories and Presbyterian stories; she told me city stories and country stories; she told me political stories and religious stories. She told me stories about living and stories about dying. And in all of those stories she told me who I was, who I was supposed to be, whom I came from, and who would follow me. In this way she taught me the meaning of the words she said, that all life is a circle and everything has a place within it. That's what she said and what she showed me in the things she did and the way she lives.

Of course, through my formal, white, Christian education, I discovered that other people had stories of their own—about women, about Indians, about fact, about reality—and I was amazed by a number of startling suppositions that others made about tribal customs and beliefs. According to the un-Indian, non-Indian view, for instance, Indians barred menstruating women from ceremonies and indeed segregated them from the rest of the people, consigning them to some space specially designed for them. This showed that Indians considered menstruating women unclean and not fit to enjoy the company of decent (nonmenstruating) people, that is, men. I was surprised and confused to hear this because my mother had taught me that white people had strange attitudes toward menstruation: they thought something was bad about it, that it meant you were sick, cursed, sinful, and weak and that you had to be very careful during that time. She taught me that menstruation was a normal occurrence, that I could go swimming or hiking or whatever else I wanted to do during my period. She actively scorned women who took to their beds, who were incapacitated by cramps, who "got the blues."

As I struggled to reconcile these very contradictory interpretations of American Indians' traditional beliefs concerning menstruation, I realized that the menstrual taboos were about power, not about sin or filth. My conclusion was later borne out by some tribes' own explanations, which, as you may well imagine, came as quite a relief to me.

The truth of the matter as many Indians see it is that women who 12 are at the peak of their fecundity are believed to possess power that throws male power totally out of kilter. They emit such force that, in their presence, any male-owned or -dominated ritual or sacred object cannot do its usual task. For instance, the Lakota say that a menstruating woman anywhere near a yuwipi man, who is a special sort of psychic, spirit-empowered healer, for a day or so before he is to do his ceremony will effectively disempower him. Conversely, among many if not most tribes, important ceremonies cannot be held without the presence of women. Sometimes the ritual woman who empowers the ceremony must be unmarried and virginal so that the power she channels is unalloyed, unweakened by sexual arousal and penetration by a male. Other ceremonies require tumescent women, others the presence of mature women who have borne children, and still others depend for empowerment on postmenopausal women. Women may be segregated from the company of the whole band or village on certain occasions, but on certain occasions men are also segregated. In short, each ritual depends on a certain balance of power, and the positions of women within the phases of womanhood are used by tribal people to empower certain rites. This does not derive from a male-dominant view; it is not a ritual observance imposed on women by men. It derives from a tribal view of reality that distinguishes tribal people from feudal and industrial people.

Among the tribes, the occult power of women, inextricably bound to our hormonal life, is thought to be very great; many hold that we possess innately the blood-given power to kill—with a glance, with a step, or with a judicious mixing of menstrual blood into somebody's soup. Medicine women among the Pomo of California cannot practice until they are sufficiently mature; when they are immature, their power is diffuse and is likely to interfere with their practice until time and experience have it under control. So women of the tribes are not especially inclined to see themselves as poor helpless victims of male domination. Even in those tribes where something akin to male domination was present, women are perceived as powerful, socially, physically, and metaphysically. In times past, as in times present, women carried enormous burdens with aplomb. We were far indeed from the "weaker sex," the designation that white aristocratic sisters unhappily earned for us all.

I remember my mother moving furniture all over the house when she wanted it changed. She didn't wait for my father to come home and help—she just went ahead and moved the piano, a huge upright from the old days, the couch, the refrigerator. Nobody had told her she was too weak to do such things. In imitation of her, I would delight in loading trucks at my father's store with cases of pop or fifty-pound sacks of flour. Even when I was quite small I could do it, and it gave me a belief in my own physical strength that advancing middle age can't quite erase. My mother used to tell me about the Acoma Pueblo women she had seen as a child carrying huge ollas (water pots) on their heads as they wound their way up the tortuous stairwell carved into the face of the "Sky City" mesa, a feat I tried to imitate with books and tin buckets. ("Sky City" is the term used by the chamber of commerce for the mother village of Acoma, which is situated atop a high sandstone table mountain.) I was never very successful, but even the attempt reminded me that I was supposed to be strong and balanced to be a proper girl.

Of course, my mother's Laguna people are Keres Indian, reputed to be the last extreme mother-right people on earth. So it is no wonder that I got notably nonwhite notions about the natural strength and prowess of women. Indeed, it is only when I am trying to get non-Indian approval, recognition, or acknowledgment that my "weak sister" emotional and intellectual ploys get the better of my tribal woman's good sense. At such times I forget that I just moved the piano or just wrote a competent paper or just completed a financial transaction satisfactorily or have supported myself and my children for most of my adult life.

Nor is my contradictory behavior atypical. Most Indian women I   16 know are in the same bicultural bind: we vacillate between being dependent and strong, self-reliant and powerless, strongly motivated and hopelessly insecure. We resolve the dilemma in various ways: some of us party all the time; some of us drink to excess; some of us travel and move around a lot; some of us land good jobs and then quit them; some of us engage in violent exchanges; some of us blow our brains out. We act in these destructive ways because we suffer from the societal conflicts caused by having to identify with two hopelessly opposed cultural definitions of women. Through this destructive dissonance we are unhappy prey to the self-disparagement common to, indeed demanded of, Indians living in the United States today. Our situation is caused by the exigencies of a history of invasion, conquest, and colonization whose searing marks are probably ineradicable. A popular bumper sticker on many Indian cars proclaims: "If You're Indian You're In," to which I always find myself adding under my breath, "Trouble."

III

No Indian can grow to any age without being informed that her people were "savages" who interfered with the march of progress pursued by respectable, loving, civilized white people. We are the villains of the scenario when we are mentioned at all. We are absent from much of white history except when we are calmly, rationally, succinctly, and systematically dehumanized. On the few occasions we are noticed in any way other than as howling, bloodthirsty beings, we are acclaimed for our noble quaintness. In this definition, we are exotic curios. Our ancient arts and customs are used to draw tourist money to state coffers, into the pocketbooks and bank accounts of scholars, and into support of the American-in-Disneyland promoters' dream.

As a Roman Catholic child I was treated to bloody tales of how the savage Indians martyred the hapless priests and missionaries who went among them in an attempt to lead them to the one true path. By the time I was through high school I had the idea that Indians were people who had benefited mightily from the advanced knowledge and superior morality of the Anglo-Europeans. At least I had, perforce, that idea to lay beside the other one that derived from my daily experience of Indian life, an idea less dehumanizing and more accurate because it came from my mother and the other Indian people who raised me. That idea was that Indians are a people who don't tell lies, who care for their children and their old people. You never see an Indian orphan, they said. You always know when you're old that someone will take care of you—one of your children will. Then they'd list the old folks who were being taken care of by this child or that. No child is ever considered illegitimate among the Indians, they said. If a girl gets pregnant, the baby is still part of the family, and the mother is too. That's what they said, and they showed me real people who lived according to those principles.

Of course the ravages of colonization have taken their toll; there are orphans in Indian country now, and abandoned, brutalized old folks; there are even illegitimate children, though the very concept still strikes me as absurd. There are battered children and neglected children, and there are battered wives and women who have been raped by Indian men. Proximity to the "civilizing" effects of white Christians has not improved the moral quality of life in Indian country, though each group, Indian and white, explains the situation differently. Nor is there much yet in the oral tradition that can enable us to adapt to these inhuman changes. But a force is growing in that direction, and it is helping Indian women reclaim their lives. Their power, their sense of direction and of self will soon be visible. It is the force of the women who speak and work and write, and it is formidable.

Through all the centuries of war and death and cultural and psy- 20 chic destruction have endured the women who raise the children and tend the fires, who pass along the tales and the traditions, who weep and bury the dead, who are the dead, and who never forget. There are always the women, who make pots and weave baskets, who fashion clothes and cheer their children on at powwow, who make fry bread and piki bread, and corn soup and chili stew, who dance and sing and remember and hold within their hearts the dream of their ancient peoples—that one day the woman who thinks will speak to us again, and everywhere there will be peace. Meanwhile we tell the stories of fun and scandal and laugh over all manner of things that happen every day. We watch and we wait.

My great-grandmother told my mother: Never forget you are Indian. And my mother told me the same thing. This, then, is how I have gone about remembering, so that my children will remember too.   *1986*

Scott Russell Sanders

The Men We Carry in Our Minds

"This must be a hard time for women," I say to my friend Anneke. "They have so many paths to choose from, and so many voices calling them."

"I think it's a lot harder for men," she replies.

"How do you figure that?"

"The women I know feel excited, innocent, like crusaders in a just cause. The men I know are eaten up with guilt."   4

We are sitting at the kitchen table drinking sassafras tea, our hands wrapped around the mugs because this April morning is cool and drizzly. "Like a Dutch morning," Anneke told me earlier. She is Dutch herself, a writer and midwife and peacemaker, with the round face and sad eyes of a woman in a Vermeer painting who might be waiting for the rain to stop, for a door to open. She leans over to sniff a sprig of lilac, pale lavender, that rises from a vase of cobalt blue.

"Women feel such pressure to be everything, do everything," I say. "Career, kids, art, politics. Have their babies and get back to the office a week later. It's as if they're trying to overcome a million years' worth of evolution in one lifetime."

"But we help one another. We don't try to lumber on alone, like so many wounded grizzly bears, the way men do." Anneke sips her tea. I gave her the mug with the owls on it, for wisdom. "And we have this deep-down sense that we're in the *right*—we've been held back, passed

over, used—while men feel they're in the wrong. Men are the ones
who've been discredited, who have to search their souls."

I search my soul. I discover guilty feelings aplenty—toward the   8
poor, the Vietnamese, Native Americans, the whales, an endless list of
debts—a guilt in each case that is as bright and unambiguous as a neon
sign. But toward women I feel something more confused, a snarl of
shame, envy, wary tenderness, and amazement. This muddle troubles
me. To hide my unease I say, "You're right, it's tough being a man these
days."

"Don't laugh." Anneke frowns at me, mournful-eyed, through the
sassafras steam. "I wouldn't be a man for anything. It's much easier
being the victim. All the victim has to do is break free. The persecutor
has to live with his past."

How deep is that past? I find myself wondering after Anneke has
left. How much of an inheritance do I have to throw off? Is it just the
beliefs I breathed in as a child? Do I have to scour memory back through
father and grandfather? Through St. Paul? Beyond Stonehenge and into
the twilit caves? I'm convinced the past we must contend with is deeper
even than speech. When I think back on my childhood, on how I
learned to see men and women, I have a sense of ancient, dizzying
depths. The back roads of Tennessee and Ohio where I grew up were
probably closer, in their sexual patterns, to the campsites of Stone Age
hunters than to the genderless cities of the future into which we are
rushing.

The first men, besides my father, I remember seeing were black
convicts and white guards, in the cottonfield across the road from our
farm on the outskirts of Memphis. I must have been three or four. The
prisoners wore dingy gray-and-black zebra suits, heavy as canvas, sod-
den with sweat. Hatless, stooped, they chopped weeds in the fierce heat,
row after row, breathing the acrid dust of boll-weevil poison. The
overseers wore dazzling white shirts and broad shadowy hats. The oiled
barrels of their shotguns flashed in the sunlight. Their faces in memory
are utterly blank. Of course those men, white and black, have become
for me an emblem of racial hatred. But they have also come to stand for
the twin poles of my early vision of manhood—the brute toiling animal
and the boss.

When I was a boy, the men I knew labored with their bodies. They   12
were marginal farmers, just scraping by, or welders, steelworkers, carpenters; they swept floors, dug ditches, mined coal, or drove trucks,
their forearms ropy with muscle; they trained horses, stoked furnaces,
built tires, stood on assembly lines wrestling parts onto cars and re-
frigerators. They got up before light, worked all day long whatever the
weather, and when they came home at night they looked as though
somebody had been whipping them. In the evenings and on weekends
they worked on their own places, tilling gardens that were lumpy with

clay, fixing broken-down cars, hammering on houses that were always too drafty, too leaky, too small.

The bodies of the men I knew were twisted and maimed in ways visible and invisible. The nails of their hands were black and split, the hands tattooed with scars. Some had lost fingers. Heavy lifting had given many of them finicky backs and guts weak from hernias. Racing against conveyor belts had given them ulcers. Their ankles and knees ached from years of standing on concrete. Anyone who had worked for long around machines was hard of hearing. They squinted, and the skin of their faces was creased like the leather of old work gloves. There were times, studying them, when I dreaded growing up. Most of them coughed, from dust or cigarettes, and most of them drank cheap wine or whiskey, so their eyes looked bloodshot and bruised. The fathers of my friends always seemed older than the mothers. Men wore out sooner. Only women lived into old age.

As a boy I also knew another sort of men, who did not sweat and break down like mules. They were soldiers, and so far as I could tell they scarcely worked at all. During my early school years we lived on a military base, an arsenal in Ohio, and every day I saw GIs in the guardshacks, on the stoops of barracks, at the wheels of olive drab Chevrolets. The chief fact of their lives was boredom. Long after I left the Arsenal I came to recognize the sour smell the soldiers gave off as that of souls in limbo. They were all waiting—for wars, for transfers, for leaves, for promotions, for the end of their hitch—like so many braves waiting for the hunt to begin. Unlike the warriors of older tribes, however, they would have no say about when the battle would start or how it would be waged. Their waiting was broken only when they practiced for war. They fired guns at targets, drove tanks across the churned-up fields of the military reservation, set off bombs in the wrecks of old fighter planes. I knew this was all play. But I also felt certain that when the hour for killing arrived, they would kill. When the real shooting started, many of them would die. This was what soldiers were *for*, just as a hammer was for driving nails.

Warriors and toilers: those seemed, in my boyhood vision, to be the chief destinies for men. They weren't the only destinies, as I learned from having a few male teachers, from reading books, and from watching television. But the men on television—the politicians, the astronauts, the generals, the savvy lawyers, the philosophical doctors, the bosses who gave orders to both soldiers and laborers—seemed as remote and unreal to me as the figures in tapestries. I could no more imagine growing up to become one of these cool, potent creatures than I could imagine becoming a prince.

A nearer and more hopeful example was that of my father, who had 16 escaped from a red-dirt farm to a tire factory, and from the assembly line to the front office. Eventually he dressed in a white shirt and tie.

He carried himself as if he had been born to work with his mind. But his body, remembering the earlier years of slogging work, began to give out on him in his fifties, and it quit on him entirely before he turned sixty-five. Even such a partial escape from man's fate as he had accomplished did not seem possible for most of the boys I knew. They joined the army, stood in line for jobs in the smoky plants, helped build highways. They were bound to work as their fathers had worked, killing themselves or preparing to kill others.

A scholarship enabled me not only to attend college, a rare enough feat in my circle, but even to study in a university meant for the children of the rich. Here I met for the first time young men who had assumed from birth that they would lead lives of comfort and power. And for the first time I met women who told me that men were guilty of having kept all the joys and privileges of the earth for themselves. I was baffled. What privileges? What joys? I thought about the maimed, dismal lives of most of the men back home. What had they stolen from their wives and daughters? The right to go five days a week, twelve months a year, for thirty or forty years to a steel mill or a coal mine? The right to drop bombs and die in war? The right to feel every leak in the roof, every gap in the fence, every cough in the engine, as a wound they must mend? The right to feel, when the lay-off comes or the plant shuts down, not only afraid but ashamed?

I was slow to understand the deep grievances of women. This was because, as a boy, I had envied them. Before college, the only people I had ever known who were interested in art or music or literature, the only ones who read books, the only ones who ever seemed to enjoy a sense of ease and grace were the mothers and daughters. Like the menfolk, they fretted about money, they scrimped and made-do. But, when the pay stopped coming in, they were not the ones who had failed. Nor did they have to go to war, and that seemed to me a blessed fact. By comparison with the narrow, ironclad days of fathers, there was an expansiveness, I thought, in the days of mothers. They went to see neighbors, to shop in town, to run errands at school, at the library, at church. No doubt, had I looked harder at their lives, I would have envied them less. It was not my fate to become a woman, so it was easier for me to see the graces. Few of them held jobs outside the home, and those who did filled thankless roles as clerks and waitresses. I didn't see, then, what a prison a house could be, since houses seemed to me brighter, handsomer places than any factory. I did not realize—because such things were never spoken of—how often women suffered from men's bullying. I did learn about the wretchedness of abandoned wives, single mothers, widows; but I also learned about the wretchedness of lone men. Even then I could see how exhausting it was for a mother to cater all day to the needs of young children. But if I had been asked, as a boy, to choose between tending a baby and tending a machine, I think I would have chosen the baby. (Having now tended both, I know I would choose the baby.)

So I was baffled when the women at college accused me and my sex of having cornered the world's pleasures. I think something like my bafflement has been felt by other boys (and by girls as well) who grew up in dirt-poor farm country, in mining country, in black ghettos, in Hispanic barrios, in the shadows of factories, in Third World nations—any place where the fate of men is as grim and bleak as the fate of women. Toilers and warriors. I realize now how ancient these identities are, how deep the tug they exert on men, the undertow of a thousand generations. The miseries I saw, as a boy, in the lives of nearly all men I continue to see in the lives of many—the body-breaking toil, the tedium, the call to be tough, the humiliating powerlessness, the battle for a living and for territory.

When the women I met at college thought about the joys and 20 privileges of men, they did not carry in their minds the sort of men I had known in my childhood. They thought of their fathers, who were bankers, physicians, architects, stockbrokers, the big wheels of the big cities. These fathers rode the train to work or drove cars that cost more than any of my childhood houses. They were attended from morning to night by female helpers, wives, and nurses and secretaries. They were never laid off, never short of cash at month's end, never lined up for welfare. These fathers made decisions that mattered. They ran the world.

The daughters of such men wanted to share in this power, this glory. So did I. They yearned for a say over their future, for jobs worthy of their abilities, for the right to live at peace, unmolested, whole. Yes, I thought, yes yes. The difference between me and these daughters was that they saw me, because of my sex, as destined from birth to become like their fathers, and therefore as an enemy to their desires. But I knew better. I wasn't an enemy, in fact or in feeling. I was an ally. If I had known, then, how to tell them so, would they have believed me? Would they now?   *1974*

Enduring Issues

24

Declarations of Independence

Thomas Jefferson, The Declaration
of Independence

Ho Chi Minh, Declaration of Independence
of the Democratic Republic of Viet-Nam

Elizabeth Cady Stanton, Declaration of
Sentiments and Resolutions

Martin Luther King, Jr., I Have a Dream

Men being, as has been said, by Nature, all free, equal and independent, no one can be put out of this Estate, and subjected to the Political Power of another, without his own *Consent.* The only way whereby any one devests himself of his Natural Liberty, and *puts on the bonds of Civil Society* is by agreeing with other Men to join and unite into a Community, for their comfortable, safe, and peaceable living one amongst another, in a secure Enjoyment of their Properties, and a greater Security against any that are not of it. This any number of Men may do, because it injures not the Freedom of the rest; they are left as they were in the Liberty of the State of Nature. When any number of Men have so *consented to make one Community* or Government, they are thereby presently incorporated, and make *one Body Politic* wherein the *Majority* have a Right to act and conclude the rest.

John Locke, from *Two Treatises of Government*

"We, the people." It is a very eloquent beginning. But when that document was completed on the seventeenth of September in 1787 I was not included in that "We, the people." I felt somehow for many years that George Washington and Alexander Hamilton, just left me out by mistake. But through the process of amendment, interpretation and court decision I have finally been included in "We, the people."

Barbara C. Jordan, from *Statement at Debate on*
Articles of Impeachment July 25, 1974

It is vain to expect virtue from women till they are in some degree independent of men; nay, it is vain to expect that strength of natural affection which would make them good wives and mothers. Whilst they are absolutely dependent on their husbands they will be cunning, mean, and selfish, and the men who can be gratified by the fawning fondness of spaniel-like affection have not much delicacy, for love is not to be bought, in any sense of the words; its silken wings are instantly shriveled up when anything beside a return in kind is sought.

Mary Wollstonecraft, from *Pernicious Effects which Arise*
from the Unnatural Distinctions Established in Society

Thomas Jefferson

The Declaration of Independence

When in the course of human events, it becomes necessary for one people to dissolve the political bands which have connected them with another, and to assume among the Powers of the earth, the separate and equal station to which the Laws of Nature and of Nature's God entitle them, a decent respect to the opinions of mankind requires that they should declare the causes which impel them to the separation.

We hold these truths to be self-evident, that all men are created equal, that they are endowed by their Creator with certain unalienable Rights, that among these are Life, Liberty and the pursuit of Happiness.

That to secure these rights, Governments are instituted among Men, deriving their just powers from the consent of the governed.

That whenever any Form of Government becomes destructive of 4
these ends, it is the Right of the People to alter or to abolish it, and to
institute a new Government, laying its foundation on such principles
and organizing its powers in such form, as to them shall seem most
likely to effect their Safety and Happiness. Prudence, indeed, will
dictate that Governments long established should not be changed for
light and transient causes; and accordingly all experience hath shown
that mankind are more disposed to suffer, while evils are sufferable,
than to right themselves by abolishing the forms to which they are
accustomed. But when a long train of abuses and usurpations pursuing
invariably the same Object evinces a design to reduce them under
absolute Despotism, it is their right, it is their duty, to throw off such
government, and to provide new Guards for their future security.

Such has been the patient sufferance of these Colonies; and such is
now the necessity which constrains them to alter their former Systems
of Government. The history of the present King of Great Britain is a
history of repeated injuries and usurpations, all having in direct object
the establishment of an absolute Tyranny over these States. To prove
this, let Facts be submitted to a candid world.

He has refused his Assent to Laws, the most wholesome and necessary for the public good.

He has forbidden his Governors to pass Laws of immediate and
pressing importance, unless suspended in their operation till his Assent
should be obtained; and when so suspended, he has utterly neglected to
attend to them.

He has refused to pass other Laws for the accommodation of large 8
districts of people, unless those people would relinquish the right of
Representation in the Legislature, a right inestimable to them and
formidable to tyrants only.

He has called together legislative bodies at places unusual, uncomfortable, and distant from the depository of their Public Records, for
the sole purpose of fatiguing them into compliance with his measures.

He has dissolved Representative Houses repeatedly, for opposing
with manly firmness his invasions on the rights of the people.

He has refused for a long time, after such dissolutions, to cause
others to be elected; whereby the Legislative Powers, incapable of Annihilation, have returned to the People at large for their exercise; the State
remaining in the mean time exposed to all the dangers of invasion from
without, and convulsions within.

He has endeavored to prevent the population of these States, for 12
that purpose obstructing the Laws of Naturalization of Foreigners;
refusing to pass others to encourage their migration hither, and raising
the conditions of new Appropriations of Lands.

He has obstructed the Administration of Justice, by refusing his Assent to Laws for establishing Judiciary Powers.

He has made Judges dependent on his Will alone, for the tenure of their offices, and the amount and payment of their salaries.

He has erected a multitude of New Offices, and sent hither swarms of Officers to harass our People, and eat out their substance.

He has kept among us, in time of peace, Standing Armies without 16 the consent of our Legislature.

He has affected to render the Military independent of and superior to the Civil Power.

He has combined with others to subject us to jurisdictions foreign to our constitution, and unacknowledged by our laws; giving his Assent to their acts of pretended Legislation:

For quartering large bodies of armed troops among us:

For protecting them, by a mock Trial, from Punishment for any 20 Murders which they should commit on the Inhabitants of these States:

For cutting off our Trade with all parts of the world:

For imposing Taxes on us without our Consent:

For depriving us in many cases, of the benefits of Trial by Jury:

For transporting us beyond Seas to be tried for pretended offenses: 24

For abolishing the free System of English Laws in a Neighbouring Province, establishing therein an Arbitrary government, and enlarging its boundaries so as to render it at once an example and fit instrument for introducing the same absolute rule into these Colonies:

For taking away our Charters, abolishing our most valuable Laws, and altering fundamentally the Forms of our Governments.

For suspending our own Legislatures, and declaring themselves invested with Power to legislate for us in all cases whatsoever.

He has abdicated Government here, by declaring us out of his 28 Protection and waging War against us.

He has plundered our seas, ravaged our Coasts, burnt our towns and destroyed the Lives of our people.

He is at this time transporting large Armies of foreign Mercenaries to compleat the works of death, desolation and tyranny, already begun with circumstances of Cruelty & perfidy scarcely paralleled in the most barbarous ages, and totally unworthy the Head of a civilized nation.

He has constrained our fellow Citizens taken Captive on the high Seas to bear Arms against their Country, to become the executioners of their friends and Brethren, or to fall themselves by their Hands.

He has excited domestic insurrections amongst us, and has endeav- 32 ored to bring on the inhabitants of our frontiers, the merciless Indian Savages, whose known rule of warfare, is an undistinguished destruction of all ages, sexes and conditions.

In every stage of these Oppressions We Have Petitioned for Redress in the most humble terms: Our repeated petitions have been answered only by repeated injury. A Prince, whose character is thus marked by every act which may define a Tyrant, is unfit to be the ruler of a free People.

Nor have We been wanting in attention to our British brethren. We have warned them from time to time of attempts by their legislature to extend an unwarrantable jurisdiction over us. We have reminded them of the circumstances of our emigration and settlement here. We have appealed to their native justice and magnanimity and we have conjured them by the ties of our common kindred to disavow these usurpations, which would inevitably interrupt our connections and correspondence. They too have been deaf to the voice of justice and consanguinity. We must, therefore, acquiesce in the necessity, which denounces our Separation, and hold them, as we hold the rest of mankind, Enemies in War, in Peace Friends.

We, therefore, the Representatives of the United States of America, in General Congress, Assembled, appealing to the Supreme Judge of the world for the rectitude of our intentions, do, in the Name, and by Authority of the good People of these Colonies, solemnly publish and declare, That these United Colonies are, and of Right ought to be, Free and Independent States; that they are Absolved from all Allegiance to the British Crown, and that all political connection between them and the State of Great Britain, is and ought to be totally dissolved; and that as Free and Independent States, they have full power to levy War, conclude Peace, contract Alliances, establish Commerce, and to do all other Acts and Things which Independent States may of right do. And for the support of this Declaration, with a firm reliance on the protection of Divine Providence, we mutually pledge to each other our lives, our Fortunes, and our sacred Honor.   *1776*

Ho Chi Minh

Declaration of Independence of the Democratic Republic of Viet-Nam

All men are created equal; they are endowed by their Creator with certain unalienable Rights; among these are Life, Liberty, and the pursuit of Happiness.

This immortal statement was made in the Declaration of Independence of the United States of America in 1776. In a broader sense, this means: All the peoples on the earth are equal from birth, all the peoples have a right to live, to be happy and free.

The Declaration of the French Revolution made in 1791 on the Rights of Man and the Citizen also states: "All men are born free and with equal rights, and must always remain free and have equal rights."

Those are undeniable truths. 4

Nevertheless, for more than eighty years, the French imperialists, abusing the standard of Liberty, Equality, and Fraternity have violated our Fatherland and oppressed our fellow citizens. They have acted contrary to the ideals of humanity and justice.

In the field of politics, they have deprived our people of every democratic liberty.

They have enforced inhuman laws; they have set up three distinct political regimes in the North, the Center, and the South of Viet-Nam in order to wreck our national unity and prevent our people from being united.

They have built more prisons than schools. They have mercilessly 8 slain our patriots; they have drowned our uprisings in rivers of blood.

They have fettered public opinion; they have practiced obscurantism against our people.

To weaken our race they have forced us to use opium and alcohol.

In the field of economics, they have fleeced us to the backbone, impoverished our people and devastated our land.

They have robbed us of our rice fields, our mines, our forests, and 12 our raw materials. They have monopolized the issuing of bank notes and the export trade.

They have invented numerous unjustifiable taxes and reduced our people, especially our peasantry, to a state of extreme poverty.

They have hampered the prospering of our national bourgeoisie; they have mercilessly exploited our workers.

In the autumn of 1940, when the Japanese fascists violated Indochina's territory to establish new bases in their fight against the Allies, the French imperialists went down on their bended knees and handed over our country to them.

Thus, from that date, our people were subjected to the double yoke 16 of the French and the Japanese. Their sufferings and miseries increased. The result was that, from the end of last year to the beginning of this year, from Quang Tri Province to the North of Viet-Nam, more than two million of our fellow citizens died from starvation. On March 9 [1945], the French troops were disarmed by the Japanese. The French colonialists either fled or surrendered, showing that not only were they incapable of "protecting" us, but that, in the span of five years, they had twice sold our country to the Japanese.

On several occasions before March 9, the Viet Minh League urged the French to ally themselves with it against the Japanese. Instead of agreeing to this proposal, the French colonialists so intensified their terrorist activities against the Viet Minh members that before fleeing they massacred a great number of our political prisoners detained at Yen Bay and Cao Bang.

Notwithstanding all this, our fellow citizens have always manifested toward the French a tolerant and humane attitude. Even after the Japanese *Putsch*[1] of March, 1945, the Viet Minh League helped many Frenchmen to cross the frontier, rescued some of them from Japanese jails, and protected French lives and property.

From the autumn of 1940, our country had in fact ceased to be a French colony and had become a Japanese possession.

After the Japanese had surrendered to the Allies, our whole people 20 rose to regain our national sovereignty and to found the Democratic Republic of Viet-Nam.

The truth is that we have wrested our independence from the Japanese and not from the French.

The French have fled, the Japanese have capitulated, Emperor Bao Dai has abdicated. Our people have broken the chains which for nearly a century have fettered them and have won independence for the Fatherland. Our people at the same time have overthrown the monarchic regime that has reigned supreme for dozens of centuries. In its place has been established the present Democratic Republic.

For these reasons, we, members of the Provisional Government, representing the whole Vietnamese people, declare that from now on we break off all relations of a colonial character with France; we repeal all the international obligation that France has so far subscribed to on behalf of Viet-Nam, and we abolish all the special rights the French have unlawfully acquired in our Fatherland.

---

[1]***Putsch***: A sudden revolt or uprising—Eds.

The whole Vietnamese people, animated by a common purpose, are 24
determined to fight to the bitter end against any attempt by the French
colonialists to reconquer their country.

We are convinced that the Allied nations, which at Teheran and San
Francisco have acknowledged the principles of self-determination and
equality of nations, will not refuse to acknowledge the independence of
Viet-Nam.

A people who have courageously opposed French domination for
more than eighty years, a people who have fought side by side with the
Allies against the fascists during these last years, such a people must be
free and independent.

For these reasons, we, members of the Provisional Government of
the Democratic Republic of Viet-Nam, solemnly declare to the world
that Viet-Nam has the right to be a free and independent country—and
in fact it is so already. The entire Vietnamese people are determined to
mobilize all their physical and mental strength, to sacrifice their lives
and property in order to safeguard their independence and liberty.

1945

Elizabeth Cady Stanton

Declaration of Sentiments and Resolutions

When, in the course of human events, it becomes necessary for one
portion of the family of man to assume among the people of the earth a
position different from that which they have hitherto occupied, but one
to which the laws of nature and of nature's God entitle them, a decent
respect to the opinions of mankind requires that they should declare
the causes that impel them to such a course.

We hold these truths to be self-evident: that all men and women are
created equal; that they are endowed by their Creator with certain
inalienable rights; that among these are life, liberty, and the pursuit of
happiness; that to secure these rights governments are instituted, deriving their just powers from the consent of the governed. Whenever any
form of government becomes destructive of these ends, it is the right of
those who suffer from it to refuse allegiance to it, and to insist upon the
institution of a new government, laying its foundation on such principles, and organizing its powers in such form, as to them shall seem most

likely to effect their safety and happiness. Prudence, indeed, will dictate that governments long established should not be changed for light
and transient causes; and accordingly all experience hath shown that
mankind are more disposed to suffer, while evils are sufferable, than to
right themselves by abolishing the forms to which they were accustomed. But when a long train of abuses and usurpations, pursuing
invariably the same object, evinces a design to reduce them under
absolute despotism, it is their duty to throw off such government, and to
provide new guards for their future security. Such has been the patient
sufferance of the women under this government, and such is now the
necessity which constrains them to demand the equal station to which
they are entitled.

The history of mankind is a history of repeated injuries and usurpations on the part of man toward woman, having in direct object the
establishment of an absolute tyranny over her. To prove this, let facts be
submitted to a candid world.

He has never permitted her to exercise her inalienable right to the   4
elective franchise.

He has compelled her to submit to laws, in the formation of which
she had no voice.

He has withheld from her rights which are given to the most ignorant and degraded men—both natives and foreigners.

Having deprived her of this first right of a citizen, the elective
franchise, thereby leaving her without representation in the halls of
legislation, he has oppressed her on all sides.

He has made her, if married, in the eye of the law, civilly dead.   8

He has taken from her all right in property, even to the wages she
earns.

He has made her, morally, an irresponsible being, as she can commit many crimes with impunity, provided they be done in the presence
of her husband. In the covenant of marriage, she is compelled to
promise obedience to her husband, he becoming to all intents and
purposes, her master—the law giving him power to deprive her of her
liberty, and to administer chastisement.

He has so framed the laws of divorce, as to what shall be the proper
causes, and in case of separation, to whom the guardianship of the
children shall be given, as to be wholly regardless of the happiness of
women—the law, in all cases, going upon a false supposition of the
supremacy of man, and giving all power into his hands.

After depriving her of all rights as a married woman, if single, and   12
the owner of property, he has taxed her to support a government which
recognizes her only when her property can be made profitable to it.

He has monopolized nearly all the profitable employments, and
from those she is permitted to follow, she receives but a scanty re-

muneration. He closes against her all the avenues to wealth and distinction which he considers most honorable to himself. As a teacher of theology, medicine, or law, she is not known.

He has denied her the facilities for obtaining a thorough education, all colleges being closed against her.

He allows her in Church, as well as State, but a subordinate position, claiming Apostolic authority for her exclusion from the ministry, and, with some exceptions, from any public participation in the affairs of the Church.

He has created a false public sentiment by giving to the world a   16
different code of morals for men and women, by which moral delinquencies which exclude women from society, are not only tolerated, but deemed of little account in man.

He has usurped the prerogative of Jehovah himself, claiming it as his right to assign for her a sphere of action, when that belongs to her conscience and to her God.

He has endeavored, in every way that he could, to destroy her confidence in her own powers, to lessen her self-respect, and to make her willing to lead a dependent and abject life.

Now, in view of this entire disfranchisement of one-half the people of this country, their social and religious degradation—in view of the unjust laws above mentioned, and because women do feel themselves aggrieved, oppressed, and fraudulently deprived of their most sacred rights, we insist that they have immediate admission to all the rights and privileges which belong to them as citizens of the United States.

In entering upon the great work before us, we anticipate no small   20
amount of misconception, misrepresentation, and ridicule; but we shall use every instrumentality within our power to effect our object. We shall employ agents, circulate tracts, petition the State and National legislatures, and endeavor to enlist the pulpit and the press in our behalf. We hope this Convention will be followed by a series of Conventions embracing every part of this country.

[The following resolutions were discussed by Lucretia Mott, Thomas and Mary Ann McClintock, Amy Post, Catharine A. F. Stebbins, and others, and were adopted:]

Whereas, The great precept of nature is conceded to be, that "man shall pursue his own true and substantial happiness." Blackstone in his Commentaries remarks, that this law of Nature being coeval with mankind, and dictated by God himself, is of course superior in obligation to any other. It is binding over all the globe, in all countries, and at all times; no human laws are of any validity if contrary to this, and such of them as are valid, derive all their force, and all their validity, and all their authority, mediately and immediately, from this original; therefore,

Resolved, That such laws as conflict, in any way, with the true and substantial happiness of woman, are contrary to the great precept of nature and of no validity, for this is "superior in obligation to any other."

Resolved, That all laws which prevent woman from occupying such a station in society as her conscience shall dictate, or which place her in a position inferior to that of man, are contrary to the great precept of nature, and therefore of no force or authority.

Resolved, That woman is man's equal—was intended to be so by the 24 Creator, and the highest good of the race demands that she should be recognized as such.

Resolved, That the women of this country ought to be enlightened in regard to the laws under which they live, that they may no longer publish their degradation by declaring themselves satisfied with their present position, nor their ignorance, by asserting that they have all the rights they want.

Resolved, That inasmuch as man, while claiming for himself intellectual superiority, does accord to woman moral superiority, it is preeminently his duty to encourage her to speak and teach, as she has an opportunity, in all religious assemblies.

Resolved, That the same amount of virtue, delicacy, and refinement of behavior that is required of woman in the social state, should also be required of man, and the same transgressions should be visited with equal severity on both man and woman.

Resolved, That the objection of indelicacy and impropriety, which is 28 so often brought against woman when she addresses a public audience, comes with a very ill-grace from those who encourage, by their attendance, her appearance on the stage, in the concert, or in feats of the circus.

Resolved, That woman has too long rested satisfied in the circumscribed limits which corrupt customs and a perverted application of the Scriptures have marked out for her, and that it is time she should move in the enlarged sphere which her great Creator has assigned her.

Resolved, That it is the duty of the women of this country to secure to themselves their sacred right to the elective franchise.

Resolved, That the equality of human rights results necessarily from the fact of the identity of the race in capabilities and responsibilities.

Resolved, therefore, That, being invested by the Creator with the same 32 capabilities, and the same consciousness of responsibility for their exercise, it is demonstrably the right and duty of woman, equally with man, to promote every righteous cause by every righteous means; and especially in regard to the great subjects of morals and religion, it is self-evidently her right to participate with her brother in teaching them, both in private and in public, by writing and by speaking, by any instrumentalities proper to be used, and in any assemblies proper to be held; and this being a self-evident truth growing out of the divinely implanted principles of human nature, any custom or authority adverse to it, whether modern or wearing the hoary sanction of antiquity, is to be regarded as a self-evident falsehood, and at war with mankind.

[At the last session Lucretia Mott offered and spoke to the following resolution:]

Resolved, That the speedy success of our cause depends upon the zealous and untiring efforts of both men and women, for the overthrow of the monopoly of the pulpit, and for the securing to woman an equal participation with men in the various trades, professions, and commerce.   *1848*

Martin Luther King, Jr.

I Have a Dream

I am happy to join with you today in what will go down in history as the greatest demonstration for freedom in the history of our nation.

Five score years ago, a great American, in whose symbolic shadow we stand today, signed the Emancipation Proclamation. This momentous decree came as a great beacon light of hope to millions of Negro slaves who had been seared in the flames of withering injustice. It came as a joyous daybreak to end the long night of their captivity. But one hundred years later, the Negro still is not free. One hundred years later, the life of the Negro is still sadly crippled by the manacles of segregation and the chains of discrimination. One hundred years later, the Negro lives on a lonely island of poverty in the midst of a vast ocean of material prosperity. One hundred years later, the Negro is still anguished in the corners of American society and finds himself in exile in his own land. And so we have come here today to dramatize a shameful condition.

In a sense we have come to our nation's capital to cash a check. When the architects of our republic wrote the magnificent words of the Constitution and the Declaration of Independence, they were signing a promissory note to which every American was to fall heir. This note was the promise that all men—yes, black men as well as white men—would be guaranteed the inalienable rights of life, liberty, and the pursuit of happiness.

It is obvious today that America has defaulted on this promissory 4 note insofar as her citizens of color are concerned. Instead of honoring this sacred obligation, America has given the Negro people a bad check, a check which has come back marked "insufficient funds." But we refuse to believe that the bank of justice is bankrupt. We refuse to believe that there are insufficient funds in the great vaults of opportunity of this nation; and so we have come to cash this check, a check that will give us upon demand the riches of freedom and the security of justice.

We have also come to this hallowed spot to remind America of the fierce urgency of *now*. This is no time to engage in the luxury of cooling off or to take the tranquilizing drug of gradualism. *Now* is the time to make real the promises of democracy. *Now* is the time to rise from the dark and desolate valley of segregation to the sunlit path of racial justice. *Now* is the time to lift our nation from the quicksands of racial injustice to the solid rock of brotherhood. *Now* is the time to make justice a reality for all of God's children.

It would be fatal for the nation to overlook the urgency of the moment. This sweltering summer of the Negro's legitimate discontent will not pass until there is an invigorating autumn of freedom and equality. Nineteen sixty-three is not an end, but a beginning. And those who hope that the Negro needed to blow off steam and will now be content will have a rude awakening if the nation returns to business as usual. There will be neither rest nor tranquility in America until the Negro is granted his citizenship rights. The whirlwinds of revolt will continue to shake the foundations of our nation until the bright day of justice emerges.

But there is something that I must say to my people who stand on the warm threshold which leads into the palace of justice. In the process of gaining our rightful place, we must not be guilty of wrongful deeds. Let us not seek to satisfy our thirst for freedom by drinking from the cup of bitterness and hatred. We must forever conduct our struggle on the high plane of dignity and discipline. We must not allow our creative protest to degenerate into physical violence. Again and again we must rise to the majestic heights of meeting physical force with soul force. And the marvelous new militancy which has engulfed the Negro community must not lead us to a distrust of all white people; for many of our white brothers, as evidenced by their presence here today, have come to realize that their destiny is tied up with our destiny, and they have come to realize that their freedom is inextricably bound to our freedom.

We cannot walk alone. And as we walk we must make the pledge that   8 we shall always march ahead. We cannot turn back. There are those who are asking the devotees of civil rights, "When will you be satisfied?" We can never be satisfied as long as the Negro is the victim of the unspeakable horrors of police brutality. We can never be satisfied as long as our bodies, heavy with the fatigue of travel, cannot gain lodging in the motels of the highways and the hotels of the cities. We cannot be satisfied as long as the Negro's basic mobility is from a smaller ghetto to a larger one. We can never be satisfied as long as our children are stripped of their selfhood and robbed of their dignity by signs stating "For Whites Only." We cannot be satisifed as long as the Negro in Mississippi cannot vote and a Negro in New York believes he has nothing for which to vote. No, no, we are not satisfied, and we will not be satisfied until justice rolls down like waters and righteousness like a mighty stream.

I am not unmindful that some of you have come here out of great trials and tribulations. Some of you have come fresh from narrow jail cells. Some of you have come from areas where your quest for freedom left you battered by the storms of persecution and staggered by the winds of police brutality. You have been the veterans of creative suffering. Continue to work with the faith that unearned suffering is redemptive.

Go back to Mississippi, and go back to Alabama. Go back to South Carolina. Go back to Georgia. Go back to Louisiana. Go back to the slums and ghettos of our Northern cities, knowing that somehow this situation can and will be changed. Let us not wallow in the valley of despair.

I say to you today, my friends, even though we face the difficulties of today and tomorrow, I still have a dream. It is a dream deeply rooted in the American dream. I have a dream that one day this nation will rise up and live out the true meaning of its creed: "We hold these truths to be self-evident, that all men are created equal." I have a dream that one day, on the red hills of Georgia, sons of former slaves and the sons of former slave owners will be able to sit down together at the table of brotherhood. I have a dream that one day even the state of Mississippi, a state sweltering with the heat of injustice, sweltering with the heat of oppression, will be transformed into an oasis of freedom and justice. I have a dream that my four little children will one day live in a nation where they will not be judged by the color of their skin, but by the content of their character.

I have a dream today. I have a dream that one day down in Alabama—with its vicious racists, with its governor's lips dripping with the words of interposition and nullification—one day right there in Alabama, little black boys and black girls will be able to join hands with little white boys and white girls as sisters and brothers.

I have a dream today. I have a dream that one day every valley shall be exalted and every hill and mountain shall be made low, the rough places will be made plain and the crooked places will be made straight, and the glory of the Lord shall be revealed, and all flesh shall see it together.

This is our hope. This is the faith that I go back to the South with. And with this faith we will be able to hew out of the mountain of despair a stone of hope. With this faith we will be able to transform the jangling discords of our nation into a beautiful symphony of brotherhood. With this faith we will be able to work together, to play together, to struggle together, to go to jail together, to stand up for freedom together, knowing that we will be free one day.

And this will be the day—this will be the day when all of God's children will be able to sing with new meaning.

My country, 'tis of thee,
Sweet land of liberty,
Of thee I sing;
Land where my fathers died,
Land of the Pilgrims' pride,
From every mountainside
Let freedom ring.

And if America is to be a great nation, this must become true.

And so let freedom ring from the prodigious hilltops of New Hampshire. Let freedom ring from the mighty mountains of New York. Let freedom ring from the heightening Alleghenies of Pennsylvania. Let freedom ring from the snow-capped Rockies of Colorado. Let freedom ring from the curvaceous slopes of California.

But not only that. Let freedom ring from Stone Mountain of Georgia. Let freedom ring from Lookout Mountain of Tennessee. Let freedom ring from every hill and molehill of Mississippi. "From every mountainside let freedom ring."

And when this happens—when we allow freedom to ring, when we let it ring from every village and every hamlet, from every state and every city—we will be able to speed up that day when all of God's children, black men and white men, Jews and Gentiles, Protestants and Catholics, will be able to join hands and sing in the words of the old Negro spiritual: "Free at last! Free at last! Thank God Almighty. We are free at last!"   *1963*

25

The Debate on Abortion

Judith Jarvis Thomson, A Defense
of Abortion

Richard Selzer, What I Saw at the Abortion

Ellen Willis, Putting Women Back into the
Abortion Debate

Of the many actual points of view, it is widely held—especially in the
media, which rarely have the time or the inclination to make fine
distinctions—that there are only two: "pro-choice" and "pro-life." This
is what the two principal warring camps like to call themselves, and
that's what we'll call them here. In the simplest characterization, a pro-
choicer would hold that the decision to abort a pregnancy is to be made
only by the woman; the state has no right to interfere. And a pro-lifer
would hold that, from the moment of conception, the embryo or fetus is
alive; that this life imposes on us a moral obligation to preserve it; and
that abortion is tantamount to murder. Both names—pro-choice and
pro-life—were picked with an eye toward influencing those whose
minds are not yet made up: Few people wish to be counted as being
against freedom of choice or as opposed to life. Indeed, freedom and
life are two of our most cherished values, and here they seem to be in
fundamental conflict.

Carl Sagan and Ann Druyan, from *Is It Possible to Be Pro-Life* and *Pro-Choice?*

Once I believed that there was a little blob of formless protoplasm in
there and a gynecologist went after it with a surgical instrument, and
that was that. Then I got pregnant myself—eagerly, intentionally, by the
right man, at the right time—and I began to doubt. My abdomen still

flat, my stomach roiling with morning sickness, I felt not that I had protoplasm inside but instead a complete human being in miniature to whom I could talk, sing, make promises. Neither of these views was accurate; instead, I think, the reality is something in the middle. And that is where I find myself now, in the middle, hating the idea of abortions, hating the idea of having them outlawed.

Anna Quindlen, from "Hers," *The New York Times*

"It's really an awfully simple operation, Jig," the man said. "It's not really an operation at all."

The girl looked at the ground the table legs rested on.

"I know you wouldn't mind it, Jig. It's really not anything. It's just to let the air in."

The girl did not say anything.

"I'll go with you and I'll stay with you all the time. They just let the air in and then it's all perfectly natural."

"Then what will we do afterward?"

"We'll be fine afterward. Just like we were before."

"What makes you think so?"

Ernest Hemingway, from *Hills like White Elephants*

If men could get pregnant, abortion would be a sacrament.

Florynce C. Kennedy, from *The Verbal Karate*
of Florynce C. Kennedy, Esq.

Judith Jarvis Thomson
A Defense of Abortion

Most opposition to abortion relies on the premise that the fetus is a human being, a person, from the moment of conception. The premise is argued for, but, as I think, not well. Take, for example, the most common argument. We are asked to notice that the development of a human being from conception through birth into childhood is continuous; then it is said that to draw a line, to choose a point in this development and say "before this point the thing is not a person, after this point it is a person" is to make an arbitrary choice, a choice for which in the nature of things no good reason can be given. It is concluded that the fetus is, or anyway that we had better say it is, a person from the moment of conception. But this conclusion does not follow. Similar things might be said about the development of an acorn into an oak tree, and it does not follow that acorns are oak trees, or that we had better say they are. Arguments of this form are sometimes called "slippery slope arguments"—the phrase is perhaps self-explanatory—and it is dismaying that opponents of abortion rely on them so heavily and uncritically.[1]

I am inclined to agree, however, that the prospects for "drawing a line" in the development of the fetus look dim. I am inclined to think also that we shall probably have to agree that the fetus has already become a human person well before birth. Indeed, it comes as a surprise when one first learns how early in its life it begins to acquire human characteristics. By the tenth week, for example, it already has a face, arms and legs, fingers and toes; it has internal organs, and brain activity is detectable.[2] On the other hand, I think that the premise is false, that the fetus is not a person from the moment of conception. A newly fertilized ovum, a newly implanted clump of cells, is no more a person than an acorn is an oak tree. But I shall not discuss any of this. For it seems to me to be of great interest to ask what happens if, for the sake of argument, we allow the premise. How, precisely, are we supposed to get from there to the conclusion that abortion is morally impermissible? Opponents of abortion commonly spend most of their time establishing that the fetus is a person, and hardly any time explaining the step from there to the impermissibility of abortion. Perhaps they think the step too simple and obvious to require much comment. Or perhaps instead they are simply being economical in argument. Many of those who defend abortion rely on the premise that the fetus is not a person, but only a bit of tissue that will become a person at birth; and why pay out more arguments than you have to? Whatever the explanation, I suggest that the step they take is neither easy nor obvious, that it calls for closer examination than it is commonly given, and that when we do give it this closer examination we shall feel inclined to reject it.

---

[1] I am very much indebted to James Thomson for discussion, criticism, and many helpful suggestions.

[2] Daniel Callahan, *Abortion: Law, Choice and Morality* (New York, 1970), p. 373. This book gives a fascinating survey of the available information on abortion. The Jewish tradition is surveyed in David M. Feldman, *Birth Control in Jewish Law* (New York, 1968), Part 5; the Catholic tradition in John T. Noonan, Jr., "An Almost Absolute Value in History," in *The Morality of Abortion*, ed. John T. Noonan, Jr. (Cambridge, Mass., 1970).

I propose, then, that we grant that the fetus is a person from the moment of conception. How does the argument go from here? Something like this, I take it. Every person has a right to life. So the fetus has a right to life. No doubt the mother has a right to decide what shall happen in and to her body; everyone would grant that. But surely a person's right to life is stronger and more stringent than the mother's right to decide what happens in and to her body, and so outweighs it. So the fetus may not be killed; an abortion may not be performed.

It sounds plausible. But now let me ask you to imagine this. You   4 wake up in the morning and find yourself back to back in bed with an unconscious violinist. A famous unconscious violinist. He has been found to have a fatal kidney ailment, and the Society of Music Lovers has canvassed all the available medical records and found that you alone have the right blood type to help. They have therefore kidnapped you, and last night the violinist's circulatory system was plugged into yours, so that your kidneys can be used to extract poisons from his blood as well as your own. The director of the hospital now tells you, "Look, we're sorry the Society of Music Lovers did this to you—we would never have permitted it if we had known. But still, they did it, and the violinist now is plugged into you. To unplug you would be to kill him. But never mind, it's only for nine months. By then he will have recovered from his ailment, and can safely be unplugged from you." Is it morally incumbent on you to accede to this situation? No doubt it would be very nice of you if you did, a great kindness. But do you *have* to accede to it? What if it were not nine months, but nine years? Or longer still? What if the director of the hospital says, "Tough luck, I agree, but you've now got to stay in bed, with the violinist plugged into you, for the rest of your life. Because remember this. All persons have a right to life, and violinists are persons. Granted you have a right to decide what happens in and to your body, but a person's right to life outweighs your right to decide what happens in and to your body. So you cannot ever be unplugged from him." I imagine you would regard this as outrageous, which suggests that something really is wrong with the plausible-sounding argument I mentioned a moment ago.

In this case, of course, you were kidnapped; you didn't volunteer for the operation that plugged the violinist into your kidneys. Can those who oppose abortion on the ground I mentioned make an exception for a pregnancy due to rape? Certainly. They can say that persons have a right to life only if they didn't come into existence because of rape; or they can say that all persons have a right to life, but that some have less of a right to life than others, in particular, that those who came into existence because of rape have less. But these statements have a rather unpleasant sound. Surely the question of whether you have a right to life at all, or how much of it you have, shouldn't turn on the question of whether or not you are the product of a rape. And in fact the people who oppose abortion on the ground I mentioned do not make this distinction, and hence do not make an exception in case of rape.

Nor do they make an exception for a case in which the mother has to spend the nine months of her pregnancy in bed. They would agree that would be a great pity, and hard on the mother; but all the same, all persons have a right to life, the fetus is a person, and so on. I suspect, in fact, that they would not make an exception for a case in which, miraculously enough, the pregnancy went on for nine years, or even the rest of the mother's life.

Some won't even make an exception for a case in which continuation of the pregnancy is likely to shorten the mother's life; they regard abortion as impermissible even to save the mother's life. Such cases are nowadays very rare, and many opponents of abortion do not accept this extreme view. All the same, it is a good place to begin; a number of points of interest come out in respect to it.

1. Let us call the view that abortion is impermissible even to save   8
the mother's life "the exteme view." I want to suggest first that it does not issue from the argument I mentioned earlier without the addition of some fairly powerful premises. Suppose a woman has become pregnant, and now learns that she has a cardiac condition such that she will die if she carries the baby to term. What may be done for her? The fetus, being a person, has a right to life, but as the mother is a person too, so has she a right to life. Presumably they have an equal right to life. How is it supposed to come out that an abortion may not be performed? If mother and child have an equal right to life, shouldn't we perhaps flip a coin? Or should we add to the mother's right to life her right to decide what happens in and to her body, which everybody seems to be ready to grant—the sum of her rights now outweighing the fetus' right to life?

The most familiar argument here is the following. We are told that performing the abortion would be directly killing[3] the child, whereas doing nothing would not be killing the mother, but only letting her die. Moreover, in killing the child, one would be killing an innocent person, for the child has committed no crime, and is not aiming at his mother's death. And then there are a variety of ways in which this might be continued. (1) But as directly killing an innocent person is always and absolutely impermissible, an abortion may not be performed. Or, (2) as

[3]The term "direct" in the arguments I refer to is a technical one. Roughly, what is meant by *direct killing* is either killing as an end in itself, or killing as a means to some end; for example, the end of saving someone else's life. See note 6, below, for an example of its use.

directly killing an innocent person is murder, and murder is always and absolutely impermissible, an abortion may not be performed.[4] Or, (3) as one's duty to refrain from directly killing an innocent person is more stringent than one's duty to keep a person from dying, an abortion may not be performed. Or, (4) if one's only options are directly killing an innocent person or letting a person die, one must prefer letting the person die, and thus an abortion may not be performed.[5]

Some people seem to have thought that these are not further premises which must be added if the conclusion is to be reached, but that they follow from the very fact that an innocent person has a right to life.[6] But this seems to me to be a mistake, and perhaps the simplest way to show this is to bring out that while we must certainly grant that innocent persons have a right to life, the theses in (1) through (4) are all false. Take (2), for example. If directly killing an innocent person is murder, and thus is impermissible, then the mother's directly killing the innocent person inside her is murder, and thus is impermissible. But it cannot seriously be thought to be murder if the mother performs an abortion on herself to save her life. It cannot seriously be said that she *must* refrain, that she *must* sit passively by and wait for her death. Let us look again at the case of you and the violinist. There you are, in bed with the violinist, and the director of the hospital says to you, "It's all most distressing, and I deeply sympathize, but you see this is putting an additional strain on your kidneys, and you'll be dead within the month. But you have to stay where you are all the same. Because unplugging you would be directly killing an innocent violinist, and that's murder, and that's impermissible." If anything in the world is true, it is that you do not commit murder, you do not do what is impermissible, if you

---

[4]Cf. *Encyclical Letter of Pope Pius XI on Christian Marriage*, St. Paul Editions (Boston, n.d.), p. 32: "however much we may pity the mother whose health and even life is gravely imperiled in the performance of the duty allotted to her by nature, nevertheless what could ever be a sufficient reason for excusing in any way the direct murder of the innocent? This is precisely what we are dealing with here." Noonan (*The Morality of Abortion*, p. 43) reads this as follows: "What cause can ever avail to excuse in any way the direct killing of the innocent? For it is a question of that."

[5]The thesis in (4) is in an interesting way weaker than those in (1), (2), and (3): they rule out abortion even in cases in which both mother *and* child will die if the abortion is not performed. By contrast, one who held the view expressed in (4) could consistently say that one needn't prefer letting two persons die to killing one.

[6]Cf. the following passage from Pius XII, *Address to the Italian Catholic Society of Midwives*: "The baby in the maternal breast has the right to life immediately from God—Hence there is no man, no human authority, no science, no medical, eugenic, social, economic or moral 'indication' which can establish or grant a valid juridical ground for a direct deliberate disposition of an innocent human life, that is a disposition which looks to its destruction either as an end or as a means to another end perhaps in itself not illicit.— The baby, still not born, is a man in the same degree and for the same reason as the mother" (quoted in Noonan, *The Morality of Abortion*, p. 45).

reach around to your back and unplug yourself from that violinist to save your life.

The main focus of attention in writings on abortion has been on what a third party may or may not do in answer to a request from a woman for an abortion. This is in a way understandable. Things being as they are, there isn't much a woman can safely do to abort herself. So the question asked is what a third party may do, and what the mother may do, if it is mentioned at all, is deduced, almost as an afterthought, from what it is concluded that third parties may do. But it seems to me that to treat the matter in this way is to refuse to grant to the mother that very status of person which is so firmly insisted on for the fetus. For we cannot simply read off what a person may do from what a third party may do. Suppose you find yourself trapped in a tiny house with a growing child. I mean a very tiny house, and a rapidly growing child— you are already up against the wall of the house and in a few minutes you'll be crushed to death. The child on the other hand won't be crushed to death; if nothing is done to stop him from growing he'll be hurt, but in the end he'll simply burst open the house and walk out a free man. Now I could well understand it if a bystander were to say, "There's nothing we can do for you. We cannot choose between your life and his, we cannot be the ones to decide who is to live, we cannot intervene." But it cannot be concluded that you too can do nothing, that you cannot attack it to save your life. However innocent the child may be, you do not have to wait passively while it crushes you to death. Perhaps a pregnant woman is vaguely felt to have the status of house, to which we don't allow the right of self-defense. But if the woman houses the child, it should be remembered that she is a person who houses it.

I should perhaps stop to say explicitly that I am not claiming that 12 people have a right to do anything whatever to save their lives. I think, rather, that there are drastic limits to the right of self-defense. If someone threatens you with death unless you torture someone else to death, I think you have not the right, even to save your life, to do so. But the case under consideration here is very different. In our case there are only two people involved, one whose life is threatened, and one who threatens it. Both are innocent: the one who is threatened is not threatened because of any fault, the one who threatens does not threaten because of any fault. For this reason we may feel that we bystanders cannot intervene. But the person threatened can.

In sum, a woman surely can defend her life against the threat to it posed by the unborn child, even if doing so involves its death. And this shows not merely that the theses in (1) through (4) are false; it shows also that the extreme view of abortion is false, and so we need not canvass any other possible ways of arriving at it from the argument I mentioned at the outset.

2. The extreme view could of course be weakened to say that while abortion is permissible to save the mother's life, it may not be per-formed by a third party, but only by the mother herself. But this cannot be right, either. For what we have to keep in mind is that the mother and the unborn child are not like two tenants in a small house which has, by an unfortunate mistake, been rented to both: the mother *owns* the house. The fact that she does adds to the offensiveness of deducing that the mother can do nothing from the supposition that third parties can do nothing. But it does more than this: it casts a bright light on the supposition that third parties can do nothing. Certainly it lets us see that a third party who says "I cannot choose between you" is fooling himself if he thinks this is impartiality. If Jones has found and fastened on a certain coat, which he needs to keep him from freezing, but which Smith also needs to keep him from freezing, then it is not impartiality that says "I cannot choose between you" when Smith owns the coat. Women have said again and again "This body is *my* body!" and they have reason to feel angry, reason to feel that it has been like shouting into the wind. Smith, after all, is hardly likely to bless us if we say to him, "Of course it's your coat, anybody would grant that it is. But no one may choose between you and Jones who is to have it."

We should really ask what it is that says "no one may choose" in the face of the fact that the body that houses the child is the mother's body. It may be simply a failure to appreciate this fact. But it may be some-thing more interesting, namely the sense that one has a right to refuse to lay hands on people, even where it would be just and fair to do so, even where justice seems to require that somebody do so. Thus justice might call for somebody to get Smith's coat back from Jones, and yet you have a right to refuse to be the one to lay hands on Jones, a right to refuse to do physical violence to him. This, I think, must be granted. But then what should be said is not "no one may choose," but only "*I* cannot choose," and indeed not even this, but "*I* will not *act*," leaving it open that somebody else can or should, and in particular that anyone in a position of authority, with the job of securing people rights, both can and should. So this is no difficulty. I have not been arguing that any given third party must accede to the mother's request that he perform an abortion to save her life, but only that he may.

I suppose that in some views of human life the mother's body is only on loan to her, the loan not being one which gives her any prior claim to it. One who held this view might well think it impartiality to say "I cannot choose." But I shall simply ignore this possibility. My own view is that if a human being has any just, prior claim to anything at all, he has a just, prior claim to his own body. And perhaps this needn't be argued for here anyway, since, as I mentioned, the arguments against abortion we are looking at do grant that the woman has a right to decide what happens in and to her body.

But although they do grant it, I have tried to show that they do not take seriously what is done in granting it. I suggest the same thing will reappear even more clearly when we turn away from cases in which the mother's life is at stake, and attend, as I propose we now do, to the vastly more common cases in which a woman wants an abortion for some less weighty reason than preserving her own life.

3. Where the mother's life is not at stake, the argument I mentioned at the outset seems to have a much stronger pull. "Everyone has a right to life, so the unborn person has a right to life." And isn't the child's right to life weightier than anything other than the mother's own right to life, which she might put forward as ground for an abortion?

This argument treats the right to life as if it were unproblematic. It is not, and this seems to me to be precisely the source of the mistake.

For we should now, at long last, ask what it comes to, to have a right 20 to life. In some views having a right to life includes having a right to be given at least the bare minimum one needs for continued life. But suppose that what in fact *is* the bare minimum a man needs for continued life is something he has no right at all to be given? If I am sick unto death, and the only thing that will save my life is the touch of Henry Fonda's cool hand on my fevered brow, then all the same, I have no right to be given the touch of Henry Fonda's cool hand on my fevered brow. It would be frightfully nice of him to fly in from the West Coast to provide it. It would be less nice, though no doubt well meant, if my friends flew out to the West Coast and carried Henry Fonda back with them. But I have no right at all against anybody that he should do this for me. Or again, to return to the story I told earlier, the fact that for continued life that violinist needs the continued use of your kidneys does not establish that he has a right to be given the continued use of your kidneys. He certainly has no right against you that *you* should give him continued use of your kidneys. For nobody has any right to use your kidneys unless you give him such a right; and nobody has the right against you that you shall give him this right—if you do allow him to go on using your kidneys, this is a kindness on your part, and not something he can claim from you as his due. Nor has he any right against anybody else that *they* should give him continued use of your kidneys. Certainly he had no right against the Society of Music Lovers that they should plug him into you in the first place. And if you now start to unplug yourself, having learned that you will otherwise have to spend nine years in bed with him, there is nobody in the world who must try to prevent you, in order to see to it that he is given something he has a right be given.

Some people are rather stricter about the right to life. In their view, it does not include the right to be given anything, but amounts to, and only to, the right not to be killed by anybody. But here a related difficulty arises. If everybody is to refrain from killing that violinist, then everybody must refrain from doing a great many different sorts of things. Everybody must refrain from slitting his throat, everybody must refrain from shooting him—and everybody must refrain from unplugging you from him. But does he have a right against everybody that they shall refrain from unplugging you from him? To refrain from doing this is to allow him to continue to use your kidneys. It could be aruged that he has a right against us that *we* would should allow him to continue to use your kidneys. That is, while he had no right against us that we should give him the use of your kidneys, it might be argued that he anyway has a right against us that we shall not now intervene and deprive him of the use of your kidneys. I shall come back to third-party interventions later. But certainly the violinist has no right against you that *you* shall allow him to continue to use your kidneys. As I said, if you do allow him to use them, it is a kindness on your part, and not something you owe him.

The difficulty I point to here is not peculiar to the right to life. It reappears in connection with all the other natural rights; and it is something which an adequate account of rights must deal with. For present purposes it is enough just to draw attention to it. But I would stress that I am not arguing that people do not have a right to life—quite to the contrary, it seems to me that the primary control we must place on the acceptability of an account of rights is that it should turn out in that account to be a truth that all persons have a right to life. I am arguing only that having a right to life does not guarantee having either a right to be given the use of or a right to be allowed continued use of another person's body—even if one needs it for life itself. So the right to life will not serve the opponents of abortion in the very simple and clear way in which they seem to have thought it would.

4. There is another way to bring out the difficulty. In the most ordinary sort of case, to deprive someone of what he has a right to is to treat him unjustly. Suppose a boy and his small brother are jointly given a box of chocolates for Christmas. If the older boy takes the box and refuses to give his brother any of the chocolates, he is unjust to him, for the brother has been given a right to half of them. But suppose that, having learned that otherwise it means nine years in bed with that violinist, you unplug yourself from him. You surely are not being unjust to him, for you gave him no right to use your kidneys, and no one else can have given him any such right. But we have to notice that in unplugging yourself, you are killing him; and violinists, like everybody else, have a right to life, and thus in the view we are considering just now, the right not to be killed. So here you do what he supposedly has a right you shall not do, but you do not act unjustly to him in doing it.

The emendation which may be made at this point is this: the right 24
to life consists not in the right not to be killed, but rather in the right
not to be killed unjustly. This runs a risk of circularity, but never mind:
it would enable us to square the fact that the violinist has a right to life
with the fact that you do not act unjustly toward him in unplugging
yourself, thereby killing him. For if you do not kill him unjustly, you do
not violate his right to life, and so it is no wonder you do him no
injustice.

But if this emendation is accepted, the gap in the argument against
abortion stares us plainly in the face: it is by no means enough to show
that the fetus is a person, and to remind us that all persons have a right
to life—we need to be shown also that killing the fetus violates its right
to life, i.e., that abortion is unjust killing. And is it?

I suppose we may take it as a datum that in a case of pregnancy due
to rape the mother has not given the unborn person a right to the use of
her body for food and shelter. Indeed, in what pregnancy could it be
supposed that the mother has given the unborn person such a right? It is
not as if there were unborn persons drifting about the world, to whom a
woman who wants a child says "I invite you in."

But it might be argued that there are other ways one can have
acquired a right to the use of another person's body than by having
been invited to use it by that person. Suppose a woman voluntarily
indulges in intercourse, knowing of the chance it will issue in pregnancy, and then she does become pregnant; is she not in part responsible for the presence, in fact the very existence, of the unborn person
inside her? No doubt she did not invite it in. But doesn't her partial
responsibility for its being there itself give it a right to the use of her
body?[7] If so, then her aborting it would be more like the boy's taking
away the chocolates, and less like your unplugging yourself from the
violinist—doing so would be depriving it of what it does have a right to,
and thus would be doing it an injustice.

And then, too, it might be asked whether or not she can kill it even 28
to save her own life: If she voluntarily called it into existence, how can
she now kill it, even in self-defense?

The first thing to be said about this is that it is something new.
Opponents of abortion have been so concerned to make out the independence of the fetus, in order to establish that it has a right to life, just
as its mother does, that they have tended to overlook the possible
support they might gain from making out that the fetus is *dependent* on
the mother, in order to establish that she has a special kind of responsibility for it, a responsibility that gives it rights against her which are

[7]The need for a discussion of this argument was brought home to me by members of the
Society for Ethical and Legal Philosophy, to whom this paper was originally presented.

not possessed by any independent person—such as an ailing violinist who is a stranger to her.

On the other hand, this argument would give the unborn person a right to its mother's body only if her pregnancy resulted from a voluntary act, undertaken in full knowledge of the chance a pregnancy might result from it. It would leave out entirely the unborn person whose existence is due to rape. Pending the availability of some further argument, then, we would be left with the conclusion that unborn persons whose existence is due to rape have no right to the use of their mothers' bodies, and thus that aborting them is not depriving them of anything they have a right to and hence is not unjust killing.

And we should also notice that it is not at all plain that this argument really does go even as far as it purports to. For there are cases and cases, and the details make a difference. If the room is stuffy, and I therefore open a window to air it, and a burglar climbs in, it would be absurd to say, "Ah, now he can stay, she's given him a right to the use of her house—for she is partially responsible for his presence there, having voluntarily done what enabled him to get in, in full knowledge that there are such things as burglars, and that burglars burgle." It would be still more absurd to say this if I had had bars installed outside my windows, precisely to prevent burglars from getting in, and a burglar got in only because of a defect in the bars. It remains equally absurd if we imagine it is not a burglar who climbs in, but an innocent person who blunders or falls in. Again, suppose it were like this: people-seeds drift about in the air like pollen, and if you open your windows, one may drift in and take root in your carpets or upholstery. You don't want children, so you fix up your windows with fine mesh screens, the very best you can buy. As can happen, however, and on very, very rare occasions does happen, one of the screens is defective; and a seed drifts in and takes root. Does the person-plant who now develops have a right to the use of your house? Surely not—despite the fact that you voluntarily opened your windows, you knowingly kept carpets and upholstered furniture, and you knew that screens were sometimes defective. Someone may argue that you are responsible for its rooting, that it does have a right to your house, because after all you *could* have lived out your life with bare floors and furniture, or with sealed windows and doors. But this won't do—for by the same token anyone can avoid a pregnancy due to rape by having a hysterectomy, or anyway by never leaving home without a (reliable!) army.

It seems to me that the argument we are looking at can establish at 32 most that there are *some* cases in which the unborn person has a right to the use of its mother's body, and therefore some cases in which abortion is unjust killing. There is room for much discussion and argument as to precisely which, if any. But I think we should sidestep this issue and leave it open, for at any rate the argument certainly does not establish that all abortion is unjust killing.

5. There is room for yet another argument here, however. We surely must all grant that there may be cases in which it would be morally indecent to detach a person from your body at the cost of his life. Suppose you learn that what the violinist needs it not nine years of your life, but only one hour: all you need do to save his life is to spend one hour in that bed with him. Suppose also that letting him use your kidneys for that one hour would not affect your health in the slightest. Admittedly you were kidnapped. Admittedly you did not give anyone permission to plug him into you. Nevertheless it seems to me plain you *ought* to allow him to use your kidneys for that hour—it would be indecent to refuse.

Again, suppose pregnancy lasted only an hour, and constituted no threat to life or health. And suppose that a woman becomes pregnant as a result of rape. Admittedly she did not voluntarily do anything to bring about the existence of a child. Admittedly she did nothing at all which would give the unborn person a right to the use of her body. All the same it might well be said, as in the newly emended violinist story, that she ought to allow it to remain for that hour—that it would be indecent in her to refuse.

Now some people are inclined to use the term "right" in such a way that it follows from the fact that you ought to allow a person to use your body for the hour he needs, that he has a right to use your body for the hour he needs, even though he has not been given that right by any person or act. They may say that it follows also that if you refuse, you act unjustly toward him. This use of the term is perhaps so common that it cannot be called wrong; nevertheless it seems to me to be an unfortu-nate loosening of what we would do better to keep a tight rein on. Suppose that box of chocolates I mentioned earlier had not been given to both boys jointly, but was given only to the older boy. There he sits, stolidly eating his way through the box, his small brother watching enviously. Here we are likely to say "You ought not to be so mean. You ought to give your brother some of those chocolates." My own view is that it just does not follow from the truth of this that the brother has any right to any of the chocolates. If the boy refuses to give his brother any, he is greedy, stingy, callous—but not unjust. I suppose that the people I have in mind will say it does follow that the brother has a right to some of the chocolates, and thus that the boy does act unjustly if he refuses to give his brother any. But the effect of saying this is to obscure what we should keep distinct, namely the difference between the boy's refusal in this case and the boy's refusal in the earlier case, in which the box was given to both boys jointly, and in which the small brother thus had what was from any point of view clear title to half.

A further objection to so using the term "right" that from the fact 36 that A ought to do a thing for B, it follows that B has a right against A that A do it for him, is that it is going to make the question of whether or not a man has a right to a thing turn on how easy it is to provide him with it; and this seems not merely unfortunate, but morally unacceptable. Take the case of Henry Fonda again. I said earlier that I had no right to the touch of his cool hand on my fevered brow, even though I needed it to save my life. I said it would be frightfully nice of him to fly in from the West Coast to provide me with it, but that I had no right against him that he should do so. But suppose he isn't on the West Coast. Suppose he has only to walk across the room, place a hand briefly on my brow—and lo, my life is saved. Then surely he ought to do it, it would be indecent to refuse. Is it to be said "Ah, well, it follows that in this case she has a right to the touch of his hand on her brow, and so it would be an injustice in him to refuse?" So that I have a right to it when it is easy for him to provide it, though no right when it's hard? It's rather a shocking idea that anyone's rights should fade away and disappear as it gets harder and harder to accord them to him.

So my own view is that even though you ought to let the violinist use your kidneys for the one hour he needs, we should not conclude that he has a right to do so—we would say that if you refuse, you are, like the boy who owns all the chocolates and will give none away, self-centered and callous, indecent in fact, but not unjust. And similarly, that even supposing a case in which a woman pregnant due to rape ought to allow the unborn person to use her body for the hour he needs, we should not conclude that he has a right to do so; we should conclude that she is self-centered, callous, indecent, but not unjust, if she refuses. The complaints are no less grave; they are just different. However, there is no need to insist on this point. If anyone does wish to deduce "he has a right" from "you ought," then all the same he must surely grant that there are cases in which it is not morally required of you that you allow that violinist to use your kidneys, and in which he does not have a right to use them, and in which you do not do him an injustice if you refuse. And so also for mother and unborn child. Except in such cases as the unborn person has a right to demand it—and we were leaving open the possibility that there may be such cases—nobody is morally *required* to make large sacrifices, of health, of all other interests and concerns, of all other duties and commitments, for nine years, or even for nine months, in order to keep another person alive.

6. We have in fact to distinguish between two kinds of Samaritan: the Good Samaritan and what we might call the Minimally Decent Samaritan. The story of the Good Samaritan, you will remember, goes like this:

> A certain man went down from Jerusalem to Jericho, and fell among thieves, which stripped him of his raiment, and wounded him, and departed, leaving him half dead.
>
> And by chance there came down a certain priest that way; and when he saw him, he passed by on the other side.
>
> And likewise a Levite, when he was at the place, came and looked on him, and passed by on the other side.
>
> But a certain Samaritan, as he journeyed, came where he was; and when he saw him he had compassion on him.
>
> And went to him, and bound up his wounds, pouring in oil and wine, and set him on his own beast, and brought him to an inn, and took care of him.
>
> And on the morrow, when he departed, he took out two pence, and gave them to the host, and said unto him, "Take care of him; and whatsoever thou spendest more, when I come again, I will repay thee."
>
> (Luke 10:30–35)

The Good Samaritan went out of his way, at some cost to himself, to help one in need of it. We are not told what the options were, that is, whether or not the priest and the Levite could have helped by doing less than the Good Samaritan did, but assuming they could have, then the fact they did nothing at all shows they were not even Minimally Decent Samaritans, not because they were not Samaritans, but because they were not even minimally decent.

These things are a matter of degree, of course, but there is a difference, and it comes out perhaps most clearly in the story of Kitty Genovese, who, as you will remember, was murdered while thirty-eight people watched or listened, and did nothing at all to help her. A Good Samaritan would have rushed out to give direct assistance against the murderer. Or perhaps we had better allow that it would have been a Splendid Samaritan who did this, on the ground that it would have involved a risk of death for himself. But the thirty-eight not only did not do this, they did not even trouble to pick up a phone to call the police. Minimally Decent Samaritanism would call for doing at least that, and their not having done it was monstrous.

After telling the story of the Good Samaritan, Jesus said "Go, and 40 do thou likewise." Perhaps he meant that we are morally required to act as the Good Samaritan did. Perhaps he was urging people to do more than is morally required of them. At all events it seems plain that it was not morally required of any of the thirty-eight that he rush out to give direct assistance at the risk of his own life, and that it is not morally required of anyone that he give long stretches of his life—nine years or nine months—to sustaining the life of a person who has no special right (we were leaving open the possibility of this) to demand it.

Indeed, with one rather striking class of exceptions, no one in any country in the world is *legally* required to do anywhere near as much as this for anyone else. The class of exceptions is obvious. My main concern here is not the state of the law in respect to abortion, but it is worth drawing attention to the fact that in no state in this country is any man compelled by law to be even a Minimally Decent Samaritan to any person; there is no law under which charges could be brought against the thirty-eight who stood by while Kitty Genovese died. By contrast, in most states in this country women are compelled by law to be not merely Minimally Decent Samaritans, but Good Samaritans to unborn persons inside them. This doesn't by itself settle anything one way or the other, because it may well be argued that there should be laws in this country—as there are in many European countries—compelling at least Minimally Decent Samaritanism.[8] But it does show that there is a gross injustice in the existing state of the law. And it shows also that the groups currently working against liberalization of abortion laws, in fact working toward having it declared unconstitutional for a state to permit abortion, had better start working for the adoption of Good Samaritan laws generally, or earn the charge that they are acting in bad faith.

I should think, myself, that Minimally Decent Samaritan laws would be one thing, Good Samaritan laws quite another, and in fact highly improper. But we are not here concerned with the law. What we should ask is not whether anybody should be compelled by law to be a Good Samaritan, but whether we must accede to a situation in which some-body is being compelled—by nature, perhaps—to be a Good Samaritan. We have, in other words, to look now at third-party interventions. I have been arguing that no person is morally required to make large sacrifices to sustain the life of another who has no right to demand them, and this even where the sacrifices do not include life itself; we are not morally required to be Good Samaritans or anyway Very Good Samaritans to one another. But what if a man cannot extricate himself from such a situation? What if he appeals to us to extricate him? It seems to me plain that there are cases in which we can, cases in which a Good Samaritan would extricate him. There you are, you were kid-napped, and nine years in bed with that violinist lie ahead of you. You have your own life to lead. You are sorry, but you simply cannot see giving up so much of your life to the sustaining of his. You cannot

---

[8]For a discussion of the difficulties involved and a survey of the European experience with such laws, see *The Good Samaritan and the Law*, ed. James M. Ratcliffe (New York, 1966).

extricate yourself, and ask us to do so. I should have thought that—in light of his having no right to the use of your body—it was obvious that we do not have to accede to your being forced to give up so much. We can do what you ask. There is no injustice to the violinist in our doing so.

7. Following the lead of the opponents of abortion, I have throughout been speaking of the fetus merely as a person, and what I have been asking is whether or not the argument we began with, which proceeds only from the fetus's being a person, really does establish its conclusion. I have argued that it does not.

But of course there are arguments and arguments, and it may be 44 said that I have simply fastened on the wrong one. It may be said that what is important is not merely the fact that the fetus is a person, but that it is a person for whom the woman has a special kind of responsibility issuing from the fact that she is its mother. And it might be argued that all my analogies are therefore irrelevant—for you do not have that special kind of responsibility for that violinist, Henry Fonda does not have that special kind of responsibility for me. And our attention might be drawn to the fact that men and women both *are* compelled by law to provide support for their children.

I have in effect dealt (briefly) with this argument in section 4 above; but a (still briefer) recapitulation now may be in order. Surely we do not have any such "special responsibility" for a person unless we have assumed it, explicitly or implicitly. If a set of parents do not try to prevent pregnancy, do not obtain an abortion, and then at the time of birth of the child do not put it out for adoption, but rather take it home with them, then they have assumed responsibility for it, they have given it rights, and they cannot *now* withdraw support from it at the cost of its life because they now find it difficult to go on providing for it. But if they have taken all reasonable precautions against having a child, they do not simply by virtue of their biological relationship to the child who comes into existence have a special responsibility for it. They may wish to assume responsibility for it, or they may not wish to. And I am suggesting that if assuming responsibility for it would require large sacrifices, then they may refuse. A Good Samaritan would not refuse—or anyway, a Splendid Samaritan, if the sacrifices that had to be made were enormous. But then so would a Good Samaritan assume responsibility for that violinist; so would Henry Fonda, if he is a Good Samaritan, fly in from the West Coast and assume responsibility for me.

8. My argument will be found unsatisfactory on two counts by many of those who want to regard abortion as morally permissible. First, while I do argue that abortion is not impermissible, I do not argue that

it is always permissible. There may well be cases in which carrying the child to term requires only Minimally Decent Samaritanism of the mother, and this is a standard we must not fall below. I am inclined to think it a merit of my account precisely that it does *not* give a general yes or a general no. It allows for and supports our sense that, for example, a sick and desperately frightened fourteen-year-old schoolgirl, pregnant due to rape, may *of course* choose abortion, and that any law which rules this out is an insane law. And it also allows for and supports our sense that in other cases resort to abortion is even positively indecent. It would be indecent in the woman to request an abortion, and indecent in a doctor to perform it, if she is in her seventh month, and wants the abortion just to avoid the nuisance of postponing a trip abroad. The very fact that the arguments I have been drawing attention to treat all cases of abortion, or even all cases of abortion in which the mother's life is not at stake, as morally on a par ought to have made them suspect at the outset.

Secondly, while I am arguing for the permissibility of abortion in some cases, I am not arguing for the right to secure the death of the unborn child. It is easy to confuse these two things in that up to a certain point in the life of the fetus it is not able to survive outside the mother's body; hence removing it from her body guarantees its death. But they are importantly different. I have argued that you are not morally required to spend nine months in bed, sustaining the life of that violinist; but to say this is by no means to say that if, when you unplug yourself, there is a miracle and he survives, you then have a right to turn around and slit his throat. You may detach yourself even if this costs him his life; you have no right to be guaranteed his death, by some other means, if unplugging yourself does not kill him. There are some people who will feel dissatisfied by this feature of my argument. A woman may be utterly devastated by the thought of a child, a bit of herself, put out for adoption and never seen or heard of again. She may therefore want not merely that the child be detached from her, but more, that it die. Some opponents of abortion are inclined to regard this as beneath contempt—thereby showing insensitivity to what is surely a powerful source of despair. All the same, I agree that the desire for the child's death is not one which anybody may gratify, should it turn out to be possible to detach the child alive.

At this place, however, it should be remembered that we have only been pretending throughout that the fetus is a human being from the moment of conception. A very early abortion is surely not the killing of a person, and so is not dealt with by anything I have said here.   *1971*

Richard Selzer

What I Saw at the Abortion

I am a surgeon. Particularities of sick flesh is everyday news. Escaping blood, all the outpourings of disease—phlegm, pus, vomitus, even those occult meaty tumors that terrify—I see as blood, disease, phlegm, and so on. I touch them to destroy them. But I do not make symbols of them.

What I am saying is that I have seen and I am used to seeing. We are talking about a man who has a trade, who has practiced it long enough to see no news in any of it. Picture this man, then. A professional. In his forties. Three children. Lives in a university town—so, necessarily, well—enlightened? Enough, anyhow. Successful in his work, yes. No overriding religious posture. Nothing special, then, your routine fellow, trying to do his work and doing it well enough. Picture him, this professional, a sort of scientist, if you please, in possession of the standard admirable opinions, positions, convictions, and so on—on this and that matter—on *abortion*, for example.

All right.

Now listen. 4

It is the western wing of the fourth floor of a great university hospital. I am present because I asked to be present. I wanted to see what I had never seen. An abortion.

The patient is Jamaican. She lies on the table in that state of notable submissiveness I have always seen in patients. Now and then she smiles at one of the nurses as though acknowledging a secret.

A nurse draws down the sheet, lays bare the abdomen. The belly mounds gently in the twenty-fourth week of pregnancy. The chief surgeon paints it with a sponge soaked in red antiseptic. He does this three times, each time a fresh sponge. He covers the area with a sterile sheet, an aperture in its center. He is a kindly man who teaches as he works, who pauses to reassure the woman.

He begins. 8

A little pinprick, he says to the woman.

He inserts the point of a tiny needle at the midline of the lower portion of her abdomen, on the downslope. He infiltrates local anesthetic into the skin, where it forms a small white bubble.

The woman grimaces.

That is all you will feel, the doctor says. Except for a little pressure. 12 But no more pain.

She smiles again. She seems to relax. She settles comfortably on the table. The worst is over.

The doctor selects a three-and-one-half-inch needle bearing a cen-tral stylet. He places the point at the site of the previous injection. He aims it straight up and down, perpendicular. Next he takes hold of her abdomen with his left hand, palming the womb, steadying it. He thrusts with his right hand. The needle sinks into the abdominal wall.

Oh, says the woman quietly.

But I guess it is not pain that she feels. It is more a recognition that 16 the deed is being done.

Another thrust and he has speared the uterus.

We are in, he says.

He has felt the muscular wall of the organ gripping the shaft of his needle. A further slight pressure on the needle advances it a bit more. He takes his left hand from the woman's abdomen. He retracts the filament of the stylet from the barrel of the needle. A small geyser of pale yellow fluid erupts.

We are in the right place, says the doctor. Are you feeling any pain? 20 he says.

She smiles, shakes her head. She gazes at the ceiling.

In the room we are six: two physicians, two nurses, the patient, and me.

The participants are busy, very attentive. I am not at all busy—but I am no less attentive. I want to see.

I see something!　　　　　　　　24

It is unexpected, utterly unexpected, like a disturbance in the earth, a tumultuous jarring. I see something other than what I expected here. I see a movement—a small one. But I have seen it.

And then I see it again. And now I see that it is the hub of the needle in the woman's belly that has jerked. First to one side. Then to the other side. Once more it wobbles, is *tugged*, like a fishing line nibbled by a sunfish.

Again! And I *know!*

It is the *fetus* that worries thus. It is the fetus struggling against the 28 needle. Struggling? How can that be? I think: *That cannot be.* I think: The fetus feels no pain, cannot feel fear, has no *motivation.* It is merely reflex.

I point to the needle.

It is a reflex, says the doctor.

By the end of the fifth month, the fetus weighs about one pound, is about twelve inches long. Hair is on the head. There are eyebrows, eyelashes. Pale pink nipples show on the chest. Nails are present, at the fingertips, at the toes.

At the beginning of the sixth month, the fetus can cry, can suck, can 32 make a fist. He kicks, he punches. The mother can feel this, can *see* this.

His eyelids, until now closed, can open. He may look up, down, side-ways. His grip is very strong. He could support his weight by holding with one hand.

A reflex, the doctor says.

I hear him. But I saw something. I saw *something* in that mass of cells *understand* that it must bob and butt. And I see it again! I have an impulse to shove to the table—it is just a step—seize that needle, pull it out.

We are not six, I think. I think we are *seven*.

Something strangles *there*. An effort, its effort, binds me to it.   36

I do not shove to the table. I take no little step. It would be . . . well, madness. Everyone here wants the needle where it is. Six do. No, *five* do.

I close my eyes. I see the inside of the uterus. It is bathed in ruby gloom. I see the creature curled upon itself. Its knees are flexed. Its head is bent upon its chest. It is in fluid and gently rocks to the rhythm of the distant heartbeat.

It resembles . . . a sleeping infant.

Its place is entered by something. It is sudden. A point coming. A   40 needle!

A spike of *daylight* pierces the chamber. Now the light is ex-tinguished. The needle comes closer in the pool. The point grazes the thigh, and I stir. Perhaps I wake from dozing. The light is there again. I twist and straighten. My arms and legs *push*. My hand finds the shaft—grabs! I *grab*. I bend the needle this way and that. The point probes, touches on my belly. My mouth opens. Could I cry out? All is a commo-tion and a churning. There is a presence in the pool. An activity! The pool colors, reddens, darkens.

I open my eyes to see the doctor feeding a small plastic tube through the barrel of the needle into the uterus. Drops of pink fluid overrun the rim and spill onto the sheet. He withdraws the needle from around the plastic tubing. Now only the little tube protrudes from the woman's body. A nurse hands the physician a syringe loaded with a colorless liquid. He attaches it to the end of the tubing and injects it.

Prostaglandin, he says.

Ah, well, prostaglandin—a substance found normally in the body.   44 When given in concentrated dosage, it throws the uterus into vigorous contraction. In eight to twelve hours, the woman will expel the fetus.

The doctor detaches the syringe but does not remove the tubing.

In case we must do it over, he says.

He takes away the sheet. He places gauze pads over the tubing. Over all this he applies adhesive tape.

I know. We cannot feed the great numbers. There is no more room. I   48
know, I know. It is woman's right to refuse the risk, to decline the pain of
childbirth. And an unwanted child is a very great burden. An unwanted
child is a burden to himself. I know.

And yet . . . there is the flick of that needle. I *saw* it. I saw . . . I *felt*—
in that room, a pace away, life prodded, life fending off. I saw life
avulsed—swept by flood, blackening—then *out*.

There, says the doctor. It's all over. It wasn't too bad, was it? he says
to the woman.

She smiles. It is all over. Oh, yes.

And who would care to imagine that from a moist and dark com-   52
mencement six months before there would ripen the cluster and
globule, the sprout and pouch of man?

And who would care to imagine that trapped within the laked pearl
and a dowry of yolk would lie the earliest stuff of dream and memory?

It is a persona carried here as well as person, I think. I think it is a
signed piece, engraved with a hieroglyph of human genes.

I did not think this until I saw. The flick. The fending off.

We leave the room, the three of us, the doctors.   56

"Routine procedure," the chief surgeon says.

"All right," I say.

"Scrub nurse says first time you've seen one, Dick. First look at a
purge," the surgeon says.

"That's right," I say. "First look."   60

"Oh, well," he says, "I guess you've seen everything else."

"Pretty much," I say.

"I'm not prying, Doctor," he says, "but was there something on your
mind? I'd be delighted to field any questions. . . ."

"No," I say. "No, thanks. Just simple curiosity."   64

"Okay," he says, and we all shake hands, scrub, change, and go to
our calls.

I know, I know. The thing is normally done at sixteen weeks. Well,
I've since seen it performed at that stage, too. And seen . . . the flick. But
I also know that in the sovereign state of my residence it is hospital
policy to warrant the procedure at twenty-four weeks. And that in the
great state that is adjacent, policy is enlarged to twenty-eight weeks.

Does this sound like argument? I hope not. I am not trying to argue.
I am only saying I've *seen*. The flick. Whatever else may be said in
abortion's defense, the vision of that other defense will not vanish from
my eyes.

What I saw I saw as that: a *defense*, a motion *from*, and effort *away*. 68
And it has happened that you cannot reason with me now. For what can
language do against the truth of what I saw?   *1976*

Ellen Willis

Putting Women Back into the Abortion Debate

Some years ago I attended a New York Institute for the Humanities
seminar on the new right. We were a fairly heterogeneous group of
liberals and lefties, feminists and gay activists, but on one point nearly
all of us agreed: the right-to-life movement was a dangerous antifeminist crusade. At one session I argued that the attack on abortion had
significance far beyond itself, that it was the linchpin of the right's social
agenda. I got a lot of supporting comments and approving nods. It was
too much for Peter Steinfels, a liberal Catholic, author of *The Neoconserv-*
atives, and executive editor of *Commonweal*. Right-to-lifers were not all
right-wing fanatics, he protested. "You have to understand," he said
plaintively, "that many of us see abortion as a *human life issue*." What I
remember best was his air of frustrated isolation. I don't think he came
back to the seminar after that.

Things are different now. I often feel isolated when I insist that
abortion is, above all, a *feminist issue*. Once people took for granted that
abortion was an issue of sexual politics and morality. Now, abortion is
most often discussed as a question of "life" in the abstract. Public
concern over abortion centers almost exclusively on fetuses; women and
their bodies are merely the stage on which the drama of fetal life and
death takes place. Debate about abortion—if not its reality—has become sexlessly scholastic. And the people most responsible for this turn
of events are, like Peter Steinfels, on the left.

The left wing of the right-to-life movement is a small, seemingly
eccentric minority in both "progressive" and antiabortion camps. Yet it
has played a critical role in the movement: by arguing that opposition to
abortion can be separated from the right's antifeminist program,
it has given antiabortion sentiment legitimacy in left-symp and
(putatively) profeminist circles. While left antiabortionists are hardly

alone in emphasizing fetal life, their innovation has been to claim that a consistent "pro-life" stand involves opposing capital punishment, supporting disarmament, demanding government programs to end poverty, and so on. This is of course a leap the right is neither able nor willing to make. It's been liberals—from Garry Wills to the Catholic bishops—who have supplied the mass media with the idea that prohibiting abortion is part of a "seamless garment" of respect for human life.

Having invented this countercontext for the abortion controversy, 4 left antiabortionists are trying to impose it as the only legitimate context for debate. Those of us who won't accept their terms and persist in seeing opposition to abortion, antifeminism, sexual repression, and religious sectarianism as the real seamless garment have been accused of obscuring the issue with demagoguery. Last year *Commonweal*—perhaps the most important current forum for left antiabortion opinion—ran an editorial demanding that we shape up: "Those who hold that abortion is immoral believe that the biological dividing lines of birth or viability should no more determine whether a developing member of the species is denied or accorded essential rights than should the biological dividing lines of sex or race or disability or old age. This argument is open to challenge. Perhaps the dividing lines are sufficiently different. Pro-choice advocates should state their reasons for believing so. They should meet the argument on its own grounds. . . ."

In other words, the only question we're allowed to debate—or the only one *Commonweal* is willing to entertain—is "Are fetuses the moral equivalent of born human beings?" And I can't meet the argument on its own grounds because I don't agree that this is the key question, whose answer determines whether one supports abortion or opposes it. I don't doubt that fetuses are alive, or that they're biologically human—what else would they be? I do consider the life of a fertilized egg less precious than the well-being of a woman with feelings, self-consciousness, a history, social ties; and I think fetuses get closer to being human in a moral sense as they come closer to birth. But to me these propositions are intuitively self-evident. I wouldn't know how to justify them to a "nonbeliever," nor do I see the point of trying.

I believe the debate has to start in a different place—with the recognition that fertilized eggs develop into infants inside the bodies of women. Pregnancy and birth are active processes in which a woman's body shelters, nourishes, and expels a new life; for nine months she is immersed in the most intimate possible relationship with another being. The growing fetus makes considerable demands on her physical and emotional resources, culminating in the cataclysmic experience of birth. And childbearing has unpredictable consequences; it always entails some risk of injury or death.

For me all this has a new concreteness: I had a baby last year. My much-desired and relatively easy pregnancy was full of what antiabortionists like to call "inconveniences." I was always tired, short of breath; my digestion was never right; for three months I endured a state of hormonal siege; later I had pains in my fingers, swelling feet, numb spots on my legs, the dread hemorrhoids. I had to think about everything I ate. I developed borderline glucose intolerance. I gained fifty pounds and am still overweight; my shape has changed in other ways that may well be permanent. Psychologically, my pregnancy consumed me—though I'd happily bought the seat on the roller coaster, I was still terrified to be so out of control of my normally tractable body. It was all bearable, even interesting—even, at times, transcendent—because I wanted a baby. Birth was painful, exhausting, and wonderful. If I hadn't wanted a baby it would only have been painful and exhausting—or worse. I can hardly imagine what it's like to have your body and mind taken over in this way when you not only don't look forward to the result, but positively dread it. The thought appalls me. So as I see it, the key question is "Can it be moral, under any circumstances, to make a woman bear a child against her will?"

From this vantage point, *Commonweal*'s argument is irrelevant, for in   8 a society that respects the individual, no "member of the species" in *any* stage of development has an "essential right" to make use of someone else's body, let alone in such all-encompassing fashion, without that person's consent. You can't make a case against abortion by applying a general principle about everybody's human rights; you have to show exactly the opposite—that the relationship between fetus and pregnant woman is an exception, one that justifies depriving women of their right to bodily integrity. And in fact all antiabortion ideology rests on the premise—acknowledged or simply assumed—that women's unique capacity to bring life into the world carries with it a unique obligation that women cannot be allowed to "play God" and launch only the lives they welcome.

Yet the alternative to allowing women this power is to make them impotent. Criminalizing abortion doesn't just harm individual women with unwanted pregnancies, it affects all women's sense of themselves. Without control of our fertility we can never envision ourselves as free, for our biology makes us constantly vulnerable. Simply because we are female our physical integrity can be violated, our lives disrupted and transformed, at any time. Our ability to act in the world is hopelessly compromised by our sexual being.

Ah, sex—it does have a way of coming up in these discussions, despite all. When pressed, right-to-lifers of whatever political persuasion invariably point out that pregnancy doesn't happen by itself. The leftists often give patronizing lectures on contraception (though some find only "natural birth control" acceptable), but remain unmoved when reminded that contraceptives fail. Openly or implicitly they argue that people shouldn't have sex unless they're prepared to procreate. (They are quick to profess a single standard—men as well as women should be sexually "responsible." Yes, and the rich as well as the poor should be allowed to sleep under bridges.) Which amounts to saying that if women want to lead heterosexual lives they must give up any claim to self-determination, and that they have no right to sexual pleasure without fear.

Opposing abortion, then, means accepting that women must suffer sexual disempowerment and a radical loss of autonomy relative to men: if fetal life is sacred, the self-denial basic to women's oppression is also basic to the moral order. Opposing abortion means embracing a conservative sexual morality, one that subordinates pleasure to repro-duction: if fetal life is sacred, there is no room for the view that sexual passion—or even sexual love—for its own sake is a human need and a human right. Opposing abortion means tolerating the inevitable dou-ble standard, by which men may accept or reject sexual restrictions in accordance with their beliefs, while women must bow to them out of fear . . . or defy them at great risk. However much *Commonweal*'s editors and those of like mind want to believe their opposition to abortion is simply about saving lives, the truth is that in the real world they are shoring up a particular sexual culture, whose rules are stacked against women. I have yet to hear any left right-to-lifers take full responsibility for that fact or deal seriously with its political implications.

Unfortunately, their fuzziness has not lessened their appeal—if anything it's done the opposite. In increasing numbers liberals and leftists, while opposing antiabortion laws, have come to view abortion as an "agonizing moral issue" with some justice on both sides, rather than an issue—however emotionally complex—of freedom versus re-pression, or equality versus hierarchy, that affects their political self-definition. This above-the-battle stance is attractive to leftists who want to be feminist good guys but are uneasy or ambivalent about sexual issues, not to mention those who want to ally with "progressive" fac-tions of the Catholic church on Central America, nuclear disarmament, or populist economics without that sticky abortion question getting in the way.

Such neutrality is a way of avoiding the painful conflict over cultural issues that continually smolders on the left. It can also be a way of coping with the contradictions of personal life at a time when liberation is a dream deferred. To me the fight for abortion has always been the cutting edge of feminism, precisely because it denies that anatomy is destiny, that female biology dictates women's subordinate status. Yet recently I've found it hard to focus on the issue, let alone summon up the militance needed to stop the antiabortion tanks. In part that has to do with second-round weariness—do we really have to go through all these things twice?—in part with my life now.

Since my daughter's birth my feelings about abortion—not as a political demand but as a personal choice—have changed. In this society, the difference between the situation of a childless woman and of a mother is immense; the fear that having a child will dislodge one's tenuous hold on a nontraditional life is excruciating. This terror of being forced into the sea-change of motherhood gave a special edge to my convictions about abortion. Since I've made that plunge voluntarily, with consequences still unfolding, the terror is gone; I might not want another child, for all sorts of reasons, but I will never again feel that my identity is at stake. Different battles with the culture absorb my energy now. Besides, since I've experienced the primal, sensual passion of caring for an infant, there will always be part of me that does want another. If I had an abortion today, it would be with conflict and sadness unknown to me when I had an abortion a decade ago. And the antiabortionists' imagery of dead babies hits me with new force. Do many women—left, feminist women—have such feelings? Is this the sort of "ambivalence about abortion" that in the present atmosphere slides so easily into self-flagellating guilt?

Some left antiabortionists, mainly pacifists—Juli Loesch, Mary Meehan, and other "feminists for life"; Jim Wallis and various writers for Wallis's radical evangelical journal *Sojourners*—have tried to square their position with concern for women. They blame the prevalence of abortion on oppressive conditions—economic injustice, lack of child care and other social supports for mothers, the devaluation of childrearing, men's exploitative sexual behavior and refusal to take equal responsibility for children. They disagree on whether to criminalize abortion now (since murder is intolerable no matter what the cause) or to build a long-term moral consensus (since stopping abortion requires a general social transformation), but they all regard abortion as a desperate solution to desperate problems, and the women who resort to it as more sinned against than sinning.

This analysis grasps an essential feminist truth: that in a male-[16] supremacist society no choice a woman makes is genuinely free or entirely in her interest. Certainly many women have had abortions they didn't want or wouldn't have wanted if they had any plausible means of caring for a child; and countless others wouldn't have gotten pregnant in the first place were it not for inadequate contraception, sexual confusion and guilt, male pressure, and other stigmata of female powerlessness. Yet forcing a woman to bear a child she doesn't want can only add injury to insult, while refusing to go through with such a pregnancy can be a woman's first step toward taking hold of her life.

And many women who have abortions are "victims" only of ordinary human miscalculation, technological failure, or the vagaries of passion, all bound to exist in any society, however utopian. There will always be women who, at any given moment, want sex but don't want a child; some of these women will get pregnant; some of them will have abortions. Behind the victim theory of abortion is the implicit belief that women are always ready to be mothers, if only conditions are right, and that sex for pleasure rather than procreation is not only "irresponsible" (i.e., bad) but something men impose on women, never something women actively seek. Ironically, left right-to-lifers see abortion as always co-erced (it's "exploitation" and "violence against women"), yet regard motherhood—which for most women throughout history has been ines-capable, and is still our most socially approved role—as a positive choice. The analogy to the feminist antipornography movement goes beyond borrowed rhetoric: the antiporners, too, see active female lust as surrender to male domination and traditionally feminine sexual atti-tudes as expressions of women's true nature.

This Orwellian version of feminism, which glorifies "female values" and dismisses women's struggles for freedom—particularly sexual freedom—as a male plot, has become all too familiar in recent years. But its use in the abortion debate has been especially muddleheaded. Somehow we're supposed to leap from an oppressive patriarchal society to the egalitarian one that will supposedly make abortion obsolete without ever allowing women to see themselves as people entitled to control their reproductive function rather than be controlled by it. How women who have no power in this most personal of areas can effectively fight for power in the larger society is left to our imagination. A "New Zealand feminist" quoted by Mary Meehan in a 1980 article in *The Progressive* says, "Accepting short-term solutions like abortion only de-lays the implementation of real reforms like decent maternity and paternity leaves, job protection, high-quality child care, community responsibility for dependent people of all ages, and recognition of the economic contribution of childminders"—as if these causes were pro-gressing nicely before legal abortion came along. On the contrary, the fight for reproductive freedom is the foundation of all the others, which is why antifeminists resist it so fiercely.

As "pro-life" pacifists have been particularly concerned with refut-ing charges of misogyny, the liberal Catholics at *Commonweal* are most exercised by the claim that antiabortion laws violate religious freedom. The editorial quoted above hurled another challenge at the proabortion forces:

> It is time, finally, for the pro-choice advocates and editorial writers to abandon, once and for all, the argument that abortion [*sic*] is a re-

ligious "doctrine" of a single or several churches being imposed on those of other persuasions in violation of the First Amendment. . . . Catholics and their bishops are accused of imposing their "doctrine" on abortion, but not their "doctrine" on the needs of the poor, or their "doctrine" on the arms race, or their "doctrine" on human rights in Central America. . . .

The briefest investigation into Catholic teaching would show that the church's case against abortion is utterly unlike, say, its belief in the Real Presence, known with the eyes of faith alone, or its insistence on a Sunday obligation, applicable only to the faithful. The church's moral teaching on abortion. . . . is for the most part like its teaching on racism, warfare, and capital punishment, based on ordinary reasoning common to believers and nonbelievers. . . .

This is one more example of right-to-lifers' tendency to ignore the sexual ideology underlying their stand. Interesting, isn't it, how the editorial neglects to mention that the church's moral teaching on abortion jibes neatly with its teaching on birth control, sex, divorce, and the role of women. The traditional, patriarchal sexual morality common to these teachings is explicitly religious, and its chief defenders in modern times have been the more conservative churches. The Catholic and evangelical Christian churches are the backbone of the organized right-to-life movement and—a few Nathansons and Hentoffs[1] notwithstanding—have provided most of the movement's activists and spokespeople.

Furthermore, the Catholic hierarchy has made opposition to abor- 20 tion a litmus test of loyalty to the church in a way it has done with no other political issue—witness Archbishop O'Connor's harassment of Geraldine Ferraro during her vice-presidential campaign. It's unthinkable that a Catholic bishop would publicly excoriate a Catholic officeholder or candidate for taking a hawkish position on the arms race or Central America or capital punishment. Nor do I notice anyone trying to read William F. Buckley out of the church for his views on welfare. The fact is there is no accepted Catholic "doctrine" on these matters comparable to the church's absolutist condemnations of abortion. While differing attitudes toward war, racism, and poverty cut across religious and secular lines, the sexual values that mandate opposition to abortion are the bedrock of the traditional religious world view, and the source of the most bitter conflict with secular and religious modernists. When churches devote their considerable political power, organizational resources, and money to translating those values

---

[1]**Nathansons and Hentoffs:** Dr. Bernard Nathanson created the controversial pro-life film of an abortion, *The Silent Scream*; the journalist, Nat Hentoff, has argued the pro-life position from a leftist position.—Eds.

into law, I call that imposing their religious beliefs on me—whether or not they're technically violating the First Amendment.

Statistical studies have repeatedly shown that people's views on abortion are best predicted by their opinions on sex and "family" issues, not on "life" issues like nuclear weapons or the death penalty. That's not because we're inconsistent but because we comprehend what's really at stake in the abortion fight. It's the antiabortion left that refuses to face the contradiction in its own position: you can't be wholeheartedly for "life"—or for such progressive aspirations as freedom, democracy, equality—and condone the subjugation of women. The seamless garment is full of holes.   *1985*

26

Freedom of Expression

Walter Lippmann, The Indispensable
Opposition

Henry Louis Gates, Jr., 2 Live Crew, Decoded

Susan Brownmiller, Let's Put Pornography
Back in the Closet

I enter into discussion and argument with great freedom and ease, inasmuch as opinion finds in me a bad soil to penetrate and take deep roots in. No propositions astonish me, no belief offends me, whatever contrast it offers my own. There is no fancy so frivolous and so extravagant that it does not seem to me quite suitable to the production of the human mind. We who deprive our judgment of the right to make decisions look mildly on opinions different from ours; and if we do not lend them our judgment, we easily lend them our ears.

Michel de Montaigne, from *On the Art of Discussion*

A good many years ago, when Mussolini was much admired for clearing the streets of beggars and making the trains run on time, a good lady said to me that she couldn't understand all this palaver about freedom of speech and of the press. Isn't everyone, she asked, always free to say what he thinks? Of course, she added, one must be prepared to take the consequences. I was unable on the spur of the moment to find an answer to that one. But it has since occurred to me that the good lady was more profoundly right than she realized. Democratic government

rests on the assumption that the people are capable of governing themselves better than any one or any few can do it for them; but this in turn
rests on the further assumption that if the people are free to think,
speak, and publish their sentiments on any subject, the consequences
will be good. Well, sometimes they are and sometimes not. If we have
faith in democracy, we get over this inconvenient fact by saying that by
and large and in the long run the consequences will be good. But the
point is that if we accept democracy we must accord to everyone the
right to think, speak, and publish his sentiments on any subject; and in
that case we must indeed be prepared to take the consequences, whatever they may turn out to be.

Carl L. Becker, from *Freedom of Speech and Press*

A man or woman who is to hold a teaching post under the state should
not be required to express majority opinions, though naturally a majority of teachers will do so. Uniformity in the opinions expressed by
teachers is not only not to be sought but is, if possible, to be avoided,
since diversity of opinion among preceptors is essential to any sound
education. No man can pass as educated who had heard only one side
on questions as to which the public is divided. One of the most important things to teach in the educational establishments of a democracy is
the power of weighing arguments, and the open mind which is prepared
in advance to accept whichever side appears the more reasonable. As
soon as a censorship is imposed upon the opinions which teachers may
avow, education ceases to serve this purpose and tends to produce,
instead of a nation of men, a herd of fanatical bigots.

Bertrand Russell, from *Freedom and the Colleges*

If all mankind minus one were of one opinion, and only one person
were of the contrary opinion, mankind would be no more justified in
silencing that one person, than he, if he had the power, would be
justified in silencing mankind. Were an opinion a personal possession
of no value except to the owner; if to be obstructed in the enjoyment of
it were simply a private injury, it would make some difference whether
the injury was inflicted only on a few persons or on many. But the
peculiar evil of silencing the expression of an opinion is, that it is
robbing the human race; posterity as well as the existing generation;
those who dissent from the opinion, still more than those who hold it. If
the opinion is right, they are deprived of the opportunity of exchanging

error for truth: if wrong, they lose, what is almost as great a benefit, the clearer perception and livelier impression of truth, produced by its collision with error.

John Stuart Mill and Harriet Taylor, from *On Liberty*

Walter Lippmann
The Indispensable Opposition

Were they pressed hard enough, most men would probably confess that political freedom—that is to say, the right to speak freely and to act in opposition—is a noble ideal rather than a practical necessity. As the case for freedom is generally put today, the argument lends itself to this feeling. It is made to appear that, whereas each man claims his freedom as a matter of right, the freedom he accords to other men is a matter of toleration. Thus, the defense of freedom of opinion tends to rest not on its substantial, beneficial, and indispensable consequences, but on a somewhat eccentric, a rather vaguely benevolent, attachment to an abstraction.

It is all very well to say with Voltaire, "I wholly disapprove of what you say, but will defend to the death your right to say it," but as a matter of fact most men will not defend to the death the rights of other men: if they disapprove sufficiently what other men say, they will somehow suppress those men if they can.

So, if this is the best that can be said for liberty of opinion, that a man must tolerate his opponents because everyone has a "right" to say what he pleases, then we shall find that liberty of opinion is a luxury, safe only in pleasant times when men can be tolerant because they are not deeply and vitally concerned.

Yet actually, as a matter of historic fact, there is a much stronger   4 foundation for the great constitutional right of freedom of speech, and as a matter of practical human experience there is a much more compelling reason for cultivating the habits of free men. We take, it seems to me, a naïvely self-righteous view when we argue as if the right of our opponents to speak were something that we protect because we are magnanimous, noble, and unselfish. The compelling reason why, if liberty of opinion did not exist, we should have to invent it, why it will eventually have to be restored in all civilized countries where it is now suppressed, is that we must protect the right of our opponents to speak because we must hear what they have to say.

We miss the whole point when we imagine that we tolerate the freedom of our political opponents as we tolerate a howling baby next door, as we put up with the blasts from our neighbor's radio because we are too peaceable to heave a brick through the window. If this were all there is to freedom of opinion, that we are too good-natured or too timid to do anything about our opponents and our critics except to let them talk, it would be difficult to say whether we are tolerant because we are magnanimous or because we are lazy, because we have strong principles or because we lack serious convictions, whether we have the hospitality of an inquiring mind or the indifference of an empty mind. And so, if we truly wish to understand why freedom is necessary in a civilized society, we must begin by realizing that, because freedom of discussion improves our own opinions, the liberties of other men are our own vital necessity.

We are much closer to the essence of the matter, not when we quote Voltaire, but when we go to the doctor and pay him to ask us the most embarrassing questions and to prescribe the most disagreeable diet. When we pay the doctor to exercise complete freedom of speech about the cause and cure of our stomachache, we do not look upon ourselves as tolerant and magnanimous, and worthy to be admired by ourselves. We have enough common sense to know that if we threaten to put the doctor in jail because we do not like the diagnosis and the prescription it will be unpleasant for the doctor, to be sure, but equally unpleasant for our own stomachache. That is why even the most ferocious dictator would rather be treated by a doctor who was free to think and speak the truth than by his own Minister of Propaganda. For there is a point, the point at which things really matter, where the freedom of others is no longer a question of their right but of our own need.

The point at which we recognize this need is much higher in some men than in others. The totalitarian rulers think they do not need the freedom of an opposition: they exile, imprison, or shoot their opponents. We have concluded on the basis of practical experience, which goes back to Magna Carta and beyond, that we need the opposition. We pay the opposition salaries out of the public treasury.

In so far as the usual apology for freedom of speech ignores this experience, it becomes abstract and eccentric rather than concrete and human. The emphasis is generally put on the right to speak, as if all that mattered were that the doctor should be free to go out into the park and explain to the vacant air why I have a stomachache. Surely that is a miserable caricature of the great civic right which men have bled and died for. What really matters is that the doctor should tell *me* what ails me, that I should listen to him; that if I do not like what he says I should be free to call in another doctor; and that then the first doctor should have to listen to the second doctor; and that out of all the speaking and listening, the give-and-take of opinions, the truth should be arrived at.

This is the creative principle of freedom of speech, not that it is a system for the tolerating of error, but that it is a system for finding the truth. It may not produce the truth, or the whole truth all the time, or often, or in some cases ever. But if the truth can be found, there is no other system which will normally and habitually find so much truth. Until we have thoroughly understood this principle, we shall not know why we must value our liberty, or how we can protect and develop it.

Let us apply this principle to the system of public speech in a totalitarian state. We may, without any serious falsification, picture a condition of affairs in which the mass of the people are being addressed through one broadcasting system by one man and his chosen subordinates. The orators speak. The audience listens but cannot and dare not speak back. It is a system of one-way communication; the opinions of the rulers are broadcast outwardly to the mass of the people. But nothing comes back to the rulers from the people except the cheers; nothing returns in the way of knowledge of forgotten facts, hidden feelings, neglected truths, and practical suggestions.

But even a dictator cannot govern by his own one-way inspiration alone. In practice, therefore, the totalitarian rulers get back the reports of the secret police and of their party henchmen down among the crowd. If these reports are competent, the rulers may manage to remain in touch with public sentiment. Yet that is not enough to know what the audience feels. The rulers have also to make great decisions that have enormous consequences, and here their system provides virtually no help from the give-and-take of opinion in the nation. So they must either rely on their intuition, which cannot be permanently and continually inspired, or, if they are intelligent despots, encourage their trusted advisers and their technicians to speak and debate freely in their presence.

On the walls of the houses of Italian peasants one may see inscribed 12 in large letters the legend, "Mussolini is always right." But if that legend is taken seriously by Italian ambassadors, by the Italian General Staff, and by the Ministry of Finance, then all one can say is heaven help Mussolini, heaven help Italy, and the new Emperor of Ethiopia.

For at some point, even in a totalitarian state, it is indispensable that there should exist the freedom of opinion which causes opposing opinions to be debated. As time goes on, that is less and less easy under a despotism; critical discussion disappears as the internal opposition is liquidated in favor of men who think and feel alike. That is why the early successors of despots, of Napoleon I and of Napoleon III, have usually been followed by an irreparable mistake. For in listening only to his yes men—the others being in exile or in concentration camps, or terrified—the despot shuts himself off from the truth that no man can dispense with.

We know all this well enough when we contemplate the dictatorships. But when we try to picture our own system, by way of contrast, what picture do we have in our minds? It is, is it not, that anyone may stand up on his own soapbox and say anything he pleases, like the individuals in Kipling's poem who sit each in his separate star and draw the Thing as they see it for the God of Things as they are. Kipling, perhaps, could do this, since he was a poet. But the ordinary mortal isolated on his separate star will have an hallucination, and a citizenry declaiming from separate soapboxes will poison the air with hot and nonsensical confusion.

If the democratic alternative to the totalitarian one-way broadcasts is a row of separate soap boxes, then I submit that the alternative is unworkable, is unreasonable, and is humanly unattractive. It is above all a false alternative. It is not true that liberty has developed among civilized men when anyone is free to set up a soapbox, is free to hire a hall where he may expound his opinions to those who are willing to listen. On the contrary, freedom of speech is established to achieve its essential purpose only when different opinions are expounded in the same hall to the same audience.

For, while the right to talk may be the beginning of freedom, the 16 necessity of listening is what makes the right important. Even in Russia and Germany a man may still stand in an open field and speak his mind. What matters is not the utterance of opinions. What matters is the confrontation of opinions in debate. No man can care profoundly that every fool should say what he likes. Nothing has been accomplished if the wisest man proclaims his wisdom in the middle of the Sahara Desert. This is the shadow. We have the substance of liberty when the fool is compelled to listen to the wise man and learn; when the wise man is compelled to take account of the fool, and to instruct him; when the wise man can increase his wisdom by hearing the judgment of his peers.

That is why civilized men must cherish liberty—as a means of promoting the discovery of truth. So we must not fix our whole attention on the right of anyone to hire his own hall, to rent his own broadcasting station, to distribute his own pamphlets. These rights are incidental; and thought they must be preserved, they can be preserved only by regarding them as incidental, as auxiliary to the substance of liberty that must be cherished and cultivated.

Freedom of speech is best conceived, therefore, by having in mind the picture of a place like the American Congress, an assembly where opposing views are represented, where ideas are not merely uttered but debated, or the British Parliament, where men who are free to speak are also compelled to answer. We may picture the true condition of freedom as existing in a place like a court of law, where witnesses testify and are cross-examined, where the lawyer argues against the opposing lawyer before the same judge and in the presence of one jury. We may picture freedom as existing in a forum where the speaker must respond to questions; in a gathering of scientists where the data, the hypothesis, and the conclusion are submitted to men competent to judge them; in a reputable newspaper which not only will publish the opinions of those who disagree but will reexamine its own opinion in the light of what they say.

Thus the essence of freedom of opinion is not in mere toleration as such, but in the debate which toleration provides: it is not in the venting of opinion, but in the confrontation of opinion. That this is the practical substance can readily be understood when we remember how differently we feel and act about the censorship and regulation of opinion purveyed by different media of communication. We find then that, in so far as the medium makes difficult the confrontation of opinion in debate, we are driven toward censorship and regulation.

There is, for example, the whispering campaign, the circulation of 20 anonymous rumors by men who cannot be compelled to prove what they say. They put the utmost strain on our tolerance, and there are few who do not rejoice when the anonymous slanderer is caught, exposed and punished. At a higher level there is the moving picture, a most powerful medium for conveying ideas, but a medium which does not permit debate. A moving picture cannot be answered effectively by another moving picture; in all free countries there is some censorship of the movies, and there would be more if the producers did not recognize their limitations by avoiding political controversy. There is then the radio. Here debate is difficult: it is not easy to make sure that the speaker is being answered in the presence of the same audience. Inevitably, there is some regulation of the radio.

When we reach the newspaper press, the opportunity for debate is so considerable that discontent cannot grow to the point where under normal conditions there is any disposition to regulate the press. But when newspapers abuse their power by injuring people who have no means of replying, a disposition to regulate the press appears. When we arrive at Congress we find that, because the membership of the House is so large, full debate is impracticable. So there are restrictive rules. On the other hand, in the Senate, where the conditions of full debate exist, there is almost absolute freedom of speech.

This shows us that the preservation and development of freedom of opinion are not only a matter of adhering to abstract legal rights, but also, and very urgently, a matter of organizing and arranging sufficient debate. Once we have a firm hold on the central principle, there are many practical conclusions to be drawn. We then realize that the defense of freedom of opinion consists primarily in perfecting the opportunity for an adequate give-and-take of opinion; it consists also in regulating the freedom of those revolutionists who cannot or will not permit or maintain debate when it does not suit their purposes.

We must insist that free oratory is only the beginning of free speech; it is not the end, but a means to an end. The end is to find the truth. The practical justification of civil liberty is not that self-expression is one of the rights of man. It is that the examination of opinion is one of the necessities of man. For experience tells us that it is only when freedom of opinion becomes the compulsion to debate that the seed which our fathers planted has produced its fruit. When that is understood, freedom will be cherished not because it is a vent for our opinions but because it is the surest method of correcting them.

The unexamined life, said Socrates, is unfit to be lived by man. This 24 is the virtue of liberty, and the ground on which we may best justify our belief in it, that it tolerates error in order to serve the truth. When men are brought face to face with their opponents, forced to listen and learn and mend their ideas, they cease to be children and savages and begin to live like civilized men. Then only is freedom a reality, when men may voice their opinions because they must examine their opinions.

The only reason for dwelling on all this is that if we are to preserve democracy we must understand its principles. And the principle which distinguishes it from all other forms of government is that in a democracy the opposition not only is tolerated as constitutional but must be maintained because it is in fact indispensable.

The democratic system cannot be operated without effective opposition. For, in making the great experiment of governing people by consent rather than by coercion, it is not sufficient that the party in power should have a majority. It is just as necessary that the party in power should never outrage the minority. That means that it must listen to the minority and be moved by the criticisms of the minority. That means that its measures must take account of the minority's objections, and that in administering measures it must remember that the minority may become the majority.

The opposition is indispensable. A good statesman, like any other sensible human being, always learns more from his opponents than from his fervent supporters. For his supporters will push him where the dangers are. So if he is wise he will often pray to be delivered from his friends, because they will ruin him. But, though it hurts, he ought to pray never to be left without opponents; for they keep him on the path of reason and good sense.

The national unity of a free people depends upon a sufficiently 28
even balance of political power to make it impracticable for the administration to be arbitrary and for the opposition to be revolutionary and
irreconcilable. Where that balance no longer exists, democracy perishes.
For unless all the citizens of a state are forced by circumstances to
compromise, unless they feel that they can affect policy but that no one
can wholly dominate it, unless by habit and necessity they have to give
and take, freedom cannot be maintained.   *1939*

Henry Louis Gates, Jr.

2 Live Crew, Decoded

The rap group 2 Live Crew and their controversial hit recording
"As Nasty as They Wanna Be" may well earn a signal place in the history
of First Amendment rights. But just as important is how these lyrics will
be interpreted and by whom.

For centuries, African-Americans have been forced to develop
coded ways of communicating to protect them from danger. Allegories
and double meanings, words redefined to mean their opposites ("bad"
meaning "good," for instance), even neologisms ("bodacious") have
enabled blacks to share messages only the initiated understood.

Many blacks were amused by the transcripts of Marion Barry's sting
operation, which reveals that he used the traditional black expression
about one's "nose being opened." This referred to a love affair and not,
as Mr. Barry's prosecutors have suggested, to the inhalation of drugs.
Understanding this phrase could very well spell the difference (for the
Mayor) between prison and freedom.

2 Live Crew is engaged in heavy-handed parody, turning the stereo- 4
types of black and white American culture on their heads. These young
artists are acting out, to lively dance music, a parodic exaggeration of
the age-old stereotypes of the oversexed black female and male. Their
exuberant use of hyperbole (phantasmagoric sexual organs, for example) undermines—for anyone fluent in black cultural codes—a too
literal-minded hearing of the lyrics.

This is the street tradition called "signifying" or "playing the
dozens," which has generally been risqué, and where the best signifier

or "rapper" is the one who invents the most extravagant images, the biggest "lies," as the culture says. (H. "Rap" Brown earned his nickname in just this way.) In the face of racist stereotypes about black sexuality, you can do one of two things: You can disavow them or explode them with exaggeration.

2 Live Crew, like many "hip-hop" groups, is engaged in sexual carnivalesque. Parody reigns supreme, from a take-off of standard blues to a spoof of the black power movement; their off-color nursery rhymes are part of a venerable Western tradition. The group even satirizes the culture of commerce when it appropriates popular advertising slogans ("Tastes great!" "Less filling!") and puts them in a bawdy context.

2 Live Crew must be interpreted within the context of black culture generally and of signifying specifically. Their novelty, and that of other adventuresome rap groups, is that their defiant rejection of euphemism now voices for the mainstream what before existed largely in the "race record" market—where the records of Redd Foxx and Rudy Ray Moore once were forced to reside.

Rock songs have always been about sex but have used elaborate   8 subterfuges to convey that fact. 2 Live Crew uses Anglo-Saxon words and is self-conscious about it: a parody of a white voice in one song refers to "private personal parts," as a coy counterpart to the group's bluntness.

Much more troubling than its so-called obscenity is the group's overt sexism. Their sexism is so flagrant, however, that it almost cancels itself out in a hyperbolic war between the sexes. In this, it recalls the inter-sexual jousting in Zora Neale Hurston's novels. Still, many of us look toward the emergence of more female rappers to redress sexual stereotypes. And we must not allow ourselves to sentimentalize street culture: the appreciation of verbal virtuosity does not lessen one's obligation to critique bigotry in all of its pernicious forms.

Is 2 Live Crew more "obscene" than, say, the comic Andrew Dice Clay? Clearly, this rap group is seen as more threatening than others that are just as sexually explicit. Can this be completely unrelated to the specter of the young black male as a figure of sexual and social disruption, the very stereotypes 2 Live Crew seems determined to undermine?

This question—and the very large question of obscenity and the First Amendment—cannot even be addressed until those who would answer them become literate in the vernacular traditions of African-Americans. To do less is to censor through the equivalent of intellectual prior restraint—and censorship is to art what lynching is to justice.

1990

Susan Brownmiller

Let's Put Pornography Back in the Closet

Free speech is one of the great foundations on which our democracy rests. I am old enough to remember the Hollywood Ten, the screen-writers who went to jail in the late 1940s because they refused to testify before a congressional committee about their political affiliations. They tried to use the First Amendment as a defense, but they went to jail because in those days there were few civil liberties lawyers around who cared to champion the First Amendment right to free speech, when the speech concerned the Communist party.

The Hollywood Ten were correct in claiming the First Amendment. Its high purpose is the protection of unpopular ideas and political dissent. In the dark, cold days of the 1950s, few civil libertarians were willing to declare themselves First Amendment absolutists. But in the brighter, though frantic, days of the 1960s, the principle of protecting unpopular political speech was gradually strengthened.

It is fair to say now that the battle has largely been won. Even the American Nazi party has found itself the beneficiary of the dedicated, tireless work of the American Civil Liberties Union. But—and please notice the quotation marks coming up—"To equate the free and robust exchange of ideas and political debate with commercial exploitation of obscene material demeans the grand conception of the First Amend-ment and its high purposes in the historic struggle for freedom. It is a misuse of the great guarantees of free speech and free press."

I didn't say that, although I wish I had, for I think the words are   4
thrilling. Chief Justice Warren Burger said it in 1973, in the United States Supreme Court's majority opinion in *Miller v. California*. During the same decades that the right to political free speech was being strengthened in the courts, the nation's obscenity laws also were under-going extensive revision.

It's amazing to recall that in 1934 the question of whether James Joyce's *Ulysses* should be banned as pornographic actually went before the Court. The battle to protect *Ulysses* as a work of literature with redeeming social value was won. In later decades, Henry Miller's *Tropic* books, *Lady Chatterley's Lover* and the *Memoirs of Fanny Hill* also were adjudged not obscene. These decisions have been important to me. As the author of *Against Our Will*, a study of the history of rape that does contain explicit sexual material, I shudder to think how my book would have fared if James Joyce, D. H. Lawrence, and Henry Miller hadn't gone before me.

I am not a fan of *Chatterley* or the *Tropic* books, I should quickly mention. They are not to my literary taste, nor do I think they represent female sexuality with any degree of accuracy. But I would hardly suggest that we ban them. Such a suggestion wouldn't get very far anyway. The battle to protect these books is ancient history. Time does march on, quite methodically. What, then, is unlawfully obscene, and what does the First Amendment have to do with it?

In the Miller case of 1973 (not Henry Miller, by the way, but a porn distributor who sent unsolicited stuff through the mails), the Court came up with new guidelines that it hoped would strengthen obscenity laws by giving more power to the states. What it did in actuality was throw everything into confusion. It set up a three-part test by which materials can be adjudged obscene. The materials are obscene if they depict patently offensive, hard-core sexual conduct; lack serious scientific, literary, artistic, or political value; and appeal to the prurient interest of an average person—as measured by contemporary community standards.

"Patently offensive," "prurient interest," and "hard-core" are indeed words to conjure with. "Contemporary community standards" are what we're trying to redefine. The feminist objection to pornography is not based on prurience, which the dictionary defines as lustful, itching desire. We are not opposed to sex and desire, with or without the itch, and we certainly believe that explicit sexual material has its place in literature, art, science, and education. Here we part company rather swiftly with old-line conservatives who don't want sex education in the high schools, for example. 8

No, the feminist objection to pornography is based on our belief that pornography represents hatred of women, that pornography's intent is to humiliate, degrade, and dehumanize the female body for the purpose of erotic stimulation and pleasure. We are unalterably opposed to the presentation of the female body being stripped, bound, raped, tortured, mutilated, and murdered in the name of commercial entertainment and free speech.

These images, which are standard pornographic fare, have nothing to do with the hallowed right of political dissent. They have everything to do with the creation of a cultural climate in which a rapist feels he is merely giving in to a normal urge and a woman is encouraged to believe that sexual masochism is healthy, liberated fun. Justice Potter Stewart once said about hard-core pornography, "You know it when you see it," and that certainly used to be true. In the good old days, pornography looked awful. It was cheap and sleazy, and there was no mistaking it for art.

Nowadays, since the porn industry has become a multimillion dollar business, visual technology has been employed in its service. Pornographic movies are skillfully filmed and edited, pornographic still shots using the newest tenets of good design artfully grace the covers of *Hustler, Penthouse,* and *Playboy,* and the public—and the courts—are sadly confused.

The Supreme Court neglected to define "hard-core" in the Miller 12 decision. This was a mistake. If "hard-core" refers only to explicit sexual intercourse, then that isn't good enough. When women or children or men—no matter how artfully—are shown tortured or terrorized in the service of sex, that's obscene. And "patently offensive," I would hope, to our "contemporary community standards."

Justice William O. Douglas wrote in his dissent to the Miller case that no one is "compelled to look." This is hardly true. To buy a paper at a corner newsstand is to subject oneself to a forcible immersion in pornography, to be demeaned by an array of dehumanized, chopped-up parts of the female anatomy, packaged like cuts of meat at the super-market. I happen to like my body and I work hard at the gym to keep it in good shape, but I am embarrassed for my body and for the bodies of all women when I see the fragmented parts of us so frivolously, and so flagrantly, displayed.

Some constitutional theorists (Justice Douglas was one) have main-tained that any obscenity law is a serious abridgment of free speech. Others (and Justice Earl Warren was one) have maintained that the First Amendment was never intended to protect obscenity. We live quite compatibly with a host of free-speech abridgments. There are restraints against false and misleading advertising or statements—shouting "fire" without cause in a crowded movie theater, etc.—that do not threaten, but strengthen, our societal values. Restrictions on the public display of pornography belong in this category.

The distinction between permission to publish and permission to display publicly is an essential one and one which I think consonant with First Amendment principles. Justice Burger's words which I quoted above support this without question. We are not saying "Smash the presses" or "Ban the bad ones," but simply "Get the stuff out of our sight." Let the legislatures decide—using realistic and humane contem-porary community standards—what can be displayed and what cannot. The courts, after all, will be the final arbiters.   *1979*

Denigrating the Species

Jonathan Swift, A Modest Proposal
Fyodor Dostoyevsky, Confession of Faith
Mark Twain, The Damned Human Race

So long as we want to enjoy the excitement of democracy we must be prepared to endure its curses, and one of them is the fact that when two men stand up before a mob, the one honest and the other a fraud, the mob always prefers the fraud. He is always longer on promises and readier with soothing and hence can be more charming to persons incapable of thought.

H. L. Mencken, from *Why Nobody Loves a Politician*

Mankind is the most selfish species this world has ever spewed up from hell, and it demands, constantly, that neighbors and politicians be "unselfish," and allow themselves to be plundered—for its benefit Nobody howls more against "public selfishness," or even private selfishness, as much as a miser, just as whores are the strongest supporters of public morality, and robbers of the people extol philanthropy. I've lived a long time, but my fellow man baffles me more and more, which no doubt is naïve of me.

Taylor Caldwell, from *Captains and the Kings*

It is manifest, that during the time men live without a common power to keep them all in awe, they are in that condition which is called war; and such a war, as is of every man, against every man. . . . In such condition, there is no place for industry; because the fruit thereof is uncertain: and consequently no culture of the earth; no navigation, nor use of the commodities that may be imported by sea; no commodious building; no instruments of moving, and removing such things as require much force; no knowledge of the face of the earth; no account of time; no arts; no letters; no society; and which is worst of all, continual fear, and danger of violent death; and the life of man, solitary, poor, nasty, brutish, and short.

Thomas Hobbes, from *Leviathan*

Jonathan Swift

A Modest Proposal

For Preventing the Children of Poor People in Ireland
from Being a Burden to Their Parents or Country,
and for Making Them Beneficial to the Public

It is a melancholy object to those who walk through this great town[1] or travel in the country, when they see the streets, the roads, and cabin doors, crowded with beggars of the female sex, followed by three, four, or six children, all in rags and importuning every passenger for an alms. These mothers, instead of being able to work for their honest livelihood, are forced to employ all their time in strolling to beg sustenance for their helpless infants: who as they grow up either turn thieves for want of work, or leave their dear native country to fight for the pretender in Spain,[2] or sell themselves to the Barbadoes.[3]

I think it is agreed by all parties that this prodigious number of children in the arms, or on the backs, or at the heels of their mothers, and frequently of their fathers, is in the present deplorable state of the

---

[1]**this great town**: Dublin.—Eds.

[2]**pretender in Spain**: James Stuart (1688–1766); exiled in Spain, he laid claim to the English crown and had the support of many Irishmen who had joined an army hoping to restore him to the throne.—Eds.

[3]**the Barbadoes**: Inhabitants of the British colony in the Caribbean where Irishmen emigrated to work as indentured servants in exchange for their passage.—Eds.

kingdom a very great additional grievance; and, therefore, whoever could find out a fair, cheap, and easy method of making these children sound, useful members of the commonwealth, would deserve so well of the public as to have his statue set up for a preserver of the nation.

But my intention is very far from being confined to provide only for the children of professed beggars; it is of a much greater extent, and shall take in the whole number of infants at a certain age who are born of parents in effect as little able to support them as those who demand our charity in the streets.

As to my own part, having turned my thoughts for many years upon   4
this important subject, and maturely weighed the several schemes of our projectors,[4] I have always found them grossly mistaken in their computation. It is true, a child just dropped from its dam may be supported by her milk for a solar year, with little other nourishment; at most not above the value of 2s.,[5] which the mother may certainly get, or the value in scraps, by her lawful occupation of begging; and it is exactly at one year old that I propose to provide for them in such a manner as instead of being a charge upon their parents or the parish, or wanting food and raiment for the rest of their lives, they shall on the contrary contribute to the feeding, and partly to the clothing, of many thousands.

There is likewise another great advantage in my scheme, that it will prevent those voluntary abortions, and that horrid practice of women murdering their bastard children, alas! too frequent among us! sacrificing the poor innocent babes I doubt more to avoid the expense than the shame, which would move tears and pity in the most savage and inhuman breast.

The number of souls in this kingdom being usually reckoned one million and a half, of these I calculate there may be about 200,000 couple whose wives are breeders; from which number I subtract 30,000 couple who are able to maintain their own children (although I apprehend there cannot be so many, under the present distress of the kingdom); but this being granted, there will remain 170,000 breeders. I again subtract 50,000 for those women who miscarry, or whose children die by accident or disease within the year. There only remain 120,000 children of poor parents annually born. The question therefore is, how this number shall be reared and provided for? which, as I have already said, under the present situation of affairs, is utterly impossible by all the methods hitherto proposed. For we can neither employ them in

---

4projectors: Planners.—Eds.

52s.: Two shillings; in Swift's time one shilling was worth less than twenty-five cents. Other monetary references in the essay are to pounds sterling ("£."), pence ("d."), a crown, and a groat. A pound consisted of twenty shillings; a shilling of twelve pence; a crown was five shillings; a groat was worth a few cents.—Eds.

handicraft or agriculture; we neither build houses (I mean in the country) nor cultivate land; they can very seldom pick up a livelihood by stealing, till they arrive at six years old, except where they are of towardly parts;[6] although I confess they learn the rudiments much earlier; during which time they can, however, be properly looked upon only as probationers; as I have been informed by a principal gentleman in the county of Cavan, who protested to me that he never knew above one or two instances under the age of six, even in a part of the kingdom so renowned for the quickest proficiency in that art.

I am assured by our merchants, that a boy or a girl before twelve years old is no salable commodity; and even when they come to this age they will not yield above 3£. or 3£. 2s. 6d. at most on the exchange; which cannot turn to account either to the parents or kingdom, the charge of nutriment and rags having been at least four times that value.

I shall now therefore humbly propose my own thoughts, which I hope will not be liable to the least objection.   8

I have been assured by a very knowing American of my acquaintance in London, that a young healthy child well nursed is at a year old a most delicious, nourishing, and wholesome food, whether stewed, roasted, baked, or broiled; and I make no doubt that it will equally serve in a fricassee or a ragout.[7]

I do therefore humbly offer it to public consideration that of the 120,000 children already computed, 20,000 may be reserved for breed, whereof only one-fourth part to be males; which is more than we allow to sheep, black cattle, or swine; and my reason is, that these children are seldom the fruits of marriage, a circumstance not much regarded by our savages; therefore one male will be sufficient to serve four females. That the remaining 100,000 may, at a year old, be offered in sale to the persons of quality and fortune through the kingdom; always advising the mother to let them suck plentifully in the last month, so as to render them plump and fat for a good table. A child will make two dishes at an entertainment for friends; and when the family dines alone, the fore and hind quarter will make a reasonable dish, and seasoned with a little pepper or salt will be very good boiled on the fourth day, especially in winter.

I have reckoned upon a medium that a child just born will weigh 12 pounds, and in a solar year, if tolerably nursed, will increase to 28 pounds.

I grant this food will be somewhat dear, and therefore very proper for landlords, who, as they have already devoured most of the parents, seem to have the best title to the children.   12

[6]**towardly parts**: Natural abilities.—Eds.
[7]**ragout**: A stew.—Eds.

Infants' flesh will be in season throughout the year, but more plentiful in March, and a little before and after: for we are told by a grave author, an eminent French physician,[8] that fish being a prolific diet, there are more children born in Roman Catholic countries about nine months after Lent than at any other season; therefore, reckoning a year after Lent, the markets will be more glutted than usual, because the number of popish infants is at least three to one in this kingdom: and therefore it will have one other collateral advantage, by lessening the number of papists among us.

I have already computed the charge of nursing a beggar's child (in which list I reckon all cottagers, laborers, and four-fifths of the farmers) to be about 2s. per annum, rags included; and I believe no gentleman would repine to give 10s. for the carcass of a good fat child, which, as I have said, will make four dishes of excellent nutritive meat, when he has only some particular friend or his own family to dine with him. Thus the squire will learn to be a good landlord, and grow popular among the tenants; the mother will have 8s. net profit, and be fit for work till she produces another child.

Those who are more thrifty (as I must confess the times require) may flay the carcass; the skin of which artificially[9] dressed will make admirable gloves for ladies, and summer boots for fine gentlemen.

As to our city of Dublin, shambles[10] may be appointed for this purpose in the most convenient parts of it, and butchers we may be assured will not be wanting: although I rather recommend buying the children alive, and dressing them hot from the knife as we do roasting pigs. 16

A very worthy person, a true lover of his country, and whose virtues I highly esteem, was lately pleased in discoursing on this matter to offer a refinement upon my scheme. He said that many gentlemen of this kingdom, having of late destroyed their deer, he conceived that the want of venison might be well supplied by the bodies of young lads and maidens, not exceeding fourteen years of age nor under twelve; so great a number of both sexes in every country being now ready to starve for want of work and service; and these to be disposed of by their parents, if alive, or otherwise by their nearest relations. But with due deference to so excellent a friend and so deserving a patriot, I cannot be altogether in his sentiments; for as to the males, my American acquaintance assured me from frequent experience that their flesh was generally

[8]**French physician**: François Rabelais (c. 1494–1553), the great Renaissance humanist and author of the comic masterpiece *Gargantua and Pantagruel*. Swift is being ironic in calling Rabelais "grave."—Eds.

[9]**artificially**: Artfully.—Eds.

[10]**shambles**: Slaughterhouses.—Eds.

tough and lean, like that of our schoolboys by continual exercise, and their taste disagreeable; and to fatten them would not answer the charge. Then as to the females, it would, I think, with humble submission be a loss to the public, because they soon would become breeders themselves: and besides, it is not improbable that some scrupulous people might be apt to censure such a practice (although indeed very unjustly), as a little bordering upon cruelty; which, I confess, has always been with me the strongest objection against any project, how well soever intended.

But in order to justify my friend, he confessed that this expedient was put into his head by the famous Psalmanazar[11] a native of the island Formosa, who came from thence to London about twenty years ago: and in conversation told my friend, that in his country when any young person happened to be put to death, the executioner sold the carcass to persons of quality as a prime dainty; and that in his time the body of a plump girl of fifteen, who was crucified for an attempt to poison the emperor, was sold to his imperial majesty's prime minister of state, and other great mandarins of the court, in joints from the gibbet, at 400 crowns. Neither indeed can I deny, that if the same use were made of several plump young girls in this town, who without one single groat to their fortunes cannot stir abroad without a chair,[12] and appear at the playhouse and assemblies in foreign fineries which they never will pay for, the kingdom would not be the worse.

Some persons of a desponding spirit are in great concern about the vast number of poor people, who are aged, diseased, or maimed, and I have been desired to employ my thoughts what course may be taken to ease the nation of so grievous an encumbrance. But I am not in the least pain upon that matter, because it is very well known that they are every day dying and rotting by cold and famine, and filth and vermin, as fast as can be reasonably expected. And as to the young laborers, they are now in as hopeful a condition: They cannot get work, and consequently pine away for want of nourishment, to a degree that if at any time they are accidentally hired to common labor, they have not strength to perform it; and thus the country and themselves are happily delivered from the evils to come.

I have too long digressed, and therefore shall return to my subject. I 20 think the advantages by the proposal which I have made are obvious and many, as well as of the highest importance.

For first, as I have already observed, it would greatly lessen the number of papists, with whom we are yearly overrun, being the princi-

---

[11]**Psalmanazar**: George Psalmanazar (c. 1679–1763) was a Frenchman who tricked London society into believing he was a native of Formosa (now Taiwan).—EDS.

[12]**a chair**: A sedan chair in which one is carried about.—EDS.

pal breeders of the nation as well as our most dangerous enemies; and who stay at home on purpose to deliver the kingdom to the Pretender, hoping to take their advantage by the absence of so many good Protestants, who have chosen rather to leave their country than stay at home and pay tithes against their conscience to an Episcopal curate.

Secondly, The poor tenants will have something valuable of their own, which by law may be made liable to distress[13] and help to pay their landlord's rent, their corn and cattle being already seized, and money a thing unknown.

Thirdly, Whereas the maintenance of 100,000 children from two years old and upward, cannot be computed at less than 10s. a-piece per annum, the nation's stock will be thereby increased £50,000 per annum, beside the profit of a new dish introduced to the tables of all gentlemen of fortune in the kingdom who have any refinement in taste. And the money will circulate among ourselves, the goods being entirely of our own growth and manufacture.

Fourthly, The constant breeders beside the gain of 8s. sterling per annum by the sale of their children, will be rid of the charge of maintaining them after the first year.

Fifthly, This food would likewise bring great custom to taverns, where the vintners will certainly be so prudent as to procure the best receipts[14] for dressing it to perfection, and consequently have their houses frequented by all the fine gentlemen, who justly value themselves upon their knowledge in good eating; and a skilful cook who understands how to oblige his guests, will contrive to make it as expensive as they please.

Sixthly, This would be a great inducement to marriage, which all wise nations have either encouraged by rewards or enforced by laws and penalties. It would increase the care and tenderness of mothers toward their children, when they were sure of a settlement for life to the poor babes, provided in some sort by the public, to their annual profit instead of expense. We should see an honest emulation among the married women, which of them would bring the fattest child to the market. Men would become as fond of their wives during the time of their pregnancy as they are now of their mares in foal, their cows in calf, their sows when they are ready to farrow; nor offer to beat or kick them (as is too frequent a practice) for fear of a miscarriage.

Many other advantages might be enumerated. For instance, the addition of some thousand carcasses in our exportation of barreled beef, the propagation of swine's flesh, and improvement in the art of making good bacon, so much wanted among us by the great destruction

---

[13]**distress**: Seizure for payment of debt.—EDS.
[14]**receipts**: Recipes.—EDS.

of pigs, too frequent at our table; which are no way comparable in taste or magnificence to a well-grown, fat, yearling child, which roasted whole will make a considerable figure at a lord mayor's feast or any other public entertainment. But this and many others I omit, being studious of brevity.

Supposing that 1,000 families in this city would be constant customers for infants' flesh, besides others who might have it at merry-meetings, particularly at weddings and christenings, I compute that Dublin would take off annually about 20,000 carcasses; and the rest of the kingdom (where probably they will be sold somewhat cheaper) the remaining 80,000. 28

I can think of no one objection that will possibly be raised against this proposal, unless it should be urged that the number of people will be thereby much lessened in the kingdom. This I freely own, and it was indeed one principal design in offering it to the world. I desire the reader will observe, that I calculate my remedy for this one individual kingdom of Ireland and for no other that ever was, is, or I think ever can be upon earth. Therefore let no man talk to me of other expedients: of taxing our absentees at 5s. a pound: of using neither clothes nor household furniture except what is of our own growth and manufacture: of utterly rejecting the materials and instruments that promote foreign luxury: of curing the expensiveness of pride, vanity, idleness, and gaming in our women: of introducing a vein of parsimony, prudence, and temperance: of learning to love our country, in the want of which we differ even from Laplanders and the inhabitants of Topinamboo:[15] of quitting our animosities and factions, nor acting any longer like the Jews, who were murdering one another at the very moment their city was taken:[16] of being a little cautious not to sell our country and conscience for nothing: of teaching landlords to have at least one degree of mercy toward their tenants: lastly, of putting a spirit of honesty, industry, and skill into our shopkeepers; who, if a resolution could now be taken to buy only our native goods, would immediately unite to cheat and exact upon us in the price the measure, and the goodness, nor could ever yet be brought to make one fair proposal of just dealing, though often and earnestly invited to it.

Therefore I repeat, let no man talk to me of these and the like expedients, till he has at least some glimpse of hope that there will be ever some hearty and sincere attempt to put them in practice.

But as to myself, having been wearied out for many years with

---

[15]**Laplanders and the inhabitants of Topinamboo**: Lapland is the area of Scandanavia above the Arctic Circle; Topinamboo, in Brazil, was known in Swift's time for the savagery of its tribes.—EDS.

[16]**was taken**: A reference to the Roman seizure of Jerusalem (A.D. 70).—EDS.

offering vain, idle, visionary thoughts, and at length utterly despairing of success, I fortunately fell upon this proposal; which, as it is wholly new, so it has something solid and real, of no expense and little trouble, full in our own power, and whereby we can incur no danger in disobliging England. For this kind of commodity will not bear exportation, the flesh being of too tender a consistence to admit a long continuance in salt, although perhaps I could name a country which would be glad to eat up our whole nation without it.

After all, I am not so violently bent upon my own opinion as to 32 reject any offer proposed by wise men, which shall be found equally innocent, cheap, easy, and effectual. But before something of that kind shall be advanced in contradiction to my scheme, and offering a better, I desire the author or authors will be pleased maturely to consider two points. First, as things now stand, how they will be able to find food and raiment for 100,000 useless mouths and backs. And secondly, there being a round million of creatures in human figure throughout this kingdom, whose subsistence put into a common stock would leave them in debt 2,000,000£. sterling, adding those who are beggars by profession to the bulk of farmers, cottagers, and laborers, with the wives and children who are beggars in effect; I desire those politicians who dislike my overture, and may perhaps be so bold as to attempt an answer, that they will first ask the parents of these mortals, whether they would not at this day think it a great happiness to have been sold for food at a year old in the manner I prescribe, and thereby have avoided such a perpetual scene of misfortunes as they have since gone through by the oppression of landlords, the impossibility of paying rent without money or trade, the want of common sustenance, with neither house nor clothes to cover them from the inclemencies of the weather, and the most inevitable prospect of entailing the like or greater miseries upon their breed for ever.

I profess, in the sincerity of my heart, that I have not the least personal interest in endeavoring to promote this necessary work, having no other motive than the public good of my country, by advancing our trade, providing for infants, relieving the poor, and giving some pleasure to the rich. I have no children by which I can propose to get a single penny; the youngest being nine years old, and my wife past childbearing.   *1729*

Fyodor Dostoyevsky

Confession of Faith

"I must make one confession," Ivan began.[1] "I could never under-stand how one can love one's neighbors. It's just one's neighbors, to my mind, that one can't love, though one might love those who live at a distance. I once read somewhere of the saint, John the Merciful. When a hungry, frozen beggar came to him, he took him into his bed, held him in his arms, and began breathing into his mouth, which was putrid and loathsome from some awful disease. I am convinced that he did that from "self-laceration," from the self-laceration of falseness, for the sake of the charity imposed by duty, as a penance laid on him. For anyone to love a man, he must be hidden, for as soon as he shows his face, love is gone."

"Father Zossima has talked of that more than once," observed Al-yosha. "He, too, said that the face of a man often hinders people not practiced in love, from loving him. But yet there's a great deal of love in mankind, an almost Christ-like love. I know that myself, Ivan."

"Well, I know nothing of it so far, and can't understand it, and the mass of mankind are with me there. The question is, whether this lack of ability to love is due to men's bad qualities or whether it's inherent in their nature. To my thinking, Christ-like love for men is a miracle impossible on earth. He was God. But we are not gods. Suppose I, for instance, suffer intensely. Another can never know how much I suffer, because he is another and not I. And what's more, a man is rarely ready to admit another's suffering. Why won't he admit it, do you think? Because I smell unpleasant, because I have a stupid face, because I once trod on his foot. Besides there is suffering and suffering; degrading, humiliating suffering such as humbles me—hunger, for instance. But when you come to higher suffering—for an idea, for instance—he will very rarely admit it, perhaps because my face he thinks is not the face of a man who suffers for an idea. And so he deprives me instantly of his favor, and not at all from badness of heart. Beggars, especially genteel beggars, should never show themselves, but ask for charity through the newspapers.

[1]In this famous chapter of Dostoyevsky's classic novel *The Brothers Karamozov*, Ivan and Alyosha—two of the book's four brothers—meet at a restaurant. Though both in their early twenties, the brothers possess dramatically different personalities. Ivan, who is a few years older, is a brilliant and cynical author; the spiritual and innocent Alyosha is a novice at a monastery, where he has become attached to the holy Father Zossima, a celebrated religious figure. Alyosha has just asked Ivan the question: "Will you explain why you don't accept the world?" What follows is Ivan's answer.

"One can love one's neighbors in the abstract, or even at a distance,   4
but at close quarters it's almost impossible. If it were as on the stage, in
the ballet, where if beggars come in, they wear silken rags and tattered
lace and beg for alms dancing gracefully, then one might enjoy looking
at them. But even then we should not love them. But enough of that. I
simply wanted to show you my point of view. I meant to speak of the
suffering of mankind generally. But we had better confine ourselves to
the sufferings of children. That reduces the scope of my argument to a
tenth of what it would be. Still we'd better keep to children, though it
does weaken my case. But, in the first place, children can be loved even
at close quarters, even when they are dirty, even when they are ugly. The
second reason why I won't speak of grown-up people is that, besides
being disgusting and unworthy of love, they have a compensation—
they've eaten the apple and know good and evil, and they have become
'like God.' They go on eating it still. But children haven't eaten anything, and are innocent. Are you fond of children, Alyosha? I know you
are, and you will understand why I prefer to speak of them. If they, too,
suffer horribly on earth, they must suffer for their fathers' sins, they
must be punished for their fathers, who have eaten the apple. But that
reasoning is of the other world and is incomprehensible for the heart of
man here on earth. The innocent must not suffer for another's sins, and
especially such innocents! You may be surprised at me, Alyosha, but I
am awfully fond of children, too. And remember, cruel people, the
violent, the rapacious, the Karamazovs are sometimes very fond of
children. Children while they are quite little—up to seven, for
instance—are so remote from grown-up people; they are different creatures, as it were, of a different species. I knew a criminal in prison who
had murdered whole families, including several children. But when he
was in prison, he had a strange affection for them. He spent all his time
at his window watching the children playing in the prison yard. He
trained one little boy to come up to his window and made friends with
him. . . . You don't know why I am telling you all this, Alyosha? My head
aches and I am sad."

"You speak in such a strange way," observed Alyosha uneasily, "as
though you were not quite yourself."

"By the way, a Bulgarian I met lately in Moscow," Ivan went on,
seeming not to hear his brother's words, "told me about the crimes
committed by Turks and Circassians in Bulgaria through fear of a
general uprising of the Slavs. They burned villages, murdered, outraged
women and children, they nailed their prisoners by the ears to the
fences, left them till morning, and in the morning they hanged them—
all sorts of things you can't imagine. People talk sometimes of bestial
cruelty, but that's a great injustice and insult to the beasts; a beast can
never be so cruel as a man, so artistically cruel. The tiger only tears and

gnaws, that's all he can do. He would never think of nailing people by the ears, even if he were able to do it. These Turks took pleasure in torturing children, too; cutting the unborn child from the mother's womb, and tossing babies up in the air and catching them on the points of their bayonets before their mother's eyes. Doing it before the mother's eyes was what gave zest to the amusement. Here is another scene that I thought very interesting. Imagine a trembling mother with her baby in her arms, a circle of invading Turks around her. They've planned a game; they pet the baby, laugh to make it laugh. They succeed, the baby laughs. At that moment a Turk points a pistol four inches from the baby's face. The baby laughs, holds out its little hands to the pistol, and the Turk pulls the trigger in the baby's face and blows out its brains. Artistic, wasn't it? By the way, Turks are particularly fond of sweet things, they say."

"Ivan, what are you driving at?" asked Alyosha.

"I think if the devil doesn't exist, then man has created him. He has 8 created him in his own image and likeness."

"Just as man created God, then?" observed Alyosha.

" 'It's wonderful how you can turn words,' as Polonius says in *Hamlet*," laughed Ivan. "You turn my words against me. Well, I am glad. Yours must be a fine God, if man created Him in His image and likeness. You asked just now what I was driving at. You see, I like to collect certain facts, and, would you believe, I even copy anecdotes of a certain sort from newspapers and books. I've already got a fine collection. The Turks, of course, are included, but they are foreigners. I have Russian examples that are even better than the Turks. You know we prefer beating—rods and scourges—that's our national institution. Nailing ears is unthinkable for us, for we are, after all, Europeans. But the rod and the scourge we have always with us and they cannot be taken from us. Abroad now they scarcely do any beating. Manners are more humane, or laws have been passed, so that they don't dare to flog men now. But they make up for it in another way just as national as ours. It is so national that it would be practically impossible among us, though I believe we are being inoculated with it, since the religious movement began in our aristocracy.

"I have a charming pamphlet translated from the French describing how, quite recently, five years ago, a murderer, Richard, was executed— a young man, I believe, of twenty-three, who repented and was converted to the Christian faith at the scaffold. This Richard was illegitimate and had been given as a child of six by his parents to some shepherds on the Swiss mountains. They brought him up to work for them. He grew up like a wild beast among them. The shepherds taught him nothing, and scarcely fed or clothed him, but sent him out at seven to herd the flock in cold and wet, and no one hesitated to treat him in

this way. On the contrary, they thought they had every right, for Richard
had been given to them as chattel, and they did not even see the
necessity of feeding him. Richard himself described how in those years,
like the Prodigal Son in the Gospel, he longed to eat of the mash given
to the pigs, which were fattened for sale. But they wouldn't even give
him that, and beat him when he stole from the pigs. And that was how
he spent all his childhood and his youth, till he grew up and was strong
enough to go away and be a thief. The savage began to earn his living as
a day laborer in Geneva. He drank what he earned, he lived like a brute,
and finished by killing and robbing an old man. He was caught, tried,
and condemned to death. They are not sentimentalists there. And in
prison he was immediately surrounded by pastors, members of Christian brotherhoods, philanthropic ladies, and the like. They taught him
to read and write in prison, and expounded the Gospel to him. They
exhorted him, worked upon him, drummed at him incessantly, till at
last he solemnly confessed his crime. He was converted. He wrote to the
court himself that he was a monster, but that in the end God had given
him light and shown grace.

"All Geneva was excited about him—all philanthropic and re- 12
ligious Geneva. All the aristocratic and well-bred society of the town
rushed to the prison, kissed Richard and embraced him: 'You are our
brother, you have found grace.' And Richard did nothing but weep with
emothon: 'Yes, I've found grace! All my youth and childhood I was glad
of pigs' food, but now even I have found grace. I am dying in the Lord.'
'Yes, Richard, die in the Lord; you have shed blood and must die.
Though it's not your fault that you knew not the Lord, when you coveted
the pigs' food and were beaten for stealing it (which was very wrong of
you, for stealing is forbidden); but you've shed blood and you must die.'
And on the last day, Richard, perfectly limp, did nothing but cry and
repeat every minute: 'This is my happiest day. I am going to the Lord.'
'Yes,' cried the pastors and the judges and philanthropic ladies. 'This is
the happiest day of your life, for you are going to the Lord!' They all
walked or drove to the scaffold behind the prison van. At the scaffold
they called to Richard: 'Die, brother, die in the Lord, for even thou hast
found grace!' And so, covered with his brothers' kisses, Richard was
dragged to the scaffold, and led to the guillotine. And they chopped off
his head in brotherly fashion, because he had found grace. Yes, that's
characteristic. That pamphlet is translated into Russian by some Russian philanthropists of aristocratic rank and evangelical aspirations,
and has been distributed gratis for the enlightenment of our people.

"Richard's case is interesting because it's national. Though to us it's
absurd to cut off a man's head, because he has become our brother and
has found grace, yet we have our own specialty, which is worse. Our
historical pastime is the direct satisfaction of inflicting pain. There are

lines in Nekrassov describing how a peasant lashes a horse on the eyes, 'on its meek eyes,' everyone must have seen it. It's typically Russian. He describes how a feeble little nag had foundered under too heavy a load and could not move. The peasant beats it, beats it savagely, beats it at last not knowing what he is doing in the intoxication of cruelty. He thrashes it mercilessly over and over again. 'However weak you are, you must pull, even if you die doing it.' The nag strains, and then he begins lashing the poor defenseless creature on its weeping, on its 'meek eyes.' The frantic beast tugs and draws the load, trembling all over, gasping for breath, moving sideways, with a sort of unnatural spasmodic action—it's awful. But that's only a horse, and God has given horses to be beaten. So the Tatars have taught us, and they left us the knout as a remembrance of it.

"But men, too, can be beaten. A well-educated, cultured man and his wife beat their own child with a birch rod, a girl of seven. I have an account of it. The father was glad that the birch was covered with twigs. 'It stings more,' said he, and so he began stinging his daughter. I know for a fact that there are people who at every blow are worked up to sensuality, to literal sensuality, which increases progressively at every blow they inflict. They beat for a minute, for five minutes, for ten minutes, more often and more savagely. The child screams. At last the child cannot scream, it gasps, 'Daddy! Daddy!' By some diabolical unseemly chance the case was brought into court. A lawyer is engaged. The Russian people have long called a lawyer 'a conscience for hire.' The lawyer protests in his client's defense. 'It's such a simple thing,' he says, 'an everyday occurrence. A father punishes his child. To our shame be it said, it is brought into court.' The jury, convinced by him, give a favorable verdict. The public roars with delight that the torturer is acquitted. Ah, pity I wasn't there! I would have proposed to raise a subscription in his honor! . . . Charming pictures.

"But I've still better things about children. I've collected a great, great deal about Russian children, Alyosha. There was a little girl of five who was hated by her father and mother, 'most worthy and respectable people, of good education and breeding.' You see, I must repeat again, it is a peculiar characteristic of many people, this love of torturing children, and children only. To all other types of humanity these torturers behave mildly and kindly, like cultivated and humane Europeans. But they are very fond of tormenting children. It's just their defenselessness that tempts the tormentor, just the angelic confidence of the child who has no refuge and no appeal, that sets the tormentor's vile blood on fire. In every man, of course, a demon lies hidden—the demon of rage, the demon of lustful heat at the screams of the tortured victim, the demon of lawlessness let off the chain, the demon of diseases that follow on vice, gout, kidney disease, and so on.

"This poor child of five was subjected to every possible torture by 16 those cultivated parents. They beat her, kicked her for no reason till her body was one bruise. Then, they went to greater refinements of cruelty—shut her up all night in the cold and frost in a privy, because she didn't ask to be taken up at night (as though a child of five sleeping its sound sleep could be trained to wake and ask), they smeared her face and filled her mouth with excrement. It was her mother, her mother who did this. And that mother could sleep, hearing the poor child's groans! Can you understand why a little creature, who can't even understand what's done to her, should beat her little aching heart with her tiny fist in the dark and the cold, and weep her meek unresentful tears to dear, kind God to protect her? Do you understand that, Alyosha, you pious and humble novice? Do you understand why this infamy must be and is permitted? Without it, I am told, man could not have existed on earth, for he could not have known good and evil. Why should he know that diabolical good and evil when it costs so much? Why, the whole world of knowledge is not worth that child's prayer to 'dear, kind God'! I say nothing of the sufferings of grown-up people, they have eaten the apple, damn them, and the devil take them all! But these little ones! . . . I am making you suffer, Alyosha. I'll stop if you like."

"Never mind. I want to suffer too," muttered Alyosha.

"One picture, only one more, because it's so curious, so characteristic, and I have only just read it in some collection of Russian antiquities. I've forgotten the name. I must look it up. It was in the darkest days of serfdom at the beginning of the century, and long live the Liberator of the People! There was in those days a general of aristocratic connections, the owner of great estates, one of those men—somewhat exceptional, I believe, even then—who, retiring from the service into a life of leisure, are convinced that they've earned absolute power over the lives of their subjects. There were such men then. So our general, settled on his property of two thousand souls, lives in pomp, and dominates his poor neighbors as though they were dependents. He has kennels of hundreds of hounds and nearly a hundred dog-boys—all mounted, and in uniform. One day a serf boy, a little child of eight, threw a stone in play and hurt the paw of the general's favorite hound. 'Why is my favorite dog lame?' He is told that the boy threw a stone that hurt the dog's paw. 'So you did it.' The general looked the child up and down. 'Take him.' He was taken—taken from his mother and kept shut up all night. Early the next morning the general comes out on horseback, with the hounds, his dependents, dog-boys, and huntsmen, all mounted around him in full hunting parade. The servants are summoned for their edification, and in front of them all stands the mother of the child. The child is brought forward. It's a gloomy, cold, foggy autumn day, a perfect day for hunting. The general orders the child to be undressed.

The child is stripped naked. He shivers, numb with terror, not daring to cry. . . . 'Make him run,' commands the general. 'Run, run!' shout the dog-boys. The boy runs. . . . 'At him!' yells the general, and he sets the whole pack of hounds after the child. The hounds catch him, and tear him to pieces before his mother's eyes! . . . I believe the general was afterwards declared incapable of administering his estates. Well—what did he deserve? To be shot? To be shot for the satisfaction of our moral feelings? Speak, Alyosha!"

"To be shot," murmured Alyosha, lifting his eyes to Ivan with a pale, twisted smile.

"Good!" cried Ivan delighted. "If even you say so . . . You're a pretty 20 monk! So there is a little devil sitting in your heart, Alyosha Karamazov!"

"What I said was absurd, but . . . "

"That's just the point that 'but'!" cried Ivan. "Let me tell you, novice, that the absurd is only too necessary on earth. The world stands on absurdities, and perhaps nothing would have come to pass in it without them. We know what we know!"

"What do you know?"

"I understand nothing," Ivan went on, as though delirious. "I don't 24 want to understand anything now. I want to stick to the facts. I made up my mind long ago not to understand. If I try to understand anything, I will be false to the facts and I have determined to stick to the facts."

"Why are you testing me?" Alyosha cried. "Will you say what you mean?"

"Of course, I will. That's what I've been leading up to. You are dear to me. I don't want to let you go. And I won't give you up to your Zossima."

Ivan was silent for a minute. His face became all at once very sad.

"Listen! I spoke of children only to make my case clearer. Of the 28 other tears of humanity with which the earth is soaked from its crust to its center, I will say nothing. I have narrowed my subject on purpose. And I recognize in all humility that I cannot understand why the world is arranged as it is. Men are themselves to blame, I suppose: They were given paradise, they wanted freedom, and stole fire from heaven, though they knew they would become unhappy. So there is no need to pity them. With my earthly, Euclidian understanding, all I know is that there is suffering and that there are none guilty; that cause follows effect, simply and directly; that everything flows and finds its level— but that's only Euclidian nonsense, I know that, and I can't consent to live by it! What comfort is it to me that there are none guilty and that cause follows effect simply and directly, and that I know it—I must have justice, or I will destroy myself. And not justice in some remote infinite time and space, but here on earth. Justice that I can see myself. I have believed in it. I want to see it. And if I am dead by then, let me rise again, for if it all happens without me, it will be too unfair. Surely I haven't suffered, simply that I, my crimes and my sufferings, may manure the soil of future harmony for somebody else. I want to see with my own eyes the lamb lie down with the lion and the victim rise up and embrace his murderer. I want to be there when everyone suddenly understands what it has all been about. All the religions of the world are built on this longing, and I am a believer.

"But then there are the children, and what am I to do about them? That's a question I can't answer. For the hundredth time I repeat, there are numbers of questions, but I've only taken the children, because in their case what I mean is so unanswerably clear. Listen! If all must suffer to pay for eternal harmony, what have children to do with it? Tell me, please. It's beyond all comprehension why they should suffer and why they should pay for the harmony. Why should they, too, furnish material to enrich the soil for the harmony of the future? I understand solidarity in sin among men. I understand solidarity in retribution, too; but there can be no such solidarity with children. And if it is really true that they must share responsibility for all their fathers' crimes, such a truth is not of this world and is beyond my comprehension. Some jester will say, perhaps, that the child would have grown up and have sinned, but you see he didn't grow up, he was torn to pieces by the dogs, at eight years of age.

"Oh, Alyosha, I am not blaspheming! I understand, of course, what an upheaval of the universe it will be, when everything in heaven and earth blends in one hymn of praise and everything that lives and has lived cries aloud: 'Thou art just, O Lord, for Thy ways are revealed.' When the mother embraces the fiend who threw her child to the dogs, and all three cry aloud with tears, 'Thou art just, O Lord!' then, of course, the crown of knowledge will be reached and all will be made clear. But what troubles me is that I can't accept that harmony. And while I am on earth, I hurry to take my own measures. You see, Alyosha, perhaps it really may happen that if I live to that moment, or rise again to see it, I, too, perhaps, may cry aloud with the rest, looking at the mother embracing the child's torturer: 'Thou art just, O Lord!' But I don't want to cry aloud then. While there is still time, I want to protect myself and so I renounce the higher harmony altogether. It's not worth the tears of that one tortured child who beat itself on the breast with its little fist and prayed in its stinking outhouse, with its tears to 'dear, kind God'! It's not worth it, because those tears are unatoned for. They must be atoned for, or there can be no harmony. But how? How are you going to atone for them? Is it possible? By their being avenged? But what do I care for avenging them? What do I care for a hell for oppressors? What good can hell do, since those children have already been tortured? And what becomes of harmony, if there is hell? I want to forgive. I want to embrace. I don't want more suffering. And if the sufferings of children go to swell the sum of sufferings which was necessary to pay for truth, then I protest that the truth is not worth such a price. I don't want the mother to embrace the oppressor who threw her sons to the dogs! She dare not forgive him! Let her forgive him for herself, if she will. Let her forgive the torturer for the immeasurable suffering of her mother's heart. But the sufferings of her tortured child she has no right to forgive; she dare not forgive the torturer, even if the child were to forgive him! And if that is so, if they dare not forgive, what becomes of harmony? Is there in the whole world a person who would have the right to forgive and could forgive? I don't want harmony. From love for humanity I don't want it. I would rather be left with unavenged suffering. I would rather remain with my unavenged suffering and unsatisfied indignation, *even if I were wrong*. Besides, too high a price is asked for harmony; it's beyond our means to pay so much. And so I give back my entrance ticket, and if I am an honest man I give it back as soon as possible. And that I am doing. It's not God that I don't accept, Alyosha, only I most respectfully return the ticket to Him."

"That's rebellion," murmured Alyosha, looking down.

"Rebellion? I am sorry you call it that," said Ivan earnestly. "One 32 can hardly live in rebellion, and I want to live. Tell me yourself, I challenge you—answer. Imagine that you are creating a fabric of human destiny with the object of making men happy in the end, giving them peace and rest at last. Imagine that you are doing this but that it is essential and inevitable to torture to death only one tiny creature—that child beating its breast with its fist, for instance—in order to found that edifice on its unavenged tears. Would you consent to be the architect on those conditions? Tell me. Tell the truth."

"No, I wouldn't consent," said Alyosha softly.   *1880*

Mark Twain

The Damned Human Race

I have been studying the traits and dispositions of the "lower animals" (so-called), and contrasting them with the traits and dispositions of man. I find the result humiliating to me. For it obliges me to renounce my allegiance to the Darwinian[1] theory of the Ascent of Man from the Lower Animals; since it now seems plain to me that that theory ought to be vacated in favor of a new and truer one, this new and truer one to be named the *Descent* of Man from the Higher Animals.

In proceeding toward this unpleasant conclusion I have not guessed or speculated or conjectured, but have used what is commonly called the scientific method. That is to say, I have subjected every postulate that presented itself to the crucial test of actual experiment, and have adopted it or rejected it according to the result. Thus I verified and established each step of my course in its turn before advancing to the next. These experiments were made in the London Zoological Gardens, and covered many months of painstaking and fatiguing work.

Before particularizing any of the experiments, I wish to state one or two things which seem to more properly belong in this place than further along. This in the interest of clearness. The massed experiments established to my satisfaction certain generalizations, to wit:

1. That the human race is of one distinct species. It exhibits slight 4 variations— in color, stature, mental caliber, and so on—due to climate, environment, and so forth; but it is a species by itself, and not to be confounded with any other.

2. That the quadrupeds are a distinct family, also. This family exhibits variations—in color, size, food preferences and so on; but it is a family by itself.

3. That the other families—the birds, the fishes, the insects, the reptiles, etc.—are more or less distinct, also. They are in the procession. They are links in the chain which stretches down from the higher animals to man at the bottom.

Some of my experiments were quite curious. In the course of my reading I had come across a case where, many years ago, some hunters on our Great Plains organized a buffalo hunt for the entertainment of an English earl—that, and to provide some fresh meat for his larder. They had charming sport. They killed seventy-two of those great animals; and ate part of one of them and left the seventy-one to rot. In order to determine the difference between an anaconda and an earl—if any—I caused seven young calves to be turned into the anaconda's cage. The grateful reptile immediately crushed one of them and swallowed it, then lay back satisfied. It showed no further interest in the calves, and no disposition to harm them. I tried this experiment with other anacondas; always with the same result. The fact stood proven that the difference between an earl and an anaconda is that the earl is cruel and the anaconda isn't; and that the earl wantonly destroys what he has no

---

[1]Charles Darwin (1809–1882) published *The Descent of Man* in 1871, a highly controversial book in which he argued that humankind had descended from "lower" forms of life.—EDS.

use for, but the anaconda doesn't. This seemed to suggest that the anaconda was not descended from the earl. It also seemed to suggest that the earl was descended from the anaconda, and had lost a good deal in the transition.

I was aware that many men who have accumulated more millions of money than they can ever use have shown a rabid hunger for more, and have not scrupled to cheat the ignorant and the helpless out of their poor servings in order to partially appease that appetite. I furnished a hundred different kinds of wild and tame animals the opportunity to accumulate vast stores of food, but none of them would do it. The squirrels and bees and certain birds made accumulations, but stopped when they had gathered a winter's supply, and could not be persuaded to add to it either honestly or by chicane. In order to bolster up a tottering reputation the ant pretended to store up supplies, but I was not deceived. I know the ant. These experiments convinced me that there is this difference between man and the higher animals: he is avaricious and miserly, they are not. 8

In the course of my experiments I convinced myself that among the animals man is the only one that harbors insults and injuries, broods over them, waits till a chance offers, then takes revenge. The passion of revenge is unknown to the higher animals.

Roosters keep harems, but it is by consent of their concubines; therefore no wrong is done. Men keep harems, but it is by brute force, privileged by atrocious laws which the other sex were allowed no hand in making. In this matter man occupies a far lower place than the rooster.

Cats are loose in their morals, but not consciously so. Man, in his descent from the cat, has brought the cat's looseness with him but has left the unconsciousness behind—the saving grace which excuses the cat. The cat is innocent, man is not.

Indecency, vulgarity, obscenity—these are strictly confined to man; he invented them. Among the higher animals there is no trace of them. They hide nothing; they are not ashamed. Man, with his soiled mind, covers himself. He will not even enter a drawing room with his breast and back naked, so alive are he and his mates to indecent suggestion. Man is "The Animal that Laughs." But so does the monkey, as Mr. Darwin pointed out; and so does the Australian bird that is called the laughing jackass. No—Man is the Animal that Blushes. He is the only one that does it—or has occasion to. 12

At the head of this article[2] we see how "three monks were burnt to

---

[2]In his nonfiction Twain often introduced newsclippings as evidence of human atrocity. In this instance the article has been lost, but Twain is most likely referring to the religious persecutions that followed the 1897 Cretan revolt.—Eds.

death" a few days ago, and a prior "put to death with atrocious cruelty." Do we inquire into the details? No; or we should find out that the prior was subjected to unprintable mutilations. Man—when he is a North American Indian—gouges out his prisoner's eyes; when he is King John, with a nephew to render untroublesome, he uses a red-hot iron; when he is a religious zealot dealing with heretics in the Middle Ages, he skins his captive alive and scatters salt on his back; in the first Richard's time he shuts up a multitude of Jew families in a tower and sets fire to it; in Columbus's time he captures a family of Spanish Jews and—but *that* is not printable; in our day in England a man is fined ten shillings for beating his mother nearly to death with a chair, and another man is fined forty shillings for having four pheasant eggs in his possession without being able to satisfactorily explain how he got them. Of all the animals, man is the only one that is cruel. He is the only one that inflicts pain for the pleasure of doing it. It is a trait that is not known to the higher animals. The cat plays with the frightened mouse; but she has this excuse, that she does not know that the mouse is suffering. The cat is moderate—unhumanly moderate: she only scares the mouse, she does not hurt it; she doesn't dig out its eyes, or tear off its skin, or drive splinters under its nails—man-fashion; when she is done playing with it she makes a sudden meal of it and puts it out of its trouble. Man is the Cruel Animal. He is alone in that distinction.

The higher animals engage in individual fights, but never in organized masses. Man is the only animal that deals in that atrocity of atrocities, War. He is the only one that gathers his brethren about him and goes forth in cold blood and with calm pulse to exterminate his kind. He is the only animal that for sordid wages will march out, as the Hessians did in our Revolution,[3] and as the boyish Prince Napoleon did in the Zulu war,[4] and help to slaughter strangers of his own species who have done him no harm and with whom he has no quarrel.

Man is the only animal that robs his helpless fellow of his country—takes possession of it and drives him out of it or destroys him. Man has done this in all the ages. There is not an acre of ground on the globe that is in possession of its rightful owner, or that has not been taken away from owner after owner, cycle after cycle, by force and bloodshed.

Man is the only Slave. And he is the only animal who enslaves. He has always been a slave in one form or another, and has always held other slaves in bondage under him in one way or another. In our day he   16

[3]**Revolution**: Approximately 17,000 mercenaries from Hesse, a part of Germany, fought for the British during the American Revolution.—Eds.
[4]**Zulu war**: Napolean III's son died while fighting for the British during the 1879 Zulu rebellion in what is now the Republic of South Africa. Great Britain annexed the Zulu territory shortly after, and that is the context for Twain's remarks in the next paragraph.—Eds.

is always some man's slave for wages, and does that man's work; and this slave has other slaves under him for minor wages, and they do *his* work. The higher animals are the only ones who exclusively do their own work and provide their own living.

Man is the only Patriot. He sets himself apart in his own country, under his own flag, and sneers at the other nations, and keeps multi-tudinous uniformed assassins on hand at heavy expense to grab slices of other people's countries, and keep *them* from grabbing slices of *his*. And in the intervals between campaigns he washes the blood off his hands and works for "the universal brotherhood of man"—with his mouth.

Man is the Religious Animal. He is the only Religious Animal. He is the only animal that has the True Religion—several of them. He is the only animal that loves his neighbor as himself, and cuts his throat if his theology isn't straight. He has made a graveyard of the globe in trying his honest best to smooth his brother's path to happiness and heaven. He was at it in the time of the Caesars, he was at it in Mahomet's time, he was at it in the time of the Inquisition, he was at it in France a couple of centuries, he was at it in England in Mary's day,[5] he has been at it ever since he first saw the light, he is at it today in Crete—as per the telegrams quoted above—he will be at it somewhere else tomorrow. The higher animals have no religion. And we are told that they are going to be left out, in the Hereafter. I wonder why? It seems questionable taste.

Man is the Reasoning Animal. Such is the claim. I think it is open to dispute. Indeed, my experiments have proven to me that he is the Unreasoning Animal. Note his history, as sketched above. It seems plain to me that whatever he is he is *not* a reasoning animal. His record is the fantastic record of a maniac. I consider that the strongest count against his intelligence is the fact that with that record back of him he blandly sets himself up as the head animal of the lot: whereas by his own standards he is the bottom one.

In truth, man is incurably foolish. Simple things which the other 20 animals easily learn, he is incapable of learning. Among my experiments was this. In an hour I taught a cat and a dog to be friends. I put them in a cage. In another hour I taught them to be friends with a rabbit. In the course of two days I was able to add a fox, a goose, a squirrel and some doves. Finally a monkey. They lived together in peace; even affectionately.

Next, in another cage I confined an Irish Catholic from Tipperary, and as soon as he seemed tame I added a Scotch Presbyterian from Aberdeen. Next a Turk from Constantinople; a Greek Christian from Crete; an Armenian; a Methodist from the wilds of Arkansas; a Buddhist

---

[5]**Mary's day**: Mary Stuart (1542–1587), known as Mary, Queen of Scots, was convicted of conspiracy and beheaded in 1587.—EDS.

from China; a Brahman from Benares. Finally, a Salvation Army Colonel from Wapping. Then I stayed away two whole days. When I came back to note results, the cage of Higher Animals was all right, but in the other there was but a chaos of gory odds and ends of turbans and fezzes and plaids and bones and flesh—not a specimen left alive. These Reasoning Animals had disagreed on a theological detail and carried the matter to a Higher Court.

One is obliged to concede that in true loftiness of character, Man cannot claim to approach even the meanest of the Higher Animals. It is plain that he is constitutionally incapable of approaching that altitude; that he is constitutionally afflicted with a Defect which must make such approach forever impossible, for it is manifest that this defect is permanent in him, indestructible, ineradicable.

I find this Defect to be *the Moral Sense*. He is the only animal that has it. It is the secret of his degradation. It is the quality *which enables him to do wrong*. It has no other office. It is incapable of performing any other function. It could never have been intended to perform any other. Without it, man could do no wrong. He would rise at once to the level of the Higher Animals.

Since the Moral Sense has but the one office, the one capacity—to 24 enable man to do wrong—it is plainly without value to him. It is as valueless to him as is disease. In fact, it manifestly *is* a disease. *Rabies* is bad, but it is not so bad as this disease. Rabies enables a man to do a thing which he could not do when in a healthy state: kill his neighbor with a poisonous bite. No one is the better man for having rabies. The Moral Sense enables a man to do wrong. It enables him to do wrong in a thousand ways. Rabies is an innocent disease, compared to the Moral Sense. No one, then, can be the better man for having the Moral Sense. What, now, do we find the Primal Curse to have been? Plainly what it was in the beginning: the infliction upon man of the Moral Sense; the ability to distinguish good from evil; and with it, necessarily, the ability to *do* evil; for there can be no evil act without the presence of consciousness of it in the doer of it.

And so I find that we have descended and degenerated, from some far ancestor—some microscopic atom wandering at its pleasure between the mighty horizons of a drop of water perchance—insect by insect, animal by animal, reptile by reptile, down the long highway of smirchless innocence, till we have reached the bottom stage of development—namable as the Human Being. Below us—nothing. Nothing but the Frenchman.

There is only one possible stage below the Moral Sense; that is the Immoral Sense. The Frenchman has it. Man is but little lower than the angels. This definitely locates him. He is between the angels and the French.

Man seems to be a rickety poor sort of a thing, any way you take him; a kind of British Museum of infirmities and inferiorities. He is always undergoing repairs. A machine that was as unreliable as he is would have no market. On top of his specialty—the Moral Sense—are piled a multitude of minor infirmities; such a multitude, indeed, that one may broadly call them countless. The higher animals get their teeth without pain or inconvenience. Man gets his through months and months of cruel torture; and at a time of life when he is but ill able to bear it. As soon as he has got them they must all be pulled out again, for they were of no value in the first place, not worth the loss of a night's rest. The second set will answer for a while, by being reinforced occasionally with rubber or plugged up with gold; but he will never get a set which can really be depended on till a dentist makes him one. This set will be called "false" teeth—as if he had ever worn any other kind.

In a wild state—a natural state—the Higher Animals have a few 28 diseases; diseases of little consequence; the main one is old age. But man starts in as a child and lives on diseases till the end, as a regular diet. He has mumps, measles, whooping cough, croup, tonsillitis, diphtheria, scarlet fever, almost as a matter of course. Afterward, as he goes along, his life continues to be threatened at every turn: by colds, coughs, asthma, bronchitis, itch, cholera, cancer, consumption, yellow fever, bilious fever, typhus fevers, hay fever, ague, chilblains, piles, inflammation of the entrails, indigestion, toothache, earache, deafness, dumbness, blindness, influenza, chicken pox, cowpox, smallpox, liver complaint, constipation, bloody flux, warts, pimples, boils, carbuncles, abscesses, bunions, corns, tumors, fistulas, pneumonia, softening of the brain, melancholia and fifteen other kinds of insanity; dysentery, jaundice, diseases of the heart, the bones, the skin, the scalp, the spleen, the kidneys, the nerves, the brain, the blood; scrofula, paralysis, leprosy, neuralgia, palsy, fits, headache, thirteen kinds of rheumatism, forty-six of gout, and a formidable supply of gross and unprintable disorders of one sort and another. Also—but why continue the list? The mere names of the agents appointed to keep this shackly machine out of repair would hide him from sight if printed on his body in the smallest type known to the founder's art. He is but a basket of pestilent corruption provided for the support and entertainment of swarming armies of bacilli—armies commissioned to rot him and destroy him, and each army equipped with a special detail of the work. The process of waylaying him, persecuting him, rotting him, killing him, begins with his first breath, and there is no mercy, no pity, no truce till he draws his last one.

Look at the workmanship of him, in certain of its particulars. What are his tonsils for? They perform no useful function; they have no value. They have no business there. They are but a trap. They have but the one office, the one industry: to provide tonsillitis and quinsy and such things

for the possessor of them. And what is the vermiform appendix for? It
has no value; it cannot perform any useful service. It is but an am-
buscaded enemy whose sole interest in life is to lie in wait for stray
grapeseeds and employ them to breed strangulated hernia. And what
are the male's mammals for? For business, they are out of the question;
as an ornament, they are a mistake. What is his beard for? It performs
no useful function; it is a nuisance and a discomfort; all nations hate it;
all nations persecute it with a razor. And because it is a nuisance and a
discomfort, Nature never allows the supply of it to fall short, in any
man's case, between puberty and the grave. You never see a man bald-
headed on his chin. But his hair! It is a graceful ornament, it is a
comfort, it is the best of all protections against certain perilous ail-
ments, man prizes it above emeralds and rubies. And because of these
things Nature puts it on, half the time, so that it won't stay. Man's sight,
smell, hearing, sense of locality—how inferior they are. The condor sees
a corpse at five miles; man has no telescope that can do it. The blood-
hound follows a scent that is two days old. The robin hears the earth-
worm burrowing his course under the ground. The cat, deported in a
closed basket, finds its way home again through twenty miles of country
which it has never seen.

Certain functions lodged in the other sex perform in a lamentably
inferior way as compared with the performance of the same functions in
the Higher Animals. In the human being, menstruation, gestation and
parturition are terms which stand for horrors. In the Higher Animals
these things are hardly even inconveniences.

For style, look at the Bengal tiger—that ideal of grace, beauty,
physical perfection, majesty. And then look at Man—that poor thing.
He is the Animal of the Wig, the Trepanned Skull, the Ear Trumpet, the
Glass Eye, the Pasteboard Nose, the Porcelain Teeth, the Silver Wind-
pipe, the Wooden Leg—a creature that is mended and patched all over,
from top to bottom. If he can't get renewals of his bric-a-brac in the next
world, what will he look like?

He has just one stupendous superiority. In his intellect he is su- 32
preme. The Higher Animals cannot touch him there. It is curious, it is
noteworthy, that no heaven has ever been offered him wherein his one
sole superiority was provided with a chance to enjoy itself. Even when
he himself has imagined a heaven, he has never made provision in it for
intellectual joys. It is a striking omission. It seems a tacit confession that
heavens are provided for the Higher Animals alone. This is matter for
thought; and for serious thought. And it is full of a grim suggestion: that
we are not as important, perhaps, as we had all along supposed we were.

1938

28

Visions of the Land

Henry David Thoreau, *From*
The Maine Woods
Wendell Berry, The Journey's End
N. Scott Momaday, A First American
Views His Land

The earth was created by the assistance of the sun, and it should be left
as it was. . . . The country was made without lines of demarcation, and it
is no man's business to divide it. . . . I see the whites all over the country
gaining wealth, and see their desire to give us lands which are worthless.
. . . The earth and myself are of one mind. The measure of the land and
the measure of our bodies are the same. Say to us if you can say it, that
you were sent by the Creative Power to talk to us. Perhaps you think the
Creator sent you here to dispose of us as you see fit. If I thought you
were sent by the Creator I might be induced to think you had a right to
dispose of me. Do not misunderstand me, but understand me fully with
reference to my affection for the land. I never said the land was mine to
do with it as I chose. The one who has the right to dispose of it is the one
who has created it. I claim a right to live on my land, and accord you the
privilege to live on yours.

Heinmot Tooyalaket (Chief Joseph) of the Nez Percés,
as quoted in Dee Brown's *Bury My Heart at Wounded Knee*

Wilderness threatened became wilderness desirable—for the handful
of converts. Thoreau was, as far as I know, the first American who
publicly concluded that wilderness as wilderness—that is, pure
nature—was a good thing to have around. In the 1850s he made a
proposal that each town in Massachusetts save a five hundred–acre piece

of woods which would be forever wild: no lumbering, no changes at all. Needless to say, he got nowhere, not even in Concord itself. It was still too much like going down to McDonald's and suggesting to the manager that he put five hundred ice cubes in permanent deep freeze, against the time when ice may be scarce.

Noel Perrin, from *Forever Virgin: The American View of America*

I am not trying to abolish the countryside. (I *state* this because it is true; I emphasize it because I don't want the lynch mob outside my window.) I'm not such a pig as to want the country built on or littered up with bottles and plastic bags merely because it doesn't appeal to *me*. As it happens, my own taste for countryside, though small, is existent. I've found the country very pleasant to be driven through in a tolerably fast car by someone whose driving I trust and whose company I like. But I admit that landscape as such bores me—to the extent that I have noticed myself in picture galleries automatically pausing to look at "Landscape with Ruins" or "Bandits in a Landscape" but walking straight past the pure landscapes at a speed which is obviously trying to simulate the effect of being driven past in a car.

Brigid Brophy, from *The Menace of Nature*

Henry David Thoreau

From The Maine Woods

At mid-afternoon we embarked on the Penobscot.[1] Our birch was nineteen and a half feet long by two and a half at the widest part, and fourteen inches deep within, both ends alike, and painted green, which Joe thought affected the pitch and made it leak. This, I think, was a middling-sized one. That of the explorers[2] was much larger, though

---

[1]**Penobscot:** The selection describes an episode during the 325-mile canoe trip Thoreau, then forty years old, and a companion (Ed Hoar) made in 1857 along the Penobscot and Allagash rivers in northwest Maine. They hired as a guide a prominent 48-year-old Penobscot Indian, Joe Polis, who represented his people in Washington and knew Daniel Webster. Thoreau portrays Polis as "stoutly built, perhaps a little above the middle height, with a broad face, and, as others said, perfect Indian features and complexion."—EDS.

[2]**explorers:** Logging surveyors that Thoreau had met earlier on the trip.—EDS.

probably not much longer. This carried us three with our baggage, weighing in all between five hundred and fifty and six hundred pounds. We had two heavy, though slender, rock-maple paddles, one of them of bird's-eye maple. Joe placed birch-bark on the bottom for us to sit on, and slanted cedar splints against the cross-bars to protect our backs, while he himself sat upon a cross-bar in the stern. The baggage occupied the middle or widest part of the canoe. We also paddled by turns in the bows, now sitting with our legs extended, now sitting upon our legs, and now rising upon our knees; but I found none of these positions endurable, and was reminded of the complaints of the old Jesuit missionaries of the torture they endured from long confinement in constrained positions in canoes, in their long voyages from Quebec to the Huron country; but afterward I sat on the cross-bars, or stood up, and experienced no inconvenience.

It was dead-water for a couple of miles. The river had been raised about two feet by the rain, and lumberers were hoping for a flood sufficient to bring down the logs that were left in the spring. Its banks were seven or eight feet high, and densely covered with white and black spruce—which, I think, must be the commonest trees thereabouts—fir, arbor-vitæ, canoe, yellow, and black birch, rock, mountain, and a few red maples, beech, black and mountain ash, the large-toothed aspen, many civil-looking elms, now imbrowned, along the stream, and at first a few hemlocks also. We had not gone far before I was startled by seeing what I thought was an Indian encampment, covered with a red flag, on the bank, and exclaimed, "Camp!" to my comrades. I was slow to discover that it was a red maple changed by the frost. The immediate shores were also densely covered with the speckled alder, red osier, shrubby-willows or sallows, and the like. There were a few yellow-lily-pads still left, half-drowned, along the sides, and sometimes a white one. Many fresh tracks of moose were visible where the water was shallow, and on the shore, and the lily-stems were freshly bitten off by them.

After paddling about two miles, we parted company with the explorers, and turned up Lobster Stream, which comes in on the right, from the southeast. This was six or eight rods wide, and appeared to run nearly parallel with the Penobscot. Joe said that it was so called from small fresh-water lobsters found in it. It is the Matahumkeag of the maps. My companion wished to look for moose signs, and intended, if it proved worth the while, to camp up that way, since the Indian advised it. On account of the rise of the Penobscot the water ran up this stream quite to the pond of the same name, one or two miles. The Spencer Mountains, east of the north end of Moosehead Lake, were now in plain sight in front of us. The kingfisher flew before us, the pigeon wood-pecker was seen and heard, and nuthatches and chicadees close at hand. Joe said that they called the chicadee *kecunnilessu* in his language. I will not vouch for the spelling of what possibly was never spelt before, but I pronounced after him till he said it would do. We passed close to a woodcock, which stood perfectly still on the shore, with feathers puffed up, as if sick. This Joe said they called *nipsquecohossus*. The kingfisher was *skuscumonsuck*; bear was *wassus*; Indian Devil, *lunxus*; the mountain-ash, *upahsis*. This was very abundant and beautiful. Moose-tracks were not so fresh along this stream, except in a small creek about a mile up it, where a large log had lodged in the spring, marked "W—cross—girdle—crow-foot." We saw a pair of moose-horns on the shore, and I asked Joe if a moose had shed them; but he said there was a head attached to them, and I knew that they did not shed their heads more than once in their lives.

After ascending about a mile and a half, to within a short distance   4 of Lobster Lake, we returned to the Penobscot. Just below the mouth of the Lobster we found quick water, and the river expanded to twenty or thirty rods in width. The moose-tracks were quite numerous and fresh here. We noticed in a great many places narrow and well-trodden paths by which they had come down to the river, and where they had slid on the steep and clayey bank. Their tracks were either close to the edge of the stream, those of the calves distinguishable from the others, or in shallow water; the holes made by their feet in the soft bottom being visible for a long time. They were particularly numerous where there was a small bay, or *pokelogan*, as it is called, bordered by a strip of meadow, or separated from the river by a low peninsula covered with coarse grass, wool-grass, etc., wherein they had waded back and forth and eaten the pads. We detected the remains of one in such a spot. At one place, where we landed to pick up a summer duck, which my companion had shot, Joe peeled a canoe-birch for bark for his hunting-horn. He then asked if we were not going to get the other duck, for his sharp eyes had seen another fall in the bushes a little farther along, and my companion obtained it. I now began to notice the bright red berries of the tree-cranberry, which grows eight or ten feet high, mingled with the alders and cornel along the shore. There was less hard wood than at first.

After proceeding a mile and three-quarters below the mouth of the Lobster, we reached, about sun-down, a small island at the head of what Joe called the Moosehorn Dead-water (the Moosehorn, in which he was going to hunt that night, coming in about three miles below), and on the upper end of this we decided to camp. On a point at the lower end lay the carcass of a moose killed a month or more before. We concluded merely to prepare our camp, and leave our baggage here, that all might be ready when we returned from moose-hunting. Though I had not come a-hunting, and felt some compunctions about accompanying the hunters, I wished to see a moose near at hand, and was not sorry to learn how the Indian managed to kill one. I went as reporter or chaplain to the hunters—and the chaplain has been known to carry a gun himself. After clearing a small space amid the dense spruce and fir trees, we covered the damp ground with a shingling of fir-twigs, and, while Joe was preparing his birch-horn and pitching his canoe—for this had to be done whenever we stopped long enough to build a fire, and was the principal labor which he took upon himself at such times—we collected fuel for the night, large wet and rotting logs, which had lodged at the head of the island, for our hatchet was too small for effective chopping; but we did not kindle a fire, lest the moose should smell it. Joe set up a couple of forked stakes, and prepared half a dozen poles, ready to cast one of our blankets over in case it rained in the night, which precaution, however, was omitted the next night. We also plucked the ducks which had been killed for breakfast.

While we were thus engaged in the twilight, we heard faintly, from far down the stream, what sounded like two strokes of a woodchopper's axe, echoing dully through the grim solitude. We are wont to liken many sounds, heard at a distance in the forest, to the stroke of an axe, because they resemble each other under those circumstances, and that is the one we commonly hear there. When we told Joe of this, he exclaimed, "By George, I'll bet that was a moose! They make a noise like that." These sounds affected us strangely, and by their very resemblance to a familiar one, where they probably had so different an origin, enchanced the impression of solitude and wildness.

At starlight we dropped down the stream, which was a dead-water for three miles, or as far as the Moosehorn; Joe telling us that we must be very silent, and he himself making no noise with his paddle, while he urged the canoe along with effective impulses. It was a still night, and suitable for this purpose—for if there is wind, the moose will smell you—and Joe was very confident that he should get some. The harvest moon had just risen, and its level rays began to light up the forest on our right, while we glided downward in the shade on the same side, against the little breeze that was stirring. The lofty, spiring tops of the spruce and fir were very black against the sky, and more distinct than by day, close bordering this broad avenue on each side; and the beauty of the scene, as the moon rose above the forest, it would not be easy to describe. A bat flew over our heads, and we heard a few faint notes of birds from time to time, perhaps the myrtle-bird for one, or the sudden plunge of a musquash, or saw one crossing the stream before us, or heard the sound of a rill emptying in, swollen by the recent rain. About a mile below the island, when the solitude seemed to be growing more complete every moment, we suddenly saw the light and heard the crackling of a fire on the bank, and discovered the camp of the two explorers; they standing before it in their red shirts, and talking aloud of the adventures and profits of the day. They were just then speaking of a bargain, in which, as I understood, somebody had cleared twenty-five dollars. We glided by without speaking, close under the bank, within a couple of rods of them; and Joe, taking his horn, imitated the call of the moose, till we suggested that they might fire on us. This was the last we saw of them, and we never knew whether they detected or suspected us.

I have often wished since that I was with them. They search for timber over a given section, climbing hills and often high trees to look off—explore the streams by which it is to be driven, and the like— spend five or six weeks in the woods, they two alone, a hundred miles or more from any town—roaming about, and sleeping on the ground where night overtakes them—depending chiefly on the provisions they carry with them, though they do not decline what game they come across—and then in the fall they return and make report to their employers, determining the number of teams that will be required the following winter. Experienced men get three or four dollars a day for this work. It is a solitary and adventurous life, and comes nearest to that of the trapper of the West, perhaps. They work ever with a gun as well as an axe, let their beards grow, and live without neighbors, not on an open plain, but far within a wilderness.

This discovery accounted for the sounds which we had heard, and destroyed the prospect of seeing moose yet awhile. At length, when we had left the explorers far behind, Joe laid down his paddle, drew forth his birch horn—a straight one, about fifteen inches long and three or four wide at the mouth, tied round with strips of the same bark—and standing up, imitated the call of the moose—*ugh-ugh-ugh*, or *oo-oo-oo-oo*, and then a prolonged *oo-o-o-o-o-o-o-o*, and listened attentively for several minutes. We asked him what kind of noise he expected to hear. He said, that, if a moose heard it, he guessed we should find out; we should hear him coming half a mile off; he would come close to, perhaps into, the water, and my companion must wait till he got fair sight, and then aim just behind the shoulder.

The moose venture out to the river-side to feed and drink at night. Earlier in the season the hunters do not use a horn to call them out, but steal upon them as they are feeding along the sides of the stream, and often the first notice they have of one is the sound of the water dropping from its muzzle. An Indian whom I heard imitate the voice of the moose, and also that of the caribou and the deer, using a much longer horn than Joe's, told me that the first could be heard eight or ten miles, sometimes; it was a loud sort of bellowing sound, clearer and more sonorous than the lowing of cattle—the caribou's a sort of snort—and the small deer's like that of a lamb.

At length we turned up the Moosehorn, where the Indians at the carry had told us that they killed a moose the night before. This is a very meandering stream, only a rod or two in width, but comparatively deep, coming in on the right, fitly enough named Moosehorn, whether from its windings or its inhabitants. It was bordered here and there by narrow meadows between the stream and the endless forest, affording favorable places for the moose to feed, and to call them out on. We proceeded half a mile up this, as through a narrow, winding canal, where the tall, dark spruce and firs and arbor-vitæ towered on both sides in the moonlight, forming a perpendicular forest-edge of great height, like the spires of a Venice in the forest. In two places stood a small stack of hay on the bank, ready for the lumberer's use in the winter, looking strange enough there. We thought of the day when this might be a brook winding through smooth-shaven meadows on some gentleman's grounds; and seen by moonlight then, excepting the forest that now hems it in, how little changed it would appear!

Again and again Joe called the moose, placing the canoe close by some favorable point of meadow for them to come out on, but listened in vain to hear one come rushing through the woods and concluded that they had been hunted too much thereabouts. We saw, many times, what to our imaginations looked like a gigantic moose, with his horns peering from out the forest-edge; but we saw the forest only, and not its inhabitants, that night. So at last we turned about. There was now a little fog on the water, though it was a fine, clear night above. There were very few sounds to break the stillness of the forest. Several times we heard the hooting of a great horned-owl, as at home, and told Joe that he would call out the moose for him, for he made a sound considerably like the horn—but Joe answered, that the moose had heard that sound a thousand times, and knew better; and oftener still we were startled by the plunge of a musquash. Once, when Joe had called again, and we were listening for moose, we heard, come faintly echoing, or creeping from far, through the moss-clad aisles, a dull, dry, rushing sound, with a solid core to it, yet as if half smothered under the grasp of the luxuriant and fungus-like forest, like the shutting of a door in some distant entry of the damp and shaggy wilderness. If we had not been there, no mortal had heard it. When we asked Joe in a whisper what it was, he answered—"Tree fall." There is something singularly grand and impressive in the sound of a tree falling in a perfectly calm night like this, as if the agencies which overthrow it did not need to be excited, but worked with a subtle, deliberate, and conscious force, like a boa-constrictor, and more effectively then than even in a windy day. If there is any such difference, perhaps it is because trees with the dews of the night on them are heavier than by day.

Having reached the camp, about ten o'clock, we kindled our fire and went to bed. Each of us had a blanket, in which he lay on the fir-twigs, with his extremities toward the fire, but nothing over his head. It was worth the while to lie down in a country where you could afford such great fires; that was one whole side, and the bright side of our world. We had first rolled up a large log some eighteen inches through and ten feet long, for a back-log, to last all night, and then piled on the trees to the height of three or four feet, no matter how green or damp. In fact, we burned as much wood that night as would, with economy and an air-tight stove, last a poor family in one of our cities all winter. It was very agreeable, as well as independent, thus lying in the open air, and the fire kept our uncovered extremities warm enough. The Jesuit missionaries used to say, that, in their journeys with the Indians in Canada, they lay on a bed which had never been shaken up since the creation, unless by earthquakes. It is surprising with what impunity and comfort one who has always lain in a warm bed in a close apartment, and studiously avoided drafts of air, can lie down on the ground without a shelter, roll himself in a blanket, and sleep before a fire, in a frosty, autumn night, just after a long rain-storm, and even come soon to enjoy and value the fresh air.

I lay awake awhile, watching the ascent of the sparks through the firs, and sometimes their descent in half-extinguished cinders on my blanket. They were as interesting as fireworks, going up in endless, successive crowds, each after an explosion, in an eager, serpentine course, some to five or six rods above the tree-tops before they went out. We do not suspect how much our chimneys have concealed; and now air-tight stoves have come to conceal all the rest. In the course of the night, I got up once or twice and put fresh logs on the fire, making my companions curl up their legs.

When we awoke in the morning (Saturday, September 17), there was considerable frost whitening the leaves. We heard the sound of the chicadee, and a few faintly lisping birds, and also of ducks in the water about the island. I took a botanical account of stock of our domains before the dew was off, and found that the ground-hemlock, or American yew, was the prevailing under-shrub. We breakfasted on tea, hard bread, and ducks.

Before the fog had fairly cleared away, we paddled down the stream 16 again, and were soon past the mouth of the Moosehorn. These twenty miles of the Penobscot, between Moosehead and Chesuncook Lakes, are comparatively smooth, and a great part dead-water; but from time to time it is shallow and rapid, with rocks or gravel-beds, where you can wade across. There is no expanse of water, and no break in the forest, and the meadow is a mere edging here and there. There are no hills near the river nor within sight, except one or two distant mountains seen in a few places. The banks are from six to ten feet high, but once or twice rise gently to higher ground. In many places the forest on the bank was but a thin strip, letting the light through from some alder-swamp or meadow behind. The conspicuous berry-bearing bushes and trees along the shore were the red osier, with its whitish fruit, hobble-bush, mountain-ash, tree-cranberry, choke-cherry, now ripe, alternate cornel, and naked viburnum. Following Joe's example, I ate the fruit of the last, and also of the hobble-bush, but found them rather insipid and seedy. I looked very narrowly at the vegetation, as we glided along close to the shore, and frequently made Joe turn aside for me to pluck a plant, that I might see by comparison what was primitive about my native river. Hore-hound, horsemint, and the sensitive fern grew close to the edge, under the willows and alders, and wool-grass on the islands, as along the Assabet River in Concord. It was too late for flowers, except a few asters, golden-rods, etc. In several places we noticed the slight frame of a camp, such as we had prepared to set up, amid the forest by the river-side, where some lumberers or hunters had passed a night—and sometimes steps cut in the muddy or clayey bank in front of it.

We stopped to fish for trout at the mouth of a small stream called Ragmuff, which came in from the west, about two miles below the Moosehorn. Here were the ruins of an old lumbering-camp, and a small space, which had formerly been cleared and burned over, was now densely overgrown with the red cherry and raspberries. While we were trying for trout, Joe, Indian-like, wandered off up the Ragmuff on his own errands, and when we were ready to start was far beyond call. So we were compelled to make a fire and get our dinner here, not to lose time. Some dark reddish birds, with grayer females (perhaps purple finches), and myrtle-birds in their summer dress, hopped within six or eight feet of us and our smoke. Perhaps they smelled the frying pork. The latter bird, or both, made the lisping notes which I had heard in the forest. They suggested that the few small birds found in the wilderness are on more familiar terms with the lumberman and hunter than those of the orchard and clearing with the farmer. I have since found the Canada jay, and partridges, both the black and the common, equally tame there, as if they had not yet learned to mistrust man entirely. The chicadee, which is at home alike in the primitive woods and in our wood-lots, still retains its confidence in the towns to a remarkable degree.

Joe at length returned, after an hour and a half, and said that he had been two miles up the stream exploring, and had seen a moose, but, not having the gun, he did not get him. We made no complaint, but concluded to look out for Joe the next time. However, this may have been a mere mistake, for we had no reason to complain of him afterward. As we continued down the stream, I was surprised to hear him whistling "O Susanna," and several other such airs, while his paddle urged us along. Once he said, "Yes, Sir-ee." His common word was "Sartain."[3] He pad-

---

[3]**"Sartain"**: Period slang for "certain."—EDS.

dled, as usual, on one side only, giving the birch an impulse by using the side as a fulcrum. I asked him how the ribs were fastened to the side rails. He answered, "I don't know, I never noticed." Talking with him about subsisting wholly on what the woods yielded, game, fish, berries, etc., I suggested that his ancestors did so; but he answered, that he had been brought up in such a way that he could not do it. "Yes," said he, "that's the way they got a living, like wild fellows, wild as bears. By George! I shan't go into the woods without provision—hard bread, pork, etc." He had brought on a barrel of hard bread and stored it at the carry for his hunting. However, though he was a Governor's son, he had not learned to read.

At one place below this, on the east side, where the bank was higher and drier than usual, rising gently from the shore to a slight elevation, some one had felled the trees over twenty or thirty acres, and left them drying in order to burn. This was the only preparation for a house between the Moosehead carry and Chesuncook, but there was no hut nor inhabitants there yet. The pioneer thus selects a site for his house, which will, perhaps, prove the germ of a town.

My eyes were all the while on the trees, distinguishing between the 20 black and white spruce and the fir. You paddle along in a narrow canal through an endless forest, and the vision I have in my mind's eye, still, is of the small, dark, and sharp tops of tall fir and spruce trees, and pagoda-like arbor-vitæs, crowded together on each side, with various hard woods, intermixed. Some of the arbor-vitæs were at least sixty feet high. The hard woods, occasionally occurring exclusively, were less wild to my eye. I fancied them ornamental grounds, with farm-houses in the rear. The canoe and yellow birch, beech, maple, and elm are Saxon and Norman; but the spruce and fir, and pines generally, are Indian. The soft engravings which adorn the annuals give no idea of a stream in such a wilderness as this. The rough sketches in Jackson's Reports on the Geology of Maine answer much better. At one place we saw a small grove of slender sapling white-pines, the only collection of pines that I saw on this voyage. Here and there, however, was a fully-grown, tall and slender, but defective one, what lumbermen call a *konchus* tree, which they ascertain with their axes, or by the knots. I did not learn whether this word was Indian or English. It reminded me of the Greek κόγχη, a conch or shell, and I amused myself with fancying that it might signify the dead sound which the trees yield when struck. All the rest of the pines had been driven off.

How far men go for the material of their houses! The inhabitants of the most civilized cities, in all ages, send into far, primitive forests, beyond the bounds of their civilization, where the moose and bear and savage dwell, for their pine-boards for ordinary use. And, on the other hand, the savage soon receives from cities, iron arrow-points, hatchets, and guns, to point his savageness with.

The solid and well-defined fir-tops, like sharp and regular spear-heads, black against the sky, gave a peculiar, dark, and sombre look to the forest. The spruce-tops have a similar, but more ragged outline—their shafts also merely feathered below. The firs were somewhat oftener regular and dense pyramids. I was struck by this universal spiring upward of the forest evergreens. The tendency is to slender, spiring tops, while they are narrower below. Not only the spruce and fir, but even the arbor-vitæ and white-pine, unlike the soft, spreading second-growth, of which I saw none, all spire upward, lifting a dense spear-head of cones to the light and air, at any rate, while their branches struggle after as they may; as Indians lift the ball over the heads of the crowd in their desperate game. In this they resemble grasses, as also palms somewhat. The hemlock is commonly a tent-like pyramid from the ground to its summit.

After passing through some long rips, and by a large island, we reached an interesting part of the river called the Pine Stream Dead-Water, about six miles below Ragmuff, where the river expanded to thirty rods in width and had many islands in it, with elms and canoe-birches, now yellowing, along the shore, and we got our first sight of Ktaadn.[4]

Here, about two o'clock, we turned up a small branch three or four rods wide, which comes in on the right from the south, called Pine Stream, to look for moose signs. We had gone but a few rods before we saw very recent signs along the water's edge, the mud lifted up by their feet being quite fresh, and Joe declared that they had gone along there but a short time before. We soon reached a small meadow on the east side, at an angle in the stream, which was, for the most part, densely covered with alders. As we were advancing along the edge of this, rather more quietly than usual, perhaps, on account of the freshness of the signs—the design being to camp up this stream, if it promised well—I heard a slight crackling of twigs deep in the alders, and turned Joe's attention to it; whereupon he began to push the canoe back rapidly; and we had receded thus half a dozen rods, when we suddenly spied two moose standing just on the edge of the open part of the meadow which we had passed, not more than six or seven rods distant, looking round the alders at us. They made me think of great frightened rabbits, with their long ears and half-inquisitive, half-frightened looks; the true denizens of the forest (I saw at once), filling a vacuum which now first I

[4] **Ktaadn**: Mt. Katahdin, the highest peak in Maine (5,270 feet); Thoreau had climbed it in 1846.—Eds.

discovered had not been filled for me—moose-men, *wood-eaters*, the word is said to mean—clad in a sort of Vermont gray, or homespun. Our Nimrod, owing to the retrograde movement, was now the farthest from the game; but being warned of its neighborhood, he hastily stood up, and, while we ducked, fired over our heads one barrel at the foremost, which alone he saw, though he did not know what kind of creature it was; whereupon this one dashed across the meadow and up a high bank on the northeast, so rapidly as to leave but an indistinct impression of its outlines on my mind. At the same instant, the other, a young one, but as tall as a horse, leaped out into the stream, in full sight, and there stood cowering for a moment, or rather its disproportionate lowness behind gave it that appearance, and uttering two or three trumpeting squeaks. I have an indistinct recollection of seeing the old one pause an instant on the top of the bank in the woods, look toward its shivering young, and then dash away again. The second barrel was levelled at the calf, and when we expected to see it drop in the water, after a little hesitation, it, too, got out of the water, and dashed up the hill, though in a somewhat different direction. All this was the work of a few seconds, and our hunter, having never seen a moose before, did not know but they were deer, for they stood partly in the water, nor whether he had fired at the same one twice or not. From the style in which they went off, and the fact that he was not used to standing up and firing from a canoe, I judged that we should not see anything more of them. The Indian said that they were a cow and her calf—a yearling, or perhaps two years old, for they accompany their dams so long; but, for my part, I had not noticed much difference in their size. It was but two or three rods across the meadow to the foot of the bank, which, like all the world thereabouts, was densely wooded; but I was surprised to notice, that, as soon as the moose had passed behind the veil of the woods, there was no sound of footsteps to be heard from the soft, damp moss which carpets that forest, and long before we landed, perfect silence reigned. Joe said, "If you wound 'em moose, me sure get 'em."

We all landed at once. My companion reloaded; the Indian fastened his birch, threw off his hat, adjusted his waistband, seized the hatchet, and set out. He told me afterward, casually, that before we landed he had seen a drop of blood on the bank, when it was two or three rods off. He proceeded rapidly up the bank and through the woods, with a peculiar, elastic, noiseless, and stealthy tread, looking to right and left on the ground, and stepping in the faint tracks of the wounded moose, now and then pointing in silence to a single drop of blood on the handsome, shining leaves of the Clintonia Borealis, which, on every side, covered the ground, or to a dry fern-stem freshly broken, all the while chewing some leaf or else the spruce gum. I followed, watching his motions more than the trail of the moose. After following the trail about forty rods in a pretty direct course, stepping over fallen trees and winding between standing ones, he at length lost it, for there were many other moose-tracks there, and returning once more to the last blood-stain, traced it a little way and lost it again, and, too soon, I thought, for a good hunter, gave it up entirely. He traced a few steps, also, the tracks of the calf; but, seeing no blood, soon relinquished the search.

I observed, while he was tracking the moose, a certain reticence or moderation in him. He did not communicate several observations of interest which he made, as a white man would have done, though they may have leaked out afterward. At another time, when we heard a slight crackling of twigs and he landed to reconnoitre, he stepped lightly and gracefully, stealing through the bushes with the least possible noise, in a way in which no white man does—as it were, finding a place for his foot each time.

About half an hour after seeing the moose, we pursued our voyage up Pine-Stream, and soon, coming to a part which was very shoal and also rapid, we took out the baggage, and proceeded to carry it round, while Joe got up with the canoe alone. We were just completing our portage and I was absorbed in the plants, admiring the leaves of the aster macrophyllus, ten inches wide, and plucking the seeds of the great round-leaved orchis, when Joe exclaimed from the stream that he had killed a moose. He had found the cow-moose lying dead, but quite warm, in the middle of the stream, which was so shallow that it rested on the bottom, with hardly a third of its body above water. It was about an hour after it was shot, and it was swollen with water. It had run about a hundred rods and sought the stream again, cutting off a slight bend. No doubt, a better hunter would have tracked it to this spot at once. I was surprised at its great size, horse-like, but Joe said it was not a large cow-moose. My companion went in search of the calf again. I took hold of the ears of the moose, while Joe pushed his canoe down stream toward a favorable shore, and so we made out, though with some difficulty, its long nose frequently sticking in the bottom, to drag it into still shallower water. It was a brownish black, or perhaps a dark iron-gray, on the back and sides, but lighter beneath and in front. I took the cord which served for the canoe's painter, and with Joe's assistance measured it carefully, the greatest distances first, making a knot each time. The painter being wanted, I reduced these measures that night with equal care to lengths and fractions of my umbrella, beginning with the smallest measures, and untying the knots as I proceeded; and when we arrived at Chesuncook the next day, finding a two-foot rule there, I reduced the last to feet and inches; and, moreover, I made myself a two-foot rule of a thin and narrow strip of black ash which would fold up conveniently to six inches. All this pains I took because I did not wish to be obliged to say merely that the moose was very large. Of the various dimensions which I obtained I will mention only two. The distance from the tips of the hoofs of the fore-feet, stretched out, to the top of the back between the shoulders, was seven feet and five inches. I can hardly believe my own measure, for this is about two feet greater than the height of a tall horse. [Indeed, I am now satisfied that this measurement was incorrect, but the other measures given here I can warrant to be correct, having proved them in a more recent visit to those woods.] The extreme length was eight feet and two inches. Another cow-moose, which I have since measured in those woods with a tape, was just six feet from the tip of the hoof to the shoulders, and eight feet long as she lay.

When afterward I asked an Indian at the carry how much taller the male was, he answered, "Eighteen inches," and made me observe the height of a cross-stake over the fire, more than four feet from the ground, to give me some idea of the depth of his chest. Another Indian, at Oldtown, told me that they were nine feet high to the top of the back, and that one which he tried weighed eight hundred pounds. The length of the spinal projections between the shoulders is very great. A white hunter, who was the best authority among hunters that I could have, told me that the male was *not* eighteen inches taller than the female; yet he agreed that he was sometimes nine feet high to the top of the back, and weighed a thousand pounds. Only the male has horns, and they rise two feet or more above the shoulders—spreading three or four, and sometimes six feet—which would make him in all, sometimes, eleven feet high! According to this calculation, the moose is as tall, though it may not be as large, as the great Irish elk, Megaceros Hibernicus, of a former period, of which Mantell says that it "very far exceeded in magnitude any living species, the skeleton" being "upward of ten feet high from the ground to the highest point of the antlers." Joe said, that, though the moose shed the whole horn annually, each new horn has an additional prong; but I have noticed that they sometimes have more prongs on one side than on the other. I was struck with the delicacy and tenderness of the hoofs, which divide very far up, and the one half could be pressed very much behind the other, thus probably making the animal surer-footed on the uneven ground and slippery moss-covered logs of the primitive forest. They were very unlike the stiff and battered feet of our horses and oxen. The bare, horny part of the fore-foot was just six inches long, and the two portions could be separated four inches at the extremities.

The moose is singularly grotesque and awkward to look at. Why should it stand so high at the shoulders? Why have so long a head? Why have no tail to speak of? For in my examination I overlooked it entirely. Naturalists say it is an inch and a half long. It reminded me at once of the camelopard, high before and low behind—and no wonder, for, like it, it is fitted to browse on trees. The upper lip projected two inches

28

beyond the lower for this purpose. This was the kind of man that was at home there; for, as near as I can learn, that has never been the residence, but rather the hunting-ground, of the Indian. The moose will perhaps one day become extinct; but how naturally then, when it exists only as a fossil relic, and unseen as that, may the poet or sculptor invent a fabulous animal with similar branching and leafy horns—a sort of fucus or lichen in bone—to be the inhabitant of such a forest as this!

Here, just at the head of the murmuring rapids, Joe now proceeded to skin the moose with a pocket-knife, while I looked on; and a tragical business it was—to see that still warm and palpitating body pierced with a knife, to see the warm milk stream from the rent udder, and the ghastly naked red carcass appearing from within its seemly robe, which was made to hide it. The ball had passed through the shoulder-blade diagonally and lodged under the skin on the opposite side, and was partially flattened. My companion keeps it to show to his grandchildren. He has the shanks of another moose which he has since shot, skinned and stuffed, ready to be made into boots by putting in a thick leather sole. Joe said, if a moose stood fronting you, you must not fire, but advance toward him, for he will turn slowly and give you a fair shot. In the bed of this narrow, wild, and rocky stream, between two lofty walls of spruce and firs, a mere cleft in the forest which the stream had made, this work went on. At length Joe had stripped off the hide and dragged it trailing to the shore, declaring that it weighed a hundred pounds, though probably fifty would have been nearer the truth. He cut off a large mass of the meat to carry along, and another, together with the tongue and nose, he put with the hide on the shore to lie there all night, or till we returned. I was surprised that he thought of leaving this meat thus exposed by the side of the carcass, as the simplest coure, not fearing that any creature would touch it; but nothing did. This could hardly have happened on the bank of one of our rivers in the eastern part of Massachusetts; but I suspect that fewer small wild animals are prowling there than with us. Twice, however, in this excursion I had a glimpse of a species of large mouse.

This stream was so withdrawn, and the moose-tracks were so fresh, that my companions, still bent on hunting, concluded to go farther up it and camp, and then hunt up or down at night. Half a mile above this, at a place where I saw the aster puniceus and the beaked hazel, as we paddled along, Joe, hearing a slight rustling amid the alders, and seeing something black about two rods off, jumped up and whispered, "Bear!" but before the hunter had discharged his piece, he corrected himself to "Beaver!"—"Hedgehog!" The bullet killed a large hedgehog more than two feet and eight inches long. The quills were rayed out and flattened on the hinder part of its back, even as if it had lain on that part, but were erect and long between this and the tail. Their points, closely examined, were seen to be finely bearded or barbed, and shaped like an awl, that is, a little concave, to give the barbs effect. After about a mile of still water, we prepared our camp on the right side, just at the foot of a considerable fall. Little chopping was done that night, for fear of scaring the moose. We had moose-meat fried for supper. It tasted like tender beef, with perhaps more flavor—sometimes like veal.

After supper, the moon having risen, we proceeded to hunt a mile 32 up this stream, first "carrying" about the falls. We made a picturesque sight, wending single-file along the shore, climbing over rocks and logs—Joe, who brought up the rear, twirling his canoe in his hands as if it were a feather, in places where it was difficult to get along without a burden. We launched the canoe again from the ledge over which the stream fell, but after half a mile of still water, suitable for hunting, it became rapid again, and we were compelled to make our way along the shore, while Joe endeavored to get up in the birch alone, though it was still very difficult for him to pick his way amid the rocks in the night. We on the shore found the worst of walking, a perfect chaos of fallen and drifted trees, and of bushes projecting far over the water, and now and then we made our way across the mouth of a small tributary on a kind of net-work of alders. So we went tumbling on in the dark, being on the shady side, effectually scaring all the moose and bears that might be thereabouts. At length we came to a standstill, and Joe went forward to reconnoitre; but he reported that it was still a continuous rapid as far as he went, or half a mile, with no prospect of improvement, as if it were coming down from a mountain. So we turned about, hunting back to the camp through the still water. It was a splendid moonlight night, and I, getting sleepy as it grew late—for I had nothing to do—found it diffi- cult to realize where I was. This stream was much more unfrequented than the main one, lumbering operations being no longer carried on in this quarter. It was only three or four rods wide, but the firs and spruce through which it trickled seemed yet taller by contrast. Being in this dreamy state, which the moonlight enhanced, I did not clearly discern the shore, but seemed, most of the time, to be floating through orna- mental grounds—for I associated the fir-tops with such scenes—very high up some Broadway, and beneath or between their tops I thought I saw an endless succession of porticos and columns, cornices and fa- çades, verandas and churches. I did not merely fancy this, but in my drowsy state such was the illusion. I fairly lost myself in sleep several times, still dreaming of that architecture and the nobility that dwelt behind and might issue from it; but all at once I would be aroused and brought back to a sense of my actual position by the sound of Joe's birch horn in the midst of all this silence calling the moose, *ugh, ugh, oo-oo-oo- oo-oo-oo,* and I prepared to hear a furious moose come rushing and crashing through the forest, and see him burst out on to the little strip of meadow by our side.

But, on more accounts than one, I had had enough of moose-hunting. I had not come to the woods for this purpose, nor had I foreseen it, though I had been willing to learn how the Indian manœuvred; but one moose killed was as good, if not as bad, as a dozen. The afternoon's tragedy, and my share in it, as it affected the innocence, destroyed the pleasure of my adventure. It is true, I came as near as is possible to come to being a hunter and miss it, myself; and as it is, I think that I could spend a year in the woods, fishing and hunting, just enough to sustain myself, with satisfaction. This would be next to living like a philosopher on the fruits of the earth which you had raised, which also attracts me. But this hunting of the moose merely for the satisfaction of killing him—not even for the sake of his hide—without making any extraordinary exertion or running any risk yourself, is too much like going out by night to some woodside pasture and shooting your neighbor's horses. These are God's own horses, poor, timid creatures, that will run fast enough as soon as they smell you, though they *are* nine feet high. Joe told us of some hunters who a year or two before had shot down several oxen by night, somewhere in the Maine woods, mistaking them for moose. And so might any of the hunters; and what is the difference in the sport, but the name? In the former case, having killed one of God's and *your own* oxen, you strip off its hide—because that is the common trophy, and, moreover, you have heard that it may be sold for moccasins—cut a steak from its haunches, and leave the huge carcass to smell to heaven for you. It is no better, at least, than to assist at a slaughter-house.

This afternoon's experience suggested to me how base or coarse are the motives which commonly carry men into the wilderness. The explorers and lumberers generally are all hirelings, paid so much a day for their labor, and as such they have no more love for wild nature than wood-sawyers have for forests. Other white men and Indians who come here are for the most part hunters, whose object is to slay as many moose and other wild animals as possible. But, pray, could not one spend some weeks or years in the solitude of this vast wilderness with other employments than these—employments perfectly sweet and innocent and ennobling? For one that comes with a pencil to sketch, or sing, a thousand come with an axe or rifle. What a coarse and imperfect use Indians and hunters make of Nature! No wonder that their race is so soon exterminated. I already, and for weeks afterward, felt my nature the coarser for this part of my woodland experience, and was reminded that our life should be lived as tenderly and daintily as one would pluck a flower.

With these thoughts, when we reached our camping-ground, I decided to leave my companions to continue moose-hunting down the stream, while I prepared the camp, though they requested me not to chop much nor make a large fire, for fear I should scare their game. In the midst of the damp fir-wood, high on the mossy bank, about nine o'clock of this bright moonlight night, I kindled a fire, when they were gone, and, sitting on the fir-twigs, within sound of the falls, examined by its light the botanical specimens which I had collected that afternoon, and wrote down some of the reflections which I have here expanded; or I walked along the shore and gazed up the stream, where the whole space above the falls was filled with mellow light. As I sat before the fire on my fir-twig seat, without walls above or around me, I remembered how far on every hand that wilderness stretched, before you came to cleared or cultivated fields, and wondered if any bear or moose was watching the light of my fire; for Nature looked sternly upon me on account of the murder of the moose.

Strange that so few ever come to the woods to see how the pine lives and grows and spires, lifting its evergreen arms to the light—to see its perfect success; but most are content to behold it in the shape of many broad boards brought to market, and deem *that* its true success! But the pine is no more lumber than man is, and to be made into boards and houses is no more its true and highest use than the truest use of a man is to be cut down and made into manure. There is a higher law affecting our relation to pines as well as to men. A pine cut down, a dead pine, is no more a pine than a dead human carcass is a man. Can he who has discovered only some of the values of whalebone and whale oil be said to have discovered the true use of the whale? Can he who slays the elephant for his ivory be said to have "seen the elephant"? These are petty and accidental uses; just as if a stronger race were to kill us in order to make buttons and flageolets[5] of our bones; for everything may serve a lower as well as a higher use. Every creature is better alive than dead, men and moose and pine-trees, and he who understands it aright will rather preserve its life than destroy it.

Is it the lumberman, then, who is the friend and lover of the pine, stands nearest to it, and understands its nature best? Is it the tanner who has barked it, or he who has boxed it for turpentine, whom posterity will fable to have been changed into a pine at last? No! no! it is the poet; he it is who makes the truest use of the pine—who does not fondle it with an axe, nor tickle it with a saw, nor stroke it with a plane—who knows whether its heart is false without cutting into it—who has not brought the stumpage of the township on which it stands. All the pines shudder and heave a sigh when *that* man steps on the forest floor. No, it

[5]**flageolets**: Small flutes—Eds.

is the poet, who loves them as his own shadow in the air, and lets them stand. I have been into the lumberyard, and the carpenter's shop, and the tannery, and the lampblack-factory, and the turpentine clearing; but when at length I saw the tops of the pines waving and reflecting the light at a distance high over all the rest of the forest, I realized that the former were not the highest use of the pine. It is not their bones or hide or tallow that I love most. It is the living spirit of the tree, not its spirit of turpentine, with which I sympathize, and which heals my cuts. It is as immortal as I am, and perchance will go to as high a heaven, there to tower above me still.

Erelong, the hunters returned, not having seen a moose, but, in consequence of my suggestions, bringing a quarter of the dead one, which, with ourselves, made quite a load for the canoe.   *1864*

Wendell Berry

The Journey's End

Early in 1968 the state's newspapers were taking note of the discovery, in one of the rock houses in the Gorge, of a crude hut built of short split planks overlaying a framework of poles. The hut was hardly bigger than a pup tent, barely large enough, I would say, to accommodate one man and a small stone fireplace. One of its planks bore the carved name: "D. boon." There was some controversy over whether or not it really was built by Daniel Boone. Perhaps it does not matter. But the news of the discovery and of the controversy over it had given the place a certain fame.

The find interested me, for I never cease to regret the scarcity of knowledge of the first explorations of the continent. Some hint, such as the "Boone hut" might provide, of the experience of the Long Hunters would be invaluable. And so one of my earliest visits to the Gorge included a trip to see the hut.

The head of the trail was not yet marked, but once I found the path leading down through the woods it was clear to me that I had already had numerous predecessors. And I had not gone far before I knew their species: scattered more and more thickly along the trail the nearer I got to the site of the hut was the trash that has come to be more characteris-

tic than shoeprints of the race that produced (as I am a little encouraged
to remember) such a man as D. boon. And when I came to the rock
house itself I found the mouth of it entirely closed, from the ground to
the overhanging rock some twenty-five feet above, by a chain-link fence.
Outside the fence the ground was littered with Polaroid negatives, film
spools, film boxes, food wrappers, cigarette butts, a paper plate, a Coke
bottle.

And inside the fence, which I peered through like a prisoner, was   4
the hut, a forlorn relic overpowered by what had been done to protect it
from collectors of mementos, who would perhaps not even know what it
was supposed to remind them of. There it was, perhaps a vital clue to
our history and our inheritance, turned into a curio. Whether because
of the ignorant enthusiasm of souvenir hunters, or because of the
strenuous measures necessary to protect it from them, Boone's hut had
become a doodad—as had Boone's name, which now stood for a men-
dacious TV show and a brand of fried chicken.

I did not go back to that place again, not wanting to be associated
with the crowd whose vandalism had been so accurately foreseen and so
overwhelmingly thwarted. But I did not forget it either, and the memory
of it seems to me to bear, both for the Gorge and for ourselves, a heavy
premonition of ruin. For are those who propose damming the Gorge,
arguing *convenience*, not the same as these who can go no place, not even
a few hundred steps to see the hut of D. boon, without the trash of
convenience? Are they not the same who will use the proposed lake as a
means of transporting the same trash into every isolated cranny that the
shoreline will penetrate? I have a vision (I don't know if it is nightmare
or foresight) of a time when our children will go to the Gorge and find
there a webwork of paved, heavily littered trails passing through tunnels
of steel mesh. When people are so ignorant and destructive that they
must be divided by a fence from what is vital to them, whether it is their
history or their world, they are imprisoned.

On a cold drizzly day in the middle of October I walk down the side
of a badly overgrazed ridge into a deep, steep hollow where there
remains the only tiny grove of virgin timber still standing in all the Red
River country. It is a journey backward through time, from the freeway
droning both directions through 1969, across the old ridge denuded by
the agricultural policies and practices of the white man's era, and down
into such a woods as the Shawnees knew before they knew white men.

Going down, the sense that it is a virgin place comes over you slowly.
First you notice what would be the great difficulty of getting in and out,
were it not for such improvements as bridges and stairways in the trail.
It is this difficulty that preserved the trees, and that even now gives the
hollow a feeling of austerity and remoteness. And then you realize that

you are passing among poplars and hemlocks of a startling girth and height, the bark of their trunks deeply grooved and moss-grown. And finally it comes to you where you are; the virginity, the uninterrupted wildness, of the place comes to you in a clear strong dose like the first breath of a wind. Here the world is in its pure state, and such men as have been here have all been here in their pure state, for they have destroyed nothing. It has lived whole into our lifetime out of the ages. Its life is a vivid link between us and Boone and the Long Hunters and their predecessors, the Indians. It stands, brooding upon its continuance, in a strangely moving perfection, from the tops of the immense trees down to the leaves of the partridge berries on the ground. Standing and looking, moving on and looking again, I suddenly realize what is missing from nearly all the Kentucky woodlands I have known: the summit, the grandeur of these old trunks that lead the eyes up through the foliage of the lesser trees toward the sky.

At the foot of the climb, over the stone floor of the hollow, the 8 stream is mottled with the gold leaves of the beeches. The water has taken on a vegetable taste from the leaves steeping in it. It has become a kind of weak tea, infused with the essence of the crown of the forest. By spring the fallen leaves on the stream bed will all have been swept away, and the water, filtered once again through the air and the ground, will take back the clear taste of the rock. I drink the cool brew of the autumn.

And then I wander some more among the trees. There is a thought repeating itself in my mind: This is a great Work, this is a great Work. It occurs to me that my head has gone to talking religion, that it is going ahead more or less on its own, assenting to the Creation, finding it good, in the spirit of the first chapters of Genesis. For no matter the age or the hour, I am celebrating the morning of the seventh day. I assent to my mind's assent. It *is* a great Work. It is a *great* Work—begun in the beginning, carried on until now, to be carried on, not by such processes as men make or understand, but by "the kind of intelligence that enables grass seed to grow grass; the cherry stone to make cherries."

Here is the place to remember D. boon's hut. Lay aside all questions of its age and ownership—whether or not he built it, he undoubtedly built others like it in similar places. Imagine it in a cave in a cliff overlooking such a place as this. Imagine it separated by several hundred miles from the nearest white men and by two hundred years from the drone, audible even here, of the parkway traffic. Imagine that the great trees surrounding it are part of a virgin wilderness still nearly as large as the continent, vast rich unspoiled distances quietly peopled by scattered Indian tribes, its ways still followed by buffalo and bear and panther and wolf. Imagine a cold gray winter evening, the wind loud in the branches above the protected hollows. Imagine a man dressed in skins coming silently down off the ridge and along the cliff face into the shelter of the rock house. Imagine his silence that is unbroken as he enters, crawling, a small hut that is only a negligible detail among the stone rubble of the cave floor, as unobtrusive there as the nest of an animal or bird, and as he livens the banked embers of a fire on the stone hearth, adding wood, and holds out his chilled hands before the blaze. Imagine him roasting his supper meat on a stick over the fire while the night falls and the darkness and the wind enclose the hollow. Imagine him sitting on there, miles and months from words, staring into the fire, letting its warmth deepen in him until finally he sleeps. Imagine his sleep.

When I return again it is the middle of December, getting on toward the final shortening, the first lengthening of the days. The year is ending, and my trip too has a conclusive feeling about it. The ends are gathering. The things I have learned about the Gorge, my thoughts and feelings about it, have begun to have a sequence, a pattern. From the start of the morning, because of this sense of the imminence of connections and conclusions, the day has both an excitement and a comfort about it.

As I drive in I see small lots staked off and a road newly graveled in   12
one of the creek bottoms. And I can hear chain saws running in the vicinity of another development on Tunnel Ridge. This work is being done in anticipation of the lake, but I know that it has been hastened by the publicity surrounding the effort to keep the Gorge unspoiled. I consider the ironic possibility that what I will write for love of it may also contribute to its destruction, enlarging the hearsay of it, bringing in more people to drive the roads and crowd the "points of interest" until they become exactly as interesting as a busy street. And yet I might as well leave the place anonymous, for what I have learned here could be learned from any woods and any free-running river.

I pull off the road near the mouth of a hollow I have not yet been in. The day is warm and overcast, but it seems unlikely to rain. Taking only a notebook and a map, I turn away from the road and start out. The woods closes me in. Within a few minutes I have put the road, and where it came from and is going, out of mind. There comes to be a wonderful friendliness, a sort of sweetness I have not known here before, about this day and this solitary walk—as if, having finally understood this country well enough to accept it on its terms, I am in turn accepted. It is as though, in this year of men's arrival on the moon, I have completed my own journey at last, and have arrived, an exultant traveler, here on the earth.

I come around a big rock in the stream and two grouse flush in the open not ten steps away. I walk on more quietly, full of the sense of ending and beginning. At any moment, I think, the forest may reveal itself to you in a new way. Some intimate insight, that all you have known has been secretly adding up to, may suddenly open into the clear—like a grouse, that one moment seemed only a part of the forest floor, the next moment rising in flight. Also it may not.

Where I am going I have never been before. And since I have no destination that I know, where I am going is always where I am. When I come to good resting places, I rest. I rest whether I am tired or not because the places are good. Each one is an arrival. I am where I have been going. At a narrow place in the stream I sit on one side and prop my feet on the other. For a while I content myself to be a bridge. The water of heaven and earth is flowing beneath me. While I rest a piece of the world's work is continuing here without my help.

Since I was here last the leaves have fallen. The forest has been at work, dying to renew itself, covering the tracks of those of us who were here, burying the paths and the old campsites and the refuse. It is showing us what to hope for. And that we can hope. And *how* to hope. It will always be a new world, if we will let it be.

The place as it was is gone, and we are gone as we were. We will never be in that place again. Rejoice that it is dead, for having received that death, the place of next year, a new place, is lying potent in the ground like a deep dream.

Somewhere, somewhere behind me that I will not go back to, I have lost my map. At first I am sorry, for on these trips I have always kept it with me. I brood over the thought of it, the map of this place rotting into it along with its leaves and its fallen wood. The image takes hold of me, and I suddenly realize that it is the culmination, the final insight, that I have felt impending all through the day. It is the symbol of what I have learned here, and of the process: the gradual relinquishment of maps, the yielding of knowledge before the new facts and the mysteries of growth and renewal and change. What men know and presume about the earth is part of it, passing always back into it, carried on by it into what they do not know. Even their abuses of it, their diminishments and dooms, belong to it. The tragedy is only ours, who have little time to be here, not the world's whose creation bears triumphantly on and on from the fulfillment of catastrophe to the fulfillment of hepatica blossoms. The thought of the lost map, the map fallen and decaying like a leaf among the leaves, grows in my mind to the force of a cleansing vision. As though freed of a heavy weight, I am light and exultant here in the end and the beginning. *1971*

N. Scott Momaday

A First American Views His Land

First Man
behold:
the earth
glitters
with leaves;
the sky
glistens
with rain.
Pollen
is borne
on winds
that low
and lean
upon
mountains.
Cedars
blacken
the slopes—
and pines.[1]

One hundred centuries ago. There is a wide, irregular landscape in what is now northern New Mexico. The sun is a dull white disk, low in the south; it is a perfect mystery, a deity whose coming and going are inexorable. The gray sky is curdled, and it bears very close upon the earth. A cold wind runs along the ground, dips and spins, flaking drift from a pond in the bottom of a ravine. Beyond the wind the silence is acute. A man crouches in the ravine, in the darkness there, scarcely visible. He moves not a muscle; only the wind lifts a lock of his hair and lays it back along his neck. He wears skins and carries a spear. These things in particular mark his human intelligence and distinguish him as the lord of the universe. And for him the universe is especially *this* landscape; for him the landscape is an element like the air. The vast, virgin wilderness is by and large his whole context. For him there is no possibility of existence elsewhere.

Directly there is a blowing, a rumble of breath deeper than the wind, above him, where some of the hard clay of the bank is broken off and the clods roll down into the water. At the same time there appears on the skyline the massive head of a long-horned bison, then the hump,

---

[1]The poem woven into this selection is drawn from Momaday's book, *The Gourd Dancer* (1976).—EDS.

then the whole beast, huge and black on the sky, standing to a height of seven feet at the hump, with horns that extend six feet across the shaggy crown. For a moment it is poised there; then it lumbers obliquely down the bank to the pond. Still the man does not move, though the beast is now only a few steps upwind. There is no sign of what is about to happen; the beast meanders; the man is frozen in repose.

Then the scene explodes. In one and the same instant the man springs to his feet and bolts forward, his arm cocked and the spear held high, and the huge animal lunges in panic, bellowing, its whole weight thrown violently into the bank, its hooves churning and chipping earth into the air, its eyes gone wide and wild and white. There is a moment in which its awful, frenzied motion is wasted, and it is mired and helpless in its fear, and the man hurls the spear with his whole strength, and the point is driven into the deep, vital flesh, and the bison in its agony staggers and crashes down and dies.

This ancient drama of the hunt is enacted again and again in the   4 landscape. The man is preeminently a predator, the most dangerous of all. He hunts in order to survive; his very existence is simply, squarely established upon that basis. But he hunts also because he can, because he has the means; he has the ultimate weapon of his age, and his prey is plentiful. His relationship to the land has not yet become a moral equation.

But in time he will come to understand that there is an intimate, vital link between the earth and himself, a link that implies an intricate network of rights and responsibilities. In some unimagined future he will understand that he has the ability to devastate and perhaps destroy his environment. That moment will be one of extreme crisis in his evolution.

The weapon is deadly and efficient. The hunter has taken great care in its manufacture, especially in the shaping of the flint point, which is an extraordinary thing. A larger flake has been removed from each face, a groove that extends from the base nearly to the tip. Several hundred pounds of pressure, expertly applied, were required to make these grooves. The hunter then is an artisan, and he must know how to use rudimentary tools. His skill, manifest in the manufacture of this artifact, is unsurpassed for its time and purpose. By means of this weapon is the Paleo-Indian hunter eminently able to exploit his environment.

Thousands of years later, about the time that Columbus begins his first voyage to the New World, another man, in the region of the Great Lakes, stands in the forest shade on the edge of a sunlit brake. In a while a deer enters into the pool of light. Silently the man fits an arrow to a bow, draws aim, and shoots. The arrow zips across the distance and strikes home. The deer leaps and falls dead.

But this latter-day man, unlike his ancient predecessor, is only 8
incidentally a hunter; he is also a fisherman, a husbandman, even a
physician. He fells trees and builds canoes; he grows corn, squash, and
beans, and he gathers fruits and nuts; he uses hundreds of species of
wild plants for food, medicine, teas, and dyes. Instead of one animal, or
two or three, he hunts many, none to extinction as the Paleo-Indian may
have done. He has fitted himself far more precisely into the patterns of
the wilderness than did his ancient predecessor. He lives on the land; he
takes his living from it; but he does not destroy it. This distinction
supports the fundamental ethic that we call conservation today. In
principle, if not yet in name, this man is a conservationist.

These two hunting sketches are far less important in themselves
than is that long distance between them, that whole possibility within
the dimension of time. I believe that in that interim there grew up in
the mind of man an idea of the land as sacred.

At dawn
eagles
lie and
hover
above
the plain
where light
gathers
in pools.
Grasses
shimmer
and shine.
Shadows
withdraw
and lie
away
like smoke.

"The earth is our mother. The sky is our father." This concept of nature,
which is at the center of the Native American world view, is familiar to
us all. But it may well be that we do not understand entirely what the
concept is in its ethical and philosophical implications.

I tell my students that the American Indian has a unique investment
in the American landscape. It is an investment that represents perhaps
thirty thousand years of habitation. That tenure has to be worth something in itself—a great deal, in fact. The Indian has been here a long
time; he is at home here. That simple and obvious truth is one of the
most important realities of the Indian world, and it is integral in the
Indian mind and spirit.

How does such a concept evolve? Where does it begin? Perhaps it begins with the recognition of beauty, the realization that the physical world *is* beautiful. We don't know much about the ancient hunter's sensibilities. It isn't likely that he had leisure in his life for the elaboration of an aesthetic ideal. And yet the weapon he made was beautiful as well as functional. It has been suggested that much of the minute chipping along the edges of his weapon served no purpose but that of aesthetic satisfaction.

A good deal more is known concerning that man of the central 12 forests. He made beautiful boxes and dishes out of elm and birch bark, for example. His canoes were marvelous, delicate works of art. And this aesthetic perception was a principle of the whole Indian world of his time, as indeed it is of our time. The contemporary Native American is a man whose strong aesthetic perceptions are clearly evident in his arts and crafts, in his religious ceremonies, and in the stories and songs of his rich oral tradition. This, in view of the pressures that have been brought to bear upon the Indian world and the drastic changes that have been effected in its landscape, is a blessing and an irony.

Consider for example the Navajos of the Four Corners area. In recent years an extensive coal-mining operation has mutilated some of their most sacred land. A large power plant in that same region spews a contamination into the sky that is visible for many miles. And yet, as much as any people of whom I have heard, the Navajos perceive and celebrate the beauty of the physical world.

There is a Navajo ceremonial song that celebrates the sounds that are made in the natural world, the particular voices that beautify the earth:

> *Voice above,*
> *Voice of thunder,*
> *Speak from the*
> *dark of clouds;*
> *Voice below,*
> *Grasshopper voice,*
> *Speak from the*
> *green of plants;*
> *So may the earth*
> *be beautiful.*

There is in the motion and meaning of this song a comprehension of the world that is peculiarly native, I believe, that is integral in the Native American mentality. Consider: The singer stands at the center of the natural world, at the source of its sound, of its motion, of its life. Nothing of that world is inaccessible to him or lost upon him. His song is filled with reverence, with wonder and delight, and with confidence as well. He knows something about himself and about the things around him—and he knows that he knows. I am interested in what he sees and hears; I am interested in the range and force of his perception. Our immediate impression may be that his perception is narrow and deep—vertical. After all, "voice above . . . voice below," he sings. But is it vertical only? At each level of his expression there is an extension of his awareness across the whole landscape. The voice above is the voice of thunder, and thunder rolls. Moreover, it issues from the impalpable dark clouds and runs upon their horizontal range. It is a sound that integrates the whole of the atmosphere. And even so, the voice below, that of the grasshopper, issues from the broad plain and multiplicity of plants. And of course the singer is mindful of much more than thunder and insects; we are given in his song the wide angle of his vision and his hearing—and we are given the testimony of his dignity, his trust, and his deep belief.

This comprehension of the earth and air is surely a matter of morality, for it brings into account not only man's instinctive reaction to his environment but the full realization of his humanity as well, the achievement of his intellectual and spiritual development as an individual and as a race.

In my own experience I have seen numerous examples of this 16 regard for nature. My grandfather Mammedaty was a farmer in his mature years; his grandfather was a buffalo hunter. It was not easy for Mammedaty to be a farmer; he was a Kiowa, and the Kiowas never had an agrarian tradition. Yet he had to make his living, and the old, beloved life of roaming the plains and hunting the buffalo was gone forever. Even so, as much as any man before him, he fitted his mind and will and spirit to the land; there was nothing else. He could not have conceived of living apart from the land.

In *The Way to Rainy Mountain* I set down a small narrative that belongs in the oral tradition of my family. It indicates something essential about the Native American attitude toward the land:

"East of my grandmother's house, south of the pecan grove, there is buried a woman in a beautiful dress. Mammedaty used to know where she is buried, but now no one knows. If you stand on the front porch of the house and look eastward towards Carnegie, you know that the woman is buried somewhere within the range of your vision. But her grave is unmarked. She was buried in a cabinet, and she wore a beautiful dress. How beautiful it was! It was one of those fine buckskin dresses, and it was decorated with elk's teeth and beadwork. That dress is still there, under the ground."

It seems to me that this statement is primarily a declaration of love for the land, in which the several elements—the woman, the dress, and this plain—are at last become one reality, one expression of the beautiful in nature. Morever, it seems to me a peculiarly Native American expression in this sense: that the concentration of things that are explicitly remembered—the general landscape, the simple, almost abstract nature of the burial, above all the beautiful dress, which is wholly singular in kind (as well as in its function within the narrative)—is especially Indian in character. The things that are *not* explicitly remembered—the woman's name, the exact location of her grave—are the things that matter least in the special view of the storyteller. What matters here is the translation of the woman into the landscape, a translation particularly signified by means of the beautiful and distinctive dress, an *Indian* dress.

When I was a boy, I lived for several years at Jemez Pueblo, New 20 Mexico. The Pueblo Indians are perhaps more obviously invested in the land than are other people. Their whole life is predicated upon a thorough perception of the physical world and its myriad aspects. When I first went there to live, the cacique, or chief, of the Pueblos was a venerable old man with long, gray hair and bright, deep-set eyes. He was entirely dignified and imposing—and rather formidable in the eyes of a boy. He excited my imagination a good deal. I was told that this old man kept the calendar of the tribe, that each morning he stood on a certain spot of ground near the center of the town and watched to see where the sun appeared on the skyline. By means of this solar calendar did he know and announce to his people when it was time to plant, to harvest, to perform this or that ceremony. This image of him in my mind's eye— the old man gazing each morning after the ranging sun—came to represent for me the epitome of that real harmony between man and the land that signifies the Indian world.

One day when I was riding my horse along the Jemez River, I looked up to see a long caravan of wagons and people on horseback and on foot. Men, women, and children were crossing the river ahead of me, moving out to the west, where most of the cultivated fields were, the farmland of the town. It was a wonderful sight to see, this long procession, and I was immediately deeply curious. I wanted to investigate, but it was not in me to do so at once, for that racial reserve, that sense of propriety that is deep-seated in Native American culture, stayed me, held me up. Then I saw someone coming toward me on horseback, galloping. It was a friend of mine, a boy of my own age. "Come on," he said. "Come with us," "Where are you going?" I asked casually. But he would not tell me. He simply laughed and urged me to come along, and of course I was very glad to do so. It was a bright spring morning, and I had a good horse under me, and the prospect of adventure was delicious. We moved far out across the eroded plain to the farthest fields at the foot of a great red mesa, and there we planted two large fields of corn. And afterward, on the edge of the fields, we sat on blankets and ate a feast in the shade of a cottonwood grove. Later I learned it was the cacique's fields we planted. And this is an ancient tradition at Jemez. The people of the town plant and tend and harvest the cacique's fields, and in the winter the hunters give to him a portion of the meat that they bring home from the mountains. It is as if the cacique is himself the translation of man, every man, into the landscape.

I have not forgotten that day, nor shall I forget it. I remember the warm earth of the fields, the smooth texture of seeds in my hands, and the brown water moving slowly and irresistibly among the rows. Above all I remember the spirit in which the procession was made, the work was done, and the feasting was enjoyed. It was a spirit of communion, of the life of each man in relation to the life of the planet and of the infinite distance and silence in which it moves. We made, in concert, an appropriate expression of that spirit.

One afternoon an old Kiowa woman talked to me, telling me of the place in Oklahoma in which she had lived for a hundred years. It was the place in which my grandparents, too, lived; and it is the place where I was born. And she told me of a time even further back, when the Kiowas came down from the north and centered their culture in the red earth of the southern plains. She told wonderful stories, and as I listened, I began to feel more and more sure that her voice proceeded from the land itself. I asked her many things concerning the Kiowas, for I wanted to understand all that I could of my heritage. I told the old woman that I had come there to learn from her and from people like her, those in whom the old ways were preserved. And she said simply: "It is good that you have come here." I believe that her word "good" meant many things; for one thing it meant *right*, or *appropriate*. And indeed it was appropriate that she should speak of the land. She was eminently qualified to do so. She had a great reverence for the land, and an ancient perception of it, a perception that it acquired only in the course of many generations.

It is this notion of the appropriate, along with that of the beautiful, 24 that forms the Native American perspective on the land. In a sense these considerations are indivisible; Native American oral tradition is rich with songs and tales that celebrate natural beauty, the beauty of the natural world. What is more appropriate to our world than that which is beautiful:

> *At noon*
> *turtles*
> *enter*
> *slowly*
> *into*
> *the warm*

dark loam.
Bees hold
the swarm.
Meadows
recede
through planes
of heat
and pure
distance.

Very old in the Native American world view is the conviction that the earth is vital, that there is a spiritual dimension to it, a dimension in which man rightly exists. It follows logically that there are ethical imperatives in this matter. I think: Inasmuch as I am in the land, it is appropriate that I should affirm myself in the spirit of the land. I shall celebrate my life in the world and the world in my life. In the natural order man invests himself in the landscape and at the same time incorporates the landscape into his own most fundamental experience. This trust is sacred.

The process of investment and appropriation is, I believe, preeminently a function of the imagination. It is accomplished by means of an act of the imagination that is especially ethical in kind. We are what we imagine ourselves to be. The Native American is someone who thinks of himself, imagines himself in a particular way. By virtue of his experience his idea of himself comprehends his relationship to the land.

And the quality of this imagining is determined as well by racial and cultural experience. The Native American's attitudes toward this landscape have been formulated over a long period of time, a span that reaches back to the end of the Ice Age. The land, *this* land, is secure in his racial memory.

In our society as a whole we conceive of the land in terms of ownership and use. It is a lifeless medium of exchange; it has for most of us, I suspect, no more spirituality than has an automobile, say, or a refrigerator. And our laws confirm us in this view, for we can buy and sell the land, we can exclude each other from it, and in the context of ownership we can use it as we will. Ownership implies use, and use implies consumption.

But this way of thinking of the land is alien to the Indian. His 28 cultural intelligence is opposed to these concepts; indeed, for him they are all but inconceivable quantities. This fundamental distinction is easier to understand with respect to ownership than to use, perhaps. For obviously the Indian does use, and has always used, the land and the available resources in it. The point is that *use* does not indicate in any real way his idea of the land. "Use" is neither his word nor his idea. As an Indian I think: "You say that I *use* the land, and I reply, yes, it is true; but it is not the first truth. The first truth is that I *love* the land; I see that it is beautiful; I delight in it; I am alive in it."

In the long course of his journey from Asia and in the realization of himself in the New World, the Indian has assumed a deep ethical regard for the earth and sky, a reverence for the natural world that is antipodal to that strange tenet of modern civilization that seemingly has it that man must destroy his environment. It is this ancient ethic of the Native American that must shape our efforts to preserve the earth and the life upon and within it.

At dusk
the gray
foxes
stiffen
in cold;
blackbirds
are fixed
in white
branches.
Rivers
follow
the moon,
the long
white track
of the
full moon.   *1976*

29

Environmental Action

Lewis Thomas, Natural Man

Charlene Spretnak, Ecofeminism: Our Roots
and Flowering

Cynthia Hamilton, Women, Home,
and Community:
The Struggle in an Urban Environment

The ecological crisis cannot be resolved by politics. It cannot be solved by science or technology. It is a crisis caused by culture and character, and a deep change in personal consciousness is needed. Your fundamental attitudes toward the earth have become twisted. You have made only brutal contact with Nature, you cannot comprehend its grace. You must change. Have few desires and simple pleasures. Honor nonhuman life. Control yourself, become more authentic. Live lightly upon the earth and treat it with respect. Redefine the word *progress* and dismiss the managers and masters. Grow inwardly and with knowledge become truly wiser. Make connections. Think differently, behave differently. For this is essentially a moral issue we face and moral decisions must be made.

Joy Williams, from *Save the Whales, Screw the Shrimp*

All ethics so far evolved rest upon a single premise: that the individual is a member of a community of interdependent parts. His instincts prompt him to compete for his place in that community, but his ethics prompt him also to cooperate (perhaps in order that there may be a place to compete for).

The land ethic simply enlarges the boundaries of the community to include soils, waters, plants, and animals, or collectively, the land.

This sounds simple: do we not already sing our love for and obligation to the land of the free and the home of the brave? Yes, but just what
and whom do we love? Certainly not the soil, which we are sending
helter-skelter downriver. Certainly not the waters, which we assume
have no function except to turn turbines, float barges, and carry off
sewage. Certainly not the plants, of which we exterminate whole communities without batting an eye. Certainly not the animals, of which we
have already extirpated many of the largest and most beautiful species.
A land ethic of course cannot prevent the alteration, management, and
use of these "resources," but it does affirm their right to continued
existence, and, at least in spots, their continued existence in a natural
state.

In short, a land ethic changes the role of *Homo sapiens* from conqueror of the land-community to plain member and citizen of it. It
implies respect for his fellow-members, and also respect for the community as such.

In human history, we have learned (I hope) that the conqueror role
is eventually self-defeating. Why? Because it is implicit in such a role
that the conqueror knows, *ex cathedra*, just what makes the community
clock tick, and just what and who is valuable, and what and who is
worthless, in community life. It always turns out that he knows neither,
and this is why his conquests eventually defeat themselves.

Aldo Leopold, from *A Sand County Almanac*

The pangs that many people now feel at the sight of dunes, salt
marshes, woodlands, and even villages brutally destroyed and erased
from the face of the Earth by bulldozers are very real. It is no comfort to
be told that this attitude is reactionary and that the new urban development will provide jobs and opportunities for young people. The fact
that this answer is partly true increases the sense of pain and outrage
by denying a right to express it. In such circumstances it is hardly surprising that the environmental movement, although powerful, has no
clear-cut objective. It tends to attack quite viciously such inappropriate
targets as the fluorocarbon industry and fox hunting, while turning
a blind eye to the potentially more serious problems posed by most
methods of agriculture.

The strong but confused emotions aroused by the worst excesses of
public works and private enterprise provide ripe material for exploitation by unscrupulous manipulators. Environmental politics is a lush
new pasture for demagogues and therefore an increasing source of
anxiety to responsible governments and industries alike. Attaching that

overworked adjective "environmental" to the names of departments and agencies dealing with various aspects of the problem seems unlikely to stem the rising tide of anger and protest.

J. E. Lovelock, from *Gaia: A New Look at Life on Earth*

Lewis Thomas

Natural Man

The social scientists, especially the economists, are moving deeply into ecology and the environment these days, with disquieting results. It goes somehow against the grain to learn that cost-benefit analyses can be done neatly on lakes, meadows, nesting gannets, even whole oceans. It is hard enough to confront the environmental options ahead, and the hard choices, but even harder when the price tags are so visible. Even the new jargon is disturbing: it hurts the spirit, somehow, to read the word *environments*, when the plural means that there are so many alternatives there to be sorted through, as in a market, and voted on. Economists need cool heads and cold hearts for this sort of work, and they must write in icy, often skiddy prose.

The degree to which we are all involved in the control of the earth's life is just beginning to dawn on most of us, and it means another revolution for human thought.

This will not come easily. We've just made our way through inconclusive revolutions on the same topic, trying to make up our minds how we feel about nature. As soon as we arrive at one kind of consensus, like an enormous committee, we found it was time to think it through all over, and now here we are, at it again.

The oldest, easiest-to-swallow idea was that the earth was man's 4 personal property, a combination of garden, zoo, bank vault, and energy source, placed at our disposal to be consumed, ornamented, or pulled apart as we wished. The betterment of mankind was, as we understood it, the whole point of the thing. Mastery over nature, mystery and all, was a moral duty and social obligation.

In the last few years we were wrenched away from this way of looking at it, and arrived at something like general agreement that we had it wrong. We still argue the details, but it is conceded almost everywhere that we are not the masters of nature that we thought ourselves; we are as dependent on the rest of life as are the leaves or midges or fish. We are part of the system. One way to put it is that the earth is a loosely formed, spherical organism, with all its working parts linked in symbiosis. We are, in this view, neither owners nor operators; at best, we might see ourselves as motile tissue specialized for receiving information—perhaps, in the best of all possible worlds, functioning as a nervous system for the whole being.

There is, for some, too much dependency in this view, and they prefer to see us as a separate, qualitatively different, special species, unlike any other form of life, despite the sharing around of genes, enzymes, and organelles. No matter, there is still the underlying idea that we cannot have a life of our own without concern for the ecosystem in which we live, whether in majesty or not. This idea has been strong enough to launch the new movements for the sustenance of wilderness, the protection of wildlife, the turning off of insatiable technologies, the preservation of "whole earth."

But now, just when the new view seems to be taking hold, we may be in for another wrench, this time more dismaying and unsettling than anything we've come through. In a sense, we shall be obliged to swing back again, still believing in the new way but constrained by the facts of life to live in the old. It may be too late, as things have turned out.

We are, in fact, the masters, like it or not.   8

It is a despairing prospect. Here we are, practically speaking twenty-first-century mankind, filled to exuberance with our new understanding of kinship to all the family of life, and here we are, still nineteenth-century man, walking boot-shod over the open face of nature, subjugating and civilizing it. And we cannot stop this controlling, unless we vanish under the hill ourselves. If there were such a thing as a world mind, it should crack over this.

The truth is, we have become more deeply involved than we ever dreamed. The fact that we sit around as we do, worrying seriously about how best to preserve the life of the earth, is itself the sharpest measure of our involvement. It is not human arrogance that has taken us in this direction, but the most natural of natural events. We developed this way, we grew this way, we are this kind of species.

We have become, in a painful, unwished-for way, nature itself. We have grown into everywhere, spreading like a new growth over the entire surface, touching and affecting every other kind of life, *incorporating* ourselves. The earth risks being eutrophied by us. We are now the dominant feature of our own environment. Humans, large terrestrial metazoans, fired by energy from microbial symbionts lodged in their cells, instructed by tapes of nucleic acid stretching back to the earliest live membranes, informed by neurons essentially the same as all the other neurons on earth, sharing structures with mastodons and lichens, living off the sun, are now in charge, running the place, for better or worse.

Or is it really this way? It could be, you know, just the other way 12 around. Perhaps we are the invaded ones, the subjugated, used.

Certain animals in the sea live by becoming part-animal, part-plant. They engulf algae, which then establish themselves as complex plant tissues, essential for the life of the whole company. I suppose the giant clam, if he had more of a mind, would have moments of dismay on seeing what he has done to the plant world, incorporating so much of it, enslaving green cells, living off the photosynthesis. But the plant cells would take a different view of it, having captured the clam on the most satisfactory of terms, including the small lenses in his tissues that focus sunlight for their benefit; perhaps algae have bad moments about what they may collectively be doing to the world of clams.

With luck, our own situation might be similar, on a larger scale. This might turn out to be a special phase in the morphogenesis of the earth when it is necessary to have something like us, for a time anyway, to fetch and carry energy, look after new symbiotic arrangements, store up information for some future season, do a certain amount of ornamenting, maybe even carry seeds around the solar system. That kind of thing. Handyman for the earth.

I would much prefer this useful role, if I had any say, to the essentially unearthly creature we seem otherwise on the way to becoming. It would mean making some quite fundamental changes in our attitudes toward each other, if we were really to think of ourselves as indispensable elements of nature. We would surely become the environment to worry about the most. We would discover, in ourselves, the sources of wonderment and delight that we have discerned in all other manifestations of nature. Who knows, we might even acknowledge the fragility and vulnerability that always accompany high specialization in biology, and movements might start up for the protection of ourselves as a valuable, endangered species. We couldn't lose. *1973*

Charlene Spretnak

Ecofeminism: Our Roots and Flowering

Our roots, our beginning, the increasing allure of "eco" for feminists offer some answers to a question of great immediacy: *What are the
experiences through which humans raised in industrialized, modern society connect on a deep level with nature?* Our flowering, our insights, our growing
impact on political philosophy and practice offer answers to another key
question of our time: *What is the purpose of cultivating ecological wisdom at
this postmodern moment in human history?*

OUR ROOTS

Our situation as a species is the following: the life-support systems
of this almost impossibly beautiful planet are being violated and degraded, causing often irreparable damage, yet only a small proportion
of humans have focused on this crisis. In our own country, our farms are
losing 4 billion tons of topsoil a year; the groundwater and soil are
being poisoned by pesticide runoff and toxic dumping; the groundwater table itself, accumulated over thousands of years, is being recklessly depleted to serve the profits of agribusiness and developers; the
nuclear power industry has generated much more than enough plutonium to poison every creature and ecosystem on Earth and has no
idea how to store it safely; we're losing 200,000 to 300,000 acres of
wetland habitat every year; and the songbirds, which used to herald the
coming of spring, are now perishing in large numbers every winter
when they migrate to the devastated land in Central and South America
that formerly was majestic tropical rain forest.

Is this many-faceted ecocrisis a focus of awareness in our society?
Hardly. In the 1987 State of the Union address, our president did not
mention the present and pending environmental disasters at all. When
the opposition party was given response time on national television and
radio, no one mentioned this absence in the president's account of our
problems. When members of the media, female and male, commented
on the address, the glaring absence of ecological concern, let alone
ecological wisdom, again went unmentioned. In the State of the Union
addresses for the previous two years, the story was the same, except
for the president's brief tip of the hat in 1986 to the Superfund
(ridiculously underfunded for the cleanup of toxic dump sites) and his
promising the previous year not to grant drilling and mining leases
inside the national park system!

That politicians, the media, and the public barely noticed the cru- 4
cial omission in the president's annual assessment of our national

situation is merely one indication of pervasive alienation from the realities of nature. A powerful industrial giant like us lives on *top* of nature, it is understood, free to do with it what we will. The arrogance and ignorance behind that deadly folly are being challenged to varying extents by environmentalist organizations and to a much deeper extent by a loose aggregate of movements whose members are sometimes called the "new" ecologists: ecofeminism, deep ecology, Green politics, bioregionalism, creation-centered spirituality, animal rights, and others. Their numbers are not a large portion of our 242 million, but they are carrying on extremely significant work, feeling their way out of alienation toward a way of being that is infused with ecological wisdom. *Something* connected those people with nature; some event or accumulation of experiences woke them up to the centrality of ecology.

In the case of ecofeminism, there are many paths into our rich and fertile garden, each with its own occasions for awakening. What cannot be said, though, is that women are drawn to ecology and ecofeminism simply because we are female. The very first issue of *Audubon Magazine* in 1887 contained an article by Celia Thaxter titled "Woman's Heartlessness," on the resistance she and other activists met in trying to get women to stop wearing on their hats the feathers and stuffed bodies of birds: "Not among the ignorant and uncultured so much as the educated and enlightened do we find the indifference and hardness that perplexes us . . . I think I may say in two-thirds of the cases to which we appeal. One lady said to me, 'I think there is a great deal of sentiment wasted on the birds. There are so many of them, they will never be missed, any more than mosquitoes.'" Clearly those ladies were team players, defenders of patriarchal, anthropocentric values, which is exactly what we were raised to be, too—until we figured out that the game was dreadfully wrong.

Ecofeminism grew out of radical, or cultural, feminism (rather than from liberal feminism or socialist feminism), which holds that identifying the dynamics—largely fear and resentment—behind the dominance of male over female is the key to comprehending every expression of patriarchal culture with its hierarchical, militaristic, mechanistic, industrialist forms. The first tendrils of ecofeminism appeared not in the exuberant season of Earth Day 1970—for feminists were quite preoccupied with the birthing of our own movement then—but in mid-decade. Our sources of inspiration at the time were not Thoreau, John Muir, or even Rachel Carson (though we have certainly come to appreciate those beacons since then) but, rather, our own experiential explorations.

One path into ecofeminism was the study of political theory and history. Radical/cultural feminists who had been exposed to Marxist analysis in the 1960s as well as those who had gone on to study critical

theory and social ecology in the early 1970s built upon the framework
of dominance theory. They rejected the Marxist assertion that domination is based solely on money and class: if there is a universally
dominated class, surely it is women. Experiencing and naming the
inadequacies of classical dominance theory, which ignores nature as
well as women, such radical feminists moved in the direction of ecofeminism. Another source of radical/cultural feminist dominance theory
was the work of cultural historians who explored the roots of patriarchy.[1]

A second path into ecofeminism is exposure to nature-based religion, usually that of the Goddess. In the mid-1970s many radical/
cultural feminists experienced the exhilarating discovery, through historic and archaeological sources, of a religion that honored the female
and seemed to have as its "good book" nature itself. We were drawn to it
like a magnet, but only, I feel, because both of those features were
central. We would not have been interested in "Yahweh with a skirt," a
distant, detached, domineering godhead who happened to be female.
What was cosmologically wholesome and healing was the discovery of
the Divine as immanent in and around us. What was intriguing was the
sacred link between the Goddess in her many guises and totemic animals and plants, sacred groves, and womblike caves, in the moon-
rhythm blood of menses, the ecstatic dance—the experience of *knowing*
Gaia, her voluptuous contours and fertile plains, her flowing waters
that give life, her animal teachers. For who among us would ever again
see a snake coiled around the arms of an ancient Goddess statue,
teaching lessons of cyclic renewal and regeneration with its shedding
of skins, as merely a member of the ophidian order in the reptilian class
of the vertebrate phylum? That period of discovery—which would
certainly not have been news to primal peoples, but was utterly earth-
shaking for us Judeo-Christian women of a thoroughly modern culture—
inspired art, music, poetry, and the resurrection of long-forgotten sacred myth and ritual, usually held out of doors, of course, often on the
Earth's holy days of cosmic alignment, the solstices and equinoxes. They
are rituals of our own creation that express our deepest feelings of a
spirituality infused with ecological wisdom and wholeness. At the beginning of that period, ecology was not on our minds; since moving out of
that period into activism, ecology has never left our minds. Today we
work for ecopeace, ecojustice, ecoeconomics, ecopolitics, ecoeducation,
ecophilosophy, ecotheology, and for the evolution of ecofeminism.

A third path into ecofeminism comes from environmentalism. For
many women with careers in public policy, science and technology,

---

[1]See, for example, the introduction and essays in Charlene Spretnak (ed.), *The Politics of
Women's Spirituality* (Garden City, NY: Doubleday/Anchor, 1982).

public-interest environmental organizations, and environmental studies programs in universities, their initial connection with feminism was
the liberal-feminist attention to how and why their progress on the
career ladder was blocked. From there they eventually encountered a
book, an article, or a lecture with ecofeminist analysis—and suddenly
their career work was framed with a radically different meaning. Similarly, women and men who become involved with Green politics for
environmental reasons discover ecofeminism and deep ecology there.
College students, male and female, who feel that feminism was merely
an issue for their mothers' generation and who enroll in an environmental studies course are often exposed to ecofeminist analysis and
recognize a depth not present in their textbooks.

There are many variations of these three well-trodden paths into
our garden, and perhaps other paths altogether. I have delineated them
in order to acknowledge our diversity, which brings strength, but also in
the hope that the social and political theory evolving within ecofeminism will address not only the interlinked dynamics in patriarchal
culture of the terror of nature and the terror of the elemental power of
the female but also the ways *out* of the mesmerizing conditioning that
keeps women and men so cut off from our grounding in the natural
world, so alienated from our larger sense of self in the unfolding story
of the universe. If we look into this matter further, I think we'll find that
many people connected with nature on a deep level through a ritual
moment of awakening, or perhaps several of them. These moments may
have occurred in the context of spiritual practice. They may have
occurred in childhood. They are the precious moments we need to
acknowledge and to cultivate, to refuse to let the dominant culture pave
them over any longer with a value system made of denial, distancing,
fear, and ignorance.

The moment of awakening, however, is only the beginning. After
that comes a great deal of work if we really want to transform patriarchal culture into new possibilities infomed by justice, wisdom, and
compassion. We have to be willing to do intellectual work—to explore
the books and articles, the speeches and debates that contribute to the
evolving social and political theory of ecofeminism. We have to be
willing to seek a holistic understanding of ecofeminism, to make an
effort to learn about the priorities and experiential wisdom of ecofeminists who came from paths different from our own. We have to be
willing to pursue self-education in ecology since our schooling for the
most part failed us in that, to read an ecology textbook, for instance.[2]
We have to be willing to educate ourselves about the major ecological

---

[2]My favorite is G. Tyler Miller, *Living in the Environment*, 4th ed. (Belmont, CA: Wadsworth,
1985).

issues of our day and to understand the economic and political forces at work.

Extremely important is a willingness to deepen our experience of 12 communion with nature. This can be done in the mountains, at the ocean, in a city park, or a backyard garden. My own life is a rather embarrassing example of how long one can be absorbed in ecofeminist intellectual thought, political activism, and ritual honoring of nature *after* the moment of awakening and still know almost nothing of the richness and profound depth of communion that nature can offer. Several years ago I was invited to a conference on bioregionalism and Green politics in Santa Fe and met the environmental editor of the journal that was then called *CoEvolution Quarterly*. We went for a walk, conversing all the while, and when we returned a colleague asked if the editor, who was wearing a large pair of binoculars on a strap around his neck, had seen any birds. "I didn't see any, but I heard four," he replied. "What?!" I thought to myself, "Four birds? On that walk? Just now? I didn't hear anything. Four birds?!" It was at that moment that I realized that, despite my intellectual and political understanding of ecofeminism, I was a tourist in the natural world. In the intervening years, I have gone on many birding hikes, which I love, as well as canoe and backpacking trips into the wilderness. Nature has given me gifts, teachings, and revelations, but none more intense than those times in the wilderness I approached in silence, simply observing and being aware of the sensations I was experiencing, until eventually I was enfolded by the deep, deep silence and the oneness that is almost palpable. At that moment the distinction between inner and outer mind dissolves, and we meet our larger self, the One Mind, the cosmic unfolding. I feel that various intensities of that mystery are revealed to us during the postorgasmic state and during certain kinds of meditation and also ritual, but the grandeur and majesty of oneness I have found only in nature. A starting point for ecofeminists who are as backward in their direct knowledge of nature as I certainly was might be to learn about ten birds and ten plants native to their bioregion. The rest will come quite naturally.

All these kinds of work are the nutrient-rich compost that has yielded the vibrant flowering of ecofeminism today. Composting good soil takes time, and the work of ecofeminism goes back more than a dozen years. In fact, it goes back to a number of feminist writers (including Simone de Beauvoir in 1947) who mentioned in passing the attitudes of men (under patriarchy) to nature and to women and the connection between the two. The first conference to address this idea was "Women and the Environment," organized by Sandra Marburg and Lisa Watson at the University of California, Berkeley, in 1974. In 1980, spurred by the Three Mile Island catastrophe, Ynestra King, Celeste

Wesson, Grace Paley, Anna Gyorgy, Christina Rawley, Nancy Jack Todd, and Deborah Gaventa organized a conference in Amherst, Massachusetts, on "Women and Life on Earth: Ecofeminism in the 1980s." Prior to learning of that gathering, Susan Adler and other spiritually aware women at Sonoma State University in California began planning a 1981 conference entitled "Women and the Environment: The First West Coast Ecofeminist Conference." In London, an ecofeminist conference called "Women and Life on Earth" was also held that year. The number of ecofeminist books and articles as well as running debates in anthologies and journals is far too great to cite here, but certainly *Woman and Nature* by Susan Griffin (New York: Harper & Row, 1978) and *The Death of Nature* by Carolyn Merchant (San Francisco: Harper & Row, 1980) were particularly important contributions. Both of those books were begun many years earlier, but they were immediately recognized as the ecofeminist classics that they are because so many radical/cultural feminists had moved in that direction during the second half of the 1970s.

OUR FLOWERING

So those are our roots. Today ecofeminists address the crucial issues of our time, from reproductive technology to Third World development, from toxic poisoning to the vision of a new politics and economics—and much more. We support and join our sisters fighting for equal pay, for battered women's shelters, for better child care, and for all the efforts to stop the daily exploitation and suffering of women. But we see those efforts as bandages on a very unhealthy system. Radical/cultural feminism is sometimes called "big-picture" feminism because we examine the deepest assumptions, values, and fears that inform the structures and expectations of patriarchal culture. The reason we insist on integrating radical analysis with ecological perspective is best understood in the larger framework of the fate of our species and all life on Earth: *What is the purpose of cultivating ecological wisdom at this postmodern moment in human history?*

Our society is facing a crisis in agriculture, a crisis in education and literacy, a crisis in national security and the arms race, a crisis in the international debt situation, and a crisis in the state of the global environment. For the first time in the modern era, there is widespread agreement that something is very wrong. The assumptions of modernity, the faith in technological "progress" and rapacious industrialism, along with the militarism necessary to support it, have left us very lost indeed. The quintessential malady of the modern era is free-floating anxiety, and it is clear to ecofeminists that the whole culture is free floating—from the lack of grounding in the natural world, from the lack of a sense of belonging in the unfolding story of the universe, from the lack of a healthy relationship between the males and females of the species. We are entangled in the hubris of the patriarchal goal of dominating nature and the female. On August 29, 1986, the *New York Times* published a lead editorial titled "Nature as Demon," reminding everyone that the proper orientation of civilization is to advance itself *in opposition* to nature. The editorial advised that disasters such as "Hiroshima, DDT, Bhopal, and now Chernobyl" simply require "improving the polity," that is, fine-tuning the system. Such smugness, of course, is the common response of guardians of the status quo: retrenchment and Band-Aids.

But ecofeminists say that the system is leading us to ecocide and 16 species suicide because it is based on ignorance, fear, delusion, and greed. We say that people, male or female, enmeshed in the *values* of that system are incapable of making rational decisions. They pushed nuclear power plants when they did not have the slightest idea what to do with the plutonium wastes—because, after all, someone always comes along later to clean up like Mom. They pushed the nuclear arms race because those big phallic missiles are so "technologically sweet." They are pushing reproductive technology with the gleeful prediction that children of the future, a result of much genetic selection, will often have a donor mother, an incubator mother, and social mother who raises them—making motherhood as disembodied and discontinuous as fatherhood, at last! They are pushing high-tech petroleum-based agriculture, which makes the soil increasingly brittle and lifeless and adds millions of tons of toxic pesticides to our food as well as our soil and water, because *they* know how to get what they want from the Earth—a far cry from the peasant rituals that persisted in parts of Europe even up to World War I where women would encircle the fields by torchlight and symbolically transfer their fertility to the land they touched. Women and men in those cultures participated in the cycles of nature with respect and gratitude.

Such attitudes have no place in a modern, technocratic society fueled by the patriarchal obsessions of dominance and control. They have been replaced by the managerial ethos, which holds efficiency of production and short-term gains above all else—above ethics or moral standards, above the health of community life, and above the integrity of all biological processes, especially those constituting the elemental power of the female. The experts guiding our society seek deliverance from their fears of nature, with which they have no real communion or deep connection, through their seeming victories over the great forces: their management of the vast watersheds and forests of the planet and its perilously thin layer of topsoil; their management of the economics and daily conditions of people of color throughout the Third World (the so-called developing nations) and the Fourth World (the indigenous

peoples); their management of "improved animal tools" for agribusiness; their management of women's economic status; and finally—so
very technologically sweet—their management of women's birthing
power, beginning first with control over labor and delivery, then control
over breastfeeding (which the AMA almost succeeded in phasing out
between the 1930s and the mid-1970s), and now control over conception
and gestation, with the prediction that they will one day colonize the
universe by sending frozen human embryos or cells for clones into
space to colonize planets.

The technological experts of the modern era, with their colleagues
in business, government, and the military, are waging an antibiological
revolution in human contact. The moral systems of Western ethics and
religion are nearly powerless in this struggle because those systems
themselves are largely devoid of ecological wisdom. The crying need
right now—if we have any hope of charting a postmodern, posthuman-
ist, and postpatriarchal transition to the Age of Ecology—is for a new
philosophical underpinning of civilization. We need an ecophilosophy
that speaks the truth with great immediacy in language that everyone
can understand.

That work has already been started by ecofeminists and by the
deep ecology movement, many of whose pioneering members are philosophy professors drawing on ecology, ethics, philosophy, and religion.
There has been little serious contact between these two movements, a
situation that I hope both parties will work to change, for ecofeminism
has a great deal to add to the evolution of ecophilosophy. The following
are a few examples. Deep ecologists write that Western philosophy,
religion, and culture in general are estranged from nature, being anthropocentric. Ecofeminists say, "Yes, but surely you've noticed something else about them, haven't you? They're intensely *andro*centric. And
surely you've noticed that Western conquest and degradation of nature
are based on fear and resentment; we can demonstrate that that
dynamic is linked closely to patriarchal fear and resentment of the elemental power of the female." Deep ecologists write that our estrangement from nature began with classic Greek humanism and the rise of
Judeo-Christian culture. But ecofeminists say, "Actually, it began
around 4500 B.C. with the Indo-European invasions of nomadic tribes
from the Eurasian steppes, who replaced the nature-based and female-
honoring religion of the Goddess in Europe, the Near East, Persia, and
India with their thunderbolt God, removing that which is held sacred
and revered from the life processes of the Earth to the distant realm of
an omnipotent, male Sky-God. It is in the Indo-European Revolution,
not in the Scientific Revolution of the sixteenth and seventeenth centuries, that one finds the earliest sources of desacralized nature, the
foundation of a mechanistic worldview." Deep ecologists write that the

only incidence of ecological wisdom in Christianity was Saint Francis of Assisi. But ecofeminists say, "There were many other creation-centered great mystics of the medieval era, including Hildegard of Bingen, Mechtild of Mageburg, Julian of Norwich, and Meister Eckhart, who said he learned much from the Beguines, a female lay order." Deep ecologists write that the well-being and flourishing of human and nonhuman life on Earth has value in itself and that humans have no right to reduce the richness and diversity of life forms except to satisfy vital human needs. Ecofeminists agree but wonder how much one's concept of "vital needs" is shaped by the values of patriarchal culture.

There are also some philosophical ecologists who favor abstract 20 schemes such as "ecological process analysis" to explain the natural world. But ecofeminists find such approaches alone to be sterile and inadequate, a veiled attempt, yet again, to distance oneself from wonder and awe, from the emotional involvement and caring that the natural world calls forth.

To care empathetically about the person, the species, and the great family of all beings, about the bioregion, the biosphere, and the universe is the framework within which ecofeminists wish to address the issues of our time. The problem of world population, for example, is one that attracts no dearth of single-minded solutions. The New Left claims that any population-control program proposed for the Third World is genocide of people of color. The Reagan administration cut off U.S. money for abortion operations in Third World countries and talked of cutting off support for contraception on the grounds that growth always brings prosperity—meaning, I suspect, that Third World fetuses are viewed as future markets. Ecologists point out that the Earth's ecosystems are strained almost beyond their carrying capacity and that a major collapse is imminent if human population continues to soar. Radical feminists say that any population control is patriarchal domination of women's wombs.

The reality that many Third World countries are facing is one with half of their populations under age 18, roaming shanty towns in overcrowded cities looking for food and work while ecosystems die around them. An ecofeminist response to this suffering would involve the following elements: (1) the health of the biosphere demands that the rate of population growth level off *everywhere* and then decline (with the exception of tribal peoples in danger of extinction); (2) Third World women have made it clear that they are not interested in contraception unless health and economic conditions are improved (studies have shown that when the death rate of children goes down, the birth rate goes down); (3) women at the regional level must be involved with the planning of population-control programs, health care, education, and nonexploitative small-scale economic opportunities; (4) the political struggles between indigenous cultural nations and the capitalist or socialist states that have been created around them (a freedom fight that accounts for 78 percent of the current wars globally, according to one study) must be resolved so that the women of the ethnic nations are no longer pressured to have many babies in order to outnumber their oppressors; (5) governments and institutions must address the patriarchal attitudes that condition men to demand a large number of offspring in order to prove their virility—as well as the patriarchal attitudes that bring such misery, and sometimes death, to young mothers who give birth to a female under China's "successful" one-child-only policy.

It is our refusal to banish feelings of interrelatedness and caring from the theory and practice of ecofeminism that will save our efforts from calcifying into well-intentioned reformism, lacking the vitality and wholeness that our lives contain. We need to find our way out of the technocratic alienation and nihilism surrounding us by cultivating and honoring our direct connections with nature.

In my own life I have found that many of those connections have 24 been long since buried. In thinking about ecofeminism recently, I remembered an event that took place sixteen years ago, which I had nearly lost from memory. When my daughter was about three days old and we were still in the hospital, I wrapped her up one evening and slipped outside to a little garden in the warmth of late June. I introduced her to the pine trees and the plants and the flowers, and they to her, and finally to the pearly moon wrapped in a soft haze and to the stars. I, knowing nothing then of nature-based religious ritual or eco-feminist theory, had felt an impulse for my wondrous little child to meet the rest of cosmic society. Perhaps it was the ultimate coming-out party! The interesting thing is that that experience, although lovely and rich, was so disconnected from life in a modern, technocratic society that I soon forgot all about it. Last year when I heard about a ritual of the Omaha Indians in which the infant is presented to the cosmos, I waxed enthusiastic and made copies of the prayer for friends who were planning a baptism—but forgot completely that I, too, had once been there, so effective is our cultural denial of nature.

I cannot imagine a challenge greater than that addressed by ecofeminism. We know that we are of one fabric with all life on this glorious blue-green planet, that the elements in our bodies and in the world around us were forged by the fireball at the moment the universe was born, and that we have no right to destroy the integrity of the Earth's delicately balanced ecosystems, whose histories are far longer than our own. Around us we see the immensely destructive thrashing of patriarchal leaders *who cannot even name the pain and ignorance that drive their greed.* In their frenzy, they push 10,000 species into extinction each year, a figure that is ever increasing. Can ecofeminism and the related grassroots movements heal those people, heal ourselves, and heal the planet?

Our society is lost and very confused. Perhaps the most effective strategy for us—and certainly the most difficult—is to lead by example: to contribute to the new philosophical base and to work in its new ecopolitics and ecoeconomics; to organize around the concrete issues of suffering and exploitation; to speak out clearly but without malice against those who further policies of injustice and ecological ignorance; to nurture the relationships with our colleagues, never feeling that we must ridicule and crush those with whom we disagree—but most of all, to unlock our memories; to follow the "body parables" of our sexuality; to cultivate our spiritual impulses; to act, as best we can, with pure mind/pure heart; to celebrate with gratitude the wonders of life on Earth; and to seek intimate communion with the natural world. All of these are the flowering of ecofeminism.   *1990*

Cynthia Hamilton

Women, Home, and Community: The Struggle in an Urban Environment

In 1956, women in South Africa began an organized protest against the pass laws. As they stood in front of the office of the prime minister, they began a new freedom song with the refrain "now you have touched the women, you have struck a rock." This refrain provides a description of the personal commitment and intensity women bring to social change. Women's actions have been characterized as "spontaneous and dramatic," women in action portrayed as "intractable and uncompromising."[1] Society has summarily dismissed these as negative attributes. When in 1986 the City Council of Los Angeles decided that a 13-acre incinerator called LANCER (for Los Angeles City Energy Recovery Project), burning 2,000 tons a day of municipal waste, should be built in a poor residential, black, and Hispanic community, the women

[1]See Cynthia Cockburn, "When Women Get Involved in Community Action," in Marjorie Mayo (ed.), *Women in the Community* (London: Routledge & Kegan Paul, 1977).

there said "No." Officials had indeed dislodged a boulder of opposition. According to Charlotte Bullock, one of the protestors, "I noticed when we first started fighting the issue how the men would laugh at the women . . . they would say, 'Don't pay no attention to them, that's only one or two women . . . they won't make a difference.' But now since we've been fighting for about a year the smiles have gone."[2]

Minority communities shoulder a disproportionately high share of the by-products of industrial development: waste, abandoned factories and warehouses, leftover chemicals and debris. These communities are also asked to house the waste and pollution no longer acceptable in white communities, such as hazardous landfills or dump sites. In 1987, the Commission for Racial Justice of the United Church of Christ published *Toxic Wastes and Race*. The commission concluded that race is a major factor related to the presence of hazardous wastes in residential communities throughout the United States. Three out of every five black and Hispanic Americans live in communities with uncontrolled toxic sites; 75 percent of the residents in rural areas in the Southwest, mainly Hispanics, are drinking pesticide-contaminated water; more than 2 million tons of uranium tailings are dumped on Native-American reservations each year, resulting in Navajo teenagers having seventeen times the national average of organ cancers; more than 700,000 inner city children, 50 percent of them black, are said to be suffering from lead poisoning, resulting in learning disorders. Working-class minority women are therefore motivated to organize around very pragmatic environmental issues, rather than those associated with more middle-class organizations. According to Charlotte Bullock, "I did not come to the fight against environmental problems as an intellectual but rather as a concerned mother. . . . People say, 'But you're not a scientist, how do you know it's not safe?' I have common sense. I know if dioxin and mercury are going to come out of an incinerator stack, somebody's going to be affected."

When Concerned Citizens of South Central Los Angeles came together in 1986 to oppose the solid waste incinerator planned for the community, no one thought much about environmentalism or feminism. These were just words in a community with a 78 percent unemployment rate, an average income ($8,158) less than half that of the general Los Angeles population, and a residential density more than twice that of the whole city. In the first stages of organization, what motivated and directed individual actions was the need to protect home and children; for the group this individual orientation emerged as a community-centered battle. What was left in this deteriorating district

[2]All of the quotes from Charlotte Bullock and Robin Cannon are personal communications, 1986.

on the periphery of the central business and commercial district had to be defended—a "garbage dump" was the final insult after years of neglect, watching downtown flourish while residents were prevented from borrowing enough to even build a new roof.

The organization was never gender restricted but it became appar- 4
ent after a while that women were the majority. The particular kind of organization the group assumed, the actions engaged in, even the content of what was said, were all a product not only of the issue itself, the waste incinerator, but also a function of the particular nature of women's oppression and what happens as the process of consciousness begins.

Women often play a primary part in community action because it is about things they know best. Minority women in several urban areas have found themselves part of a new radical core as the new wave of environmental action, precipitated by the irrationalities of capital-intensive growth, has catapulted them forward. These individuals are responding not to "nature" in the abstract but to the threat to their homes and to the health of their children. Robin Cannon, another activist in the fight against the Los Angeles incinerator, says, "I have asthma, my children have asthma, my brothers and sisters have asthma, there are a lot of health problems that people living around an incinerator might be subjected to and I said, 'They can't do this to me and my family.'"

Women are more likely than men to take on these issues precisely because the home has been defined and prescribed as a woman's domain. According to British sociologist Cynthia Cockburn, "In a housing situation that is a health hazard, the woman is more likely to act than the man because she lives there all day and because she is impelled by fear for her children. Community action of this kind is a significant phase of class struggle, but it is also an element of women's liberation."[3]

This phenomenon was most apparent in the battle over the Los Angeles incinerator. Women who had had no history of organizing responded as protectors of their children. Many were single parents, others were older women who had raised families. While the experts were convinced that their smug dismissal of the validity of the health concerns these women raised would send them away, their smugness only reinforced the women's determination. According to Charlotte Bullock:

> People's jobs were threatened, ministers were threatened . . . but I said, "I'm not going to be intimidated." My child's health comes first, . . . that's more important than my job.

³Cockburn, "When Women," p. 62.

> In the 1950s the city banned small incinerators in the yard and yet they want to build a big incinerator . . . the Council is going to build something in my community which might kill my child. . . . I don't need a scientist to tell me that's wrong.

None of the officials were prepared for the intensity of concern or the consistency of agitation. In fact, the consultants they hired had concluded that these women did not fit the prototype of opposition. The consultants had concluded:

> Certain types of people are likely to participate in politics, either by virtue of their issue awareness or their financial resources, or both. Members of middle or higher socioeconomic strata (a composite index of level of education, occupational prestige, and income) are more likely to organize into effective groups to express their political interests and views. All socioeconomic groupings tend to resent the nearby siting of major facilities, but the middle and upper socioeconomic strata possess better resources to effectuate their opposition. Middle and higher socioeconomic strata neighborhoods should not fall at least within the one mile and five mile radii of the proposed site.
>
> . . . although environmental concerns cut across all subgroups, people with a college education, young or middle aged, and liberal in philosophy are most likely to organize opposition to the siting of a major facility. Older people, with a high school education or less, and those who adhere to a free market orientation are least likely to oppose a facility.[4]

The organizers against the incinerator in South Central Los Angeles are the antithesis of the prototype: they are high school educated or less, above middle age and young, nonprofessionals and unemployed and low-income, without previous political experience. The consultants and politicians thus found it easy to believe that opposition from this group could not be serious.

The intransigence of the City Council intensified the agitation, and the women became less willing to compromise as time passed. Each passing month gave them greater strength, knowledge, and perseverance. The council and its consultants had a more formidable enemy than they had expected, and in the end they have had to compromise. The politicians have backed away from their previous embrace of incineration as a solution to the trash crisis, and they have backed away from this particular site in a poor, black and Hispanic, residential area. While the issues are far from resolved, it is important that the willingness to compromise has become the official position of the city as a result of the determination of "a few women."

8

---

[4]Cerrell Associates, *Political Difficulties Facing Waste to Energy Conversion Plant Siting* (Los Angeles: California Waste Management Board, 1984), pp. 42–43.

The women in South Central Los Angeles were not alone in their battle. They were joined by women from across the city, White, middle-class, and professional women. As Robin Cannon puts it, "I didn't know we all had so many things in common . . . millions of people in the city had something in common with us—the environment." These two groups of women, together, have created something previously unknown in Los Angeles—unity of purpose across neighborhood and racial lines. According to Charlotte Bullock, "We are making a difference . . . when we come together as a whole and stick with it, we can win because we are right."

This unity has been accomplished by informality, respect, tolerance of spontaneity, and decentralization. All of the activities that we have been told destroy organizations have instead worked to sustain this movement. For example, for a year and a half the group functioned without a formal leadership structure. The unconscious acceptance of equality and democratic process resulted practically in rotating the chair's position at meetings. Newspeople were disoriented when they asked for the spokesperson and the group responded that everyone could speak for the neighborhood.

It may be the case that women, unlike men, are less conditioned to see the value of small advances.[5] These women were all guided by their vision of the possible: that it *was* possible to completely stop the construction of the incinerator, that it is possible in a city like Los Angeles to have reasonable growth, that it is possible to humanize community structures and services. As Robin Cannon says, "My neighbors said, 'You can't fight City Hall . . . and besides, you work there.' I told them I would fight anyway."

None of these women was convinced by the consultants and their traditional justifications for capital-intensive growth: that it increases property values by intensifying land use, that it draws new businesses and investment to the area, that it removes blight and deterioration—and the key argument used to persuade the working class—that growth creates jobs. Again, to quote Robin Cannon, "They're not bringing real development to our community. . . . They're going to bring this incinerator to us, and then say 'We're going to *give* you fifty jobs when you get this plant.' Meanwhile they're going to shut down another factory [in Riverside] and eliminate two hundred jobs to buy more pollution rights. . . . They may close more shops."

Ironically, the consultants' advice backfired. They had suggested that emphasizing employment and a gift to the community (of $2 million for a community development fund for park improvement) would

12

[5]See Cockburn, "When Women," p. 63.

persuade the opponents. But promises of heated swimming pools, air-conditioned basketball courts and fifty jobs at the facility were more insulting than encouraging. Similarly, at a public hearing, an expert witness's assurance that health risks associated with dioxin exposure were less than those associated with "eating peanut butter" unleashed a flurry of derision.

The experts' insistence on referring to congenital deformities and cancers as "acceptable risks" cut to the hearts of women who rose to speak of a child's asthma, or a parent's influenza, or the high rate of cancer, heart disease, and pneumonia in this poverty-stricken community. The callous disregard of human concerns brought the women closer together. They came to rely on each other as they were subjected to the sarcastic rebuffs of men who referred to their concerns as "irrational, uninformed, and disruptive." The contempt of the male experts was directed at professionals and the unemployed, at Whites and Blacks—all the women were castigated as irrational and uncompromising. As a result, new levels of consciousness were sparked in these women.

The reactions of the men backing the incinerator provided a very 16 serious learning experience for the women, both professionals and nonprofessionals, who came to the movement without a critique of patriarchy. They developed their critique in practice. In confronting the need for equality, these women forced the men to a new level of recognition—that working-class women's concerns cannot be simply dismissed.

Individual transformations accompanied the group process. As the struggle against the incinerator proceeded to take on some elements of class struggle, individual consciousness matured and developed. Women began to recognize something of their own oppression as women. This led to new forms of action not only against institutions but to the transformation of social relations in the home as well. As Robin Cannon explains:

> My husband didn't take me seriously at first either. . . . He just saw a whole lot of women meeting and assumed we wouldn't get anything done. . . . I had to split my time . . . I'm the one who usually comes home from work, cooks, helps the kids with their homework, then I watch a little TV and go to bed to get ready for the next morning. Now I would rush home, cook, read my materials on LANCER . . . now the kids were on their own . . . I had my own homework. . . . My husband still wasn't taking me seriously. . . . After about 6 months everyone finally took me seriously. My husband had to learn to allocate more time for baby sitting. Now on Saturdays, if they went to the show or to the park, I couldn't attend . . . in the evening there were hearings . . . I was using my vacation time to go to hearings during the workday.

As parents, particularly single parents, time in the home was strained for these women. Children and husbands complained that meetings and public hearings had taken priority over the family and relations in the home. According to Charlotte Bullock, "My children understand, but then they don't want to understand. . . . They say, 'You're not spending time with me.'" Ironically, it was the concern for family, their love of their families, that had catapulted these women into action to begin with. But, in a pragmatic sense, the home did have to come second in order for health and safety to be preserved. These were hard learning experiences. But meetings in individual homes ultimately involved children and spouses alike—everyone worked and everyone listened. The transformation of relations continued as women spoke up at hearings and demonstrations and husbands transported children, made signs, and looked on with pride and support at public forums.

The critical perspective of women in the battle against LANCER went far beyond what the women themselves had intended. For these women, the political issues were personal and in that sense they became feminist issues. These women, in the end, were fighting for what they felt was "right" rather than what men argued might be reasonable. The coincidence of the principles of feminism and ecology that Carolyn Merchant explains in *The Death of Nature* (San Francisco: Harper & Row, 1981) found expression and developed in the consciousness of these women: the concern for Earth as a home, the recognition that all parts of a system have equal value, the acknowledgment of process, and, finally, that capitalist growth has social costs. As Robin Cannon says, "This fight has really turned me around, things are intertwined in ways I hadn't realized. . . . All these social issues as well as political and economic issues are really intertwined. Before, I was concerned only about health and then I began to get into the politics, decision making, and so many things."

In two years, what started as the outrage of a small group of mothers has transformed the political climate of a major metropolitan area. What these women have aimed for is a greater level of democracy, a greater level of involvement, not only in their organization but in the development process of the city generally. They have demanded accountability regarding land use and ownership, very subversive concerns in a capitalist society. In their organizing, the group process, collectivism, was of primary importance. It allowed the women to see their own power and potential and therefore allowed them to consolidate effective opposition. The movement underscored the role of principles. In fact, we citizens have lived so long with an unquestioning acceptance of profit and expediency that sometimes we forget that our objective is to do "what's right." Women are beginning to raise moral concerns in a very forthright manner, emphasizing that experts have left us no other choice but to follow our own moral convictions rather than accept neutrality and capitulate in the face of crisis.

The environmental crisis will escalate in this decade and women are 20 sure to play pivotal roles in the struggle to save our planet. If women are able to sustain for longer periods some of the qualities and behavioral forms they have displayed in crisis situations (such as direct participatory democracy and the critique of patriarchal bureaucracy), they may be able to reintroduce equality and democracy into progressive action. They may also reintroduce the value of being moved by principle and morality. Pragmatism has come to dominate all forms of political behavior and the results have often been disastrous. If women resist the "normal" organizational thrust to barter, bargain, and fragment ideas and issues, they may help set new standards for action in the new environment movement.   *1990*

The Power of Language

30

The Languages of Home

John Edgar Wideman, The Language
of Home

Paule Marshall, From the Poets in
the Kitchen

Maxine Hong Kingston, *From* A Song for a
Barbarian Reed Pipe

Grace Paley, The Loudest Voice

Two years ago, when I started writing this paper, trying to bring order out of chaos, my ten-year-old daughter was suffering from an acute attack of boredom. She drifted in and out of the room complaining that she had nothing to do, no one to "be with" because none of her friends were at home. Patiently I explained that I was working on something special and needed peace and quiet, and I suggested that she paint, read, or work with her computer. None of these interested her. Finally, she pulled up a chair to my desk and watched me, now and then heaving long, loud sighs. After two or three minutes (nine or ten sighs), I lost my patience. "Looka here, Allie," I said, "you too old for this kinda carryin' on. I done told you this is important. You wronger than dirt to be in here haggin' me like this and you know it. Now git on outta here and leave me off before I put my foot all the way down."

Barbara Mellix, from *From Outside, In*

My mother! My father! After English became my primary language, I no longer knew what words to use in addressing my parents. The old Spanish words (those tender accents of sound) I had earlier used— *mamá* and *papá*—I couldn't use anymore. They would have been all-too-painful reminders of how much had changed in my life. On the other hand, the words I heard neighborhood kids call their parents seemed unsatisfactory. "Mother" and "father," "ma," "papa," "pa," "dad," "pop" (how I hated the all-American sound of that last word)—all these I felt were unsuitable terms of address for *my* parents. As a result, I never used them at home. Whenever I'd speak to my parents, I would try to get their attention by looking at them. In public conversations, I'd refer to them as my "parents" or my "mother" and "father."

Richard Rodriguez, from *Aria: A Memoir of a Bilingual Childhood*

Vietnamese is not my language. The people are not my people. Outside the family, the Vietnamese language is yet more complicated for me because all the natives speak with the southern accent, whereas I have been raised on my parents' northern dialect. This fluid, melodic learned language immediately identifies them as northern upper class. It is that of the ancient emperors and scholars. It is that of Hồ Chí Minh. It is also that of the evening. When my mother puts us to bed, tucking in the mosquito net, she will then sing to my baby brother. Lying drowsily beside the trembling air conditioner, it seems to me that my mother's songs don't actually have *meaning*. I guess that she simply takes the softest, most undulating sounds of her language and smooths them together. Her voice rises and falls, following sinuous accents, suggesting subtle smells, caresses, visions. It is the language of the night which she speaks to my father. Their voices drift through the thin walls, accompanied by the droning of their fan. The low, relaxed rumbling of my father, an occasional chuckle, and my mother's higher, lighter stream.

An-Thu Quang Nguyen, from *Tai Con*

Some years after my father's death, I began making notes of his vocabulary and his characteristic phrases, and for the first time I took account of how old-fashioned his English was. He would say, for example, "It rains" or "It snows"—as the characters in Jane Austen do—instead of "It is raining," "It is snowing"; "It makes no matter" for "It doesn't matter." He would sometimes correct himself if he fell into the current usage of "*a* hotel" and make it "*an* hotel." He was the only living person I have ever known who used the exclamation "Zounds!" He was incapable of any other profanity, never even said, "Good God!" or "Damn!" and his "Zounds" had a nuance of humor, but he did not regard it as a period piece. He was especially fond of such metaphors as "weltering around in a Dead Sea of mediocrity"—something I was warned not to do, when my school marks were not up to scratch—it was the worst fate with which he could threaten me. He was very much annoyed one day when, on our way home from one of his speeches, I undertook to inform him that the word he had wanted to use was *cataclysm*, not *cataclasm*. *Cataclasm* was then so archaic that I did not even know it existed and that it differed in meaning from *cataclysm*. I decided, in any case, at the moment of discovering in the writing of his papers the model for my literary style that this model was a valuable heritage, like the table pieces of silver of the Paul Revere silversmith period which had come to me from his side of the family.

Edmund Wilson, from *The Problem of English*

John Edgar Wideman

The Language of Home

Why do writers write about the same place over and over again? There are probably as many answers to this question as there are writers obsessed with a city, a county, a village, or a community. Rather than try to speak for others whose one certified virtue is speaking well for themselves, I'll focus my thoughts on the turn my own work has taken, my excursions home again, home again in fiction and nonfiction, to Homewood, a black neighborhood in Pittsburgh.

In the green woods of Maine, beside a lake, 2,300 miles from my present home in Wyoming, even farther in most ways from the city-scapes of my imagination, there is a gray wooden lawn chair perched on the edge of a dock. The setting is crucial. Like most writers, I observe rituals. A meticulously arranged scenario, certain pens, paper, a time of day, an alignment of furniture, particular clothing, coffee cooled to a precise temperature—the variations are infinite, but each writer knows his or her version of the preparatory ritual must be exactly duplicated if writing is to begin, prosper.

Repetition dignifies these rituals. My return home begins with a ceremony. Early morning is my time. Bundled in a hooded sweatshirt, more of a protection against mosquitoes than weather, I slouch in my gray chair at the end of the dock facing Long Lake. The morning play of water, wind, and light has never been the same once in the eighteen summers I've watched. From where I sit, it's almost two miles to the opposite shore. Picture a long, dark, ominous spine, low-hanging mist, white birches leaning over the water, a stillness so profound you can hear fish breaking the surface to catch insects. Whatever kind of weather they happen to be producing, the elements are always perfectly harmonized, synchronized.

The trick is to borrow, to internalize for a few quiet instants, the   4 peace of the elements at play. Whatever mood or scene I'm attempting to capture, the first condition is inner calm, a simultaneous grasping and letting go that allows me to be a witness, a mirror. This state has gradually become more accessible to me only after fighting for years to believe again in my primal perceptions, my primal language, the words, gestures, and feelings of my earliest memories. At some point I taught myself to stop translating from one language to another. I've learned I can say the things I want to say using the words and telling the stories of Homewood people. The blackness of my writing inheres in its history, its bilingual, Creole, maroon, bastardized, miscegenated, cross-cultural acceptance of itself in the mirror only it can manufacture.

I was once a paperboy. To deliver the *Pittsburgh Post-Gazette*, I had to climb Negley Avenue Hill. On bad days, with a sack of newspapers slung over my back, the cobbled hill seemed almost vertical, and I mounted it hand over hand with the help of an invisible rope anchored at the crest. Because rich white people resided at the top of Negley, the climb was almost worthwhile. They tipped royally, compensating me for the rigors of the ascent, the enormous distances separating their houses. I whistled a lot as I made my rounds. The turf atop Negley Hill remained foreign. Immense houses of stone and brick, long curving driveways, sculpted trees and shrubberies, lawns cleaner than most people's living-room floors. If I wasn't whistling, I was singing inside my head. The music of the Drifters, Dells, Turbans, Spaniels, Miracles, Flamingos, Louis Berry, Jerry Butler, all the quartets and stars in whose songs I could imagine a shape for my feelings.

On those lily-white streets bordering the Squirrel Hill section of Pittsburgh, I knew I was an intruder. Would I be discovered, punished? The songs were protection, a talisman, but they also could betray me. If anybody ever heard the music inside my head, I'd be in real trouble. Though I couldn't have articulated it at the time, I sensed that my music wove an alternate version of reality, one that included me and incriminated me, one that could sweep away the stones. Some evenings I was buoyed by the danger, the trespass I was committing, walking those sleepy streets, carrying doowop and "Oh, What a Night" and "For Your Precious Love," contraband in my skull.

Thirty years later, and things haven't changed much. I return to Pittsburgh again and again in my writing. Three books of fiction, a nonfiction narrative, "Brothers and Keepers," a pair of new novels in the works, all rooted in Homewood, the actual black community where I was raised, the imaginary landscape I dream up as I go along. Every book a voyage home, each a struggle up a steep incline whose familiarity makes it more rather than less difficult. I find myself, each time a book is finished, in an alien place, whistling, singing to keep away the strangers who own the hilltop and everything else.

On our way back and forth to Peabody High School, my partner   8
Scott Payne and I crossed Penn Avenue, the main drag of East Liberty, which was in those days a thriving pocket of stores, theaters, banks, and restaurants. On Penn Avenue was a confectioner's we liked to ogle. One day as we stared at the windlowload of fanciful sweets, I said to Scott in my best stuck-up, siddity white folks' voice, "The prices here are exorbitant," emphasizing the final exotic word, precisely chopping it into four syllables, the orotund "or" deep in my throat the way I'd heard somebody somewhere say it. A nicely dressed white lady who would have been quite at home on Negley Hill laying that extra twenty-five or fifty cents on me when I collected at the end of the week heard me say "exorbitant" and did a wide-eyed double take. If I'd yelled an obscenity at her, she couldn't have looked more shocked, outraged. She regarded her companion, another middle-aged, coifed-for-shopping matron, and the two of them wagged their heads in dismay. *Did you hear that? Did you hear what he said? . . .*

Not until years later did I begin to guess at the nature of my offense. I'd stolen a piece of their language. Not only was it in my possession, I also had the nerve to flaunt it in a public place, in their righteous faces. To them a colored kid with a big word instead of a watermelon in his mouth wasn't even funny. I was peeking under their clothes, maybe even shouting that they, like the emperor, weren't wearing any.

Language is power. I was fighting skirmishes in a battle still engaging me—legitimizing the language of my tribe. The songs in my head on Negley Hill, the fancy word I appropriated and mocked surveying in a shop window sweets I couldn't afford were means I had developed to create sense in a world that insistently denied me. When my family moved to Shadyside so I could attend "better" schools and we were one of only three or four black families in the neighborhood, I learned to laugh with the white guys when we hid in a stairwell outside Liberty School gym and passed around a "nigarette." I hated it when a buddy took a greedy, wet puff, "nigger-lipping" a butt before he passed it on to me. Speaking out, identifying myself with the group being slurred by these expressions, was impossible. I had neither the words nor the heart. I talked the talk and walked the walk of the rest of my companions.

When Lavinia, my first love, on leave one summer from Harlem to visit her grandfather, who boarded in my grandparents' house, urged me to wear my jeans slung low on my hips like the black boys and Spanish boys she'd left behind on Convent Avenue, her distaste for the white kids' style, her assertion that another way was both possible and better, struck me with the force of revelation. At 13 Lavinia possessed a woman's body, and the fact that she would let me, only thirteen myself, touch it kept me in a constant state of agitation and awe. She was larger than life and grew more fascinating, more like a goddess as she described Harlem's black ways, its authority to be what it wished to be. Lavinia didn't exactly hate whites; they were beneath her contempt. It dawned on me that there was a Negley Hill where my white buddies, those unconscious kings of the earth, would be scared to deliver papers.

I've taught Ralph Ellison's *Invisible Man* to many classes, lots of 12 people, including Lois, a fundamentalist Christian from Wyoming who was so shocked by the language and situations dramatized in the books of my Afro-American literature class that she threatened to report me to my chairman unless I allowed her to skip the readings her husband, a one-man board of censors, found objectionable. There was also David Bradley, who sat through one of my first fumbling attempts to teach black writing at the University of Pennsylvania and went on to produce a prizewinning novel, *The Chaneysville Incident*, which absorbed and extended the traditions Mr. Ellison affirms. I return to *Invisible Man* not because of a scarcity of good books by black authors but because without Mr. Ellison's work in the mix—monumental, prophetic, bristling with flashes of light—something necessary has been left unsaid, something's missing no matter what combination of books and authors I select for a course.

Mr. Ellison's vision is indispensable because it makes tangible so much of the fiber, the nuance, connecting other Afro-American writers to him and one another. *Invisible Man* is a home, and Afro-American writers predictably return to it. Although its faults—a protagonist whose abstractness inhibits a reader's emotional identification with him, episodes brilliant in themselves but too long, too allegorical, too distracting from the narrative sequence, minor stereotypical roles for its female characters—cause the novel to be like any home, less than perfect, it also has the incalculable advantages of home cooking. For many of us, "Invisible Man" came first, educating our palates, defining what's good, stamping our tastes for a lifetime.

My wife, Judy, has spent almost every summer of her life in Maine. For her the lake and pinewoods of Camp Takajo are a special place. She's found no other spot on earth that duplicates the haunting dance of sunlight as it seeps down through the dark trunks of the pine trees. Because she taught me to see this indwelling spirit that animates the green woods, it lives now, not only in trees but in her. Certain affinities, constellations of meaning are triggered for me by arrangements and rearrangements of green, light, and shadow. A green robe Judy wears, a path fringed with greenery winding from cabin to lake, feathery pine branches a hundred feet up that crackle with light when wind stirs them, all these images connect, permeate each other.

Words, objects, rituals have the power to shine forth. They accumulate this power, this endless string of associations presiding Januslike backward and forward in time, because by circumstance of choice we must return to them. We live many lives, and the confusion, the chaos of a splintered existence is lessened a bit by the riveting flashes that connect our multiple selves to one another and to other lives. When I write I want to show how simple acts, simple words can be transformed to release their spiritual force. This is less a conscious esthetic to be argued or analyzed than a determination to draw from the unique voices of Homewood's people the means for documenting the reality of their attitudes and emotions. I want to trace the comings and goings of my people on the invisible plane of existence where so much of the substance of black life resides.

Everyone lives a significant portion of life below the surface. Art 16 records and elaborates this unseen dimension. A minority culture systematically prevented from outward expression of its dreams, wishes, and aspirations must evolve ways for both individuals and the group to sustain its underground life. Afro-Americans have become experts at living in at least two places simultaneously, cultivating a sensitivity to the distance—comic, ironic, tragic—between our outer and inner lives. For us music, speech, and body movement are repositories for preserving history, values, dignity, a sense of ourselves as separate, whole. Double-entendre, signifying, mimicry, call-and-response patterns of storytelling, oratory, and song, style as cutting edge, as a weapon against enforced anonymity have been honed to display and protect our secrets.

One of the earliest lessons I learned as a child was that if you looked away from something, it might not be there when you looked back. I feared loss, feared turning to speak to someone and finding no one there. Being black and poor reinforced the wisdom of a tentative purchase on experience. Don't get too close, doubt what you think you see. Need, commitment set you up for a fall, create the conditions for disaster. If you let your eyes touch lightly, rely on an impressionistic touch and go, then you may achieve the emotional economy of faint gains, faint losses. Writing forces me to risk ignoring the logic of this lesson. Another legacy from Mr. Ellison, the implicit challenge he poses—who will write our history?—has helped turn me around. The stance, the habit of looking long and hard, especially at those things—a face, a hand, a home—that matter, makes them matter more and more. I examine minutely the place I come from, repeat its stories, sing its songs, preserve its language and values, because they make me what I am and because if I don't, who will?   *1985*

Paule Marshall

From the Poets in the Kitchen

Some years ago, when I was teaching a graduate seminar in fiction at Columbia University, a well-known male novelist visited my class to speak on his development as a writer. In discussing his formative years, he didn't realize it but he seriously endangered his life by remarking that women writers are luckier than those of his sex because they usually spend so much time as children around their mothers and their mothers' friends in the kitchen.

What did he say that for? The women students immediately forgot about being in awe of him and began readying their attack for the question and answer period later on. Even I bristled. There again was that awful image of women locked away from the world in the kitchen with only each other to talk to, and their daughters locked in with them.

But my guest wasn't really being sexist or trying to be provocative or even spoiling for a fight. What he meant—when he got around to examining himself more fully—was that, given the way children are (or were) raised in our society, with little girls kept closer to home and their mothers, the woman writer stands a better chance of being exposed, while growing up, to the kind of talk that goes on among women, more often than not in the kitchen; and that this experience gives her an edge over her male counterpart by instilling in her an appreciation for ordinary speech.

It was clear that my guest lecturer attached great importance to this,   4 which is understandable. Common speech and the plain, workaday words that make it up are, after all, the stock in trade of some of the best fiction writers. They are the principal means by which a character in a novel or story reveals himself and gives voice sometimes to profound feelings and complex ideas about himself and the world. Perhaps the proper measure of a writer's talent is his skill in rendering everyday speech—when it is appropriate to his story—as well as his ability to tap, to exploit, the beauty, poetry, and wisdom it often contains.

"If you say what's on your mind in the language that comes to you from your parents and your street and friends you'll probably say something beautiful." Grace Paley tells this, she says, to her students at the beginning of every writing course.

It's all a matter of exposure and a training of the ear for the would-be writer in those early years of his or her apprenticeship. And, according to my guest lecturer, this training, the best of it, often takes place in as unglamorous a setting as the kitchen.

He didn't know it, but he was essentially describing my experience as a little girl. I grew up among poets. Now they didn't look like poets—whatever that breed is supposed to look like. Nothing about them suggested that poetry was their calling. They were just a group of ordinary housewives and mothers, my mother included, who dressed in a way (shapeless housedresses, dowdy felt hats and long, dark, solemn coats) that made it impossible for me to imagine they had ever been young.

Nor did they do what poets were supposed to do—spend their days 8 in an attic room writing verses. They never put pen to paper except to write occasionally to their relatives in Barbados. "I take my pen in hand hoping these few lines will find you in health as they leave me fair for the time being," was the way their letters invariably began. Rather, their day was spent "scrubbing floor," as they described the work they did.

Several mornings a week these unknown bards would put an apron and a pair of old house shoes in a shopping bag and take the train or streetcar from our section of Brooklyn out to Flatbush. There, those who didn't have steady jobs would wait on certain designated corners for the white housewives in the neighborhood to come along and bargain with them over pay for a day's work cleaning their houses. This was the ritual even in the winter.

Later, armed with the few dollars they had earned, which in their vocabulary became "a few raw-mouth pennies," they made their way back to our neighborhood, where they would sometimes stop off to have a cup of tea or cocoa together before going home to cook dinner for their husbands and children.

The basement kitchen of the brownstone house where my family lived was the usual gathering place. Once inside the warm safety of its walls the women threw off the drab coats and hats, seated themselves at the large center table, drank their cups of tea or cocoa, and talked. While my sister and I sat at a smaller table over in a corner doing our homework, they talked—endlessly, passionately, poetically, and with impressive range. No subject was beyond them. True, they would indulge in the usual gossip: whose husband was running with whom, whose daughter looked slightly "in the way" (pregnant) under her bridal gown as she walked down the aisle. That sort of thing. But they also tackled the great issues of the time. They were always, for example, discussing the state of the economy. It was the mid and late thirties then, and the aftershock of the Depression, with its soup lines and suicides on Wall Street, was still being felt.

Some people, they declared, didn't know how to deal with adversity. 12
They didn't know that you had to "tie up your belly" (hold in the pain, that is) when things got rough and go on with life. They took their image from the bellyband that is tied around the stomach of a newborn baby to keep the navel pressed in.

They talked politics. Roosevelt was their hero. He had come along and rescued the country with relief and jobs, and in gratitude they christened their sons Franklin and Delano and hoped they would live up to the names.

If F.D.R. was their hero, Marcus Garvey was their God. The name of the fiery, Jamaican-born black nationalist of the twenties was constantly invoked around the table. For he had been their leader when they first came to the United States from the West Indies shortly after World War I. They had contributed to his organization, the United Negro Improvement Association (UNIA), out of their meager salaries, bought shares in his ill-fated Black Star Shipping Line, and at the height of the movement they had marched as members of his "nurses' brigade" in their white uniforms up Seventh Avenue in Harlem during the great Garvey Day parades. Garvey: He lived on through the power of their memories.

And their talk was of war and rumors of wars. They raged against World War II when it broke out in Europe, blaming it on the politicians. "It's these politicians. They're the ones always starting up all this lot of war. But what they care? It's the poor people got to suffer and mothers with their sons." If it was *their* sons, they swore they would keep them out of the Army by giving them soap to eat each day to make their hearts sound defective. Hitler? He was for them "the devil incarnate."

Then there was home. They reminisced often and at length about 16
home. The old country. Barbados—or Bimshire, as they affectionately called it. The little Caribbean island in the sun they loved but had to leave. "Poor—poor but sweet" was the way they remembered it.

And naturally they discussed their adopted home. America came in for both good and bad marks. They lashed out at it for the racism they encountered. They took to task some of the people they worked for, especially those who gave them only a hard-boiled egg and a few spoonfuls of cottage cheese for lunch. "As if anybody can scrub floor on an egg and some cheese that don't have no taste to it!"

Yet although they caught H in "this man country," as they called America, it was nonetheless a place where "you could at least see your way to make a dollar." That much they acknowledged. They might even one day accumulate enough dollars, with both them and their husbands working, to buy the brownstone houses which, like my family, they were only leasing at that period. This was their consuming ambition: to "buy house" and to see the children through.

There was no way for me to understand it at the time, but the talk that filled the kitchen those afternoons was highly functional. It served as therapy, the cheapest kind available to my mother and her friends. Not only did it help them recover from the long wait on the corner that morning and the bargaining over their labor, it restored them to a sense of themselves and reaffirmed their self-worth. Through language they were able to overcome the humiliations of the work-day.

But more than therapy, that freewheeling, wide-ranging, exuberant 20 talk functioned as an outlet for the tremendous creative energy they possessed. They were women in whom the need for self-expression was strong, and since language was the only vehicle readily available to them they made of it an art form that—in keeping with the African tradition in which art and life are one—was an integral part of their lives.

And their talk was a refuge. They never really ceased being baffled and overwhelmed by America—its vastness, complexity, and power. Its strange customs and laws. At a level beyond words they remained fearful and in awe. Their uneasiness and fear were even reflected in their attitude toward the children they had given birth to in this country. They referred to those like myself, the little Brooklyn-born Bajans (Barbadians), as "these New York children" and complained that they couldn't discipline us properly because of the laws here. "You can't beat these children as you would like, you know, because the authorities in this place will dash you in jail for them. After all, these is New York children." Not only were we different, American, we had, as they saw it, escaped their ultimate authority.

Confronted therefore by a world they could not encompass, which even limited their rights as parents, and at the same time finding themselves permanently separated from the world they had known, they took refuge in language. "Language is the only homeland," Czeslaw Milosz, the emigré Polish writer and Nobel Laureate, has said. This is what it became for the women at the kitchen table.

It served another purpose also, I suspect. My mother and her friends were after all the female counterpart of Ralph Ellison's invisible man. Indeed, you might say they suffered a triple invisibility, being black, female, and foreigners. They really didn't count in American society except as a source of cheap labor. But given the kind of women they were, they couldn't tolerate the fact of their invisibility, their powerlessness. And they fought back, using the only weapon at their command: the spoken word.

Those late afternoon conversations on a wide range of topics were a 24
way for them to feel they exercised some measure of control over their
lives and the events that shaped them. "Soully-gal, talk yuh talk!" they
were always exhorting each other. "In this man world you got to take
yuh mouth and make a gun!" They were in control, if only verbally and
if only for the two hours or so that they remained in our house.

For me, sitting over in the corner, being seen but not heard, which
was the rule for children in those days, it wasn't only what the women
talked about—the content—but the way they put things—their style.
The insight, irony, wit, and humor they brought to their stories and
discussions and their poet's inventiveness and daring with language—
which of course I could only sense but not define back then.

They had taken the standard English taught them in the primary
schools of Barbados and transformed it into an idiom, an instrument
that more adequately described them—changing around the syntax and
imposing their own rhythm and accent so that the sentences were more
pleasing to their ears. They added the few African sounds and words
that had survived, such as the derisive suck-teeth sound and the word
"yam," meaning to eat. And to make it more vivid, more in keeping with
their expressive quality, they brought to bear a raft of metaphors,
parables, biblical quotations, sayings, and the like:

"The sea ain' got no back door," they would say, meaning that it
wasn't like a house where if there was a fire you could run out the back.
Meaning that it was not to be trifled with. And meaning perhaps in a
larger sense that man should treat all of nature with caution and
respect.

"I has read hell by heart and called every generation blessed!" They 28
sometimes went in for hyperbole.

A woman expecting a baby was never said to be pregnant. They
never used that word. Rather, she was "in the way" or, better yet,
"tumbling big." "Guess who I butt up on in the market the other day
tumbling big again!"

And a woman with a reputation of being too free with her sexual
favors was known in their book as a "thoroughfare"—the sense of men
like a steady stream of cars moving up and down the road of her life. Or
she might be dubbed "a free-bee," which was my favorite of the two. I
liked the image it conjured up of a woman scandalous perhaps but
independent, who flitted from one flower to another in a garden of
male beauties, sampling their nectar, taking her pleasure at will, the
roles reversed.

And nothing, no matter how beautiful, was ever described as simply
beautiful. It was always "beautiful-ugly": the beautiful-ugly dress, the
beautiful-ugly house, the beautiful-ugly car. Why the word "ugly," I used
to wonder, when the thing they were referring to was beautiful, and they

knew it. Why the antonym, the contradiction, the linking of opposites? It used to puzzle me greatly as a child.

There is the theory in linguistics which states that the idiom of a 32 people, the way they use language, reflects not only the most fundamental views they hold of themselves and the world but their very conception of reality. Perhaps in using the term "beautiful-ugly" to describe nearly everything, my mother and her friends were expressing what they believed to be a fundamental dualism in life: the idea that a thing is at the same time its opposite, and that these opposites, these contradictions make up the whole. But theirs was not a Manichaean[1] brand of dualism that sees matter, flesh, the body, as inherently evil, because they constantly addressed each other as "soully-gal"—soul: spirit; gal: the body, flesh, the visible self. And it was clear from their tone that they gave one as much weight and importance as the other. They had never heard of the mind/body split.

As for God, they summed up His essential attitude in a phrase. "God," they would say, "don' love ugly and He ain' stuck on pretty."

Using everyday speech, the simple commonplace words—but always with imagination and skill—they gave voice to the most complex ideas. Flannery O'Connor would have approved of how they made ordinary language work, as she put it, "double-time," stretching, shading, deepening its meaning. Like Joseph Conrad they were always trying to infuse new life in the "old old words worn thin . . . by . . . careless usage." And the goals of their oral art were the same as his: "to make you hear, to make you feel . . . to make you *see*." This was their guiding esthetic.

By the time I was eight or nine, I graduated from the corner of the kitchen to the neighborhood library, and thus from the spoken to the written word. The Macon Street Branch of the Brooklyn Public Library was an imposing half block long edifice of heavy gray masonry, with glass-paneled doors at the front and two tall metal torches symbolizing the light that comes of learning flanking the wide steps outside.

The inside was just as impressive. More steps—of pale marble with 36 gleaming brass railings at the center and sides—led up to the circulation desk, and a great pendulum clock gazed down from the balcony stacks that faced the entrance. Usually stationed at the top of the steps like the guards outside Buckingham Palace was the custodian, a stern-faced West Indian type who for years, until I was old enough to obtain an adult card, would immediately shoo me with one hand into the Children's Room and with the other threaten me into silence, a finger to

---

[1]**Manichaean**: Pertaining to the dualistic religion of the Persian prophet Manes (A.D. 216?–276?), whose basic doctrine consists of a universal conflict between light and dark, good and evil.—EDS.

his lips. You would have thought he was the chief librarian and not just someone whose job it was to keep the brass polished and the clock wound. I put him in a story called "Barbados" years later and had terrible things happen to him at the end.

I was sheltered from the storm of adolescence in the Macon Street library, reading voraciously, indiscriminately, everything from Jane Austen to Zane Grey, but with a special passion for the long, full-blown, richly detailed eighteenth- and nineteenth-century picaresque tales: *Tom Jones. Great Expectations. Vanity Fair.*

But although I loved nearly everything I read and would enter fully into the lives of the characters—indeed, would cease being myself and become them—I sensed a lack after a time. Something I couldn't quite define was missing. And then one day, browsing in the poetry section, I came across a book by someone called Paul Laurence Dunbar, and opening it I found the photograph of a wistful, sad-eyed poet who to my surprise was black. I turned to a poem at random. "Little brown-baby wif spa'klin' / eyes / Come to yo' pappy an' set on his knee." Although I had a little difficulty at first with the words in dialect, the poem spoke to me as nothing I had read before of the closeness, the special relationship I had had with my father, who by then had become an ardent believer in Father Divine and gone to live in Father's "kingdom" in Harlem. Reading it helped to ease somewhat the tight knot of sorrow and longing I carried around in my chest that refused to go away. I read another poem. "Lias! Lias! Bless de Lawd! Don' you know de day's / erbroad? / Ef you don' get up, you scamp / Dey'll be trouble in dis camp." I laughed. It reminded me of the way my mother sometimes yelled at my sister and me to get out of bed in the mornings.

And another: "Seen my lady home las' night / Jump back, honey, jump back. / Hel' huh han' an' sque'z it tight . . ." About love between a black man and a black woman. I had never seen that written about before and it roused in me all kinds of delicious feelings and hopes.

And I began to search then for books and stories and poems about 40 "The Race" (as it was put back then), about my people. While not abandoning Thackeray, Fielding, Dickens, and the others, I started asking the reference librarian, who was white, for books by Negro writers, although I must admit I did so at first with a feeling of shame—the shame I and many others used to experience in those days whenever the word "Negro" or "colored" came up.

No grade school literature teacher of mine had ever mentioned Dunbar or James Weldon Johnson or Langston Hughes. I didn't know that Zora Neale Hurston existed and was busy writing and being published during those years. Nor was I made aware of people like Frederick Douglass and Harriet Tubman—their spirit and example—or the great nineteenth-century abolitionist and feminist Sojourner Truth.

There wasn't even Negro History Week when I attended P.S. 35 on Decatur Street!

What I needed, what all the kids—West Indian and native black American alike—with whom I grew up needed, was an equivalent of the Jewish shul, someplace where we could go after school—the schools that were shortchanging us—and read works by those like ourselves and learn about our history.

It was around that time also that I began harboring the dangerous thought of someday trying to write myself. Perhaps a poem about an apple tree, although I had never seen one. Or the story of a girl who could magically transplant herself to wherever she wanted to be in the world—such as Father Divine's kingdom in Harlem. Dunbar—his dark, eloquent face, his large volume of poems—permitted me to dream that I might someday write, and with something of the power with words my mother and her friends possessed.

When people at readings and writers' conferences ask me who my 44 major influences were, they are sometimes a little disappointed when I don't immediately name the usual literary giants. True, I am indebted to those writers, white and black, whom I read during my formative years and still read for instruction and pleasure. But they were preceded in my life by another set of giants whom I always acknowledge before all others: the group of women around the table long ago. They taught me my first lesson in the narrative art. They trained my ear. They set a standard of excellence. This is why the best of my work must be attributed to them; it stands as testimony to the rich legacy of language and culture they so freely passed on to me in the wordshop of the kitchen.   *1983*

Maxine Hong Kingston

From A Song for a Barbarian Reed Pipe

Long ago in China, knot-makers tied string into buttons and frogs, and rope into bell pulls. There was one knot so complicated that it blinded the knotmaker. Finally an emperor outlawed this cruel knot, and the nobles could not order it anymore. If I had lived in China, I would have been an outlaw knotmaker.

Maybe that's why my mother cut my tongue. She pushed my tongue up and sliced the frenum. Or maybe she snipped it with a pair of nail scissors. I don't remember her doing it, only her telling me about it, but all during childhood I felt sorry for the baby whose mother waited with scissors or knife in hand for it to cry—and then, when its mouth was wide open like a baby bird's, cut. The Chinese say "a ready tongue is an evil."

I used to curl up my tongue in front of the mirror and tauten my frenum into a white line, itself as thin as a razor blade. I saw no scars in my mouth. I thought perhaps I had had two frena, and she had cut one. I made other children open their mouths so I could compare theirs to mine. I saw perfect pink membranes stretching into precise edges that looked easy enough to cut. Sometimes I felt very proud that my mother committed such a powerful act upon me. At other times I was terrified—the first thing my mother did when she saw me was to cut my tongue.

"Why did you do that to me, Mother?"   4

"I told you."

"Tell me again."

"I cut it so that you would not be tongue-tied. Your tongue would be able to move in any language. You'll be able to speak languages that are completely different from one another. You'll be able to pronounce anything. Your frenum looked too tight to do those things, so I cut it."

"But isn't 'a ready tongue an evil'?"   8

"Things are different in this ghost country."

"Did it hurt me? Did I cry and bleed?"

"I don't remember. Probably."

She didn't cut the other children's. When I asked cousins and other 12 Chinese children whether their mothers had cut their tongues loose, they said, "What?"

"Why didn't you cut my brothers' and sisters' tongues?"

"They didn't need it."

"Why not? Were theirs longer than mine?"

"Why don't you quit blabbering and get to work?"   16

If my mother was not lying she should have cut more, scraped away the rest of the frenum skin, because I have a terrible time talking. Or she should not have cut at all, tampering with my speech. When I went to kindergarten and had to speak English for the first time, I became silent. A dumbness—a shame—still cracks my voice in two, even when I want to say "hello" casually, or ask an easy question in front of the check-out counter, or ask directions of a bus driver. I stand frozen, or I hold up the line with the complete, grammatical sentence that comes squeaking out at impossible length. "What did you say?" says the cab driver, or "Speak up," so I have to perform again, only weaker the second time. A telephone call makes my throat bleed and takes up that day's courage. It spoils my day with self-disgust when I hear my broken voice come skittering out into the open. It makes people wince to hear it. I'm getting better, though. Recently I asked the postman for special-issue stamps; I've waited since childhood for postmen to give me some of their own accord. I am making progress, a little every day.

My silence was thickest—total—during the three years that I covered my school paintings with black paint. I painted layers of black over houses and flowers and suns, and when I drew on the blackboard, I put a layer of chalk on top. I was making a stage curtain, and it was the moment before the curtain parted or rose. The teachers called my parents to school, and I saw they had been saving my pictures, curling and cracking, all alike and black. The teachers pointed to the pictures and looked serious, talked seriously too, but my parents did not understand English. ("The parents and teachers of criminals were executed," said my father.) My parents took the pictures home. I spread them out (so black and full of possibilities) and pretended the curtains were swinging open, flying up, one after another, sunlight underneath, mighty operas.

During the first silent year I spoke to no one at school, did not ask before going to the lavatory, and flunked kindergarten. My sister also said nothing for three years, silent in the playground and silent at lunch. There were other quiet Chinese girls not of our family, but most of them got over it sooner than we did. I enjoyed the silence. At first it did not occur to me I was supposed to talk or to pass kindergarten. I talked at home and to one or two of the Chinese kids in class. I made motions and even made some jokes. I drank out of a toy saucer when the water spilled out of the cup, and everybody laughed, pointing at me, so I did it some more. I didn't know that Americans don't drink out of saucers.

I liked the Negro students (Black Ghosts) best because they laughed 20 the loudest and talked to me as if I were a daring talker too. One of the Negro girls had her mother coil braids over her ears Shanghai-style like mine; we were Shanghai twins except that she was covered with black like my paintings. Two Negro kids enrolled in Chinese school, and the teachers gave them Chinese names. Some Negro kids walked me to school and home, protecting me from the Japanese kids, who hit me and chased me and stuck gum in my ears. The Japanese kids were noisy and tough. They appeared one day in kindergarten, released from concentration camp, which was a tic-tac-toe mark, like barbed wire, on the map.

It was when I found out I had to talk that school became a misery, that the silence became a misery. I did not speak and felt bad each time that I did not speak. I read aloud in first grade, though, and heard the barest whisper with little squeaks come out of my throat. "Louder," said the teacher, who scared the voice away again. The other Chinese girls did not talk either, so I knew the silence had to do with being a Chinese girl.

Reading out loud was easier than speaking because we did not have to make up what to say, but I stopped often, and the teacher would think I'd gone quiet again. I could not understand "I." The Chinese "I" has seven strokes, intricacies. How could the American "I," assuredly wearing a hat like the Chinese, have only three strokes, the middle so straight? Was it out of politeness that this writer left off strokes the way a Chinese has to write her own name small and crooked? No, it was not politeness; "I" is a capital and "you" is lower-case. I stared at that middle line and waited so long for its black center to resolve into tight strokes and dots that I forgot to pronounce it. The other troublesome word was "here," no strong consonant to hang on to, and so flat, when "here" is two mountainous ideographs. The teacher, who had already told me every day how to read "I" and "here," put me in the low corner under the stairs again, where the noisy boys usually sat.

When my second grade class did a play, the whole class went to the auditorium except the Chinese girls. The teacher, lovely and Hawaiian, should have understood about us, but instead left us behind in the classroom. Our voices were too soft or nonexistent, and our parents never signed the permission slips anyway. They never signed anything unnecessary. We opened the door a crack and peeked out, but closed it again quickly. One of us (not me) won every spelling bee, though.

I remember telling the Hawaiian teacher, "We Chinese can't sing 'land where our fathers died.' " She argued with me about politics, while I meant because of curses. But how can I have that memory when I couldn't talk? My mother says that we, like the ghosts, have no memories.

After American school, we picked up our cigar boxes, in which we had arranged books, brushes, and an inkbox neatly, and went to Chinese school, from 5:00 to 7:30 P.M. There we chanted together, voices rising and falling, loud and soft, some boys shouting, everybody reading together, reciting together and not alone with one voice. When we had a memorization test, the teacher let each of us come to his desk and say the lesson to him privately, while the rest of the class practiced copying or tracing. Most of the teachers were men. The boys who were so well behaved in the American school played tricks on them and talked back to them. The girls were not mute. They screamed and yelled during recess, when there were no rules; they had fistfights. Nobody was afraid of children hurting themselves or of children hurting school property. The glass doors to the red and green balconies with the gold job symbols were left wide open so that we could run out and climb the fire escapes. We played capture-the-flag in the auditorium, where Sun Yat-sen and Chiang Kai-shek's pictures hung at the back of the stage, the Chinese flag on their left and the American flag on their right. We climbed the teak ceremonial chairs and made flying leaps off the stage. One flag headquarters was behind the glass door and the other on stage right. Our feet drummed on the hollow stage. During recess the teachers locked themselves up in their office with the shelves of books, copybooks, inks from China. They drank tea and warmed their hands at a stove. There was no play supervision. At recess we had the school to ourselves, and also we could roam as far as we could go—downtown, Chinatown stores, home—as long as we returned before the bell rang.

At exactly 7:30 the teacher again picked up the brass bell that sat on his desk and swung it over our heads, while we charged down the stairs, our cheering magnified in the stairwell. Nobody had to line up.

Not all of the children who were silent at American school found voice at Chinese school. One new teacher said each of us had to get up and recite in front of the class, who was to listen. My sister and I had memorized the lesson perfectly. We said it to each other at home, one chanting, one listening. The teacher called on my sister to recite first. It was the first time a teacher had called on the second-born to go first. My sister was scared. She glanced at me and looked away; I looked down at my desk. I hoped that she could do it because if she could, then I would have to. She opened her mouth and a voice came out that wasn't a whisper, but it wasn't a proper voice either. I hoped that she would not cry, fear breaking up her voice like twigs underfoot. She sounded as if she were trying to sing though weeping and strangling. She did not pause or stop to end the embarrassment. She kept going until she said the last word, and then she sat down. When it was my turn, the same voice came out, a crippled animal running on broken legs. You could hear splinters in my voice, bones rubbing jagged against one another. I was loud, though. I was glad I didn't whisper. There was one little girl who whispered.

You can't entrust your voice to the Chinese, either; they want to 28 capture your voice for their own use. They want to fix up your tongue to speak for them. "How much less can you sell it for?" we have to say. Talk the Sales Ghosts down. Make them take a loss.

We were working at the laundry when a delivery boy came from the Rexall drugstore around the corner. He had a pale blue box of pills, but nobody was sick. Reading the label we saw that it belonged to another Chinese family, Crazy Mary's family. "Not ours," said my father. He pointed out the name to the Delivery Ghost, who took the pills back. My mother muttered for an hour, and then her anger boiled over. "That ghost! That dead ghost! How dare he come to the wrong house?" She could not concentrate on her marking and pressing. "A mistake! Huh!" I was getting angry myself. She fumed. She made her press crash and hiss.

"Revenge. We've got to avenge this wrong on our future, on our health, and on our lives. Nobody's going to sicken my children and get away with it." We brothers and sisters did not look at one another. She would do something awful, something embarrassing. She'd already been hinting that during the next eclipse we slam pot lids together to scare the frog from swallowing the moon. (The word for "eclipse" is *frog-swallowing-the-moon*.) When we had not banged lids at the last eclipse and the shadow kept receding anyway, she'd said, "The villagers must be banging and clanging very loudly back home in China."

("On the other side of the world, they aren't having an eclipse, Mama. That's just a shadow the earth makes when it comes between the moon and the sun."

"You're always believing what those Ghost Teachers tell you. Look at the size of the jaws!")

"Aha!" she yelled. "You! The biggest." She was pointing at me. "You go to the drugstore." 32

"What do you want me to buy, Mother?" I said.

"But nothing. Don't bring one cent. Go and make them stop the curse."

"I don't want to go. I don't know how to do that. There are no such things as curses. They'll think I'm crazy."

If you don't go, I'm holding you responsible for bringing a plague on this family." 36

"What am I supposed to do when I get there?" I said, sullen, trapped. "Do I say, 'Your delivery boy made a wrong delivery'?"

"They know he made a wrong delivery. I want you to make them rectify their crime."

I felt sick already. She'd make me swing stinky censers around the counter, at the druggist, at the customers. Throw dog blood on the druggist. I couldn't stand her plans.

"You get reparation candy," she said. "You say, 'You have tainted my house with sick medicine and must remove the curse with sweetness.' He'll understand." 40

"He didn't do it on purpose. And no, he won't, Mother. They don't understand stuff like that. I won't be able to say it right. He'll call us beggars."

"You just translate." She searched me to make sure I wasn't hiding any money. I was sneaky and bad enough to buy the candy and come back pretending it was a free gift.

"Mymotherseztagimmesomecandy," I said to the druggist. Be cute and small. No one hurts the cute and small.

"What? Speak up. Speak English," he said, big in his white druggist coat. 44

"Tatatagimme somecandy."

The druggist leaned way over the counter and frowned. "Some free candy," I said. "Sample candy."

"We don't give sample candy, young lady," he said.

"My mother said you have to give us candy. She said that is the way 48 the Chinese do it."

"What?"

"That is the way the Chinese do it."

"Do what?"

"Do things." I felt the weight and immensity of things impossible to 52 explain to the druggist.

"Can I give you some money?" he asked.

"No, we want candy."

He reached into a jar and gave me a handful of lollipops. He gave us candy all year round, year after year, every time we went into the drugstore. When different druggists or clerks waited on us, they also gave us candy. They had talked us over. They gave us Halloween candy in December, Christmas candy around Valentine's day, candy hearts at Easter, and Easter eggs at Halloween. "See?" said our mother. "They understand. You kids just aren't very brave." But I knew they did not understand. They thought we were beggars without a home who lived in back of the laundry. They felt sorry for us. I did not eat their candy. I did not go inside the drugstore or walk past it unless my parents forced me to. Whenever we had a prescription filled, the druggist put candy in the medicine bag. This is what Chinese druggists normally do, except they give raisins. My mother thought she taught the Druggist Ghosts a lesson in good manners (which is the same word as "traditions").

My mouth went permanently crooked with effort, turned down on 56 the left side and straight on the right. How strange that the emigrant villagers are shouters, hollering face to face. My father asks, "Why is it I can hear Chinese from blocks away? Is it that I understand the language? Or is it they talk loud?" They turn the radio up full blast to hear the operas, which do not seem to hurt their ears. And they yell over the singers that wail over the drums, everybody talking at once, big arm gestures, spit flying. You can see the disgust on American faces looking at women like that. It isn't just the loudness. It is the way Chinese sounds, chingchong ugly, to American ears, not beautiful like Japanese sayonara words with the consonants and vowels as regular as Italian. We make guttural peasant noise and have Ton Duc Thang names you can't remember. And the Chinese can't hear Americans at all; the language is too soft and western music unhearable. I've watched a Chinese audience laugh, visit, talk-story, and holler during a piano recital, as if the musician could not hear them. A Chinese-American, somebody's son, was playing Chopin, which has no punctuation, no cymbals, no gongs. Chinese piano music is five black keys. Normal Chinese women's voices are strong and bossy. We American-Chinese girls had to whisper to make ourselves American-feminine. Apparently we whispered even more softly than the Americans. Once a year the teachers referred my sister and me to speech therapy, but our voices would straighten out, unpredictably normal, for the therapists. Some of us gave up, shook our heads, and said nothing, not one word. Some of us could not even shake our heads. At times shaking my head no is more self-assertion than I can manage. Most of us eventually found some voice, however faltering. We invented an American-feminine speaking personality, except for that one girl who could not speak up even in Chinese school.

She was a year older than I and was in my class for twelve years. During all those years she read aloud but would not talk. Her older sister was usually beside her; their parents kept the older daughter back to protect the younger one. They were six and seven years old when they began school. Although I had flunked kindergarten, I was the same age as most other students in our class; my parents had probably lied about my age, so I had had a head start and came out even. My younger sister was in the class below me; we were normal ages and normally separated. The parents of the quiet girl, on the other hand, protected both daughters. When it sprinkled, they kept them home from school. The girls did not work for a living the way we did. But in other ways we were the same.

We were similar in sports. We held the bat on our shoulders until we walked to first base. (You got a strike only when you actually struck at the ball.) Sometimes the pitcher wouldn't bother to throw to us. "Automatic walk," the other children would call, sending us on our way. By fourth or fifth grade, though, some of us would try to hit the ball. "Easy out," the other kids would say. I hit the ball a couple of times. Baseball was nice in that there was a definite spot to run to after hitting the ball. Basketball confused me because when I caught the ball I didn't know whom to throw it to. "Me. Me." the kids would be yelling. "Over here." Suddenly it would occur to me I hadn't memorized which ghosts were on my team and which were on the other. When the kids said, "Automatic walk," the girl who was quieter than I kneeled with one end of the bat in each hand and placed it carefully on the plate. Then she dusted her hands as she walked to first base, where she rubbed her hands softly, fingers spread. She always got tagged out before second base. She would whisper-read but not talk. Her whisper was as soft as if she had no muscles. She seemed to be breathing from a distance. I heard no anger or tension.

I joined in at lunchtime when the other students, the Chinese too, talked about whether or not she was mute, although obviously she was not if she could read aloud. People told how *they* had tried *their* best to be friendly. *They* said hello, but if she refused to answer, well, they didn't see why they had to say hello anymore. She had no friends of her own but followed her sister everywhere, although people and she herself probably thought I was her friend. I also followed her sister about, who was fairly normal. She was almost two years older and read more than anyone else.

I hated the younger sister, the quiet one. I hated her when she was 60 the last chosen for her team and I, the last chosen for my team. I hated her for her China doll haircut. I hated her at music time for the wheezes that came out of her plastic flute.

One afternoon in the sixth grade (that year I was arrogant with talk, not knowing there were going to be high school dances and college seminars to set me back), I and my little sister and the quiet girl and her big sister stayed late after school for some reason. The cement was cooling, and the tetherball poles made shadows across the gravel. The hooks at the rope ends were clinking against the poles. We shouldn't have been so late; there was laundry work to do and Chinese school to get to by 5:00. The last time we had stayed late, my mother had phoned the police and told them we had been kidnapped by bandits. The radio stations broadcast our descriptions. I had to get home before she did that again. But sometimes if you loitered long enough in the schoolyard, the other children would have gone home and you could play with the equipment before the office took it away. We were chasing one another through the playground and in and out of the basement, where the playroom and lavatory were. During air raid drills (it was during the Korean War, which you knew about because every day the front page of the newspaper printed a map of Korea with the top part red and going up and down like a window shade), we curled up in this basement. Now everyone was gone. The playroom was army green and had nothing in it but a long trough with drinking spigots in rows. Pipes across the ceiling led to the drinking fountains and to the toilets in the next room. When someone flushed you could hear the water and other matter, which the children named, running inside the big pipe above the drinking spigots. There was one playroom for girls next to the girls' lavatory and one playroom for boys next to the boys' lavatory. The stalls were open and the toilets had no lids, by which we knew that ghosts have no sense of shame or privacy.

Inside the playroom the lightbulbs in cages had already been turned off. Daylight came in x-patterns through the caging at the windows. I looked out and, seeing no one in the schoolyard, ran outside to climb the fire escape upside down, hanging on to the metal stairs with fingers and toes.

I did a flip off the fire escape and ran across the schoolyard. The day was a great eye, and it was not paying much attention to me now. I could disappear with the sun; I could turn quickly sideways and slip into a different world. It seemed I could run faster at this time, and by evening I would be able to fly. As the afternnon wore on we could run into the forbidden places—the boys' big yard, the boys' playroom. We could go into the boys' lavatory and look at the urinals. The only time during school hours I had crossed the boys' yard was when a flatbed truck with a giant thing covered with canvas and tied down with ropes had parked across the street. The children had told one another that it was a gorilla in captivity; we couldn't decide whether the sign said "Trail of the Gorilla" or "Trial of the Gorilla." The thing was as big as a house. The teachers couldn't stop us from hysterically rushing to the fence and clinging to the wire mesh. Now I ran across the boys' yard clear to the Cyclone fence and thought about the hair that I had seen sticking out of the canvas. It was going to be summer soon, so you could feel that freedom coming on too.

I ran back into the girls' yard, and there was the quiet sister all by 64 herself. I ran past her, and she followed me into the girls' lavatory. My footsteps rang hard against cement and tile because of the taps I had nailed into my shoes. Her footsteps were soft, padding after me. There was no one in the lavatory but the two of us. I ran all around the rows of twenty-five open stalls to make sure of that. No sisters. I think we must have been playing hide-and-seek. She was not good at hiding by herself and usually followed her sister, they'd hide in the same place. They must have gotten separated. In this growing twilight, a child could hide and never be found.

I stopped abruptly in front of the sinks, and she came running toward me before she could stop herself, so that she almost collided with me. I walked closer. She backed away, puzzlement, then alarm in her eyes.

"You're going to talk," I said, my voice steady and normal, as it is when talking to the familiar, the weak, and the small. "I am going to make you talk, you sissy-girl." She stopped backing away and stood fixed.

I looked into her face so I could hate it close up. She wore black bangs, and her cheeks were pink and white. She was baby-soft. I thought that I could put my thumb on her nose and push it bonelessly in, indent her face. I could poke dimples into her cheeks. I could work her face around like dough. She stood still, and I did not want to look at her face anymore; I hated fragility. I walked around her, looked her up and down the way the Mexican and Negro girls did when they fought, so tough. I hated her weak neck, the way it did not support her head but let it droop; her head would fall backward. I stared at the curve of her nape. I wished I was able to see what my own neck looked like from the back and sides. I hoped it did not look like hers; I wanted a stout neck. I grew my hair long to hide it in case it was a flower-stem neck. I walked around to the front of her to hate her face some more.

I reached up and took the fatty part of her cheek, not dough, but 68 meat, between my thumb and finger. This close, and I saw no pores. "Talk," I said. "Are you going to talk?" Her skin was fleshy, like squid out of which the glassy blades of bones had been pulled. I wanted tough skin, hard brown skin. I had callused my hands; I had scratched dirt to blacken the nails, which I cut straight across to make stubby fingers. I gave her face a squeeze. "Talk." When I let go, the pink rushed back into my white thumbprint on her skin. I walked around to her side. "Talk!" I shouted into the side of her head. Her straight hair hung, the same all these years, no ringlets or braids or permanents. I squeezed her other cheek. "Are you? Huh? Are you going to talk?" She tried to shake her head, but I had hold of her face. She had no muscles to jerk away. Her skin seemed to stretch. I let go in horror. What if it came away in my hand? "No, huh?" I said, rubbing the touch of her off my fingers. "Say 'No,' then," I said. I gave her another pinch and a twist. "Say 'No.'" She shook her head, her straight hair turning with her head, not swinging side to side like the pretty girls'. She was so neat. Her neatness bothered me. I hated the way she folded the wax paper from her lunch; she did not wad her brown paper bag and her school papers. I hated her clothes—the blue pastel cardigan, the white blouse with the collar that lay flat over the cardigan, the homemade flat, cotton skirt she wore when everybody else was wearing flared skirts. I hated pastels; I would wear black always. I squeezed again, harder, even though her cheek had a weak rubbery feeling I did not like. I squeezed one cheek, then the other, back and forth until the tears ran out of her eyes as if I had pulled them out. "Stop crying," I said, but although she habitually followed me around, she did not obey. Her eyes dripped; her nose dripped. She wiped her eyes with her papery fingers. The skin on her hands and arms seemed powdery-dry, like tracing paper, onion paper. I hated her fingers. I could snap them like breadsticks. I pushed her hands down. "Say 'Hi,'" I said. "'Hi.' Like that. Say your name. Go ahead. Say it. Or are you stupid? You're so stupid, you don't know your own name, is that it? When I say, 'What's your name?' you just blurt it out, OK? What's your name?" Last year the whole class had laughed at a boy who couldn't fill out a form because he didn't know his father's name. The teacher sighed, exasperated and was very sarcastic, "Don't you notice things? What does your mother call him?" she said. The class laughed at how dumb he was not to notice things. "She calls him father of me," he said. Even we laughed although we knew that his mother did not call his father by name, and a son does not know his father's name. We laughed and were relieved that our parents had had the foresight to tell us some names we could give the teachers. "If you're not stupid," I said to the quiet girl, "what's your name?" She shook her head, and some hair caught in the tears; wet black hair stuck to the side of the pink and white face. I reached up (she was taller than I) and took a strand of hair. I pulled it. "Well, then, let's honk your hair," I said. "Honk. Honk." Then I pulled the other side—"ho-o-n-nk"—a long pull; "ho-o-n-n-nk"—a longer pull. I could see her little white ears, like white cutworms curled underneath the hair. "Talk!" I yelled into each cutworm.

I looked right at her. "I know you talk," I said. "I've heard you." Her eyebrows flew up. Something in those black eyes was startled, and I pursued it. "I was talking past your house when you didn't know I was there. I heard you yell in English and in Chinese. You weren't just talking. You were shouting. I heard you shout. You were saying, 'Where are you?' Say that again. Go ahead, just the way you did at home." I yanked harder on the hair, but steadily, not jerking. I did not want to pull it out. "Go ahead. Say, 'Where are you?' Say it loud enough for your sister to come. Call her. Make her come help you. Call her name. I'll stop if she comes. So call. Go ahead."

She shook her head, her mouth curved down, crying. I could see her tiny white teeth, baby teeth. I wanted to grow big strong yellow teeth. "You do have a tongue," I said. "So use it." I pulled the hair at her temples, pulled the tears out of her eyes. "Say, 'Ow.' " I said. "Just 'Ow.' Say, 'Let go.' Go ahead. Say it. I'll honk you again if you don't say, 'Let me alone.' Say, 'Leave me alone,' and I'll let you go. I will. I'll let go if you say it. You can stop this anytime you want to, you know. All you have to do is tell me to stop. Just say, 'Stop.' You're just asking for it, aren't you? You're just asking for another honk. Well then, I'll have to give you another honk. Say, 'Stop,' " But she didn't. I had to pull again and again.

Sounds did come out of her mouth, sobs, chokes, noises that were almost words. Snot ran out of her nose. She tried to wipe it on her hands, but there was too much of it. She used her sleeve. "You're disgusting," I told her. "Look at you, snot streaming down your nose, and you won't say a word to stop it. You're such a nothing." I moved behind her and pulled the hair growing out of her weak neck. I let go. I stood silent for a long time. Then I screamed, "Talk!" I would scare the words out of her. If she had had little bound feet, the toes twisted under the balls, I would have jumped up and landed on them—crunch!—stomped on them with my iron shoes. She cried hard, sobbing aloud. "Cry, 'Mama,' " I said. "Come on. Cry, 'Mama.' Say, 'Stop it.' "

I put my finger on her pointed chin. "I don't like you. I don't like 72 the weak little toots you make on your flute. Wheeze. Wheeze. I don't like the way you don't swing at the ball. I don't like the way you're the last one chosen. I don't like the way you can't make a fist for tetherball. Why don't you make a fist? Come on. Get tough. Come on. Throw fists." I pushed at her long hands; they swung limply at her sides. Her fingers were so long, I thought maybe they had an extra joint. They couldn't possibly make fists like other people's. "Make a fist," I said. "Come on.

Just fold those fingers up; fingers on the inside, thumbs on the outside. Say something. Honk me back. You're so tall, and you let me pick on you.

"Would you like a hanky? I can't get you one with embroidery on it or crocheting along the edges, but I'll get you some toilet paper if you tell me to. Go ahead. Ask me. I'll get it for you if you ask." She did not stop crying. "Why don't you scream, 'Help'?" I suggested. "Say, 'Help.' Go ahead." She cried on. "OK. OK. Don't talk. Just scream, and I'll let you go. Won't that feel good? Go ahead. Like this." I screamed not too loudly. My voice hit the tile and rang it as if I had thrown a rock at it. The stalls opened wider and the toilets wider and darker. Shadows leaned at angles I had not seen before. I was very late. Maybe a janitor had locked me in with this girl for the night. Her black eyes blinked and stared, blinked and stared. I felt dizzy from hunger. We had been in this lavatory together forever. My mother would call the police again if I didn't bring my sister home soon. "I'll let you go if you say just one word," I said. "You can even say 'a' or 'the,' and I'll let you go. Come on. Please." She didn't shake her head anymore, only cried steadily, so much water coming out of her. I could see the two duct holes where the tears welled out. Quarts of tears but no words. I grabbed her by the shoulder. I could feel bones. The light was coming in queerly through the frosted glass with the chicken wire embedded in it. Her crying was like an animal's—a seal's—and it echoed around the basement. "Do you want to stay here all night?" I asked. "Your mother is wondering what happened to her baby. You wouldn't want to have her mad at you. You'd better say something." I shook her shoulder. I pulled her hair again. I squeezed her face. "Come on! Talk! Talk! Talk!" She didn't seem to feel it anymore when I pulled her hair. "There's nobody here but you and me. This isn't a classroom or a playground or a crowd. I'm just one person. You can talk in front of one person. Don't make me pull harder and harder until you talk." But her hair seemed to stretch; she did not say a word. "I'm going to pull harder. Don't make me pull anymore, or your hair will come out and you're going to be bald. Do you want to be bald? You don't want to be bald, do you?"

Far away, coming from the edge of town, I heard whistles blow. The cannery was changing shifts, letting out the afternoon people, and still we were here at school. It was a sad sound—work done. The air was lonelier after the sound died.

"Why won't you talk?" I started to cry. What if I couldn't stop, and everyone would want to know what happened? "Now look what you've done," I scolded. "You're going to pay for this. I want to know why. And you're going to tell me why. You don't see I'm trying to help you out, do you? Do you want to be like this, dumb (do you know what dumb means?), your whole life? Don't you ever want to be a cheerleader? Or a pompon girl? What are you going to do for a living? Yeah, you're going to have to work because you can't be a housewife. Somebody has to marry you before you can be a housewife. And you, you are a plant. Do you know that? That's all you are if you don't talk. If you don't talk, you can't have a personality. You'll have no personality and no hair. You've got to let people know you have a personality and a brain. You think somebody is going to take care of you all your stupid life? You think you'll always have your big sister? You think somebody's going to marry you, is that it? Well, you're not the type that gets dates, let alone gets married. Nobody's going to notice you. And you have to talk for interviews, speak right up in front of the boss. Don't you know that? You're so dumb. Why do I waste my time on you?" Sniffling and snorting, I couldn't stop crying and talking at the same time. I kept wiping my nose on my arm, my sweater lost somewhere (probably not worn because my mother said to wear a sweater). It seemed as if I had spent my life in that basement, doing the worst thing I had yet done to another person. "I'm doing this for your own good," I said. "Don't you dare tell anyone I've been bad to you. Talk. Please talk."

I was getting dizzy from the air I was gulping. Her sobs and my sobs 76 were bouncing wildly off the tile, sometimes together, sometimes alternating. "I don't understand why you won't say just one word," I cried, clenching my teeth. My knees were shaking, and I hung on to her hair to stand up. Another time I'd stayed too late, I had had to walk around two Negro kids who were bonking each other's head on the concrete. I went back later to see if the concrete had cracks in it. "Look. I'll give you something if you talk. I'll give you my pencil box. I'll buy you some candy. OK? What do you want? Tell me. Just say it, and I'll give it to you. Just say, 'yes,' or, 'OK,' or, 'Baby Ruth.'" But she didn't want anything.

I had stopped pinching her cheek because I did not like the feel of her skin. I would go crazy if it came away in my hands. "I skinned her," I would have to confess.

Suddenly I heard footsteps hurrying through the basement, and her sister ran into the lavatory calling her name. "Oh, there you are," I said. "We've been waiting for you. I was only trying to teach her to talk. She wouldn't cooperate, though." Her sister went into one of the stalls and got handfuls of toilet paper and wiped her off. Then we found my sister, and we walked home together. "Your family really ought to force her to speak," I advised all the way home. "You mustn't pamper her."

The world is sometimes just, and I spent the next eighteen months sick in bed with a mysterious illness. There was no pain and no symptoms, though the middle line in my left palm broke in two. Instead of starting junior high school, I lived like the Victorian recluses I read about. I had a rented hospital bed in the living room, where I watched soap operas on TV, and my family cranked me up and down. I saw no one but my family, who took good care of me. I could have no visitors, no other relatives, no villagers. My bed was against the west window, and I watched the seasons change the peach tree. I had a bell to ring for help. I used a bedpan. It was the best year and a half of my life. Nothing happened.   *1975*

Grace Paley

The Loudest Voice

There is a certain place where dumbwaiters boom, doors slam, dishes crash; every window is a mother's mouth bidding the street shut up, go skate somewhere else, come home. My voice is the loudest.

There, my own mother is still as full of breathing as me and the grocer stands up to speak to her. "Mrs. Abramowitz," he says, "people should not be afraid of their children."

"Ah, Mr. Bialik," my mother replies, "if you say to her or her father 'Ssh,' they say, 'In the grave it will be quiet.' "

"From Coney Island to the cemetery," says my papa. "It's the same   4
subway; it's the same fare."

I am right next to the pickle barrel. My pinky is making tiny whirlpools in the brine. I stop a moment to announce: "Campbell's Tomato Soup. Campbell's Vegetable Beef Soup. Campbell's S-c-otch Broth . . ."

"Be quiet," the grocer says, "the labels are coming off."

"Please, Shirley, be a little quiet," my mother begs me.

In that place the whole street groans: Be quiet! Be quiet! but steals   8
from the happy chorus of my inside self not a tittle or a jot.

There, too, but just around the corner, is a red brick building that has been old for many years. Every morning the children stand before it in double lines which must be straight. They are not insulted. They are waiting anyway.

I am usually among them. I am, in fact, the first, since I begin with "A."

One cold morning the monitor tapped me on the shoulder. "Go to Room 409, Shirley Abramowitz," he said. I did as I was told. I went in a hurry up a down staircase to Room 409, which contained sixth-graders.

I had to wait at the desk without wiggling until Mr. Hilton, their teacher, had time to speak.

After five minutes he said, "Shirley?"   12

"What?" I whispered.

He said, "My! My! Shirley Abramowitz! They told me you had a particularly loud, clear voice and read with lots of expression. Could that be true?"

"Oh, yes," I whispered.

"In that case, don't be silly; I might very well be your teacher   16
someday. Speak up, speak up."

"Yes," I shouted.

"More like it," he said. "Now, Shirley, can you put a ribbon in your hair or a bobby pin? It's too messy."

"Yes!" I bawled.

"Now, now, calm down." He turned to the class. "Children, not a   20
sound. Open at page 39. Read till 52. When you finish, start again." He looked me over once more. "Now, Shirley, you know, I suppose, that Christmas is coming. We are preparing a beautiful play. Most of the parts have been given out. But I still need a child with a strong voice, lots of stamina. Do you know what stamina is? You do? Smart kid. You know, I heard you read 'The Lord is my shepherd' in Assembly yesterday. I was very impressed. Wonderful delivery. Mrs. Jordan, your teacher, speaks highly of you. Now listen to me, Shirley Abramowitz, if you want to take the part and be in the play, repeat after me, 'I swear to work harder than I ever did before.'"

I looked to heaven and said at once, "Oh, I swear." I kissed my pinky and looked at God.

"That is an actor's life, my dear," he explained. "Like a soldier's, never tardy or disobedient to his general, the director. Everything," he said, "absolutely everything will depend on you."

That afternoon, all over the building, chidren scraped and scrubbed the turkeys and the sheaves of corn off the schoolroom windows. Goodbye Thanksgiving. The next morning a monitor brought red paper and green paper from the office. We made new shapes and hung them on the walls and glued them to the doors.

The teachers became happier and happier. Their heads were ring-   24
ing like the bells of childhood. My best friend Evie was prone to evil, but she did not get a single demerit for whispering. We learned "Holy Night" without an error. "How wonderful!" said Miss Glacé, the student teacher. "To think that some of you don't even speak the language!" We learned "Deck the Halls" and "Hark! The Herald Angels." . . . They weren't ashamed and we weren't embarrassed.

Oh, but when my mother heard about it all, she said to my father: "Misha, you don't know what's going on there. Cramer is the head of the Tickets Committee."

"Who?" asked my father. "Cramer? Oh yes, an active woman."

"Active? Active has to have a reason. Listen," she said sadly, "I'm surprised to see my neighbors making tra-la-la for Christmas."

My father couldn't think of what to say to that. Then he decided: 28 "You're in America! Clara, you wanted to come here. In Palestine the Arabs would be eating you alive. Europe you had pogroms. Argentina is full of Indians. Here you got Christmas. . . . Some joke, ha?"

"Very funny, Misha. What is becoming of you? If we came to a new country a long time ago to run away from tyrants, and instead we fall into a creeping pogrom, that our children learn a lot of lies, so what's the joke? Ach, Misha, your idealism is going away."

"So is your sense of humor."

"That I never had, but idealism you had a lot of."

"I'm the same Misha Abramovitch, I didn't change an iota. Ask 32 anyone."

"Only ask me," says my mama, may she rest in peace. "I got the answer."

Meanwhile the neighbors had to think of what to say too.

Marty's father said: "You know, he has a very important part, my boy."

"Mine also," said Mr. Sauerfeld.   36

"Not my boy!" said Mrs. Klieg. "I said to him no. The answer is no. When I say no! I mean no!"

The rabbi's wife said, "It's disgusting!" But no one listened to her. Under the narrow sky of God's great wisdom she wore a strawberry-blond wig.

Every day was noisy and full of experience. I was Right-hand Man. Mr. Hilton said: "How could I get along without you, Shirley?"

He said: "Your mother and father ought to get down on their knees 40 every night and thank God for giving them a child like you."

He also said: "You're absolutely a pleasure to work with, my dear, dear child."

Sometimes he said: "For God's sakes, what did I do with the script? Shirley! Shirley! Find it."

Then I answered quietly: "Here it is, Mr. Hilton."

Once in a while, when he was very tired, he would cry out: "Shirley, 44 I'm just tired of screaming at those kids. Will you tell Ira Pushkov not to come in till Lester points to that star the second time?"

Then I roared: "Ira Pushkov, what's the matter with you? Dope! Mr. Hilton told you five times already, don't come in till Lester points to that star the second time."

"Ach, Clara," my father asked, "what does she do there till six o'clock she can't even put the plates on the table?"

"Christmas," said my mother coldly.

"Ho! Ho!" my father said. "Christmas. What's the harm? After all, 48 history teaches everyone. We learn from reading this is a holiday from pagan times also, candles, lights, even Chanukah. So we learn it's not altogether Christian. So if they think it's a private holiday, they're only ignorant, not patriotic. What belongs to history, belongs to all men. You want to go back to the Middle Ages? Is it better to shave your head with a secondhand razor? Does it hurt Shirley to learn to speak up? It does not. So maybe someday she won't live between the kitchen and the shop. She's not a fool."

I thank you, Papa, for your kindness. It is true about me to this day. I am foolish but I am not a fool.

That night my father kissed me and said with great interest in my career, "Shirley, tomorrow's your big day. Congrats."

"Save it," my mother said. Then she shut all the windows in order to prevent tonsillitis.

In the morning it snowed. On the street corner a tree had been 52 decorated for us by a kind city administration. In order to miss its chilly shadow our neighbors walked three blocks east to buy a loaf of bread. The butcher pulled down black window shades to keep the colored lights from shining on his chickens. Oh, not me. On the way to school, with both my hands I tossed it a kiss of tolerance. Poor thing, it was a stranger in Egypt.

I walked straight into the auditorium past the staring children. "Go ahead, Shirley!" said the monitors. Four boys, big for their age, had already started work as propmen and stagehands.

Mr. Hilton was very nervous. He was not even happy. Whatever he started to say ended in a sideward look of sadness. He sat slumped in the middle of the first row and asked me to help Miss Glacé. I did this, although she thought my voice too resonant and said, "Show-off!"

Parents began to arrive long before we were ready. They wanted to make a good impression. From among the yards of drapes I peeked out at the audience. I saw my embarrassed mother.

Ira, Lester, and Meyer were pasted to their beards by Miss Glacé. 56 She almost forgot to thread the star on its wire, but I reminded her. I coughed a few times to clear my throat. Miss Glacé looked around and saw that everyone was in costume and on line waiting to play his part. She whispered, "All right . . ." Then:

Jackie Sauerfeld, the prettiest boy in first grade, parted the curtains with his skinny elbow and in a high voice sang out:

"Parents dear
We are here
To make a Christmas play in time.
It we give
In narrative
And illustrate with pantomime."

He disappeared.

My voice burst immediately from the wings to the great shock of Ira, Lester, and Meyer, who were waiting for it but were surprised all the same.

"I remember, I remember, the house where I was born . . ."   60

Miss Glacé yanked the curtain open and there it was, the house—an old hayloft, where Celia Kornbluh lay in the straw with Cindy Lou, her favorite doll. Ira, Lester, and Meyer moved slowly from the wings toward her, sometimes pointing to a moving star and sometimes ahead to Cindy Lou.

It was a long story and it was a sad story. I carefully pronounced all the words about my lonesome childhood, while little Eddie Braunstein wandered upstage and down with his shepherd's stick, looking for sheep. I brought up lonesomeness again, and not being understood at all except by some women everybody hated. Eddie was too small for that and Marty Groff took his place, wearing his father's prayer shawl. I announced twelve friends, and half the boys in the fourth grade gathered round Marty, who stood on an orange crate while my voice harangued. Sorrowful and loud, I declaimed about love and God and Man, but because of the terrible deceit of Abie Stock we came suddenly to a famous moment. Marty, whose remembering tongue I was, waited at the foot of the cross. He stared desperately at the audience. I groaned, "My God, my God, why hast thou forsaken me?" The soldiers who were shieks grabbed poor Marty to pin him up to die, but he wrenched free, turned again to the audience, and spread his arms aloft to show despair and the end. I murmured at the top of my voice, "The rest is silence, but as everyone in this room, in this city—in this world—now knows, I shall have life eternal."

That night Mrs. Kornbluh visited our kitchen for a glass of tea.

"How's the virgin?" asked my father with a look of concern.   64

"For a man with a daughter, you got a fresh mouth, Abramovitch."

"Here," said my father kindly, "have some lemon, it'll sweeten your disposition."

They debated a little in Yiddish, then fell in a puddle of Russian and Polish. What I understood next was my father, who said, "Still and all, it was certainly a beautiful affair, you have to admit, introducing us to the beliefs of a different culture."

"Well, yes," said Mrs. Kornbluh. "The only thing . . . you know   68 Charlie Turner—that cute boy in Celia's class—a couple others? They got very small parts or no part at all. In very bad taste, it seemed to me. After all, it's their religion."

"Ach," explained my mother, "what could Mr. Hilton do? They got very small voices; after all, why should they holler? The English language they know from the beginning by heart. They're blond like angels.

You think it's so important they should get in the play? Christmas . . .
the whole piece of goods . . . they own it."

I listened and listened until I couldn't listen any more. Too sleepy, I
climbed out of bed and kneeled. I made a little church of my hands and
said, "Hear, O Israel . . ." Then I called out in Yiddish, "Please, good
night, good night. Ssh." My father said, "Ssh yourself," and slammed the
kitchen door.

I was happy. I fell asleep at once. I had prayed for everybody: my
talking family, cousins far away, passersby, and all the lonesome Christians. I expected to be heard. My voice was certainly the loudest.

1956

31

Bilingualism

Richard Rodriguez, Toward an American Language
James Fallows, Viva Bilingualism

The two extreme solutions to the question of how to educate non-native speakers of English are these: (1) "immersion," in which the students hear and speak only English in school, and (2) bilingualism, in which students study major subjects in their native language and study English as a second language. The first approach—until recently the only approach—is based on the idea that America is a "melting pot" in which Russians, Germans, Italians, Chinese, and all others who come here should become "Americans." The method is sink or swim; the failure of the method cannot be calculated—we can hardly measure the psychological pain that some people endured—but the success can be. The history of the United States is, on the whole, a history of the success of immigrants.

Tina Bakka, from *Locking Students Out*

As an immigrant to this nation, I am keenly aware of the things that bind us as Americans and unite us as a single people. Foremost among these unifying forces is the common language we share. While it is certainly true that our love of freedom and devotion to democratic principles help to unite and give us a mutual purpose, it is English, our common language, that enables us to discuss our views and allows us to maintain a well-informed electorate, the cornerstone of democratic government.

S. I. Hayakawa, from *Bilingualism in America:*
English Should Be the Only Language

Hector, being a little Cuban, didn't speak much English. The nurses figured they would help him by teaching him English. After all, he was blond and fair and didn't look Spanish. There was one nurse who took special care of him: meals, bedpans, injections, tubes.

"Do you know something," she said to him, "you're very stupid for not speaking in English. This is your country. You live here and should know the languge."

To teach him English she would lock him up in a closet. He would be quiet for a while then get scared and start banging on the door. She'd say, "Not until you say, 'Please let me out!'" But he wouldn't even try. He'd pull on the door of the closet and cry out in Spanish. He was afraid: All the clothes on the shelves were haunted. They had belonged at one time or another to children now dead, and they seemed to be puffed up and to move around, as if hundreds of invisible kids had crawled into them. Dead children were like normal children except their eyes were closed. He would bang on the door and scream out in Spanish, "¡Abra la puerta! ¡Abra la puerta!"—"Open the door! Open the door!" wishing in his deep dreams to open the door to Aunt Luisa's kitchen in Cuba and find a glass of the magic concoction, or to see Alejo as he went down the hall to work. He kept on saying it, in a panic, crazy, as if on fire inside. Then the voice on the other side would return, "Say it in English. *Let me out!*" Then she would shout it. "Now don't be stupid," she would tell him, "say it!"

The hours would drag and the door would not open.

Oscar Hijuelos, from *Our House in the Last World*

Richard Rodriguez

Toward an American Language

For a hundred years Americans have resorted to Huckleberry Finn's American summer for refreshment. As much as Huck, Americans resist the coming of fall, the chill in the woods, the starched shirt, the inimical expectation of the schoolmarm. All city ways. Individualism is the source of America, the source of our greatness. But America is a city now and individualism has become our national dilemma.

America's individualism derives from low-church Protestantism. They taught us well, those old Puritans. Distrust the tyranny of the plural. Seek God with a singular pronoun. They didn't stop there. Puritans advised fences. Build a fence around what you hold dear and respect other fences.

TO SUIT ANY TASTE

The antisocial inclination of eighteenth-century Puritans paradoxically allowed for the immigrant America of the nineteenth century. Lacking a communal sense of itself—there was no "we" here—how could America resist the coming of strangers? America became a multiracial, multireligious society because a small band of Puritans didn't want the world.

The outsider is not the exception to America, rather the outsider is   4 the archetypal citizen. In him, and only in him, in her—suitcase in hand, foreign-speaking, bewildered by the crowd—can Americans recognize ourselves. We recognize the stranger in us. For we are a nation of immigrants, we are accustomed to remind ourselves. We see ourselves as strangers to one another, all of us bewildered by the city.

Immigrants may be appalled by the individualism they find when they get here—skateboards; slang; disrespect; Daisy Miller; Deadheads—it's all the same. But this same individualism allows the immigrant to purchase a new life. Each new immigrant has a stake in the perpetuation of American individualism. Here the immigrant is freed from the collective fate of his village. Once here, the immigrant has already eluded the destiny of his father.

The limits of American generosity are the limits of Puritan individualism. We accept the stranger, sure we do, but we are suspicious of any assimilationist insinuation such as that the stranger might eventually change us: Two in their meeting are changed.

With the exception of the army, the classroom is the most subversive institution of America. The classroom works against our historical inclination by chipping away at any tangible distance between us. In the classroom, children are taught that they belong to a group. Children are taught that there is a national culture, a public language, a plural pronoun implied by the singular assertion of the Pledge of Allegiance.

About fifteen years ago, I got involved in the national debate over   8 bilingual education. Proponents of bilingual classrooms argued that non-English speaking children would have an easier time of it in school if they could keep a hold on heritage as a kind of trainer-wheel; if they would be allowed to use their "family language" in classrooms.

What I knew from my own education was that such a scheme would betray public education. There is no way for a child to use her family language in a classroom unless we diminish the notion of public school, unless we confuse the child utterly about what is expected of her. Bilingual classrooms imply we are going to expect less.

BECAUSE IT'S GOOD FOR YOU

Family language distinguishes one child from all others. Classroom language, on the other hand, is unyielding, impersonal, blind, public—there are rules, there are limits, there are inevitable embarrassments, but there are no exceptions. The child is expected to speak up, to make himself understood to an audience of boys and girls. It is an unsentimental business.

At the time—in the mid-1970s—I took bilingual enthusiasts to be a romantic lot, a fringe of the Ethnic Left. Fifteen years have passed and bilingual education has become a bureaucracy. I still believe that bilingualism is a confused ideology. But I now believe the confusion is willful and characteristically American. Americans have always been at war with the idea of school. We shrink from the idea of uniformity—as our Puritan fathers would shrink—as from the image of the melting pot. We say we want the advantages of public life, but we do not want to relinquish our separateness for it. We want to coexist, not change.

In my mind, bilingual education belongs to those sentimental and   12 violent American years, the sixties, when my generation imagined we had discovered individualism. There was a conveniently dishonorable war to protest. But Americans went to war against the idea of America. We went to war against anyone over thirty, against our parents, against memory. We marched in the name of "the people," exclusive of at least half the population.

The radical sixties were not such an isolated time. In the nineteenth century there were nativist riots against an expanding notion of America, against any idea of a plural pronoun. Should we now, in retrospect, be surprised that the black civil rights movement (the heroic march toward integration) was undermined, finally, by subsequent cries for black separatism? Another example of American ambivalence.

We think we are united only by a clean consent, and yet the rest of the world can spot us a mile off. America exists. Americans end up behaving more like each other alive, even in disagreement, than we resemble dead ancestors. There is a discernible culture about us, tangible in the spaces between us, that connects Thomas Jefferson with Martin Luther King, Jr. Trouble is, the lesson of that culture, the indoctrination of that culture in schools, implies that we form a "we." Our professors have lost the conviction of it. A unifying canon—an intellectual line which might implicate us all by virtue of our arrival here—seems an impossibility. Our professors have begun to fish in other streams, seeking alternatives to Western Civ.

In 1989 the majority of immigrants do not come from Europe. Now Americans describe the distance we maintain from one another as "diversity." The problem of our national diversity becomes, with a little choke on logic, the solution to itself. "We should celebrate diversity," teachers, bureaucrats, join to tell us—that is what America means, they say. And they are right.

FAVORITE FLAVORS

Traditionally it has been pragmatism that forced Americans to 16 yield to the fiction of a nation indivisible. War, for example. The U.S. Army took your darling boy, with his allergies and his moles and his favorite flavor and reduced him to a uniform. The workplace is very nearly as unsentimental.

In the nineteenth century, America compromised Puritanism with pragmatism. In order to work, to continue existing as a country, America required some uniform sense of itself.

In the nineteenth century, even as the American city was building, Samuel Clemens romanced the nation with a celebration of the wildness of the American river. But in the redbrick cities, and on streets without trees, the river became an idea, a learned idea, a civilizing idea, taking all to itself. Women, usually women, tireless, overworked women, stood in front of rooms filled with the children of immigrants, teaching those children a common language. For language is not just another classroom skill, as today's bilingualists would have it. Language is the lesson of *grammar* school. And from the schoolmarm's achievement came the possibility of a shared history and a shared future. To my mind, this achievement of the nineteenth century classroom was an honorable one, comparable to the opening of the plains, the building of bridges. Grammar school teachers forged a nation.

My own first attempts to read *Huckleberry Finn* ended in defeat. I entered the classroom as a Spanish-speaking boy. I learned English with difficulty, but rightly enough. Huck spoke a dialect English, not the English I learned. ("You don't know about me without you have read. . . .") Eventually, but this was long after, I was able to discern in Huck's dilemma—how he chafed so at school!—a version of my own. And, later still, to discern in him a version of the life of our nation: Huck as the archetypal bilingual child!

My fear is that today Huck Finn would emerge as the simple winner.   20 The schoolmarm would be shown up as a tyrannical supremacist. I tell you the schoolmarm is the hero of America. My suspicion is that many of our children—dropouts and graduates alike—are learning the lesson of communality remedially, from the workplace. At the bank or behind the counter at McDonald's, or in the switch room of the telephone company, people from different parts of town and different parts of the country, and different countries of the world learn that they have one thing or another in common. Initially, a punch clock. A supervisor. A paycheck. A shared irony. A takeout lunch. Some nachos, some bagels, a pizza. And here's a fortune cookie for you: Two in their meeting are changed.

All the while the professors speak limply of diversity, which is truly our strength. But diversity which is not shared is no virtue. Diversity which is not shared is a parody nation.

The river owes its flux and its swell and its entire strength to its tributaries. But America was created in autumn by the schoolmarm, mistress of all she surveyed.   *1989*

James Fallows
Viva Bilingualism

In his classic work of crackpot anthropology, *The Japanese Brain*, Dr. Tadanobu Tsunoda told his Japanese readers not to feel bad about their difficulties learning other languages, especially English. "Isn't it remarkable," he said (I am paraphrasing), "that whenever you meet someone who speaks English really well, he turns out to be a drip?" The Japanese have their own reasons for seeking such reassurance.

Their students learn English exactly the way Americans (used to) learn Latin: through long, boring analyses of antique written passages. Not surprisingly, most of them feel about as comfortable making English conversation as I would if Julius Caesar strolled up for a chat. The few Japanese who do speak good English have generally lived overseas— and to that extent have become less Japanese and, by local standards, more like drips.

Still, for all the peculiar Japaneseness of his sentiment, the spirit of Dr. Tsunoda is alive in America today. It is reflected in the general disdain for bilingualism and bilingual education, and in campaigns like the one on California's ballot last week, sponsored by the group called U.S. English, to declare that English is America's "official" language.

Yes, yes, everyone needs to learn English. America doesn't want to   4 become Quebec. We have enough other forces pulling us apart that we don't want linguistic divisions too. But is there any reason to get so worked up about today's Spanish-speaking immigrants, even if they keep learning Spanish while in school? I will confess that I once shared U.S. English-type fears about Spanish language separatism. But having spent a long time reporting among immigrants and seeing how much their children wanted to learn English, I'm not worried anymore. And, having been out of the country most of the year, I've come to think that the whole American language scare rests on two bogus and amazingly parochial assumptions.

The first is a view of bilingualism as a kind of polygamy. That is, according to Western standards it just doesn't work to have two wives. The partners in a marriage require a certain exclusive commitment from each other. If a man gives it to one wife, there's not enough left over to give to someone else. Similarly with language: there's only so much room in a person's brain, and if he speaks one language—let us say Spanish—really well, he'll be all filled up and won't learn English. And if his brain were not a problem, his heart would be, since he can be truly loyal to only one language. I'm burlesquing the argument a little, but not much. Why would anyone worry about students taking "mainte-nance" courses in Spanish, if not for the fear that Spanish would somehow use up the mental and emotional space English should fill?

In the American context, it's easy to see why people might feel this way. Ninety-nine percent of all Americans can happily live their lives speaking and thinking about no language but English. Foreign-language education has been falling off, and except in unusual circumstances— wars, mainly—it has never had much practical reinforcement anyway. When we come across people in the United States who obviously know a foreign language, the main signal is usually that their English is so poor.

But suppose that mastering a second language is less like having two wives than like having two children. Maybe there's not really a limit in the brain or heart, and spreading attention among several languages—like spreading love among several children—may actually enrich everyone involved. Without going through all the linguistic arguments showing that bilingualism is possible and natural (one impressive recent summary was *Mirror of Language* by Kenji Hakuta, published this year) I will merely say that after about five seconds of talking with someone who really is bilingual, the two-child, rather than two-wife, view comes to make much more sense.

Everyone has heard about the Scandinavians and Swiss, who grow   8 up in a big swirl of languages and can talk easily to anyone they meet. Their example may seem too high-toned to be persuasive in connection with today's Spanish-speaking immigrants, so consider the more down-to-earth illustrations of multilingualism to be found all over Asia.

Seven years ago, the government of Singapore launched a "Speak Mandarin!" campaign, designed to supplant various southern Chinese dialects with Mandarin. (This is roughly similar to a "Speak Like Prince Charles!" campaign being launched in West Virginia.) Since then, competence in Mandarin has gone up—and so has mastery of English. At the beginning of the Speak Mandarin campaign, the pass rate for O-level (high school) exams in English was 41 percent. Now it's 61 percent. During the same period, the O-level pass rate for Mandarin went from 84 percent to 92 percent. The children managed to get better at both languages at once.

Just north of Singapore is Malaysia, another one-time British colony whose main political problem is managing relations among three distinct ethnic groups: Malays, Chinese, and Indians. Each of the groups speaks a different language at home—Malay for the Malays, Cantonese or Hokkien for the Chinese, Tamil for the Indians. But if you put any two Malaysians together in a room, it's almost certain that they'll be able to speak to each other, in either Malay or English, since most people are bilingual and many speak three or more languages. (The Chinese generally speak one or two Chinese dialects, plus English and/or Malay. The Indians speak English or Malay on top of Tamil, and many or most Malays speak English.) Neither Tamil nor the Chinese dialects travel well outside the ethnic group, and Malay doesn't travel anywhere else but Indonesia, so most Malaysians have a strong incentive to learn another language.

I should emphasize that I'm talking about people who in no way fit modern America's idea of a rarefied intellectual elite. They are wizened Chinese shopkeepers, unschooled Indian night guards, grubby Malay food hawkers, in addition to more polished characters who've traveled around the world. Yet somehow they all find room in their brains for more than one language at a time. Is it so implausible that Americans can do the same?

The second antibilingual assumption, rarely stated but clearly 12 there, is that English is some kind of fragile blossom, about to be blown apart by harsh blasts from the Spanish-speaking world. Come on! Never before in world history has a language been as dominant as English is now. In every corner of the world, people realize that their chances to play on the big stage—to make money, have choices, travel—depend on learning English. They don't always succeed, but more and more of them try. In Malaysia, in South China, even in linguophobic Japan, my family's main problem as we travel has been coping with people who spring from behind every lamppost and tofu stand, eager to practice the English they've picked up from the shortwave radio. Malaysia ships out tens of thousands of young people each year for studies in the United States, Australia, and England. Guess what language they have to learn before they go.

It may seem that modern America shamelessly coddles its immigrants, with all those Spanish-language street signs and TV broadcasts and "maintenance" courses, which together reduce the incentive to learn English. Well, I've spent most of this year in a position similar to the immigrants', and it's not as comfortable or satisfactory as it may look. Japan makes many more accommodations to the English language than America does to Spanish. Tokyo has four English-language daily newspapers—more than most American cities—plus several magazines. The major train and subway routes have English signs, most big-city restaurants have English menus, all major hotels have English-speaking staff. Students applying for university admission must pass tests in (written) English. Most shopkeepers, policemen, and passersby can make sense of written-down English messages. Even the Shinkansen, or bullet train, makes its announcements in both Japanese and English— which is comparable to the Eastern shuttle giving each "Please have your fares ready" message in Spanish as well as English. The nighttime TV news broadcasts now come in a bilingual version—you push a button on your set to switch from Japanese to English. It is as if the "CBS Evening News" could be simultaneously heard in Spanish.

Does all of this reduce the incentive to learn Japanese, or the feeling of being left out if you don't? Hah! Even though Japanese society is vastly more permeated by English than American society is by Spanish, each day brings ten thousand reminders of what you're missing if you don't know the language. You can't read the mainstream newspapers, can't follow most shows on TV, can't communicate above the "please-give-me-a-ticket-to-Kyoto" level. Without learning the language, you could never hope to win a place as anything but a fringe figure. Some adults nonetheless live out a ghettoized, English-only existence, because Japanese is no cinch, but foreign children raised in Japan pick up the language as the only way to participate.

   The incentives for America's newcomers to learn English are even stronger. How are an immigrant's children going to go to any college, get any kind of white-collar job, live anything but a straitened, ghetto existence unless they speak English? When are the SATs, Bruce Spring-steen songs, and the David Letterman show going to be in Spanish—or Korean, or Tagalog? If Malaysians and rural Chinese can see that En-glish is their route to a wider world, are Guatemalans and Cubans who've made it to America so much more obtuse? And if they keep up their Spanish at the same time, even through the dreaded "mainte-nance" courses, why don't we count that as a good thing? It's good for them, in making their lives richer and their minds more flexible, and it's good for the country, in enlarging its ability to deal with the rest of the world.

   The adult immigrants themselves don't usually succeed in learning   16
English, any more than my wife and I have become fluent in Japanese. But that has been true of America's immigrants for two hundred years. (The main exception were the Eastern European Jewish immigrants of the early twentieth century, who moved into English faster than Italians, Germans, Poles, or today's Latin Americans.) The Cubans' and Mexi-cans' children are the ones who learn, as previous immigrants' children have. When someone can find large numbers of children who are being raised in America but don't see English as a necessity, then I'll start to worry.

   We don't want to become Quebec—and we're not about to. Quebec, Belgium, Sri Lanka, and other places with language problems have old, settled groups who've lived alongside each other, in mutual dislike, for many years—not new groups of immigrants continually being ab-sorbed. We don't need to declare English our official language, because it already is that—as no one knows better than the immigrants and their children. Anywhere else in the world, people would laugh at the idea that English is in any way imperiled. Let's calm down and enjoy the joke too.   *1986*

32

Language and Politics

George Orwell, Politics and the
English Language

Václav Havel, Words on Words

June Jordan, Nobody Mean More to
Me than You
and the Future Life of Willie Jordan

Language, be it remembered, is not an abstract construction of the
learned, or of dictionary makers, but is something arising out of the
work, needs, ties, joys, affections, tastes, of long generations of humanity, and has its bases broad and low, close to the ground. Its final
decisions are made by the masses, people nearest the concrete, having
most to do with actual land and sea. It impermeates all, the Past as well
as the Present, and is the grandest triumph of the human intellect.

Walt Whitman, from *Slang in America*

The greatest American industry—why has no one ever said so?—is the
industry of using words. We pay tens of millions of people to spend
their lives lying to us, or telling us the truth, or supplying us with a
nourishing medicinal compound of the two. All of us are living in the
middle of a dark wood—a bright Technicolored forest—of words,
words, words. It is a forest in which the wind is never still: there isn't a
tree in the forest that is not, for every moment of its life and our lives,
persuading or ordering or seducing or overawing us into buying this,
believing that, voting for the other.

Randall Jarrell, from *The Taste of the Age*

It goes without saying, then, that language is also a political instrument, means, and proof of power. It is the most vivid and crucial key to identity: It reveals the private identity, and connects one with, or divorces one from, the larger public, or communal identity. There have been, and are, times, and places, when to speak a certain language could be dangerous, even fatal. Or, one may speak the same language, but in such a way that one's antecedents are revealed, or (one hopes) hidden. This is true in France, and is absolutely true in England: The range (and reign) of accents on that damp little island make England coherent for the English and totally incomprehensible for everyone else. To open your mouth in England is (if I may use black English) to "put your business in the street": You have confessed your parents, your youth, your school, your salary, your self-esteem, and, alas, your future.

James Baldwin, from *If Black English Isn't a Language,*
Then Tell Me, What Is?

George Orwell

Politics and the English Language

Most people who bother with the matter at all would admit that the English language is in a bad way, but it is generally assumed that we cannot by conscious action do anything about it. Our civilization is decadent and our language—so the argument runs—must inevitably share in the general collapse. It follows that any struggle against the abuse of language is a sentimental archaism, like preferring candles to electric light or hansom cabs to airplanes. Underneath this lies the half-conscious belief that language is a natural growth and not an instrument which we shape for our own purposes.

Now, it is clear that the decline of a language must ultimately have political and economic causes: It is not due simply to the bad influence of this or that individual writer. But an effect can become a cause, reinforcing the original cause and producing the same effect in an intensified form, and so on indefinitely. A man may take to drink because he feels himself to be a failure, and then fail all the more completely because he drinks. It is rather the same thing that is happening to the English language. It becomes ugly and inaccurate because our thoughts are foolish, but the slovenliness of our language makes it easier for us to have foolish thoughts. The point is that the process is reversible. Modern English, especially written English, is full of bad habits which spread by imitation and which can be avoided if one is willing to take the necessary trouble. If one gets rid of these habits one can think more clearly, and to think clearly is a necessary first step towards political regeneration: so that the fight against bad English is not frivolous and is not the exclusive concern of professional writers. I will come back to this presently, and I hope that by that time the meaning of what I have said here will have become clearer. Meanwhile, here are five specimens of the English language as it is now habitually written.

These five passages have not been picked out because they are especially bad—I could have quoted far worse if I had chosen—but because they illustrate various of the mental vices from which we now suffer. They are a little below the average, but are fairly representative samples. I number them so that I can refer back to them when necessary:

(1) I am not, indeed, sure whether it is not true to say that the Milton who once seemed not unlike a seventeenth-century Shelley had not become, out of an experience ever more bitter in each year, more alien [*sic*] to the founder of that Jesuit sect which nothing could induce him to tolerate.   Professor Harold Laski (Essay in *Freedom of Expression*).

(2) Above all, we cannot play ducks and drakes with a native battery of idioms which prescribes such egregious collections of vocables as the Basic *put up with* for *tolerate* or *put at a loss* for *bewilder.*
          Professor Lancelot Hogben (*Interglossa*).

(3) On the one side we have the free personality: By definition it is not neurotic, for it has neither conflict nor dream. Its desires, such as they are, are transparent, for they are just what institutional approval keeps in the forefront of consciousness; another institutional pattern would alter their number and intensity; there is little in them that is natural, irreducible, or culturally dangerous. But *on the other side*, the social bond itself is nothing but the mutual reflection of these self-secure integrities. Recall the definition of love. Is not this the very picture of a small academic? Where is there a place in this hall of mirrors for either personality or fraternity?   Essay on psychology in *Politics* (New York).

(4) All the "best people" from the gentlemen's clubs, and all the frantic fascist captains, united in common hatred of Socialism and bestial horror of the rising tide of the mass revolutionary movement, have turned to acts of provocation, to foul incendiarism, to medieval legends of poisoned wells, to legalize their own destruction of proletarian organizations, and rouse the agitated petty-bourgeoisie to chauvinistic

fervor on behalf of the fight against the revolutionary way out of the
crisis.   Communist pamphlet.

(5) If a new spirit *is* to be infused into this old country, there is one
thorny and contentious reform which must be tackled, and that is the
humanization and galvanization of the B.B.C. Timidity here will be-
speak cancer and atrophy of the soul. The heart of Britain may be
sound and of strong beat, for instance, but the British lion's roar at
present is like that of Bottom in Shakespeare's *Midsummer Night's
Dream*—as gentle as any sucking dove. A virile new Britain cannot
continue indefinitely to be traduced in the eyes or rather ears, of the
world by the effete languors of Langham Place, brazenly masquerading as "standard English." When the Voice of Britain is heard at nine
o'clock, better far and infinitely less ludicrous to hear aitches honestly
dropped than the present priggish, inflated, inhibited, school-
ma'amish arch braying of blameless bashful mewing maidens!
                                                   Letter in *Tribune*.

Each of these passages has faults of its own, but, quite apart from   4
avoidable ugliness, two qualities are common to all of them. The first is
staleness of imagery: The other is lack of precision. The writer either
has a meaning and cannot express it, or he inadvertently says something
else, or he is almost indifferent as to whether his words mean anything
or not. This mixture of vagueness and sheer incompetence is the most
marked characteristic of modern English prose, and especially of any
kind of political writing. As soon as certain topics are raised, the
concrete melts into the abstract and no one seems able to think of turns
of speech that are not hackneyed: Prose consists less and less of *words*
chosen for the sake of their meaning, and more and more of *phrases*
tacked together like the sections of a prefabricated hen-house. I list
below, with notes and examples, various of the tricks by means of which
the work of prose-construction is habitually dodged:

Dying Metaphors. A newly invented metaphor assists thought by
evoking a visual image, while on the other hand a metaphor which is
technically "dead" (e.g., *iron resolution*) has in effect reverted to being an
ordinary word and can generally be used without loss of vividness. But
in between these two classes there is a huge dump of worn-out metaphors which have lost all evocative power and are merely used because
they save people the trouble of inventing phrases for themselves. Examples are: *Ring the changes on, take up the cudgels for, toe the line, ride
roughshod over, stand shoulder to shoulder with, play into the hands of, no axe to
grind, grist to the mill, fishing in troubled waters, rift within the lute, on the
order of the day, Achilles' heel, swan song, hotbed.* Many of these are used
without knowledge of their meaning (what is a "rift," for instance?), and
incompatible metaphors are frequently mixed, a sure sign that the

writer is not interested in what he is saying. Some metaphors now current have been twisted out of their original meaning without those who use them even being aware of the fact. For example, *toe the line* is sometimes written *tow the line*. Another example is *the hammer and the anvil*, now always used with the implication that the anvil gets the worst of it. In real life it is always the anvil that breaks the hammer, never the other way about: a writer who stopped to think what he was saying would be aware of this, and would avoid perverting the original phrase.

Operators or Verbal False Limbs. These save the trouble of picking out appropriate verbs and nouns, and at the same time pad each sentence with extra syllables which give it an appearance of symmetry. Characteristic phrases are *render inoperative, militate against, make contact with, be subjected to, give rise to, give grounds for, have the effect of, play a leading part (role) in, make itself felt, take effect, exhibit a tendency to, serve the purpose of,* etc., etc. The keynote is the elimination of simple verbs. Instead of being a single word, such as *break, stop, spoil, mend, kill,* a verb becomes a *phrase*, made up of a noun or adjective tacked on to some general-purpose verb such as *prove, serve, form, play, render.* In addition, the passive voice is wherever possible used in preference to the active, and noun constructions are used instead of gerunds (*by examination of* instead of *by examining*). The range of verbs is further cut down by means of the *-ize* and *de-* formation, and the banal statements are given an appearance of profundity by means of the *not un-* formation. Simple conjunctions and prepositions are replaced by such phrases as *with respect to, having regard to, the fact that, by dint of, in view of, in the interests of, on the hypothesis that;* and the ends of sentences are saved from anticlimax by such resounding commonplaces as *greatly to be desired, cannot be left out of account, a development to be expected in the near future, deserving of serious consideration, brought to a satisfactory conclusion,* and so on and so forth.

Pretentious Diction. Words like *phenomenon, element, individual* (as noun), *objective, categorical, effective, virtual, basic, primary, promote, constitute, exhibit, exploit, utilize, eliminate, liquidate,* are used to dress up simple statements and give an air of scientific impartiality to biased judgments. Adjectives like *epoch-making, epic, historic, unforgettable, triumphant, age-old, inevitable, inexorable, veritable,* are used to dignify the sordid processes of international politics, while writing that aims at glorifying war usually takes on an archaic color, its characteristic words being: *realm, throne, chariot, mailed fist, trident, sword, shield, buckler, banner, jackboot, clarion.* Foreign words and expressions such as *cul de sac, ancien régime, deus ex machina, mutatis mutandis, status quo, gleichschaltung, weltanschauung,* are used to give an air of culture and elegance. Except for the useful abbreviations *i.e., e.g.,* and *etc.,* there is no real need for any of the hundreds of foreign phrases now current in English. Bad writers, and especially scientific, political, and sociological writers, are nearly always haunted by the notion that Latin or Greek words are grander than Saxon ones, and unnecessary words like *expedite, ameliorate, predict, extraneous, deracinated, clandestine, subaqueous,* and hundreds of others constantly gain ground from their Anglo-Saxon opposite numbers.[1] The jargon peculiar to Marxist writing (*hyena, hangman, cannibal, petty bourgeois, these gentry, lackey, flunkey, mad dog, White Guard, etc.*) consists largely of words and phrases translated from Russian, German, or French; but the normal way of coining a new word is to use a Latin or Greek root with the appropriate affix and, where necessary, the *-ize* formation. It is often easier to make up words of this kind (*deregionalize, impermissible, extramarital, nonfragmentatory,* and so forth) than to think up the English words that will cover one's meaning. The result, in general, is an increase in slovenliness and vagueness.

Meaningless Words. In certain kinds of writing, particularly in art 8 criticism and literary criticism, it is normal to come across long passages which are almost completely lacking in meaning.[2] Words like *romantic, plastic, values, human, dead, sentimental, natural, vitality,* as used in art criticism, are strictly meaningless, in the sense that they not only do not point to any discoverable object, but are hardly ever expected to do so by the reader. When one critic writes, "The outstanding feature of Mr. X's work is its living quality," while another writes, "The immediately striking thing about Mr. X's work is its peculiar deadness," the reader accepts this as a simple difference of opinion. If words like *black* and *white* were involved, instead of the jargon words *dead* and *living,* he would see at once that language was being used in an improper way. Many political words are similarly abused. The word *Fascism* has now no meaning except in so far as it signifies "something not desirable." The words *democracy, socialism, freedom, patriotic, realistic, justice,* have each of them several different meanings which cannot be reconciled with one another. In the case of a word like *democracy,* not only is there no agreed definition, but the attempt to make one is resisted from all sides. It is

•

[1]An interesting illustration of this is the way in which the English flower names which were in use till very recently are being ousted by Greek ones, *snapdragon* becoming *antirrhinum, forget-me-not* becoming *myosotis,* etc. It is hard to see any practical reason for this change of fashion: It is probably due to an instinctive turning-away from the more homely word and a vague feeling that the Greek word is scientific.

[2]Example: Comfort's catholicity of perception and image, strangely Whitmanesque in range, almost the exact opposite in aesthetic compulsion, continues to evoke that trembling atmospheric accumulative hinting at a cruel, an inexorably serene timelessness. . . . Wrey Gardiner scores by aiming at simple bull's-eyes with precision. Only they are not so simple, and through this contented sadness runs more than the surface bitter-sweet of resignation." (*Poetry Quarterly.*)

almost universally felt that when we call a country democratic we are praising it: Consequently the defenders of every kind of regime claim that it is a democracy, and fear that they might have to stop using the word if it were tied down to any one meaning. Words of this kind are often used in a consciously dishonest way. That is, the person who uses them has his own private definition, but allows his hearer to think he means something quite different. Statements like *Marshal Pétain[3] was a true patriot, The Soviet Press is the freest in the world, The Catholic Church is opposed to persecution*, are almost always made with intent to deceive. Other words used in variable meanings, in most cases more or less dishonestly, are: *class, totalitarian, science, progressive, reactionary, bourgeois, equality.*

Now that I have made this catalogue of swindles and perversions, let me give another example of the kind of writing that they lead to. This time it must of its nature be an imaginary one. I am going to translate a passage of good English into modern English of the worst sort. Here is a well-known verse from *Ecclesiastes*:

> I returned and saw under the sun, that the race is not to the swift, nor the battle to the strong, neither yet bread to the wise, nor yet riches to men of understanding, nor yet favor to men of skill; but time and chance happeneth to them all.

Here it is in modern English:

> Objective consideration of contemporary phenomena compels the conclusion that success or failure in competitive activities exhibits no tendency to be commensurate with innate capacity, but that a consider-able element of the unpredictable must invariably be taken into ac-count.

This is a parody, but not a very gross one. Exhibit (3), above, for instance, contains several patches of the same kind of English. It will be seen that I have not made a full translation. The beginning and ending of the sentence follow the original meaning fairly closely, but in the middle the concrete illustrations—race, battle, bread—dissolve into the vague phrase "success or failure in competitive activities." This had to be so, because no modern writer of the kind I am discussing—no one capable of using phrases like "objective consideration of contemporary phenomena"—would ever tabulate his thoughts in that precise and

---

[3]*Pétain*: Henri Phillipe Pétain was a World War I French military hero who served as chief of state in France from 1940 to 1945, after France surrendered to Germany. A controver-sial figure, Pétain was regarded by some to be a patriot who had sacrificed himself for his country, while others considered him to be a traitor. He was sentenced to life imprison-ment in 1945, the year before Orwell wrote this essay.—EDS.

detailed way. The whole tendency of modern prose is away from concreteness. Now analyze these two sentences a little more closely. The
first contains forty-nine words but only sixty syllables, and all its words
are those of everyday life. The second contains thirty-eight words of
ninety syllables: eighteen of its words are from Latin roots, and one
from Greek. The first sentence contains six vivid images, and only one
phrase ("time and chance") that could be called vague. The second
contains not a single fresh, arresting phrase, and in spite of its ninety
syllables it gives only a shortened version of the meaning contained in
the first. Yet without a doubt it is the second kind of sentence that is
gaining ground in modern English. I do not want to exaggerate. This
kind of writing is not yet universal, and outcrops of simplicity will occur
here and there in the worst-written page. Still, if you or I were told to
write a few lines on the uncertainty of human fortunes, we should
probably come much nearer to my imaginary sentence than to the one
from *Ecclesiastes*.

As I have tried to show, modern writing at its worst does not consist
in picking out words for the sake of their meaning and inventing images
in order to make the meaning clearer. It consists in gumming together
long strips of words which have already been set in order by someone
else, and making the results presentable by sheer humbug. The attraction of this way of writing is that it is easy. It is easier—even quicker
once you have the habit—to say *In my opinion it is a not unjustifiable
assumption that* than to say *I think*. If you use ready-made phrases, you not
only don't have to hunt about for words; you also don't have to bother
with the rhythms of your sentences, since these phrases are generally so
arranged as to be more or less euphonious. When you are composing in
a hurry—when you are dictating to a stenographer, for instance, or
making a public speech—it is natural to fall into a pretentious, Lat-
inized style. Tags like *a consideration which we should do well to bear in mind*
or *a conclusion to which all of us would readily assent* will save many a
sentence from coming down with a bump. By using stale metaphors,
similes, and idioms, you save much mental effort, at the cost of leaving
your meaning vague, not only for your reader but for yourself. This is
the significance of mixed metaphors. The sole aim of a metaphor is to
call up a visual image. When these images clash—as in *The Fascist octopus
has sung its swan song, the jackboot is thrown into the melting pot*—it can be
taken as certain that the writer is not seeing a mental image of the
objects he is naming; in other words he is not really thinking. Look
again at the examples I gave at the beginning of this essay. Professor
Laski (1) uses five negatives in fifty-three words. One of these is superfluous, making nonsense of the whole passage, and in addition there is
the slip—*alien* for akin—making further nonsense, and several avoidable pieces of clumsiness which increase the general vagueness. Pro-

fessor Hogben (2) plays ducks and drakes with a battery which is able to write prescriptions, and, while disapproving of the everyday phrase *put up with*, is unwilling to look *egregious* up in the dictionary and see what it means; (3), if one takes an uncharitable attitude towards it, is simply meaningless: Probably one could work out its intended meaning by reading the whole of the article in which it occurs. In (4), the writer knows more or less what he wants to say, but an accumulation of stale phrases chokes him like tea leaves blocking a sink. In (5), words and meaning have almost parted company. People who write in this manner usually have a general emotional meaning—they dislike one thing and want to express solidarity with another—but they are not interested in the detail of what they are saying. A scrupulous writer, in every sentence that he writes, will ask himself at least four questions, thus: What am I trying to say? What words will express it? What image or idiom will make it clearer? Is this image fresh enough to have an effect? And he will probably ask himself two more: Could I put it more shortly? Have I said anything that is avoidably ugly? But you are not obliged to go to all this trouble. You can shirk it by simply throwing your mind open and letting the ready-made phrases come crowding in. They will construct your sentences for you—even think your thoughts for you, to a certain extent—and at need they will perform the important service of par- tially concealing your meaning even from yourself. It is at this point that the special connection between politics and the debasement of language becomes clear.

In our time it is broadly true that political writing is bad writing. 12 Where it is not true, it will generally be found that the writer is some kind of rebel, expressing his private opinions and not a "party line." Orthodoxy, of whatever color, seems to demand a lifeless, imitative style. The political dialects to be found in pamphlets, leading articles, manifestos, White Papers, and the speeches of under-secretaries do, of course, vary from party to party, but they are all alike in that one almost never finds in them a fresh, vivid, home-made turn of speech. When one watches some tired hack on the platform mechanically repeating the familiar phrases—*bestial atrocities, iron heel, bloodstained tyranny, free peoples of the world, stand shoulder to shoulder*—one often has a curious feeling that one is not watching a live human being but some kind of dummy: a feeling which suddenly becomes stronger at moments when the light catches the speaker's spectacles and turns them into blank discs which seem to have no eyes behind them. And this is not al- together fanciful. A speaker who uses that kind of phraseology has gone some distance towards turning himself into a machine. The appropriate noises are coming out of his larynx, but his brain is not involved as it would be if he were choosing his words for himself. If the speech he is making is one that he is accustomed to make over and over again, he may be almost unconscious of what he is saying, as one is when one utters the responses in church. And this reduced state of consciousness, if not indispensable, is at any rate favorable to political conformity.

In our time, political speech and writing are largely the defense of the indefensible. Things like the continuance of British rule in India, the Russian purges and deportations, the dropping of the atom bombs on Japan, can indeed be defended, but only by arguments which are too brutal for most people to face, and which do not square with the professed aims of political parties. Thus political language has to consist largely of euphemism, question-begging and sheer cloudy vagueness. Defenseless villages are bombarded from the air, the inhabitants driven out into the countryside, the cattle machine-gunned, the huts set on fire with incendiary bullets: This is called *pacification*. Millions of peasants are robbed of their farms and sent trudging along the roads with no more than they can carry: This is called *transfer of population* or *rectification of frontiers*. People are imprisoned for years without trial, or shot in the back of the neck or sent to die of scurvy in Arctic lumber camps: This is called *elimination of unreliable elements*. Such phraseology is needed if one wants to name things without calling up mental pictures of them. Consider for instance some comfortable English professor defending Russian totalitarianism. He cannot say outright, "I believe in killing off your opponents when you can get good results by doing so." Probably, therefore, he will say something like this:

"While freely conceding that the Soviet régime exhibits certain features which the humanitarian may be inclined to deplore, we must, I think, agree that a certain curtailment of the right to political opposition is an unavoidable concomitant of transitional periods, and that the rigors which the Russian people have been called upon to undergo have been amply justified in the sphere of concrete achievement."

The inflated style is itself a kind of euphemism. A mass of Latin words falls upon the facts like soft snow, blurring the outlines and covering up all the details. The great enemy of clear language is insincerity. When there is a gap between one's real and one's declared aims, one turns as it were instinctively to long words and exhausted idioms, like a cuttlefish squirting out ink. In our age there is no such thing as "keeping out of politics." All issues are political issues, and politics itself is a mass of lies, evasions, folly, hatred, and schizophrenia. When the general atmosphere is bad, language must suffer. I should expect to find—this is a guess which I have not sufficient knowledge to verify— that the German, Russian, and Italian languages have all deteriorated in the last ten or fifteen years, as a result of dictatorship.

But if thought corrupts language, language can also corrupt 16 thought. A bad usage can spread by tradition and imitation, even among people who should and do know better. The debased language that I have been discussing is in some ways very convenient. Phrases like *a not unjustifiable assumption, leaves much to be desired, would serve no good purpose, a consideration which we should do well to bear in mind,* are a continuous temptation, a packet of aspirins always at one's elbow. Look back through this essay, and for certain you will find that I have again and again committed the very faults I am protesting against. By this morning's post I have received a pamphlet dealing with conditions in Germany. The author tells me that he "felt impelled" to write it. I open it at random, and here is almost the first sentence that I see: "(The Allies) have an opportunity not only of achieving a radical transformation of Germany's social and political structure in such a way as to avoid a nationalistic reaction in Germany itself, but at the same time of laying the foundations of a co-operative and unified Europe." You see, he "feels impelled" to write—feels, presumably, that he has something new to say—and yet his words, like cavalry horses answering the bugle, group themselves automatically into the familiar dreary pattern. This invasion of one's mind by ready-made phrases (*lay the foundations, achieve a radical transformation*) can only be prevented if one is constantly on guard against them, and every such phrase anaesthetizes a portion of one's brain.

I said earlier that the decadence of our language is probably curable. Those who deny this would argue, if they produced an argument at all, that language merely reflects existing social conditions, and that we cannot influence its development by any direct tinkering with words and constructions. So far as the general tone or spirit of a language goes, this may be true, but it is not true in detail. Silly words and expressions have often disappeared, not through any evolutionary process but owing to the conscious action of a minority. Two recent examples were *explore every avenue* and *leave no stone unturned,* which were killed by the jeers of a few journalists. There is a long list of flyblown metaphors which could similarly be got rid of if enough people would interest themselves in the job; and it should also be possible to laugh the *not un-* formation out of existence,[4] to reduce the amount of Latin and Greek in the average sentence, to drive out foreign phrases and strayed scientific words, and, in general, to make pretentiousness unfashionable. But all these are minor points. The defense of the English language implies more than this, and perhaps it is best to start by saying what it does *not* imply.

To begin with it has nothing to do with archaism, with the salvaging of obsolete words and turns of speech, or with the setting up of a "standard English" which must never be departed from. On the con-

---

[4]One can cure oneself of the *not un-* formation by memorizing this sentence: *A not unblack dog was chasing a not unsmall rabbit across a not ungreen field.*

trary, it is especially concerned with the scrapping of every word or idiom which has outworn its usefulness. It has nothing to do with correct grammar and syntax, which are of no importance so long as one makes one's meaning clear, or with the avoidance of Americanisms, or with having what is called a "good prose style." On the other hand it is not concerned with fake simplicity and the attempt to make written English colloquial. Nor does it even imply in every case preferring the Saxon word to the Latin one, though it does imply using the fewest and shortest words that will cover one's meaning. What is above all needed is to let the meaning choose the word, and not the other way about. In prose, the worst thing one can do with words is to surrender to them. When you think of a concrete object, you think wordlessly, and then, if you want to describe the thing you have been visualizing you probably hunt about till you find the exact words that seem to fit. When you think of something abstract you are more inclined to use words from the start, and unless you make a conscious effort to prevent it, the existing dialect will come rushing in and do the job for you, at the expense of blurring or even changing your meaning. Probably it is better to put off using words as long as possible and get one's meaning as clear as one can through pictures or sensations. Afterwards one can choose—not simply *accept*—the phrases that will best cover the meaning, and then switch round and decide what impression one's words are likely to make on another person. This last effort of the mind cuts out all stale or mixed images, all prefabricated phrases, needless repetitions, and humbug and vagueness generally. But one can often be in doubt about the effect of a word or a phrase, and one needs rules that one can rely on when instinct fails. I think the following rules will cover most cases:

(i) Never use a metaphor, simile, or other figure of speech which you are used to seeing in print.
(ii) Never use a long word where a short one will do.
(iii) If it is possible to cut a word out, always cut it out.
(iv) Never use the passive where you can use the active.
(v) Never use a foreign phrase, a scientific word or a jargon word if you can think of an everyday English equivalent.
(vi) Break any of these rules sooner than say anything outright barbarous.

These rules sound elementary, and so they are, but they demand a deep change in attitude in anyone who has grown used to writing in the style now fashionable. One could keep all of them and still write bad English, but one could not write the kind of stuff that I quoted in those five specimens at the beginning of this article.

I have not here been considering the literary use of language, but merely language as an instrument for expressing and not for concealing or preventing thought. Stuart Chase and others have come near to claiming that all abstract words are meaningless, and have used this as a pretext for advocating a kind of political quietism. Since you don't know what Fascism is, how can you struggle against Fascism? One need not swallow such absurdities as these, but one ought to recognize that the present political chaos is connected with the decay of language, and that one can probably bring about some improvement by starting at the verbal end. If you simplify your English, you are freed from the worst follies of orthodoxy. You cannot speak any of the necessary dialects, and when you make a stupid remark its stupidity will be obvious, even to yourself. Political language—and with variations this is true of all political parties, from Conservatives to Anarchists—is designed to make lies sound truthful and murder respectable, and to give an appearance of solidity to pure wind. One cannot change this all in a moment, but one can at least change one's own habits, and from time to time one can even, if one jeers loudly enough, send some worn-out and useless phrase—some *jackboot, Achilles' heel, hotbed, melting pot, acid test, veritable inferno*, or other lump of verbal refuse—into the dustbin where it belongs.   *1946*

Václav Havel

Words on Words

The prize which it is my honor to receive today is called a peace prize and has been awarded to me by booksellers, in other words, people whose business is the dissemination of words. It is therefore appropriate, perhaps, that I should reflect here today on the mysterious link between words and peace, and in general on the mysterious power of words in human history.

In the beginning was the Word; so it states on the first page of one of the most important books known to us. What is meant in that book is that the Word of God is the source of all creation. But surely the same could be said, figuratively speaking, of every human action? And indeed, words can be said to be the very source of our being, and in fact the very substance of the cosmic life-form we call Man. Spirit, the human soul, our self-awareness, our ability to generalize and think in concepts, to perceive the world as the world (and not just as our locality), and lastly, our capacity for knowing that we will die—and living in spite of that knowledge: Surely all these are mediated or actually created by words?

If the Word of God is the source of God's entire creation then that part of God's creation which is the human race exists as such only thanks to another of God's miracles—the miracle of human speech. And if this miracle is the key to the history of mankind, then it is also the key to the history of society. Indeed it might well be the former just because it is the latter. For the fact is that if there were not a means of communication between two or more human "I"s, then words would probably not exist at all.

All these things have been known to us—or people have at least   4
suspected them—since time immemorial. There has never been a time when a sense of the importance of words was not present in human consciousness.

But that is not all: Thanks to the miracle of speech, we know probably better than the other animals that we actually know very little, in other words we are conscious of the existence of mystery. Confronted by mystery—and at the same time aware of the virtually constitutive power of words for us—we have tried incessantly to address that which is concealed by mystery, and influence it with our words. As believers, we pray to God, as magicians we summon up or ward off spirits, using words to intervene in natural or human events. As subjects of modern civilization—whether believers or not—we use words to construct scientific theories and political ideologies with which to tackle or redirect the mysterious course of history—successfully or otherwise.

In other words, whether we are aware of it or not, and however we explain it, one thing would seem to be obvious: we have always believed in the power of words to change history—and rightly so, in a sense.

Why "rightly so"?

Is the human word truly powerful enough to change the world and   8
influence history? And even if there were epochs when it did exert such a power, does it still do so today?

You live in a country with considerable freedom of speech. All citizens without exception can avail themselves of that freedom for whatever purpose, and no one is obliged to pay the least attention, let alone worry their heads over it. You might, therefore, easily get the impression that I overrate the importance of words quite simply because I live in a country where words can still land people in prison.

Yes, I do live in a country where the authority and radioactive effect of words are demonstrated every day by the sanctions which free speech attracts. Just recently, the entire world commemorated the bicentenary of the great French Revolution. Inevitably we recalled the famous Declaration of the Rights of Man and of Citizens, which states that every citizen has the right to own a printing press. During the same period, i.e., exactly two hundred years after that Declaration, my friend Frantisek Stárek was sent to prison for two-and-a-half years for producing the independent cultural journal *Vokno*—not on some private printing press but with a squeaky, antediluvian duplicator. Not long before, my friend Ivan Jirous was sentenced to sixteen months' imprisonment for berating, on a typewriter, something that is common knowledge: that our country has seen many judicial murders and that even now it is possible for a person unjustly convicted to die from ill-treatment in prison. My friend Petr Cibulka is in prison for distributing samizdat texts[1] and recordings of nonconformist singers and bands.

Yes, all that is true. I do live in a country where a writers' congress or some speech at it is capable of shaking the system. Could you conceive of something of the kind in the Federal Republic of Germany? Yes, I live in a country which, twenty-one years ago, was shaken by a text from the pen of my friend Ludvík Vaculík. And as if to confirm my conclusions about the power of words, he entitled his statement: "Two Thousand Words." Among other things, that manifesto served as one of the pretexts for the invasion of our country one night by five foreign armies. And it is by no means fortuitous that as I write these words, the present regime in my country is being shaken by a single page of text entitled—again as if to illustrate what I am saying—"A few words." Yes, I really do inhabit a system in which words are capable of shaking the entire structure of government, where words can prove mightier than ten military divisions, where Solzhenitsyn's words of truth were regarded as something so dangerous that it was necessary to bundle their author into an airplane and transport him. Yet, in the part of the world I inhabit the word Solidarity was capable of shaking an entire power bloc.

All that is true. Reams have been written about it and my distinguished predecessor in this place, Lev Kopelev,[2] spoke about it also. 12

But it is a slightly different matter that concerns me here. It is not my intention solely to speak about the incredible importance that unfettered words assume in totalitarian conditions. Nor do I wish to demonstrate the mysterious power of words by pointing exclusively to those countries where a few words can count for more than a whole train of dynamite somewhere else.

I want to talk in more general terms and consider the wider and more controversial aspects of my topic.

---

[1]**samizdat texts**: Prohibited writing that is privately circulated in the Soviet Union.—Eds.
[2]Lev Kopelev received the Peace Prize of the German Booksellers Association in 1981.

We live in a world in which it is possible for a citizen of Great
Britain to find himself the target of a lethal arrow aimed—publicly and
unashamedly—by a powerful individual in another country merely
because he had written a particular book.[3] That powerful man apparently did it in the name of millions of his fellow believers. And moreover, it is possible in this world that some portion of those millions—
one hopes only a small portion—will identify with the death sentence
pronounced.

What's going on? What does it mean? Is it no more than an icy blast   16
of fanaticism, oddly finding a new lease on life in the era of the various
Helsinki agreements, and oddly resuscitated by the rather crippling
results of the rather crippling Europeanization of worlds which initially
had no interest in the import of foreign civilization, and on account of
that ambivalent commodity ended up saddled with astronomical debts
they can never repay?

It certainly is all that.

But it is something else as well. It is a symbol.

It is a symbol of the mysteriously ambiguous power of words.

In truth, the power of words is neither unambiguous nor clear-cut.   20
It is not merely the liberating power of Walesa's words or the alarm-
raising power of Sakharov's. It is not just the power of Rushdie's—
clearly misconstrued—book.

The point is that alongside Rushdie's words we have Khomeini's.
Words that electrify society with their freedom and truthfulness are
matched by words that mesmerize, deceive, inflame, madden, beguile,
words that are harmful—lethal, even. The word as arrow.

I don't think I need to go to any lengths to explain to you of all
people the diabolic power of certain words: You have fairly recent firsthand experience of what indescribable historical horrors can flow, in
certain political and social constellations, from the hypnotically spell-
binding, though totally demented, words of a single, average, petit
bourgeois.[4] Admittedly I fail to understand what it was that transfixed a
large number of your fathers and mothers, but at the same time I realize
that it must have been something extremely compelling as well as
extremely insidious if it was capable of beguiling, albeit only briefly,
even that great genius[5] who lent such modern and penetrating meaning
to the words: *Sein, Da-Sein,* and *Existenz.*

---

[3]**particular book**: The reference is to the writer Salman Rushdie, whose novel, *The Satanic
Verses* (1988), resulted in a call by the Ayatollah Khomeini to Moslems to kill Rushdie and
his publishers.—Eds.

[4]**petit bourgeois**: Havel is referring to Adolf Hitler.—Eds.

[5]**great genius**: The German philosopher Martin Heidegger (1889–1976); *Sein, Da-Sein,* and
Existenz are key terms of his metaphysics and refer to "Being," "Being-there," and "Existence." He was drafted by the Nazis in 1944.—Eds.

The point I am trying to make is that words are a mysterious, ambiguous, ambivalent, and perfidious phenomenon. They are capable of being rays of light in a realm of darkness, as Belinsky once described Ostrovsky's *Storm*. They are equally capable of being lethal arrows. Worst of all, at times they can be the one and the other. And even both at once!

The words of Lenin—what were they? Liberating or, on the con-   24 trary, deceptive, dangerous, and ultimately enslaving? This is still a bone of contention among aficionados of the history of communism and the controversy is likely to go on raging for a good while yet. My own impression of these words is that they were invariably frenzied.

And what about Marx's words? Did they serve to illuminate an entire hidden plane of social mechanisms, or were they just the inconspicuous germ of all the subsequent appalling gulags? I don't know: Most likely they are both at once.

And what about Freud's words? Did they disclose the secret cosmos of the human soul, or were they no more than the fountainhead of the illusion now benumbing half of America that it is possible to shed one's torments and guilt by having them interpreted away by some well-paid specialist?

But I'd go further and ask an even more provocative question: What was the true nature of Christ's words? Were they the beginning of an era of salvation and among the most powerful cultural impulses in the history of the world—or were they the spiritual source of the crusades, inquisitions, the cultural extermination of the Americas, and, later, the entire expansion of the white race that was fraught with so many contradictions and had so many tragic consequences, including the fact that most of the human world has been consigned to that wretched category known as the "Third World"? I still tend to think that His words belonged to the former category, but at the same time I cannot ignore the umpteen books that demonstrate that, even in its purest and earliest form, there was something unconsciously encoded in Christianity which, when combined with a thousand and one other circumstances, including the relative permanence of human nature, could in some way pave the way spiritually, even for the sort of horrors I mentioned.

Words can have histories too.   28

There was a time, for instance, when, for whole generations of the downtrodden and oppressed, the word socialism was a mesmerizing synonym for a just world, a time when, for the ideal expressed in that word, people were capable of sacrificing years and years of their lives, and their very lives even. I don't know about your country, but in mine, that particular word—*socialism*—was transformed long ago into just an ordinary truncheon used by certain cynical, parvenu bureaucrats to bludgeon their liberal-minded fellow citizens from morning until night, labeling them *enemies of socialism* and *antisocialist forces*. It's a fact: In my country, for ages now, that word has been no more than an incantation that should be avoided if one does not wish to appear suspect. I was recently at an entirely spontaneous demonstration, not dissident-organized, protesting the sell-off of one of the most beautiful parts of Prague to some Australian millionaires. When one of the speakers there, loudly decrying the project, sought to bolster his appeal to the government by declaring that he was fighting for his home in the name of socialism, the crowd started to laugh. Not because they had anything against a just social order, but quite simply because they heard a word which has been incanted for years and years in every possible and impossible context by a regime that only knows how to manipulate and humiliate people.

What a weird fate can befall certain words! At one moment in history, courageous, liberal-minded people can be thrown into prison because a particular word means something to them, and at another moment, people of the selfsame variety can be thrown into prison because that word has ceased to mean anything to them, because it has changed from a symbol of a better world into the mumbo jumbo of a doltish dictator.

No word—at least not in the rather metaphorical sense I am employing the word *word* here—comprises only the meaning assigned to it by an etymological dictionary. The meaning of every word also reflects the person who utters it, the situation in which it is uttered, and the reason for its utterance. The selfsame word can, at one moment, radiate great hopes, at another, it can emit lethal rays. The selfsame word can be true at one moment and false the next, at one moment illuminating, at another, deceptive. On one occasion it can open up glorious horizons, on another, it can lay down the tracks to an entire archipelago of concentration camps. The selfsame word can at one time be the cornerstone of peace, while at another, machine-gun fire resounds in its every syllable.

Gorbachev wants to save socialism through the market economy 32 and free speech, while Li Peng protects socialism by massacring students, and Ceauşescu by bulldozing his people. What does that word actually mean on the lips of the one and the lips of the other two? What is this mysterious thing that is being rescued in such disparate ways?

I referred to the French Revolution and that splendid declaration that accompanied it. That declaration was signed by a gentleman who was later among the first to be executed in the name of that superbly humane text. And hundreds and possibly thousands followed him.

Liberté Egalité, Fraternité—what superb words! And how terrifying their meaning can be. Freedom: the shirt unbuttoned before execution. Equality: the constant speed of the guillotine's fall on different necks. Fraternity: some dubious paradise ruled by a Supreme Being!

The world now reechoes to the wonderfully promising word *perestroika*.[6] We all believe that it harbors hopes for Europe and the whole world.

I am bound to admit, though, that I sometimes shudder at the thought that this word might become just one more incantation, and in the end turn into yet another truncheon for someone to beat us with. It is not my own country I am thinking of: When our rulers utter that word it means about the same as the word *our monarch* when uttered by the Good Soldier Svejk. No, what I have in mind is the fact that even the intrepid man who now sits in the Kremlin occasionally, and possibly only from despair, accuses striking workers, rebellious nations or national minorities, or holders of rather too unusual minority opinions, of "jeopardizing perestroika." I can understand his feelings. It is terribly difficult to fulfill the enormous task he has undertaken. It all hangs by the finest of threads and almost anything could break that thread. Then we would all fall into the abyss. But even so I cannot help wondering whether all this "new thinking" does not contain some disturbing relics of the old. Does it not contain some echoes of former stereotyped thinking and the *ancien régime*'s verbal rituals? Isn't the word *perestroika* starting to resemble the word socialism, particularly on the odd occasion when it is discreetly hurled at the very people who, for so long, were unjustly lambasted with the word *socialism*?

Your country made an enormous contribution to modern European 36 history. I refer to the first wave of détente: the celebrated *Ostpolitik*.[7]

But even that word managed at times to be well and truly ambivalent. It signified, of course, the first glimmer of hope of a Europe without cold wars or iron curtains. At the same time—unhappily—there were also occasions when it signified the abandonment of freedom: the basic precondition for all real peace. I still vividly recall how, at the beginning of the Seventies, a number of my West German colleagues and friends avoided me for fear that contact with me—someone out of favor with the government here—might needlessly provoke that government and thereby jeopardize the fragile foundations of nascent détente.

---

[6]*perestroika*: The Soviet program of economic restructuring.—Eds.

[7]*Ostpolitik*: West German Chancellor Willy Brandt's "opening to the East" policy that led to economic and political agreements with the Soviet Union, Poland, and East Germany in the early 1970s; the policy eventually led to East Germany's recognition by the Western powers.—Eds.

Naturally I am not mentioning it on account of myself personally, let alone out of any sort of self-pity. After all, even in those days it was rather I who pitied them, since it was not I but they who were voluntarily renouncing their freedom. I mention it only in order to demonstrate yet again from another angle how easy it is for a well-intentioned cause to be transformed into the betrayal of its own good intentions—and yet again because of a word whose meaning does not seem to have been kept under adequate observation. Something like that can happen so easily that it almost takes you unawares: It happens inconspicuously, quietly, by stealth—and when at last you realize it, there is only one option left to you—belated astonishment.

However, that is precisely the fiendish way that words are capable of betraying us—unless we are constantly circumspect about their use. And frequently—alas—even a fairly minor and momentary lapse in this respect can have tragic and irreparable consequences, consequences far transcending the nonmaterial world of mere words and penetrating deep into a world that is all too material.

I'm finally getting around to that beautiful word *peace*.

For forty years now I have read it on the front of every building and 40 in every shop window in my country. For forty years, an allergy to that beautiful word has been engendered in me as in every one of my fellow citizens because I know what the word has meant here for the past forty years: ever mightier armies ostensibly to defend peace.

In spite of that lengthy process of systematically divesting the word *peace* of all meaning—worse than that, investing it instead with quite the opposite meaning to that given in the dictionary—a number of Don Quixotes in Charter 77 and several of their younger colleagues in the Independent Peace Association have managed to rehabilitate the word and restore its original meaning. Naturally, though, they had to pay a price for their "semantic perestroika"—i.e., standing the word *peace* back on its feet again: almost all the youngsters who fronted the Independent Peace Association were obliged to spend a few months inside for their pains. It was worth it, though. One important word has been rescued from total debasement. And it is not just a question of saving a word, as I have been trying to explain throughout my speech. Something far more important is saved.

The point is that all important events in the real world—whether admirable or monstrous—are always spearheaded in the realm of words.

As I've already stated, my intention here today is not to convey to you the experience of one who has learned that words still count for something when you can still go to prison for them. My intention was to share with you another lesson that we in this corner of the world have learned about the importance of words. I am convinced it is a lesson which has universal application: Namely, that it always pays to be suspicious of words and to be wary of them, and that we can never be too careful in this respect.

There can be no doubt that distrust of words is less harmful than 44 unwarranted trust in them.

Besides, to distrust words, and indict them for the horrors that might slumber unobtrusively within them—isn't this, after all, the true vocation of the intellectual? I recall that André Glucksmann, the dear colleague who preceded me here today, once spoke in Prague about the need for intellectuals to emulate Cassandra: to listen carefully to the words of the powerful, to be watchful of them, to forewarn of their danger, and to proclaim their dire implications or the evil they might invoke.

There is something that should not escape our attention and it concerns the fact that for centuries we—the Germans and the Czechs— had all sorts of problems with living together in Central Europe. I cannot speak for you, but I think I can rightly say that as far as we Czechs are concerned, the age-old animosities, prejudices and passions, constantly fueled and fanned in numerous ways over the centuries, have evaporated in the course of recent decades. And it is by no means coincidental that this has happened at a time when we have been saddled with a totalitarian regime. Thanks to this regime we have developed a profound distrust of all generalizations, ideological plati- tudes, clichés, slogans, intellectual stereotypes, and insidious appeals to various levels of our emotions, from the baser to the loftier. As a result, we are now largely immune to all hypnotic enticements, even of the traditionally persuasive national or nationalistic variety. The stifling pall of hollow words that have smothered us for so long has cultivated in us such a deep mistrust of the world of deceptive words that we are now better equipped than ever before to see the human world as it really is: a complex community of thousands of millions of unique, individual human beings in whom hundreds of beautiful characteristics are matched by hundreds of faults and negative tendencies. They must never be lumped together into homogeneous masses beneath a welter of hollow clichés and sterile words and then en bloc—as "classes," "nations," or "political forces"—extolled or denounced, loved or hated, maligned or glorified.

This is just one small example of the good that can come from treating words with caution. I have chosen the example especially for the occasion, i.e., for the moment when a Czech has the honor to address an audience that is overwhelmingly German.

In the beginning of everything is the word.   48

It is a miracle to which we owe the fact that we are human.

But at the same time it is a pitfall and a test, a snare and a trial.

More so, perhaps, than it appears to you who have enormous freedom of speech, and might therefore assume that words are not so important.

They are.   52

They are important everywhere.

The selfsame word can be humble at one moment and arrogant the next. And a humble word can be transformed quite easily and imperceptibly into an arrogant one, whereas it is a very difficult and protracted process to transform an arrogant word into one that is humble. I tried to demonstrate this by referring to the fate of the word *peace* in my country.

As we approach the end of the second millennium, the world, and particularly Europe, finds itself at a peculiar crossroads. It is a long time since there were so many grounds for hoping that everything will turn out well. At the same time, there have never been so many reasons for us to fear that if everything went wrong the catastrophe would be final.

It is not hard to demonstrate that all the main threats confronting   56
the world today, from atomic war and ecological disaster to social and civilizational catastrophe—by which I mean the widening gulf between rich and poor individuals and nations—have hidden within them just one root cause: the imperceptible transformation of what was originally a humble message into an arrogant one.

Arrogantly, Man started to believe that, as the pinnacle and lord of creation, he had a total understanding of nature and could do what he liked with it.

Arrogantly, he started to think that as the possessor of reason he was capable of understanding totally his own history and therefore of planning a life of happiness for all. This even gave him the right, in the name of an ostensibly better future for all—to which he had found the one and only key—to sweep from his path all those who did not fall for his plan.

Arrogantly he started to think that since he was capable of splitting the atom he was now so perfect that there was no longer any danger of nuclear arms rivalry, let alone nuclear war.

In all those cases he was fatally mistaken. That is bad. But in each   60
case he is already beginning to realize his mistake. And that is good.

Having learned all those lessons, we should all fight together against arrogant words and keep a weather eye out for any insidious germs of arrogance in words that are seemingly humble.

Obviously this is not just a linguistic task. Responsibility for and toward words is a task which is intrinsically ethical.

As such, however, it is situated beyond the horizon of the visible world, in that realm wherein dwells the Word that was in the beginning and is not the word of Man.

I won't explain why this is so. It has been explained far better than I 64 ever could by your great forebear Immanuel Kant.   *1989*

June Jordan

Nobody Mean More to Me than You[1] and the Future Life of Willie Jordan

Black English is not exactly a linguistic buffalo; as children, most of the thirty-five million Afro-Americans living here depend on this language for our discovery of the world. But then we approach our maturity inside a larger social body that will not support our efforts to become anything other than the clones of those who are neither our mothers nor our fathers. We begin to grow up in a house where every true mirror shows us the face of somebody who does not belong there, whose walk and whose talk will never look or sound "right," because that house was meant to shelter a family that is alien and hostile to us. As we learn our way around this environment, either we hide our original word habits, or we completely surrender our own voice, hoping to please those who will never respect anyone different from themselves: Black English is not exactly a linguistic buffalo, but we should understand its status as an endangered species, as a perishing, irreplaceable system of community intelligence, or we should expect its extinction, and, along with that, the extinguishing of much that constitutes our own proud, and singular identity.

What we casually call "English," less and less defers to England and its "gentlemen." "English" is no longer a specific matter of geography or an element of class privilege; more than thirty-three countries use this tool as a means of "intranational communication."[2] Countries as

---

[1]Black English aphorism crafted by Monica Morris, a Junior at S.U.N.Y. at Stony Brook, October, 1984.

[2]*English Is Spreading, But What Is English?* A presentation by Professor S. N. Sridahr, Dept. of Linguistics, S.U.N.Y. at Stonybrook, April 9, 1985: Dean's Conversation Among the Disciplines.

disparate as Zimbabwe and Malaysia, or Israel and Uganda, use it as their non-native currency of convenience. Obviously, this tool, this "English," cannot function inside thirty-three discrete societies on the basis of rules and values absolutely determined somewhere else, in a thirty-fourth other country, for example.

In addition to that staggering congeries of non-native users of English, there are five countries, or 333,746,000 people, for whom this thing called "English" serves as a native tongue.[3] Approximately ten percent of these native speakers of "English" are Afro-American citizens of the U.S.A. I cite these numbers and varieties of human beings dependent on "English" in order, quickly, to suggest how strange and how tenuous is any concept of "Standard English." Obviously, numerous forms of English now operate inside a natural, an uncontrollable, continuum of development. I would suppose "the standard" for English in Malaysia is not the same as "the standard" in Zimbabwe. I know that standard forms of English for Black people in this country do not copy that of whites. And, in fact, the structural differences between these two kinds of English have intensified, becoming more Black, or less white, despite the expected homogenizing effects of television[4] and other mass media.

Nonetheless, white standards of English persist, supreme and unquestioned, in these United States. Despite our multilingual population, and despite the deepening Black and white cleavage within that conglomerate, white standards control our official and popular judgments of verbal proficiency and correct, or incorrect, language skills, including speech. In contrast to India, where at least fourteen languages co-exist as legitimate Indian languages, in contrast to Nicaragua, where all citizens are legally entitled to formal school instruction in their regional or tribal languages, compulsory education in America compels accommodation to exclusively white forms of "English." White English, in America, is "Standard English."

4

This story begins two years ago. I was teaching a new course, "In Search of the Invisible Black Woman," and my rather large class seemed evenly divided between young Black women and men. Five or six white students also sat in attendance. With unexpected speed and enthusiasm we had moved through historical narratives of the 19th century to literature by and about Black women, in the 20th. I had assigned the first forty pages of Alice Walker's *The Color Purple*, and I came, eagerly, to class that morning:

[3]Ibid.
[4]*New York Times*, March 15, 1985, Section One, p. 14: Report on study by Linguistics at the University of Pennsylvania.

"So!" I exclaimed, aloud. "What did you think? How did you like it?" The students studied their hands, or the floor. There was no response. The tense, resistant feeling in the room fairly astounded me. At last, one student, a young woman still not meeting my eyes,   8 muttered something in my direction:

"What did you say?" I prompted her.

"Why she have them talk so funny. It don't sound right."

"You mean the language?"

Another student lifted his head: "It don't look right, neither. I 12 couldn't hardly read it."

At this, several students dumped on the book. Just about unanimously, their criticisms targeted the language. I listened to what they wanted to say and silently marvelled at the similarities between their casual speech patterns and Alice Walker's written version of Black English.

But I decided against pointing to these identical traits of syntax; I wanted not to make them self-conscious about their own spoken language—not while they clearly felt it was "wrong." Instead I decided to swallow my astonishment. Here was a negative Black reaction to a prize winning accomplishment of Black literature that white readers across the country had selected as a best seller. Black rejection was aimed at the one irreducibly Black element of Walker's work: the language—Celie's Black English. I wrote the opening lines of *The Color Purple* on the blackboard and asked the students to help me translate these sentences into Standard English:

> *You better not never tell nobody but God. It'd kill your mammy.*
> Dear God,
>   I am fourteen years old. I have always been a good girl. Maybe you can give me a sign letting me know what is happening to me.
>   Last spring after Little Lucious come I heard them fussing. He was pulling on her arm. She say it too soon, Fonso. I aint well. Finally he leave her alone. A week go by, he pulling on her arm again. She say, Naw, I ain't gonna. Can't you see I'm already half dead, an all of the children.[5]

Our process of translation exploded with hilarity and even hysterical, shocked laughter: The Black writer, Alice Walker, knew what she was doing! If rudimentary criteria for good fiction includes the manipulation of language so that the syntax and diction of sentences will tell you the identity of speakers, the probable age and sex and class of speakers, and even the locale—urban/rural/southern/western—then Walker had

[5]Alice Walker, *The Color Purple*, p. 11, Harcourt Brace, N.Y.

written, perfectly. This is the translation into Standard English that our
class produced:

Absolutely, one should never confide in anybody besides God. Your secrets could
prove devastating to your mother.
Dear God,
        I am fourteen years old. I have always been good. But now, could
you help me to understand what is happening to me?
        Last spring, after my little brother, Lucious, was born, I heard my
parents fighting. My father kept pulling at my mother's arm. But she
told him, "It's too soon for sex, Alfonso. I am still not feeling well."
Finally, my father left her alone. A week went by, and then he began
bothering my mother, again: Pulling her arm. She told him, "No, I
won't! Can't you see I'm already exhausted from all of these children?"

(Our favorite line was "It's too soon for sex, Alphonso.")
Once we could stop laughing, once we could stop our exponentially   16
wild improvisations on the theme of Translated Black English, the
students pushed me to explain their own negative first reactions to
their spoken language on the printed page. I thought it was probably
akin to the shock of seeing yourself in a photograph for the first time.
Most of the students had never before seen a written facsimile of the
way they talk. None of the students had ever learned how to read and
write their own verbal system of communication: Black English. Alternatively, this fact began to baffle or else bemuse and then infuriate my
students. Why not? Was it too late? Could they learn how to do it, now?
And, ultimately, the final test question, the one testing my sincerity:
Could I teach them? Because I had never taught anyone Black English
and, as far as I knew, no one, anywhere in the United States, had ever
offered such a course, the best I could say was "I'll try."

He looked like a wrestler.
He sat dead center in the packed room and, every time our eyes
met, he quickly nodded his head as though anxious to reassure, and
encourage, me.
Short, with strikingly broad shoulders and long arms, he spoke with
a surprisingly high, soft voice that matched the soft bright movement of
his eyes. His name was Willie Jordan. He would have seemed even more
unlikely in the context of Contemporary Women's Poetry, except that
ten or twelve other Black men were taking the course, as well. Still,
Willie was conspicuous. His extreme fitness, the muscular density of his
presence underscored the riveted, gentle attention that he gave to
anything anyone said. Generally, he did not join the loud and rowdy
dialogue flying back and forth, but there could be no doubt about his
interest in our discussions. And, when he stood to present an argument

he'd prepared, overnight, that nervous smile of his vanished and an irregular stammering replaced it, as he spoke with visceral sincerity, word by word.

That was how I met Willie Jordan. It was in between "In Search of 20 the Invisible Black Woman" and "The Art of Black English." I was waiting for Departmental approval and I supposed that Willie might be, so to speak, killing time until he, too, could study Black English. But Willie really did want to explore Contemporary Women's poetry and, to that end, volunteered for extra research and never missed a class.

Towards the end of that semester, Willie approached me for an independent study project on South Africa. It would commence the next semester. I thought Willie's writing needed the kind of improvement only intense practice will yield. I knew his intelligence was outstanding. But he'd wholeheartedly opted for "Standard English" at a rather late age, and the results were stilted and frequently polysyllabic, simply for the sake of having more syllables. Willie's unnatural formality of language seemed to me consistent with the formality of his research into South African apartheid. As he projected his studies, he would have little time, indeed, for newspapers. Instead, more than 90 percent of his research would mean saturation in strictly historical, if not archival, material. I was certainly interested. It would be tricky to guide him into a more confident and spontaneous relationship both with language and apartheid. It was going to be wonderful to see what happened when he could catch up with himself, entirely, and talk back to the world.

September, 1984: Breezy fall weather and much excitement! My class, "The Art of Black English," was full to the limit of the fire laws. And, in Independent Study, Willie Jordan showed up, weekly, fifteen minutes early for each of our sessions. I was pretty happy to be teaching, altogether!

I remember an early class when a young brother, replete with his ever present pork-pie hat, raised his hand and then told us that most of what he'd heard was "all right" except it was "too clean." "The brothers on the street," he continued, "they mix it up more. Like 'fuck' and 'motherfuck.' Or like 'shit.' " He waited. I waited. Then all of us laughed a good while, and we got into a brawl about "correct" and "realistic" Black English that led to Rule 1.

Rule 1: *Black English is about a whole lot more than mothafuckin.* 24

As a criterion, we decided, "realistic" could take you anywhere you want to go. Artful places. Angry places. Eloquent and sweetalkin places. Polemical places. Church. And the local Bar & Grill. We were checking out a language, not a mood or a scene or one guy's forgettable mouthing off.

It was hard. For most of the students, learning Black English required a fallback to patterns and rhythms of speech that many of their parents had beaten out of them. I mean *beaten*. And, in a majority of cases, correct Black English could be achieved only by striving for *incorrect* Standard English, something they were still pushing at, quite uncertainly. This state of affairs led to Rule 2.

Rule 2: *If it's wrong in Standard English it's probably right in Black English, or, at least, you're hot.*

It was hard. Roommates and family members ridiculed their stud-   28
ies, or remained incredulous, "You *studying* that shit? At school?" But we were beginning to feel the companionship of pioneers. And we decided that we needed another rule that would establish each one of us as equally important to our success. This was Rule 3.

Rule 3: *If it don't sound like something that come out somebody mouth then it don't sound right. If it don't sound right then it ain't hardly right. Period.*

This rule produced two weeks of compositions in which the students agonizingly tried to spell the sound of the Black English sentence they wanted to convey. But Black English is, preeminently, an oral/spoken means of communication. *And spelling don't talk.* So we needed Rule 4.

Rule 4: *Forget about the spelling. Let the syntax carry you.*

Once we arrived at Rule 4 we started to fly because syntax, the   32
structure of an idea, leads you to the world view of the speaker and reveals her values. The syntax of a sentence equals the structure of your consciousness. If we insisted that the language of Black English adheres to a distinctive Black syntax, then we were postulating a profound difference between white and Black people, *per se*. Was it a difference to prize or to obliterate?

There are three qualities of Black English—the presence of life, voice, and clarity—that testify to a distinctive Black value system that we became excited about and self-consciously tried to maintain.

1. Black English has been produced by a pre-technocratic, if not anti-technological, culture. More, our culture has been constantly threatened by annihilation or, at least, the swallowed blurring of assimilation. Therefore, our language is a system constructed by people constantly needing to insist that we exist, that we are present. Our language devolves from a culture that abhors all abstraction, or anything tending to obscure or delete the fact of the human being who is here and now/the truth of the person who is speaking or listening. Consequently, *there is no passive voice construction possible in Black English.* For example, you cannot say, "Black English is being eliminated." You must say, instead, "White people eliminating Black English." The assumption of the presence of life governs all of Black English. Therefore, overwhelmingly, *all action takes place in the language of the present indicative.*

And every sentence assumes the living and active participation of at least two human beings, the speaker and the listener.

2. A primary consequence of the person-centered values of Black English is the delivery of voice. If you speak or write Black English, your ideas will necessarily possess that otherwise elusive attribute, *voice*.

3. One main benefit following from the person-centered values of 36 Black English is that of *clarity*. If your idea, your sentence, assumes the presence of at least two living and active people, you will make it understandable because the motivation behind every sentence is the wish to say something real to somebody real.

As the weeks piled up, translation from Standard English into Black English or vice versa occupied a hefty part of our course work.

> Standard English (hereafter S.E.): "In considering the idea of studying Black English those questioned suggested—"
> (What's the subject? Where's the person? Is anybody alive in there, in that idea?)
> Black English (hereafter B.E.): "I been asking people what you think about somebody studying Black English and they answer me like this."

But there were interesting limits. You cannot "translate" instances of Standard English preoccupied with abstraction or with nothing/nobody evidently alive, into Black English. That would warp the language into uses antithetical to the guiding perspective of its community of users. Rather you must first change those Standard English sentences, themselves, into ideas consistent with the person-centered assumptions of Black English.

GUIDELINES FOR BLACK ENGLISH

1. Minimal number of words for every idea: This is the source for the aphoristic and/or poetic force of the language; eliminate every possible word.

2. Clarity: If the sentence is not clear it's not Black English.

3. Eliminate use of the verb *to be* whenever possible. This leads to 40 the deployment of more descriptive and therefore, more precise verbs.

4. Use *be* or *been* only when you want to describe a chronic, ongoing state of things.

> He *be* at the office, by 9. (He is always at the office by 9.)
> He *been* with her since forever.

5. Zero copula: Always eliminate the verb *to be* whenever it would combine with another verb, in Standard English.

S.E.: She is going out with him.
B.E.: She going out with him.

6. Eliminate *do* as in:

S.E.: What do you think? What do you want?
B.E.: What you think? What you want?

Rules number 3, 4, 5, and 6 provide for the use of the minimal 44
number of verbs per idea and, therefore, greater accuracy in the choice
of verb.

7. In general, if you wish to say something really positive, try to
formulate the idea using emphatic negative structure.

S.E.: He's fabulous.
B.E.: He bad.

8. Use double or triple negatives for dramatic emphasis.

S.E.: Tina Turner sings out of this world.
B.E.: Ain nobody sing like Tina.

9. Never use the *-ed* suffix to indicate the past tense of a verb.

S.E.: She closed the door.
B.E.: She close the door. Or, she have close the door.

10. Regardless of intentional verb time, only use the third person 48
singular, present indicative, for use of the verb *to have*, as an auxiliary.

S.E.: He had his wallet then he lost it.
B.E.: He have him wallet then he lose it.
S.E.: He had seen that movie.
B.E.: We seen that movie. Or, we have see that movie.

11. Observe a minimal inflection of verbs. Particularly, never
change from the first person singular forms to the third person singular.

S.E.: Present Tense Forms: He goes to the store.
B.E.: He go to the store.
S.E.: Past Tense Forms: He went to the store.
B.E.: He go to the store. Or, he gone to the store. Or, he been to the
     store.

12. The possessive case scarcely ever appears in Black English.
Never use an apostrophe ('s) construction. If you wander into a possessive case component of an idea, then keep logically consistent: ours, *his*,
theirs, mines. But, most likely, if you bump into such a component, you
have wandered outside the underlying world-view of Black English.

S.E.: He will take their car tomorrow.
B.E.: He taking they car tomorrow.

13. Plurality: Logical consistency, continued: If the modifier indicates plurality then the noun remains in the singular case.

S.E.: He ate twelve doughnuts.
B.E.: He eat twelve doughnut.
S.E.: She has many books.
B.E.: She have many book.

14. Listen for, or invent, special Black English forms of the past 52
tense, such as: "He losted it. That what she felted." If they are clear and
readily understood, then use them.

15. Do not hesitate to play with words, sometimes inventing them:
e.g. "astropotomous" means huge like a hippo plus astronomical and,
therefore, signifies real big.

16. In Black English, unless you keenly want to underscore the past
tense nature of an action, stay in the present tense and rely on the
overall context of your ideas for the conveyance of time and sequence.

17. Never use the suffix -ly form of an adverb in Black English.

S.E.: The rain came down rather quickly.
B.E.: The rain come down pretty quick.

18. Never use the indefinite article an in Black English. 56

S.E.: He wanted to ride an elephant.
B.E.: He want to ride him a elephant.

19. Invarient syntax: in correct Black English it is possible to formulate an imperative, an interogative, and a simple declarative idea with
the same syntax:

B.E.: You going to the store?
    You going to the store.
    You going to the store!

Where was Willie Jordan? We'd reached the mid-term of the semester. Students had formulated Black English guidelines, by consensus,
and they were now writing with remarkable beauty, purpose, and enjoyment:

I ain hardly speakin for everybody but myself so understan that.—Kim Parks

Samples from student writings:

Janie have a great big ole hole inside her. Tea Cake the only thing that
fit that hole . . .
    That pear tree beautiful to Janie, especial when bees fiddlin with
the blossomin pear there growin large and lovely. But personal
speakin, the love she get from starin at that tree ain the love what starin
back at her in them relationship. (Monica Morris)

Love is a big theme in, *They Eye Was Watching God.* Love show people new corners inside theyself. It pull out good stuff and stuff back bad stuff. . . Joe worship the doing uh his own hand and need other people to worship him too. But he ain't think about Janie that she a person and ought to live like anybody common do. Queen life not for Janie. (Monica Morris)

In both life and writin, Black womens have varietous experience of love that be cold like a iceberg or fiery like a inferno. Passion got for the other partner involve, man or woman, seem as shallow, ankle-deep water or the most profoundest abyss. (Constance Evans)

Family love another bond that ain't never break under no pressure. (Constance Evans)

You know it really cold / When the friend you / Always get out the fire / Act like they don't know you / When you in the heat. (Constance Evans)

Big classroom discussion bout love at this time. I never take no class where us have any long arguin for and against for two or three day. New to me and great. I find the class time talkin a million time more interestin than detail bout the book. (Kathy Esseks)

As these examples suggest, Black English no longer limited the students, in any way. In fact, one of them, Philip Garfield, would shortly "translate" a pivotal scene from Ibsen's *Doll House*, as his final term paper.

NORA: I didn't gived no shit. I thinked you a asshole back then, too, you make it so hard for me save mines husband life.
KROGSTAD: Girl, it clear you ain't any idea what you done. You done exact what once done, and I losed my reputation over it.
NORA: You asks me believe you once act brave save you wife life?
KROGSTAD: Law care less why you done it.
NORA: Law must suck.
KROGSTAD: Suck or no, if I wants, judge screw you wid dis paper.
NORA: No way, man. (Philip Garfield)

But where was Willie? Compulsively punctual, and always thor- 60 oughly prepared with neatly typed compositions, he had disappeared. He failed to show up for our regularly scheduled conference, and I received neither a note nor a phone call of explanation. A whole week went by. I wondered if Willie had finally been captured by the extremely current happenings in South Africa: passage of a new constitution that did not enfranchise the Black majority, and militant Black South African reaction to that affront. I wondered if he'd been hurt, somewhere. I wondered if the serious workload of weekly readings and writings had overwhelmed him and changed his mind about independent study. Where was Willie Jordan?

One week after the first conference that Willie missed, he called: "Hello, Professor Jordan? This is Willie. I'm sorry I wasn't there last week. But something has come up and I'm pretty upset. I'm sorry but I really can't deal right now."

I asked Willie to drop by my office and just let me see that he was okay. He agreed to do that. When I saw him I knew something hideous had happened. Something had hurt him and scared him to the marrow. He was all agitated and stammering and terse and incoherent. At last, his sadly jumbled account let me surmise, as follows: Brooklyn police had murdered his unarmed, twenty-five-year-old brother, Reggie Jordan. Neither Willie nor his elderly parents knew what to do about it. Nobody from the press was interested. His folks had no money. Police ran his family around and around, to no point. And Reggie was really dead. And Willie wanted to fight, but he felt helpless.

With Willie's permission I began to try to secure legal counsel for the Jordan family. Unfortunately Black victims of police violence are truly numerous while the resources available to prosecute their killers are truly scarce. A friend of mine at the Center for Constitutional Rights estimated that just the preparatory costs for bringing the cops into court normally approaches $180,000. Unless the execution of Reggie Jordan became a major community cause for organizing, and protest, his murder would simply become a statistical item.

Again, with Willie's permission, I contacted every newspaper and 64 media person I could think of. But the William Bastone feature article in *The Village Voice* was the only result from that canvassing.

Again, with Willie's permission, I presented the case to my class in Black English. We had talked about the politics of language. We had talked about love and sex and child abuse and men and women. But the murder of Reggie Jordan broke like a hurricane across the room.

There are few "issues" as endemic to Black life as police violence. Most of the students knew and respected and liked Jordan. Many of them came from the very neighborhood where the murder had occurred. All of the students had known somebody close to them who had been killed by police, or had known frightening moments of gratuitous confrontation with the cops. They wanted to do everything at once to avenge death. Number One: They decided to compose personal statements of condolence to Willie Jordan and his family written in Black English. Number Two: They decided to compose individual messages to the police, in Black English. These should be prefaced by an explanatory paragraph composed by the entire group. Number Three: These individual messages, with their lead paragraph, should be sent to *Newsday*.

The morning after we agreed on these objectives, one of the young women students appeared with an unidentified visitor, who sat through the class, smiling in a peculiar, comfortable way.

Now we had to make more tactical decisions. Because we wanted the   68 messages published, and because we thought it imperative that our outrage be known by the police, the tactical question was this: Should the opening, group paragraph be written in Black English or Standard English?

I have seldom been privy to a discussion with so much heart at the dead heat of it. I will never forget the eloquence, the sudden haltings of speech, the fierce struggle against tears, the furious throwaway, and useless explosions that this question elicited.

That one question contained several others, each of them extraordinarily painful to even contemplate. How best to serve the memory of Reggie Jordan? Should we use the language of the killers—Standard English—in order to make our ideas acceptable to those controlling the killers? But wouldn't what we had to say be rejected, summarily, if we said it in our own language, the language of the victim, Reggie Jordan? But if we sought to express ourselves by abandoning our language wouldn't that mean our suicide on top of Reggie's murder? But if we expressed ourselves in our own language wouldn't that be suicidal to the wish to communicate with those who, evidently, did not give a damn about us/Reggie/police violence in the Black community?

At the end of one of the longest, most difficult hours of my own life, the students voted, unanimously, to preface their individual messages with a paragraph composed in the language of Reggie Jordan. "*At least we don't give up nothing else. At least we stick to the truth: Be who we been. And stay all the way with Reggie.*"

It was heartbreaking to proceed, from that point. Everyone in the   72 room realized that our decision in favor of Black English had doomed our writings, even as the distinctive reality of our Black lives always has doomed our efforts to "be who we been" in this country.

I went to the blackboard and took down this paragraph, dictated by the class:

... YOU COPS!
WE THE BROTHER AND SISTER OF WILLIE JORDAN, A FEL-
LOW STONY BROOK STUDENT WHO THE BROTHER OF THE
DEAD REGGIE JORDAN. REGGIE, LIKE MANY BROTHER AND
SISTER, HE A VICTIM OF BRUTAL RACIST POLICE, OCTOBER 25,
1984. US APPALL, FED UP, BECAUSE THAT ANOTHER SENSELESS
DEATH WHAT OCCUR IN OUR COMMUNITY. THIS WHAT WE
FEEL, THIS, FROM OUR HEART, FOR WE AIN'T STAYIN' SILENT
NO MORE:

With the completion of this introduction, nobody said anything. I asked for comments. At this invitation, the unidentified visitor, a young Black man, ceaselessly smiling, raised his hand. He was, it so happens, a rookie cop. He had just joined the force in September and, he said, he thought he should clarify a few things. So he came forward and sprawled easily into a posture of barroom, or fireside, nostalgia:

"See," Officer Charles enlightened us, "Most times when you out on the street and something come down you do one of two things. Over-react or under-react. Now, if you under-react then you can get yourself kilt. And if you over-react then maybe you kill somebody. Fortunately it's about nine times out of ten and you will over-react. So the brother got kilt. And I'm sorry about that, believe me. But what you have to understand is what kilt him: Over-reaction. That's all. Now you talk about Black people and white police but see, now, I'm a cop myself. And (big smile) I'm Black. And just a couple months ago I was on the other side. But see it's the same for me. You a cop, you the ultimate authority: the Ultimate Authority. And you on the street, most of the time you can only do one of two things: over-react or under-react. That's all it is with the brother. Over-reaction. Didn't have nothing to do with race."

That morning Officer Charles had the good fortune to escape 76 without being boiled alive. But barely. And I remember the pride of his smile when I read about the fate of Black policemen and other collaborators, in South Africa. I remember him, and I remember the shock and palpable feeling of shame that filled the room. It was as though that foolish, and deadly, young man had just relieved himself of his foolish, and deadly, explanation, face to face with the grief of Reggie Jordan's father and Reggie Jordan's mother. Class ended quietly. I copied the paragraph from the blackboard, collected the individual messages and left to type them up.

Newsday rejected the piece.

The Village Voice could not find room in their "Letters" section to print the individual messages from the students to the police.

None of the tv news reporters picked up the story.

Nobody raised $180,000 to prosecute the murder of Reggie Jordan. 80

Reggie Jordan is really dead.

I asked Willie Jordan to write an essay pulling together everything important to him from that semester. He was still deeply beside himself with frustration and amazement and loss. This is what he wrote, unedited, and in its entirety:

Throughout the course of this semester I have been researching the effects of oppression and exploitation along racial lines in South Africa and its neighboring countries. I have become aware of South

African police brutalization of native Africans beyond the extent of
the law, even though the laws themselves are catalyst affliction upon
Black men, women and children. Many Africans die each year as a
result of the deliberate use of police force to protect the white power
structure.

Social control agents in South Africa, such as policemen, are also
used to force compliance among citizens through both overt and
covert tactics. It is not uncommon to find bold-faced coercion and
cold-blooded killings of Blacks by South African police for undeter-
mined and/or inadequate reasons. Perhaps the truth is that the only
reasons for this heinous treatment of Blacks rests in racial differences.
We should also understand that what is conveyed through the media is
not always accurate and may sometimes be construed as the tip of the
iceberg at best.

I recently received a painful reminder that racism, poverty, and
the abuse of power are global problems which are by no means unique
to South Africa. On October 25, 1984 at approximately 3:00 p.m. my
brother, Mr. Reginald Jordan, was shot and killed by two New York City
policemen from the 75th precinct in the East New York section of
Brooklyn. His life ended at the age of twenty-five. Even up to this
current point in time the Police Department has failed to provide my
family, which consists of five brothers, eight sisters, and two parents,
with a plausible reason for Reggie's death. Out of the many stories that
were given to my family by the Police Department, not one of them
seems to hold water. In fact, I honestly believe that the Police Department's assessment of my brother's murder is nothing short of ABSO-
LUTE BULLSHIT, and thus far no evidence had been produced to
alter perception of the situation.

Furthermore, I believe that one of three cases may have occurred
in this incident. First, Reggie's death may have been the desired outcome of the police officer's action, in which case the killing was
premeditated. Or, it was a case of mistaken identity, which clarifies the
fact that the two officers who killed my brother and their commanding
parties are all grossly incompetent. Or, both of the above cases are
correct, i.e., Reggie's murderers intended to kill him and the Police
Department behaved insubordinately.

Part of the argument of the officers who shot Reggie was that he
had attacked one of them and took his gun. This was their major claim.
They also said that only one of them had actually shot Reggie. The
facts, however, speak for themselves. According to the Death Certificate and autopsy report, Reggie was shot eight times from point-blank
range. The Doctor who performed the autopsy told me himself that
two bullets entered the side of my brother's head, four bullets were
sprayed into his back, and two bullets struck him in the back of his
legs. It is obvious that unnecessary force was used by the police and
that it is extremely difficult to shoot someone in his back when he is
attacking or approaching you.

After experiencing a situation like this and researching South Africa I believe that to a large degree, justice may only exist as rhetoric. I find it difficult to talk of true justice when the oppression of my people both at home and abroad attests to the fact that inequality and injustice are serious problems whereby Blacks and Third World people are perpetually short-changed by society. Something has to be done about the way in which this world is set up. Although it is a difficult task, we do have the power to make a change.

—Willie J. Jordan, Jr.
EGL 487, Section 58, November 14, 1984

It is my privilege to dedicate this book to the future life of Willie J. Jordan, Jr. *August 8, 1985*

33

The Power of Metaphor

George Lakoff and Mark Johnson,
From Metaphors We Live By
Susan Sontag, *From* AIDS and Its Metaphors

It is a great thing, indeed, to make a proper use of these poetical forms, as also of compounds and strange words. But the greatest thing by far is to be a master of metaphor. It is the one thing that cannot be learnt from others; and it is also a sign of genius, since a good metaphor implies an intuitive perception of the similarity in dissimilars.

Aristotle, from *Poetics*

Man has only one means to discovery, and that is to find *likenesses* between two things. To him, two trees are like two shouts and like two parents, and on this likeness he has built all mathematics. A lizard is like a bat and like a man, and on such likenesses he has built the theory of evolution and all biology. A gas behaves like a jostle of billiard balls, and on this and kindred likenesses rests much of our atomic picture of matter.

In looking for intelligibility in the world, we look for unity; and we find this (in the arts as well as in science) in its unexpected likenesses. This indeed is man's creative gift, to find or make a likeness where none was seen before—a likeness between mass and energy, a link between time and space, an echo of all our fears in the passion of Othello.

Jacob Bronowski, from *What Is Science?*

Through metaphor, the past has the capacity to imagine us, and we it. Through metaphorical concentration, doctors can imagine what it is to be their patients. Those who have no pain can imagine those who suffer. Those at the center can imagine what it is to be outside. The strong can imagine what it is to be weak. Illuminated lives can imagine the dark. Poets in their twilight can imagine the borders of stellar fire. We strangers can imagine the familiar hearts of strangers.

Cynthia Ozick, from *The Moral Necessity of Metaphor*

I will tell my brother about the time I took ten sacks of oranges into a school so that I could teach metaphor. The school was for special students—those who were socially or intellectually impaired. I had planned to have them peel the oranges as I spoke about how much the world is like the orange. I handed out the oranges. The students refused to peel them, not because they wanted to make life difficult for me— they were enchanted with the gift. One child asked if he could have an orange to take home to his little brother. Another said he would bring me ten dollars the next day if I would give him a sack of oranges. And I knew I was at home, that these children and I shared something that *makes* the leap of mind the metaphor attempts. And something in me healed.

Judy Ruiz, from *Oranges and Sweet Sister Boy*

George Lakoff and Mark Johnson
From Metaphors We Live By

Metaphor is for most people a device of the poetic imagination and the rhetorical flourish—a matter of extraordinary rather than ordinary language. Moreover, metaphor is typically viewed as characteristic of language alone, a matter of words rather than thought or action. For this reason, most people think they can get along perfectly well without metaphor. We have found, on the contrary, that metaphor is pervasive in everyday life, not just in langauge but in thought and action. Our ordinary conceptual system, in terms of which we both think and act, is fundamentally metaphorical in nature.

The concepts that govern our thought are not just matters of the intellect. They also govern our everyday functioning, down to the most mundane details. Our concepts structure what we perceive, how we get around in the world, and how we relate to other people. Our conceptual system thus plays a central role in defining our everyday realities. If we are right in suggesting that our conceptual system is largely metaphorical, then the way we think, what we experience, and what we do every day is very much a matter of metaphor.

But out conceptual system is not something we are normally aware of. In most of the little things we do every day, we simply think and act more or less automatically along certain lines. Just what these lines are is by no means obvious. One way to find out is by looking at language. Since communication is based on the same conceptual system that we use in thinking and acting, language is an important source of evidence for what that system is like.

Primarily on the basis of linguistic evidence, we have found that 4 most of our ordinary conceptual system is metaphorical in nature. And we have found a way to begin to identify in detail just what the metaphors are that structure how we perceive, how we think, and what we do.

To give some idea of what it could mean for a concept to be metaphorical and for such a concept to structure an everyday activity, let us start with the concept ARGUMENT and the conceptual metaphor ARGUMENT IS WAR. This metaphor is reflected in our everyday language by a wide variety of expressions:

ARGUMENT IS WAR

Your claims are *indefensible*.
He *attacked every weak point* in my argument.
His criticisms were *right on target*.
I *demolished* his argument.
I've never *won* an argument with him.
You disagree? Okay, *shoot!*
If you use that *strategy*, he'll *wipe you out*.
He *shot down* all of my arguments.

It is important to see that we don't just *talk* about arguments in terms of war. We can actually win or lose arguments. We see the person we are arguing with as an opponent. We attack his positions and we defend our own. We gain and lose ground. We plan and use strategies. If we find a position indefensible, we can abandon it and take a new line of attack. Many of the things we *do* in arguing are partially structured by the concept of war. Thought there is no physical battle, there is a verbal battle, and the structure of an argument—attack, defense, counter-attack, etc.—reflects this. It is in this sense that the ARGUMENT IS WAR metaphor is one that we live by in this culture; it structures the actions we perform in arguing.

Try to imagine a culture where arguments are not viewed in terms of war, where no one wins or loses, where there is no sense of attacking or defending, gaining or losing ground. Imagine a culture where an argument is viewed as a dance, the participants are seen as performers, and the goal is to perform in a balanced and aesthetically pleasing way. In such a culture, people would view arguments differently, experience them differently, carry them out differently, and talk about them differently. But *we* would probably not view them as arguing at all: they would simply be doing something different. It would seem strange even to call what they were doing "arguing." Perhaps the most neutral way of describing this difference between their culture and ours would be to say that we have a discourse form structured in terms of battle and they have one structured in terms of dance.

This is an example of what it means for a metaphorical concept, 8 namely, ARGUMENT IS WAR, to structure (at least in part) what we do and how we understand what we are doing when we argue. *The essence of metaphor is understanding and experiencing one kind of thing in terms of another*. It is not that arguments are a subspecies of war. Arguments and wars are different kinds of things—verbal discourse and armed conflict—and the actions performed are different kinds of actions. But ARGUMENT is partially structured, understood, performed, and talked about in terms of WAR. The concept is metaphorically structured, the activity is metaphorically structured, and, consequently, the language is metaphorically structured.

Moreover, this is the *ordinary* way of having an argument and talking about one. The normal way for us to talk about attacking a position is to use the words "attack a position." Our conventional ways of talking about arguments presuppose a metaphor we are hardly ever conscious of. The metaphor is not merely in the words we use—it is in our very concept of an argument. The language of argument is not poetic, fanciful, or rhetorical; it is literal. We talk about arguments that way because we conceive of them that way—and we act according to the way we conceive of things.

The most important claim we have made so far is that metaphor is not just a matter of language, that is, of mere words. We shall argue that, on the contrary, human *thought processes* are largely metaphorical. This is what we mean when we say that the human conceptual system is metaphorically structured and defined. Metaphors as linguistic expressions are possible precisely because there are metaphors in a person's conceptual system. Therefore, whenever . . . we speak of metaphors, such as ARGUMENT IS WAR, it should be understood that *metaphor* means *metaphorical concept*. . . .

We have been claiming that metaphors partially structure our everyday concepts and that this structure is reflected in our literal language. Before we can get an overall picture of the philosophical implications of these claims, we need a few more examples. In each of the ones that follow we give a metaphor and a list of ordinary expressions that are special cases of the metaphor. The English expressions are two sorts: simple literal expressions and idioms that fit the metaphor and are part of the normal everyday way of talking about the subject.

THEORIES (AND ARGUMENTS) ARE BUILDINGS

Is that the *foundation* for your theory? The theory needs more *support.* 12
The argument is *shaky.* We need some more facts or the argument will *fall apart.* We need to *construct* a *strong* argument for that. I haven't figured out yet what the *form* of the argument will be. Here are some more facts to *shore up* the theory. We need to *buttress* the theory with *solid* arguments. The theory will *stand* or *fall* on the *strength* of that argument. The argument *collapsed.* They *exploded* his latest theory. We will show that theory to be without *foundation.* So far we have put together only the *framework* of the theory.

IDEAS ARE FOOD

What he said *left a bad taste in my mouth.* All this paper has in it are *raw facts, half-baked ideas, and warmed-over theories.* There are too many facts here for me to *digest* them all. I just can't *swallow* that claim. That argument *smells fishy.* Let me *stew* over that for a while. Now there's a theory you can really *sink your teeth into.* We need to let that idea *percolate* for a while. That's *food for thought.* He's a *voracious* reader. We don't need to *spoon-feed* our students. He *devoured* the book. Let's let that idea *simmer on the back burner* for a while. This is the *meaty* part of the paper. Let that idea *jell* for a while. That idea has been *fermenting* for years.

With respect to life and death IDEAS ARE ORGANISMS, either PEOPLE OR PLANTS.

IDEAS ARE PEOPLE

The theory of relativity *gave birth to* an enormous number of ideas in physics. He is the *father* of modern biology. Whose *brainchild* was that? Look at what his ideas have *spawned.* Those ideas *died off* in the Middle Ages. His ideas will *live on* forever. Cognitive psychology is still in its *infancy.* That's an idea that ought to be *resurrected.* Where'd you *dig up* that idea? He *breathed new life into* that idea.

IDEAS ARE PLANTS

His ideas have finally come to *fruition.* That idea *died on the vine.* That's 16
a *budding* theory. It will take years for that idea to *come to full flower.* He views chemistry as a mere *offshoot* of physics. Mathematics has many

branches. The *seeds* of his great ideas were *planted* in his youth. She has a *fertile* imagination. Here's an idea that I'd like to *plant* in your mind. He has a *barren* mind.

IDEAS ARE PRODUCTS

We're really *turning* (*churning, cranking, grinding*) *out* new ideas. We've *generated* a lot of ideas this week. He *produces* new ideas at an astound-ing rate. His *intellectual productivity* has decreased in recent years. We need to *take the rough edges off* that idea, *hone it down, smooth it out*. It's a rough idea; it needs to be *refined*.

IDEAS ARE COMMODITIES

It's important how you *package* your ideas. He won't *buy* that. That idea just won't *sell*. There is always a *market* for good ideas. That's a *worthless* idea. He's been a source of *valuable* ideas. I wouldn't *give a plugged nickel for* that idea. Your ideas don't have a chance in the *intellectual market-place*.

IDEAS ARE RESOURCES

He *ran out of* ideas. Don't *waste* your thoughts on small projects. Let's *pool* our ideas. He's a *resourceful* man. We've *used up* all our ideas. That's a *useless* idea. That idea will *go a long way*.

IDEAS ARE MONEY

Let me put in my *two cents' worth*. He's *rich* in ideas. That book is a *treasure trove* of ideas. He has a *wealth* of ideas.

20

IDEAS ARE CUTTING INSTRUMENTS

That's an *incisive* idea. That *cuts right to the heart of* the matter. That was a *cutting* remark. He's *sharp*. He has a *razor* wit. He has a *keen* mind. She *cut* his argument *to ribbons*.

IDEAS ARE FASHIONS

That idea went *out of style* years ago. I hear sociobiology *is in* these days. Marxism is currently *fashionable* in western Europe. That idea is *old hat*! That's an *outdated* idea. What are the new *trends* in English criticism? *Old-fashioned* notions have no place in today's soceity. He keeps *up-to-date* by reading the New York Review of Books. Berkeley is a center of *avant-garde* thought. Semiotics has become quite *chic*. The idea of revolution is no longer *in vogue* in the United States. The transforma-tional grammar *craze* hit the United States in the mid-sixties and has just made it to Europe.

UNDERSTANDING IS SEEING; IDEAS ARE LIGHT-SOURCES; DISCOURSE IS A LIGHT-MEDIUM

I *see* what you're saying. It *looks* different from my *point of view*. What is your *outlook* on that? I *view* it differently. Now I've got the *whole picture*. Let me *point something out* to you. That's an *insightful* idea. That was a *brilliant* remark. The argument is *clear*. It was a *murky* discussion. Could you *elucidate* your remarks? It's a *transparent* argument. The discussion was *opaque*.

LOVE IS A PHYSICAL FORCE (ELECTROMAGNETIC, GRAVITATIONAL, ETC.)

I could feel the *electricity* between us. There were *sparks*. I was *magnet-*   24
ically drawn to her. They are uncontrollably *attracted* to each other. They
gravitated to each other immediately. His whole life *revolves* around her.
The *atmosphere* around them is always *charged*. There is incredible *energy*
in their relationship. They lost their *momentum*.

LOVE IS A PATIENT

This is a *sick* relationship. They have a *strong, healthy* marriage. The
marriage is *dead*—it can't be *revived*. Their marriage is *on the mend*.
We're getting *back on our feet*. Their relationship is *in really good shape*.
They've got a *listless* marriage. Their marriage is *on its last legs*. It's a *tired*
affair.

LOVE IS MADNESS

I'm *crazy* about her. She *drives me out of my mind*. He constantly *raves*
about her. He's gone *mad* over her. I'm just *wild* about Harry. I'm *insane*
about her.

LOVE IS MAGIC

She *cast her spell* over me. The *magic* is gone. I was *spellbound*. She had
me *hypnotized*. He has me *in a trance*. I was *entranced* by him. I'm *charmed*
by her. She is *bewitching*.

LOVE IS WAR

He is known for his many rapid *conquests*. She *fought for* him, but his   28
mistress *won out*. He *fled from* her *advances*. She *pursued* him *relentlessly*.
He is slowly *gaining ground* with her. He *won* her hand in marriage. He
overpowered her. She is *besieged* by suitors. He had to *fend* them *off*. He
enlisted the aid of her friends. He *made an ally* of her mother. Theirs is a
misalliance if I've ever seen one.

WEALTH IS A HIDDEN OBJECT

He's *seeking* his fortune. He's flaunting his *new-found* wealth. He's a
fortune-hunter. She's a *gold-digger*. He *lost* his fortune. He's *searching for*
wealth.

SIGNIFICANT IS BIG

He's a *big* man in the garment industry. He's a *giant* among writers.
That's the *biggest* idea to hit advertising in years. He's *head and shoulders
above* everyone in the industry. It was only a *small* crime. That was only
a *little* white lie. I was astounded at the *enormity* of the crime. That was
one of the *greatest* moments in World Series history. His accomplishments *tower over* those of *lesser* men.

SEEING IS TOUCHING; EYES ARE LIMBS

I can't *take* my eyes *off* her. He sits with his eyes *glued to* the TV. Her eyes *picked out* every detail of the pattern. Their eyes *met*. She never *moves* her eyes *from* his face. She *ran* her eyes *over* everything in the room. He wants everything *within reach of* his eyes.

THE EYES ARE CONTAINERS FOR THE EMOTIONS

I could see the fear *in* his eyes. His eyes were *filled* with anger. There was passion *in* her eyes. His eyes *displayed* his compassion. She couldn't *get* the fear out of her eyes. Love *showed* in his eyes. Her eyes *welled* with emotion.   32

EMOTIONAL EFFECT IS PHYSICAL CONTACT

His mother's death *hit* him *hard*. That idea *bowled me over*. She's a *knockout*. I was *struck* by his sincerity. That really *made an impression* on me. He *made his mark on* the world. I was *touched* by his remark. That *blew me away*.

PHYSICAL AND EMOTIONAL STATES ARE ENTITIES WITHIN A PERSON

He has a pain *in* his shoulder. Don't *give* me the flu. My cold has *gone from my head to my chest*. His pains *went away*. His depression *returned*. Hot tea and honey will *get rid of* your cough. He could barely *contain* his joy. The smile *left* his face. *Wipe* that sneer *off* your face, private! His fears *keep coming back*. I've got to *shake off* this depression—it keeps *hanging on*. If you've got a cold, drinking lots of tea will *flush it out* of your system. There isn't a *trace* of cowardice *in* him. He hasn't got *an honest bone in his body*.

VITALITY IS A SUBSTANCE

She's *brimming* with vim and vigor. She's *overflowing* with vitality. He's *devoid* of energy. I don't *have* any energy *left* at the end of the day. I'm *drained*. That *took a lot out of* me.

LIFE IS A CONTAINER

I've had a *full* life. Life is *empty* for him. There's *not much left* for him *in* life. Her life is *crammed* with activities. *Get the most out of* life. His life *contained* a great deal of sorrow. Live your life *to the fullest*.   36

LIFE IS A GAMBLING GAME

I'll *take my chances*. The *odds are against* me. I've got an *ace up my sleeve*. He's *holding all the aces*. It's a *toss-up*. If you *play your cards right*, you can do it. He *won big*. He's a real *loser*. Where is he when the *chips are down*? That's my *ace in the hole*. He's *bluffing*. The president is *playing it close to his vest*. Let's *up the ante*. Maybe we need to *sweeten the pot*. I think we should *stand pat*. That's *the luck of the draw*. Those are *high stakes*.

In this last group of examples we have a collection of what are called "speech formulas," or "fixed-form expressions," or "phrasal lexical items." These function in many ways like single words, and the language has thousands of them. In the examples given, a set of such phrasal lexical items is coherently structured by a single metaphorical concept. Although each of them is an instance of the LIFE IS A GAMBLING GAME metaphor, they are typically used to speak of life, not of gambling situations. They are normal ways of talking about life situations, just as using the word "construct" is a normal way of talking about theories. It is in this sense that we include them in what we have called literal expressions structured by metaphorical concepts. If you say "The odds are against us" or "We'll have to take our chances," you would not be viewed as speaking metaphorically but as using the normal everyday language appropriate to the situation. Nevertheless, your way of talking about, conceiving, and even experiencing your situation would be metaphorically structured.

1980

Susan Sontag

From AIDS and Its Metaphors

"Plague" is the principal metaphor by which the AIDS epidemic is understood. And because of AIDS, the popular misidentification of cancer as an epidemic, even a plague, seems to be receding: AIDS has banalized cancer.

Plague, from the Latin *plaga* (stroke, wound), has long been used metaphorically as the highest standard of collective calamity, evil, scourge—Procopius, in his masterpiece of calumny, *The Secret History*, called the Emperor Justinian worse than the plague ("fewer escaped")—as well as being a general name for many frightening diseases. Although the disease to which the word is permanently affixed produced the most lethal of recorded epidemics, being experienced as a pitiless slayer is not necessary for a disease to be regarded as plague-like. Leprosy, very rarely fatal now, was not much more so when at its greatest epidemic strength, between about 1050 and 1350. And syphilis has been regarded as a plague—Blake speaks of "the youthful Harlot's curse" that "blights with plagues the Marriage hearse"—not because it killed often, but because it was disgracing, disempowering, disgusting.

It is usually epidemics that are thought of as plagues. And these mass incidences of illness are understood as inflicted, not just endured.

Considering illness as a punishment is the oldest idea of what causes illness, and an idea opposed by all attention to the ill that deserves the noble name of medicine. Hippocrates, who wrote several treatises on epidemics, specifically ruled out "the wrath of God" as a cause of bubonic plague. But the illnesses interpreted in antiquity as punishments, like the plague in *Oedipus*, were not thought to be shameful, as leprosy and subsequently syphilis were to be. Diseases, insofar as they acquired meaning, were collective calamities, and judgments on a community. Only injuries and disabilities, not diseases, were thought of as individually merited. For an analogy in the literature of antiquity to the modern sense of a shaming, isolating disease, one would have to turn to Philoctetes and his stinking wound.

The most feared diseases, those that are not simply fatal but transform the body into something alienating, like leprosy and syphilis and cholera and (in the imagination of many) cancer, are the ones that seem particularly susceptible to promotion to "plague." Leprosy and syphilis were the first illnesses to be consistently described as repulsive. It was syphilis that, in the earliest descriptions by doctors at the end of the fifteenth century, generated a version of the metaphors that flourish around AIDS: of a disease that was not only repulsive and retributive but collectively invasive. Although Erasmus, the most influential European pedagogue of the early sixteenth century, described syphilis as "nothing but a kind of leprosy" (by 1529 he called it "something worse than leprosy"), it had already been understood as something different, because sexually transmitted. Paracelsus speaks (in Donne's paraphrase) of "that foule contagious disease which then had invaded mankind in a few places, and since overflowes in all, that for punishment of generall licentiousnes God first inflicted that disease." Thinking of syphilis as a punishment for an individual's transgression was for a long time, virtually until the disease became easily curable, not really distinct from regarding it as retribution for the licentiousness of a community—as with AIDS now, in the rich industrial countries. In contrast to cancer, understood in a modern way as a disease incurred by (and revealing of) individuals, AIDS is understood in a premodern way, as a disease incurred by people both as individuals and as members of a "risk group"—that neutral-sounding, bureaucratic category which also revives the archaïc idea of a tainted community that illness has judged.

Not every account of plague or plague-like diseases, of course, is a vehicle for lurid stereotypes about illness and the ill. The effort to think critically, historically, about illness (about disaster generally) was attempted throughout the eighteenth century: say, from Defoe's *A Journal of the Plague Year* (1722) to Alessandro Manzoni's *The Betrothed* (1827). Defoe's historical fiction, purporting to be an eyewitness account of bubonic plague in London in 1665, does not further any understanding of the plague as punishment or, a later part of the script, as a transforming experience. And Manzoni, in his lengthy account of the passage of plague through the duchy of Milan in 1630, is avowedly committed to presenting a more accurate, less reductive view than his historical sources. But even these two complex narratives reinforce some of the perennial, simplifying ideas about plague.

One feature of the usual script for plague: The disease invariably comes from somewhere else. The names for syphilis, when it began its epidemic sweep through Europe in the last decade of the fifteenth century, are an exemplary illustration of the need to make a dreaded disease foreign.[1] It was the "French pox" to the English, *morbus Germanicus* to the Parisians, the Naples sickness to the Florentines, the Chinese disease to the Japanese. But what may seem like a joke about the inevitability of chauvinism reveals a more important truth: that there is a link between imagining disease and imagining foreignness. It lies perhaps in the very concept of wrong, which is archaically identical with the non-us, the alien. A polluting person is always wrong, as Mary Douglas has observed. The inverse is also true: A person judged to be wrong is regarded as, at least potentially, a source of pollution.

The foreign place of origin of important illnesses, as of drastic changes in the weather, may be no more remote than a neighboring country. Illness is a species of invasion, and indeed is often carried by soldiers. Manzoni's account of the plague of 1630 (chapters 31 to 37) begins:

> The plague which the Tribunal of Health had feared might enter the Milanese provinces with the German troops had in fact entered, as is well known; and it is also well known that it did not stop there, but went on to invade and depopulate a large part of Italy.

[1]As noted in the first accounts of the disease: "This malady received from different peoples whom it affected different names," writes Giovanni di Vigo in 1514. Like earlier treatises on syphilis, written in Latin—by Nicolo Leoniceno (1497) and by Juan Almenar (1502)—the one by di Vigo calls it *morbus Gallicus*, the French disease. (Excerpts from this and other accounts of the period, including *Syphilis: Or a Poetical History of the French Disease* [1530] by Girolamo Fracastoro, who coined the name that prevailed, are in *Classic Descriptions of Disease*, edited by Ralph H. Major [1932].) Moralistic explanations abounded from the beginning. In 1495, a year after the epidemic started, the Emperor Maximilian issued an edict declaring syphilis to be an affliction from God for the sins of men.

The theory that syphilis came from even farther than a neighboring country, that it was an entirely new disease in Europe, a disease of the New World brought back to the Old by sailors of Columbus who had contracted it in America, became the accepted explanation of the origin of syphilis in the sixteenth century and is still widely credited. It is worth noting that the earliest medical writers on syphilis did not accept the dubious theory. Leoniceno's *Libellus de Epidemia, quam vulgo morbum Gallicum vocant* starts by taking up the question of whether "the French disease under another name was common to the ancients," and says he believes firmly that it was.

Defoe's chronicle of the plague of 1665 begins similarly, with a flurry of ostentatiously scrupulous speculation about its foreign origin:

> It was about the beginning of September, 1664, that I, among the rest of my neighbours, heard in ordinary discourse that the plague was returned again in Holland; for it had been very violent there, and particularly at Amsterdam and Rotterdam, in the year 1663, whither, they say, it was brought, some said from Italy, others from the Levant, among some goods which were brought home by their Turkey fleet; others said it was brought from Candia; others from Cyprus. It mattered not from whence it came; but all agreed it was come into Holland again.

The bubonic plague that reappeared in London in the 1720s had arrived from Marseilles, which was where plague in the eighteenth century was usually thought to enter Western Europe: brought by seamen, then transported by soldiers and merchants. By the nineteenth century the foreign origin was usually more exotic, the means of transport less specifically imagined, and the illness itself had become phantasmagorical, symbolic.

At the end of *Crime and Punishment* Raskolnikov dreams of plague: 8 "He dreamt that the whole world was condemned to a terrible new strange plague that had come to Europe from the depths of Asia." At the beginning of the sentence it is "the whole world,"which turns out by the end of the sentence to be "Europe," afflicted by a lethal visitation from Asia. Dostoevsky's model is undoubtedly cholera, called Asiatic cholera, long endemic in Bengal, which had rapidly become and remained through most of the nineteenth century a worldwide epidemic disease. Part of the centuries-old conception of Europe as a privileged cultural entity is that it is a place which is colonized by lethal diseases coming from elsewhere. Europe is assumed to be by rights free of disease. (And Europeans have been astoundingly callous about the far more devastating extent to which they—as invaders, as colonists—have introduced *their* lethal diseases to the exotic, "primitive" world: Think of the ravages of smallpox, influenza, and cholera on the aboriginal populations of the Americas and Australia.) The tenacity of the connection of exotic origin with dreaded disease is one reason why cholera, of which there were four great outbreaks in Europe in the nineteenth century, each with a lower death toll than the preceding one, has continued to be more memorable than smallpox, whose ravages increased as the century went on (half a million died in the European smallpox pandemic of the early 1870s) but which could not be construed as, plague-like, a disease with a non-European origin.

Plagues are no longer "sent," as in Biblical and Greek antiquity, for the question of agency has blurred. Instead, peoples are "visited" by plagues. And the visitations recur, as is taken for granted in the subtitle of Defoe's narrative, which explains that it is about that "which happened in London during the Last Great Visitation in 1665." Even for non-Europeans, lethal disease may be called a visitation. But a visitation on "them" is invariably described as different from one on "us." "I believe that about one half of the whole people was carried off by this visitation," wrote the English traveler Alexander Kinglake, reaching Cairo at a time of the bubonic plague (sometimes called "oriental plague"). "The Orientals, however, have more quiet fortitude than Europeans under afflictions of this sort." Kinglake's influential book *Eothen* (1844)—suggestively subtitled "Traces of Travel Brought Home from the East"—illustrates many of the enduring Eurocentric presumptions about others, starting from the fantasy that peoples with little reason to expect exemption from misfortune have a lessened capacity to *feel* misfortune. Thus it is believed that Asians (or the poor, or blacks, or Africans, or Moslems) don't suffer or don't grieve as Europeans (or whites) do. The fact that illness is associated with the poor—who are, from the perspective of the privileged, aliens in one's midst—reinforces the association of illness with the foreign: with an exotic, often primitive place.

Thus, illustrating the classic script for plague, AIDS is thought to have started in the "dark continent," then spread to Haiti, then to the United States and to Europe, then . . . It is understood as a tropical disease: another infestation from the so-called Third World, which is after all where most people in the world live, as well as a scourge of the *tristes tropiques*. Africans who detect racist stereotypes in much of the speculation about the geographical origin of AIDS are not wrong. (Nor are they wrong in thinking that depictions of Africa as the cradle of AIDS must feed anti-African prejudices in Europe and Asia.) The subliminal connection made to notions about a primitive past and the many hypotheses that have been fielded about possible transmission from animals (a disease of green monkeys? African swine fever?) cannot help but activate a familiar set of stereotypes about animality, sexual license, and blacks. In Zaire and other countries in Central Africa where AIDS is killing tens of thousands, the counterreaction has begun. Many doctors, academics, journalists, government officials, and other educated people believe that the virus was sent to Africa from the United States, an act of bacteriological warfare (whose aim was to decrease the African birth rate) which got out of hand and has returned to afflict its perpetrators. A common African version of this belief about the disease's provenance has the virus fabricated in a CIA–Army laboratory in Maryland, sent from there to Africa, and brought back to its country of origin by American homosexual missionaries returning from Africa to Maryland.[2]

At first it was assumed that AIDS must become widespread elsewhere in the same catastrophic form in which it has emerged in Africa, and those who still think this will eventually happen invariably invoke the Black Death. The plague metaphor is an essential vehicle of the most pessimistic reading of the epidemiological prospects. From classic fiction to the latest journalism, the standard plague story is of inexorability, inescapability. The unprepared are taken by surprise; those observing the recommended precautions are struck down as well. *All* succumb when the story is told by an omniscient narrator, as in Poe's parable "The Masque of the Red Death" (1842), inspired by an account of a ball held in Paris during the cholera epidemic of 1832. Almost all— if the story is told from the point of view of a traumatized witness, who will be a benumbed survivor, as in Jean Giono's Stendhalian novel *Horseman on the Roof* (1951), in which a young Italian nobleman in exile wanders through cholera-stricken southern France in the 1830s.

Plagues are invariably regarded as judments on society, and the   12 metaphoric inflation of AIDS into such a judgment also accustoms people to the inevitability of global spread. This is a traditional use of sexually transmitted diseases: to be described as punishments not just of individuals but of a group ("generall licentiousnes"). Not only vene- real diseases have been used in this way, to identify transgressing or vicious populations. Interpreting any catastrophic epidemic as a sign of moral laxity or political decline was as common until the later part of the last century as associating dreaded diseases with foreignness. (Or with despised and feared minorities.) And the assignment of fault is not contradicted by cases that do not fit. The Methodist preachers in En-

---

[2]The rumor may not have originated as a KGB-sponsored "disinformation" campaign, but it received a crucial push from Soviet propaganda specialists. In October 1985 the Soviet weekly *Literaturnaya Gazeta* published an article alleging that the AIDS virus had been engineered by the U.S. government during biological-warfare research at Fort Detrick, Maryland, and was being spread abroad by U.S. servicemen who had been used as guinea pigs. The source cited was an article in the Indian newspaper *Patriot*. Repeated on Moscow's "Radio Peace and Progress" in English, the story was taken up by newspapers and magazines throughout the world. A year later it was featured on the front page of London's conservative, mass-circulation *Sunday Express*. ("The killer AIDS virus was ar- tificially created by American scientists during laboratory experiments which went disas- trously wrong—and a massive cover-up has kept the secret from the world until today.") Though ignored by most American newspapers, the *Sunday Express* story was recycled in virtually every other country. As recently as the summer of 1987, it appeared in news- papers in Kenya, Peru, Sudan, Nigeria, Senegal, and Mexico. Gorbachev-era policies have since produced an official denial of the allegations by two eminent members of the Soviet Academy of Sciences, which was published in *Izvestia* in late October 1987. But the story is still being repeated—from Mexico to Zaire, from Australia to Greece.

gland who connected the cholera epidemic of 1832 with drunkenness (the temperance movement was just starting) were not understood to be claiming that *everybody* who got cholera was a drunkard: There is always room for "innocent victims" (children, young women). Tuberculosis, in its identity as a disease of the poor (rather than of the "sensitive"), was also linked by late-nineteenth-century reformers to alcoholism. Re-sponses to illnesses associated with sinners and the poor invariably recommended the adoption of middle-class values: the regular habits, productivity, and emotional self-control to which drunkenness was thought the chief impediment.[3] Health itself was eventually identified with these values, which were religious as well as mercantile, health being evidence of virtue as disease was of depravity. The dictum that cleanliness is next to godliness is to be taken quite literally. The succes-sion of cholera epidemics in the nineteenth century shows a steady waning of religious interpretations of the disease; more precisely, these increasingly coexisted with other explanations. Although, by the time of the epidemic of 1866, cholera was commonly understood not simply as a divine punishment but as the consequence of remediable defects of sanitation, it was still regarded as the scourge of the sinful. A writer in the *New York Times* declared (April 22, 1866): "Cholera is especially the punishment of neglect of sanitary laws; it is the curse of the dirty, the intemperate, and the degraded."[4]

That it now seems unimaginable for cholera or a similar disease to be regarded in this way signifies not a lessened capacity to moralize about diseases but only a change in the kind of illnesses that are used didactically. Cholera was perhaps the last major epidemic disease fully qualifying for plague status for almost a century. (I mean cholera as a European and American, therefore a nineteenth-century, disease; until 1817 there had never been a cholera epidemic outside the Far East.) Influenza, which would seem more plague-like than any other epidemic in this century if loss of life were the main criterion, and which struck as suddenly as cholera and killed as quickly, usually in a few days, was never viewed metaphorically as a plague. Nor was a more recent epi-demic, polio. One reason why plague notions were not invoked is that these epidemics did not have enough of the attributes perenially as-cribed to plagues. (For instance, polio was construed as typically a

[3]According to the more comprehensive diagnosis favored by secular reformers, cholera was the result of poor diet and "indulgence in irregular habits." Officials of the Central Board of Health in London warned that there were no specific treatments for the disease, and advised paying attention to fresh air and cleanliness, though "the true preventatives are a healthy body and a cheerful, unruffled mind." Quoted in R. J. Morris, *Cholera 1832* (1976).

[4]Quoted in Charles E. Rosenberg, *The Cholera Years: The United States in 1832, 1849, and 1866* (1962).

disease of children—of the innocent.) The more important reason is that there has been a shift in the focus of the moralistic exploitation of illness. This shift, to diseases that can be interpreted as judgments on the individual, makes it harder to use epidemic disease as such. For a long time cancer was the illness that best fitted this secular culture's need to blame and punish and censor through the imagery of disease. Cancer was a disease of an individual, and understood as the result not of an action but rather of a failure to act (to be prudent, to exert proper self-control, or to be properly expressive). In the twentieth century it has become almost impossible to moralize about epidemics—except those which are transmitted sexually.

The persistence of the belief that illness reveals, and is a punishment for, moral laxity or turpitude can be seen in another way, by noting the persistence of descriptions of disorder or corruption as a disease. So indispensable has been the plague metaphor in bringing summary judgments about social crisis that its use hardly abated during the era when collective diseases were no longer treated so moralistically—the time between the influenza and encephalitis pandemics of the early and mid-1920s and the acknowledgment of a new, mysterious epidemic illness in the early 1980s—and when great infectious epidemics were so often and confidently proclaimed a thing of the past.[5] The plague metaphor was common in the 1930s as a synonym for social and psychic catastrophe. Evocations of plague of this type usually go with rant, with antiliberal attitudes: Think of Artaud on theater and plague, of Wilhelm Reich on "emotional plague." And such a generic "diagnosis" necessarily promotes antihistorical thinking. A theodicy as well as a demonology, it not only stipulates something emblematic of evil but makes this the bearer of a rough, terrible justice. In Karel Čapek's *The White Plague* (1937), the loathsome pestilence that has appeared in a state where fascism has come to power afflicts only those over the age of forty, those who could be held morally responsible.

Written on the eve of the Nazi takeover of Czechoslovakia, Čapek's allegorical play is something of an anomaly—the use of the plague metaphor to convey the menace of what is defined as barbaric by a mainstream European liberal. The play's mysterious, grisly malady is something like leprosy, a rapid, invariably fatal leprosy that is supposed to have come, of course, from Asia. But Čapek is not interested in identifying political evil with the incursion of the foreign. He scores his

[5]As recently as 1983, the historian William H. McNeill, author of *Plagues and Peoples*, started his review of a new history of the Black Death by asserting: "One of the things that separate us from our ancestors and make contemporary experience profoundly different from that of other ages is the disappearance of epidemic disease as a serious factor in human life" (*The New York Review of Books*, July 21, 1983). The Eurocentric presumption of this and many similar statements hardly needs pointing out.

didactic points by focusing not on the disease itself but on the management of information about it by scientists, journalists, and politicians.
The most famous specialist in the disease harangues a reporter ("The
disease of the hour, you might say. A good five million have died of it to
date, twenty million have it and at least three times as many are going
about their business, blithely unaware of the marble-like, marble-sized
spots on their bodies"); chides a fellow doctor for using the popular
terms, "the white plague" and "Peking leprosy," instead of the scientific
name, "the Cheng Syndrome"; fantasizes about how his clinic's work on
identifying the new virus and finding a cure ("every clinic in the world
has an intensive research program") will add to the prestige of science
and win a Nobel Prize for its discoverer; revels in hyperbole when it is
thought a cure has been found ("it was the most dangerous disease in all
history, worse than the bubonic plague"); and outlines plans for sending
those with symptoms to well-guarded detention camps ("Given that
every carrier of the disease is a potential spreader of the disease, we
must protect the uncontaminated from the contaminated. All sentimentality in this regard is fatal and therefore criminal"). However car-
toonish Čapek's ironies may seem, they are a not improbable sketch of
catastrophe (medical, ecological) as a managed public event in modern
mass society. And however conventionally he deploys the plague metaphor, as an agency of retribution (in the end the plague strikes down the
dictator himself), Čapek's feel for public relations leads him to make
explicit in the play the understanding of disease *as* a metaphor. The
eminent doctor declares the accomplishments of science to be as
nothing compared with the merits of the dictator, about to launch a war,
"who has averted a far worse scourge: the scourge of anarchy, the
leprosy of corruption, the epidemic of barbaric liberty, the plague of
social disintegration fatally sapping the organism of our nation."

Camus's *The Plague*, which appeared a decade later, is a far less [16]
literal use of plague by another great European liberal, as subtle as
Čapek's *The White Plague* is schematic. Camus's novel is not, as is sometimes said, a political allegory in which the outbreak of bubonic plague
in a Mediterranean port city represents the Nazi occupation. This
plague is not retributive. Camus is not protesting anything, not corruption or tyranny, not even mortality. The plague is no more or less than
an exemplary event, the irruption of death that gives life its seriousness.
His use of plague, more epitome than metaphor, is detached, stoic,
aware—it is not about bringing judgment. But, as in Čapek's play,
characters in Camus's novel declare how unthinkable it is to have a
plague in the twentieth century . . . as if the belief that such a calamity
could not happen, could not happen *anymore*, means that it must.

The emergence of a new catastrophic epidemic, when for several
decades it had been confidently assumed that such calamities belonged

to the past, would not be enough to revive the moralistic inflation of an epidemic into a "plague." It was necessary that the epidemic be one whose most common means of transmission is sexual.

Cotton Mather called syphilis a punishment "which the Just Judgment of God has reserved for our Late Ages." Recalling this and other nonsense uttered about syphilis from the end of the fifteenth to the early twentieth centuries, one should hardly be surprised that many want to view AIDS metaphorically—as, plague-like, a moral judgment on society. Professional fulminators can't resist the rhetorical opportunity offered by a sexually transmitted disease that is lethal. Thus, the fact that AIDS is predominantly a heterosexually transmitted illness in the countries where it first emerged in epidemic form has not prevented such guardians of public morals as Jesse Helms and Norman Podhoretz from depicting it as a visitation specially aimed at (and deservedly incurred by) Western homosexuals, while another Reagan-era celebrity, Pat Buchanan, orates about "AIDS and Moral Bankruptcy," and Jerry Falwell offers the generic diagnosis that "AIDS is God's judgment on a society that does not live by His rules." What is surprising is not that the AIDS epidemic has been exploited in this way but that such cant has been confined to so predictable a sector of bigots; the official discourse about AIDS invariably includes admonitions against bigotry.

The pronouncements of those who claim to speak for God can mostly be discounted as the rhetoric regularly prompted by sexually transmitted illness—from Cotton Mather's judgment to recent statements by two leading Brazilian clerics, Bishop Falcão of Brasilia, who declares AIDS to be "the consequence of moral decadence," and the Cardinal of Rio de Janeiro, Eugenio Sales, who wants it both ways, describing AIDS as "God's punishment" and as "the revenge of nature." More interesting, because their purposes are more complex, are the secular sponsors of this sort of invective. Authoritarian political ideologies have a vested interest in promoting fear, a sense of the imminence of takeover by aliens—and real diseases are useful material. Epidemic diseases usually elicit a call to ban the entry of foreigners, immigrants. And xenophobic propaganda has always depicted immigrants as bearers of disease (in the late nineteenth century: cholera, yellow fever, typhoid fever, tuberculosis). It seems logical that the political figure in France who represents the most extreme nativist, racist views, Jean-Marie Le Pen, has attempted a strategy of fomenting fear of this new alien peril, insisting that AIDS is not just infectious but contagious, and calling for mandatory nationwide testing and the quarantine of everyone carrying the virus. And AIDS is a gift to the present regime in South Africa, whose Foreign Minister declared recently, evoking the incidence of the illness among the mine workers imported from neighboring all-

black countries: "The terrorists are now coming to us with a weapon
more terrible than Marxism: AIDS."

The AIDS epidemic serves as an ideal projection for First World   20
political paranoia. Not only is the so-called AIDS virus the quintessential invader from the Third World. It can stand for any mythological
menace. In this country, AIDS has so far evoked less pointedly racist
reactions than in Europe, including the Soviet Union, where the African
origin of the disease is stressed. Here it is as much a reminder of
feelings associated with the menace of the Second World as it is an
image of being overrun by the Third. Predictably, the public voices in
this country most committed to drawing moral lessons from the AIDS
epidemic, such as Norman Podhoretz, are those whose main theme is
worry about America's will to maintain its bellicosity, its expenditures
on armaments, its firm anti-Communist stance, and who find everywhere evidence of the decline of American political and imperial
authority. Denunciations of "the gay plague" are part of a much larger
complaint, common among antiliberals in the West and many exiles
from the Russian bloc, about contemporary permissiveness of all kinds:
a now-familiar diatribe against the "soft" West, with its hedonism, its
vulgar sexy music, its indulgence in drugs, its disabled family life, which
have sapped the will to stand up to communism. AIDS is a favorite
concern of those who translate their political agenda into questions of
group psychology: of national self-esteem and self-confidence. Although these specialists in ugly feelings insist that AIDS is a punishment for deviant sex, what moves them is not just, or even principally,
homophobia. Even more important is the utility of AIDS in pursuing
one of the main activities of the so-called neoconservatives, the Kultur-
kampf against all that is called, for short (and inaccurately), the 1960s.
A whole politics of "the will"—of intolerance, of paranoia, of fear of
political weakness—has fastened on this disease.

AIDS is such an apt goad to familiar, consensus-building fears that
have been cultivated for several generations, like fear of "subversion"—
and to fears that have surfaced more recently, of uncontrollable pollution and of unstoppable migration from the Third World—that it would
seem inevitable that AIDS be envisaged in this society as something
total, civilization-threatening. And raising the disease's metaphorical
stature by keeping alive fears of its easy transmissibility, its imminent
spread, does not diminish its status as, mainly, a consequence of illicit
acts (or of economic and cultural backwardness). That it is a punishment for deviant behavior and that it threatens the innocent—these two
notions about AIDS are hardly in contradiction. Such is the extraordinary potency and efficacy of the plague metaphor: It allows a disease to
be regarded both as something incurred by vulnerable "others" and as
(potentially) everyone's disease.

Still, it is one thing to emphasize how the disease menaces every-body (in order to incite fear and confirm prejudice), quite another to argue (in order to defuse prejudice and reduce stigma) that eventually AIDS will, directly or indirectly, affect everybody. Recently these same mythologists who have been eager to use AIDS for ideological mobiliza-tion against deviance have backed away from the most panic-inspiring estimates of the illness. They are among the most vocal of those who insist that infection will *not* spread to "the general population" and have turned their attention to denouncing "hysteria" or "frenzy" about AIDS. Behind what they now consider the excessive publicity given the disease, they discern the desire to placate an all-powerful minority by agreeing to regard "their" disease as "ours"—further evidence of the sway of nefarious "liberal" values and of America's spiritual decline. Making AIDS everyone's problem and therefore a subject on which everyone needs to be educated, charge the antiliberal AIDS mytholo-gists, subverts our understanding of the difference between "us" and "them"; indeed, exculpates or at least makes irrelevant moral judg-ments about "them." (In such rhetoric the disease continues to be identified almost exclusively with homosexuality, and specifically the practice of sodomy.) "Has America become a country where classroom discussion of the Ten Commandments is impermissible but teacher instructions in safe sodomy are to be mandatory?" inquires Pat Bu-chanan, protesting the "foolish" proposal made in the report of the recent Presidential Commission on the epidemic, chaired by Admiral Watkins, to outlaw discrimination against people with AIDS. Not the disease but the appeals heard from the most official quarters "to set aside prejudice and fear in favor of compassion" (the words of the Watkins Report) have become a principal target, suggesting as they do a weakening of this society's power (or willingness) to punish and segre-gate through judgments about sexual behavior.

More than cancer, but rather like syphilis, AIDS seems to foster ominous fantasies about a disease that is a marker of both individual and social vulnerabilities. The virus invades the body; the disease (or, in the newer version, the fear of the disease) is described as invading the whole society. In late 1986 President Reagan pronounced AIDS to be spreading—"insidiously" of course—"through the length and breadth of our society."[6] But AIDS, while the pretext for expressing dark intima-tions about the body politic, has yet to seem credible as a political

---

[6]Reagan's affirmation through cliché of the frightening reality of a disease of other people contrasts with his more original denial of the reality of his own illness. When asked how he felt after his cancer operation, he declared: "I didn't have cancer. I had something inside of me that had cancer in it and it was removed."

metaphor for internal enemies, even in France, where AIDS—in French *le sida*—was quickly added to the store of political invective. Le Pen has dismissed some of his opponents as "AIDS-ish" (*sidatique*), and the antiliberal polemicist Louis Pauwels said that lycée students on strike last year were suffering from "mental AIDS" (*sont atteint d'un sida mental*). Neither has AIDS proved of much use as a metaphor for international political evil. True, Jeane Kirkpatrick once couldn't resist comparing international terrorism to AIDS, but such sallies are rare—perhaps because for that purpose the cancer metaphor has proved so fecund.

This doesn't mean that AIDS is not used, preposterously, as a   24 metaphor, but only that AIDS has a metaphoric potential different from that of cancer. When the movie director in Alain Tanner's film *La Vallée Fantôme* (1987) muses, "Cinema is like a cancer," and then corrects himself, "No, it's infectious, it's more like AIDS," the comparison seems lumberingly self-conscious as well as a decided underuse of AIDS. Not its infectiousness but its characteristic latency offers a more distinctive use of AIDS as a metaphor. Thus, the Palestinian Israeli writer Anton Shammas in the Jerusalem weekly *Ko Ha'ir*, in a fit of medical, sexual, and political fantasy, recently described Israel's Declaration of Independence of 1948 as

> the AIDS of "the Jewish State in the Land of Israel," whose long incubation has produced Gush Emunim and . . . [Rabbi Meir] Kahane. That is where it all began, and that is where it all will end. AIDS, I am sorry to say, despite my sympathy for homosexuals, affects mainly monoerotics, and a mononational Jewish State contains by definition the seeds of its own destruction: the collapse of the political immune system that we call democracy. . . . Rock Hudson, who once was as beautiful as a Palmachnik, now lies dying long after the dissolution of the Palmach. The State of Israel (for Jews, of course) was indeed once beautiful. . . .

And even more promising than its connection with latency is the potential of AIDS as a metaphor for contamination and mutation. Cancer is still common as a metaphor for what is feared or deplored, even if the illness is less dreaded than before. If AIDS can eventually be drafted for comparable use, it will be because AIDS is not only invasive (a trait it shares with cancer) or even because it is infectious, but because of the specific imagery that surrounds viruses.

Virology supplies a new set of medical metaphors independent of AIDS which nevertheless reinforce the AIDS mythology. It was years before AIDS that William Burroughs oracularly declared, and Laurie Anderson echoed, "Language is a virus." And the viral explanation is invoked more and more often. Until recently, most of the infections recognized as viral were ones, like rabies and influenza, that have very rapid effects. But the category of slow-acting viral infections is growing.

Many progressive and invariably fatal disorders of the central nervous system and some degenerative diseases of the brain that can appear in old age, as well as the so-called auto-immune diseases, are now suspected of being, in fact, slow virus diseases. (And evidence continues to accumulate for a viral cause of at least some human cancers.) Notions of conspiracy translate well into metaphors of implacable, insidious, infinitely patient viruses. In contrast to bacteria, which are relatively complex organisms, viruses are described as an extremely primitive form of life. At the same time, their activities are far more complex than those envisaged in the earlier germ models of infection. Viruses are not simply agents of infection, contamination. They transport genetic "information," they transform cells. And they themselves, many of them, evolve. While the smallpox virus appears to stay constant for centuries, influenza viruses evolve so rapidly that vaccines need to be modified every year to keep up with changes in the "surface coat" of the virus.[7] The virus or, more accurately, viruses thought to cause AIDS are at least as mutable as the influenza viruses. Indeed, "virus" is now a synonym for change. Linda Ronstadt, recently explaining why she prefers doing Mexican folk music to rock 'n' roll, observed: "We don't have any tradition in contemporary music except change. Mutate, like a virus."

So far as "plague" still has a future as a metaphor, it is through the ever more familiar notion of the virus. (Perhaps no disease in the future caused by a bacillus will be considered as plague-like). Information itself, now inextricably linked to the powers of computers, is threatened by something compared to a virus. Rogue or pirate programs, known as software viruses, are described as paralleling the behavior of biological viruses (which can capture the genetic code of parts of an organism and effect transfers of alien genetic material). These programs, deliberately planted onto a floppy disk meant to be used with the computer or introduced when the computer is communicating over telephone lines or data networks with other computers, copy themselves onto the computer's operating system. Like their biological namesakes, they won't produce immediate signs of damage to the computer's memory, which gives the newly "infected" program time to spread to other computers. Such metaphors drawn from virology, partly stimulated by the omnipresence of talk of AIDS, are turning up everywhere. (The virus that

[7]The reason that a vaccine is considered the optimal response to viruses has to do with what makes them "primitive." Bacteria have many metabolic differences from mammalian cells and can reproduce outside the cells of their host, which makes it possible to find substances that target them specifically. With viruses, which bond with their host cells, it is a much more difficult problem to distinguish viral functions from normal cellular ones. Hence, the main strategy for controlling viral infections has been the development of vaccines, which do not "attack" a virus directly (as penicillin attacks infectious bacteria) but "forestall" infection by stimulating the immune system in advance.

destroyed a considerable amount of data at the student computer center at Lehigh University in Bethlehem, Pennsylvania, in 1987, was given the name PC AIDS. In France, computer specialists already speak of the problem of *le sida informatique*.) And they reinforce the sense of the omnipresence of AIDS.

It is perhaps not surprising that the newest transforming element in the modern world, computers, should be borrowing metaphors drawn from our newest transforming illness. Nor is it surprising that descriptions of the course of viral infection now often echo the language of the computer age, as when it is said that a virus will normally produce "new copies of itself." In addition to the mechanistic descriptions, the way viruses are animistically characterized—as a menace in waiting, as mutable, as furtive, as biologically innovative—reinforces the sense that a disease can be something ingenious, unpredictable, novel. These metaphors are central to ideas about AIDS that distinguish this illness from others that have been regarded as plague-like. For though the fears AIDS represents are old, its status as that unexpected event, an entirely new disease—a new judgment, as it were—adds to the dread.   *1988*

34

Fighting Words

S. I. Hayakawa, Words with
Built-in Judgments

Gloria Naylor, A Question of Language

Anne Roiphe, The WASP Sting

To deny women their biological identity, their individuality, their humanness, is such an important aspect of obscene language that one can
only marvel at how seldom, in an era preoccupied with definitions of
obscenity, this fact is brought to our attention. One problem, of course,
is that many of the people in the best position to do this (critics,
teachers, writers) are so reluctant today to admit that they are angered
or shocked by obscenity. Bored, maybe, unimpressed, aesthetically dis-
pleased, but—no matter how brutal or denigrating the material—never
angered, never shocked.

And yet how eloquently angered, how piously shocked many of
these same people become if denigrating language is used about any
minority group other than women; if the obscenities are racial or ethnic,
that is, rather than sexual. Words like *coon, kike, spic, wop*, after all,
deform identity, deny individuality and humanness in almost exactly
the same way that sexual vulgarisms and obscenities do.

Barbara Lawrence, from *Four Letter Words Can Hurt You*

University officials who have formulated policies to respond to incidents of racial harassment have been characterized in the press as
"thought police," but such policies generally do nothing more than
impose sanctions against intentional face-to-face insults. When racist
speech takes the form of face-to-face insults, catcalls, or other assaultive
speech aimed at an individual or small group of persons, it falls directly

within the "fighting words" exception to First Amendment protection. The Supreme Court has held that words which "by their very utterance inflict injury or tend to incite an immediate breach of the peace" are not protected by the First Amendment.

Charles R. Lawrence, from *The Debates over Placing Limits on Racist Speech*

I have come to one vital conclusion: In our post–1960s obsession with social justice among class, ethnic, and racial (as well as gender) categories, we have witnessed a steady decline in personal morality. Today, it is far worse to be accused of being anti-Semitic, anti-black, sexist, or elitist than to be known as a consummate liar or adulterer. The J-word and the B-word are now more taboo than the F-word, which is now firmly ensconced in liberal living rooms.

E. Digby Baltzell, from *Philadelphia* **magazine, "The Wasp's Last Gasp"**

S. I. Hayakawa

Words with Built-in Judgments

The fact that some words arouse both informative and affective connotations simultaneously gives a special complexity to discussions involving religious, racial, national, and political groups. To many people, the word "communist" means simultaneously "one who believes in communism" (informative connotations) *and* "one whose ideals and purposes are altogether repellent" (affective connotations). Words applying to occupations of which one disapproves ("pickpocket," "racketeer," "prostitute"), like those applying to believers in philosophies of which one may disapprove ("atheist," "heretic," "materialist," "Holy Roller," "radical," "liberal"), likewise often communicate *simultaneously* a fact and a judgment on the fact.

In some parts of the southwestern United States there is strong prejudice against Mexicans, both immigrant and American-born. The strength of this prejudice is indirectly revealed by the fact that newspapers and polite people have stopped using the word "Mexican" altogether, using the expression "Spanish-speaking person" instead.

"Mexican" has been used with contemptuous connotations for so long that it has become, in the opinion of many people in the region, unsuitable for polite conversation. In some circles, the word is reserved for lower-class Mexicans, while the "politer" term is used for the upper class. There are also terms, such as "chicano" and "Latino," that Mexican-American and Spanish-speaking groups have chosen to describe themselves.

In dealing with subjects about which strong feelings exist, we are compelled to talk in roundabout terms if we wish to avoid traditional prejudices, which hinder clear thinking. Hence we have not only such terms as "Spanish-speaking persons" but also, in other contexts, "problem drinkers" instead of "drunkards," and "Hansen's disease" instead of "leprosy."

These verbal stratagems are necessitated by the strong affective 4 connotations as well as by the often misleading implications of their blunter alternatives, they are not merely a matter of giving things fancy names in order to fool people, as the simple-minded often believe. Because the old names are "loaded," they dictate traditional patterns of behavior toward those to whom they are applied. When everybody "knew" what to do about "little hoodlums," they threw them in jail and "treated 'em rough." Once in jail, little hoodlums showed a marked tendency to grow up into big hoodlums. When thoughtful people began to observe such facts, they started rethinking the problem, using different terminologies. What is the best way of describing these troubled and troublesome youths? Shall they be described as "defectives" or "psychopathic personalities"? Or as "maladjusted" or "neurotic"? Shall we say they are "deprived," "disadvantaged," "frustrated," or "socially displaced"? Shall we say they are "troubled by problems of identity"? Are they in need of "confinement," "punishment," "treatment," "education," or "rehabilitation"? It is through trying out many, many possible terms such as these that new ways of dealing with the problem are discovered and devised.

The meaning of words, as we have observed, changes from speaker to speaker and from context to context. The words "Japs" and "niggers," for instance, although often used both as a designation and an insult, are sometimes used with no intent to offend. In some classes of society and in some geographical areas, there are people who know no other words for Japanese, and in other areas there are people who know no other words for blacks. Ignorance of regional and class differences of dialect often results in feelings being needlessly hurt. Those who believe that the meaning of a word is *in the word* often fail to understand this simple point of differences in usage. For example, an elderly Japanese woman of my acquaintance used to squirm at the mention of the word "Jap," even when used in an innocuous or complimentary context. "Whenever I hear the word," she used to say, "I feel dirty all over."

The word "nigger" has a similar effect on most blacks. A distinguished black sociologist tells of an incident in his adolescence when he was hitchhiking far from home in regions where blacks are hardly ever seen. He was befriended by an extremely kindly white couple who fed him and gave him a place to sleep in their home. However, they kept calling him "little nigger"—a fact which upset him profoundly, even while he was grateful for their kindness. He finally got up courage to ask the man not to call him by that "insulting term."

> "Who's insultin' you, son?" said the man.
> "You are, sir—that name you're always calling me."
> "What name?"
> "Uh . . . you know."
> "I ain't callin' you no names, son."
> "I mean your calling me 'nigger.' "
> "Well, what's insultin' about that? You are a nigger, ain't you?"

As the sociologist says now in telling the story, "I couldn't think of an answer then, and I'm not sure I can now."

In case the sociologist reads this book, we are happy to provide him with an answer, although it may be twenty-five years late. He might have said to his benefactor, "Sir, in the part of the country I come from, white people who treat colored people with respect call them blacks, while those who wish to show their contempt for colored people call them niggers. I hope the latter is not your intention." And the man might have replied, had he been kindly in thought as he was in deed, "Well, you don't say! Sorry I hurt your feelings, son, but I didn't know." And that would have been that. Many black people now have rejected the term "Negro" as itself an insulting term and prefer to be called blacks or Afro-Americans. Some "hip" terms that they use for themselves are "moulenjam," "splib," "member," "blood," and "boots."

Blacks, having for a long time been victims of unfair persecution because of race, are often even more sensitive about racial appellations than the Japanese woman previously mentioned. It need hardly be said that blacks suffer from the confusion of informative and affective connotations just as often as white people—or Japanese. Such blacks, and those white sympathizers with their cause who are equally naive in linguistic matters, tend to feel that the entire colored "race" is vilified whenever and wherever the word "nigger" occurs. They bristle even when it occurs in such expressions as "niggertoe" (the name of an herb; also a dialect term for Brazil nut), "niggerhead" (a type of chewing tobacco), "niggerfish" (a kind of fish found in West Indian and Floridian waters)—and even the word "niggardly" (of Scandinavian origin,

unrelated, of course, to "Negro") has to be avoided before some audiences.

Such easily offended people sometimes send delegations to visit
dictionary offices to demand that the word "nigger" be excluded from
future editions, being unaware that dictionaries . . . perform a historical, rather than legislative, function. To try to reduce racial discrimination by getting dictionaries to stop including the word "nigger" is like
trying to cut down the birth rate by shutting down the office of the
county register of births. When racial discrimination against blacks is
done away with, the word will either disappear or else lose its present
connotations. By losing its present connotations, we mean, first, that
people who need to insult their fellow men will have found more
interesting grounds on which to base their insults and, second, that
people who are called "niggers" will no longer fly off the handle any
more than a person from New England does at being called a "Yankee."

One other curious fact needs to be recorded about words applied to
such hotly debated issues as race, religion, political heresy, and economic dissent. Every reader is acquainted with certain people who,
according to their own flattering descriptions of themselves, "believe in
being frank" and like to "tell it like [sic] it is." By "telling it like it is,"
they usually mean calling anything or anyone by the term which has the
strongest and most disagreeable affective connotations. Why people
should pin medals on themselves for "candor" for performing this nasty
feat has often puzzled me. Sometimes it is necessary to violate verbal
taboos as an aid to clearer thinking, but more often "calling a spade a
spade" is to provide our minds with a greased runway down which we
may slide back into old *and discredited* patterns of evaluation and behavior.   *1972*

Gloria Naylor

A Question of Language

Language is the subject. It is the written form with which I've
managed to keep the wolf away from the door and, in diaries, to keep
my sanity. In spite of this, I consider the written word inferior to the
spoken, and much of the frustration experienced by novelists is the
awareness that whatever we manage to capture in even the most tran-

scendent passages falls far short of the richness of life. Dialogue achieves its power in the dynamics of a fleeting moment of sight, sound, smell, and touch.

I'm not going to enter the debate here about whether it is language that shapes reality or vice versa. That battle is doomed to be waged whenever we seek intermittent reprieve from the chicken and egg dispute. I will simply take the position that the spoken word, like the written word, amounts to a nonsensical arrangement of sounds or letters without a consensus that assigns "meaning." And building from the meanings of what we hear, we order reality. Words themselves are innocuous; it is the consensus that gives them true power.

I remember the first time I heard the word *nigger*. In my third-grade class, our math tests were being passed down the rows, and as I handed the papers to a little boy in back of me, I remarked that once again he had received a much lower mark than I did. He snatched his test from me and spit out that word. Had he called me a nymphomaniac or a necrophiliac, I couldn't have been more puzzled. I didn't know what a nigger was, but I knew that whatever it meant, it was something he shouldn't have called me. This was verified when I raised my hand, and in a loud voice repeated what he had said and watched the teacher scold him for using a "bad" word. I was later to go home and ask the inevitable question that every black parent must face—"Mommy, what does 'nigger' mean?"

And what exactly did it mean? Thinking back, I realize that this 4 could not have been the first time the word was used in my presence. I was part of a large extended family that had migrated from the rural South after World War II and formed a close-knit network that gravitated around my maternal grandparents. Their ground-floor apartment in one of the buildings they owned in Harlem was a weekend mecca for my immediate family, along with countless aunts, uncles, and cousins who brought along assorted friends. It was a bustling and open house with assorted neighbors and tenants popping in and out to exchange bits of gossip, pick up an old quarrel or referee the ongoing checkers game in which my grandmother cheated shamelessly. They were all there to let down their hair and put up their feet after a week of labor in the factories, laundries, and shipyards of New York.

Amid the clamor, which could reach deafening proportions—two or three conversations going on simultaneously, punctuated by the sound of a baby's crying somewhere in the back rooms or out on the street— there was still a rigid set of rules about what was said and how. Older children were sent out of the living room when it was time to get into the juicy details about "you-know-who" up on the third floor who had gone and gotten herself "p-r-e-g-n-a-n-t!" But my parents, knowing that I could spell well beyond my years, always demanded that I follow the others out to play. Beyond sexual misconduct and death, everything else was considered harmless for our young ears. And so among the anec-dotes of the triumphs and disappointments in the various workings of their lives, the word *nigger* was used in my presence, but it was set within contexts and inflections that caused it to register in my mind as some-thing else.

In the singular, the word was always applied to a man who had distinguished himself in some situation that brought their approval for his strength, intelligence, or drive:

"Did Johnny really do that?"

"I'm telling you, that nigger pulled in $6,000 of overtime last year. 8 Said he got enough for a down payment on a house."

When used with a possessive adjective by a woman—"my nigger"— it became a term of endearment for husband or boyfriend. But it could be more than just a term applied to a man. In their mouths it became the pure essence of manhood—a disembodied force that channeled their past history of struggle and present survival against the odds into a victorious statement of being: "Yeah, that old foreman found out quick enough—you don't mess with a nigger."

In the plural, it became a description of some group within the community that had overstepped the bounds of decency as my family defined it: Parents who neglected their children, a drunken couple who fought in public, people who simply refused to look for work, those with excessively dirty mouths or unkempt households were all "trifling nig-gers." This particular circle could forgive hard times, unemployment, the occasional bout of depression—they had gone through all of that themselves—but the unforgivable sin was lack of self-respect.

A woman could never be a *nigger* in the singular, with its connota-tion of confirming worth. The noun *girl* was its closest equivalent in that sense, but only when used in direct address and regardless of the gender doing the addressing. *Girl* was a token of respect for a woman. The one-syllable word was drawn out to sound like three in recognition of the extra ounce of wit, nerve or daring that the woman had shown in the situation under discussion.

"G-i-r-l, stop. You mean you said that to his face?" 12

But if the word was used in a third-person reference or shortened so that it almost snapped out of the mouth, it always involved some ele-ment of communal disapproval. And age became an important factor in these exchanges. It was only between individuals of the same genera-tion, or from an older person to a younger (but never the other way around), that "girl" would be considered a compliment.

I don't agree with the argument that use of the word *nigger* at this social stratum of the black community was an internalization of racism. The dynamics were the exact opposite: the people in my grandmother's living room took a word that whites used to signify worthlessness or degradation and rendered it impotent. Gathering there together, they transformed *nigger* to signify the varied and complex human beings they knew themselves to be. If the word was to disappear totally from the mouths of even the most liberal of white society, no one in that room was naïve enough to believe it would disappear from white minds. Meeting the word head-on, they proved it had absolutely nothing to do with the way they were determined to live their lives.

So there must have been dozens of times that the word *nigger* was spoken in front of me before I reached the third grade. But I didn't "hear" it until it was said by a small pair of lips that had already learned it could be a way to humiliate me. That was the word I went home and asked my mother about. And since she knew that I had to grow up in America, she took me in her lap and explained.   *1986*

Anne Roiphe

The WASP Sting

When I was a teenager I was invited for lunch at the home of a Protestant classmate. Her mother turned to me at the end of the meal and said, "You have such good manners for a Jewish girl." Not knowing what to do and not wanting to feed into her stereotype of Jews, I said, "Thank you." I should have left. I should have turned over my water glass and stuck my elbow in the butter plate.

The summer before, in 1950, I had been to camp in Maine—a camp for Jewish girls run by Aunt Kitty and Aunt Caroline, also Jewish. They called a meeting before we went out on our canoe and hiking trips and told us that we had to be very quiet when going through towns or in public places because Jews were known to be loud and conspicuous and we didn't want to give the natives of Maine a reason to hate us, did we? Another stereotype, this time one about Jews passed on by Jews, believed by Jews about themselves. True, we weren't fourth-generation Yankees and, true, we yelled a lot, but was it our Jewishness that led us into the temptation of noisiness or was it our youth? Jews have been the butt of so many stereotypes—we are greedy, miserly, loud, ugly—yet sadly this has not stopped us from developing and enjoying our own brutal stereotypes of others. WASP[1] is the word I am worrying about now.

WASP is an acronym for white Anglo-Saxon Protestant and as such is a neutral description, but in its acronym form it carries the natural hostility of the generations of immigrants who found their way blocked by the unwelcoming establishment. A wasp stings and a wasp is an insect, a thing lower than a human being, and the joke and the satisfaction in the acronym is that the mighty Anglo-Saxon is, in one verbal swipe, reduced to a small and unpleasant bug.

The term WASP describes to the knowing listener a cold, blocked, dry, stiff person, capable of limited family warmth, limited sexual joy, pale of skin, pale in originality, invention, passion. There are myriad WASP jokes that tell that tale. WASPs play golf, they don't play the piano. WASPs drink, they don't eat. WASPs can hardly recognize their children and all their sisters are nicknamed Bitsy or BooBoo.   4

There is nothing neutral or sociologically descriptive in the term WASP as we have woven it into our conversations. The word has proved so adaptable that it has even reached into the general culture, and there probably isn't a literate person in America who doesn't know its meaning. I have Christian friends now who will say to me, with an apologetic shrug, "I have to go visit my WASP mother in South Carolina." Just as some Jews believed the going cultural word about themselves, so now some WASPs believe that their parents are cold and unimaginative and their hometowns places to despise because they lack the ethnic mix, the wonderful color of warm and happy Jews who never drink, beat their wives, or leave their families a note on the fireplace saying they have moved to California.

So what have we done with this wonderful word WASP? We have won a limited public relations battle. In that battle the Jewish culture—with its Woody Allens and Barbra Streisands, its Milton Berles and Eddie Cantors and Lenny Bruces, its Hollywood moguls, its Albert Einsteins and Mischa Ellmans, its Jonas Salks and Philip Roths—has made the others, the ones who were here first, feel no good, not up to par, not up to us with our warm, huggy capacity to eat foods of all kinds and express everything the moment we feel it.

Well, maybe they deserve it. Turnabout is just deserts, and in the war of words on the playgrounds the guy with the best insult, who gets his in last, wins.

---

[1] **WASP**: This now derogatory acronym was coined by the prominent Philadelphia sociologist of upper-class American life, E. Digby Baltzell, whose books include *The Protestant Establishment* (1966) and *Philadelphia Gentlemen* (1979).—Eds.

Or does he? In fact when Jews use the word WASP they are demean-   8
ing themselves, doing something fundamentally non-Jewish. They are
attempting to shame someone else in public, a thing our rabbis told us
was a great sin, back in the days before the Second Temple fell. Jews who
should have developed an allergy to stereotypes, to words that lump all
of a people together in some derogatory image, are willing to use that
very same weapon against someone else. That is moral progress.

We know that all Jews have individual faces and that our attitudes
toward money vary and that our economic roles in the culture have
been determined most often by what has been permitted us. How, then,
can we turn around and lump all the Protestants of America, the
farmers and the bankers, the workers and the lawyers, under one label,
one that insults their capacity for love and human warmth? Revenge is a
good clean motive, but it has its pitfalls.

In today's world, where so many of us have non-Jewish friends,
colleagues, business partners, not to mention non-Jewish sons- and
daughters-in-law, when so many Jews-by-choice are joining our syn-
agogues and participating in our community affairs, our casual use of
the word WASP risks offending, just as the mother of my friend did
when she commented on my table manners. She revealed an unpleasant
assumption about my behavior based on my Jewish identity, just as the
word WASP reveals an equally unpleasant assumption about the Gentile who may be sitting in the seat next to you, may be a Jew-by-choice in
your synagogue, or a tennis partner on your public court.

I was told by a group of women converts who were the pillars of
their synagogue and the best teachers in their Hebrew school that when
they heard the word WASP they cringed. "It makes us feel," said one, "as
if our mothers and fathers were bad in some way. It makes me feel
disloyal to them and I want to be able to be Jewish without looking
down on my family, the one I came from." Well, that seems reasonable.

Now what about the idea that the nasty implications of the word   12
WASP are, after all, true, and therefore we should be free to express
them? What are we doing more than speaking the truth? All stereotypes,
including those about Jews, reflect something of reality. Jews did deal
with money. Jewish manners and mores as they came out of the shtetls
and into the suburbs were at odds with suburban cultural norms. Jews
had accents. They did speak in less modulated tones in public places,
some of them, some of the time.

And it is true that Protestant America has problems with drinking,
with enjoyment and open expression. But these are broad generalizations. While stereotypes catch cultural trends and reflect impressions,
they exaggerate them and in doing so add new heights to the walls
between people, the walls behind which we stand as we throw stones at
one another.

In a pluralistic democratic society our best protection lies in a generous and respectful attitude toward all other groups, and of course we wish to be respected in turn. If in every Jewish home the Anglo-Saxon Protestant is made the butt of a joke, the end of a sneer, then we can expect that in every Protestant home the anti-Semitic stereotypes will be continued, and who can blame them?

Of course, anti-Protestant feeling on the part of Jews has never led to a Holocaust or a pogrom, or even to exclusion from hotels or universities. But Jews know, know very well, that this acceptable intergroup contempt can easily escalate into something actually dangerous and truly evil. Therefore it serves our best interests as well as our moral souls to catch ourselves now and end the indiscriminate use of prejudicial language. I don't want to become like the mother of my friend who complimented my good Jewish manners. That victory I don't want to give her. Good-bye to the word WASP. It was fun to use you for a while, but enough is enough.   *1989*

The Pleasures of the Mind

35

Sight into Insight

Annie Dillard, Seeing
Barry Lopez, The Stone Horse
Walker Percy, The Loss of the Creature

If I were the president of a university I should establish a compulsory course in "How to Use Your Eyes." The professor would try to show his pupils how they could add joy to their lives by really seeing what passes unnoticed before them. He would try to awake their dormant and sluggish faculties.

Perhaps I can best illustrate by imagining what I should most like to see if I were given the use of my eyes, say, for just three days. And while I am imagining, suppose you, too, set your mind to work on the problem of how you would use your own eyes if you had only three more days to see. If with the oncoming darkness of the third night you knew that the sun would never rise for you again, how would you spend those three precious intervening days? What would you most want to let your gaze rest upon?

Helen Keller, from *Three Days to See*

What we observe is not nature in itself but nature exposed to our method of questioning.

Werner Heisenberg, from *Physics and Philosophy*

At another point, I wished to describe the appearance of my mother's face after several years of looking after three young children, on her own with very little money and in a bronchitic condition. Again, many words came into my mind . . . grey, bloodless, matt, lined, and so on. They were unexceptionable but vague and distant; and I had again the irritable feeling that I needed to push through. Then I remembered something particular. I did not invent it; I remembered it: but I only remembered it after working through other possibilities. I remembered that, if I saw my mother's face in a certain light, I saw not only the lines scored into it—but saw that the lines were embedded with fine dirt. It is the kind of thing a child photographs in close-up—unsentimentally, perhaps a little put-off, but with no desire to tone it down. I saw now that those dirt-lines went with a whole way of living, with years of snatching quick washes in cold water, using coarse yellow soap or no soap at all, under the one tap in the back kitchen. This was the face of a woman only just over forty. As I remembered and understood all this I knew it was the detail I wanted—but that I would have to be careful not to over-emphasize it, not to exploit it.

Richard Hoggart, from *A Question of Tone*

Annie Dillard

Seeing

When I was six or seven years old, growing up in Pittsburgh, I used to take a precious penny of my own and hide it for someone else to find. It was a curious compulsion; sadly, I've never been seized by it since. For some reason I always "hid" the penny along the same stretch of sidewalk up the street. I would cradle it at the roots of a sycamore, say, or in a hole left by a chipped-off piece of sidewalk. Then I would take a piece of chalk, and, starting at either end of the block, draw huge arrows leading up to the penny from both directions. After I learned to write I labeled the arrows: SURPRISE AHEAD or MONEY THIS WAY. I was greatly excited, during all this arrow-drawing, at the thought of the first lucky passer-by who would receive in this way, regardless of merit, a free gift from the universe. But I never lurked about. I would go straight home and not give the matter another thought, until, some months later, I would be gripped again by the impulse to hide another penny.

It is still the first week in January, and I've got great plans. I've been thinking about seeing. There are lots of things to see, unwrapped gifts and free surprises. The world is fairly studded and strewn with pennies cast broadside from a generous hand. But—and this is the point—who gets excited by a mere penny? If you follow one arrow, if you crouch motionless on a bank to watch a tremulous ripple thrill on the water and are rewarded by the sight of a muskrat kit paddling from its den, will you count that sight a chip of copper only, and go your rueful way? It is dire poverty indeed when a man is so malnourished and fatigued that he won't stoop to pick up a penny. But if you cultivate a healthy poverty and simplicity, so that finding a penny will literally make your day, then, since the world is in fact planted in pennies, you have with your poverty bought a lifetime of days. It is that simple. What you see is what you get.

I used to be able to see flying insects in the air. I'd look ahead and see, not the row of hemlocks across the road, but the air in front of it. My eyes would focus along that column of air, picking out flying insects. But I lost interest, I guess, for I dropped the habit. Now I can see birds. Probably some people can look at the grass at their feet and discover all the crawling creatures. I would like to know grasses and sedges—and care. Then my least journey into the world would be a field trip, a series of happy recognitions. Thoreau, in an expansive mood, exulted, "What a rich book might be made about buds, including, perhaps, sprouts!" It would be nice to think so. I cherish mental images I have of three perfectly happy people. One collects stones. Another—an Englishman, say—watches clouds. The third lives on a coast and collects drops of seawater which he examines microscopically and mounts. But I don't see what the specialist sees, and so I cut myself off, not only from the total picture, but from the various forms of happiness.

Unfortunately, nature is very much a now-you-see-it, now-you-don't 4 affair. A fish flashes, then dissolves in the water before my eyes like so much salt. Deer apparently ascend bodily into heaven; the brightest oriole fades into leaves. These disappearances stun me into stillness and concentration; they say of nature that it conceals with a grand nonchalance, and they say of vision that it is a deliberate gift, the revelation of a dancer who for my eyes only flings away her seven veils. For nature does reveal as well as conceal: now-you-don't-see-it, now-you-do. For a week last September migrating red-winged blackbirds were feeding heavily down by the creek at the back of the house. One day I went out to investigate the racket; I walked up to a tree, an Osage orange, and a hundred birds flew away. They simply materialized out of the tree. I saw a tree, then a whisk of color, then a tree again. I walked closer and another hundred blackbirds took flight. Not a branch, not a twig budged: The birds were apparently weightless as well as invisible. Or, it was as if the leaves of the Osage orange had been freed from a spell in the form of red-winged blackbirds; they flew from the tree, caught my eye in the sky, and vanished. When I looked again at the tree the leaves had reassembled as if nothing had happened. Finally I walked directly to the trunk of the tree and a final hundred, the real diehards, appeared, spread, and vanished. How could so many hide in the tree without my seeing them? The Osage orange, unruffled, looked just as it had looked from the house, when three hundred red-winged blackbirds cried from its crown. I looked downstream where they flew, and they were gone. Searching, I couldn't spot one. I wandered downstream to force them to play their hand, but they'd crossed the creek and scattered. One show to a customer. These appearances catch at my throat; they are the free gifts, the bright coppers at the roots of trees.

It's all a matter of keeping my eyes open. Nature is like one of those line drawings of a tree that are puzzles for children: Can you find hidden in the leaves a duck, a house, a boy, a bucket, a zebra, and a boot? Specialists can find the most incredibly well-hidden things. A book I read when I was young recommended an easy way to find caterpillars to rear: You simply find some fresh caterpillar droppings, look up, and there's your caterpillar. More recently an author advised me to set my mind at ease about those piles of cut stems on the ground in grassy fields. Field mice make them; they cut the grass down by degrees to reach the seeds at the head. It seems that when the grass is tightly packed, as in a field of ripe grain, the blade won't topple at a single cut through the stem; instead, the cut stem simply drops vertically, held in the crush of grain. The mouse severs the bottom again and again, the stem keeps dropping an inch at a time, and finally the head is low enough for the mouse to reach the seeds. Meanwhile, the mouse is positively littering the field with its little piles of cut stems into which, presumably, the author of the book is constantly stumbling.

If I can't see these minutiae, I still try to keep my eyes open. I'm always on the lookout for antlion traps in sandy soil, monarch pupae near milkweed, skipper larvae in locust leaves. These things are utterly common, and I've not seen one. I bang on hollow trees near water, but so far no flying squirrels have appeared. In flat country I watch every sunset in hopes of seeing the green ray. The green ray is a seldom-seen streak of light that rises from the sun like a spurting fountain at the moment of sunset; it throbs into the sky for two seconds and disappears. One more reason to keep my eyes open. A photography professor at the University of Florida just happened to see a bird die in midflight; it jerked, died, dropped, and smashed on the ground. I squint at the wind because I read Stewart Edward White: "I have always maintained that if you looked closely enough you could *see* the wind—the dim, hardly-made-out, fine débris fleeing high in the air." White was an excellent observer, and devoted an entire chapter of *The Mountains* to the subject of seeing deer: "As soon as you can forget the naturally obvious and construct an artificial obvious, then you too will see deer."

But the artificial obvious is hard to see. My eyes account for less than one percent of the weight of my head; I'm bony and dense; I see what I expect. I once spent a full three minutes looking at a bullfrog that was so unexpectedly large I couldn't see it even though a dozen enthusiastic campers were shouting directions. Finally I asked, "What color am I looking for?" and a fellow said, "Green." When at last I picked out the frog, I saw what painters are up against: The thing wasn't green at all, but the color of wet hickory bark.

The lover can see, and the knowledgeable. I visited an aunt and   8 uncle at a quarter-horse ranch in Cody, Wyoming. I couldn't do much of anything useful, but I could, I thought, draw. So, as we all sat around the kitchen table after supper, I produced a sheet of paper and drew a horse. "That's one lame horse," my aunt volunteered. The rest of the family joined in: "Only place to saddle that one is his neck"; "Looks like we better shoot the poor thing, on account of those terrible growths." Meekly, I slid the pencil and paper down the table. Everyone in that family, including my three young cousins, could draw a horse. Beautifully. When the paper came back it looked as though five shining, real quarter horses had been corraled by mistake with a papier-mâché moose; the real horses seemed to gaze at the monster with a steady, puzzled air. I stay away from horses now, but I can do a creditable goldfish. The point is that I just don't know what the lover knows; I just can't see the artificial obvious that those in the know construct. The herpetologist asks the native, "Are there snakes in that ravine?" "Nosir." And the herpetologist comes home with, yessir, three bags full. Are there butterflies on that mountain? Are the bluets in bloom, are there arrowheads here, or fossil shells in the shale?

Peeping through my keyhole I see within the range of only about thirty percent of the light that comes from the sun; the rest is infrared and some little ultraviolet, perfectly apparent to many animals, but invisible to me. A nightmare network of ganglia, charged and firing without my knowledge, cuts and splices what I do see, editing it for my brain. Donald E. Carr points out that the sense impressions of one-celled animals are *not* edited for the brain: "This is philosophically interesting in a rather mournful way, since it means that only the simplest animals perceive the universe as it is."

A fog that won't burn away drifts and flows across my field of vision. When you see fog move against a backdrop of deep pines, you don't see the fog itself, but streaks of clearness floating across the air in dark shreds. So I see only tatters of clearness through a pervading obscurity. I can't distinguish the fog from the overcast sky; I can't be sure if the light is direct or reflected. Everywhere darkness and the presence of the unseen appalls. We estimate now that only one atom dances alone in every cubic meter of intergalactic space. I blink and squint. What planet or power yanks Halley's Comet out of orbit? We haven't seen that force yet; it's a question of distance, density, and the pallor of reflected light. We rock, cradled in the swaddling band of darkness. Even the simple darkness of night whispers suggestions to the mind. Last summer, in August, I stayed at the creek too late.

Where Tinker Creek flows under the sycamore log bridge to the tear-shaped island, it is slow and shallow, fringed thinly in cattail marsh. At this spot an astonishing bloom of life supports vast breeding populations of insects, fish, reptiles, birds, and mammals. On windless summer evenings I stalk along the creek bank or straddle the sycamore log in absolute stillness, watching for muskrats. The night I stayed too late I was hunched on the log staring spellbound at spreading, reflected stains of lilac on the water. A cloud in the sky suddenly lighted as if turned on by a switch; its reflection just as suddenly materialized on the water upstream, flat and floating, so that I couldn't see the creek bottom, or life in the water under the cloud. Downstream, away from the cloud on the water, water turtles smooth as beans were gliding down with the current in a series of easy, weightless push-offs, as men bound on the moon. I didn't know whether to trace the progress of one turtle I was sure of, risking sticking my face in one of the bridge's spider webs made invisible by the gathering dark, or take a chance on seeing the carp, or scan the mudbank in hope of seeing a muskrat, or follow the last of the swallows who caught at my heart and trailed it after them like streamers as they appeared from directly below, under the log, flying upstream with the tails forked, so fast.

But shadows spread, and deepened, and stayed. After thousands of years we're still strangers to darkness, fearful aliens in an enemy camp with our arms crossed over our chests. I stirred. A land turtle on the bank, startled, hissed the air from its lungs and withdrew into its shell. An uneasy pink here, an unfathomable blue there, gave great suggestion of lurking beings. Things were going on. I couldn't see whether that sere rustle I heard was a distant rattlesnake, slit-eyed, or a nearby sparrow kicking in the dry flood debris slung at the foot of a willow. Tremendous action roiled the water everywhere I looked, big action, inexplicable. A tremor welled up beside a gaping muskrat burrow in the bank and I caught my breath, but no muskrat appeared. The ripples continued to fan upstream with a steady, powerful thrust. Night was knitting over my face an eyeless mask, and I still sat transfixed. A distant airplane, a delta wing out of nightmare, made a gliding shadow on the creek's bottom that looked like a stingray cruising upstream. At once a black fin slit the pink cloud on the water, shearing it in two. The two halves merged together and seemed to dissolve before my eyes. Darkness pooled in the cleft of the creek and rose, as water collects in a well. Untamed, dreaming lights flickered over the sky. I saw hints of hulking underwater shadows, two pale splashes out of the water, and round ripples rolling close together from a blackened center.

At last I stared upstream where only the deepest violet remained of the cloud, a cloud so high its underbelly still glowed feeble color reflected from a hidden sky lighted in turn by a sun halfway to China. And out of that violet, a sudden enormous black body arced over the water. I saw only a cylindrical sleekness. Head and tail, if there was a head and tail, were both submerged in cloud. I saw only one ebony fling, a headlong dive to darkness; then the waters closed, and the lights went out.

I walked home in a shivering daze, up hill and down. Later I lay open-mouthed in bed, my arms flung wide at my sides to steady the whirling darkness. At this latitude I'm spinning 836 miles an hour round the earth's axis; I often fancy I feel my sweeping fall as a breakneck arc like the dive of dolphins, and the hollow rushing of wind raises hair on my neck and the side of my face. In orbit around the sun I'm moving 64,800 miles an hour. The solar system as a whole, like a merry-go-round unhinged, spins, bobs, and blinks at the speed of 43,200 miles an hour along a course set east of Hercules. Someone has piped, and we are dancing a tarantella until the sweat pours. I open my eyes and I see dark, muscled forms curl out of water, with flapping gills and flattened eyes. I close my eyes and I see stars, deep stars giving way to deeper stars, deeper stars bowing to deepest stars at the crown of an infinite cone.

"Still," wrote van Gogh in a letter, "a great deal of light falls on everything." If we are blinded by darkness, we are also blinded by light. When too much light falls on everything, a special terror results. Peter Freuchen describes the notorious kayak sickness to which Greenland Eskimos are prone. "The Greenland fjords are peculiar for the spells of completely quiet weather, when there is not enough wind to blow out a match and the water is like a sheet of glass. The kayak hunter must sit in his boat without stirring a finger so as not to scare the shy seals away. . . . The sun, low in the sky, sends a glare into his eyes, and the landscape around moves into the realm of the unreal. The reflex from the mirror-like water hypnotizes him, he seems to be unable to move, and all of a sudden it is as if he were floating in a bottomless void, sinking, sinking, and sinking. . . . Horror-stricken, he tries to stir, to cry out, but he cannot, he is completely paralyzed, he just falls and falls." Some hunters are especially cursed with this panic, and bring ruin and sometimes starvation to their families.

Sometimes here in Virginia at sunset low clouds on the southern or 16 northern horizon are completely invisible in the lighted sky. I only know one is there because I can see its reflection in still water. The first time I discovered this mystery I looked from cloud to no-cloud in bewilderment, checking my bearings over and over, thinking maybe the ark of the covenant was just passing by south of Dead Man Mountain. Only much later did I read the explanation: Polarized light from the sky is very much weakened by reflection, but the light in clouds isn't polarized. So invisible clouds pass among visible clouds, till all slide over the mountains; so a greater light extinguishes a lesser as though it didn't exist.

In the great meteor shower of August, the Perseid, I wail all day for the shooting stars I miss. They're out there showering down, committing hara-kiri in a flame of fatal attraction, and hissing perhaps at last into the ocean. But at dawn what looks like a blue dome clamps down over me like a lid on a pot. The stars and planets could smash and I'd never know. Only a piece of ashen moon occasionally climbs up or down the inside of the dome, and our local star without surcease explodes on our heads. We have really only that one light, one source for all power, and yet we must turn away from it by universal decree. Nobody here on the planet seems aware of this strange, powerful taboo, that we all walk about carefully averting our faces, this way and that, lest our eyes be blasted forever.

Darkness appalls and light dazzles; the scrap of visible light that doesn't hurt my eyes hurts my brain. What I see sets me swaying. Size and distance and the sudden swelling of meanings confuse me, bowl me over. I straddle the sycamore log bridge over Tinker Creek in the summer. I look at the lighted creek bottom: Snail tracks tunnel the mud in quavering curves. A crayfish jerks, but by the time I absorb what has happened, he's gone in a billowing smokescreen of silt. I look at the water: minnows and shiners. If I'm thinking minnows, a carp will fill my brain till I scream. I look at the water's surface: skaters, bubbles, and leaves sliding down. Suddenly, my own face, reflected, startles me witless. Those snails have been tracking my face! Finally, with a shuddering wrench of the will, I see clouds, cirrus clouds. I'm dizzy, I fall in. This looking business is risky.

Once I stood on a humped rock on nearby Purgatory Mountain, watching through binoculars the great autumn hawk migration below, until I discovered that I was in danger of joining the hawks on a vertical migration of my own. I was used to binoculars, but not, apparently, to balancing on humped rocks while looking through them. I staggered. Everything advanced and receded by turns; the world was full of unexplained foreshortenings and depths. A distant huge tan object, a hawk the size of an elephant, turned out to be the browned bough of a nearby loblolly pine. I followed a sharp-shinned hawk against a featureless sky, rotating my head unawares as it flew, and when I lowered the glass a glimpse of my own looming shoulder sent me staggering. What prevents the men on Palomar from falling, voiceless and blinded, from their tiny, vaulted chairs?

I reel in confusion; I don't understand what I see. With the naked 20 eye I can see two million light-years to the Andromeda galaxy. Often I slop some creek water in a jar and when I get home I dump it in a white china bowl. After the silt settles I return and see tracings of minute snails on the bottom, a planarian or two winding round the rim of water, roundworms shimmying frantically, and finally, when my eyes have adjusted to these dimensions, amoebae. At first the amoebae look like muscae volitantes, those curled moving spots you seem to see in your eyes when you stare at a distant wall. Then I see the amoebae as drops of water congealed, bluish, translucent, like chips of sky in the bowl. At length I choose one individual and give myself over to its idea of an evening. I see it dribble a grainy foot before it on its wet, unfathomable way. Do its unedited sense impressions include the fierce focus of my eyes? Shall I take it outside and show it Andromeda, and blow its little endoplasm? I stir the water with a finger, in case it's running out of oxygen. Maybe I should get a tropical aquarium with motorized bubblers and lights, and keep this one for a pet. Yes, it would tell its fissioned descendants, the universe is two feet by five, and if you listen closely you can hear the buzzing music of the spheres.

Oh, it's mysterious lamplit evenings, here in the galaxy, one after the other. It's one of those nights when I wander from window to window, looking for a sign. But I can't see. Terror and a beauty insoluble are a ribband of blue woven into the fringes of garments of things both great and small. No culture explains, no bivouac offers real haven or rest. But it could be that we are not seeing something. Galileo thought comets were an optical illusion. This is fertile ground: Since we are certain that they're not, we can look at what our scientists have been saying with fresh hope. What if there are *really* gleaming, castellated cities hung upside-down over the desert sand? What limpid lakes and cool date palms have our caravans always passed untried? Until, one by one, by the blindest of leaps, we light on the road to these places, we must stumble in darkness and hunger. I turn from the window. I'm blind as a bat, sensing only from every direction the echo of my own thin cries.

I chanced on a wonderful book by Marius von Senden, called *Space and Light*. When Western surgeons discovered how to perform safe cataract operations, they ranged across Europe and America operating on dozens of men and women of all ages who had been blinded by cataracts since birth. Von Senden collected accounts of such cases; the histories are fascinating. Many doctors had tested their patients' sense perceptions and ideas of space both before and after the operations. The vast majority of patients, of both sexes and all ages, had, in von Senden's opinion, no idea of space whatsoever. Form, distance, and size were so many meaningless syllables. A patient "had no idea of depth, confusing it with roundness." Before the operation a doctor would give a blind patient a cube and a sphere; the patient would tongue it or feel it with his hands, and name it correctly. After the operation the doctor would show the same objects to the patient without letting him touch them; now he had no clue whatsoever what he was seeing. One patient called lemonade "square" because it pricked on his tongue as a square shape pricked on the touch of his hands. Of another postoperative patient, the doctor writes, "I have found in her no notion of size, for example, not even within the narrow limits which she might have encompassed with the aid of touch. Thus when I asked her to show me how big her mother was, she did not stretch out her hands, but set her two index-fingers a few inches apart." Other doctors reported their patients' own statements to similar effect. "The room he was in . . . he knew to be but part of the house, yet he could not conceive that the whole house could look bigger"; "Those who are blind from birth . . . have no real conception of height or distance. A house that is a mile away is thought of as nearby, but requiring the taking of a lot of steps. . . . The elevator that whizzes him up and down gives no more sense of vertical distance than does the train of horizontal."

For the newly sighted, vision is pure sensation unencumbered by meaning: "The girl went through the experience that we all go through and forget, the moment we are born. She saw, but it did not mean anything but a lot of different kinds of brightness." Again, "I asked the patient what he could see; he answered that he saw an extensive field of light, in which everything appeared dull, confused, and in motion. He could not distinguish objects." Another patient saw "nothing but a confusion of forms and colours." When a newly sighted girl saw photographs and paintings, she asked, " 'Why do they put those dark marks all over them?' 'Those aren't dark marks,' her mother explained, 'those are shadows. That is one of the ways the eye knows that things have shape. If it were not for shadows many things would look flat.' 'Well, that's how things do look,' Joan answered. 'Everything looks flat with dark patches.' "

But it is the patients' concepts of space that are most revealing. One 24
patient, according to his doctor, "practiced his vision in a strange
fashion; thus he takes off one of his boots, throws it some way off in
front of him, and then attempts to gauge the distance at which it lies; he
takes a few steps toward the boot and tries to grasp it; on failing to reach
it, he moves on a step or two and gropes for the boot until he finally gets
hold of it." "But even at this stage, after three weeks' experience of
seeing," von Senden goes on, " 'space,' as he conceives it, ends with
visual space, i.e., with color-patches that happen to bound his view. He
does not yet have the notion that a larger object (a chair) can mask a
smaller one (a dog), or that the latter can still be present even though it
is not directly seen."

In general the newly sighted see the world as a dazzle of color-
patches. They are pleased by the sensation of color, and learn quickly to
name the colors, but the rest of seeing is tormentingly difficult. Soon
after his operation a patient "generally bumps into one of these color-
patches and observes them to be substantial, since they resist him as
tactual objects do. In walking about it also strikes him—or can if he pays
attention—that he is continually passing in between the colors he sees,
that he can go past a visual object, that a part of it then steadily
disappears from view; and that in spite of this, however he twists and
turns—whether entering the room from the door, for example, or
returning back to it—he always has a visual space in front of him. Thus
he gradually comes to realize that there is also a space behind him,
which he does not see."

The mental effort involved in these reasonings proves overwhelming for many patients. It oppresses them to realize, if they ever do at all,
the tremendous size of the world, which they had previously conceived
of as something touchingly manageable. It oppresses them to realize
that they have been visible to people all along, perhaps unattractively
so, without their knowledge or consent. A disheartening number of
them refuse to use their new vision, continuing to go over objects with
their tongues, and lapsing into apathy and despair. "The child can see,
but will not make use of his sight. Only when pressed can he with
difficulty be brought to look at objects in his neighborhood; but more
than a foot away it is impossible to bestir him to the necessary effort."
Of a twenty-one-year-old girl, the doctor relates, "Her unfortunate father, who had hoped for so much from this operation, wrote that his
daughter carefully shuts her eyes whenever she wishes to go about the
house, especially when she comes to a staircase, and that she is never
happier or more at ease than when, by closing her eyelids, she relapses
into her former state of total blindness." A fifteen-year-old boy, who was
also in love with a girl at the asylum for the blind, finally blurted out,

"No, really, I can't stand it any more; I want to be sent back to the asylum again. If things aren't altered, I'll tear my eyes out."

Some do learn to see, especially the young ones. But it changes their lives. One doctor comments on "the rapid and complete loss of that striking and wonderful serenity which is characteristic only of those who have never yet seen." A blind man who learns to see is ashamed of his old habits. He dresses up, grooms himself, and tries to make a good impression. While he was blind he was indifferent to objects unless they were edible; now, "a sifting of values sets in . . . his thoughts and wishes are mightily stirred and some few of the patients are thereby led into dissimulation, envy, theft and fraud."

On the other hand, many newly sighted people speak well of the 28 world, and teach us how dull is our own vision. To one patient, a human hand, unrecognized, is "something bright and then holes." Shown a bunch of grapes, a boy calls out, "It is dark, blue and shiny. . . . It isn't smooth, it has bumps and hollows." A little girl visits a garden. "She is greatly astonished, and can scarcely be persuaded to answer, stands speechless in front of the tree, which she only names on taking hold of it, and then as 'the tree with the lights in it.'" Some delight in their sight and give themselves over to the visual world. Of a patient just after her bandages were removed, her doctor writes, "The first things to attract her attention were her own hands; she looked at them very closely, moved them repeatedly to and fro, bent and stretched the fingers, and seemed greatly astonished at the sight." One girl was eager to tell her blind friend that "men do not really look like trees at all," and astounded to discover that her every visitor had an utterly different face. Finally, a twenty-two-year-old girl was dazzled by the world's brightness and kept her eyes shut for two weeks. When at the end of that time she opened her eyes again, she did not recognize any objects, but, "the more she now directed her gaze upon everything about her, the more it could be seen how an expression of gratification and astonishment overspread her features; she repeatedly exclaimed: 'Oh God! How beautiful!'"

I saw color-patches for weeks after I read this wonderful book. It was summer; the peaches were ripe in the valley orchards. When I woke in the morning, color-patches wrapped round my eyes, intricately, leaving not one unfilled spot. All day long I walked among shifting color-patches that parted before me like the Red Sea and closed again in silence, transfigured, wherever I looked back. Some patches swelled and loomed, while others vanished utterly, and dark marks flitted at random over the whole dazzling sweep. But I couldn't sustain the illusion of flatness. I've been around for too long. Form is condemned to an eternal danse macabre with meaning: I couldn't unpeach the peaches. Nor can I remember ever having seen without understanding; the color-patches of infancy are lost. My brain then must have been smooth as any balloon. I'm told I reached for the moon; many babies do. But the color-patches of infancy swelled as meaning filled them; they arrayed themselves in solemn ranks down distance which unrolled and stretched before me like a plain. The moon rocketed away. I live now in a world of shadows that shape and distance color, a world where space makes a kind of terrible sense. What gnosticism is this, and what physics? The fluttering patch I saw in my nursery window—silver and green and shape-shifting blue—is gone; a row of Lombardy poplars takes its place, mute, across the distant lawn. That humming oblong creature pale as light that stole along the walls of my room at night, stretching exhilaratingly around the corners, is gone, too, gone the night I ate of the bittersweet fruit, put two and two together and puckered forever my brain. Martin Buber tells this tale: "Rabbi Mendel once boasted to his teacher Rabbi Elimelekh that evenings he saw the angel who rolls away the light before the darkness, and mornings the angel who rolls away the darkness before the light. 'Yes,' said Rabbi Elimelekh, 'in my youth I saw that too. Later on you don't see these things any more.' "

Why didn't someone hand those newly sighted people paints and brushes from the start, when they still didn't know what anything was? Then maybe we all could see color-patches too, the world unraveled from reason, Eden before Adam gave names. The scales would drop from my eyes; I'd see trees like men walking; I'd run down the road against all orders, hallooing and leaping.

Seeing is of course very much a matter of verbalization. Unless I call my attention to what passes before my eyes, I simply won't see it. It is, as Ruskin says, "not merely unnoticed, but in the full, clear sense of the word, unseen." My eyes alone can't solve analogy tests using figures, the ones which show, with increasing elaborations, a big square, then a small square in a big square, then a big triangle, and expect me to find a small triangle in a big triangle. I have to say the words, describe what I'm seeing. If Tinker Mountain erupted, I'd be likely to notice. But if I want to notice the lesser cataclysms of valley life, I have to maintain in my head a running description of the present. It's not that I'm obser-vant; it's just that I talk too much. Otherwise, especially in a strange place, I'll never know what's happening. Like a blind man at the ball game, I need a radio.

When I see this way I analyze and pry. I hurl over logs and roll away 32 stones; I study the bank a square foot at a time, probing and tilting my head. Some days when a mist covers the mountains, when the muskrats won't show and the microscope's mirror shatters, I want to climb up the blank blue dome as a man would storm the inside of a circus tent, wildly, dangling, and with a steel knife claw a rent in the top, peep, and, if I must, fall.

But there is another kind of seeing that involves a letting go. When I see this way I sway transfixed and emptied. The difference between the two ways of seeing is the difference between walking with and without a camera. When I walk with a camera I walk from shot to shot, reading the light on a calibrated meter. When I walk without a camera, my own shutter opens, and the moment's light prints on my own silver gut. When I see this second way I am above all an unscrupulous observer.

It was sunny one evening last summer at Tinker Creek; the sun was low in the sky, upstream. I was sitting on the sycamore log bridge with the sunset at my back, watching the shiners the size of minnows who were feeding over the muddy sand in skittery schools. Again and again, one fish, then another, turned for a split second across the current and flash! the sun shot out from its silver side. I couldn't watch for it. It was always just happening somewhere else, and it drew my vision just as it disappeared: flash, like a sudden dazzle of the thinnest blade, a spark-ing over a dun and olive ground at chance intervals from every direc-tion. Then I noticed white specks, some sort of pale petals, small, floating from under my feet on the creek's surface, very slow and steady. So I blurred my eyes and gazed toward the brim of my hat and saw a new world. I saw the pale white circles roll up, roll up, like the world's turning, mute and perfect, and I saw the linear flashes, gleaming silver, like stars being born at random down a rolling scroll of time. Some-thing broke and something opened. I filled up like a new wineskin. I breathed an air like light; I saw a light like water. I was the lip of a fountain the creek filled forever; I was ether, the leaf in the zephyr; I was flesh-flake, feather, bone.
When I see this way I see truly. As Thoreau says, I return to my senses. I am the man who watches the baseball game in silence in an empty stadium. I see the game purely; I'm abstracted and dazed. When it's all over and the white-suited players lope off the green field to their shadowed dugouts, I leap to my feet; I cheer and cheer.

But I can't go out and try to see this way. I'll fail, I'll go mad. All I 36 can do is try to gag the commentator, to hush the noise of useless interior babble that keeps me from seeing just as surely as a newspaper dangled before my eyes. The effort is really a discipline requiring a lifetime of dedicated struggle; it marks the literature of saints and monks of every order East and West, under every rule and no rule, discalced and shod. The world's spiritual geniuses seem to discover universally that the mind's muddy river, this ceaseless flow of trivia and trash, cannot be dammed, and that trying to dam it is a waste of effort that might lead to madness. Instead you must allow the muddy river to flow unheeded in the dim channels of consciousness; you raise your sights; you look along it, mildly, acknowledging its presence without interest and gazing beyond it into the realm of the real where subjects and objects act and rest purely, without utterance. "Launch into the deep," says Jacques Ellul, "and you shall see."

The secret of seeing is, then, the pearl of great price. If I thought he could teach me to find it and keep it forever I would stagger barefoot across a hundred deserts after any lunatic at all. But although the pearl may be found, it may not be sought. The literature of illumination reveals this above all: Although it comes to those who wait for it, it is always, even to the most practiced and adept, a gift and a total surprise. I return from one walk knowing where the killdeer nests in the field by the creek and the hour the laurel blooms. I return from the same walk a day later scarcely knowing my own name. Litanies hum in my ears; my tongue flaps in my mouth Ailinon, alleluia! I cannot cause light; the most I can do is try to put myself in the path of its beam. It is possible, in deep space, to sail on solar wind. Light, be it particle or wave, has force: you rig a giant sail and go. The secret of seeing is to sail on solar wind. Hone and spread your spirit till you yourself are a sail, whetted, translucent, broadside to the merest puff.

When her doctor took her bandages off and led her into the garden, the girl who was no longer blind saw "the tree with the lights in it." It was for this tree I searched through the peach orchards of summer, in the forests of fall and down winter and spring for years. Then one day I was walking along Tinker Creek thinking of nothing at all and I saw the tree with the lights in it. I saw the backyard cedar where the mourning doves roost charged and transfigured, each cell buzzing with flame. I stood on the grass with the lights in it, grass that was wholly fire, utterly focused and utterly dreamed. It was less like seeing than like being for the first time seen, knocked breathless by a powerful glance. The flood of fire abated, but I'm still spending the power. Gradually the lights went out in the cedar, the colors died, the cells unflamed and disappeared. I was still ringing. I had been my whole life a bell, and never knew it until at that moment I was lifted and struck. I have since only very rarely seen the tree with the lights in it. The vision comes and goes, mostly goes, but I live for it, for the moment when the mountains open and a new light roars in spate through the crack, and the mountains slam.   *1974*

Barry Lopez

The Stone Horse

I

The deserts of southern California, the high, relatively cooler and wetter Mojave and the hotter, dryer Sonoran to the south of it, carry the signatures of many cultures. Prehistoric rock drawings in the Mojave's Coso Range, probably the greatest concentration of petroglyphs in North America, are at least three thousand years old. Big-game-hunting cultures that flourished six or seven thousand years before that are known from broken spear tips, choppers, and burins left scattered along the shores of great Pleistocene lakes, long since evaporated. Weapons and tools discovered at China Lake may be thirty thousand years old; and worked stone from a quarry in the Calico Mountains is, some argue, evidence that human beings were here more than 200,000 years ago.

Because of the long-term stability of such arid environments, much of this prehistoric stone evidence still lies exposed on the ground, accessible to anyone who passes by—the studious, the acquisitive, the indifferent, the merely curious. Archaeologists do not agree on the sequence of cultural history beyond about twelve thousand years ago, but it is clear that these broken bits of chalcedony, chert, and obsidian, like the animal drawings and geometric designs etched on walls of basalt throughout the desert, anchor the earliest threads of human history, the first record of human endeavor here.

Western man did not enter the California desert until the end of the eighteenth century, 250 years after Coronado brought his soldiers into the Zuni pueblos in a bewildered search for the cities of Cibola. The earliest appraisals of the land were cursory, hurried. People traveled *through* it, en route to Santa Fe or the California coastal settlements. Only miners tarried. In 1823 what had been Spain's became Mexico's, and in 1848 what had been Mexico's became America's; but the bare, jagged mountains and dry lake beds, the vast and uniform plains of creosote bush and yucca plants, remained as obscure as the northern Sudan until the end of the nineteenth century.

Before 1940 the tangible evidence of twentieth-century man's pas- 4
sage here consisted of very little—the hard tracery of travel corridors; the widely scattered, relatively insignificant evidence of mining operations; and the fair expanse of irrigated fields at the desert's periphery. In the space of a hundred years or so the wagon roads were paved, railroads were laid down, and canals and high-tension lines were built to bring water and electricity across the desert to Los Angeles from the

Colorado River. The dark mouths of gold, talc, and tin mines yawned from the bony flanks of desert ranges. Dust-encrusted chemical plants stood at work on the lonely edges of dry lake beds. And crops of grapes, lettuce, dates, alfalfa, and cotton covered the Coachella and Imperial valleys, north and south of the Salton Sea, and the Palo Verde Valley along the Colorado.

These developments proceeded with little or no awareness of earlier human occupations by cultures that preceded those of the historic Indians—the Mohave, the Chemehuevi, the Quechan. (Extensive irrigation began actually to change the climate of the Sonoran Desert, and human settlements, the railroads, and farming introduced many new, successful plants into the region.)

During World War II, the American military moved into the desert in great force, to train troops and to test equipment. They found the clear weather conducive to year-round flying, the dry air and isolation very attractive. After the war, a complex of training grounds, storage facilities, and gunnery and test ranges was permanently settled on more than three million acres of military reservations. Few perceived the extent or significance of the destruction of the aboriginal sites that took place during tank maneuvers and bombing runs or in the laying out of highways, railroads, mining districts, and irrigated fields. The few who intuited that something like an American Dordogne Valley lay exposed here were (only) amateur archaeologists; even they reasoned that the desert was too vast for any of this to matter.

After World War II, people began moving out of the crowded Los Angeles basin into homes in Lucerne, Apple, and Antelope valleys in the western Mojave. They emigrated as well to a stretch of resort land at the foot of the San Jacinto Mountains that included Palm Springs, and farther out to old railroad and military towns like Twentynine Palms and Barstow. People also began exploring the desert, at first in military-surplus jeeps and then with a variety of all-terrain and off-road vehicles that became available in the 1960s. By the mid-1970s, the number of people using such vehicles for desert recreation had increased exponentially. Most came and went in innocent curiosity; the few who didn't wreaked a havoc all out of proportion to their numbers. The disturbance of previously isolated archaeological sites increased by an order of magnitude. Many sites were vandalized before archaeologists, themselves late to the desert, had any firm grasp of the bounds of human history in the desert. It was as though in the same moment an Aztec library had been discovered intact various lacunae had begun to appear.

The vandalism was of three sorts: the general disturbance usually 8 caused by souvenir hunters and by the curious and the oblivious; the wholesale stripping of a place by professional thieves for black-market sale and trade; and outright destruction, in which vehicles were actually used to ram and trench an area. By 1980, the Bureau of Land Management estimated that probably 35 percent of the archaeological sites in the desert had been vandalized. The destruction at some places by rifles and shotguns, or by power winches mounted on vehicles, was, if one cared for history, demoralizing to behold.

In spite of public education, land closures, and stricter law enforcement in recent years, the BLM estimates that, annually, about 1 percent of the archaeological record in the desert continues to be destroyed or stolen.

2

A BLM archaeologist told me, with understandable reluctance, where to find the intaglio. I spread my Automobile Club of Southern California map of Imperial County out on his desk, and he traced the route with a pink felt-tip pen. The line crossed Interstate 8 and then turned west along the Mexican border.

"You can't drive any farther than about here," he said, marking a small X. "There's boulders in the wash. You walk up past them."

On a separate piece of paper he drew a route in a smaller scale that 12 would take me up the arroyo to a certain point where I was to cross back east, to another arroyo. At its head, on higher ground just to the north, I would find the horse.

"It's tough to spot unless you know it's there. Once you pick it up . . ." He shook his head slowly, in a gesture of wonder at its existence.

I waited until I held his eye. I assured him I would not tell anyone else how to get there. He looked at me with stoical despair, like a man who had been robbed twice, whose belief in human beings was offered without conviction.

I did not go until the following day because I wanted to see it at dawn. I ate breakfast at four A.M. in El Centro and then drove south. The route was easy to follow, though the last section of road proved difficult, broken and drifted over with sand in some spots. I came to the barricade of boulders and parked. It was light enough by then to find my way over the ground with little trouble. The contours of the landscape were stark, without any masking vegetation. I worried only about rattlesnakes.

I traversed the stone plain as directed, but, in spite of the frankness 16 of the land, I came on the horse unawares. In the first moment of recognition I was without feeling. I recalled later being startled, and that I held my breath. It was laid out on the ground with its head to the east, three times life size. As I took in its outline I felt a growing concentration of all my senses, as though my attentiveness to the pale rose color of the morning sky and other peripheral images had now ceased to be important. I was aware that I was straining for sound in the windless air, and I felt the uneven pressure of the earth hard against my feet. The horse, outlined in a standing profile on the dark ground, was as vivid before me as a bed of tulips.

I've come upon animals suddenly before, and felt a similar tension, a precipitate heightening of the senses. And I have felt the inexplicable but sharply boosted intensity of a wild moment in the bush, where it is not until some minutes later that you discover the source of electricity— the warm remains of a grizzly bear kill, or the still moist tracks of a wolverine.

But this was slightly different. I felt I had stepped into an unoc-cupied corridor. I had no familiar sense of history, the temporal struc-ture in which to think: this horse was made by Quechan people three hundred years ago. I felt instead a headlong rush of images: people hunting wild horses with spears on the Pleistocene veld of southern California; Cortés riding across the causeway into Montezuma's Ten-ochtitlán; a short-legged Comanche, astride his horse like some sort of ferret, slashing through cavalry lines of young men who rode like farmers; a hoof exploding past my face one morning in a corral in Wyoming. These images had the weight and silence of stone.

When I released by breath, the images softened. My initial feeling, of facing a wild animal in a remote region, was replaced with a calm sense of antiquity. It was then that I became conscious, like an ordinary tourist, of what was before me, and thought: this horse was probably laid out by Quechan people. But when? I wondered. The first horses they saw, I knew, might have been those that came north from Mexico in 1692 with Father Eusebio Kino. But Cocopa people, I recalled, also came this far north on occasion, to fight with their neighbors, the Quechan. And *they* could have seen horses with Melchior Díaz, at the mouth of the Colorado River in the fall of 1540. So, it could be four hundred years old. (No one in fact knows.)

I still had not moved. I took my eyes off the horse for a moment to 20 look south over the desert plain into Mexico, to look east past its head at the brightening sunrise, to situate myself. Then, finally, I brought my trailing foot slowly forward and stood erect. Sunlight was running like a thin sheet of water over the stony ground and it threw the horse into relief. It looked as though no hand had ever disturbed the stones that gave it its form.

The horse had been brought to life on ground called desert pave-ment, a tight, flat matrix of small cobbles blasted smooth by sand-laden winds. The uniform, monochromatic blackness of the stones, a patina of iron and magnesium oxides called desert varnish, is caused by long-term exposure to the sun. To make this type of low-relief ground glyph, or intaglio, the artist either selectively turns individual stones over to their lighter side or removes areas of stone to expose the lighter soil underneath, creating a negative image. This horse, about eighteen feet from brow to rump and eight feet from withers to hoof, had been made in the latter way, and its outline was bermed at certain points with low ridges of stone a few inches high to enhance its three-dimensional qualities. (The left side of the horse was in full profile; each leg was extended at 90 degrees to the body and fully visible, as though seen in three-quarter profile.)

I was not eager to move. The moment I did I would be back in the flow of time, the horse no longer quivering in the same way before me. I did not want to feel again the sequence of quotidian events—to be drawn off into deliberation and analysis. A human being, a four-footed animal, the open land. That was all that was present—and a "thought-less" understanding of the very old desires bearing on this particular animal: to hunt it, to render it, to fathom it, to subjugate it, to honor it, to take it as a companion.

What finally made me move was the light. The sun now filled the shallow basin of the horse's body. The weighted line of the stone berm created the illusion of a mane and the distinctive roundness of an equine belly. The change in definition impelled me. I moved to the left, circling past its rump, to see how the light might flesh the horse out from various points of view. I circled it completely before squatting on my haunches. Ten or fifteen minutes later I chose another view. The third time I moved, to a point near the rear hooves, I spotted a stone tool at my feet. I stared at it a long while, more in awe than disbelief, before reaching out to pick it up. I turned it over in my left palm and took it between my fingers to feel its cutting edge. It is always difficult, especially with something so portable, to rechannel the desire to steal.

I spent several hours with the horse. As I changed positions and as 24 the angle of the light continued to change I noticed a number of things. The angle at which the pastern carried the hoof away from the ankle was perfect. Also, stones had been placed within the image to suggest at precisely the right spot the left shoulder above the foreleg. The line that joined thigh and hock was similarly accurate. The muzzle alone seemed distorted—but perhaps these stones had been moved by a later hand. It was an admirably accurate representation, but not what a breeder would call perfect conformation. There was the suggestion of a bowed neck and an undershot jaw, and the tail, as full as a winter coyote's, did not appear to be precisely to scale.

The more I thought about it, the more I felt I was looking at an individual horse, a unique combination of generic and specific detail. It was easy to imagine one of Kino's horses as a model, or a horse that ran off from one of Coronado's columns. What kind of horses would these have been? I wondered. In the sixteenth century the most sought-after horses in Europe were Spanish, the offspring of Arabian stock and Barbary horses that the Moors brought to Iberia and bred to the older, eastern European strains brought in by the Romans. The model for this horse, I speculated, could easily have been a palomino, or a descendant of horses trained for lion hunting in North Africa.

A few generations ago, cowboys, cavalry quartermasters, and draymen would have taken this horse before me under consideration and not let up their scrutiny until they had its heritage fixed to their satisfaction. Today, the distinction between draft and harness horses is arcane knowledge, and no image may come to mind for a blue roan or a claybank horse. The loss of such refinement in everyday conversation leaves me unsettled. People praise the Eskimo's ability to distinguish among forty types of snow but forget the skill of others who routinely differentiate between overo and tobiano pintos. Such distinctions are made for the same reason. You have to do it to be able to talk clearly about the world.

For parts of two years I worked as a horse wrangler and packer in Wyoming. It is dim knowledge now; I would have to think to remember if a buckskin was a kind of dun horse. And I couldn't throw a double-diamond hitch over a set of panniers—the packer's basic tie-down—without guidance. As I squatted there in the desert, however, these more personal memories seemed tenuous in comparison with the sweep of this animal in human time. My memories had no depth. I thought of the Hittite cavalry riding against the Syrians 3,500 years ago. And the first of the Chinese emperors, Ch'in Shih Huang, buried in Shensi Province in 210 B.C. with thousands of life-size horses and soldiers, a terra-cotta guardian army. What could I know of what was in the mind of whoever made this horse? Was there some racial memory of it as an animal that had once fed the artist's ancestors and then disappeared from North America? And then returned in this strange alliance with another race of men?

Certainly, whoever it was, the artist had observed the animal very 28 closely. Certainly the animal's speed had impressed him. Among the first things the Quechan would have learned from an encounter with Kino's horses was that their own long-distance runners—men who could run down mule deer—were no match for this animal.

From where I squatted I could look far out over the Mexican plain. Juan Bautista de Anza passed this way in 1774, extending El Camino Real into Alta California from Sinaloa. He was followed by others, all of them astride the magical horse; gente de razón, the people of reason, coming into the country of los primitivos. The horse, like the stone animals of Egypt, urged these memories upon me. And as I drew them up from some forgotten corner of my mind—huge horses carved in the white chalk downs of southern England by an Iron Age people; Spanish horses rearing and wheeling in fear before alligators in Florida—the images seemed tethered before me. With this sense of proportion, a memory of my own—the morning I almost lost my face to a horse's hoof—now had somewhere to fit.

I rose up and began to walk slowly around the horse again. I had taken the first long measure of it and was now looking for a way to depart, a new angle of light, a fading of the image itself before the rising sun, that would break its hold on me. As I circled, feeling both heady and serene at the encounter, I realized again how strangely vivid it was. It had been created on a barren bajada between two arroyos, as nondescript a place as one could imagine. The only plant life here was a few wands of ocotillo cactus. The ground beneath my shoes was so hard it wouldn't take the print of a heavy animal even after a rain. The only sounds I heard here were the voices of quail.

The archaeologist had been correct. For all its forcefulness, the horse is inconspicuous. If you don't care to see it you can walk right past it. That pleases him, I think. Unmarked on this bleak shoulder of the plain, the site signals to no one; so he wants no protective fences here, no informative plaque, to act as beacons. He would rather take a chance that no motorcyclist, no aimless wanderer with a flair for violence and a depth of ignorance, will ever find his way here.

The archaeologist had given me something before I left his office 32 that now seemed peculiar—an aerial photograph of the horse. It is widely believed that an aerial view of an intaglio provides a fair and accurate depiction. It does not. In the photograph the horse looks somewhat crudely constructed; from the ground it appears far more deftly rendered. The photograph is of a single moment, and in that split second the horse seems vaguely impotent. I watched light pool in the intaglio at dawn; I imagine you could watch it withdraw at dusk and sense the same animation I did. In those prolonged moments its shape and so, too, its general character changed—noticeably. The living quality of the image, its immediacy to the eye, was brought out by the light-in-time, not, at least here, in the camera's frozen instant.

Intaglios, I thought, were never meant to be seen by gods in the sky above. They were meant to be seen by people on the ground, over a long period of shifting light. This could even be true of the huge figures on the Plain of Nazca in Peru, where people could walk for the length of a day beside them. It is our own impatience that leads us to think otherwise.

This process of abstraction, almost unintentional, drew me gradually away from the horse. I came to a position of attention at the edge of the sphere of its influence. With a slight bow I paid my respects to the horse, its maker, and the history of us all, and departed.

3

A short distance away I stopped the car in the middle of the road to make a few notes. I could not write down what I was thinking when I was with the horse. It would have seemed disrespectful, and it would have required another kind of attention. So now I patiently drained my memory of the details it had fastened itself upon. The road I'd stopped on was adjacent to the All American Canal, the major source of water for the Imperial and Coachella valleys. The water flowed west placidly. A disjointed flock of coots, small, dark birds with white bills, was paddling against the current, foraging in the rushes.

I was peripherally aware of the birds as I wrote, the only movement in the desert, and of a series of sounds from a village a half-mile away. The first sounds from this collection of ramshackle houses in a grove of cottonwoods were the distracted dawn voices of dogs. I heard them intermingled with the cries of a rooster. Later, the high-pitched voices of children calling out to each other came disembodied through the dry desert air. Now, a little after seven, I could hear someone practicing on the trumpet, the same rough phrases played over and over. I suddenly remembered how as children we had tried to get the rhythm of a galloping horse with hands against our thighs, or by fluttering our tongues against the roofs of our mouths.

After the trumpet, the impatient calls of adults summoning children. Sunday morning. Wood smoke hung like a lens in the trees. The first car starts—a cold eight-cylinder engine, of Chrysler extraction perhaps, goosed to life, then throttled back to murmur through dual mufflers, the obbligato music of a shade-tree mechanic. The rote bark of mongrel dogs at dawn, the jagged outcries of men and women, an engine coming to life. Like a thousand villages from West Virginia to Guadalajara.

I finished my notes—where was I going to find a description of the horses that came north with the conquistadors? Did their manes come forward prominently over the brow, like this one's, like the forelocks of Blackfeet and Assiniboin men in nineteenth-century paintings? I set the notes on the seat beside me.

The road followed the canal for a while and then arced north, toward Interstate 8. It was slow driving and I fell to thinking how the desert had changed since Anza had come through. New plants and animals—the MacDougall cottonwood, the English house sparrow, the chukar from India—have about them now the air of the native born. Of the native species, some—no one knows how many—are extinct. The populations of many others, especially the animals, have been sharply reduced. The idea of a desert impoverished by agricultural poisons and varmint hunters, by off-road vehicles and military operations, did not seem as disturbing to me, however, as this other horror, now that I had been those hours with the horse. The vandals, the few who crowbar rock art off the desert's walls, who dig up graves, who punish the ground that holds intaglios, are people who devour history. Their self-centered scorn, their disrespect for ideas and images beyond their ken, create the awful atmosphere of loose ends in which totalitarianism thrives, in which the past is merely curious or wrong.

I thought about the horse sitting out there on the unprotected plain.   40
I enumerated its qualities in my mind until a sense of its vulnerability receded and it became an anchor for something else. I remembered that history, a history like this one, which ran deeper than Mexico, deeper than the Spanish, was a kind of medicine. It permitted the great breadth of human expression to reverberate, and it did not urge you to locate its apotheosis in the present.

Each of us, individuals and civilizations, has been held upside down like Achilles in the River Styx. The artist mixing his colors in the dim light of Altamira; an Egyptian ruler lying still now, wrapped in his byssus,[1] stored against time in a pyramid; the faded Dorset culture of the Arctic; the Hmong and Samburu and Walbiri of historic time; the modern nations. This great, imperfect stretch of human expression is the clarification and encouragement, the urging and the reminder, we call history. And it is inscribed everywhere in the face of the land, from the mountain passes of the Himalayas to a nameless bajada in the California desert.

Small birds rose up in the road ahead, startled, and flew off. I prayed no infidel would ever find that horse.   *1986*

Walker Percy

The Loss of the Creature

I

Every explorer names his island Formosa, beautiful. To him it is beautiful because, being first, he has access to it and can see it for what it is. But to no one else is it ever as beautiful—except the rare man who manages to recover it, who knows that it has to be recovered.

Garcia López de Cárdenas discovered the Grand Canyon and was

---

[1]**byssus**: Ancient cloth.—EDS.

amazed at the sight. It can be imagined: One crosses miles of desert, breaks through the mesquite, and there it is at one's feet. Later the government set the place aside as a national park, hoping to pass along to millions the experience of Cárdenas. Does not one see the same sight from the Bright Angel Lodge that Cárdenas saw?

The assumption is that the Grand Canyon is a remarkably interesting and beautiful place and that if it had a certain value P for Cárdenas, the same value P may be transmitted to any number of sightseers—just as Banting's discovery of insulin can be transmitted to any number of diabetics. A counterinfluence is at work, however, and it would be nearer the truth to say that if the place is seen by a million sightseers, a single sightseer does not receive value P but a millionth part of value P.

It is assumed that since the Grand Canyon has the fixed interest value P, tours can be organized for any number of people. A man in Boston decides to spend his vacation at the Grand Canyon. He visits his travel bureau, looks at the folder, signs up for a two-week tour. He and his family take the tour, see the Grand Canyon, and return to Boston. May we say that this man has seen the Grand Canyon? Possibly he has. But it is more likely that what he has done is the one sure way not to see the canyon.

Why is it almost impossible to gaze directly at the Grand Canyon under these circumstances and see it for what it is—as one picks up a strange object from one's back yard and gazes directly at it? It is almost impossible because the Grand Canyon, the thing as it is, has been appropriated by the symbolic complex which has already been formed in the sightseer's mind. Seeing the canyon under approved circumstances is seeing the symbolic complex head on. The thing is no longer the thing as it confronted the Spaniard; it is rather that which has already been formulated—by picture postcard, geography book, tourist folders, and the words *Grand Canyon*. As a result of this preformulation, the source of the sightseer's pleasure undergoes a shift. Where the wonder and delight of the Spaniard arose from his penetration of the thing itself, from a progressive discovery of depths, patterns, colors, shadows, etc., now the sightseer measures his satisfaction *by the degree to which the canyon conforms to the preformed complex*. If it does so, if it looks just like the postcard, he is pleased; he might even say, "Why it is every bit as beautiful as a picture postcard!" He feels he has not been cheated. But if it does not conform, if the colors are somber, he will not be able to see it directly; he will only be conscious of the disparity between what it is and what it is supposed to be. He will say later that he was unlucky in not being there at the right time. The highest point, the term of the sightseer's satisfaction, is not the sovereign discovery of the thing before him; it is rather the measuring up of the thing to the criterion of the preformed symbolic complex.

Seeing the canyon is made even more difficult by what the sightseer does when the moment arrives, when sovereign knower confronts the thing to be known. Instead of looking at it, he photographs it. There is no confrontation at all. At the end of forty years of preformulation and with the Grand Canyon yawning at his feet, what does he do? He waives his right of seeing and knowing and records symbols for the next forty years. For him there is no present; there is only the past of what has been formulated and seen and the future of what has been formulated and not seen. The present is surrendered to the past and the future.

The sightseer may be aware that something is wrong. He may simply be bored; or he may be conscious of the difficulty: that the great thing yawning at his feet somehow eludes him. The harder he looks at it, the less he can see. It eludes everybody. The tourist cannot see it; the bellboy at the Angel Lodge cannot see it: For him it is only one side of the space he lives in, like one wall of a room; to the ranger it is a tissue of everyday signs relevant to his own prospects—the blue haze down there means that he will probably get rained on during the donkey ride.

How can the sightseer recover the Grand Canyon? He can recover it   8
in any number of ways, all sharing in common the stratagem of avoiding the approved confrontation of the tour and the Park Service.

It may be recovered by leaving the beaten track. The tourist leaves the tour, camps in the back country. He arises before dawn and ap- proaches the South Rim through a wild terrain where there are no trails and no railed-in lookout points. In other words, he sees the canyon by avoiding all the facilities for seeing the canyon. If the benevolent Park Service hears about this fellow and thinks he has a good idea and places the following notice in the Bright Angel Lodge: *Consult ranger for infor- mation on getting off the beaten track*—the end result will only be the closing of another access to the canyon.

It may be recovered by a dialectical movement which brings one back to the beaten track but at a level above it. For example, after a lifetime of avoiding the beaten track and guided tours, a man may deliberately seek out the most beaten track of all, the most com- monplace tour imaginable: he may visit the canyon by a Greyhound tour in the company of a party from Terre Haute—just as a man who has lived in New York all his life may visit the Statue of Liberty. (Such dialectical savorings of the *familiar* as the familiar are, of course, a favorite stratagem of *The New Yorker* magazine.) The thing is recovered from familiarity by means of an exercise in familiarity. Our complex friend stands behind the fellow tourists at the Bright Angel Lodge and sees the canyon through them and their predicament, their picture taking and busy disregard. In a sense, he exploits his fellow tourists; he stands on their shoulders to see the canyon.

Such a man is far more advanced in the dialectic than the sightseer who is trying to get off the beaten track—getting up at dawn and approaching the canyon through the mesquite. This stratagem is, in fact, for our complex man the weariest, most beaten track of all.

It may be recovered as a consequence of a breakdown of the sym- 12 bolic machinery by which the experts present the experience to the consumer. A family visits the canyon in the usual way. But shortly after their arrival, the park is closed by an outbreak of typhus in the south. They have the canyon to themselves. What do they mean when they tell the home folks of their good luck: "We had the whole place to our-selves"? How does one see the thing better when the others are absent? Is looking like sucking: the more lookers, the less there is to see? They could hardly answer, but by saying this they testify to a state of affairs which is considerably more complex than the simple statement of the schoolbook about the Spaniard and the millions who followed him. It is a state in which there is a complex distribution of sovereignty, of zoning.

It may be recovered in a time of national disaster. The Bright Angel Lodge is converted into a rest home, a function that has nothing to do with the canyon a few yards away. A wounded man is brought in. He regains consciousness; there outside his window is the canyon.

The most extreme case of access by privilege conferred by disaster is the Huxleyan[1] novel of the adventures of the surviving remnant after the great wars of the twentieth century. An expedition from Australia lands in Southern California and heads east. They stumble across the Bright Angel Lodge, now fallen into ruins. The trails are grown over, the guard rails fallen away, the dime telescope at Battleship Point rusted. But there is the canyon, exposed at last. Exposed by what? By the decay of those facilities which were designed to help the sightseer.

This dialectic of sightseeing cannot be taken into account by plan-ners, for the object of the dialectic is nothing other than the subversion of the efforts of the planners.

The dialectic is not known to objective theorists, psychologists, and 16 the like. Yet it is quite well known in the fantasy-consciousness of the popular arts. The devices by which the museum exhibit, the Grand Canyon, the ordinary thing, is recovered have long since been stumbled upon. A movie shows a man visiting the Grand Canyon. But the movie-maker knows something the planner does not know. He knows that one cannot take the sight frontally. The canyon must be approached by the stratagems we have mentioned: the Inside Track, the Familiar Revisited, the Accidental Encounter. Who is the stranger at the Bright Angel Lodge? Is he the ordinary tourist from Terre Haute that he makes himself out to be? He is not. He has another objective in mind, to

---

[1]**Huxleyan:** A reference to the English novelist Aldous Huxley (1894–1963), best known for his anti-utopian novel, *Brave New World* (1932).—EDS.

revenge his wronged brother, counterespionage, etc. By virtue of the fact that he has other fish to fry, he may take a stroll along the rim after supper and then we can see the canyon through him. The movie accomplishes its purpose by concealing it. Overtly the characters (the American family marooned by typhus) and we the onlookers experience pity for the sufferers, and the family experience anxiety for themselves; covertly and in truth they are the happiest of people and we are happy through them, for we have the canyon to ourselves. The movie cashes in on the recovery of sovereignty through disaster. Not only is the canyon now accessible to the remnant: the members of the remnant are now accessible to each other; a whole new ensemble of relations becomes possible—friendship, love, hatred, clandestine sexual adventures. In a movie when a man sits next to a woman on a bus, it is necessary either that the bus break down or that the woman lose her memory. (The question occurs to one: Do you imagine there are sightseers who see sights just as they are supposed to? a family who live in Terre Haute, who decide to take the canyon tour, who go there, see it, enjoy it immensely, and go home content? a family who are entirely innocent of all the barriers, zones, losses of sovereignty I have been talking about? Wouldn't most people be sorry if Battleship Point fell into the canyon, carrying all one's fellow passengers to their death, leaving one alone on the South Rim? I cannot answer this. Perhaps there are such people. Certainly a great many American families would swear they had no such problems, that they came, saw, and went away happy. Yet it is just these families who would be happiest if they had gotten the Inside Track and been among the surviving remnant.)

It is now apparent that as between the many measures which may be taken to overcome the opacity, the boredom, of the direct confrontation of the thing or creature in its citadel of symbolic investiture, some are less authentic than others. That is to say, some stratagems obviously serve other purposes than that of providing access to being—for example, various unconscious motivations which it is not necessary to go into here.

Let us take an example in which the recovery of being is ambiguous, where it may under the same circumstances contain both authentic and unauthentic components. An American couple, we will say, drives down into Mexico. They see the usual sights and have a fair time of it. Yet they are never without the sense of missing something. Although Taxco and Cuernavaca are interesting and picturesque as advertised, they fall short of "it." What do the couple have in mind by "it"? What do they really hope for? What sort of experience could they have in Mexico so that upon their return, they would feel that "it" had happened? We have a clue: Their hope has something to do with their own role as tourists in a foreign country and the way in which they conceive this role. It has something to do with other American tourists. Certainly they feel that they are very far from "it" when, after traveling five thousand miles, they arrive at the plaza in Guanajuato only to find themselves surrounded by a dozen other couples from the Midwest.

Already we may distinguish authentic and unauthentic elements. First, we see the problem the couple faces and we understand their efforts to surmount it. The problem is to find an "unspoiled" place. "Unspoiled" does not mean only that a place is left physically intact; it means also that it is not encrusted by renown and by the familiar (as in Taxco), that it has not been discovered by others. We understand that the couple really want to get at the place and enjoy it. Yet at the same time we wonder if there is not something wrong in their dislike of their compatriots. Does access to the place require the exclusion of others?

Let us see what happens.   20

The couple decide to drive from Guanajuato to Mexico City. On the way they get lost. After hours on a rocky mountain road, they find themselves in a tiny valley not even marked on the map. There they discover an Indian village. Some sort of religious festival is going on. It is apparently a corn dance in supplication of the rain god.

The couple know at once that this is "it." They are entranced. They spend several days in the village, observing the Indians and being themselves observed with friendly curiosity.

Now may we not say that the sightseers have at last come face to face with an authentic sight, a sight which is charming, quaint, picturesque, unspoiled, and that they see the sight and come away rewarded? Possibly this may occur. Yet it is more likely that what happens is a far cry indeed from an immediate encounter with being, that the experience, while masquerading as such, is in truth a rather desperate impersonation. I use the word *desperate* advisedly to signify an actual loss of hope.

The clue to the spuriousness of their enjoyment of the village and   24 the festival is a certain restiveness in the sightseers themselves. It is given expression by their repeated exclamations that "this is too good to be true," and by their anxiety that it may not prove to be so perfect, and finally by their downright relief at leaving the valley and having the experience in the bag, so to speak—that is, safely embalmed in memory and movie film.

What is the source of their anxiety during the visit? Does it not mean that the couple are looking at the place with a certain standard of performance in mind? Are they like Fabre,[2] who gazed at the world about him with wonder, letting it be what it is; or are they not like the overanxious mother who sees her child as one performing, now doing

---

[2]**Fabre**: Jean-Henri Fabre (1823–1913), French scientist who wrote numerous books on insects (*The Life of the Fly*, *The Life of the Spider*, etc.) based on careful observation.—EDS.

badly, now doing well? The village is their child and their love for it is an anxious love because they are afraid that at any moment it might fail them.

We have another clue in their subsequent remark to an ethnologist friend. "How we wished you had been there with us! What a perfect goldmine of folkways! Every minute we would say to each other, if only you were here! You must return with us." This surely testifies to a generosity of spirit, a willingness to share their experience with others, not at all like their feelings toward their fellow Iowans on the plaza at Guanajuato!

I am afraid this is not the case at all. It is true that they longed for their ethnologist friend, but it was for an entirely different reason. They wanted him, not to share their experience, but to certify their experience as genuine.

"This is it" and "Now we are really living" do not necessarily refer 28 to the sovereign encounter of the person with the sight that enlivens the mind and gladdens the heart. It means that now at last we are having the acceptable experience. The present experience is always measured by a prototype, the "it" of their dreams. "Now I am really living" means that now I am filling the role of sightseer and the sight is living up to the prototype of sights. This quaint and picturesque village is measured by a Platonic ideal of the Quaint and the Picturesque.

Hence their anxiety during the encounter. For at any minute something could go wrong. A fellow Iowan might emerge from a 'dobe hut; the chief might show them his Sears catalogue. (If the failures are "wrong" enough, as these are, they might still be turned to account as rueful conversation pieces: "There we were expecting the chief to bring us a churinga and he shows up with a Sears catalogue!") They have snatched victory from disaster, but their experience always runs the danger of failure.

They need the ethnologist to certify their experience as genuine. This is borne out by their behavior when the three of them return for the next corn dance. During the dance, the couple do not watch the goings-on; instead they watch the ethnologist! Their highest hope is that their friend should find the dance interesting. And if he should show signs of true absorption, an interest in the goings-on so powerful that he becomes oblivious of his friends—then their cup is full. "Didn't we tell you?" they say at last. What they want from him is not ethnological explanations; all they want is his approval.

What has taken place is a radical loss of sovereignty over that which is as much theirs as it is the ethnologist's. The fault does not lie with the ethnologist. He has no wish to stake a claim to the village; in fact, he desires the opposite: he will bore his friends to death by telling them about the village and the meaning of the folkways. A degree of sovereignty has been surrendered by the couple. It is the nature of the loss, moreover, that they are not aware of the loss, beyond a certain uneasiness. (Even if they read this and admitted it, it would be very difficult for them to bridge the gap in their confrontation of the world. Their consciousness of the corn dance cannot escape their consciousness of their consciousness, so that with the onset of the first direct enjoyment, their higher consciousness pounces and certifies: "Now you are doing it! Now you are really living!" and, in certifying the experience, sets it at nought.)

Their basic placement in the world is such that they recognize a 32 priority of title of the expert over his particular department of being. The whole horizon of being is staked out by "them," the experts. The highest satisfaction of the sightseer (not merely the tourist but any layman seer of sights) is that his sight should be certified as genuine. The worst of this impoverishment is that there is no sense of impoverishment. The surrender of title is so complete that it never even occurs to one to reassert title. A poor man may envy the rich man, but the sightseer does not envy the expert. When a caste system becomes absolute, envy disappears. Yet the caste of layman-expert is not the fault of the expert. It is due altogether to the eager surrender of sovereignty by the layman so that he may take up the role not of the person but of the consumer.

I do not refer only to the special relation of layman to theorist. I refer to the general situation in which sovereignty is surrendered to a class of privileged knowers, whether these be theorists or artists. A reader may surrender sovereignty over that which has been written about, just as a consumer may surrender sovereignty over a thing which has been theorized about. The consumer is content to receive an experience just as it has been presented to him by theorists and planners. The reader may also be content to judge life by whether it has or has not been formulated by those who know and write about life. A young man goes to France. He too has a fair time of it, sees the sights, enjoys the food. On his last day, in fact as he sits in a restaurant in Le Havre waiting for his boat, something happens. A group of French students in the restaurant get into an impassioned argument over a recent play. A riot takes place. Madame la concierge joins in, swinging her mop at the rioters. Our young American is transported. This is "it." And he had almost left France without seeing "it"!

But the young man's delight is ambiguous. On the one hand, it is a pleasure for him to encounter the same Gallic temperament he had heard about from Puccini and Rolland.[3] But on the other hand, the source of his pleasure testifies to a certain alienation. For the young

---

[3]**Puccini**: Giacomo Puccini (1853–1924), the Italian composer of such well-known operas as *La Bohème* (1896) and *Madame Butterfly* (1904); **Rolland**: Romain Rolland (1866–1944), Nobel-prize-winning French novelist and dramatist.—EDS.

man is actually barred from a direct encounter with anything French excepting only that which has been set forth, authenticated by Puccini and Rolland—those who know. If he had encountered the restaurant scene without reading Hemingway, without knowing that the performance was so typically, charmingly French, he would not have been delighted. He would only have been anxious at seeing things get out of hand. The source of his delight is the sanction of those who know.

This loss of sovereignty is not a marginal process, as might appear from my example of estranged sightseers. It is a generalized surrender of the horizon to those experts within whose competence a particular segment of the horizon is thought to lie. Kwakiutls are surrendered to Franz Boas;[4] decaying Southern mansions are surrendered to Faulkner and Tennessee Williams. So that, although it is by no means the intention of the expert to expropriate sovereignty—in fact he would not even know what sovereignty meant in this context—the danger of theory and consumption is a seduction and deprivation of the consumer.

In the New Mexican desert, natives occasionally come across strange-looking artifacts which have fallen from the skies and which are stenciled: *Return to U.S. Experimental Project, Alamogordo. Reward.* The finder returns the object and is rewarded. He knows nothing of the nature of the object has found and does not care to know. The sole role of the native, the highest role he can play, is that of finder and returner of the mysterious equipment.

The same is true of the layman's relation to *natural* objects in a modern technical society. No matter what the object or event is, whether it is a star, a swallow, a Kwakiutl, a "psychological phenomenon," the layman who confronts it does not confront it as a sovereign person, as Crusoe confronts a seashell he finds on the beach. The highest role he can conceive himself as playing is to be able to recognize the title of the object, to return it to the appropriate expert and have it certified as a genuine find. He does not even permit himself to see the thing—as Gerard Hopkins[5] could see a rock or a cloud or a field. If anyone asks him why he doesn't look, he may reply that he didn't take that subject in college (or he hasn't read Faulkner).

This loss of sovereignty extends even to oneself. There is the neurotic who asks nothing more of his doctor than that his symptoms should prove interesting. When all else fails, the poor fellow has nothing to offer but his own neurosis. But even this is sufficient if only the doctor will show interest when he says, "Last night I had a curious

[4]**Boas**: Franz Boas (1858–1942), influential German-born American anthropologist who specialized in the languages of and cultures of Native Americans; in 1886 he began studying the Kwakiutl tribe of British Columbia.—Eds.

[5]**Hopkins**: Gerard Manly Hopkins (1844–1889), English poet admired for his observations of nature and his innovative use of rhythm and metrics.—Eds.

sort of dream; perhaps it will be significant to one who knows about such things. It seems I was standing in a sort of alley—" (I have nothing else to offer you but my own unhappiness. Please say that it, at least, measures up, that it is a *proper* sort of unhappiness.)

II

A young Falkland Islander walking along a beach and spying a dead dogfish and going to work on it with his jackknife has, in a fashion wholly unprovided in modern educational theory, a great advantage over the Scarsdale high-school pupil who finds the dogfish on his laboratory desk. Similarly the citizen of Huxley's *Brave New World* who stumbles across a volume of Shakespeare in some vine-grown ruins and squats on a potsherd to read it is in a fairer way of getting at a sonnet than the Harvard sophomore taking English Poetry II.

The educator whose business it is to teach students biology or 40 poetry is unaware of a whole ensemble of relations which exist between the student and the dogfish and between the student and the Shakespeare sonnet. To put it bluntly: A student who has the desire to get at a dogfish or a Shakespeare sonnet may have the greatest difficulty in salvaging the creature itself from the educational package in which it is presented. The great difficulty is that he is not aware that there is a difficulty; surely, he thinks, in such a fine classroom, with such a fine textbook, the sonnet must come across! What's wrong with me?

The sonnet and the dogfish are obscured by two different processes. The sonnet is obscured by the symbolic package which is formulated not by the sonnet itself but by the *media* through which the sonnet is transmitted, the media which the educators believe for some reason to be transparent. The new textbook, the type, the smell of the page, the classroom, the aluminum windows and the winter sky, the personality of Miss Hawkins—these media which are supposed to transmit the sonnet may only succeed in transmitting themselves. It is only the hardiest and cleverest of students who can salvage the sonnet from this many-tissued package. It is only the rarest student who knows that the sonnet must be salvaged from the package. (The educator is well aware that something is wrong, that there is a fatal gap between the student's learning and the student's life: The student reads the poem, appears to understand it, and gives all the answers. But what does he recall if he should happen to read a Shakespeare sonnet twenty years later? Does he recall the poem or does he recall the smell of the page and the smell of Miss Hawkins?)

One might object, pointing out that Huxley's citizen reading his sonnet in the ruins and the Falkland Islander looking at his dogfish on the beach also receive them in a certain package. Yes, but the difference lies in the fundamental placement of the student in the world, a placement which makes it possible to extract the thing from the package. The pupil at Scarsdale High sees himself placed as a consumer receiving an experience-package; but the Falkland Islander exploring his dogfish is a person exercising the sovereign right of a person in his lordship and mastery of creation. He too could use an instructor and a book and a technique, but he would use them as his subordinates, just as he uses his jackknife. The biology student does not use his scalpel as an instrument; he uses it as a magic wand! Since it is a "scientific instrument," it should do "scientific things."

The dogfish is concealed in the same symbolic package as the sonnet. But the dogfish suffers an additional loss. As a consequence of this double deprivation, the Sarah Lawrence student who scores A in zoology is apt to know very little about a dogfish. She is twice removed from the dogfish, once by the symbolic complex by which the dogfish is concealed, once again by the spoliation of the dogfish by theory which renders it invisible. Through no fault of zoology instructors, it is nevertheless a fact that the zoology laboratory at Sarah Lawrence College is one of the few places in the world where it is all but impossible to see a dogfish.

The dogfish, the tree, the seashell, the American Negro, the dream, 44 are rendered invisible by a shift of reality from concrete thing to theory which Whitehead[6] has called the fallacy of misplaced concreteness. It is the mistaking of an idea, a principle, an abstraction, for the real. As a consequence of the shift, the "specimen" is seen as less real than the theory of the specimen. As Kierkegaard[7] said, once a person is seen as a specimen of a race or a species, at that very moment he ceases to be an individual. Then there are no more individuals but only specimens.

To illustrate: A student enters a laboratory which, in the pragmatic view, offers the student the optimum conditions under which an educational experience may be had. In the existential view, however—that view of the student in which he is regarded not as a receptacle of experience but as a knowing being whose peculiar property it is to see himself as being in a certain situation—the modern laboratory could not have been more effectively designed to conceal the dogfish forever.

The student comes to his desk. On it, neatly arranged by his instructor, he finds his laboratory manual, a dissecting board, instruments, and a mimeographed list:

Exercise 22: Materials

1 dissecting board

1 scalpel

[6]**Whitehead:** Alfred North Whitehead (1861–1947), prominent British philosopher and mathematician.—EDS.
[7]**Kierkegaard:** Sören Aabye Kierkegaard (1813–1855), Danish philosopher and theologian.—EDS.

1 forceps

1 probe

1 bottle india ink and syringe

1 specimen of *Squalus acanthias*

The clue to the situation in which the student finds himself is to be found in the last item: 1 specimen of *Squalus acanthias*.

The phrase *specimen of* expresses in the most succinct way imagin- 48 able the radical character of the loss of being which has occurred under his very nose. To refer to the dogfish, the unique concrete existent before him, as a "specimen of *Squalus acanthias*" reveals by its grammar the spoliation of the dogfish by the theoretical method. This phrase, *specimen of*, example of, instance of, indicates the ontological status of the individual creature in the eyes of the theorist. The dogfish itself is seen as a rather shabby expresson of an ideal reality, the species *Squalus acanthias*. The result is the radical devaluation of the individual dogfish. (The *reductio ad absurdum*[8] of Whitehead's shift is Toynbee's[9] employ-ment of it in his historical method. If a gram of NaCl is referred to by the chemist as a "sample of" NaCl, one may think of it as such and not much is missed by the oversight of the act of being of this particular pinch of salt, but when the Jews, and the Jewish religion are understood as—in Toynbee's favorite phrase—a "classical example of" such and such a kind of *Voelkerwanderung*,[10] we begin to suspect that something is being left out.)

If we look into the ways in which the student can recover the dogfish (or the sonnet), we will see that they have in common the stratagem of avoiding the educator's direct presentation of the object as a lesson to be learned and restoring access to sonnet and dogfish as beings to be known, reasserting the sovereignty of knower over known.

In truth, the biography of scientists and poets is usually the story of the discovery of the indirect approach, the circumvention of the educa-tor's presentation—the young man who was sent to the *Technikum*[11] and on his way fell into the habit of loitering in book stores and reading poetry; or the young man dutifully attending law school who on the way became curious about the comings and goings of ants. One remembers the scene in *The Heart Is a Lonely Hunter*[12] where the girl hides in the bushes to hear the Capehart in the big house play Beethoven. Perhaps

---

[8]*reductio ad absurdum*: "A reduction to absurdity" (Latin); the argumentative method by which one shows that a statement carried to its logical conclusion leads to an absurd-ity.—Eds.

[9]**Toynbee**: Arnold Toynbee (1889–1975), British historian who believed that civilizations were formed out of responses to adversity.—Eds.

[10]*Voelkerwanderung*: Barbarian invasion (German).—Eds.

[11]*Technikum*: Technical school (German).—Eds.

[12]*The Heart Is a Lonely Hunter*: A 1940 novel by Carson McCullers (1917–1967).—Eds.

she was the lucky one after all. Think of the unhappy souls inside, who
see the record, worry about scratches, and most of all worry about
whether they are *getting it*, whether they are bona fide music lovers.
What is the best way to hear Beethoven: sitting in a proper silence
around the Capehart or eavesdropping from an azalea bush?

However it may come about, we notice two traits of the second
situation: (1) an openness of the thing before one—instead of being an
exercise to be learned according to an approved mode, it is a garden of
delights which beckons to one; (2) a sovereignty of the knower—instead
of being a consumer of a prepared experience, I am a sovereign way-
farer, a wanderer in the neighborhood of being who stumbles into the
garden.

One can think of two sorts of circumstances through which the 52
thing may be restored to the person. (There is always, of course, the
direct recovery: A student may simply be strong enough, brave enough,
clever enough to take the dogfish and the sonnet by storm, to wrest
control of it from the educators and the educational package.) First by
ordeal: The Bomb falls; when the young man recovers consciousness in
the shambles of the biology laboratory, there not ten inches from his
nose lies the dogfish. Now all at once he can see it, directly and without
let, just as the exile or the prisoner or the sick man sees the sparrow at
his window in all its inexhaustibility; just as the commuter who has had
a heart attack sees his own hand for the first time. In these cases, the
simulacrum of everydayness and of consumption has been destroyed by
disaster; in the case of the bomb, literally destroyed. Secondly, by
apprenticeship to a great man: One day a great biologist walks into the
laboratory; he stops in front of our student's desk; he leans over, picks
up the dogfish, and ignoring instruments and procedure, probes with a
broken fingernail into the little carcass. "Now here is a curious business," he says, ignoring also the proper jargon of the specialty. "Look
here how this little duct reverses its direction and drops into the pelvis.
Now if you would look into a coelacanth, you would see that it—" And
all at once the student can see. The technician and the sophomore who
loves his textbooks are always offended by the genuine research man
because the latter is usually a little vague and always humble before the
thing; he doesn't have much use for the equipment or the jargon.
Whereas the technician is never vague and never humble before the
thing; he holds the thing disposed of by the principle, the formula, the
textbook outline; and he thinks a great deal of equipment and jargon.

But since neither of these methods of recovering the dogfish is
pedagogically feasible—perhaps the great man even less so than the
Bomb—I wish to propose the following educatonal technique which
should prove equally effective for Harvard and Shreveport High
School. I propose that English poetry and biology should be taught as

usual, but that at irregular intervals, poetry students should find dog-fishes on their desks and biology students should find Shakespeare sonnets on their dissection boards. I am serious in declaring that a Sarah Lawrence English major who began poking about in a dogfish with a bobby pin would learn more in thirty minutes than a biology major in a whole semester; and that the latter upon reading on her dissecting board

> That time of year Thou may'st in me behold
> When yellow leaves, or none, or few, do hang
> Upon those boughs which shake against the cold—
> Bare ruin'd choirs where late the sweet birds sang.[13]

might catch fire at the beauty of it.

The situation of the tourist at the Grand Canyon and the biology student are special cases of a predicament in which everyone finds himself in a modern technical society—a society, that is, in which there is a division between expert and layman, planner and consumer, in which experts and planners take special measures to teach and edify the consumer. The measures taken are measures appropriate to the consumer: The expert and the planner *know* and *plan*, but the consumer *needs* and *experiences*.

There is a double deprivation. First, the thing is lost through its packaging. The very means by which the thing is presented for consumption, the very techniques by which the thing is made available as an item of need-satisfaction, these very means operate to remove the thing from the sovereignty of the knower. A loss of title occurs. The measures which the museum curator takes to present the thing to the public are self-liquidating. The upshot of the curator's efforts are not that everyone can see the exhibit but that no one can see it. The curator protests: Why are they so indifferent? Why do they even deface the exhibit? Don't they know it is theirs? But it is not theirs. It is his, the curator's. By the most exclusive sort of zoning, the museum exhibit, the park oak tree, is part of an ensemble, a package, which is almost impenetrable to them. The archaeologist who puts his find in a museum so that everyone can see it accomplishes the reverse of his expectations. The result of his action is that no one can see it now but the archaeologist. He would have done better to keep it in his pocket and show it now and then to strangers.

The tourist who carves his initials in a public place, which is 56 theoretically "his" in the first place, has good reasons for doing so, reasons which the exhibitor and planner know nothing about. He does

---

[13]The opening lines of William Shakespeare's Sonnet 73.—Eds.

so because in his role of consumer of an experience (a "recreational experience" to satisfy a "recreational need") he knows that he is disinherited. He is deprived of his title over being. He knows very well that he is in a very special sort of zone in which his only rights are the rights of a consumer. He moves like a ghost through schoolroom, city streets, trains, parks, movies. He carves his initials as a last desperate measure to escape his ghostly role of consumer. He is saying in effect: I am not a ghost after all; I am a sovereign person. And he establishes title the only way remaining to him, by staking his claim over one square inch of wood or stone.

Does this mean that we should get rid of museums? No, but it means that the sightseer should be prepared to enter into a struggle to recover a sight from a museum.

The second loss is the spoliation of the thing, the tree, the rock, the swallow, by the layman's misunderstanding of scientific theory. He believes that the thing is *disposed of* by theory, that it stands in the Platonic relation of being a *specimen of* such and such an underlying principle. In the transmission of scientific theory from theorist to layman, the expectation of the theorist is reversed. Instead of the marvels of the universe being made available to the public, the universe is disposed of by theory. The loss of sovereignty takes this form: As a result of the science of botany, trees are not made available to every man. On the contrary. The tree loses its proper density and mystery as a concrete existent and, as merely another *specimen of* a species, becomes itself nugatory.

Does this mean that there is no use taking biology at Harvard and Shreveport High? No, but it means that the student should know what a fight he has on his hands to rescue the specimen from the educational package. The educator is only partly to blame. For there is nothing the educator can do to provide for this need of the student. Everything the educator does only succeeds in becoming, for the student, part of the educational package. The highest role of the educator is the maieutic role of Socrates: to help the student come to himself not as a consumer of experience but as a sovereign individual.

The thing is twice lost to the consumer. First, sovereignty is lost: It is 60 theirs, not his. Second, it is radically devalued by theory. This is a loss which has been brought about by science but through no fault of the scientist and through no fault of scientific theory. The loss has come about as a consequence of the seduction of the layman by science. The layman will be seduced as long as he regards beings as consumer items to be experienced rather than prizes to be won, and as long as he waives his sovereign rights as a person and accepts his role of consumer as the highest estate to which the layman can aspire.

As Mounier said, the person is not something one can study and provide for; he is something one struggles for. But unless he also struggles for himself, unless he knows that there is a struggle, he is going to be just what the planners think he is.   *1975*

36

The Unexpected Universe

Stephen Jay Gould, Sex, Drugs, Disasters, and the Extinction of Dinosaurs

Loren Eiseley, The Star Thrower

K. C. Cole, Much Ado about Nothing

To know that what is impenetrable to us really exists, manifesting itself as the highest wisdom and the most radiant beauty, which our dull facilities can comprehend only in the most primitive forms—this knowledge, this feeling, is at the center of true religiousness. In this sense, and in this sense only, I belong to the ranks of the devoutly religious men. *Ib.*

Albert Einstein, from *What I Believe*

It is interesting to contemplate a tangled bank, clothed with many plants of many kinds, with birds singing on the bushes, with various insects flitting about, and with worms crawling through the damp earth, and to reflect that these elaborately constructed forms, so different from each other, and dependent upon each other in so complex a manner, have all been produced by laws acting around us. These laws, taken in the largest sense, being Growth with Reproduction; Inheritance which is almost implied by reproduction; Variability from the indirect and direct action of the conditions of life, and from use and disuse: a Ratio of Increase so high as to lead to a Struggle for Life, and as a consequence to Natural Selection, entailing Divergence of Character and the Extinction of less-improved forms. Thus, from the war of nature, from famine and death, the most exalted object which we are capable of conceiving, namely, the production of the higher animals, directly follows. There is grandeur in this view of life, with its several powers, having been originally breathed by the Creator into a few forms or into one; and that, whilst this planet has gone cycling on according to the fixed law of gravity, from so simple a beginning endless forms most beautiful and most wonderful have been, and are being evolved.

Charles Darwin, conclusion to *The Origin of Species*

The white man drew a small circle in the sand and told the red man, "This is what the Indian knows," and drawing a big circle around the small one, "This is what the white man knows." The Indian took the stick and swept an immense ring around both circles: "This is where the white man and the red man know nothing."

Carl Sandburg, from *The People, Yes*

Stephen Jay Gould

Sex, Drugs, Disasters, and the Extinction of Dinosaurs

Science, in its most fundamental definition, is a fruitful mode of inquiry, not a list of enticing conclusions. The conclusions are the consequence, not the essence.

My greatest unhappiness with most popular presentations of science concerns their failure to separate fascinating claims from the methods that scientists use to establish the facts of nature. Journalists, and the public, thrive on controversial and stunning statements. But science is, basically, a way of knowing—in P. B. Medawar's apt words, "the art of the soluble." If the growing corps of popular science writers would focus on *how* scientists develop and defend those fascinating claims, they would make their greatest possible contribution to public understanding.

Consider three ideas, proposed in perfect seriousness to explain that greatest of all titillating puzzles—the extinction of dinosaurs. Since these three notions invoke the primally fascinating themes of our culture—sex, drugs, and violence—they surely reside in the category of fascinating claims. I want to show why two of them rank as silly speculation, while the other represents science at its grandest and most useful.

Science works with testable proposals. If, after much compilation   4
and scrutiny of data, new information continues to affirm a hypothesis,
we may accept it provisionally and gain confidence as further evidence
mounts. We can never be completely sure that a hypothesis is right,
though we may be able to show with confidence that it is wrong. The
best scientific hypotheses are also generous and expansive: they suggest
extensions and implications that enlighten related, and even far distant, subjects. Simply consider how the idea of evolution has influenced
virtually every intellectual field.

Useless speculation, on the other hand, is restrictive. It generates no
testable hypothesis, and offers no way to obtain potentially refuting
evidence. Please note that I am not speaking of truth or falsity. The
speculation may well be true; still, if it provides, in principle, no
material for affirmation or rejection, we can make nothing of it. It must
simply stand forever as an intriguing idea. Useless speculation turns in
on itself and leads nowhere; good science, containing both seeds for its
potential refutation and implications for more and different testable
knowledge, reaches out. But, enough preaching. Let's move on to dinosaurs, and the three proposals for their extinction.

1. *Sex*: Testes function only in a narrow range of temperature (those
   of mammals hang externally in a scrotal sac because internal
   body temperatures are too high for their proper function). A
   worldwide rise in temperature at the close of the Cretaceous
   period caused the testes of dinosaurs to stop functioning and led
   to their extinction by sterilization of males.
2. *Drugs*: Angiosperms (flowering plants) first evolved toward the
   end of the dinosaurs' reign. Many of these plants contain psychoactive agents, avoided by mammals today as a result of their
   bitter taste. Dinosaurs had neither means to taste the bitterness
   nor livers effective enough to detoxify the substances. They died
   of massive overdoses.
3. *Disasters*: A large comet or asteroid struck the earth some 65
   million years ago, lofting a cloud of dust into the sky and blocking sunlight, thereby suppressing photosynthesis and so drastically lowering world temperatures that dinosaurs and hosts of
   other creatures became extinct.

Before analyzing these three tantalizing statements, we must establish a basic ground rule often violated in proposals for the dinosaurs'
demise. *There is no separate problem of the extinction of dinosaurs.* Too often
we divorce specific events from their wider contexts and systems of
cause and effect. The fundamental fact of dinosaur extinction is its
synchrony with the demise of so many other groups across a wide range
of habitats, from terrestrial to marine.

The history of life has been punctuated by brief episodes of mass extinction. A recent analysis by University of Chicago paleontologists Jack Sepkoski and Dave Raup, based on the best and most exhaustive tabulation of data ever assembled, shows clearly that five episodes of mass dying stand well above the "background" extinctions of normal times (when we consider all mass extinctions, large and small, they seem to fall in a regular 26-million-year cycle). The Cretaceous debacle, occurring 65 million years ago and separating the Mesozoic and Cenozoic eras of our geological time scale, ranks prominently among the five. Nearly all the marine plankton (single-celled floating creatures) died with geological suddenness; among marine invertebrates, nearly 15 percent of all families perished, including many previously dominant groups, especially the ammonites (relatives of squids in coiled shells). On land, the dinosaurs disappeared after more than 100 million years of unchallenged domination.

In this context, speculations limited to dinosaurs alone ignore the larger phenomenon. We need a coordinated explanation for a system of events that includes the extinction of dinosaurs as one component. Thus it makes little sense, though it may fuel our desire to view mammals as inevitable inheritors of the earth, to guess that dinosaurs died because small mammals ate their eggs (a perennial favorite among untestable speculations). It seems most unlikely that some disaster peculiar to dinosaurs befell these massive beasts—and that the debacle happened to strike just when one of history's five great dyings had enveloped the earth for completely different reasons.

The testicular theory, an old favorite from the 1940s, had its root in an interesting and thoroughly respectable study of temperature tolerances in the American alligator, published in the staid *Bulletin of the American Museum of Natural History* in 1946 by three experts on living and fossil reptiles—E. H. Colbert, my own first teacher in paleontology; R. B. Cowles; and C. M. Bogert.

The first sentence of their summary reveals a purpose beyond alligators: "This report describes an attempt to infer the reactions of extinct reptiles, especially the dinosaurs, to high temperatures as based upon reactions observed in the modern alligator." They studied, by rectal thermometry, the body temperatures of alligators under changing conditions of heating and cooling. (Well, let's face it, you wouldn't want to try sticking a thermometer under a 'gator's tongue.) The predictions under test go way back to an old theory first stated by Galileo in the 1630s—the unequal scaling of surfaces and volumes. As an animal, or any object, grows (provided its shape doesn't change), surface areas must increase more slowly than volumes—since surfaces get larger as length squared, while volumes increase much more rapidly, as length cubed. Therefore, small animals have high ratios of surface to volume, while large animals cover themselves with relatively little surface.

Among cold-blooded animals lacking any physiological mechanism
for keeping their temperatures constant, small creatures have a hell of a
time keeping warm—because they lose so much heat through their
relatively large surfaces. On the other hand, large animals, with their
relatively small surfaces, may lose heat so slowly that, once warm, they
may maintain effectively constant temperatures against ordinary fluctuations of climate. (In fact, the resolution of the "hot-blooded dinosaur" controversy that burned so brightly a few years back may simply
be that, while large dinosaurs possessed no physiological mechanism
for constant temperature, and were not therefore warm-blooded in the
technical sense, their large size and relatively small surface area kept
them warm.)

Colbert, Cowles, and Bogert compared the warming rates of small   12
and large alligators. As predicted, the small fellows heated up (and
cooled down) more quickly. When exposed to a warm sun, a tiny 50-
gram (1.76-ounce) alligator heated up one degree Celsius every minute
and a half, while a large alligator, 260 times bigger at 13,000 grams (28.7
pounds), took seven and a half minutes to gain a degree. Extrapolating
up to an adult 10-ton dinosaur, they concluded that a one-degree rise in
body temperature would take eighty-six hours. If large animals absorb
heat so slowly (through their relatively small surfaces), they will also be
unable to shed any excess heat gained when temperatures rise above a
favorable level.

The authors then guessed that large dinosaurs lived at or near their
optimum temperatures; Cowles suggested that a rise in global temperatures just before the Cretaceous extinction caused the dinosaurs to heat
up beyond their optimal tolerance—and, being so large, they couldn't
shed the unwanted heat. (In a most unusual statement within a scientific paper, Colbert and Bogert then explicitly disavowed this speculative extension of their empirical work on alligators.) Cowles conceded
that this excess heat probably wasn't enough to kill or even to enervate
the great beasts, but since testes often function only within a narrow
range of temperature, he proposed that this global rise might have
sterilized all the males, causing extinction by natural contraception.

The overdose theory has recently been supported by UCLA psychiatrist Ronald K. Siegel. Siegel has gathered, he claims, more than 2,000
records of animals who, when given access, administer various drugs to
themselves—from a mere swig of alcohol to massive doses of the big H.
Elephants will swill the equivalent of twenty beers at a time, but do not
like alcohol in concentrations greater than 7 percent. In a silly bit of
anthropocentric speculation, Siegel states that "elephants drink, perhaps, to forget . . . the anxiety produced by shrinking rangeland and the
competition for food."

Since fertile imaginations can apply almost any hot idea to the
extinction of dinosaurs, Siegel found a way. Flowering plants did not

evolve until late in the dionosaurs' reign. These plants also produced an array of aromatic, amino-acid-based alkaloids—the major group of psychoactive agents. Most mammals are "smart" enough to avoid these potential poisons. The alkaloids simply don't taste good (they are bitter); in any case, we mammals have livers happily supplied with the capacity to detoxify them. But, Siegel speculates, perhaps dinosaurs could neither taste the bitterness nor detoxify the substances once ingested. He recently told members of the American Psychological Association: "I'm not suggesting that all dinosaurs OD'd on plant drugs, but it certainly was a factor." He also argued that death by overdose may help explain why so many dinosaur fossils are found in contorted positions. (Do not go gentle into that good night.)

Extraterrestrial catastrophes have long pedigrees in the popular 16 literature of extinction, but the subject exploded again in 1979, after a long lull, when the father-son, physicist-geologist team of Luis and Walter Alvarez proposed that an asteroid, some 10 km in diameter, struck the earth 65 million years ago (comets, rather than asteroids, have since gained favor. Good science is self-corrective).

The force of such a collision would be immense, greater by far than the megatonnage of all the world's nuclear weapons. In trying to reconstruct a scenario that would explain the simultaneous dying of dinosaurs on land and so many creatures in the sea, the Alvarezes proposed that a gigantic dust cloud, generated by particles blown aloft in the impact, would so darken the earth that photosynthesis would cease and temperatures drop precipitously. (Rage, rage against the dying of the light.) The single-celled photosynthetic oceanic plankton, with life cycles measured in weeks, would perish outright, but land plants might survive through the dormancy of their seeds (land plants were not much affected by the Cretaceous extinction, and any adequate theory must account for the curious pattern of differential survival). Dinosaurs would die by starvation and freezing; small, warm-blooded mammals, with more modest requirements for food and better regulation of body temperature, would squeak through. "Let the bastards freeze in the dark," as bumper stickers of our chauvinistic neighbors in sunbelt states proclaimed several years ago during the Northeast's winter oil crisis.

All three theories, testicular malfunction, psychoactive overdosing, and asteroidal zapping, grab our attention mightily. As pure phenomenology, they rank about equally high on any hit parade of primal fascination. Yet one represents expansive science, the others restrictive and untestable speculation. The proper criterion lies in evidence and methodology; we must probe behind the superficial fascination of particular claims.

How could we possibly decide whether the hypothesis of testicular frying is right or wrong? We would have to know things that the fossil record cannot provide. What temperatures were optimal for dinosaurs? Could they avoid the absorption of excess heat by staying in the shade, or in caves? At what temperatures did their testicles cease to function? Were late Cretaceous climates ever warm enough to drive the internal temperatures of dinosaurs close to this ceiling? Testicles simply don't fossilize, and how could we infer their temperature tolerances even if they did? In short, Cowles's hypothesis is only an intriguing speculation leading nowhere. The most damning statement against it appeared right in the conclusion of Colbert, Cowles, and Bogert's paper, when they admitted: "It is difficult to advance any definite arguments against the hypothesis." My statement may seem paradoxical—isn't a hypothesis really good if you can't devise any arguments against it? Quite the contrary. It is simply untestable and unusable.

Siegel's overdosing has even less going for it. At least Cowles extrap- 20 olated his conclusion from some good data on alligators. And he didn't completely violate the primary guideline of siting dinosaur extinction in the context of a general mass dying—for rise in temperature could be the root cause of a general catastrophe, zapping dinosaurs by testicular malfunction and different groups for other reasons. But Siegel's speculation cannot touch the extinction of ammonites or oceanic plankton (diatoms make their own food with good sweet sunlight; they don't OD on the chemicals of terrestrial plants). It is simply a gratuitous, attention-grabbing guess. It cannot be tested, for how can we know what dinosaurs tasted and what their livers could do? Livers don't fossilize any better than testicles.

The hypothesis doesn't even make any sense in its own context. Angiosperms were in full flower ten million years before dinosaurs went the way of all flesh. Why did it take so long? As for the pains of a chemical death recorded in contortions of fossils, I regret to say (or rather I'm pleased to note for the dinosaurs' sake) that Siegel's knowledge of geology must be a bit deficient: muscles contract after death and geological strata rise and fall with motions of the earth's crust after burial—more than enough reason to distort a fossil's pristine appearance.

The impact story, on the other hand, has a sound basis in evidence. It can be tested, extended, refined, and, if wrong, disproved. The Alvarezes did not just construct an arresting guess for public consumption. They proposed their hypothesis after laborious geochemical studies with Frank Asaro and Helen Michael had revealed a massive increase of iridium in rocks deposited right at the time of extinction. Iridium, a rare metal of the platinum group, is virtually absent from indigenous rocks of the earth's crust; most of our iridium arrives on extraterrestrial objects that strike the earth.

The Alvarez hypothesis bore immediate fruit. Based originally on evidence from two European localities, it led geochemists throughout the world to examine other sediments of the same age. They found abnormally high amounts of iridium everywhere—from continental rocks of the western United States to deep sea cores from the South Atlantic.

Cowles proposed his testicular hypothesis in the mid-1940s. Where has it gone since then? Absolutely nowhere, because scientists can do nothing with it. The hypothesis must stand as a curious appendage to a solid study of alligators. Siegel's overdose scenario will also win a few press notices and fade into oblivion. The Alvarezes' asteroid falls into a different category altogether, and much of the popular commentary has missed this essential distinction by focusing on the impact and its attendant results, and forgetting what really matters to a scientist—the iridium. If you talk just about asteroids, dust, and darkness, you tell stories no better and no more entertaining than fried testicles or terminal trips. It is the iridium—the source of testable evidence—that counts and forges the crucial distinction between speculation and science.

The proof, to twist a phrase, lies in the doing. Cowles's hypothesis has generated nothing in thirty-five years. Since its proposal in 1979, the Alvarez hypothesis has spawned hundreds of studies, a major conference, and attendant publications. Geologists are fired up. They are looking for iridium at all other extinction boundaries. Every week exposes a new wrinkle in the scientific press. Further evidence that the Cretaceous iridium represents extraterrestrial impact and not indigenous volcanism continues to accumulate. As I revise this essay in November 1984 (this paragraph will be out of date when the book is published),[1] new data include chemical "signatures" of other isotopes indicating unearthly provenance, glass spherules of a size and sort produced by impact and not by volcanic eruptions, and high-pressure varieties of silica formed (so far as we know) only under the tremendous shock of impact.

My point is simply this: Whatever the eventual outcome (I suspect it will be positive), the Alvarez hypothesis is exciting, fruitful science because it generates tests, provides us with things to do, and expands outward. We are having fun, battling back and forth, moving toward a resolution, and extending the hypothesis beyond its original scope.

As just one example of the unexpected, distant cross-fertilization that good science engenders, the Alvarez hypothesis made a major contribution to a theme that has riveted public attention in the past few months—so-called nuclear winter. In a speech delivered in April 1982, Luis Alvarez calculated the energy that a ten-kilometer asteroid would release on impact. He compared such an explosion with a full nuclear exchange and implied that all-out atomic war might unleash similar consequences.

This theme of impact leading to massive dust clouds and falling 28 temperatures formed an important input to the decision of Carl Sagan and a group of colleagues to model the climatic consequences of nuclear holocaust. Full nuclear exchange would probably generate the same kind of dust cloud and darkening that may have wiped out the dinosaurs. Temperatures would drop precipitously and agriculture might become impossible. Avoidance of nuclear war is fundamentally an ethical and political imperative, but we must know the factual consequences to make firm judgments. I am heartened by a final link across disciplines and deep concerns—another criterion, by the way, of science at its best.[2] A recognition of the very phenomenon that made our evolution possible by exterminating the previously dominant dinosaurs and clearing a way for the evolution of large mammals, including us, might actually help to save us from joining those magnificent beasts in contorted poses among the strata of the earth.   *1984*

Loren Eiseley

The Star Thrower

Who is the man walking in the Way? An eye glaring in the skull.
—Seccho

I

It has ever been my lot, though formally myself a teacher, to be taught surely by none. There are times when I have thought to read lessons in the sky, or in books, or from the behavior of my fellows, but in the end my perceptions have frequently been inadequate or betrayed. Nevertheless, I venture to say that of what man may be I have caught a fugitive glimpse, not among multitudes of men, but along an endless wave-beaten coast at dawn. As always, there is this apparent break, this rift in nature, before the insight comes. The terrible question has to translate itself into an even more terrifying freedom.

---

[2]This quirky connection so tickles my fancy that I break my own strict rule about eliminating redundancies from [this essay]. . . .—Gould's note.

If there is any meaning to this book [*The Unexpected Universe*], it began on the beaches of Costabel with just such a leap across an unknown abyss. It began, if I may borrow the expression from a Buddhist sage, with the skull and the eye. I was the skull. I was the inhumanly stripped skeleton without voice, without hope, wandering alone upon the shores of the world. I was devoid of pity, because pity implies hope. There was, in this desiccated skull, only an eye like a pharos light, a beacon, a search beam revolving endlessly in sunless noonday or black night. Ideas like swarms of insects rose to the beam, but the light consumed them. Upon that shore meaning had ceased. There were only the dead skull and the revolving eye. With such an eye, some have said, science looks upon the world. I do not know. I know only that I was the skull of emptiness and the endlessly revolving light without pity.

Once, in a dingy restaurant in the town, I had heard a woman say: "My father reads a goose bone for the weather." A modern primitive, I had thought, a diviner, using a method older than Stonehenge, as old as the arctic forests.

"And where does he do that?" the woman's companion had asked 4 amusedly.

"In Costabel," she answered complacently, "in Costabel." The voice came back and buzzed faintly for a moment in the dark under the revolving eye. It did not make sense, but nothing in Costabel made sense. Perhaps that was why I had finally found myself in Costabel. Perhaps all men are destined at some time to arrive there as I did.

I had come by quite ordinary means, but I was still the skull with the eye. I concealed myself beneath a fisherman's cap and sunglasses, so that I looked like everyone else on the beach. This is the way things are managed in Costabel. It is on the shore that the revolving eye begins its beam and the whispers rise in the empty darkness of the skull.

The beaches of Costabel are littered with the debris of life. Shells are cast up in windrows; a hermit crab, fumbling for a new home in the depths, is tossed naked ashore, where the waiting gulls cut him to pieces. Along the strip of wet sand that marks the ebbing and flowing of the tide, death walks hugely and in many forms. Even the torn fragments of green sponge yield bits of scrambling life striving to return to the great mother that has nourished and protected them.

In the end the sea rejects its offspring. They cannot fight their 8 way home through the surf which casts them repeatedly back upon the shore. The tiny breathing pores of starfish are stuffed with sand. The rising sun shrivels the mucilaginous bodies of the unprotected. The seabeach and its endless war are soundless. Nothing screams but the gulls.

In the night, particularly in the tourist season, or during great storms, one can observe another vulturine activity. One can see, in the hour before dawn on the ebb tide, electric torches bobbing like fireflies along the beach. This is the sign of the professional shellers seeking to outrun and anticipate their less aggressive neighbors. A kind of greedy madness sweeps over the competing collectors. After a storm one can see them hurrying along the bundles of gathered starfish, or, toppling and overburdened, clutching bags of living shells whose hidden occupants will be slowly cooked and dissolved in the outdoor kettles provided by the resort hotels for the cleaning of specimens. Following one such episode I met the star thrower.

As soon as the ebb was flowing, as soon as I could make out in my sleeplessness the flashlights on the beach, I arose and dressed in the dark. As I came down the steps to the shore I could hear the deeper rumble of the surf. A gaping hole filled with churning sand had cut sharply into the breakwater. Flying sand as light as powder coated every exposed object like snow. I made my way around the altered edges of the cove and proceeded on my morning walk up the shore. Now and then a stooping figure moved in the gloom or a rain squall swept past me with light pattering steps. There was a faint sense of coming light somewhere behind me in the east.

Soon I began to make out objects, up-ended timbers, conch shells, sea wrack wrenched from the far-out kelp forests. A pink-clawed crab encased in a green cup of sponge lay sprawling where the waves had tossed him. Long-limbed starfish were strewn everywhere, as though the night sky had showered down. I paused once briefly. A small octopus, its beautiful dark-lensed eyes bleared with sand, gazed up at me from a ragged bundle of tentacles. I hesitated, and touched it briefly with my foot. It was dead. I paced on once more before the spreading whitecaps of the surf.

The shore grew steeper, the sound of the sea heavier and more 12 menacing, as I rounded a bluff into the full blast of the offshore wind. I was away from the shellers now and strode more rapidly over the wet sand that effaced my footprints. Around the next point there might be a refuge from the wind. The sun behind me was pressing upward at the horizon's rim—an ominous red glare amidst the tumbling blackness of the clouds. Ahead of me, over the projecting point, a gigantic rainbow of incredible perfection had sprung shimmering into existence. Somewhere toward its foot I discerned a human figure standing, as it seemed to me, within the rainbow, though unconscious of his position. He was gazing fixedly at something in the sand.

Eventually he stooped and flung the object beyond the breaking surf. I labored toward him over a half-mile of uncertain footing. By the time I reached him the rainbow had receded ahead of us, but something of its color still ran hastily in many changing lights across his features. He was starting to kneel again.

In a pool of sand and silt a starfish had thrust its arms up stiffly and was holding its body away from the stifling mud.

"It's still alive," I ventured.

"Yes," he said, and with a quick yet gentle movement he picked up 16 the star and spun it over my head and far out into the sea. It sank in a burst of spume, and the waters roared once more.

"It may live," he said, "if the offshore pull is strong enough." He spoke gently, and across his bronzed worn face the light still came and went in subtly altering colors.

"There are not many come this far," I said, groping in a sudden embarrassment for words. "Do you collect?"

"Only like this," he said softly, gesturing amidst the wreckage of the shore. "And only for the living." He stooped again, oblivious of my curiosity, and skipped another star neatly across the water.

"The stars," he said, "throw well. One can help them."   20

He looked full at me with a faint question kindling in his eyes, which seemed to take on the far depths of the sea.

"I do not collect," I said uncomfortably, the wind beating at my garments. "Neither the living nor the dead. I gave it up a long time ago. Death is the only successful collector." I could feel the full night blackness in my skull and the terrible eye resuming its indifferent journey. I nodded and walked away, leaving him there upon the dune with that great rainbow ranging up the sky behind him.

I turned as I neared a bend in the coast and saw him toss another star, skimming it skillfully far out over the ravening and tumultuous water. For a moment, in the changing light, the sower appeared magnified, as though casting larger stars upon some greater sea. He had, at any rate, the posture of a god.

But again the eye, the cold world-shriveling eye, began its inevitable 24 circling in my skull. He is a man, I considered sharply, bringing my thought to rest. The star thrower is a man, and death is running more fleet than he along every seabeach in the world.

I adjusted the dark lens of my glasses and, thus disguised, I paced slowly back by the starfish gatherers, past the shell collectors, with their vulgar little spades and the stick-length shelling pincers that eased their elderly backs while they snatched at treasures in the sand. I chose to look full at the steaming kettles in which beautiful voiceless things were being boiled alive. Behind my sunglasses a kind of litany began and refused to die down. *"As I came through the desert thus it was, as I came through the desert."*

In the darkness of my room I lay quiet with the sunglasses removed, but the eye turned and turned. In the desert, an old monk had once advised a traveler, the voices of God and the Devil are scarcely distinguishable. Costabel was a desert. I lay quiet, but my restless hand at

the bedside fingered the edge of an invisible abyss. "Certain coasts"—
the remark of a perceptive writer came back to me—"are set apart for
shipwreck." With unerring persistence I had made my way thither.

II

There is a difference in our human outlook, depending on whether
we have been born on level plains, where one step reasonably leads to
another, or whether, by contrast, we have spent our lives amidst glacial
crevasses and precipitous descents. In the case of the mountaineer, one
step does not always lead rationally to another save by a desperate leap
over a chasm, or by an even more hesitant tiptoeing across precarious
snow bridges.

Something about these opposed landscapes has its analogue in the 28
mind of man. Our prehistoric life, one might say, began amidst en-
forested gloom with the abandonment of the protected instinctive life
of nature. We sought, instead, an adventurous existence amidst the
crater lands and ice fields of self-generated ideas. Clambering onward,
we have slowly made our way out of a maze of isolated peaks into the
level plains of science. Here, one step seems definitely to succeed
another, the universe appears to take on an imposed order, and the
illusions through which mankind has painfully made its way for many
centuries have given place to the enormous vistas of past and future
time. The encrusted eye in the stone speaks to us of undeviating
sunlight; the calculated elliptic of Halley's comet no longer forecasts
world disaster. The planet plunges on through a chill void of star years,
and there is little or nothing that remains unmeasured.

Nothing, that is, but the mind of man. Since boyhood I had been
traveling across the endless coordinated realms of science, just as, in the
body, I was a plains dweller, accustomed to plodding through distances
unbroken by precipes. Now that I come to look back, there was one
contingent aspect of that landscape I inhabited whose significance, at
the time, escaped me. "Twisters," we called them locally. They were a
species of cyclonic, bouncing air funnel that could suddenly loom out of
nowhere, crumpling windmills or slashing with devastating fury
through country towns. Sometimes, by modest contrast, more harmless
varieties known as dust devils might pursue one in a gentle spinning
dance for miles. One could see them hesitantly stalking across the alkali
flats on a hot day, debating, perhaps, in their tall, rotating columns,
whether to ascend and assume more formidable shapes. They were the
trickster part of an otherwise pedestrian landscape.

Infrequent though the visitations of these malign creations of the
air might be, all prudent homesteaders in those parts had provided
themselves with cyclone cellars. In the careless neighborhood in which

I grew up, however, we contented ourselves with the queer yarns of cyclonic folklore and the vagaries of weather prophecy. As a boy, aroused by these tales and cherishing a subterranean fondness for caves, I once attempted to dig a storm cellar. Like most such projects this one was never completed. The trickster element in nature, I realize now, had so buffeted my parents that they stoically rejected planning. Unconsciously, they had arrived at the philosophy that foresight merely invited the attention of some baleful intelligence that despised and persecuted the calculating planner. It was not until many years later that I came to realize that a kind of maleficent primordial power persists in the mind as well as in the wandering dust storms of the exterior world.

A hidden dualism that has haunted man since antiquity runs across his religious conceptions as the conflict between good and evil. It persists in the modern world of science under other guises. It becomes chaos versus form or antichaos. Form, since the rise of the evolutionary philosophy, has itself taken on an illusory quality. Our apparent shapes no longer have the stability of a single divine fiat. Instead, they waver and dissolve into the unexpected. We gaze backward into a contracting cone of life until words leave us and all we know is dissolved into the simple circuits of a reptilian brain. Finally, sentience subsides into an animalcule.

Or we revolt and refuse to look deeper, but the void remains. We are rag dolls made out of many ages and skins, changelings who have slept in wood nests or hissed in the uncouth guise of waddling amphibians. We have played such roles for infinitely longer ages than we have been men. Our identity is a dream. We are process, not reality, for reality is an illusion of the daylight—the light of our particular day. In a fortnight, as aeons are measured, we may lie silent in a bed of stone, or, as has happened in the past, be figured in another guise. Two forces struggle perpetually in our bodies: Yam, the old sea dragon of the original Biblical darkness, and, arrayed against him, some wisp of dancing light that would have us linger, wistful, in our human form. "Tarry thou, till I come again"—an old legend survives among us of the admonition given by Jesus to the Wandering Jew. The words are applicable to all of us. Deep-hidden in the human pysche there is a similar injunction, no longer having to do with the longevity of the body but, rather, a plea to wait upon some transcendent lesson preparing in the mind itself.

Yet the facts we face seem terrifyingly arrayed against us. It is as if at our backs, masked and demonic, moved the trickster as I have seen his role performed among the remnant of a savage people long ago. It was that of the jokester present at the most devout of ceremonies. This creature never laughed; he never made a sound. Painted in black, he followed silently behind the officiating priest, mimicking, with the added flourish of a little whip, the gestures of the devout one. His timed and stylized posturings conveyed a derision infinitely more formidable than actual laughter.

In modern terms, the dance of contingency, of the indeterminable, outwits us all. The approaching fateful whirlwind on the plain had mercifully passed me by in youth. In the moment when I witnessed that fireside performance I knew with surety that primitive man had lived with a dark message. He had acquiesced in the admission into his village of a cosmic messenger. Perhaps the primitives were wiser in the ways of the trickster universe than ourselves; perhaps they knew, as we do not, how to ground or make endurable the lightning.

At all events, I had learned, as I watched that half-understood drama by the leaping fire, why man, even modern man, reads goose bones for the weather of his soul. Afterward I had gone out, a troubled unbeliever, into the night. There was a shadow I could not henceforth shake off, which I knew was posturing and would always posture behind me. That mocking shadow looms over me as I write. It scrawls with a derisive pen and an exaggerated flourish. I know instinctively it will be present to caricature the solemnities of my deathbed. In a quarter of a century it has never spoken.

Black magic, the magic of the primeval chaos, blots out or trans- 36 mogrifies the true form of things. At the stroke of twelve the princess must flee the banquet or risk discovery in the rags of a kitchen wench; coach reverts to pumpkin. Instability lies at the heart of the world. With uncanny foresight folklore has long toyed symbolically with what the nineteenth century was to proclaim a reality—namely, that form is an illusion of the time dimension, that the magic flight of the pursued hero or heroine through frogskin and wolf coat has been, and will continue to be, the flight of all men.

Goethe's genius sensed, well before the publication of the *Origin of Species*, the thesis and antithesis that epitomize the eternal struggle of the immediate species against its dissolution into something other: in modern terms, fish into reptile, ape into man. The power to change is both creative and destructive—a sinister gift, which, unrestricted, leads onward toward the formless and inchoate void of the possible. This force can only be counterbalanced by an equal impulse toward specificity. Form, once arisen, clings to its identity. Each species and each individual holds tenaciously to its present nature. Each strives to contain the creative and abolishing maelstrom that pours unseen through the generations. The past vanishes; the present momentarily persists; the future is potential only. In this specious present of the real, life struggles to maintain every manifestation, every individuality, that exists. In the end, life always fails, but the amorphous hurrying stream is held and diverted into new organic vessels in which form persists, though the form may not be that of yesterday.

The evolutionists, piercing beneath the show of momentary stability, discovered, hidden in rudimentary organs, the discarded rubbish of the past. They detected the reptile under the lifted feathers of the bird, the lost terrestrial limbs dwindling beneath the blubber of the giant cetaceans. They saw life rushing outward from an unknown center, just as today the astronomer senses the galaxies fleeing into the infinity of darkness. As the spinning galactic clouds hurl stars and worlds across the night, so life, equally impelled by the centrifugal powers lurking in the germ cell, scatters the splintered radiance of consciousness and sends it prowling and contending through the thickets of the world.

All this devious, tattered way was exposed to the ceaselessly turning eye within the skull that lay hidden upon the bed in Costabel. Slowly that eye grew conscious of another eye that searched it with equal penetration from the shadows of the room. It may have been a projection from the mind within the skull, but the eye was, nevertheless, exteriorized and haunting. It began as something glaucous and blind beneath a web of clinging algae. It altered suddenly and became the sand-smeared eye of the dead cephalopod I had encountered upon the beach. The transformations became more rapid with the concentration of my attention, and they became more formidable. There was the beaten, bloodshot eye of an animal from somewhere within my childhood experience. Finally, there was an eye that seemed torn from a photograph, but that looked through me as though it had already raced in vision up to the steep edge of nothingness and absorbed whatever terror lay in that abyss. I sank back again upon my cot and buried my head in the pillow. I knew the eye and the circumstance and the question. It was my mother. She was long dead, and the way backward was lost.

III

Now it may be asked, upon the coasts that invite shipwreck, why the ships should come, just as we may ask the man who pursues knowledge why he should be left with a revolving search beam in the head whose light falls only upon disaster or the flotsam of the shore. There is an answer, but its way is not across the level plains of science, for the science of remote abysses no longer shelters man. Instead, it reveals him in vaporous metamorphic succession as the homeless and unspecified one, the creature of the magic flight.

Long ago, when the future was just a simple tomorrow, men had cast intricately carved game counters to determine its course, or they had traced with a grimy finger the cracks on the burnt shoulder blade of a hare. It was a prophecy of tomorrow's hunt, just as was the old farmer's anachronistic reading of the weather from the signs on the breastbone of a goose. Such quaint almanacs of nature's intent had sufficed mankind since antiquity. They would do so no longer, nor would formal apologies to the souls of the game men hunted. The hunters had come, at last, beyond the satisfying supernatural world that had always surrounded the little village, into a place of homeless frontiers and precipitous edges, the indescribable world of the natural. Here tools increasingly revenged themselves upon their creators and tomorrow became unmanageable. Man had come in his journeying to a region of terrible freedoms.

It was a place of no traditional shelter, save those erected with the aid of tools, which had also begun to achieve a revolutionary independence from their masters. Their ways had grown secretive and incalculable. Science, more powerful than the magical questions that might be addressed by a shaman to a burnt shoulder blade, could create these tools but had not succeeded in controlling their ambivalent nature. Moreover, they responded all too readily to that urge for tampering and dissolution which is part of our primate heritage.

We had been safe in the enchanted forest only because of our weakness. When the powers of that gloomy region were given to us, immediately, as in a witch's house, things began to fly about unbidden. The tools, if not science itself, were linked intangibly to the subconscious poltergeist aspect of man's nature. The closer man and the natural world drew together, the more erratic became the behavior of each. Huge shadows leaped triumphantly after every blinding illumination. It was a magnified but clearly recognizable version of the black trickster's antics behind the solemn backs of the priesthood. Here, there was one difference. The shadows had passed out of all human semblance; no societal ritual safely contained their posturings, as in the warning dance of the trickster. Instead, unseen by many because it was so gigantically real, the multiplied darkness threatened to submerge the carriers of the light.

Darwin, Einstein, and Freud might be said to have released the shadows. Yet man had already entered the perilous domain that henceforth would contain his destiny. Four hundred years ago Francis Bacon had already anticipated its dual nature. The individuals do not matter. If they had not made their discoveries, others would have surely done so. They were good men, and they came as enlighteners of mankind. The tragedy was only that at their backs the ritual figure with the whip was invisible. There was no longer anything to subdue the pride of man. The world had been laid under the heavy spell of the natural; henceforth, it would be ordered by man.

Humanity was suddenly entranced by light and fancied it reflected light. Progress was its watchword, and for a time the shadows seemed to recede. Only a few guessed that the retreat of darkness presaged the emergence of an entirely new and less tangible terror. Things, in the words of G. K. Chesterton, were to grow incalculable by being calculated. Man's powers were finite; the forces he had released in nature recognized no such limitations. They were the irrevocable monsters conjured up by a completely amateur sorcerer.

But what, we may ask, was the nature of the first discoveries that now threaten to induce disaster? Pre-eminent among them was, of course, the perception to which we have already referred: the discovery of the interlinked and evolving web of life. The great Victorian biologists saw, and yet refused to see, the war between form and formlessness, chaos and antichaos, which the poet Goethe had sensed contesting beneath the smiling surface of nature. "The dangerous gift from above," he had termed it, with uneasy foresight.

By contrast, Darwin, the prime student of the struggle for existence, sought to visualize in a tangled bank of leaves the silent and insatiable war of nature. Still, he could imply with a veiled complacency that man might "with some confidence" look forward to a secure future "of inappreciable length." This he could do upon the same page in the *Origin of Species* where he observes that "of the species now living very few will transmit progeny to a far distant futurity." The contradiction escaped him; he did not wish to see it. Darwin, in addition, saw life as a purely selfish struggle, in which nothing is modified for the good of another species without being directly advantageous to its associated form.

If, he contended, one part of any single species had been formed for 48 the exclusive good of another, "it would annihilate my theory." Powerfully documented and enhanced though the statement has become, famine, war, and death are not the sole instruments biologists today would accept as the means toward that perfection of which Darwin spoke. The subject is subtle and intricate; let it suffice to say here that the sign of the dark cave and the club became so firmly fixed in human thinking that in our time it has been invoked as signifying man's true image in books selling in the hundreds of thousands.

From the thesis and antithesis contained in Darwinism we come to Freud. The public knows that, like Darwin, the master of the inner world took the secure, stable, and sunlit province of the mind and revealed it as a place of contending furies. Ghostly transformations, flitting night shadows, misshapen changelings existed there, as real as anything that haunted the natural universe of Darwin. For this reason, appropriately, I had come as the skull and the eye to Costabel—the coast demanding shipwreck. Why else had I remembered the phrase, except for a dark impulse toward destruction lurking somewhere in the subconscious? I lay on the bed while the agonized eye in the remembered photograph persisted at the back of my closed lids.

It had begun when, after years of separation, I had gone dutifully

home to a house from which the final occupant had departed. In a
musty attic—among old trunks, a broken aquarium, and a dusty heap of
fossil shells collected in childhood—I found a satchel. The satchel was
already a shabby antique, in whose depths I turned up a jackknife and a
"rat" of hair such as women wore at the beginning of the century.
Beneath these lay a pile of old photographs and a note—two notes,
rather, evidently dropped into the bag at different times. Each, in a
thin, ornate hand, reiterated a single message that the writer had
believed important. "This satchel belongs to my son, Loren Eiseley." It
was the last message. I recognized the trivia. The jackknife I had carried
in childhood. The rat of hair had belonged to my mother, and there
were also two incredibly pointed slippers that looked as though they
had been intended for a formal ball, to which I knew well my mother
would never in her life have been invited. I undid the rotted string
around the studio portraits.

Mostly they consisted of stiff, upright bearded men and heavily
clothed women equally bound to the formalities and ritual that attended upon the photography of an earlier generation. No names
identified the pictures, although here and there a reminiscent family
trait seemed faintly evident. Finally I came upon a less formal photograph, taken in the eighties of the last century. Again no names identified the people, but a commercial stamp upon the back identified the
place: Dyersville, Iowa. I had never been in that country town, but I
knew at once it was my mother's birthplace.

Dyersville, the thought flashed through my mind, making the con- 52
nection now for the first time: the dire place. I recognized at once the
two sisters at the edge of the photograph, the younger clinging reluctantly to the older. Six years old, I thought, turning momentarily away
from the younger child's face. Here it began, her pain and mine. The
eyes in the photograph were already remote and shadowed by some
inner turmoil. The poise of the body was already that of one miserably
departing the peripheries of the human estate. The gaze was mutely
clairvoyant and lonely. It was the gaze of a child who knew unbearable
difference and impending isolation.

I dropped the notes and pictures once more into the bag. The last
message had come from Dyersville: "my son." The child in the photograph had survived to be an ill-taught prairie artist. She had been deaf.
All her life she had walked the precipice of mental breakdown. Here on
this faded porch it had begun—the long crucifixion of life. I slipped
downstairs and out of the house. I walked for miles through the streets.

Now at Costabel I put on the sunglasses once more, but the face
from the torn photograph persisted behind them. It was as though I, as
man, was being asked to confront, in all its overbearing weight, the
universe itself. "Love not the world," the Biblical injunction runs, "nei-

ther the things that are in the world." The revolving beam in my mind had stopped, and the insect whisperings of the intellect. There was, at last, an utter stillness, a waiting as though for a cosmic judgment. The eye, the torn eye, considered me.

"But I *do* love the world," I whispered to a waiting presence in the empty room. "I love its small ones, the things beaten in the strangling surf, the bird, singing, which flies and falls and is not seen again." I choked and said, with the torn eye still upon me, "I love the lost ones, the failures of the world." It was like the renunciation of my scientific heritage. The torn eye surveyed me sadly and was gone. I had come full upon one of the last great rifts in nature, and the merciless beam no longer was in traverse around my skull.

But no, it was not a rift but a joining: the expression of love projected beyond the species boundary by a creature born of Darwinian struggle, in the silent war under the tangled bank. "There is no boon in nature," one of the new philosophers had written harshly in the first years of the industrial cities. Nevertheless, through war and famine and death, a sparse mercy had persisted, like a mutation whose time had not yet come. I had seen the star thrower cross that rift and, in so doing, he had reasserted the human right to define his own frontier. He had moved to the utmost edge of natural being, if not across its boundaries. It was as though at some point the supernatural had touched hesitantly, for an instant, upon the natural.

Out of the depths of a seemingly empty universe had grown an eye, like the eye in my room, but an eye on a vastly larger scale. It looked out upon what I can only call itself. It searched the skies and it searched the depths of being. In the shape of man it had ascended like a vaporous emanation from the depths of night. The nothing had miraculously gazed upon the nothing and was not content. It was an intrusion into, or a projection out of, nature for which no precedent existed. The act was, in short, an assertion of value arisen from the domain of absolute zero. A little whirlwind of commingling molecules had succeeded in confronting its own universe.

Here, at last, was the rift that lay beyond Darwin's tangled bank. For a creature, arisen from that bank and born of its contentions, had stretched out its hand in pity. Some ancient, inexhaustible, and patient intelligence, lying dispersed in the planetary fields of force or amidst the inconceivable cold of interstellar space, had chosen to endow its desolation with an apparition as mysterious as itself. The fate of man is to be the ever-recurrent, reproachful Eye floating upon night and solitude. The world cannot be said to exist save by the interposition of that inward eye—an eye various and not under the restraints to be apprehended from what is vulgarly called the natural.

I had been unbelieving. I had walked away from the star thrower in the hardened indifference of maturity. But thought mediated by the eye is one of nature's infinite disguises. Belatedly, I arose with a solitary mission. I set forth in an effort to find the star thrower.

IV

Man is himself, like the universe he inhabits, like the demoniacal 60
stirrings of the ooze from which he sprang, a tale of desolations. He walks in his mind from birth to death the long resounding shores of endless disillusionment. Finally, the commitment to life departs or turns to bitterness. But out of such desolation emerges the awesome freedom to choose—to choose beyond the narrowly circumscribed circle that delimits the animal being. In that widening ring of human choice, chaos and order renew their symbolic struggle in the role of titans. They contend for the destiny of a world.

Somewhere far up the coast wandered the star thrower beneath his rainbow. Our exchange had been brief because upon that coast I had learned that men who ventured out at dawn resented others in the greediness of their compulsive collecting. I had also been abrupt because I had, in the terms of my profession and experience, nothing to say. The star thrower was mad, and his particular acts were a folly with which I had not chosen to associate myself. I was an observer and a scientist. Nevertheless, I had seen the rainbow attempting to attach itself to earth.

On a point of land, as though projecting into a domain beyond us, I found the star thrower. In the sweet rain-swept morning, that great many-hued rainbow still lurked and wavered tentatively beyond him. Silently I sought and picked up a still-living star, spinning it far out into the waves. I spoke once briefly. "I understand," I said. "Call me another thrower." Only then I allowed myself to think, He is not alone any longer. After us there will be others.

We were part of the rainbow—an unexplained projection into the natural. As I went down the beach I could feel the drawing of a circle in men's minds, like that lowering, shifting realm of color in which the thrower labored. It was a visible model of something toward which man's mind had striven, the circle of perfection.

I picked and flung another star. Perhaps far outward on the rim of 64
space a genuine star was similarly seized and flung. I could feel the movement in my body. It was like a sowing—the sowing of life on an infinitely gigantic scale. I looked back across my shoulder. Small and dark against the receding rainbow, the star thrower stooped and flung once more. I never looked again. The task we had assumed was too immense for gazing. I flung and flung again while all about us roared the insatiable waters of death.

But we, pale and alone and small in that immensity, hurled back the living stars. Somewhere far off, across bottomless abysses, I felt as though another world was flung more joyfully. I could have thrown in a frenzy of joy, but I set my shoulders and cast, as the thrower in the rainbow cast, slowly, deliberately, and well. The task was not to be assumed lightly, for it was men as well as starfish that we sought to save. For a moment, we cast on an infinite beach together beside an unknown hurler of suns. It was, unsought, the destiny of my kind since the rituals of the Ice Age hunters, when life in the Northern Hemisphere had come close to vanishing. We had lost our way, I thought, but we had kept, some of us, the memory of the perfect circle of compassion from life to death and back again to life—the completion of the rainbow of existence. Even the hunters in the snow, making obeisance to the souls of the hunted, had known the cycle. The legend had come down and lingered that he who gained the gratitude of animals gained help in need from the dark wood.

I cast again with an increasingly remembered sowing motion and went my lone way up the beaches. Somewhere, I felt, in a great atavistic surge of feeling, somewhere the Thrower knew. Perhaps he smiled and cast once more into the boundless pit of darkness. Perhaps he, too, was lonely, and the end toward which he labored remained hidden—even as with ourselves.

I picked up a star whose tube feet ventured timidly among my fingers while, like a true star, it cried soundlessly for life. I saw it with an unaccustomed clarity and cast far out. With it, I flung myself as forfeit, for the first time, into some unknown dimension of existence. From Darwin's tangled bank of unceasing struggle, selfishness, and death, had arisen, incomprehensibly, the thrower who loved not man, but life. It was the subtle cleft in nature before which biological thinking had faltered. We had reached the last shore of an invisible island—yet, strangely, also a shore that the primitives had always known. They had sensed intuitively that man cannot exist spiritually without life, his brother, even if he slays. Somewhere, my thought persisted, there is a hurler of stars, and he walks, because he chooses, always in desolation, not in defeat.

In the night the gas flames under the shelling kettles would continue to glow. I set my clock accordingly. Tomorrow I would walk in the storm. I would walk against the shell collectors and the flames. I would walk remembering Bacon's forgotten words "for the uses of life." I would walk with the knowledge of the discontinuities of the unexpected universe. I would walk knowing of the rift revealed by the thrower, a hint that there looms, inexplicably, in nature something above the role men give her. I knew it from the man at the foot of the rainbow, the starfish thrower on the beaches of Costabel.   *1969*

K. C. Cole

Much Ado about Nothing

What's nothing? And why should anyone care? Physicists, it turns out, care very much—because nothing is a deep and mysterious kind of something. The vacuum, the very dictionary definition of nothing, is the scene of continuous creation, a churning sea of invisible vibrating fields that continually erupt with particles—particles that effervesce in and out of existence like bubbles in a cosmic foam. The structure of the vacuum offers insights into the evolution of the universe and into the sizes and properties of every particle within it. There are ideal vacuums, false vacuums, liquid vacuums, and frozen vacuums. There is even a concentrated bit of nothing—the Higgs particle (named for British physicist Peter Higgs)—that Frank Wilczek calls "a chip off the old vacuum." Wilczek, a physicist at the University of California at Santa Barbara, along with many of his colleagues, would like to construct a theory of matter that "blames everything on the vacuum."

If all this strikes you as so much nonsense, you aren't alone. Physicists themselves have only just begun to take it seriously. The new view of nothing has amounted to an "invisible revolution"—one that "permits the working scientist today to undertake projects only very recently considered the province of science fiction writers," say University of Capetown physicists B. Müller and J. Rafelski in their new book, *The Structured Vacuum*. Not so surprisingly, Chapter I deals with the difficulty of writing about the vacuum, because no subject is quite as hard to deal with as nothing.

So, what is nothing? Nothing is what you can't tell you're in because it looks the same no matter which way you look at it. It looks the same from the left or from the right. It even looks the same whether you're moving in it or not. It is so uniform that one bit of nothing can't be distinguished from another bit of nothing. This is the kind of idea that physicists like to call nontrivial—which is their way of saying it's a lot more subtle than it seems. It's a definition of nothing that applies to ideal vacuums and false vacuums alike—even to false vacuums containing occasional particles. But it hardly implies that nothing is . . . well, nothing.

Consider a fish. To a fish, nothing is water—a medium so pervasive   4 and featureless that it's all but unsensible. Food floats within the water, currents run through it, its temperature changes, but the water itself is the very structure of the fish's space. A fish can't imagine (if a fish could imagine) that the surface of the water marks the end of his water universe any more than we can contemplate an edge to our universe, a beginning or an end to time. Fish evolved in the backdrop of water, just as human beings evolved in the equally unsensible backdrop of four-dimensional space, of our own peculiar vacuum. Is it any wonder that nothing is unthinkable? Or that when we do try to think about it, we're like fish out of water?

Imaginable or not, the vacuum we live in is alive with the rippling of invisible fields. There is a field for every kind of force and every kind of matter. The fields interlock in complex ways—sometimes interfering with each other to produce, for example, a force (one field) on a particle (another field). "Now we believe that the entire universe is nothing but a field theory," says Harvard physicist Sidney Coleman.

Fields are the stuff of the vacuum. "You can think of a field as a kind of jelly," says Wilczek. "If you tweak it at one end, a wiggle moves through it." If an electron wiggles in the sun, it tweaks the electromagnetic field, and eight minutes later the ripple in the field arrives on earth to tickle an electron in your eye—allowing you to see the light. A light particle is nothing but a large tweak in the electromagnetic jelly (field). "Of course," says Wilczek, "these are very peculiar jellies. They can interpenetrate each other. Also, they look the same whether you're moving through them or not—that's certainly not true of ordinary jelly."

If nothing tweaks the fields, they don't go away. They *can't* go away, because they're part of the structure of the vacuum itself. The fields in their quietest possible state *are* the vacuum. "A vacuum is what you have when you take everything possible away," says Wilczek.

Reconsider the fish. Say he swims in a bathtub. If you take every- 8 thing possible away—waves, ripples, currents, eddies, soap bubbles, and dust particles, you still have something: a volume of water. You can't take the water away because that's the fish's universe, his space-time. A vacuum for the fish is very, very still water.

"The vacuum means that nothing more can be removed," says Coleman. "It's an empty box. But that doesn't mean that the empty box has no structure."

Physicists these days spend a good deal of time thinking about what you have when you take everything else away (or when you get as far away from everything else as you can, which amounts to the same thing). In April 1983 a small sturdy spacecraft called Pioneer, much admired by its parent earthlings for the spectacular photographs it sent back during the 1973 Jupiter fly-by, finally swept past the farthest planet in our solar system. For good. What will Pioneer find out there? Even in interstellar space, a thimbleful of vacuum might contain an atom or two. Discounting that, however, you also have to consider that energy is a kind of matter (and vice versa). That's the meaning of Einstein's $E = mc^2$: energy equals mass times the speed of light squared. So the energy of starlight counts as "something," too.

"Say you get as far away from everything as you can get, and you set up an imaginary telescope," says Wilczek. "If you can see stars, that's still not a vacuum. So say you put a box around yourself and exclude the starlight. You still have to worry about neutrinos, cosmic rays, the microwave background, and so forth. At least you can imagine that you could turn those off, too. But even when you've taken everything away, the vacuum still isn't as empty as it seems."

What could possibly be left? Well, there are the fields—the quiet 12 structure of the vacuum. But in addition there seems to be something that isn't necessarily in its quietest possible state. It has some value, some strength, even in the vacuum. The thing is called the Higgs field, and it can't be taken away because it seems to account for the properties of matter.

"Imagine that the entire universe was permeated with a constant magnetic field," Wilczek suggests. "You would notice certain things that you couldn't explain unless you assumed the presence of the field. The Higgs field is similar to that situation. We see things—the particle masses—that we can't explain, and assuming the presence of the Higgs field explains them." If you couldn't get rid of this mythical magnetic field, it would be part of what you had left when you took everything else away. In other words, it would be part of the structure of the vacuum.

"If we could turn the Higgs field off, we would get a nicer, more vacuumy vacuum," says Wilczek. "There's this ideal vacuum that we can aspire to with the Higgs field turned off, but the world we live in seems to have it." Wilczek is hopeful that the new generation of atom smashers will be able to tweak the Higgs field with sufficient force to produce the hitherto undetected Higgs particle. "Then the theory would be fertile," he says, "and not just talk."

Higgs, schmiggs, it seems clear to physicists that some kind of structure in the vacuum is responsible for giving the particles masses and other properties. Even more bizarre, the vacuum, as noted, is literally popping with particles that appear and disappear—tweaks in the fields too brief to be properly called particles, and so known by the eerie appellation "virtual particles." And, strange as they may seem to us, these "vacuum fluctuations" are old hat to physicists, who've known about them since the early 1920s. They've been proven experimentally "down to the last decimal point," says MIT Institute Professor Victor Weisskopf, who was involved in the discoveries. "You calculate it and it shows up just right."

The fields, that is, are always in some state of motion—even without 16 tweaks. If a field gets enough energy, a piece can break off and take on a life of its own, becoming a particle. But it's obvious by now that what's nothing, and what's something, isn't black and white—not at all as clear cut as "to be or not to be." There seems to be a great chain of being that links vacuums, virtual particles, and "real" particles. There's no clear separation between space and what's in it. Even the "real" particles—the large tweaks in the fields—are linked to each other so that it's impossible ever to single out just one. "What is a particle?" seems like a simple question. "But if you pose that to twelve different physicists," says MIT physicist Alan Guth, "you'll probably get twelve different answers."

Very recent theories presume an even more complicated vacuum—a vacuum popping not only with virtual particles but also with real gluon-antigluon pairs. Gluons are particles that bind other particles, called quarks, together to form protons and neutrons, the constituents of the atomic nucleus. (An antigluon is the antimatter counterpart of a gluon.) Physicists have never been able to fathom why quarks are bound so tightly. A single quark has never been seen. In fact, the force between two quarks seems to increase infinitely as they pull apart—as if they were held together by a powerful spring.

At least one solution to this puzzle has been found lurking in the depths of the "liquid" vacuum. This vacuum is a sea of gluons and antigluons. Like water molecules, gluons prefer to stick together. If you put a quark inside, it would be trapped like air in a bubble. If you looked closely enough at an atom, say Müller and Rafelski, "the nucleus would resemble Swiss cheese." A nucleus is a cluster of bubbles, each bubble being a proton or a neutron filled with quarks that can't escape, just as air can't escape from a bubble in water.

By now you're probably wondering where the vacuum gets the energy to do all this stuff. The vacuum is supposed to be the absolute lowest energy state possible. But if there's all this going on, there has to be energy, and energy is stuff, so how can it be a vacuum? Take heart, the physicists are just as worried as you are. "It's one of the great unsolved problems in physics," says Weisskopf, in his Anglo-Viennese. "One does the following swindle: One calls the energy of the vacuum zero, but with a big red face and a bad conscience. We pull it under the rug." Even Coleman agrees that setting the vacuum energy at zero is somewhat arbitrary. "It's a starting point," he says.

There is, however, one force in the universe that's a neutral judge on 20 matters of energy. It's the one thing we've omitted from our vacuum: gravity. Gravity is a measure of energy, because (according to Einstein) it is the curvature of space-time caused by matter/energy. If there's energy in the vacuum, space should curve. On the other hand, "if you have no gravitational field," says Coleman, "you can be sure you have no energy inside that box. And that's true of our universe. Space is pretty flat. There's no way of understanding it."

Flat or not, "space-time is definitely a kind of stuff," as Guth says. Guth should know. Less than five years ago he proposed an outrageous idea for the creation of the universe based on the rapid inflation of space-time stuff (*Discover*, June 1983). Even he has been amazed to see it embraced like an old friend, and quickly adorned with embellishments. The plot (or at least one of the versions) goes something like this:

Once upon a time (about twenty billion years ago), there was nothing—although not the kind of nothing we're used to today. To be specific, there was something (or nothing?) called a false vacuum, which was packed to the brim with energy and even speckled with occasional particles. (It was still a vacuum because you couldn't tell whether you were moving in it or not.) Like the true vacuum (our vacuum), the false vacuum rippled with tiny fluctuations. One day (eon? millisecond? what do you call time before time began?) a particularly large fluctuation jarred the false vacuum with such force that it began to disintegrate. Whoosh went the universe, inflating from a billionth the size of a proton to the size of grapefruit in less than a millionth of a trillionth of a trillionth of a second. The time was now one trillion trillion trillionth (or so) of a second after the universe began. The universe has been expanding ever since, but at a more stately pace. (Of course, it doesn't expand *into* anything, because it already *is* everything.) All the particles and energy within it come from the energy of the false vacuum.

How can physicists take such an absurd scenario seriously? The truth (which rhymes with Guth) is that it's all based on a few very familiar principles. But as Coleman points out, so is a jet plane. "And if I try to explain the whole jet plane at once, I'll go crazy." So one piece at a time.

Once more, let's reconsider our fish. Say his water vacuum is false. 24 That is, it isn't at its lowest possible energy state. In fact, this happens to be true, because liquid water contains heat, which is energy. When the water drops to its true lowest energy state, it freezes (along with the poor fish). And when water freezes, it releases energy.

But say the fish survives (or a new kind of fish evolves to live in this frozen vacuum). We know that ice is a crystal, it has structure. Would the fish know it had structure? No, because it's the fish's vacuum. How would the fish account for the fact that the crystal wasn't uniform—that is, if he looked up he would see something different from what he would see if he looked sideways or diagonally? Of course, he couldn't actually *see* the crystal, but he could see that things behaved differently depending on how they were oriented in the crystal. He might find, for example, that if he swam in certain directions he would be repelled by mysterious forces. "If he was very smart," says Guth (who wasn't talking about a fish but a little person living in a crystal), "he might notice that if he went backward in time, he could see that his crystal was once water at very high temperature. Our current view of physics is that we live in such an ice crystal."

You can see right away why physicists like this story so well. "The ingredients aren't really new," says Guth. "And it fits together very nicely." The evolution of the universe explains the nature of our present vacuum; the nature of vacuums explains the evolution of the universe. There is much about this that's extremely speculative, of course. So speculative, in fact, that you wouldn't be out of line to ask: Is this stuff science? Or is it the kind of thing a bunch of students might have cooked up one night over a case of beer after watching *Twilight Zone* reruns? What, in the end, is the poor lay reader to make of all this?

The ideas are worth talking about because they seem like good ways of solving long-standing problems. "They're things that need to be pursued to the end," says Coleman. "It doesn't mean they'll last." Weisskopf, who has spent much of his formidable career pushing the importance of popularization, is afraid that these subjects may be too speculative even to *try* to explain to laymen. "A frontier of science like this is extremely unsafe thin ice," he says. "We don't understand it, and you shouldn't be trying to explain things that you don't understand. It's not explainable, because it's not understood."

Physicists, in other words, are engaged in a very serious and impor- 28 tant kind of theoretical play, and the rest of us needn't feel left out if we don't understand all the rules. Neither do they—entirely. "But the only way we can find out the truth," says Weisskopf "is to play with it."

As Mark Twain once remarked, the fascinating thing about science is the wholesale returns of conjecture one gets out of such a trifling investment of fact. And when it comes to vacuums, the conjecture has barely begun. Is it possible, for example, that we're living in another false vacuum? Is there a still more vacuumy vacuum?

Think about a stick of dynamite. Like water, it can exist in various states. As a stick of dynamite on a table, it's in a high energy state, but it's stuck there until something comes along to trigger it—say, a lighted match. Then it releases a lot of energy (and noise!) and turns into a gas. Gas is a lower energy state for the dynamite, even though it's still the same "stuff." In the same way, the original melted vacuum stuck around for a considerable time before something caused it to start freezing into our present-day ice crystal vacuum. Then it turned into a lower energy state of essentially the same stuff.

Now what if a particularly energetic cosmic ray or a fast particle created in one of the new superpowerful accelerators tweaked our present vacuum? It isn't inconceivable, say Müller and Rafelski, that "our vacuum is a big stick of dynamite, and that if we are not careful with it we might destroy our world."

Or take something else familiar to physicists: the fact that particles 32 are created at random in a vacuum. If particles, why not a whole universe? This is the theory of Hunter College physicist Edward Tryon, who in 1973 proposed that the entire universe sprang—literally—from nothing. "I realized," he says, "that if there were any scientific explanation of creation—if the universe had been created as a result of physical law rather than in defiance of it—this had to be it."

It used to be considered an unbreachable law of nature that you couldn't get something from nothing. You could get electric charge, for example, because each bit of positive charge in the universe is balanced by an equal bit of negative charge, so the net amount is zero. The same is true of other quantities, like spin. If you add up all the opposite spins in the universe, they cancel out.

Matter is a different matter, and so is energy. Yet in recent years all the cases in which physicists thought you couldn't get something from nothing have fallen by the wayside. Says Guth, "People are talking about questions that five years ago were considered outside physics." For the first time, scientists are dealing seriously with a subject that until now has been strictly hands off: the *reasons* behind creation. And all because nothing may well turn out to be the source of everything.

In the end, says Wilczek, "physics has totally turned around: now it's accepted that most things started out as nothing. Now we have to explain why certain things aren't nothing any more."   *1985*

37

Understanding Horror

Edgar Allan Poe, The Tell-Tale Heart

Harper's Magazine, In Pursuit of
Pure Horror

The mythic horror movie, like the sick joke, has a dirty job to do. It deliberately appeals to all that is worst in us. It is morbidity unchained, our most base instincts let free, our nastiest fantasies realized . . . and it all happens, fittingly enough, in the dark. For those reasons, good liberals often shy away from horror films. For myself, I like to see the most aggressive of them—*Dawn of the Dead*, for instance—as lifting a trap door in the civilized forebrain and throwing a basket of raw meat to the hungry alligators swimming around in that subterranean river beneath.

Stephen King, from *Why We Crave Horror Movies*

The normal process of life contains moments as bad as any of those which insane melancholy is filled with, moments in which radical evil gets its innings and takes its solid turn. The lunatic's visions of horror are all drawn from the material of daily fact. Our civilization is founded on the shambles, and every individual existence goes out in a lonely spasm of helpless agony. If you protest, my friend, wait till you arrive there yourself! To believe in the carnivorous reptiles of geologic times is hard for our imagination—they seem too much like mere museum specimens. Yet there is no tooth in any one of those museum-skulls that did not daily through long years of the foretime hold fast to the body struggling in despair of some fated living victim. Forms of horror just as dreadful to their victims, if on a smaller spatial scale, fill the world about us today. Here on our very hearths and in our gardens the infernal cat plays with the panting mouse, or holds the hot bird flutter-

ing in her jaws. Crocodiles and rattlesnakes and pythons are at this
moment vessels of life as real as we are; their loathsome existence fills
every minute of every day that drags its length along; and whenever
they or other wild beasts clutch their living prey, the deadly horror
which an agitated melancholiac feels is the literally right reaction on the
situation.

William James, from *Varieties of Religious Experience*

If Poe were alive, he would not have to invent horror; horror would
invent him.

Richard Wright, from *How "Bigger" Was Born*

Edgar Allan Poe
The Tell-Tale Heart

True!—nervous—very, very dreadfully nervous I had been and am;
but why *will* you say that I am mad? The disease had sharpened my
senses—not destroyed—not dulled them. Above all was the sense of
hearing acute. I heard all things in the heaven and in the earth. I heard
many things in hell. How, then, am I mad? Hearken! and observe how
healthily—how calmly I can tell you the whole story.

It is impossible to say how first the idea entered my brain; but once
conceived, it haunted me day and night. Object there was none. Passion
there was none. I loved the old man. He had never wronged me. He had
never given me insult. For his gold I had no desire. I think it was his eye!
yes, it was this! One of his eyes resembled that of a vulture—a pale blue
eye, with a film over it. Whenever it fell upon me, my blood ran cold;
and so by degrees—very gradually—I made up my mind to take the life
of the old man, and thus rid myself of the eye for ever.

Now this is the point. You fancy me mad. Madmen know nothing.
But you should have seen *me*. You should have seen how wisely I
proceeded—with what caution—with what foresight—with what dissimulation I went to work! I was never kinder to the old man than

during the whole week before I killed him. And every night, about midnight, I turned the latch of his door and opened it—oh, so gently! And then, when I had made an opening sufficient for my head, I put in a dark lantern, all closed, closed, so that no light shone out, and then I thrust in my head. Oh, you would have laughed to see how cunningly I thrust it in! I moved it slowly—very, very slowly, so that I might not disturb the old man's sleep. It took me an hour to place my whole head within the opening so far that I could see him as he lay upon his bed. Ha!—would a madman have been so wise as this? And then, when my head was well in the room, I undid the lantern cautiously—oh, so cautiously—cautiously (for the hinges creaked)—I undid it just so much that a single thin ray fell upon the vulture eye. And this I did for seven long nights—every night just at midnight—but I found the eye always closed; and so it was impossible to do the work; for it was not the old man who vexed me, but his Evil Eye. And every morning, when the day broke, I went boldly into the chamber, and spoke courageously to him, calling him by name in a hearty tone, and inquiring how he had passed the night. So you see he would have been a very profound old man, indeed, to suspect that every night, just at twelve, I looked in upon him while he slept.

Upon the eighth night I was more than usually cautious in opening the door. A watch's minute hand moves more quickly than did mine. Never before that night had I *felt* the extent of my own powers—of my sagacity. I could scarcely contain my feelings of triumph. To think that there I was, opening the door, little by little, and he not even to dream of my secret deeds or thoughts. I fairly chuckled at the idea; and perhaps he heard me; for he moved on the bed suddenly, as if startled. Now you may think that I drew back—but no. His room was as black as pitch with the thick darkness (for the shutters were close fastened, through fear of robbers), and so I knew that he could not see the opening of the door, and I kept pushing it on steadily, steadily. 4

I had my head in, and was about to open the lantern, when my thumb slipped upon the tin fastening, and the old man sprang up in the bed, crying out—"Who's there?"

I kept quite still and said nothing. For a whole hour I did not move a muscle, and in the meantime I did not hear him lie down. He was still sitting up in the bed listening—just as I have done, night after night, hearkening to the death watches in the wall.

Presently I heard a slight groan, and I knew it was the groan of mortal terror. It was not a groan of pain or of grief—oh, no!—it was the low stifled sound that arises from the bottom of the soul when over-charged with awe. I knew the sound well. Many a night, just at midnight, when all the world slept, it has welled up from my own bosom, deepening, with its dreadful echo, the terrors that distracted me. I say I knew it well. I knew what the old man felt, and pitied him, although I chuckled at heart. I knew that he had been lying awake ever since the first slight noise, when he had turned in the bed. His fears had been ever since growing upon him. He had been trying to fancy them causeless, but could not. He had been saying to himself—"It is nothing but the wind in the chimney—it is only a mouse crossing the floor," or "it is merely a cricket which has made a single chirp." Yes, he has been trying to comfort himself with these suppositions; but he had found all in vain. *All in vain*; because Death, in approaching him, had stalked with his black shadow before him, and enveloped the victim. And it was the mournful influence of the unperceived shadow that caused him to feel—although he neither saw nor heard—to *feel* the presence of my head within the room.

When I had waited a long time, very patiently, without hearing him 8 lie down, I resolved to open a little—a very very little crevice in the lantern. So I opened it—you cannot imagine how stealthily, stealthily— until, at length, a single dim ray, like the thread of the spider, shot from out the crevice and full upon the vulture eye.

It was open—wide, wide open—and I grew furious as I gazed upon it. I saw it with perfect distinctness—all a dull blue, with a hideous veil over it that chilled the very marrow in my bones; but I could see nothing else of the old man's face or person: for I had directed the ray as if by instinct, precisely upon the damned spot.

And now have I not told you that what you mistake for madness is but over-acuteness of the senses?—now, I say, there came to my ears a low, dull, quick sound, such as a watch makes when enveloped in cotton. I knew *that* sound well too. It was the beating of the old man's heart. It increased my fury, as the beating of a drum stimulates the soldier into courage.

But even yet I refrained and kept still. I scarcely breathed. I held the lantern motionless. I tried how steadily I could maintain the ray upon the eye. Meantime the hellish tattoo of the heart increased. It grew quicker and quicker, and louder and louder every instant. The old man's terror *must* have been extreme! It grew louder, I say, louder every moment!—do you mark me well? I have told you that I am nervous: so I am. And now at the dead hour of the night, amid the dreadful silence of that old house, so strange a noise as this excited me to uncontrollable terror. Yet, for some minutes longer I refrained and stood still. But the beating grew louder, louder! I thought the heart must burst. And now a new anxiety seized me—the sound would be heard by a neighbor! The old man's hour had come! With a loud yell, I threw open the lantern and leaped into the room. He shrieked once—once only. In an instant I dragged him to the floor, and pulled the heavy bed over him. I then smiled gaily, to find the deed so far done. But, for many minutes, the heart beat on with a muffled sound. This, however, did not vex me; it would not be heard through the wall. At length it ceased. The old man was dead. I removed the bed and examined the corpse. Yes, he was stone, stone dead. I placed my hand upon the heart and held it there many minutes. There was no pulsation. He was stone dead. His eye would trouble me no more.

If still you think me mad, you will think no longer when I describe 12 the wise precautions I took for the concealment of the body. The night waned, and I worked hastily, but in silence. First of all I dismembered the corpse. I cut off the head and the arms and the legs.

I then took up three planks from the flooring of the chamber, and deposited all between the scantlings. I then replaced the boards so cleverly, so cunningly, that no human eye—not even *his*—could have detected any thing wrong. There was nothing to wash out—no stain of any kind—no blood-spot whatever. I had been too wary for that. A tub had caught all—ha! ha!

When I had made an end of these labors, it was four o'clock—still dark as midnight. As the bell sounded the hour, there came a knocking at the street door. I went down to open it with a light heart—for what had I *now* to fear? There entered three men, who introduced themselves, with perfect suavity, as officers of the police. A shriek had been heard by a neighbor during the night; suspicion of foul play had been aroused; information had been lodged at the police office, and they (the officers) had been deputed to search the premises.

I smiled—for *what* had I to fear? I bade the gentlemen welcome. The shriek, I said, was my own in a dream. The old man, I mentioned, was absent in the country. I took my visitors all over the house. I bade them search—search *well*. I led them, at length, to *his* chamber. I showed them his treasures, secure, undisturbed. In the enthusiasm of my confidence, I brought chairs into the room, and desired them *here* to rest from their fatigues, while I myself, in the wild audacity of my perfect triumph, placed my own seat upon the very spot beneath which reposed the corpse of the victim.

The officers were satisfied. My *manner* had convinced them. I was 16 singularly at ease. They sat, and while I answered cheerily, they chatted familiar things. But, ere long, I felt myself getting pale and wished them gone. My head ached, and I fancied a ringing in my ears: but still they sat and still chatted. The ringing became more distinct—it continued and became more distinct: I talked more freely to get rid of the feeling: but it continued and gained definitiveness—until, at length, I found that the noise was *not* within my ears.

No doubt I now grew *very* pale—but I talked more fluently, and with a heightened voice. Yet the sound increased—and what could I do? It was *a low, dull, quick sound—much such a sound as a watch makes when enveloped in cotton.* I gasped for breath—and yet the officers heard it not. I talked more quickly—more vehemently; but the noise steadily in-creased. I arose and argued about trifles, in a high key and with violent gesticulations, but the noise steadily increased. Why *would* they not be gone? I paced the floor to and fro with heavy strides, as if excited to fury by the observation of the men—but the noise steadily increased. Oh God! what *could* I do? I foamed—I raved—I swore! I swung the chair upon which I had been sitting, and grated it upon the boards, but the noise arose over all and continually increased. It grew louder—louder—*louder!* And still the men chatted pleasantly, and smiled. Was it possible they heard not? Almighty God!—no, no! They heard!—they suspected!—they *knew!*—they were making a mockery of my horror!—this I thought, and this I think. But any thing was better than this agony! Any thing was more tolerable than this derision! I could bear those hypocritical smiles no longer! I felt that I must scream or die!—and now—again!—hark! louder! louder! louder! *louder!*—

"Villains!" I shrieked, "dissemble no more! I admit the deed!—tear up the planks!—here, here!—it is the beating of his hideous heart!"

1843

Harper's Magazine

In Pursuit of Pure Horror

Judging by the success of the horror story in all of its forms, it appears that Americans crave few sensations as much as the shudder of dread. Other societies fear monsters or vampires or inexorable plagues. But we seem to be most terrified by the spectacle of a seemingly ordinary character—whether presented under the name of Roderick Usher, Norman Bates, or Jason—driven to the point of gro-tesque crime. What does it suggest that during the 1980s this Ur-character almost exclusively has pursued partially clad, cowering young women? Perhaps we are not as reconciled to the ambitions of feminism as we had thought.

Now that the popularity of the slasher film is waning, Hollywood and the publishing syndicates are testing new narratives, hoping to discover the way the all-American murderer will be dressed for the 1990s. To assist in this effort, Harper's Magazine *asked four masters of horror to convene a story-development meeting and plot an updating of the earliest incarnation of this character: the edgy killer of Poe's masterpiece "The Tell-Tale Heart." Were he to reappear among us today, what would he be like? What would goad him to murder? On what victims would he prey?*

The following forum is based on a discussion held at 60 East Fifty-fourth Street. Near here, in 1934, one of New York City's most frightening murderers was apprehended. Albert Fish, an old man described in a contemporary newspaper account as an "undersized, wizened house painter with restless eyes and thin, nervous hands," confessed to eating more than a dozen young children "by the light of a full moon." During his trial, one of Fish's own children testified that his dad was given to reading the Bible while setting fires in the family bathroom and to eating raw steaks by moonlight. During his cannibalistic binge, Fish indulged in severe mortification of the flesh: He inserted sewing needles into his abdomen until they disappeared—after he was captured, X rays revealed twenty-nine of them—and he regularly beat himself with a paddle or tree branches. Fish especially horrified the public with a creepy cheerfulness that he maintained right up to the end. Minutes before his execution, Fish observed how eager he was to try out the electric chair. "What a thrill that will be," he told his guards. "The only one I haven't tried." Jack Hitt served as moderator of this forum.

JACK HITT
is a senior editor of Harper's Magazine.

ROBERT BLOCH
is the author of many books, including Psycho. *His most recent novel,* Lori, *is published by Tor Books.*

SUZY MCKEE CHARNAS
is a Nebula Award-winning science-fiction and fantasy writer. She is best known in the horror genre for her novel The Vampire Tapestry.

HARLAN ELLISON
is the author of dozens of books, teleplays, and motion-picture scripts. His most recent book, Harlan Ellison's Watching, *was published last month by* Underwood-Miller. *He recently completed a screenplay for NBC and Roger Corman.*

GAHAN WILSON
is a cartoonist whose work appears in The New Yorker *and* Playboy *magazines and is the author of* Eddie Deco's Last Caper. *His most recent work is the unillustrated novel* Everybody's Favorite Duck, *which is published by the Mysterious Press.*

I

JACK HITT: I want to talk about Edgar Allan Poe's "The Tell-Tale Heart," and how we might recast that story for a modern audience. Assume that Poe's narrator has been released. To make the story truly contemporary, let's say he gets off on a Fourth Amendment technicality. He's out. It's "The Tell-Tale Heart, Part II." How would we open the story for today's audience?

HARLAN ELLISON: Here's what I'd do. What if the "killer" in Poe's story didn't actually kill the old man? What if he only *thought* he'd done it? What if the old man had died of a heart attack? Our guy gets out because he confessed to a murder he didn't commit! The old man was dead before our guy ever cut him up. What could they arrest him for?

ROBERT BLOCH: Maybe make a cardiac arrest?

HITT: Doc Severinsen, a rimshot, please?   4

ELLISON: Okay. So let's put him in a large city, maybe Detroit. He's been relocated. Now, not only has he been let out but—because he's innocent—he has inherited the old man's money. His picture has been in the paper. Open the story with the old landlady realizing who it is that's living in the back apartment. Also in the area is, perhaps, a Hispanic street gang. They say, "This guy up there, he's got a lot of money." And you reverse the situation. They come after him. So you open with a completely crazy character who believes he's murdered somebody, and you've got these kids who are trying to take him out. I would make *him* the victim.

GAHAN WILSON: I think you're throwing away a great villain.

ELLISON: Now he's a victim *and* a villain. Because eventually he starts taking out the kids.

SUZY MCKEE CHARNAS: I would pick up on Poe's theme of sound. I like the   8
idea of somebody who's supersensitive to sound, going back to the heartbeat in Poe's story. Suppose, in his new life, he can't get away from the noises of everyday life. They drive him crazy.

So maybe he locks up a fire station and torches the place, with the firemen inside, because he can't stand sirens. Maybe the gang members have boom boxes. And he can't stand it, so—an ice pick right through the ears! You did it to my ears; now I'm doing it to yours.

WILSON: Sweet.

CHARNAS: Our guy should work in a very quiet place. Maybe in a beautiful, ornate library.

BLOCH: Where the rule is silence, quiet. Very nice.   12

CHARNAS: Exactly. It's a safe place. But it gets invaded by noisy people, and so he goes for them. Eventually, he gets into a situation where everything backfires, and he ends up paralyzed. He's trapped in a wheelchair, and there are noises all around. He can't get away. He opens his mouth and screams, and the scream begins to crack the wall and break the place apart: He's got a sound inside him that is *that* destructive. That's why sound was so integral to him.

ELLISON: I love the library idea. Maybe he hollows out books. And one day somebody picks up a copy of Halliburton's account of his adventures, opens it, and finds a piece of a face in the book.

BLOCH: And maybe the book is Conrad's *Heart of Darkness*?

HITT: Okay, if this were a movie, what would be the opening scene 16 establishing that this is Poe's character and grabbing the audience?

WILSON: I like Suzy's idea. The overriding obsession of this guy is that life is intolerable. Poe would love this. In "The Fall of the House of Usher," one encounters this supersensitivity. Our guy can't stand the world. It is *too* painful.

I'd kick it off with his release. He is marched out of prison, and he winces frightfully at all these new sounds. Every noise pains him. You could have a short comic scene in front of the judge, and it's a quiet discussion among lawyers. Then the judge finally hits the gavel. And our guy's face is an explosion of tics.

CHARNAS: Say he worked in the prison library, so we can segue our guy straight into a real job when he gets out.

ELLISON: I would start on a long shot—simple credits with white on 20 black. Then you see a little square light, with the camera dollying in smoothly. You begin to hear the voices of a coroner's inquest. You hear a voice saying, "He clearly could not have done it." Another guy says, "But he *thinks* he did it. What's the difference? He's dangerous." Another says, "We can't legislate that. The old man died of a heart attack." "Yes, but he cut the old man up." "All right. That's the desecration of a corpse at most, and he's been in prison for three years already."

As the square of light gets closer, you realize that it's a window, and, closer, it's a madhouse. The camera moves through the window, and he's down below. You shoot straight down on him, and he looks up at you, and you hear the voices say, "We have to let him go."

Then quick cut to a mundane building, a brownstone. You come in on the window, and he is making himself tea on a little hot plate. Then banging on the door. It's the landlady, shaking a newspaper and saying, "I knew there was something about you. Your name isn't Thomas, your name is, uh, uh, Kropotnik! You're the guy who murdered that old man. I want you the hell out of here." The idea is to establish all of the back story as quickly as possible so that you can get into the new material.

CHARNAS: I'd open on a dark street, with the sound of a heartbeat. His heartbeat. My experience with movies is that the visual is not scary. *Sound* is scary. That's why I like this idea. The times I have walked out of movies are when I can close my eyes but not my ears. In *Bonnie and Clyde*, when Gene Hackman has been shot in the head and he's making grotesque sounds, I had to leave. And at the end of

Lina Wertmuller's *Love and Anarchy*, a prison official types, "He died by banging his head against the wall." And you know what's going to happen. They grab this guy with his hands tied behind him, and they start banging his head against the wall. I couldn't stand the sound.

WILSON: I agree. I remember Arch Oboler, the guy who did horror radio   24
shows. One time there was the problem of someone being thrown out a window and landing—swack!—on the sidewalk. So they built a marble slab, miked it, and then the soundman climbed a stepladder and heaved a grapefruit straight down and—swack! The sound was an initial splitting, then a squirting, and then—this is the beautiful part—it made this hideous little slurp as the grapefruit resumed its regular spherical shape, sucking in air. It was a fine, fine sound.

HITT: Has what scares us changed over time?

ELLISON: Everything that scares us today dates back to Jack the Ripper. He is still the operative icon of terror. He may be small potatoes by current standards—a guy mowing down twenty-five people in McDonald's with an Uzi—but the Ripper started it. He created the form.

WILSON: Just as no one paints landscapes the same way since Turner, a creative monster like the Ripper changed the landscape of what scares us. He inspired generations.

ELLISON: He had all the appurtenances of show biz: a name, a style, a   28
media approach. He once mailed a piece of a victim's kidney and claimed that he had eaten the other half.

WILSON: Or he signed his notes, "From hell, Mr. Lusk"—Lusk being the head of the London Vigilance Committee.

ELLISON: "Yours truly, Jack the Ripper" is how he signed the notes that went to the London *Times*. Or when he wrote, "My next victim—to be sure you know who I am—I'm going to nick her ears good and proper." That kind of charming behavior gets you media attention.

WILSON: The prettiest murder he did had a *horse* as a witness. As the murder was occurring, this horse sensed it, reared up, and scared Jackie off. You just don't get details like that too often.

HITT: "Jackie"? That's somewhat familiar, isn't it?   32

WILSON: He gave himself that name. Jackie was very droll, and that's the point. He *changed* the way we were scared. There had been horrible murders aplenty, but he pioneered the grotesque dismemberment of the victim, always with overtones of sexual violence. He culmi-nated one killing by decorating the victim's apartment with her viscera. He set the standard.

ELLISON: At a place called M'Carthy's Rents, he removed the fetus of a pregnant victim and hung her veins on picture hooks. Hardened members of Scotland Yard vomited on the spot.

WILSON: Another aspect of horror that has changed is the extent of documentation in the papers. I remember Ed Gein, on whom Bob based *Psycho*, in the Fifties. When his activities were first reported, the newspapers told you everything: A piece of liver was found in a frying pan, or whatever. Then suddenly this kind of detail stopped, and we got very circumspect announcements.

ELLISON: "The woman was defiled."   36

WILSON: Or "A body was discovered." Now it's gone full circle, and you have a quickly published pocket book that lovingly retells all.

BLOCH: Okay. Where were we in our story? We've gotten to the point where he is living in this rooming house, and we have introduced the gang menace. The landlady has discovered his identity. Now, in order for the plot to advance, we first have to dispose of the land-lady as a menace. I'm talking in technical, workshop terms: Since he lives with her and would be immediately suspected if she died, *he* cannot be the one who kills the landlady. So one of the gang members is after him and kills her by mistake. That takes her out and leaves him where he is.

 With Suzy's idea of sound as the principal leitmotiv and harking back to the original story, it's the heartbeat that sets him off. He removes the hearts of the kids—in different ways—one by one. In the end, of course, after multiple killings, he realizes that the sound that has driven him crazy all this time is the sound of his *own* heart, and he must stop it as well.

CHARNAS: Lovely. I would like the venue to be the library and not some   40
spooky house. The library is his kind of place—quiet. Then it's invaded by these kids.

WILSON: The sequence I see is one in which these kids are doing their damnedest to sneak around, but they can't sneak quietly enough because our guy hears everything.

HITT: Maybe you have a scene in which he stabs through the wall, nailing the kid perfectly.

WILSON: Exactly. When the kid is creeping along, you—the viewer—can't hear a thing. But cut to our guy's point of view, and you hear the crunch, crunch, crunch of someone walking.

ELLISON: Yeah. The kids think he's got this money. That's what is motivat-   44
ing them. One of the toughs says, "You guys have been trying to take out one guy! What's the matter with you?" And they say, "Go ahead and do it." So the gang member knocks out the light bulbs in the hall, thinking this will put our guy at a disadvantage.

 The kid is coming down the hall for him in the dark of night. The kid takes off his shoes so that our guy won't hear him. But, of course, our guy can hear everything and has planted razor blades in the floor.

CHARNAS: Aaah. Pretty farfetched.

ELLISON: Getting cut is one of the most terrifying things. Have you ever gotten a paper cut in the soft folds between your fingers?

CHARNAS: Definitely the worst. 48

ELLISON: So let's cut the soft folds of his toes. What could be worse? Then our guy is on top of him.

WILSON: What if the kid breaks the bulbs, but our guy, like so many Poe characters, is meticulous and prissy. Somehow he knows the bulbs are broken, and he has gathered them up neatly, old-maidishly. He knows the kid is coming and scatters the broken bulb glass in the hall.

ELLISON: Except bulb glass won't cut you that well.

WILSON: In my film it will. 52

ELLISON: One has to strive for verisimilitude.

CHARNAS: Harlan, our guy shouldn't start out as a cut killer. Remember, he *smothered* the old man. What I'd like to see him do is take on a dog. Barking is an effective sound. He's got to get rid of it, but he doesn't know how.

ELLISON: He smothers him in a garbage can?

CHARNAS: I was thinking of drowning. 56

ELLISON: In a dumpster full of rainwater?

CHARNAS: It could be. It should be a physical thing. That's where he gets his taste for actually doing it with his *hands*, not just using a pillow.

ELLISON: First of all, make it a little rat dog. Everybody despises those things—the only animals in the world that go through menopause their entire life. He starts to kill the little rat dog, and our guy's wearing a leather vest. So you hear the dog's paws scrabbling against the vest.

WILSON: No. No. The dog is scratching the wall; that's what sets him off. 60

CHARNAS: No. You've got to have the dog facing him. What sets him off is the yap-yapping.

ELLISON: You've got to get that scrabbling sound against the guy's clothes.

WILSON: I think you're right, Harlan. He grabs the dog and holds it. The dog's going yap, yap, yap. He clamps the dog's mouth shut with one hand; the other hand holds the dog in the air by the neck. You still hear the dog's muffled yaps. So he just takes two fingers, and he slowly and easily pinches the dog's nostrils and suffocates him.

ELLISON: That's horrible, Gahan! 64

CHARNAS: But so delicate. Very nice.

WILSON: And as the dog's muffled yaps die down, you see our guy, and an expression of relief, of bliss, blooms on his face.

II

BLOCH: It's interesting how easily we have moved from the quill pen to the camera. There is no question at this table that this story should be done for the big screen. Cinema is where the enthusiasm is these days. Visualizing. It's much simpler that way. You easily overcome problems that Poe didn't overcome in the original: motivation, rationale—

CHARNAS: —and who tells the story.   68

HITT: If you wrote this story, who *would* tell it?

CHARNAS: Well, it couldn't be Poe's narrator. He's such a blithering psychotic that you can stand him only for the three pages it takes Poe to tell his story. But for something the length we're talking about, he would drive you crazy. You'd have to go to third-person omniscient.

HITT: If you were writing it for today's audience, what events drawn from reality might you use?

WILSON: I think of New York recently, with those kids who just wander   72 around and go wilding. You haven't got a specific villain; you can't track down the killer; and there's no geographical fix. These mobs just suddenly emerge from a subway or spring up in the park.

CHARNAS: That's a monster story, essentially. A monster is a juggernaut.

WILSON: But this is such a modern, Eighties monster: It comes right out of the new chaos theory of the physicists. Out of the general tumult of urban life, this thing suddenly takes form, coalesces—a mob, gathering like a storm.

CHARNAS: Always terrifying is the dead, a fresh corpse. In fact, many cultures so feared lifeless flesh that the burial customs were designed to keep a corpse confined and harmless until the flesh had decayed. Then the bones were dug up and removed to an ossuary. In some cultures, you actually received a second, "final" burial. In other cultures, there existed a special caste of people whose duty was to strip the flesh from the bones of the recently deceased. No matter how sophisticated we have become, we fear few things more than a lifeless body.

WILSON: One of the most horrific things of late involved the serial   76 murderer Ted Bundy. Do you remember a journalist who quit interviewing Bundy several years ago because he thought that everything Bundy uttered was a con? The journalist said, "This son of a bitch Bundy is going to die *conning* someone right up to the end."

Now, do you remember the last interview Bundy gave to that preacher, just hours before his execution? Bundy, with a straight face, blamed everything he did on reading pornography—porn would make Bundys of us all!—and the preacher ate it up. Mean-while, everyone's waiting for the governor to call and say "halt" or "proceed." Bundy is working his con on this preacher—minutes from death—and the phone rings. You can see this on the tape: Bundy locks momentarily in mid-sentence, trembling slightly. But does he turn to look at the guard who answers the phone? To discover his fate? No, he doesn't even glance over, but rather he *carries on* with the con! My blood ran cold when I saw that. It's straight out of Poe.

BLOCH: I think the most horrifying thing that most people can imagine is persistence: something you can't stop, that inexorably continues. In Poe's story—after all, conscience doth make cowards of us all—the heart's beating was what forced the protagonist to confess. Jack the Ripper captured that essence: When would these murders ever end? That's what scares us.

WILSON: The persistence of our protagonist is thematically related to the original: It's the heartbeat that drives our guy mad. In each scene, he is driven to *muffle* his victim.

ELLISON: So if he kills the kid in the hall—   80

WILSON: —he rolls the kid in a carpet!

ELLISON: Or he grabs the landlady's cleaning bucket from the hall closet and stuffs the kid's head into a bucket filled with rags redolent of English polish and carbolic acid. The tools he uses should always be things at hand. That's where you find terror. You're not going to find terror with *Dr. No* superweapons.

WILSON: Maybe he's grabbing a shawl from the table to kill one of the kids and he inadvertently knocks over a bust of Napoleon. It crashes, and he halts momentarily—winces at the noise, furious that he made this sound—and then resumes his killing.

BLOCH: Everything should be done manually. Even in the end, he should   84
use the Aztec technique—in which you cut open the chest with an obsidian knife and scoop out the heart—to cut out his own offend-ing heart!

ELLISON: Have you ever tried to rip a heart out?

BLOCH: Only halfheartedly.

HITT: All right. What about locations? *Alien* took place in deep space—where "no one can hear you scream"—essentially resetting the little-girl-gets-lost-in-the-woods story. And *Psycho* made brilliant use of the shower, that last sanctuary, sensual, private, and safe.

WILSON: What about the toilet?   88

HITT: Well, a shower is sublime; a toilet is farce.

WILSON: I disagree.

HITT: You think a toilet is sublime?

ELLISON: I disagree with you both. *Alien* is terrifying because of the   92
sets—purely sexual images. You enter the ship; you enter a vagina—

WILSON: —it did look like someone's guts.

ELLISON: Remember how the ship was always wet and moist? And the
reason Bob's shower scene works so well is because it is so mundane.
When you take an ordinary object—say, a spoon—and suddenly
this ordinary object is cutting someone's heart out, then it becomes
horrible.

HITT: Is there any longer a place like Bob's shower?

ELLISON: There's the confessional, the bed, the bathroom. They've all   96
been done.

CHARNAS: That's why I like the library. Like Bob's shower, it's peaceful,
safe, and controlled.

WILSON: The charm of our movie is not visual but aural. We should be
thinking about sound.

ELLISON: You know how one scene might work? He's sitting behind the
checkout desk in a two-story library with a wrought-iron balcony
inside. It's very mundane. You've got two guys—avoid the cliché of
two high-school kids giggling and tittering—a couple of pro-
fessorial types. They are softly whispering and flipping through the
card catalogue. That's reality. Then you cut to his perspective. And
the voices are thundering throughout the place, and the riffling
cards sould like the wind.

But you have to build it as the film goes. You cannot start at that   100
pitch.

WILSON: One nice touch might be that he moves very quietly. Everything
he does is quiet. When he removes his keys, it is done carefully.

CHARNAS: Or he wraps them in a handkerchief; or he has each key
wrapped separately. Wait a minute, Harlan. You want to start off
slowly. What if he's taking medication in the institution? We know
he has to take certain drugs. As the plot develops, he stops taking
these drugs, and his senses begin to heighten.

ELLISON: I've got a great scene. He's sitting at the desk, and there's a pile
of books to be checked out. Instead of stamping them, he rests the
stamp gently on a book and then presses quietly.

Suddenly there's a sh-sh-sh. He doesn't know what it is. But it's   104
something very commonplace. It's, maybe, a cricket in the waste-
basket with a half-dozen popcorn balls of paper.

WILSON: Yeah. First he picks up a ball of paper and slowly squeezes it
until he can't squeeze anymore. But he still hears the sound. So he
does this a couple of times, until he squeezes one ball of paper and
the cricket's chirping stops. And that smile plays across his face.

BLOCH: Let me play devil's advocate. If all sounds cause such a reaction,

we might lose the significance of *why* he is killing off these tormen-
tors. Let us say that his rage to suffocate occurs only when he gets
extremely annoyed. Take the cricket. It's a beautiful thing. This is an
introduction. This is what tells the audience that when he hears a
certain kind of sound, he kills the source. It's like *Jaws*. Only we
don't need the rinky-tink music. When he hears the sound that
upsets him, the audience will know.

HITT: Are you saying that only *rhythmic* sounds reminiscent of a heartbeat set him off—the rhythmic chirp of the cricket or a song on the
boom box that has a heartbeat-like bass or the yap-yap of the dog?

WILSON: You're right, Bob. He can't be perpetually pissed off at this   108
painful, noisy world.

CHARNAS: I think we have another problem, though. I'm concerned
about this gang of kids as our victims. I'm fed up with women and
kids always being the victims, even though that reflects reality. I
would like to see, well, one of your professors get it, Harlan. Some
comfortable, secure, white, rich male. Harlan's right that there are
no safe places—no showers—left to violate. But there are *people* we
think of as safe—like white guys with property.

ELLISON: And that's a person we all know—arrogant, supercilious
beyond belief.

CHARNAS: I was thinking of Bill Buckley.

WILSON: Would you like to snuff Bill?   112

ELLISON: Absolutely. I've always hated his nostrils. Have you ever
noticed them? Terrible nostrils, like Judd Nelson's. Roomy enough
to take in boarders. True horror for me is a Judd Nelson movie with
a tight close-up of his face.

HITT: This might be off the subject.

ELLISON: Actually, it isn't. Everything is grist for a good writer. If Suzy's
supercilious character is a victim, then one of the sounds the professor makes constantly is that disdainful sniff-sniff characteristic
of Buckley. Maybe our guy is driven crazy by this rhythmic sniffing.

HITT: Not too comical?   116

ELLISON: Why not have fun? Something commonplace but irritating that
activates his rage.

BLOCH: What do you do if this guy walks down the hall and encounters a
grandfather clock?

CHARNAS: It's not alive.

BLOCH: We have to establish that difference, because that relieves the   120
story of so many questions. He goes off only when the sound comes
from the living.

ELLISON: We can make the psychosis affect him any way we want. It's
easy. He's coming down the hall, and the clock is ticking. He stands
and listens. It's metronomic; in fact, he likes it.

CHARNAS: And then you hear the little dog yapping in the distance and he starts to twitch.

WILSON: Wait, I want to kill the professor. How do we do it? Pile pages of paper over his face?

ELLISON: Bludgeoned by books?   124

WILSON: No, he must be smothered.

HITT: Press his nose into the spine of an open book?

ELLISON: That's ridiculous. You couldn't really kill someone that way. You don't need reality, but you must strive for verisimilitude.

WILSON: Come on, gang, let's kill the professor. How would we do it?   128

ELLISON: We pull his tweed jacket up over his head and tighten it. It's muffling; and it kills him.

WILSON: Tweed is good.

ELLISON: And what if he's carrying his tweed, fresh from the dry cleaner's? It is covered in a plastic bag.

WILSON: Our guy takes the plastic bag and pops it over the professor's   132
head. His gasps are a grotesque version of his sniffing. And we've cast this professor to look as much like Buckley as possible—those bulging eyes looking out of the bag coming into view when he sucks in the bag for air, sniff-sniff, and the bag blowing out sniff-sniff.

III

HITT: We've wiped out the professor, the kids, the old lady. Now, it is often said that the response of fear is related to the sexual response. Is it? And should there be any sexuality in our story?

ELLISON: It's always there.

BLOCH: The Marquis de Sade made that connection; so did Jack the Ripper.

WILSON: The profile of these killers is always one of an enormously sexy   136
person. Ted Bundy. Robert Chambers.

BLOCH: The sexual component operates on several levels. I was robbed in Paris once by Gypsies. They came out of nowhere; it lasted thirty seconds. I felt I'd been raped. This fear, the victim's fear, is sexual. The aggressor—with all the symbols of knives, guns, what have you—is, of course, phallic; he is violating you.

ELLISON: That's one thing the cops, particularly, never understand. They dismiss burglary as nothing too traumatizing since it's only a stolen stereo. What they do not understand is that for most people crime operates on the level of personal revulsion you describe, Bob. It's not your stereo or silverware you care about. It's that they came into your home. They looked in your drawers. They *felt* your underwear.

WILSON: A lot of burglars understand this notion of violation. Many of them physically or biologically violate the place after the burglary. Often they urinate, or defecate, or masturbate.

ELLISON: Or it's banal. They eat half a candy bar and put the other half 140 back in the refrigerator.

HITT: Just to terrify you? Sort of a signature?

ELLISON: Absolutely. Turkish commandos in World War II used to sneak into German camps in sub-zero temperatures. The soldiers would be sleeping together, two guys in one bag, to keep warm. They would cut the throat of *one* guy but leave the other guy alive. If they killed both, they're both dead. But if they left one alive, that guy would need fifteen people to handle him after he wakes up next to his dead buddy. It's the same impulse with burglars. There was one recently in L.A. who would use your toothbrush and then leave it for you with toothpaste on it. And he would prove that he had used it by spitting and leaving a gobbet in the sink.

WILSON: I know this fascinating guy, a Brit. He was with the OSS and the French Resistance. They had a piano wire tied to little sticks, and they'd almost decapitate a guy with this thing. *Then* the violation part came. Because collaborating officers all carried these little dandy hankies in their cuffs—an Erich von Stroheim touch—the members of the Resistance would wipe their piano wire off on this hankie and leave it.

ELLISON: Sometimes they would stuff the hankie into the mouth and out 144 through the neck opening. Sex, religion, and death: They all aspire to the same physical response.

Remember Angela Cartwright in *Alien*? In one scene she is trapped between two corridors with Yaphet Koto, and the alien is coming after her. The shot is low, from behind her, and she's standing with her legs apart. The beast is suddenly in front, hovering over her. The camera shows that scorpion tail coming around and striking up between her legs. Death, terror, and sexuality—all in one.

BLOCH: This connection between fear and sexuality is very physical. Go to your nearest slaughterhouse and watch the cattle being pushed down the ramp to their doom. They will couple. The realization of imminent death evokes sexuality the same way a man has an orgasm when he is hanged by the neck. I believe the reaction is psychological as well as physical—not that I'm personally all that eager to find out.

CHARNAS: The feeling is a physical excitation; whether it's fear or sexuality or whatever, they are biologically related.

BLOCH: I'd like to draw a distinction between these killers and burglars 148 we've been talking about and great horror. What is truly monstrous about any monster is a total innocence of what he is doing, an ignorance of his own monstrosity.

WILSON: That's right. You have to be totally unaware, you have to be solipsistic.

CHARNAS: In *Silence of the Lambs*, one psychiatrist says, "These serial murderers treat people like dolls. They are not real people."

WILSON: One of the Ripper's letters to the commissioner of police has this incredible line in it: "Saw you, box of toys."

HITT: What does that mean? 152

WILSON: He considered people a box of toys.

ELLISON: These attitudes are no different in depth and kind from those of the Ayatollah, who thought nothing about saying, "I'll kill that man; he said something bad." Or kids you see walking the streets who pull out a shake knife and do you for your pocket change.

WILSON: Bundy hardly ever had sex with a living victim. He had to turn this person into an object by killing her. Then he would have his way with her. He said, in much filthier language, "They're not really mine until I've killed them." In other words, he had to remove this distracting element of their being human beings.

BLOCH: You know what he was trying to remove, I think? The judgmen- 156 tal element. That's one of the reasons child molesters go for children. Their sexual performance will not be judged.

ELLISON: There's another great case that's breaking in L.A. A man and a woman who killed. Carol Bundy is the woman's name—no relation to Ted. It's so horrific, it makes Ted look mild by comparison. After the guy killed one woman, who had been one of his lovers, Carol Bundy put the head in her freezer. To Carol, the dead woman had caused the guy to kill her. So every day Carol would remove the head and cry sentimentally over it. She would kiss the head's lips and cry over it.

WILSON: Sentimentality, of course, is a perverse emotion. It takes something real and renders it artificial.

HITT: Let's discuss the end of the story for a minute. How would we actually pull this off? What would be the final gripping scene?

BLOCH: When our guy realizes the sound is coming from within. 160

CHARNAS: For that scene I want to put him in the library—that safe place he has cleansed of the maddening noise caused by others.

ELLISON: You have to build logically to this conclusion, when he actually tears out his own heart. You have him holding the thing, and it's still attached and beating. He's still alive and he says, "Now it will be quiet." And you hear "bump-bump," and you pull back, as the camera—bump-bump—tightens to an iris, and—

WILSON: —a saintly peace comes over his face as he looks at his heart, and his coloration grows paler and paler, and more blissful—

ELLISON: —and the camera irises in—bump-bump—and closes tight on 164 full-screen black and—bump. The end.

HITT: If you knew that this book or movie was going to do quite well, could you end it in a satisfying way that still leaves the door open for *The Tell-Tale Heart III*?

WILSON: The sequel starts with the doctor finishing the last suture, biting the cord and saying, "I think he'll live." Bump-bump. Bump-bump.

ELLISON: I would nail the story shut.

BLOCH: It was a black day in Hollywood when producers discovered Roman numerals. 168

WILSON: You don't have to worry about it, because Hollywood could resurrect this guy no matter what you did to him. You crush him with a cement truck and roll him flat. You could burn him alive. Whatever you do, next year you'll have *The Tell-Tale Heartbreaker*!

ELLISON: *The Beat Goes On?*

BLOCH: *The Tell-Tale Heart Transplant?*

ELLISON: I hate the idea of sequels. As Samuel Johnson said, "What we cannot resist, we must at least attempt to palliate." I won't even discuss it. This story ends right here. 172

1989

38

Origins

Plato, *From* Symposium

Genesis, Chapters One, Two, and Three

Bering Strait Eskimo Creation Myth,
The Time When There Were
No People on the Earth Plain

Mythology is the study of whatever religious or heroic legends are so foreign to a student's experience that he cannot believe them to be true. Hence the English adjective "mythical," meaning "incredible"; and hence the omission from standard European mythologies of all Biblical narratives even when closely paralleled by myths from Persia, Babylonia, Egypt, and Greece, and of all hagiological legends.

Myth has two main functions. The first is to answer the sort of awkward questions that children ask, such as: "Who made the world? How will it end? Who was the first man? Where do souls go after death?" The answers, necessarily graphic and positive, confer enormous power on the various deities credited with the creation and care of souls—and incidentally on their priesthoods.

The second function of myth is to justify an existing social system and account for traditional rites and customs.

Robert Graves, from *Mythology*

Creation myths attempt to reveal the absolute dimension of the relative world. They proclaim the Holy as the ground of being and, taking into account the human experience of alienation from this ground, proclaim it also as the goal of all being. They encourage people to understand themselves, physically, mentally, and spiritually, in the context of the cyclic flow of being and not-being and ultimately in the absolute union of these two.

In a time when old myths are being rejected and "faith" is under attack, these myths rise above the dogmatism and institutionalism which plague all established religions to serve as a testament of their common concern. While showing the provinciality of each religion, they demonstrate the universality of the religious. And they vividly express the fundamental religious point that, while the worldly is meaningless, the world is full of meaning: people, their cultures, and nature itself are all revelations of the Holy, occasions in which the transcendent absolute is immanently manifest. The myths are still valid, because they show how life is a symbol to be lived.

Barbara C. Sproul, from *Primal Myth: Creating the World*

I recall my father saying, "Well, who created the world? You? Who made the sky, the stars, the sun, the moon, man, the animals?" My brother's answer was that everything evolved. He mentioned Darwin. "But," my mother wanted to know, "how can a creature with eyes, ears, lungs, and a brain, evolve from earth and water?" My father used to say, "You can spatter ink, but it won't write a letter by itself." My brother never had an answer for this. As yet none has been found.

Isaac Bashevis Singer, from *Yes*

Plato

From Symposium[1]

Well then, Eryximachus, Aristophanes began, I propose, as you suggested, to take quite a different line from you and Pausanias. I am convinced that mankind has never had any conception of the power of Love, for if we had known him as he really is, surely we should have

---

[1]**Symposium:** In ancient Greece and Rome, a symposium was usually an after-dinner party for drinking and conversation. One of Plato's greatest dialogues, the *Symposium* consists of a discussion on the topic of love by various speakers, including Socrates who delivers the culminating speech. In this excerpt, Aristophanes, who follows Pausanias and Eryximachus, delivers an eloquent myth on the origins of the sexes.—Eps.

raised the mightiest temples and altars, and offered the most splendid sacrifices, in his honor, and not—as in fact we do—have utterly neglected him. Yet he of all the gods has the best title to our service, for he, more than all the rest, is the friend of man; he is our great ally, and it is he that cures us of those ills whose relief opens the way to man's highest happiness. And so, gentlemen, I will do my best to acquaint you with the power of Love, and you in your turn shall pass the lesson on.

First of all I must explain the real nature of man, and the change which it has undergone—for in the beginning we were nothing like we are now. For one thing, the race was divided into three; that is to say, besides the two sexes, male and female, which we have at present, there was a third which partook of the nature of both, and for which we still have a name, though the creature itself is forgotten. For though "hermaphrodite" is only used nowadays as a term of contempt, there really was a man-woman in those days, a being which was half male and half female.

And secondly, gentlemen, each of these beings was globular in shape, with rounded back and sides, four arms and four legs, and two faces, both the same, on a cylindrical neck, and one head, with one face one side and one the other, and four ears, and two lots of privates, and all the other parts to match. They walked erect, as we do ourselves, backward or forward, whichever they pleased, but when they broke into a run they simply stuck their legs straight out and went whirling round and round like a clown turning cartwheels. And since they had eight legs, if you count their arms as well, you can imagine that they went bowling along at a pretty good speed.

The three sexes, I may say, arose as follows. The males were descended from the Sun, the females from the Earth, and the hermaphrodites from the Moon, which partakes of either sex, and they were round and they *went* round, because they took after their parents. And such, gentlemen, were their strength and energy, and such their arrogance, that they actually tried—like Ephialtes and Otus in Homer— to scale the heights of heaven and set upon the gods.

At this Zeus took counsel with the other gods as to what was to be done. They found themselves in rather an awkward position; they didn't want to blast them out of existence with thunderbolts as they did the giants, because that would be saying good-bye to all their offerings and devotions, but at the same time they couldn't let them get altogether out of hand. At last, however, after racking his brains, Zeus offered a solution.

I think I can see my way, he said, to put an end to this disturbance by weakening these people without destroying them. What I propose to do is to cut them all in half, thus killing two birds with one stone, for each one will be only half as strong, and there'll be twice as many of them, which will suit us very nicely. They can walk about, upright, on their two legs, and if, said Zeus, I have any more trouble with them, I shall split them up again, and they'll have to hop about on one.

So saying, he cut them all in half just as you or I might chop up sorb apples[2] for pickling, or slice an egg with a hair. And as each half was ready he told Apollo to turn its face, with the half-neck that was left, toward the side that was cut away—thinking that the sight of such a gash might frighten it into keeping quiet—and then to heal the whole thing up. So Apollo turned their faces back to front, and, pulling in the skin all the way round, he stretched it over what we now call the belly—like those bags you pull together with a string—and tied up the one remaining opening so as to form what we call the navel. As for the creases that were left, he smoothed most of them away, finishing off the chest with the sort of tool a cobbler uses to smooth down the leather on the last, but he left a few puckers round about the belly and the navel, to remind us of what we suffered long ago.

Now, when the work of bisection was complete it left each half with a   8
desperate yearning for the other, and they ran together and flung their arms around each other's necks, and asked for nothing better than to be rolled into one. So much so, that they began to die of hunger and general inertia, for neither would do anything without the other. And whenever one half was left alone by the death of its mate, it wandered about questing and clasping in the hope of finding a spare half-woman—or a whole woman, as we should call her nowadays—or half a man. And so the race was dying out.

Fortunately, however, Zeus felt so sorry for them that he devised another scheme. He moved their privates round to the front, for of course they had originally been on the outside—which was now the back—and they had begotten and conceived not upon each other, but, like the grasshoppers, upon the earth. So now, as I say, he moved their members round to the front and made them propagate among themselves, the male begetting upon the female—the idea being that if, in all these clippings and claspings, a man should chance upon a woman, conception would take place and the race would be continued, while if man should conjugate with man, he might at least obtain such satisfaction as would allow him to turn his attention and his energies to the everyday affairs of life. So you see, gentlemen, how far back we can trace our innate love for one another, and how this love is always trying to reintegrate our former nature, to make two into one, and to bridge the gulf between one human being and another.

And so, gentlemen, we are all like pieces of the coins that children break in half for keepsakes—making two out of one, like the flatfish—

---

[2]**sorb apples**: European fruit related to both the apple and the pear.—Eds.

and each of us is forever seeking the half that will tally with himself. The man who is a slice of the hermaphrodite sex, as it was called, will naturally be attracted by women—the adulterer, for instance—and women who run after men are of similar descent—as, for instance, the unfaithful wife. But the woman who is a slice of the original female is attracted by women rather than by men—in fact she is a Lesbian—while men who are slices of the male are followers of the male, and show their masculinity throughout their boyhood by the way they make friends with men, and the delight they take in lying beside them and being taken in their arms. And these are the most hopeful of the nation's youth, for theirs is the most virile constitution.

I know there are some people who call them shameless, but they are wrong. It is not immodesty that leads them to such pleasures, but daring, fortitude, and masculinity—the very virtues that they recognize and welcome in their lovers—which is proved by the fact that in after years they are the only men who show any real manliness in public life. And so, when they themselves have come to manhood, their love in turn is lavished upon boys. They have no natural inclination to marry and beget children. Indeed, they only do so in deference to the usage of society, for they would just as soon renounce marriage altogether and spend their lives with one another.

Such a man, then, gentlemen, is of an amorous disposition, and 12 gives his love to boys, always clinging to his like. And so, when this boy lover—or any lover, for that matter—is fortunate enough to meet his other half, they are both so intoxicated with affection, with friendship, and with love, that they cannot bear to let each other out of sight for a single instant. It is such reunions as these that impel men to spend their lives together, although they may be hard put to it to say what they really want with one another, and indeed, the purely sexual pleasures of their friendship could hardly account for the huge delight they take in one another's company. The fact is that both their souls are longing for a something else—a something to which they can neither of them put a name, and which they can only give an inkling of in cryptic sayings and prophetic riddles.

Now, supposing Hephaestus were to come and stand over them with his tool bag as they lay there side by side, and suppose he were to ask, Tell me, my dear creatures, what do you really want with one another?

And suppose they didn't know what to say, and he went on, How would you like to be rolled into one, so that you could always be together, day and night, and never be parted again? Because if that's what you want, I can easily weld you together, and then you can live your two lives in one, and, when the time comes, you can die a common death and still be two-in-one in the lower world. Now, what do you say? Is that what you'd like me to do? And would you be happy if I did?

We may be sure, gentlemen, that no lover on earth would dream of refusing such an offer, for not one of them could imagine a happier fate. Indeed, they would be convinced that this was just what they'd been waiting for—to be merged, that is, into an utter oneness with the beloved.

And so all this to-do is a relic of that original state of ours, when we 16 were whole, and now, when we are longing for and following after that primeval wholeness, we say we are in love. For there was a time, I repeat, when we were one, but now, for our sins, God has scattered us abroad, as the Spartans scattered the Arcadians.[3] Moreover, gentlemen, there is every reason to fear that, if we neglect the worship of the gods, they will split us up again, and then we shall have to go about with our noses sawed asunder, part and counterpart, like the basso-relievos on the tombstones. And therefore it is our duty one and all to inspire our friends with reverence and piety, for so we may ensure our safety and attain that blessed union by enlisting in the army of Love and marching beneath his banners.

For Love must never be withstood—as we do, if we incur the displeasure of the gods. But if we cling to him in friendship and reconciliation, we shall be among the happy few to whom it is given in these latter days to meet their other halves. Now, I don't want any coarse remarks from Eryximachus. I don't mean Pausanias and Agathon, though for all I know they may be among the lucky ones, and both be sections of the male. But what I am trying to say is this—that the happiness of the whole human race, women no less than men, is to be found in the consummation of our love, and in the healing of our dissevered nature by finding each his proper mate. And if this be a counsel of perfection, then we must do what, in our present circumstances, is next best, and bestow our love upon the natures most congenial to our own.

And so I say that Love, the god who brings all this to pass, is worthy of our hymns, for his is the inestimable and present service of conducting us to our true affinities, and it is he that offers this great hope for the future—that, if we do not fail in reverence to the gods, he will one day heal us and restore us to our old estate, and establish us in joy and blessedness.

Such, Eryximachus, is my discourse on Love—as different as could be from yours. And now I must ask you again. Will you please refrain from making fun of it, and let us hear what all the others have to say—or rather, the other two, for I see there's no one left but Agathon and Socrates.

c. 370 B.C.

---

[3]**Arcadians**: Sparta and Arcadia were two districts of Ancient Greece with a longstanding rivalry.—Eds.

Genesis

Chapters One, Two, and Three

THE CREATION

CHAPTER 1

1 In the beginning God created the heaven and the earth.

2 And the earth was without form, and void; and darkness was upon the face of the deep. And the Spirit of God moved upon the face of the waters.

3 And God said, Let there be light, and there was light.

4 And God saw the light, that *it was* good: and God divided the light from the darkness.

5 And God called the light Day, and the darkness he called Night. And the evening and the morning were the first day.

6 And God said, Let there be a firmament in the midst of the waters, and let it divide the waters from the waters.

7 And God made the firmament, and divided the waters which *were* under the firmament from the waters which *were* above the firmament: and it was so.

8 And God called the firmament Heaven. And the evening and the morning were the second day.

9 And God said, Let the waters under the heaven be gathered together unto one place, and let the dry *land* appear: and it was so.

10 And God called the dry *land* Earth; and the gathering together of the waters called he Seas: and God saw that *it was* good.

11 And God said, Let the earth bring forth grass, the herb yielding seed, *and* the fruit tree yielding fruit after his kind, whose see *is* in itself, upon the earth: and it was so.

12 And the earth brought forth grass, *and* herb yielding seed after his kind, and the tree yielding fruit, whose seed *was* in itself, after his kind: and God saw that *it was* good.

13 And the evening and the morning were the third day.

14 And God said, Let there be lights in the firmament of the heaven to divide the day from the night; and let them be for signs, and for seasons, and for days, and years:

15 And let them be for lights in the firmament of the heaven to give light upon the earth: and it was so.

16 And God made two great lights; the greater light to rule the day, and the lesser light to rule the night: *he made* the stars also.

17 And God set them in the firmament of the heaven to give light upon the earth.

18 And to rule over the day and over the night, and to divide the light from the darkness: and God saw that *it was* good.

19 And the evening and the morning were the fourth day.

20 And God said, Let the waters bring forth abundantly the moving creature that hath life, and fowl *that* may fly above the earth in the open firmament of heaven.

21 And God created great whales, and every living creature that moveth, which the waters brought forth abundantly, after their kind, and every winged fowl after his kind: and God saw that *it was* good.

22 And God blessed them, saying, Be fruitful, and multiply, and fill the waters in the seas, and let fowl multiply in the earth.

23 And the evening and the morning were the fifth day.

24 And God said, Let the earth bring forth the living creature after his kind, cattle, and creeping thing, and beast of the earth after his kind: and it was so.

25 And God made the beast of the earth after his kind, and cattle after their kind, and every thing that creepeth upon the earth after his kind: and God saw that *it was* good.

26 And God said, Let us make man in our image, after our likeness: and let them have dominion over the fish of the sea, and over the fowl of the air, and over the cattle, and over all the earth, and over every creeping thing that creepeth upon the earth.

27 So God created man in his *own* image, in the image of God created he him; male and female created he them.

28 And God blessed them, and God said unto them, Be fruitful, and multiply, and replenish the earth, and subdue it: and have dominion over the fish of the sea, and over the fowl of the air, and over every living thing that moveth upon the earth.

29 And God said, Behold, I have given you every herb bearing seed, which *is* upon the face of all the earth, and every tree, in the which *is* the fruit of a tree yielding seed; to you it shall be for meat.

30 And to every beast of the earth, and to every fowl of the air, and to every thing that creepeth upon the earth, wherein *there is* life, *I have given* every green herb for meat: and it was so.

31 And God saw every thing that he had made, and, behold, *it was* very good. And the evening and the morning were the sixth day.

CHAPTER 2

1 Thus the heavens and the earth were finished, and all the host of them.

2 And on the seventh day God ended his work which he had made; and he rested on the seventh day from all his work which he had made.

3 And God blessed the seventh day, and sanctified it: because that in it he had rested from all his work which God created and made.

4 These *are* the generations of the heavens and of the earth when they were created, in the day that the LORD God made the earth and the heavens,

5 And every plant of the field before it was in the earth, and every herb of the field before it grew: for the LORD God had not caused it to rain upon the earth, and *there was* not a man to till the ground.

6 But there went up a mist from the earth, and watered the whole face of the ground.

7 And the LORD God formed man *of* the dust of the ground, and breathed into his nostrils the breath of life; and man became a living soul.

8 And the LORD God planted a garden eastward in Eden; and there he put the man whom he had formed.

9 And out of the ground made the LORD God to grow every tree that is pleasant to the sight, and good for food; the tree of life also in the midst of the garden, and the tree of knowledge of good and evil.

10 And a river went out of Eden to water the garden; and from thence it was parted, and became into four heads.

11 The name of the first *is* Pison: that *is* it which compasseth the whole land of Havilah, where *there is* gold;

12 And the gold of that land *is* good: there *is* bdellium and the onyx stone.

13 And the name of the second river *is* Gihon: the same *is* it that compasseth the whole land of Ethiopia.

14 And the name of the third river *is* Hiddekel: that *is* it which goeth toward the east of Assyria. And the fourth river *is* Euphrates.

15 And the LORD God took the man, and put him into the garden of Eden to dress it and to keep it.

16 And the LORD God commanded the man, saying, Of every tree of the garden thou mayest freely eat:

17 But of the tree of knowledge of good and evil, thou shalt not eat of it: for in the day that thou eatest thereof thou shalt surely die.

18 And the LORD God said, *It is* not good that the man should be alone; I will make him an help meet for him.

19 And out of the ground the LORD God formed every beast of the field, and every fowl of the air; and brought *them* unto Adam to see what he would call them: and whatsoever Adam called every living creature, that *was* the name thereof.

20 And Adam gave names to all cattle, and to the fowl of the air, and to every beast of the field; but for Adam there was not found an help meet for him.

21 And the LORD God caused a deep sleep to fall upon Adam, and he slept: and he took one of his ribs, and closed up the flesh instead thereof;

22 And the rib, which the LORD God had taken from man, made he a woman, and brought her unto the man.

23 And Adam said, This *is* now bone of my bones, and flesh of my flesh: she shall be called Woman, because she was taken out of Man.

24 Therefore shall a man leave his father and his mother, and shall cleave unto his wife: and they shall be one flesh.

25 And they were both naked, the man and his wife, and were not ashamed.

THE FALL

CHAPTER 3

1 Now the serpent was more subtil than any beast of the field which the LORD God had made. And he said unto the woman, Yea, hath God said, Ye shall not eat of every tree of the garden?

2 And the woman said unto the serpent, We may eat of the fruit of the trees of the garden:

3 But of the fruit of the tree which *is* in the midst of the garden, God hath said, Ye shall not eat of it, neither shall ye touch it, lest ye die.

4 And the serpent said unto the woman, Ye shall not surely die:

5 For God doth know that in the day ye eat thereof, then your eyes shall be opened, and ye shall be as gods, knowing good and evil.

6 And when the woman saw that the tree *was* good for food, and that it *was* pleasant to the eyes, and a tree to be desired to make *one* wise, she took of the fruit thereof, and did eat, and gave also unto her husband with her; and he did eat.

7 And the eyes of them both were opened, and they knew that they *were* naked; and they sewed fig leaves together, and made themselves aprons.

8 And they heard the voice of the LORD God walking in the garden in the cool of the day: and Adam and his wife hid themselves from the presence of the LORD God amongst the trees of the garden.

9 And the LORD God called unto Adam, and said unto him, Where *art* thou?

10 And he said, I heard thy voice in the garden, and I was afraid, because I *was* naked; and I hid myself.

11 And he said, Who told thee that thou *wast* naked? Hast thou eaten of the tree, whereof I commanded thee that thou shouldest not eat?

12 And the man said, The woman whom thou gavest *to be* with me, she gave me of the tree, and I did eat.

13 And the LORD God said unto the woman, What *is* this *that* thou hast done? And the woman said, The serpent beguiled me, and I did eat.

14 And the LORD God said unto the serpent, Because thou hast

done this, thou *art* cursed above all cattle, and above every beast of the field; upon thy belly shalt thou go, and dust shalt thou eat all the days of thy life:

15 And I will put enmity between thee and the woman, and between thy seed and her seed; it shall bruise thy head, and thou shalt bruise his heel.

16 Unto the woman he said, I will greatly multiply thy sorrow and thy conception; in sorrow thou shalt bring forth children; and thy desire *shall be* to thy husband, and he shall rule over thee.

17 And unto Adam he said, Because thou hast hearkened unto the voice of thy wife, and hast eaten of the tree, of which I commanded thee, saying, Thou shalt not eat of it: cursed *is* the ground for thy sake; in sorrow shalt thou eat *of* it all the days of thy life;

18 Thorns also and thistles shall it bring forth to thee; and thou shalt eat the herb of the field;

19 In the sweat of thy face shalt thou eat bread, till thou return unto the ground; for out of it wast thou taken: for dust thou *art*, and unto dust shalt thou return.

20 And Adam called his wife's name Eve; because she was the mother of all living.

21 Unto Adam also and to his wife did the Lord God make coats of skins, and clothed them.

22 And the Lord God said, Behold, the man is become as one of us, to know good and evil: and now, lest he put forth his hand, and take also of the tree of life, and eat, and live for ever:

23 Therefore the Lord God sent him forth from the garden of Eden, to till the ground from whence he was taken.

24 So he drove out the man; and he placed at the east of the garden of Eden Cherubims, and a flaming sword which turned every way, to keep the way of the tree of life.

Bering Strait Eskimo Creation Myth

The Time When There Were No People on the Earth Plain

It was in the time when there were no people on the earth plain. During four days the first man lay coiled up in the pod of a beach-pea. On the fifth day he stretched out his feet and burst the pod, falling to the ground, where he stood up, a full-grown man. He looked about him, and then moved his hands and arms, his neck and legs, and examined himself curiously. Looking back, he saw the pod from which he had fallen, still hanging to the vine, with a hole in the lower end, out of which he had dropped. Then he looked about him again and saw that he was getting farther away from his starting place, and that the ground moved up and down under his feet and seemed very soft. After a while he had an unpleasant feeling in his stomach, and he stooped down to take some water into his mouth from a small pool at his feet. The water ran down into his stomach and he felt better. When he looked up again he saw approaching, with a waving motion, a dark object which came on until just in front of him, when it stopped, and, standing on the ground, looked at him. This was a raven, and, as soon as it stopped, it raised one of its wings, pushed up its beak, like a mask, to the top of its head, and changed at once into a man. Before he raised his mask Raven had stared at the man, and after it was raised he stared more than ever, moving about from side to side to obtain a better view. At last he said: "What are you? Whence did you come? I have never seen anything like you." Then Raven looked at Man, and was still more surprised to find that this strange new being was so much like himself in shape.

Then he told Man to walk away a few steps, and in astonishment exclaimed again: "When did you come? I have never seen anything like you before." To this Man replied: "I came from the pea-pod." And he pointed to the plant from which he came. "Ah!" exclaimed Raven, "I made that vine, but did not know that anything like you would ever come from it. Come with me to the high ground over there; this ground I made later, and it is still soft and thin, but it is thicker and harder there."

In a short time they came to the higher land, which was firm under their feet. Then Raven asked Man if he had eaten anything. The latter answered that he had taken some soft stuff into him at one of the pools. "Ah!" said Raven, "you drank some water. Now wait for me here."

Then he drew down the mask over his face, changing again into a 4 bird, and flew far up into the sky where he disappeared. Man waited where he had been left until the fourth day, when Raven returned, bringing four berries in his claws. Pushing up his mask, Raven became a man again and held out two salmonberries and two hearthberries, saying, "Here is what I have made for you to eat. I also wish them to be plentiful over the earth. Now eat them." Man took the berries and placed them in his mouth one after the other and they satisfied his hunger, which had made him feel uncomfortable. Raven then led Man to a small creek near by and left him while he went to the water's edge and molded a couple of pieces of clay into the form of a pair of mountain sheep, which he held in his hand, and when they became dry he called Man to show him what he had done. Man thought they were very pretty, and Raven told him to close his eyes. As soon as Man's eyes were closed Raven drew down his mask and waved his wings four times over the images, when they became endowed with life and bounded away as full-grown mountain sheep. Raven then raised his mask and told Man to look. When Man saw the sheep moving away, full of life, he cried out with pleasure. Seeing how pleased Man was, Raven said, "If these animals are numerous, perhaps people will wish very much to get them." And Man said he thought they would. "Well," said Raven, "it will be better for them to have their home among the high cliffs, so that every one can not kill them, and there only shall they be found."

Then Raven made two animals of clay which he endowed with life as before, but as they were dry only in spots when they were given life, they remained brown and white, and so originated the tame reindeer with mottled coat. Man thought these were very handsome, and Raven told him that they would be very scarce. In the same way a pair of wild reindeer were made and permitted to get dry and white only on their bellies, then they were given life; in consequence, to this day the belly of the wild reindeer is the only white part about it. Raven told Man that these animals would be very common, and people would kill many of them.

"You will be very lonely by yourself," said Raven. "I will make you a companion." He then went to a spot some distance from where he had made the animals, and looking now and then at Man, made an image very much like him. Then he fastened a lot of fine water grass on the back of the head for hair, and after the image had dried in his hands, he waved his wings over it as before and a beautiful young woman arose and stood beside Man. "There," cried Raven, "is a companion for you," and he led them back to a small knoll near by.

In those days there were no mountains far or near, and the sun never ceased shining brightly; no rain ever fell and no winds blew. When they came to the knoll, Raven showed the pair how to make a bed in the dry moss, and they slept there very warmly; Raven drew down his mask and slept near by in the form of a bird. Waking before the others, Raven went back to the creek and made a pair each of sticklebacks, graylings, and blackfish. When these were swimming about in the water, he called Man to see them. When the latter looked at them and saw the sticklebacks swim up the stream with a wriggling motion he was so surprised that he raised his hand suddenly and the fish darted away. Raven then showed him the graylings and told him that they would be found in clear mountain streams, while the sticklebacks would live along the seacoast and that both would be good for food. Next the shrew-mouse was made, Raven saying that it would not be good for food but would enliven the ground and prevent it from seeming barren and cheerless.

In this way Raven continued for several days making birds, fishes, 8 and animals, showing them to Man, and explaining their uses. . . .

1899

39

The Search for Truth

Francis Bacon, Idols of the Mind

René Descartes, Stripping the Mind
of Its Beliefs

Shunryu Suzuki, Emptiness

We know the truth not only through our reason but also through our heart. It is through the latter than we know first principles, and reason, which has nothing to do with it, tries in vain to refute them. The sceptics have no other object than that, and they work at it to no purpose. We know that we are not dreaming, but, however unable we may be to prove it rationally, our inability proves nothing but the weakness of our reason, and not the uncertainty of all our knowledge, as they maintain.

Blaise Pascal, from *Pensées*

Convictions are more dangerous enemies of truth than lies.

Friedrich Nietzsche, from *Human, All Too Human*

Can we actually "know" the universe? My God, it's hard enough finding your way around in Chinatown. The point, however, is: Is there anything out there? And why? And must they be so noisy? Finally, there can be no doubt that the one characteristic of "reality" is that it lacks essence. That is not to say it has no essence, but merely lacks it. (The reality I speak of here is the same one Hobbes described, but a little smaller.) Therefore the Cartesian dictum "I think, therefore I am" might better be expressed "Hey, there goes Edna with a saxophone!" So, then, to know a substance or an idea we must doubt it, and thus, doubting it, come to perceive the qualities it possesses in its finite state, which are truly "in the thing itself," or "of the thing itself," or of something or nothing. If this is clear, we can leave epistemology for the moment.

Woody Allen, from *Getting Even*

Francis Bacon

Idols of the Mind

1

There are four classes of Idols which beset men's minds. To these for distinction's sake I have assigned names—calling the first class *Idols of the Tribe*; the second, *Idols of the Cave*; the third, *Idols of the Market-place*; the fourth, *Idols of the Theatre*.

2

The formation of ideas and axioms by true induction is no doubt the proper remedy to be applied for the keeping off and clearing away of idols. To point them out, however, is of great use, for the doctrine of Idols is to the Interpretation of Nature what the doctrine of the refutation of Sophisms is to common Logic.

3

The Idols of the Tribe have their foundation in human nature itself, and in the tribe or race of men. For it is a false assertion that the sense of man is the measure of things. On the contrary, all perceptions as well of the sense as of the mind are according to the measure of the individual and not according to the measure of the universe. And the human understanding is like a false mirror, which, receiving rays irregularly, distorts and discolours the nature of things by mingling its own nature with it.

4

The Idols of the Cave are the idols of the individual man. For every one (besides the errors common to human nature in general) has a cave or den of his own, which refracts and discolours the light of nature; owing either to his own proper and peculiar nature; or to his education and conversation with others; or to the reading of books, and the authority of those whom he esteems and admires; or to the differences of impressions, accordingly as they take place in a mind preoccupied and predisposed or in a mind indifferent and settled; or the like. So that the spirit of man (according as it is meted out to different individuals) is in fact a thing variable and full of perturbation, and governed as it were by chance. Whence it was well observed by Heraclitus[1] that men look for sciences in their own lesser worlds, and not in the greater or common world.

5

There are also Idols formed by the intercourse and association of men with each other, which I call Idols of the Market-place, on account of the commerce and consort of men there. For it is by discourse that men associate, and words are imposed according to the apprehension of the vulgar. And therefore the ill and unfit choice of words wonderfully obstructs the understanding. Nor do the definitions or explanations wherewith in some things learned men are wont to guard and defend themselves, by any means set the matter right. But words plainly force and overrule the understanding, and throw all into confusion, and lead men away into numberless empty controversies and idle fancies.

6

Lastly, there are Idols which have immigrated into men's minds from the various dogmas of philosophies, and also from wrong laws of demonstration. These I call Idols of the Theatre, because in my judgement all the received systems are but so many stage-plays, representing worlds of their own creation after an unreal and scenic fashion. Nor is it only of the systems now in vogue, or only of the ancient sects and philosophies, that I speak; for many more plays of the same kind may yet be composed and in like artificial manner set forth, seeing that errors the most widely different have nevertheless causes for the most part alike. Neither again do I mean this only of entire systems, but also of many principles and axioms in science, which by tradition, credulity, and negligence have come to be received.

But of these several kinds of Idols I must speak more largely and exactly, that the understanding may be duly cautioned.

---

[1]**Heraclitus**: Ancient Greek philosopher (c. 540–c. 470 B.C.).—EDS.

7

The human understanding is of its own nature prone to suppose the existence of more order and regularity in the world than it finds. And though there be many things in nature which are singular and unmatched, yet it devises for them parallels and conjugates and relatives which do not exist. Hence the fiction that all celestial bodies move in perfect circles; spirals and dragons being (except in name) utterly rejected. Hence too the element of Fire with its orb is brought in, to make up the square with the other three which the sense perceives. Hence also the ratio of density of the so-called elements is arbitrarily fixed at ten to one. And so on of other dreams. And these fancies affect not dogmas only, but simple notions also.

8

The human understanding when it has once adopted an opinion (either as being the received opinion or as being agreeable to itself) draws all things else to support and agree with it. And though there be a greater number and weight of instances to be found on the other side, yet these it either neglects and despises, or else by some distinction sets aside and rejects; in order that by this great and pernicious predetermination the authority of its former conclusions may remain inviolate. And therefore it was a good answer that was made by one who when they showed him hanging in a temple a picture of those who had paid their vows as having escaped shipwreck, and would have him say whether he did not now acknowledge the power of the gods—"Aye," asked he again, "but where are they painted that were drowned after their vows?" And such is the way of all superstition, whether in astrology, dreams, omens, divine judgements, or the like; wherein men, having a delight in such vanities, mark the events where they are fulfilled, but where they fail, though this happen much oftener, neglect and pass them by. But with far more subtlety does this mischief insinuate itself into philosophy and the sciences, in which the first conclusion colours and brings into conformity with itself all that come after, though far sounder and better. Besides, independently of that delight and vanity which I have described, it is the peculiar and perpetual error of the human intellect to be more moved and excited by affirmatives than by negatives; whereas it ought properly to hold itself indifferently disposed towards both alike. Indeed in the establishment of any true axiom, the negative instance is the more forcible of the two.

9

The human understanding is moved by those things most which strike and enter the mind simultaneously and suddenly, and so fill the imagination; and then it feigns and supposes all other things to be somehow, though it cannot see how, similar to those few things by which it is surrounded. But for that going to and fro to remote and hetero-geneous instances, by which axioms are tried as in the fire, the intellect is altogether slow and unfit, unless it be forced thereto by severe laws and overruling authority.

10

The human understanding is unquiet; it cannot stop or rest, and still presses onward, but in vain. Therefore it is that we cannot conceive of any end or limit to the world, but always as of necessity it occurs to us that there is something beyond. Neither again can it be conceived how eternity has flowed down to the present day, for that distinction which is commonly received of infinity in time past and in time to come can by no means hold; for it would thence follow that one infinity is greater than another, and that infinity is wasting away and tending to become finite. The like subtlety arises touching the infinite divisibility of lines, from the same inability of thought to stop. But this inability interferes more mischievously in the discovery of causes: for although the most general principles in nature ought to be held merely positive, as they are discovered, and cannot with truth be referred to a cause; neverthe-less the human understanding being unable to rest still seeks something prior in the order of nature. And then it is that in struggling towards that which is further off it falls back upon that which is more nigh at hand, namely, on final causes: which have relation clearly to the nature of man rather than to the nature of the universe, and from this source have strangely defiled philosophy. But he is no less an unskilled and shallow philosopher who seeks causes of that which is most general, than he who in things subordinate and subaltern omits to do so.

11

The human understanding is no dry light, but receives an infusion from the will and affections, whence proceed sciences which may be called "sciences as one would." For what a man had rather were true he more readily believes. Therefore he rejects difficult things from impa-tience of research; sober things, because they narrow hope; the deeper things of nature, from superstition; the light of experience, from ar-rogance and pride, lest his mind should seem to be occupied with things mean and transitory; things not commonly believed, out of defer-ence to the opinion of the vulgar. Numberless in short are the ways, and sometimes imperceptible, in which the affections colour and infect the understanding.

12

But by far the greatest hindrance and aberration of the human understanding proceeds from the dullness, incompetency, and deceptions of the senses; in that things which strike the sense outweigh things which do not immediately strike it, though they be more important. Hence it is that speculation commonly ceases where sight ceases, insomuch that of things invisible there is little or no observation. Hence all the working of the spirits inclosed in tangible bodies lies hid and unobserved of men. So also all the more subtle changes of form in the parts of coarser substances (which they commonly call alteration, though it is in truth local motion through exceedingly small spaces) is in like manner unobserved. And yet unless these two things just mentioned be searched out and brought to light, nothing great can be achieved in nature, as far as the producton of works is concerned. So again the essential nature of our common air, and of all bodies less dense than air (which are very many), is almost unknown. For the sense by itself is a thing infirm and erring; neither can instruments for enlarging or sharpening the senses do much; but all the truer kind of interpretation of nature is effected by instances and experiments fit and apposite; wherein the sense decides touching the experiment only, and the experiment touching the point in nature and the thing itself.

13

The human understanding is of its own nature prone to abstractions and gives a substance and reality to things which are fleeting. But to resolve nature into abstractions is less to our purpose than to dissect her into parts; as did the school of Democritus,[2] which went further into nature than the rest. Matter rather than forms should be the object of our attention, its configurations and changes of configuration, and simple action, and law of action or motion; for forms are figments of the human mind, unless you will call those laws of action forms.

14

Such then are the idols which I call *Idols of the Tribe*, and which take their rise either from the homogeneity of the substance of the human spirit, or from its preoccupation, or from its narrowness, or from its restless motion, or from an infusion of the affections, or from the incompetency of the senses, or from the mode of impression.

[2]**Democritus**: Ancient Greek philosopher (c. 460–370 B.C.) who believed that the world was composed of atoms brought together randomly.—EDS.

15

The *Idols of the Cave* take their rise in the peculiar constitution, mental or bodily, of each individual, and also in education, habit, and accident. Of this kind there is a great number and variety, but I will instance those the pointing out of which contains the most important caution, and which have most effect in disturbing the clearness of the understanding.

16

Men become attached to certain particular sciences and speculations, either because they fancy themselves the authors and inventors thereof, or because they have bestowed the greatest pains upon them and become most habituated to them. But men of this kind, if they betake themselves to philosophy and contemplations of a general character, distort and colour them in obedience to their former fancies: a thing especially to be noticed in Aristotle, who made his natural philosophy a mere bond-servant to his logic, thereby rendering it contentious and well nigh useless. The race of chemists[3] again out of a few experiments of the furnace have built up a fantastic philosophy, framed with reference to a few things; and Gilbert[4] also, after he had employed himself most laboriously in the study and observation of the loadstone, proceeded at once to construct an entire system in accordance with his favourite subject.

17

There is one principal and as it were radical distinction between different minds, in respect of philosophy and the sciences, which is this: that some minds are stronger and apter to mark the differences of things, others to mark their resemblances. The steady and acute mind can fix its contemplations and dwell and fasten on the subtlest distinctions: the lofty and discursive mind recognizes and puts together the finest and most general resemblances. Both kinds however easily err in excess, by catching the one at gradations, the other at shadows.

18

There are found some minds given to an extreme admiration of antiquity, others to an extreme love and appetite for novelty; but few so

---

[3]**chemists**: Bacon is referring to alchemists who were searching for a way to turn base metal into gold.—Eds.
[4]**Gilbert**: William Gilbert (c. 1540–1603), English scientist and physician who wrote the earliest accounts of magnetism.—Eds.

duly tempered that they can hold the mean, neither carping at what has been well laid down by the ancients, nor despising what is well introduced by the moderns. This however turns to the great injury of the sciences and philosophy, since these affectations of antiquity and novelty are the humours of partisans rather than judgements; and truth is to be sought for not in the felicity of any age, which is an unstable thing, but in the light of nature and experience, which is eternal. These factions therefore must be abjured, and care must be taken that the intellect be not hurried by them into ascent.

19

Contemplations of nature and of bodies in their simple form break up and distract the understanding, while contemplations of nature and bodies in their composition and configuration overpower and dissolve the understanding: a distinction well seen in the school of Leucippus and Democritus as compared with the other philosophies. For that school is so busied with the particles that it hardly attends to the structure, while the others are so lost in admiration of the structure that they do not penetrate to the simplicity of nature. These kinds of contemplation should therefore be alternated and taken by turns; that so the understanding may be rendered at once penetrating and comprehensive, and the inconveniences above mentioned, with the idols which proceed from them, may be avoided.

20

Let such then be our provision and contemplative prudence for keeping off and dislodging the *Idols of the Cave*, which grow for the most part either out of the predominance of a favourite subject, or out of an excessive tendency to compare or to distinguish, or out of partiality for particular ages, or out of the largeness or minuteness of the objects contemplated. And generally let every student of nature take this as a rule—that whatever his mind seizes and dwells upon with peculiar satisfaction is to be held in suspicion, and that so much the more care is to be taken in dealing with such questions to keep the understanding even and clear.

21

But the *Idols of the Market-place* are the most troublesome of all: idols which have crept into the understanding through the alliances of words and names. For men believe that their reason governs words, but it is also true that words react on the understanding; and this it is that has rendered philosophy and the sciences sophistical and inactive. Now words, being commonly framed and applied according to the capacity of the vulgar, follow those lines of division which are most obvious to the vulgar understanding. And whenever an understanding of greater acuteness or a more diligent observation would alter those lines to suit the true divisions of nature, words stand in the way and resist the change. Whence it comes to pass that the high and formal discussions of learned men end oftentimes in disputes about words and names; with which (according to the use and wisdom of the mathematicians) it would be more prudent to begin, and so by means of definitions reduce them to order. Yet even definitions cannot cure this evil in dealing with natural and material things, since the definitions themselves consist of words, and those words beget others: so that it is necessary to recur to individual instances, and those in due series and order; as I shall say presently when I come to the method and scheme for the formation of notions and axioms.

22

The idols imposed by words on the understanding are of two kinds. They are either names of things which do not exist (for as there are things left unnamed through lack of observation, so likewise are there names which result from fantastic suppositions and to which nothing in reality corresponds), or they are names of things which exist, but yet confused and ill-defined, and hastily and irregularly derived from realities. Of the former kind are Fortune, the Prime Mover, Planetary Orbits, Element of Fire, and like fictions which owe their origin to false and idle theories. And this class of idols is more easily expelled, because to get rid of them it is only necessary that all theories should be steadily rejected and dismissed as obsolete.

But the other class, which springs out of a faulty and unskillful abstraction, is intricate and deeply rooted. Let us take for example such a word as *humid*, and see how far the several things which the word is used to signify agree with each other; and we shall find the word *humid* to be nothing else than a mark loosely and confusedly applied to denote a variety of actions which will not bear to be reduced to any constant meaning. For it both signifies that which easily spreads itself round any other body; and that which in itself is indeterminate and cannot solidize; and that which readily yields in every direction; and that which easily divides and scatters itself; and that which easily unites and collects itself; and that which readily flows and is put in motion; and that which readily clings to another body and wets it; and that which is easily reduced to a liquid, or being solid easily melts. Accordingly when you come to apply the word, if you take it in one sense, flame is humid; if in another, air is not humid; if in another, fine dust is humid; if in another, glass is humid. So that it is easy to see that the notion is taken by abstraction only from water and common and ordinary liquids, without any due verification.

There are however in words certain degrees of distortion and error. One of the least faulty kinds is that of names of substances, especially of lowest species and well-deduced (for the notion of *chalk* and of *mud* is good, of *earth* bad); a more faulty kind is that of actions, as to *generate, to corrupt, to alter*; the most faulty is of qualities (except such as are the immediate objects of the sense) and *heavy, light, rare, dense,* and the like. Yet in all these cases some notions are of necessity a little better than others, in proportion to the greater variety of subjects that fall within the range of the human sense.

23

But the *Idols of the Theatre* are not innate, nor do they steal into the understanding secretly, but are plainly impressed and received into the mind from the play-books of philosophical systems and the perverted rules of demonstration. To attempt refutations in this case would be merely inconsistent with what I have already said: for since we agree neither upon principles nor upon demonstrations there is no place for argument. And this is so far well, inasmuch as it leaves the honour of the ancients untouched. For they are no wise disparaged—the question between them and me being only as to the way. For as the saying is, the lame man who keeps the right road outstrips the runner who takes a wrong one. Nay it is obvious that when a man runs the wrong way, the more active and swift he is the further he will go astray.

But the course I propose for the discovery of sciences is such as leaves but little to the acuteness and strength of wits, but places all wits and understandings nearly on a level. For as in the drawing of a straight line or a perfect circle, much depends on the steadiness and practice of the hand, if it be done by aim of hand only, but if with the aid of rule or compass, little or nothing; so is it exactly with my plan. But though particular confutations would be of no avail, yet touching the sects and general divisions of such systems I must say something; something also touching the external signs which show that they are unsound; and finally something touching the causes of such great infelicity and of such lasting and general agreement in error; that so the access to truth may be made less difficult, and the human understanding may the more willingly submit to its purgation and dismiss its idols.   *1620*

René Descartes

Stripping the Mind of Its Beliefs

PART ONE

Good sense is the most equitably distributed thing in the world, for each man considers himself so well provided with it that even those who are most difficult to satisfy in everything else do not usually wish to have more of it than they have already. It is not likely that everyone is mistaken in this; it shows, rather, that the ability to judge rightly and separate the true from the false, which is essentially what is called good sense or reason, is by nature equal in all men, and thus that our opinions differ not because some men are better endowed with reason than others, but only because we direct our thoughts along different paths, and do not consider the same things. For it is not enough to have a good mind: what is most important is to apply it rightly. The greatest souls are capable of the greatest vices; and those who walk very slowly can advance much further, if they always keep to the direct road, than those who run and go astray.

For my part, I have never presumed my mind to be more perfect than average in any way; I have, in fact, often wished that my thoughts were as quick, or my imagination as precise and distinct, or my memory as capacious or prompt, as those of some other men. And I know of no other qualities than these which make for the perfection of the mind; for as to reason, or good sense, inasmuch as it alone makes us men and distinguishes us from the beasts, I am quite willing to believe that it is whole and entire in each of us, and to follow in this the common opinion of the philosophers who say that there are differences of more or less only among the accidents, and not among the forms, or natures, of individuals of a single species.

But I am not afraid to say that I think I was very fortunate in my early youth to have entered upon certain paths that have led me to the considerations and maxims from which I have formed a method which, it seems to me, has given me a means of increasing my knowledge step by step, and gradually raising it to the highest point which the mediocrity of my mind and the short duration of my life will allow it to reach. For I have already gathered such fruits from this method that, although in the judgments I make of myself I always try to lean toward mistrust rather than presumption, and although, when I look with a philosophical eye upon the various actions and enterprises of all men, there are scarcely any which do not seem to me vain and futile, I nevertheless receive extreme satisfaction from the progress I think I have already made in the search for truth, and I conceive such hopes for the future that if, among the occupations of men who are purely and simply men, there is one which is of solid worth and importance, I venture to believe that it is the one I have chosen.

I may be mistaken, however, and what I take for gold and diamonds   4 may be only a little copper and a few bits of glass. I know how subject we are to error in what concerns ourselves, and also how suspicious we ought to be of our friends' judgments when they are in our favor. But I shall be glad to point out, in this discourse, the paths I have followed, and to depict my life in it as though in a picture, in order that everyone may form his own judgment, and so that, in learning from common report the opinions that will be held with regard to what I have said, I shall have a new means of instructing myself which I shall add to those I am already accustomed to using.

Thus my intention is not to teach here the method which everyone ought to follow in order to conduct his reason correctly, but only to point out how I have tried to conduct my own. Those who take it upon themselves to give precepts ought to regard themselves as cleverer than those to whom they give them; and if they are lacking in the slightest thing, they must bear the blame for it. But in presenting this work only as a story, or, if you prefer, as a fable, in which, among some examples which may be followed, there may also be others which will be rightly avoided, I hope that it will be useful to some without being harmful to anyone, and that everyone will be grateful to me for my frankness.

I was nourished on books in my childhood, and since I had been persuaded that by means of them one could acquire clear and assured knowledge of everything that is useful in life, I was eager to learn from them. But as soon as I had completed that whole course of study at the end of which it is customary to be admitted into the ranks of the learned, I changed my opinion entirely, for I found myself entangled in so many doubts and errors that it seemed to me that the only benefit I had derived from my efforts to educate myself was a progressive discovery of my ignorance. And yet I had attended one of the most famous schools in Europe, where I thought there must be learned men if any were to be found on the face of the earth. I had learned there all that the others learned, and, not content with the sciences that had been taught to us, I had perused all the books dealing with those deemed to be rarest and strangest which happened to fall into my hands. Furthermore, I knew how others judged me, and it did not seem to me that I was regarded as inferior to my fellow students, even though some of them were already being prepared to replace our masters. And finally, the age in which we live seemed to me as flourishing, and as fertile in great minds, as any preceding age. I therefore took the liberty of judging all others by myself, and of deciding that there was no doctrine in the world which was such as I had been led to expect it to be.

I nevertheless continued to respect the training that is received in the schools. I knew that the languages learned there are necessary for the understanding of ancient books; that the graciousness of the fables awakens the mind; that it is exalted by the accounts of memorable deeds contained in books of history, and that, read with discretion, they help to form the judgment; that the reading of all good books is like a conversation with the finest men of the past who wrote them, a studied conversation, in fact, in which they reveal to us only the best of their thoughts; that eloquence has incomparable powers and beauties; that poetry has enchanting delicacy and sweetness; that mathematics has very subtle inventions which can be of great use in satisfying curious minds, as well as in furthering all the arts and crafts, and in diminishing the work of mankind; that moral treatises contain many teachings and exhortations to virtue which are very useful; that theology teaches us how to gain heaven; that philosophy enables us to speak plausibly of all things, and win the admiration of the least learned; that jurisprudence, medicine and the other sciences bring honors and wealth to those who cultivate them; and, finally, that it is good to have examined them all, even those most tainted with superstition and falsehood, in order to know their true worth and avoid being deceived by them.

But I thought I had already given enough time to the study of languages, and even to the reading of ancient books, with their histories and fables. For conversing with men of other centuries is almost the same as traveling. It is good to know something about the ways of various peoples, so that we can judge our own more soundly, and not think that anything contrary to our own customs is ridiculous and irrational, as is usually assumed by those who have seen nothing. But a man who spends too much time in traveling eventually becomes a foreigner in his own country; and a man who is too curious about what was done in the past usually remains extremely ignorant of what is being done in the present. Moreover, fables make us imagine many impossible events to be possible, and the most faithful histories, even if they do not change or enhance the value of the facts to make them worthier of being read, at least nearly always omit the basest and least glorious incidents and circumstances, so that what remains does not appear as it really was, and those who regulate their conduct by the examples they draw from it are prone to fall into the extravagances of the knights-errant in our romances, and to conceive designs which exceed their powers.

I held eloquence in high esteem, and I was in love with poetry, but I thought that both were gifts of the mind, rather than fruits of study. Those who have the strongest powers of reasoning, and who best digest their thoughts in order to make them clear and intelligible, are always best able to convince others of what they put forward, even if they speak only a Breton dialect and have never studied rhetoric. And those who have the most pleasing fancies, and know how to express themselves with the most grace and sweetness, will still be the best poets even if they are ignorant of the canons of poetry.

I took the greatest pleasure in mathematics, because of the certainty and clarity of its reasoning; but I was not yet aware of its true use, and, thinking that it served only the mechanical arts, I was surprised that no loftier edifice had been built on such a firm and solid foundation. On the other hand, I compared the moral treatises of the ancient pagans to splendid and magnificent palaces built only on sand and mud. They raise virtues to great heights and make them seem more worthy of esteem than anything else in the world, but they do not teach us enough about them, and often what they call by such a fine name is nothing but insensitivity, or pride, or despair, or parricide.

I revered our theology and was as desirous as anyone else of reaching heaven; but, having learned as a certainty that the way to heaven is open to the most ignorant no less than to the most learned, and that the revealed truths which lead us there are above our intelligence, I would not have dared to submit them to the weakness of my reasoning, and I thought that, in order for anyone to undertake to examine them, and to do so successfully, he would need some extraordinary aid from heaven, and would have to be more than a man.

I shall say nothing of philosophy except that, seeing that it had been 12
cultivated by the most excellent minds in the world for many centuries, and that there was nevertheless nothing in it which was not in dispute and therefore doubtful, I was not presumptuous enough to hope that I might be more fortunate in it than others had been. And when I considered how many different opinions could be held by learned men with respect to a single topic, whereas only one of those opinions could ever be true, I regarded almost as false anything that was merely plausible.

As for the other sciences, inasmuch as they borrow their principles from philosophy, I judged that nothing solid could be built on such insecure foundations. And neither the honor nor the gain which they promise was enough to incite me to learn them, for I felt that, by the grace of God, my worldly situation was such that I was not obliged to make a trade of science in order to improve my fortune, and although I did not profess to despise glory in the manner of the Cynics, I cared very little for the kind of glory which I could hope to acquire only on false pretenses. And finally, I thought I already knew enough about unsound doctrines not to be deceived by the promises of an alchemist, the predictions of an astrologer, the impostures of a magician or the tricks and boasting of any of those who profess to know more than they do.

For these reasons, as soon as my age allowed me to free myself from subjection to my teachers, I entirely abandoned the study of letters. Resolving henceforth to seek no other knowledge than that which I might find within myself or in the great book of the world, I spent the rest of my youth in traveling, observing courts and armies, frequenting people of diverse character and rank, gathering various experiences, testing myself in the situations that chance brought my way, and every-where reflecting on the things I encountered in such a way as to derive some benefit from them. For it seemed to me that I could find much more truth in the reasonings which each man makes with regard to matters that are important to him, and whose outcome will quickly punish him if he has judged badly, than in those made by a man of letters in his study, with regard to speculations which produce no effect, and which are of no consequence except insofar as he may draw all the more vanity from them the further they are removed from common sense, because he has had to employ all the more wit and ingenuity in making them appear plausible. And I always had a strong desire to learn to distinguish the true from the false, so that I could see my own actions clearly and walk with assurance in this life.

It is true that while I was doing nothing except considering the behavior of other men I found very little grounds for assurance in it, and that I observed almost as much diversity in it as I had previously observed in the opinions of philosophers. And so the greatest benefit I derived from this was that, seeing many things which, although they seem extremely immoderate and ridiculous to us, are nevertheless commonly accepted and approved by other great nations, I learned not to believe too firmly in anything whose validity rested only on example and custom; and thus I gradually freed myself from many of the errors which may obscure our natural light and make us less capable of listening to reason. But after I had spent several years in thus studying the book of the world and trying to acquire experience, I resolved one day to study within myself as well, and to use all the resources of my mind in choosing the paths I ought to follow. I succeeded much better in this, I believe, than I would have done if I had never left either my country or my books.

PART TWO

I was then in Germany, where I had been drawn by the wars which 16 are not yet ended. As I was on my way to rejoin the army after attending the Emperor's coronation, the beginning of winter detained me in a place where, finding no conversation to divert me, and fortunately having no cares or passions to trouble me, I remained alone all day in a stove-heated room where I was completely free to concern myself with my own thoughts. One of the first thoughts that came to me was that there is often less perfection in works composed of several pieces, and carried out by various hands, than in those carried out by a single man. Thus we see that buildings which a single architect has undertaken and completed are usually more beautiful and better designed than those which many have tried to restore by making use of old walls that were built for different purposes. The same is true of those ancient towns which, having originally been only villages, have in the course of time become great cities. They are usually badly laid out, compared to those orderly designs which an engineer can trace at will on a plain, and although their buildings considered separately often display as much art as those of other cities, or even more, when we see how they are arranged, with a big one here and a little one there, and how crooked and uneven they make the streets, we are inclined to say that these cities have been designed by chance, rather than by the will of men making use of reason. And if we consider that there have nevertheless always been officials responsible for making private edifices contribute to public beauty, we can easily understand how difficult it is to achieve any kind of perfection by working with what has already been done by others. Thus I reflected that nations that were once half savage and, having become civilized only little by little, have made their laws piece-meal as they were forced to do so by the ill effects of crimes and disputes, cannot be so well regulated as those which, from the time when they first assembled, have always observed the laws laid down by some wise legislator. Similarly, it is certain that the true religion, whose ordinances come from God alone, must be incomparably better ordered than any other. And to speak of human things, I think that Sparta flourished not because each of its laws was good in itself, for many of them were strange and even contrary to morality, but because, having been devised by one man, they all tended toward a single end. And so I thought that the teachings contained in books, at least those whose grounds are merely probable, and which have no demonstrations, hav-ing been composed by many different persons and gradually built up from their opinions, do not come so close to the truth as the simple reasonings of a man of good sense concerning the things he encounters. And finally I thought that, considering that we were all children before becoming men, that for a long time we were necessarily governed by our desires and our teachers, that they were often in opposition to each other, and that perhaps neither of them always advised us wisely, it was nearly impossible that our judgments should be as pure or sound as they would have been if we had had the full use of our reason from birth and had always been guided by it alone.

It is true that all the buildings in a city are never torn down for the sole purpose of rebuilding them in a different way and making the streets more beautiful, but it does happen that certain individuals tear down their own houses in order to rebuild them, and that sometimes they are even forced to do so, when their houses are in danger of collapsing and the foundations are insecure. From this example I concluded that it would be truly senseless for an individual to set out to reform a State by changing everything from the foundations upward and tearing it down in order to build it up again, or even to reform the body of the sciences or the established order of teaching them in the schools, but that, with regard to all the opinions I had hitherto accepted, I could do no better than to undertake to reject them entirely in order to replace them with better ones later, or else accept the same ones again after bringing them to the level of reason. And I firmly believed that in this way I would succeed in conducting my life much better than if I built only on old foundations and relied only on the principles I had been persuaded to accept in my youth, without ever examining them to determine whether or not they were true. For although I saw various difficulties in this, they were not without remedy, nor were they comparable to the difficulties involved in reforming anything concerning the public. Those great bodies are too difficult to lift when they have been brought down, or even to hold up when they have been shaken, and their falls cannot fail to be violent. As for their imperfections, if they have any—and their diversity alone is enough to ensure that many of them do—they have no doubt been softened by use, which has even imperceptibly avoided or corrected many of them which could not have been so easily remedied by prudence. And finally, these imperfections are always more bearable than their alternatives, just as the roads which wind their way among the mountains become so smooth and convenient from long use that it is much better to follow them than to try to take a more direct route by climbing over rocks and down precipices.

That is why I could in no way approve of those rash and restless individuals who, having been called by neither birth nor fortune to the management of public affairs, are nevertheless constantly reforming them in their minds. And if I thought there was anything in what I have written that might make me be suspected of such madness, I would deeply regret its publication. My intentions have never gone beyond the attempt to reform my own thoughts, and to build on a foundation that is mine alone. If, since my work has pleased me well enough, I here present its pattern to you, that does not mean that I wish to advise anyone to copy it. Those on whom God has more lavishly bestowed His gifts will perhaps have loftier designs, although I fear that even mine will be too bold for many. The decision to rid oneself of all the opinions to which one has previously given credence is not an example that ought to be followed by everyone, and the world is made up almost entirely of two kinds of minds for whom it is thoroughly unsuitable.

First there are those who, believing themselves to be cleverer than they are, cannot help making hasty judgments and do not have enough patience to conduct all their thoughts in an orderly manner, so that if they ever took the liberty of doubting the principles they have been taught, and of departing from the common path, they would never be able to keep to the road that would take them more directly toward their goal, and would remain lost for the rest of their lives. Then there are those who, having enough good sense or modesty to realize that they are less capable of distinguishing the true from the false than are certain others from whom they can learn, ought to content themselves with following the opinions of these others, rather than seeking better ones themselves.

As for myself, I would no doubt have been included among the latter if I had never had more than one teacher, or if I had not known the differences that have always existed among the opinions of the most learned. But I learned in school that one cannot imagine anything so strange and incredible that it has not been said by some philosopher, and later, in the course of my travels, I observed that all those who have sentiments strongly opposed to our own are not necessarily barbarians or savages, but that many of them use their reason as much as we do, or even more. And I considered the fact that if a man has been raised among Frenchmen or Germans, he becomes quite different from what he would have been, even with the same natural endowments, if he had always lived among Chinese or cannibals. I further considered that even in our fashions of dress, the same thing which pleased us ten years ago, and may please us again within another ten years, now seems excessive and ridiculous to us. From all this I concluded that we are swayed much more by custom and example than by certain knowledge, and that nevertheless a preponderance of opinion is worthless as a criterion for truths that are rather difficult to discover, since they are much more likely to be encountered by a single man than by a whole people. For these reasons, I could select no one whose opinions seemed preferable to those of others, and I found myself with little choice but to undertake to be my own guide.

But, like a man walking alone and in darkness, I decided to proceed 20 so slowly, and with so much circumspection in all things, that while I might make little progress, I would at least avoid falling. I was even unwilling to begin entirely rejecting any of the opinions that might have slipped in among my beliefs, without having been placed there by my reason, before I had first spent enough time in planning the work I was undertaking, and in seeking the true method of attaining knowledge of everything within the capacity of my mind.

In my early youth I had made some study of logic (in philosophy) and of geometrical analysis and algebra (in mathematics), and it seemed to me that these three arts or sciences should contribute something to my design. But when I examined them I found that, in the case of logic, its syllogisms and most of its other teachings are useful not in acquiring knowledge, but in explaining to others what one knows already, or, as in the art of Lully,[1] in speaking without judgment about things one does not know. And although logic does contain many true and good precepts, they are mingled with so many others which are either harmful or superfluous that it is as difficult to separate them as to draw a Diana or a Minerva from an unshaped block of marble. As for the geometrical analysis of the ancients and the algebras of the moderns, aside from the fact that they deal only with highly abstract matters which have no apparent practical use, the former is always so tightly bound to the consideration of figures that it cannot exercise the understanding without greatly tiring the imagination, and the latter is so subject to certain rules and notations that it has been made into a confused and obscure art which encumbers the mind, rather than into a science which cultivates it. I therefore decided that I must seek another method which would include the advantages of these three, yet be free of their defects. And just as a multiplicity of laws often provides excuses for vices, so that a State is much better governed if it has only a few laws and these are strictly observed, so, instead of the great number of precepts of which logic is composed, I believed that the four following ones would be enough for me, provided I maintained a firm and constant resolution never once to depart from them.

The first was never to accept anything as true which I did not know to be manifestly so, that is, carefully to avoid precipitancy and bias, and to include nothing in my judgments except what presented itself so clearly and distinctly to my mind that I would never have occasion to doubt it.

The second, to divide each difficulty I examined into as many parts as possible, and as would be required in order to resolve it better.

The third, to conduct my thoughts in an orderly manner, beginning 24 with those objects which are simplest and easiest to know, then rising little by little, as though by steps, to knowledge of the most complex, even assuming order to exist among those which have no natural order of precedence.

And the last, always to make such complete enumerations and comprehensive reviews that I could be sure I had overlooked nothing.

Those long chains of reasoning, each link of which is simple and easy, that geometers employ in reaching their most difficult demonstrations, had given me occasion to imagine that all things which may be

---

[1]**Lully**: Raymund Lully or Ramon Lull (c. 1236–1315), an Italian philosopher and theologian who argued that all articles of the Catholic faith could be demonstrated with logic.—Eds.

known by men are interconnected in the same way, and that, provided we refrain from accepting any of them as true which are not so, and always maintain the order required for deducing them one from another, there can be none so remote that it cannot be eventually reached, or so hidden that it cannot be discovered. . . .

PART FOUR

I do not know whether I ought to tell you about the first meditations with which I concerned myself here, for they are so metaphysical and so far out of the ordinary that they may not be to everyone's taste. And yet, to make it possible for others to judge whether or not the foundations I have chosen are firm enough, I feel that I am more or less obliged to speak of them. I had long ago observed that in matters of custom and morality it is sometimes necessary to follow opinions that we know to be extremely uncertain as though they were unquestionably true, as I have already said; but since I now wished to occupy myself only with the search for truth, I thought I ought to do exactly the opposite and reject as absolutely false anything in which I could imagine the slightest doubt, in order to see whether anything completely indubitable would afterward remain. And so, because our senses sometimes deceive us, I decided to assume that nothing in the world was such as they presented it to me. Having observed that some men went astray in their reasoning and made logical errors, even in the simplest geometrical matters, and having judged that I was as fallible as anyone else, I rejected as false all the reasonings I had previously accepted as demonstrations. And finally, considering that all the thoughts which come to us when we are awake can also come to us when we are asleep, without one of them then being true, I resolved to pretend that everything which had ever entered my mind was no more true than the illusions of my dreams. But then I immediately realized that while I was thinking of everything as false, I, who was so thinking, necessarily had to be something. Noting that this truth: *I think, therefore I am*, was so firm and assured that all of the most extravagant suppositions of the skeptics were incapable of shaking it, I judged that I could accept it without misgivings as the first principle of philosophy which I had been seeking.

Next I attentively examined what I was, and I saw that while I could pretend that I had no body and that there was no world or any place in which I was, I could not pretend that I did not exist; on the contrary, from the very fact that I was thinking of doubting the truth of other things, it followed manifestly and certainly that I existed, whereas if I had ceased to think, even though all the rest of what I had imagined were true, I had no reason to believe that I would have existed. From this I knew that I was a thinking substance whose whole essence or nature was only to think, and which, in order to exist, had no need of any location and did not depend on any material thing. Thus the self, that is, the soul by which I am what I am, is entirely distinct from the body, is even easier to know than the body, and would still be all that it is if the body did not exist.

After this, I considered in general what is required of a proposition in order that it be true and certain, for since I had just discovered one which I knew to be such, I thought that I ought also to know in what its certainty consists. Having observed that there is nothing at all in the proposition, *"I think, therefore I am"* which assures me that I am speaking the truth, except that I see very clearly that, in order to think, it is necessary to be, I concluded that I could take it as a general rule that those things which we apprehend very clearly and distinctly are all true, but that there is some difficulty in determining which ones we apprehend distinctly.

Then, reflecting on the fact that I doubted, and that my being was therefore not entirely perfect, for I saw clearly that it was a greater perfection to know than to doubt, I decided to try to determine how I had learned to think of something more perfect than myself, and it became obvious to me that I must have learned it from some nature which was in fact more perfect. As for the thoughts I had of many other things outside myself, such as the sky, the earth, light, heat and countless others, I was less concerned to know from where they came, for since I saw nothing in them that seemed to make them superior to me, I could believe that, if they were true, they were dependencies of my nature, insofar as it had some perfection, and that, if they were not true, I had acquired them from nothing, that is, that I had them because of some deficiency in myself. But this could not be the case with the idea of a being more perfect than myself, for it was manifestly impossible that I should have acquired it from nothing, and since it is as contradictory to suppose that the more perfect follows from and is dependent upon the less perfect as it is to suppose that something comes from nothing, I could not have acquired it from myself. Thus it could only have been placed in me by a nature truly more perfect than myself, and possessing all the perfections of which I could have any idea; in short, it had been placed in me by God. I further reflected that, since I knew some perfections which I did not possess, I was not the only being in existence (here I shall, with your permission, freely use the terms of the School), but that there must necessarily be a more perfect being on which I depended and from which I had acquired everything I possessed. For if I had been alone and independent of any other being, so that I would have acquired from myself what little perfection I shared with the perfect being, I could also have given myself, by the same reasoning, all the other perfections which I knew to be lacking in me, and thus I myself could have been infinite, eternal, immutable, all-knowing and all-powerful; that is, I could have had all the perfections I could see in God. For, according to the reasoning I have just set forth, in order to know the nature of God insofar as my own nature was capable of doing so, I had only to consider, with regard to each thing of which I had any idea, whether or not it was a perfection to possess it, and I could be sure that those which indicated any imperfection were not in Him, and that all the others were. I saw that doubt, inconstancy, sadness and other such things could not be in Him, for I myself would have been glad to be free of them. Furthermore, I had ideas of many perceptible and corporeal things, and even if I supposed that I was dreaming and that all the things I saw or imagined were false, I still could not deny that the ideas of them were really in my mind. But I had already seen very clearly, in examining myself, that intellectual nature is distinct from corporeal nature, and so, considering that all composition implies dependency, and that dependency is manifestly a defect, I concluded that it could not be a perfection in God to be composed of those two natures, and that consequently He was not so composed, but that if there were any bodies in the world, or any intelligences or other natures not entirely perfect, their existence must depend on His power in such a way that they could not subsist without Him for a single moment.

I next sought to discover other truths. Turning my attention to the object studied by geometers, which I conceived to be a continuous body, or a space indefinitely extended in length, breadth, and height or depth, divisible into various parts capable of having various shapes and sizes and being moved and transposed in all sorts of ways, for the geometers assume all this in the object of their study, I went through some of their simplest demonstrations. And having noted that the great certainty which everyone attributes to these demonstrations is based only on the fact that they are apprehended as manifestly true, in accordance with the rule I have stated above, I also noted that there was nothing in them which assured me of the existence of their object. I saw clearly that, given a triangle, for example, its three angles had to be equal to two right angles, but I saw nothing in this which gave me any assurance that there were any triangles in the world. But when I again began to examine the idea I had of a perfect being, I found that existence is included in it just as manifestly, or even more so, as having its three angles equal to two right angles is included in the idea of a triangle, or having all its parts equidistant from its center is included in the idea of a sphere, and that consequently it is at least as certain as any geometrical demonstration can be that God, who is this perfect being, is or exists.

But what causes many people to be convinced that it is difficult to 32 know God, or even to know what their own souls are, is that they never

raise their minds above the objects of their senses, and are so accustomed to considering nothing without imagining it, which is a way of
thinking used exclusively for material things, that anything not imaginable seems to them unintelligible. This is obvious from the fact that, in
the schools, the philosophers regard it as a maxim that there is nothing
in the understanding which was not first in the senses, even though it is
certain that the ideas of God and of the soul have never been in the
senses. And it seems to me that those who try to understand them by
means of their imagination are doing exactly the same as if they tried to
use their eyes to hear sounds or smell odors, with this difference,
however, that the sense of sight gives us no less assurance of the truth of
its objects than do the senses of smell and hearing, whereas neither our
imagination nor our senses can ever assure us of anything without the
intervention of our understanding.

Finally, if there are still some people who have not been sufficiently
convinced of the existence of God and the soul by the reasons I have
brought forward, I would like them to know that all the other things
which they may consider to be more certain, such as that they have a
body, that there are stars and an earth. and so on, are actually less
certain. For while we have a moral assurance of these things which
makes it seem impossible to doubt them without being absurd, if we are
concerned with metaphysical certainty we cannot rationally deny that
we have sufficient grounds for not being entirely certain of them when
we have noted that we can, in the same way, imagine while we are asleep
that we have another body, and that we see other stars and another
earth, without this actually being the case at all. For how do we know
that the thoughts which come to us in dreams are false rather than the
others, since they are no less vivid and definite? Let the best minds
study this as long as they please; I do not think that they will ever be able
to give any reason that will be sufficient to remove this doubt, unless
they presuppose the existence of God. For, first of all, what I was taking
as a rule, namely, that the things which we apprehend very clearly and
distinctly are all true, is assured only by the fact that God is or exists,
that He is a perfect being, and that everything that is in us comes from
Him. Hence it follows that our ideas, being real things which come from
God, insofar as they are clear and distinct, must be true. If we often have
ideas which contain falsity, they can only be those which are to some
extent confused and obscure because they partake of nothingness, that
is, they are thus confused in us because we are not entirely perfect. It is
obvious that it would be as contradictory for falsity or imperfection, as
such, to come from God as it would be for truth or perfection to come
from nothing. But if we do not know that everything real and true that is
in us comes from a perfect and infinite being, we shall have no reason
to be certain that our ideas have the perfection of being true, no matter
how clear and distinct they may be.

Now once the knowledge of God and the soul has made us certain of this rule, it is quite easy to understand that the dreams we have when we are asleep should in no way make us doubt the truth of the thoughts we have when we are awake. For if anyone should happen to have a very distinct idea even while asleep—if, for example, a geometer should invent some new demonstration—his sleep would not prevent it from being true. As for the most common error of our dreams, which consists in their representing various objects to us in the same way as our external senses, it does not matter that it gives us occasion to be suspicious of the truth of such ideas, because they can deceive us rather often when we are awake, as when those who have jaundice see every-thing as yellow, or when stars and other distant objects appear to be much smaller than they are. For whether we are awake or asleep, we ought never to let ourselves be convinced of anything except by the evidence of our reason. And I wish to stress that I am speaking of our reason, not of our imagination or our senses. Although we see the sun very clearly, we must not conclude from this that its size is no greater than we see it to be; and we can distinctly imagine the head of a lion grafted onto the body of a goat without being forced to conclude that a chimera exists. Reason does not tell us that everything we thus see or imagine is true, but it does tell us that all our ideas or notions must have some foundation of truth, for otherwise it would not be possible that they had been placed in us by God, who is completely perfect and veracious. And because our reasonings are never so manifest or com-plete when we are asleep as they are when we are awake, although sometimes in sleep our imaginings are even more vivid and definite, reason also tells us that since our thoughts cannot all be true, inasmuch as we are not entirely perfect, the truth that is in them must necessarily be found in those we have when we are awake, rather than in our dreams.   *1637*

Shunryu Suzuki

Emptiness

EMPTINESS

"When you study Buddhism you should have a general house cleaning of your mind."

If you want to understand Buddhism it is necessary for you to forget all about your preconceived ideas. To begin with, you must give up the idea of substantiality or existence. The usual view of life is firmly rooted in the idea of existence. For most people everything exists; they

think whatever they see and whatever they hear exists. Of course the
bird we see and hear exists. It exists, but what I mean by that may not be
exactly what you mean. The Buddhist understanding of life includes
both existence and non-existence. The bird both exists and does not
exist at the same time. We say that a view of life based on existence
alone is heretical. If you take things too seriously, as if they existed
substantially or permanently, you are called a heretic. Most people may
be heretics.

We say true existence comes from emptiness and goes back again
into emptiness. What appears from emptiness is true existence. We have
to go through the gate of emptiness. This idea of existence is very
difficult to explain. Many people these days have begun to feel, at least
intellectually, the emptiness of the modern world, or the self-
contradiction of their culture. In the past, for instance, the Japanese
people had a firm confidence in the permanent existence of their
culture and their traditional way of life, but since they lost the war, they
have become very skeptical. Some people think this skeptical attitude is
awful, but actually it is better than the old attitude.

As long as we have some definite idea about or some hope in the
future, we cannot really be serious with the moment that exists right
now. You may say, "I can do it tomorrow, or next year," believing that
something that exists today will exist tomorrow. Even though you are
not trying so hard, you expect that some promising thing will come, as
long as you follow a certain way. But there is no certain way that exists
permanently. There is no way set up for us. Moment after moment we
have to find our own way. Some idea of perfection, or some perfect way
which is set up by someone else, is not the true way for us.

Each one of us must make his own true way, and when we do, that
way will express the universal way. This is the mystery. When you
understand one thing through and through, you understand everything. When you try to understand everything, you will not understand
anything. The best way is to understand yourself, and then you will
understand everything. So when you try hard to make your own way,
you will help others, and you will be helped by others. Before you make
your own way you cannot help anyone, and no one can help you. To be
independent in this true sense, we have to forget everything which we
have in our mind and discover something quite new and different
moment after moment. This is how we live in this world.

So we say true understanding will come out of emptiness. When you
study Buddhism, you should have a general house cleaning of your
mind. You must take everything out of your room and clean it thoroughly. If it is necessary, you may bring everything back in again. You
may want many things, so one by one you can bring them back. But if
they are not necessary, there is no need to keep them.

We see the flying bird. Sometimes we see the trace of it. Actually we cannot see the trace of a flying bird, but sometimes we feel as if we could. This is also good. If it is necessary, you should bring back in the things you took from your room. But before you put something in your room, it is necessary for you to take out something. If you do not, your room will become crowded with old, useless junk.

We say, "Step by step I stop the sound of the murmuring brook." When you walk along the brook you will hear the water running. The sound is continuous, but you must be able to stop it if you want to stop it. This is freedom; this is renunciation. One after another you will have various thoughts in your mind, but if you want to stop your thinking you can. So when you are able to stop the sound of the murmuring brook, you will appreciate the feeling of your work. But as long as you have some fixed idea or are caught by some habitual way of doing things, you cannot appreciate things in their true sense.

If you seek for freedom, you cannot find it. Absolute freedom itself 8 is necessary before you can acquire absolute freedom. That is our practice. Our way is not always to go in one direction. Sometimes we go east; sometimes we go west. To go one mile to the west means to go back one mile to the east. Usually if you go one mile to east it is the opposite of going one mile to the west. But if it is possible to go one mile to the east, that means it is possible to go one mile to the west. This is freedom. Without this freedom you cannot be concentrated on what you do. You may think you are concentrated on something, but before you obtain this freedom, you will have some uneasiness in what you are doing. Because you are bound by some idea of going east or west, your activity is in dichotomy or duality. As long as you are caught by duality you cannot attain absolute freedom, and you cannot concentrate.

Concentration is not to try hard to watch something. In zazen[1] if you try to look at one spot you will be tired in about five minutes. This is not concentration. Concentration means freedom. So your effort should be directed at nothing. You should be concentrated on nothing. In zazen practice we say your mind should be concentrated on your breathing, but the way to keep your mind on your breathing is to forget all about yourself and just to sit and feel your breathing. If you are concentrated on your breathing you will forget yourself, and if you forget yourself you will be concentrated on your breathing. I do not know which is first. So actually there is no need to try too hard to be concentrated on your breathing. Just do as much as you can. If you continue this practice, eventually you will experience the true existence which comes from emptiness.

---

[1]**zazen:** Pertains to zen meditation in the prescribed cross-legged posture.—EDS.

READINESS, MINDFULNESS

"It is the readiness of the mind that is wisdom."

In the Prajna Paramita Sutra[2] the most important point, of course, is the idea of emptiness. Before we understand the idea of emptiness, everything seems to exist substantially. But after we realize the emptiness of things, everything becomes real—not substantial. When we realize that everything we see is a part of emptiness, we can have no attachment to any existence; we realize that everything is just a tentative form and color. Thus we realize the true meaning of each tentative existence. When we first hear that everything is a tentative existence, most of us are disappointed; but this disappointment comes from a wrong view of man and nature. It is because our way of observing things is deeply rooted in our self-centered ideas that we are disappointed when we find everything has only a tentative existence. But when we actually realize this truth, we will have no suffering.

This sutra says, "Bodhisattva Avalokitesvara observes that every-thing is emptiness, thus he forsakes all suffering." It was not *after* he realized this truth that he overcame suffering—to realize this fact is itself to be relieved from suffering. So realization of the truth is salva-tion itself. We say, "to realize," but the realization of the truth is always near at hand. It is not after we practice zazen that we realize the truth; even before we practice zazen, realization is there. It is not after we understand the truth that we attain enlightenment. To realize the truth is to live—to exist here and now. So it is not a matter of understanding or of practice. It is an ultimate fact. In this sutra Buddha is referring to the ultimate fact that we always face moment after moment. This point is very important. This is Bodhidharma's[3] zazen. Even before we prac-tice it, enlightenment is there. But usually we understand the practice of zazen and enlightenment as two different things: here is practice, like a pair of glasses, and when we use the practice, like putting the glasses on, we see enlightenment. This is the wrong understanding. The glasses themselves are enlightenment, and to put them on is also enlighten-ment. So whatever you do, or even though you do not do anything, enlightenment is there, always. This is Bodhidharma's understanding of enlightenment.

You cannot practice true zazen, because *you* practice it; if you do not, then there is enlightenment, and there is true practice. When you do it, you create some concrete idea of "you" or "I," and you create some particular idea of practice or zazen. So here you are on the right side, 12

---

[2]**Sutra:** A notable Buddhist discourse known as "The Perfection of Wisdom."—EDS.
[3]**Bodhidharma:** Indian Buddhist philosopher (died A.D. c. 530) who founded Zen Bud-dhism.—EDS.

and here is zazen on the left. So zazen and you become two different things. If the combination of practice and you is zazen, it is the zazen of a frog. For a frog, his sitting position is zazen. When a frog is hopping, that is not zazen. This kind of misunderstanding will vanish if you really understand emptiness means everything is always here. One whole being is not an accumulation of everything. It is impossible to divide one whole existence into parts. It is always here and always working. This is enlightenment. So there actually is no particular practice. In the sutra it says, "There are no eyes, no ears, no nose, no tongue, no body or mind. . . ." This "no mind" is Zen mind, which includes everything.

The important thing in our understanding is to have a smooth, free-thinking way of observation. We have to think and to observe things without stagnation. We should accept things as they are without difficulty. Our mind should be soft and open enough to understand things as they are. When our thinking is soft, it is called imperturbable thinking. This kind of thinking is always stable. It is called mindfulness. Thinking which is divided in many ways is not true thinking. Concentration should be present in our thinking. This is mindfulness. Whether you have an object or not, your mind should be stable and your mind should not be divided. This is zazen.

It is not necessary to make an effort to think in a particular way. Your thinking should not be one-sided. We just think with our whole mind, and see things as they are without any effort. Just to see, and to be ready to see things with our whole mind, is zazen practice. If we are prepared for thinking, there is no need to make an effort to think. This is called mindfulness. Mindfulness is, at the same time, wisdom. By wisdom we do not mean some particular faculty or philosophy. It is the readiness of the mind that is wisdom. So wisdom could be various philosophies and teachings, and various kinds of research and studies. But we should not become attached to some particular wisdom, such as that which was taught by Buddha. Wisdom is not something to learn. Wisdom is something which will come out of your mindfulness. So the point is to be ready for observing things, and to be ready for thinking. This is called emptiness of your mind. Emptiness is nothing but the practice of zazen. *1970*

40

Why We Write

Joan Didion, Why I Write

Bernice Johnson Reagon,
Nurturing Resistance

Francine du Plessix Gray, I Write for
Revenge against Reality

Rudolfo A. Anaya, B. Traven Is Alive and
Well in Cuernavaca

What I have most wanted to do throughout the past ten years is to make
political writing into an art. My starting point is always a feeling of
partisanship, a sense of injustice. When I sit down to write a book, I do
not say to myself, "I am going to produce a work of art." I write it
because there is some lie that I want to expose, some fact to which I
want to draw attention, and my initial concern is to get a hearing. But I
could not do the work of writing a book, or even a long magazine article,
if it were not also an esthetic experience.

George Orwell, from *Why I Write*

Writing is one of the ways I participate in struggle—one of the ways I
help to keep vibrant and resilient that vision that has kept the Family
going on. Through writing I attempt to celebrate the tradition of resistance, attempt to tap black potential, and try to join the chorus of voices
that argues that exploitation and misery are neither inevitable nor
necessary. Writing is one of the ways I participate in the transformation—one of the ways I practice the commitment to explore bodies of
knowledge for the usable wisdoms they yield. In writing, I hope to
encourage the fusion of those disciplines whose split (material science

versus metaphysics versus aesthetics versus politics versus . . .) pre-
disposes us to accept fragmented truths and distortions as the whole.
Writing is one of the ways I do my work in the world.

Toni Cade Bambara, from *What It Is I Think I'm Doing Anyhow*

A well-known writer got collared by a university student who asked,
"Do you think I could be a writer?"
"Well," the writer said, "I don't know. . . . Do you like sentences?"
The writer could see the student's amazement. Sentences? Do I like
sentences? I am twenty years old and do I like sentences? If he had liked
sentences, of course, he could begin, like a joyful painter I knew. I asked
him how he came to be a painter. He said, "I liked the smell of the
paint."

Annie Dillard, from *The Writing Life*

Joan Didion
Why I Write

Of course I stole the title for this talk, from George Orwell. One
reason I stole it was that I like the sound of the words: Why I Write.
There you have three short unambiguous words that share a sound, and
the sound they share is this:

I

I

I   4

In many ways writing is the act of saying *I*, of imposing oneself upon
other people, of saying *listen to me, see it my way, change your mind*. It's an
aggressive, even a hostile act. You can disguise its aggressiveness all you
want with veils of subordinate clauses and qualifiers and tentative sub-
junctives, with ellipses and evasions—with the whole manner of intimating rather than claiming, of alluding rather than stating—but
there's no getting around the fact that setting words on paper is the
tactic of a secret bully, an invasion, an imposition of the writer's sensibility on the reader's most private space.

I stole the title not only because the words sounded right but because they seemed to sum up, in a no-nonsense way, all I have to tell you. Like many writers I have only this one "subject," this one "area": the act of writing. I can bring you no reports from any other front. I may have other interests: I am "interested," for example, in marine biology, but I don't flatter myself that you would come out to hear me talk about it. I am not a scholar. I am not in the least an intellectual, which is not to say that when I hear the word "intellectual" I reach for my gun, but only to say that I do not think in abstracts. During the years when I was an undergraduate at Berkeley I tried, with a kind of hopeless late-adolescent energy, to buy some temporary visa into the world of ideas, to forge for myself a mind that could deal with the abstract.

In short I tried to think. I failed. My attention veered inexorably back to the specific, to the tangible, to what was generally considered, by everyone I knew then and for that matter have known since, the peripheral. I would try to contemplate the Hegelian dialectic and would find myself concentrating instead on a flowering pear tree outside my window and the particular way the petals fell on my floor. I would try to read linguistic theory and would find myself wondering instead if the lights were on in the bevatron up the hill. When I say that I was wondering if the lights were on in the bevatron you might immediately suspect, if you deal in ideas at all, that I was registering the bevatron as a political symbol, thinking in shorthand about the military-industrial complex and its role in the university community, but you would be wrong. I was only wondering if the lights were on in the bevatron, and how they looked. A physical fact.

I had trouble graduating from Berkeley, not because of this inability   8
to deal with ideas—I was majoring in English, and I could locate the house-and-garden imagery in *The Portrait of a Lady*[1] as well as the next person, "imagery" being by definition the kind of specific that got my attention—but simply because I had neglected to take a course in Milton. For reasons which now sound baroque I needed a degree by the end of that summer, and the English department finally agreed, if I would come down from Sacramento every Friday and talk about the cosmology of *Paradise Lost*,[2] to certify me proficient in Milton. I did this. Some Fridays I took the Greyhound bus, other Fridays I caught the Southern Pacific's City of San Francisco on the last leg of its transcontinental trip. I can no longer tell you whether Milton put the sun or the earth at the center of his universe in *Paradise Lost*, the central question of at least one century and a topic about which I wrote 10,000 words that summer, but I can still recall the exact rancidity of the butter in the City

---

[1] *The Portrait of a Lady*: The 1881 American novel by Henry James.—Eds.
[2] *Paradise Lost*: John Milton's epic poem, published in 1667.—Eds.

of San Francisco's dining car, and the way the tinted windows on the Greyhound bus cast the oil refineries around Carquinez Straits into a grayed and obscurely sinister light. In short my attention was always on the periphery, on what I could see and taste and touch, on the butter, and the Greyhound bus. During those years I was traveling on what I knew to be a very shaky passport, forged papers: I knew that I was no legitimate resident in any world of ideas. I knew I couldn't think. All I knew then was what I couldn't do. All I knew then was what I wasn't, and it took me some years to discover what I was.

Which was a writer.

By which I mean not a "good" writer or a "bad" writer but simply a writer, a person whose most absorbed and passionate hours are spent arranging words on pieces of paper. Had my credentials been in order I would never have become a writer. Had I been blessed with even limited access to my own mind there would have been no reason to write. I write entirely to find out what I'm thinking, what I'm looking at, what I see and what it means. What I want and what I fear. Why did the oil refineries around Carquinez Straits seem sinister to me in the summer of 1956? Why have the night lights in the bevatron burned in my mind for twenty years? *What is going on in these pictures in my mind?*

When I talk about pictures in my mind I am talking, quite specifically, about images that shimmer around the edges. There used to be an illustration in every elementary psychology book showing a cat drawn by a patient in varying stages of schizophrenia. This cat had a shimmer around it. You could see the molecular structure breaking down at the very edges of the cat: the cat became the background and the background the cat, everything interacting, exchanging ions. People on hallucinogens describe the same perception of objects. I'm not a schizophrenic, nor do I take hallucinogens, but certain images do shimmer for me. Look hard enough, and you can't miss the shimmer. It's there. You can't think too much about these pictures that shimmer. You just lie low and let them develop. You stay quiet. You don't talk to many people and you keep your nervous system from shorting out and you try to locate the cat in the shimmer, the grammar in the picture.

Just as I meant "shimmer" literally I mean "grammar" literally. 12 Grammar is a piano I play by ear, since I seem to have been out of school the year the rules were mentioned. All I know about grammar is its infinite power. To shift the structure of a sentence alters the meaning of that sentence, as definitely and inflexibly as the position of a camera alters the meaning of the object photographed. Many people know about camera angles now, but not so many know about sentences. The arrangement of the words matters, and the arrangement you want can be found in the picture in your mind. The picture dictates the arrangement. The picture dictates whether this will be a sentence with or

without clauses, a sentence that ends hard or a dying-fall sentence, long or short, active or passive. The picture tells you how to arrange the words and the arrangement of the words tells you, or tells me, what's going on in the picture. *Nota bene.*[3]
     It tells you.
     You don't tell it.
     Let me show you what I mean by pictures in the mind. I began *Play It as It Lays* just as I have begun each of my novels, with no notion of "character" or "plot" or even "incident." I had only two pictures in my mind, more about which later, and a technical intention, which was to write a novel so elliptical and fast that it would be over before you noticed it, a novel so fast that it would scarcely exist on the page at all. About the pictures, the first was of white space. Empty space. This was clearly the picture that dictated the narrative intention of the book—a book in which anything that happened would happen off the page, a "white" book to which the reader would have to bring his or her own bad dreams—and yet this picture told me no "story," suggested no situation. The second picture did. This second picture was of something actually witnessed. A young woman with long hair and a short white halter dress walks through the casino at the Riviera in Las Vegas at one in the morning. She crosses the casino alone and picks up a house telephone. I watch her because I have heard her paged, and recognize her name: she is a minor actress I see around Los Angeles from time to time, in places like Jax and once in a gynecologist's office in the Beverly Hills Clinic, but have never met. I know nothing about her. Who is paging her? Why is she here to be paged? How exactly did she come to this? It was precisely this moment in Las Vegas that made *Play It as It Lays* begin to tell itself to me, but the moment appears in the novel only obliquely, in a chapter which begins:

> "Maria made a list of things she would never do. She would never: walk through the Sands or Caesar's alone after midnight. She would never: ball at a party, do S-M unless she wanted to, borrow furs from Abe Lipsey, deal. She would never: carry a Yorkshire in Beverly Hills."

     That is the beginning of the chapter and that is also the end of the 16 chapter, which may suggest what I meant by "white space."
     I recall having a number of pictures in my mind when I began the novel I just finished, *A Book of Common Prayer.* As a matter of fact one of these pictures was of that bevatron I mentioned, although I would be hard put to tell you a story in which nuclear energy figures. Another was a newspaper photograph of a hijacked 707 burning on the desert in the Middle East. Another was the night view from a room in which I

---

[3]"Note well."

once spent a week with paratyphoid, a hotel room on the Colombian coast. My husband and I seemed to be on the Colombian coast representing the United States of America at a film festival (I recall invoking the name "Jack Valenti" a lot, as if its reiteration could make me well), and it was a bad place to have fever, not only because my indisposition offended our hosts but because every night in this hotel the generator failed. The lights went out. The elevator stopped. My husband would go to the event of the evening and make excuses for me and I would stay alone in this hotel room, in the dark. I remember standing at the window trying to call Bogotá (the telephone seemed to work on the same principle as the generator) and watching the night wind come up and wondering what I was doing eleven degrees off the equator with a fever of 103. The view from that window definitely figures in *A Book of Common Prayer*, as does the burning 707, and yet none of these pictures told me the story I needed.

The picture that did, the picture that shimmered and made these other images coalesce, was the Panama airport at 6 A.M. I was in this airport only once, on a plane to Bogotá that stopped for an hour to refuel, but the way it looked that morning remained superimposed on everything I saw until the day I finished *A Book of Common Prayer*. I lived in that airport for several years. I can still feel the hot air when I step off the plane, can see the heat already rising off the tarmac at 6 A.M. I can feel my skirt damp and wrinkled on my legs. I can feel the asphalt stick to my sandals. I remember the big tail of a Pan American plane floating motionless down at the end of the tarmac. I remember the sound of a slot machine in the waiting room. I could tell you that I remember a particular woman in the airport, an American woman, *a norteamericana*,[4] a thin *norteamericana* about forty who wore a big square emerald in lieu of a wedding ring, but there was no such woman there.

I put this woman in the airport later. I made this woman up, just as I later made up a country to put the airport in, and a family to run the country. This woman in the airport is neither catching a plane nor meeting one. She is ordering tea in the airport coffee shop. In fact she is not simply "ordering" tea but insisting that the water be boiled, in front of her, for twenty minutes. Why is this woman in this airport? Why is she going nowhere, where has she been? Where did she get that big emerald? What derangement, or disassociation, makes her believe that her will to see the water boiled can possibly prevail?

"She had been going to one airport or another for four months, one could see it, looking at the visas on her passport. All those airports where Charlotte Douglas's passport had been stamped would have looked alike. Sometimes the sign on the tower would say "Bienvenidos" 20

---

[4]*norteamericana*: Sp. North American.—Eds.

and sometimes the sign on the tower would say "Bienvenue," some places were wet and hot and others dry and hot, but at each of these airports the pastel concrete walls would rust and stain and the swamp off the runway would be littered with the fuselages of cannibalized Fairchild F-227's and the water would need boiling.

"I knew why Charlotte went to the airport even if Victor did not.

"I knew about airports."

These lines appear about halfway through *A Book of Common Prayer*, but I wrote them during the second week I worked on the book, long before I had any idea where Charlotte Douglas had been or why she went to airports. Until I wrote these lines I had no character called "Victor" in mind: the necessity for mentioning a name, and the name "Victor," occurred to me as I wrote the sentence. *I knew why Charlotte went to the airport* sounded incomplete. *I knew why Charlotte went to the airport even if Victor did not* carried a little more narrative drive. Most important of all, until I wrote these lines I did not know who "I" was, who was telling the story. I had intended until then that the "I" be no more than the voice of the author, a nineteenth-century omniscient narrator. But there it was:

"I knew why Charlotte went to the airport even if Victor did not.   24

"I knew about airports."

This "I" was the voice of no author in my house. This "I" was someone who not only knew why Charlotte went to the airport but also knew someone called "Victor." Who was Victor? Who was this narrator? Why was this narrator telling me this story? Let me tell you one thing about why writers write: had I known the answer to any of these questions I would never have needed to write a novel.   *1976*

Bernice Johnson Reagon

Nurturing Resistance

There is money going overseas
To buy changes that will never come
Dollar-backed contras spill the blood of the people
In small nations we won't leave alone

There are contras in Nicaragua
U.S. trained death squads in El Salvador
I hear Jonas Savimbe holding hands with apartheid
Is being led to drink at the trough

U.S.A. sponsored violence
Creates refugees all over the world
They pour into LA, DC, and Arizona
Seeking Sanctuary from our guns

Meanwhile in the corporate board rooms
They talk about the debt as if it could be paid
But money borrowed and loaned for:
Guns you can't eat
And buildings you can't live
And trinkets you can't wear
It is a debt not owed by the people

There is money going overseas. . . .
To buy changes that will never come
Dollar-backed contras spill the blood of the people
In small nations we won't leave alone
—"Ode to the International Debt"

"Ode to the International Debt" is one of a group of songs I wrote when I spent a year at the Institute for Policy Studies. When I was asked to present something for their annual winter festival, I asked several of the research fellows to give me some of their latest papers on the state of the world from their particular area of research and analysis. I wanted to see if I could sing progressive contemporary analysis. I did a suite of six pieces; Sweet Honey in the Rock (the vocal group I work with), moved two of those works to performance level one year later. We continue to work on several others.

Socially conscious artists are not born. We are culturally oriented and trained. As an activist in the Civil Rights Movement I learned about the relationship between organizing for change and being a cultural artist. Most of us who became known during that time as singers or songleaders saw ourselves as organizers, specifically, SNCC (The Student Nonviolent Coordinating Committee) field secretaries. I saw again and again the connections between being an effective leader and a cultural artist. Participating in that struggle for change taught me about being challenged to trust my inner voice about how I and my people were doing in the world. The movement gave me the opportunity to use my own perception of how things were as the foundation upon which to base my actions and to make my decisions. It was here that I learned about the sweetness of struggle in my life. That, in the midst of standing against opposition, even when at great risks, there is a satisfaction of knowing on the deepest level that who you are to yourself is the same essence you offer to the world in which you move.

CULTURE OF STRUGGLE

I grew up in a culture of struggle where, without any specific spoken warning, I received clear messages of boundaries in all aspects of my life that were not to be crossed, rules that were not to be broken. I internalized these messages, thus setting up a control mechanism to protect myself against acting freely. I went around in life with this inner warning light or buzzer that would be triggered if I considered any action that was considered inappropriate behavior. There was a tape in my head that chanted, "If you do that you are going to be killed." This warning system worked to control my actions at home, in school, in church, and in the larger society. I am not here talking about a physical murder. I am talking about a fear of being shut out, cut off if you behaved in unacceptable ways. Within the home, the school, and the church, you had a sense that this structure of boundaries was set up by people who cared about you and wanted you to do well. They organized community structures so that all pressures would be applied to make you make the right choices. In the larger society, with its blatant racism, there were clearly marked places for you to live and function. When one considered challenging those narrow, twisted spaces, the inner buzzer system went crazy. You felt inside that you would be inviting total destruction if you considered behavior that was outside the parameters drawn by whites who controlled your community.

There was a life inside the boundaries. There were ways of being fed   4 and centered on a worldview that made us know somewhere deep inside that life based on racism was wrong. That white people were not supe- rior. We knew this best because we cleaned their homes, we took care of their children, we knew how they treated each other, we knew how they treated us. We knew they were not superior. Everywhere—in church, in school—we were drawn into powerful creative experiences that said that we were worthwhile, that there was a reason for us being alive, and it was not to serve white men and women. I had teachers who talked to us between the prescribed lessons to tell us in a hundred ways that things could change. I heard old men and women sing in church, "I'm so glad trouble don't last always." I thus also internalized the perspec- tive that we as a people were living through a time that had to change, and we had to be prepared for functioning and living productive, respectable lives.

It was the Civil Rights Movement that taught me that one did not always get killed for going up against the powers that controlled your life. The movement taught me that if you went across the line, you were offering your life, but it was not always taken. The space between being alive and becoming conscious of my own beliefs and being killed belonged to me. I could, once I put my life where my beliefs were, really stand for what I felt deeply about. It was the first time my life really made sense as an empowered person. It was the first time I felt what I said and did made a difference. I could affect the space I operated in if I offered my life to back up my actions.

The relationship between singing and that struggle was crucial for me. The training for being a singing fighter had begun with learning about the role of music in African-American culture and the role of the artist in the leadership of the community.

Growing up in a traditionally based home and community, I had seen that it was important for leaders to also be cultural artists of great power. Content went beyond text; the virtuosity of delivery of a talk, sermon, or speech included both what was said and whether the speaker could tune her or his words with feelings. Information passed within the traditional forms of the African-American culture is concrete reality. It helps if one lives "the life one sings about," but the singing itself is a concrete offering that can be and is used by those gathered within the sound of the expression. Our people respond when information is heard and felt. We are culturally socialized to test experiences by how we feel when we sit under the power of someone's voice. This is talk that goes far beyond an aural experience. Exchanges between leaders and their constituents had to be transforming experiences where a bonding was created by all gathered, a community was formed in the process of giving and receiving through talk and song.

My central training was as a singer. I learned very early that I had to   8 affect the space I sang in. The air that people breathed carried the sound of my voice as songleader joined by their own. I am now describing a feast of song, where that which is consumed is also created by the consumers, and what you take in is more than you give out because when you put it out, it is enlarged by the sounds of others who commit themselves to participate in the creation. Creating a congregational song means creating sound images that so affect the environment that people walk into you several blocks before they get to you as a source of the sound. Black people singing together is a pulling sound; when you hear it you want to go to it and to get in it. You want to belong to that group that is being born in that singing.

Having been trained in African-American southern communities to sing, I then was charged to go to schools to learn the way of the larger society. I trained in Western-structured institutions run by my people to be a scholar and scientist in the history of this nation. It was my experience in the Civil Rights Movement coming in the middle of these two learning systems that made me reshape how I would try to operate in the world.

As a scholar at the Smithsonian Institution, I have made every effort to do work that validates the presence of my people in this world as a vital and central part of who this country is. I have produced programs that through research, analysis, and public presentations make clear that African Americans belong to a world family of culture based in Africa and that the most prolific sacred music form created in the twentieth century in the United States of America is the gospel music of the urban Black church.

"AMERICA"

I operate out of the assumption that I am the United States of America and that I am central to anything that is really happening in this country that is worthwhile. I recognize that I am a secret. I also recognize that among the people who do pay attention to the fact of my existence and the existence of my people—our history, our contributions, and our culture—we are presented as being subcultural, as if we are outside, the other—a tangent, a limb or something that if lost by the main body, life would not be threatened. The inference is that if you, the United States of America, lose us, you would still be. This is a lie, I know that without me, there would not be a United States of America to talk about. My people are central to what is the main cultural power and fabric of this society. The distortion and outright denial of that fact are central to the lie perpetuated as myth that the culture of this country is not African-American at her core.

It is the same kind of mythology that is wrapped up in the owner- 12 ship of terms like "America." Most of us say the word and we only see the United States of America. We do not see the Americas and all of its peoples and their cultures and their histories. The collective pysche of this society is based on denying the existence of a society that is multi-cultural and composed of many peoples and classes, existing in a world that is very small and dominated by women, children, and peoples of color. We steal the identity of being American from millions of others throughout the hemisphere who should share that identity equally in our minds and thus in our daily practice. When we use the term America as a synonym for the United States of America, we are denying other peoples their space, reality, hope, and territory.

Re-imagining America for me is smashing the mythology, and end-ing the robbery that is so basic to the general collective consciousness. Re-imaging America is to embrace the reality of the human community and life on the planet and to try to understand partnering with responsibility and love for all that makes up our universe as we understand it, as well as that which is still beyond our knowing.

CULTURALLY GROUNDED INTERNATIONALISM

All of my work has to do with my sense of being very central and being part of a larger constituency that is the heart of what this society can be. When I think of the future, I think of myself as being a part of laying the foundation for the evolution of a society where many peoples can live and share the same world without killing, exploiting, and ruling each other. Whenever I offer an image as a singer, as a scholar, it is that vision that drives my efforts. I also make clear that in this living and sharing the world with many peoples and cultures, I will always be an African American woman, and all my offerings will come from that base. That being in the world as a daughter of daughters of daughters of African parents is not a contradiction to being able to live in a multicultural society.

In the context of the African American community experience, there are all of these songs that are about church or praying—information that says that black people are very conscious of what is going on in the larger world we live in and how it impacts on us. We are not a cocoon people. Our culture is constructed with internal boundaries; there are always ways to enter and leave. In doing my work, I have continued to operate from that perspective. You don't have to move from your base in order to participate in the larger world; you don't have to obscure or go beyond your cultural soundings in order for peoples of other soundings to make use of your offerings.

The community I celebrate is that universe of progressive peoples 16 who share with others a loose collection of values and ideals about human and environmental society. In my mind most of these people are culturally united. They do not in local communities always work together. They may not really like each other. However, they do share a vision of a less oppressive society. They dream of a less violent world; they care intensively about whether there will be a tomorrow. When I speak through my singing and my research, it is that constituency I try to nurture and validate.

> *We come to you*
> *You in every color of the rainbow*
> *With your freedom and struggle stances*
> *In every position of the moon and sun*
>
> *We come to you*
> *Offering our songs and the sounds of our mothers' mothers*
> *In libation*
> *To everyone of us*

There really is a community
We have seen and felt and been held by you these ten years
There is a community we belong to without geographical boundaries
D.C., Atlanta, Berea, Chicago, East St. Louis, L.A., Toronto, Chiba, the Bay
area, Newark, Seattle, Chapel Hill, Boston, Frankfurt, London, Richmond, Little
Rock, NYC, Denver, Albuquerque, Nashville, Brixton, New Orleans, Vancouver,
Portland, Berlin, Albany, Durham, Tokyo, St. Louis, Detroit, St. Paul, Dallas, Peoria,
Jamaica . . .
There really is a community
Lovers
Searchers
Movers into life
Fighters and builders
Of a place where military machines, hatred of women, abuse of children, homophobia,
societal male suicide, racial bigotry, starvation, work that kills and cripples, social
orders driven by greed, the U.S.A. invading whoever . . . this week.
Where this dying and acting out of fear, anger, and terror
will find no feeding ground
I wanna be there.

(written July 1983 for the tenth anniversary album release
of Sweet Honey in the Rock, "We All . . . Everyone of Us.")

This community is everywhere . . . in order to do the nurturing, others like me must share in the ownership of the airwaves so that the food we offer can be received from those who would eat from our palettes. Our visions of the world, the universe, and the future have every right to ride the waves and be accessible to all who would choose.

COMMUNITY OF ORGANIZERS

I sing to those who will listen. It is important to talk to the convinced. I am often asked if when Sweet Honey sings, "Aren't you singing to yourself?" The progressive community of this country is one of the most fragile in the world. We suffer from illusions of being in better shape than we are because we think it follows that if we are Americans, we must be great! We are in great need of understanding our vulnerability, our need for validation, maintenance, nurturing, and celebration. We need to learn how to be longtimers and not be forever limited by operating ahistorically and responding to crisis after crisis.

I like to think of the life of a woman I call my political mother, Ella Jo Baker. Before her death in 1986, she put in over a half century of consistent organizing, full-time no matter what her specific job was. She understood that in being an organizer, she had to also be a creator or trainer of organizers. I offer this life's work, which is really more than fifty years, for as a child Ella Baker had to be sent to live with her grandmother after her resistance to abuse by a white boy made her unsafe in her own community. Often we get involved in a struggle for change that affects our immediate lives, and rather than that being a beginning, after ten years or so, we float away. Some of us say that what we do at that point is go on with our lives. We are still decent people, but we are not able to sustain forty to fifty years as organizers. I happen to believe, as with Ella Baker, you can fight for change anywhere and for as long as there is the breath of life.

It is important to gather together to nurture and feed as a com- 20 munity committed to being a presence in a society beyond our own meager lives. When moving in new territories as an organizer I use the model I learned in the Black church and as a field secretary for SNCC. First, there is a home base; there is a place that you can go back to for shelter, rest, and re-orientation. It is from there that you move into the world offering your message and work sometimes to people who will throw rocks at you, throw you in jail, or slam doors in your face. Facing the work of this intensity, we do not have to apologize for needing to return to home base. There must be a strategy for going out, organizing, speaking, and raising issues and then coming in to yourself and your community for a check-in. It is important to have a safety zone to refuel where you can eat your dinner with others who understand and will protect your need to be vulnerable.

MULTI-ISSUE STRUGGLES

We live in a time when we have to be able to function across issues. Sometimes I sing before audiences that give great responses to one verse in a song because that verse calls their name; the next verse goes placidly by because they have not developed as organizers and socially conscious people to celebrate the struggle for a world where we can exist together.

I wrote a song with my daughter, Toshi, for the film "On Becoming a Woman," produced by the National Black Women's Health Project. The film speaks to the need to fill the communication gap between mother and daughter when young Black women move into puberty and begin monthly periods. This personal issue may not seem like a political one, but I say that knowledge and the control of knowledge goes hand-in-hand with being able to control people's lives. The lives of women are shaped and placed by definitions of who we are and what we should be used for in our families and in our communities. Information about how we function as physical units is so highly charged with taboos that we only whisper about ourselves to those we trust and will not tell others that we think things that happen to us are important enough to

talk about with somebody else. The song is Toshi and I talking across
generations about our bodies changing and thus our position in society:

Mama sister I wake up my body's not the same
My feelings run deeper than they ever run before
I am feeling so strange about changes in my life
Can I sit awhile with you and ease my changing times

Are you here by my side
I am here, I will listen while you tell me
About the ways of the woman rising in your life

Daughter, woman I'm aware of what you're moving through
You see I have walked the same road only yesterday
I came to my mama as you have come to me
I will sit awhile with you and ease your troubled times

I am here by your side
Are you here, will you listen while I tell you
About the ways of the woman rising in my life

CHOOSING

I once wrote a song that said "You have to choose to be a sister of
mine." It was my way of saying that I come into my space loaded down
with the experiences and changes of my life. I have chosen a path and I
am picky about my company. I want to walk with those who will claim a
different world and will hold real space daily through real living. To do
this we have to choose.

You have to choose and keep on choosing. Every day we are offered   24
opportunities to sell out ourselves and our principles. I count it as a
rare blessing to have developed as a young adult around people like
Ella Jo Baker and Septima Clark. With fighters like this I had examples
of people who really worked for a living, paid their bills, and were
always in every part of their lives taking a stand for the things they
believed in. It made me have the feeling that I could live that kind of
life, where my life's work was working for what I believed in for myself
and my communities. You can choose to stand. You only have your life
to lose, if they take it you may not even know it because you'll be dead,
or if you do know it you can just begin to strategize to come back again.
I urge people to take risks. I urge myself to go beyond those boundaries
that say stop. In my stancing, I have never been alone.

I heard Ron Dellums say that progressives are the majority in this
country, but we do not often speak as the majority. Many of us are very
much taken with being a minority. Many of us who work very hard for
change also participate in denying the impact of our efforts. Even as we
challenge the forces that try to keep us down, we keep waiting for
someone to come so we can really get started.

Well, I see you all the time, and find it unbelievable how many of us don't know we exist. Sometimes artists are the only people who can announce to you that you're okay. It is our work to show you what we see and to nurture, cradle, and change these images. At our best, we are your mirrors. We show that we really do exist and are enough for the work we have before us.   *1990*

Francine du Plessix Gray

I Write for Revenge against Reality

A nightmare recurs since childhood:

Facing a friend, I struggle for words and emit no sound. I have an urgent message to share but am struck dumb, my jaw is clamped shut as in a metal vise, I gasp for breath and cannot set my tongue free. At the dream's end my friend has fled and I am locked into the solitude of silence.

The severe stutter I had as a child, my father's impatience and swiftness of tongue, his constant interruption of me when I tried to speak?

Or perhaps another incident which also has to do with the threat of   4 the Father and the general quirkiness of my French education: One day when I was 9 I was assigned my first free composition. From infancy I had been tutored at home in Paris by a tyrannical governess, the two of us traveling once a week to a correspondence school whose Gallically rigid assignments (memorization of Asian capitals and Latin verbs, codifying of sentence parts) were hardly conducive to a fertile imagination. "Write a Story About Anything You Wish," Central Bureau suddenly ordered. Filled with excitement and terror by this freedom, I began as a severe minimalist:

"The little girl was forbidden by her parents to walk alone to the lake at the other end of the long lawn. But she wished to visit a luminous green-eyed frog who would offer her the key to freedom. One day she disobeyed her parents and walked to the lake and immediately drowned." (The End)

"Pathetic dribble!" the Father stormed on his daily visit to my study room. "You dare call that a story! What will become of you if you can't ever finish anything!"

It was a warm May evening of 1939, the year before he died in the Resistance. The love of my life (my father was himself an occasional scribbler) was warning me that I should never write again. I still remember the hours I spent honing those meager sentences, the square white china inkwell into which I squeezed the rubber filler of a Waterman pen, the awkwardness of ink-stained fingers as I struggled to shape my letters (I was born left-handed and had been forced to use my right), the tears, the sense that my writing was doomed to be sloppy, abortive, good for naught.

So it may have begun, the central torment of my life, my simul-   8 taneous need to commit fantasies to paper and the terror that accompanies that need, the leaden slowness of the words' arrival, my struggle with the clamped metal jaws of mouth and mind. An affliction deepened by that infatuation with the written word that possesses most solitary children. For books had been the only companions of my childhood prison, particularly such stirring tales of naval adventure as *Captains Courageous* or *Two Years Before the Mast*, which fueled dreams of running away to sea and never being seen again.

Then came the war, the flight to America, the need to learn a new language. English was learned as a means of survival and became a lover to be seduced and conquered as swiftly as possible, to be caressed and rolled on the tongue in a continuous ecstacy of union. English words, from the time I was 11 on, were my medium of joy and liberation. I fondled them by memorizing twenty lines of Blake when ten had been assigned; I wooed them so assiduously that I won the Lower School Spelling Bee within 10 months of having come to the United States. (I was the only foreign scholarship student at the Spence School; shortly after the contest a delegation of Spence parents descended on my mother, who was supporting us by designing hats at Henri Bendel's, to verify that we were true emigrés and not usurpers from Brooklyn.)

I continued to court my new tongue by struggling for A's in English, by being elected editor of the school paper, which a predecessor had artfully named Il Spenceroso. Omens of a "literary gift" continued to accrete—a prize in Bryn Mawr's Freshman Essay Contest, the Creative Writing Award at Barnard for three stories of a strictly autobiographical nature. Such portents brought no security. I fled from myself by being a compulsive talker, a bureaucrat, polemicist, hack journalist. I had taken no more than two courses in literature beyond Freshman English, thinking I was smartass enough to learn it for myself. One of the other courses had been a creative writing class that earned me a C− for first-person fictions about situations I knew nothing about—I seemed always to be a middle-aged alcoholic actor seeking salvation in a Bowery church. After that fiasco I had sought refuge in rigor and formalism— physics, philosophy, medieval history. There was a curious furtiveness about the way I continued to carry on my love affair with literature. I copied entire paragraphs from Henry James or T. S. Eliot into private notebooks out of sheer delectation in the texture of their prose. In a stretch of a few solitary vacation weeks I would memorize two hundred lines of Marvell for the pleasure of speaking them to myself during nights of insomnia. Why all this reluctance and convertness?

"You're writing pure junk," Charles Olson[1] had stormed at me during a summer workshop at Black Mountain when I'd handed him my prize-winning college stories. "If you want to be a writer keep it to a journal." The giant walrus rising from his chair, 6 feet 7 inches of him towering. ". . . AND ABOVE ALL DON'T TRY TO PUBLISH ANYTHING FOR TEN YEARS!" Another paternal figure had censored me into silence, perhaps this time for the best.

I followed Big Charles's advice. I kept my journal in New Orleans 12 where I dallied as if I had 10 lives to squander, drinking half a bottle of gin a night as I followed a jazz clarinetist on the rounds of Bourbon Street. I remained faithful to my secret vice in the dawns of New York when I worked the night shift at United Press, writing World in Briefs about Elks' Meetings and watermelon-eating contests in Alabama. I remained loyal to my journal through a myriad of failed aspirations while flirting with the thought of entering Harvard's Department of Architecture, of going to Union Theological Seminary for a degree in divinity. I persevered with it when I moved to Paris to earn my living as a fashion reporter, dallying with a succession of consummate narcissists to whom I eventually gave their literary due. I continued to write it when I fulfilled one of my life's earliest dreams and spent five years as a painter of meticulously naturalistic landscapes and still lifes.

By then I was married and had two children. And since I lived in deep country and in relative solitude, encompassed by domestic duties, the journal became increasingly voluminous, angry, introspective. The nomad, denied flight and forced to turn inward, was beginning to explode. One day when I was thirty-three, after I'd cooked and smiled for a bevy of weekend guests whom I never wished to see again, I felt an immense void, great powerlessness, the deepest loneliness I'd ever known. I wept for some hours, took out a notebook, started rewriting one of the three stories that had won me my Barnard prize. It was the one about my governess. It was published a short time later in *The New Yorker*, one year past the deadline Charles Olson had set me. It was to become, 12 years and two books of nonfiction later, the first chapter of *Lovers and Tyrants*. The process of finishing that book was as complex and lengthy as it was painful. It entailed a solid and delicate psycho-

---

[1]**Olson**: Charles Olson (1910–1970), the influential American poet who taught at the experimental Black Mountain College.—Eds.

analysis which forced me to accept my father's death. Epiphany achieved, I was able to write the novel's three last chapters—my first genuine attempt at fiction—in a mere six months. I may have had to bury my father to set my tongue free.

And yet what kind of writer have I become, six years and two novels later? Few scribblers I know have struggled so hard for so little. I am too many things I do not wish to be—a Jane of all trades shuttling back and forth between scant fiction, voluminous reporting, innumerable and unmemorable literary essays. I feel honored by yet undeserving of the appellation "novelist." I am merely a craftsperson, a cabinetmaker of texts and occasionally, I hope, a witness to our times. My terror of fictional invention has denied me that activity which from childhood on has been the most furtively longed for, which has proved to be (when I finally began to tackle it) the most deeply satisfying.

Might I remain brainwashed, along with many of my generation, by the notion that fiction is the noblest, the most "creative" of all genres of prose? No avocation has better clarified that issue or my identity as a writer than the business of teaching. I stress to young colleagues that some of the greatest masterpieces of our time have been works of nonfiction or hybrid forms which defy classification—James Agee's *Let Us Now Praise Famous Men*, Edmund Wilson's criticism, Peter Handke's *A Sorrow Beyond Dreams*, all of Roland Barthes's work. I urge them to shake loose from the peculiarly American fixation on novel-writing. I tell them that the obsession to write The Great American Novel might have done more harm to generations of Americans than all the marijuana in Mexico. The syllabus for the course I taught at Yale last fall sums it all up:

THE WRITING OF THE TEXT: This is a seminar in the reading   16 and writing of literature which I hope can remain untainted by the word "creative." It is dedicated to the premise that a distinction be-tween "fiction" and "nonfiction" is potentially harmful to many aspir-ing writers who will progress more fruitfully if they are encouraged to think of their writing as pure "text" without worrying about what "form" or "genre" it will fall into.

Reading Assignments: F. Scott Fitzgerald's *Crack-Up*, Max Frisch's *Sketchbooks*, Flaubert's *Dictionary of Accepted Ideas*, Elizabeth Hardwick's *Sleepless Nights*, Boris Pasternak's *Safe Conduct*, William Gass's *On Being Blue*, Maureen Howard's *Facts of Life*.

The first thing we must do when we set out to write, I also tell my classes, is to shed all narcissism. My own decades of fear came from my anxiety that my early drafts were ugly, sloppy, not promising enough. We must persevere and scrawl atrocities; persevere dreadful draft after dreadful draft in an unhindered stream of consciousness, persevere, if need be, in Breton's technique of automatic writing, of mindless trance.

And within that morass of words there may be an ironic turn of phrase, a dislocation that gives us a key to the voice, the tone, the structure we're struggling to find. I am a witness to the lateness of my own vocation, the hesitation and terrors that still haunt all my beginnings, the painful slowness with which I proceed through a minimum of four drafts in both fiction and nonfiction.

Question:
Why do I go on writing, seeing the continuing anguish of the act, 20 the dissatisfaction I feel toward most results?

Flannery O'Connor said it best: "I write because I don't know what I think until I read what I say."

I write out of a desire for revenge against reality, to destroy forever the stuttering powerless child I once was, to gain the love and attention that silenced child never had, to allay the dissatisfaction I still have with myself, to be something other than what I am. I write out of hate, out of a desire for revenge against all the men who have oppressed and humiliated me.

I also write out of love and gratitude for a mother and stepfather who made me feel worthy by hoarding every scrap of correspondence I ever sent them; love and gratitude for a husband of exquisite severity who still edits every final draft that leaves my typewriter. I write out of an infantile dread of ever disappointing them again.

I write because in the act of creation there comes that mysterious, 24 abundant sense of being both parent and child; I am giving birth to an Other and simultaneously being reborn as child in the playground of creation.

I write on while continuing to despair that I can't ever achieve the inventiveness, irreverence, complexity of my favorite contemporary authors—Milan Kundera, Italo Calvino, Günter Grass, Salman Rushdie, to name only the foreign ones. They are certain enough of their readers' love (or indifferent enough to it, since the great Indifferents are the great Seducers) to indulge in that shrewd teasing and misguiding of the reader, that ironic obliqueness which is the marrow of the best modernist work. It is not only my lesser gift that is at fault. Behind my impulsive cataloguing, my Slavic unleashing of emotion, my Quaker earnestness to inform my readers guilelessly of all I know, there still lurks the lonely, stuttering child too terrified of losing the reader's love to take the necessary risks.

Yet, I remain sustained by a definition of faith once offered me by Ivan Illich: "Faith is a readiness for the Surprise." I write because I have faith in the possibility that I can eventually surprise myself. I am still occasionally plagued by that recurring nightmare of my jaw being clamped shut, my mouth frozen in silence. But I wake up from it with less dread, with the hope that some day my tongue will loosen and emit a surprising new sound which even I, at first, shall not be able to understand.

1982

Rudolfo A. Anaya

B. Traven Is Alive and Well in Cuernavaca

I didn't go to Mexico to find B. Traven.[1] Why should I? I have enough to do writing my own fiction, so I go to Mexico to write, not to search out writers. B. Traven? you ask. Don't you remember THE TREA-SURE OF THE SIERRA MADRE? A real classic. They made a movie from the novel. I remember seeing it when I was a kid. It was set in Mexico, and it had all the elements of a real adventure story. B. Traven was an adventurous man, travelled all over the world, then disappeared into Mexico and cut himself off from society. He gave no interviews and allowed few photographs. While he lived he remained unapproachable, anonymous to his public, a writer shrouded in mystery.

He's dead now, or they say he's dead. I think he's alive and well. At any rate, he has become something of an institution in Mexico, a man honored for his work. The cantineros[2] and taxi drivers in Mexico City know about him as well as the cantineros of Spain knew Hemingway, or they claim to. I never mention I'm a writer when I'm in a cantina, because inevitably some aficionado will ask, "Do you know the work of B. Traven?" And from some dusty niche will appear a yellowed, thumb-worn novel by Traven. Thus if the cantinero knows his business, and they all do in Mexico, he is apt to say, "Did you know that B. Traven used to drink here?" If you show the slightest interest, he will follow with, "Sure, he used to sit right over here. In this corner. . . ." And if you don't leave right then you will wind up hearing many stories about the mysterious B. Traven while buying many drinks for the local patrons.

[1]Traven, whose real name may have been Berick (or Bruno) Traven Torsvan, was probably born in Chicago sometime between 1890 and 1901; he died in 1969. Presumably he did live for most of his adult life in Mexico, where he wrote numerous novels, the most famous of which is *The Treasure of the Sierra Madre* (1935).
[2]Spanish: "bartender."

Everybody reads his novels, on the buses, on street corners; if you look closely you'll spot one of his titles. One turned up for me, and that's how this story started. I was sitting in the train station in Juárez, waiting for the train to Cuernavaca, which would be an exciting title for this story except that there is no train to Cuernavaca. I was drinking beer to kill time, the erotic and sensitive Mexican time which is so different from the clean-packaged, well-kept time of the Americanos. Time in Mexico can be cruel and punishing, but it is never indifferent. It permeates everything, it changes reality. Einstein would have loved Mexico because there time and space are one. I stare more often into empty space when I'm in Mexico. The past seems to infuse the present, and in the brown, wrinkled faces of the old people one sees the presence of the past. In Mexico I like to walk the narrow streets of the cities and the smaller pueblos, wandering aimlessly, feeling the sunlight which is so distinctively Mexican, listening to the voices which call in the streets, peering into the dark eyes which are so secretive and proud. The Mexican people guard a secret. But in the end, one is never really lost in Mexico. All streets lead to a good cantina. All good stories start in a cantina.

At the train station, after I let the kids who hustle the tourists know   4 that I didn't want chewing gum or cigarettes, and I didn't want my shoes shined, and I didn't want a woman at the moment, I was left alone to drink my beer. Luke-cold Dos Equis. I don't remember how long I had been there or how many Dos Equis I had finished when I glanced at the seat next to me and saw a book which turned out to be a B. Traven novel, old and used and obviously much read, but a novel nevertheless. What's so strange about finding a B. Traven novel in that dingy little corner of a bar in the Juárez train station? Nothing, unless you know that in Mexico one never finds anything. It is a country that doesn't waste anything, everything is recycled. Chevrolets run with patched up Ford engines and Chrysler transmissions, buses are kept together, and kept running, with baling wire and home-made parts, yesterday's Traven novel is the pulp on which tomorrow's Fuentes[3] story will appear. Time recycles in Mexico. Time returns to the past, and the Christian finds himself dreaming of ancient Aztec rituals. He who does not believe that Quetzalcoatl[4] will return to save Mexico has little faith.

So the novel was the first clue. Later there was Justino. "Who is Justino?" you want to know. Justino was the jardinero[5] who cared for the garden of my friend, the friend who had invited me to stay at his home in Cuernavaca while I continued to write. The day after I arrived I was

[3]**Fuentes**: Carlos Fuentes (b. 1928), prominent Mexican novelist.—Eds.
[4]**Quetzalcoatl**: Aztec god and hero, usually depicted as a plumed serpent.—Eds.
[5]**jardinero**: "Gardener."—Eds.

sitting in the sun, letting the fatigue of the long journey ooze away, thinking nothing, when Justino appeared on the scene. He had finished cleaning the swimming pool and was taking his morning break, so he sat in the shade of the orange tree and introduced himself. Right away I could tell that he would rather be a movie actor or an adventurer, a real free spirit. But things didn't work out for him. He got married, children appeared, he took a couple of mistresses, more children appeared, so he had to work to support his family. "A man is like a rooster," he said after we talked awhile, "the more chickens he has the happier he is." Then he asked me what I was going to do about a woman while I was there, and I told him I hadn't thought that far ahead, that I would be happy if I could just get a damned story going. This puzzled Justino, and I think for a few days it worried him. So on Saturday night he took me out for a few drinks and we wound up in some of the bordellos of Cuernavaca in the company of some of the most beautiful women in the world. Justino knew them all. They loved him, and he loved them.

I learned something more of the nature of this jardinero a few nights later when the heat and an irritating mosquito wouldn't let me sleep. I heard music from a radio, so I put on my pants and walked out into the Cuernavacan night, an oppressive, warm night heavy with the sweet perfume of the dama de la noche[6] bushes which lined the wall of my friend's villa. From time to time I heard a dog cry in the distance, and I remembered that in Mexico many people die of rabies. Perhaps that is why the walls of the wealthy are always so high and the locks always secure. Or maybe it was because of the occasional gunshots that explode in the night. The news media tell us that Mexico is the most stable country in Latin America and, with the recent oil finds, the bankers and the oil men want to keep it that way. I sense, and many know, that in the dark the revolution does not sleep. It is a spirit kept at bay by the high fences and the locked gates, yet it prowls the heart of every man. "Oil will create a new revolution," Justino had told me, "but it's going to be for our people. Mexicans are tired of building gas stations for the Gringos from Gringolandia." I understood what he meant: there is much hunger in the country.

I lit a cigarette and walked toward my friend's car, which was parked in the driveway near the swimming pool. I approached quietly and peered in. On the back seat with the legs propped on the front seat-back and smoking a cigar sat Justino. Two big, luscious women sat on either side of him running their fingers through his hair and whispering in his ears. The doors were open to allow a breeze. He looked content. Sitting there he was that famous artist on his way to an afternoon reception in Mexico City, or he was a movie star on his way to the

---

[6]**dama de la noche**: "Lady of the night," a prostitute.—Eds.

premiere of his most recent movie. Or perhaps it was Sunday and he
was taking a Sunday drive in the country, towards Tepoztlán. And why
shouldn't his two friends accompany him? I had to smile. Unnoticed I
backed away and returned to my room. So there was quite a bit more
than met the eye to this short, dark Indian from Ocosingo.

In the morning I asked my friend, "What do you know about   8
Justino?"

"Justino? You mean Vitorino."

"Is that his real name?"

"Sometimes he calls himself Trinidad."

"Maybe his name is Justino Vitorino Trinidad," I suggested.   12

"I don't know, don't care," my friend answered. "He told me he used
to be a guide in the jungle. Who knows? The Mexican Indian has an
incredible imagination. Really gifted people. He's a good jardinero, and
that's what matters to me. It's difficult to get good jardineros, so I don't
ask questions."

"Is he reliable?" I wondered aloud.

"As reliable as a ripe mango," my friend nodded.

I wondered how much he knew, so I pushed a little further. "And the   16
radio at night?"

"Oh, that. I hope it doesn't bother you. Robberies and break-ins are
increasing here in the colonia. Something we never used to have.
Vitorino said that if he keeps the radio on low the sound keeps thieves
away. A very good idea, don't you think?"

I nodded. A very good idea.

"And I sleep very soundly," my friend concluded, "so I never hear it."

The following night when I awakened and heard the soft sound of   20
music from the radio and heard the splashing of water, I had only to
look from my window to see Justino and his friends in the pool,
swimming nude in the moonlight. They were joking and laughing softly
as they splashed each other, being quiet so as not to awaken my friend,
the patrón[7] who slept so soundly. The women were beautiful. Brown
skinned and glistening with water in the moonlight they reminded me
of ancient Aztec maidens, swimming around Chac, their god of rain.
They teased Justino, and he smiled as he floated on a rubber mattress in
the middle of the pool, smoking his cigar, happy because they were
happy. When he smiled the gold fleck of a filling glinted in the moonlight.

"¡Qué cabrón!"[8] I laughed and closed my window.

Justino said a Mexican never lies. I believed him. If a Mexican says
he will meet you at a certain time and place, he means he will meet you

---

[7]**patron:** Landlord or master.—Eds.

[8]**¡Qué cabrón!":** "What a man!"—Eds.

sometime at some place. Americans who retire in Mexico often complain of maids who swear they will come to work on a designated day,
then don't show up. They did not lie, they knew they couldn't be at
work, but they knew to tell the señora otherwise would make her sad or
displease her, so they agree on a date so everyone would remain happy.
What a beautiful aspect of character. It's a real virtue which Norteamericanos[9] interpret as a fault in their character, because we are used
to asserting ourselves on time and people. We feel secure and comfortable only when everything is neatly packaged in its proper time and
place. We don't like the disorder of a free-flowing life.

Some day, I thought to myself, Justino will give a grand party in the
sala of his patrón's home. His three wives, or his wife and two mistresses,
and his dozens of children will be there. So will the women from the
bordellos. He will preside over the feast, smoke his cigars, request his
favorite beer-drinking songs from the mariachis,[10] smile, tell stories and
make sure everyone has a grand time. He will be dressed in a tuxedo,
borrowed from the patrón's closet of course, and he will act gallant and
show everyone that a man who has just come into sudden wealth should
share it with his friends. And in the morning he will report to the
patrón that something has to be done about the poor mice that are
coming in out of the streets and eating everything in the house.

"I'll buy some poison," the patrón will suggest. 24

"No, no," Justino will shake his head, "a little music from the radio
and a candle burning in the sala[11] will do."

And he will be right.

I liked Justino. He was a rogue with class. We talked about the
weather, the lateness of the rainy season, women, the role of oil in
Mexican politics. Like other workers, he believed nothing was going to
filter down to the campesinos.[12] "We could all be real Mexican greasers
with all that oil," he said, "but the politicians will keep it all."

"What about the United States?" I asked. 28

"Oh, I have traveled in the estados unidos[13] to the north. It's a
country that's going to the dogs in a worse way than Mexico. The thing I
liked the most was your cornflakes."

"Cornflakes?"

"Sí. You can make really good cornflakes."

"And women?" 32

---

[9]**Norteamericanos**: "North Americans."—Eds.
[10]**mariachis**: Musicians who perform mariachi, a lively popular music.—Eds.
[11]**sala**: Drawing room or parlor.—Eds.
[12]**campesinos**: Peasants, farmers.—Eds.
[13]**estados unidos**: "The United States."—Eds.

"Ah, you better keep your eyes open, my friend. Those gringas are going to change the world just like the Suecas[14] changed Spain."

"For better or for worse?"

"Spain used to be a nice country," he winked.

We talked, we argued, we drifted from subject to subject. I learned 36 from him. I had been there a week when he told the story which eventually led me to B. Traven. One day I was sitting under the orange tree reading the B. Traven novel I had found in the Juárez train station, keeping one eye on the ripe oranges which fell from time to time, my mind wandering as it worked to focus on a story so I could begin to write. After all, that's why I had come to Cuernavaca, to get some writing done, but nothing was coming, nothing. Justino wandered by and asked what I was reading and I replied it was an adventure story, a story of a man's search for the illusive pot of gold at the end of a make-believe rainbow. He nodded, thought awhile and gazed toward Popo, Popocatepetl,[15] the towering volcano which lay to the south, shrouded in mist, waiting for the rains as we waited for the rains, sleeping, gazing at his female counterpart, Itza, who lay sleeping and guarding the valley of Cholula,[16] there, where over four-hundred years ago Cortés[17] showed his wrath and executed thousands of Cholulans.

"I am going on an adventure," he finally said and paused. "I think you might like to go with me."

I said nothing, but I put my book down and listened.

"I have been thinking about it for a long time, and now is the time to go. You see, it's like this. I grew up on the hacienda[18] of Don Francisco Jimenez, it's to the south, just a day's drive on the carretera.[19] In my village nobody likes Don Francisco, they fear and hate him. He has killed many men and he has taken their fortunes and buried them. He is a very rich man, muy rico. Many men have tried to kill him, but Don Francisco is like the devil, he kills them first."

I listened as I always listen, because one never knows when a word 40 or phrase or an idea will be the seed from which a story sprouts, but at first there was nothing interesting. It sounded like the typical patrón-peón story I had heard so many times before. A man, the patrón, keeps the workers enslaved, in serfdom, and because he wields so much power

[14]**Suecas**: "Swedes."—EDS.

[15]**Popocatepetl**: A volcano near Mexico City.—EDS.

[16]**Cholula**: An ancient city in central Mexico.—EDS.

[17]**Cortés**: Hernán Cortés (1485–1547), Spanish explorer who led the conquest of Mexico in 1519.—EDS.

[18]**hacienda**: Farm or country property.—EDS.

[19]**carretera**: Highway.—EDS.

soon stories are told about him and he begins to acquire super-human powers. He acquires a mystique, just like the divine right of old. The patrón wields a mean machete, like old King Arthur swung Excalibur. He chops off heads of dissenters and sits on top of the bones and skulls pyramid, the king of the mountain, the top macho.[20]

"One day I was sent to look for lost cattle," Justino continued. "I rode back into the hills where I had never been. At the foot of a hill, near a ravine, I saw something move in the bush. I dismounted and moved forward quietly. I was afraid it might be bandidos who steal cattle, and if they saw me they would kill me. When I came near the place I heard a strange sound. Somebody was crying. My back shivered, just like a dog when he sniffs the devil at night. I thought I was going to see witches, brujas who like to go to those deserted places to dance for the devil, or la Llorona.[21]

"La Llorona," I said aloud. My interest grew. I had been hearing Llorona stories since I was a kid, and I was always ready for one more. La Llorona was that archetypal woman of ancient legends who murdered her children then, repentant and demented, she has spent the rest of eternity searching for them.

"Sí, la Llorona. You know that poor woman used to drink a lot. She played around with men, and when she had babies she got rid of them by throwing them into la barranca.[22] One day she realized what she had done and went crazy. She started crying and pulling her hair and running up and down the side of cliffs of the river looking for her children. It's a very sad story."

A new version, I thought, and yes, a sad story. And what of the men who made love to the woman who became la Llorona, I wondered? Did they ever cry for their children? It doesn't seem fair to have only her suffer, only her crying and doing penance. Perhaps a man should run with her, and in our legends we would call him "El Mero Chingón,"[23] he who screwed up everything. Then maybe the tale of love and passion and the insanity it can bring will be complete. Yes, I think someday I will write that story.

"What did you see?" I asked Justino.

"Something worse than la Llorona," he whispered.

To the south a wind mourned and moved the clouds off Popo's crown. The bald, snow-covered mountain thrust its power into the blue Mexican sky. The light glowed like liquid gold around the god's head.

[20]**macho:** Mule.—Eps.
[21]**la Llorona:** "The mourner" or weeper.—Eps.
[22]**la barranca:** "The ravine."—Eps.
[23]**"El Mero Chingón":** "The utter failure."—Eps.

Popo was a god, an ancient god. Somewhere at his feet Justino's story had taken place.

"I moved closer, and when I parted the bushes I saw Don Francisco. 48 He was sitting on a rock, and he was crying. From time to time he looked at the ravine in front of him, the hole seemed to slant into the earth. That pozo[24] is called el Pozo de Mendoza. I had heard stories about it before, but I had never seen it. I looked into the pozo, and you wouldn't believe what I saw."

He waited, so I asked, "What?"

"Money! Huge piles of gold and silver coins! Necklaces and bracelets and crowns of gold, all loaded with all kinds of precious stones! Jewels! Diamonds! All sparkling in the sunlight that entered the hole. More money than I have every seen! A fortune, my friend, a fortune which is still there, just waiting for two adventurers like us to take it!"

"Us? But what about Don Francisco! It's his land, his fortune."

"Ah," Justino smiled, "that's the strange thing about this fortune. 52 Don Francisco can't touch it, that's why he was crying. You see, I stayed there, and watched him closely. Every time he stood up and started to walk into the pozo the money disappeared. He stretched out his hand to grab the gold, and poof, it was gone! That's why he was crying! He murdered all those people and hid their wealth in the pozo, but now he can't touch it. He is cursed."

"El Pozo de Mendoza," he said aloud. Something began to click in my mind. I smelled a story.

"Who was Mendoza?" I asked.

"He was a very rich man. Don Francisco killed him in a quarrel they had over some cattle. But Mendoza must have put a curse on Don Francisco before he died, because now Don Francisco can't get to the money."

"So Mendoza's ghost haunts old Don Francisco," I nodded.   56

"Many ghosts haunt him," Justino answered. "He has killed many men."

"And the fortune, the money. . . ."

He looked at me and his eyes were dark and piercing. "It's still there. Waiting for us!"

"But it disappears as one approaches it, you said so yourself. Per- 60 haps it's only an hallucination."

Justino shook his head. "No, it's real gold and silver, not hallucination money. It disappears for Don Francisco because the curse is on him, but the curse is not on us." He smiled. He knew he had drawn me into his plot. "We didn't steal the money, so it won't disappear for us. And

---

[24]**pozo**: Spring.—EDS.

you are not connected with the place. You are innocent. I've thought very carefully about it, and now is the time to go. I can lower you into the pozo with a rope, in a few hours we can bring out the entire fortune. All we need is a car. You can borrow the patrón's car, he is your friend. But he must not know where we're going. We can be there and back in one day, one night." He nodded as if to assure me, then he turned and looked at the sky. "It will not rain today. It will not rain for a week. Now is the time to go."

He winked and returned to watering the grass and flowers of the jardín,[25] a wild Pan among the bougainvillea and the roses, a man possessed by a dream. The gold was not for him, he told me the next day, it was for his women, he would buy them all gifts, bright dresses, and he would take them on vacation to the United States, he would educate his children, send them to the best colleges. I listened and the germ of the story cluttered my thoughts as I sat beneath the orange tree in the mornings. I couldn't write, nothing was coming, but I knew that there were elements for a good story in Justino's tale. In dreams I saw the lonely hacienda to the south. I saw the pathetic tormented figure of Don Francisco as he cried over the fortune he couldn't touch. I saw the ghosts of the men he had killed, the lonely women who mourned over them and cursed the evil Don Francisco. In one dream I saw a man I took to be B. Traven, a grey-haired distinguished looking gentleman who looked at me and nodded approvingly. "Yes, there's a story there, follow it, follow it. . . ."

In the meantime, other small and seemingly insignificant details came my way. During a luncheon at the home of my friend, a woman I did not know leaned toward me and asked me if I would like to meet the widow of B. Traven. The woman's hair was tinged orange, her complexion was ashen grey. I didn't know who she was or why she would mention B. Traven to me. How did she know Traven had come to haunt my thoughts? Was she a clue, which would help unravel the mystery? I didn't know, but I nodded. Yes, I would like to meet her. I had heard that Traven's widow, Rosa Elena, lived in Mexico City. But what would I ask her? What did I want to know? Would she know Traven's secret? Somehow he had learned that to keep his magic intact he had to keep away from the public. Like the fortune in the pozo, the magic feel for the story might disappear if unclean hands reached for it. I turned to look at the woman, but she was gone. I wandered to the terrace to finish my beer. Justino sat beneath the orange tree. He yawned. I knew the literary talk bored him. He was eager to be on the way to el Pozo de Mendoza.

I was nervous, too, but I didn't know why. The tension for the story 64 was there, but something was missing. Or perhaps it was just Justino's

---

[25] **jardín**: Garden.—Eds.

insistence that I decide whether I was going or not that drove me out of the house in the mornings. Time usually devoted to writing found me in a small cafe in the center of town. From there I could watch the shops open, watch the people cross the zócalo, the main square. I drank lots of coffee, I smoked a lot, I daydreamed, I wondered about the significance of the pozo, the fortune, Justino, the story I wanted to write about B. Traven. In one of these moods I saw a friend from whom I hadn't heard in years. Suddenly he was there, trekking across the square, dressed like an old rabbi, moss and green algae for a beard, and followed by a troop of very dignified Lacandones, Mayan Indians from Chiapas.

"Victor," I gasped, unsure if he was real or a part of the shadows which the sun created as it flooded the square with its light.

"I have no time to talk," he said as he stopped to munch on my pan dulce and sip my coffee. "I only want you to know, for purposes of your story, that I was in a Lacandonian village last month, and a Hollywood film crew descended from the sky. They came in helicopters. They set up tents near the village, and big-bosomed bikinied actresses emerged from them, tossed themselves on the cut trees which are the atrocity of the giant American lumber companies, and they cried while the direc-tor shot his film. Then they produced a grey-haired old man from one of the tents and took shots of him posing with the Indians. Herr Traven, the director called him."

He finished my coffee, nodded to his friends and they began to walk away.

"B. Traven?" I asked.

He turned. "No, an imposter, an actor. Be careful for imposters. Remember, even Traven used many disguises, many names!"

"Then he's alive and well?" I shouted. People around me turned to stare.

"His spirit is with us," were the last words I heard as they moved across the zócalo, a strange troop of near naked Lacandon Mayans and my friend the Guatemalan Jew, returning to the rain forest, returning to the primal, innocent land.

I slumped in my chair and looked at my empty cup. What did it mean? As their trees fall the Lacandones die. Betrayed as B. Traven was betrayed. Does each one of us also die as the trees fall in the dark depths of the Chiapas jungle? Far to the north, in Aztlán, it is the same where the earth is ripped open to expose and mine the yellow uranium. A few poets sing songs and stand in the way as the giant machines of the corporations rumble over the land and grind everything into dust. New holes are made in the earth, pozos full of curses, pozos with fortunes we cannot touch, should not touch. Oil, coal, uranium, from holes in the earth through which we suck the blood of the earth.

There were other incidents. A telephone call late one night, a voice with a German accent called my name, and when I answered the line went dead. A letter addressed to B. Traven came in the mail. It was dated March 26, 1969. My friend returned it to the post office. Justino grew more and more morose. He was under the orange tree and stared into space, my friend complained about the garden drying up. Justino looked at me and scowled. He did a little work then went back to daydreaming. Without the rains the garden withered. His heart was set on the adventure which lay at el pozo. Finally I said yes, dammit, why not, let's go, neither one of us is getting anything done here, and Justino cheering like a child, ran to prepare for the trip. But when I asked my friend for the weekend loan of the car he reminded me that we were invited to a tertulia, an afternoon reception, at the home of Señora Ana R. Many writers and artists would be there. It was in my honor, so I could meet the literati of Cuernavaca. I had to tell Justino I couldn't go.

Now it was I who grew morose. The story growing within would not let me sleep. I awakened in the night and looked out the window, hoping to see Justino and women bathing in the pool, enjoying themselves. But all was quiet. No radio played. The still night was warm and heavy. From time to time gunshots sounded in the dark, dogs barked, and the presence of a Mexico which never sleeps closed in on me.

Saturday morning dawned with a strange overcast. Perhaps the rains will come, I thought. In the afternoon I reluctantly accompanied by friend to the reception. I had not seen Justino all day, but I saw him at the gate as we drove out. He looked tired, as if he, too, had not slept. He wore the white shirt and baggy pants of a campesino. His straw hat cast a shadow over his eyes. I wondered if he had decided to go to the pozo alone. He didn't speak as we drove through the gate, he only nodded. When I looked back I saw him standing by the gate, looking after the car, and I had a vague, uneasy feeling that I had lost an opportunity.

The afternoon gathering was a pleasant affair, attended by a num- 76 ber of affectionate artists, critics, and writers who enjoyed the refreshing drinks which quenched the thirst.

But my mood drove me away from the crowd. I wandered around the terrace and found a foyer surrounded by green plants, huge fronds and ferns and flowering bougainvillea. I pushed the green aside and entered a quiet, very private alcove. The light was dim, the air was cool, a perfect place for contemplation. At first I thought I was alone, then I saw the man sitting in one of the wicker chairs next to a small, wrought iron table. He was an elderly white-haired gentleman. His face showed he had lived a full life, yet he was still very distinguished in his manner and posture. His eyes shone brightly.

"Perdón,"[26] I apologized and turned to leave. I did not want to intrude.

"No, no, please," he motioned to the empty chair, "I've been waiting for you." He spoke English with a slight German accent. Or perhaps it was Norwegian, I couldn't tell the difference. "I can't take the literary gossip. I prefer the quiet."

I nodded and sat. He smiled and I felt at ease. I took the cigar he   80
offered and we lit up. He began to talk and I listened. He was a writer also, but I had the good manners not to ask his titles. He talked about the changing Mexico, the change the new oil would bring, the lateness of the rains and how they affected the people and the land, and he talked about how important a woman was in a writer's life. He wanted to know about me, about the Chicanos of Aztlán, about our work. It was the workers, he said, who would change society. The artist learned from the worker. I talked, and sometime during the conversation I told him the name of the friend with whom I was staying. He laughed and wanted to know if Vitorino was still working for him.

"Do you know Justino?" I asked.

"Oh, yes, I know that old guide. I met him many years ago, when I first came to Mexico," he answered. "Justino knows the campesino very well. He and I traveled many places together, he in search of adventure, I in search of stories."

I thought the coincidence strange, so I gathered the courage and asked, "Did he ever tell you the story of the fortune at el Pozo de Mendoza?"

"Tell me?" the old man smiled. "I went there."   84

"With Justino?"

"Yes, I went with him. What a rogue he was in those days, but a good man. If I remember correctly I even wrote a story based on that adventure. Not a very good story. Never came to anything. But we had a grand time. People like Justino are the writer's source. We met interesting people and saw fabulous places, enough to last me a lifetime. We were supposed to be gone for one day, but we were gone nearly three years. You see, I wasn't interested in the pots of gold he kept saying were just over the next hill, I went because there was a story to write."

"Yes, that's what interested me," I agreed.

"A writer has to follow a story if it leads him to hell itself. That's our   88
curse. Ay, and each one of us knows our own private hell."

I nodded. I felt relieved. I sat back to smoke the cigar and sip from my drink. Somewhere to the west the sun bronzed the evening sky. On a clear afternoon, Popo's crown would glow like fire.

[26]**Perdón**: "Excuse me."—EDS.

"Yes," the old man continued, "a writer's job is to find and follow people like Justino. They're the source of life. The ones you have to keep away from are the dilettantes like the ones in there." He motioned in the general direction of the noise of the party. "I stay with people like Justino. They may be illiterate, but they understand our descent into the pozo of hell, and they understand us because they're willing to share the adventure with us. You seek fame and notoriety and you're dead as a writer."

I sat upright. I understood now what the pozo meant, why Justino had come into my life to tell me the story. It was clear. I rose quickly and shook the old man's hand. I turned and parted the palm leaves of the alcove. There, across the way, in one of the streets that led out of the maze of the town towards the south, I saw Justino. He was walking in the direction of Popo, and he was followed by women and children, a rag-tail army of adventurers, all happy, all singing. He looked up to where I stood on the terrace, and he smiled as he waved. He paused to light the stub of a cigar. The women turned, and the children turned, and all waved to me. They they continued their walk, south, towards the foot of the volcano. They were going to the Pozo de Mendoza, to the place where the story originated.

I wanted to run after them, to join them in the glorious light which 92 bathed the Cuernavaca valley and the majestic snow-covered head of Popo. The light was everywhere, a magnetic element which flowed from the clouds. I waved as Justino and his followers disappeared in the light. Then I turned to say something to the old man, but he was gone. I was alone in the alcove. Somewhere in the background I heard the tinkling of glasses and the laughter which came from the party, but that was not for me. I left the terrace and crossed the lawn, found the gate and walked down the street. The sound of Mexico filled the air. I felt light and happy. I wandered aimlessly through the curving, narrow streets, then I quickened my pace because suddenly the story was overflowing and I needed to write. I needed to get to my quiet room and write the story about B. Traven being alive and well in Cuernavaca.   *1982*

41

The Act of Reading

Richard Wright, *From* Black Boy

Eudora Welty, A Sweet Devouring

Donald Hall, Four Kinds of Reading

Lin Yutang, The Art of Reading

I have often reflected upon the new vistas that reading opened to me. I knew right there in prison that reading had changed forever the course of my life. As I see it today, the ability to read awoke inside me some long dormant craving to be mentally alive. I certainly wasn't seeking any degree, the way a college confers a status symbol upon its students. My homemade education gave me, with every additional book that I read, a little bit more sensitivity to the deafness, dumbness, and blindness that was afflicting the black race in America. Not long ago, an English writer telephoned me from London, asking questions. One was, "What's your alma mater?" I told him, "Books." You will never catch me with a free fifteen minutes in which I'm not studying something I feel might be able to help the black man.

Malcolm X, from *Learning to Read*

Men sometimes speak as if the study of classics would at length make way for more modern and practical studies; but the adventurous student will always study classics, in whatever language they may be written and however ancient they may be. For what are the classics but the noblest recorded thoughts of man? They are the only oracles which are not decayed, and there are such answers to the most modern inquiry in them as Delphi and Dodona never gave. We might as well omit to study Nature because she is old. To read well, that is, to read true books in a true spirit, is a noble exercise, and one that will task the reader more than any exercise which the customs of the day esteem. It requires a training such as the athletes underwent, the steady intention almost of the whole life to this object. Books must be read as deliberately and reservedly as they were written.

Henry David Thoreau, from *Walden*

Curiously enough, one cannot *read* a book: One can only reread it. A good reader, a major reader, an active and creative reader is a rereader. And I shall tell you why. When we read a book for the first time the very process of laboriously moving our eyes from left to right, line after line, page after page, this complicated physical work upon the book, the very process of learning in terms of space and time what the book is about, this stands between us and artistic appreciation. When we look at a painting we do not have to move our eyes in a special way even if, as in a book, the picture contains elements of depth and development. The element of time does not really enter in a first contact with a painting. In reading a book, we must have time to acquaint ourselves with it. We have no physical organ (as we have the eye in regard to painting) that takes in the whole picture and then can enjoy its details. But at a second, or third, or fourth reading we do, in a sense, behave towards a book as we do towards a painting.

Vladimir Nabokov, from *Good Readers and Good Writers*

My mother read to me when I was a tot. Cuddled together on a couch, we shared warmth and adventure. Stories became my passion in life. When she was too busy to read them, I looked elsewhere. The quest was constant. My grandmother, two doors away, was always delighted to see me. She always had Jell-O, with sliced bananas, in the refrigerator, but she could not read English.

So, clutching a story book, I would roam the neighborhood in search of someone who could, even beseeching the mailman to stay and "read a book-a to me?"

Edna Buchanan, from *The Corpse Had a Familiar Face*

Richard Wright

From Black Boy

One morning I arrived early at work and went into the bank lobby where the Negro porter was mopping. I stood at a counter and picked up the Memphis *Commercial Appeal* and began my free reading of the press. I came finally to the editorial page and saw an article dealing with one H. L. Mencken. I knew by hearsay that he was the editor of the *American Mercury*, but aside from that I knew nothing about him. The article was a furious denunciation of Mencken, concluding with one, hot, short sentence: Mencken is a fool.

I wondered what on earth this Mencken had done to call down upon him the scorn of the South. The only people I had ever heard denounced in the South were Negroes, and this man was not a Negro. Then what ideas did Mencken hold that made a newspaper like the *Commercial Appeal* castigate him publicly? Undoubtedly he must be advocating ideas that the South did not like. Were there, then, people other than Negroes who criticized the South? I knew that during the Civil War the South had hated the northern whites, but I had not encountered such hate during my life. Knowing no more of Mencken than I did at that moment, I felt a vague sympathy for him. Had not the South, which had assigned me the role of a non-man, cast at him its hardest words?

Now, how could I find out about this Mencken? There was a huge library near the riverfront, but I knew that Negroes were not allowed to patronize its shelves any more than they were the parks and play-grounds of the city. I had gone into the library several times to get books for the white men on the job. Which of them would now help me to get books? And how could I read them without causing concern to the white men with whom I worked? I had so far been successful in hiding my thoughts and feelings from them, but I knew that I would create hos-tility if I went about this business of reading in a clumsy way.

I weighed the personalities of the men on the job. There was Don, a   4
Jew; but I distrusted him. His position was not much better than mine and I knew that he was uneasy and insecure; he had always treated me in an offhand, bantering way that barely contained his contempt. I was afraid to ask him to help me to get books; his frantic desire to demon-strate a racial solidarity with the whites against Negroes might make him betray me.

Then how about the boss? No, he was a Baptist and I had the suspicion that he would not be quite able to comprehend why a black boy would want to read Mencken. There were other white men on the

job whose attitudes showed clearly that they were Kluxers or sympathizers, and they were out of the question.

There remained only one man whose attitude did not fit into an
anti-Negro category, for I had heard the white men refer to him as a
"Pope lover." He was an Irish Catholic and was hated by the white
Southerners. I knew that he read books, because I had got him volumes
from the library several times. Since he, too, was an object of hatred, I
felt that he might refuse me but would hardly betray me. I hesitated,
weighing and balancing the imponderable realities.

One morning I paused before the Catholic fellow's desk.

"I want to ask you a favor," I whispered to him.   8

"What is it?"

"I want to read. I can't get books from the library. I wonder if you'd
let me use your card?"

He looked at me suspiciously.

"My card is full most of the time," he said.   12

"I see," I said and waited, posing my question silently.

"You're not trying to get me into trouble, are you, boy?" he asked,
staring at me.

"Oh, no, sir."

"What book do you want?"   16

"A book by H. L. Mencken."

"Which one?"

"I don't know. Has he written more than one?"

"He has written several.   20

"I didn't know that."

"What makes you want to read Mencken?"

"Oh, I just saw his name in the newspaper," I said.

"It's good of you to want to read," he said. "But you ought to read   24
the right things."

I said nothing. Would he want to supervise my reading?

"Let me think," he said. "I'll figure out something."

I turned from him and he called me back. He stared at me
quizzically.

"Richard, don't mention this to the other white men," he said.   28

"I understand," I said. "I won't say a word."

A few days later he called me to him.

"I've got a card in my wife's name," he said. "Here's mine."

"Thank you, sir."   32

"Do you think you can manage it?"

"I'll manage fine," I said.

"If they suspect you, you'll get in trouble," he said.

"I'll write the same kind of notes to the library that you wrote when 36
you sent me for books," I told him. "I'll sign your name."

He laughed.

"Go ahead. Let me see what you get," he said.

That afternoon I addressed myself to forging a note. Now, what were the names of books written by H. L. Mencken? I did not know any of them. I finally wrote what I thought would be a foolproof note: *Dear Madam: Will you please let this nigger boy*—I used the word *nigger* to make the librarian feel that I could not possibly be the author of the note—*have some books by H. L. Mencken?* I forged the white man's name.

I entered the library as I had always done when on errands for 40 whites, but I felt that I would somehow slip up and betray myself. I doffed my hat, stood a respectful distance from the desk, looked as unbookish as possible, and waited for the white patrons to be taken care of. When the desk was clear of people, I still waited. The white librarian looked at me.

"What do you want, boy?"

As though I did not possess the power of speech, I stepped forward and simply handed her the forged note, not parting my lips.

"What books by Mencken does he want?" she asked.

"I don't know, ma'am," I said, avoiding her eyes.   44

"Who gave you this card?"

"Mr. Falk," I said.

"Where is he?"

"He's at the work, at the M—— Optical Company," I said. "I've been in 48 here for him before."

"I remember," the woman said. "But he never wrote notes like this."

Oh, God, she's suspicious. Perhaps she would not let me have the books? If she had turned her back at that moment, I would have ducked out the door and never gone back. Then I thought of a bold idea.

"You can call him up, ma'am," I said, my heart pounding.

"You're not using these books, are you?" she asked pointedly.   52

"Oh, no, ma'am. I can't read."

"I don't know what he wants by Mencken," she said under her breath.

I knew now that I had won; she was thinking of other things and the race question had gone out of her mind. She went to the shelves. Once or twice she looked over her shoulder at me, as though she was still doubtful. Finally she came forward with two books in her hand.

"I'm sending him two books," she said. "But tell Mr. Falk to come in 56 next time, or send me the names of the books he wants. I don't know what he wants to read."

I said nothing. She stamped the card and handed me the books. Not daring to glance at them, I went out of the library, fearing that the woman would call me back for further questioning. A block away from the library I opened one of the books and read a title: *A Book of Prefaces*. I

was nearing my nineteenth birthday and I did not know how to pronounce the word "preface." I thumbed the pages and saw strange words
and strange names. I shook my head, disappointed. I looked at the other
book; it was called *Prejudices*. I knew what that word meant; I had heard it
all my life. And right off I was on guard against Mencken's books. Why
would a man want to call a book *Prejudices*? The word was so stained
with all my memories of racial hate that I could not conceive of anybody
using it for a title. Perhaps I had made a mistake about Mencken? A man
who had prejudices must be wrong.

When I showed the books to Mr. Falk, he looked at me and frowned.

"That librarian might telephone you," I warned him.

"That's all right," he said. "But when you're through reading those   60
books, I want you to tell me what you get out of them."

That night in my rented room, while letting the hot water run over
my can of pork and beans in the sink, I opened *A Book of Prefaces* and
began to read. I was jarred and shocked by the style, the clear, clean,
sweeping sentences. Why did he write like that? And how did one write
like that? I pictured the man as a raging demon, slashing with his pen,
consumed with hate, denouncing everything American, extolling everything European or German, laughing at the weaknesses of people,
mocking God, authority. What was this? I stood up, trying to realize
what reality lay behind the meaning of the words . . . Yes, this man was
fighting, fighting with words. He was using words as a weapon, using
them as one would use a club. Could words be weapons? No. It frightened me. I read on and what amazed me was not what he said, but how
on earth anybody had the courage to say it.

Occasionally I glanced up to reassure myself that I was alone in the
room. Who were these men about whom Mencken was talking so pas-
sionately? Who was Anatole France? Joseph Conrad? Sinclair Lewis,
Sherwood Anderson, Dostoevski, George Moore, Gustave Flaubert,
Maupassant, Tolstoy, Frank Harris, Mark Twain, Thomas Hardy, Arnold
Bennett, Stephen Crane, Zola, Norris, Gorky, Bergson, Ibsen, Balzac,
Bernard Shaw, Dumas, Poe, Thomas Mann, O. Henry, Dreiser, H. G.
Wells, Gogol, T. S. Eliot, Gide, Baudelaire, Edgar Lee Masters, Stendhal,
Turgenev, Huneker, Nietzsche, and scores of others? Were these men
real? Did they exist or had they existed? And how did one pronounce
their names?

I ran across many words whose meanings I did not know, and I
either looked them up in a dictionary or, before I had a chance to do
that, encountered the word in a context that made its meaning clear. But
what strange world was this? I concluded the book with the conviction
that I had somehow overlooked something terribly important in life. I
had once tried to write, had once reveled in feeling, had let my crude
imagination roam, but the impulse to dream had been slowly beaten

out of me by experience. Now it surged up again and I hungered for books, new ways of looking and seeing. It was not a matter of believing or disbelieving what I read, but of feeling something new, of being affected by something that made the look of the world different.

As dawn broke I ate my pork and beans, feeling dopey, sleepy. I 64 went to work, but the mood of the book would not die; it lingered, coloring everything I saw, heard, did. I now felt that I knew what the white men were feeling. Merely because I had read a book that had spoken of how they lived and thought, I identified myself with that book. I felt vaguely guilty. Would I, filled with bookish notions, act in a manner that would make the whites dislike me?

I forged more notes and my trips to the library became frequent. Reading grew into a passion. My first serious novel was Sinclair Lewis's *Main Street*. It made me see my boss, Mr. Gerald, and identify him as an American type. I would smile when I saw him lugging his golf bags into the office. I had always felt a vast distance separating me from the boss, and now I felt closer to him, though still distant. I felt now that I knew him, that I could feel the very limits of his narrow life. And this had happened because I had read a novel about a mythical man called George F. Babbitt.

The plots and stories in the novels did not interest me so much as the point of view revealed. I gave myself over to each novel without reserve, without trying to criticize it; it was enough for me to see and feel something different. And for me, everything was something different. Reading was like a drug, a dope. The novels created moods in which I lived for days. But I could not conquer my sense of guilt, my feeling that the white men around me knew that I was changing, that I had begun to regard them differently.

Whenever I brought a book to the job, I wrapped it in newspaper—a habit that was to persist for years in other cities and under other circumstances. But some of the white men pried into my packages when I was absent and they questioned me.

"Boy, what are you reading those books for?"   68

"Oh, I don't know, sir."

"That's deep stuff you're reading, boy."

"I'm just killing time, sir."

"You'll addle your brains if you don't watch out."   72

I read Dreiser's *Jennie Gerhardt* and *Sister Carrie* and they revived in me a vivid sense of my mother's suffering; I was overwhelmed. I grew silent, wondering about the life around me. It would have been impossible for me to have told anyone what I derived from these novels, for it was nothing less than a sense of life itself. All my life had shaped me for the realism, the naturalism of the modern novel, and I could not read enough of them.

Steeped in new moods and ideas, I bought a ream of paper and tried to write; but nothing would come, or what did come was flat beyond telling. I discovered that more than desire and feeling were necessary to write and I dropped the idea. Yet I still wondered how it was possible to know people sufficiently to write about them? Could I ever learn about life and people? To me, with my vast ignorance, my Jim Crow station in life, it seemed a task impossible of achievement. I now knew what being a Negro meant. I could endure the hunger. I had learned to live with hate. But to feel that there were feelings denied me, that the very breath of life itself was beyond my reach, that more than anything else hurt, wounded me. I had a new hunger.

In buoying me up, reading also cast me down, made me see what was possible, what I had missed. My tension returned, new, terrible, bitter, surging, almost too great to be contained. I no longer *felt* that the world about me was hostile, killing; I *knew* it. A million times I asked myself what I could do to save myself, and there were no answers. I seemed forever condemned, ringed by walls.

I did not discuss my reading with Mr. Falk, who had lent me his 76 library card; it would have meant talking about myself and that would have been too painful. I smiled each day, fighting desperately to maintain my old behavior, to keep my disposition seemingly sunny. But some of the white men discerned that I had begun to brood.

"Wake up there, boy!" Mr. Olin said one day.

"Sir!" I answered for the lack of a better word.

"You act like you've stolen something," he said.

I laughed in the way I knew he expected me to laugh, but I resolved 80 to be more conscious of myself, to watch my every act, to guard and hide the new knowledge that was dawning within me.

If I went north, would it be possible for me to build a new life then? But how could a man build a life upon vague, unformed yearnings? I wanted to write and I did not even know the English language. I bought English grammars and found them dull. I felt that I was getting a better sense of the language from novels than from grammars. I read hard, discarding a writer as soon as I felt that I had grasped his point of view. At night the printed page stood before my eyes in sleep.

Mrs. Moss, my landlady, asked me one Sunday morning:

"Son, what is this you keep on reading?"

"Oh, nothing. Just novels."

"What you get out of 'em?"   84

"I'm just killing time," I said.

"I hope you know your own mind," she said in a tone which implied that she doubted if I had a mind.

I knew of no Negroes who read the books I liked and I wondered if 88 any Negroes ever thought of them. I knew that there were Negro doctors, lawyers, newspapermen, but I never saw any of them. When I read a Negro newspaper I never caught the faintest echo of my preoccupation in its pages. I felt trapped and occasionally, for a few days, I would stop reading. But a vague hunger would come over me for books, books that opened up new avenues of feeling and seeing, and again I would forge another note to the white librarian. Again I would read and wonder as only the naïve and unlettered can read and wonder, feeling that I carried a secret, criminal burden about with me each day.

That winter my mother and brother came and we set up housekeeping, buying furniture on the installment plan, being cheated and yet knowing no way to avoid it. I began to eat warm food and to my surprise found that regular meals enabled me to read faster. I may have lived through many illnesses and survived them, never suspecting that I was ill. My brother obtained a job and we began to save toward the trip north, plotting our time, setting tentative dates for departure. I told none of the white men on the job that I was planning to go north; I knew that the moment they felt I was thinking of the North they would change toward me. It would have made them feel that I did not like the life I was living, and because my life was completely conditioned by what they said or did, it would have been tantamount to challenging them.

I could calculate my chances for life in the South as a Negro fairly clearly now.

I could fight the southern whites by organizing with other Negroes, as my grandfather had done. But I knew that I could never win that way; there were many whites and there were but few blacks. They were strong and we were weak. Outright black rebellion could never win. If I fought openly I would die and I did not want to die. News of lynchings were frequent.

I could submit and live the life of a genial slave, but that was 92 impossible. All of my life had shaped me to live by my own feelings and thoughts. I could make up to Bess and marry her and inherit the house. But that, too, would be the life of a slave; if I did that, I would crush to death something within me, and I would hate myself as much as I knew the whites already hated those who had submitted. Neither could I ever willingly present myself to be kicked, as Shorty had done. I would rather have died than do that.

I could drain off my restlessness by fighting with Shorty and Harrison. I had seen many Negroes solve the problem of being black by transferring their hatred of themselves to others with a black skin and fighting them. I would have to be cold to do that, and I was not cold and I could never be.

I could, of course, forget what I had read, thrust the whites out of my mind, forget them; and find release from anxiety and longing in sex and alcohol. But the memory of how my father had conducted himself made that course repugnant. If I did not want others to violate my life, how could I voluntarily violate it myself?

I had no hope whatever of being a professional man. Not only had I been so conditioned that I did not desire it, but the fulfillment of such an ambition was beyond my capabilities. Well-to-do Negroes lived in a world that was almost as alien to me as the world inhabited by whites.

What, then, was there? I held my life in my mind, in my conscious- 96 ness each day, feeling at times that I would stumble and drop it, spill it forever. My reading had created a vast sense of distance between me and the world in which I lived and tried to make a living, and that sense of distance was increasing each day. My days and nights were one long, quiet, continuously contained dream of terror, tension, and anxiety. I wondered how long I could bear it.   *1945*

Eudora Welty

A Sweet Devouring

When I used to ask my mother which we were, rich or poor, she refused to tell me. I was then nine years old and of course what I was dying to hear was that we were poor. I was reading a book called *Five Little Peppers* and my heart was set on baking a cake for my mother in a stove with a hole in it. Some version of rich, crusty old Mr. King—up till that time not living on our street—was sure to come down the hill in his wheelchair and rescue me if anything went wrong. But before I could start a cake at all I had to find out if we were poor, and poor *enough*; and my mother wouldn't tell me, she said she was too busy. I couldn't wait too long; I had to go on reading and soon Polly Pepper got into more trouble, some that was a little harder on her and easier on me.

Trouble, the backbone of literature, was still to me the original property of the fairy tale, and as long as there was plenty of trouble for everybody and the rewards for it were falling in the right spots, reading was all smooth sailing. At that age a child reads with higher appetite and gratification, and with those two stars sailing closer together, than ever again in his growing up. The home shelves had been providing me all along with the usual books, and I read them with love—but snap, I finished them. I read everything just alike—snap. I even came to the

Tales from Maria Edgeworth and went right ahead, without feeling the bump—then. It *was* noticeable that when her characters suffered she punished them for it, instead of rewarding them as a reader had rather been led to hope. In her stories, the children had to make their choice between being unhappy and good about it and being unhappy and bad about it, and then she helped them to choose wrong. In *The Purple Jar*, it will be remembered, there was the little girl being taken through the shops by her mother and her downfall coming when she chooses to buy something beautiful instead of something necessary. The purple jar, when the shop sends it out, proves to have been purple only so long as it was filled with purple water, and her mother knew it all the time. They don't deliver the water. That's only the cue for stones to start coming through the hole in the victim's worn-out shoe. She bravely agrees she must keep walking on stones until such time as she is offered another choice between the beautiful and the useful. Her father tells her as far as he is concerned she can stay in the house. If I had been at all easy to disappoint, that story would have disappointed me. Of course, I did feel, what is the good of walking on rocks if they are going to let the water out of the jar too? And it seemed to me that even the illustrator fell down on the characters in that book, not alone Maria Edgeworth, for when a rich, crusty old gentleman gave Simple Susan a guinea for some kind deed she'd done him, there was a picture of the transaction and where was the guinea? I couldn't make out a feather. But I liked *reading* the book all right—except that I finished it.

My mother took me to the Public Library and introduced me: "Let her have any book she wants, except *Elsie Dinsmore*." I looked for the book I couldn't have and it was a row. That was how I learned about the Series Books. The *Five Little Peppers* belonged, so did *The Wizard of Oz*, so did *The Little Colonel*, so did *The Green Fairy Book*. There were many of everything, generations of everybody, instead of one. I wasn't coming to the end of reading, after all—I was saved.

Our library in those days was a big rotunda lined with shelves. A 4 copy of *V. V.'s Eyes* seemed to follow you wherever you went, even after you'd read it. I didn't know what I liked, I just knew what there was a lot of. After *Randy's Spring* there came *Randy's Summer, Randy's Fall* and *Randy's Winter*. True, I didn't care very much myself for her spring, but it didn't occur to me that I might not care for her summer, and then her summer didn't prejudice me against her fall, and I still had hopes as I moved on to her winter. I was disappointed in her whole year, as it turned out, but a thing like that didn't keep me from wanting to read every word of it. The pleasures of reading itself—who doesn't remember?—were like those of a Christmas cake, a sweet devouring. The "Randy Books" failed chiefly in being so soon over. Four seasons doesn't make a series.

All that summer I used to put on a second petticoat (our librarian wouldn't let you past the front door if she could she through you), ride my bicycle up the hill and "through the Capitol" (shortcut) to the library with my two read books in the basket (two was the limit you could take out at one time when you were a child and also as long as you lived), and tiptoe in ("Silence") and exchange them for two more in two minutes. Selection was no object. I coasted the two new books home, jumped out of my petticoat, read (I suppose I ate and bathed and answered questions put to me), then in all hope put my petticoat back on and rode those two books back to the libary to get my next two.

The librarian was the lady in town who wanted to be it. She called me by my full name and said, "Does your mother know where you are? You know good and well the fixed rule of this library: *Nobody is going to come running back here with any book on the same day they took it out.* Get both those things out of here and don't come back till tomorrow. And I can practically see through you."

My great-aunt in Virginia, who understood better about needing more to read than you *could* read, sent me a book so big it had to be read on the floor—a bound volume of six or eight issues of *St. Nicholas* from a previous year. In the very first pages a serial began: *The Lucky Stone* by Abbie Farwell Brown. The illustrations were right down my alley: a heroine so poor she was ragged, a witch with an extremely pointed hat, a rich, crusty old gentleman in—better than a wheelchair—a runaway carriage; and I set to. I gobbled up installment after installment through the whole luxurious book, through the last one, and then came the words, turning me to *unlucky* stone: "To be concluded." The book had come to an end and *The Lucky Stone* wasn't finished! The witch had it! I couldn't believe this infidelity from my aunt. I still had my secret childhood feeling that if you hunted long enough in a book's pages, you could find what you were looking for, and long after I knew books better than that, I used to hunt again for the end of *The Lucky Stone*. It never occurred to me that the story had an existence anywhere else outside the pages of that single green-bound book. The last chapter was just something I would have to do without. Polly Pepper could do it. And then suddenly I tried something—I read it again, as much as I had of it. I was in love with books at least partly for what they looked like; I loved the printed page.

In my little circle books were almost never given for Christmas, they cost too much. But the year before, I'd been given a book and got a shock. It was from the same classmate who had told me there was no Santa Claus. She gave me a book, all right—*Poems by Another Little Girl*. It looked like a real book, was printed like a real book—but it was *by her*. *Homemade* poems? Illusion-dispelling was her favorite game. She was in such a hurry, she had such a pile to get rid of—her mother's electric

8

runabout was stacked to the bud vases with copies—that she hadn't even time to say, "Merry Christmas!" With only the same raucous laugh with which she had told me, "Been filling my own stocking for years!" she shot me her book, received my Japanese pencil box with a moonlight scene on the lid and a sharpened pencil inside, jumped back into the car and was sped away by her mother. I stood right where they had left me, on the curb in my Little Nurse's uniform, and read that book, and I had no better way to prove when I got through than I had when I started that this was not a real book. But of course it wasn't. The printed page is not absolutely everything.

Then this Christmas was coming, and my grandfather in Ohio sent along in his box of presents an envelope with money in it for me to buy myself the book I wanted.

I went to Kress's. Not everybody knew Kress's sold books, but children just before Christmas know everything Kress's ever sold or will sell. My father had showed us the mirror he was giving my mother to hang above her desk, and Kress's is where my brother and I went to reproduce that by buying a mirror together to give her ourselves, and where our little brother then made us take him and he bought her one his size for fifteen cents. Kress's had also its version of the Series Books, called, exactly like another series, "The Camp Fire Girls," beginning with *The Camp Fire Girls in the Woods*.

I believe they were ten cents each and I had a dollar. But they weren't all that easy to buy, because the series stuck, and to buy some of it was like breaking into a loaf of French bread. Then after you got home, each single book was as hard to open as a box stuck in its varnish, and when it gave way it popped like a firecracker. The covers once prized apart would never close; those books once open stayed open and lay on their backs helplessly fluttering their leaves like a turned-over June bug. They were as light as a matchbox. They were printed on yellowed paper with corners that crumbled, if you pinched on them too hard, like old graham crackers, and they smelled like attic trunks, caramelized glue, their own confinement with one another and, over all, the Kress's smell—bandannas, peanuts and sandalwood from the incense counter. Even without reading them I loved them. It was hard, that year, that Christmas is a day you can't read.

What could have happened to those books?—but I can tell you 12 about the leading character. His name was Mr. Holmes. He was not a Camp Fire Girl: he wanted to catch one. Through every book of the series he gave chase. He pursued Bessie and Zara—those were the Camp Fire Girls—and kept scooping them up in his touring car, while they just as regularly got away from him. Once Bessie escaped from the second floor of a strange inn by climbing down a gutter pipe. Once she escaped by driving away from Mr. Holmes in his own automobile, which she had learned to drive by watching him. What Mr. Holmes wanted with them—either Bessie or Zara would do—didn't give me pause; I was too young to be a Camp Fire Girl; I was just keeping up. I wasn't alarmed by Mr. Holmes—when I cared for a chill, I knew to go to Dr. Fu Manchu, who had his own series in the library. I wasn't fascinated either. There was one thing I wanted from those books, and that was for me to have ten to read at one blow.

Who in the world wrote those books? I knew all the time they were the false "Camp Fire Girls" and the ones in the library were the authorized. But book reviewers sometimes say of a book that if anyone else had written it, it might not have been this good, and I found it out as a child—their warning is justified. This was a proven case, although a case of the true not being as good as the false. In the true series the characters were either totally different or missing (Mr. Holmes was missing), and there was too much time given to teamwork. The Kress's Campers, besides getting into a more reliable kind of trouble than the Carnegie Campers, had adventures that even they themselves weren't aware of: the pages were in wrong. There were transposed pages, repeated pages, and whole sections in upside down. There was no way of telling if there was anything missing. But if you knew your way in the woods at all, you could enjoy yourself tracking it down. I read the library "Camp Fire Girls," since that's what they were there for, but though they could be read by poorer light they were not as good.

And yet, in a way, the false Campers were no better either. I wonder whether I felt some flaw at the heart of things or whether I was just tired of not having any taste; but it seemed to me when I had finished that the last nine of those books weren't as good as the first one. And the same went for all Series Books. As long as they are keeping a series going, I was afraid, nothing can really happen. The whole thing is one grand prevention. For my greed, I might have unwittingly dealt with myself in the same way Maria Edgeworth dealt with the one who put her all into the purple jar—I had received word it was just colored water.

And then I went again to the home shelves and my lucky hand reached and found Mark Twain—twenty-four volumes, not a series, and good all the way through.   *1957*

Donald Hall

Four Kinds of Reading

Everywhere one meets the idea that reading is an activity desirable in itself. It is understandable that publishers and librarians—and even writers—should promote this assumption, but is strange that the idea should have general currency. People surround the idea of reading with piety, and do not take into account the purpose of reading or the value of what is being read. Teachers and parents praise the child who reads, and praise themselves, whether the text be *The Reader's Digest* or *Moby Dick.* The advent of TV has increased the false values ascribed to reading, since TV provides a vulgar alternative. But this piety is silly; and most reading is no more cultural nor intellectual nor imaginative than shooting pool or watching *What's My Line.*

It is worth asking how the act of reading became something to value in itself, as opposed for instance to the act of conversation or the act of taking a walk. Mass literacy is a recent phenomenon, and I suggest that the aura which decorates reading is a relic of the importance of reading to our great-great-grandparents. Literacy used to be a mark of social distinction, separating a small portion of humanity from the rest. The farm laborer who was ambitious for his children did not daydream that they would become schoolteachers or doctors; he daydreamed that they would learn to read, and that a world would therefore open up to them in which they did not have to labor in the fields fourteen hours a day for six days a week in order to buy salt and cotton. On the next rank of society, ample time for reading meant that the reader was free from the necessity to spend most of his waking hours making a living. This sort of attitude shades into the contemporary man's boast of his wife's cultural activities. When he says that his wife is interested in books and music and pictures, he is not only enclosing the arts in a female world, he is saying that he is rich enough to provide her with the leisure to do nothing. Reading is an inactivity, and therefore a badge of social class. Of course, these reasons for the piety attached to reading are never acknowledged. They show themselves in the shape of our attitudes toward books; reading gives off an air of gentility.

It seems to me possible to name four kinds of reading, each with a characteristic manner and purpose. The first is reading for information—reading to learn about a trade, or politics, or how to accomplish something. We read a newspaper this way, or most textbooks, or directions on how to assemble a bicycle. With most of this material, the reader can learn to scan the page quickly, coming up with what he needs and ignoring what is irrelevant to him, like the rhythm of the sentence,

or the play of metaphor. Courses in speed reading can help us read for
this purpose, training the eye to jump quickly across the page. If we
read the *New York Times* with the attention we should give a novel or a
poem, we will have time for nothing else, and our mind will be cluttered
with clichés and dead metaphor. Quick eye-reading is a necessity to
anyone who wants to keep up with what's happening, or learn much of
what has happened in the past. The amount of reflection, which interrupts and slows down the reading, depends on the material.

But it is not the same activity as reading literature. There ought to 4
be another word. If we read a work of literature properly, we read slowly,
and we *hear* all the words. If our lips do not actually move, it's only
laziness. The muscles in our throat move, and come together when we
see the word "squeeze." We hear the sounds so accurately that if a
syllable is missing in a line of poetry we hear the lack, through we may
not know what we are lacking. In prose we accept the rhythms, and hear
the adjacent sounds. We also register a track of feeling through the
metaphors and associations of words. Careless writing prevents this sort
of attention, and becomes offensive. But the great writers reward it.
Only by the full exercise of our powers to receive language can we
absorb their intelligence and their imagination. This kind of reading
goes through the ear—though the eye takes in the print, and decodes it
into sound—to the throat and the understanding, and it can never be
quick. It is slow and sensual, a deep pleasure that begins with touch and
ends with the sort of comprehension that we associate with dream.

Too many intellectuals read in order to reduce images to abstractions. One reads philosophy slowly, as if it were literature, but much
time must be spent with the eyes turned away from the page, reflecting
on the text. To read literature this way is to turn it into something it is
not—to concepts clothed in character, or philosophy sugar-coated. I
think that most literary intellectuals read this way, including brighter
professors of English, with the result that they miss literature completely, and concern themselves with a minor discipline called the
history of ideas. I remember a course in Chaucer at my University in
which the final exam required the identification of a hundred or more
fragments of Chaucer, none as long as a line. If you like poetry, and read
Chaucer through a couple of times slowly, you found yourself knowing
them all. If you were a literary intellectual, well-informed about the
great chain of being, chances are you had a difficult time. To read
literature is to be intimately involved with the words on the page, and
never to think of them as the embodiments of ideas which can be
expressed in other terms. On the other hand, intellectual writing—
closer to mathematics on a continuum that has at its opposite pole lyric
poetry—requires intellectual reading, which is slow because it is reflective and because the reader must pause to evaluate concepts.

But most of the reading which is praised for itself is neither literary nor intellectual. It is narcotic. Novels, stories, and biographies—historical sagas, monthly regurgitations of book clubs, four- and five-thousand word daydreams of the magazines—these are the opium of the suburbs. The drug is not harmful except to the addict himself, and is no more injurious to him than Johnny Carson or a bridge club, but it is nothing to be proud of. This reading is the automated daydream, the mild trip of the housewife and the tired businessman, interested not in experience and feeling but in turning off the possibilities of experience and feeling. Great literature, if we read it well, opens us up to the world, and makes us more sensitive to it, as if we acquired eyes that could see through walls and ears that could hear the smallest sounds. But by narcotic reading, one can reduce great literature to the level of *The Valley of the Dolls*. One can read *Anna Karenina* passively and inattentively, and float down the river of lethargy as if one were reading a confession magazine: "I Spurned My Husband for a Count."

I think that everyone reads for narcosis occasionally, and perhaps most consistently in late adolescence, when great readers are born. I remember reading to shut the world out, away at a school where I did not want to be; I invented a word for my disease: "bibliolepsy," on the analogy of narcolepsy. But after a while the books became a window on the world, and not a screen against it. This change doesn't always happen. I think that late adolescent narcotic reading accounts for some of the badness of English departments. As a college student, the boy loves reading and majors in English because he would be reading anyway. Deciding on a career, he takes up English teaching for the same reason. Then in graduate school he is trained to be a scholar, which is painful and irrelevant, and finds he must write papers and publish them to be a Professor—and at about this time he no longer requires reading for narcosis, and he is left with nothing but a Ph.D. and the prospect of fifty years of teaching literature; and he does not even like literature.

Narcotic reading survives the impact of television, because this type [8] of reading has even less reality than melodrama; that is, the reader is in control: once the characters reach into the reader's feelings, he is able to stop reading, or glance away, or superimpose his own daydream. The trouble with television is that it embodies its own daydream. Literature is often valued precisely because of its distance from the tangible. Some readers prefer looking into the text of a play to seeing it performed. Reading a play, it is possible to stage it oneself by an imaginative act; but it is also possible to remove it from real people. Here is Virgina Woolf, who was lavish in her praise of the act of reading, talking about reading a play rather than seeing it: "Certainly there is a good deal to be said for reading *Twelfth Night* in the book if the book can be read in a garden, with no sound but the thud of an apple falling to the earth, or of the wind ruffling the branches of the trees." She sets her own stage; the play is called *Virginia Woolf Reads Twelfth Night in a Garden*. Piety moves into narcissism, and the high metaphors of Shakespeare's lines dwindle into the flowers of an English garden; actors in ruffles wither, while the wind ruffles branches.

1968

Lin Yutang

The Art of Reading

Reading or the enjoyment of books has always been regarded among the charms of a cultured life and is respected and envied by those who rarely give themselves that privilege. This is easy to understand when we compare the difference between the life of a man who does no reading and that of a man who does. The man who has not the habit of reading is imprisoned in his immediate world, in respect to time and space. His life falls into a set routine; he is limited to contact and conversation with a few friends and acquaintances, and he sees only what happens in his immediate neighborhood. From this prison there is no escape. But the moment he takes up a book, he immediately enters a different world, and if it is a good book, he is immediately put in touch with one of the best talkers of the world. This talker leads him on and carries him into a different country or a different age, or unburdens to him some of his personal regrets, or discusses with him some special line or aspect of life that the reader knows nothing about. An ancient author puts him in communion with a dead spirit of long ago, and as he reads along, he begins to imagine what that ancient author looked like and what type of person he was. Both Mencius and Ssema Ch'ien, China's greatest historian, have expressed the same idea. Now to be able to live two hours out of twelve in a different world and take one's thoughts off the claims of the immediate present is, of course, a privilege to be envied by people shut up in their bodily prison. Such a change of environment is really similar to travel in its psychological effect.

But there is more to it than this. The reader is always carried away into a world of thought and reflection. Even if it is a book about physical events, there is a difference between seeing such events in person or living through them, and reading about them in books, for then the events always assume the quality of the spectacle and the reader becomes a detached spectator. The best reading is therefore that which leads us into this contemplative mood, and not that which is merely occupied with the report of events. The tremendous amount of time spent on newspapers I regard as not reading at all, for the average readers of papers are mainly concerned with getting reports about events and happenings without contemplative value.

The best formula for the object of reading, in my opinion, was stated by Huang Shanku, a Sung poet and friend of Su Tungp'o. He said, "A scholar who hasn't read anything for three days feels that *his talk has no flavor* (becomes insipid), *and his own face becomes hateful to look at* (in the mirror)." What he means, of course, is that reading gives a man a certain charm and flavor, which is the entire object of reading, and only reading with this object can be called an art. One doesn't read to "improve one's mind," because when one begins to think of improving his mind, all the pleasure of reading is gone. He is the type of person who says to himself: "I must read Shakespeare, and I must read Sophocles, and I must read the entire Five-foot Shelf of Dr. Eliot, so I can become an educated man." I'm sure that man will never become educated. He will force himself one evening to read Shakespeare's *Hamlet* and come away, as if from a bad dream, with no greater benefit than that he is able to say that he had "read" *Hamlet*. Anyone who reads a book with a sense of obligation does not understand the art of reading. This type of reading with a business purpose is in no way different from a senator's reading up on files and reports before he makes a speech. It is asking for business advice and information, and not reading at all.

Reading for the cultivation of personal charm of appearance and 4 flavor in speech is then, according to Huang, the only admissible kind of reading. This charm of appearance must evidently be interpreted as something other than physical beauty. What Huang means by "hateful to look at" is not physical ugliness. There are ugly faces that have a fascinating charm and beautiful faces that are insipid to look at. I have among my Chinese friends one whose head is shaped like a bomb and yet who is nevertheless always a pleasure to see. The most beautiful face among Western authors, so far as I have seen them in pictures, was that of G. K. Chesterton. There was such a diabolical conglomeration of mustache, glasses, fairly bushy eyebrows and knitted lines where the eyebrows met. One felt there were a vast number of ideas playing about inside that forehead, ready at any time to burst out from those quizzically penetrating eyes. That is what Huang would call a beautiful face, a face not made up by powder and rouge, but by the sheer force of thinking. As for flavor of speech, it all depends on one's way of reading.

Whether one has "flavor" or not in his talk, depends on his method of reading. If a reader gets the flavor of books, he will show that flavor in his conversations, and if he has flavor in his conversations, he cannot help also having a flavor in his writing.

Hence I consider flavor or taste as the key to all reading. It necessarily follows that taste is selective and individual, like the taste for food. The most hygienic way of eating is, after all, eating what one likes, for then one is sure of his digestion. In reading as in eating, what is one man's meat may be another's poison. A teacher cannot force his pupils to like what he likes in reading, and a parent cannot expect his children to have the same tastes as himself. And if the reader has no taste for what he reads, all the time is wasted. As Yüan Chunglang says, "You can leave the books that you don't like alone, *and let other people read them.*"

There can be, therefore, no books that one absolutely must read. For our intellectual interests grow like a tree or flow like a river. So long as there is proper sap, the tree will grow anyhow, and so long as there is fresh current from the spring, the water will flow. When water strikes a granite cliff, it just goes around it; when it finds itself in a pleasant low valley, it stops and meanders there a while; when it finds itself in a deep mountain pond, it is content to stay there; when it finds itself traveling over rapids, it hurries forward. Thus, without any effort or determined aim, it is sure of reaching the sea some day. There are no books in this world that everybody must read, but only books that a person must read at a certain time in a given place under given circumstances and at a given period of his life. I rather think that reading, like matrimony, is determined by fate or *yinyüan.* Even if there is a certain book that everyone must read, like the Bible, there is a time for it. When one's thoughts and experience have not reached a certain point for reading a masterpiece, the masterpiece will leave only a bad flavor on his palate. Confucius said, "When one is fifty, one may read the *Book of Changes,*" which means that one should not read it at forty-five. The extremely mild flavor of Confucius' own sayings in the *Analects* and his mature wisdom cannot be appreciated until one becomes mature himself.

I regard the discovery of one's favorite author as the most critical event in one's intellectual development. There is such a thing as the affinity of spirits, and among the authors of ancient and modern times, one must try to find an author whose spirit is akin with his own. Only in this way can one get any real good out of reading. One has to be independent and search out his masters. Who is one's favorite author, no one can tell, probably not even the man himself. It is like love at first sight. The reader cannot be told to love this one or that one, but when he has found the author he loves, he knows it himself by a kind of instinct. We have such famous cases of discoveries of authors. Scholars seem to have lived in different ages, separated by centuries, and yet their modes of thinking and feeling were so akin that their coming together across the pages of a book was like a person finding his own image. In Chinese phraseology, we speak of these kindred spirits as reincarnations of the same soul, as Su Tungp'o was said to be a reincarnation of Chuangtse or T'ao Yüanming, and Yüan Chunglang was said to be the reincarnation of Su Tungp'o. Su Tungp'o said that when he first read Chuangtse, he felt as if all the time since his childhood he had been thinking the same things and taking the same views himself. When Yüan Chunglang discovered one night Hsü Wench'ang, a contemporary unknown to him, in a small book of poems, he jumped out of bed and shouted to his friend, and his friend began to read it and shout in turn, and then they both read and shouted again until their servant was completely puzzled. George Eliot described her first reading of Rousseau as an electric shock. Nietzsche felt the same thing about Schopenhauer, but Schopenhauer was a peevish master and Nietzsche was a violent-tempered pupil, and it was natural that the pupil later rebelled against the teacher.

It is only this kind of reading, this discovery of one's favorite author, 8 that will do one any good at all. Like a man falling in love with his sweetheart at first sight, everything is right. She is of the right height, has the right face, the right color of hair, the right quality of voice and the right way of speaking and smiling. This author is not something that a young man need to be told about by his teacher. The author is just right for him; his style, his taste, his point of view, his mode of thinking, are all right. And then the reader proceeds to devour every word and every line that the author writes, and because there is a spiritual affinity, he absorbs and readily digests everything. The author has cast a spell over him, and he is glad to be under the spell, and in time his own voice and manner and way of smiling and way of talking become like the author's own. Thus he truly steeps himself in his literary lover and derives from these books sustenance for his soul. After a few years, the spell is over and he grows a little tired of this lover and seeks for new literary lovers, and after he has had three or four lovers and completely eaten them up, he emerges as an author himself. There are many readers who never fall in love, like many young men and women who flirt around and are incapable of forming a deep attachment to a particular person. They can read any and all authors, and they never amount to anything.

Such a conception of the art of reading completely precludes the idea of reading as a duty or as an obligation. In China, one often encourages students to "study bitterly." There was a famous scholar who studied bitterly and who stuck an awl in his calf when he fell asleep while studying at night. There was another scholar who had a maid stand by his side as he was studying at night, to wake him up every time he fell asleep. This was nonsensical. If one has a book lying before him and falls asleep while some wise ancient author is talking to him, he should just go to bed. No amount of sticking an awl in his calf or of shaking him up by a maid will do him any good. Such a man has lost all sense of pleasure of reading. Scholars who are worth anything at all never know what is called "a hard grind" or what "bitter study" means. They merely love books and read on because they cannot help themselves.

What, then, is the true art of reading? The simple answer is to just take up a book and read when the mood comes. To be thoroughly enjoyed, reading must be entirely spontaneous.   *1937*

The Writers

Allen, Paula Gunn (b. 1939)

A poet, essayist, novelist, and teacher, Paula Gunn Allen speaks from the experience of a contemporary Native American woman negotiating several cultures. Allen is originally from New Mexico, and her heritage includes the Laguna Pueblo, Sioux, and Chicano traditions. In addition to several volumes of poetry, Allen is the author of the novel *The Woman Who Owned the Shadows* (1983) and the editor of *The Sacred Hoop: Recovering the Feminine in American Indian Traditions* (1986), from which "Where I Come from Is Like This" is taken. She has taught at the University of California at Berkeley and currently teaches at the University of California at Los Angeles.

Allison, Dorothy (b. 1949)

Dorothy Allison was born in South Carolina and holds a degree in urban anthropology. Her first book, *The Women Who Hate Me*, was published in 1984. "Don't Tell Me You Don't Know" appears in a collection of short stories called *Trash* (1988), which won the 1989 Lambda Book Award for the best work of lesbian fiction. Allison contributes to many periodicals, including the *Advocate, Conditions, Southern Exposure,* and the *Village Voice*. Her stories have appeared in several anthologies as well. She currently teaches literature and writing in the San Francisco Bay area.

Anaya, Rudolfo A. (b. 1937)

Rudolfo A. Anaya, author of poems, essays, novels, and short stories, is a professor of English at the University of New Mexico. His writing is enriched by the oral tradition of the Mexican-American peoples of the Southwest and by Spanish, his first language. Anaya has published several novels, including *Bless Me, Ultima* (1972), which won the Premio Quinto Sol literary award, *The Legend of La Llorona* (1984), and *The Lord of the Dawn* (1987). His stories have appeared in many magazines, such as *Grito del Sol, Mother Jones,* and *Writers of the Purple Sage*. His stories are also

959

collected in *The Silence of the Llano* (1982), and "B. Traven is Alive and Well in Cuernavaca" appears in an anthology he edited, *Cuentos Chicanos* (1984). Anaya was a fellow of the National Chicano Council on Higher Education in 1978 and a National Education Association Creative Writing Fellow in 1979. He has received the University of New Mexico Mesa Chicana Literary Award (1977) and the New Mexico Governor's Public Service Award (1978).

Anderson, Sherwood (1876–1941)
Leaving formal education at the age of fourteen, Sherwood Anderson worked as a newsboy, house painter, field worker, stable hand, and soldier before taking his first writing job as an advertising copywriter. He also owned and managed a paint factory in Chicago while writing fiction in his spare time. In 1912 Anderson left his business abruptly and began to concentrate on developing his literary skills. The author of seven novels, Anderson is best remembered for his short stories, especially those collected in *Winesburg, Ohio* (1919). Among his most notable works of nonfiction are his *Memoirs* (1942), from which "Discovery of a Father" is taken, as well as *The Modern Writer* (1925), *Sherwood Anderson's Notebook* (1926), and *Tar: A Midwest Childhood* (1926). Anderson's distinctively spare and original prose style broke with contemporary norms for the short story and exerted a strong influence on Ernest Hemingway, John Steinbeck, and William Faulk-

ner, who said of Anderson, "He was the father of my generation of American writers and the tradition of American writing which our successors will carry on."

Angelou, Maya (b. 1928)
Maya Angelou is perhaps best known for the first installment of her autobiography, *I Know Why the Caged Bird Sings* (1970), but her talents also include dancing, singing, composing, and theater arts. She has acted in Genet's *The Blacks* and in the television series *Roots*, and she has written, directed, and acted in several other TV, film, and stage productions. In addition to the several volumes of her autobiography, she is the author of articles, short stories, and poetry. Maya Angelou grew up in St. Louis and in Stamps, Arkansas, a victim of poverty, discrimination, and abuse. Angelou courageously confronts the pain and injustice of her childhood in *I Know Why the Caged Bird Sings*, from which the selection "What's Your Name, Girl?" is taken. James Baldwin praised this book as the mark of the "beginning of a new era in the minds and hearts of all black men and women." Maya Angelou is currently Reynolds Professor of American Studies at Wake Forest University.

Apple, Max (b. 1941)
Max Apple is a professor of English at Rice University and the author of several novels and short stories. He has twice been the recipient of the Jesse Jones Award from the Texas Institute of Letters, in 1976 for *The Oranging of America and Other*

Stories (1976), and in 1985 for *Free Agents* (1984). The story "Bridging" appears in the latter collection of stories. His other publications include *Zip: A Novel of the Left and the Right* (1978) and *The Propheteers* (1987). Contributor to many national magazines including *Esquire, Mademoiselle, American Review,* and *Georgia Review,* in 1985 Apple won the *Hadassah* magazine–Ribalous Award for best Jewish fiction. His other honors include a fellowship from the National Endowment for the Humanities in 1971 and a Guggenheim Fellowship in 1986.

Arlen, Michael (b. 1930)
Michael Arlen was born in England and moved to the United States when he was ten years old. After finishing his education at Harvard, he worked as a reporter at *Life* magazine for four years before moving to the staff of the *New Yorker.* He has written reviews and articles for the *New Yorker* since 1966, and specializes in television criticism. Arlen has expanded some of these articles into book form, publishing *The View from Highway 1: Essays on Television* (1976), *Thirty Seconds* (1980), and *The Camera Age* (1981), in which "Ode to Thanksgiving" appears. In 1968 Michael Arlen received the Screen Director's Guild award for television criticism. He is also the author of novels, short stories, social commentary, and autobiography. Arlen won a National Book Award in contemporary affairs for *Passage to Ararat* (1975). His other publications include *Living-Room War* (1969), *Exiles* (1970), *An American Verdict*

(1973), and *Say Goodbye to Sam* (1984).

Ascher, Barbara Lazear (b. 1946)
Barbara Lazear Ascher earned her law degree from the Cardozo School of Law in 1979 and practiced law for two years. However, she has always been a writer, and now devotes herself full-time to this occupation. She has contributed essays to anthologies and many magazines, including the *New York Times,* the *Yale Review, Newsday, Vogue, Elle,* and *Saturday Review.* Her essays have been published in two collections, *Playing After Dark* (1986), and *The Habit of Loving* (1989). The selection "Mothers and Sons" comes from *Playing After Dark,* about which Eudora Welty comments, "Barbara Ascher shows herself in these impressions to have a serious mind and the gift of a light touch. That's a rare and valuable combination these days. Her timely and perceptive pieces, written with grace and a nice sense of the absurd, carry considerable substance. What a refreshing collection!"

Bacon, Francis (1561–1626)
Francis Bacon was born in London, educated at Cambridge, and after training in the law, was elected to Parliament at the age of twenty-three. A skillful politician, he rose quickly in the court of King James I and became Lord Chancellor in 1618. His close association with the King made him the target of the King's political enemies, however, and Bacon was convicted in 1621 of a trumped-up corruption charge. His sudden exit from politics left

Bacon with more time to devote to his writing, which he had pursued throughout his career. The first essayist in the English language, Bacon wrote on many subjects; however, his principle project was to establish a new method of scientific investigation. Bacon believed that inductive reasoning should replace the mixture of religious edicts, faith in traditional authority, and a priori assumptions that then characterized scientific investigation. "Idols of the Mind," taken from Book I of the *Novum Organum* (1620), is one part of this ambitious project. On the same theme, Bacon wrote *The Advancement of Learning* (1605) and *The New Atlantis* (1624); his *Essays*, published in 1597, 1612, and 1625, established the essay as a literary form in English.

Baker, Russell (b. 1925)

Since 1962, Russell Baker has written the "Observer" column in the *New York Times*, a column which is syndicated to over 450 newspapers across the nation. The selection "Happy New Year" appeared in this column in 1984. Baker's articles on contemporary American politics, culture, and language are consistently funny and often sharply satiric. Collections of his articles have been published in several volumes including *No Cause for Panic* (1964), *Poor Russell's Almanac* (1972, revised 1982), and *So This Is Depravity* (1980). He is also the author of fiction and children's literature. Among other professional honors, he has twice been awarded the Pulitzer Prize, in 1979 for commentary and in 1983 for his autobiography, *Growing Up* (1982), from which the selection "Gumption" is taken. Baker's second volume of memoirs, *The Good Times*, was published in 1989. He has received numerous honorary degrees and is also the recipient of the Frank Sullivan Memorial Award (1976) and the George Polk Award for commentary (1979).

Baldwin, James (1924–1987)

James Baldwin grew up in New York City but left for France in 1948 because he felt artistically stifled as a black, gay man in America. His first novels, *Go Tell It on the Mountain* (1953) and *Giovanni's Room* (1956), and his first collection of essays, *Notes of a Native Son* (1955), were written during Baldwin's first stay abroad, where he felt able to write critically about race, sexual identity, and social injustice in America. The essay "Stranger in the Village" appears in *Notes of a Native Son*. After nearly a decade in France, he returned to New York and became a national figure in the civil rights movement. Henry Louis Gates, Jr., eulogized Baldwin as the conscience of the nation, for he "educated an entire generation of Americans about the civil-rights struggle and the sensibility of Afro-Americans as we faced and conquered the final barriers in our long quest for civil rights." Baldwin continues to educate through his essays, collected in *Nobody Knows My Name* (1961), *The Fire Next Time* (1963), *No Name in the Street* (1971), and *The Devil Finds Work* (1976). Langston

Hughes wrote of these works, "Few American writers handle words more effectively in the essay form than James Baldwin."

Bambara, Toni Cade (b. 1939)
In her various capacities as a social worker, novelist, scriptwriter, and educator, Toni Cade Bambara has always worked to alleviate the injustices of urban poverty and racial discrimination. Bambara is the editor of *Tales and Stories for Black Folks* (1975), honored by the *New York Times* as Outstanding Book of the Year in juvenile literature. Her story "The Lesson" appears in a collection called *Gorilla, My Love* (1972). As John Wideman describes her work, Toni Cade Bambara "emphasizes the necessity for black people to maintain their best traditions, to remain healthy and whole as they struggle for political power." In 1981 her novel *The Salt Eaters* (1980) won the American Book Award, and in 1986 her television script for *The Bombing of Osage* won awards from the Philadelphia Association of Broadcasters and the National Black Programming Consortium. Among other honors, Bambara has received a Langston Hughes Medallion and a grant from the National Endowment for the Arts.

Berry, Wendell (b. 1934)
Wendell Berry lives and farms in Kentucky. His novels, short stories, poems, and essays present his love for nature and his concerns with agriculture, the environment, and the maladies of modern industrial society. During the 1960s and 1970s he taught at New York University and the University of Kentucky; he left academia in 1977 to devote himself full-time to farming and writing, but since 1987 has resumed part-time teaching. Berry's writing has been published in numerous journals, including the *Nation, New World Writing, Prairie Schooner, Contract, Chelsea Review,* and the *Quarterly Review of Literature*. His essay "The Journey's End" appears in *Recollected Essays* (1981). Berry's other works of nonfiction include *The Unsettling of America: Culture and Agriculture* (1977), *The Gift of Good Land* (1981), and *Standing by Words* (1985). His *Collected Poems* was published in 1985. Wendell Berry was a Wallace Stegner Fellow in 1957–58 and has received grants from the Guggenheim and Rockefeller foundations. He received the Bess Hokin Prize for poetry in 1967 and a National Institute of Arts and Letters Literary Award in 1971.

Bradley, David (b. 1950)
Novelist and professor of English at Temple University, David Bradley received the PEN/Faulkner Award, the American Academy and Institute of Arts and Letters award for literature, and the *New York Times Book Review* "Editor's Choice" citation for his novel *The Chaneysville Incident* (1981). He is also author of *South Street* (1975) and has contributed to *While Someone Else is Eating* (1980), *In Praise of What Persists* (1983), *From Mt. San Angelo* (1984), and *Our Roots Grow Deeper than We Know* (1981). Bradley has contributed over one hundred articles, stories, and reviews to magazines

including *Sport*, the *Nation*, *Esquire*, the *New York Times Magazine*, *Southern Review*, *Signature*, and *Quest*. "Ringgold Street" appeared in *Philadelphia Magazine* in 1985.

Brady, Judy (b. 1937)
Judy Brady studied painting at the University of Iowa and earned her B.F.A. in 1962. She married in 1960 and raised two daughters; she is now divorced. Since 1969 she has been active in the women's movement, work that has sharpened her critique of power relationships structured along gender and class lines. She has twice traveled to Cuba and written about her experience there. Brady's other free-lance writing covers topics as diverse as abortion and union organizing. Her article "I Want a Wife" appeared in the first issue of *Ms.* magazine and has been reprinted many times.

Brownmiller, Susan (b. 1935)
Susan Brownmiller has made a long and successful career in journalism, starting as an editor for *Albany Report*, working as a researcher for *Newsweek*, and writing on the staff of the *Village Voice* and ABC-TV. Since 1968 she has been a free-lance journalist and writer and has contributed to many national magazines, including *Newsweek*, *Esquire*, and the *New York Times Magazine*. She created a national sensation with her 1975 book *Against Our Will: Men, Women, and Rape*. Exploring the history and politics of rape, this book made Brownmiller famous throughout the country, and *Time* magazine

elected her one of the twelve Women of the Year for 1975. She is the founder of Women Against Pornography. "Let's Put Pornography Back in the Closet" is taken from *Take Back the Night* (1980). Brownmiller has been honored with grants from the Alicia Patterson Foundation and the Louis M. Rabinowitz Foundation.

Cofer, Judy Ortiz (b. 1952)
Born in Puerto Rico, Judy Ortiz Cofer moved to the United States in 1960. She challenged herself to learn English well enough not only to teach it, but to write poetry in it, and has been very successful in both. Her poetry has appeared in *Prairie Schooner, New Letters, Southern Poetry Review*, and *Poetry Miscellany*, among other literary magazines. Collections of her poems have also been published: *The Native Dancer* (1981), *Peregrina* (1986), and *Reaching for the Mainland* (1986). "Casa: A Partial Remembrance of a Puerto Rican Childhood" appeared in *Prairie Schooner* in 1989. Cofer has taught at Broward Community College, the University of Georgia, and the University of Miami. In 1981 she was a fellow of the Fine Arts Council of Florida, and in 1977 studied at Oxford University as a scholar of the English Speaking Union.

Cole, K. C. (b. 1946)
A journalist and essayist, K. C. Cole has specialized in many areas but never restricted herself to one. She started writing as a free-lance reporter in Eastern Europe and the U.S.S.R. in 1969

and 1970. Since then she has written on education, science, health, and women's issues. Cole's articles have appeared in the *Washington Post*, the *New York Times*, and *Newsday*, and she has contributed to magazines such as *Smithsonian, Omni, Glamour, Seventeen*, and *Cosmopolitan*. The article reprinted here, "Much Ado about Nothing," originally appeared in *Discover* magazine in 1985. In 1982 Cole published a collection of essays called *Between the Lines*. Her other books include *What Only a Mother Can Tell You about Having a Baby* (1980), *Order in the Universe* (1982), and *Sympathetic Vibrations* (1985).

Crèvecoeur, J. Hector St. Jean de (1735–1813)

Born Michel-Guillaume Jean de Crèvecoeur in France, de Crèvecoeur immigrated to America and in his writings celebrated the new American national identity. He lived in New York state, and under the name J. Hector St. John he published *Letters from an American Farmer* (1782), from which the present selection is excerpted. This document contains an early articulation of an idea that has played a central role in American intellectual history—that European class structures do not function in America and that any person can succeed through hard work and determination. The ideology of the "melting pot" is evident in de Crèvecoeur, but clearly encompasses only European cultures. De Crèvecoeur believed that the "true American," born in the New World of parents from mixed European heritage, had not only a distinct identity, but in fact constituted a "new man."

Curtis, Bruce (b. 1933)

Bruce Curtis earned his Ph.D. in American intellectual history at the University of Iowa in 1964. He has taught at the University of Wichita and Kansas State College of Pittsburg, and is currently professor of American thought and language at Michigan State University. He is the author of *William Graham Sumner* (1981) and has published articles in many scholarly journals, including *Mid-America, American Studies*, the *New England Quarterly*, and the *Journal of American History*. "The Wimp Factor" appeared in *American Heritage* in 1989.

Derricotte, Toi (b. 1941)

In the 1960s Toi Derricotte worked as a teacher of the mentally and emotionally retarded; more recently she has taught poetry in the New Jersey Poet-in-the-Schools program. Derricotte has also been a guest poet and lecturer at several colleges and universities, and has served as an educational consultant to Columbia University's Sex Desegregation Assistance Center. She contributes poems to many periodicals, including *Iowa Review, Poetry Northwest, Chrysalis*, and *New York Quarterly*. Derricotte's poetry has appeared in several anthologies, including *Extended Outlooks: The Iowa Review Collection of Contemporary Women Writers* (1982) and *Home Girls: A Black Feminist Anthology* (1982). She has also published her own collections of poems. Her non-fiction appears in the anthology *Ariadne's Thread: A Collection of Contemporary Women's Journals* (1982). "Diary: At an Artist's Colony" appeared in the *Massachusetts Review* in 1988. Derricotte received first prizes from the Academy of American Poets for "Unburying the Bird" and "Natural Birth" and she is the recipient of fellowships from the MacDowell Colony (1982), the New Jersey State Council on the Arts (1982), and the National Education Association (1985).

Descartes, René (1596–1650)
A mathematician and philosopher, René Descartes is generally considered the founder of modern philosophy. Rather than accepting the precepts and employing the methods of the philosophical traditional, Descartes initiated a mode of thinking that sought to strip away the errors of previous philosophers and to arrive at definitive truths. His assertion *cogito ergo sum* (I think, therefore I am) is the most famous example of his philosophical method, which proceeds from a set of self-evident intuitions and a set of logical truths to arrive at general conclusions, such as the existence of God. His most influential writings include *Discours de la méthode* (1637), from which "Stripping the Mind of Its Beliefs" is excerpted, *Méditations philosophiques* (1641), *Principia philosophiae* (1644), and *Traité des passions de l'âme* (1649).

Didion, Joan (b. 1934)
The author of novels, short stories, and essays, Joan Didion be-

gan her career in 1956 as a staff writer at *Vogue* magazine in New York. In 1963 she published her first novel, *Run River*, and the following year returned to her native California, where she lives today. Didion's essays have appeared in periodicals ranging from *Mademoiselle* and *Life* to the *American Scholar* and the *National Review*. Her essay "Why I Write" appeared in the *New York Times Book Review* in 1976, and "On Keeping a Notebook" can be found in her collection of essays, *Slouching Towards Bethlehem* (1968). The critic Alfred Kazin remarks that in Didion's work "silence as a form and fear of imminent breakdown is a significant element . . . She refers often to her fragility in *Slouching Towards Bethlehem*, and she writes about her panics with a deliberation that is not merely disarming but that always makes a point, in perfect style, about something other than herself." Didion's other nonfiction publications include *The White Album* (1979), *Essays and Interviews* (1984), *Salvador* (1983), and *Miami* (1987). Her most recent novel is *Democracy* (1984).

Dillard, Annie (b. 1945)
In 1974 Annie Dillard was awarded the Pulitzer Prize for general nonfiction for her book *Pilgrim at Tinker Creek*, from which "Seeing" is excerpted. Dillard describes this book through reference to Henry David Thoreau, calling it "a meteorological journal of the mind." Eudora Welty writes of Dillard that "A reader's heart must go out to a young writer

with a sense of wonder so fearless and unbridled. It is this intensity of experience that she seems to live in order to declare." Annie Dillard has also published poems in *Tickets for a Prayer Wheel* (1975), literary theory in *Living by Fiction* (1982), essays in *Teaching a Stone to Talk* (1982), and autobiography in *An American Childhood* (1987). Her most recent book, *The Writing Life* (1989), contains reflections on the writing process. From 1973 to 1982 she served as contributing editor to *Harper's* magazine, and since 1979 she has taught creative writing at Wesleyan University.

Dostoyevsky, Fyodor Mikhailovich (1821–1881)

When his first novel, *Poor Folk*, was published in 1845, Dostoyevksy was hailed as the new Gogol. His fame continued to grow throughout his career, in spite of many obstacles. In 1849 Dostoyevsky was arrested for associating with a group of young intellectuals who were interested in utopian socialism, and after a last-minute reprieve from the firing squad, he spent a decade in a Siberian prison. Dostoyevsky also faced many personal problems after he was released from prison, including the deaths of his wife and brother and his gambling debts, which forced him into exile from 1867 to 1871. Nonetheless, he continued to work as a journalist, as well as writing such classic novels as *Crime and Punishment* (1866), *The Idiot* (1869), and *The Possessed* (1872). After returning to Russia in 1871, Dostoyevsky edited a conservative newspaper, *Grazhdanin*, and wrote his final masterpiece, *The Brothers Karamazov* (1880).

Douglass, Frederick (1817?–1895)

Born into slavery, Frederick Douglass was taken from his mother as an infant and denied knowledge of his father's identity. He escaped to the north at the age of twenty-one and created a new identity for himself as a free man. He educated himself and went on to become one of the most eloquent orators and persuasive writers of the nineteenth century. He was a national leader in the abolition movement and, among other activities, founded and edited the *North Star* and *Douglass' Monthly*. His public service included appointments as United States marshall and consul general to the Republic of Haiti. His most lasting literary accomplishment was his memoirs, which he revised several times before they were published as the *Life and Times of Frederick Douglass* (1881 and 1892). "Learning to Read and Write" is taken from these memoirs.

Early, Gerald (b. 1952)

Gerald Early is the author of *Tuxedo Junction: Essays on American Culture* (1989), which he wrote as a postdoctoral fellow at the University of Kansas. Currently, Early is professor of English and Afro-American studies at Washington University. He has received awards from the Whiting Foundation and CCLM-General Electric, and contributed to such journals as *Antaeus*, the *Antioch*

Review, Callaloo, Cimarron Review, the *Hudson Review*, the *Kenyon Review*, and *Obsidian II*. "Baseball: The Ineffable National Pastime" appears in *House of Ruth, House of Robinson*.

Edison, Thomas (1847–1931)

Thomas Edison left school after only three months of formal education and worked as a telegraph operator before turning his talents to invention. In 1869 he received his first patent, for an electronic voice recorder. Over the course of his life, Edison patented over one thousand inventions. The most famous of these, the phonograph (1877) and the incandescent lamp (1879), have secured his position as an American legend. Edison concerned himself with applied rather than abstract science, but is credited with one discovery in pure science–the "Edison effect," which describes the conversion of alternating current to direct current. In 1912 his essay "The Woman of the Future" appeared in *Good Housekeeping*.

Ehrlich, Gretel (b. 1946)

Although she started her career as a film-maker and poet, Gretel Ehrlich now operates a ranch in the Big Horn Basin in Wyoming. Ehrlich was educated at Bennington College, the UCLA film school, and the New School for Social Research in New York. In 1976 she arrived in Wyoming to film a documentary on sheepherders and fell in love with the open land and sky. Since moving to Wyoming Ehrlich has published essays in *Harper's* and the

Atlantic; the essay "The Solace of Open Spaces" appears in a collection of the same name, published in 1985. In 1987 she received a Whiting Award, and in 1988 published her first novel, *Heart Mountain*.

Eiseley, Loren (1907–1977)

Loren Eiseley taught at the University of Kansas, Oberlin College, and the University of Pennsylvania, where he was Franklin Professor of Anthropology and History of Science, and where he also served as provost. A versatile writer, Eiseley published fiction as well as nonfiction. He contributed to both scientific magazines such as *American Anthropologist* and *Scientific Monthly* and to popular magazines like *Harper's*, the *Saturday Evening Post, Ladies' Home Journal*, and the *Atlantic*. Because of Eiseley's special talent for making science accessible to lay readers, Edward Hoagland remarked that Eiseley's "command of the language is that of a literary man. He is one of those transcendent imaginative thinkers who are not limited to one branch of science, nor to science itself. . . . He's a writer so good he can stop you dead in your tracks for a day or a week." Among Eiseley's many acclaimed books are *Darwin's Century* (1958), *The Firmament of Time* (1960), *The Night Country* (1971), and *The Star Thrower* (1978), from which the present selection is excerpted.

Elkind, David (b. 1931)

A specialist in child and adolescent psychology, David Elkind has taught at Wheaton College, UCLA, the University of Denver, the University of Rochester, and most recently, Tufts University. In 1964 and 1965 he was a National Science Foundation postdoctoral fellow in Geneva, Switzerland. Elkind has edited translations of the Swiss psychologist Jean Piaget, and written extensively on his work. He has also edited and written several books on child development, including *A Sympathetic Understanding of the Child: Six to Sixteen* (1971), *All Grown Up and No Place to Go* (1984), from which the essay "Teenagers in Crisis" is taken, and most recently *Mis-Education: Preschoolers at Risk* (1987).

Ephron, Nora (b. 1941)
Nora Ephron started her writing career as a reporter for the *New York Post* and also worked as a free-lance reporter before joining the staff of *Esquire*, where she wrote the "Women" column in 1972 and 1973. In 1973 she became a contributing editor of *New York* magazine, and in 1974 returned as senior editor to *Esquire*. Her work has also appeared in *Oui*, *McCall's*, and *Cosmopolitan*. Ephron has published two collections of essays on popular culture, *Wallflower at the Orgy* (1970) and *Crazy Salad* (1975), from which the essay "A Few Words about Breasts" is taken. More recently, she has published *Scribble, Scribble: Notes on the Media* (1979) and *Heartburn* (1983), and with Alice Arden wrote the screenplay *Silkwood*, which was nominated for an Academy Award.

Fallows, James (b. 1949)
Educated at Harvard and Oxford, where he studied as a Rhodes Scholar from 1970 to 1972, James Fallows has contributed to numerous magazines and journals. He has worked as staff editor of the *Washington Monthly*, associate editor of the *Texas Monthly*, and Washington editor of the *Atlantic Monthly*. From 1977 to 1979 he was chief speech writer for President Carter. His publications include *Who Runs Congress?* (1972), *The System* and *Inside the System* (both 1976, edited with Charles Peters), and *National Defense* (1981). Fallows wrote the article reprinted here, "Viva Bilingualism," when he was based in Asia; it appeared in the *New Republic* in 1986.

Gates, Henry Louis, Jr. (b. 1950)
One of the foremost contemporary critics and theorists of African and African-American literature, Henry Louis Gates, Jr., has taught at Yale and Cornell and is currently the John Spencer Bassett Professor of English and Literature at Duke University. He has edited numerous books, including *Black Literature and Literary Theory* (1984), *"Race," Writing, and Difference* (1986), and *In the House of Osugbo: Critical Essays on Wole Soyinka* (1988). Gates's seminal work, *The Signifying Monkey and the Language of Signify(ing): Towards a Theory of Afro-American Literary Criticism* (1988), received an American Book Award. About his writing John Wideman comments, "Eclectic, exciting, convincing, provocative, challenging even when he's

not altogether convincing, Mr. Gates gives black literature room to breathe, invents interpretive frameworks that enable us to experience black writing rather than label it in terms of theme or ideology." In addition to his scholarly writing, Gates contributes articles and reviews to national periodicals; "2 Live Crew, Decoded" appeared in the *New York Times* in 1990.

Giovanni, Nikki (b. 1943)

Best known for her poetry, Nikki Giovanni has also received acclaim for her children's fiction, autobiography, and essays. In 1967 she received a Ford Foundation grant, and in 1968 published her first collections of poems: *Black Judgment* and *Black Feeling, Black Talk*. A leading figure of the black consciousness literary movement of the 1960s, Giovanni continues to attract large crowds to her readings and lectures. Her numerous awards and honors include several honorary degrees, awards from the National Endowment for the Arts and the Harlem Cultural Council, and a National Book Award nomination for her autobiography, *Gemini* (1971). Her nonfiction includes two collaborative efforts, *A Dialogue: James Baldwin and Nikki Giovanni* (1973) and *A Poetic Equation: Conversations Between Nikki Giovanni and Margaret Walker* (1974), as well as a recent collection of essays, *Sacred Cows* (1988), from which "On Holidays and How to Make Them Work" is excerpted. Currently, Giovanni teaches at Virginia Polytechnic Institute and State University.

Goodwin, Doris Kearns (b. 1943)

Doris Kearns Goodwin had recently cowritten an article for the *New Republic* called "How to Remove LBJ in 1968" when President Johnson asked her to work with him in the White House. Johnson found her critical voice to be an asset, and when he retired asked Goodwin to assist him in writing his official biography, *The Vantage Point: Perspectives of the Presidency*. Goodwin wrote about Johnson from her own perspective in *Lyndon Johnson and the American Dream* (1976). A contributor to several periodicals, including the *New Republic*, Goodwin wrote "From Father, with Love" for a special supplement to the *Boston Globe* in 1986. Since 1969 Goodwin has taught government and politics at Harvard University. Her most recent publication is *The Fitzgeralds and the Kennedys* (1987).

Gordon, Mary (b. 1949)

From 1974 to 1978 Mary Gordon taught English at Dutchess Community College in Poughkeepsie, New York. Since that time she has published several novels, including *Final Payments* (1978), *The Company of Women* (1981), and *Men and Angels* (1985), and a collection of stories, *Temporary Shelter* (1987). Gordon frequently contributes articles and reviews to the *New York Times*, in which the essay "More Than Just a Shrine" originally appeared. Francine du Plessix Gray observes of Gordon that "at a time when many of her contemporaries have capitulated to the chic anomie of postmodernism, she continues to grapple with some of the vast issues that have given the novel form much of its grandeur. What is redemption? What is charity? What is our specific gravity of grace? Who else, among her peers, is asking such searing questions?"

Gornick, Vivian (b. 1935)
Vivian Gornick taught English at the State University of New York at Stony Brook and Hunter College of the City University of New York in the 1960s before turning to writing full time. Gornick writes social commentary and concentrates on women's issues. In 1971 she edited, together with Barbara K. Moran, *Women in Sexist Society*, an acclaimed collection of essays by professional writers and scholars. Since that time her work has included *In Search of Ali Mahomud: An American Woman in Egypt* (1973), *The Romance of American Communism* (1977), *Essays in Feminism* (1978), *Women in Science* (1983), and *Fierce Attachments* (1987). She also contributes to such periodicals as the *New York Times Magazine*, in which "Who Says We Haven't Made a Revolution?" originally appeared.

Gould, Stephen Jay (b. 1941)
Stephen Jay Gould is professor of geology and zoology at Harvard and curator of invertebrate paleontology at Harvard's Museum of Comparative Zoology. He has published widely on evolution and other topics and has earned a reputation for making technical subjects readily comprehensible to lay readers without trivializing the material. His *The Panda's Thumb* (1980) won the

American Book Award, and *The Mismeasure of Man* (1981) won the National Book Critics Circle Award. Gould has published over one hundred articles in scientific journals, and contributes to national magazines as well. "Sex, Drugs, Disasters, and the Extinction of Dinosaurs" appeared in *Discover* magazine in 1984. More recently, Gould has written *An Urchin in the Storm* (1987) and *Time's Arrow, Time's Cycle* (1987). Among many other honors and awards, he has been a fellow of the National Science Foundation and the MacArthur Foundation. John Updike comments that "Gould, in his scrupulous explication of [other scientists'] carefully wrought half-truths, abolishes the unnecessary distinction between the humanities and science, and honors the latter as a branch of humanistic thought, fallible and poetic."

Gray, Francine du Plessix (b. 1930)
Born in France, Francine du Plessix Gray came to the United States when she was eleven years old. She has been a free-lance writer for many years, contributing to *Vogue*, the *New Yorker*, the *New Republic, Saturday Review*, the *New York Review of Books*, and the *New York Times Book Review*, in which "I Write for Revenge Against Reality" appeared in 1982. She has also taught at Yale University and Columbia University, and in 1974 served as judge of the National Book Award in philosophy and religion. Gray won the National Catholic Book Award for *Divine Disobedience: Profiles in Catholic Radicalism* (1970) and the Front

Page Award for *Hawaii: The Sugar-Coated Fortress* (1972). Gray has written the novels *Lovers and Tyrants* (1976), *World Without End* (1981), and *October Blood* (1985). In 1987 she published a collection of essays called *Adam and Eve in the City*. Her newest book, *Soviet Women*, came out in 1990.

Greene, Bob (b. 1947)

Award-winning columnist and author Bob Greene writes for the *Chicago Tribune* and his columns are syndicated nationally. Greene often covers offbeat stories rather than major news items and has a talent for revealing the humanity of any situation. He has collected his columns in *Johnny Deadline, Reporter* (1976), *American Beat* (1983), and *Cheeseburgers* (1985). His other books deal with subjects as diverse as parenting (*Good Morning, Merry Sunshine,* 1984), the rock group Alice Cooper (*Billion Dollar Baby,* 1973), and Vietnam veterans (*Homecoming,* 1989). Greene is also a contributing editor of *Esquire* magazine, in which "Mr. President" appeared in 1987. His awards include Best Newspaper Column in Illinois from the Associated Press (1975), Best Sustaining Feature in Chicago from the Chicago Newspaper Guild (1976), the National Headliner Award for best newspaper column in the United States (1977), and the Peter Lisagor Award for exemplary journalism (1981).

Gruchow, Paul

Born in Minnesota and educated at the University of Minnesota, as an undergraduate Paul Gruchow was editor of the *Minnesota Daily*, the university newspaper. After graduation he worked as a congressional aide, then became news director of Minnesota Public Radio. He has also worked as editor of *Mpls.* magazine and of the *Worthington Daily Globe*. He contributes to *Minnesota Monthly*, in which "Seeing the Elephant" appeared in 1987, and to the *Great River Review*. In 1985 he published *Journal of a Prairie Year*, and in 1988 *The Necessity of Empty Places*.

Hall, Donald (b. 1928)

Donald Hall was educated at Harvard and Oxford and began his academic career as junior fellow in the Society of Fellows at Harvard in 1954. In 1957 he became a professor at the University of Michigan at Ann Arbor, where he remained until 1975, when he left to devote himself full-time to writing. Hall has published numerous volumes of poetry over the years, as well as contributing poetry to the *Times Literary Supplement*, the *New Yorker*, the *Partisan Review*, *Poetry*, and *Harper's*, among many other magazines. His prose writing also fills many volumes, and includes biography and juvenile literature as well as writing about reading and writing. "Four Kinds of Reading" appears in *To Keep Moving: Essays 1959–1969* (1980). Hall is the recipient of the Newdigate Prize from Oxford University (1952), the Academy of American Poets' Lamont Poetry Selection Award (1955), the Edna St. Vincent Millay Award of the Poetry Society of America (1956), two Guggenheim Fellowships (1963 and 1972), the Caldecott Medal from the American Library Association (1980), and the National Book Critics Circle Award (1989).

Hamill, Pete (b. 1935)

Pete Hamill began his career in journalism as a reporter for the *New York Post*, and also wrote for the *Saturday Evening Post* before becoming a war correspondent in Vietnam in 1966. In the past two decades he has written columns for *Newsday*, the *New York Daily News*, the *Village Voice*, and *Esquire*. Hamill's journalism has earned awards from the Columbia University Graduate School of Journalism and the Newspaper Reporters Association. His newspaper columns have been collected in *Irrational Ravings* (1971) and *The Invisible City: A New York Sketchbook* (1980). Hamill also writes short stories, screenplays, and novels. His more recent novels include *Dirty Laundry* (1978), *The Deadly Piece* (1979), and *The Guns of Heaven* (1983). He contributes to many national magazines including *Cosmopolitan*, *Life*, the *New York Times Magazine*, and *Playboy*; "Crack and the Box" appeared in *Esquire* in 1990.

Hamilton, Cynthia

Cynthia Hamilton studied political science at Stanford University, where she earned her B.A., and Boston University, where she earned her Ph.D. She is a political activist as well as a scholar, and worked against the construction of a solid waste incinerator in Los Angeles, a project

which she writes about in "Women, Home, and Commnity: The Struggle in an Urban Environment." This article can be found in *Reweaving the World: The Emergence of Ecofeminism* (1990). Currently, Hamilton is a professor in the Pan African Studies Department at California State University, Los Angeles.

Havel, Václav (b. 1936)

Czechoslovakia's foremost contemporary dramatist and an outspoken critic of the former government, Václav Havel was censored, arrested, and harassed for twenty years following the Soviet invasion of Prague in 1968. Banned from the stage, Havel continued to agitate for political reform and refused to immigrate to the West. Following months of popular unrest, in 1989 Havel was elected president of the first noncommunist government of Czechoslovakia in over forty years. Even during the 1970s when his work could only be performed in private homes, Havel has never avoided including political messages in his plays, which tend to deal with universal themes. He started his theater career as a stagehand at the prestigous Theater on the Balustrade in 1960 and rose through various positions to resident playwright in 1968. Before the Soviet invasion Havel wrote a number of plays that have been translated into English: *The Garden Party* (1963, trans. 1969), *The Memorandum* (1965, trans. 1967), and *The Increased Difficulty of Concentration* (1968, trans. 1972). The short plays Havel wrote during the 1970s have been performed collectively in the West under the title *A Private View*; he is also the author of *Largo Desolato* (1986) and *Temptation* (1988). His essay "Words on Words" appeared in the *New York Review of Books* in 1989.

Hayakawa, S. I. (b. 1906)
Samuel Ichiye Hayakawa was born in Canada and earned his B.A. and M.A. degrees at Canadian universities. He earned his Ph.D. from the University of Wisconsin in 1935. A naturalized United States citizen, he has taught English at the University of Wisconsin, the University of Chicago, and San Francisco State University, where he also served as president. From 1977 to 1983 Hayakawa was a member of the U. S. Senate; since his retirement from the Senate he has campaigned to make English the official language of the United States. Hayakawa has written and edited many books on language. His first book, *Language in Action* (1941), was a best-seller. It has been revised and published as *Language in Thought and Action* (1949), and has been reissued in four editions; "Words with Built-in Judgements" appears in the 1972 edition. Hayakawa also contributes to the *New Republic*, *Harper's*, *Poetry*, *Sewanee Review*, and other periodicals. He is founder and from 1943 to 1970 was editor of *ETC: A Review of General Semantics*.

Ho Chi Minh (1890–1969)
Born Nguyen Sinh Cung, Ho Chi Minh changed his name many times to confound the security systems of the French during his lifetime struggle against colo-

nialism in Vietnam. His political ideology was strongly influenced by the progressive intellectuals and activists he encountered in France, England, and the United States, where he lived in the 1910s and 1920s. Ho Chi Minh became a journalist in Paris for the socialist newspaper *Le Populaire* and the communist newspaper *L'Humanité*, and he started anticolonial newspapers as well. In 1923 he visited Moscow for the first time and expanded his ties to the international communist movement. During the Japanese occupation of Vietnam during World War II, Ho Chi Minh lived on Vietnam's northern border, biding his time and helping to organize the Vietminh as a political and military force. After Japan's surrender, the Vietminh seized territory in northern Vietnam, and in the document reprinted here, Ho Chi Minh declared Vietnam independent. The French tried to stamp out the independence movement, but were decisively defeated at Dien Bien Phu in 1954. The Geneva Conference the same year split the nation into north and south, but the war continued and despite Ho Chi Minh's repeated offers to negotiate, the United States gradually increased its military intervention in support of the pro-Western southern government. Ho Chi Minh died of a heart attack before the war was concluded.

hooks, bell (b. 1952)
Gloria Watkins, who writes under the pseudonym "bell hooks," teaches at Oberlin College. She contributes regularly to *Zeta Mag-*

azine and has written several books including *And There We Slept: Poems* (1978), *Ain't I a Woman: Black Women and Feminism* (1981), *Feminist Theory from Margin to Center* (1984), and *Talking Back: Thinking Feminist, Thinking Black* (1989), in which "Feminism: a Transformational Politic" is found.

Hughes, Langston (1902–1967)

One of the leading figures of the Harlem Renaissance, Langston Hughes was a prolific writer. He started his career as a poet, but also wrote fiction, autobiography, biography, history, and plays, as well as working at various times as a journalist. One of his most famous poems, "The Negro Speaks of Rivers," was written while he was a high school student. Although Langston Hughes traveled widely, most of his writings are concerned with the lives of urban working-class African Americans. Hughes used the rhythms of blues and jazz to bring to his writing a distinctive expression of black culture and experience. His work continues to be popular today, especially such collections of short stories as *The Ways of White Folks* (1934), such volumes of poetry as *Montage of a Dream Deferred* (1951), and his series of vignettes on the character Jesse B. Simple, collected and published from 1950 to 1965. Hughes published two volumes of autobiography; "Salvation" is taken from the first of these, *The Big Sea* (1940).

Jacoby, Susan (b. 1946)

Susan Jacoby has been an education reporter for the *Washington Post* and has contributed to the "Hers" column in the *New York Times*. The essay "Unfair Game" appeared in the *Times* in 1978. She began to write and publish books after spending 1969 to 1971 as a free-lance writer in the U.S.S.R. Her insights and experiences of those years are recorded in *Moscow Conversations* (1972), *The Friendship Barrier* (1972), and *Inside Soviet Schools* (1974). An Alicia Patterson Fellowship enabled Jacoby to publish a collection of essays, *The Possible She* (1979).

Jefferson, Thomas (1743–1826)

Thomas Jefferson was born and raised in Virginia, and attended William and Mary College. After being admitted to the bar he entered politics and served in the Virginia House of Burgesses and the Continental Congress of 1775. During the Revolutionary War he was elected governor of Virginia, and after independence was appointed special minister to France and later secretary of state. As the nation's third president he negotiated the Louisiana Purchase. Of all his accomplishments as an inventor, architect, diplomat, scientist, and politician, Jefferson counted his work in designing the University of Virginia among the most important, along with his efforts to establish separation of church and state and the composition of the Declaration of Independence.

Johnson, Mark (b. 1949)

Mark Johnson earned his Ph.D. in philosophy from the University of Chicago in 1977. Currently, he is professor of philosophy at Southern Illinois

University at Carbondale, and his research interests include recent moral theory and the theory of the imagination. He has published articles in several scholarly journals including the *Journal of Aesthetics and Art Criticism*, the *Journal of Philosophy*, and *Cognitive Science*. He is the co-author with George Lakoff of *Metaphors We Live By* (1980).

Jordan, June (b. 1936)

June Jordan taught at the City College of the City University of New York, Sarah Lawrence College, and the State University of New York at Stony Brook before going to the University of California at Berkeley, where she is professor of Afro-American studies and women's studies. She is the author of novels, short stories, poetry, children's fiction, and biography. Her essays can be found in such collections as *Civil Wars* (1981), *On Call* (1986), and *Moving Toward Home: Political Essays* (1989). The essay "Nobody Mean More to Me than You and the Future Life of Willie Jordan" is found in *On Call*; "Waiting for a Taxi" appeared in the *Progressive* in 1989. She has also published stories and poems in numerous national magazines, ncluding *Esquire*, *Black World*, the *Nation*, the *Partisan Review*, *Essence*, and the *Village Voice*. Her numerous honors include fellowships from the National Endowment for the Arts and the New York Foundation for the Arts. Toni Cade Bambara remarks that "as a poet, novelist, journalist, scenarist, urban designer, and teacher—June Jordan has always worked hard to keep before us

the essential questions of life, death, choice, and honor. She has done it *not* from the relatively safe vantage point the writer's desk affords, but always from the danger zone, in the heated thick of things."

Kincaid, Jamaica (b. 1949)

Jamaica Kincaid was born in Antigua and immigrated to the United States. She has been a contributor and staff writer for the *New Yorker* since 1976. The story "Girl" comes from her collection of stories *At the Bottom of the River* (1984), which won the Morton Dauwen Zabel Award from the American Academy and Institute of Arts and Letters. She has also published *Annie John* (1985) and *A Small Place* (1988). Commenting on her stories, David Leavitt says that "Kincaid's particular skill lies in her ability to articulate the internal workings of a potent imagination without sacrificing the rich details of the external world on which that imagination thrives."

King, Martin Luther, Jr. (1929–1968)

Martin Luther King, Jr., was born in Atlanta, Georgia, and after training for the ministry became pastor of the Dexler Avenue Baptist Church in Montgomery, Alabama. He became active in the civil rights movement in 1956 when he was elected president of the Montgomery Improvement Association, the group which organized a transportation boycott in response to the arrest of Rosa Parks. King later became president of the Southern Christian Leadership Conference, and under his philosophy of nonviolent direct action he led marches and protests throughout the South, to Chicago, and to Washington, D.C. In 1963 King delivered his most famous speech, "I Have a Dream," before 200,000 people in front of the Lincoln Memorial in Washington, D.C., and in 1964 he was awarded the Nobel Peace Prize. King was assassinated on April 3, 1968, in Memphis, Tennessee. Martin Luther King was a masterful orator and a powerful writer. As well as his many speeches, King wrote several books, including *Why We Can't Wait* (1964), *Where Do We Go From Here: Chaos or Community?* (1967), *The Measure of a Man* (1968), and *Trumpet of Conscience* (1968).

Kingston, Maxine Hong (b. 1940)
Both of the selections reprinted here come from Maxine Hong Kingston's first book, *The Woman Warrior: Memoirs of a Girlhood Among Ghosts* (1976), which won the National Book Critics Circle Award for nonfiction. *Time* magazine named this book one of the top ten nonfiction works of the 1970s. In 1981 Kingston won the American Book Award for *China Men* (1980), and she has also received acclaim for her most recent book, *Tripmaster Monkey* (1989). Kingston is the recipient of the *Mademoiselle* award (1977), an NEA writing fellowship (1980), and a Guggenheim fellowship (1981). Her poems, short stories, and articles have appeared in numerous national. magazines, including the *New York Times Magazine, New West, Ms.*, the *New Yorker*, and *Iowa Review*. Kingston has taught at high schools in California and Hawaii and at the University of Hawaii, Eastern Michigan University and, most recently, the University of California at Berkeley.

Kowinski, William
William Kowinski studied at Knox College and spent one semester at the University of Iowa writers workshop. Since completing his B.A., he has been a writer and editor for the Boston *Phoenix* and the Washington *Newsworks*. Kowinski's articles appear in such national magazines as *Esquire, American Film, New Times*, and the *New York Times Magazine*. The selection "Kids in the Mall: Growing Up Controlled" is from his 1985 book *The Malling of America: An Inside Look at the Great Consumer Paradise*.

Kozol, Jonathan (b. 1936)
Jonathan Kozol is a writer and social critic who has worked extensively in education, especially the education of underpriviliged children. He won the National Book Award in 1967 for *Death at an Early Age*. Other publications include *Alternative Schools: A Guide for Educators and Parents* (1982), *Prisoners of Silence: Breaking the Bonds of Adult Illiteracy in the United States* (1980), and *Rachael and Her Children; Homeless Families in America* (1988). The essay "Distancing the Homeless" is adapted from the last-mentioned work and appeared in the *Yale Review* in its present form. Kozol has been a Saxton Fellow in creative writing, and has received other fellowships from the Guggenheim, Field, Ford, and Rockefeller foundations.

Lakoff, George (b. 1941)
George Lakoff earned his Ph.D. in linguistics from Indiana University in 1966. He has taught linguistics at the University of Michigan and Harvard University and is currently professor of linguistics at the University of California at Berkeley. In addition to articles in scholarly journals, his publications include *Pronouns and Reference* (1968), *Deep and Surface Grammar* (1968), *On Generative Semantics* (1969), *Irregularity in Syntax* (1970), and *Women, Fire, and Dangerous Things: What Categories Reveal about the Mind* (1987). He wrote *Metaphors We Live By* (1980) with the philosopher Mark Johnson.

Leavitt, David (b. 1961)
Born in California, David Leavitt attended Yale University, from which he graduated in 1983. He won an O. Henry Prize in 1984 for his story "Counting Months." His stories have appeared in the *New Yorker* and *Harper's*, and have been collected in *Family Dancing* (1984), which was nominated for a National Book Critics Circle Award and a PEN/Faulkner Award. The story which is reprinted here, "Territory," appears in *Family Dancing*. His other work includes the novels *The Lost Language of Cranes* (1986), *Equal Affections* (1989), and the story collection *A Place I've Never Been* (1990).

Lin Yutang (1895–1976)
Educated at St. Johns College, Harvard University, and the University of Leipzig, Lin Yutang wrote novels as well as nonfiction accounts of modern China. He was also a renowned pro-

fessor and university administrator, starting his career at Peking National University and crowning it as Chancellor of Nanyang University in Singapore. Lin Yutang lived in the West for many years, and served as the head of UNESCO's arts and letters division in 1948 and 1949. He thought his most lasting achievement to be his Chinese/English dictionary of modern usage. In his career Lin Yutang strove to bridge gaps between cultures, and he is perhaps best remembered as the author of *My Country and My People* (1935) and *The Importance of Living* (1937), two nonfiction works which describe China for western readers. "The Art of Reading" is taken from *The Importance of Living*.

Lippmann, Walter (1889–1974)
Walter Lippmann was educated at Harvard under the instruction of George Santayana and William James, and counted John Reed and T. S. Eliot among his friends and classmates. After graduation he joined the staff of *Everybody's Magazine* and began to write his own books. Over the course of the following sixty years Lippmann wrote dozens of books dealing with United States politics and foreign affairs. Together with Herbert Croly he cofounded the *New Republic* in 1914, but left the magazine to work for the federal government, where he was asked to help write President Wilson's "Fourteen Points." After World War I, Lippmann wrote columns for the *New York World* and the *New York Herald Tribune* that were syndicated to 275 papers around the world. "The Indispensable

Opposition" appeared in the *Atlantic Monthly* in 1939. By the opening of World War II, Lippmann was regarded with such high respect that when traveling abroad he was treated as a visiting dignitary. His numerous honors include the rank of Commander of the Legion of Honor in both France and Belgium, the Knight's Cross of the Order of St. Olav from Norway, Commander of the Order of Orange Nassau from the Netherlands, two Pulitzer Prizes (1958 and 1962), and a Presidential Medal of Freedom (1964).

Lopez, Barry (b. 1945)

Barry Lopez writes on nature and the environment, using both fiction and nonfiction to convey the mystery and beauty of, for example, arctic wolves. A frequent contributor to such newspapers and periodicals as the *New York Times*, the *Washington Post*, *National Geographic*, and *Antaeus*, Lopez is also the author of several books. He is currently a contributing editor to *Harper's* and *North American Review*. "The Stone Horse" appeared in *Antaeus* in 1986. In 1979 he received the John Burroughs Medal, in 1982 he was recognized by the Friends of American Writers with an award for fiction, and in 1986 he received an award in literature from the American Academy and Institute of Arts and Letters. His publications include *Of Wolves and Men* (1978), *Winter Count* (1981), and *Arctic Dreams* (1986).

Mairs, Nancy (b. 1943)

Nancy Mairs has contributed poetry, short stories, articles, and essays to numerous journals. The collection of her essays from which "A Letter to Matthew," comes, *Plaintext*, was published in 1986. She is currently working on a memoir, *House Bound: An Erotics of Place and Space*. From 1983–1985 she served as assistant director of the Southwest Institute for Research on Women in Tucson, and has also taught at the University of Arizona and at UCLA. Nancy Mairs was a William P. Sloan Fellow in nonfiction (1984) and received the Western States Book Award in 1984.

Marshall, Paule (b. 1929)

Paule Marshall's family immigrated to New York from Barbados shortly before she was born, and the themes and language of her work are influenced by her Caribbean heritage. Author of novels and short stories, Paule Marshall's books include *Brown Girl, Brownstones* (1959), *Soul Clap Hands and Sing* (1961), *The Chosen Place, The Timeless People* (1969), *Reena and Other Stories* (1983), and *Praisesong for the Widow* (1983). She also contributes to the *New York Times Book Review*, in which "From the Poets in the Kitchen" appeared in 1983. Marshall has lectured on creative writing and black literature at many universities, including Yale, Oxford, Columbia, Michigan State, and Cornell. Her honors include a Guggenheim Fellowship (1960), a Rosenthal Award from the National Institute of Arts and Letters (1962), a Ford Foundation grant (1964–65), a National Endowment for the Arts grant (1967–68), and a Before Columbus

Foundation American Book Award (1984).

McCarthy, Mary (b. 1912)
Mary McCarthy has held the Stevenson Chair in Literature at Bard College since 1986. She taught at Bard and Sarah Lawrence in the 1940s and for many years worked as editor and drama critic for the *Partisan Review*. Her short stories and essays have appeared in many national magazines, and she has published over twenty books, including novels and autobiography. Her nonfiction includes *Vietnam* (1967), *Hanoi*, (1968), *The Writing on the Wall* (1970), *Medina* (1972), *Occasional Prose* (1985), and *How I Grew* (1987). The present selection is taken from *Memories of a Catholic Girlhood* (1957). Mary McCarthy's professional honors include two Guggenheim Fellowships (1949, 1959), a Horizon Prize (1949), an Edward McDowell Medal (1984), and a National Medal for Literature (1984).

Momaday, N. Scott (b. 1934)
N. Scott Momaday was born on a Kiowa Indian reservation in Oklahoma and grew up surrounded by the cultural traditions of the Kiowa people. He earned his B.A. from the University of New Mexico in 1958 and his Ph.D. from Stanford University in 1963. Momaday has taught at the University of California at Santa Barbara and at Berkeley, and at Stanford University. Since 1982, he has been professor of English at the University of Arizona. His first novel, *House Made of Dawn* (1968), won a Pulitzer Prize. Momaday is also the au-

thor of poetry and autobiography, and has edited a collection of Kiowa oral literature. He contributes regularly to the *New York Times Book Review* and other national periodicals; "A First American Views His Land" was published in *National Geographic* in 1976. Wallace Stegner observes that "Momaday has not invented himself, as many Americans have tried to do. He has let the blood speak, looked for tracks, listened and remembered . . . He has pieced together a tradition and created his ancestors . . . They empty like feeder streams into the river of his sensibility and awareness. He comes out of them." Among other honors, Momaday has been awarded an Academy of American Poets Prize (1962), a Guggenheim Fellowship (1966–67), and a National Institute of Arts and Letters grant (1970).

Morris, Desmond (b. 1928)
A British zoologist, Desmond Morris is best known for his research and writing on human behavior. In the late 1950s Morris was a film-maker at the London Zoo, and he went on to become curator of mammals for the Zoological Society. He is also an artist and was at one time the director of London's Institute of Contemporary Arts. Presently he holds a research fellowship at Oxford. In addition to his scholarly publications, Morris is author of *The Naked Ape* (1967), *The Human Zoo* (1970), *Intimate Behaviour* (1972), *Manwatching* (from which "Territorial Behavior" is taken, 1977), and *Animal Days* (1980).

Mukherjee, Bharati (b. 1940)
Born in India, Bharati Mukherjee has lived in Canada and the United States for over thirty years. She has taught at McGill University and Columbia University and is currently professor of English at the University of California at Berkeley. A collection of her short stories, *The Middleman and Other Stories*, won the 1988 National Book Critics Circle Award. The story "Fathering" can be found in this collection. She has also written the novels *The Tiger's Daughter* (1972), *Wife* (1975), and *Jasmine* (1989). Her nonfiction works include *Days and Nights in Calcutta* (1977) and *The Sorrow and the Terror* (1987), both coauthored with her husband, Clark Blaise. Mukherjee has received awards from the Guggenheim Foundation, Canada Arts Council, and the Canadian government.

Naylor, Gloria (b. 1950)
Gloria Naylor's first novel, *The Women of Brewster Place* (1982), won an American Book Award. Her other works of fiction include *Linden Hills* (1985) and *Mama Day* (1988), and her nonfiction has been published in *Centennial* (1986). In addition to these books, Naylor contributes essays and articles to many periodicals, including *Southern Review*, *Essence*, *Ms.*, *Life*, *Callaloo*, and the *Ontario Review*. Naylor holds an M.A. in Afro-American studies from Yale University. She has worked as the "Hers" columnist for the *New York Times* and as a visiting professor and writer at Princeton University, New York University, the University of Pennsylvania, Boston University, and Brandeis University. In addition, Naylor was a cultural exchange lecturer in India in 1985 and a senior fellow at the Society for the Humanities, Cornell University, in 1988. The article "A Question of Language" first appeared in the *New York Times* in 1986.

Njeri, Itabari
Itabari Njeri won the American Book Award for her 1990 book *Every Good-bye Ain't Gone: Family Portraits and Personal Escapades*, from which "Grandaddy' is taken. Before she became a writer, Njeri was a singer, and was named best new pop vocalist of 1969 by MGM Records. Her political commitments led Njeri to become a journalist in the 1970s, and she earned degrees in communications and journalsim from Boston University and Columbia University. Njeri has published articles and essays in *Harper's*, *Essence*, and other national magazines; currently, she writes for the *Los Angeles Times*, where she specializes in immigration issues and cultural diversity. Her numerous awards include an Associated Press Award, two UNITY Awards, and the Los Angeles Press Club Certificate of Excellence.

Noda, Kesaya E. (b. 1950)
Kesaya Noda was born in California and raised in New Hampshire. She began to study Japanese after graduating from high school, and spent eighteen months living and studying in Japan. After finishing college, Noda wrote her first book, *The*

Yamato Colony (1981), a history of the community in California where her grandparents settled and where her parents grew up. "Growing Up Asian in America" is found in *Making Waves*, an anthology of Asian-American writing. Noda holds a master's degree from Harvard Divinity School and is currently working toward her doctorate in religious studies at Harvard University.

Oates, Joyce Carol (b. 1938)

Joyce Carol Oates is one of the most prolific contemporary American writers; her novels, short stories, poems, and essays fill over four dozen volumes. John Updike observes of Oates that "not since Faulkner has an American writer seemed so mesmerized by a field of imaginary material, and so headstrong in the cultivation of that field." She began to write as a child, and received her first major award in 1959 when *Mademoiselle* published "In the Old World" as part of their annual college fiction competition. Her third novel, *them*, won the National Book Award in 1970. In 1967 and 1968 she was a Guggenheim Fellow, and the same year she received an O. Henry Prize. Oates also contributes regularly to national magazines; the article "Shopping" appeared in *Ms.* in 1987. Her essays can be found in *The Edge of Impossibility* (1971), *New Heaven, New Earth* (1974), *Contraries: Essays* (1981), and *The Profane Art: Essays and Reviews* (1983). She is writer-in-residence at Princeton University, and together with her husband Raymond Smith operates the On-

tario Review Press and publishes the literary magazine *The Ontario Review*.

Orwell, George (1903–1950)

George Orwell was born Eric Arthur Blair in Bengal, India, the son of a colonial administrator. He was sent to England for his education, and attended Eton on a scholarship, but rather than go on to university in 1922 he returned to the East and served with the Indian Imperial Police in Burma. Orwell hated his work and the colonial system; published posthumuously, the essay "Shooting an Elephant" was based on his experience in Burma. The essay "Politics and the English Language," although first published in 1946, is found in the same collection, *Shooting an Elephant and Other Essays* (1950). In 1927 Orwell returned to England and began a career as a professional writer. He served briefly in the Spanish Civil War until he was wounded, then settled in Hertfordshire. Best remembered for his novels *Animal Farm* (1945) and *Nineteen Eighty-Four* (1949), Orwell also wrote articles, essays, and reviews, usually with a political point in mind. In 1969 Irving Howe honored Orwell as "the best English essayist since Hazlitt, perhaps since Dr. Johnson. He was the greatest moral force in English letters during the last several decades: craggy, fiercely polemical, sometimes mistaken, but an utterly free man."

Paley, Grace (b. 1922)

Grace Paley is a political activist and a teacher as well as a writer.

During the 1960s she gained prominence for traveling to Hanoi and Moscow with peace delegations, and for speaking out while in Moscow against human rights abuses in the Soviet Union. Her story "The Loudest Voice" comes from her first collection of stories, *The Little Disturbances of Man* (1959). Paley's stories appear in *Esquire*, the *Atlantic*, *Accent*, and *Ikon*, among other magazines. They are collected in *Enormous Changes at the Last Minute* (1974), and *Later the Same Day* (1985). Vivian Gornick remarks that "Paley is the ultimate New Yorker. She is to New York what William Faulkner is to Mississippi. Her pages are alive with the sounds of the savvy, street-smart New Yorker, and every character . . . knows his lines to perfection." In 1988 Paley was elected the first New York State Author by the state legislature; she has also received awards from the Guggenheim Foundation and the National Institute of Arts and Letters. Currently, Paley teaches at Sarah Lawrence College.

Percy, Walker (1916–1990)
Walker Percy received his M.D. in 1941 and began a career practicing and teaching medicine shortly thereafter. However, as a resident physician he contracted tuberculosis, and the disease changed the course of his life. During his recovery he read extensively in literature, philosophy, and theology, and this reading program became the basis for a new career of reading and writing. His first novel, *The Moviegoer* (1961), won a National

Book Award. He wrote a number of other novels, including *The Thanatos Syndrome* (1987), as well as works of nonfiction such as *Lost in the Cosmos* (1983) and *The Message in the Bottle* (1975). The latter work contains the essay "The Loss of the Creature." The critic Alfred Kazin called Percy a "philosopher among novelists," and commented that there "is a singularity to his life, to his manifest search for a new religious humanism, there is a closeness to pain and extreme situations, that makes him extraordinarily 'sensitive'—to the existentialist theme of life as shipwreck—without suggesting weakness."

Plato (c. 428–348 B.C.)
A student of Socrates and teacher of Aristotle, Plato is one of the three philosophers who stand at the center of the Western intellectual tradition. Born into a prominent Athenian family, Plato might have been expected to pursue a political career, but was instead inspired by Socrates to devote his life to philosophy and education. Plato believed that politicians would be incapable of establishing social justice until philosophers became rulers or rulers philosophers. He founded the Academy, the first Western institution dedicated to philosophical inquiry and teaching and the precursor of the modern university. Plato wrote in the form of dialogues, over twenty of which have survived and continue to be read today. The myth reprinted here is taken from the *Symposium*.

Poe, Edgar Allan (1809–1849)
Born the son of wandering actors, Edgar Poe was orphaned at the age of two when his drunkard father abandoned the family and his mother died. He was informally adopted into the wealthy Allan family in Richmond, Virginia, and enjoyed the privileges of European travel and the best education. While a student at the University of Virginia, Poe had a disagreement with his guardians and ran away to Boston, where he published his first poems. Eventually, the rift with his adopted family was repaired long enough for Poe to agree to enter West Point, but Poe disliked military education and was soon dismissed. Cut off from the wealth of the Allans, Poe was determined to make a living by writing and editing, and although he was successful at both, he never earned enough money to live comfortably. *Tales of the Grotesque and Arabesque* was published in 1840 to popular acclaim, and in 1843 "The Tell-Tale Heart" was published in *Pioneer* magazine. By 1845 Poe's career reached its peak with the publication of *The Raven and Other Poems*. His fans included Fyodor Dostoyevsky, who remarked that "there exists one characteristic that is singularly peculiar to Poe and which distinguishes him from every other writer, and that is the vigor of his imagination." However, Poe continued to have problems in his personal life, including drinking problems, and in 1847 his wife died. The last two years of Poe's life were spent writing and lecturing almost frantically, and then in 1849 he mysteriously got off his Philadelphia-bound train in Baltimore and was found nearly dead in the street. He died in the hospital.

Reagon, Bernice Johnson
Bernice Johnson Reagon was active in the civil rights movement during the 1960s, when she was a member of the Student Non-violent Coordinating Committee Freedom Singers. She has worked as a singer and a composer and is currently a curator at the Smithsonian's Museum of American History. In 1973 Reagon founded the African-American women's vocal group Sweet Honey in the Rock, and she continues to tour with this internationally renowned group. "Nurturing Resistance" appeared in *Reimaging America: The Arts of Social Change* in 1990.

Reed, Ishmael (b. 1938)
Ishmael Reed is a prolific writer who also finds time to support and encourage other writers; he has helped establish and manage the Yardbird Publishing Company, Reed, Cannon & Johnson (a publishing and video production company), and the Before Columbus Foundation, which supports the work of ethnic writers. He has also taught at Yale, Dartmouth, Columbia, and Harvard, and currently teaches at the University of California at Berkeley. Reed's work has been nominated for National Book Awards in both fiction (*Mumbo Jumbo*, 1972) and poetry (*Conjure: Selected Poems*, 1972). His recent novels include *Flight to Canada* (1976), *The Terrible Twos* (1982), *Reckless Eyeballing* (1986), and *The*

Terrible Threes (1989). His essays are collected in *Shrovetide in Old New Orleans* (1978), and *God Made Alaska for the Indians* (1982), and he is editor of *Writin' Is Fightin'* (1988). His essay "America: The Multinational Society" appears in *The Graywolf Annual Five: Multicultural Literacy* (1988). Reed has received awards from the National Institute of Arts and Letters (1975), the ACLU (1978), the National Endowment for the Arts (three publishing grants), the Guggenheim Foundation (1974), and the Studio Museum in Harlem, which awarded him the Lewis H. Michaux Literary Prize (1978).

Rich, Adrienne (b. 1929)
Adrienne Rich's work has appeared in numerous volumes of poetry and in several anthologies. She received her first award for poetry, a Yale Series of Younger Poets Award, while a student at Radcliffe College in 1951. Since then Adrienne Rich has received many other professional honors, including a National Institute of Arts and Letters Award (1961), a National Book Award (1974), and a Fund for Human Dignity Award from the National Gay Task Force (1981). Adrienne Rich's poetics are informed by her political work against the oppression of women and against homophobia, and her critics charge her with being overly polemical. As Margaret Atwood points out, however, Rich's politics do not limit her artistry for she "is not just one of America's best feminist poets or one of America's best woman poets, she is one of

America's best poets . . . she is eloquent, she convinces, and inspires." Besides poetry, Rich's publications include *Of Woman Born: Motherhood as Experience and Institution* (1976), *On Lies, Secrets and Silence: Selected Prose, 1966–1978* (1979), and *Blood, Bread and Poetry: Selected Prose* (1986), from which "Split at the Root" is excerpted. She has taught at many colleges and universities and since 1986 has been professor of English and Feminist Studies at Stanford University.

Rodriguez, Richard (b. 1944)
Richard Rodriguez earned his B.A. from Stanford University and did graduate work at Columbia University, the Warburg Institute in London, and the University of California at Berkeley, where he completed his Ph.D. in English Renaissance literature. Rodriguez has contributed articles to many magazines and newspapers, including *Harpers, Saturday Review, Neustro, American Scholar*, the *Los Angeles Times*, and the *New York Times*, in which "Toward an American Language" (published under a different title) appeared in 1989. His most sensational literary accomplishment, however, is his autobiography, *Hunger of Memory: The Education of Richard Rodriguez* (1981). In it, Rodriguez outlines his positions on such issues as bilingualism, affirmative action, and assimilation, and concludes that current policies in these areas are misguided and only serve to reinforce current social inequalities. Rodriguez has been honored with a Fulbright Fellowship (1972–73) and a National

Endowment for the Humanities Fellowship (1976–77). Currently, he works as an educational consultant, lecturer, and free-lance writer.

Roiphe, Anne Richardson (b. 1935)
Anne Roiphe earned her B.A. from Sarah Lawrence College in 1957 and has made a career of writing novels and psychology. Under the name of Anne Richardson she has published *Digging Out* (1967) and *Torch Song* (1977); under Anne Roiphe she has written *Up the Sandbox!* (1970), *Long Division* (1972), *Lovingkindness* (1987), and *A Season for Healing* (1988). With Herman Roiphe she has coauthored *Your Child's Mind* (1986). "The WASP Sting" appeared in *Present Tense* in 1989.

Rose, Phyllis (b. 1942)
Phyllis Rose is perhaps best known by the reading public for her book reviews and essays, which appear in the *Nation*, the *Atlantic*, the *Washington Post*, and the *New York Times*; "Shopping and Other Spiritual Adventures" appeared in the *Times* in 1984. Rose is also the author of a biography of Virginia Woolf, of *Parallel Lives* (1983), and *Jazz Cleopatra* (1989). She has taught at Harvard, Yale, and Berkeley, and since 1976 has been professor of English at Wesleyan University. Phyllis Rose was an NEH fellow in 1973 and 1974, a Rockefeller Fellow in 1984 and 1985, and a Guggenheim Fellow in 1985.

Roth, Philip (b. 1933)
Philip Roth grew up in New Jersey and studied at Rutgers University and the University of Chicago, where he earned an M.A. in 1955. His first book, *Goodbye, Columbus, and Five Short Stories* (1959), won a National Book Award. Since that time, Roth has published over a dozen novels and collections of short stories, as well as nonfiction. He writes about baseball in *The Great American Novel* (1973); "My Baseball Years" appears in *Reading Myself and Others* (1975). Roth has taught at the University of Chicago, the University of Iowa, and the State University of New York at Stony Brook, as well as serving as writer-in-residence at Princeton University and the University of Pennsylvania. He is a regular contributor to such national magazines as *Esquire*, *Harper's*, the *New Yorker*, *Commentary*, and the *Paris Review*. The appeal of Roth's writing is attested to by Joyce Carol Oates, who comments that "Roth's best work, so far, has transformed intense private experience into fiction that speaks for its era, no matter how eccentric the basic metaphor of the words might be." Roth is a member of the National Institute of Arts and Letters and has received grants from the Guggenheim and Ford foundations. His recent books include *The Counterlife* (1987) and *The Facts* (1988).

Safire, William (b. 1929)
William Safire began his career in journalism as a reporter for the *New York Herald Tribune* in 1949 and served as a correspondent for WNBC-WNBT in Europe and the Middle East in 1951. During the 1960s he worked in public relations, and

in 1968 became a chief speech writer for President Nixon. When Nixon resigned, Safire left the White House for the *New York Times*, where he writes the "Essay" column twice a week and the "On Language" column for the *Time*'s Sunday magazine. "On Keeping a Diary" appeared in the *Times* in 1974. Safire's columns are syndicated to over five hundred newspapers across the country and have earned him a Pulitzer Prize for distinguished commentary (1978). He is also the author of several books, including *Good Advice* (1982), *I Stand Corrected* (1984), *Take My Word for It* (1986), and a novel, *Freedom* (1987).

Sanders, Scott Russell (b. 1945)
Scott Russell Sanders writes in a variety of genres: science fiction, realistic fiction, folktales, children's stories, essays, and historical novels. In all his work, however, he is concerned with the ways in which people live in communities. Some of his more recent books include *Stone Country* (1986), *Bad Man Ballad* (1986), and *The Paradise of Bombs* (1987), from which "The Men We Carry in Our Minds" is excerpted. Sanders also contributes to both literary and popular magazines such as *North American Review*, *Georgia Review*, *Omni*, *Transatlantic Review*, and *New Dimensions*. For many years he wrote a column for the *Chicago-Sun Times*. Professor of English at Indiana University, Sanders has been honored as a Woodrow Wilson Fellow (1976–78), a Marshall Scholar (1967–71), a Bennett Fellow in creative writing (1974–

75), and a National Endowment for the Arts Fellow (1983–84).

Selzer, Richard (b. 1928)
Before leaving medicine to become a writer, Richard Selzer spent fifteen years teaching surgery at the Yale School of Medicine and running a private surgical practice. Selzer has published several books, including *Confessions of a Knife* (1979), *Letters to a Young Doctor* (1982), and *Taking the World in for Repairs* (1986). His essays have appeared in *Harper's, Esquire* (where "What I Saw at the Abortion" appeared in 1976), *Antaeus*, and many other magazines.

Sontag, Susan (b. 1933)
Widely recognized as one of America's leading intellectuals, Susan Sontag has written a variety of works of fiction and nonfiction, as well as teaching at several universities and directing films and plays. She established her reputation as an essayist early in her career with the collection *Against Interpretation* (1966). Her more recent essays can be found in *Illness as Metaphor* (1978), *Under the Sign of Saturn* (1980), and *AIDS and Its Metaphors* (1989), from which the selection reprinted here is excerpted. In 1978 she won the National Book Critics Circle Award for the six essays collected in *On Photography* (1976) and in 1990 she was awarded a MacArthur Foundation "genius grant."

Spretnak, Charlene
A writer and editor, Charlene Spretnak holds degrees from St. Louis University and the Univer-

sity of California at Berkeley. She is the coauthor, with Fritjof Capra, of *Green Politics* (1984) and the author of *Lost Goddesses of Early Greece* (1978) and *The Spiritual Dimension of Green Politics* (1986). "Ecofeminism: Our Roots and Flowering" comes from *Reweaving the World: The Emergence of Ecofeminism* (1990). Spretnak also contributes to *Anima*. She is the founder of the Feminist Writers Guild, and cofounder of the Green Committees of Correspondence.

Stanton, Elizabeth Cady (1815–1902)
An orator, journalist, and advocate for women's rights, Elizabeth Cady Stanton worked closely with Susan B. Anthony in the campaign for suffrage. Stanton and Anthony published the magazine *Revolution* from 1868 to 1869 and the three-volume *History of Woman Suffrage* (1881–86). Her own writings include *The Woman's Bible* (2 vols., 1895, 1898), which interprets an exhaustive number of Biblical passages from a woman's point of view, and her autobiography, *Eighty Years and More* (1898). In 1848 Stanton helped organize a convention in Seneca Falls, New York, to address the rights of women. Her "Declaration of Sentiments and Resolutions," amended and adopted by the Seneca Falls Convention, became the platform for the women's movement in the United States. Stanton went on to serve as president of the National Woman Suffrage Association.

Staples, Brent (b. 1951)
Brent Staples earned his B.A. from Widener University in 1973

and his Ph.D. in psychology from the University of Chicago in 1982, and has made his career in journalism. When he lived in Chicago, Staples wrote for *Chicago Magazine*, the *Chicago Reader*, and *Down Beat Magazine*. He also contributes to *Harper's*, *New York Woman*, the *New York Times Magazine*, and *Ms.*, in which "Just Walk on By" appeared in 1986. Since 1990 he has been on the editorial board of the *New York Times*, and currently he is writing his autobiography.

Steele, Shelby (b. 1946)
Shelby Steele earned his Ph.D. from the University of Utah in 1974, and is currently professor of English at San Jose State University. He has contributed articles and reviews to such periodicals as *Confrontation*, *Black World*, *Harper's*, and the *Western Humanities Review*. Steele's writings on race relations in the United States have placed him in the center of the national debate on affirmative action and other issues. "On Being Black and Middle Class" appeared in *Commentary* in 1988. Recently, Steele published his first book, *The Content of Our Character: A New Vision of Race in America* (1990).

Steinem, Gloria (b. 1934)
One of America's most prominent activists for women's rights, Gloria Steinem is the founding editor of *Ms.* magazine and has worked for many political organizations, including the National Women's Political Caucus, the Women's Action Alliance, and the Student Non-Violent Coordinating Committee. Steinem's

writing career began before she became involved in politics with *The Thousand Indians* (1957), based on two years spent living in India. Since 1968 Steinem's writing has focused on women's issues. She has written several books as well as scripts for TV and film, and has published articles in many magazines, including *Esquire, Show, Vogue, Life,* and *Cosmopolitan.* The selection "Ruth's Song" comes from her collection of essays, *Outrageous Acts and Everyday Rebellions* (1983).

Stone, Elizabeth (b. 1946)
Elizabeth Stone teaches English and media studies at Fordham University. "Stories Make a Family" is excerpted from *Black Sheep and Kissing Cousins: How Our Family Stories Shape Us* (1989).

Suzuki, Shunryu (1905–1971)
Shunryu Suzuki came to the United States in 1959 and founded the first Soto Zen monastery in the West, the Zen Mountain Center at Tassajara. He also established the associated Zen Center in San Francisco. "Emptiness" comes from his only book, *Zen Mind, Beginner's Mind* (1989).

Swift, Jonathan (1667–1745)
Jonathan Swift was born and raised in Ireland, son of English parents. He was ordained an Anglican priest, and although as a young man he lived a literary life in London, he was appointed against his wishes to be dean of St. Patrick's Cathedral in Dublin. Swift wrote some poetry, but is remembered principally for his essays and political pamphlets, most of which were published under pseudonyms. Swift received payment for only one work in his entire life, *Gulliver's Travels* (1726), for which he earned £200. Swift's political pamphlets were very influential in his day; among other issues, he spoke out against English exploitation of the Irish. Some of Swift's more important publications include *A Tale of a Tub* (1704), *The Importance of the Guardian Considered* (1713), *The Public Spirit of the Whigs* (1714), and *A Modest Proposal* (1729).

Tan, Amy (b. 1952)
Amy Tan was born in California shortly after her parents immigrated to the United States from China. She started writing as a child and won a writing contest at age eight. As an adult, Tan made her living as a free-lance business writer for many years, but started to write fiction in 1985. In 1987 Tan traveled to China for the first time, an experience that helped shape her consciousness of both her American and Chinese identities. In 1989 Tan published her best-selling first novel, *The Joy Luck Club,* from which "Two Kinds" is excerpted.

Thomas, Lewis (b. 1913)
Lewis Thomas was trained as a pathologist at Harvard Medical School and has pursued a distinguished career as a researcher and administrator at Tulane University, Bellevue Medical Center, and Yale University Medical School. He served as president and chancellor of Memorial Sloan-Kettering Cancer Center, and more recently as professor of pathology and medicine at

Cornell University Medical School. Aside from a few poems, Thomas published mainly scientific articles and books until 1971, when he became a regular columnist for the *New England Journal of Medicine*. In 1974 his columns were collected in *The Lives of a Cell*, which became a best-seller and won an American Book Award. The essay "Natural Man" is found in this collection. In a review of *The Lives of a Cell* Joyce Carol Oates commented that the book "anticipates the kind of writing that will appear more and more frequently, as scientists take on the language of poetry in order to communicate human truths too mysterious for old-fashioned common sense." Thomas continues to write about medical and biological issues for a general audience, and has published *The Medusa and the Snail* (1979), *Late Night Thoughts on Listening to Mahler's Ninth Symphony* (1983), *The Youngest Science* (1983), and *The Lasker Awards: Four Decades of Scientific Medical Progress* (1986).

Thomson, Judith Jarvis (b. 1929)
Judith Jarvis Thomson studied at Barnard College and Cambridge University and since the 1960s has taught philosophy at the Massachusetts Institute of Technology. She is the editor of *On Being and Saying: Essays for Richard Cartwright* (1987) and the author of *Rights, Restitution, and Risk: Essays in Moral Theory* (1986) and *Self-defense and Rights* (1977). Her essays often consider the philosophical questions raised by contemporary legal and political issues. The essay "A Defense

of Abortion" appeared in *Philosophy and Public Affairs 1*.

Thoreau, Henry David (1817–1862)
Regarded today as one of the central literary figures of the nineteenth century, in his lifetime Thoreau was for the most part viewed as a talented but largely unsuccessful disciple of Ralph Waldo Emerson. In fact, although the two men held many beliefs in common, Thoreau possessed a fiercely independent intellect together with political convictions that sometimes alienated Emerson. Thoreau articulates his thoughts on political activism in the essay "Civil Disobedience" (1849), which influenced the nonviolent strategies of both Mahatma Gandhi and Martin Luther King, Jr. Despite the considerable impact of his writing on contemporary thought, it was not until the 1930s that Thoreau's masterpiece *Walden* (1845) began to be studied widely, and only more recently that the value of his other writings has been recognized. As Emerson observed, "One would say that, as Webster could never speak without an antagonist, so Henry [David Thoreau] does not feel himself except in opposition. He wants a fallacy to expose, a blunder to pillory, requires a little sense of victory, a roll of the drums, to call his powers into full exercise." In addition to philosophical and biographical essays, Thoreau wrote poetry, speeches, and natural history. Halfway through his two-year stay on Walden Pond, Thoreau took a backwoods vacation in Maine. He wrote an account of

his journey in *The Maine Woods*, which was published serially in *Sartain's Union Magazine* in 1848.

Tisdale, Sallie (b. 1957)
A writer and part-time nurse, Sallie Tisdale has written two books on the nursing profession, *The Sorcerer's Apprentice* (1986) and *Harvest Moon* (1987). She also contributes articles to *Harper's*, in which "Neither Morons Nor Imbeciles Nor Idiots" appeared in 1990. Her most recent book is *Lot's Wife: Salt and the Human Condition* (1988).

Tocqueville, Alexis de (1805–1859)
In 1831 the young French aristocrat Alexis de Tocqueville arrived in the United States to study the American prison system for the French government. During his tour, he also conducted an informal but exhaustive survey of American political and social life. He later published his impressions of the young nation in the classic two-volume study *Democracy in America* (1835 and 1840). "How the Americans Understand the Equality of the Sexes" is excerpted from volume two of this work. The first comprehensive examination of American cultural institutions, this text is still regarded as one of the most important documents of American historical, social, and political studies.

Twain, Mark (1835–1910)
Mark Twain, the pseudonym of Samuel Clemens, was a master satirist, journalist, novelist, orator, and steamboat pilot. He grew up in Hannibal, Missouri, a frontier setting which appears in different forms in several of his novels, most notably in his masterpiece *Adventures of Huckleberry Finn* (1869). His satirical eye spared very few American political or social institutions including slavery and for this reason, as well as because it violated conventional standards of taste, *Huckleberry Finn* created a minor scandal when it was published. Nonetheless, with such books as *Roughing It* (1872), *The Innocents Abroad* (1869), *Old Times on the Mississippi* (1875), *The Adventures of Tom Sawyer* (1876), and *The Prince and the Pauper* (1882) Twain secured himself a position as one of the most popular authors in American history. "The Damned Human Race" comes from *Letters from the Earth* (1938). Twain built his career upon his experiences in the western states and his travels in Europe and the Middle East, but he eventually settled in Hartford, Connecticut. His last years were spent as one of the most celebrated public speakers and social figures in the United States.

Updike, John (b. 1932)
John Updike began his career as a staff writer for the *New Yorker*, and his stories have continued to appear in the magazine over the years. Since 1957 he has made his living as an independent writer of novels, short stories, poetry, and essays. "A & P" is found in his 1962 collection of short stories, *Pigeon Feathers*. Among his more popular novels are the "Rabbit" series, *Rabbit, Run* (1960), *Rabbit Redux* (1971), *Rabbit is Rich* (1981), and *Rabbit at*

Rest (1990). *The Centaur* (1963) won a National Book Award, and many of his other novels have met with both popular and critical success. His recent books include *The Witches of Eastwick* (1984), *Facing Nature* (poetry, 1985), *Trust Me* (stories, 1986), *S., a Novel* (1988) and *Self-Consciousness* (1989), from which "At War with My Skin" is taken. His criticism and essays have been collected in *Assorted Prose* (1965), *Picked-Up Pieces* (1975), and *Hugging the Shore* (1983), which won the National Book Critics Circle Award. John Updike has also received the Rosenthal Award from the National Institute of Arts and Letters, the O. Henry Prize, the Macdowell Medal, the Pulitzer Prize, and the American Book Award. The critic Alfred Kazin comments that "Among American novelists, John Updike is the college intellectual with genius. By genius . . . I mean someone who can brilliantly describe the adult world without conveying its depths and risks, someone wholly literary, dazzingly bright, the quickest of quick children, someone ready to understand everything and to describe anything, for nothing that can be put into words is alien to him."

Walker, Alice (b. 1944)
Alice Walker was awarded the Pulitzer Prize and the American Book Award for her second novel, *The Color Purple* (1983), which has subsequently been made into a popular film. This novel helped establish Walker's reputation as one of America's most important contemporary

writers. In both her fiction and nonfiction she shares her compassion for the black women of America whose lives have long been largely excluded from or distorted in literary representation. Walker is also the author of other novels, short stories, several volumes of poetry, a children's biography of Langston Hughes, essays, and criticism. Her work has been recognized with a Lillian Smith Award (1979), a Rosenthal Award (1973), and a Guggenheim Foundation Award (1979). Her most recent novel is *The Temple of My Familiar* (1989). The two essays reprinted here come from her 1983 collection *In Search of Our Mothers' Gardens*. In addition to writing, Alice Walker has been a civil rights activist, and has taught at numerous universities including Wellesley, Yale, Brandeis, and the University of California at Berkeley. Currently, she runs a publishing company, Wild Trees Press.

Weinberg, George
George Weinberg holds an M.A. in English literature from New York University and a Ph.D. in clinical psychology from Columbia University. In 1973 he coined the word "homophobia" in his book *Society and the Healthy Homosexual*; he has written several other books, including *The Heart of Psychotherapy* (1984), *Projection Principle* (1989), and *Self Creation* (1989), as well as articles on psychology and statistics published in professional journals. "The Madness and Myths of Homophobia" appeared in the London *Gay News* in 1973. Dr.

Weinberg practices psychology in New York City.

Welty, Eudora (b. 1909)
During the first years of the Depression Eudora Welty worked for newspapers and radio stations in her native Mississippi, and during World War II she wrote reviews for the *New York Times Book Review*. For most of her career, however, Welty has been an independent writer. Her novels, short stories, and nonfiction have earned Welty many awards, including a Guggenheim Fellowship in 1942, O. Henry Awards in 1942 and 1943, a William Dean Howells Medal in 1955 for *The Ponder Heart* (1954), a Pulitzer Prize in 1973 for *The Optimist's Daughter* (1972), a National Medal for Literature (1980), and a Presidential Medal of Freedom (1980). "A Sweet Devouring" can be found in *The Eye of the Story: Selected Essays and Reviews* (1978). Welty's other recent publications include her *Collected Stories* (1980) and *One Writer's Beginnings* (1984). Welty's highly imaginative style has been praised by Katherine Anne Porter as "the waking faculty of daylight reason recollecting and recording the crazy logic of the dream."

White, E. B. (1899–1985)
Elwyn Brooks White started contributing to the *New Yorker* soon after the magazine began publication in 1925, and in the "Talk of the Town" and other columns helped establish the magazine's reputation for precise and brilliant prose. Collections of his contributions can be found in *Every Day Is Saturday* (1934), *Quo Vadimus?* (1939), and *The Wild Flag* (1946). He also wrote essays for *Harper's* on a regular basis; these essays include "Once More to the Lake," and are collected in *One Man's Meat* (1941). In his comments on this work, the critic Jonathan Yardley observed that White is "one of the few writers of this or any century who has succeeded in transforming the ephemera of journalism into something that demands to be called literature." Capable of brilliant satire, White could also be sad and serious, as in his compilation of forty years of writing, *Essays* (1977). Among his numerous awards and honors, White received the American Academy of Arts and Letters Gold Medal (1960), a Presidential Medal of Freedom (1963), and a National Medal for Literature (1971). He made a lasting contribution to children's literature with *Stuart Little* (1945), *Charlotte's Web* (1952), and *The Trumpet of the Swan* (1970).

Wideman, John Edgar (b. 1941)
John Edgar Wideman grew up in Homewood, a Pittsburgh ghetto, and much of his fiction is concerned with issues of the black urban poor in America. Wideman is the author of several novels, including *The Lynchers* (1973), *Sent for You Yesterday* (1984), which won the PEN/Faulkner Award, and *Reuben* (1987). He has also published a collection of short stories, *Damballah* (1981), and his memoirs, *Brothers and Keepers* (1984). Wideman contributes to many magazines and journals, including *Negro Di-*

gest, Black World, American Scholar, Gentleman's Quarterly, the *Washington Post Book World*, and the *New York Times Book Review*, in which "The Language of Home" appeared. Wideman currently teaches at the University of Wyoming, and he has previously taught at Howard University and the University of Pennsylvania (where he also served as assistant basketball coach). Wideman was a Rhodes Scholar (1963) and a Kent Fellow at the University of Iowa writing workshop (1966). He is a member of the Philadelphia Big Five Basketball Hall of Fame.

Willis, Ellen (b. 1941)

Ellen Willis was educated at Barnard College and the University of California at Berkeley. She writes on a wide variety of subjects and her work has appeared in a diverse group of national magazines, including the *New York Review of Books*, *Commentary*, the *New American Review*, and the *New York Times Book Review*. From 1968 to 1975 she served as rock music critic for the *New Yorker*, and she has also worked as an editor and written for *Us*, *Ms.*, and *Rolling Stone*. Currently, Willis is a staff writer for the *Village Voice*, in which "Putting Women Back into the Abortion Debate" appeared in 1985. In 1981 she published *Beginning to See the Light*, twenty-eight essays of wide-ranging commentary on the 1970s, covering subjects from rock music to religion to feminism.

Winn, Marie (b. 1936?)

Born in Prague, Czechoslovakia, Marie Winn came to the United States in 1939. After receiving her education at Radcliffe College and Columbia University Winn became a free-lance writer specializing in children's literature. In addition to over a dozen books written for children or for parents and teachers of children, Winn is the author of *The Plug-In Drug: Television, Children, and the Family* (1977), from which "TV Addiction" is taken. More recently, Winn wrote *Children Without Childhood* (1983). She contributes articles to the *New York Times Magazine*, the *New York Times Book Review*, and *Parade*.

Woolf, Virginia (1882–1941)

One of the most important writers of the twentieth century, Woolf's innovations in indirect narration and the impressionistic use of language are now considered hallmarks of the modern novel and continue to influence novelists on both sides of the Atlantic. Together with her husband Leonard Woolf she founded the Hogarth Press, which published many experimental works that have now become classics, including her own. A central figure in the Bloomsbury group of writers, Woolf established her reputation with the novels *Mrs. Dalloway* (1925), *To the Lighthouse* (1927), and *The Waves* (1931). The feminist movement has helped to focus attention on her work, and Woolf's nonfiction has provided the basis for several important lines of argument in contemporary feminist theory. *A Room of One's Own* (1929), *Three Guineas*, (1938), and *The Common Reader* (1938) are the major works of nonfiction published in Woolf's lifetime; posthumously, her esssays have been gathered together, and "Thoughts on Peace in an Air Raid" can be found in the fourth volume of the *Collected Essays*.

Wright, Richard (1908–1960)

Richard Wright experienced the life of poor black sharecroppers as a child in Mississippi and the life of the urban poor in Chicago and New York as an adult. He spent his writing career coming to terms with the meaning of poverty, violence, and racism in America. During the 1930s Wright wrote for communist newspapers, but he eventually became disillusioned with Communism and in 1944 severed all ties with the party. In 1947 he moved to Paris and lived there until his death; during this time he began to make use of French existentialist philosophy in his fiction. Wright's first publishing success was the novel *Native Son* (1940). His autobiography, *Black Boy* (1945), from which the selection reprinted here is excerpted, was also a best-seller. Ralph Ellison compared *Black Boy* to the autobiographical writing of Joyce, Dostoyevsky, and Rousseau and found that in addition to themes common to their works "*Black Boy* is filled with blues-tempered echoes of railroad trains, the names of southern towns and cities, estrangements, fights and flights, deaths and disappointments, charged with physical and spiritual hungers and pain." After moving to Paris, Wright wrote three more novels and several works of nonfiction, including accounts of his travels to Indonesia and what is now Ghana, as well as publishing his lectures on race and literature.

Acknowledgments (continued from p. iv)

Barbara Lazear Ascher, "Mothers and Sons." From *Playing After Dark* by Barbara Lazear Ascher, copyright © 1982, 1983, 1984, 1985, 1986 by Barbara Lazear Ascher. Used by permission of Doubleday, a division of Bantam Doubleday Dell Publishing Group, Inc.

Russell Baker, "Gumption" an excerpt from *Growing Up* by Russell Baker. Copyright © 1982 by Russell Baker. Reprinted by permission of Contemporary Books, Inc., Chicago. "Happy New Year?" by Russell Baker. Copyright © 1983 by The New York Times Company. Reprinted by permission.

James Baldwin, from "If Black English Isn't a Language, Then Tell Me, What Is?" Reprinted from *The Price of the Ticket* by James Baldwin (NY: St. Martin's Press, 1985). "Stranger in the Village." From *Notes of a Native Son* by James Baldwin. Copyright © 1955, renewed 1983, by James Baldwin. Reprinted by permission of Beacon Press.

Toni Cade Bambara, "The Lesson." From *Gorilla, My Love* by Toni Cade Bambara. Copyright © 1972 by Toni Cade Bambara. Reprinted by permission of Random House Inc.

Wendell Berry, "The Journey's End." Excerpted from *Recollected Essays*, copyright © 1981 by Wendell Berry. Published by North Point Press and reprinted by permission.

David Bradley, "Ringgold Street." Copyright © 1985 by David Bradley. Reprinted by permission of The Wendy Weil Agency, Inc.

Judy Brady, "I Want a Wife." Originally appeared in *Ms.*, December 31, 1971. Reprinted by permission of the author.

Susan Brownmiller, "Let's Put Pornography Back in the Closet." Copyright © 1979 by Susan Brownmiller. Reprinted by permission of the author.

Judith Ortiz Cofer, "*Casa*: A Partial Remembrance of a Puerto Rican Childhood." From *Silent Dancing: A Partial Remembrance of a Puerto Rican Childhood*, by Judith Ortiz Cofer (Houston: Arte Publico Press of the University of Houston, 1990). First appeared in *Prairie Schooner* Volume 63, No. 3 (Fall 1989). Copyright © 1989 by The University of Nebraska Press. Reprinted by permission of the author, Arte Publico Press of the University of Houston, and The University of Nebraska Press.

K. C. Cole, "Much Ado about Nothing." Copyright © 1985 Discover Publications. Reprinted with permission.

Bruce Curtis, "The Wimp Factor." Copyright © 1989 by American Heritage, a division of Forbes, Inc. Reprinted with permission from *American Heritage*, Volume 40, Number 7.

Toi Derricotte, "Diary: At an Artist's Colony." Originally appeared in *Massachusetts Review*, Summer 1988. Reprinted by permission of the author.

René Descartes, "Stripping the Mind of Its Beliefs." From *Discourse on Method and Other Writings* by René Descartes, translated by Arthur Wollaston. Copyright © 1957 by Arthur Wollaston. Reprinted by permission of Penguin Books, Ltd.

Joan Didion, "On Keeping a Notebook." From *Slouching Towards Bethlehem* by Joan Didion. Copyright © 1966, 1968 by Joan Didion. Reprinted by permission of Farrar, Straus and Giroux, Inc. "Why I Write" by Joan Didion. Copyright © 1976 by Joan Didion. First appeared in *The New York Times Book Review*, December 5, 1976. Reprinted by permission of the Wallace Literary Agency, Inc.

Annie Dillard, "Seeing." From *Pilgrim at Tinker Creek* by Annie Dillard. Copyright © 1974 by Annie Dillard. Reprinted by permission of HarperCollins Publishers.

Gerald Early, "Baseball: The Ineffable National Pastime." Excerpted from "House of Ruth, House of Robinson: Some Observations on Baseball, Biography, and the American Myth" by Gerald Early. Copyright © 1990 by Gerald Early. Published in *Openings: Original Essays by Contemporary Soviet and American Writers*, edited by Robert Atwan and Valerie Valerivinokurov. Reprinted by permission of University of Washington Press, Seattle, Washington.

Gretel Ehrlich, "The Solace of Open Spaces." From *The Solace of Open Spaces* by Gretel Ehrlich. Copyright © 1985 by Gretel Ehrlich. Reprinted by permission of Viking Penguin, a division of Penguin Books, USA, Inc.

Loren Eiseley, "The Star Thrower." From *The Unexpected Universe*, copyright © 1969 by Loren Eiseley, reprinted by permission of Harcourt Brace Jovanovich, Inc.

David Elkind, "Teenagers in Crisis." From *All Grown Up and No Place to Go*, © 1984, by David Elkind. From pages 3–17. Reprinted with permission of Addison-Wesley Publishing Co., Inc., Reading, Massachusetts.

Nora Ephron, "A Few Words about Breasts." From *Crazy Salad: Some Things about Women* by Nora Ephron. Copyright © 1975 by Nora Ephron. Reprinted by permission of Alfred A. Knopf, Inc.

James Fallows, "Viva Bilingualism." Copyright © 1986, The New Republic, Inc. Reprinted by permission of *The New Republic*.

Henry Louis Gates, Jr., "2 Live Crew, Decoded." Copyright © 1990 by The New York Times Company. Reprinted by permission.

Nikki Giovanni, "On Holidays and How to Make Them Work." From *Sacred Cows—And Other Edibles* by Nikki Giovanni. Copyright © 1988 by Nikki Giovanni. Reprinted by permission of William Morrow and Company, Inc.

Doris Kearns Goodwin, "From Father, with Love." Copyright © 1986 by Doris Kearns Goodwin. Reprinted by permission of Sterling Lord Literistic, Inc.

Mary Gordon, "More than Just a Shrine." Copyright © 1985 by The New York Times Company. Reprinted by permission.

Vivian Gornick, "Who Says We Haven't Made a Revolution?: A Feminist Takes Stock." Copyright © 1990 by The New York Times Company. Reprinted by permission.

Stephen Jay Gould, "Sex, Drugs, Disasters, and the Extinction of Dinosaurs" is reprinted from *The Flamingo's Smile: Reflections in Natural History* by Stephen Jay Gould, by permission of W. W. Norton & Company, Inc. Copyright © 1985 by Stephen Jay Gould.

Francine du Plessix Gray, "I Write for Revenge against Reality." Reprinted by permission of Francine du Plessix Gray. Copyright © 1982 by Francine du Plessix Gray.

N. Scott Momaday, "A First American Views His Land." Copyright © 1976 by N. Scott Momaday. Reprinted by permission of the author.

Desmond Morris, "Territorial Behavior." Reprinted from the book, *Manwatching: A Field Guide to Human Behavior* by Desmond Morris. Published by Harry N. Abrams, Inc., New York, 1977. Text © 1977 by Desmond Morris. All rights reserved.

Bharati Mukherjee, "Fathering." From *The Middleman and Other Stories.* Copyright © 1988 by Bharati Mukherjee. Reprinted by permission of Grove Weidenfeld.

Gloria Naylor, "A Question of Language." Copyright © 1986 by Gloria Naylor. Reprinted by permission of Sterling Lord Literistic, Inc.

Itabari Njeri, "Grandaddy." From *Every Good-Bye Ain't Gone* by Itabari Njeri. Copyright © 1982, 1983, 1984, 1986, 1990 by Itabari Njeri. Reprinted by permission of Times Books, a Division of Random House Inc.

Kesaya Noda, "Growing Up Asian." From *Making Waves* by Asian Women United of California. Copyright © 1989 by Asian Women United of California. Reprinted by permission of Beacon Press.

Joyce Carol Oates, "Shopping." Copyright © 1987 by The Ontario Review, Inc. Reprinted by permission of the author and Blanche C. Gregory, Inc., Agent.

George Orwell, "Politics and the English Language." Copyright 1946, renewed 1974 by Sonia Orwell. "Shooting an Elephant." Copyright 1950 by Sonia Brownell Orwell and renewed 1978 by Sonia Pitt-Rivers. Reprinted from *Shooting an Elephant and Other Essays* by George Orwell, by permission of Harcourt Brace Jovanovich, Inc., and A. M. Heath, and the Estate of the late Sonia Brownell Orwell and Martin Secker and Warburg Ltd.

Grace Paley, "The Loudest Voice." From *The Little Disturbances of Man* by Grace Paley. Copyright © 1956, 1957, 1958, 1959 by Grace Paley. Reprinted by permission of Viking Penguin, a division of Penguin Books, USA, Inc.

Walker Percy, "The Loss of the Creature." From *The Message in the Bottle* by Walker Percy. Copyright © 1975 by Walker Percy. Reprinted by permission of Farrar, Straus and Giroux, Inc.

Noel Perrin, from "Forever Virgin: The American View of America." Reprinted from *Antaeus*, Autumn 1986.

Plato, from *Symposium.* From *The Collected Dialogues of Plato*, trans. Michael Joyce, ed. Edith Hamilton and Huntington Cairns. Copyright © 1961, 1989 by Princeton University Press. Reprinted with permission of Princeton University Press.

Anna Quindlen, from "Hers." Copyright © 1986 by The New York Times Company. Reprinted by permission.

Bernice Johnson Reagon, "Nurturing Resistance." From *Reimaging America: The Arts of Social Change*, eds. Mark O'Brien and Craig Little. Copyright © 1990 Mark O'Brien and Craig Little. Reprinted by permission of New Society Publishers, Philadelphia, PA; Santa Cruz, CA; and Gabriola Island, B.C., Canada.

Ishmael Reed, "America: The Multinational Society." From *Writin' Is Fightin'* by Ishmael Reed. Copyright © 1988 by Ishmael Reed. Reprinted with permission of Atheneum Publishers, an imprint of Macmillan Publishing Company.

Adrienne Rich. "Split at the Root: An Essay on Jewish Identity" abridged, from *Blood, Bread, and Poetry: Selected Prose 1979–1985*, by Adrienne Rich, with the permission of the publisher, W. W. Norton & Company, Inc. Copyright © 1986 by Adrienne Rich.

Richard Rodriguez, "Toward an American Language." Copyright © 1989 by Richard Rodriguez. Reprinted by permission of the author and Georges Borchardt, Inc.

Anne Roiphe, "The WASP Sting." Originally appeared in *Present Tense.* Copyright © 1989 by Anne Roiphe. Reprinted by permission of the author.

Phyllis Rose, "Shoping and Other Spiritual Adventures in America Today." From *Never Say Good-Bye* by Phyllis Rose. Copyright © 1991 by Phyllis Rose. Used by permission of Doubleday, a division of Bantam Doubleday Dell Publishing Group, Inc.

Philip Roth, "My Baseball Years." From *Reading Myself and Others* by Philip Roth. Copyright © 1973, 1975 by Philip Roth. Reprinted by permission of Farrar, Straus and Giroux, Inc.

William Safire, "On Keeping a Diary." Copyright © 1974 by The New York Times Company. Reprinted by permission.

Scott Russell Sanders, "The Men We Carry in Our Minds." Copyright © 1974 by Scott Russell Sanders; first appeared in *Milkweed Chronicle*; reprinted by permission of the author, the author's agent, Virginia Kidd, and the University of Georgia Press.

Richard Selzer, "What I Saw at the Abortion." From January 1976 *Esquire.* Reprinted courtesy of the Hearst Corporation.

Leslie Marmon Silko, from "Landscape, History, and the Pueblo Imagination." Reprinted from *Antaeus*, Autumn 1986.

Susan Sontag, "AIDS and Its Metaphors." From *Aids and Its Metaphors* by Susan Sontag. Copyright © 1988, 1989 by Susan Sontag. Reprinted by permission of Farrar, Straus and Giroux, Inc.

Charlene Spretnak, "Ecofeminism: Our Roots and Flowering." From *Reweaving the World: The Emergence of Ecofeminism*, eds. Irene Diamond and Gloria Feman Orenstein. Copyright © 1990 by Irene Diamond and Gloria Feman Orenstein. Reprinted by permission of Irene Diamond.

Brent Staples, "Just Walk on By: A Black Man Ponders His Power to Alter Public Space." Copyright © 1986 by Brent Staples. Reprinted by permission of the author.

Shelby Steele, "On Being Black and Middle Class." Reprinted from *Commentary*, January 1988, by permission; all rights reserved.

Gloria Steinem, "Ruth's Song (Because She Could Not Sing It)." From *Outrageous Acts and Everyday Rebellions* by Gloria Steinem. Copyright © 1983 by Gloria Steinem, © 1984 by East Toledo Productions, Inc. Reprinted by permission of Henry Holt and Company, Inc.

Elizabeth Stone, "Stories Make a Family." From *The New York Times*, copyright © 1988 by Elizabeth Stone. Reprinted by permission of the author.

Index of Authors and Titles